# Collection « Épitome musical »

## dirigée par : Philippe VENDRIX

Ministère

Culture Communication

CNRS

# Essays on Music and Culture

## in Honor of

# Herbert Kellman

Photograph by William Wiegand, Urbana, Illinois

CENTRE D'ÉTUDES SUPÉRIEURES DE LA RENAISSANCE
*Collection « Épitome musical »*

# Essays on Music and Culture

## in Honor of

# Herbert Kellman

Barbara HAGGH (ed.)

MINERVE

2001

Composition et mise en page
Patrick GILBERT

Gravure musicale
Vincent BESSON

Conception de la couverture
Mickaël ROBERT & François REYNAUD

## Ad Charibertum Septuagenarium

Bis septena tibi peracta lustra
gaudentes, Chariberte, gratulamur
quos cernis celebres adesse amicos,
mirati lepidissimosque mores
doctrinamque simul perelegantem.
nec soli colimus; uiden ut adsint
e caelo, Chariberte, te intuentes
ipsi quos penes est honor canendi?
arridere tibi uidetur uni
Pratensis solitus latere et ille
Petrus qui uoluit Mese uocari.
his plus plusque probabimus probatum:
discens uiue diutius docensque.

*Thy sev'nty years we come to celebrate,*
*Herbert, alike in charm and learning great.*
*Nor think that we alone are gathered here:*
*Methinks musicians from the heav'ns appear.*
*On thee alone the secret Josquin smiles,*
*He too, that himself Alamire styles.*
*Whom these approve, hear our approving speech:*
*Live longer, longer learn, and longer teach.*

Leofranc HOLFORD-STREVENS

# Tabula Gratulatoria

Alamire Foundation

Jonathan Bellman and Deborah Kauffman

M. Jennifer Bloxam

L. Kathryn Bumpass

Marie-Alexis Colin

Julie E. Cumming

Virginia Danielson

Jeffrey Dean

Els Delsupehe

Kathryn Duffy

Albert Dunning

Elise Ferer

Rachel Ferer

Martin Ferer

Kristine K. Forney

Richard Freedman

David Fuller

Michel and Yannick Godts

Royston Gustavson

Michel Huglo

Martin Just

Dr. Tess Knighton

J. Evan Kreider

Mary S. Lewis

Louise Litterick

Patrick Macey

Agostino Magro

Alison McFarland

Bruno Nettl

Michael Noone

Martin Picker

Willard W. Radell, Jr

Seppo Saari

Antonio Santosuosso

Anne Schnoebelen

Alexander Silbiger

Fred Stoltzfus

Henri Vanhulst

Stephen Wild

Robert (Bob) Witmer

# Table of Contents

## Spain

## Josquin Des Prez

## England

## Renaissance and Baroque Sacred Music

# PREFACE

ERBERT KELLMAN, an influential scholar and teacher with a lifelong interest in music and culture, taught at the University of Illinois in Urbana-Champaign from 1966 to 2000. Known for his scholarship on the Alamire manuscript complex and on Josquin des Prez, he joined Charles Hamm in founding the Renaissance Archives in 1968, which he has directed since 1976. He edited and brought to completion the *Census-Catalogue of Manuscript Sources of Polyphonic Music, 1400-1550* (Stuttgart, 1979-1988), the first comprehensive catalogue of 1600 extant manuscripts. To celebrate Herbert Kellman's seventieth birthday, and in honor of his career at the University of Illinois, past and present colleagues, friends, and students offer this collection of essays. We thank Herbert not only for his contribution to the study of music and culture, also the subject of this book, but especially for his teaching, collegiality, and friendship.

The preparation of this book was far more pleasant than I could have ever anticipated. Usually the most daunting tasks in preparing a festschrift are finding a publisher, coaxing papers out of contributors, and preparing camera-ready copy. I wish to thank Philippe Vendrix in first place, who agreed with enthusiasm to publish the volume in the series « Epitome musical », and managed the production process, responding to my questions promptly and completely despite his busy schedule.

As for the papers, in this case the response from contributors was overwhelming and unhesitating, and the flurry of contributions arrived on time—very few came at the last minute. The massive task of reconciling texts processed with different programs and of arranging musical examples, photos, tables, and images not conforming to page size was completed with exceptional competence and professionalism by the editorial team of the Ricercar Programme. Intelligent initiatives, experience, and patience throughout the process of preparing camera-ready copy, and devotion to the task, made this festschrift possible. I am deeply grateful to Vincent Besson, Patrick Gilbert, Mickaël Robert and to other assisting staff at the C.E.S.R. in Tours, and to the Centre for making available for this project the staff time and computer equipment necessary for the preparation of the book.

I also wish to thank Susan Parisi, who answered numerous questions, Bonnie Blackburn, Graeme Boone, Kristine Forney, and Rita Steblin, for making recommendations and answering questions, and my husband, Michel Huglo, not only for checking Latin and French texts, but also for his experience and encouragement. I am grateful to every contributor for their essays and their willingness to accommodate the unpredictable production schedule of the last months.

Finally, I wish to thank Herbert Kellman for developing in me the passion for learning and discovery that only burns stronger with time. I am not alone in this respect, as the following pages testify.

A few editorial comments are in order. Years preceding the Gregorian calendar are automatically given in New Style. The spelling of words conforms to American English, but their usage follows author preference (as in measure vs. bar). The editor nevertheless encouraged authors to avoid idioms unique to American or British English for the sake of readers whose native language might not English. To distinguish the names of churches, saints, and towns, the former but not the latter two are hyphenated.

Barbara HAGGH
College Park, Maryland
18 December 2000

# Le Dit du Maître[*]
## Biography of Herbert Kellman

Herbert Kellman was born into the troubled world of pre-war Germany, in Berlin, on 3 August 1930. His early years were difficult: he remembers watching Nazi parades on the street below his balcony, and huddling with his family in a darkened apartment on *Kristallnacht*. His schooling was sporadic. Herbert left Berlin in February 1939 by *Kindertransport*, the rescue operation that brought boatloads of Jewish children from threatened parts of the continent across the North Sea to England. He was separated from his family for almost eight years.

In England, Herbert attended first a boarding school, but when war broke out in August 1939 he was brought back to London, evacuated to the country along with most of London's children, and sent to a local elementary school. Later he entered Battersea Grammar School, a London school also evacuated to the vicinity, at which he received a classical education. He matriculated at Manchester University in 1946.

Herbert emigrated to the United States in November 1946, joining his surviving family in New York. He had already begun piano lessons in England and had been an enthusiastic concert-goer, and soon after his arrival in the city his formal training in music began at the New York College of Music. There he studied piano with Frederic Marshik, history and composition with Erich Katz, and conducting with Siegfried Landau. He graduated with a diploma in composition and conducting in 1950. In 1951 he became a U.S. citizen.

Around this time Herbert became involved in the performance of early music, influenced particularly by Erich Katz, a pioneer in that area. In concerts and recordings, he played recorders and sang with ensembles that included such musicians as LaNoue Davenport, Valerie Lamoree, Brayton Lewis, Bernard Krainis, and others who were soon to form *Pro Musica*, under Noah Greenberg. With the latter Herbert developed a warm friendship that lasted until Greenberg's death in 1966. Also in the early 1950's, he began to teach the recorder—he continued to do so for many years—and served as assistant director of the American Recorder Society; at the same time his compositions received

[*]    I am grateful to Susan Parisi for giving me factual information about Herbert's life and to all of the persons who wrote to me about him, many of whom are quoted in this account.

performances in concerts and in the festivals of American music of radio station WNYC.

In 1953, prompted in part by his contact with early music, Herbert began baccalaureate studies at the City College of New York, with a concentration in medieval civilization. He received a B.A. *magna cum laude*, and the Claflin Latin prize, in 1957.

Later that year he began graduate studies in musicology at Princeton University, where his teachers were Oliver Strunk and Arthur Mendel, and Edward Cone and Milton Babbitt. His fellow entrants to Princeton were Charles Hamm and Thor Wood, and among the senior musicology students were Paul Evans, Lewis Lockwood, and Harold Powers. Herbert completed his M.F.A. in 1959. By that time, an article that was the outgrowth of a seminar paper he had written in his first semester had been published in the *Journal of the American Musicological Society*. This was "The Origins of the Chigi Codex… Rome, Biblioteca Vaticana, Chigiana CVIII 234," now famous for its revelations about that important manuscript, for identifying almost all of the extant manuscripts from the workshops of Petrus Alamire and his predecessor, and perhaps most importantly, for pointing Renaissance manuscript studies in a new direction, that of codicological study of large manuscript "complexes". Lewis Lockwood remembers Herbert at this time in Princeton:

> I first met Herbert in the Fall of 1958 when I came back to Princeton from two years of duty in the U.S. Army, where I had served mainly as a cellist in the Seventh Army Orchestra, touring Germany and playing concerts. Deep in the lowest floor of Firestone Library was the old Seminar Room, then presided over by Oliver Strunk and Arthur Mendel, and there was Herbert, working on the Alamire manuscripts as a result of a Josquin seminar given by Mendel, whose standards for scholarship were notoriously demanding with regard to both accuracy, rationality, and common sense. Herbert's blend of intelligence, humor, and humaneness brought us together at once, and we have been close friends ever since. His command of his material was evident from the very beginning, and when he published his first article and began to give papers at AMS meetings it became clear what wonderful new territory was opening up from what had apparently been a "chance" assignment in a seminar.

The Alamire manuscripts (more properly the Burgundy-Habsburg court manuscripts), of which the Chigi codex is the earliest, eventually became Herbert's dissertation project. With fellowships from the Belgian-American Educational Foundation he lived in Brussels in the years 1959-61, working in the Bibliothèque royale and in libraries throughout Europe on the whole complex, which comprised, as he eventually established, fifty manuscripts. He was the first scholar to study the relationships among all of these sources, including their common Ghent-Bruges illumination; the first westerner after World War II to be granted access for several weeks to the manuscripts in Jena, then in East Germany; and the first altogether to examine the many lesser-known manuscripts in the complex in detail. He returned to Princeton for a final year as a Proctor Fellow, with the goal of completing the dissertation. In this he was not successful, however, and the dissertation subsequently remained unfinished. He himself has written, "The reasons for this are complicated, but to a large extent it was because the subject was immense and I was too naive—perhaps too stubborn—to make allowances for this. Of course, it has been a constant source of regret to me. Nevertheless, I have continued my research on the subject to the present, and at each stage of progress have tried to make my findings known through papers and publications."

Musical performance remained a serious enterprise for Herbert. For several years before and after living in Belgium he studied oboe at the Juilliard School with Lois Wann, and he kept up this study at the Brussels Conservatory with Louis Van Deyck. Throughout the 1960s he continued to perform in concerts, and conducted programs of early, and, occasionally, contemporary music. At Princeton he founded and directed the Princeton Consort, an ensemble performing Renaissance music. Harold Powers remembers this side of Herbert's activity at the university:

> He and Paul Evans maintained a high professional tone as performers and were not sure they wanted to hack around on antique wind instruments in public. I remember this, since I'd just bought a set of "sorduns" from Steinkopf then and was gung-ho for putting together an 'Early Music' concert."

He also writes,

> Herb is living proof that you don't need a doctorate in hand to establish a position as a great scholar; the only comparable case I know of in our generation is the late Tom Walker, and of course the prime instance is Oliver Strunk himself.

Herbert began his teaching career in 1962-63 as an instructor at his alma mater, City College. At that year's meeting of the American Musicological Society he presented the first of his series of papers analyzing the Alamire manuscripts for their codicological relationships (with the first color slides of their illuminations), their repertory, and their indebtedness to French court music. In the audience were Allen Sapp, chairman of the music department at the State University of New York at Buffalo, and Frank D'Accone, on the musicology faculty there, who eventually extended an offer to Herbert to join that department. He taught there from 1963 to 1966. Another colleague was David Fuller, who joined the department the same year and remembers Herbert as "a cosmopolitan and civilized person." Also in 1963 Herbert married Maedra Asch; they subsequently had two sons, Joshua, born in 1964, and Jordan, born in 1966. Herbert's interest in North Indian music dates from this period, and was the impetus for a week-long India festival which he organized at SUNY-Buffalo in October 1965, with concerts (featuring Ali Akbar Khan, in residence for the week), dance, films, an art exhibit, panels, and lectures.

In 1966 Herbert accepted a visiting appointment in musicology at the University of Illinois at Urbana-Champaign. He stayed on, and three years later received tenure in the School of Music, and, eventually, the rank of professor of music. He has said that he was attracted to Illinois largely because of its outstanding research facilities, and because he wanted to collaborate on Renaissance manuscript research with Charles Hamm, who was already on the faculty, a collaboration they had contemplated since Princeton days. Besides Hamm, among Herbert's contemporaries in musicology from the late 1960's on were Bruno Nettl, Alexander Ringer, Nicholas Temperley, and later Lawrence Gushee. Herbert has often remarked on how fortunate he was to be one of a group of colleagues as compatible and stable as this one for over thirty years.

In 1968 Charles Hamm and Herbert established the Musicological Archives for Renaissance Manuscript Studies (the name was recently shortened to Renaissance Archives) in the School of Music. They saw their first task to be a sweeping survey of all extant manuscripts of Renaissance polyphony, and the publication of a catalogue of these sources, a project that resulted in the five-volume *Census-Catalogue of Manuscript Sources of Polyphonic Music, 1400-1550.* By 1977, with contributions from a dedicated group of scholars in the field and the help of graduate research assistants, a typescript of volume I and a large grant from the National Endowment for the Humanities (NEH) in support of volume II were in hand. Around this time Hamm left the university, and responsibility for the enterprise fell to Herbert. However, the NEH grant made it possible to hire a graduate student (Jerry Call) as a full-time cataloguer, and under Herbert's supervision and editorship, and with three further grants from NEH and strong support from the university, all five volumes, describing over 1,600 manuscripts, were published in the years 1979-88. Much of Herbert's manuscript research found its way into the volumes.

One by-product of the compilation of the Census-Catalogue was a growing set of files containing unpublished research and other data, partially contributed by scholars from other institutions in exchange for information from the Archives. Another was the gradual acquisition of microfilms of all sources of polyphony composed before 1550. Today, three decades after the Archives were established, the collection of files and microfilms of all 1600 manuscripts in the Census-Catalogue, and of many other printed and manuscript sources of the Renaissance, is unparalleled. Its scope and depth draw researchers from throughout the world, and large numbers of scholars request and exchange information by correspondence. In the last several years, such exchanges have involved scholars in more than fifty universities. Under Herbert's guidance, too, the Archives have entered into collaborations on particular projects with such organizations as the Répertoire international des sources musicales (RISM), the Centre national de la recherche scientifique (CNRS) in France, the Alamire Foundation of the Katholieke Universiteit in Leuven, and the Koninklijke Vereniging voor Nederlandse

Muziekgeschiedenis, publisher of the critical edition of the works of Josquin des Prez. Over the years also a large number of dissertations and an equally large number of editions have been based mainly on the Archives' resources.

Concurrently with the building of the Archives, Herbert returned to research on Josquin des Prez, begun at Princeton. The immediate stimulus came from Edward Lowinsky, who invited him to participate in the 1971 Josquin Festival-Conference in New York with a paper focusing on the transmission of works by Josquin in the Burgundy-Habsburg court manuscripts. Herbert's paper ("Josquin and the Courts of the Netherlands and France: the Evidence of the Sources") did that, and more. Challenging the received belief that Josquin had worked for Margaret of Austria in the last stage of his career, it demonstrated that all the evidence for this conclusion, including that of the court manuscripts, fell away when closely tested, leaving little doubt that he had not worked for her. It ended with the suggestion that the tradition of Josquin's relationship with the French court was probably more reliable and more profitable to pursue, an insight borne out by the discoveries of recent years. From this beginning, Herbert went on through the next decade, with two fellowships from the American Council of Learned Societies, to search archives in northern France and Belgium for more documentation on Josquin's final years in the north. His discoveries, particularly concerning the composer's residence in Condé-sur-l'Escaut and position in its collegiate church are well known: new documents attested to Josquin's birth in France, visit to Condé and the church in 1483, assumption of the church's provostship in 1504, houses in Condé, deathbed bequest to the church, and endowment of regular commemorations, including the singing of his six-voice *Pater noster-Ave Maria*. There was also much new information bearing on the musical eminence of the collegiate church itself. Some of these results were appended to the article in the 1976 *Proceedings of the Josquin Festival-Conference*, and others were transmitted to the authors of the articles on Josquin in the *New Grove 6* and *The New Grove High Renaissance Masters*. More recently, Herbert has been working on a survey of the composer's life, and a collection that brings together several of his papers: "Young Josquin Emerging from the Mists of the Escaut," "It Was Not Josquin who Pulled King Louis's Leg the Second Time," "On Josquin's Authorship of Emperor Maximilian's Funeral Motet," "Music in the Renaissance Collégiale: Josquin des Prez and Notre-Dame at Condé-sur-Escaut," "The Elderly Josquin: Allegiances, Character, Compositional Style," and "Exegetical and Rhetorical Gestures in the Late Works of Josquin des Prez".

In 1976 Herbert found in England the missing altus book of the so-called "Newberry Partbooks," a book believed "irrevocably lost" when H. Colin Slim published his edition of the extant partbooks (with the altus reconstructed)in 1972. At Herbert's insistence Colin Slim announced the discovery and published a study and separate edition of the part.

From 1977 to 1980, and again in 1983 Herbert was chairman of the Division of Musicology in Urbana. His earlier marriage having ended, in 1979 he married Susan Parisi. A sabbatical leave in the following year was spent, with his family, in the south of France, where he could edit volume II of the *Census-Catalogue* undisturbed. One anecdote from that time: a colleague, wondering why Herbert had chosen this particular destination, wrote with some amusement, "are you now going to look for Josquin down there? - maybe on the Riviera?" That same year Josquin was found (by Noel Coulet and Yves Esquieu) in Aix-en-Provence, at the court of René of Anjou.

In 1982 Herbert was a member of a three-person delegation of the American Musicological Society—with Howard Smither, president of the AMS, and Howard Brown—past president, that held discussions with the Board of the Vereniging voor Nederlandse Muziekgeschiedenis concerning the disputed *New Josquin Edition*. The negotiations were successful, and resulted in the reorganization and publishing of the edition, thereafter sponsored by both societies. Herbert was subsequently appointed to the NJE editorial board, and later charged with the preparation of a key volume in the edition, *The Sources of Compositions Attributed to Josquin des Prez*. This multi-volume work is now complete: it itemizes and indexes the full contents of almost 700 printed and manuscript sources—some 27,000 compositions in all—containing one work or more attributed to Josquin.

Herbert also played a role in the genesis of another project, the Columbia University repository of archival references to music and musicians of the Renaissance (known as RENARC), directed by Leeman Perkins. At the annual meetings of AMS in 1974 and 1975, aware that a revival of archival research was bringing to light much new information about the activities of musicians within the institutions of earlier centuries, Herbert had organized the first panels on patronage of music in the Renaissance. These exchanges proved most fruitful, and prompted the main participants (Allan Atlas, Frank D'Accone, Lewis Lockwood, Jeremy Noble, Leeman Perkins, William Prizer, Richard Sherr, Craig Wright, and Herbert) to form a work group that met for a decade. Herbert remembers these gatherings as among the most stimulating of his career. The archival data collected by members of the group has been stored in a database repository at Columbia University, and awaits only additional funding and technological improvements to become operative.

Herbert had long been interested in the music of Heinrich Schütz, and in 1985, together with his colleague in the Choral Division, Chester Alwes, organized an International Heinrich Schütz Festival and Conference at Illinois, the first full-scale conference devoted to Schütz in this country. Under the auspices of AMS and several other societies, and with support from NEH, the event featured papers, panels, and seven concerts, and the participation of Roger Norrington, the ensembles *Pomerium*

*Musices* and *The Newberry Consort*, a choral delegation from Germany, and English and German as well as American scholars. It attracted visitors from throughout the U.S. and Europe, and was widely and favorably reviewed. Herbert's own paper, "The Magdalen of Heinrich Schütz and Georges de La Tour," reflected his interdisciplinary interests: it dealt with the figure of Mary Magdalen in the seventeenth century, beginning and ending with Schütz's treatment, but diverging to a broad consideration of the figure in German sermons, German and French devotional poetry, and French, Italian, and Dutch painting.

In the late 1980s Herbert returned to the Burgundy-Habsburg court manuscripts. Having been commissioned to write introductions to facsimile editions of two of these for the Garland Library series, he carried out new research, and incorporated the results in their introductory essays. In the first of these, for the facsimile of London, British Library MS Royal 8 G. vii, published in 1987, he showed the close relationship of this source to another Alamire manuscript, and conclusively laid to rest the notion—then still current in some quarters—that it had been prepared for Anne of Brittany and copied in France. In the second, for the facsimile of the Chigi Codex, published a year later, he conveyed much of the new information he had gathered since his first article.

Herbert was awarded a Guggenheim Fellowship in 1990, and began further research on the Chigi Codex, particularly on its owner, Philippe Bouton, and its miniatures. He continued the research in 1996 as a fellow in the University of Illinois' Center for Advanced Study. His paper for the Ockeghem conference in Tours in the following year, "Ockeghem and the Court of Burgundy," cast new light on Bouton's likely intersections with Ockeghem, his literary activities, and the allusions to members of his family in the miniatures. Herbert's history of the manuscript will appear with a critical edition of its contents by Edward Houghton, in the University of Chicago Press series *Monuments of Renaissance Music*.

Another sixteenth-century manuscript source was Herbert's subject at a 1993 conference on Renaissance Rome: that paper, "The Empire's Secondhand Motets: Biblioteca Vaticana, MSS Pal. lat. 1976-79," dealt with the many examples in this source of the Burgundy-Habsburg courts' curious practice of borrowing French state motets and, by merely changing proper names, adapting them to important Habsburg occasions.

When Howard Mayer Brown's death early in 1993 left a void at the University of Chicago, Herbert was asked to give a seminar there, which he devoted to Josquin's late works, much admired by Howard Brown; he also took over supervision of a dissertation Brown had been guiding. In addition, he later accepted the charge of completing *Printed Anthologies of Music, 1500-1550: Their Contents*, a volume Howard Brown had been preparing for the RISM cataloguing project. With support from the Newberry Library, work on this volume resumed, and publication is imminent. In the manner of the Josquin *Sources* volume, it itemizes and indexes the contents of around 550 anthologies, amounting to some 22,000 compositions.

In 1999 Herbert was involved in a large three-part project of the Alamire Foundation of the Katholieke Universiteit in Leuven, Belgium, to celebrate the 500th anniversary of the birth of Emperor Charles V: an exhibition of forty of the fifty extant Burgundy-Habsburg court manuscripts; an authoritative catalogue of all the manuscripts, with essays on their production and repertory; and a scholarly conference on these sources. He helped to mount the exhibition. He edited the catalogue (*The Treasury of Petrus Alamire: Music and Art in Flemish Court Manuscripts 1500-1535*), wrote half of the manuscript entries, and contributed an introductory essay. He also gave the keynote address for the conference, "Openings: The Alamire Manuscripts After Five Hundred Years" (proceedings of the conference in *Yearbook of the Alamire Foundation*, VI), in which he took stock of current knowledge about the complex, and suggested areas of investigation for the future. During the planning of these events he was also instrumental in the founding of a small vocal ensemble at the University of Illinois—*Choragós*, directed by his colleague Fred Stoltzfus—dedicated to performing the repertory of the Burgundy-Habsburg manuscripts. The ensemble gave its first concert at the Leuven conference, and has since given other concerts in the U.S. and Canada, and recorded a compact disc. Herbert advises the group in its choice of programs and matters of performance practice, and he and his students prepare the editions that are used.

In the last two years Herbert has helped to launch a program of research exchanges between Illinois faculty in medieval and Renaissance studies and similar specialists affiliated with the CNRS in France. He has already welcomed several French scholars to the Renaissance Archives, and in September 2000 was himself attached to the team *Culture, politique et société en Europe* in Paris, where he worked with Darwin Smith, a historian of medieval theater and biographer of Arnoul Greban.

✼     ✼

✼

From his first years at Illinois Herbert taught graduate seminars and tutorials, as well as undergraduate surveys - these frequently with very large enrollments. The graduate courses spanned all periods, genres, and composers. They included topics related to his research: "The Netherlands Court Manuscripts," "Renaissance Codicology," "Josquin's Motets," "Problems of Authenticity in Josquin;" other subjects of interest: "The Song Cycle in the Nineteenth Century," "Stravinsky's Paris Years;" the music of several later composers: Monteverdi, Schütz, Schubert, Tchaikovsky, Stravinsky, Berg, Copland; interdisciplinary subjects: "Mary Magdalene in Music, Literature and Art of the Twelfth to Seventeenth Centuries"; "Musical-Literary Circles in Early Nineteenth-century Vienna"; and even "French Cabaret Music since 1940." In recent years he was drawn particularly to twentieth-century opera, and offered seminars on some of his favorite works—*Pelléas* and *Lulu* for example—concurrently with university or nearby productions.

Herbert was a recipient of the University's Undergraduate Instructional Award in 1970. From Mary Ferer, his assistant then, comes this description of activities in a course for freshman music majors, at a difficult time:

> Teaching with Herbert was an adventure, particularly in fall 1970. The course that fall asked students to examine their musical values and aspirations. My task in the recitation sections was to play works and ask provocative questions. At his suggestion I performed *4'33"* and helped students deal with Salvatore Martirano's film and theater piece *L's GA*. Toward the end of the semester the students presented their own compositions, and we were treated to works played on wine glasses and to one multi-media piece which featured the exquisite sonority and visual effect of burning plastic dry-cleaning bags. On the final day of class Herbert responded in kind by reading from Charles Ives and John Cage in the darkened lecture hall lit by candles, and I manned the turntable. From Herbert I learned that teaching is not just about dispensing information and ideas, but helping students to discover and question, explore and confront.

Two courses Herbert molded became (and have remained) staples in the graduate program at Illinois: "Introduction to Musicology," required of all entering musicology students, and the analogous "Problems and Methods," required of students in performance and in theory-composition. Since the 1960's scores of first-year musicology students have traced the changes and debates in the field since its birth, read Arthur Mendel's "Evidence and Explanation," dissected poorly-reasoned arguments in the literature, and produced a final, massive paper on "The State of Research" in an area of interest. Even more students over the years in "P&M" have evaluated critical editions, investigated the genesis of works, and debated performance practice questions, demonstrating points on the spot, usually live. Assignments were never negligible—three papers in one semester in the latter, which seemed to this writer, a student in the course in 1979, very demanding indeed. Still, Herbert made us forget the workload because class meetings were always thought-provoking. Many veterans of that course recall not merely the long hours in the library, but also the animated discussions and camaraderie in the class.

Personal qualities, of course, also entered into Herbert's teaching, and affected students. Ted Solis writes:

> Having been out of the loop vis-a-vis historical musicology for quite a while, I found myself in Herbert's "Introduction to Musicology," where his witty and humane tolerance of my initial Teutonic author malapropisms ("Von Winterschnitzel" became a joke between us) gave me the courage to persevere in the program. I feel very privileged to know Herbert. He is someone who combines broad culture, humor, and compassion in rare measure.

For Marcello Sorce Keller, Herbert's control of languages—Dutch, French, German, Italian, Latin, and Spanish—and his pragmatic approach to using them, also left a mark:

> When I took Herbert's "Introduction to Musicology" he convinced me that it is possible, and actually desirable, to start reading books and articles written in languages related to one's mother tongue—even before having formally studied those languages. To this suggestion I owe my present ability to read Spanish, Portuguese, and Catalan with some fluency. A native speaker of Italian, like myself, can indeed get something out of a text written in any other romance language … with practice, little by little, one gets more than just the gist of an article …

Herbert's lessons in the written application of language have also not been forgotten. Lynn Trowbridge writes:

> Whenever I put pen to paper (or fingers to keyboard) I think of Herbert, for he taught me, among many other things, to write with precision and grace. These lessons have paid rich dividends in all my endeavors, and I am forever in his debt.

Herbert's fluency in a wide range of subjects and repertories can be seen in the variety of dissertations he has directed. They are on topics as diverse as style change in the fifteenth century chanson, patronage of music by Spanish nobility in the Renaissance, Giovanni Battista Doni, the politics of popular music in England in the 17th century, the social and economic context of music in Vienna in Schubert's day, Stravinsky's *Agon*. He was ready also to encourage students who wished to set out in new directions. Laura Bischoff, who wrote a dissertation on *Perfect Pitch: Event-Related Brain Potentials and Memory*, notes:

> Herbert was an outstanding teacher and advisor who gave high priority to the professional needs of his students. More important, however, is the friendship he extended to those he trained, and his commitment to their success. I respect him very much for his vision and willingness to support and encourage my pursuit of a non-traditional interdisciplinary pathway to my degree. Without his guidance I could not have succeeded. He will remain a role model throughout my professional career.

Herbert's support of his students extends well beyond their years at the university. Judith Radell, whose thesis examined performance implications in the sketches of Beethoven's *Diabelli Variations*, writes:

> When I contacted Herbert … about some editorial work I planned to do, it had been almost a decade since my doctoral project. Yet his attitude was one of enthusiastic support, and, of course, he had good advice about ways in which I could proceed. I am also grateful for his point of view that scholarship and performance are mutually necessary areas, not mutually exclusive ones. As a teacher he encouraged inquiry and what we now call 'critical thinking' (is there another kind?) as did only a few teachers in my experience."

Herbert has unstintingly shared his unpublished findings, not to mention the materials in the Renaissance Archives, with colleagues and students. His longtime friend and colleague Leeman Perkins writes:

> Since [1971] we have shared interests in source studies and archival work in particular, and I have learned a good deal from him in both of those areas … He made available to me the files and films in the Renaissance Archives for projects with which I was involved, and although I was able to contribute a few details, I received a good deal more than I was able to contribute … He has been an ideal colleague: generous, helpful, and, when needed, acutely but constructively critical.

In 1985, when I discovered that Du Fay was the composer of chant appearing anonymously in the service books of Cambrai cathedral, Herbert shared with me an important Cambrai antiphoner he had discovered in the municipal library there a year or two earlier, and had painstakingly photographed—all three hundred openings. The source, as he recognized, was catalogued as a manuscript but was in fact the earliest surviving antiphoner printed in France. With encouragement from Ruth Steiner and assistance from her staff, I published an introduction and indices of its contents the CANTUS series. (On a later trip Herbert photographed for me pages of an antiphoner kept in Mons; then he taught me to photograph manuscripts myself, a lesson that has served me well throughout my career). Herbert has also shared with me not only countless books from his personal library, but also his copious notes on Marian devotion in Condé and Douai and on the devotion to the Seven Sorrows of Mary in the Low Countries.

Generosity to students and colleagues also took other forms. Most academics devote time to writing letters that support requests of one kind or another. But many scholars and many students indeed, owe the success of their quests in part to the strong and meticulously crafted letters over which Herbert labored. Then there were all the field trips he organized for his students: to research centers, conferences, and AMS meetings; to the Lyric Opera and orchestral concerts in Chicago, and to the Indiana Opera in Bloomington. One of the most memorable trips occurred in 1999, when he raised the funds to take his entire graduate seminar to the Burgundy-Habsburg conference in Leuven. Finally, there is the frequent hospitality: almost every graduate student over the years, and many an undergraduate, has experienced one or another of the friendly, informal gatherings, replete with food and drink, at the Kellman residence.

*          *

*

My preface refers to Herbert Kellman as an influential scholar and teacher. On the influence of his scholarship, Albert Dunning, author of the classic *Die Staatsmotette*, is an eloquent witness:

Herbert's *Alamire* book has inspired in me a number of reflections. Essentially, it is the result of many years of profound study of Renaissance sources, above all the manuscripts. This type of study has become a branch of research in which the Americans of the post-War years truly excel, and among its many masters Herbert is surely the arch-master. What Herbert did in the *Census-Catalogue* and has now done in *The Treasury of Petrus Alamire* are things that will remain on the shelves of our public libraries (and the private libraries of scholars like ourselves) for the next 150 years. Not many in our line of business can claim to have left to our discipline things of such fundamental importance. My own *Staatsmotette* would have been a very different book if at the time I had had his studies: but in life that's often how things go. Herbert has changed the entire methodological approach to Renaissance research.

For me, the scholar and teacher come together in Herbert's insistence that music and its performance must not be studied independently of the history of culture—one might say the history of the humanities—and that interdisciplinary research on the primary sources must remain the basis for responsible historical inquiry. He recognized and explored with students and colleagues the ways in which musical compositions, while manifesting a present aesthetic condition, still recall the condition of their genesis, their patrons, and their performers, and how one can see in the sources recording those compositions contemporary artistic, devotional, and intellectual currents, understanding of which can lead to a richer comprehension of each work. These basic lessons inform the studies that here follow.

Barbara Helen HAGGH

## Publications

"The Origins of the Chigi Codex: The Date, Provenance, and Original Ownership of Rome, Biblioteca Vaticana, Chigiana C VIII 234," *Journal of the American Musicological Society* 11 (1958), 6-19.

Review of *Polyphonia Sacra. A Continential Miscellany of the Fifteenth Century*, ed. Charles VAN DEN BORREN. London, 1932. Revised edition, Pennsylvania State University Press, 1963. *Notes: Quarterly Journal of the Music Library Association* 21 (1964), 605-07.

"The Musicological Archives for Renaissance Manuscript Studies" (with Charles HAMM), *Fontes Artes Musicae* 16 (1969), 148-49.

"Communication concerning Josquin des Prez," *Journal of the American Musicological Society* 27 (1974), 367.

"Josquin and the Courts of the Netherlands and France: The Evidence of the Sources," in *Josquin des Prez*, ed. Edward E. LOWINSKY and Bonnie J. BLACKBURN. London: Oxford University Press, 1976, 181-216; reprinted in *The Garland Library of the History of Western Music*, Ellen ROSAND, General Editor. Volume 3, *Renaissance Music*. New York and London: Garland Publishing, 1985, 353-88.

*Census-Catalogue of Manuscript Sources of Polyphonic Music, 1400-1550*. Stuttgart: American Institute of Musicology/ Hänssler-Verlag.
Volume I, eds. Charles HAMM and Herbert KELLMAN, 1979. xxx + 441 pp.
Volume II, ed. Herbert KELLMAN, 1982. xxi + 493 pp.
Volume III, ed. Herbert KELLMAN, 1984. xix + 410 pp.
Volume IV, ed. Herbert KELLMAN, 1988. xxiii + 482 pp.
Volume V, ed. Herbert KELLMAN, 1988. ix + 359 pp.

"Alamire, Pierre [Petrus; Peter van der Hove]," *The New Grove Dictionary of Music and Musicians*, ed. Stanley SADIE. London: Macmillan, 1980, volume 1, 192-93.

"Sources, Manuscripts, IX, 16: Presentation Manuscripts" (with Stanley BOORMAN), *The New Grove Dictionary of Music and Musicians*, ed. Stanley SADIE. London: Macmillan, 1980, volume 17, 689-90.

*A Thematic Catalog of the Works of Pierre de la Rue*, eds. Nigel DAVISON, J. Evan KREIDER, T. Herman KEAHEY, with Herbert KELLMAN. Typescript reproduction, 1981.

*London, British Library MS Royal 8 G. vii*. Facsimile Edition with Introduction. New York and London: Garland Publishing, 1987. xvii + 126 pp.

*Vatican City, Biblioteca Apostolica Vaticana, MS Chigi C VIII 234*. Facsimile Edition with Introduction. New York and London: Garland Publishing, 1988. xv + 580 pp., 12 color pl.

*The Treasury of Petrus Alamire: Music and Art in Flemish Court Manuscripts 1500-1535*, ed. Herbert KELLMAN. Catalogue by Herbert KELLMAN and Eric JAS. With essays by Wim BLOCKMANS, Eric JAS, Herbert KELLMAN, Jacobijn KIEL, Honey MECONI, Eugeen SCHREURS, Dagmar THOSS, Flynn WARMINGTON. Ghent and Amsterdam: Ludion, 1999. Distributed by University of Chicago Press. 179 pp., 77 color pl., 27 b&w pl.

"Production, Distribution, and Symbolism of the Manuscripts - A Synopsis," in *The Treasury of Petrus Alamire*, 10-14; "Catalogue of Manuscripts and Fragments," 63-167.

"Alamire, Petrus [Pierre; Peter van der Hove]," *The New Grove Dictionary of Music and Musicians*, Second Edition. London: Macmillan, 2000, volume 1, 273-75.

"Openings: The Alamire Manuscripts After Five Hundred Years." *Yearbook of the Alamire Foundation*, vol. 6, ed. Bruno BOUCKAERT, Eugeen SCHREURS *et al.* Leuven: PEER, 2001 (in press). [Proceedings of the International Conference on Music Manuscripts from the Burgundian-Habsburg Courts, 1495-1535, Alamire Foundation/ Katholieke Universiteit, Leuven, November 25-28, 1999].

*Anthologies of Printed Music, 1500-1550: Their Contents*, compiled by Howard M. BROWN, completed and edited by Herbert KELLMAN with Stacey JOCOY and Trudie RANSON. Répertoire International des Sources Musicales, Series B. 2 vols. Munich: G. Henle, 2001 (in press).

*The Sources of Compositions Attributed to Josquin des Prez*, ed. Herbert Kellman. *New Josquin Edition*, vol. 1a.& b. Utrecht: Koninklijke Vereniging voor Nederlandse Muziekgeschiedenis, (forthcoming).

**In preparation:**

*The Chigi Codex. Volume 1: Historical Introduction*, by Herbert KELLMAN; Volume 2: *Critical Edition*, by Edward HOUGHTON. Monuments of Renaissance Music, ed. Bonnie BLACKBURN. University of Chicago Press.

*Essays on Josquin des Prez.*

**Selected Papers**

"Illuminated Choirbooks and the Manuscript Tradition in Flanders in the Early Sixteenth Century," Annual Meeting, American Musicological Society, Ohio State University, Columbus, December 1962.

"Music in the Habsburg Courts," Fall Meeting, New York State Chapter, American Musicological Society, Syracuse, October 1964.

"The Role of the Empire in the Radiation of the Northern Repertory, 1500-1530," Annual Meeting, American Musicological Society, University of Michigan, Ann Arbor, December 1965.

"Imperial Choirbooks in the Renaissance," Center for Medieval and Renaissance Studies, Ohio State University, Columbus, April 1966.

"Musical Links between France and the Empire, 1500-1530," Annual Meeting, American Musicological Society, Toronto, November 1970.

"Josquin and the Courts of the Netherlands and France: The Evidence of the Sources," International Josquin Festival-Conference, New York, June 1971.

"Scribes and Illuminators in Flemish Cities, 1450-1550," Annual Meeting, American Musicological Society, University of North Carolina, Chapel Hill, November 1971.

"Josquin in Condé: Discoveries and Revisions," Annual Meeting, American Musicological Society, Chicago, November 1973.

"Book Production and Book Distribution at the Netherlands Court, 1495-1534," Internazionales Kolloquium: Formen und Probleme der Überlieferung mehrstimmiger Musik im Zeitalter Josquins Desprez, Wolfenbüttel, September 1976.

"The Politics of Music: The Burgundian Chapel from Mary of Burgundy to Margaret of Austria," Seventh Medieval Workshop: Late Medieval Burgundy, University of British Columbia, Vancouver, November 1977.

"It was not Josquin who pulled King Louis's Leg the Second Time," Spring Meeting, Midwest Chapter, American Musicological Society, Ann Arbor, March 1975; Winter Meeting, Greater New York Chapter, American Musicological Society, New York City,1978.

"Music in the Renaissance Collégiale: Josquin des Prez and Notre-Dame at Condé-sur-Escaut," 13th Congress of the International Musicological Society, Strasbourg, August 1982.

"The Magdalen of Heinrich Schütz and Georges de La Tour (and Frescobaldi)," International Frescobaldi Quadrocentennial Conference/ Spring Meeting, Midwest Chapter, American Musicological Society, University of Wisconsin, Madison, April 1983.

"Éléments biographiques susceptibles d'intéresser l'interprétation des musiques de Josquin," International Colloquium on Music in the Era of Josquin des Prez, Saintes, April 1985.

"Die Gestalt der Maria Magdalene in Schütz's Auferstehungshistorie," Internationaler Musikwissenschaftlicher Kongress, Stuttgart, September 1985.

"The Central Scene in the Auferstehungshistorie," 30th International Henirich Schütz Festival and Conference/ Spring Meeting, Midwest Chapter, American Musicological Society, University of Illinois, Urbana, October 1985.

"On Josquin's Authorship of Emperor Maximilian's Funeral Motet," Second International Josquin Symposium, Utrecht, August 1986.

"The Elderly Josquin: Allegiances, Character, Compositional Style," Colloquium, Department of Music, Harvard University, Cambridge, September 1992.

The Empire's Secondhand Motets: Biblioteca Apostolica Vaticana, MS Pal. lat. 1976-79," International Conference on Music, Musicians, and Musical Culture in Renaissance Rome, Library of Congress, Washington, D.C., April 1993.

"Young Josquin Emerging from the Mists of the Escaut," Spring meeting, St. Lawrence and New York State Chapter, American Musicological Society, April 1995; Conference on Medieval and Renaissance Music, University of Southampton, Southampton, July 1996.

"Ockeghem and the Court of Burgundy: the Memories of Philippe Bouton," International Conference on Johannes Ockeghem, Centre d'Études Supérieures de la Renaissance, Tours, February 1997.

"Exegetical and Rhetorical Gestures in the Late Works of Josquin des Prez," 16th Congress of the International Musicological Society, London, August 1997.

"The Present State of Research on the Biography of Josquin des Prez," Colloquium, Department of Music, Brandeis University, Waltham, October 1997.

"Josquin's Career in the Absence of Judochus de Picardia," Annual Meeting, American Musicological Society, Phoenix, November 1997.

"Openings: The Alamire Manuscripts After 500 Years," Keynote address, International Conference on Music Manuscripts from the Burgundian-Habsburg Courts, 1495-1535, Alamire Foundation/ Katholieke Universiteit, Leuven, November 1999.

"Recensement et dépouillement des manuscrits de musique de la Renaissance: les Renaissance Archives à l'Université de Illinois," Institut de Recherche et d'Histoire des Textes, Paris, September 2000.

Alma Colk Santosuosso

# A *Musicus* Versus *Cantor* Debate
# in an Early 11ᵀᴴ-Century
# Norman Poem

ARLY IN THE ELEVENTH CENTURY the Norman poet Warner/Garnier[1] wrote what
may be the first *musicus* versus *cantor* debate. In his satirical poem, *Rotberto doctis ful-*
*genti semper alumnis*, two opponents—a music theorist and a performer—argue
about music. Warner's 160-line poem is interesting to musicologists, because it reveals
not only his approach to the study of music, but it also reflects his knowledge of
Boethius' *De institutione musica* and possibly Macrobius' *Commentarii in somnium Scipionis*.
Since Warner was a monk in one of the newly reformed Norman monasteries, the content of his poem sheds some light on the educational practices of the reform movement.
The text of *Rotberto doctis fulgenti semper alumnis*, which Lucien Musset published in 1954,[2]
can be subdivided into three sections: prologue (lines 1-18); the dialogue between Warner
and Franbaldus[3] (lines 19-154, with the debate on music in lines 73-138); epilogue (lines
155-160). A brief summary of the contents of the poem is in Appendix I; a full transcription of lines 73-138 is in Appendix II.

Beside *Rotberto doctis fulgenti semper alumnis*, we also have another satire by Warner,
*Contra Moriuht*.[4] Both poems are found consecutively on folios 2ʳ-11ᵛ in Paris,
Bibliothèque nationale de France, Ms. lat. 8121A.[5] This codex comprises 34 folios mea-
suring 262 x 195 mm. and has been dated by Henri Omont as either a product of "the sec-
ond half of the eleventh century, or at the latest, the early years of the twelfth century."[6]
*Rotberto doctis fulgenti semper alumnis* appears on folios 46ʳ-48ᵛ in another source, Paris,

---

1.   The Norman poet is called Warner by English
scholars and Garnier by French scholars.

2.   Lucien MUSSET, "Le satiriste Garnier de Rouen et
son milieu (début du xiᵉ siècle)," *Revue du Moyen Âge latin*
10 (1954): 237-66. Subsequent references to Musset's
edition of Warner's poem, *Rotberto doctis fulgenti semper*
*alumnis*, will be cited as *Rd*.

3.   The full name of Warner's opponent is not given
in either manuscript that contains the poem. In Ms. lat.
8121A, f. 9ᵛ, the name "Fran" appears with a space after
it. In his edition of the poem, Musset has given the

name Franbaldus (in order to complete the poetic
metre) to Warner's adversary. See MUSSET, "Le satiriste
Garnier," 255-56, 260.

4.   Henri OMONT, "Satire de Garnier de Rouen contre
le poète Moriuht (xᵉ-xiᵉ siècle)," *Annuaire-Bulletin de la*
*Société de l'Histoire de France* 31 (1894): 193-210. Subsequent
references to Omont's edition of Warner's poem, *Contra*
*Moriuht*, will be cited as *CM*.

5.   *Contra Moriuht* appears on ff. 2ʳ-9ʳ and *Rotberto doctis*
*fulgenti semper alumnis* on ff. 9ʳ-11ᵛ.

6.   OMONT, "Satire de Garnier," 194.

Bibliothèque nationale de France, Ms. lat. 8319, a composite codex, measuring 217 x 144 mm., which dates from the second half of the eleventh century.

That Warner was a member of a religious community in Normandy is suggested by several passages in *Rotberto doctis fulgenti semper alumnis* and *Contra Moriuht*. First of all, both poems open with a dedication to Robert I, the archbishop of Rouen (989-1037): *Rotberto doctis fulgenti semper alumnis* in one and *Rotberto domino subnixo presulis ostro* in the other. Secondly, Warner clearly recognized the authority of the archbishop, saying: "When I gave myself to be of service to your [archbishop Robert's] Rotomagus (Rouen),"[7] and, "Your excellency, may you thrive in your bishopric for a long time; This is the wish of Warnerius, your servant with his whole body."[8] Moreover, *Rotberto doctis fulgenti semper alumnis*, gives some indications of Warner's religious order since it reveals his intimate knowledge of the Benedictine rule. In lines 19-72 Warner scolds Franbaldus, his adversary in the poem and a former monk from the Benedictine monastery of Mont St.-Michel, for leaving the order for a life in commerce at Rouen. He admonishes him: "You do not follow truth, you do not imitate the Benedictine [rule]."[9] Within the poem, Warner alludes to specific passages found in chapters 5, 7, 8, and 55 of the Benedictine Rule.[10] Elsewhere, Warner mentions the vows of poverty and celibacy,[11] and his last words to Franbaldus are: "Remember to be willing to be mindful of Benedict who has been set forth; Change your life for the better."[12]

The monastery to which Warner belonged has been a matter of debate. In the prologue of *Rotberto doctis fulgenti semper alumnis*, Warner mentions the church of Audoene (St.-Ouen, Rouen) by name, for it was there where Franbaldus insulted Warner's teacher.[13] On the basis of this statement, Manitius concluded that Warner was a member of St.-Ouen's Benedictine community,[14] whereas Musset has expressed some doubts about Warner's relationship to St.-Ouen, because his poem disparages St. Peter, the apostolic patron of the monastery of St.-Ouen.[15] I have come to the conclusion that if we exclude St.-Ouen, Warner's most likely location was the Benedictine monastery of the Holy Trinity at Fécamp.

---

7. *CM*, 27: *Servitio vestro cum me Rotomago dedissem.*

8. *Rd*, 155-156: *Presul, episcopio vigeas in tempore longo, Optat Warnerius, corpore mente tuus.*

9. *Rd*, 37: *Non verum sequeris, Benedictum non imitaris.*

10. Direct parallels between chapters of the Benedictine Rule and the text of Warner's *Rd* are: Benedictine Rule (BR), chap. 5, *Rd*, lines 25-26, 38; BR chap. 7, *Rd*, 3-4, 9, 26-63, 38, 69-70; BR chap. 8, *Rd*, 57-58; BR chap. 55, *Rd*, 38, 42, 52, 60. *The Rule of Saint Benedict in Latin and English*, ed. and trans. by Abbot Justin McCann (London: Burns and Oates, 1952).

11. *Rd*, poverty: 43, 44, 60; celibacy: 65-6.

12. *Rd*, 153-54: *Propositique memor, Benedicti velle memento, Commuta vitam per meliora tuam.*

13. *Rd*, 4-6: *Carmina vaniloquo mitto; nec inmerito His defendo meum quem blasphemavit amicum, Audoene, tua nuper in ecclesia.* "Against the braggart do I compose poems; with these, quite rightly, do I defend my friend whom he blasphemed, Recently in your church, Audoene."

14. Max Manitius, *Geschichte der lateinischen Literatur des Mittelalters*, 2 (Munich: C.H. Beck, 1923), 493, n. 2.

15. Musset, "Le satiriste Garnier," 243. *Rd*, 143-44: *Non quibit servum judex retinere ligatum, Petrus apostolici ordine judicii.*

In the year 1001 William, abbot of St.-Bénigne, Dijon (962-1031), was invited by Richard II, Duke of Normandy, to reform and expand the Norman church.[16] Later that same year William and a small group of companions travelled to the abbey of the Holy Trinity at Fécamp, and they began instituting ecclesiastical and educational changes there and in other monasteries in the diocese of Rouen: St.-Ouen (1006), St.-Wandrille (1008), and Jumièges (1015). Soon the reforms spread to Norman houses in other ecclesiastical provinces: Mont St.-Michel (1023) and Bernay (1025).[17] In 1973 Neithard Bulst published a report that William compiled between 3 January 1015 and 30 January 1016.[18] This document lists enumerations and privileges and includes a census of the bishops, abbots, and monks in seven communities reformed by William. The accuracy of the document is enhanced because a number of prominent churchmen, including, among others, the archbishop of Rouen, Robert I, and the bishops of Bayeux, Évreux, Avranches, and Lisieux checked the lists before 1022-1025. There are over 300 monks in the census, which is systematically organized by monastic house, with the members of each listed by rank in the following order: bishop, abbot or prior, priests, deacons, subdeacons, and neophytes. There is only one Vuarnerius included among all of these names, a neophyte at the church of the Holy Trinity at Fécamp.[19] Vuarnerius, I believe, is the poet Warner, and he belonged to Fécamp, the first Norman monastery reformed by William of Dijon.

Many changes were made in the educational system in Normandy by William and his followers. Exterior and interior schools were established and libraries were expanded.[20] William's biographer, Rodulphus Glaber (c.980-1046), wrote in his *Vita domni Willelmi abbatis* (1031-c.1036):[21]

> In the meantime the most vigilant father [William], seeing that amongst the inhabitants not only of that place [the church of the Holy Trinity, Fécamp] but throughout the entire province and also all Gaul the science of reading and singing psalms had greatly declined and was becoming extinct, especially amongst the common people, founded schools in the holy ministry for clerics which brethren learned in that office were to attend assiduously for the love of God. Here indeed the benefit of teaching was to be freely bestowed on all those who converged on the monasteries entrusted to his charge; none who aspired to it was to be deprived, rather an example of uniform charity was to be given, for the slave

16. William is referred to as William of Volpiano or Dijon or Fécamp.

17. For a full discussion of William of Volpiano's reforms see Neithard BULST, *Untersuchungen zu den Klosterreformen Wilhelms von Dijon (962-1031)* (Bonn: Ludwig Röhrscheid, 1973).

18. Ibid., 222, 235-36.

19. Ibid., 234, #283.

20. See Betty BRANCH, "Inventories of the Library of Fécamp from the 11th and 12th century," *Manuscripta* 23

(1979): 159-72; BRANCH, "The Development of Script in Eleventh and Twelfth Century Manuscripts in the Norman abbey of Fécamp," (Ph.D. diss., Duke University, 1974); Geneviève NORTIER, *Les Bibliothèques médiévales des abbayes bénédictines de Normandie*, 2d. ed. (Paris: P. Lethielleux, 1971).

21. For the date of Rodulphus Glaber's Life of St. William, see *Rodulfi Glabri Historiarum libri quinque*, ed. and trans. John FRANCE (Oxford: Clarendon Press, 1989), xlv.

and the freeman, the rich and the poor ...
In fact his educational work conferred the most desirable fruit on the different churches.[22]

The ecclesiastical reforms in Normandy included improvements in the quality of performance of Gregorian chant, which must have been particularly dear to a man interested in musical accomplishments like William of Volpiano. With respect to William's role in the musical reforms of the Norman church, his biographer Glaber explains,

> As he was throughly learned in the nectar of the highest sweetness of the art of music and accomplished in teaching it, through correction and emendation he governed whatever was sung in the chanting of choirs of monks, by day or night, whether in antiphon, responsory, or hymn, to such a state of precision that there was no lovelier or correcter singing in the whole Roman church. He singled out especially the harmony of the Psalms, and more than anyone else adorned them with the sweetest melodiousness.[23]

The medieval educational system was based on the curriculum of the seven liberal arts: the *trivium* (grammar, rhetoric, and dialectic) and *quadrivium* (arithmetic, music, geometry, and astronomy). Of these seven subjects, grammar was the most important because it was the foundation of literacy and provided "the requisite first principles for learning how to deal with texts on any level—how to read, how to correct, how to interpret, how to evaluate."[24] Proficiency in grammar was then essential in places like monasteries, where knowledge and service to God were approached through an understanding of the liturgy and Scripture. As Charles Jones writes, three subjects: grammar, time (*computus*), and music (performance of the liturgy), were "always present, always fundamental;" indeed, "they were quintessential" in monasteries.[25] Music served a practical purpose—the monks sang the daily Office and Mass chants and learned them by rote—but music was also studied as a theoretical subject especially through the most thorough approach to the subject, Boethius' textbook, *De institutione musica*. Warner's poems reflect two of the three major subjects of medieval ecclesiastical learning: grammar (as expressed in poetry) and music.

In *Contra Moriuht*, he spends almost one-quarter of the poem (120 lines) ridiculing the poet Moriuht's grammatical mistakes.[26] In *Rotberto doctis fulgenti semper alumnis*, the debate on music begins when Franbaldus insults Warner by saying that he does not know the "*casus Donati*"[27] of music. Aelius Donatus (fl. fourth century) wrote two grammatical treatises, *Ars minor* and *Ars maior*. The former, the more elementary of his two books,

22. GLABER, *Vita*, 273.     23. Ibid., 289.
24. Martin IRVINE, "Bede the grammarian and the scope of grammatical studies in eighth-century Northumbria," *Anglo-Saxon England* 15 (1986): 41.
25. Charles W. JONES, ed. *Bedae venerabilis Opera. Pars I Opera didascalica* (Corpus christianorum series latina,

123A; Turnhout: Brepols, 1975), vi.
26. *CM*, 334-454. It should be mentioned that Garnier's own knowledge of Latin versification is far from perfect. The poem contains examples of intolerable hiatus, false quantities, and hypermetric lines.
27. *Rd*, 75: *Casus Donati forsan, non musice nosti.*

was the most popular textbook for the study of grammar until the twelfth century. In Warner's poem, the phrase *"casus Donati"* refers to the cases of nouns in Latin grammar, which are explained in Donatus' book. By using this metaphor, Franbaldus means that Warner does not understand the *"casus Donati"* or the basics of music. Warner replies (lines 76-88) that Franbaldus is ignorant about grammar[28] and points out a grammatical mistake made by his opponent.[29] He urges Franbaldus to study Donatus, because one must first know grammar before studying music. After mastering Donatus, says Warner to Franbaldus, you "will be able to sound your music true."[30] He concludes by telling Franbaldus "to enjoy the fruits of the first stages of grammar."[31]

Franbaldus answers (lines 89-94) that "our scholars are not ignorant about music" and they know its measure, mode and sound (*mensura, modus, sonus*).[32] He continues his reply with the definition of what a musician is, based on Boethius' *De institutione musica*, Book I, chapter 34. Boethius (*c.*480-524) introduced his views on a musician in this manner: "Now one should bear in mind that every art and also every discipline considers reason inherently more honourable than a skill which is practiced by the hand and the labor of an artisan."[33] Boethius went on to say, ". . . in fact, physical skill serves as a slave, while reason rules like a mistress. Unless the hand acts according to the will of reason, it acts in vain."[34] Franbaldus repeats similar ideas. When he hears the interval of a fifth (*diapente*), his mind, not his right hand, struggles because "with my hand I touch wood, with my mind I swallow sound."[35] He is unconcerned with the skill of playing or performing, as suggested by the hand touching wood, but focuses instead on the mind and its judgment of sounds based on thought and reason. This is what he means when he says he "swallows sounds with his mind." Franbaldus concludes by saying that mind, work, and art on the fingers are the sweet proportion of the heart, and if the habit is sweet, sweeter also is the sound (*dulcior atque sonus*).[36] For him, the habit of using one's mind will result in a sweeter sound. These lines probably relate to Boethius' statement that "reason exercises authority and leads to what is right; for unless the authority is obeyed, an act, lacking a rational basis, will falter."[37] Also, Franbaldus agrees with Boethius' statement that a musician is someone

28. *Rd*, 76-78: *Musica grammaticam sustulit ipsa tuam. Musica, grammatica, non ars tibi novimus ulla. Musicus es doctus, grammatica vacuus.*

29. *Rd*, 79-80: *Das ad discipulis, a discipulosque dedisti, Donet ut.a. monstrans, auferat.a. resonans.*

30. *Rd*, 81-82: *Do tibi consilium, Donatum discito primum; Post poteris Musas sat resonare tuas.*

31. *Rd*, 88: *Uberibus prime grammatice fruere.*

32. *Rd*, 89-90: *Musica vis nostris non est incognita doctis/Et mensura, modus, notus ubique sonus.*

33. See Gottfried FRIEDLEIN, ed., Anicius Manlius Torquatus Severinus BOETHIUS, *De institutione arithmetica* libri duo, De institutione musica libri quinque, accedit geometria quae fertur Boetii (Leipzig: B.G. Teubner, 1867; repr. Frankfurt: Minerva, 1966). Also see BOETHIUS, *Fundamentals of Music*, trans. Calvin M. BOWER (New Haven: Yale University Press, 1989), henceforth cited as BOETHIUS, *DIM*. See Book I, chap. 34, p. 50.

34. BOETHIUS, *DIM*, Book I, chap. 34, p. 50.

35. *Rd*, 91-92: *Si diapente sonat, mea mens, non dextra laborat. Tango manu lignum, haurio mente sonum.*

36. *Rd*, 93-94: *Mens, opus, ars, digitis, dulcis proportio cordis. Sit dulcis habitus, dulcior atque sonus.*

37. BOETHIUS, *DIM*, Book I, chap. 34, p. 51.

who, "has gained knowledge of making music by weighing with reason, not through the servitude of work, but through the sovereignity of speculation."[38]

Warner replies (lines 95-102) that Franbaldus is good on rationality, but that he utters his words in ignorance,[39] for when Franbaldus plays, his lack of skill is so evident that even asses who have gathered around him weep and night birds congregate when he sings "*Uppupa*."[40] Indeed, only an ape could appreciate and applaud Franbaldus' music.[41] Warner's position concerning music as an art is well stated here in his initial attack on his opponent's performing skills. He speaks of the power of music, while Franbaldus' music, governed by reason, results in sounds that only an ape could enjoy. He tells Franbaldus: "Let your voice be sweet, thus it is more pleasing to the heart."[42] In other words, if you sing sweetly, the effect on listeners will be much better.

In his response, Franbaldus presents (lines 103-21) the argument found in Boethius' *De institutione musica*, Book 1, chapter 1, that musicians should not be satisified merely by finding "pleasure in melodies without coming to know how they are structured internally by means of ratio of pitches."[43] Franbaldus then presents the Pythagorean consonances as found in Book I, chapter 10 of Boethius' treatise. Later he mentions other intervals. He states that he enjoys the Pythagorean *quaterna*. "Let the *quintus* be a castaway mallet as far as you are concerned,"[44] he tells Warner. This refers to Pythagoras' discovery, as retold by Boethius,[45] of the mathematical proportions of musical consonances at a blacksmith's workshop. Among the intervals produced from the five striking hammers were the consonances of a fourth, fifth, and octave. By considering the weight of four of the hammers in relation to each other (*ie.* 12, 9, 8, 6), the musical consonances resounded, while the fifth mallet, which was dissonant with all of the others was rejected. The Pythagoreans measured the consonances by ear, but committed them to the rules of reason. "They delegate the determination of distances to rules and reason," Boethius wrote, "as though the sense were something submissive and a servant, while reason is a judge and carries authority."[46]

Most of the musical terminology used in the poem appears in lines 103-126: *diapason* (106), *sesquitertia* (107), *epitrita* (108), *diatessaron* (110), *diapente* (110, 111, 112), *sesqualtera* (111,112), *hemiola* (114), *epogdous* (117), *comma* (119, 120, 121) *apotome* (124, 125, 126), *tonus* (119), *major* (119), *minor* (120), *modulis* (126). This vocabulary is common in medieval theoretical writings about music except for the reference to the *comma*, where the poet's reliance on

38. Ibid.
39. *Rd*, 95: *Tu ratione viges, ignorans edere voces.*
40. *Rd*, 96: *Percutis ut cordas, flere mones asinas.* lines 99-100: *Conveniunt asine te sic resonante sonore. Uppupa nocturnos congregat aligeros.*
41. *Rd*, 97-98: *Simia cum manibus, totos tibi subrigit artus, Applaudit digitis, gaudet in his modulis.*

42. *Rd*, 101: *Vox tua sit dulcis, sic est gratissima cordis.*
43. BOETHIUS, *DIM*, Book I, chap. 1, p. 8.
44. *Rd*, 103-104: *Nos Pitagoricis fruimur resonando quaternis: Quintus es abjectus sit tibi malleolus.*
45. BOETHIUS, *DIM*, Book I, chaps. 9-11.
46. Ibid., Book I, chap. 9, p. 17.

Boethius becomes apparent. Most of these terms are mentioned by Franbaldus who first states the basic musical ratios: the *diapason* (octave) has the ratio of 2:1, the *diapente* (fifth) lies in the *sesqualtera* (*hemiola*) proportion 3:2, the *diatessaron* (fourth) in the *sesquitertia* (*epitrita*) 4:3, the *epogdous* (tone) is in the *sesquioctava* proportion 9:8.[47] He then talks about the major and minor parts of a tone with the difference being a comma, but his presentation is far from clear.[48]

Warner keeps attacking Franbaldus' singing viciously, describing its devastating effect even on animals (lines 122-38). He says he hopes that Franbaldus will not be able to split a tone in two, for what will be left will "lay low an ass."[49] The *apotome* (that is the major semitone, which differs from the minor semitone by a comma in the division of a tone) will gather together rabbits and dogs, dispel gloomy fevers, and agree with his *modulis*.[50] Again this is a reference to Boethius, who discussed the impossibility of splitting a tone in *De institutione musica*, Book III, chapters 1 and 2. Warner then insults Franbaldus by saying that his voice is "consonant with crows" and that even fish are repelled by his singing.[51] Franbaldus, he says, produces a groan, a discordant lament and he uses modes and sounds of lamentation.[52] Warner suggests that St. Michael (the archangel and patron saint of Mont St.-Michel) left his mountain peaks, because he could no longer tolerate Franbaldus' singing.[53] Finally, he recommends that Franbaldus return to Mont St.-Michel, where he should "rejoice in the modes of the mind, not of the voice."[54] This concludes the argument on music.

Both Warner and Franbaldus reflect ideas found in Boethius' *De institutione musica*, the standard textbook for the study of music in the Middle Ages. Boethius placed music in the *quadrivium* along with three other mathematical disciplines, arithmetic, geometry, and astronomy, and these four disciplines served to prepare one for the study of philosophy. For Boethius, music was associated with mathematics and subject to numerical theories. He wrote "How much nobler, then, is the study of music as a rational discipline than as composition and performance!"[55] Elsewhere, he wrote on the affective quality of music "that it can ennoble or debase our character."[56] In the debate, Franbaldus, a music theorist, presents the Boethian concept that music is a mathematical science and one understands

47. BOETHIUS, Book 2, chaps. 25 and 27.

48. Ibid., Book 3, chaps. 6, 7, and 8. Warner makes some mistakes in discussing the semitones. Lucien MUSSET, "Le satiriste Garnier de Rouen," errs in his designation of the speakers. Five lines (122-26) that Musset assigned to Franbaldus should be given to Warner.

49. *Rd*, 122-23: *Non poteris medium spero secare tonum; Quod fuerit reliquum, resonando sternat asellum.*

50. *Rd*, 124-26: *Apotome lepores, congreget atque canes, Apotome tristes valeat depellere febres, Concordatque tuis apotome modulis.*

51. *Rd*, 127-28: *Musicus es verbis, tua vox bene consona corvis,*

*Vox tua non cordis consonat atque tonis. Rd*, 131-32: *Pisces namque maris, dicunt, cantando fugasti: Retia dum cernunt, voce tua fugiunt.*

52. *Rd*, 129-30: *Pro cantu gemitum, discordem fers ululatum, Flebilibus uteris modis atque sonis.*

53. *Rd*, 133-34: *Te Michael timuit, Montisque cacumina liquit; Jam sufferre tuum non potuit sonitum.*

54. *Rd*, 136: *Mentis, non vocis, conjubilando modis.*

55. BOETHIUS, *DIM*, Book I, chap. 34, p. 50.

56. Ibid., Book I, chap. 1, p. 1.

57. Ibid., Book I, chap. 1, p. 3.

aspects of music by knowing the mathematical ratios in the proportions of consonances. His presentation of the ratios of the Pythagorean consonances is correct, but he has some problems with the explanation of the semitones found in a tone. Franbaldus also reflects Boethius' view that a musician is someone who has gained the knowledge of making music, not through the servitude of work but through the sovereignty of reason.

Warner, a performing musician, maintains the importance of singing correctly. He dwells on the affective quality of music, a subject dealt with by Boethius in Book I, chapter 1 of *De institutione musica*. In the debate, Warner repeatedly attacks Franbaldus' terrible singing and describes its effect on animals, birds, and fish. Boethius wrote: "Indeed no path to the mind is as open for instruction as the sense of hearing. Thus, when rhythms and modes reach an intellect through the ears, they doubtless affect and reshape that mind according to their particular character."[57]

There is the possibility that the discussion of the power of music, as presented in the poem, was influenced by Macrobius' (*fl.* 400) *Commentarii in somnium Scipionis*. In lines 131-32, Warner says that fish are so repelled by Franbaldus' singing, that "when they perceive the nets, they flee from your voice."[58] This may be a reference to Macrobius, who says that "creatures of land, sea, and air willingly fall into nets under the spell of music ..."[59] Another connection with Macrobius could be Warner's statements: "As they say, suns move mountains with voice," (line 102) and "And when the *epogdous* is surrounded by parallel zones, the star itself as it moves bears to itself seven generations" (lines 117-18).[60] Boethius promised to discuss the harmony of the spheres, but he never did it, while Macrobius mentions the motions of the starry sphere and the seven underlying spheres and their musical harmonies. Macrobius also refers to the number seven as being the key to the universe.[61]

It is likely that Warner's position concerning music in *Roberto doctis fulgenti semper alumnis*, particularly the importance of singing correctly, is also a result of the ecclesiastical reforms of William of Dijon. The desire for perfection in singing was perhaps extended to musical notation, for in the early eleventh century, in monasteries reformed by William, the Latin letters *a-p* were employed as a system of musical notation. The *a-p* system of letter notation appears in thirty-six manuscripts, which date from the eleventh or twelfth centuries. Two-thirds of the sources are from the Benedictine monasteries that

---

58. *Rd*, 131-32: *Pisces namque maris, dicunt, cantando fugasti; Retia dum cernunt, voce tua fugiunt.*
59. See William Harris STAHL, ed., MACROBIUS, *Commentary on the Dream of Scipio* (New York: Columbia University Press, 1952), 195. Jacobus WILLIS, ed., Ambrosius Theodosius MACROBIUS, *Commentarii in somnium Scipionis* (Leipzig: Teubner, 1963), 105: ... *non nullae vero vel aves vel terrenae seu aquatiles beluae, invitante cantu in retia sponte decurrant....* Also see Michel HUGLO, "La réception de Calcidius et des *Commentarii* de Macrobe

à l'époque carolingienne," *Scriptorium* 44 (1990): 3-20.
60. *Rd*, 102: *Ut dicunt, montes voce movere soles.* Lines 117-18: *Cumque parallelis epogdous orbita zonis. Fert sibi septenos astra movendo gonos.*
61. STAHL, *Macrobius*, 185. In Book 2, chap. 1, Macrobius also presents the Pythagorean consonances and their ratios and mentions the problem of trying to divide a tone into two equal parts. His vocabulary for the latter is not used by Warner.

were reformed in the first half of the eleventh century, with twenty-four originating at reformed houses in Normandy.[62] In Ms. lat. 8121A, line 89: *Musica vis nostris non est incognita doctis* of Warner's poem is notated by letters of the *a-p* system of letter notation. It is also a clever pun—not only do the teachers know about music, but they also know a new system of notation!

Warner believes that an understanding of grammar is a prerequisite to the study of music. His association of grammar with music strengthens the connection musicologists have made in observing the close relationship between language and music in medieval theoretical writings on music. Warner organized his poem as a dialogue, a literary form that was widely used in medieval literature; indeed, the teacher-student dialogue is widely found in grammatical works including Donatus' *Ars minor*. Warner's poem, however, is not strictly a *magister-discipulus* debate, because two scholars are involved. Warner refers to himself as a disciple of his teacher (*magister*), but the name of his mentor is never given.

Warner's poem also poses another fascinating question, which can be answered only tentatively. Warner was probably a contemporary of two other authors, Dudo of St.-Quentin and Lantfridus, who each wrote a poem dealing with the same aspects of music theory found in *Rotberto doctis fulgenti semper alumnis*. Several scholars believe that Rouen was the home of a literary school that flourished during the reign of archbishop Robert I and his brother, Duke Richard II. Before his death in 996, Duke Richard I commissioned Dudo, a canon from St.-Quentin, to write a history of the early dukes, the *De moribus et actis primorum Normanniae ducum*. This task was supported by his son and successor Duke Richard II, archbishop Robert, and by another member of the ducal court, Count Rolf. Eventually Dudo became Richard II's chaplain and chancellor and "in 1011 he drew up a charter in favour of the community of St.-Ouen."[63]

Dudo's history comprises four books; each book is devoted to a duke (Hastings, Rollo, William, and Richard I). Dudo wrote his history in the form of a *prosimetrum*, where passages of prose and poetry (in various quantitative meters) alternate. In his third poem, Dudo speaks of his trepidation in doing the project "How then, can I relate with eloquence/What I am charged, all hesitant, to collect."[64] In several of his poems, Dudo worries about his ability as a poet. In poem 84 he says: "Whereas our ignorant and rustic pen adorns/This work with varying metres, of discordant sorts/Too vacuous, and impoverished, lacking artistry …"[65] Several times he apologizes for writing in a dull style but these remarks may be a requirement expected within the literary convention.[66]

62. Alma Colk Santosuosso, *Letter Notations in the Middle Ages* (Ottawa: Institute of Mediaeval Music, 1989), 83-124.

63. Jules-Auguste Lair published an edition of Dudo's *De moribus et actis primorum Normanniae ducum* (Caen: F. Le Blanc-Hardel, 1865). An English translation with and introduction and notes was prepared by Eric Christiansen. See his Dudo of St.-Quentin, *History of the Normans* (Woodbridge: Boydell, 1998), xi.

64. Christiansen, *Dudo*, 8.

65. Ibid., 154.

66. Ibid., xxx, n. 70.

Dudo mentions music theory twice in his *De moribus et actis primorum Normanniae ducum*. In his dedication to Adalbero of Laon, Dudo discusses numbers and relates some of them to music theory. After mentioning the twelve apostles, he turns to the inner meaning of the number twelve (called "oddly even" by mathematicians). He says: "What else is the total of twelve than the harmonic consonance of an octave."[67] Dudo later refers to the ratios of the fourth and fifth and to five tetrachords "interwoven with eighteen unequal strings."[68] But it is in the second instance, poem 13, the preface of Book 2 which is addressed to Rollo, that Dudo discusses music in a manner similar to that found in Warner's poem. In lines 39-54 he presents some of the basic mathematical principles of music theory. "If you understood the basics of music, which are categorized into three types," he says, "You could have played among the swans, with sweet/Melodious sound, harmonically tuned."[69] (lines 39-42) He states that the eight modes involve five tetrachords and embrace the intervals of the fourth and fifth. In the next section of the poem (lines 45-52), Dudo gives the musical ratios of the consonances. Dudo also uses a musical vocabulary similar to Warner: *diatessaron* (lines 44, 48, 51), *diapente* (44, 49, 51, 53), *tonus* (45), *limata* (45), *sesquioctava* (47), *epitrita* (48), *hemiola* (49), *diapason* (51, 53, 54). Dudo then mentions compound intervals (lines 52-54).

Like Warner, Dudo's main source must have been Boethius, but Dudo probably also used Martianus Capella's *De nuptiis philologiae et mercurii*, Book 9, *De harmonica*. This is evident for instance when he begins by saying that knowledge of the basics of music would allow a person to make beautiful music. This is an idea quite close to Boethius who wrote that "it does not suffice for musicians to find pleasure in melodies without also coming to know how they are structured internally by means of ratio of pitches,"[70] that is, the same argument presented by Franbaldus in Warner's poem. Dudo's organization of music into three categories (line 40) reflects Boethius' description in Book I, chapter 2, where he accommodates music according to its specific properties: *musica mundana*, music of the universe; *musica humana*, music of the human body and soul, and *musica instrumentalis*, music produced by instruments. Dudo's mention that the eight modes involve five tetrachords parallels Boethius' views in Book 4, chapters 15-17, and in Book 1, chapters 20 and 21, and Martianus Capella's rendering in Book 9 of his treatise. Similarities between Dudo and the two Latin authors appear also in Dudo's reference to the species of fourths and fifths; however, Dudo specifies eight modes, which is the system in which Gregorian chants are classified.[71] Two lines of Dudo resemble close passages from Martianus Capella: the phrase *dissona limata* (jarring semitones) and a refer-

67. Ibid., 4.    68. Ibid., 5.
69. BOETHIUS, *DIM*, Book 1, chap. 2, presents his famous classification of music: *musica mundana, musica humana, musica instrumentalis*.
70. Ibid., Book I, chap. 1, p. 8.

71. CHRISTIANSEN, *Dudo*, 24 (lines 43-44) "Eight modes, which each involve five tetrachords, and which/The intervals of fourth and fifth embrace." LAIR, *Dudo*, "Octomodus quinis haerentes in tetracordis,/Quos diatessaron et diapente fovet," 139.

ence to music's unequal metres.[72] Finally, Dudo's compound intervals, the double, triple, and quadruple ratios are found in Boethius' Book 1, chapter 7.

In spite of these similarities there is an important difference between the two men's approach to the topic. Warner stresses the importance of grammar to the study of music; Dudo also mentions another subject of the seven liberal arts, rhetoric, as an asset to music performance. In the middle of poem 13, Dudo moves unexpectedly into a brief soliloquy, where he again worries about the reaction to his work: "I flinch; I pant and tremble, pricked and stung./Hold fast "resist the reckless scoffing" of the mob,/Hold fast! Or thunderbolts "will lay you low,"[73] … and "There will be chatter, and much ridicule."[74] Then again, rather suddenly, he encourages Duke Rollo, to whom the book is dedicated, to turn to God and to the "sevenfold spirit's all protecting wing."[75] He goes on to say, "With Rhetoric's sweet nectar may he stir your sense,/Intoxicate you with harmonic beat,/And so enable you to chant in tones of praise/With plectrum and with strings a borrowed lay." (lines 67-70)[76]

Did Dudo and Warner know each other? Or were they familiar with each other's poems? It is possible, but not necessarily so, since their works indicate that what they have in common is the source—Boethius. On the other hand it is quite enticing to believe that there could have been a direct contact between them. They both lived in Normandy during the time of the ecclesiastical reform: Dudo was a canon who resided in Rouen at the court of Duke Richard II, whereas Warner was a monk at Fécamp. Both authors dedicated poems to archbishop Robert I. Among Dudo's 89 poems, ten (6, 7, 8, 9, 50, 51, 52, 53, 86) are addressed to archbishop Robert I and several to the city of Rouen. In two poems, Dudo humbly asks the archbishop to accept his work: "With holy hand, touch what I bring you, beseeching/— Things unattempted by masters of grammar,"[77] and "Accept what I have revealed/In the form of a treatise prosaic,/Unlearned, incompetent stuff from a/tongue-tied dull, sluggard."[78] Similarly Warner's *Rotberto doctis fulgenti semper alumnis* pleads with Robert, "Through it all [the poem], your excellency, be favorable to my pen; you will be Palaemon and you will give the subject for my poems."[79] Warner invites Robert to be his Palaemon (a celebrated grammarian under Tiberius), who was "the poetic umpire of Virgil's third eclogue."[80] Both poets clearly respect archbishop Robert I's knowledge of grammar and literature.

---

72. James WILLIS, ed., MARTIANUS CAPELLA, *De Nuptiis Philologiae et Mercuriae* (Leipzig: Teubner, 1983); *Martianus Capella and the Seven Liberal Arts*, 1: William Harris STAHL, *The Quadrivium of Martianus Capella*, (New York: Columbia University Press, 1971); *Martianus Capella and the Seven Liberal Arts*, 2: *The Marriage of Philology and Mercury*, trans. William Harris STAHL and Richard JOHNSON with E.L. BURGE, (New York: Columbia University Press, 1977). See WILLIS, 970-95; STAHL, 368, 370-71.

73. CHRISTIANSEN, *Dudo*, 24, lines 56-58.
74. Ibid., 24, line 82.
75. Ibid., line 64.
76. Ibid., lines 67-70.
77. Ibid., poem #6, p. 12.
78. Ibid., poem #7, p. 13.
79. *Rd*, 9-10: *Tu calamo nostro, presul, per cuncta faveto, Tu Palaemon eris, carmina nostra dabis.*
80. CHRISTIANSEN, *Dudo*, xxvi.

The date of composition of the two works also places the two men fairly close, although the evidence is of rather difficult interpretation. Dudo's *De moribus et actis primorum Normanniae ducum* dates from 996-*c*.1020; whereas Warner's poems were written after the death of Richard I (21 November 996) and before the death of his successor Richard II (23 August 1026).[81] In his satires Warner mentions contemporary events and the following members of the Norman ducal family: Dukes Richard I and II, duchess Gonnor, as well as archbishop Robert (who was the son of Duke Richard I). In the epilogue of *Rotberto doctis fulgenti semper alumnis*, Warner hopes that the archbishop and his brother, the Duke of Normandy, "will conquer the haughty Franks."[82] That phrase suggests, as Lucien Musset argues, that Warner's poem could have been written between 1005 and 1013, a period which witnessed a confrontation between the Normans and the Franks. The dispute originated in 1005 in the aftermath of the death of Matilda, the wife of Odo of Chartres and the sister of Duke Richard and archbishop Robert. It ended with the treaty of Coudres of 1013.[83] The *casus belli* was Odo's refusal to relinquish Matilda's dowry to the duke when Matilda died without children. Lucien Musset suggests also 1006 as one of two possible dates for Warner's other satire, *Contra Moriuht*. Warner probably met Archbishop Robert in 1006, when Robert was at Fécamp celebrating the Feast of the Ascension at the church of the Holy Trinity.[84]

Lucien Musset believes that Dudo and Warner belonged to the same literary school of Rouen and that they probably knew each other.[85] Barbara Vopelius-Holtzendorff suggests that Dudo was "the educator in chief of the Normans during this period: the master of a seminal new school of Rouen, where future bishops and upper clergy studied the seven arts and the classical authors under the patronage of archbishop Robert and count Rolf, the brother and uncle of the ruler."[86] Could Dudo have been Warner's teacher? It seems very unlikely. Dudo's first poem seems to place him in conflict with Norman scholars in general, by a contrast between "our Frankish schools" and the Norman schools,

> Should you [Dudo's book] now proceed at full speed to the Norman academies
> Or still remain in confinement to our Frankish high-schools,
> I fear all those jeers and the sneers that will arise in abundance.
> No, you impatient book; spurn not the key, nor open the doorway
> Now. Don't you fly out in the face of the keen-witted public, Or those Normans will
> shake up the poet *malgré lui* with their blows.[87]

81. MUSSET, "Le satiriste Garnier," 243.

82. *Rd*, 157: *Et vincas Francos domino cum fratre superbos.*

83. MUSSET, "Le satiriste Garnier," 245. See Elisabeth M. C. VAN HOUTS ed., *The Gesta Normannorum Ducum of William of Jumièges, Orderic Vitalis, and Robert of Torigni*, 2 (Oxford: Clarendon Press, 1995), 23-29.

84. MUSSET, "Le satiriste Garnier," 245.

85. Ibid., 247-48.

86. Barbara VOPELIUS-HOLTZENDORFF quoted by CHRISTIANSEN, *Dudo*, XII.

87. CHRISTIANSEN, *Dudo*, 7, lines 11-16.

Perhaps Dudo feared the criticism of those trained in the monastic and secular schools established by the reformer William of Dijon. Indeed, perhaps the above-mentioned passage is an oblique reference to Warner's poem, *Contra Moriuht*, where a foreign poet is mercilessly ridiculed by Warner's vicious tongue. Dudo states that Rouen, the capital of Normandy, has not had good poets to extol its merits:

> If only you had possessed chattering poets
> By whom the good deeds he [Richard I] strove to do could be composed!
> The teachers are to blame, that you lack rhetoricians;
> Educate now boys in the liberal arts,
> so that they will be able to compose in poetry of many meters
> whatever deeds the successors of the great father accomplish.[88]

Dudo's argument is too vague to allow us to identify the poets indicted by Dudo. We have only a few poems that have come down to us from this period. There are a "verse inscription commemorating the death of a certain Raoul who was killed by robbers and buried in a chapel in the cathedral of Rouen,"[89] Warner's two satires, and another two poems, *Jezebel* and *Semiramis.* The latter are both found in Ms. lat. 8121A immediately after Warner's poems. Jan Ziolkowski doubts that Warner wrote these poems but believes that they could have been written in response to his work.[90] Like Warner's satires, these poems are dialogues and written in hexameters.

Besides Dudo and Warner there is another poet who mentions music theory. In 1972 Michael Lapidge called attention to a 125-line dialogue, which he titled *Altercatio magistri et discipuli.*[91] This poem, from Æthelwold's school at Winchester, may be by Lantfridus and dates from "no later than 994."[92] It is organized as "a series of interchanges between a disgruntled student and a pompous teacher."[93] In the *Altercatio*, the *discipulis* asks the *magister* questions relating to the subjects of dialectic and music.[94] In lines 77-82, the student asks the teacher to define *diatessaron, diapente, diapason, epogdous, hemiolius, epitritus,* and to tell him how many *simphoniae* there are and what are their names. The teacher ignores all of the student's questions and gives instead "a magisterial exposition of computation."[95]

Although the musical content in the *Altercatio* is restricted to only a few unanswered questions, there are similarities in organization and content between the *Altercatio* and Warner's satire. Both poems were written as a dialogue, with the *Altercatio* being a typ-

88. For this translation, see Jan M. Ziolkowski, *Jezebel: A Norman Latin Poem of the Early Eleventh Century* (New York: P. Lang, 1989), 45-46.

89. Ziolkowski, *Jezebel*, 39.    90. Ibid., 37.

91. Michael Lapidge, "Three Latin poems from Æthelwold's school at Winchester," *Anglo-Saxon England* 1 (1972): 85-137.

92. Ibid., 94 (dating) and 106 (authorship).

93. Ibid., 95.

94. Ibid., 116-17; see lines 70-76 for dialectic and lines 77-85 for music.

95. Ibid., 101.

ical debate between a teacher and a student and Warner's, an argument between two scholars. Both poems were written in the same metre, incorporate Greek musical vocabulary, and conclude with the respective couples hurling insults at each other. Lapidge acknowledges that the similarities between these poems "are too close to be coincidental."[96] Lucien Musset has indicated even closer thematic ties between the *Altercatio* and Warner's *Contra Moriuht* and pointed out some associations between the monks of St.-Ouen and King Edgar of England.[97] As well, in 1002, Emma the sister of Duke Richard II and archbishop Robert, went to England to marry first Aethelred "the Unready" and King Cnut after Aethelred's death. Although there are clearly political and cultural relationships between England and Normandy during this period, with respect to the poetry of Lantfridus and Warner, Lapidge cautions that "in the absence of any direct and unmistakable verbal reminiscences it is impossible to conjecture what might have been the relationship between them."[98]

In summary, three poems written sometime between 994 and 1020 contain passages about music theory. The most important of these poems was written by Warner, a neophyte at the Benedictine abbey of the Holy Trinity at Fécamp, a house which was reformed by William of Dijon in 1001. He dedicated two satires to archbishop Robert I (989-1037), who was the son of Duke Richard I of Normandy. In *Rotberto doctis fulgenti semper alumnis,* Warner presents what may be the first *musicus* versus *cantor* argument. From the musical vocabulary and the positions taken by the two opponents, it is clear that Warner was familiar with Boethius' *De institutione musica* and probably Macrobius' *Commentarii in somnium Scipionis.* Franbaldus maintains Boethius' position on what a musician is, and states the ratios of the Pythagorean consonances. Warner, the practicing musician, constantly ridicules Franbaldus' singing. Warner speaks of the importance of knowing grammar before studying music and he discusses the impact of music. Warner's poem predates the famous statement of Guido of Arezzo in the opening lines of his *Regulae rhythmicae* (*c.*1030), where he pointed out the difference between the scholar and the performer:

> Musicorum et cantorum magna est distantia:
> Isti dicunt, illi sciunt, quae componit musica.
> Nam qui facit, quod non sapit, diffinitur bestia.[99]

> From the musician to the singer how immense is the distance;
> The latter's voice, the former's mind will show what music's nature is;
> But he who does, he knows not what, a beast by definition is.

96. LAPIDGE, "Three Latin poems," 102.
97. Lucien MUSSET, "Rouen et l'Angleterre vers l'an mil," *Annales de Normandie* 24 (1974): 287-90.
98. LAPIDGE, "Three Latin poems," 102.
99. Martin GERBERT, *Scriptores* (St. Blasien, 1784), 2: 25.

My research for this project was funded by grants from Wilfrid Laurier University and the Social Sciences and Humanities Research Council of Canada. My husband, Antonio Santosuosso, offered me advice and criticism, and we spent long hours discussing aspects of Warner's poem.

# Appendix

## I. Summary of Warner's Poem

| Section | Lines of text | Content |
| --- | --- | --- |
| Prologue: | 1-18 | Warner informs the archbishop of Rouen, Robert I, that he is writing a poem against Franbaldus, who recently insulted Warner's teacher |
| Debate: | 19-72 | Warner tells Franbaldus, a monk who has left the monastery of Mont St.-Michel, to return to his former life and extols the virtues of the Benedictine rule |
| | 73-75 | Franbaldus scorns Warner for his lack of knowledge of Scripture and states that Warner does not know the basics of music |
| *Music:* | 76-88 | Warner maintains that a solid foundation in grammar is necessary for the study of music |
| | 89-94 | Franbaldus claims he is aware of the power of music and that he uses his mind when he plays and listens |
| | 95-102 | Warner replies that Franbaldus makes sounds only an ape could appreciate |
| | 103-21 | Franbaldus recites the fundamentals of musical proportions |
| | 122-38 | Warner replies that Franbaldus knows the vocabulary of music, but that he cannot sing and that this was one of the reasons Franbaldus left Mont St.-Michel |
| | 139-54 | Warner and Franbaldus call upon saints to help them. Franbaldus appeals to St. Peter, while Warner calls on St. Michael, the archangel |
| Epilogue: | 155-60 | Warner addresses the archbishop and wishes him well in all his endeavors |

## II. The Debate (lines 73-138 from Paris, BnF, Ms. lat. 8319)

(FRANBALDUS)
Erras scripturis, scripturas non bene sentis,
Letargum pateris, somnia corde geris;
75 Casus Donati forsan, non musice nosti.

(WARNER)
Musica grammaticam sustulit ipsa tuam.
Musica, grammatica, non ars tibi novimus ulla.
Musicus es doctus, grammatica vacuus.
Das ad discipulis, a discipulosque dedisti,

Donet ut.a. monstrans, auferat.a. resonans.
Do tibi consilium, Donatum discito primum;
Post poteris Musas sat resonare tuas.
Nam lepus ecce cani jungetur, cerva leoni.
Si valet emissus sermo manere tuus,
85 Lac potare prius, solido nec pane cibatus,
Gengivas perdas frustra terendo tuas.
Neve teras tenerum tamquam puer ipse palatum,
Uberibus prime grammatice fruere.

(FRANBALDUS)

Musica vis nostris non est incognita doctis
Et mensura, modus, notus ubique sonus.
Si diapente sonat, mea mens, non dextra laborat.
Tango manu lignum, haurio mente sonum.
Mens, opus, ars, digitis, dulcis proportio cordis.
Sit dulcis habitus, dulcior atque sonus.

(WARNER)

95 Tu ratione viges, ignorans edere voces;
Percutis ut cordas, flere mones asinas.
Simia cum manibus, totos tibi subrigit artus,
Applaudit digitis, gaudet in his modulis.
Conveniunt asine te sic resonante sonore.
Uppupa nocturnos congregat aligeros.
Vox tua sit dulcis, sic est gratissima cordis:
Ut dicunt, montes voce movere solae.

(FRANBALDUS)

Nos Pitagoricis fruimur resonando quaternis:
Quintus et abjectus sit tibi malleolus.
105 Simplus cum duplo, bis ternus cum duodeno,
Nam diapasonicum perficiunt sonitum,
Octoque cum senis sit sesquitertia binis.
Epitrita modis constat et innumeris.
Bissenisque novem ternis superantur eodem.
Haec diatessaron est, sed diapente subest.
Si diapente sonat, sesqualtera portio surgat:
Sesqualter numerat cum diapente sonat.
Nonne novem seni succumbunt ordine ternis?
Haec hemiolia fit, pars diapente cadit,

115 Octoque bis seni succrescunt pondere quadris,
Perficiunt demum octo novemque tonum;
Cumque parallelis epogdous orbita zonis.
Fert sibi septenos astra movendo gonos.
Si tonos est major, si commata transilit octo,
Commatibus novem si minor adspeciem,
Commate progreditur pars, parte sua superatur.

(WARNER)

Non poteris medium spero secare tonum;
Quod fuerit reliquum, resonando sternat asellum.
125 Apotome lepores, congreget atque canes,
Apotome tristes valeat depellere febres,
Concordatque tuis apotome modulis.
Musicus es verbis, tua vox bene consona corvis,
Vox tua non cordis consonat atque tonis.
Pro cantu gemitum, discordem fers ululatum,
Flebilibus uteris modulis atque sonis.
Pisces namque maris, dicunt, cantando fugasti:
Retia dum cernunt, voce tua fugiunt.
Te Michael timuit, Montisque cacumina liquit;
Jam sufferre tuum non potuit sonitum.
135 Sed si vis lene potius residendo tacere,
Mentis, non vocis, conjubilando[†] modis,
Cum Michaele tuam poteris conducere vitam:
Ad Montem properet, te quoque repperiet.

[†] =8121A] cum jubilando=8319

Elizabeth Aubrey

# MEDIEVAL MELODIES
# IN THE HANDS OF BIBLIOPHILES
# OF THE *ANCIEN RÉGIME*

THE LATE THIRTEENTH-CENTURY MANUSCRIPT, Paris, Bibliothèque nationale de France, Ms f.fr. 846,[1] known as the "Chansonnier Cangé" after Jean-Pierre-Imbert Châtre de Cangé (d. 1746), who gave the codex to the Bibliothèque du Roy in 1733, transmits 351 songs of the trouvères. All but seventeen were given melodies by a single medieval scribe, who used an inconsistent mensural notation and an unusually large number of chromatic inflections. Judging from the calligraphy and certain orthographical features, the manuscript appears to have been copied in Burgundy—the only extant source of trouvère song from that region—between about 1280 and 1290.[2] The medieval scribe gave no composer attributions; he arranged the songs alphabetically by incipit and then by composer within each letter, starting with the songs of Thibaut de Navarre that begin with "A," then those by Gace Brulé that begin with "A," and so on.

As is typical for trouvère manuscripts, f.fr. 846 was produced and assembled in stages: first margins and text lines were ruled, then the text and next the staff lines and music notation were entered, and finally the initials were decorated. The left column of f. 54ʳ (Figure 1) shows that the music was entered before the decoration: note how the decorator carefully avoided covering the C-clef on the second stave with the extender of the initial "F."

Also visible on this leaf are marginal and interlinear annotations in Cangé's hand. Such glosses are found throughout the codex—rubrics with attributions, missing text to be interpolated, translations, commentary, and "corrections." Cangé openly and proudly announced his additions on a parchment bifolio at the beginning of the medieval

---

1.   Throughout this paper I will use library shelf numbers rather than sigla to refer to specific manuscripts.

2.   Facsimile edition by Jean BECK, *Les Chansonniers des troubadours et des trouvères, publiés en facsimilé et transcrits en notation modern*. I. *Reproduction phototypique du manuscrit Cangé (Paris, Bibl. Nat. fr. ms. 846)*, Corpus cantilenarum medii aevi, 1ˢᵗ ser., 1/1-2 (Paris: Honoré Champion, 1927). See also

Sylvia HUOT, *From Song to Book: The Poetics of Writing in Old French Lyric and Lyrical Narrative Poetry* (Ithaca: Cornell University Press, 1987), 74-80; Mark EVERIST, *Polyphonic Music in Thirteenth-Century France: Aspects of Sources and Distribution* (New York: Garland, 1989), 200-205; and Elizabeth AUBREY, "Sources, MS, §III, 4: Secular Monophony, French," *The New Grove*, 2d. ed., forthcoming.

volume. The left side of this bifolio is glued to the binding cover, and the right side serves as Cangé's title page. It reads:

CHANSONS

d'Anciens Poetes Francois
Rangeés par Ordre Alfabetique dans
ce MS. qui est environ de l'An 1350.
J'Ay fait nombre d'Additions & de Corrections
d'apres les MS. du Roy de M. le Duc de Noailles
et de M. de Clairembaut et me suis attaché
par preferance aux Chansons du Roy de
Navarre, et de Gaces Brullés que j'ay essaié
de rendre complettes. aussy bien que celles
du Chastelain de Coucy.

Cangé went about this work of "completing" his chansonnier deliberately and with scholarly care. His marginal commentaries include short biographical sketches (presumably taken from Claude Fauchet's *Recueil de l'origine de la langue et poésie françoise, ryme et romans* [Paris, 1581], which he cites in some glosses),[3] references to songs mentioned in Dante's *De vulgari eloquentia*, and variant attributions in other manuscripts. As the title page implies, Cangé had access to manuscripts owned by maréchal Adrien-Maurice de Noailles (now Bibliothèque nationale de France, f.fr. 12615), the genealogist Pierre de Clairambault (now Bibliothèque nationale de France, n.a.fr. 1050), the bishop of Metz, Henri-Charles du Cambout (now Bibliothèque nationale de France, f.fr. 20050) and to the "manuscrit du Roi" (now Bibliothèque nationale de France, f.fr. 844). His annotations show that at one time or another he also consulted two other manuscripts that were housed in the Bibliothèque du Roy: Bibliothèque nationale de France, f.fr. 1109 and f.fr. 1591 (to which he refers by their old numbers, 7363 and 7613 respectively). Annotations added sometime later refer to "*mon autre MSS*" [sic] [my other manuscript] and to a manuscript which he says "*m'a presté/ M. l'Abbé Sallier*" [Abbot Sallier loaned me][4]; he does not give variant readings from these manuscripts, but from his comments that cite specific features in them, they can be identified respectively as the manuscripts in the Bibliothèque nationale de France now numbered f.fr. 847 and f.fr. 845. Cangé eventually owned both of these manuscripts. After the title page of f.fr. 846 is an added parchment quinternion on which Cangé wrote an alphabetized index of authors with song incipits, followed by an alphabetized list of incipits of songs whose authors he had not identified, all keyed to his own Arabic foliation of the leaves. He marked concordances found in f.fr. 12615,

---

3. Fauchet owned the manuscript Bibliothèque nationale de France, f.fr. 765 and added attributive rubrics and other notes to its leaves. After passing through the hands of Jean-Baptiste Colbert and Charles-Éléonor, count of Seignelay, the manuscript entered the Bibliothèque du Roy in 1732.

4. Claude Sallier was director of the Department of Printed Books at the Bibliothèque du Roy from 1726-61.

Bibliothèque nationale de France, Ms. f.fr. 846, f. 54ʳ

Cliché Bibliothèque nationale de France, Paris

n.a.fr. 1050, f.fr. 1591, f.fr. 845, and f.fr. 847 next to the incipits and in the margins beside the songs themselves in f.fr. 846.

Cangé bought f.fr. 846 in 1724 for 175 *livres*, as a small note in the upper right corner of the title page indicates, apparently from the estate of Charles-César Baudelot de Dairval. Baudelot was a lawyer who, while trying a case in Dijon once, had been distracted by the curiosities to be found in old books and other antiquities there.[5] He spent the greater part of his career collecting, documenting, and studying cultural artifacts of the Middle Ages and ancient Greece and Rome. From about 1697 he served the duchesse d'Orléans as *garde du cabinet des médailles d'or et des pierres gravées*,[6] and he became a member of the Académie des Inscriptions et Belles Lettres in 1705. No extant record indicates when and how Baudelot acquired f.fr. 846, although given its Burgundian provenance, it seems probable that it was among the antiquities that he obtained in Dijon. Just before his death in 1722 Baudelot willed his books and antiquities to the Académie des Inscriptions; the documents of the Académie, which published an eloquent eulogy after his death,[7] do not mention this manuscript specifically. It is possible that f.fr. 846 was not included in his bequest and that it was sold by the heirs of his estate to Cangé.

Cangé was the son of a *valet de chambre* of the duc d'Orléans and a *femme de chambre* of the duchess.[8] From 1723-27 he served as mayor of Tours, after which time he assumed his father's position in the royal retinue at Orléans. In 1727 he was appointed *commissaire des guerres*, and he maintained a lifelong interest in military history and its records. In 1735 he became *premier valet de chambre* to Louis XV. As we have seen, Cangé obtained f.fr. 846 in 1724, and sometime afterwards he acquired f.fr. 847 and f.fr. 845. In 1733 he sold 158 manuscripts and about 7000 printed books to the Bibliothèque du Roy;[9] in that year a catalogue of Cangé's library was printed, which does not list f.fr. 846. After the sale had been arranged Cangé decided to give twelve other manuscripts to the king's collection, including the three trouvère manuscripts. A printed catalogue of the sale is now in the Department of Manuscripts of the Bibliothèque nationale de France, and at the end is an addendum written by hand before the catalogue entered the Bibliothèque du Roy (the royal seal was

5.   See entries in *Biographie Universelle, ancienne et moderne*, 3, ed. Joseph François MICHAUD (Paris: A.T. Desplaces, 1854), 276; *Nouvelle biographie générale depuis les temps les plus reculés jusqu'à nos jours*, 4, ed. Jean Chrétien Ferdinand HOEFER (Paris: Firmin Didot Frères, 1855), col. 765; and *Dictionnaire de biographie française*, 5, ed. Michel PRÉVOST and Roman d'AMAT (Paris: Letouzey et Ané, 1951), col. 840.

6.   Baudelot published several works, most notably a two-volume tract entitled *De l'utilité des voyages et de l'avantage que la recherche des antiquités procure aux savants* (Paris: Pierre Aubouin & Pierre Emery, 1686).

7.   *Histoire de l'Académie royale des Inscriptions et Belles Lettres, avec les Mémoires de Littérature tirés des Registres de cette Académie, depuis l'année M.DCCXVIII, jusques et compris l'année M.DCCXXV* (Paris: L'Imprimerie Royale, 1729), 5: 403-

11; see also Jean Pierre NICERON, *Mémoires pour servir à l'Histoire des hommes illustres dans la République des lettres*, 12 (Paris: Briasson, 1730), 272-84. The *Histoire* (p. 9) mentions his bequest: "M. Baudelot, Académicien Pensionnaire, qui mourut au mois de Juin 1722, laissa à l'Académie, par son testament, une partie de sa Bibliothèque [sic]…"

8.   See entry in *Dictionnaire de biographie française*, 8 (1959): col. 822.

9.   See Léopold DELISLE, *Le Cabinet des manuscrits de la Bibliothèque impériale*, 1 (Paris: Imprimerie Impériale, 1868), 411-12; and Eugène-Gabriel LEDOS, *Histoire des catalogues des livres imprimés de la Bibliothèque nationale* (Paris: Éditions des Bibliothèques Nationales, 1936), 67-68.

stamped atop the ink of the addendum),[10] which describes the three trouvère manuscripts, numbered 65, 66, and 67 of Cangé's collection. These volumes eventually were renumbered, respectively, 847, 846, and 845 of the *fonds français* of the library.

Cangé's annotations are obvious to the modern reader, and if they have inspired any special note among scholars, it has been to bemoan their presence in such a beautiful and well-preserved medieval book, and perhaps to suggest a lack of reverence on Cangé's part toward the authority of this manuscript's testimony to an important repertoire of medieval literature. Yet there is reason to examine Cangé's glosses more closely than has been done before, and perhaps to reevaluate the role that Cangé and other *littéraires* of his day had in collecting, preserving, and studying these ancient repositories of French literature.

In his effort to create a comprehensive anthology of the songs of the trouvères, Cangé added four texts to the end of the last medieval quaternion, ff. 142$^r$-143$^v$, and filled the leaves of an additional parchment quaternion at the end, ff. 144$^r$-151$^v$, with twenty-seven more songs. Most of the additions on these six folios were copied from n.a.fr. 1050, (which he designates "Cl" for Clairambault although as the rubric at the top of f. 142$^r$ shows (Figure 2), he also consulted the manuscript in the "Bibliothèque du Roy, No. 7222" or "R" (now f.fr. 844) and that of "N" (the duc de Noailles, now f.fr. 12615); on other leaves of this added gathering he made note of concordances with "*mon autre MSS*" [sic] (now f.fr. 847) and the manuscript he borrowed from "*M. l'Abbé Sallier*" (now f.fr. 845). With the first added song, *L'autrier par la matinee* by Thibaut de Navarre (RS 529),[11] he included music. This song is found with its melody on f. 28$^r$ of Clairambault's manuscript (n.a.fr 1050), and the shapes and spacing of the notes in the two manuscripts, one medieval, the other of the eighteenth century, are identical (see Figure 3). Note, for example, the proximity of the two longas over the paroxytonic syllables *-ee* near the beginning of the second stave of n.a.fr. 1050, scrupulously copied by Cangé in the added gathering at the end of f.fr. 846.

Cangé did not attempt to provide any more of his added texts with music; judging from the somewhat awkward appearance of the notes in this first one, he may have concluded that the result was not worth his exertion. But is it possible that he copied music elsewhere in the medieval manuscript, on those staves left tantalizingly empty by the thirteenth-century scribe, where Cangé would be saved from the trouble of drawing the lines himself?

Jean-Baptiste Beck, the editor of the chansonnier's facsimile edition, noticed that all of the melodies in f.fr. 846 were written by a single hand except for two, *Au tans plain*

---

10.  *Catalogue des livres du cabinet de M. du [sic] Cangé, acheté par le Roy au milieu de juillet 1733* (Paris: Jacques Guerin, 1733), Bibliothèque nationale de France, Département des manuscrits, Cote no. 8° 453.

11.  "RS" refers to the standard index of trouvère songs, Hans SPANKE, ed, G. *Raynauds Bibliographie des altfranzösischen Liedes* (Leiden: E. J. Brill, 1980).

FIGURE 2    Bibliothèque nationale de France, Ms. f.fr. 846, f. 142ʳ

Cliché Bibliothèque nationale de France, Paris

*de felonie* by Thibaut de Navarre (RS 1152) on f. 2ʳ and *Chanter et renvoisier seuil* by Thibaut de Blason (RS 1001) on f. 25ᵛ.[12] The notation of these two melodies is square without any

12.  BECK, ed., *Les Chansonniers*, 2: 30.

FIGURE 3   Bibliothèque nationale de France, Ms. n.a.fr. 1050, f. 28ʳ

Cliché Bibliothèque nationale de France, Paris

semblance of mensural shapes. Unlike the other melodies in the rest of the volume, where the music notation is underneath the decorative elements, the notes here lie on top, indicating that they were entered after the decoration. Beck accepted these two melodies as legitimate medieval readings, as did Hans Tischler in his edition of trouvère melodies.[13] The dark black color of the ink, as opposed to the faded brown of the other melodies, is quite similar to that of the ink of Cangé's added melody on f. 142ʳ. The note shapes have the same somewhat clumsy appearance; in fact on f. 25ᵛ some of the shapes are improbable for a thirteenth-century scribe (Figure 4): single notes with a tail on the left (sixth, seventh, and eighth staves); two-note ascending neumes with the connecting stroke on the left rather than the right (sixth stave); a slur mark over a three-note descending neume (second stave).

These two melodies are found in several other manuscripts, including the ones from which Cangé supplied his textual emendations and additions. A search of these manuscripts turns up concordances for both melodies in Clairambault's manuscript (n.a.fr. 1050), where the note shapes and spacing are strikingly similar to those of the suspicious melodies in f.fr. 846. Thibaut de Blason's song is given on f. 87ᵛ of n.a.fr. 1050, attributed by its medieval scribe to "Mesire Thiebaut de Blazon," with the same odd spelling as in Cangé's attribution in f.fr. 846 (Figure 4). A comparison of the melody given for the song by Thibaut de Navarre on f. 2ʳ of f.fr. 846 with the corresponding melody on f. 24ᵛ of Clairambault's manuscript strengthens the suspicion that Cangé copied the melody out of the latter (see Figures 5 and 6). First of all one notices the interlinear additions in f.fr. 846—"*plain*" over "*ploin*" on the first line, the expansion of the abbreviation for "*-con-*" (9) in the word "*esconmenier*" in the sixth line, the reading "*aiment*" for "*offrent*" in the seventh line—all taken from n.a.fr. 1050 (the variant "*aiment*" occurs uniquely in n.a.fr. 1050).

The placement and shapes of the neumes in the two readings are identical; notice especially the unusual rhomboid single notes in both melodies. Most of the note shapes in the melody on f. 2ʳ of f.fr. 846 (Figure 5), unlike the added melody on f. 25ᵛ (Figure 4), are plausible enough for a medieval hand, although the C-clefs have a somewhat mechanical squared-off appearance, unlike the more fluid rounded shape typical of thirteenth-century hands (compare the clefs of the last part of the melody just before this one in f.fr. 846, at the top of the left column).

All of the clefs in f.fr. 846 are on the second line from the top of each stave; in n.a.fr. 1050 the clef shifts in the middle of the fifth stave to the third line and remains there for one more stave. The corresponding place in f.fr. 846 (end of the fourth stave, over the syllable "*fa-*") includes the change of clef, but the shift is not continued on the following stave: the notes are placed at the same level as in n.a.fr. 1050, but they are now a third too low; the other extant versions of this melody (in f.fr. 844, f.fr. 1591, and Bibliothèque de l'Arsenal, Ms. 5198) agree at this spot with the reading in n.a.fr. 1050. The

13. Hans Tischler, ed., *Trouvère Lyrics with Melodies: Complete Comparative Edition*, Corpus mensurabilis musicae, 107 (American Institute of Musicology; Stuttgart: Hänssler-Verlag, 1997), vol. 8, no. 659 (RS 1152), and vol. 7, no. 545 (RS 1001); Hendrik van der Werf accepted the reading of Thibaut de Navarre's melody in *Trouvère-Melodien*, 2, Monumenta monodica medii aevi, 12 (Kassel: Bärenreiter, 1979), 146-50, 691-92.

Bibliothèque nationale de France, Ms. f.fr. 846, f. 25ᵛ

Cliché Bibliothèque nationale de France, Paris

two versions converge again on the third syllable of *"esconmenier"* (sixth stave of f.fr. 846, seventh stave of n.a.fr. 1050), just where n.a.fr. 1050 begins a new system and the clef is moved back to the second line. Clearly the notator of f.fr. 846 failed to notice that the clef change in the exemplar continued through one more stave; perhaps he drew all of the

Figure 5 Bibliothèque nationale de France, Ms. f.fr. 846, f. 2r

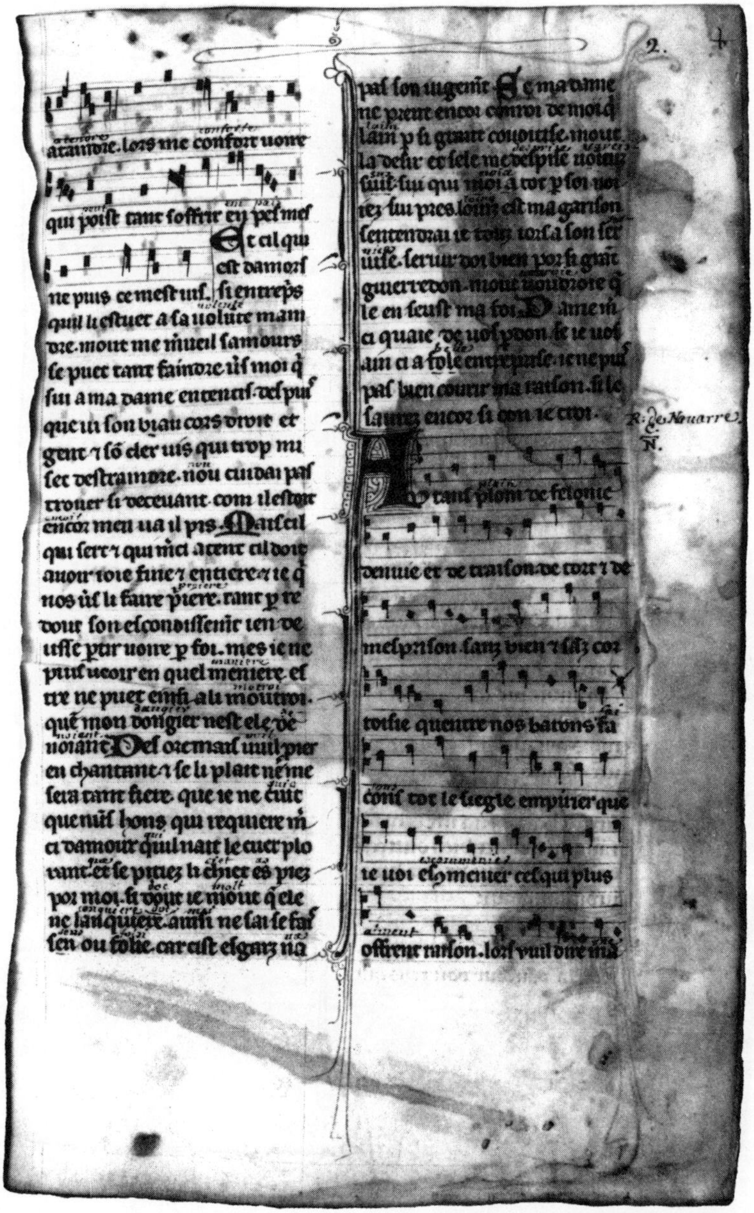

Cliché Bibliothèque nationale de France, Paris

clefs at once before entering notes. This error leaves no doubt that the notator of f.fr. 846 copied his melody from n.a.fr. 1050. The later notator may also have been responsible for the ink spilled on the end of the first system in n.a.fr. 1050 (Figure 6).

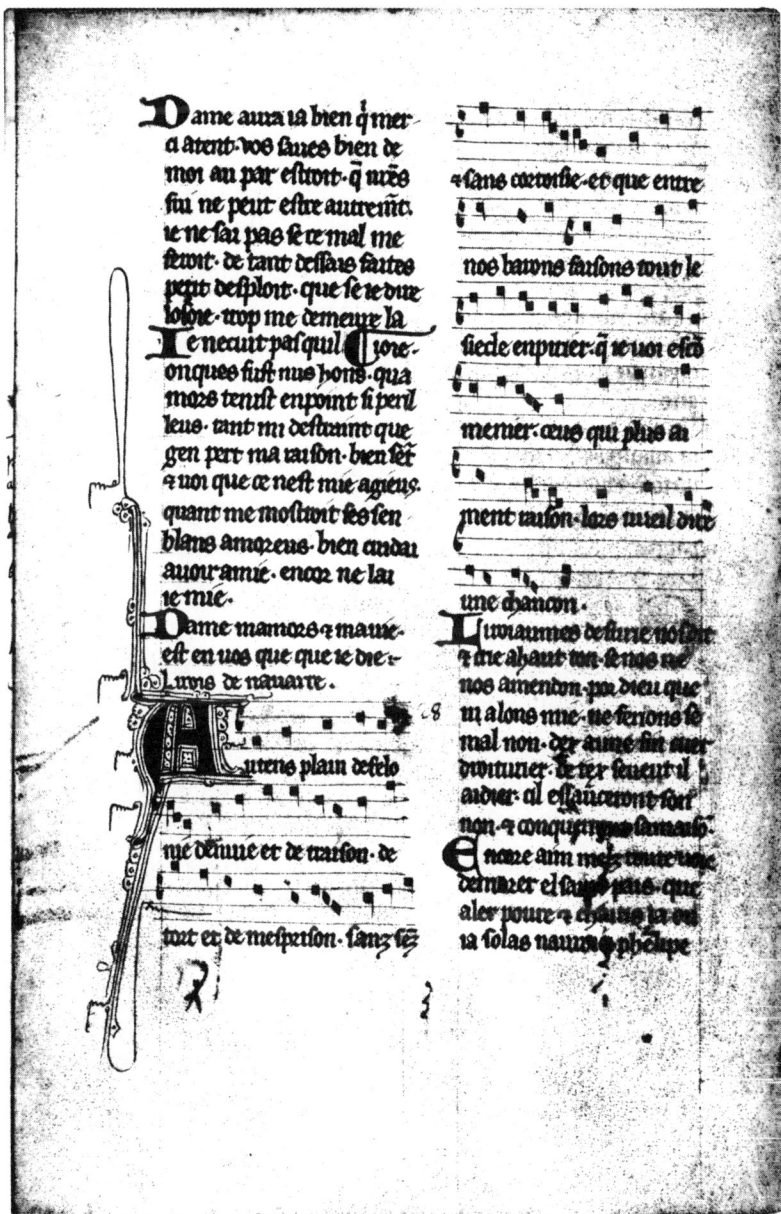

Cliché Bibliothèque nationale de France, Paris

But whether or not this person was Cangé is still not proven. If he did fill in the melody here, why did he not fill in melodies for the other fifteen songs left unnotated by the medieval scribe? Table 1 gives the incipits of these unnotated melodies in f.fr. 846 and the manuscripts in which their melodies are found. Remember that by Cangé's own account, he had access to f.fr. 844, f.fr. 1109, f.fr. 1591, f.fr. 12615, and n.a.fr. 1050, and sometime later, f.fr. 845 and f.fr. 847. As can be seen, eight of these songs are either *unica* in f.fr. 846 or have no music extant in sources that were available to Cangé. The fact that he did not copy melodies for the remaining seven can be explained in various ways. He lists RS 1463, 361, 523, and 1982 in the section of his index devoted to authors he could not identify, and he gives no marginal indication that he had located them in other manuscripts. Manuscripts f.fr. 845, f.fr. 847, f.fr. 1591, and n.a.fr. 1050 do not have incipit indexes, so Cangé would have to hunt through them leaf by leaf to find his concordances. Although f.fr. 844 does have a medieval index of incipits, it does not provide folio numbers, and since this manuscript was probably already in its mutilated and disarrayed state by the time Cangé consulted it, it would have been difficult to use and search. Furthermore, RS 361 in f.fr. 844 begins "*A la joie*" rather than "*De la joie*," further obscuring the concordance. RS 523 is in an anonymous section in f.fr. 1591, and although it is found in n.a.fr. 1050, Cangé does not cite that manuscript in the index or the margin. He indicates in the index that he had found RS 1757 in f.fr. 12615 ("N"), from which he took the attribution to Gace Brulé, but there is no melody there; in the margin next to the text he erroneously indicates n.a.fr. 1050 ("Cl") as having a concordance; there is a melody in f.fr. 844, but again Cangé gives no indication that he had located the song there. RS 1840 is attributed to Gautier d'Espinau in f.fr. 845 and f.fr. 847, but Cangé did not copy a melody from either of them, possibly because he did not own those manuscripts until later, and when he did acquire them he did not take time to copy from them into f.fr. 846; elsewhere he simply cites concordant readings but does not give variants from f.fr. 845 and f.fr. 847. RS 549 is in anonymous sections of f.fr. 845, f.fr. 847, and n.a.fr. 1050, so Cangé must have taken his attribution to Gace from f.fr. 844, but in this one case it is difficult to explain why he did not copy the melody. Perhaps he simply had lost interest in the music by the time he reached fol. 99.

One final source of evidence that points to Cangé's hand in f.fr. 846 requires us to trace the provenance of Clairambault's manuscript (n.a.fr. 1050), and in the process we catch a glimpse of the activities of a group of bibliophiles in early eighteenth-century France and of the ramifications that their actions had on the preservation of Old French songs. To track the whereabouts of n.a.fr. 1050 we must begin with François-Roger de Gaignières (1642-1715), a member of the court of Louis-Joseph de Lorraine, duc de Guise; he was appointed governor of Joinville in 1679, and he devoted his leisure hours to archeology, heraldry, genealogy, and history.[14] Much like Baudelot, Gaignières traveled throughout France hunting up documents and making copies of epitaphs, coats of arms, cartularies, and ecclesiastical doc-

14. See DELISLE, *Cabinet des manuscrits*, 1: 337-49; and entries in *Dictionnaire de biographie française*, 15 (1982): cols. 62-63, and *Dictionnaire des lettres françaises*, pp. 445-46.

| RS Linker | Folio | Incipit and composer | Concordances, with music* | Cangé notes |
|---|---|---|---|---|
| 1591 65-5 | 3ᵛ | Amours qui a son oes m'a pris (Gace Brulé) | *unicum* | index: anon., "non noté" margin: nothing |
| 294 240-57 | 15 | Baudoyn il sunt dui amant (Thibaut de Navarre) | 12615, 844 | index: Thibaut, "la note manque" margin: N, R |
| 1965 38-3 | 16ᵛ-17 | Bien cuidai vivre sans amours (Chastelain de Coucy) | none available to Cangé | index: anon. margin: nothing |
| 1463 65-13 | 27 | Chancon de plains et de sopirs (Gace Brulé) | 1591* | index: anon., "la note manque" margin: nothing |
| 1193A 65-21 | 27-27ᵛ | Contre le froit tans d'yver (Gace Brulé) | *unicum* | index: anon., "la note manque" margin: nothing |
| 1407 65-28 | 38ᵛ-39 | Des or me vuil ejoir (Gace Brulé) | 844 | index: anon., "la note manque" margin: nothing |
| 361 65-26 | 40-40ᵛ | De la joie que desir tant (Gace Brulé) | 844*, 847, 12615 | index: Gace, "la note manque" margin: N |
| 773 65-55 | 90 | Or ne puis je plus celer (Gace Brulé) | *unicum* | index: anon., "la note manque" margin: nothing |
| 477 65-57 | 98 | Pour faire l'autrui volonte (Gace Brulé) | *unicum* | index: anon., "la note manque" margin: nothing |
| 523 240-45 | 98ᵛ | Pour mal temps ne por gelee (Thibaut de Navarre) | 844*, 1591* 12615, 1050* | index: anon., "la note manque" margin: nothing |
| 549 65-59 | 99 | Pour verdure ne pour pree (Gace Brulé) | 844*, 845* 847*, 1050* | index: Gace, R margin: nothing |
| 1757 65-67 | 111 | Quant li temps renverdoie (Gace Brulé) | 844*, 12615 | index: Gace, N margin: Cl |
| 1982 38-17 | 112-112ᵛ | Quant voi venir le beau tens (Chastelain de Coucy) | 844*, 1591* 12615* | index: anon., "la note manque" margin: nothing |
| 524 265-1635 | 132-132ᵛ | Sor toutes riens sort amors honoree (anonymous) | *unicum* | index: anon. margin: nothing |
| 1840 77-21 | 136 | Tout autresi com l'aymanz (Gautier d'Espinau) | 845*, 847* | index: Gauthier d'Espinois margin: nothing |

uments. He eventually amassed an immense collection of documents and antiquities, for which he established a library and museum in the rue de Sèvres in Paris. Accompanying Gaignières in his travels and assisting with the copying was his *valet de chambre*, a paleographer named Barthélemy Remy. Remy made copies of several thirteenth-century manuscripts, including f.fr. 846, 12615, 20050, and n.a.fr. 1050, and his copies are found now in the Bibliothèque nationale de France, f.fr. 12610-12614. We will return to Remy.

In 1711 Gaignières, declining bids from such figures as the king of Prussia, and the duc d'Orléans, decided to cede his rich collection to Louis XIV in return for a lump sum plus an annuity. This arrangement turned out to be unfortunate for the hapless collector, whose dispossessed heirs attempted to contest the deal during the last four years of his life, while the king's agents acted to protect their sovereign's claim by barricading Gaignières in his hôtel behind iron bars and guarding its entrance with policemen.

Even more disastrous was the fact that Pierre de Clairambault (1651-1740), a native of Champagne, who, as previously noted, served Louis XIV as a genealogist and secretary,[15] was entrusted with the task of compiling an inventory of Gaignières' collection for the king, whose ministers were suspicious of Gaignières' honesty. This inventory of 1711 is extant (Bibliothèque nationale de France, Collection Clairambault, Ms. 1032, ff. 33rff.), as are a number of subsequent inventories created during a lengthy period of attempts to trace many of the volumes on the original list. But it is Clairambault rather than Gaignères who appears to have been duplicitous in the execution of his commission to inventory and manage the collection.

Two items in the 1711 inventory draw our attention: under the category of manuscripts of *"Belles lettres"* we find:[16]

997. Poesies d'anciens vers françois in 4° parchemin
998. Recueil de diverses poisies [sic] françoises, a la fin une mignature et des vers sur le songe de la Pucelle, papier et velin relié en veau vieux.

The parchment book of "old French poems" is probably n.a.fr. 1050, whose size (250 x 175 mm.) fits the description of in-quarto. The *"Songe de la Pucelle"* found at the end of the other collection is most likely a reference to a lengthy fifteenth-century allegorical poem about a girl's dream of a battle of words between Amour and Honte.[17] Thus the poetry in this *"recueil"* (no. 998) must date from at least the fifteenth century. More information about this collection emerges from a letter from marquis Colbert de Torcy dated 19 February 1715—a month before Gaignières' death—which requests of Clairambault that he *"examiner si les recueils des chansons se trouvent. On estime quel doit [être] envir[on] 20 vol."*[18] The 1711 inventory does not list twenty separate volumes of chansons, and so the "recueil" of no. 998 must mean literally a "collection," not a single codex. It would appear that among the

15. See entries in *Dictionnaire de biographie*, 8 (1959): cols. 1338-39, and in *Biographie universelle générale*, 10 (1855): cols. 633-734.

16. Bibliothèque nationale de France, Collection Clairambault, Ms. 1032, f. 434v. See also Ms. n.a.fr. 5737, f. 118r. Manuscript 1032 is an enormous collection of correspondence between Clairambault and various royal ministers, inventories, and other documents relating to the disposition of Gaignières' manuscripts and printed books. Other sources in the Bibliothèque nationale de France contain more such documents, including Mss. n.a.fr. 3106, 5737, 5738, 5739, 5740, and Coll. Clair., 1044.

17. Edited by Paul AEBISCHER, "Le Songe de la pucelle. Poème moral du xve siècle publié d'après le texte du manuscrit Supersaco 97 bis," *Vallesia* 16 (1961): 225-41.

18. Coll. Clair., 1032, p. 162. See DELISLE, *Cabinet des manuscrits*, 1: 352, 355.

many antiquities that he accumulated, Gaignières also collected songs both medieval and contemporary. If so, he was not alone. The Bibliothèque nationale de France possesses dozens of eighteenth-century manuscripts of songs of the sixteenth, seventeenth, and eighteenth centuries.

A few days after Gaignières' death Clairambault took possession of the collection and prepared a revised inventory. Along with the king's ministers, he proceeded to assess which items were interesting and valuable enough to be sent to the king's library and which should be disposed of otherwise. In December 1716 the designated items were delivered to the king, and ten weeks later the Council authorized a public sale of the remainder.[19] An inventory for this sale, dated 6 March 1717, lists the volumes of chansons among those that were supposed to have been deposited in the royal library in 1716.[20] But they and a number of other documents were never delivered, as is indicated by a flurry of correspondence and several inventories with marginal notations of "manquant" or "ils ne se trouvent en leurs places" next to the entries for numbers 997 and 998 and many other manuscripts. These suggest that they and perhaps as many as a hundred manuscripts, especially those relating to his avid interest in genealogy, ended up in Clairambault's hands.[21]

Clairambault prepared a catalogue of his own library in 1727 in which he included an entry for a "*chansonnier*" comprised of several volumes, beginning with "*Vol. I^er, escrit sur velin, couvert de velin, in 4°. Chansons de Thibaut, roi de Navarre, comte de Champagne, et par d'autres, faites du temps du roy saint Louis, notées en plain chant*";[22] the remaining volumes were the rest of the "recueil" listed in the Gaignières inventories. This description of "Volume I" closely matches the words on the title page of n.a.fr. 1050, which is in Clairambault's hand:

Recueil
de Chansons de Thibaut Roy de Navarre
Comte de Champagne,
& autres faites du temps de St. Louis
Roy de France,
notées.
Volume
I^er.

---

19. The sale garnered only a fraction of the sum that the collection was probably worth. See Simone BALAYÉ, *La Bibliothèque Nationale des origines à 1800* (Geneva: Librairie Droz, 1988), 132-34. Some of Gaignières' collection of 27,000 portraits, many of them of significant value, along with the porcelains, coins, funerary monuments, maps, and printed books, eventually wound up variously in the king's collections. Some 2407 manuscripts originally in Gaignières' library are now in the Bibliothèque nationale de France.

20. Ms. n.a.fr. 5738, p. 88: "Extrait de l'Inventaire du Cabinet de M. de Gaignieres donné au Roi par acte du fevrier 1711 contenant ce qui a été remis a la Bibliotèque [sic] de sa Majesté en Éxécution de l'Arrest du Conseil d'Etat du 6 mars 1717." See DELISLE, *Cabinet des manuscrits*, I: 353-55.

21. See DELISLE, *Cabinet des manuscrits*, I: 354-55.

22. Coll. Clair., 1351, 603-11. See Paul MEYER, "Henri d'Andeli et le Chancelier Philippe," *Romania* I (1872): 201; Philippe LAUER, *Bibliothèque nationale, Département des manuscrits, Catalogue des manuscrits de la Collection Clairambault*, 3, (Paris: Librairie Ernest Leroux, 1932), viii, xiii-xxi.

The remains of an older binding, which are still visible under the current binding, read "Chansons du roy Thibaut. Vol$^e$ $i^{er}$ du Chansonnier." The identification of this codex as "Volume I" is baffling without the knowledge that it was the first of many volumes of chansons—from medieval to modern—in Clairambault's (and earlier, Gaignières') library.[23] The material in these books formed the basis of a collection of seventeenth- and eighteenth-century chansons that Clairambault undertook in the 1730s at the behest of the secretary of state, Jean-Frédéric Phélippeaux, comte de Maurepas.[24] Clairambault's author index of n.a.fr. 1050 (ff. 2$^r$-3$^v$) has the heading "Table des Chansons, vaudevilles, et vers, Vol$^e$ $i^{er}$," which resembles the wording in the heading of the eighteenth-century Chansonnier de Maurepas (f.fr. 12616): "Recueil de chansons, vaudevilles, sonnets, épigrammes, épitaphes et autres vers satiriques et historiques, avec des remarques curieuses." The collection continues after volume I with songs of the year 1389—picking up almost where the medieval chansonnier leaves off.

During the period from 1715 (when n.a.fr. 1050 was delivered to Clairambault) to 1724 (after which Cangé consulted n.a.fr. 1050 in "completing" f.fr. 846), several *savants* took an active interest in these and other collections of medieval songs. The leaves of the extant manuscripts reveal a complicated web of collaboration, lending, borrowing, and copying involving besides Clairambault and Cangé, the duc de Noailles (f.fr. 12615), Baudelot (who presumably retained f.fr. 846 until his death in 1722), and Henri-Charles du Cambout, bishop of Metz and grandson of the chancelier Pierre Séguier (f.fr. 20050), as well as Barthélemy Remy, the shadowy paid scribe (there are no entries for him in any of the standard biographical dictionaries of France) who worked for Gaignières, the marquis de Torcy, Clairambault, and others.

Remy, as mentioned above, made copies of f.fr. 846, f.fr. 12615, f.fr. 20050, and n.a.fr. 1050; his copies are deposited in the Bibliothèque nationale de France, f.fr. 12610-12613. He refers to these and other manuscripts as those of Baudelot, Noailles, Séguier, and Clairambault, respectively. Thus he must have undertaken this work sometime after

---

23. Clairambault died in 1740, and his collection of manuscripts and printed books went to his nephew Nicolas-Pascal, who ceded them to the Ordre du Saint-Esprit in 1753. From there the volumes went to the convent of the Grands-Augustins in 1772, whose collections were open to the public; Jean-Benjamin de La Borde consulted n.a.fr. 1050 there in preparing his *Essai sur la musique ancienne et moderne*, 4 vols. (Paris: P.-D. Pierres, 1780). From thence the manuscripts went to the Bibliothèque nationale in 1792. During the Revolution many documents pertaining to genealogies of the French nobility were ordered burned, and n.a.fr. 1050 was believed lost until 1876 when it was discovered

safe and sound in the Bibliothèque nationale. See Gaston RAYNAUD, "Le Chansonnier Clairambault de la Bibliothèque nationale," *Bibliothèque de l'École des Chartes* 40 (1879): 48-67; and LAUER, *Collection Clairambault*, 3: IX-XI.

24. The so-called Chansonnier de Clairambault and Chansonnier de Maurepas were edited from the manuscripts (now fr. 12686-12743 and fr. 12616-12659 respectively) by Émile RAUNIÉ, *Recueil Clairambault-Maurepas, Chansonnier historique du XVIII$^e$ siècle* (Paris: A. Quantin, 1882); see LAUER, *Collection Clairambault*, 3: XIX-XX; and DELISLE, *Cabinet des manuscrits*, 1: 352, 355.

1715, when n.a.fr. 1050 wound up in the hands of Clairambault, but before 1722, when Baudelot died; in fact, his copy of the manuscript of "Séguier" (f.fr. 20050) suggests that he had completed the copying by 1720, since in that year Coislin, the bishop of Metz who owned f.fr. 20050 at that time, had placed his library in the care of the abbey of St. Germain-des-Prés.[25]

The leaves of Remy's copy of Baudelot's manuscript (f.fr. 12610) provide the definitive proof that it was Cangé who added the two melodies on ff. 2$^r$ and 25$^v$ of f.fr. 846 discussed above. Remy began his copy with the intention of including music with the texts, and he did so for the first three songs, found on f. 1$^{r-v}$ of f.fr. 846 (pp. 1-5 of his copy). When he came to the next song, *Au tans ploin de felonie*, he left the staves empty—because they were empty in the medieval exemplar. He wrote the music above the texts of the next four songs (ff. 2$^v$-4$^r$, pp. 9-18 of his copy), but he gave up the effort after this, drawing in no staves after p. 18 of his copy. Although we cannot know for certain whether the staves on f. 25$^v$ were still empty when Remy reached that leaf, there can be little doubt that they were. When Cangé obtained fr. 846 in 1724, the staves were still empty, waiting for him to fill them in.

The criss-crossing of books, bookowners, and scribes becomes dizzying: f.fr. 846 was copiously annotated by its second known modern owner, Cangé, who copied freely from f.fr. 844, f.fr. 12615, and n.a.fr. 1050, and made comparisons with f.fr. 1109, f.fr. 1591, f.fr. 845, and f.fr. 847 in constructing the indexes, adding songs, stanzas, and verses, and providing comments in the text. The previous owner of f.fr. 846, Baudelot, used his manuscript as an exemplar for songs that he added to Clairambault's manuscript, n.a.fr. 1050 (ff. 277$^r$-280$^r$). Baudelot also added to n.a.fr. 1050 (ff. 4$^r$-7$^v$) an author index collated with Fauchet, his manuscript (f.fr. 846), and f.fr. 12615. He copied a section of songs from f.fr. 845 (ff. 91$^v$-109$^v$)—which evidently was owned at that time by the abbé Claude Sallier—onto a paper gathering added in the middle of n.a.fr. 1050 (ff. 136$^r$-154$^v$). The connection between f.fr. 845 and n.a.fr. 1050 becomes more curious, in that the latter includes a short song index matching the contents of f.fr. 845, in an unidentified hand, with the heading "*A Mad$^e$. Varennes-Gode*"—evidently an owner of f.fr. 845 before it was acquired by Sallier. How this mix-up occurred has always been a mystery, but perhaps it happened in conjunction with Baudelot's copying from one manuscript into the other. Finally we have Remy's copies of f.fr. 846, f.fr. 12615, n.a.fr. 1050, and f.fr. 20050 (f.fr. 12610-12613), which Baudelot cross-referenced in a style quite similar to the system that Cangé later used in f.fr. 846—a variant followed by a manuscript siglum.

25. Roger BERGER, in *Littérature et société arrageoises au XIII$^e$ siècle: Les chansons et dits artésiens* (Arras: Commission Départementale des Monuments Historiques du Pas-de-Calais, 1981), states that the earliest verifiable date that fr. 12615 was in Noailles' possession is 1742; but its citation in these manuscripts confirm that Noailles had obtained it by 1720, and probably earlier.

The discovery of two spurious readings of trouvère melodies, though irrelevant to the history of trouvère song and probably of little note in the history of the intellectual climate of the *Ancien Régime*, is important at least to a historiography of medieval manuscripts. Its obvious lesson is that we should not trust our eyes when we look at a manuscript—all might not be as it seems. Even the most fastidious editor might err; the need for a revision of the editions of these two melodies, though real, is barely consequential, but careful scrutiny of other medieval manuscripts might necessitate more significant correctives.

A much larger story remains to be told. We still do not know how *savants* like Baudelot, the duc de Noailles, Gaignières, Pierre Séguier, Claude Fauchet, Madame Varennes-Gode, and others came upon the manuscripts which captured their imaginations, let alone where the volumes were hidden for 400 years or more after they had been copied. Nearly every extant chansonnier was annotated in some way by its owner or owners, if not in the great detail with which Cangé wrote in f.fr. 846, at least with foliations or paginations of the leaves, numerations of songs, and *manchettes* that point to songs for reasons that are lost to us. It is ironic that the eighteenth-century bibliophiles of France, whose appreciation for their literary heritage helped to establish the discipline of modern philology, treated the very manuscripts that preserve that heritage in a manner that has in some ways obscured it.[26]

26. I thank François Avril of the Department of Manuscripts of the Bibliothèque nationale de France for his kindness in allowing me to examine several Old French manuscripts for this study.

Barbara Haggh

# Plays and Music in Late Medieval Processions in the Low Countries: The Two "Joys of Mary" from Brussels

E VEN THOUGH MEDIEVAL PROCESSIONS are still very much a part of modern life in Belgium, research is only beginning to address the music of the plays that such processions once included.[1] The lack of play manuscripts with music has certainly hindered research as has the diversity and dispersion of other sources: a single procession could generate manuscripts of chant, polyphony, sacred and secular monophony, instrumental music, play libretti, and individual poems, as well as documentation in chronicles, city and church accounts, guild archives, and even paintings.[2] The vast secondary literature only touches on music in passing, for most often it is based on only one kind of source—accounts or an individual manuscript, for example—or it addresses topics related to plays, such as rhetoricians (*rederijkers*) or wind bands, but not the plays themselves.[3]

1. The most useful study remains Howard Mayer BROWN, *Music in the French Secular Theatre, 1400-1550* (Cambridge, MA: Harvard University Press, 1963), since certain features of French theatre are found in the Low Countries; also see Charles MAZOUER, *Le théâtre français du moyen âge* (Paris: Sedes, 1998). Dutch and French secular plays are compared in Wim HÜSKEN, *Noyt meerder vrucht: Compositie en structuur van het komische toneel in de Nederlanden voor de Renaissance*, Deventer Studiën, 3 (Deventer: Sub Rosa, 1987), beginning p. 20. On music for Dutch plays, see the brief but interesting discussion in Rob C. WEGMAN, *Born for the Muses* (Oxford: Clarendon Press, 1994), 156-57; Reinhard STROHM, *Music in Late Medieval Bruges* (Oxford: Clarendon Press, 1985), 68-70, 106-108 and *passim*, and idem, *The Rise of European Music* (Cambridge: Cambridge University Press, 1993), 303-304, 344, 384-86; Bart RAMAKERS, *Spelen en figuren. Toneelkunst en processiecultuur in Oudenaarde tussen middeleeuwen en moderne tijd* (Amsterdam: Amsterdam Univ. Press, 1996); and *Een theatergeschiedenis der Nederlanden. Tien eeuwen drama en theater in Nederland en Vlaanderen*, ed. Robert ERENSTEIN (Amsterdam, 1996), 42-49, 56-63, 70-78.

2. For example, many manuscripts with *rederijker* lyrics

survive, such as Brussels, Bibliothèque Royale, Ms. II 270 (*c.*1500), but it is not known whether the poems were sung during plays. On this problem, see Margaret RIERINK, "De Missing Link: Het Gruuthuseliedboek als Schakel tussen het hoofse Lied en Rederijkerskunst," *Op belofte van profijt. Stadsliteratuur en burgermoraal in de Nederlandse letterkunde van de middeleeuwen*, ed. Herman PLEIJ et al. (Amsterdam: Prometheus, 1991), 135-50.

3. Most helpful were several archival studies on town festivities: Eugeen van AUTENBOER, *Volksfeesten en rederijkers te Mechelen (1400-1600)* (Ghent, 1962); Léon de BURBURE, *De Antwerpsche ommegangen in de XIVᵉ en XVᵉ eeuw* (Antwerp: P. Kockx, 1878); Herman PLEIJ, "Volksfeest en toneel in de middeleeuwen," *De Revisor* 3 (1976): 52-63, and 4 (1977): 34-41; Frans DE POTTER, *Schets eener geschiedenis van de gemeentefeesten in Vlaanderen* (Ghent, 1870), especially chap. 1 on processions; Edmond VAN DER STRAETEN, *Le théâtre villageois en Flandre*, 2 vols., 2d. ed. (Brussels: F. Claassens, 1881); and on *rederijkers*: Dirk COIGNEAU, "Rederijkers-literatuur," *Historische letterkunde, Facetten van vakbeoefening*, Marijke SPIES ed. (Groningen, 1984), 35-37; Prudens VAN DUYSE, *De Rederijkerskamers in Nederland. Hun invloed op letterkundig, politiek en zedelijk gebied*, 2 vols. (Ghent, 1900-1902);

That such music is worthy of and indeed urgently in need of further investigation is apparent from two mid fifteenth-century Middle Dutch plays from Brussels, the *First* and *Seventh Joy of the Virgin Mary*, both performed for a century as part of the city's most magnificent procession, the *Ommegang*.[4] Comparison of these plays, their music, and their role in the procession with those of other similar events held in the Low Countries reveals widespread music-making articulating the telling of sacred stories outside of the church[5].

On 20 February 1448 the magistrates of Brussels published a new ordinance on the *Ommegang*.[6] (This procession commemorated the arrival in Brussels of the statue of *Onze Lieve Vrouw op 't stocxken*, Our Lady on the Little Branch, the principal icon of the parish church of Our Lady of the Sand, on the Sunday before Pentecost in 1348, as well as that church's Dedication, celebrated on that day.)[7] The new ordinance was intended primarily to fix in writing the respective financial contributions due from town and church, but also to introduce new features to the procession to increase its magnificence and attract a more cultured audience. One article to that purpose bears special mention: henceforth a play would be staged outdoors at 2 PM in the afternoon, a dramatic representation of one of the Joys of the Virgin Mary. A different Joy would be performed every year, with the cycle repeating every seventh year. From 1448 until 1566 the cycle was performed without documentable interruptions.[8]

Antonin VAN ELSLANDER, *Letterkundig leven in de Bourgondische tijd: de rederijkers; lijst van Nederlandse rederijker-skamers uit de XV<sup>e</sup> en XVI<sup>e</sup> eeuw*, Rederijkerstudiën, 5 (Ghent, 1969); Jacobus Johannes MAK, *De rederijkers* (Amsterdam: P. N. van Kampen, 1944); idem, "Het toneel van de rederijkers in de bloeitijd," *Cultureel jaarboek van de Provincie Oost-Vlaanderen* (1948), 124 ff.; J.B. VAN DER STRAELEN, *Geschiedenis der Antwerpsche rederykkamers* (Antwerp, 1863). On windbands, see Keith POLK's most recent "Minstrels and Music in the Low Countries in the Fifteenth Century," *Musicology and Archival Research*, ed. Barbara HAGGH, Frank DAELEMANS, and André VANRIE (Brussels: Koninklijke Bibliotheek, 1994), 392-440.

4. On music during the *Ommegang* and other processions in Brussels, see Barbara HAGGH, *Music, Liturgy, and Ceremony in Brussels, 1350-1500* (Ph.D. diss., University of Illinois at Urbana-Champaign, 1988), 422-46, especially 434-42. On vernacular mystery plays replacing sung Latin drama, see Konrad SCHOELL, "Les origines et les intentions du théâtre profane du XV<sup>e</sup> siècle en France et en Allemagne," *Rappresentazioni archaiche della tradizione popolare* (Viterbo, 1982), 485-502.

5. On plays out of doors, see, for example, Karl YOUNG, *The Drama of the Medieval Church*, 2 (Oxford: Clarendon Press, 1933), 424-25, and DE POTTER, *Schets*, 36,

who cites a charter dated 1402 of the French king, Charles VI, indicating that a Confraternity of the Passion was paid for performing a play out of doors.

6. The ordinance of 1448 is in a contemporary cartulary, Brussels, Archives de la Ville, Ms. VIII, f. 98<sup>v</sup>-99<sup>r</sup>; cf. Pierre COCKSHAW et al., *Charles le Téméraire: Exposition organisée à l'occasion du cinquième centenaire de sa mort* (Brussels: Bibliothèque royale, 1977), 106-107.

7. Beatrice Soetkens brought the icon to Brussels from Antwerp after she saw the Virgin Mary in a vision; it was destroyed by iconoclasts in 1580. The church of Our Lady of the Sand was founded in 1304 as the chapel of the guild of crossbowmen. Both churchmasters of Our Lady of the Sand were elected by the guild on the day of the *Ommegang*. The *Ommegang* was held yearly, concurrent with the Brussels fair, but was eclipsed after 1530 by a procession asking for deliverance from the plague (*sudor anglicus*) of 1529. On the procession, see Robert STEIN, "Cultuur en politiek in Brussel in de vijftiende eeuw. Wat beoogde het Brusselse stadsbestuur bij de annexatie van de plaatselijke Ommegang?" *Op belofte van profijt*, 228-43.

8. See *Die eerste bliscap van Maria*, Jacobus Johannes MAK ed. (Antwerp, 1949), XII; *Die eerste bliscap van Maria en die sevenste bliscap van onser vrouwen*, Willem Hendrik BEUKEN ed. (Culemborg: Willink, 1973; Zwolle, 1978), 50; and

Plays like the *Joys of Mary* were introduced to other town processions in increasing numbers throughout the Low Countries in the fifteenth century.[9] In the region of Brussels alone, every year, one procession of the collegiate church of St.-Peter in Anderlecht and probably three of the parish church of St.-John the Baptist in Molenbeek included outdoor plays.[10] In Mechelen near Brussels, the procession in honor of the town's patron saint, Rombaut, included plays of the Virgin Mary and of St. Rombaut on two consecutive days, and the Corpus Christi procession also included plays.[11] Other town *Ommegangen* with documented play performances were those in Aalst (1488),[12] Antwerp (1399, 1441),[13] Furnes (1516),[14] Kortrijk (1417, 1424),[15] Leuven (several),[16] Nieuwpoort (1493/4),[17] Oudenaarde (1412-14),[18] and Sluis (1442), and these are only the tip of the undocumented iceberg.[19] Processions with plays also increased the ceremony of Joyous Entries, such as, in Brussels, those of Mary of Burgundy on 4 June 1477,[20] Maximilian

Willem KUIPER and Robert RESOORT, *Maria op de markt. Middeleeuws toneel in Brussel* (Amsterdam: Querido, 1995), 128. On Franchoys van Ballaer's omissions at the 1559 performance of the *Seventh Joy*, motivated by religious tension and including some complete rondeaux, see BEUKEN, *Die eerste bliscap*, 21-22, who also discusses modern stagings of the plays on 50-51.

9. Marian plays were performed at *ommegangen* in Antwerp and Mechelen. On Marian themes in *rederijker* literature, see Hubertus AHSMANN, *Le culte de la sainte vierge et la littérature française profane du moyen âge* (Utrecht: Dekker, 1930); Antonin VAN ELSLANDER, "De Mariavereering bij de Rederijkers", *Jaarboek 'De Fonteyne'* 3 (1945), 57-74; and E.H.F. De RIDDER, "De Devotie tot O.L. Vrouw van VII Weeën, haar Ontstaan", *Handelingen van het Vlaamsch Maria-Congres te Brussel, 8-11 September 1921* (Brussels, 1922), chap. 2.

10. Minstrels played during the St. Guido procession (12 September) in Anderlecht, which included an unnamed mystery play at first and a play of St. Guido by 1491. Beginning in 1455 accounts of the parish church of St.-John the Baptist in Molenbeek list payments to persons performing plays in the church courtyard three times yearly; the three most important processions of this church were those on the festivals of the Nativity of St. John the Baptist, Corpus Christi, and the Visitation. See HAGGH, *Music*, 443-45.

11. The plays performed in Mechelen were numerous and are richly documented. They included a Magi play with camels and elephants during the procession after Easter for St. Rombaut in 1436, later Marian plays, and, at different times, plays of St. Rombaut, Mary Magdalene, the Three Marys, the Seven Sorrows of the Virgin, and the Passion. On the Mechelen plays and processions, see AUTENBOER, *Volksfeesten*.

12. See DE POTTER, *Schets*, 76, on a play performed by the *rederijkers* of Ghent in 1488.

13. This Marian *Ommegang* was held first on 17 August 1399, with *rederijkers* staging a Marian play on the market square. In 1441 the best *spel vande besniedenesse* (Circumcision) received a prize. See De BURBURE, *De Antwerpsche ommegangen*.

14. DE POTTER, *Schets*, 58-59. A play of St. Godelieve was performed, which included the *stadstrompetter* Adrianus Coels and his *gezellen* (pipers).

15. DE POTTER, *Schets*, 38: in 1417 a play of the King of the Moors, and in 1424 and later a Three Kings play, all during processions. In the afternoon on the feast of Corpus Christi in 1424 the *ghezellen* from Overbeke performed a play on the marketplace.

16. See G. VERLINDEN, *Ommegang en toneel te Leuven in de late middeleeuwen* (licence, Katholieke Universiteit Leuven, 1982).

17. DE POTTER, *Schets*, 113-14. In 1493/4 the guild of St. Barbara of Furnes performed *een spel van sinne*.

18. Ibid., 37. In 1412 and 1414 mystery plays were performed out of doors; in 1432 wagon plays. In 1413 six troupes of *rederijkers* performed a Corpus Christi play. The oldest play for a procession in Oudenaarde was *Het Paradijs (de val des Menschen)* (Paradise, the Fall of Mankind). See the study by RAMAKERS, *Spelen en figuren*.

19. RAMAKERS, 113, notes that *vredefeesten* (festivals of peace) often included processions with mystery plays performed by *rederijkers*. A vast literature on local *ommegangen* can also be found in local historical journals.

20. The 1476/7 accounts of the Fabric of the collegiate church of St.-Gudula in Brussels, Algemeen Rijksarchief, Archief Sint-Goedele, 1390, f. 248ᵛ, record a payment *totten coste vanden speele in dinnecompst van Maria gened. Joffre*. See HAGGH, *Music*, 451.

in early June 1486,[21] and Philip the Fair and Juana of Aragon on 9 January 1497,[22] to name but a few.[23] Finally, some exceptional plays on similar themes were performed without the processions but in the same town square location, such as the play of the Seven Sorrows of the Virgin, performed twice for Philip the Fair on 25 March 1493 in Mechelen, and a passion play in eight episodes performed from 5 to 12 July 1501 in Mons.[24]

Yet few manuscripts survive in proportion to the many plays that are documented, even fewer can be attributed to an author or traced to a locale, and most date from the sixteenth century.[25] For these reasons, two manuscripts from Brussels with the plays of the *First* and *Seventh Joy of the Virgin* are of uncommon interest, Brussels, Royal Library, Mss. IV 192 and II 478.[26] Probably dating from around 1455 according to Beuken, and certainly from 1448 or later, they were used as director's manuals in the sixteenth century, when marginalia were added assigning actors to parts and giving brief instructions. The plays have fascinated historians and literary scholars for more than a century, and debates still surround their authors and literary context, but no study has given detailed consideration to what is surely their most interesting and elusive feature—the indications they give (and suggest) for numerous musical interpolations, both vocal and instrumental.[27]

21. HAGGH, *Music*, 452 and cf. 450-53. Maximilian's Entry included a play and *personnagie* and playing by Cole de pypere and Adaem de sot *stadpipers*. A trumpeter announced the procession and a shawmist played from atop the spire of the town hall. The choirboys of the church of St.-Gudula were paid for the Entry.

22. The chambers of rhetoric of Brussels devised pageants to welcome them. See HAGGH, 454, and Jean MOLINET, *Chroniques*, Georges DOUTREPONT and Omer JODOGNE eds., 3 vols (Brussels: Palais des Académies, 1935-37), chap. 266.

23. On Entries, also see H. JOLY, "Plechtige intochten in de steden van de zuidelijke nederlanden tijdens de overgang van middeleeuwen naar nieuwe tijd: communicatie, propaganda, spektakel," *Tijdschrift voor geschiedenis* 97 (1984): 341-61.

24. Only a summary description of Henri Maes' Seven Sorrows play survives. See AUTENBOER, *Volksfeesten*, 151-52. The Mons play is edited by Gustave COHEN as *Le Mystère de la Passion joué à Mons en Juillet 1501. Livre des Prologues. Matinée III*ᵉ (Gembloux, 1957).

25. On plays, see H. VAN DIJK et al., "A Survey of Dutch Drama before the Renaissance," *Dutch Crossing* 22 (1984): 97-131; sources for French plays are listed in BROWN, *Music*, 13-20. Editions and lists of dramas include: *Drie schandaleuse spelen (Brussel 1559)*, W. VAN EEGHEM ed. (Antwerp, 1937); Else ELLERBROEK-FORTUIN, *Amsterdamse rederijkersspelen in de zestiende eeuw* (Groningen: Wolters, 1937); M.C.A. VAN DER HEIJDEN, *Hoort wat men u spelen zal: Toneelstukken uit de middel-*

eeuwen (Utrecht, 1968); Willem HUMMELEN, *Repertorium van het rederijkersdrama 1500-ca. 1620* (Assen: Van Gorcum, 1968); Nicolaas VAN DER LAAN, *Noordnederlandse rederijkers-spelen* (Amsterdam: Elsevier, 1941); idem, "Rederijkers- spelen in de bibliotheek van het Leidsche gemeentearchief," *Tijdschrift voor nederlandsche taalen en letterkunde*, 49 (1930), 127-55; idem, *Rederijkersspelen naar een handschrift ter bibliotheek van het Leidsche gemeentearchief* (The Hague: Nijhoff, 1932).

26. None of the "Joys" were ever printed as far as we know. Modern editions are: *Die eerste bliscap*, BEUKEN ed. (the best); *Die eerste bliscap van Maria*, Willem Lodewijk DE VREESE ed. (The Hague, 1931); *Die eerste bliscap*, MAK ed.; *Die eerste bliscap van Marie: vijftiend'eeuwsch mysteriespel*, Willebrord SMULDERS ed. (Nijmegen, 1932); *Die eerste bliscap van Maria: Mysteriespel van het jaar 1444*, J.F. WILLEMS ed. (Hulst, 1976); *De sevenste bliscap van Maria*, Karl STALLAERT ed. (Gent, 1887); also among *De seven bliscapen*, 2 vols., W. VAN EEGHEM ed. (Brussels, 1963); and *Vijf geestelijke toneelspelen*, Hubert ENDEPOLS ed. (Amsterdam, 1940).

27. On the date and authorship of the plays, see, most recently, Robert STEIN, "Nogmaals de datering van de Bliscapen van Maria," *Spiegel der letteren* 33 (1991): 73-78; also BEUKEN, *Die eerste Bliscap van Maria en die sevenste Bliscap van Onser Vrouwen*, 2d ed. (Zwolle, 1978), 12-15 on dates, 48-51 on authorship, favoring an anonymous author, and 26-28 on music. Candidates proposed as authors are Jan Smeken, Colijn Cailleau (city poet from 1474-85) and Jan Amoers (a Benedictine monk). The earliest evidence of an *Ommegang* play is a payment of 1413 to *"den gesellen die*

The *First* and *Seventh Joy of the Virgin Mary* are mystery plays with some allegorical characters—devils, emotions, and virtues—which lend color to the events from Mary's life that are portrayed.[28] The *First Joy* is the more moving play and develops characters and situations with greater skill. The *Seventh Joy* ends the cycle and is appropriately spectacular and entertaining, treating its subject matter in a lighter tone. The *First Joy* begins in Paradise with the Fall of Man and leads to Mary's happiness at being chosen above all women to save mankind by bearing the Saviour. The *Seventh Joy* reinacts Mary's Assumption, God's reward for the successful apostolate.

The nearly identical prologues of the two plays include prayers for the dukes of Burgundy and Brabant and their families, who were present for some of the performances, as well as for townspeople from all walks of life: lay and clergy, rich and poor.[29] By the mid fifteenth century, the local populace was educated if not literate and had at least a rudimentary understanding of music. Public education had been available to most boys and girls in Brussels since 1320, when Duke John III of Brabant ratified an ordinance on public education. That it included provisions for increasing the number of schools to match population growth implies mandatory attendance even though this is not stated explicitly. Item four in the 1320 ordinance states that boys and girls were to be taught grammar, music, and morals, but that girls could not be instructed in Latin.[30] (Both Marian plays are in Dutch.)

The two play manuscripts suggest at first glance that the role of music was peripheral. The dialogue is unbroken except for the prologue and epilogue, with seven notices for *sanc of spel* during interludes in the *First Joy* and none in the *Seventh* (see Appendix I). (The town wind band played from the spire of the town hall, as well as on the platform serving as the stage, constructed at the town's expense.)[31] On the surface the plays seem entirely

speelden te Brussel voir minen voirs. heeren, doe men de processie aldaer dede" (STEIN, "Cultuur," 237). From 1485 to 1507 the *Joys of Mary* were performed exclusively by the crossbowmen.

28. Endepols interprets the *Seventh Joy* as a miracle play. See BEUKEN, *Die eerste bliscap*, 39.

29. The presence of the dukes was desired as part of the political agenda of the event, whose procession included a living geneology of past dukes of Brabant. See Herman PLEIJ, "Geladen vermaak: Rederijkerstoneel als politiek instrument van een élite-cultuur," *Jaarboek 'De Fonteine'* 25 (1975): 75-103. Rulers present in Brussels for the *Ommegang* included King Louis XI (for whom the 1456 procession was moved), Margaret of Austria, and, in 1510, Charles, later Emperor Charles V, with the dukes of Saxony, Milan and the Margrave of Brandenburg. The prologues are compared in BEUKEN, *Die eerste bliscap*, 15-16.

30. The ordinance and education in Brussels are dis-

cussed in HAGGH, *Music*, 149-54.

31. See Jesus Francesc MASSIP, "The Staging of the Assumption in Europe," *Iconographic and Comparative Studies in Medieval Drama*, ed. C. DAVIDSON and J. H. STROUPE, Comparative Drama, 25 (Kalamazoo, 1991), 17-28, especially 20-21 on the report of a Spanish chronicler, who saw the fourth play of the set in Brussels in 1549, observing that the market place was "enclosed by many platforms richly embellished" and that the drama was played "on a platform built in the manner of a coliseum" in front of the splendid Gothic town hall from which the more important authorities and their retinue watched. Massip cites Juan Christóbal CALVETE DE ESTRELLA, *El felicíssimo viaje del muy alto y muy poderoso Príncipe Don Phelipe* (Antwerp, 1552), f. 74r-78r [f. 75r-76v do not exist]. I thank Mr. Massip for bringing his study to my attention. On the *alta cappella*, see the discussion below.

representative of the new vernacular religious play devoid of all but a few musical interludes and unworthy of serious musicological interest. Such impressions explain why the history of music in liturgical drama only gives token coverage to the fifteenth century.

The play may well have included vocal as well as instrumental music, however, since poems are interpolated throughout both plays.[32] The prologue of the first play embeds a one-stanza virelai, *Sijt willecome, edele en gemeyne* (Be welcome, nobility and commoners), a four-line poem, ABCA. That the virelai was sung even though it bears no such rubric seems possible, since it is set off from the preceding text by a colon and follows a change in the object of address from Mary to the audience. Moreover, the imperative acclamation, "Be welcome," joins this song to several poems in rondeau form beginning with similar acclamations that are interspersed throughout the two plays.[33] (Appendix I summarizes the content and structure of the plays and gives full texts and English translations of the virelai, rondeaux, and indications for interludes. Appendix II represents the poetic structure of the two plays in a table.)

The presence of poetic texts in song forms within longer poems has a long and much discussed history.[34] In relation to fifteenth-century French plays, of which none survive with musical notation, Howard Brown has urged caution in interpreting the evidence given by song texts, and Dirk Coigneau has recently argued that the poetic variety they introduced served rhetorical requirements well enough without song.[35] Yet even in the absence of rubrics indicating how the rondeaux of the two *Joys* were to be performed, their content, poetic context, placement, and function within the play strongly suggest that they would have been more effective if sung, as do historical precedents with music, such as the fourteenth-century *Miracles de Nostre Dame*, not to mention the similarity of the genre to the *historiae* of Matins with their interpolated responsories. The lack of surviving music is also not an argument against it, since surprisingly little survives from Brussels, even though well-known composers and singers worked there.[36]

In the *First Joy*, twelve poems in eight-line rondeau form gradually move the listener from the sounds of hell to the singing of young men.[37] The first, *Lof, rechter*, is a dialogue

32. On music in the *Bliscappen*, see BEUKEN, *Die eerste blis-cap*, 26-28 and 47-48.

33. Many of the theater songs discussed by Brown begin with imperatives or acclamations: "Adieu, Allez, Allons, Hau!, Hélas!, Hy!, Hé!, Las."

34. On this procedure, see Maria V. COLDWELL, "*Guillaume de Dole* and Medieval Romances with Musical Interpolations," *Musica disciplina* 35 (1981): 55-86, and Susan RANKIN, "The Divine Truth of Scripture: Chant in the *Roman de Fauvel*," *Journal of the American Musicological Society* 47 (1994): 203-43, especially 208-209 on musical interpolations in poems.

35. BROWN, *Music*, 92. His views are shared by others for some plays. On the debate, see Dirk COIGNEAU, "Strofische vormen in het rederijkerstoneel," 17-44, and W. HÜSKEN, "Strofische vormen in het rederijkerstoneel in historisch perspectief," 45-58, both in *Spel in de verte. Tekst, structuur en opvoeringspraktijk van het rederijkerstoneel*, B.A.M. RAMAKERS ed. (Ghent, 1994). Also see Nigel WILKENS, "Rondeau (i)," *The New Grove*, 16:166-70.

36. See HAGGH, *Music, Liturgy, and Ceremony*, especially chap. 4.

37. This is the oldest rondeau form and is not used in fifteenth-century polyphonic song. I am grateful to

between Lucifer as the Devil, a character found especially in plays from northern Europe, and the *Nijt* or Envy.[38] They praise God for judging and punishing Adam, who will now be sent to keep them company and suffer the torments of hell. Their rondeau is set off clearly from God's preceding monologue by the change in character, a procedure, which, like the dialogue rondeau itself, is common in French plays.[39] After the rondeau, Lucifer describes in horrific detail the loud rumbles, stirrings, and screeches of hell (reminding of *charivari*), which actually sound after his speech, noises made more impressive by the immediately following *selete*, in this instance undoubtedly silence.[40] That the audience should be left with a truly frightening aural impression of hell is essential to the play and indeed the entire cycle, since the noise serves as a backdrop against which the remaining music, especially the music of the angels praising Mary in heaven, can then stand out.

The second rondeau, *Verhuecht u, vriende*, is also set off from its surrounding text by a change in character. Here it ends a section of dialogue and is followed immediately by *sanc of spel*. This rondeau is another exultation sung in hell, here by a trio of condemned Biblical personalities, Adam, an unidentified other, and David. They rejoice because Isaiah, speaking from his place in hell, has prophesied that a child would save them from their present torment. What is new here is the disposition of the three characters in the rondeau. Adam has the refrain twice; in the previous rondeau one character sang it, then another. Similar changes among characters in the rondeaux continue throughout the play. (We see their counterpart inside the church in the performance of plainchant responsories, whose verses were customarily sung by different performers.)

The central musical moment follows Jesus' monologue, in which he agrees to die to save mankind. At this point, three characters have three rondeaux in a row praising Mary, rotating places for each one.[41] These rondeaux, *Lof, specie*; *Ghi wert gebloeit*; and *Bi u soe wert*, and the single line following them also end one of the longest dialogues in the play, another reason why three were thought necessary. Then, once an angel has announced that the girl should be named Mary, a priest and a pastor praise her in the rondeau *Lof, salich kint*, which is followed by three lines and a *selete*. This cheerful rondeau ends a brief scene in the play.

David Fallows for sending me his list of fifteenth-century Flemish polyphonic songs, none of which set these rondeau texts, however.

38. Cf. Edward Johannes HASLINGHUIS, *De duivel in het drama der middeleeuwen* (Leiden: Gebroeders Van der Hoeck, 1912); Maximilian Josef RUDWIN, *Der Teufel in den deutschen geistlichen Spielen des Mittelalters und der Reformationszeit* (Göttingen, 1915); J. B. HIRSCHFELD, Heinrich WIECK, *Die Teufel auf der mittelalterlichen Mysterienbühne Frankreichs* (Leipzig, 1887); and Herman PLEIJ, *De sneeuwpoppen van 1511: Stadscultuur in de late middeleeuwen* (Amsterdam: Meulenhoff, 1988), 80, on a play for the birth of prince Charles in 1500, *Pluyto die helsche dief*, and 336, on associates

of Lucifer in a Limburg play of *c*.1430. Devils and even all of Hell (Oudenaarde, 1544) marched in processions. See DE POTTER, *Schets*, passim.

39. On rondeaux in dialogue, see BROWN, *Music*, chap. 3; on dialogue songs in the Gruuthuse manuscript, see J. REYNAERT, "Onhoofse liederen: Thematische genres en types in het Gruuthuseliedboek," *Een zoet akkoord*, 159.

40. On *charivari*, see *Le charivari: actes de la table ronde organisée à Paris (25-27 avril 1977)*, Jacques LE GOFF and Jean-Claude SCHMITT eds. (Paris: EHESS, 1981). On sound effects for hell, see BROWN, *Music*, 46.

41. On trios in chansons in plays, see BROWN, *Music*, 87-88.

Now Mary and her parents go to the temple, where Mary is received by the bishop. On departing, her parents, Anna and Joachim, bid her farewell with *Nu ga wi, Joachim*. It opens a longer dialogue between the parents, which ends with their second rondeau, *Lof, goddelijc wesen*, a self-contained praise of God followed by three concluding lines. The next two rondeaux, *Balseme van gracien* and *Lof, cracht*, are sung almost in succession by the two priests and bishop at the temple. The end of the first, a praise of Mary, does not correspond to the end of a sentence, lacking the subject. This seems deliberate—a way of representing mankind's incapability of praising the Virgin sufficiently. Indeed, the line of verse after the rondeau, which reads, "Whom no one can praise fully," completes the sentence. Then the angel addresses the bishop briefly, whereafter the same ensemble sings another rondeau, a self-contained poem.

Soon thereafter, three boys sing the last two rondeaux of the play, *Gods werken sijn wonderlijc* and *Sijn roede sal bloyen*, which begin and end a section of dialogue and are self-contained.[42] The first praises God; the second the blooming staff of Mary's future husband, a hint of the subject matter of the *Second Joy*.

Remarkably, the final scene of Mary's *First Joy*, a representation of the Annunciation, which could have served as the culminating moment of the play, is entirely without music, including neither rondeaux nor musical interludes. The lack of music may have been intended to represent the mystery of Christ's conception or even to stop the play (in music) *in medias res*, saving it for Christ's birth, the subject of the Second Joy. The omission of music points backwards as well, lending more emphasis to the central moment in this play, the *First Joy* or Mary's birth and the promise she holds for mankind.

This emphasis is also underscored by the configuration of rondeaux, which form a palindrome centered on Mary and her parents. The play has only two rondeau sets, first the three of Pity, Justice, and Truth and then the two of the priests and bishop, all praises of Mary but the last praising God's power. Between these sets are three rondeaux—the outer two praising Mary; the inner rondeau a conversation between the parents leaving Mary, the central subjects of the play. By contrast, the outer rondeaux each praise God and Christ successively.

The *Seventh Joy* includes seven rondeaux, an appropriate number, since it symbolized the Virgin's Joys and Sorrows. Again, all but one are hymns of praise. The first, *Nu, gawy met anderen voort*, is not: it encapsulates the seventh joy, which is Mary's Assumption, not only in its text but also in representing the characters—it is a dialogue between Mary and the apostle John. Here they depart to begin her journey to heaven. This rondeau ends in mid-sentence, "since he [God] brings us." The next line completes it—"out of

---

42. BROWN, 100, notes a performance by three *petits enfants chantres* in a play in 1556; cf. 52-53 on choirboys     singing during plays.

this miserable earthly valley"—and returns abruptly to earth and mortal existence, which would have been an inappropriate ending for a song about heaven.

The second rondeau *O laes! God Heere!* is Mary's prayer to God for relief from her sadness, expressing the opening theme of the play. The self-contained rondeau ends with a question, "What may happen?," whereupon Mary's monologue continues. Once Gabriel has arrived, Mary sings a hymn of praise about her great joy at receiving his message, *Lof deser bliscap*. It ends mid-sentence in order to leave a mention of sin until after the rondeau. Then five further lines end the dialogue.

The next three rondeaux, all praises, end in mid-sentence in the same way. The apostles have two rondeaux, a praise of Mary, *Lof hebt, oetmoedege Vrou*, and, once Lucifer has been frightened away, a praise to God, *Lof, Heere, dat U did geweerde!* Then Peter's prayer to God, *O Heere, alder menscen confoort*, comes immediately after a silence and moves into dialogue seamlessly. This rondeau is self-contained, but also open-ended: the exclamation mark of the first refrain becomes a question mark in the second, leading to an extra line, which then eases into the following sentence. The last rondeau, a trio, is Peter, Paul and John's self-contained farewell, *Orlof, lieve brueders*. Then five lines end the play.

It is surely significant that, unlike the rondeaux of the *First Joy*, which all end with completed sentences (except for the incomplete human praise of the Virgin, *Balseme van gracien*), those of the *Seventh Joy* that precede Mary's Assumption are all incomplete. This may again express the impossibility of praising God or the Mother of God enough, but was intended, more likely, to point forward to Mary's Assumption. Once Mary is in heaven and her joy and the salvation of mankind have been realized, the two final rondeaux of the play are complete: in *O Heere, alder menscen confoort*, Peter marvels at the Assumption that has just occurred; then, later, the three apostles sing a farewell, *Orlof, lieve brueders*, and take leave of each other.

Of the seventeen rondeaux in the two *Joys*, all correspond to a change in character and all but two (I-4,5) to a change in the object of address. Most end sections of dialogue, but for contrast, some begin scenes (I-1,7,11; VII-2,5). In these ways, the rondeaux are highlighted and separated from the surrounding text.[43] That such differentiation from the text was intended is also shown by their logical distribution throughout the poetry. (Indeed, differentiation marks the poetry as well, which alternates patterned rhyme with paired rhyme, the former applied to passages highlighting the ineffable, God or the Virgin, as shown in Appendix II).[44] In both plays, the function of the rondeaux strongly resembles that of the formally similar responsorial chants, whose texts and music often reflect on preceding texts.[45] This separation of the rondeaux, their emotive

43. Cf. BEUKEN, *Die eerste bliscap*, 47-48.

44. Ibid., 42-46, for a different analysis, and, on rhyme in *rederijker* plays, *De Gentse spelen van 1539*, 1, B. H. ERNÉ and L.

M. VAN DIS eds. (The Hague: Nijhoff, 1982), 17-18.

45. See A. RÜCKER, "Das Responsorium in Liturgie und Volkskunde," *Volk und Volkstum* 3 (1938): 251-56.

language, as well as the references to *accords* and singing elsewhere in the play, suggest that they were not just recited differently, but were sung.

Unfortunately, there is no other corroborating evidence from the archives of Brussels, and although we know that the crossbowmen performed the plays, we have no knowledge of any members being singers.[46] Other documents do suggest that such interpolations would have been sung, however. In 1496/7, the accounts of the city of Ghent record a payment to master Jacop Doykin, singer, for "diverse verses of rhetoric put to music and song and for other beautiful things he made for the Joyous Entry [of Philip the Fair in Ghent in 1497]."[47] Such "diverse verses" might well have been performed during a play, since plays are documented at Joyous Entries and cities often paid for them. Here the city paid Doykin. If the songs of the Joys were sung, it was most likely to simple, easily remembered tunes. Polyphony seems virtually out of the question; the eight-line form argues strongly against it. Nor does it seem likely that actor-singers accompanied themselves with instruments.[48]

An organ and perhaps polyphony were heard elsewhere, however, during the central moment in the *Seventh Joy*, Mary's Assumption, when a lift raised the Virgin, angels, and musicians to heaven.[49] When Mary arrives in Heaven, following the instructions in the manuscript, "the angels in the tower should also sing and play the organ" (*dinglen in den trone selen oec singen ende orglen*), the dramatic realization of angel musicians depicted so often in paintings. Later in the play, the text suggests that this heavenly music included polyphony. Peter, recalling to Thomas the marvellous events of Mary's Assumption, says, "We have heard such great fruits of melodious accords that no person ever heard." (*Wi hebben soo groten vruecht gehoort Van sange ende melodiosen acoorde dat noyt mensce tsgelijcs en hoorde.*)[50]

46. See AUTENBOER, *Volksfeesten*, beginning at 79, who argues that *rederijker* guilds, found in the Low Countries especially after 1440, developed from the guilds of crossbowmen, whose festivities, with processions, banquets, church ceremonies, marksmanship contests, prizes and plays were not unlike the *ommegangen*. Pleij points out that the *rederijkers* belonged to the social elite as did the crossbowmen (*Op belofte*, 183-85). Chambers of rhetoric, most dating from after 1440, are listed in ELSLANDER, *Letterkundig leven*, 21-52. Het Boeck, the first Brussels guild, was founded in 1401. On *rederijkers* in Brussels, see W. VAN EEGHEM, "Rhetores Bruxellenses," *Revue belge de philologie et d'histoire* 14 (1935): 427-48, and 15 (1936): 47-78; Joseph CUVELIER, *Een viertal onbekende werken van de Brusselse 15e- eeuwse rederijkers Colijn en Smeken, en van de Bruggeling Anthonis de Roover* (Brussels, 1937); Cyriel de BAERE, "Het aandeel der Gilden in de ontwikkeling van het Nederlandsch Toneel te Brussel," *Eigen Schoon en de Brabander* 27 (1944): 1-4; idem, "De Brusselse kamers van rhetorica," ibid., 29 (1946): 1-16; idem, "De bedrijvigheid der oude kamers van rhetorica te Brussel," ibid.: 97-116;

idem, "De deelneming der Brusselse rederijkers aan rhetoricale feesten en wedstrijden," ibid., 31 (1948): 8-24 and 49-61; idem, "De organisatie der oude kamers van rhetorica te Brussel," ibid., 32 (1949): 1-16, 72-83.
47. "*Item betaelt meester Jacop Doykin, cantere, van diversschen veersen van rhetoriicken ghestelt thebbene in musyke ende zanghe ende voor diverssche andere moyten bij hem ghebadt ter blijde incomst-5 s.g.*" (Ghent, Stadsarchief, Stadsrekeningen 1496/7), cited in Frans DE POTTER, *Gent van den oudsten tijt tot heden*, 3 (Ghent 1885): 280-81, cf. 284-85. I thank Daniël Lievois for bringing this notice to my attention. The passage is also discussed by Dirk COIGNEAU, "Een vreughdich liedt moet ick vermanen: Positie en gebruikswijzen van het rederijkerslied," *Een zoet akkoord*, 257, who nevertheless argues that music was usually incidental to *rederijker* verse.
48. Cf. BROWN, *Music*, 98-99.
49. BEUKEN, *Die eerste bliscap*, 25, concludes that the play required three upper platforms (*hemelhuisjes*), for God, the angels, and the martyrs and confessors.
50. Cf. Hubert Joseph Edmund ENDEPOLS, *Het dekoratief en de opvoering van het middelnederlandsche toneelstukken*

In any case, this was the most dramatic musical moment of the entire cycle and the only one to include organ playing. That was probably conventional, as is suggested by many paintings, since organists are paid in Mechelen for plays representing the Assumption.[51]

The Assumption scene also included the only plainsong of the entire play.[52] After Peter, John, and Paul discuss who is worthiest to carry the bier with Mary's corpse, all raise it up and sing *Exit de Egypto. Alleluia.* This is surely Ps. 113, *In exitu Israel,* one of very few texts assigned to the *tonus peregrinus* or wandering tone.[53] What is interesting here is the appearance of precisely the same incipit for the psalm in the account of Mary's Assumption in the Golden Legend, whose content matches that of the play closely: both describe John's preaching in Ephesus, the Jewish plot to steal the corpse and Thomas receiving the Virgin's girdle.[54]

Whereas any vocal music performed during the play would have been sung by amateur musicians, such as the crossbowmen, professionals were responsible for the instrumental music. Loud instruments played during several interludes of the Joys, because the Brussels' city accounts record payments to the town *alta cappella* "for playing during the pauses of the *Ommegang* plays" and both Joys have interludes during which there was to be playing (*spelen*).[55] These explicit references to singing or playing are nearly all associated either with hell or with angels and acts of God. A *selete* with singing or playing follows the Cherubim's speech in the *First Joy.* Later, singing or playing concludes Seth's praise of God, which was probably also intended to make Lucifer's arrival just afterwards more jolting. After a scene in hell, singing or playing frames a dialogue between Misery and Meditation, probably calling for somber music. The next singing and play-

(Amsterdam, 1903), and n. 31 above. On high places built on stages for singers and instruments, mainly for paradise or heaven, and found in most plays, see BROWN, *Music,* 75; on angels singing polyphony, 44–45; and on improvised part singing, 101–105. On instruments and the Assumption in particular, see Reinhold HAMMERSTEIN, *Die Musik der Engel: Untersuchungen zur Musikanschauung des Mittelalters* (Bern: Francke Verlag, 1962), 232–36; and Baron Alexandre DE LA FONS-MÉLICOCQ, *Cérémonies dramatiques et anciens usages dans les églises du nord de la France* (Paris: V. Didron, 1850), 9, on the celebration of the Assumption in Béthune in 1414, when wine was given *"aux menestreurs qui jouèrent quand Dieu monta es cieulx."* Also see Emanuel WINTERNITZ, "On Angel Concerts in the 15th Century: A Critical Approach to Realism and Symbolism in Sacred Painting," *The Musical Quarterly* 49 (1963): 450–63.

51. See AUTENBOER, *Volksfeesten,* 169, on the organist playing for the Marian play, documented from 1442/3 to 1472/3 in town accounts. In 1530 the instrumentalist *speelman* Jan van Liekerke was paid for the play. The city of Brussels did not pay an organist. Cf. BROWN, *Music,*

49–50, on organists.

52. Sacred music is rare in French plays (BROWN, *Music,* 169).

53. *In exitu Israel* is the psalm following the antiphon *Chorus angelorum* in the Cistercian burial ritual. Cf. GHENT, University Library, Ms. 233, f. 136ʳ. On the *tonus peregrinus* and settings of *In exitu,* see Rhabanus ERBACHER, *Tonus Peregrinus: Aus der Geschichte eines Psalmtons,* Münsterschwarzacher Studien, 12 (Münsterschwarzach: Vier-Türme-Verlag, 1971).

54. On the influence of the Golden Legend on the plays, see BEUKEN, *Die eerste bliscap,* 34–38.

55. In 1485/6 and 1486/7 four city minstrels were paid: "Betaelt den piperen van deser stadt van op te voerpuye ende op het voirs. speelhuys tusschen de pauseringe van den voirs. spele te pypene" (HAGGH, *Music,* 459). Cf. BEUKEN, *Die eerste bliscap,* 25–26, and Edmond VANDER STRAETEN, *Les ménéstrels aux Pays-Bas du XIIIᵉ au XVIIIᵉ siècle* (Brussels, A. & F. Mahillon, 1878). Brown observes that the instruments used in plays before the sixteenth century were usually loud (*Music,* 70–71).

ing comes at a joyous moment, just before God is revealed, who orders the angel to be sent to Anna and Joachim. And *sanc et spel opt lanxte* ends the scene between Joachim and Anna, the central moment in the play when Mary is conceived. A pause with singing or playing is the final interlude of this kind and precedes Joachim's arrival, once Anna has praised God for her joy. Such interludes are entirely absent from the *Seventh Joy*.

The most frequent interludes, found in both plays, are *seletes* and *pauses*. Howard Brown argues that *pauses* were instrumental flourishes and that *selete* could refer to music played to quiet the spectators.[56] He cites a stage indication for a 1547 production, *Lieu pour jouer silete*, that assumes the playing of music.[57] From the use of these terms in the *Joys*, it appears that *pauses* might well have meant playing, but that the content of *seletes* depended on their context. The *seletes* in both *Joys* mark changes of dialogue or character. In the *First Joy*, music would have been highly inappropriate at the *selete cort* and *selete opt cortste* before the appearance of God and the *selete* before Anna's praise of God.[58] And some *seletes* came just after rondeaux, favoring silence. Two other *seletes* suggest silence: one occurring while Mary grows up and the other preceding the epilogue to the play. The *pauses* could have included music. The first *selete pause* marks a transition to hell, a scene ending with noise. (Noise punctuates the second scene in hell, too.) Another *pause* accompanies Joachim's offering, a moment where music would have been expected; a short pause precedes Anne's appearance, and a last short pause marks the moment of the Annunciation. The *Seventh Joy* places *seletes* at scene changes consistently, but four exceptional *pauses* are indicated in the margins: two when John preaches in Ephesus and another two as the apostles appear in the clouds. Like the rondeaux, the *pauses* are spaced logically throughout the plays. Their music would have contrasted agreeably with sung rondeaux.

The Brussels' *Ommegang* included other plays that were performed by *rederijkers*, some who may have been musicians. In 1497/8, during the fair (*kermes*) held that evening, the guilds known as the Violet and the Book performed entertainments, and the Lily and Cornflower guilds performed a *wysen spele* at some point. That year, Jan Smeken, a prominent member of the Lily and a poet, was among three judges giving out prizes.[59] There is no archival evidence for music in these plays, but the Lily, who performed the *wysen spele*, did include leading priests and musicians among its membership in 1498/9: Willem Bouwens, priest and curate of the parish church of St.-Géry; Anthonis de Vos,

---

56. BROWN, *Music*, chap. 4. Brown considers the music that might have been used during such interludes, concluding that what survives would have been too complex, with the possible exception of a lute piece, "Factie", from *Carminum quae chely vel testudine canuntur, Liber primus* (Louvain: Phalèse, 1549, f. 14ʳ; transcribed by BROWN, *Music*, 154), meaning *sottie* in Flemish and thus perhaps appropriate for a dramatic pause. He also sug-

gests dance music as possible, 148-68.
57. BROWN, *Music*, 42.
58. BROWN, *Music*, 141, notes that in the mystery play *La Création, la Passion, la Résurrection*, Paris, Bibliothèque Nationale, Ms. f.f. 904, *siletes* are associated with solemn moments, especially preceding God's speeches.
59. HAGGH, *Music*, 440 (Brussels, Algemeen Rijksarchief, Rekenkamer, city accounts of Brussels, Ms. 30948).

a member of the *cotidiane* of the wealthy parish church of St.-Nicholas and responsible for the singers at St.-Gudula in 1490/91; Aert Volkaert, the priest and minor canon responsible for the choirboys trained to sing polyphony at the collegiate church of St.-Gudula; and two organists, Gielis and Claes Brugman. It is no wonder that one of the Lily's two mottos was *Rhetorica musica*.[60]

Music also accompanied the *Ommegang* procession itself, which left the church of Our Lady of the Sand on the morning of the play to arrive at the town square. Like similar processions such as the *ommegangen* of Mechelen and Antwerp, the Brussels *Ommegang* included wagons carrying recreations of Biblical or allegorical scenes, often matching the subject matter of scenes in plays. Those most widely represented were of Adam and Eve, David and Goliath, the Tree of Jesse, St. George and the dragon, Paradise, the Annunciation, Assumption, Crucifixion, Christ on Mount Olivet, and the Stable in Bethlehem. In 1549 one wagon in the Brussels *Ommegang* carried an "organ" with cats instead of pipes.[61] Such wagons did often carry human musicians. In 1469 the Ghent St. Livinus procession included a wagon with two clerks singing the song of St. Livinus (*twee clercxkins die songhen het liedekin van Sint Lievin*).[62]

The same scenes were represented by *tableaux vivants* in Joyous Entries, by *entremets* at banquets, and even in paintings.[63] A vivid description of the music that was part of *entremets* is the well-known account of the Feast of the Pheasant in Lille in 1454.[64] Elaborate *tableaux vivants* include those at the splendid Entry of Philip the Good into Bruges in 1440, when music filled the streets. At the end of the *Peperstraat*, a stage had the four prophets preaching and singing together, thus probably in polyphony "unusually happily and melodiously" (*uutnemende lustelick ende melodieuselick*); elsewhere in front of the almshouse of St.-Obrecht, the story of Abraham and Isaac was shown. There musicians played "a harp very pleasantly, a lute and a dulcian" (*zeer playsantelick up een harpe, een lute ende een doulchanye*). At the end of the *Zegherstraat*, a *tableau vivant* revealed Queen Esther and King Assueris surrounded by musicians playing "melodiously on an organ, harp and lute" (*melodieuselick up een orghele, harpe ende lute*). And at the fountain of the Dominican convent, Christ's Nativity was represented with angels coming from heaven with sweet prayers, playing an organ, harp, and lute. On a raised platform on top of the convent,

---

60. On the *cotidiane* or choir of daily singers at the church of St.-Nicholas in Brussels, see Barbara HAGGH, "Crispijne and Abertijne: Two Tenors at the Church of St. Niklaas, Brussels," *Music & Letters* 76 (1995): 325-44. See ELSLANDER, *Letterkundig leven*, on the Lily.

61. See Frédéric FABER, *Histoire du théâtre français en Belgique depuis son origine jusqu'à nos jours*, 1 (Brussels: F. J. Olivier, 1878), 4-5. Numerous descriptions of wagons are found in DE POTTER, *Schets*.

62. DE POTTER, *Schets*, 16-20.

63. Some examples are given in FABER, *Histoire du théâtre*, 1-11. Cf. Gustave COHEN, "Scènes de théâtre dans les peintures et gravures de l'école hollandaise," *Miscellanea Leo van Puyvelde* (Brussels, 1949): 317-20; Leo VAN PUYVELDE, *Schilderkunst en toneelvertooningen op het einde van de middeleeuwen* (Ghent, 1912); PLEIJ, *De sneeuwpoppen*, 88-89.

64. See the accounts of the banquet published in *Chronique de Mathieu d'Escouchy*, Gaston DU FRESNE DE BEAUCOURT, ed., 2 (Paris: Veuve Renouard, 1864), 116-237.

choirboys sang *Gloria in excelsis*. A few steps further stood the Virgin Mary and St. Dominic, with harpists, lutenists and shawmists playing. Another *tableau* set up by the merchants of Bruges showed King David with his harp singing about Bruges. On the corners of *Bogaard*, *Ridder* and the next two streets, the Seven Works of Mercy were depicted, the last showing the Almighty God surrounded by musicians playing organ, harp and lute. Finally, at the Halle gate, there were not less than 80 trumpeters and clarions.[65]

That almost identical scenes were recreated within entirely different events: plays, banquets, contests, and processions, that some required similar instruments or types of music, is evidence that accepted stereotypes governed secular as well as sacred festivals, which included a predetermined content and sequence of events. Even the finale of the Brussels *Ommegang*, an archery contest, the last event to include music, was prescribed by stereotypes. After the plays, once the procession had returned to the church of Our Lady of the Sand, the archery contest took place, which was sponsored by the crossbowmen. Whoever hit the wooden parrot tied to the spire of the church would become the new King of the guild and Emperor or perpetual king if he won three years in a row. Often sovereigns participated in this contest. In 1500 singers from Our Lady of the Sand were paid for singing discant during it. This same archery contest was part of many other processions in the Low Countries and in France into the eighteenth century and was consistently associated with the upper classes and the nobility.[66]

That late medieval town processions in the Low Countries, like the Brussels *Ommegang*, consisted of a predictable sequence of stereotypes gives evidence that they had their own ritual, which was prescribed by social convention, as was the ritual of the Church. Thus secular and ecclesiastical ritual in this time were undoubtedly less separated from one another than we have been led to believe. Many modern writers have sought to define the nature of late-medieval sacred ritual, particularly of events, such as dramas or certain votive devotions, that seem to belong outside the liturgy. It is important to remember, however, that the word "liturgy" was a Humanist reinvention, was never applied to ecclesiastical ritual after the patristic writers and before the sixteenth century, and acquired many shades of its modern meaning only in the twentieth century. Removing this word from discussions of the Middle Ages would free us to investigate the medieval language for and understanding of sacred ritual.[67]

Sacred and secular ritual also shared common sources of inspiration: saints' lives

---

65. Fuller discussion in Strohm, *Music in Late Medieval Bruges*, 80-83.
66. On processions including this game, see Robert Darnton, *The Great Cat Massacre and Other Episodes in French Cultural History* (New York: Basic Books, 1984), chap. 3, 107-109.
67. Young, *The Medieval Drama*, 2, 408-409, discusses medieval words used to describe plays: *officium, similitudo, repraesentatio, ludus, miraculum, mysterium*, the latter dating from the fourteenth century. On the history of the word "liturgy" see Barbara Haggh, "Foundations or Institutions? On Bringing the Middle Ages into the History of Medieval Music," *Acta musicologica* 60/1 (1996): 22-55.

and the *Golden Legend*, in particular. This latter collection of saints' lives supplemented other lectionaries in the choirs of many churches by the fifteenth century, Cambrai Cathedral and some of the parish churches in Ghent being examples. The subjects of plays in processions like the *Ommegang* of Brussels often matched those of offices sung in the church: lives of saints and the Joys or miracles of the Virgin were frequently performed.[68]

Even though debate will continue on the performance and function of interpolated song texts in plays, this reading of the two *Bliscappen* nevertheless suggests that late-medieval processions in the Low Countries were filled with more vocal and instrumental music than has been acknowledged, not only in plays but also in scenes on wagons, during contests, as well as during the processions themselves.[69] (Unfortunately, no chant for the Brussels *Ommegang* survives in the only processional from that city.)[70] Moreover, the processions were governed by ritual practices no less strict than those of the church. Processions did offer greater possibilities, however. Scenes presented out of doors by familiar townspeople with sounding music were vivid reminders of the validity of religious messages for everyday life. Such intersections of sacred and secular, in the Low Countries and elsewhere, as well as the meaning of music therein are urgently in need of further investigation.[71]

---

68. See BROWN, *Music*, 24, on dramatized lives of St. Martin and St. Fiacre, and 44 on a motet for a Flemish miracle play on the life of St. Trudon, performed in 1555/6. The plays performed during the 1502/3 *ommegang* of Mechelen included a life of St. Augustine, miracles of the Virgin, and a play of David. See AUTENBOER, *Volksfeesten*, 222.

69. Large numbers of musicians marched in some processions. In Antwerp in 1398, 27 trumpeters were paid for the Marian *ommegang*, and, for the Corpus Christi procession, *menistrelen, trompers, pypers ende alrehande menistrelen die metten processien gingen ende haer spel ende conste daden ende toenden*. The numbers of musicians present was greatest in Mechelen: in 1391 the city paid 190 instrumentalists for the St. Rombaut *ommegang*, the next year 130; in 1408 there were 168, and in 1419 not less than 215. The players came from Brussels, Aalst, Leuven, Antwerp, and Dendermonde especially. See AUTENBOER, *Volksfeesten*;

DE BURBURE, *De Antwerpsche ommegangen*; Edmund BOWLES, "Musical Instruments in Civic Processions during the Middle Ages," *Acta musicologica* 33 (1961): 147-61; idem, "Musical Instruments in the Medieval Corpus Christi Procession," *Journal of the American Musicological Society* 17 (1964): 251-60.

70. Cambridge, University Library, Syn 7.53.9, *Processionale ad usum insignis ecclesie dive Gudile* of 1531, the only surviving processional from the church, only includes chant for the Sunday processions, not for the *Ommegang* or other outdoor processions.

71. I wish to the thank Marie-Noël Colette; the Leverhulme Foundation; and Royal Holloway, University of London, for supporting my research; and Dirk Coigneau for bringing several recent studies to my attention and for his comments, although our conclusions differ on some points.

# Appendix I

## Rondeau Texts and Summaries

(based on the editions of BEUKEN, DE VREESE, and STALLAERT, with my translations in brackets)[72]

### Brussels, Royal Library, Ms. IV 192:
### Anon., *Die eerste bliscap van Maria* [The First Joy of Mary]. Brussels, 1444-1462

Prologue (lines 1-75)

VIRELAI (20-23):

| | |
|---|---|
| *Sijt willecome, edele en gemeyne,* | Be welcome, nobility and commoners, |
| *Die hier dus minlic sijt versaemt* | Who are gathered here in such friendship, |
| *In desen melodyosen pleyne.* | In this beautiful square, |
| *Sijt willecome, edele en gemeyne!* | Be welcome ... |

Dialogue: NIJT [Envy], LUCIFER (76-163)

Dialogue: SERPENT, NIJT (163-193)

Dialogue: SERPENT, YEVE [Eve], ADAM (194-257)

Selete cort [short silence] (257-258)

Monologue: GOD (258-271)

Dialogue: GOD, ADAM, YEVE (272-281)

Dialogue: GOD, INGEL [Angel], INGEL CHERUBIN (281-342)

Selete; sanc of spel [silence; song or playing] (342-343)

Dialogue: ADAM, YEVE (343-379)

Selete; pause [silence; pause] (379-380)

Dialogue: NIJT, LUCIFER, 1 DUVEL [Devil] (380-453)

Dialogue: NIJT, ADAM, LUCIFER, GOD (453-587)

RONDEAU (588-595):

| | | |
|---|---|---|
| LUCIFER: | *Lof, rechter, van uwen rechte vercoren.* | Praise, O Judge, chosen by your own law. |
| | *Wi dancken ons uwer weerdicheien!* | We are thankful for your favor! |
| NIJT: | *Ghi hebt gemindert onsen toren,* | You have lessened our anger. |
| | *Lof, rechter, van uwen rechte vercoren!* | Praise, Judge ... |
| LUCIFER: | *Wy selen gaen stampen en smoren,* | We will go make a racket, |
| | *Ende tegen hem lieden ons coken bereyen.* | And prepare our boiling liquid against these people. |
| NIJT: | *Lof, rechter, van uwen rechte vercoren.* | Praise, Judge ... |
| | *Wi bedancken ons uwer werdicheyen!* | We are thankful ... |

Dialogue: LUCIFER, NIJT (596-616)

LUCIFER [on the sounds of hell] (605-616): [edited elsewhere as prose]

| | |
|---|---|
| *Ghi helle, hoert wes ic doe bekint:* | You, hell, hear what I make known to you: |
| *Doet maken alrande instrumint* | Have all kinds of instruments made |
| *Van ruesters, van trydents en van tangen,* | Of grills, tridents, and pincers, |
| *Daer ghi den mensce met selt ontfangen;* | With which you shall welcome people; |
| *Van cupen, van pannen ende van ketelen,* | Of tubs, of pans and of kettles, |
| *Van pecke en van gloyende zeetelen, ...* | Of tar and of glowing seats, ... |
| *Om yegeliken nae sinen state* | In order to receive each according to his rank, |

72. I thank Jaap van Benthem for his assistance with the translations.

| | |
|---|---|
| *Tontfane, coninge en prelate.* | kings and prelates: |
| *Al saelter comen, rijf en raf!* | All shall come, without distinction |
| *Maect u bereescap, en comes af,* | Prepare yourselves, and carry it off! |
| *Sijt blide en vro! Helle, maect feeste:* | Be happy and joyful! Hell, be festive: |
| *Het wert al onse, beide minste en meeste!* | it will all be ours, both the least and the most! |
| *Groet gerommel ende geruusch salmen* | One should make great |
| *inde helle maken,* | rumblings and noises in hell, |
| *met alrehande geruchte.* | with all kinds of screeches. |
| *Ende dan selete.* | And then silence. (616-617) |

Dialogue: ADAM, EEN KINT [One Child], DANDER KINT [The Other Child], SET [Seth] (617-690)

Dialogue: SET, *Ingel vor tparadijs* [Angel before Paradise] (691-738)

| | |
|---|---|
| *Hier salmen singen of spelen,* | Here one shall sing or play. |
| *Ende dan comt Lucifer.* | And then Lucifer comes. (738-739) |

Dialogue: LUCIFER, NIJT (739-771)

| | |
|---|---|
| *Groet geruchte inde helle.* | Loud screeches in hell. (766) |
| *Gheruchte.* | Noises. |
| *Dits tclagen ende tkermen* | This is the wailing and moaning |
| *inde helle vanden vaders.* | in hell of [our] predecessors. (770-771) |

Dialogue: ADAM, YEVE, EEN Ander [One Other], DAVID, JOB, YSAYAS (772-838)

RONDEAU (831-838):

| | | |
|---|---|---|
| ADAM: | *Verhuecht u, vriende, ende blijft in hopen:* | Rejoice friends, and remain hopeful |
| | *Die prophecie en mach niet liegen.* | This prophecy cannot deceive |
| EEN ANDER: | *De gracie Gods steet al noch open.* | The grace of God is still available |
| | *Verhuecht u, vriende, ende blijft in hopen.* | Rejoice ... |
| DAVID: | *Hoe ons dees demsterheit mach nopen,* | However much this darkness may depress us |
| | *Gods woert en sal ons niet bedriegen.* | God's word shall not betray us |
| ADAM: | *Verhuecht u, vriende, ende blijft in hopen:* | Rejoice ... |
| | *Die prophecie en mach niet liegen.* | The prophecy ... |

*Sanc of spel* [Song or playing] (838-839)

Dialogue: BITTER ELLENDE [Bitter Misery], INNICH GEBET [Meditation], ELLINDICHEIT [Misery] (839-916)

*Sanc of spel* (916-917)

Dialogue: INNICH GEBET, ONTFERMICHEIT [Pity] (917-960)

*Selete opt cortste* [The shortest silence] (960-961)

Dialogue (continues): ONTFERMICHEIT, GHERECHTICHEIT [Justice], GOD, DE WAERHEIT [Truth], EEN INGEL, DE SOEN GODS [The Son of God], DE HEILEGE GEEST [The Holy Ghost], DE VREDE [Peace] (961-1400)

*Hier swigen sy alle* [Here they are all silent; moment immediately following the recommendation that Christ should die for man] (1182-1183)

RONDEAU (1376-1383):

| | | |
|---|---|---|
| ONTFERMICHEIT: | *Lof, specie edel, vruchtbarich tac,* | Praise, O precious spice, fruitful branch |
| | *Sonder nommer soe es u weerde!* | Your value cannot be counted! |
| GHERECHTICHEIT: | *Lof, bloyende rijs, dat Adam brac,* | Praise, blooming sprig, that Adam broke |
| | *Lof, specie, edel, vruchtbarich tac!* | Praise, O precious countenance ... |
| WAERHEIT: | *U vruchten sijn reyn ende sonder lac;* | Your fruits are pure and without stain; |
| | *Noyt edelre vrucht en wies op eerde.* | Never did more precious fruit grow on earth. |
| ONTFERMICHEIT: | *Lof, specie, edel, vruchtbarich tac,* | Praise, O precious countenance ... |
| | *Sonder nommer soe es u weerde!* | It cannot be counted ... |

Rondeau (1384-1391):

| | | |
|---|---|---|
| Gherechticheit: | *Ghi wert gebloeit uut Yessen geerde,* | You bloom from Jesse's garden, |
| | *Also ons Balam heeft vorsproken.* | As Balam promised us. |
| Waerheit: | *Ende ons inder scrifturen vercleerde,* | And explained to us in Scripture, |
| | *Werdi gebloyt uut Yessen geerde.* | You bloom … |
| Ontfermicheit: | *Gheen edelre bloeme noch soe vermeerde* | No more precious flower did multiply thus |
| | *En stont ter werelt noit ontploken.* | Nor stand in the world, never in full bloom. |
| Gherechticheit: | *Ghi wert gebloeyt uut Yessen geerde,* | You bloom … |
| | *Alsoe ons Balam heeft vorsproken.* | As Balam promised … |

Rondeau (1392-1400):

| | | |
|---|---|---|
| Waerheyt: | *Bi u soe wert de helle te broken!* | By you hell will be broken! |
| | *Voetsel van vramen leit in u keerne.* | Beneficial nourishment leads to your essence. |
| Ontfermicheit: | *U grote genaden staen wide ontploken,* | Your great mercies are ready to bloom, unfolding widely, |
| | *Bi u soe wert de helle te broken!* | By you … |
| Gherechticheit: | *Ghi sult sorcoersen met uwen roeken* | You will bring comfort to your friends; |
| | *U vrienden, Lucifer te deerne!* | You, friends, to the misfortune of Lucifer! |
| Waerheit: | *Bi u soe wert de helle te broken.* | By you … |
| | *Voetsel van vramen leit in u keerne.* | You will bring comfort… |
| | *Al onduecht steet tot uwen beweerne!* | All vices are under your control! |

  *Selete* [Silence] (1400-1401)

Dialogue: Joachim, 2 Priester [2 Priests], De Bisscop [The Bishop] (1401-1460)
  Pause (1411-1412)
  *Hier singen ende spelen inden trone* [Here singing and playing in the tower] (1460-1461)
Dialogue: God, Dingel, Joachim (1461-1527)
  *Pause lutter* [Small pause] (1527-1528)
Dialogue: Joachim, Anne (1528-1545)
  *Sanc; spel opt lanxste* [Song; playing for the longest time] (1545-1546)
Dialogue: 2 Gebueren [2 Relatives] (1546-1571)
  *Selete* (1571-1572)
Monologue: Anna (1572-1585)
  *Pause: sanc of spel* (margin in other hand: *nota* [possibly the term used by Johannes de Grocheo describing lai form and applied to dances]) (1585-1586)
Dialogue: Joachim, Een Priester, Dander Priester, Deerste Pape [The First Pastor] (1586-1631)
Dialogue: Angel, Een Priester, Dander Pape [The Other Pastor] (1632-1654)
Rondeau (1644-1651):

| | | |
|---|---|---|
| Een Priester: | *Lof, salich kint, gebenedijt* | Praise, holy child, blessed |
| | *Van Gode, die ons dees boetscap brachte!* | By God, who brought us this message! |
| Dander Pape: | *In uwer moeder lichame gewijt,* | In your mother's body anointed |
| | *Lof, salich kint gebenedijt.* | Praise … |
| Een Priester: | *Ghespruyt, geboren dat ghi sijt* | Born that you are |
| | *Uut Yesse, den edelen gheslachte.* | From Jesse, the noble race |
| Dander Pape: | *Lof, salich kint gebenedijt* | Praise … |
| | *Van Gode, die ons dees bootscap brachte!* | By God … |
| | *Ghespruyt, geboren dat ghi sijt* | Born that you are |

  *Selete; wech* [Silence; away] (1654-1655)

Dialogue: ANNE, JOACHIM, ONS VROUWE [Our Lady—as child], BISSCOP (1655-1717)

RONDEAU (1701-1708):

| | | |
|---|---|---|
| ANNA: | *Nu ga wi, Joachim, vercorne man,* | Now we go, Joachim, chosen man, |
| | *Maria es inden tempel bleven.* | Mary has stayed in the temple. |
| JOACHIM: | *God wilse met duechden verlichten voort an.* | God wants to enlighten her with virtues henceforth. |
| ANNA: | *Nu ga wi, Joachim, vercorne man.* | Now we go … |
| JOACHIM: | *Die hemel ende erde heeft int gespan,* | [He] who has heaven and earth in his yoke, |
| | *Die wille haer salegen voortganc geven.* | He will give her holy precedence. |
| ANNA: | *Nu ga wi, Joachim, vercorne man,* | Now we go … |
| | *Maria es inden tempel bleven.* | Mary stayed … |

*Selete* (1717-1718)

Dialogue: BISSCOP, EEN PRIESTER, DANDER PRIESTER (1718-1755)

*Selete. Dan sal Ons Vrouwe groot sijn* [Silence. Then Our Lady shall become large with child] (1755-1756)

Dialogue: JOACHIM, ANNA, BISSCOP, MARIA (1756-1815)

RONDEAU (1782-1789):

| | | |
|---|---|---|
| JOACHIM: | *Lof, goddelijc wesen, diet al verblijt,* | Praise, godly being, who makes all happy |
| | *Ingelen, menscen, hemel ende erde.* | Angels, Mankind, Heaven and Earth. |
| ANNA: | *Lof, specie vol duechden, der yngelen jolijt.* | Praise, spice full of virtue, joy of the angels. |
| JOACHIM: | *Lof, goddelijc wesen gebenedijt.* | Praise, godly being … |
| ANNA: | *Lof, die fonteyne van gracien sijt,* | Praise, [you] who are the fountain of grace, |
| | *Onsprekelic es u hoge weerde.* | Your high value cannot be expressed. |
| JOACHIM: | *Lof, godlijc wesen diet al verblijt,* | Praise, godly being … |
| | *Ingelen, menscen, hemel ende erde.* | Angels … |

Dialogue: 1 PRIESTER, 2 PRIESTER, BISSCOP, DINGELE (1816-1849)

RONDEAU (1816-1826):

| | | |
|---|---|---|
| 1 PRIESTER: | *Balseme van gracien, suet honichrate,* | Balsam of grace, sweet honeycomb, |
| | *Wilt u grote genadicheit hier bewisen.* | Will you prove your great mercy here. |
| 2 PRIESTER: | *Verwerft ons in glorien de hemelsce sate,* | Obtain the heavenly residence for us in glory, |
| | *Daer men de sielen mach ewich spisen.* | Where one may nourish the souls for ever. |
| BISSCOP: | *Soe datter elc confoort van duechden in vate,* | By which everybody obtains moral comfort, |
| | *Balseme van gracien, reyn honichrate.* | Balsam … |
| 2 PRIESTER: | *Verwerft ons inder glorien de hemelsce gesate,* | Obtain … |
| | *Daer men de sielen mach ewich spisen.* | Where one … |
| BISSCOP: | *Balseme van duechden, reyn honichrate,* | Balsam … |
| | *Wilt u grote genadicheit haer bewisen,* | Will you … |
| | *Wyens lof dat niemen en can volprisen.* | Which praise nobody can complete. |

RONDEAU (1833-1840):

| | | |
|---|---|---|
| BISSCOP: | *Lof, cracht, des alle crachten cracht hebben,* | O mightiness from which all mightiness derives, |
| | *Dat ghi u vrienden aldus versiet.* | That you can take care of your friends. |
| 1 PRIESTER: | *Wel hem, die u in haer gedacht hebben.* | May he [be glad] who has you in his mind. |
| | *Lof, cracht, des alle crachten cracht hebben.* | Praise, power … |
| BISSCOP: | *Wat dat wi, menscen, in duechden gewracht hebben,* | What that we, mankind, in virtue have wrought, |
| | *Bi uwer duecht soe en eest al niet.* | Is nothing at all [when compared] with your virtue. |
| 2 PRIESTER: | *Lof, cracht, des alle crachten cracht hebben,* | Praise, power … |
| | *Dat ghi u vrienden aldus versiet.* | That you … |

Dialogue: 1 JONGELINC, 2 JONGELINC, 3 JONGELINC (1850-1912)

RONDEAU (1850-1857):

| 1 JONGELINC: | Gods werken sijn wonderlijc te verstane. | God's works are startling to behold |
| 2 JONGELINC: | Wie sal sijn wijsheit dan gronderen? | Who shall then fathom his wisdom? |
| 3 JONGELINC: | Het gaet verre buten minen vermane. | It goes far beyond my wording. |
| 1 JONGELINC: | Gods werken sijn wonderlijc te verstane. | God's works ... |
| 3 JONGELINC: | Nu pinen wi, na sbisscops bevel, te gane | Now we prepare, according to the bishop's order, to go |
| | Ten tempel, daer elc mach veryubileren. | To the temple, where each [person] may enjoy him- or herself. |
| 1 JONGELINC: | Gods werken sijn wonderlijc te verstane. | God's works ... |
| 2 JONGELINC: | Wie sal sijn wijsheit dan gronderen? | Who shall then fathom ... |

RONDEAU (1904-1911):

| 1 JONGELINC: | Sijn roede sal bloyen, die brudegoem wesen sal. | His staff shall bloom, who shall be bridegroom. |
| | Ga wi ten temple de maecht aenscouwen. | Let us go to the temple to behold the Virgin. |
| 2 JONGELINC: | Tes messelic wie ons meskief genesen sal, | It is uncertain who shall cure us of our mischief, |
| | Sijn roede sal bloyen, die brudegoem wesen sal. | His rod shall bloom ... |
| 3 JONGELINC: | Sijn aventuere es groet, die in desen sal | His undertaking is great, who in this [way] shall |
| | Gode behagen ende de maget trouwen. | Help God and marry the Virgin. |
| 1 JONGELINC: | Sijn roede sal bloyen, die brudegoem wesen sal. | His rod shall bloom ... |
| | Ga wi ten temple de maegt aenscouwen. | Let us go ... |

Dialogue: BISSCOP, 1 VAN DAVIDS GESLECHTE [of David's lineage], JOSEPH, 1 PRIESTER, MARIA (1913-1964)
Dialogue: GOD, GABRIEL (1965-2012)
    *Pause cort* [Short pause] (2012-2013)
Dialogue: GABRIEL, MARIA, DINGEL (2013-2050)
    *Selete* (2050-2051)
*Naprologhe* [Epilogue] (2051-2081)

## Brussels, Royal Library, Ms. II 478:
### Anon., *Die sevenste bliscap van onser vrouwen* [The Seventh Joy of Our Lady] Brussels, 1444-1462

*Prologe* (1-60)
Dialogue: JAN, MARIA (61-165)
RONDEAU (157-164):

| JAN: | Nu, gawy met anderen voort in minnen, | Now let us go forth with the others in neighborly love, |
| | Tot Gode gelieft dat Hi ons hale. | Until God wants to collect us. |
| MARIA: | Sijn heilege gracie laet Hi ons kinnen, | He lets us recognize his holy grace |
| | Gawy met anderen voort in minnen. | Let us go forth with the others in neighborly love. |
| JAN: | Sijn godheit doe ons genade gewinnen, | His godliness lets us win mercy, |
| | Dat wi ontvlien der helscer quale. | So that we flee the hellish pain. |
| MARIA: | Nu gawi met anderen voort in minnen, | Now let us go ... |
| | Tot Gode gelieft dat Hi ons hale ... | Until God ... |
| | Uut dezen ellendichen eerdscendalen. | Out of this miserable earthly valley. |

    *Silete cort* (164-165)
Dialogue: 1 JODE [Jew], 2 JODE, POTESTAET [Potentate], DOUWERE [Elder] (165-304)
    *Selete* (304-305)
Monologue: MARIA (305-325)
RONDEAU (306-313):

| MARIA: | O laes! God Heere! Wat sal ic bestaen? | Alas! God, Lord! What shall I withstand? |
| | Sal ic van troeste dus bliven versteken? | Shall I thus remain banished from comfort? |

| | |
|---|---|
| Mijn herte mocht my in drucke ontgaen. | My courage fails me under pressure |
| Ay laes! God Here! Wat sal ic bestaen? | Alas! … |
| Ic ben in sulken rouwe bevaen! | I am caught in such grief! |
| Mi dunct al soude mi therte breken. | It seems as if my heart should break |
| O laes! God Heere! Wat sal ic bestaen? | Alas! … |
| Sal ic van troeste dus bliven versteken? | Shall I thus remain banished? |

*Selete. Die wile sal men den hemel opdoen, daer God sit, ende seggen toten ingel Gabriel …* [Silence. During which one should open the heavens, where God sits, and say to the angel Gabriel …] (325-326)

Dialogue: GOD, GABRIEL (326-383)

Dialogue: GABRIEL, MARIA (384-505)

RONDEAU (493-500):

| MARIA: | Lof deser bliscap in mi gemaect | Praise this Joy made in me |
|---|---|---|
| | Bi des yngels sueten ingevene! | By the angel's sweet infusion! |
| | Nu ben ic met alder vruecht ontstaect. | Now I am inflamed with all the fruit. |
| | Lof deser bliscap in mi gemaect! | Praise this Joy … |
| | Lof hebt, die mi ontbiet, dus naect | Have praise, [to him] who notifies me, thus naked |
| | Dat ic sal comen ten ewigen levene! | That I shll come to eternal life! |
| | Lof deser bliscap in my gemaect, | Praise this Joy … |
| | Bi des yngels sueten ingevene, | By the angel's … |
| | [continues] | |

*Selete. Hier sal Jan staen predeken den volke in der stat van Ephesen* [Silence. Here John shall stand preaching to the townspeople of the city of Ephesus] [Left margin has above this text "1. Pausa" and below "2. Pausa"] (505-506)

Monologue: Jan (506-570)

*Hier selen comen 2 ingle met enen cleede ende omslaen Sint Janne: ende tcleet sal scinen als een wolke. Ende soe bedect, selen sine voeren vor Marien dore, oft anderssins, soet best es.* [Here two angels shall come with a dress and wrap it around St. John: and the dress shall shine as a cloud. And covered in this way, he shall appear before Mary's door, or elsewhere, as it is best.]

Dialogue: 1 GEBUER [Relative], 2 GEBUER, 3 GEBUERINNE (571-638)

Dialogue: JAN, MARIA (639-758)

*Selete* (758-759)

Dialogue: PETER, ANDRIES, PAUWELS, MATHIJS, MARIE, JAN, BERTELMEEUS, JACOP, PHILIPS, SYMON (759-989)

RONDEAU (981-989):

| JAN: | Lof hebt, oetmoedege Vrou vercoren! | Be praised, discouraged chosen Woman! |
|---|---|---|
| | U groot begeren wort Gode bequame. | Your great desire pleases God |
| PETER: | Want ghi en vreest noch wee noch toren; | Because you fear neither harm nor anger from him |
| | Lof hebt, oetmoedege Vrou vercoren! | Be praised … |
| PAUL: | Ghi sijt de rose als onder doren, | You are the rose among thorns |
| | Ende moeder en maecht tot onser vrame. | And mother and Virgin to our advantage |
| JAN: | Lof hebt, oetmoedege Vrou vercoren! | Be praised … |
| | U groot begeren wert Gode bequame, | Your great desire … |

*Selete* (989-990)

Dialogue: LUCIFER, 1 VIANT [Monster], 2 VIANT (990-1049)

Dialogue: MICHAEL, 1 VIANT, 2 VIANT (1049-1136)

*Selete* (1136-1137)

Dialogue: GOD, INGEL (1137-1178)

Dialogue: CONFESSOR, MARIA, PETER, GOD, JAN (1179-1262)

> *Hier selen dapostelen alle cnielen oft si haer gebet lasen* [Here the apostles shall all kneel as if they are reading their prayer]

Dialogue: JAN, PETER, 1 MAECHT, 2 MAECHT, 3 MAECHT, PAUWELS, ANDRIES, BERTELMEEUS, GOD (1263-1343)

RONDEAU (1330-1337):

| JAN: | *Lof, Heere, dat U dit geweerde!* | Praise, Lord, that you let this happen! |
|---|---|---|
|  | *Wes wi vermogen, wort tuwer eeren.* | What we dispose of, is for your honor |
| PETER: | *Lof hebt, die ons dit selve vercleerde!* | Praise has [the one] who clarified this to us! |
|  | *Lof, Heere, dat U dit geweerde!* | Praise, Lord ... |
| PAUWELS: | *Lof U gescie in hemel ende erde!* | Praise your actions in heaven and earth! |
|  | *Glorie moet ewich in U vermeeren!* | Glory must be multiplied in you forever! |
| JAN: | *Lof, Heere, dat U dit geweerde!* | Praise, Lord ... |
|  | *Wes wi vermogen wort tUwer eeren,* | What we dispose of ... |

Dialogue: PETER, JAN, PAUWELS (1338-1385)

> *Hier heffen se de bare op ende singen: Exit de Egypto. Alleluia. Ende dinglen in den trone selen oec singen ende orglen* (1385-1386) [Here they lift up the bier and sing: Exit ... And the angels in the tower shall also sing and play organ]

Dialogue: 1 JODE, 2 JODE, POTESTAET, DOUWERE (1386-1503)

> First Jew: *Al singen se nu, si mochten wel weenen; Eerlanc, wi mochten van haren sange Wel droefheit maken* [Now they are all singing, they may as well whine; before long, we would like to make melancholy of their song] (1413-1415)

Dialogue: 1 GEBUER, THOMAS (1503-1527)

> *Selete* (1527-1528)

Dialogue: PETER, JAN, PAUWELS, ANDRIES, THOMAES, BERTELMEEUS, MATHIJS (1528-1680)

RONDEAU (1528-1535):

| PETER: | *O Heere, alder menscen confoort,* | O Lord, comfort to all mankind |
|---|---|---|
|  | *Wat vruechden mach in den hemel risen!* | What fruits may rise into heaven! |
|  | *Ic hebt seer lange wile gehoort.* | I have heard for a very long time. |
|  | *Lof alder creatueren confoort,* | Praise the comfort to all creatures, |
|  | *Tes al in vrouden, suyt ende noort,* | They are all in joy, south and north, |
|  | *Al themelsce heer wilt verjolisen;* | The whole heavenly army wants to rejoice; |
|  | *O Heere, alder menscen confoort,* | O Lord ... |
|  | *Wat vruechden mach in den hemel risen?* | What fruits ... |

| PETER [commenting on the music just heard] (1568-1572): | | |
|---|---|---|
|  | *Doets ons vermaen;* | Do advise us; |
|  | *Lieve Thomaes, om cort recoort,* | Dear Thomas, about a short report, |
|  | *Wi hebben soo groten vruecht gehoort* | We have heard such great fruits |
|  | *Van sange ende melodiosen acoorde,* | Of song and melodious accords, |
|  | *Dat noyt mensce tsgelijcs en hoorde; ...* | Such as men have never heard; ... |

RONDEAU (1668-1675):

| PETER: | *Orlof, lieve brueders, wi moeten sceyen,* | Goodbye, dear brothers, we must take leave |
|---|---|---|
|  | *Niet langere en mogen wi tsamen bliven.* | We may not stay together longer. |
| PAUWELS: | *Wi moeten gaen Gods wege bereyen.* | We must go to prepare God's way. |
|  | *Orlof, lieve brueders, wi moeten sceyen.* | Goodbye ... |
| JAN: | *Elc bidde den Heere met weerdicheyen,* | We each pray to the Lord with honesty, |
|  | *Dat ons sijn gracie wille verstiven.* | That he may sow his grace upon us. |
| PETER: | *Orlof, live brueders, wi moeten sceyen,* | Goodbye ... |
|  | *Niet langer en mogen wi tsamen bliven.* | We may ... |

*Naprologhe* [Epilogue] (1681-1721)

# Appendix II

## Summary of Poetic Rhyme Schemes

### *First Joy*

| Lines | Rhyme | Characters |
|---|---|---|
| 1-40 | pattern | Prologue, addressing Mary |
| | (20-23 virelai) | |
| 41-68 | pairs | Prologue |
| 69-73 | pattern | Prologue, addressing God |
| 74-75 | pairs | Prologue |
| 76-331 | pairs | |
| 332-379 | pattern | Angel, Adam and Eve |
| 380-523 | pairs | |
| 524-549 | pattern | God, Adam |
| 550-569 | pairs | |
| 570-587 | pattern | God |
| | (588-595 rondeau) | |
| 596-602 | prose | Lucifer, Envy |
| 603-674 | pairs | |
| 675-679 | pattern | other child [of Adam and Eve] |
| 680-695 | pairs | |
| 696-736 | pattern | Angel, Seth |
| 737-770 | pairs | |
| 771-830 | pattern | Adam, Eve, Another, David, Job, Isaiah (beseeching God) |
| | (831-838 rondeau) | |
| 839-1139 | pairs | |
| 1140-1216 | pattern | God, Pity, Angel, Justice, Truth |
| 1217-1248 | pairs | |
| 1249-1271 | pattern | God, Pity, Son of God |
| 1272-1333 | pairs | |
| 1334-1407 | pattern | Son, Peace, Pity, Truth, Joachim |
| | (1376-1383 rondeau) | |
| | (1384-1391 rondeau) | |
| | (1392-1400 rondeau) | |
| 1408-1447 | pairs | except 1414, which refers to God |
| 1448-1523 | pattern | Joachim, God, Angel, Anne |
| 1524-1573 | pairs | |
| 1574-1579 | pattern | Anna conceives Mary by God |
| 1580-1631 | pairs | |
| 1632-1643 | pattern | Angel, Priest, 2 Pastors |
| | (1644-1651 rondeau) | |

| | | |
|---|---|---|
| 1651-1700 | pairs | |
| | (1701-1708 rondeau) | |
| 1708-1757 | pairs | |
| 1758-1781 | pattern | Joachim, Anna |
| | (1782-1789 rondeau) | |
| 1789-1816 | pairs | |
| | (1816-1826 rondeau) | |
| 1826-1832 | pattern | Priests, Bishop (then rondeaux) |
| | (1833-1840 rondeau) | |
| 1840-1849 | pairs | |
| | (1850-1857 rondeau) | |
| 1857-1966 | pairs | |
| | (1904-1911 rondeau) | |
| 1967-1978 | pattern | God |
| 1979-2012 | pairs | |
| 2013-2075 | pattern | Gabriel, Mary, Epilogue |
| 2076-2081 | pairs | |

*Seventh Joy*

| | | |
|---|---|---|
| 1-164 | pattern | Mary, John |
| | (157-164 rondeau) | |
| 165-305 | pairs | |
| | (306-313 rondeau) | |
| 313-570 | pattern | Mary, God, Gabriel, John |
| | (493-500 rondeau) | |
| 571-710 | pairs | |
| 711-758 | pattern | John, Mary |
| 759-864 | pairs | |
| 865-980 | pattern | Mary, Apostles |
| | (981-989 rondeau) | |
| 990-1136 | pairs | |
| 1137-1262 | pattern | God, Angel, Confessor, Mary, Peter |
| 1263-1312 | pairs | |
| 1313-1343 | pattern | God |
| | (1330-1337 rondeau) | |
| 1344-1506 | pairs | |
| 1507-1536 | pattern | Thomas, Peter |
| | (1528-1535 rondeau) | |
| 1537-1626 | pairs | |
| 1627-1721 | pattern | John, Andrew, Peter, Paul, Epilogue |
| | (1668-1675 rondeau) | |

Richard Wexler

# IN SEARCH
## OF THE MISSING MOVEMENTS
## OF OCKEGHEM'S REQUIEM

W HAT did the French court chapel sing after completing the five extant movements of Ockeghem's Requiem: an introit, a Kyrie, a gradual, a tract, and an offertory?[1] Without a doubt the service proceeded in some manner with a Sanctus and an Agnus Dei, and concluded with a communion. Were these movements sung in chant?

In a recent article, I suggested that the chapel probably sang chant rather more often than we suppose.[2] The chants paraphrased in the existing movements of Ockeghem's Requiem correspond for the most part to those in the Roman and Sarum graduals.[3] But these easily accessible graduals do not provide us with definitive information.

A case in point: offertories appear more and more often in chant books written in the high middle ages without the verses previously associated with them, the one exception being the offertory for the Missa pro defunctis, *Domine Jesu Christe*.[4] The standard chant books all supply a verse for it, beginning *Hostias et preces*. The Chigi Codex,[5] the sole source transmitting all five extant movements of Ockeghem's Requiem, offers two different musical settings of the verse's first half. At the top left of the opening this section of the offertory occupies, *Hostias et preces* is set to a monophonic intonation in Renaissance-style chant notation (See Example 1a). At the bot-

1. *Johannes Ockeghem: Collected Works*, 2, ed. Dragan PLAMENAC (New York: American Musicological Society, 1966), Second, Corrected Edition, 83-97; also *Johannes Ockeghem: Missa pro defunctis*, ed. Bruno TURNER (London: Mappa Mundi, 1978). The formulary adopted by Ockeghem is shown in the left-hand column of Table 2, below.

2. "Ockeghem and Politics," *Tijdschrift van de koninklijke vereniging voor nederlandse muziekgeschiedenis* 47 (1997): 16.

3. *Graduale sacrosanctae romanae ecclesiae* (Paris: Desclée, 1961), hereafter referred to as GR; Walter H. FRERE, ed. *Graduale Sarisburiense: A Reproduction in Facsimile of a Manuscript of the Thirteenth Century* (London: Bernard Quaritch, 1894; repr. Farnborough: Gregg Press, 1966),

hereafter referred to as GS.

In his doctoral dissertation, "The Structure of the Ockeghem *Requiem*" (University of Chicago, 1977), 55-74, Michael ECKERT provides a complete transcription of the work. He accompanies each system with a staff containing the chant as it appears in one (or at times both) of the graduals cited above, showing its relationship to the voice bearing the cantus firmus. I am very grateful to him for making a copy of his dissertation available to me.

4. Ruth STEINER, "Some Questions about the Gregorian Offertories and Their Verses," *Journal of the American Musicological Society* 19 (1966): 163.

5. Rome, Vatican City, Biblioteca Apostolica Vaticana, Ms. Chigi C VIII 234, ff. 125ᵛ-136ʳ.

tom of the same opening, *Hostias et preces* receives a two-voice setting in measured polyphony (Example 1b). One would expect that the duo, generally thought to be an alternative to the intonation, should somehow incorporate the intonation's melody. However, it is nowhere to be found,[6] and the duo has seemed for this reason to be the only portion of Ockeghem's Requiem not based on chant.

Another early Requiem Mass was composed by Ockeghem's probable successor as *maître de chapelle* at the French court, Johannes Prioris,[7] and ultimately printed by Attaingnant in 1532.[8] Prioris' setting of the offertory verse begins with a chant intonation (Example 1c) that differs markedly from Ockeghem's. This intonation turns out to be the cantus firmus of the *Hostias* duo in Ockeghem's Requiem, indicated with crosses in the lower voice of Example 1b.

One might expect that the differences between the intonations resulted from the composers' having employed different chants in their offertory settings. But both Ockeghem and Prioris use the same chant melody in the antiphon and in the remainder of the verse, one that corresponds very closely to what is printed in the *Graduale Romanum*.[9] Thus, *Domine Jesu Christe* must have had more than one verse in times past, especially since there are reports concerning elaborate processions in connection with this offertory.[10]

Turning to Ott's *Offertoriale*,[11] I found four verses rather than one,[12] and the end of the third (Example 1d) somewhat resembles the chant borrowed for Prioris's intonation and the duo of the Chigi Codex. The melody in Ott is rather more melismatic, but it begins on d, rises immediately to a', descends to d and then on to c, rises through d to f, and descends again to c, ending on d.[13]

6.   Eckert attempts to relate the settings of the verse found in the GR and GS to the duo, which he also labels, "Free variation of chant," op. cit., 73.

7.   *Johannes Prioris: Opera omnia*, 2, ed. T. Herman KEAHEY and Conrad M. DOUGLAS, Corpus mensurabilis musicae, 90 (Neuhausen-Stuttgart: American Institute of Musicology, 1982), 1-28. See also Richard WEXLER, "Prioris," *The New Grove*, 15: 275.

8.   Pierre ATTAINGNANT, *Quintus liber tres missas continet, ...* (Paris, 1532), ff. 165ᵛ-176ʳ. Other sources include Casale Monferrato, Archivio capitolare, Ms. N (4), ff. 132ᵛ-134ʳ and 136ᵛ-138ʳ (anon.); and Adrian LE ROY and Robert BALLARD, *Liber primus sex missas continens* (Paris, 1553) (superius only), ff. 11ᵛ-13ᵛ (Prioris).

9.   GR, pp. 100*-101*.

10.  See Claude GAY, "Formulaires anciens pour la messe des défunts," *Études grégoriennes* 2 (1957): 96-97, and Barbara HAGGH, "The Archives of the Order of the Golden Fleece and Music," *Journal of the Royal Musical Association* 120 (1995): 12.

11.  Carolus OTT, *Offertoriale sive versus offertoriorum* (Paris: Desclée, 1935), 189-91.

12.  Containing offertory verses not in the editions of the Roman chant, Ott's book is based on the graduals Montpellier, Ms. H 159, and Paris, BnF, Ms. lat. 903 (see *Paléographie musicale*, 7-8, 13).

13.  But something still does not quite fit here: Why would a duo incorporating a melody associated with the end of the third verse of an offertory serve as something leading to the conclusion of the first verse? And how much like Ockeghem is it for there to be eight major thirds in a row (in effect, gymel in the English manner) from the third measure of Example 1b to the ninth. As attractive as this duo is, one has to wonder if Ockeghem actually composed it. On the other hand, the Requiem often seems unlike other works by Ockeghem in so many ways, that one feels hesitant about questioning the authenticity of any given portion of it.

**Example 1a**  Ockeghem, Requiem, Offertory verse incipit (after Ms. Chigi, ff. cxxviiᵛ-cxxviiiʳ)

Hostias    et preces tibi domine    offerimus

**Example 1b**  Ockeghem, Requiem, alternative (?) duo Hostias, mm. 116-42 (of Offertory)

Duo

Hostias    et    Ho - sti - as,    ho - sti - as    et

Hostias    et preces    Hos - sti - - - as _____ et

*123*

pre - ces _____ ti - - bi    Do - mi - ne    of -

pre - - - ces    ti - bi _____ Do - -

*133*

- - - - fe - ri - - - mus.

- - mi - ne _____ of - - fe - ri - - mus.

**Example 1c**  Johannes Prioris, Requiem, Offertory verse incipit (after RISM 1532⁵)

Hostias    et    preces    tibi    domine    offerimus.

**Example 1d**  C. Ott, *Offertoriale*, No. 110.—Domine Jesu Christe, last third, verse 3

et li- be- ra e- as    de lo- cis tormen- to- rum.

Having received some assistance from Prioris, I then turned to other early
Franco-Netherlandish Requiem Masses by Antoine Brumel,[14] Pierre de La Rue,[15] and,
depending on which manuscript prepared by the famous scribe Petrus Alamire one
chooses to believe, either Antoine de Févin or Antonius Divitis.[16] (It appears Alamire
may have confused his French court Anthonys at some point.)

Also pertinent is the work included under the rubric "Basurto in agendis mortuorum" in the Spanish manuscript Tarazona 5,[17] mainly because it incorporates the
opening duo of Ockeghem's tract.[18] However, even though Juan García de Basurto
supplied an introit, a Kyrie, a gradual, a tract—in fact two, since Ockeghem's is preceded by another partial setting for three voices attributed to [Pedro de] Pastrana[19]—,

14. *Antoine Brumel: Missa pro defunctis*, ed. Albert SEAY, Das
Chorwerk, 68 (Wolfenbüttel: Möseler, 1959); and *Antoine
Brumel: Opera omnia*, ed. Barton HUDSON. Corpus mensu-
rabilis musicae, 5 (n.p.: American Institute of
Musicology, 1970), 65-79.
15. *Pierre de La Rue: Requiem und eine Motette*, ed. Friedrich
BLUME. Das Chorwerk, 11 (Wolfenbüttel: Möseler, 1931);
and *Pierre de La Rue: Opera omnia*, 5, ed. Nigel St. John
DAVISON, Corpus mensurabilis musicae, 97 (Neuhausen-
Stuttgart: American Institute of Musicology, 1996),
102-25 (*Missa pro fidelibus defunctis*).
16. Edward CLINKSCALE, ed., *Les Oeuvres complètes d'Antoine de
Févin*, 1 (Henryville, PA: Institute of Mediæval Music, 1980),
1-32. Petrus Alamire was the pen name of Peter van den
Hove, one of the chief scribes at the court of Burgundy. See
Herbert KELLMAN, "Alamire, Pierre," *The New Grove*, 1: 192-93.
The *Missa pro fidelibus defunctis* is attributed to Févin in Vienna,
Österreichische Nationalbibliothek, Musiksammlung, Ms.
Mus. 15495 (f. 68ᵛ); and Jena, Universitäts-Bibliothek, Cod.
5 (f. 73ᵛ). However, the "Occo Codex," Brussels,
Bibliothèque royale Albert I, Ms. IV. 922, gives it to Divitis
(f. 133ᵛ). All three sources are in Alamire's hand. See further,
Bernard HUYS, ed. *Occo Codex*, Facsimilia musica neer-
landica, 1, Willem ELDERS, gen. ed. (Buren: Vereniging voor
nederlandse muziekgeschiedenis, 1979), xxvi. Also see,
*Antonius Divitis: Collected Works*, ed. William A. NUGENT.
Recent Researches in the Music of the Renaissance, 94
(Madison: A-R Editions, 1993), xiv-xv.
Both the Févin/Divitis and the La Rue settings bear the
designation *pro fidelibus defunctis* (for the faithful departed) in original sources, the standard means of
referring to a Requiem mass, which may suggest that
they are not occasional pieces but rather works for routine liturgical use. On the other hand, all of the sources
containing this designation were written at the
Burgundian scriptorium and therefore may merely
reflect what the scribes of that particular institution

considered an appropriate title, regardless of usage.
Although Jean Richafort's Requiem is sometimes
thought of as being among the earliest, I have decided
against considering it for a variety of reasons: First,
Richafort, who lived *c.*1480-*c.*1547 (Howard Mayer
BROWN, "Richafort, Jean," *The New Grove*, 15: 839), was perhaps as a much as a generation younger than Brumel,
Févin/Divitis, La Rue, and Prioris. Also, although chant
paraphrase is present at times, Richafort based his
Requiem on the canonic voices from Josquin's(?) *Christus
mortuus—Circumdederunt me*. For this reason, and because
Richafort also quoted from Josquin's *Faulte d'argent* where
the text is "c'est douleur non pareille," Gustave Reese suggested that Richafort composed it upon the death of
Josquin. (See *Music in the Renaissance*, revised ed. [New York:
Norton, 1959], 336.) If Reese was right, then Richafort's
Requiem would have been written after 1521, making it the
youngest of the several Masses mentioned here, and, on
account of its structure incorporating pre-existent canon,
a very different kind of piece from the others. For what it
is worth, however, Richafort also included a Sanctus, an
Agnus Dei, and a communion. For editions, see *Jean
Richafort: Requiem zu 6 Stimmen*, ed. Albert SEAY, Das
Chorwerk, 124 (Wolfenbüttel: Möseler, 1976); and
*Johannes Richafort: Opera omnia*, 1, ed. Harry ELZINGA, Corpus
mensurabilis musicae, 81 (Neuhausen-Stuttgart:
American Institute of Musicology, 1979), 59-101.
17. Tarazona, Archivo Capitular de la Catedral, Ms. 5,
ff. 68ᵛ-73ʳ.
18. See Eleanor RUSSELL, "The *Missa in agendis mortuorum*
of Juan García de Basurto: Johannes Ockeghem,
Antoine Brumel, and an Early Spanish Polyphonic
Requiem Mass," *Tijdschrift van de koninklijke vereniging voor
nederlandse muziekgeschiedenis* 29 (1979): 1-37. Russell provides transcriptions of the introit, the Kyrie, and the
gradual (*Requiem eternam*) on 32-36.
19. *Idem*, "Pastrana, Pedro de," *The New Grove*, 14: 297.

**Example 2**  Agnus Dei, "Basurto in agendis mortuorum"

1)  Dot missing erroneously
2)  Originally a breve
3)  A single barline in Tarazona 5. (Repeat all, including the intonation, twice.)

a Sanctus, an Agnus Dei (Example 2[20]), and a communion, I suspect the work may have found more varied uses, not only as a Requiem for a funeral, but perhaps also for anniversaries or other commemorations. The rubric "in agendis mortuorum" is common in printed liturgical books, including agendas and manuals, and usually signals an office and mass for the dead that could be used for many different purposes, as opposed to that prescribed for All Soul's Day, 2 November, or one prepared for a specific funeral. In fact, Basurto's communion is from Brumel's Requiem, and it is not certain that Basurto, whose other known works include only a few motets and a magnificat,[21] necessarily composed any of it.[22]

There would hardly be much point in examining the style of Basurto's motets to see if it might resemble what is found in this apparent anthology of music for funerals. The style of the latter is so simple, especially in the final three movements (the last of which is in any event the same as the communion in Brumel's Requiem), that anyone who knew a bit of counterpoint could have composed most of it. Indeed, the same could be said of the Requiems by Brumel, Févin/Divitis, and Prioris, which are often so elementary, that one is hard pressed to recognize these musicians' normal styles of composition (Examples 3a, b, and c).[23]

These composers paraphrased the melodies they borrowed so lightly, that it becomes relatively easy to discern the underlying chant, and thereby to know what Ockeghem's might have been. The first staff in Example 4 provides the reading of Agnus I common to all three standard chant books,[24] followed by the melodies distilled from the cantus firmi of the Agnus Dei movements under discussion here. Considering how many Agnus Dei chants are known that are not accounted for in these chant publications,[25] none of the composers' melodies matches exactly.[26]

20. My transcription. I owe a debt of gratitude to Grayson Wagstaff for providing me with copies of the relevant folios of Tarazona 5 from a microfilm belonging to him.

21. See Robert STEVENSON, "García de Basurto, Juan," *The New Grove*, 7: 155, for a list of works.

22. As Wagstaff has pointed out, Basurto's introit begins with a short intonation, consisting of the word "Requiem" only, as found in the northern tradition. In surviving masses for the dead known to be by Spanish composers, the intonation of the introit customarily incorporates the second word of the chant, "aeternam." See WAGSTAFF, "Music for the Dead: Polyphonic Settings of the *Officium* and *Missa pro defunctis* by Spanish and Latin American composers before 1630" (Ph.D. dissertation, University of Texas at Austin, 1995), 273f. This suggests that Basurto may have borrowed his introit from an otherwise unknown northern Requiem Mass.

23. I have not included an excerpt from La Rue's Requiem, because it stands apart from the others, being in more florid polyphony almost throughout.

24. The melodies of both the Sanctus and the Agnus Dei in the Mass for the Dead are substantially the same as those in the modern cycle bearing the rubric "For the ferias of Advent and Lent as well as for vigils, Ember Days, and Rogation Days" (which is to say, for use on weekdays in penitential seasons and on penitential days), Mass XVIII, in *The Liber Usualis with Introduction and Rubrics in English*, ed. Benedictines of Solesmes (Tournai: Desclée, 1963 hereafter referred to as LU), 62-63.

In Example 4, the clefs indicate which voices bear the cantus firmus. In point of fact, the first four notes of Prioris's version of the chant are an octave lower. This is because he presents all intonations in the tenor voice, although in the polyphony he most often paraphrases the chant in the superius.

**Example 3a**  Johannes Prioris, Requiem, Agnus Dei II

25. In his *Das einstimmige Agnus Dei und seine handschriftliche Überlieferung vom 10. bis zum 16. Jahrhundert* (Erlangen: J. Hogl, 1967), Martin Schildbach lists a total of 270, not counting numerous variants.

26. Except for being transposed down a fifth, La Rue's comes the closest. Brumel's is similar, although with a different modal flavor, which may have something to do with the fact that his *Missa pro defunctis* was published by Antico in Rome, in 1516 (*Liber quindecim missarum electarum quæ per excellentissimos musicos compositae fuerunt*, ff. 155ᵛ-61ᵛ), and perhaps was intended for Italian use. Basurto's version appears to have its B's and F's in the wrong places,

but in any event we cannot be sure where his Agnus comes from or who might have composed it.

The style of Basurto's Sanctus is substantially the same. Because Basurto took over one of his tracts from Ockeghem and his communion from Brumel without crediting either composer, one might be tempted to advance the possibility that his Sanctus and Agnus Dei are two of the missing movements from Ockeghem's Requiem. But attempting to make such a claim on stylistic grounds would extend well beyond the bounds of reason, and any such possibility must be considered extremely remote.

**Example 3b**    Antoine BRUMEL, *Missa pro defunctis*, Agnus Dei III
(after Albert SEAY, ed., Das Chorwerk, 68)

**Example 3c** Agnus II, "Missa pro fidelibus defunctis. Anthonius divitis [? fevin?] pie memorie +"

**Example 4**  The Agnus Dei melodies of five Requiems written after Ockeghem's

*Liber Usualis*, p. 1815; *Graduale Romanum*, p. 101\*; *Graduale Sarisburiense*, p. 18\*

A - gnus De - i, \* qui tol - lis pec - ca - ta     mun - di:  do - na    e - is    re - qui - em.

Juan García de Basurto(?)

A - gnus De - i,  qui tol - lis pec - ca - ta    mun - di:  do - na  e - is   re - qui - em.

Antoine Brumel

A - gnus De - i,  qui tol - lis pec - ca - ta    mun - di:  do - na    e - is   re - qui - em.

Antoine de Févin? / Antonius Divitis?

A - gnus De - i,  qui tol - lis pec - ca - ta    mun - di:  do - na    e - is   re - qui - em.

Pierre de La Rue

A - gnus De - i,  qui tol - lis pec - ca - ta   mun - di:  do - na   e - is   re - qui - em.

Johannes Prioris

A - gnus De - i,  qui tol - lis pec - ca - ta    mun - di:  do - na    e - is   re - qui - em.

The Févin/Divitis and Prioris melodies for the Agnus Dei, however, are almost identical to one another, if not precisely the same as the chant in the standard books.[27] Because both (or maybe it should be said, all three) were composers at the French court, there is a fair degree of probability that this melody was the Agnus Dei chant known to Ockeghem, the ferial Agnus Dei XVIII in the Liber Usualis. This same Agnus common to their settings appears in an ordinal prepared in 1471 once belonging to the Sainte-Chapelle in Paris.[28] In the ordinal, the rubric for this Agnus reads, "[For] feasts of three lessons not during solemn octaves; mass for the dead."[29]

27.  SCHILDBACH, *Das einstimmige Agnus Dei*, 103, No. 101, is essentially the melody in LU, GR, and GS shown at the top of Example 4. It is possible to see the melody used by Févin/Divitis and Prioris, otherwise unrecorded by Schildbach, as a variant of his No. 101.

28.  The incipits are published in Barbara HAGGH, "An Ordinal of Ockeghem's Time from the Sainte-Chapelle

of Paris: Paris, Bibliothèque de l'Arsenal, Ms. 114," *Tijdschrift van de koninglijke vereniging voor nederlandse muziekgeschiedenis* 47 (1997): 62-67. Schildbach lists other French sources of this melody, op. cit., 103-04.

29.  HAGGH, op. cit., 65. See also Craig WRIGHT. *Music and Ceremony at Notre Dame of Paris, 500-1550* (Cambridge: Cambridge University Press, 1989), 89. The same deduc-

Returning now to the unadorned, unpretentious, note-against-note style of the final three movements of the Requiems by Brumel, Févin/Divitis, and Prioris: In Example 3a, by the last named, the "chords" are almost without exception in root position, and the intervals between the tenor and the superius are mainly sixths. This matches the description of the four-voice fauxbourdon, which we have come to call "falsobordone," discussed by Guillelmus Monachus in his late fifteenth-century treatise *De preceptis artis musicae*.[30] Example 3b, the third Agnus from Brumel's *Missa pro defunctis*, resembles Prioris's Agnus in most respects, although in the approach to the first signum, mm. 11-13, the counterpoint seems momentarily not quite so rigid. A closer examination of this brief passage reveals that the three lower voices cadence in the manner typical in fauxbourdon. (I have marked the first-inversion sonorities with "6" figures.) At least half of the Févin/Divitis Agnus II in Example 3c, scored for three voices, is in rather strict, written-out fauxbourdon.

It appears that all three of these examples reflect one kind or another of extemporized counterpoint. In other words, all of these movements, and also each composer's Sanctus and communion, may well represent somewhat refined versions, cleaned up for the sake of recording them in written form, of what a skilled chapel could have created while singing *"super librum."*[31]

Based on the foregoing observations, I would suggest that the French royal chapel completed Ockeghem's Requiem not in chant, but in quasi-improvised polyphony.[32] And it seems to me that the five movements that have come down to us

tive process can be applied to the five Sanctus movements and also to the five communions, which, as it happens, are all based on the communion *Lux æterna* found in the standard books, LU, 1815; GR, 102*; GS, 233.

30. Albert SEAY, ed., Corpus scriptorum de musica, 11 (n. p.: American Institute of Musicology, 1965), 38-43.

31. Without a doubt, Ockeghem would have been acquainted with three-voice fauxbourdon, but would he have known of falsobordone, which we are accustomed to associating with sixteenth-century Italian and Spanish psalm settings? The answer is probably yes, because he could very well have been aware of compositions like Prioris's Mass based on Hayne van Ghizeghem's well-known chanson *Allez regrets*, which survives today in a Vatican Ms. written in the 1480s, Cappella Sistina 35. See *Johannes Prioris: Opera omnia*, 1: 47-70. For another edition, see Richard WEXLER, "The Complete Works of Johannes Prioris" (Ph.D. diss., New York University, 1974), 397-443, esp. 402-404, 406, 413, and 417-18, all passages in which falsobordone texture predominates. Also see Craig WRIGHT, "Performance Practices at the Cathedral of Cambrai, 1475-1550," *The Musical Quarterly*

49 (1978): 315-22, concerning direct evidence that both fauxbourdon and falsobordone were sung at Cambrai in the latter part of the fifteenth century.

32. In his *Deploration dudit Cretin sur le trespas de feu Okergan, Tresorier de Sainct Martin de Tours*, the French poet and court chronicler Guillaume de Crétin calls the work

La messe aussi exquise et tresparfaicte
De Requiem par ledict deffunct [Ockeghem] faicte

and also wrote:

Enfans de cueur ne faictes plus leçons
De fleuretiz, mais note contre note
Sur Requiem en doulcettes façons,
Puis accordez voz chantz en piteux sons.

*(Choirboys, do no more lessons*
*in florid counterpoint, but note against note*
*on Requiem in agreeable ways*
*then join your songs and mourning sounds.)*

(Translation, Michael Eckert)

Ernest THOINAN, ed. *Déploration de Guillaume Crétin sur le trépas de Jean Ockeghem* (Paris: A. Claudin, 1864; repr. London: H. Baron, 1965), 34 and 41, respectively. See also ECKERT, op. cit., 28-29; and Fabrice FITCH, *Johannes*

indicate themselves which type of singing *super librum* it was. The sound of three-voice fauxbourdon becomes very apparent beginning in the sixth measure of Ockeghem's introit (Example 5).[33] One also encounters fauxbourdon texture in the section that

*Ockeghem: Masses and Models*, Collection Ricercar, 2 (Paris: Honoré Champion, 1997), 204. For another edition of the 420-line poem, see Kathleen CHESNEY, ed. *Œuvres poétiques de Guillaume de Crétin* (Paris: Firmin Didot, 1932; repr. Geneva: Slatkine, 1977), No. XXXI, pp. 60-73.
Crétin may be referring directly to Ockeghem's introit setting, but in any event he is making a clear distinction between florid and note-against-note counterpoint. Eckert interprets these four verses to mean that the poet considered the latter style more "appropriate for the 'piteux' character of a *Requiem*" (op. cit., 29), which is probably undeniable. Fitch takes this one step further, suggesting (*loc. cit.*), "The Introit represents a rare instance of a composer putting to paper a slightly more complex version of what might have been expected of performers improvising in the musical vernacular of the period."
But how actually rare is it? Considering the movements discussed above from Masses for the Dead by Brumel, Févin/Divitis, and Prioris, as well as the pieces collected by Basurto, writing of that kind must have been quite common in the genre. One might also argue that virtually every surviving piece of written-out fauxbourdon represents a somewhat developed version of what competent singers could have created *ex tempore*. (For a catalogue of 175 such pieces, see Ernest TRUMBLE. *Fauxbourdon: An Historical Survey*, 1 [Brooklyn, NY: Instititue of Mediæval Music, 1959], 68-80.) Moreover, the underlying premise of Heinrich Besseler's *Bourdon und Fauxbourdon* (Leipzig: Breitkopf & Härtel, 1950) is that extemporized counterpoint should be seen as a basic component of the Franco-Netherlandish style. Cf. his subtitle: *Studien zum Ursprung der niederländischen Musik.*
We, who are so thoroughly accustomed to thinking of the creation of music as inseparable from the process of writing it down, run the risk of misunderstanding how music was made before writing materials became more widely used and freely available to composers. But our shortsightedness of the present seems remarkably strange, considering how surrounded we are in our day-to-day lives by music that can be quite complex and accomplished, even though not set down in writing. Cf. Margaret BENT, "*Resfacta* and *Cantare Super Librum*," *Journal of the American Musicological Society* 36 (1983): 378.
As Bonnie J. BLACKBURN has said, "If we conceive of singing *super librum* as analogous to realizing a basso continuo, it will not seem so mysterious and difficult to us. Nor is it irrelevant to think of the sophisticated impro-

visations of jazz musicians in our day." ("On Compositional Process in the Fifteenth Century," *Journal of the American Musicological Society* 40 [1987]: 258.) The three-voice music that she reproduces (Example 4, p. 257) from Tinctoris's *Liber de arte contrapuncti* (III.iv [2:149]), which is said by the theorist to represent what could be created singing *super librum*, looks astonishingly like what we normally assume was composed entirely in writing.
33.  Concerning fauxbourdon, see Ernest TRUMBLE, op. cit.; Brian TROWELL, "Faburden and Fauxbourdon," *Musica Disciplina* 13 (1959): 43-78; Suzanne CLERX, "Aux Origines du faux-bourdon," *Revue de musicologie* 40 (1957): 151-65; Ann Besser SCOTT, "The Beginnings of Fauxbourdon: a New Interpretation," *Journal of the American Musicological Society* 24 (1971): 345-63; Willem ELDERS, "Guillaume Dufay's Concept of Faux-Bourdon," *Revue belge de musicologie* 43 (1989): 173-95; and Andrew KIRKMAN, "Some early fifteenth-century fauxbourdons by Dufay and his contemporaries: A study in liturgically-motivated musical style," *Tijdschrift van de koninglijke vereniging voor nederlandse muziekgeschiedenis* 40 (1990): 3-35. Although these authors are often in substantial disagreement with one another, it is at least clear that fauxbourdon is one of several possible outcomes of singing *super librum*.
After examining the apparent meanings of the expressions "res facta" and "cantare super librum" as Tinctoris uses them in his *Liber de arte contrapuncti* (1477; Johannes Tinctoris, *Opera theoretica*, 2, ed. Albert SEAY, Corpus scriptorum de musica, 22 [n.p.: American Institute of Musicology, 1975], II) and his *Terminorum musicae diffinitorium* (*c.*1472, printed 1495; Johannes Tinctoris. *Dictionary of Musical Terms ... Together with the Latin Text*, transl. and annotated, Carl PARRISH [London: The Free Press of Glencoe, 1963]), Margaret Bent concludes ("*Resfacta* and *Cantare Super Librum*," 390):

> The "important difference" between *resfacta* and *cantare super librum* is that the parts of *resfacta* are "mutually obliged" with respect to the law and ordering of consonances, while the minimum requirement for *cantare super librum* is that each voice be consonant with the tenor, not needing to be subject to other voices. Having made the distinction in principle, Tinctoris goes on to say that it is better if singers upon the book do in fact arrange among themselves to avoid similar successions of consonances, that their singing may be sweeter.

serves as Kyries I and III (Example 6). There is only a small amount of fauxbourdon texture in the gradual[34] and none at all in the tract, but it makes an appreciable reappearance in the offertory, both at "Tu suscipe" (Example 7), which is the conclusion of the verse following "Hostias et preces," and in the part of the antiphon setting that repeats to end the five movements (Example 8).[35]

But in many respects, the three-voice fauxbourdon texture sounds out of place in the offertory, which otherwise represents Ockeghem at his most "learned." This is the movement of Ockeghem's Requiem that, aside perhaps from the fantastical duo beginning in m. 19, seems the least improvisatory in character. It contains much florid counterpoint, as well as intricate sequences of rapidly changing proportions indicated by almost every known mensuration sign. (See Example 9 and Table 1.) Could Ockeghem have returned to fauxbourdon texture at the end of the offertory in order to prepare his auditors for three-voice extemporized counterpoint in the movements to follow? I know of no theoretical statements from Ockeghem's time indicating that musicians prized this kind of unity, but what in the end, for example, is the cyclic mass all about if not the adoption of strategies for creating a better unified work of music? (See Example 10.[36])

If in suggesting this Tinctoris adhered to a very narrow definition of consonance and by "similar successions of consonances" meant parallel unisons, fifths, or octaves, then it does not appear he was being altogether consistent. For it seems unlikely that he would have considered parallel thirds and sixths with the tenor (as occurs in basic fauxbourdon) dissonant. Or could he have meant to suggest that contrary motion is preferable to parallel? In any event, Tinctoris's train of thought may help to clarify certain otherwise puzzling aspects of the counterpoint in Ockeghem's Requiem. For example, very near the beginning of the introit, mm. 17-20 of Example 5, one hears four consecutive sets of parallel fifths between the superius and the contra. Might this passage be representative of counterpoint in which the parts are *not* mutually obliged, but are each only consonant with the tenor? Could the introit in an earlier guise have been something sung *super librum*? Did Ockeghem later choose not to "arrange" away the parallel fifths in order to retain the flavor of extemporized counterpoint? Or did he deliberately commit the flagrant series of "contrapuntal errors" as he composed the introit in order to simulate the sound of singing *super librum*? These may not be the only parallel fifths in Ockeghem's works (see FITCH, op. cit., 156, for a list of others), but they certainly would seem to be the most conspicuous.

34. See also Ockeghem's gradual, mm. 69-71 and 86-92.
35. But (with apologies to René Magritte), this is not a fauxbourdon! Ockeghem paraphrases the chant in the *lowest* of the three sounding voices. Also, there is virtually no chant present at all in the extensive fauxbourdon passage at the end of the offertory verse, mm. 111-13 (Eckert, op. cit., 10). Could he have intended to create no more than the illusion of fauxbourdon in this instance?
36. This doggedly homorhythmic, bare-bones setting of the communion (LU, 1815; GR, 102*; GS, 233) in fauxbourdon by me is furnished purely for purposes of illustration. Surely the French court chapel singers had the ability to extemporize something much less literal-minded and vastly more creative. For one thing, written-out fauxbourdon pieces from the period usually contain far more rhythmic diversity. See Andrew KIRKMAN, op. cit., 8-10. The singing of a communion chant in fauxbourdon was far from unprecedented; the communion in Dufay's *Missa Sancti Jacobi, Vos qui secuti estis me*, is generally considered to have been the first fauxbourdon setting recorded in writing. See David FALLOWS, *Dufay*, The Master Musicians (London: J. M. Dent, revised edition 1987), 170. Dufay's communion is printed in *Guglielmi Dufay: Opera omnia*, 2, ed. Heinrich BESSELER, Corpus mensurabilis musicae, 1 (n.p.: American Institute of Musicology, 1960), 44.

**Example 5**  OCKEGHEM, Requiem, Introit, mm. 1-21

**Example 6**  OCKEGHEM, Requiem, Kyrie I and III, mm. 1-17

**Example 6 (cont'd)**

**Example 7** Ockeghem, Requiem, Offertory, mm. 85-90

**Example 8** Ockeghem, Requiem, Offertory, mm. 77-79

**Example 9**  Ockeghem, Requiem, Offertory, mm. 1-24

**Example 9 (cont'd)**

**Table 1**  Mensuration signs in Ockeghem 's Requiem

| | | | |
|---|---|---|---|
| INTROIT (throughout) | ¢ | TRACT | |
| | | Sicut cervus | O |
| KYRIE (throughout) | ¢ | Sitivit anima | C |
| | | Fuerunt michi lacrime | O* |
| GRADUAL (throughout) | ¢ | Ubi est Deus tuus? | O |

OFFERTORY

| | | |
|---|---|---|
| Domine Jhesu Christe | O2 | (S, B) |
| | O 3 ℭ 2 φ O | (Ct) |
| | ¢ | (T) |
| Sed signifer | O | |
| Quam olim | O2 | (S, T, B) |
| | ⊙ φ ℭ ¢ O φ C ¢ 2 | (Ct) |
| Hostias et preces | ¢ | |
| Tu suscipe | φ | |

*φ erroneously(?) in S.

**Example 10**  Communion—Missa pro defunctis (hypothetical extemporized setting)

**Example 10 (cont'd)**

qui - a  pi - us _____ es.  Requi-em æternam dona e-is Domine,

qui - a  pi - us _____ es.

qui - a  pi - us _____ es.

et  lux  per - pe - tu - a  lu - ce - at  e - - - is.

et  lux  per - pe - tu - a  lu - ce - at  e - - - is.

et  lux  per - pe - tu - a  lu - ce - at  e - - - is.

"Cum sanctis" *ut supra*

I propose now to edge still further out on the proverbial limb by delineating hypothetically the process by which Ockeghem composed his Requiem Mass. (See Table 2.[37])

37. The entry "2½" in the column "Number of Voices" for the "Fuerunt michi lacrime" section of the tract is not merely facetious; it is meant to call attention to one of the most unusual examples of scoring in fifteenth-century music. The three voices sing together only three times, briefly: in m. 121; mm. 136-138, the approach to the most prominent internal cadence; and mm. 151-154, the approach to the final cadence. Otherwise the tenor rests while the contratenor sings and vice versa. But it seems as though everything the tenor sings could be thought of as a continuation of the contratenor's line. There is no better demonstration of this than mm. 143-44, where the tenor rests after singing the leading tone (assuming a musica-ficta sharp should be applied) of a cadence, and the contratenor resumes, after having rested, with the note of resolution. Style characteristics were selected for inclusion in Table 2 mainly in terms of their potential for indicating the presence of early or late style. The question of what may be early or late is no easy one where Ockeghem is concerned, since it is possible to date only one of his works with any degree of certainty. (See the discussion of his lament for Gilles Binchois that follows.) Therefore, the stylistic traits chosen refer instead to what generally could be considered early or late in fifteenth-century music. But they should be regarded with a fair degree of caution. For example, two-voice counterpoint all but excludes the possibility of cadence types other than the 7-8, 2-1 variety, and, on the whole, it is more difficult to differentiate between early and late style in music for two voices.

"Under-Third Cadences" could be another somewhat misleading category. The type of cadence in which the voice having the 7-8 motion sings instead 7-6-8 (or a variant) was already in use as early as the thirteenth century and continued to be employed in the sixteenth. Under-third cadences seem to occur with rather less frequency at the end of the fifteenth than at the beginning. But the the sixth degree appears, in any event, to be ornamental, perhaps even something added in performance.

**Table 2**  Selected style characteristics of Ockeghem's Requiem

| | Number of Voices | Cantus Firmus Voice Location | Tessitura (Clefs) | Crossing of Voices | Note-Against-Note Partwriting | Faux-bourdon Texture | 7-8,2-1 Cadences | Double Leading-Tone Cadences | Under-Third Cadences | Octave-Leap Cadences | Authentic Cadences | Presence of Imitation | "Drive to the Cadence" |
|---|---|---|---|---|---|---|---|---|---|---|---|---|---|
| Requiem eternam (Introit Antiphon) | 3 | Superius | S, T, T | 3 times | occasionally | mm. 6-20 | 7 (all) | 5 | 0 | 0 | 0 | mm. 25-30 | none |
| Te decet hymnus (Introit Verse) | 3 | Superius | S, T, T | once | mostly | mm. 84-6 | 3 (all) | 2 | 0 | 0 | 0 | none | slight |
| Kyrie I and III | 3 | Superius | S, T, T | once | prevalently | none | 2 (all) | 1 | 0 | 1 | 0 | none | none |
| Kyrie II | 2 | both | S, S | twice | c. 25% | none | 2 (all) | 0 | 1 | 0 | 0 | frequent | none |
| Christe I and III | 2 | Superius | S, S | twice | c. 25% | none | 2 (all) | 0 | 0 | 0 | 0 | none | slight |
| Christe II | 3 | Superius | S, T, T | twice | rarely | none | 2 (all) | 0 | 0 | 1 | 0 | none | none |
| Kyrie I (=IV) | 3 | Superius | S, T-Bar, T | twice | c. 50% | none | 2 (all) | 0 | 0 | 0 | 0 | none | none |
| Kyrie II (=V) | 2 | both | S, S | 3 times | mostly | none | 2 (all) | 0 | 0 | 0 | 0 | canonic | none |
| Kyrie III (=VI) | 4 | Superius | S, A, T, Bar | 3 times | mostly | none | 1 | 0 | 0 | 1 | 1 | mm. 125-32 | none |
| Si ambulem (Gradual Respond) | 3 | Superius & Tenor | S, T, Bar | 10 times | rarely | mm. 69-71, 86-92 | 8 (all) | 1 | 0 | 1 | 0 | mm. 65-8, 86-90 | noticeable |
| Virga tua (Gradual Verse) | 2 (S & Ct), then 4 | Superius & Contra | S, T, Bar, Bass | twice (in 4-vc. section) | rarely (2 vcs.) mostly (4) | none | 9 (all, 2 vcs.) 1 (4 vcs.) | 0 | 0 | 1 | 1 (and•) | mm. 105-10, 114-17,149-55 | none |
| Sicut cervus (Tract) | 2 | Superius | S, S | 10 times | rarely | none | 7 (all) | 0 | 0 | 0 | 0 | throughout | none |
| Sitivit anima (Tract, continued) | 2 | Tenor | T, B | 4 times | very rarely | none | 13 (all) | 0 | 0 | 0 | 0 | frequent | none |
| Fuerunt michi lacrime (Tract, cont.) | 2½ | Superius | S, S, (T) | 7 times | very rarely | none | 12 (all) | 0 | 0 | 0 | 0 | frequent | none |
| Ubi est Deus tuus? (Tract, cont.) | 4 | Superius | S, S, T, B | 3 times | rarely | none | 2 | 1(?) | 0 | 0 | 3•• | mm. 164-65 | none |
| Domine Jhesu Christe (Offertory Antiphon) | 4 | Superius | S†, T, Bar, B | 7 times | rarely | none | 7 | 2 | 0 | 1 | 6•• | none | definite |
| Sed signifer (Offertory Ant., cont.) | 3 | Tenor | Mezzo-S, T, B | once | very rarely | none | 3 | 0 | 0 | 0 | 3•• | none | slight |
| Quam olim (Offertory Ant., cont.) | 4 | Tenor | Mezzo-S, T, Bar, B | once | rarely | mm. 77-79 | 3 | 0 | 0 | 1 | 3•• | none | slight |
| Hostias et preces‡ (Offertory Verse) | 2 | ? | S, S | twice | c. 30% | none | 2 (all) | 0 | 0 | 0 | 0 | none | none |
| Tu suscipe (Offertory Verse, cont.) | 3 | Superius | Mezzo-S, T, Bar | 4 times | c. 12% | mm. 85-88, 111-13 | 9 (all) | 3 | 0 | 0 | 0 | none | definite |

•Final cadence of "Virga tua" is plagal.  •••Some with delayed or avoided resolutions in the bassus.  †Clef changes to mezzo-soprano after seven measures.  ‡Both plainchant and duo in MS Chigi.

I have identified only one clear-cut under-third cadence in the entire Requiem. Does this suggest that Ockeghem composed the work at the end of his career? Or could it mean instead that he regarded such ornamentation in the context of a Mass for the Dead frivolous and therefore excluded it? Or could it be that the scribe of the Chigi Codex took it upon himself to "modernize" the cadences, for whatever reason?

Similarly, the presence or absence of imitation may not have a great deal of significance. It appears that, after

I continue to think, as I wrote a good number of years ago,[38] that the Requiem was intended for use at the 1461 obsequies of Charles VII.[39] My principal evidence is *Mort, tu as navré*, Ockeghem's lament for Gilles Binchois,[40] who died in 1460, one year before the French king. The opening melodic idea in the contratenor of the lament[41] is also heard prominently in the introit of the Requiem, mm. 61-65.[42] (See Examples 11a and 11b.) This, by itself, would not seem to count for much, even considering the fact that the same idea reappears several other times in the Mass.[43] But, in addition, the cambiata-like figure sung by the tenor and bassus voices in the lament (Example 11a, m. 2), makes its first appearance at the opening of the introit (see Example 5, mm. 5-7) and then pervades the Kyrie.[44] (See the last five measures of Example 6,

---

around 1460, some composers employed it more often than others, and those composers who used it did so in some works but not in others. The most one can say is that it was somewhat more progressive to employ imitation than not. On the other hand, I have the impression that Ockeghem made more use of it in his earlier works than in his later ones. This notion would be greatly reinforced, if it could be shown that the *Missa sine nomine* for three voices is indeed authentic. (But see Andrew Kirkman. *The Three-Voice Masses in the Later Fifteenth and Early Sixteenth Centuries: Style, Distribution and Case-Studies* [New York: Garland, 1995], 249-60.) It would certainly seem to be so on account of Antoine Busnois' having apparently drawn upon mm. 24-26 of its Sanctus for the melodic point of imitation to which he set the words "Haec Okeghem" at the beginning of the *secunda pars* of his motet composed in Ockeghem's honor, *In Hydraulis*. The passage of the Sanctus in question is printed in *Ockeghem: Collected Works*, 1: 25. For Busnois' motet, see *Antoine Busnoys: Collected Works*, 5/2, ed. Richard Taruskin, Masters and Monuments of the Renaissance (New York: Broude Trust, 1990), 151-65, esp. 158.

38. "Which Franco-Netherlander Composed the First Polyphonic Requiem Mass?" *Papers from the First Interdisciplinary Conference on Netherlandic Studies*, ed. William Fletcher (Lanham, MD: University Press of America, 1985), 171-76. According to Fabrice Fitch (op. cit., 204), "Richard Wexler's proposal of a dating *c.*1461 (for the obsequies of king Charles VII) rests entirely on nonmusical grounds, ... " But in actual fact my statement concerning this dating (p. 173) read, "In Ockeghem's Requiem, as one music historian has recently written, 'The plainchant melodies are treated in a manner reminiscent of the early part of the [fifteenth] century, being presented in the superius and lightly embellished [Leeman L. Perkins, "Johannes Ockeghem," *The New Grove*, 13: 492-93].' Other early fifteenth-century style

traits include predominance of three-voice texture, fauxbourdon-like partwriting, frequent double-leading-tone and octave-leap cadences, and a generally high tessitura. A consideration of the work on the basis of its style alone suggests that it was composed before 1470."

39.  By this time, it had become the custom for the king to have at least two identical full-length funeral services, the first in Notre-Dame de Paris and the second on the following day in the abbey-church of Saint-Denis, where the corpse was also finally laid to rest. See Ralph E. Giesey, *The Royal Funeral Ceremony in Renaissance France* (Geneva: E. Droz, 1960), 35-36.

40. Printed in *Ockeghem: Collected Works*, 3: 77-78. Ockeghem obviously knew the sequence for the Mass for the Dead, *Dies irae, dies illa*, because he quotes both words and music from it in mm. 50-60 of *Mort, tu as navré*. See Wexler, "Ockeghem and Politics," 6. However, the only one of the surviving early Requiem Masses to contain a setting of the sequence is Brumel's.

41.  Not only does this idea occupy a prominent place at the opening of the piece, but one hears it again five times on account of the ballade form.

42.  See also, the superius, mm. 115-16, and the contratenor, mm. 190-95, of the gradual. It was Michael Eckert who first pointed to a connection between the opening of the lament's contratenor and melodic ideas in the Requiem (op. cit., 10-11), calling attention to the superius at the end of the tract (presumably mm. 162-63) and at the openings of the "Sed signifer" and "Quam olim" sections in the offertory, and also mentioning the tenor at mm. 25-26 of the offertory's first section.

43.  To the melodies resembling the lament that Eckert lists might also be added the bassus of the tract, mm. 88-91.

44.  Eckert acknowledged the importance of this melodic idea in the Requiem, devoting an appendix to the occurrences of it and its permutations, op. cit., 75.

**Example 11a**   OCKEGHEM, *Mort tu as navré*, opening

**Example 11b**   OCKEGHEM, Requiem, Introit, mm. 61-65

mm. 5-7 of Example 11c, and Example 11d, throughout, for illustrations of a few of the most obvious occurences.) Moreover, fauxbourdon texture, which is quite rare in Ockeghem's known works aside from the Requiem,[45] is present in the second and third measures of the lament (Example 11a).

I do not mean to suggest that Ockeghem was quoting himself, something he does not do very often, if at all, except when borrowing from one of his own chansons for cantus-firmus material. He appears to have regarded, perhaps even unconsciously, these two melodic figures together with fauxbourdon texture as a kind of motif that expressed grief. The fact that these three relatively discrete devices are conjoined in the lament, which must have been composed not long after Binchois' death in 1460, and also occur in the Requiem, strongly suggests to me that the two works were conceived at approximately the same time.

45.  *Credo sine nomine, Ockeghem: Collected Works*, 2, Second, Corrected Edition, 61, mm. 93-100; and *Intemerata Dei mater, Ockeghem: Collected Works*, 3, 10, mm. 50-54.

For the Requiem, that time may have been after 1457-58, when Charles VII's health took a very noticeable turn for the worse,[46] and Ockeghem perhaps began thinking about what role the French court chapel would play in a royal Mass for the Dead.[47] It is somewhat doubtful that he would have sketched his ideas in writing.

**Figure 1**    Jean FOUQUET, *Livre d'heures de maistre Estienne Chevalier*, Funeral Procession

46. WEXLER, "Ockeghem and Politics," 11-12.

47. As BRENET reports (*Musique et musiciens de la vieille France* [Paris: Librairie Félix Alcan, 1911], 32), Ockeghem "figure parmi les 'officiers de la maison du roy Charles VII [d. 22 July 1461] qui ont eu robes et chaperons faits de drap noir pour les obsèques et funérailles du corps du feu roy,'" (See also Leeman L. PERKINS, "Musical Patronage at the Royal Court of France Under Charles VII and Louis XI (1422-83)," *Journal of the American Musicological Society* 37 [1984], Appendix I-6, 551.)

There is a miniature (Fig. 1) by Jean Fouquet, the great French painter who was Ockeghem's tenant in Tours

Instead, he might have worked on them together with his singers, in the manner once proposed by Margaret Bent.[48] Without a doubt they were well versed in the art of

(*Ockeghem and Politics*, 13-16) depicting a funeral procession. It comes from a series of miniatures executed by Fouquet for the *Livre d'Heures de maistre Estienne Chevalier*, now separated from its original binding and preserved, in the main, at the Musée Condé, Chantilly.

The mourners process through a courtyard, with four or five men of apparently noble birth supporting the casket of a dignitary (whose initials are "E. C."; see below) by means of rolled up sheets, surrounded by torchbearers. The latter were perhaps recruited from among the poor for the occasion, which appears to have been a custom, for the first of them wears torn hosiery and shoes with holes in them. At the left are two "officers of the household," as the document quoted above suggests, wearing black robes and hoods. The clerics at the head of the procession have entered the church, as can be seen from the processional cross that extends upward from the top of the portal, its bearer having already gone inside. A priest emerges who holds a long staff in his left hand and an aspergillum in his right, from which he dispenses holy water onto the richly embroidered pall. The legend at the base of the panel reads, "Dilexi q(uonia)m exavdiet d(omi)n(u)s vocem oratcionis," the opening of Psalm 114, the first psalm of the Office for the Dead (LU, 1772).

This is not a representation of an actual event, inasmuch as Étienne Chevalier (*c.*1410-1474), Trésorier de France (from 1452), owned the book and undoubtedly utilized it in his private devotions. The scene, illustrating, as suggested, the Office for the Dead, was probably meant to rouse in Chevalier a humble sense of his eventual demise. His monogram is everywhere: on the poles of all the torches, on the pall, and in the initial "D" of the legend. But Fouquet probably drew upon vivid, detailed memories of real funeral processions he had witnessed in Tours or elsewhere. See *Jean Fouquet: The Hours of Etienne Chevalier*, preface by Charles STERLING, introduction by Claude SCHAEFER (New York: G. Braziller, 1971), passim; and Trenchard Cox, *Jehan Foucquet, Native of Tours* (London: Faber & Faber, 1931), 125-26.

The motif of mourners in hoods (*pleurants*) is quite common in medieval funerary painting and sculpture. With particular relevance to Fouquet's miniature, see the funeral monument of Philippe Pot (d. 1495), Chamberlain of Charles VIII, in the Louvre, which includes eight figures in black robes and hoods bearing the corpse on a litter. Jean-René GABORIT, *Le Louvre: La sculpture européenne* (Paris: France-Loisir, 1995), 39. See also, Otto CARTELLIERI, *Am Hofe der Herzöge von Burgund: Kulturhistorische Bilder* (Basel: B. Schwabe, 1926), plate 5,

depicting *pleurants* on the tomb of the dukes of Burgundy in the Musée des Beaux-Arts of Dijon.

Surviving documents indicate that Jean Fouquet, as the leading painter of the realm, was expected in 1461 to create, from a death mask, the face for an effigy of Charles VII, which was to be carried in the king's funeral procession. Gaston du Fresne de Beaucourt, "Extraits du compte des obsèques de Charles VII." *Annuaire-bulletin de la Société de l'Histoire de France* 2/2 (1864), 180. Some doubt concerning whether he actually ever carried out the assignment exists. Cf. Paul VIOLLET, "Jehan Fouquet," *Gazette des Beaux-Arts*, 23 (1867), 101.

According to a reconstruction based on documents of Charles VII's funeral procession, the officers of the household in their black robes and hoods, including presumably Ockeghem, occupied places of honor at the sides of the coffin. Ralph E. GIESEY, op. cit.,[211]. See also ibid., 40, 76, and 108. Giesey reproduces two miniatures from a manuscript (Paris, Bibliothèque nationale de France, Ms. f.fr. 5054) dating from the time of Charles VII's funeral, as plates 9 and 10. The first of these shows the coffin in the procession, but the depiction is evidently somewhat fanciful. One sees the four presidents of the parlement, one at each corner, holding the pall, and also underneath the feet of the hanouars, salt carriers of Paris, who were privileged to bear the body of the king. But no wearers of robes and hoods are present, perhaps to permit an unobstructed view of the effigy on top of the pall. Also, several bishops follow the coffin in the miniature, although the documents make it clear that all ecclesiastics were near the head of the procession in 1461, as was customary, and it was "princes of deep mourning" who came after the coffin.

The second of the two miniatures depicts Charles VII's burial in Saint-Denis (8 August). Five bishops, the middle one with his right hand raised in benediction, stand before the tomb. Two men in work clothes, perhaps two of the hanouars, are placing the slab on top. Three men, two on the bishops' left and one on their right, wear short coats covered with fleurs-de-lis and carry maces. More than likely they are the heralds who proclaimed, "Le roi est mort! Vive le roy!" or something similar at this point in the ceremony. (The surviving chronicles differ with respect to the exact wording; see ibid., 135-36.) On either side of the heralds are princes, and behind them on the bishops' left is a group of monks of Saint-Denis. In back of the heralds, monks, and princes, one can see only the tops of what may well be three or four black hoods. Finally, the rear of the miniature is lined

counterpoint, and probably, with guidance from their master and a thoroughgoing familiarity with his idiom, they were capable of creating music in three voices *ex tempore* that went several steps beyond the most basic fauxbourdon.[49] It stands to reason that they could also extemporize in two voices, since everyone who studied counterpoint at that time began with the singing of two-voice discant.[50]

with torches to which are affixed the arms of France. The as yet uncrowned new king, Louis XI, was absent, according to tradition and very possibly his own inclinations, since he and his father had been bitterly estranged for the better part of a decade and a half.

48. Margaret Bent first proposed this in "Some Factors in the Control of Consonance and Sonority: Successive Composition and the Solus Tenor," *International Musicological Society: Report of the Twelfth Congress, Berkeley 1977*, ed. Daniel HEARTZ and Bonnie WADE (Kassel: Bärenreiter, 1981), 626, and subsequently elaborated on it in "*Resfacta* and *Cantare Super Librum*," 371-91, in which on p. 376 she wrote:

> There is no evidence that fifteenth-century composers used scores in the process of composition. A composer could work out his ideas, and/or realize his mental conceptions, by communicating the succesively-conceived parts, either orally or in writing, to singers who then substituted for the function of a written score by providing aural, not visual, control over simultaneities.

49. A surviving payment record from that same year, 1458, reads:

> M. Jehan Okeghan, premier chapelain de chant de la chapelle du roy, pour lui et ses compagnons, le 5 novembre, en faveur que par ordre du roy ils ont chanté solennellement le *Te Deum* pour les premières nouvelles pour la création du pape Pie, en l'église du chastel de Vendomme, 8 l[ivres] 5 s[ols]

Michel BRENET. op. cit., 31. Perhaps not coincidentally, the so-called Scottish Anonymous treatise of one hundred years later ("The Airt of Musick," London, British Library, Additional Ms. 4911, f. 94ff; discussed extensively in Frank HARRISON, "Faburden in Practice," *Musica Disciplina* 16 [1962]: 11-34) illustrates fauxbourdon using the hymn *Te Deum* (f. 97ᵛ) (see LU, 1832ff); see Manfred F. BUKOFZER, "Fauxbourdon Revisited," *The Musical Quarterly* 38 (1952): 29-30. Also, a fauxbourdon setting of *Te Deum* by Binchois survives; see Jeanne MARIX, *Les Musiciens de la cour de Bourgogne au XVᵉ siècle (1420-1467)* (Paris: Oiseau-Lyre, 1937; repr. New York: AMS Press, 1976), 219. See also Winfried KIRSCH, *Die Quellen der mehrstimmigen Magnificat- und Te Deum-Vertonungen bis zur Mitte des 16. Jahrhunderts* (Tutzing: Hans Schneider, 1966), 281, n. 621.

The French royal chapel normally included around eighteen members, not all of whom were necessarily singers. See PERKINS, op. cit., 521, 534, and 542. In 1458, seven, including Ockeghem, were designated "chantre." (ibid., Appendix II, 553-54.) Among them were Martin Courtois, who was identified as a "teneur" in 1466 and had served in the chapel since 1451 (ibid., 521), and perhaps another tenor, David de Lannoy, whose name does not appear until 1461 but who may have been present earlier.

By 1461 Jehan Escatefer dit Cousin, the composer of a polyphonic mass, had probably joined the chapel. (Tom R. WARD, "Cousin, Jean," *The New Grove*, 5: 4.) It is also possible that Jehan Sohier dit Fedé participated in the king's obsequies, if he was by then a member of the separate chapel of the queen, Marie d'Anjou, although he is not listed there until 1462 (PERKINS, op. cit., Appendix I-5, 549.) Fedé was the composer of a handful of works, among them an antiphon, *Magne pater sancte Domine*, in fauxbourdon (TRUMBLE, op. cit., 76, n. 123). Eventually, in 1473-74 he joined the chapel of the king (PERKINS, op. cit., Appendix II, 555). Still another minor composer, Jehan Fresneau, became a member of the chapel in 1469-70 (ibid., 534).

There is a lamentable gap in the records beginning in *c*.1475 and extending to *c*.1515 (ibid., 542-43), but a group of letters executed at the Vatican in 1486 on behalf of French court chaplains seeking prebends allows us to know who had joined since 1475. Among them were Loyset Compère and Guillaume Crétin. The presence of Crétin has interesting implications, since he seems to have been in possession of a firsthand knowledge of the Requiem, as suggested by the enthusiastic description he gave of it in his *Déploration* (see n. 29 above), possibly from having sung it at the obsequies of Louis XI (d. 30 August 1483). If in fact Crétin was born around 1465 (too late?), as reported by J. M. DAUWE in *Johannes Ockeghem en zijn tijd* (Dendermonde: A de Cuyper, 1970), 126, joined the chapel after 1475, and participated in a performance of the work, then we have direct evidence that the Requiem was part of the chapel's repertory and in use during the last quarter of the century.

50. Concerning the role of extemporization in two voices in the learning of counterpoint, see Rob C.

Therefore, I suspect that the earliest version of the Requiem consisted of a series of settings for two and three voices, some of which may have been the same as or at least resembled sections in the Requiem we know today but which may or may not have been written down at first. That is, they could have been part of a perhaps sizeable repertory the singers of the chapel routinely performed from memory.[51] The chapel may well have needed to keep music for the Mass for the Dead at the ready, if only for obits, but especially after Louis XI founded the Order of St. Michael in 1469, which he patterned directly after the Burgundian Order of the Golden Fleece, established in 1429 by Philip the Good.[52]

It was customary at meetings of the Order of the Golden Fleece, which were held annually if circumstances permitted, to devote part of the third day to a Requiem in honor of deceased members,[53] and one might well expect that the Order of

WEGMAN, "From Maker to Composer: Improvisation and Musical Authorship in the Low Countries, 1450-1500," *Journal of the American Musicological Society* 49 (1996): 413-26, esp. 423. Craig Wright has brought forward a series of documents, one of which specifically mentions discant, revealing that the canons of Cambrai required singers whose skills were considered deficient to study singing *super librum*. See his "Performance Practices at Cambrai," 313-14.

51. This proposal is not nearly as farfetched as it may seem, when one considers that the music world is teeming with oral traditions that support repertories containing some quite complex music, to mention one prominent and not particularly exotic example: the jazz big-band head arrangement. Gunther Schuller has defined this as follows:

> Such "arrangements" are generally not written down (though in some cases they are partially written or sketched out in notation) but are assembled instead from the ideas (as it were, out of the heads) of an entire band or perhaps some of its leading members. Widespread in jazz, this form of arrangement results from a conceptually simple yet technically complex combining of players' suggestions, the working out of individual parts in rehearsals, intuitive spontaneous contributions, memorization, and, sometimes, the group leader's final arbitration concerning all these elements. Many of the finest arrangements by orchestras such as Count Basie's and Duke Ellington's were achieved in this collective, collaborative way.

Both of these organizations included three or four trumpets, four or five saxophones, three trombones, rhythm guitar, piano, bass, and drums—as many as sixteen instrumentalists, each playing a different, often unique part. See SCHULLER's article "Arrangement" in *The New*

*Grove Dictionary of Jazz*, 1, ed. Barry KERNFELD (London: Macmillan, 1988), 33. For a detailed description of Ellington's collaborative method of composition, see in particular Mark TUCKER, ed., *The Duke Ellington Reader* (New York: Oxford University Press, 1993), 100-101. It is interesting that if and when a head arrangement is finally committed to paper, one individual, usually the leader, customarily receives the entire credit for it. Cf. Gunther SCHULLER, *Early Jazz: Its Roots and Musical Development* (New York: Oxford University Press, 1968), 326, n. 11. For something perhaps even closer to home, see also Deane L. ROOT, "Barbershop harmony," *The New Grove*, 2: 137.

52. See WEXLER, "Ockeghem and Politics," 13.

53. William F. PRIZER, "Music and Ceremonial in the Low Countries: Philip the Fair and the Order of the Golden Fleece," *Early Music History* 5 (1985): 119-20. Prizer has shown that the statutes of the order required the presence of the ducal chapel, provision was made for its attendance and participation, and it can be inferred that it sang the Mass for the Dead in polyphony. If so, then one can only wonder what polyphonic Mass for the Dead the chapel sang from the year of its first meeting, 1431 (ibid., 118), until Dufay composed his Requiem (which is not extant), perhaps as late as 1470 or 1471. In any event, it would not have been Dufay's. Prizer has discovered a letter of 1501 revealing that Dufay's Requiem was for three voices, it was sung at the order's meeting of that year in Brussels, and the Burgundian chapel probably did not obtain the use of it until after the composer's death in 1474 (ibid., 133-34 and 142). See also HAGGH, "The Archives of the Order of the Golden Fleece," 10-11. On p. 12, she reports that according to the *acta* of several meetings the chapel sang *De profundis* at the end of the offertory procession of the Mass for the Dead.

St. Michael adopted similar observances.[54] It is conceivable, then, that a process of evolution set in, whereby Ockeghem and his chapel revised the Requiem somewhat for each subsequent performance, whether to account for departed singers, to accommodate newly enlisted ones,[55] or to introduce new music.[56] Perhaps, for example, it was

Concerning the dating of Dufay's lost Requiem, the music scribe Simon Mellet received payment in 1470 for copying such a Mass, said to be "de novo compilata," into books belonging to the cathedral of Cambrai. See Jules HOUDOY. *Histoire artistique de la cathédrale de Cambrai, ancienne église métropolitaine Notre-Dame* (Lille: L. Danel, 1880; repr. 1972), 198. This may mean the Mass was newly composed, but it could also mean that it was set down for the first time in a form, perhaps in writing, that facilitated the copying of it.

54. Barbara HAGGH has discovered a copy of the statutes of the Order of St. Michael in the archives of the Order of the Golden Fleece. She reports, "The St. Michael statutes are taken almost word for word from those of the Order of the Golden Fleece" (op. cit., 37). The statutes of the Order of St. Michael are printed in the Marquis de PASTORET, ed. *Ordonnances des rois de France de la troisième race*, 21 vols. (Paris: Imprimerie royale, 1820), 17: 236-55.

Recent scholarship suggests, rather extraordinarily, that the knights of the Order of St. Michael did not assemble in full at all until Michaelmas of 1548, at Lyon, during the reign of Henri II (r. 1547-1559). (See D'Arcy Jonathan Dacre BOULTON. *Knights of the Crown: The Monarchial Orders of Knighthood in Later Medieval Europe, 1325-1520* [Woodbridge, Suffolk: Boydell, 1987], 435.) However, elaborate preparations for a meeting, including the painting of armorial panels by Jean Fouquet and the fashioning of costumes for the participants, were begun in December of 1470. (Ibid., p. 432.) One can scarcely imagine that the rehearsal of suitable music failed to take place. But the assembly never was held. (See also Philippe CONTAMINE, "L'Ordre de Saint-Michel au temps de Louis XI et de Charles VIII," *Bulletin de la Société nationale des antiquaires de France*, 1976 [1978], 217-21.)

When several years passed subsequent to the founding of the order and no meetings had been held, certain influential charter members complained to the king regarding what they considered to be a violation of the order's statutes. The king sought to placate them by issuing further ordinances (22 December 1476) in which he spelled out how the order's business could be carried out despite the absence of assemblies. (See the Marquis de PASTORET, op. cit., 18: 217-23.) His solution was to create

the additional office of *prevost maistre de ceremonies.* The provost would be authorized to schedule events, such as the induction of a new knight or funeral services for a deceased member, and then oblige those present at court belonging to the order to attend. To facilitate such duties, the king stipulated that the provost should be an officer of his household and an ordinary councillor—in other words a domestic official of the same kind as Ockeghem.

One may readily suppose that the *prevost* and the *premier chapelain* were familiar colleagues. But the new ordinances are silent concerning the role of the royal chapel, saying only, with regard to ceremonies for the deceased (Ibid., 219):

> 12) Item. Quant aucun desdits chevaliers ou officiers dudit order ira de vie à trespas, ledit prevost sera tenu avoir veritable certiffication de la mort et trespassement, du jour, du mois et an, par quel inconvenient naturel ou autre accident, et de estat de sa derreniere fin, pour le tout remettre en veritable escripture et nous en advertir, *pour faire le service du trepassé tel qui appartient estre fait,* et après le redigera en veritable escript et le fera enregistrer par ledit greffier de l'ordre [emphasis mine].

It would seem, therefore, that the singers of the chapel did have occasion to perform Requiem masses in connection with ceremonies of the Order of St. Michael, even though the knights never assembled formally. And, in fact, several distinguished members of the order, including, among others, René d'Anjou, Charles de France (the king's younger brother), Georges de la Trémoille, Tanguy du Châtel, and Louis XI himself, died before 1484. See CONTAMINE, op. cit., 230, n. 2. Concerning related ceremonies held in the basilica of Saint-Martin, see Agostino MAGRO, "Basilique, pouvoir et dévotion: Ockeghem à Saint-Martin de Tours," *Johannes Ockeghem: Actes du XIᵉ Colloque international d'études humanistes*, ed. Philippe VENDRIX (Paris: Klincksieck, 1998), 82-83.

55. With the loss of several chaplains who had served since the early 1450s, there were numerous changes of personnel in the 1460s and 70s. PERKINS, op. cit., 534.

56. According to Leeman PERKINS (op. cit., 535), citing information obtained from Paula Higgins, two large parchment choirbooks were compiled at the French court in 1471. One contained 245 folios and the other

during the 1470s that Ockeghem substituted the four-voice settings that now conclude the Kyrie, the gradual, and the tract for whatever had been sung previously.

Continuing in this vein, I wish to propose that Ockeghem composed a new setting of the offertory's antiphon for the obsequies in 1483 of Louis XI.[57] As mentioned previously, I cannot see how the practice of singing *super librum* could have played a part in the conception of this section (Example 9), except perhaps in the passage in discant, mm. 19-23. To my way of thinking this is a composition in the modern sense of the word, a study of the mensural system that adopts a somewhat different direction from that taken in the *Missa prolationum*.[58] It constitutes both a demonstration of Ockeghem's unexcelled learnedness as a musician and what also could be a solemn and, because it incorporates a prayer for the intercession of St. Michael,[59] a most fitting tribute to his monarch and employer of the previous twenty-two years.[60]

246. (For the sake of comparison, the Chigi Codex, in its present form, has 287.) Might the preparation of these manuscripts, now lost, have provided an occasion for the writing down of an early redaction of Ockeghem's Requiem?

57. The funeral of Louis XI was one of the most unusual in the history of French royalty. The king declined to be buried at Saint-Denis, preferring instead Notre-Dame de Cléry near Orléans (see "Ockeghem and Politics," 12), where Sixtus IV had appointed him *prothocanonicus* in 1471. Therefore, his funeral was not a state occasion, but an ecclesiastical one. (GIESEY, op. cit., 46, n. 25.) Nevertheless, it is likely that he had a dual service of the kind described in note 39, above. Since he died at Plessis-lès-Tours, west of the city, his corpse probably was borne through Tours, where a ceremony would have been held at the cathedral, Saint-Maurice, or else at the abbey-church of Saint-Martin, where the king was titular abbot, on the way to Orléans. Concerning a service at Saint-Martin, see MAGRO, op. cit., 83-84. Then another full service, plus the interment, would have taken place at Notre-Dame de Cléry. Even though Louis XI abdicated the throne to his son, Charles VIII, on his deathbed and dissolved his household (ibid., 74), Ockeghem, as the king's *premier chapelain*, undoubtedly participated in the rites, along with the singers of the chapel.

58. WEGMAN (op. cit., 428) has observed, "Unlike the practice of counterpoint, which could be and was widely popularized, mensural theory was essentially intellectual in its conception, involving specialized Latin terminology and modes of thought whose underlying rationale could not be fully comprehended except through university training in the liberal arts." While we know nothing of Ockeghem's education, he was highly

respected for the quality of his intellect. The poem of 1523 by Nicolle Le Vestu that accompanies the famous miniature of Ockeghem surrounded by his singers begins:

> Okhem, tresdocte en art mathématique
> Arithméticque, aussy géometrie,
> Astrologie, et mesment musique
> Qui fantastique ennuy chasse et maistrie
> Par industrie en fleurtys et deschant …

See DAUWE, *Johannes Ockeghem en zijn tijd*, 113-14. (Might the final word of the last line quoted above refer to Ockeghem's ability to *cantare super librum* in two voices?)

59. "Sed signifer sanctus Michael representet eas in lucem sanctam (But let thy standard-bearer, blessed Michael, bring them into that holy light)." Here as translated by Alec ROBERTSON, *Requiem: Music of Mourning and Consolation* (New York: Praeger, 1967), 21. This section of Ockeghem's offertory, for three voices and in tempus perfectum, is noteworthy for its austerity in the midst of the erudite four-voice mensural discourse.

60. It should be noted that Ockeghem's offertory setting may have had an independent existence, since it apparently survived separately in Leuven Ms. 163, a contra partbook dated 1546, destroyed, along with the university library that housed it, in 1914. See *Census-Catalogue of Manuscript Sources of Polyphonic Music, 1400-1550*, 2, ed. Herbert KELLMAN and Charles HAMM, Renaissance Manuscript Studies, 1 (Neuhausen-Stuttgart: American Institute of Musicology, 1982), 37-38. According to Jacques-Gabriel PROD'HOMME ("Les Institutions musicales [bibliothèques et archives] en Belgique et en Hollande," *Sammelbände der Internationalen Musik-Gesellschaft* 15 [1913-14]: 486-87), it contained a *Rex Gloria* (*sic*) attributed to Ockeghem. (The opening words of Ockeghem's offertory, "Domine Jesu Christe," are sung

But the verse of the offertory, it seems, was left unchanged and in the improvisatory style. And this, I am proposing, was done to provide a smooth transition to the singing *super librum* of the simple and austere chants of the Sanctus, Agnus Dei, and communion from the Mass for the Dead in enhanced fauxbourdon.[61]

in chant; the polyphony begins with "Rex gloriae.") FITCH (op. cit., 195, n. 1) casts doubt on whether the work in question is the same as the offertory in Ockeghem's Requiem, because "the voice part was labelled '*alti sex*,' which may imply a six-voice composition." However, the manuscript was burned, so one cannot really say what the label was. We have only Prod'homme's transcription of the partbook's tabula, either one of which could have been in error. For whatever this information is worth, it does not come even remotely close to describing any other known work by Ockeghem, and it is more than likely that it was the offertory of Ockeghem's Requiem, if in six voices, then with parts added at a later date by someone else.

Certain evidence suggests that Ockeghem was close to the king, but, as always where Louis XI was concerned, the relationship would have been a complicated one. See "Ockeghem and Politics," passim; and my "The Politics of Ockeghem's Canonicate," *Johannes Ockeghem*, op. cit., 65-78.

61.   The following represents an attempt to summarize the diverging views concerning whether or not the various movements of Ockeghem's Requiem were composed at the same time: The possibility that Ockeghem composed the offertory subsequent to the other movements was first proposed by Edward F. HOUGHTON in his Ph.D. dissertation, "Rhythmic Structure in the Masses and Motets of Johannes Ockeghem" (University of California, Berkeley, 1971). Houghton suggests that the Requiem could be a composite work on account of "an internal disparity of mensural style" (p. 136). Michael ECKERT (op. cit.) set out to demonstrate by means of style analysis that Ockeghem's Requiem "was conceived as a totality" (p. 14); and he ultimately concludes (p. 52), "The 'disparity of style' in the Requiem is more apparent than real; an analysis has shown that Ockeghem's compositional *technique* [emphasis Eckert's] is consistent throughout his work."

Eckert does allow, however, that at times the work has an evolutionary quality about it. On p. 19 he writes, "It is possible to see in the Requiem the whole development of fifteenth century cadential structures and progressions, in a kind of musical 'ontogeny recapitulates phylogeny.'" And he seems well aware of the offertory's stylistic anomalies (p. 14): "Only in the antiphon of the Offertory do we find long passages for four voices. The

thickness of the texture is emphasized there by the low range of all parts." Eckert also recognizes that (p. 29) "Ockeghem's Introit reflects this (that is, note-against-note partwriting) simple improvised type of counterpoint, which seems to have been considered most appropriate for the 'piteux' character of a *Requiem*." But finally he sees the offertory as being (p. 51):

> not, then, incongruous with the rest of the *Requiem*; it is the summation—and not only symbolically—of all that has gone before ... These conclusions suggest that Ockeghem intended the Offertory to be the final movement of the *Requiem*. The lack of a polyphonic *Sanctus, Agnus Dei*, and *Communio* does not require an extramusical explanation; in terms of both text and music the Offertory is the climax of the whole setting.

Fabrice FITCH (op. cit.) largely follows Eckert with respect to the question of the Requiem's unity, but his analysis of the physical structure of its source leads him to conclude that the Requiem "as transmitted in Chigi is incomplete (p. 27)." He finds (p. 28), not implausibly, that "six blank openings left by the Chigi scribe might well suffice for a Sanctus, an Agnus Dei, a Communion, and possibly also a Sequence between the Offertory and the Sanctus." (This last suggestion seems rather doubtful, however, inasmuch as the sequence would have followed the tract and preceded the offertory. In addition, there are in fact seven blank openings, if one counts the verso ending the eighteenth gathering and the recto beginning the nineteenth. Of the seventeen breaks between gatherings containing Masses by Ockeghem, the Chigi scribe filled thirteen.) Fitch's explanation for why the last three movements were not copied on to the openings he believes were left for them in the Chigi Codex is as follows (p. 12):

> When the order for a manuscript laying special emphasis on Ockeghem's Masses (and perhaps also Regis's motets) was placed with the workshop, exemplars of works may have been sent for from different quarters, and were then copied *as they came available* [emphasis Fitch's] ... Provision was made for additional movements that may never have materialised.

Fitch eventually concludes that (p. 201-02):

> The hypothesis concerning the work's incomplete state in Chigi appears at first glance to lend credence to Houghton's theory [that the Requiem is a composite

work], for if the scribes of Chigi received their exemplars in fragments, those bits and pieces may conceivably reflect different stages in the work's elaboration. However, the evidence of the empty openings in Chigi suggests the existence of a final movement [not three?] (probably a three-voice setting of the Communion) that would act as a pendant to the Introit ...

It seems, then, that the opening movements are the most difficult to explain in terms of Ockeghem's style. Nevertheless, I believe that their stylistic disparity in relation to the other movements reflects a deliberate compositional decision rather than a hiatus in the chronology of the various movements.

As insightful as Fitch's analysis of the structure of the Chigi Codex with respect to Ockeghem's Requiem may be, other interpretations of his findings are possible: 1) Perhaps the manuscript was not as planned as Fitch supposes (op. cit., p. 13), and the blank openings were simply left over when the Ockeghem Mass series, which the Requiem ends, was completed. To a certain extent, his argument for the existence at one time of movements now missing from the Requiem depends on his perceiving other Masses in the series as incomplete. Therefore Fitch makes a case for the partial transmission in Chigi of Ockeghem's *Missa Fors seulement* (three movements, ff. 45ᵛ-53ʳ) and *Missa Ma maistresse* (two movements, ff. 60ᵛ-63ʳ); ibid., 23-25. But he is of the opinion that at least Ockeghem's *Missa sine nomine* (a 5), which has only three movements, is complete as Chigi transmits it (ff. 55ᵛ-60ʳ); ibid., 25. All three of these Masses are unique to the Chigi Codex, so one is unable to confirm in some other source that any of them had more movements at one time than the Chigi Codex contains.

Or 2) with the Mass series finished, the scribe planned to copy some or all of Ockeghem's motets. (But see FITCH, op. cit., 27, where he dismisses this possibility.) The so-called "Spanish" scribe eventually added three French-court motets on the originally blank folios, Mouton's *Quis dabit oculis nostris*, a lament for the French queen Anne of Brittany (d. 1514), *Costanzo Festa: Sacrae cantiones 3-6 vocibus*, 2, ed. Eduardo DAGNINO, Monumenta polyphoniae italicae (Rome: Pontif. Institutum Musicae Sacrae, 1936), 113ff; Ockeghem's *Ave Maria*, *Ockeghem: Collected Works*, 3, 6-7; and Compère's *Ave Maria*, the *secunda pars* of which begins, "Sancte Michael ora pro nobis" (in the context of parts of the Litany of the Saints), *Loyset Compère: Opera omnia*, ed. Ludwig FINSCHER. Corpus mensurabilis musicae, 15 (n.p.: American Institute of

Musicology, 1961): 8-10. Concerning the presence of the litany, see ibid., p. II; it is printed in LU, pp. 776ᵛ-776ʷ. Or 3) the scribe intended to end the Ockeghem Mass series with a further work now lost to us, such as the *Missa La belle se siet*, but was unable to obtain a copy of it. (But see FITCH, op. cit., 27, where he precludes the possibility of a new Mass, perhaps too hastily.) Johannes Tinctoris reproduces the opening of the Credo of this otherwise unknown work in his *Liber de arte contrapuncti*, chap. XXXII; see *Ockeghem: Collected Works*, 2: XLII. Ockeghem's *Missa Au travail suis* occupies exactly seven openings in Chigi (ff. 89ᵛ-96ʳ), and so also might have another Mass based on a chanson.

Or 4) the Chigi scribe, who worked at or in the vicinity of the Burgundian court, knowing that the Sanctus, Agnus Dei, and communion of Pierre de La Rue's *Missa pro fidelibus defunctis* occupy together five openings, left that many plus one or two extra for analogous movements by Ockeghem, which, however, may or may not have existed. In their unpublished prospectus for the edition, "A Thematic Catalog of the Works of Pierre de La Rue," dated 1981, the editors of La Rue's works listed his Mass for the Dead among "Other Early Four-Part Masses." But the commentary of the published edition (see n. 14 above) contains no mention of a possible date. In one of its sources, Jena, Universitäts-Bibliothek, Chorbuch 12, written by a Burgundian court scribe, (Herbert KELLMAN, "Josquin and the Courts of the Netherlands and France," *Josquin des Prez: Proceedings of the International Josquin Festival Conference ... 1971*, ed. Edward E. LOWINSKY in collaboration with Bonnie J. BLACKBURN [London: Oxford University Press, 1976], 209) the three movements in question fill ff. 117ᵛ-122ʳ. See Karl Erich ROEDIGER, *Die geistlichen Musikhandschriften der Universitäts-Bibliothek Jena* (Jena: Frommanssche Buchhandlung, 1935), Notenverzeichnis, p. 28ˣ, No. 58.

Or 5) the scribe, having left room for them, ultimately received a Sanctus, Agnus Dei, and communion for Ockeghem's Requiem, and found them to be set down in simple, straightforward fauxbourdon style. Therefore he perhaps declined to expend precious ink and parchment on recording them in writing, assuming that any reasonably competent group of singers such as would have participated in a performance of a Mass for the Dead at a meeting of the Order of the Golden Fleece or the obsequies of an illustrious person could have created something almost identical *ex tempore*.

Edward F. Houghton

# A Close Reading of
# Compère's Motet *Sile Fragor*

L OYSET COMPÈRE's four-voice setting of *Sile fragor* is found in the Chigi Codex
(Vatican City, Biblioteca Apostolica Vaticana, Ms. Chigi C VIII 234),[1] a manuscript which Herbert Kellman has studied and written about extensively.[2] This
relatively short motet is placed near the end of the collection of motets that concludes
the Codex. It stands out in the collection primarily because of the unusual character
of its text, but also because of its advanced musical style. Unlike the other works in
the Codex, the text is not a liturgical work, conventional prayer, or paraphrase of
either. It begins with a peremptory command for silence, extols the power of music,
and combines a prayer to the Virgin Mary with an invitation to approach Bacchus. The
text alone merits a close reading. The musical style and historical origins of the motet,
however, also deserve special consideration.

   *Sile fragor* may well be the latest composition in the original corpus of the Chigi
Codex copied by the principal scribe. Its musical style has more in common with
Antoine Fevin's widely disseminated motet *Sancta trinitas unus deus*, added to the Codex
by a later scribe,[3] than with other works in the original layer. The graceful integration

1.   Ff. 279ᵛ-281ʳ. A transcription of the motet is published in Loyset COMPÈRE, *Opera omnia*, 4, ed. Ludwig
FINSCHER, Corpus mensurabilis musicae, 15 ([Rome]:
American Institute of Musicology, 1958), 49-51.
2.   Its origins and history have been studied and documented by Herbert Kellman in a series of publications: first in his article "The Origins of the Chigi
Codex: The Date, Provenance, and Ownership of
Rome, Biblioteca Vaticana, Chigiana, C VIII 234,"
*Journal of the American Musicological Society* 11 (1958): 6-9; in
his paper at the international Josquin conference in
1971, "Josquin and the Courts of the Netherlands and
France: The Evidence of the Sources," *Josquin des Prez:*

*Proceedings of the International Josquin Festival-Conference held
at the Juilliard School at Lincoln Center in New York City, 21-25
June 1971*, ed. Edward E. LOWINSKY and Bonnie J.
BLACKBURN (London: Oxford University Press, 1976),
185-216; and in the introduction to the Garland facsimile edition, *Vatican City, Biblioteca Apostolica Vaticana, MS
Chigi C VIII 234*, Renaissance Music in Facsimile, 22
(New York: Garland Publishing, 1987), v-xi.
3.   Ff. 87ᵛ-88ʳ. This and the other additions are often
attributed to the "Spanish hand" because of the calligraphic similarities among the added motets and the
table of contents in Spanish, *Tabla de missas y motetes*.
Fevin's motet is found in 36 other sources.

of independent lines in *Sile fragor*, its effective use of vertical sonorities, and its clear declamation contrast sharply with the dense and complex textures of Ockeghem and Regis. *Sile fragor* also seems more developed in the treatment of text and texture than the motets in the original layer of the Codex by the generation of composers after Ockeghem and Regis, namely Josquin, Isaac, and Gaspar van Weerbecke.

*Sile fragor* is also found in several other sources of the late fifteenth and early sixteenth centuries, given here with sigla from the *Census-Catalogue* for manuscript sources or *RISM* for printed sources:[4]

| | |
|---|---|
| **BarcBC 454** | Barcelona, Biblioteca Central, Ms. 454, ff. 131$^v$-133$^r$: Anonymous. |
| **HradKM 7** | Hradec Kralove, Krajske Muzeum Knihovna (Regional Museum Library). Ms. II A 7 ("Speciálník Codex"), pp. 112-15: Anonymous. |
| **VatS 15** | Vatican City, Biblioteca Apostolica Vaticana, Ms. Cappella Sistina 15, ff. 183$^v$-185$^r$: Anonymous. |
| **VerBC 768** | Verona, Biblioteca Capitolare, Ms. DCCLVIII, ff. 17$^v$-19$^r$: Anonymous. |
| **1502$^1$** | Motetti A. *numero trentatre*, Venice: O. Petrucci, 1502, pp. 26$^v$-28$^r$: Compere. |

## The Text

The text in Chigi is as follows:[5]

Sile[6] fragor/ ac rerum[7] tumultus/ fuge[8] pavor/ qui pectore[9] raucus anelas/ psallere nos sine/ et nostros equare modos/[10] urget amor muse/ oprimens iurgia ire/ Cum[11] ecclesia resonat dulcore carminis nostri/ et voces solide/[12] audiencium aures demulcent/[13] Suscipe deitatis[14] mater/[15] vocum[16] precordia[17] nostra/ et nato refunde vota/[18] que

---

4. *Census-Catalogue of Manuscript Sources of Polyphonic Music: 1400-1550*, 5 vols., ed. Charles HAMM and Herbert KELLMAN, Renaissance Manuscript Studies, 1 (Neuhausen-Stuttgart: Hänssler-Verlag, 1979-1988); *Répertoire international des sources musicales* (Kassel: Bärenreiter, 1971-).

5. The solidus (slash) is used to indicate musical articulations which probably reflect the composer's view of the textual phrasing. Significant variants are given in the footnotes. Voices are abbreviated as follows: S, Ct, T, and B for Superius, Contratenor altus, Tenor, and Bassus respectively.

6. *Scile* in Verona and Petrucci.

7. *verborum* in Verona and Petrucci.

8. *fugor* in B in Chigi. This and several other textual errors in Chigi (noted below in the textual variants) suggest that the scribe was not skilled in Latin. In most respects, however, the scribal execution is of high quality. Both pieces of information point to the transition in some places from part-time copyists, well-schooled singer-clerics who copied pieces in addition to their

normal duties, to the professional scriptorium.

9. *peccatore* in B in Chigi; *pectora* in Hradec.

10. *modus* in the S with an *o* above the *u* in Chigi, apparently a correction.

11. *nam* in S, Ct, and B in Hradec.

12. *nam et voces audiencium solide ...* in Barcelona.

13. *demultent* in B in Chigi, an apparent error or confusion between the letters *c* and *t*; otherwise it would stem from the verb *multare* "to punish." Thrashing, rather than caressing, the ears of the listeners would prompt a different character for *voces solidae*.

14. *dei* in Verona and Petrucci.

15. *lumen* in Hradec.

16. *voce* in Ct in Chigi.

17. *vocum amor precordia ...* in Ct in Barcelona.

18. *preces* in T and B of Barcelona but *vota* in S and T, an alteration which suggests a general reading of *vota* as "prayers" in the Barcelona source at least, rather than "vows" or "solemn promises," such as those exchanged by King Charles VIII and Pope Alexander VI in January of 1495.

psallimus omnes/ nunc fontem adire[19] decet/[20] quo bachus insedet ipse/ et discedat lympha/ Liberos/[21] dum carpimus rivos/ amen[22]

I offer this translation:[23]

> Be silent, noise and uproar of the world; flee, fear, hoarse and panting in our breasts; let us sing and modulate our tones.[24] Love of the Muse impels (us), suppressing angry quarrels, when the church resounds with the sweetness of our song and our clear voices caress the ears of the listeners.
> Receive, mother of the divinity, the expression of our hearts and refer to your Son the vows that we all sing. Now it is fitting to approach the spring where Bacchus himself dwells; and let water be gone, while we enjoy (his) free-flowing streams. Amen.

The references to the Muse and to Bacchus are obvious neo-classical elements that prompt a search for others. The use of *psallere* (to make music, to sing to the lyre) and *psallimus* instead of *cantare*, though not unusual, does invoke the image of Homer and the ancient poets.[25] On the other hand, the words *dulcore* and *deitatis* are neologisms.

What about the textual structure: is it quantitative and does it show other humanistic influence? Ludwig Finscher[26] asserts that it is scarcely coincidental that the first words of Compère's text are strongly reminiscent of an ode by Francesco Filelfo: *Pulsat fragor: tumultus en populi furit.* [27]

Filelfo (1398-1481) was a leading humanistic writer at the Milanese court of the Visconti after 1439 and enjoyed continuing favor later under the Sforzas. Filelfo may have been in Milan at the beginning of Compère's tenure there. The earliest mention of Compère at the court is a record of payment dated 15 July 1474, as a singer in the service of Galeazzo Maria Sforza.[28] Filelfo left Milan for an academic appointment

---

19. *audire* in Ct in Chigi.

20. *fontem nunc haurimus* in Hradec, a unique and interesting variant in all voices.

21. *et discedens liberos liberas . . .* in Hradec.

22. No *Amen* in Hradec and Petrucci, although Petrucci provides the repeated notes of the finals without text.

23. I am greatly indebted to John F. Collins, a specialist in classical and ecclesiastical Latin, who has assisted me in understanding the meaning and structure of the texts in the Codex.

24. *Modos* might refer to general habits and customs or, more specifically, to rhythm (the mensural modes), to melody (the melodic modes), or to intervals (cf., *The New Grove* 12: 376 ff.). The verb *equare*, "to equalize," in the context of making music (*psallere*) suggests a specific meaning for *modos*. Mensural levels of mode are at least obsolescent in Compère's time. The term *tonos* or *tonus* is

more commonly used for the melodic modes by musical theorists of the time. The process of tuning intervals and balancing voices, however, is a common concern of singers. The tuning of sonorities and balancing of voices in a reverberant space are central elements in the effective presentation of the repertory at hand.

25. While *Psallere nos sine* by itself might be translated as "Let us make music," the later context of *psallimus* links the verb with *vota* (vows or prayers) and strongly suggests singing for both uses of *psallere*, a translation supported by the subsequent association of *carminis* (song) and *voces* (voices).

26. Ludwig FINSCHER, *Loyset Compère (c.1450-1518), Life and Works*, Musicological Studies and Documents, 12 (n.p.: American Institute of Musicology, 1964), 191 (hereafter cited as FINSCHER, *Compère*).

27. Cf., Francesco FILELFO, *Odae* (Venice: Angelus Britannicus, 1497), f. diii[r].

in Rome in the same year and began teaching there in January, 1475.[29] Compère was probably at court before the payment of 15 July. Although personal contact between Compère and Filelfo remains only a possibility, Compère may well have encountered Filelfo's writings and influence in the humanistic circle of the Milanese court. If Filelfo's language and style shaped Compère's later effort to produce a motet of humanistic character, however, the influence does not seem to extend beyond the use of the words *fragor* and *tumultus* in the first line. Finscher describes the text as "written in clumsy hexameters,"[30] but my efforts to discern a recognizable poetic structure based on a scansion of syllabic quantities or dynamic accent proved fruitless.

John Collins sees the structure and word order of *Sile fragor* as that of very good prose, albeit rather colored. He has arranged the text to bring out the apparent structural device of *homoeoteleuton* (similar ending). This is close to but not quite rhyme, used since Gorgias (427 B.C.E.), an ancient precedent probably unknown to the author of Compère's original text.

Text of *Sile fragor* arranged to emphasize the *homoeoteleuton*[31]

(1) Sile, Fragor,
ac rerum Tumultus,
fuge, Pavor,
qui pectore raucus
anhelas: psallere nos
sine et nostros
aequare modos.

(2) Urget amor Musae,
opprimens iurgia irae,
cum ecclesia resonat dulcore

carminis nostri et voces solidae
audientium aures demulcent.

(3) Suscipe, Deitatis Mater,
vocum praecordia nostra,
et Nato refunde vota,
quae psallimus omnes.

(4) Nunc fontem adire decet,
quo Bacchus insidet ipse; et
discedat lympha, liberos
dum carpimus rivos.

The most extensive textual variant is the substitution in VerBC 758 and Petrucci of the last lines, which begin with the words *Nunc fontem* ..., a substitution that eliminates the reference to Bacchus and extends the prayer to the Mother of God, *dei mater* in both sources.[32]

tu sacrum templum tu fons uberimus ille es
cuius inexhausta detrahit unda sitim. Amen.[33]

*You are the holy temple; you are that abundant spring whose inexhaustible water takes away thirst. Amen.*

28. Finscher, *Compère*, 17.
29. Roberto Weiss, "Francesco Filelfo e il costume umanistico" in *Dizionario critico della letteratura italiana, 2*, under the direction of Vittore Branca (Turin: Unione Tipografico-Editrice Torinese, 1974), 2: 85-87.
30. Finscher, *Compère*, 191.
31. This is highly colored prose—a prose poem. It is

neither accentual nor quantitative. In this arrangement of the text, spelling is standardized and punctuation is provided.
32. Note the substitution of *dei* for the neologism *deitatis*.
33. The substitution in Petrucci and VerBC 758 is an elegiac couplet, in which the first line is a dactylic

Ludwig Finscher, who was apparently not aware of the Verona concordance at the time of his writing, speculates that Petrucci's reading is intended for as large a public as possible, a version suitable "for private services and devotional hours in every 'middle class' home"[34] rather than for an elite circle of humanists.

Though it is also possible that Petrucci simply copied the version transmitted in VerBC 758, the reason for the variant might be similar to Finscher's suggestion: neither Petrucci's patrons nor ecclesiastical circles in northern Italy would readily understand or appreciate the association of the Virgin Mary and Bacchus in the text or the literary fashion of Christianizing pagan traditions. On the other hand, the reference may have been too specific to Rome, the "Holy See," the seat (*insedet*) or chair of Peter where Christ (Bacchus) himself resides in the person of his representative, the pope, and the source (*fontem*) from which flow the divine streams (*liberos rivos*), the water of life and revelation.

The obvious skill of the author in writing a respectable elegiac couplet and the generally high Latin literacy evident in the readings of VerBC 758 and Petrucci suggest a low probability for Finscher's hypothesis. One skilled enough to produce quantitative verse in dactylic hexameter would probably have been informed about humanistic issues. The allegorical designation of God by the name of Bacchus, the pagan deity of classical Rome, may have been strange to many but not to those clerics and humanists who delighted in classical allusions. Indeed, the use of allegory to interpret classical writings in terms of Christian ideals may be seen as early as the twelfth century in the *Integumenta* of Johannes, in Chrétien Legouais' *Ovide moralisé* (thirteenth century), and in Petrus Berchorius' *Reductorium morale* (Paris, 1342).[35] By means of allegory, classical writings, such as Ovid's *Metamorphoses*, were reinterpreted in literate circles as repositories of Christian truth. And if humanistic allegory was used to glorify the secular nobility of Milan and Florence, in Rome it took on an ecclesiastical character that is well documented in John D'Amico's book, *Renaissance Humanism in Papal Rome*.[36] If the textual references were understood as specific to Rome, they would probably not be appropriate for general use or much appreciated by the clerics of Verona or by Petrucci's clientele.

Whatever the reason for the substitution, the couplet clearly differs in structure from the rest of the text. Its differences reinforce the critical preference for the more difficult reading and argue that the text with the reference to Bacchus is the original one. At the same time, the level of literary skill demonstrated in the variant highlights the limitations of the original text. While the original may be viewed as addressing an

hexameter, but the second has lost enough to be termed a pentameter. The second scans as a dactylic hexameter up to the strong caesura of the third foot, but then the remaining part of the third foot (either two shorts or one long) is lacking; the final syllable of the sixth foot is likewise omitted. Thanks again to John Collins for this analysis.

34. FINSCHER, *Compère*, 192.

35. Cf., Edward KENNARD RAND, *Ovid and his Influence* (New York: Cooper Square Publishers, 1963), 134-37.

36. John F. D'AMICO, *Renaissance Humanism in Papal Rome* (Baltimore: Johns Hopkins University, 1983).

audience of ecclesiastical humanists, it shows little that would suggest more than a limited knowledge of classical style.

## The Sources

Only Petrucci attributes the motet to Compère. The other sources present it anonymously.

VatS 15 may well be the earliest surviving source of *Sile fragor* and, if the hypothesis developed below is correct, it is most proximate to the origin of the composition.[37] Based on a comparative study of paper, watermarks, heraldry, scribal characteristics, and other evidence in the early Sistine manuscripts, Richard Sherr dates the copying of the motet in VatS 15 to the period between 1495 and 1497. He argues persuasively that the manuscript was copied in Rome for the papal singers. His evidence suggests, furthermore, that the copying of the various pieces that were eventually brought together to form VatS 15 began in connection with the occupation of the city by the French during the campaign of Charles VIII in late 1494 and early 1495 to assert his hereditary claim to the kingdom of Naples.[38] We know from the letter of Ferrante d'Este to his father, Ercole, Duke of Ferrara, dated 7 October 1494, that Compère participated in the expedition.[39] The letter also recounts Compère's apology to the Duke that he was unable to send to him any suitable music because he had left his recent compositions behind in France. This information provides a basis for speculating that works of Compère from around this period and copied in Italy were composed there.

The readings in VerBC 458 and Petrucci's Motetti A are closely related. They share distinguishing textual variants (*Scile, verborum, dei*) and the concluding couplet discussed above.

All sources except Chigi contain an extended cadence in the Tenor and Contra at the end of the Prima pars, though the Tenor in VerBC 758 is abbreviated. The readings of this cadence in Chigi and VatS 15 are given in Examples 1-2.[40]

HradKM 7 is the farthest removed from the other readings. Several unique errors or variants, both musical and textual, set it apart from the others. VatS 15 and HradKM 7 share an erroneous pitch, semibreve G in the Contra against D, F, and A in the other voices.[41] In the text of HradKM 7, *deitatis lumen*, "light of God," replaces *deitatis mater*; the word order is changed for *voces audiencium solidae*; and the approach to Bacchus is less allegorical: *fontem nunc haurimus*, "now let us drink from (draw from,

37. Ludwig Finscher regards Chigi as "the best and probably original version." See Compère, *Opera omnia*, 4.

38. Richard SHERR, *Papal Music Manuscripts in the Late Fifteenth and Early Sixteenth Centuries*, Renaissance Manuscript Studies, 5 (American Institute of Musicology; Neuhausen-Stuttgart: Hänssler-Verlag, 1996), 11-20.

39. The letter is published by Lewis LOCKWOOD in "Music at Ferrara in the Period of Ercole I d'Este," *Studi musicali* 1 (1972): 129f.

40. In the musical examples, original note values are reduced 2:1; ligatures are marked by horizontal brackets, black coloration by broken brackets.

**Example 1**

**Example 2**

consume, drain dry) the spring" where Bacchus himself dwells. The less specific role of Mary (light, rather than mother, of God), though she is still present in the reference to her son (*nato*), the more specific meaning of *haurimus*, and the absence of *Amen*, as well as the notes for it,[42] encourage the speculation that *Sile fragor* is a drinking song: "having silenced the uproar, settled our quarrels, sung our music, and said our prayers, let's drink pure wine—no water!"[43]

Thus, the reading in HradKM 7 contrasts sharply with the version transmitted in VerBC 758 and Petrucci, which ends as a prayer to Mary. In the latter version, not only did the author omit the reference to Bacchus and expand the role of Mary, who

41. See FINSCHER's transcription, 50, Contra, measure 42, the sixth note, an A in the transcription, which follows the reading in Chigi.

42. Petrucci omits the word *Amen* but provides a place

for it at the finals, repeated twice in all voices, after the last word of the text.

43. Once again, I acknowledge John Collins for pointing out this possible interpretation.

acquires the attribute of *fons* (source, spring) from the original reading, but in so doing he also manages to reverse the miracle at Cana by transforming wine (Bacchus's free-flowing streams) into water (*inexhausta unda*).

If *Sile fragor* in its original text and in HradKM 7 is a drinking song, it is certainly among the most elegant ones of that genre. But if it is, such an interpretation might also supply a motivation for the excision of Bacchus and the transformation of the motet into a more conventional prayer in VerBC 758 and Petrucci. It may be even more difficult to explain the presence of Mary in a drinking song than it is to explain the presence of Bacchus in a Marian prayer to an ecclesiastical humanist.

## The Music

*Sile fragor* is a short, four-voice setting, approximately four to five minutes in duration. It is divided into two principal parts, both in *tempus imperfectum diminutum*.[44] The second part ends in a ternary proportion, most probably *sesquialtera*.[45] The setting is notable for its close relationship between music and text, its clear textual declamation, its dramatic use of vertical synchronization and sonority, and its effective exploration of textural variety and contrast.

The close relationship between music and text is clear in all the sources. Except for some melismatic passages, the placement of words in all voices is typically unequivocal; the number of available notes often matches the number of syllables. Even in melismatic phrases, the placement of text is often clear. Thus, when Ludwig Finscher observes the expressive upward leap of a minor sixth on the word *mater*, the relationship is evident in all sources.[46]

Clear declamation, the rhythmic synchronization of all voices, and the juxtaposition of vertical sonorities combine to deliver the text with striking effect at several points: *ac rerum tumultus, Psallere nos sine, Urget amor musae, quae psallimus omnes, Suscipe deitatis mater, quo Bacchus insedet,* and *et discedat lympha . . . .*

Textural contrasts heighten the homophonic effect but may also form an important structural feature. From this perspective, the motet opens with a point of imitation at the fifth and octave involving all voices, follows with homophonic declamation that dissolves into polyphony in four voices, then with a series of S-Ct and T-B polyphonic duos. A schematic representation of text and texture for the motet might appear as follows:[47]

---

44. ¢ in all sources except VatS 15, where the sign is C2.

45. Indicated in Chigi by the cipher "3" and some black coloration.

46. Even in HradKM 7, where *mater* is replaced by *lumen*, the relationship of the replacement to the melodic leap remains. FINSCHER's observation is found in *Compère*, 193.

47. The left column shows the beginning of the textual phrase, based on the reading in Chigi.

| Table 1 | *Sile fragor*: Text and Texture |
|---|---|

### prima pars

| | |
|---|---|
| Sile fragor | opening point of imitation (Ct, S, T, B) to cadence on B♭ |
| ac rerum | 4v synchronous declamation dissolving into polyphony to cadence on D |
| fuge pavor | S-Ct and T-B polyphonic duos |
| qui pectore | S-Ct and T-B polyphonic duos, cadencing on B♭ |
| Psallere nos | 4v synchronous declamation |
| et nostros aequare | 4v synchronous declamation dissolving into polyphony, cadencing on B♭ |
| Urget amor | 4v synchronous declamation |
| opprimens | S-Ct and T-B polyphonic duos, cadencing on D |
| cum ecclesia | S-Ct and T-B polyphonic duos, overlapping with the next section |
| dulcore | short 4v point of imitation |
| audientium | 4v declamation dissolving into polyphony to an extended cadence on D |

### secunda pars

| | |
|---|---|
| Suscipe | 4v synchronous declamation dissolving into polyphony, cadencing on G |
| et nato | S-Ct and T-B polyphonic duos, B imitates S |
| quae psallimus | 4v synchronous declamation |
| nunc fontem | S-Ct and T-B polyphonic duos, imitation in all voices |
| quo Bacchus | 4v synchronous declamation |
| et discedat | 4v synchronous declamation in sesquialtera to the end of the piece |
| liberos | T-B and S-Ct duos, second duo echoes the first |
| dum carpimus | T-B and S-Ct duos, second duo echoes the first |
| rivos | 4v polyphony |
| Amen | 4v homophony, final cadence on G |

Sometimes textural changes are sharp and sudden; sometimes the transition is gradual. The treatment of *Psallere nos sine ...* ("Let us sing ...") illustrates the motet's textural variety and control. Preceded by two pairs of polyphonic duos, the texture suddenly changes and the textual phrase appears in a four-voice synchronous declamation that thrusts the words into immediate prominence. The voices then gradually assert their polyphonic independence: see Example 3.

Two aspects of texture are quite sophisticated: the subtle dissolution of homophonic effect as the voices go their independent ways; and an equally subtle imitative technique where the identity of repeated material, veiled by melodic and rhythmic changes or buried in a complex texture, is not readily apparent.

**Example 3** Homophony dissolves into polyphony

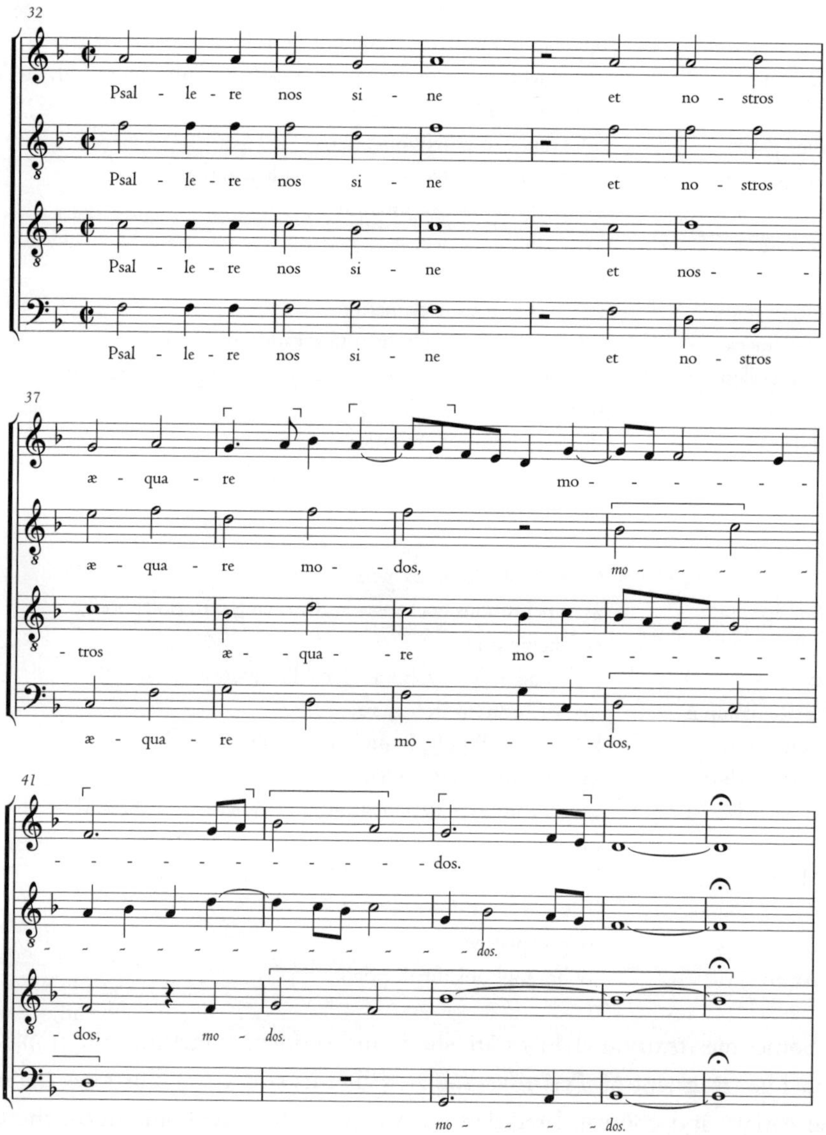

## Historical Circumstances

The text exhibits a number of unusual features that may point to the origin of the motet. The first part is an exorcism of noise, confusion, fear, and the suppression of angry contentions through the power of music. The second part of the motet begins with a prayer to Mary to receive and convey to her son (Jesus) the vows which all sing. Such vows having been made, it is fitting to approach the source where Bacchus dwells and to enjoy his free-flowing streams.

The information provided by Richard Sherr that the Magnificats and motets of VatS 15 were copied for the papal singers sometime between 1495 and 1497 and in connection with the French occupation of Rome considerably narrows the search for circumstances that match the text. We should also keep in mind the information, mentioned above, that Compère did not have any recent compositions with him.

The most likely occasion for the text of *Sile fragor* was presented by the negotiations in Rome and the ensuing agreement between Charles VIII and Pope Alexander VI in January of 1495. The humanistic character of the papal court was well known and may account for the unusual textual elements in *Sile fragor*. Charles entered Rome on 31 December 1494, and departed for Naples on 28 January 1495. His agreement of 15 January with Alexander was central to his Italian policies and to his campaign to manifest his claim to the Kingdom of Naples. Johannes Burchard, Alexander VI's Master of Ceremonies, gives the most detailed contemporary account of the events surrounding the French occupation of Rome.[48] Other first hand accounts of the events are found in the *Memoirs of Philippe de Commynes* and the poetic diary of André de la Vigne, *Le Voyage de Naples*.[49]

Negotiations between Charles and Alexander were protracted and difficult, complicated by the pope's alliance with Alfonso II of Aragon, King of Naples, which was the target of Charles' invasion, by Alexander's resentment of Charles' ultimatums and occupation of papal lands, by Alexander's own political insecurity and his uncertainty about the French king's intentions, and by the polarization of leading Romans for or against the pope or the French. Although possessing overwhelming military forces and able to dictate terms to the pope, who was virtually besieged behind the weak defenses of Castel Sant'Angelo, Charles seems to have respected the spiritual office and political authority of the papacy. He disappointed those who sought to

48. Johannes BURCHARD, *Diarium sive rerum urbanarum commentarii* (1483-1506), 2, ed. L. THUASNE (Paris: Ernest Leroux, 1884), 216-37. See also Johannes BURCHARD, *At the Court of the Borgia, being an Account of the Reign of Pope Alexander VI written by his Master of Ceremonies Johann Burchard*, ed. and trans. Geoffrey PARKER (London: The Folio Society, 1958), 90-120.

49. For Commynes' brief account, see *Memoirs of Philippe de Commynes*, 2, ed. Samuel KINSER, trans. Isabelle CAZEAUX (Columbia, SC: University of South Carolina Press, 1973): 481-82. André DE LA VIGNE, *Le Voyage de Naples*, critical ed. Anna SLERCA, Contributi del 'Centro studi sulla letteratura medio-francese,' 2 (Milan: Università Cattolica, 1981): 229-39.

invalidate Alexander's election and depose him, though Alexander may well have feared French support for these actions most of all. After considerable negotiation and strategic scheming on both sides, each achieved his immediate goals in a limited way: Charles received the pope's acquiescence, grudging though it was, in his campaign to seize Naples; Alexander publicly received the allegiance of the king and ended the French occupation of Rome with his own power for the most part undiminished.

Compère's text may reflect the confrontations of power in the French occupation of Rome, the tension of the extended negotiations, the treaty of 15 January, 1495, and Charles' formal approach to the pope with a pledge of obedience and reverence in the Consistory of 19 January. The solemn Mass in St. Peter's on the following day would have been the grandest of several possible occasions for a special motet, although it has no place in the liturgy. The ceremonial Consistory of 19 January, however, may have been the most appropriate occasion for Compère's motet, a gesture of conciliation and celebration designed to flatter the humanistic papal court. Papal Master of Ceremonies Johannes Burchard notes that the Consistory, ordered by the pope to receive the king formally, was unique and outside the usual ceremonial order.[50] Compère would probably have had sufficient time to prepare a special work because Charles knew what he wanted in the negotiations and was in a good position to determine the outcome. Even the length of the motet seems appropriate: long enough to demonstrate the musical forces of the royal chapel and its excellence in the latest musical style but not so long that it strains royal or papal attention or detracts from the principal business at hand.

While celebration of the agreement was extensive, descriptions of the events, aside from the politically significant words and actions of the king and the pope, are absent. Richard Sherr argues, as noted above, that the Magnificats and motets of Cappella Sistina Ms. 15, which include *Sile fragor*, were copied for the papal singers in connection with Charles' visit.[51] The music of Compère is prominent in this collection, and the manuscript also contains heraldic decorations identified with the French royal family.

The text of *Sile fragor* relates well to these historical circumstances. The classical allusions are directed at an audience of ecclesiastical humanists. In particular, the invocation of Bacchus, the Roman god of wine, of the harvest, of the earth, as a reference to God the Creator, to the risen Christ or his representative (the pope), seems appropriate only to Rome. A reading of Burchard and Commynes indicates that noise, uproar, and fear were palpable in Rome with the arrival of the French

50. BURCHARD, *At the Court of the Borgia*, 111.
51. Richard SHERR, "The Papal Chapel *c*.1492-1513 and Its Polyphonic Sources" (Ph.D. diss., Princeton University, 1975), 161. See also SHERR, *Papal Music Manuscripts*, 11-20.

forces. The *vota* (vows, solemn promises) in the secunda pars might refer to the pledges made by Charles and Alexander in the accord of January 15 and the formal Consistory of January 19. The final idea of the text, " Now it is fitting to approach the spring where Bacchus himself dwells; and let water be gone, while we enjoy (his) free-flowing streams," may be read as an allusion to approaching the Holy See, where God in his representative presides (literally "sits," *insedet*) and from which flows the life of the Church (*liberos rivos*). It is conceivable, in addition, that the final allusion, the approach to Bacchus, might have simultaneously sustained the other meaning, the invitation to enjoy undiluted wine to celebrate the historic accord between Charles and Alexander.

Why is *Sile fragor* in the Chigi Codex? One can speculate that Compère's piece must have been a recent arrival in the workshops of Ghent-Bruges when the Codex was being copied and assembled.[52] Why was it included in this manuscript, a retrospective collection of works by Ockeghem and Regis assembled shortly after their deaths and a series of pieces, as Herbert Kellman has argued, with special significance to Philippe Bouton.[53]

Herbert Kellman has developed our acquaintance with Philippe Bouton, Seigneur de Corberon, in a paper presented at the Ockeghem Conference in Tours in early February of 1997, "Ockeghem and the court of Burgundy: the memoires of Philippe Bouton." Among Philippe's notable achievements was his success in securing and sustaining the favor of both the French kings and the Burgundian-Habsburg aristocracy, in aligning his sons Claude and Jean on either side, thus assuring the patrimony of his heirs and avoiding the confiscation of family holdings that followed the changing fortunes of war and politics between these often adversarial dynasties.[54] The reconciliation of Louis XI and Maximilian of Austria in 1483 had allowed Philippe to enter the service of the king of France, to retain most of his titles, and to receive others. Although Philippe was thus allied with the French court, he also retained important connections in the Low Countries, principal among them his cousin Olivier de la Marche, *grand maitre d'hôtel*, knight, and captain of the guard for Charles the Bold and his successors. Around 1488 he placed his son Claude as a squire at the Austro-Burgundian court. Claude eventually rose in position under Philip the Fair and Charles V and lived most of his life in proximity to the court, some distance both politically and geographically from his ancestral home of Corberon in the region near

---

52. Between 1498 and 1503 according to Kellman, "Introduction" to the facsimile edition cited above, p. v.
53. Ibid., vi.
54. This strategy is outlined by Eugène BEAUVOIS, *Un agent politique de Charles-Quint, le Bourguignon Claude Bouton,* *seigneur de Corberon* (Geneva: Slatkine Reprints, 1971; reprint of Paris, 1882). The details and unfolding of the strategy can be seen in the documentary evidence (*Pièces justificatives*, 31-173), including many legal documents.

Beaune. Nevertheless, Claude's preferred title, visible in many surviving documents, is Seigneur de Corberon.[55] Jean, on the other hand, was clearly identified with the French royal court, an affiliation which proved beneficial to the family on several occasions. A canon of St. Ladre in Autun,[56] Jean preferred the title of papal prothonotary (*Prothonotaire du St. Siège apostolique*), also visible in many legal documents.[57]

Herbert Kellman has suggested Philippe's association with the French royal court, particularly those of Louis XI and Charles VIII, as a reason for the inclusion of a French repertoire, most notably the works of Ockeghem, in the collection. In his Introduction to the Garland facsimile of the Codex, Professor Kellman posits specific connections of other pieces with aspects of Philippe's life, such as Isaac's motet *Angeli archangeli*, whose text is proper to All Saints Day, Philippe's birthday. Might a special connection also exist for *Sile fragor*, or was Philippe only generally associated with Compère at the French court?

If *Sile fragor* were written in Rome in January of 1495 for the encounters between King Charles VIII and Pope Alexander VI, how could Philippe Bouton have been involved? Although Philippe's epitaph notes that he lived more than 96 years with all his teeth, one would assume that at age 75 in 1494 at the beginning of Charles' campaign he was probably too old to undertake the rigors of the military expedition to Italy. Since he describes himself as a man-at-arms, moreover, one would expect him to mention among his exploits, some of which he recounts, any participation in this historic campaign. Indeed, a contingent from Burgundy was led by the governor of Burgundy, Monsieur de Bauldicourt.[58]

If Philippe did not participate in the expedition, what of his sons, Claude and Jean? In view of his Burgundian/Habsburg alignment, Claude would not be expected in the company of Charles VIII, and payment accounts clearly place Claude with the young Duke Philip the Fair in 1495. Claude notes in his last will and testament, dated 24 May 1556, that he served the houses of Burgundy, Austria, and Spain for more than 68 years—no mention of France.[59]

---

55. The titles of both Claude and Jean are confirmed in a notarized declaration in the jurisdiction of the bailiff of Dijon on 1 March 1542: "noble seigneur messire Claude Bouton, chevalier, et messire Iehan Bouton, prothonotaire du S‌ᵗ Siège apostolique, frères, chanoine d'Ostun et de Beaune, seigneurs de Corberon, Villy le Bruslé, Marrigny, Glannon et Laiz ..." BEAUVOIS, *Un agent*, 120. Most of the titles seem to refer to Jean, who resided in the region while Claude did not.

56. The Cathedral of St.-Lazarus.

57. See for example BEAUVOIS, *Un agent*, 46: Claude's delegation of power of attorney to Jean of 1515. A pro-thonotary apostolic is a member of the highest college of prelates in the Roman Curia. Since the sixteenth century the popes had also appointed honorary prothonotaries, who enjoyed the same privileges as the seven real members of the college, and titular prothonotaries, who held a corresponding position in the administration of the episcopal ordinariate in the collegiate chapter. See *The Catholic Encyclopedia*, "Prothonotary Apostolic" (Online Edition, 1999, URL: http://www.newadvent.org/cathen).

58. André DE LA VIGNE, *Le voyage*, 141.

59. BEAUVOIS, *Un agent*, 167.

Jean Bouton, younger brother of Claude, remained a French subject all his life. The papal connections of Jean remain a subject of exploration. A reading of the documentary evidence published by Eugène Beauvois indicates that Jean and his family were proud of his rank as Apostolic Prothonotary. How did he achieve this rank, normally a papal appointment? Both his French connections and his high papal office prompt the speculation that he, undoubtedly a young cleric in 1495, may have participated in the expedition of Charles VIII to Italy. Indeed, the king was accompanied by a retinue of ecclesiastical dignitaries. His initial request to Pope Alexander VI at their first and most historic meeting, a request to which the pope acceded, was to confer immediately on Guillaume Briçonnet of Tours, Bishop of St. Malo, the rank of cardinal.[60]

For subjects of the French king, the expedition of Charles VIII to Italy must have been an enormous undertaking and among the most significant developments of the century, even though in hindsight it fell considerably short of its clear political objectives and of Charles' occasional and, perhaps, rhetorical suggestions that it was the beginning of a great crusade to the Holy Land. While it is unlikely that Philippe participated personally in the undertaking, the noble neighbors of Corberon and, perhaps, even his son Jean witnessed the historic encounters between King Charles VIII and Pope Alexander VI—circumstances for which Compère's motet may have been intended. Jean's participation, like his subsequent appointment as apostolic prothonotary, would have been a matter of family pride and might account for the presence of *Sile fragor* in the musical collection commissioned by or for Philippe Bouton.

---

60. Burchard, *At the Court of the Borgia*, 109; see also André DE LA VIGNE, *Le voyage*, 235.

Bruno Bouckaert

# An Anonymous Letter from Lille of *c.*1536
## about the Organization of Musicians
## in the Collegiate Church of St.-Bavo in Ghent

"No city anywhere in the whole Christian world surpasses Ghent in splendour and magnificence." Thus Erasmus described in 1529 (albeit not without polite exaggeration) the native town of the Emperor Charles V, the administrative and judicial capital of Flanders.[1] Just a few years after Erasmus' words some important religious changes took place: the monks of the old and venerable abbey of St. Bavo were converted into a secular chapter, and shortly thereafter, the chapter (situated at first on the outskirts of the town) was transferred to the (parish) church of St. Jan, in the very center of the city. These events had far-reaching consequences for musical life in Ghent.

All important cities of the Low Countries had one or more collegiate churches. The religious structure of Ghent was quite unique. It was dominated by two very rich Benedictine abbeys. Both abbeys, St. Peters and St. Bavo, were situated at the outskirts of the city, with, in their immediate vicinity, the churches of Heilige Kerst [St.-Savior] and Onze Lieve Vrouw. The parish churches within the city boundary (St.-Jacob, St.-Jan, St.-Niklaas, St.-Michiel) and the collegiate church of St.-Veerle (Pharaïlde) were subject to the patronage of one of the abbeys.[2] The plans for the conversion of the abbey of St.-Bavo into a secular chapter were first drawn up shortly after the accession of abbot Lucas Munich in 1535.[3] The authorities wanted to establish a chapter with great prestige in Ghent.[4]

1. M. Nauwelaerts, "Erasme et Gand," *De Gulden Passer,* 47 (1969): 152-78.
2. See Jan Art & Johan Decavele, art. "Gand," in *Dictionnaire d'histoire et de géographie ecclésiastiques,* 10, ed. Roger Aubert (Paris: Letouzey et Ané, 1981), cols. 1005-58.
3. For the history of the chapter see Emmanuel August Hellin, *Histoire chronologique des evêques et du chapitre exemt de l'eglise cathédrale de S. Bavon à Gand, suivie d'un recueil des epitaphes modernes et anciennes de cette eglise* (Ghent, 1772). For the foundation phase, see Geert Berings & Ch. Lebbe, *Abbaye de Saint-Bavon,* Monasticon Belge 7/1, (Liège,

1988), 65-67, Maurits Gysseling, "De proosten van Sint-Baafs en Sint-Amands," *Jaarboek van de Heemkundige Kring De Oost-Oudburg* 28 (1991): 6-9; Maurits Gysseling, *Inventaris van het archief van Sint-Baafs en Bisdom Gent. Deel I. Sint-Baafsabdij en Sint-Baafskapittel als instelling (nrs. 1-7534),* Rijksarchief te Gent, Toegangen in beperkte oplage, 64 (Brussels, 1997): 4-8.
4. Ghent-Rijksarchief, Fonds Sint-Baafs en Bisdom, K 10520. (The St.-Veerle chapter developed from the count's castle, but led an uneventful existence in the fifteenth and sixteenth centuries.)

Both the governess, Mary of Hungary, and Emperor Charles supported the request, and Pope Paul III secularized the persons and goods of the abbey on 24 July 1536. The monastic rule as well as the vow of poverty were abolished. The conversion was completed in 1537.[5]

The conversion from abbey to chapter also entailed a change of functions for all persons involved. The abbot became provost of the chapter, the prior became dean, the treasurer retained his post and title, the provost became cantor, and the provost of Papingloo became scholaster. The monks left behind their monastic attire and became canons. In the course of the sixteenth century the chapter of 24 canons included two composers: Roger Pathie, organist at the court of Mary of Hungary in Brussels by 1535 at the latest, and Cornelis Canis, chapelmaster at the imperial chapel from 1542 onwards. Their intimate connection with the court is significant. At the time of the foundation of the St.-Bavo chapter, it was agreed that half of the benefices would be at the collation of the Emperor. It may therefore be assumed that the composers obtained their canonicate by the intercession of the court, as a reward for services rendered and for security in their old age. Pathie had his prebend granted in 1540, but he may have never resided in Ghent. Canis, on the other hand, was more closely connected with the chapter. He received his canonicate on 19 June 1551. After the abdication of Emperor Charles, he preferred to spend the last years of his life in his homeland and retired to Ghent with his father and mother, living from his prebend at St.-Bavo.[6]

The higher offices in the chapter originated primarily from the new interpretation of the existing functions in the old abbey. Even though the chapter was in essence a religious institution, the real interests of many canons (like Pathie) lay outside the chapter and there was no strict obligation of residence. So the group of persons that now assumed responsibility for daily singing were all new appointments: chaplains, vicars, a choirmaster (*zangmeester*), and others not formerly at the abbey. For the organization of a professional musical ensemble, the new chapter followed the example of other chapters. An undated letter of advice provides, thanks to its anonymous author's evident familiarity with chapters in Bruges (St.-Donatian), Arras, Cambrai, Tournai, and Lille, new insights into the contemporary organization of several important collegiate churches of the Low Countries. The author of this letter cannot be determined, but is most probably someone who served as a choirmaster and knew the collegiate churches in question from personal experience. Strangely enough, little or nothing is said of the position of choirmaster, as if the writer took that for granted. The document is written in rather poor French. At the end, the author apologizes for this to his Ghent commissioner. I summarize the pertinent sections of this document, which is edited in full in Appendix 1.

---

5.   The (former) monks agreed with these changes and with the first statutes of the new chapter, dated 31 July 1537.

6.   See Bruno BOUCKAERT, *Het muziekleven aan de collegiale kerken van Sint-Baafs en Sint-Veerle in Ghent (ca. 1350-ca. 1600)*, Ph.D. diss. Katholieke Universiteit Leuven, 1998, 125-43.

## An Ideal Model

Once employed, both the vicars and the singers are expected to reside, like the choirboys, in the same house. The chapter would do best to purchase a block of houses large enough for a common kitchen, dining room, latrines, and a public dormitory. Each vicar and singer could have his own room, but without a hearth. One small room with fireplace was to be reserved for the ill or for a visitor. Since the upper floor of the house (with the dormitory) had to be rather large, the author proposes to use the ground floor for the chapter school. Ideally the choirboys' house should also be in the immediate vicinity. According to the author, the choirboys' school of St.-Donatian in Bruges was located under the dining room, and in Lille on the chapter's upper floor. The house of the vicars and singers must be supervised by a *minister*, as that post was called in Lille. Only a dutiful and experienced curate is eligible for this responsability. He keeps the accounts of the choirmaster and the vicars, takes care of the choirboys' attire, and purchases food daily, etc. With a concrete example, the author again refers to the situation in the church of St.-Peter in Lille. There the vicars and the singers annually receive three or four *rasieren* of grain, which they must use to pay for their share of the provisions of bread and beer. With the money they receive each week, they must pay for their own food (meat, butter, and cheese, for example). Besides the minister, a (married) man must be taken into employ, who, together with his wife, is responsible for cooking, setting the table, buying food, lighting the fire, and other such tasks. The picture painted by this anonymous author is quite unique: he intersperses his account with concrete examples from, among other places, Bruges and especially Lille, where a vicar could be found willing to introduce all good usages and customs in Ghent. Although there is no real reason to doubt the veracity of this account, the literature has preserved virtually no data on such houses in which the vicars and the singers lived communally.[7]

With regard to the singers, the author always distinguishes clearly between the vicars (*vicariotz, vicaires*) and the singers (*chantres*), although most of his suggestions apply to both groups. One passage, in which he adduces a concrete example from the collegiate church in Lille, makes it clear that the distinction between the two categories is partly of a financial nature.[8] The singers earn considerably more than the vicars, who are apparently still dependent on the financial support of their parents. The difference does not seem to be due to the degree of ordination, as might be assumed on the basis of the situation in some other collegiate churches (lay singers vs. clerical vicars), for at the end of his text,

---

7.   Only for Lille do we know that the house in which the choirboys resided since 1518 was built in the courtyard of the *maison des clercs* (Édouard HAUTCOEUR, *Histoire de l'église collégiale et du chapitre de Saint-Pierre de Lille*, 2 (Lille, 1896-1899), 145-50).

8.   *Avec layde de leurs parens sentretiennent le vicariotz ont en gaiges toutes les sepmaines sans leur bled et les obitz IIII, V ou VI patars ... Les chantres ont en gaiges toutes les sepmaines XV, XVI, XVIII et XX patars selon quilz le vallent et quy servent...*

the author says that the vicars do not necessarily have to be priests.[9] From a second passage in which the vicars and the singers are not mentioned separately, it can be deduced that the vicars are responsible for the the holy office and the singers for the performance of polyphonic music, even though they too participate in the holy office by joining in the singing of plainchant.[10] And whenever there is talk of a foreign singer (*chantre estrangier*) or a bass, he is never associated with the vicars.

All the same, a good vicar, in the author's opinion, must also have an excellent voice. He does not necessarily have to be able to sing the office from memory, which he says was the custom in the Lille chapter. This is an interesting indication. Apparently, in some collegiate churches the office was not sung systematically from notated liturgical manuscripts, which existed from Carolingian times on, but rather on the basis of an oral tradition. This implies that the music was (and is) more than the mere reproduction of the written notes. For other churches too we know that a large number of services were sung from memory and that this was sometimes even a prerequisite for employment as a singer.[11] But according to our author, the disadvantage of the practice is that those who do not know the office are more a burden than a benefit to the others. He holds that such singers will do better by remaining silent, and he claims to speak from personal experience. Perhaps that is why he counsels that choirboys should learn the psalms and hymns *quasi memoriter*. It is especially regrettable if for that reason the basses cannot take part in church singing, because their powerful voices provide solid support. By placing books in the choir the problem could be resolved. They would mainly be an aid for any "foreign" singers, which confirms that the liturgy could differ considerably from church to church. Each collegiate church apparently had its own chants and presumably its own performance style as well. With his remarks on "foreign" singers the author also implicitly testifies to the migrations and mobility of musicians so typical of the period. Yet he does not have much sympathy for such "foreigners." Thus he holds that the choirboys must always do their very best to get the "strangers" to follow their lead and adapt themselves to the prevailing standards of the collegiate church. He unabashedly states that the local church servants fulfil their task with more emotional involvement and pleasure, whereas

9.    *Il vous fauldra au commencement prendre telz vicaires que polrez trouver presbitre ou non presbitre et sur tout quilz ayent bonne voix et bien accordee...* This could also be taken to mean that it was most important to find good singers as quickly as possible, and that the priesthood was not important in this respect, because a whole new group of singers had to be installed.

10.    *Pour exemple il alleghe que a Lille les vicariotz chantent loffice memoriter. Il est bon pour ceulx qui le sceuent, mais ceulx qui ne le sceuent sont constraint de eulx taire, et silz ont livres au coeur les non scavantz ladite office, donnent ayde et assistence aux aultres.*

*Pareillement pour le present sont constraint eulx servir pour la musicque des chantres estrangier lesquelz ne sceuent ladite office par memoire. Et ayant ut super des livres au cueur chanteront et assisteront les aultres et maxime les bascontres qui sont plus oys et ont les plus fortes voix.*

11.    Craig Wright, *Music and Ceremony at Notre Dame of Paris, 500-1550* (Cambridge: Cambrigde University Press, 1989), 325-29, concerning Notre-Dame in Paris, with references to the same practice in, among others, the cathedrals of Chartres, Rouen, and Amiens.

extraneous singers are motivated instead by their salary (*serviront plus par affection et pour com-plaire que ung estrangier pour bons gaiges*).

One of the most illuminating aspects of this text is the recommendation to create a structure in which the vicars could progress by step to higher, and therefore better-paid functions in the collegiate church. The wages of the vicars would be reviewed every year. Those who perform well could get a yearly raise, but *les inutilles et mal servans* might incur a pay cut. In that way malfunctioning and incompetent servants could be eliminated.

In the course of a singer's career there is also a possibility of promotion. After some time a vicar (possibly a former choirboy himself) could become the holder of a chaplaincy. Within the chaplaincies, there is a three-step scale in importance and payment (*petittes, moyennes, grandes*). The great vicars (*grandz vicaires*) then form the next step. Like the canons, they take part in the Holy Office, are clothed in the same way, but do not attend the meetings of the chapter. It is their job to sing the *messe de prime*, in which the choirboys perform the plainchant with them. When a vicar-chaplain becomes great vicar, he must abandon his chaplaincy and leave the communal house of vicars, thus creating a vacancy for a new and young talent. Thus a system was in place for a transfer from lower to higher positions.

The letter does not dwell in detail on the duties of the vicars. It is notable that the succentor, when necessary and provided a compensation is paid, can call upon the assistance of one or two vicars to train the choirboys. This undoubtedly concerns the teaching of plainchant, not polyphony, and once again confirms that the vicars, according to this author, are primarily concerned with the performance of plainchant.[12]

In the letter the author does not discuss the position of the choirmaster, probably because the latter was himself responsible for the letter. If it was drawn up by a choirmaster, he apparently took his own duties for granted and therefore gave them no further comment. The author makes a clear distinction between the posts of choirmaster and succentor. The term succentor is derived from sub-cantor (*sous-chantre*), which immediately explains the extent of his duties. He was an assistant to the cantor, who was responsible for all liturgical and ceremonial activities within the chapter. In the absence of the cantor, the succentor took over his responsibilities. The choirmaster's task focused more on the instruction of the choirboys in the singing of polyphony. Like the teaching of chant, this took place daily at set times. Lille regulations for the choirboys stipulate that the choirmaster had to accompany the choirboys on their way to and from the church, as well as to the school where they received instruction from the succentor and his submonitors in

---

12. St.-Gudula in Brussels also knew a division of duties in which the choirmaster (here synonymous with succentor) brought in singers to teach the choirboys plainchant; see Kaat VAN WONTERGHEM & Eugeen SCHREURS, "De 16de- en vroeg 17de-eeuwse zangers verbonden aan het Sint-Goedelekapittel in Brussel," *Musica Antiqua* 14 (1997): 16.

plainchant and where the schoolmaster taught them *lechons de grammaire* [Latin]. It was his reponsibility to ensure that the boys *soient instruitz en bonne meurs*[13]. Whereas the choirmaster was concerned primarily with the schooling of the choirboys and with polyphony, the succentor's main task was the daily supervision of the various liturgical services. Only a person with experience, familiar with the choral services and the ceremonies of a good collegiate church, could be considered eligible for this position, because he would have to initiate the choirboys in ecclesiastical usage and teach them plainchant.

The anonymous author predicts at the end of his text that it will take some time before everything is straightened out. As regards the singing itself, he remarks that a too lengthy office is not conducive to good musical performance. A shorter office is preferable, because it can be executed more attractively and with greater devotion (*affin que on la chante plus attret en plus grande reverence et devotion*). Again Lille is cited as a model to be emulated, and he proposes that an experienced person should copy the office according to Lille usage. He also counsels the enlisting of five or six vicars from Lille, Tournai, or Cambrai (Lille, in particular, he says, has a surplus of vicars). For they know the customs of a collegiate church well and can teach the others *la maniere de bien chanter et officier selon les accentz que les notes requierent commes les penultismes longues*. Especially this last sentence is intriguing. The author seems to hint at a more mensural execution of plainchant following text accent, and whereby the penultimate note in cadences may be held longer. Presumably this should be envisaged as a somewhat slower and more stately performance. The singers had to take the trouble not to sing the chant routinely, but attentively and with feeling (*que le chant et loffice. . . soit bien visitee et corrigee en beau chant*).[14]

## The Actual Situation

The above counsel may be only a theoretical or ideal model, but it still paints a general picture of the various duties and functions, as well as of their desired implementation. The actual situation in Ghent can be only partially reconstructed. The accounts of the church fabric of the newly founded chapter between 1537 and 1541 offer the most information.[15] They indicate that the Lille model would be imitated. In the account for 1537/38, we read that *meester* Jacop de la Cathoÿre was reimbursed for expenses in bringing the choirboys from Lille to Ghent. The choirboys were therefore recruited in Lille, where they probably received their training. In 1425 Philip the Good had provided a significant financial incentive for the support of four choirboys and their choirmaster, and in the course of time the

---

13. Lille, Archives départementales du Nord: 16 G 537, 16 G 81 (regulations for the choirboys).

14. Cf. Jean LE MUNERAT, *In Defense of Music: The Case for Music as Argued by a Singer and Scholar of the Late Fifteenth Century*, ed. Don HARRÁN (Lincoln: University of Nebraska Press, 1989).

15. Ghent, Rijksarchief, Fonds Sint-Baafs en Bisdom: R223, R224/1-2-3. The *acta capituli* are only preserved from 1540, but with a lacuna between 1542 and 1557. These accounts, together with the accounts of the new cotidiane from 1542, are accordingly a necessary source for the reconstruction of musical life in that early period.

school for choirboys must have established a firm reputation. Twice, choirboys from Lille were invited for Charles V's own chapel at the court: in 1542 by Roger Pathie and in 1543 by Cornelis Canis.[16] In the early years of the Ghent chapter, there is talk of four choirboys. This is considerably less than the aforementioned "ideal" of twelve to sixteen, but the latter numbers are actually rather exceptional. In the chapter of St.-Peter in Lille, for example, there were eight choirboys by 1524, in St.-Donatian in Bruges also eight, and six in Mary of Hungary's court chapel.[17] Later in the sixteenth century, the number of choirboys at St.-Bavo increase from eight to twelve. Upon their arrival in Ghent the four young choirboys were provided with appropriate garments: *lakin and voeringhe* were purchased to make four black *keerlen* (a long outer garment, also called a tabard), four *capproenen* (caps), eight *supplysen* (a surplice worn by persons under the rank of priest) and four winter *cappen*. Cathoÿre himself, accompanied by Jehan Cobbau, came from Lille at the request of the chapter. Some adult singers, too, were recruited from beyond Ghent. One, Jan Catti, came with two or three singers from Bruges, to present them. In September 1538, a *basconter* presented himself, but was not accepted and had to be content with alms. Unfortunately, there is no listing of singers by name. In 1539, Cornelis Diemes is mentioned, the first succentor. He is paid for, among other things, the production of a book that was used in the choir on the occasion of duplex feasts. In the scriptorium of the Hieronymites, various books were also repaired or (re)bound: in 1538-1539 an antiphonary, a missal, several procession books, the *martyrologie* and a *boucke daer de choraulen tgraduael uut singhen*. In August 1537, all is apparently made ready for the arrival of the choirmaster. In that month, two stucco-workers work seven days on *den camere vanden sanghemeestere*, with some assistance from the carpenter Clais Hebscaep and his crew. Two helpers receive 3 groats because they have *thuys en thovekin gheruumpt* for three days. In the church fabric account of 1537/38, we also find the name Mr. Jan Dormont, *sanghemeester*,[18] in connection with the payment of an excessive salary. The distinction between choirmaster and succentor (see above) is therefore respected. In the other church fabric accounts there is no mention of Dormont or of any other choirmaster.

In the years after the foundation of the chapter and the installation of the musical staff political shifts occur which cause some revolutionary changes.[19] Since 1515, the

16.  Henry DUBRULLE, "Bulle de Martin V en faveur des choraux de Saint-Pierre de Lille," *Bulletin de la Société d'Études de la Province de Cambrai* 10 (1907): 147-49; Homer RUDOLF, *The Life and Works of Cornelius Canis*, (Ph.D. diss., University of Illinois, 1977), 18.

17.  For Lille, Archives départementales du Nord, 16 G 537, 16 G 81, with an excerpt from the *acta capituli*. 2 July 1524 is given as the exact date of the foundation for four new choirboys. Alfons DEWITTE, "Gegevens betreffende het muziekleven in de voormalige Sint-Donaaskerk te Brugge (1251-1600)," *Handelingen van het Genootschap voor*

*Geschiedenis Brugge* 111 (1934): 129-74. See Glenda Goss THOMPSON, *Benedictus Appenzeller: Maître de la chapelle to Mary of Hungary*, 2 (Ph.D.diss., University of North Carolina, 1975), 469-74.

18.  Ghent, Rijksarchief, Fonds Sint-Baafs en Bisdom: R 233.

19.  See *Keizer tussen stropdragers. Karel V 1500-1558*, ed. Johan DECAVELE (Leuven, 1990), 121-92; and *Maria van Hongarije (1505-1558). Koningin tussen keizers en kunstenaars*, ed. A.M. KOLDEWEIJ (Zwolle, 1993), 118-26.

city of Ghent was at odds with Emperor Charles V, who considerably restricted the privileges of the particularistic citizens of Ghent when they obstinately refused to approve
his *beden* (taxes). The war against the French king, Francis I, compelled Mary of Hungary
to impose a new *bede* in 1537. Again the city refused to approve it, which in 1539 resulted
in open rebellion. Charles decided to come and repress the revolt of his native city himself. The *Concessio Carolina* of 1540 deprived the city of its self-government and
profoundly reformed the political and judicial institutions. At the same time, Charles
wanted to construct a fortress to keep the city under permanent control. The notorious
Gravensteen did not meet the requirements of this purpose because of its location in a
densely populated area. But the location of the old abbey (the newly founded chapter)
on the edge of the city appeared ideal for the construction of the new Spanish castle, and
therefore the old abbey had to be demolished. Despite loud protest, the recently founded chapter had to move. Three venues qualified for the new location of the chapter: the
small *begijnhof* ter Hooie, the church of St.-Michael, and that of St.-Jan. Ultimately, the
latter was chosen: it was the most important parish church in Ghent, being the church
where Charles V was baptised in 1500 and one of the few parish churches where a chapter of the Order of the Golden Fleece had taken place. The few surviving accounts of
the *cotidiane* (which literally means "what happens every day", i.e. the choral service) contain sufficient indications that there was already considerable musical activity before
1540.[20] In the fifteenth century, mention is made, for example, of the performance of
polyphony (*musycke, in discante*) and the singing of motets, and the presence of nine bell-
ringers. The murals in the crypt show that the guild of the trumpeters had its altar there.
There were also choirboys and singers under the direction of a choirmaster, but we have
no precise idea of the composition and size of this music ensemble.[21]

   The accounts of the "new cotidiane" (after 1540) provide precise information
about the actual composition of the music ensemble: eight (instead of four) choirboys
and twelve vicars, among them a choirmaster, two *grandz vicaires*, and nine singers.[22] In an
account of expenses for the various offices, we find further details: there are three bass
singers, three tenors, and three countertenors.[23] The doubling of the number of choirboys may have resulted from the collocation of the choirboys of both churches of
St.-Bavo and St.-Jan. The choirmaster Jacob Bracquemers had held the same post in St.-

20. Ghent, Rijksarchief, fonds Sint-Baafs en Bisdom: K3957 (1484/1485).
21. On musical life in the church of St.-Jan, see Paul TRIO & Barbara HAGGH, "The Archives of Confra-ternities in Ghent," *Musicology and Archival Research*, ed. Barbara HAGGH, Frank DAELEMANS and André VANRIE (Brussels: Koninklijke Bibliotheek, 1994); Bruno BOUCKAERT, *Het muziekleven*.

22. Ghent, Rijksarchief, Fonds Sint-Baafs en Bisdom: K5568 (1542-1561), K3742 (1561-1562). From 1550 separate accounts are even kept for the choirboys (RAG, SBAB: K3526 ff.). For the sixteenth century both the chorister accounts and those of the *cotidiane* have been preserved with few gaps.
23. Ghent, Rijksarchief, Fonds Sint-Baafs en Bisdom: K12578, document 2.

Jan. So the staffs of both churches may well have been combined . There is also a new succentor (Anthonius Nemmegheer). That the organ of the old abbey was dismantled and partially re-used for the building of a new organ can be concluded from the accounts, where it is reported that on 4 July 1541 a *positijf uuten huuse vanden france organiste* was moved to the church, with the mention that *someghe stoffe* various materials belonging to the organ of St.-Bavo were brought to the church of St.-Jan. Shortly after the transferral, the bellfounder Jacobus Waghevens was asked to melt ten new bells.[24]

For the period after 1540 we have a few unique regulations for the *cotidianisten*, to which the vicar-singers belonged, as well as for the choirmaster, the sacristans, the gospel singers, the epistle singers, and others. The regulations include minute details, and are mostly formulated in the negative, which seems to indicate the prevalence of abuses and therefore the need for a code of conduct. For that matter, in the Low Countries, a lack of dedication on the part of singers seems to have been endemic.[25] A first important codification is provided by the statutes of the chapter, which deal extensively with the vicars; but these were drawn up without any knowledge of the transfer that was to take place three years later.[26] The stipulations of the statutes were formulated separately in some unique ordinances. A first regulation dates from shortly after the transfer to the church of St.-Jan. On 3 October 1543 the canons issued a series of orders applicable to all officers (*officiers*) of the church, including the curates, the vicars, the choirmaster, the sacristans, among others.[27] This was probably the first time the chapter drafted separate regulations.[28] The *cotidianisten* were urged to be present before the beginning of the holy offices in suitable attire. The observances should be solemn, discrete without noise, without singers sleeping, walking around, scolding, or cursing. The chants should not be performed hurriedly, and the recitation should be perfect. The visiting of suspect taverns and concubinage with unchaste women were obviously strictly forbidden. This regulation may have come into existence as a reaction against actual abuses, but strikingly some of the passages from these ordinances almost literally resemble the regulations for the *cotidianisten* from the (old) church of St.-Jan in the fifteenth century.[29]

## Conclusions

The anonymous letter determined to a considerable extent the organization of musical life of St.-Bavo. Most of the recommendations were put into practice, and they

24. See BOUCKAERT, *Het muziekleven in de collegiale kerken van Sint-Baafs en Sint-Veerle.*

25. See Eric JAS, *De koorboeken van de Pieterskerk te Leiden. Het zestiende-eeuwse muzikale erfgoed van een Hollands getijdencollege,* (Ph.D. diss, Universiteit Utrecht, 1997), 56-58 (about Leiden).

26. Ghent, Rijksarchief, Fonds Sint-Baafs en Bisdom:

B4840 (see especially an enumeration of 51 *statuta generalia*).

27. Ghent, Rijksarchief, Fonds Sint-Baafs en Bisdom: K10628.

28. See BOUCKAERT, *Het muziekleven aan de collegiale kerken van Sint-Baafs en Sint-Veerle,* 97-101.

29. Ghent, Rijksarchief, Fonds Sint-Baafs en Bisdom: B5637 (1471).

defined the framework within which the musicians had to function to the end of the eighteenth century. Thus a distinction was made between succentor and choirmaster, which was not the case in most other collegiate churches. Singers charged with the performance of polyphony were employed as vicars. In contrast with what the anonymous author says, there seems to have been no distinction between singers and vicars (cf. *chantres* versus *vicariotz*). However, many singers were employed for only a short time and must be regarded as merely occasional members. Besides the vicars, two great vicars were installed who concerned themselves primarily with plainchant. The Lille model was preferred to that of Cambrai and Arras, where several great vicars were in service. The recommendations that vicars could, in due course and after years of good service, become curate or "great" vicar, appear to have also been applied in the sixteenth century, as well as the varying pay scales. The chaplaincy was for the singers an extra function (with added income), and was in most cases combined with the office of vicar.

The newly discovered information about Ghent also shows clearly how a flourishing musical life in the Low Countries was closely connected with the chapters. Institutional changes in the ecclesiastical geography had their impact on musical life. For the chapter of St.-Bavo, we were able to establish this for the earliest period of the new foundation, but similar events had equal influence in the sixteenth century: the organisation of the diocese of Ghent and the transition from chapter to cathedral, the Council of Trent, the far-reaching influence of the two sixteenth-century iconoclastic raids, and the Calvinist administration of the city. These aspects make research into the musical life of the rebellious city of Ghent extremely fascinating.

* A version of this article was delivered as a paper at the meeting *Musique et rituels dans les cathédrales d'Europe* in Royaumont (May 1997), where I met Herbert Kellman for the first time. My sincere thanks go to Peter Van Dessel of Leuven for the translation into English. See also Bruno BOUCKAERT, "De Gentse Sint-Baafs in de 16de eeuw. Enkele bemerkingen over het muziekleven bij de oprichting van een nieuw kapittel," *Musica Antica*, 11 (1994), 61-67 and idem, *Het muziekleven aan de collegiale kerken van Sint-Baafs en Sint-Veerle in Ghent (ca. 1350-ca. 1600)*, Ph.D. diss., Katholieke Universiteit Leuven, 1998.

# Appendix

## An Anonymous Letter about the Organization of Musicians in the Collegiate Church of St.-Bavo in Ghent, *c.*1536

### (Ghent, Rijksarchief, Fonds Sint-Baafs en Bisdom: K10594)

*Mon treshonore Seigneur,*

*Depuis avoir escript par ordre ce qui sensuyt, jay leu ung ordonnance faite et escripte par ung chanoine de Lille selon lordonnance et coustume de Lille, laquelle est bien faite et a la verite, mais mon advis ne seroit point de entierement son arrester selon ladite coustume sinon aultant que elle seroit bonne de loffice et cerimonies du coeur, mais aussy se conformer et regler selon aucunes ordonnances daultres colleges ou nonnelles si plus savies sont et commodes. Pour exemple il alleghe que a Lille les vicariotz chantent loffice memoriter. Il est bon pour ceulx qui le sceuent, mais ceulx qui ne le sceuent sont constraint de eulx taire, et silz ont livres au coeur les non scavantz ladite office, donnent ayde et assistence aux aultres. Et de faict de mon temps moy pour le premier et plusieurs de mes compaignons ne scavienes ladite office par memoire, parquoy donniesme plus dempeschement que dayde aux aultres. Pareillement pour le present sont constraint eulx servir pour la musicque des chantres estrangier lesquelz ne sceuent ladite office par memoire. Et ayant ut supra des livres au cueur chanteront et assisteront les aultres et maxime les bascontres qui sont plus oys et ont les plus fortes voix.*

*Semblablement des enffans venans au cueur qui sont tonsurez et acoustrez comme prestres. Il seroit difficille en mettre la possession en la ville de Gand. Aussy uest bon quil y en vienne sans nombre, cars les inutilles se vueillent comparer aux utilles et semble a leurs parens quon leur faict grand tort si on ne les faict egaulx. Aussy servent tant quil leur plaist ou que bon leur samble.*

*Mon treshonnore Seigneur, humblement et de bien bon cueur en vostre bonne grace je me recommande.*

*En accomplissant vostre commandement (daultant que voz prieres me sont commandemens) jay icy escript en ordre par forme de texte et en brief che quil me samble estre utille voire necessaire pour le service de vostre eglise. Pour (avec le temps) estre bien devotement et honorablement servie en reverence, obedience et a peu de despens, assavoir pour les heures canonicalles, unde canonici nomen acceperunt.*

*Premierement se pourveoir dung homme de bien, bien instruit au service et cerimonies dune eglise collegialle comme Cambray, Tournay, Arras ou Lille. Et luy donner charge du cueur (quant a loffice), tenir lordinaire, les heures de sonner et chanter etc. et luy donner tiltre de succentor et lauctorite du chantre en son absence quant a ladite office du cueur.*

*[margin: Pour parvenir a bonne consequence]*

*Que ledit succentor tienque escolle de chant publicque en lescolle publicque ou on aprent les lettres et aye ses heures ordinaires et cotidianes deputees ascavoir depuis le micaresme jusque a la Toussain apres le service des vespres et complies acompliez jusques au Salve et depuis la Toussain jusque au micaresme et les samedis et veiles des festes depuis VII heures le matin jusques a huit heures ou lheure de prime.*

*Que en ladite escolle du chant le maistre des enffans de coeur soit oblige amener ausditz heures ses enffans de coeur (ditz coraulx) pour illes les aprendre. Et si ledit succentor est trop grave de grand nombre denfantz peult prendre ayde dung ou deux vicariotz en les salariant du stipende que les enfans donneront pour leur escolle du chant. Que ledit succentor eslise entre lesdits enfans venans au chant le nombre de XII ou XVI enfans les plus ydoines de voix et plus elegans de personne pour servir au coeur de lire lecons a matines, respons et verses (ordonnez en nombre selon la sollempnite du jour), graduaulx et lecons et respons aux vigilles des mortz, pour supporter les coraulx lesquelz officeroient III triplicibus duplicibus et diebus dominicis.*

*Instruire lesdits enfans aux cerimonies du coeur, leur aprendre bien le chant gregorian selon la coustume dudit coeur, aussy le psaultier et les hymnes quasi memoriter.*

*Ne laisser porter habit ne entrer au cueur aultres enfans que lesdits XII ou XVI et les coraulx en leur lieux deputez et que lesdits XII ou XVI soyent tous les ans salariez du drap dune robe de couleur et moyennant ladite robe et aucuns petitz gaigna-*

ges comme servir messe, tenir des torses aux services des maisons mortuaires etc. Et apres devenir vicariot, de vicariot chapellain et presbitre et consequament homme de bien. Les parens desditz enfans seront joyeulx que leurs enfans soÿent eslus au nombre desditz XII ou XVI et les assisteront a leur povoir jusques a ce quilz soient parvenu hors du dangier.

Pour bonne consequence est necessaire ordonner ung quartier de maisons ascavoir une maison pour les vicariotz et chantres pour illec avoir ung dortoir public ou chacun vicariot et chantres auront une chambre particuliere sans cheminee, aupres desditz chambres des latrines communes, embas une cuisine commune et une salle pour menger en commun, aussy une chambrette a cheminee pour subvenir a quelque malade ou festoier en particulier quelque amy estrangier par le consetement du ministre. Et pour ce que le dortoir de hault comprenderoit plus de longeur et dheritage que le bas se pourroit faire de la reste le lieu de lescolle publicque embas, aupres ladite maison seroit bon y faire de lung ou laultre coste la maison des enffans de coeur.

[margin:] Selon la maniere de Lille laquelle est trouvee tressinguliere et commode.

Ladite escolle est a Lille dessus le chapitre et a Saint Donas dessoubs le refertoir.

Ainsi est elle a Lille.

En ladite maison des vicaires y fauldra constituer ung chapelain homme de bien et bon ancien serviteur ayant pres de la porte une chambre pour tenir de nuit enferme lesdits vicariotz et chantres, et de matin les appeller ou faire appeller aux matines. Ledit chapellain se nomme a Lille ministre et preside a table dict benedicite et graces, et en son absence le plus vieulx vicaire, et entre le benedicite et graces ne se peult faire aucune question ne dire injure ou quelque parolle vilaine sus amende a ce ordonnee au prouffit de la table.

[margin:] lamende est de II lotz de biere pour les obstinez, mais qui prie de grace eschappe pour I lot.

Ledit ministre recoit, paye et tient compte des gaiges du maistre, des chantres et des vicariotz. Aussy poulroit des accoustremens des coraulx et des draps de robe desditz XII ou XVI enffans. Aussy des despens ordinaire de la provision de la maison des vicaires qui est telle depuis la Toussain jusques a Pacques au disner et souper une bourree et ung fassel, de une brassie de bois en commun, tout le boix de la cuisine, le potage au disner, tous le vinaigre moustarde et sel. Les vicariotz et chantres de Lille demorans en ladite maison commune ont entre leur gaiges chacun trois ou IIII rasieres de bled par annee, dont ilz payent leur pain et leur bierre. La reste en argent toutes les sepmaines dont chacun achapte ou faict achapter sa provision lung une piece de beuf, laultre une piece de mouton, de beure, du fromage etc. Avec layde de leurs parens sentretiennent les vicariotz ont en gaiges toutes les sepmaines sans leur bled et les obitz IIII, V ou VI patars.

Les chantres ont en gaiges toutes les sepmaines XV, XVI, XVII et XX patars selon quilz le vallent et quy servent.

[margin: ] les bascontres dessus les aultres sont recommandez.

Tous les ans les gaiges des vicaires (qui se disent les graces) sont renouvellees a la saint Jehan. Ceulx qui sont idoine et servent bien demeurent en leur entier. Les plus idoines et mieulx servans sont augmentez, et les inutilles et mal servans diminuez. Par ce moyen chacun rend paine de bien servir et par honneur lon se faict quicte de ceulx que par experience on a congneu inutilles.

[margin:] Pour denoncer les graces desditz vicaires en leur salle commune sont tousiours deputez monsieur le chantre, ung chanoine, III desditz vicaires, le succentor et leur ministre.

En ladite maison est proveu dung bon preudhomme marie lequel achate et cuit et cuisine les portions et provisions des vicaires, les garde, et a leure de disner couvre la table commune, allume le feu, les sert a table et leur baille pain et bierre par compte et par taille. Toutes les sepmaines sarreste le compte du pain et de la bierre tous les mois et au bout de lan se rabat dessus leur bled comme dessus est dit. Et si le bled ny peult furnir le ministre le rabat dessus les gaiges aussi chacun advise de soy gouverner saigement et faire sa robe selon ce quil a drap.

[margin:] le pain se tient par compte en une table de cire et la bierre par chacun une taille de bois.

Aucunes menues, coustumes ou cerimonies quilz ont encores entre eulx, ung seul vicariot de Lille le apprendera bien aux aultres.

Pour la provision des serviteures vicaires et chantres seroit bon et utilles de faire de trois prebendes VI demies prebendes que a Cambray, Arras et Tournay lon nomme grandz vicaires lesquelz officent en cueur comme chanoines et portent lhabit de chanoine, mais ilz ne vont point en chapitre, ne sont point aussy collateurs. A Lille il y a deux prebendes, lesquelles se donnent capitularitor au bons et anciens serviteurs de leglise et sont a deux subietz de tous les jours chanter la messe de prime que les enffans de cueur chantent en plain chant gregorian. Et sont lesdits deux chanonoines capitulaires mais tousiours les plus jeusnes et non collateurs. La maniere de Cambray, Arras et Tournay en cest endroit me samble meilleure daultant que plus servent IIII que deux et VI que trois et aussy plus de serviteurs sont prouvenz et le coeur remply de plus de personnes.

Aussy est utile et necessaire avoir des chapelles de divers valleur comme petites, moyennes et grandes. Et pour recollection quand ung des grandz vicaire (lequel par longuement servir seroit vieulx et mortel) viendroit a morir ung chapellain (lequel par bien servir ou par estre ydosne seroit pourveu dune des bonnes chapelles) laisseroit ladite bonne chapelle pour avoir ladite grand vicarie, la bonne chapelle seroit donnee a ung chapelain ayant une moyenne, et la moyenne a une petite, et la petite a ung vicaire et tousiours moyennant bien continuer au service du coeur. Par ainsi le coeur seroit tousiours bien servy et remply de personnes tant de chapellains, grandz vicaires que vicariotz.

Lesdits vicariotz prouvenz et estans presbitres deslogeroient de la maison commune des vicaires et se rempliroit ladite maison et le nombre des vicariotz de ces XII ou XVI enffans assavoir des plus grandz et plus ydoines et le nombre desditz enffans se racompliroit daultres josnes a ce utilles et ydoines. Par ceste ordonnance leglise seroit tousiours bien servie en obedience en reverence et devotion et a peu de despens car enffans de la ville auront crainte de leurs parens aussy assistence pour lespoir de parvenir, ensemble nourris en josnesse et instruitz au service et ceremonies du coeur, saccorderont ensemble tant en faisant ledit service que en conversation et donneront bon exemple aux chantres estrangiers, lesquelz seront constraintz vivre a leur mode et en obedience comme eulx.

[margin:] Et serviront plus par affection et pour complaire que ung estrangier poour bons gaiges.

Mon treshonnore Seigneur, Je vous supplie que nayez regard au bien dicter ou ortografier de ce present escript mais seullement a la substance et matiere et plaise a vostre seigneurie le lire et relire tant que ayez le contenu bien entendu, et vous trouverez le moyen par lequel (avec le temps) vostre eglise sera bien servie et continuer a le service de bien en mieulx. Et pour ce quil y fault du temps pour le tout mettre en ordre et que le commencement est mal prest, il vous fauldra au commencement prendre telz vicaires que polrez trouver presbitres ou non presbitres et sur tout quilz ayent bonne voix et bien accordee et seroit bon (voire necessaire) en avoir (quant on les debvroit achepter) ung nombre de V ou VI lesquelz eussent vicaries a Cambray, a Tournay ou a Lille. Especiallement a Lille pource quil en y a grand nombre qui seullement officent en chant gregorian et phalmodier affin quilz aprinssent les aultres la maniere de bien chanter et officier selon les accentz que les notes requierent comme les penultismes longues etc.

Dessus tout et avant toutes choses il est necessaire que le chant et loffice (maxime des sainctz) soit bien visitee et corrigee en beau chant. Et du premier commencement prendre la possession de le bien chanter attret selon les plus ou moins jours sollempnelz.

Quant aux cerimonies du coeur en officiant tant pour les chanoines, chapelains, vicaires que enffans, la maniere de Lille est fort bonne et tient la moyenne voye. Ce qui est lourd se declare de soy mesme et facillement le peult on au commenchement amender.

[margin:] Une personne bien experimentee es cerimonies de plusieurs eglises quy coppieroit lordinaire de Lille quant il trouveroit ce qui est moins que souffisant il le pourroit permuer a la mainiere dung aultre bon college.

La plus briefve office est la meilleure affin que on la chante plus attret en plus grande reverence et devotion. Au temps present lon cognoit assez par experience que la prolixite de loffice et les plusieurs suffrages et stations sont cause que le principal ascavoir la messe grande et les heures canonicalles sont moins que bien et devottement chantees et non seullement fastidie les officians mais aussy les escoutans et en lieu de devotion leur donne nausiam et en plusieurs (voire tous) colleges vouldroient bien par bon moyen et par ung accord povoir, oster, demettre et changer plusieurs desditz cerimonies ou superstitions.

Quant aux fondations et rentes de leglie ce men faitz mention car elles sont faictes avec le temps aussy les terres et coustumes des pays ne sont point semblables, mais tant est que a Lille y a plusieurs receptes et aultres offices dont aucuns chapellains en sont pourveus aussy aucuns vicariotz lesditz offices sont bien dessines et les officiers ont ayde et subside pour vivre plus aisement. Entre lesditz offices ou receptes il y a la recepte des bledz qui se nomme lesparse, la recepte des vicariotz, loffice de la cave au vin, et les deservent les chapelains, les vicariotz deservent la recepte des obitz, de la diette et loffice du bachin dargent et par dessus eulx ont chacun ung maistre chanoine auquel ilz rendent compte. Pareillement le grand coustre se faict ordinairement dung vicaire a ce idoine et a sa chambre en leglise parquoy donne lieu a ung aultre en la maison ordinaire des vicariotz.

Eugeen Schreurs

# THREE FRAGMENTS
# OF 16ᵀᴴ-CENTURY MUSIC PRINTS
# NOW IN ST. TRUIDEN AND TONGEREN

THE MUSICAL CULTURE in the province of Belgian Limburg during the *Ancien Régime* in general and during the Renaissance in particular has until recently received little attention from musicologists. One explanation for this is that the region belonged largely to the Dutch-speaking part of the independent prince-bishopric of Liège, which steered a course different from that of Flanders and Brabant. Another reason is the somewhat peripheral place the region continues to hold within present-day Flanders. Besides several more general nineteenth-century studies by local historians (C. Thys of Tongeren, F.E. Straven of St. Truiden, J. Daris of Borgloon), in which music receives scant attention,[1] the standard twentieth-century work is Antoine Auda's book on music in the Liège region.[2] Yet his general overview is based almost exclusively on secondary literature. The information on musical life in the larger Dutch-speaking cities (Hasselt, Tongeren, St. Truiden) of the prince-bishopric is, however, extremely minimal and incomplete, because almost no archival research was carried out.

As the twentieth century progressed, a number of partial studies appeared – especially on St. Truiden – such as Roger Bragard's study of a four-voice motet by Johannes Vrancken, choirmaster at the collegiate church of Our Lady; the motet was part of a play based on the life of St. Trudo, the latter dating from 1566.[3] A first, interesting step towards

---

1.   See respectively Charles Thys, *Le Chapitre de Notre-Dame à Tongres,(Académie d'archéologie de Belgique)*, 3 vols. (Antwerp, 1888-89); François Egide Straven, *Inventaire analytique et chronologique des archives de la ville de Saint-Trond*, 6 vols. (St. Truiden, 1886-95); Jozef Grauwels, *Inventaris van de verzameling F. E. Straven* (Brussels, 1978); Joseph Daris, *Histoire de la bonne ville, de l'église et des comtes de Looz*, 3 vols. (Liège, 1864-67). For a recent bibliography on the cities of Limburg, see Jan Gerits, *Historische steden in Limburg* (Brussels, 1989).

2.   Antoine Auda, *La Musique et les musiciens de l'ancien pays de Liège. Essai bio-bibliographique sur la musique liégeoise depuis ses origines jusqu'à la fin de la Principauté (1800)* (Brussels: Librairie Saint-Georges, 1930). On the musical culture in the former county of Loon in the eighteenth century, see Eugeen Schreurs, "Het muzikale landschap in het graafschap Loon in de 18de eeuw," *Musica Antiqua* 4 (1987): 119-29.

3.   Roger Bragard, "Contribution à l'histoire de la musique au pays de Liège. Une Composition Musicale de 1565 provenant de l'Abbaye de Saint-Trond," *Bulletin de l'Institut archéologique Liégeois* 15 (1931): 184-204. For a fac-simile see Eugeen Schreurs, "J. Vrancken: In fata dum concesserit," *Musica Antiqua* 5 (1988): 23-26.

a monograph on musical culture in St. Truiden was a study on music at the collegiate church of St. Truiden by its dean, Jan Rutten.[4] A 1988 exhibition of manuscripts accompanied by a catalogue showed that the abbey of St. Truiden must have been a thriving cultural center, including musical as well as liturgical activities, but it also showed how little is known at present.[5] In the course of the twentieth century, almost no musicological studies have been published on Hasselt or the smaller Borgloon, although preliminary study has shown that even in Borgloon an interesting musical culture blossomed.[6]

It is the musical culture of Tongeren about which we know the most. A ten-year-long systematic study (1981-90) of sources in archives and libraries resulted in a doctoral dissertation in which the musical life of the collegiate church of Our Lady was situated within its urban context.[7] Preparatory research situated Tongeren within the broader context of the music history of the Low Countries. This research included the sampling of selected documents that point clearly to a thriving and by no means isolated musical culture, especially in southern Limburg. The comparative study of the musical culture of the collegiate churches in the area delineated by present-day Flanders that was carried out by the Alamire Foundation from 1991 to 2000, also showed clearly that an important network of musicians extended beyond the former borders. The cities of Borgloon, St. Truiden, and Tongeren, in southern Limburg, were an important part of this network.[8]

---

4. Jan RUTTEN, "De cantorie of sangherije bij het kapittel van Onze-Lieve-Vrouw te Sint-Truiden (1451-1797)," *Historische bijdragen opgedragen aan pater Archangelus Houbaert o.f.m.* (St. Truiden, 1980), 175-203.

5. *Handschriften uit de abdij van Sint-Truiden* (Leuven, 1986). In connection with the office of St. Trudo, see Antoine AUDA, *L'école liégeoise au XIIᵉ siècle. L'office de saint Trudon* (Brussels: Lamertin, 1923).

6. Christophe Libberecht studied the archive of the collegiate church of St.-Odulphus and demonstrated that a professional ensemble had existed there for centuries. The presence of an eight-voice Requiem by Henricus Remouchamp and of a ten-voice *Battaglia* by Tilman Botton had previously suggested this possibility. See Joseph DARIS, *Notices sur les églises du diocèse de Liège*, 1, (Liège, 1867), 262-65.

7. Eugeen SCHREURS, *Het muziekleven in de Onze-Lieve-Vrouwekerk van Tongeren (circa 1400-1797)* (Ph.D. diss., Katholieke Universiteit Leuven, 1990). Part of this study is to be published by the Koninklijke Academie of Belgium; a selection of the music will appear in the series *Monumenta Musicae Flandria* (in press).

8. See, for instance, the case of the singer, choirmaster and composer Lambertus de Monte, active in Liège (St.-Martinus after Petit Jean de Lattre in 1565), Ghent (St.-Bavo, 1567-75), Aachen (Our Lady, possibly *c.*1574-

79) and Borgloon (St.-Odulphus, 1582-92) as discussed in Eugeen SCHREURS, "Bronnen en methodologie voor de studie van het muziekleven in de collegiales van de Lage Landen tijdens het ancien régime: een oriëntatie en enkele voorbeelden," *Musicology and Archival Research*, ed. Barbara HAGGH, Frank DAELEMANS, and André VANRIE (Brussels: Koninklijke Bibliotheek, 1994), 168-69 and Bruno BOUCKAERT, *Het muziekleven aan de collegiale kerken van Sint-Baafs en Sint-Veerle (ca. 1350- ca. 1600)* (Ph.D. diss., Katholieke Universiteit Leuven, 1998), 121, 397-99. For the biographies of four musicians active in several cities, see SCHREURS (*Muziekleven*, vol. 2) on the biographies of Henricus Buckenberch (Ab Olmen), *basconter* in Diest (St-Sulpitius, 1578-79) and Tongeren (Our Lady, 1579-1603), Arnoldus Bullinx, vicar/singer in Tongeren (Our Lady, 1520) and Hasselt (St.-Quintinus, 1554-58), Henricus Falcon, choirmaster in Tongeren (1450-61) and Brussels (St.-Goedele, 1467), and Petrus de Roest, choirmaster in Tongeren (Our Lady, 1440, 1445-49) and singer in Antwerp (Our Lady, 1449). The spread of the local offices of saints (e.g., of Landoaldus, celebrated in Wintershoven and Ghent, and Lambertus, celebrated in, among other places, Liège, Maastricht and Tongeren, but also in Leuven and even in Anderlecht, near Brussels) also places this regional music within a broader context.

The lack of a more extensive musicological study on Limburg is partly a result of the fact that many primary sources kept in archives and libraries have not been systematically examined until recently. Accordingly, for the comparative study that formed part of my research into the musical culture of Tongeren, we depended on others or had to search by ourselves for musical sources that had not yet been catalogued. Although very time-consuming, this resulted in a number of remarkable discoveries, even if the rediscovered music was not always of local origin or use.[9] So it was, in 1984, when we were shown two fragmentary music prints from the abbey of St. Truiden by Raf Van Laere, head of the Provincial Archives and Documentation Centre of Limburg. Similarly, while investigating the library of the basilica in Tongeren, (the former collegiate church of Our Lady), and the most important old collections of the Tongeren City Archives, we came across a great deal of music, some only fragmentary but including manuscripts and prints of both Gregorian chant and polyphony dating from the Middle Ages to *c*.1800.[10] A third printed fragment was found in the collection of the archives of the city of Tongeren. These three fragments are here the subject of our discussion.

### The Seminary Library in St. Truiden

The first two documents come from the Seminary Library of the abbey of St. Truiden. The history of this library is rather complex. Originally (1831-39), the Kleinseminarie (small seminary) was established in the former abbey of Rolduc, in present-day Dutch Limburg. After the eastern part of Limburg was conceded to the Netherlands in 1839, the Kleinseminarie moved to the former Benedictine abbey of St. Truiden. The heart of this collection is formed by books that came from the Grootseminarie (large seminary) in Liège, which included, among other items, books originally from the collection of canon S.P. Ernst, who had been able to take possession of a major portion of the library of the noble abbey of Rolduc when it was abolished in 1797; the rest of his collection had been acquired through auctions and private sales.[11] A second part of the collection came from a number of other religious institutions, also

9. With the aim of making governments aware of the issue of the conservation of early music, the Alamire Foundation organized an exhibition in the former *Landcommanderij* of Alden Biesen in 1995. For a short description of the polyphonic fragments, see Eugeen SCHREURS, *An Anthology of Music Fragments from the Low Countries (Middle Ages-Renaissance). Polyphony, Monophony and Slate Fragments in Facsimile* (Peer: Alamire, 1995), which also includes handwritten music fragments likely originating in the collegiate churches of Our Lady in St. Truiden and Tongeren. Only a few music prints have thus far been discovered; they include those presented in this article. The array of Gregorian chant books and frag-

ments found to date is a good deal larger. An inventory of these latter sources from Tongeren is forthcoming.
10. In connection with these fragments, see also SCHREURS, *Muziekleven* and Bruno BOUCKAERT and Eugeen SCHREURS, *Bedreigde klanken. Muziekfragmenten uit de Lage Landen. (Middeleeuwen – Renaissance)*, exhibition catalogue (Leuven: Alamire, 1995)
11. For the history of the seminary library of St. Truiden, see Karel VERHELST and Raf VAN LAERE, *Catalogus van de 16de-eeuwse drukken bewaard in Limburgse bibliotheken*, (Brussels, 1997): in particular 10-11. See also Karel VERHELST, "De bibliotheek van het voormalig Kleinseminaire van Sint-Truiden," *Sint-Truiden 1300* (n.p., 1993): 28 ff.

disbanded in 1797, as well as nineteenth-century donations, including those made by G. Lonay, professor of philosophy at the Kleinseminarie, N. Schwartz, professor at the University of Liège, and J. Lupus, canon at the cathedral in Liège. Through various purchases of books and even of whole collections, the library grew over the course of the nineteenth century and the first half of the twentieth.

Music is not generally found in this collection, which is dominated by theology, philosophy, history, classical languages, and French, and to a lesser degree ecclesiastical law, Dutch, German, and scientific works.[12] The two pages to be discussed here are thus exceptional and moreover contain no marks of ownership. Since they have been preserved as isolated items, without any mention of their origins, it has been almost impossible to glean any further information concerning their background, unless it is accepted that these St. Truiden fragments can be related to the waste-paper reinforcement from a bookbinding preserved under the shelf mark D-0018.[13] Considering the geographical position of Rolduc (in the eastern part of the Dutch province of Limburg, only a few kilometers from Aachen), Liège, and St. Truiden, the German origin of these two musical editions is surprising.

At present, the library is still located at the site of the Abbey of St. Truiden, but in 1985, together with the administrative wing of which it was a part, a long lease was taken out on it by the Belgian province of Limburg from the board of governors of the Episcopal Seminary of Hasselt. In 1993 the lease was taken over by the city of St. Truiden, which subsequently assumed the administration in 1997. The transfer of the collection was likely reponsible in part for the fact that by 1990, the two documents identified by Raf Van Laere could no longer be found, and that despite extensive searches by the present archivist, they have yet to be located.[14]

## Fragments From Galliculus' Treatise *Libellus de compositione cantus*

The first set of fragments from the St. Truiden Seminary Library consists of two sheets of paper in octavo, printed on both sides, measuring approximately 175 mm

12. VERHELST, *Bibliotheek*, 29-31.

13. With thanks to Karel Verhelst (Hasselt) for this information. Mr. Verhelst knows this collection better than anyone, having been its curator until 1997. See also Karel VERHELST, *Catalogus*, no. 391: 210, Theocritus SYRACUSANUS, *Theokritou Eidullia, toutesti mikra poiemata...*, (Frankfurt: Petrus Brubacchius, 1545), a volume comprising nineteen half-pages of printed paper of German origin, used as binding reinforcement, including four sheets with music, dating from between 1517 and 1544. Considering that the block measures 17 cm and both fragments are of approximately the same length, it is quite possible that these pages may have come from this

volume. The book had formerly belonged to Petrus Christophorus Scheiblerus (1675) and to the Kleinseminarie of Rolduc in the nineteenth century.

14. In December 1999, M. Van Laere informed me only that the documents were to be found in a brown envelope. Els De Coninck, who succeeded Van Laere, was not able to help me any further; nor has the search been successful under the present archivist, F. Duchateau. According to Karel Verhelst, in a communication of February 2000, the music fragments were still present in 1997. I wish here to thank all of these persons for their help in my quest for the lost originals.

(length) by 105 mm (width). There are thus four complete pages (see Table 1, pages 33, 34, 35, 36). Since the folios have been cut off too high, likely because they were used to reinforce the binding of a larger book, four upper margins of four other pages (see Table 1: respectively pages 17, 18 and 27, 28) have also been preserved. Judging by the large outer and lower margins, these are clearly two outer edges of one sheet.

We were able to identify the pages as originating in an edition of Johannes Galliculus' treatise *Libellus de compositione cantus*, Wittenberg, Georg Rhau, 1538.[15] Table 1 offers an overview of the composition of the St. Truiden fragments, and also shows the concordance with the 1538 edition. The consecutive, completely preserved pages are numbered in the overview as pages 1 to 4 and correspond with pages 17, 18, 27, 28, and 33 to 36 in the 1538 edition.[16]

**Table 1** J. GALLICULUS, overview of the preserved pages from St. Truiden with gathering signatures, text incipit of the page in question, and concordant page in the Rhau 1538 edition.

| Fragments from St. Truiden | | Brussels, Koninklijke Bibliotheek, Fétis, no. 6669 (RISM, Galliculus, 1538) | |
|---|---|---|---|
| Page | Gathering signature | Text incipit | Page[17] |
| [p. 1] | C iiij$^r$ | DE CLAVSVLIS FORMALIBVS | p. 33 |
| [p. 1/above] | [B i$^v$] | SECVNDA. | p. 18 |
| [p. 2] | [C iiij$^v$] | CANTVS. | p. 34 |
| [p. 2/above] | [B i$^r$] | CAPVT OCTAVVM. | p. 17 |
| [p. 3] | B v$^r$ | [-]tiam supra Tenorem | p. 35 |
| [p. 3/above] | None | [-]tae difficilem positionem | p. 28 |
| [p. 4] | [B v$^v$] | Est & alius | p. 36 |
| [p. 4/above] | None | [-]tilenae partem, diuersia | p. 27 |

15. Searches in *Thesavrvs Mvsicarvm Latinarvm* (TML), of the Center for the History of Music Theory and Literature at the School of Music, Indiana University, Bloomington, directed by Thomas J. Mathiesen and available on the Internet <http://www.music.indiana.edu/tml/> resulted in identification of textual concordances with Friedrich Beurhaus' *Erotematum Musicae Libri Duo* (Nuremberg, 1580, especially pp. 116-17); several phrases wer found again in Franchinus GAFFURIUS's *Practica musicae*, Milan, 1496. I would like to thank Prof. Mathiesen for his help. Knowing that Beurhaus was chiefly a compiler, I was able to search more precisely using the afterword in the facsimile by Walther THOENE, *Friedrich Beurhaus. Erotematum musicae Libri Duo*, Beiträge zur Rheinischen Musikgeschichte, 47 (Cologne, 1961), which led me to a facsimile edition on microfiche (ed. Inter Documentation Zug) of Galliculus's treatise *Isagoge Ioannis Galliculi de composicione cantus* (Leipzig: Valentin Schumann, 1520).

16. According to RISM and the inventory of the Fétis-collection (François Joseph FÉTIS, *Catalogue de la Bibiothèque de F.J. Fétis acquise par l'Etat Belge*, Bibliotheca musica Bononiensis. Sezione 1, 7 (Brussels, 1877; reprint Bologna, 1969), the Royal Library in Brussels holds two copies of Galliculus's treatise. I consulted the 1538 edition (Fétis, no. 6669). Unfortunately the 1553 edition (Fétis, no. 6670) could no longer be found in the library. According to information found both in the general reading room and in the rare books collection, the treatise should have been found in the music section. A thorough search there was without success, neither in the place where the book normally should have been nor on the shelves of oversized books. The handwritten question mark in the inventory of the Fétis collection used in the music section also suggests that the work has been missing for some time.

17. The pagination, made by the author, begins from the title page. The gathering signature is identical in both versions (i.e. the St. Truiden and Brussels copies).

**Example 1**    J. GALLICULUS, music example, f. Ciiij[v]

In their music printing technique—by woodcut—and their text, the two sheets from St. Truiden are identical with the 1538 version.[18] A comparison of the earliest editions of 1520 (*Isagoge Joannis Galliculi de composicione cantus*) printed in Leipzig by Valentin Schumann[19] with those printed by Rhau (*Libellus de compositione cantus Joannis Galliculi*, Wittenberg, 1538 and 1546) and his heirs (also in Wittenberg, 1551 and 1553), reveals that the

18. With thanks to doctoral student Katelijne SCHILTZ for looking up Galliculus' prints in the Bayerische Staatsbibliothek in Munich. On Rhau, see Willy WOELBING, *Der Drucker und Musikverleger Georg Rhau: Ein* *Beitrag zur Drucker-und Verlegerstätigkeit im Zeitalter der Reformation* (Ph.D. diss., Friedrich-Wilhelms-Universität, Berlin, 1922).

19. In connection with the printer Valentin Schumann,

music examples are identical, in content and in engraving (compare Fig. 1a and 1b). Rhau's apparently direct borrowing of the woodcuts of the music examples from Schumann was a not uncommon practice in music printing.[20] A comparison between the editions of 1520 and 1538 also shows clearly that the nature, scope, and arrangement of the texts are different.[21] For example, there are more abbreviations in the earlier edition, the gathering signature is different, and the initial letters are often not filled in or are set in a smaller type. That the 1520 print has more pages (23 folios in the 1520 edition and only 20 in the editions of 1538 to 1553) is simply a result of the more compact typesetting of the later editions.[22] The St. Truiden fragment as well as the edition of 1538 have an erroneous gathering signature on page 33: f. Ciiij[r] should be f. Biiij[r], then followed logically by f. B[v]).

Both the 1520 edition and that of 1538-53 conclude with a four-voice composition that serves as a model for the application of various rules of composition (*Sequitur exemplum omnium regularum*). It is remarkable that both in the 1520 editions and the later editions in this four-part composition, the term *tenor acutus*, used throughout the treatise is replaced by *altus*, and *baritonans* by the more modern *bassus*.[23] A last, additional curiosity is that in music example 1 (f. C iiij[v]), the *tenor acutus* makes a remarkable leap downward of an octave on the final chord; this is preserved in all editions.

## Fragments of the German Song *Wyr glawben all*

Besides the treatise just discussed, a paper fragment, printed on one side only, was also shown to me in 1984. The following measurements could be deduced from the photocopies I received: *c*.175 mm (length: comparable with the previous print) x 214 mm (width). Like the two previous folios preceding this fragment, it was trimmed with no respect for the music, most likely (as with the two previously discussed folios) to be used as the reinforcement of the same binding. The music that has remained visible (the end of the song) shows the tenor of a version of the widely distributed German sacred Tenorlied, *Wir glauben all an einen Gott*, a German version of the Credo set in three ten-line verses by Martin Luther.[24] The three verses are all printed after the music which is probably a part of a cantus firmus.[25] The ligatures suggest a polyphonic setting.

see Günther HEMPEL and Peter KRAUSE, "Leipzig," *Die Musik in Geschichte und Gegenwart* 5: 1050-75.

20. See for example WOELBING, *Drucker und Musikverleger*, 86-87.

21. RISM, *Ecrits imprimés concernant la musique* 1, ed. François LESURE (Munich: Henle, 1971): 345-46.

22. In the pagination made by the author for the copy in Brussels (edition of 1538), pages 33 to 36 should be inserted between pages 22 and 23. The whole thus ends with pages 37 to 39. The later editions are corrected.

23. Also striking is that even Beurhaus takes over the

term *Baritonans* in 1580, even though this term generally fell out of use after the first quarter of the sixteenth century. See Owen JANDER, "Baritone", *The New Grove*, 2: 160.

24. See A.F.W. FISCHER, *Kirchenlieder-Lexikon. Hymnologisch-literarische Nachweisungen über ca. 4500 der wichtigsten und verbreitetsten Kirchenliede*, 1 (Reprint, Hildesheim: Olms, 1967), 399-400.

25. I wish to thank Harald Heckmann (Universität Frankfurt) and Edith Weber (Université Paris-Sorbonne) for information on this song.

**CANTVS.**

**TENOR.**

**TENOR ACVTVS.**

**BARITONANS.**

Si aũt Tenor cũ Cantu in mi claudit. Tũc penultima Baritonantis notula/ex tertia in quintã desiliet Etsi his tribus coniunctis par‑ tibus/Cõtra tenorẽ coaptare tentaueris. Tũc contratenor / in tertiã supra Tenorẽ ductus/ & vltima notula / per quartã siue etiam sex‑ ram/ipsi Tenori ꝗ̃ optime respondebit.

Figure 1a    J. GALLICULUS, edition by Schumann, 1520, p. 28

**Figure 1b** J. Galliculus, edition by Rhau (version St.-Truiden), f. Ciiijᵛ [sic; = f. Biiijᵛ]

Unfortunately, the beginning of the melody is missing, more the pity as this version is divergent from those published in *Das Tenorlied* (see Fig. 2).[26]

### Fragments of Jean Louys' Psalm Setting *A toy mon Dieu* (1555)

In the city archives of Tongeren (Beguinage Collection), a register of accounts pertaining to the infirmary (dated 1573-75) is catalogued as number 513.[27] In the flap of the cover there are two clearly visible, consecutive pages, not yet cut off, of a contratenor partbook.[28] The oblong folios are not completely visible, measuring *c.*135 mm (width) x 295 mm (the height of two uncut pages) in their visible and uncut state. The music on page 14 and 15 is part of Jean Louys, *Pseavlmes cinqvante de David composeez mvsicalement ensvyuant le chant vulgaire à cincq parties, deuxiesme liure contenant xvj. Pseaulmes*, printed in Antwerp in 1555 by Hubert Waelrant and Jan Laet (RISM L 2889).[29] The back of the sheets is not visible. Copies of this print are preserved in Munich (Bayerische Staatsbibliothek); Poland (Biblioteka Jagiellonska), and Stockholm (Kungliga Biblioteket—superius only).[30] No modern edition of this chanson has been published.[31]

### Conclusion

Although these three modest fragments of printed music are not spectacular per se, they do suggest that a systematic inventory of musical sources in Limburg and adjacent regions would be useful, considering the many libraries, archives, and private

26. Norbert BÖKER-HEIL and Harald HECKMANN, *Das Tenorlied: Mehrstimmige Lieder in deutschen Quellen 1450 – 1580*, Catalogus musicus, 9-11, RISM Sonderbände (Kassel: Bärenreiter, 1979-1986) offers the following variants: *Wir glauben all, Wir gleuben al, Wir gleubenn all, Wir glewben al, Wjr glauben all, Wjr Gleuben all, Wyr gleuben all* but not *Wyr glawben all*.

27. The infirmary of the beguinage was a hospital with a chapel where sick beguines could be treated. My thanks go to city archivist Johan Helsen for the facilities put at my disposal and for advice on my research. For an inventory of the collection, see H. BAILLIEN, *Inventaris van de fondsen van het Sint-Jacobsgasthuis en van het Begijnhof* (Brussels, 1969), 266.

28. As the right hand of the first page is hidden in the volume, we could not read the original pagination, nor the number of the psalm. Annie Coeurdevey (Paris) was able to inform me that it was a setting of Psalm 25, in a translation by Clement Marot, and that the chance was good that it was a work by Jean Louys, printed by Waelrant and Laet in Antwerp. On the basis of this information, I established that the two Tongeren sheets did indeed come from this Antwerp edition (microfilm from the Bayerische Staatsbibliothek, Munich, held by the Koninklijke Bibliotheek, Brussels; with thanks to Henri

Vanhulst from Brussels for this reference). Almost at the same time as this identification, Robert Lee Weaver (Michigan) faxed me a printout of all the voices of this five-voice psalm setting, for which I am very grateful.

29. Robert Lee WEAVER, *A descriptive bibliographical catalogue of the music printed by Hubert Waelrant and Jan de Laet*, Detroit studies in music bibliography, 73 (Ann Arbor, 1994), 30-35. The Tongeren fragments contain the seventh chanson from the 1555 collection.

30. Robert Lee WEAVER, *Additions and Corrections to A Descriptive Bibliographical Catalog of the Music Printed by Hubert Waelrant and Jan de Laet* (Ann Arbor: UMI Research Press, 1998), 1-6, and idem, *Additions and Corrections to Waelrant and Laet Music Publishers in Antwerp's Golden Age* (Ann Arbor, 1998), 4.

31. This bookbinding may contain more unknown music: because of damage to the sheets of the Waelrant print, traces of a printed lute tablature are visible. At present it has not been deemed possible to have the binding restored and thereby to identify the lute print. If the Koninklijk Instituut voor het Kunstpatrimonium in Brussels offers its collaboration and the Tongeren city council gives permission for the paper sheets in the volume to be extracted, we shall be able to begin further research.

**Figure 2**  Incomplete end of the German song *Wyr glawben all an eynen Got*

collections that have received little or no attention from researchers. Moreover, these fragments show that a great deal of music (especially music without rich illumination) was ingloriously recycled into bookbindings, but that at the same time fragments of music that might otherwise have been lost have now been preserved.[32] In this connection, as well as in the context of this *Festschrift*, I am particularly reminded of the "Alamire choirbooks" from the St. Goedele archives, first described by Herbert Kellman.[33] Such documents, be they handwritten or printed music, fragments or complete books, recently unearthed or not, can teach us much about the dissemination of music.

Transl.: Stratton BULL (Katholieke Universiteit Leuven)

32. For more on the sorry fate of early music in days gone by, see the history of the music library of the Tongeren collegiate church of Our Lady, where the sales of the old music books financed the purchases of new music books. SCHREURS, *Muziekleven*, 214.

33. *Census-Catalogue of Manuscript Sources of Polyphonic Music, 1400-1550*, 1 (Neuhausen-Stuttgart: Hänssler-Verlag, 1979), 104.

Bonnie J. Blackburn

# LEONARDO AND GAFFURIO ON HARMONY
# AND THE PULSE OF MUSIC

L EONARDO, in his famous comparison of the arts, seeks to vindicate for painting the same elevated status enjoyed by music because of its position in the Quadrivium. While he cannot deny the mathematical foundation that justifies music's placement with arithmetic, geometry, and astronomy, he seeks to undermine music's prestige by comparing it unfavourably with painting on a number of points. The main argument takes place in his *Paragone*, but scattered remarks are found elsewhere; these show that Leonardo has thought much more deeply about the nature of music, especially polyphonic music, than most music theorists, if we can judge from their treatises—which, of course, we cannot really do, but that is the evidence we have. For all their treatment of consonance and dissonance and the intricacies of mensural notation, we find very little theoretical discussion about the most fundamental aspect of all: how music operates in time. It is the element of motion that Leonardo returns to again and again, and it is the concept of time that plays a crucial role in the redefinition of harmony at the end of the fifteenth century. Leonardo frequently appeals to two concepts that have a technical musical meaning: harmonic proportionality and harmonic tempo. In this article I investigate what those concepts meant to him, and whether his understanding of them agrees with contemporary music theory, especially as expounded by Franchino Gaffurio, his colleague in Milan.

Leonardo believed that painting was not numbered among the sciences for lack of writers on the subject; but since painting "is the sole imitator of all the manifest works of nature" and "nothing can be found in nature that is not part of science," and furthermore, since it draws upon the lines and points of geometry, and perspective depends on arithmetic (discontinuous quantity) and geometry (continuous quantity), painting can rightly be considered a science.[1] In the *Paragone* Leonardo compared the arts of poetry, painting, and music.

---

1.  *Leonardo on Painting*, ed. Martin KEMP, selected and trans. Martin KEMP and Margaret WALKER (New Haven: Yale University Press, 1989), 13-14, hereafter referred to as Kemp and Walker.

Because the eye, "which is said to be the window of the soul," is superior to the ear, painting is superior to poetry and to music. The poet is limited because his descriptive words "are separated from one another by time, which leaves voids between them and dismembers the proportions."[2] Music, by contrast, "composes harmony from the conjunction of her proportional parts sounded simultaneously," but is "constrained to arise and die in one or more harmonic beats (*tempi armonici*)."[3] Thus painting "excels and is superior in rank to music, because it does not perish immediately after its creation"; moreover, the eye can grasp the whole simultaneously. Therefore, if music is among the liberal arts, "either you should place painting there or remove music."[4]

Statements such as these show that Leonardo was thinking in terms of musical performance: the sound of music is continuous—unlike poetry, where there are gaps between words in recitation—but it cannot be grasped as a whole, and when the piece finishes, the music is gone. Some writers on music *were* concerned with this phenomenon, but from a somewhat different point of view: is music evanescent and lost after performance, or is there such a thing as a work of art that remains? Tinctoris makes a distinction between music that arises in the process of singing *super librum*, "on the book," that is, improvising a melodic line over a written melody taken from chant or polyphony, which he calls counterpoint, and music that is composed according to rules regulating the relations between all the voices, which he calls *res facta*, a "made thing," and which I have proposed to call "harmonic composition."[5] A *res facta* is fixed in writing; later authors called it an *opus perfectum et absolutum*. After performance it did not vanish, although it existed in another dimension.[6] A *res facta* was also a visual object, and often a very beautiful one, but in that form it is not music. (On Leonardo's admiration of a *res facta* as a work of art, see the Appendix.)

---

2.    Ibid., 20, 24 (Urb 11ᵛ: "il tempo le divide l'un da l'altro & infra mette la oblivione et divide le proportioni"). I cite the Italian from the earliest version of the treatise on painting, prepared by Leonardo's pupil Francesco Melzi, now in the Vatican Library (MS Urb. lat. 1270), known as the Codex Urbinas. A facsimile has been published in vol. 2 of *Treatise on Painting by Leonardo da Vinci*, ed. and trans. A. Philip McMahon, intro. Ludwig Heydenreich, 2 vols. (Princeton: Princeton University Press, 1956).

3.    Ibid., 34, but Kemp and Walker translate *operate nel medesimo tempo* as "which make their effect instantaneously" and *armonici tempi* as "harmonic intervals" (Urb 16ʳ: "compone armonia con le congiontioni delle sue parti proportionali operate nel medesimo tempo costrette a nascere e morire in uno o piu tempi armonici").

4.    Ibid., 35 (Urb 16ᵛ: "ma la pittura eccelle & signoreggia la musica perch'essa non more immediate dopo la sua creatione") and 37. Luca Pacioli makes much the

same claim for perspective's equal right to belong to the Quadrivium in *De divina proportione* (Milan, 1497), Part I, chap. 3. See Arnaldo Bruschi, Corrado Maltese, Manfredo Tafuri, and Renato Bonelli, eds., *Scritti rinascimentali di architettura* (Milan: Il polifilo, 1978), 67-68. On the role of music in the *Paragone*, see also Emanuel Winternitz, *Leonardo da Vinci as a Musician* (New Haven: Yale University Press, 1982), chap. 12.

5.    See Bonnie J. Blackburn, "On Compositional Process in the Fifteenth Century," *Journal of the American Musicological Society* 40 (1987): 210-84, esp. 246-68.

6.    Leonardo anticipated this riposte from the musician, but answers not quite to the point: "If you should say that music lasts for ever by being written down, we are doing the same here with letters"; Kemp and Walker, 35 (Urb 17ᵛ: "et se tu dicessi la musica s'eterna con lo scriverla el medesimo facciamo noi qui con le lettere").

Let us consider the words Leonardo used to describe music: it composes harmony from the conjunction of proportional parts in one or more harmonic *tempi*. Just what did Leonardo mean by harmony, the conjunction of proportional parts, and *tempi armonici*? There is no easy answer to this question, because the definition of harmony was a matter of considerable controversy in his time. In the 1470s Tinctoris could define *armonia* as "a certain pleasantness caused by a combining of sound" and, given that general definition, he could also claim that melody is the same as harmony.[7] This same general meaning is the one we use today when we speak of something being harmonious because we think the parts fit together well, sometimes appealing to proportion, sometimes to symmetry. But at a certain point harmony began to develop a specifically musical use. Did Leonardo use "harmony" in a general or a technical sense?

Our modern understanding of harmony—the relationship of tones sounded simultaneously—brings us up short when we are confronted by some fifteenth-century definitions. In 1482 Bartolomé Ramos stated that many people believed that harmony and music were the same thing. He disagreed, defining harmony as "the mixture of concordant voices," but music as the intellectual investigation of these concords, recalling Boethius' definition of the *musicus*.[8] It has been suggested that theorists of the late fifteenth century "reserved the term 'harmony' for a chord of three pitches; chords of two pitches were concords or discords."[9] This is true of Niccolò Burzio, who, in 1487, gives a definition of harmony that specifies music of three or four parts: "It is a modulation of the voice and a concord of many sounds, as is very evident in mensural music, especially when we sing in three or four concordant parts."[10]

Franchino Gaffurio differs: for him only the harmonic division of a consonance produces what is called harmony. This view is set forth most clearly in his *Angelicum ac divinum opus musice* (Milan, 1508).[11] In his *Practica musice* (Milan, 1496) he notes that the

7. *Terminorum musicae diffinitorium* [Treviso, ca. 1495]: "Armonia est amenitas quedam ex convenienti sono causata" and "Melodia idem est quod armonia."

8. "Harmoniam atque musicam idem esse multi credunt, verum nos longe aliter sentimus. Ex quorundam enim musicorum sententiis longa investigatione collegimus harmoniam concordium vocum esse commixtionem, musicam vero ipsius concordiae rationem sive perpensam et subtilem cum ratione indaginem." *Musica practica* (Bologna, 1482); ed. Johannes WOLF (Publikationen der Internationalen Musikgesellschaft, Beihefte, 2; Leipzig: Breitkopf & Härtel, 1901), 3. The following section is based on the more extensive discussion in Blackburn, "On Compositional Process," 224-28. See also BLACKBURN, "The Dispute about Harmony *c*.1500 and the Creation of a New Style," to be published in a volume of papers given at the conference "Théorie et analyse musicales 1450–1650" (Louvain-la-Neuve, 23-25 September 1999).

9. Richard L. CROCKER, in his seminal article "Discant, Counterpoint, and Harmony," *Journal of the American Musicological Society* 15 (1962): 1-21 at 18.

10. "est modulatio vocis et concordia plurium sonorum, quod in cantu figurato latissime patet maxime dum cantus triplici concordia vel quadruplici cantamus"; *Florum libellus*, ed. Giuseppe MASSERA ("Historiae musicae cultores" Biblioteca, 28; Florence: Olschki, 1975), 74-75.

11. "Ma la harmonica e dicta proprie mediocrita: perche la chorda de mezo in questa consyderatione conduce et conclude con le extreme sue quello suave concento che e dicto harmonia" (sig. D2ᵛ), referring to Pietro d'Abano's exposition of the 12th problem of Pseudo-Aristotle: "Medium est constitutivum harmonie." Furthermore,

octave is the first of the intervals that can be divided according to a harmonic ratio, and this "harmony" imparts a more pleasing movement (*modulatio*) to all musical compositions.[12] The mediated fifth (a triad) and mediated sixth (a sixth or first-inversion chord) achieve the same effect, but he hastens to say that they are produced by *almost* harmonic divisions. The fifth mediated to produce a major and minor triad "brings about a sweeter concord of the extremes as if it adhered to the harmonic mean by a kind of imitation"; the mediated sixth makes a concord "as if it were neighbor and partaker of the harmonic mean."[13] But in the *De harmonia musicorum instrumentorum opus* (completed by 1500 but not published till 1518) Gaffurio appears to relax his strict understanding of the term "harmony": a marginal note in chapter 10 of Book III summarizes: "What harmony is. Harmony differs from consonance: consonance consists of two sounds, harmony of three." The text explains that a consonance forms only one proportion, but a harmony has at least two. Therefore every harmony is a consonance, but not every consonance a harmony.[14] In the next chapter, however, we discover that Gaffurio is using both a loose and a strict definition of harmony: "Having disposed three tones according to a harmonic division . . . a melody is thus produced that we properly call harmony."[15] Having conceded this much, he feels bound to invent a term for other pleasant three-voice sonorities that are not "proper" harmonies. His solution is to characterize them as consonances divided by a "sonorous mean," which accounts

"aben che La consonantia corresponda in li soi extremi soni bona concordia como e diapason: niente dimanco *non se po dire harmonia per non esser mediata de uno sono conditionato ali soy extremi secundo la convenientia harmonica.*" (Ibid.; italics added, and in all of the following quotations.)

12.  *Practica musice*, Bk. III, chap. 2: "Octava qua aequisonantem diapason . . . perfecta est contrapuncti species: et *prima quidem harmonica mediate consistens* . . ." (sig. cc7ᵛ). "Est Itaque *octava harmonice mediata prima ac simplex illa harmonia qua musicus omnis concentus gratiore atque suaviore modulatione perfulget* . . ." (sig. cc8ʳ). An English translation is available in Franchinus Gaffurius, *Practica musicae*, trans. Clement A. MILLER (Musicological Studies and Documents, 20; n.p.: American Institute of Musicology, 1968).

13.  *Practica musice*, sig. cc7ᵛ: "Quinta autem quam diapente integra tribus s. tonis ac minore semitonio ducta sesqualtera dimensione producit: mediam obtinet concordem chordam cum extremis. Componitur enim ex duabus primis simplicibus s. tertia minore atque tertia maiore concordi medietate servata. Inde suaviorem ducit extremitatum concordiam *quasi quae certa imitatione harmonicae adhaereat medietati.*" "Habet enim sexta solam chordam mediam et concinnam quae s. tertia est ad graviorem et diatessaron subsonat ad acutam. Diatessaron

enim consonantia et si simplex ducta dissona sit: coniuncta tamen concordi commixtioni concordem efficit cum extremis medietatem: *quasi harmonicae medietatis proxima sit et particeps* . . ."

14.  "Quid sit harmonia. A consonantia differt harmonia[;] duobus sonis fit consonantia. Tribus vero harmonia." "Ea enim est extremarum contrariumque vocum communi medio consonantias complectentium suavis et congrua sonoritas. quam iccirco a consonantia differre constat. Haec namque sola proportione: duabus saltem Illa producitur. Hinc falso sunt arbitrati qui consonantiam et harmoniam idem esse posuerunt. nam quamquam harmonia consonantia est: omnis tamen consonantia non facit harmoniam. Consonantia namque ex acuto et gravi generatur sono: *Harmoniam vero ex acuto et gravi conficiunt atque medio*" (f. 80ᵛ). An English translation is available in Franchinus GAFFURIUS, *De Harmonia Musicorum Instrumentorum Opus*, trans. Clement A. MILLER (Musicological Studies and Documents, 33; Neuhausen-Stuttgart: American Institute of Musicology – Hänssler-Verlag, 1977).

15.  "Dispositis vero tribus chordis secundum harmonicam medietatem . . . ea tunc producetur melodia: quam proprie harmoniam vocamus" (ibid., ff. 80ᵛ-81ʳ).

for the not quite harmonic division of major and minor sixths and tenths.[16] Similarly, Ptolemy's adjustment of the intervals to superparticular ratios is deemed to produce a pleasing but not a harmonic division.[17]

Gaffurio does not have a word for "chord"; the concept certainly exists for him, as we can see from his remarks, but it has to be ferreted out from circumlocutions. (It could trap the unwary reader that he uses the term *chorda* to describe the mediating note; here, however, it means "string" and goes back to the Greek nomenclature for the notes of the Greater Perfect System, deriving ultimately from the strings of the lyre. Leonardo, incidentally, uses the word *chorda* to mean nerve, tendon, or ligament.)

There has been much speculation on Leonardo's acquaintance with Gaffurio, which is likely but not supported by direct evidence.[18] Given Leonardo's intense interest in music, as demonstrated by scattered remarks in his notebooks, his acoustic experi-

16. Bk. III, chap. 12, headed "De sonora medietate sextae et decimae maioris atque minoris": "Est quoque alia in sonis mediocritas quae neque eisdem et terminorum et differentiarum proportionibus commixta est ut Geometrica: neque aequalibus differentiis ut Arythmetica: neque aequalibus extremorum terminorum proportionibus ac differentiarum ut harmonica: sed his penitus tribus noscitur aliena quippe quae coniungitur ex communi chorda, s. *concinna et consona*" (f. 82ᵛ).

17. "At Ditono huiusmodi coniuncta Diatessaron in acutum Sextam ipsam maiorem mediabit et *concinnam (non tamen harmonice)*" (f. 78ʳ). The major and minor third in Ptolemy's syntonic diatonic, the basis of just intonation, are in fact harmonic divisions, and Gaffurio's reluctance to recognize them as such drew him into an argument with Giovanni Spataro. For a summary, see the introduction to Clement Miller's translation of the *De harmonia*, p. 21.

18. Cf. WINTERNITZ, *Leonardo da Vinci*, 5-8, who offers a perhaps too optimistic assessment of the circumstantial evidence, which in fact is mainly that Leonardo and Gaffurio were in Milan at the same time (1484-99 and 1506-13; Leonardo had arrived in 1483). On p. 6 Winternitz claims that "They lent each other books," without documentation. As far as I can see, he may have had in mind the following: Leonardo refers to Plutarch's *Lives* in a marginal note; Gaffurio owned a copy of the 1491 edition, which he purchased in Milan in 1494. On this copy, see Kate TRAUMAN STEINITZ, "Two Books from the Environment of Leonardo da Vinci in the Elmer Belt Library of Vinciana: Gaffurio and Plutarch," *Libri* 2 (1951-52): 1-14; figs. 1 and 2 show Gaffurio's inscriptions on the colophon and title-page.

Some authors (including WINTERNITZ in *New Grove*,

10:671, but not in his book; see his Preface, p. xviii) believe that Leonardo refers to Gaffurio's *De harmonia musicorum instrumentorum* in a passage in his notes on anatomy discussing pitch in relation to the length and width of a pipe or tube, written ca. 1508-10. Leonardo remarks "And I do not go into this at greater length because it is fully treated in the book about harmonical instruments"; see Edward MacCURDY, *The Notebooks of Leonardo da Vinci, Arranged, Rendered into English and Introduced*, 2 vols. (2d. ed., London: Jonathan Cape, 1956), 1: 171. Earlier it had been thought that Leonardo was referring to a book written by himself, "ne ho trattato," but the wording is actually "ne [= n'è] trattato," as MacCurdy has translated it, according to Carlo PEDRETTI, *The Literary Works of Leonardo da Vinci, Commentary*, 2 vols. (Oxford: Phaidon, 1977), 1:107, who commented: "This is probably a reference to Franchino Gafurio's *De harmonia musicorum instrumentorum opus quadripartitum*, published in 1508 [*sic*], rather than a reference to a book 'delli strumenti armonici' written by Leonardo himself." It is a common misunderstanding of Gaffurio's title to believe that the book deals with musical instruments; in fact it refers to the harmonies of the universe and the harmonious relations of the human mind and body. (There is, however, a brief passage on the pitch of organ pipes at the end of the last chapter of Bk. II [ff. 69ᵛ-70], but it does not appear in the *Angelicum opus*.)

I agree with Winternitz (p. 8) that the "Portrait of a Musician" in the Pinacoteca Ambrosiana, once ascribed to Ambrogio de Predis but now accepted as by Leonardo, cannot be of Gaffurio; it is much more likely to be of one of the Sforza court musicians. (In *The New Grove*, 10:671, written earlier, he had suggested that Gaffurio was "probably the subject of Leonardo's painting.")

ments, and his sketches of the mechanics of musical instruments—in addition to his known ability as a performer on the lira da braccio—it would seem fruitful to investigate his acquaintance with music theory of the time. Emanuel Winternitz, in his wide-ranging book on Leonardo and music, barely mentioned Gaffurio's theoretical writings as of possible interest to Leonardo; instead he concentrated on acoustics, improvisation, and musical instruments, apart from the discussion of the *Paragone*. This omission was noted with regret by Martin Kemp in his review of Winternitz's book.[19] In particular, Kemp wondered about the basis of Gaffurio's musical thought and the association between harmonic systems and the science of nature, and whether Leonardo's ideas had any impact on Gaffurio. This, of course, would require a very wide-ranging investigation; in the present article I shall limit myself to Leonardo's notions of harmony and "tempi armonici," especially as they relate to polyphonic music.

Leonardo frequently uses the term "proportionalità armonica" in his writings on painting.[20] "Proportionality" is a technical mathematical term; as Boethius and, following him, numerous music theorists explain, a proportion consists of two terms (e.g. the octave, 1:2), but a proportionality consists of three (e.g. a fifth-octave chord, 3:4:6). Simple proportions become proportionalities when divided by an arithmetic, geometric, or harmonic mean. The terms are in harmonic proportion if the greatest is to the least as the difference between the greatest and the mean is to the difference between the mean and the least, i.e. if the greatest term be $a$, and mean $b$, and the least $c$, $a : c :: a - b : b - c$. The harmonic mean may be found by the following formula:

$$b = \frac{2ac}{a + c}$$

Leonardo is aware of the technical meaning, as can be seen in the following statement:

> The eye is the true intermediary between the objects and the *imprensiva*, which immediately transmits with the highest fidelity the true surfaces and shapes of whatever is in front of it. And from these is born the proportionality called harmony, which delights the sense with sweet concord, no differently from the proportionality made by different musical notes to the sense of hearing.[21]

Nevertheless, he seems to use "proportionalità armonica" in a looser sense, more equivalent to "a harmonious proportion." Indeed it would not be possible to compose a "dolce concento" using only harmonic proportionalities: in Gaffurio's strict definition, based on Pythagorean intonation, one could not have any triads.

19. In the *Journal of the American Musicological Society* 36 (1983): 312-16.
20. See e.g. KEMP and WALKER, 23, 24, 26, 37, mostly translated as "proportional harmonies."
21. KEMP and WALKER, 23 (Urb 11ʳ: "l'occhio vero mezzo infra l'obbietto & la impressiva il quale immedia-

te conferisse con somma verita le vere superficie e figure di quel che dinanzi se gli apresenta delle quale ne nasce la proportionalita detta armonia che con dolce concento contenta il senso non altrimente che si faciano le proportionalita de diverse voci al senso dello audito").

Harmonic proportionality is applied to painting in the same loose sense: music and painting are sister disciplines because they both make use of it. The great failure of poetry is that it lacks proportionality, since words are spoken successively. Leonardo relates an anecdote of King Matthias' dispute with a poet to illustrate this point. The king says:

> Do you not know that our soul is composed of harmony, and that harmony cannot be generated other than when the proportions of the form [*le proportionalita delli obbietti*] are seen and heard instantaneously? Can you not see that in your science, proportionality is not created in an instant, but each part is born successively after the other, and the succeeding one is not born if the previous one has not died? From this I judge that your invention is markedly inferior to that of the painter, solely because it cannot compose a proportional harmony [*non componesi proportionalita armonica*].[22]

The same criticism applies to monophonic music, or voice parts sung singly:

> The poet may be regarded as equivalent to a musician who sings by himself a song composed for four choristers, singing first the soprano, then the tenor, and following with the contralto and then the bass. Such singing cannot result in that grace of harmonic proportionality which is contained within harmonic beats [*tempi armonici*].... Yet music, in its harmonic beat [*tempo armonico*], makes its suave melodies, which are composed from varied notes. The poet is deprived of this harmonic option, and although poetry enters the seat of judgement through the sense of hearing, like music, the poet is unable to describe the harmony of music [*l'armonia della musica*], because he has not the power to say different things at the same time. However, the harmonic proportionality of painting is composed simultaneously from various components, the sweetness of which may be judged instantaneously.[23]

In the comparison of painting with music, the argument from harmonic proportionality draws these two disciplines together, likening optical to harmonic space. Indeed, Leonardo seems in both cases to be using harmonic proportionality to indicate depth or volume, whereas poetry can produce no more than surface. It should be emphasized that Leonardo is not talking about music *per se* but specifically about polyphonic

---

22. KEMP and WALKER, 26 (Urb 14ᵛ-15ʳ: "non sai tu che la nostra anima e composta d'armonia ed armonia non singenera se non in istanti ne quali le proportionalita delli obbietti si fan vedere o udire[;] non vedi che nella tua scientia non e proportionalita creata in istante anzi l'una parte nasce dallaltra successivamente e non nasce la succedente se l'antecedente non more. Per questo giudico la tua inventione essere assai inferiore a quella del pictore solo perche da quella non componesi proportionalita armonica").

23. KEMP and WALKER, 37 (translation slightly changed, as noted above) (Urb 18ʳ-19ʳ: "et al poeta accade il medesimo come al musico che canta sol'un canto composto di quatro cantori et canta prima il canto poi il tenore, e cosi seguita il contro alto e poi il basso e di costui non risulta la gracia della proportionalita armonica la quale si rinchiude in tempi armonici ... et la musica ancora fa nel suo tempo armonico le soavi melodie composte delle sue varie voci delle quali il poeta e privato della loro discretione armonica et ben che la poesia entri per il senso dell'audito alla sedia del giuditio si come la musica, esso poeta non puo descrivere l'armonia della musica perche non ha potesta in un medesimo tempo di dire diverse cose, come la porportionalita harmonica della pittura composta di diverse membra in un medesimo tempo").

music. Music "composes harmony from the conjunction of her proportional parts sounded simultaneously."[24] "Conjunction of proportional parts sounded simultaneously" must be Leonardo's circumlocution for "chord." Gaffurio had described only specific chords, in terminology that does not lend itself to a general description, except perhaps as "consonantia mediata"; later writers will use the word "a harmony" to describe two or more superimposed consonances.[25] I shall return to this below.

We now come to the more difficult passage in the *Paragone* where Leonardo uses the expression "tempi armonici." It comes directly after the above passage in the following context:

> Music is not to be regarded as other than the sister of painting, in as much as she is depen-
> dent on hearing, second sense behind that of sight. She composes harmony from the con-
> junction of her proportional parts sounded simultaneously, constrained to arise and die
> in one or more *tempi armonici*. These *tempi* surround the proportionality of the component
> parts of which such harmony is composed no differently from the linear contours of the
> limbs from which human beauty is generated.[26]

Here Leonardo turns from the aspect shared by painting and music—harmonic proportionality—to the aspect that separates them, the dimension of time. A painting can be grasped as a whole; music unfolds in time and is evanescent. This is a point he returns to several times because it is the linchpin of his argument for the superiority of painting: music perishes immediately after its creation, painting endures.[27]

---

24. See above, n. 3.

25. See BLACKBURN, "The Dispute about Harmony."

26. KEMP and WALKER, 34, with the change in translation noted above (n. 3); (Urb 16ʳ-16ᵛ: "La musica non e da essere chiamata altro che sorella della pictura conciosia ch'essa e subiecto dell'audito 2.ᵈᵒ senso al occhio e compone armonia con le congiontioni delle sue parti proportionali operate nel medesimo tempo costrette a nascere e morire in uno o piu tempi armonici liquali tempi circondano la proporcionalita de membri di che tale armonia si compone non altrimente che si faccia la linea circonferentiale le membra di che si genera la bellezza humana"). Kemp and Walker give the last sentence as "These intervals may be said to circumscribe the proportionality of the component parts of which such harmony is composed—no differently from the linear contours of the limbs from which human beauty is generated." In Latin *circumdare* means to surround and does not have the geometrical implications of circumscribe.

27. Urb 16ᵛ: "ma la pittura eccelle & sinoreggia la musica perch'essa non more immediate dopo la sua creatione come fa la sventurata musica anzi resta in essere" (KEMP and WALKER, 35).

Emanuel Winternitz translated *tempi armonici* as "harmonic sections" and interpreted the passage not as chords moving in time but as the proportional relationships between sections of a musical composition, though he saw the text as "obscure or at least inconsistent" (*Leonardo*, 211). Thus he credits Leonardo with having "applied the concept of proportion to the relation between successive portions of Music and thus established the notion of a quasi-spatial structure of portions balanced against one another" (ibid.). In another section Winternitz translates *in tanti tempi armonici* as "in as many sections of musical time" (p. 212), and elsewhere as "moments of harmony," interpreted as chords, and *tempo armonico* as "harmonious flow [time]" (p. 217). Leonardo certainly was acquainted with the proportionability of sections of a composition (the subject is covered thoroughly in Gaffurio's *Practica musice*, Bk. IV, and Tinctoris' *Proportionale*), since he discusses the proportionability of time in the Codex Arundel (the passage is cited by Winternitz on p. 221), but I do not believe that this is what he means by *tempi armonici*. Winternitz did not take into account Leonardo's use of the term in other contexts that do not refer to musical compositions.

*Tempi armonici* is a term Leonardo uses many times, also in other contexts.[28] Often *tempo armonico* is used to indicate a regular beat, which can be employed to measure the velocity of moving objects since, Leonardo says, it is more reliable than the pulse. He uses it to ascertain how far water travels in an hour:

> This is done by means of harmonic time [*tempo armonico*], and it could be done by a pulse if the time of its beat were uniform; but musical time is more reliable in such a case, for by means of it it is possible to calculate the distance that an object carried by this water travels in ten or twelve of these beats of time; and by this means it is possible to make a general rule for every level canal.[29]

As a musician himself, Leonardo was familiar with the concept of a regular musical beat. Since harmony or harmonic proportionality is not relevant in this context, *tempo armonico* means no more than musical beat; in the early Codex B he in fact says "tempo di musica." How fast is this beat? In Codex Arundel one hour is said to contain 1080 *tempi*, based on human respiration, making one *tempo* equal to 3.33 seconds, or 18 per minute.[30] This is quite slow; thus it is likely that Leonardo is using the word *tempo* in its technical musical sense: *tempus* = breve.[31] In *tempus perfectum* 1080 *tempi* per hour would come to 54 semibreves per minute.

Placing the musical beat on the breve reflects early fifteenth-century thought: in his treatise of 1434, Giorgio Anselmi, one of the earliest authors to discuss the musical beat, states:

> And this notated *mensura* is called one *tempus*. Still, this *mensura* is not fixed, not exceeding limits, but according to the judgement of the singer [is] here more broad and now more strict ... the *mensura* is near enough to a moderate tempo in which the singer, not much accelerating the song or extending the note-lengths, stamps the front part of the foot, keeping the heel still, or claps one hand to the other or the back of the student as regularly as possible.[32]

By Leonardo's time, however, the musical beat, called *mensura*, *battuta*, or (in Germany) *tactus*, was considered to fall on the semibreve. Like Leonardo, both Bartolomé

---

28. Leonardo's *tempo armonico* is the subject of an article by Augusto MARINONI, "'Tempo armonico' o 'musicale' in Leonardo da Vinci," *Lingua nostra* 16 (1955): 45–48, from which the following quotations are taken.

29. MacCURDY, *The Notebooks of Leonardo*, 2:165 (Codex Leicester 13ᵛ: "Modo di sapere quanto un'acqua corre per ora. —Questo si fa col tempo armonico, e potrebbesi fare col polso, se 'l tempo del suo battere fussi uniforme; ma è più securo, in tal caso, il tempo musicale, col quale si noterà quanto spazio cammina una cosa portata da essa acqua per dieci o dodici d'essi tempi e con questo tal modo si farà regola generale in qualunche canale equale"; quoted by Marinoni, 46).

30. "1080 son quelli li quali universalmente l'omo trapassa nel suo spirare e respirare, e l'ora è composta di 1080 de' medesimi tempi" (f. 223ᵛ; quoted in Marinoni, 46). This is the standard division in the Jewish calendar; the connection remains to be explained.

31. In Greek rhythmic doctrine, *chrónos* indicates minimum measure of time, corresponding to our "beat in the bar."

32. Quoted in Anna Maria BUSSE BERGER, *Mensuration and Proportion Signs: Origins and Evolution* (Oxford: Clarendon Press, 1993), 78, from Giorgio Anselmi, *De musica*, ed. Giuseppe MASSERA ("Historiae musicae cultores" Biblioteca, 14; Florence: Olschki, 1961), 171. In n. 80 she lists later theorists who mention the former placement of the beat on the breve.

Ramos and Gaffurio liken the musical beat to the beat of the pulse.[33] Ramos considers the *mensura* to be the interval between the diastole and the systole;[34] Gaffurio, however, says that the *mensura* comprises both the diastole and systole.[35] (The discrepancy will be explained below.) When discussing the permissible length of dissonances in composition, Gaffurio states that a dissonance cannot last the length of a semibreve, calculated as the full *mensura* of time "in modum scilicet pulsus aeque respirantis."[36] There has been some disagreement as to how this phrase is to be understood: is Gaffurio equating the length of the semibreve with the time between beats of a normal pulse, allowing thereby an approximate indication of the tempo at his time, or is he simply likening a regular musical beat to a regular pulse? Clement Miller translated this passage as "For a semibreve, equal to a complete measurement of time [a tactus], like the pulse of a man breathing evenly, cannot be given to a dissonance," noting that "aeque respirantis" had frequently been mistranslated as "quietly breathing."[37] Irwin Young translated it as "a normal semibreve occupying a full measure of time, in the manner of a pulse throbbing evenly, cannot support a discord."[38] Dale Bonge, pointing out that the pulse and respiration were considered to be linked in contemporary medical thought, believes that Gaffurio intended no more than the analogy of the regularity of musical beat and pulse. He would therefore translate it: "For a regular semibreve equalling a full measure of time, namely, in the manner of a pulse *dilating and contracting evenly*, cannot lie under a dissonance in counterpoint."[39]

It would indeed seem that Gaffurio's statement emphasizes regularity of beat, not the particular length of the semibreve. However, the restatement of this passage in his Italian treatise, the *Angelicum ac divinum opus musice* of 1508, clearly makes the equation of tempo between semibreve and pulse:

33.   They are writing about the pulse of music, not the music of pulse. Since antiquity physicians had sought to discern musical proportions in the uneven rhythms of the pulse as a diagnostic tool. The discussions were still very much alive in the Middle Ages. See Nancy G. SIRAISI, "The Music of Pulse in the Writings of Italian Academic Physicians (Fourteenth and Fifteenth Centuries)," *Speculum* 50 (1975): 689-710. For Greek sources, some transmitted through Latin and Arabic writings, see Leofranc HOLFORD-STREVENS, "The Harmonious Pulse," *Classical Quarterly* NS 43 (1993): 475-79.

34.   "Mensura enim, ut diximus, est illud tempus sive intervallum inter diastolen et systolen corporis eucraton comprehensum." *Musica practica*, ed. WOLF, 83. A translation is available by Clement A. MILLER: Bartolomeo Ramis de Pareia, *Musica practica* (Musicological Studies and Documents, 44; Neuhausen-Stuttgart: American Institute of Musicology – Hänssler-Verlag, 1993).

35.   "Neoterici postremo rectae semibrevi temporis unius mensuram ascripserunt: diastolen et sistolen uniuscuiusque semibrevis sono concludentes. Cumque Diastole et Sistole seu Arsis et Thesis quae contrariae sunt ac minimae quidem in pulsu: solius temporis mensura consyderentur: semibrevem ipsam integra temporis mensura dispositam: duas in partes aequas distinxere: quasi altera Diastoles in mensura pulsus tanquam in sono: altera Sistoles quantitatem contineat." *Practica musice*, Bk. II, chap. 3, sig. aaiii.

36.   "Semibrevis enim recta plenam temporis mensuram consequens: in modum scilicet pulsus aeque respirantis: in contrapuncto discordantiae subiacere non potest" (ibid., Bk. III, chap. 4, sig. ddiijᵛ).

37.   *Practica musicae*, 129 and n. 10.

38.   *The Practica musicae of Franchinus Gafurius*, trans. Irwin YOUNG (Madison: University of Wisconsin Press, 1969), 137.

39.   "Gaffurius on Pulse and Tempo: A Reinterpretation," *Musica disciplina* 36 (1982): 167-74 at 171-72.

For just as the *mensura* of the human pulse is considered to be one *tempo* divided into two motions, that is in one ascending and the other descending, which physicians call systole and diastole, and musicians arsis and thesis, so have the scholars of later ages ascribed the *mensura* of a sonorous *tempo* to the semibreve equal to the *tempo* of the pulse: and it is divided into two equal motions of *tempo* that are dedicated and applied to two minims.[40]

The *Angelicum ac divinum opus musice*, a compendium derived from all of Gaffurio's treatises, including the as yet unpublished *De harmonia musicorum instrumentorum opus*, was written in Italian for the benefit of practical musicians (and nuns) who were not able to read Latin, or who found the sometimes ornate and obscure style (such as Gaffurio's own humanistic Latin) difficult to understand.[41] The decision to write in the vernacular must reflect Gaffurio's experience in speaking with many musicians in Milan, and quite possibly Leonardo himself, whose Latin was rudimentary at best.

Leonardo clearly does give a length to the *tempo armonico*. This was necessary for his purpose: he needed to calculate how fast an object was moving, and therefore the measurement had to be based on exact units of time. He calculated the length not from the pulse, rejected for its irregularity, but from human respiration: "1080 are those [*tempi armonici*] that man universally passes in breathing in and out." As mentioned above, this tempo is quite slow and must correspond to the breve, not the semibreve. At some later point Leonardo changed the calculation of the *tempo armonico* so that an hour was equal to 3000 *tempi*.[42] Augusto Marinoni believed that the reason for the substitution was that 3.33 seconds per beat was too large for measurement, leaving too many fractions; at 3000 *tempi* per hour the unit is 1.2 seconds. He also believed that just as the previous measurement had had its origin in a natural rhythm (respiration), so must the new one, which he took to be the rhythm of the pulse, but a rather slow one, 50 beats per minute (Leonardo does not clarify his change from 1080 to 3000). Marinoni wondered how Leonardo became accustomed to the new tempo, and posited the need for an instrument to mea-

---

40. "Nam secundo che la mensura del pulso humano se consydera in uno tempo diviso in duy moti: cioe in uno ascendente et l'altro descendente: quali son dicti da Physici sistole et diastole: da Musici Arsis et thesis: cosi li Curiosi posteri hano ascripto la mensura de uno tempo sonoro a la semibreve aequale al tempo del pulso: et e distincto in duy moti aequali de tempo quali son dicati et applicati a doe minime" (Tr. III, chap. 1; sig. Fiᵛ). Here Gaffurio uses the word *tempo* to mean unit of time, not breve.

41. The book begins: "Perche molti illiterati fano professione de musica: et con grande difficultade pervengano a la vera coginitione de li praecepti harmonici per non intendere le opere nostre et de altri degni auctori latini quale son scripte con qualche ornato et alquanto obscuro stillo: havemo consyderato subvenire non solamente a lor voti et desiderii: ma anchora a la devotione de molte donne religiose intente ad laudare lo eterno Dio con tuta la corte celeste" (sig. Biʳ). There is a facsimile edition (Antiquae musicae italicae scriptores, 1; Bologna: A.M.I.S., 1971), but no translation. Gaffurio had already published, under the name of his pupil Francesco Caza, a short Italian version of his treatise on notation, which eventually became Book II of the *Practica musice*. See Francesco CAZA, *Tractato vulgare de canto figurato* [Milan, 1492], facs. and trans. by Johannes WOLF (Veröffentlichungen der Musik-Bibliothek Paul Hirsch, 1; Berlin: Martin Breslauer, 1922).

42. In the Codex Arundel, on f. 191ʳ, he first wrote "essendo un'ora 1080 tempi," then crossed out 1080, writing 3000 above it. See MARINONI, p. 47.

sure time.[43] But a musician would have had no difficulty with the alteration in tempo: instead of placing the beat on the breve, Leonardo has in effect changed it, in line with contemporary music theory, to the semibreve. Still, this semibreve is even slower than before, 50 rather than 54 per minute. Scholars assume that the normal tempo of music ranged between 60 and 80 beats per minute.[44] Rather than attempting to reproduce any exact rate of musical time, then, Leonardo chose a mathematically convenient figure close to that of the length of the semibreve, which, after all, was not fixed. Moreover, musicians were used to changing the speed of the beat even within a composition, when a proportion was encountered.

In calculating the length of the semibreve according to Leonardo's figure of 1080 *tempi armonici* per hour, I have assumed *tempus perfectum*, three imperfect semibreves per breve. If we were to assume *tempus imperfectum*, the beat of the semibreve would be even slower, at 36 per minute. But this difference holds true only if we consider the breve to have the same temporal value in all mensurations. Such was the theoretical position held by Bartolomé Ramos (and his disciple Giovanni Spataro) and the great majority of theorists in the fifteenth century: the breve is the central unit of mensuration; it is multiplied to achieve *modus* (longs and maximas) and divided to achieve *prolatio* (semibreves and minims).[45] Thus a semibreve in *tempus perfectum* will be 1/3 of a breve, but in *tempus imperfectum* 1/2, producing a proportion between semibreves of 3:2.[46] Not all theorists agreed: Franchino Gaffurio—and Johannes Tinctoris, by whom Gaffurio was heavily influenced in his younger years—held instead that the minim, the smallest of the five figures of mensuration, was the invariable unit, and that all larger notes were multiples of minims. Thus the breve that contains nine minims (*tempus perfectum, prolatio maior*) will be one-half longer than the breve that contains six minims (*tempus perfectum, prolatio minor, or tempus imperfectum, prolatio maior*).[47]

Herein lies the explanation for the discrepancy between Ramos and Gaffurio with regard to the analogy between the *mensura* (semibreve) and the pulse. Ramos, unlike Gaffurio, took into account the unequal parts of the pulse: he equates the *mensura* with the time between diastole and systole; the interval between diastole and diastole (or systole and systole) is equated with the breve. Therefore he can extend his analogy by liken-

---

43. Ibid. Indeed, on the same page Leonardo had noted that one could divide the hour into 3000 parts "coll'oriolo alleggerendo e aggravando il contrappeso," which to Marinoni suggested that he had anticipated Maelzel's metronome.

44. There is even greater variation in the rate of pulse, which differs with age, physical condition, and even country.

45. "Consideratione temporis accepta, quae in pulsus noscitur palpitatione, scire nos oportet, utrum duplari aut triplari aut quadruplari eam contingat aut etiam dimidiare aut trifariam sive quadrifariam dividere" (*Musica practica*, ed. WOLF, 77). *Tempus* here means breve, not time.

46. This phenomenon allows mensuration signs to be used as signs of proportion.

47. On the controversy and its historical background, see BUSSE BERGER, *Mensuration and Proportion Signs*, chap. 3.

ing the unequal movements of the pulse to unequal musical proportions.[48] Gaffurio, however, considers the diastole and systole to be equal in length (except in a fevered state), and therefore he equates the length of the semibreve with the whole pulse, which conveniently makes the arsis and thesis on the minims equivalent to the systole and diastole.[49] Thus, even though both theorists place the *mensura* on the semibreve, the regular invariable unit for Ramos is the breve and for Gaffurio the minim.

Leonardo's use of *tempo armonico* as a unit of measurement stresses the aspect of *tempo*; when he uses it in a musical context more weight is given to *armonico*. "Harmonic time" is a unit of time encompassing a harmonic simultaneity: music "composes harmony from the conjunction of her proportional parts sounded simultaneously, constrained to arise and die in one or more *tempi armonici*." So much is clear. The continuation, however, is somewhat obscure: "These *tempi* surround the proportionality of the component parts of which such harmony is composed no differently from the linear contours of the limbs from which human beauty is generated."[50] Here Leonardo seems to be attempting a visual image of an auditory phenomenon. Time envelops sound just as a line may be drawn around the members of a human body. Does he have in mind here the famous image of the Vitruvian man, whose outstretched limbs fit exactly within a circle? Or does he mean the outline of a human figure? The proportions of the human body greatly occupied Leonardo,[51] as did outlines, contours, and boundaries, not only of the human figure but also objects of nature, including landscape. Outlines define the wholeness of a figure, the conjunction of proportional parts, which might be likened to a chord in music.

By attaching *tempo* so firmly to *armonia* and stressing the successive nature of musical sounds, Leonardo underlines another aspect of music that has a counterpart in painting: motion. The painter, of course, has much the more difficult task: he must convey the appearance of motion, not motion itself. Time is frozen in painting, and yet everything that happens in that frozen moment can be conveyed at once. Music, by contrast, is continually in motion and can never be grasped as a whole.

Motion plays a very important role in the dispute concerning harmony in the late fifteenth century. While all theorists agreed that two-note chords formed either conso-

---

48. "De cuius inaequali alteratione insurgunt inaequales musicae proportiones" (*Musica practica*, ed. WOLF, 83).

49. See above, n. 35, for one passage. Earlier he had stated: "Rectam autem brevis temporis mensuram Physici aequis pulsuum motibus accomodandam esse consentiunt: Arsim et thesim quas Diastolen et Sistolen vocant in uniuscuiusque pulsus mensura aequaliter comprobantes: Constat tamen febricitantium pulsus inaequali diastoles et sistoles proportione accessionem seu alterationem suscipere quod ipsis physicis curae est. Diastole

graece dilatatio seu ellevatio interpretatur latine: Sistole vero contractio" (*Practica musice*, Bk. II, chap. 1, sig. aaiᵛ).

50. See above, n. 26. Cf. a similar remark in Gaffurio, *De harmonia*, Bk. IV, end of chap. 18: "Quod quum corporis partes consyderaveris: eas quae pulchritudinem participant consonis diastematibus senties proportione convenire (pulchritudinem inquam)…"

51. See the section on proportions in KEMP and WALKER, 119-43.

nances or dissonances, they did not agree on the classification of three-voice chords.[52] Gaffurio, as we saw above, limits the strict use of the term "harmony" to consonances mediated by a harmonic division, although he also uses it in a looser sense to describe other divisions that produce a pleasant concord. Burzio was willing to describe any three- or four-voice chord made of up consonant parts as a harmony, and he probably reflects the attitude of contemporary musicians as well as other theorists who did not have as great a stake in ancient Greek theory as did Gaffurio. But there was one theorist who accepted neither of these definitions of harmony, Giovanni Spataro. In his polemical answer of 1491 to Burzio's equally polemical treatise against Spataro's teacher, Bartolomé Ramos, he was scathing about Burzio's knowledge in general and his discussion of harmony in particular. For Spataro, harmony was something quite different. He agreed with Burzio that "consonance is only the consideration of the interval between a low and a high note and vice versa," but insisted that the addition of one or more voices does not turn consonance into harmony. To have harmony, movement is necessary: "it is called harmony when considering the process they make by concording together (*il procedere che fanno inseme concordando*), because if they do not move (*se non se moveno*), even if there are four voices, it is not called harmony, but consonances. . . . Let harmony be defined as the mixture of consonances and dissonances in a composition, because it is quite true that good composers exert themselves to make dissonances marvellously consonant in harmony."[53]

Here, then, is that elusive view of music as a process that unfolds in time, a process sometimes called by another term that has a different meaning today: modulation. *Now*, modulation indicates a change of key area; originally it simply meant measurement of any kind: measured or rhythmical in respect of music, or singing or playing, whether melody alone or a whole composition. Burzio had used "modulation" in his definition of harmony, calling it a *modulatio vocis*, a modulation or movement of the voice. Leonardo understood this very well: for him, harmony is a conjoining of proportional parts, and this conjoining is described as arising and dying in harmonic *tempi*: we have here a description of the process chords make in musical time.

Musical notions and musical terminology have a central position in Leonardo's discussion of painting. In fact, if the subject is not stated, one would sometimes be hard put to know whether Leonardo is talking about painting or music: "thus *x* simultaneously conveys the proportional harmony of which the parts of the whole are com-

---

52. The special position of a fourth, which is not allowed in two-part counterpoint but is permitted in composition if the interval is between upper voices, will not be considered here. Apart from this, the theorists assume all chords of more than two voices to be consonant.

53. *Honesta defensio in Nicolai Burtii parmensis opusculum* (Bologna, 1491), sig. EIII[r–v]. Quoted and translated in BLACKBURN, "On Compositional Process," 224–25, where I discussed the passage as adumbrating functional harmony.

posed, and delights the senses." The subject here is painting.[54] Indeed, the parts of a painting can have the same "proportione armonica" as music, and when viewed together, they can make a "armonico concento."[55] "Concento" could be interpreted in the general sense of sounding together, but it is also a technical term at this time for a polyphonic composition; Gaffurio calls his musical examples *concentus*.

It has been suggested with some plausibility that Leonardo based the *Last Supper* on musical proportions,[56] even that the four groups of disciples resemble the four vocal ranges.[57] To be a truly *armonico concento*, however, the parts of this painting would have to move in harmonic time, that is, harmony in Spataro's definition: dissonance resolving into consonance, which in modern parlance could be termed "functional harmony." I would submit that this happens in the *Last Supper*. Leonardo has captured the moment where the disciples react with harsh gestures to Jesus' words, "One of you will betray me," as if he had portrayed a dissonant suspension. The painting is alive with harmonic movement, resolving in the calm, central figure of Jesus.

Quite possibly Gaffurio saw Leonardo at work on the *Last Supper* in the refectory of Santa Maria delle Grazie. Did he remark on its musicality? So far I have considered only whether Leonardo discussed music with Gaffurio. Did Gaffurio discuss art with Leonardo? There is a passage in the *De harmonia* that would gladden the heart of Leonardo, for it pays tribute to the mathematical basis of painting. It comes in a chapter entitled "Consonant numbers offer much to other arts":

> Again, if attention is paid to other arts, how much utility has accrued precisely from numbers may easily be perceived; for when you look at painting, you will discover that nothing has been done in it without numerical proportions, but you will see that both the measurements of bodies and the mixtures of colours, and thus the beauties of painting, have

54. KEMP and WALKER, 23 (Urb 11ʳ: "La pittura ti rapresenta in un subito la sua essentia . . . et anchora nel medesimo tempo nel quale si compone l'armonicha proportionalita delle parti che compongono il tutto che contenta il senso").

55. Urb 10ʳ: "molto piu farà le proportionali bellezze d'un angelico viso posto in pittura della quale proportionalità ne risulta un'armonico concento."

56. Thomas BRACHERT, "A Musical Canon of Proportion in Leonardo da Vinci's *Last Supper*," *Art Bulletin* 53 (1971): 461-66. A reconsideration is offered in Martin KEMP, *Leonardo da Vinci: The Marvellous Works of Nature and Man* (London: Dent, 1981), 189-99, who recognizes a "substratum of mathematical intervals" in the treatment of the ceiling coffers and in the diminution in size of the tapestries approximating the ratios 12:6:4:3, noting that Leonardo's jottings show that he was interested in musical ratios in this period (p. 198). Indeed Kemp

goes so far as to suggest that "Gaffurio may well have introduced Leonardo to the definitive theory of musical harmonics" (p. 170). In a later book Kemp discusses the incongruencies in the painting and concludes that Leonardo was using a pictorial effect of perspective rather than orthodox perspective: "Leonardo's space looks logical but actively resists unequivocal translation into an actual space"; *The Science of Art: Optical Themes in Western Art from Brunelleschi to Seurat* (New Haven: Yale University Press, 1990), 49. The same might be said, mutatis mutandis, of Gaffurio's recognition of the "concinnity" and "concord" of triads and sixth chords that are not "proper" harmonies.

57. John ONIANS, *Bearers of Meaning: The Classical Orders in Antiquity, the Middle Ages, and the Renaissance* (Cambridge: Cambridge University Press, 1988), 233. For Onians, Judas is the figure "expressively jarring the harmony of the whole."

been determined according to numbers and symmetries, and that it is thus that the beauties of the paintings have been arranged, and that in turn it is through numbers that the art itself imitates primary nature. For whatever proportion has created beauty in natural bodies, such proportion has also ensued in the measurements of shapes and the comparisons of colours; for which reason, by colours, form, and shape painters themselves meant character and life to be understood.[58]

What a generous compliment to contemporary artists, one thinks! But in fact, these are not Gaffurio's words at all. He has taken the whole passage, verbatim and unacknowledged, from a Latin translation made for him in 1494 of the *Peri mousikēs* of Aristides Quintilianus, a writer of the late third or early fourth century AD.[59] It was Gaffurio's habit—and not only his—to incorporate passages from many ancient sources without specifically crediting them. We need to be aware of this in evaluating theoretical statements, even those that have a contemporary ring. The habit was surely common among teachers, who taught by explicating texts.

That Gaffurio viewed himself above all as a teacher is made clear in the woodcut that graces his two last treatises, where he is shown expounding music *ex cathedra*, as holder of the chair in music at the University of Milan, to twelve disciples (see Plate 1). From his mouth issues the famous saying, "Harmonia est discordia concors," "harmony is concordant discord," or harmony is concord brought forth from disparate parts. This is not merely a play on words, or even only a statement about the nature of music: it places music at the heart of the universe. The phrase *discordia concors* comes from the *Astronomica* of Manilius, an author of Augustus' and Tiberius' time who after centuries of neglect had been discovered during the Council of Constance and copied many times over in the

---

58. "Rursus exhibita in alias artes consyderatione quanta ex ipsis numeris prodierit utilitas facile percipi potest: Namque dum picturam animadvertis: nihil absque numerorum proportionibus in ea factum comperies: sed et corporum mensuras: colorumque mixtiones per numeros et symetrias: atque ita picturae ornamenta conspicies esse disposita: rursus per numeros ipsam artem primam imitari naturam. Qualis namque proportio in naturalibus corporibus fecerit pulchritudinem talis et in figurarum mensuris et colorum comparationibus est subsecuta: ob quam causam coloribus forma atque figura Pictores ipsi mores atque vitam intelligi voluerunt." *De harmonia musicorum instrumentorum*, Bk. IV, chap. 16 (fol. 96ᵛ). The English translation is by Leofranc HOLFORD-STREVENS.

59. The passage quoted by Gaffurio appears in Bk. III, chap. 8, which is entirely based on Aristides. The borrowing was noticed by Clement Miller; see his translation of the *De harmonia*, 204, n. 88. Aristides has been edited most recently by R. P. WINNINGTON-INGRAM (Leipzig: B. G.

Teubner, 1963). Leofranc Holford-Strevens has kindly provided the following translation from the Greek: "It will be plain to one who has examined the other arts how much benefit they gather from numbers. Should anyone care to consider painting, he will discover that it does nothing without numbers and proportions, but even seeks out the symmetries of bodies and blendings of colours through numbers and from these creates beauty in the paintings. One can also see that it is through numbers that this same art is also imitative of primary nature; at any rate, whatever proportion applied in natural bodies has created beauty it is this proportion that [painters] pursue both in the measurements of shapes and in the mixtures of colours. They too have shapes, colours, and figures that express ways of life and character . . ."

For an English translation of the treatise, see Aristides QUINTILIANUS, *On Music, in Three Books*, trans. Thomas J. MATHIESEN (Music Theory Translation Series, New Haven: Yale University Press, 1983). Concerning Aristides' dates see pp. 10-14.

**Plate 1**    Gaffurio lecturing *ex cathedra*, in his *Angelicum ac divinum opus musice*
Bodleian Library, University of Oxford, E.1.13(2) Art.Seld., sig. Aii recto

course of the Quattrocento; there are six or seven incunable editions (including one published by Dulcinius at Milan in 1489 with an enthusiastic preface on the rebirth of letters).
Reviewing the various competing theories of the universe, Manilius comes to Empedocles' view that it is the product of four elements in the two relations of love and strife:

> aut neque terra patrem novit nec flamma nec aer
> aut umor, faciuntque deum per quattuor artus
> et mundi struxere globum prohibentque requiri
> ultra se quicquam, cum per se cuncta crearint,                    140
> frigida nec calidis desint aut umida siccis,
> spiritus aut solidis, sitque haec discordia concors
> quae nexus habilis et opus generabile fingit
> atque omnis partus elementa capacia reddit:[60]

60.  Bk. I, ll. 137-44; "else it may be that neither earth
nor fire nor air nor water acknowledges a begetter, but
themselves constitute a godhead of four elements,
which have formed the sphere of the universe and ban all

Seneca similarly declares (*Naturales quaestiones* 7. 27. 4): "tota haec mundi concordia ex discordibus constat," this entire universal concord is formed out of discordant elements. The same notion is expressed by Horace (*Epistles* 1. 12. 19), with explicit mention of Empedocles, as "rerum concordia discors," the discordant concord of things, and by Ovid, *Metamorphoses* 1. 430–33:

> quippe ubi temperiem sumpsere umorque calorque,
> concipiunt, et ab his oriuntur cuncta duobus;
> cumque sit ignis aquae pugnax, vapor umidus omnes
> res creat, et discors concordia fetibus apta est.[61]

Gaffurio acknowledges Ovid as his source and quotes these four lines in Bk. I, chap. 1 of the *De harmonia*, though he has them indirectly, from Lactantius, *Divinae institutiones* ("2. 10" = 2. 9. 20).

In the woodcut this concord is illustrated in the harmonic division of the octave, 3:4:6, shown in string lengths on the right, and in organ pipes on the left. A pair of compasses underlines the geometrical aspects of music as continuous quantity. An hourglass is set at Gaffurio's left elbow: this might have been used to time his lectures, but it is also a reminder of the temporal aspect of music. His listeners are, on the left, monks and clergy; in the center, young laymen who wish to learn about music; and on the right, adolescents who are probably choirboys. Not included here are men and women in the wider social world of Milan, especially those associated with the court, with whom Gaffurio must have come in contact. "Harmonia discordia concors" is a concept that would have had particular resonance for one of them, Leonardo.

---

search for a source beyond them, having created all things from themselves, so that cold combines with hot, wet with dry, and airy with solid, and the discord is one of harmony, allowing apt unions and generative activity and enabling the elements to produce all things"; trans. G. P. GOOLD in the Loeb ed. (Cambridge, Mass.: Harvard University Press, 1977), 15. The parallel passages cited here are taken from Housman's note on Manilius 1. 142 in his edition: Marcus MANILIUS, *Astronomicon*, ed. A. E. HOUSMAN, 2 vols. (London: Grant Richards, 1903-30; repr. Hildesheim: Olms, 1972). I am grateful to Leofranc Holford-Strevens for bringing Manilius to my attention and supplying the translated passages.

61. See the translation by Arthur GOLDING (1567), *Ovid's Metamorphoses*, ed. John Frederick NIMS (New York: Macmillan, 1965), 17:

For when that moysture with the heate is tempred equally,
They doe conceyve: and of them twaine engender by and by
All kinde of things. For though that fire with water aye debateth
Yet moysture mixt with equall heate all living things createth.
And so those discordes in their kinde, one striving with the other,
In generation doe agree and make one perfect mother.

# Appendix

## A Musical Silhouette at the Sforza Court

"The first picture was merely a line, drawn round the shadow of a man cast by the sun upon a wall."[62] As commonplace as this notion was, for Leonardo it had particular meaning because of his continuing involvement with pictorial boundaries, outlines, and contours. Thus one can understand his astonishment and delight at a demonstration of the art of paper-cutting at the court of Milan in 1499. In his youth, the Spanish chronicler Gonzalo Fernández de Oviedo visited Milan and met Leonardo. In his memoirs, written some fifty years later, he relates the following story:

> In 1499 in Milan I cut a polyphonic motet for four voices with the arms of the Duke, who was at that time Ludovico Sforza, also called El Moro, who, astonished at the subtlety of that work, wanted to see me cut, and in his presence I cut everything he wished to give me. Marveling at what he saw, he asked his great painter and sculptor named Leonardo de Avince, whose art, as some said, was unique in Italy, what he thought about what I was doing. And Leonardo said: "Your Excellency may believe that of all the things I have seen in the world, this is the one that has impressed me the most, and if I myself had not seen him cut, I would not believe that a man could do something so subtle with scissors alone, without any drawing, but moving the hands solely by memory." Then the Duke said: "If this Spaniard had lived at the time of the ancient Romans, he would have been crowned God of the Scissors."[63]

I know of no motet on the arms of Ludovico, and it is a puzzle how they might have been shown in polyphony. Ghiselin Danckerts's *Tua est potentia* was written using a representation of the arms of Paul III in the tenor part; the arrangement of the six lilies

---

62. Kemp and Walker, 193.

63. "Corté en Milán, el año de 1499, un motete de canto de órgano puntado a cuatro voces, con las armas del Duque, que era a la sazón el señor Ludovico Esforza, que por otro nombre le llamaban *el Moro*, el cual, maravillado de la sotileza de aquella obra, quiso verme cortar, y en su presencia corté todo lo que él quiso mandarme; e maravillándose de lo que veía, preguntó a un su grandísimo pintor y escultar llamado Leonardo de Avince, que era su arte, según algunos decían, el único en Italia, que qué le parecía de lo que yo hacía; y el Leonardo dijo: 'Crea Su Excelencia que ésta es la cosa del mundo que hasta hoy he visto que más me haya maravillado, y si no lo viera cortar yo, no creyera que hombre podía hacer cosa tan sutil con solas las tijeras y sin dibujo alguno, más de solamente a memoria mental mover las manos.' Entonces dijo el Duque: 'Si questo spañol fuora al tempo de aquei anti-

qui romani, fuora laureato per Dió de le forfectie.'" Gonzalo Fernández de Oviedo, *Historia general y natural de las Indias*, ed. Juan Pérez de Tudela Bueso, 5 vols. (Biblioteca de Autores Españoles, 117-21; Madrid: Ediciones Atlas, 1959), 1:xix-xx. The passage was quoted in Pedretti, *Literary Works*, 1:372, wrongly translating "canto de órgano" as "organ motet." The memoirs have been partially published in *Las memorias de Gonzalo Fernández de Oviedo*, ed. Juan Bautista Avalle-Arce, 2 vols. (Chapel Hill: University of North Carolina Press, 1974), who unfortunately omitted "todas (o casi todas) las muestras de gárrula ancianidad," including the present anecdote. The memoirs, entitled *Batallas y Quincuagenas*, exist in several manuscript sources; Pérez de Tudela used one in the Real Academia de la Historia (without signature); see p. xi, n. 13. They were written in Fernández de Oviedo's last years.

superimposed on a staff can be read as the six initial notes of the *Da pacem*.[64] Perhaps there was some such device in the tenor of the motet.[65]

Like many men who became famous in later life, Fernández de Oviedo regretted the time wasted in his youth on frivolities. He is known today as the great chronicler of the Indies (he was officially appointed in 1532), author of *Historia general y natural de las Indias*, the first part of which was published in Seville in 1535, the second part in 1557. It was based on five trips to the New World, between 1514 and 1546.[66] He was born in Madrid in 1478, and at about the age of 12 became a page in the household of the Duke of Villahermosa, nephew of Ferdinand the Catholic. Three years later he became a *mozo de cámara* in the household of Prince John, only son of Ferdinand and Isabella, who at the time of his early death in 1497 was married to Margaret of Austria. In 1499 he went to Italy, serving various patrons until his return to Spain in 1501. Details of his career are vague until the point where he became deputy to Lope Conchillos, Secretary for Indian Affairs, and left for the New World in 1514. From the time he published a novel on chivalry in 1519 he continued to write and to translate from Italian.[67]

Obviously Fernández de Oviedo had some musical knowledge. What little we know of the musical establishment of Prince John is based on his *Libro de la Camara Real del Prínçipe Don Juan e offiçios de su casa e serviçio ordinario*. In it he recalls Prince John's inclination to music, his instruments, his musicians, and the master of his chapel, Johannes de Anchieta.[68]

Fernández de Oviedo's memoirs reveal that his skill with scissors was not unique: there were others who had learned the art, both in Spain and outside it, but he held that none surpassed him. He disapproved of those who drew their patterns first, with rulers

64. The cryptic version was in the lost Treviso Ms. 30; for a sketch of the tenor and an explanation see Bonnie J. BLACKBURN, *Music for Treviso Cathedral in the Late Sixteenth Century: A Reconstruction of the Lost Manuscripts 29 and 30* (Royal Musical Association Monographs, 3; London: Royal Musical Association, 1987), 112 and 40-43. The motet was printed by Kriesstein in 1540 with the tenor resolved. Other compositions on coats of arms by Isaac (*Palle palle*) and Costanzo Porta (*Missa ducalis*) are discussed ibid. See also Mitchell P. Brauner's interpretation of the two cantus firmi in Carlet's seven-voice motet *Vidit Dominus* in "The Manuscript Verona, Accademia Filarmonica, B 218 and its Political Motets," *Studi musicali* 16 (1987): 3-12.
65. The Sforza arms are a crowned eagle quartered with the Visconti *biscia*. Jeffrey Dean has suggested to me that the arms might have been separate from the music, say within the soprano initial. If so, there is a good candidate for the composition (though the piece is rather long): Gaffurio wrote a motet addressing Ludovico, *Salve decus genitoris*, found in Milan, Archivio della Veneranda Fabbrica del Duomo, Sezione Musicale, Librone 1 (*olim*

2269), ff. 82ᵛ-84ʳ, facsimile edited by Howard Mayer BROWN (Renaissance Music in Facsimile, 12a; New York: Garland Publishing, 1987). There is a modern edition of the piece in Franchino Gaffurio, *Motetti*; ed. Luciano MIGLIAVACCA (Archivium musices metropolitanum mediolanense, 5; Milan: Veneranda Fabbrica del Duomo di Milano, 1959), 69-74.
66. See Daymond TURNER, *Gonzalo Fernández de Oviedo y Valdés: An Annotated Bibliography* (University of North Carolina Studies in the Romance Languages and Literatures, 66; Chapel Hill: University of North Carolina Press, 1966), introduction.
67. Ibid., pp. x-xv.
68. See Higinio ANGLÉS, *La música en la Corte de los Reyes Católicos*, I (Monumentos de la Música Española, 1; Madrid: Consejo Superior de Investigaciones Científicas, 1941), 74-75, and Mary Kay DUGGAN, "Queen Joanna and her Musicians," *Musica disciplina* 30 (1976): 73-95 at 74-76. The *Libro de la camara real* was edited by J. M. ESCUDERO DE LA PEÑA (Sociedad de Bibliófilos Españoles, 7; Madrid: Viuda é hijos de Galiano, 1870).

and compasses, and used gouges and tools in addition to scissors (making the technique more similar to wood-cutting). He recalls cutting the arms of Prince John and Margaret, some in size no larger than a small coin.[69] With such a skill he must have found an easy entry into the Italian courts.

The history of the art of paper-cutting is badly in need of study. Although related to the silhouette, paper-cuts are much more ornate since they involve cutting not only around the edges to create an outline but cutting inside; the result can be reminiscent of filigree technique. The art has not died out; I have seen extremely elaborate modern Chinese paper-cuts. The English term "silhouette" derives from the name of Étienne de Silhouette (1709–67), and the technique became extremely popular in the later eighteenth century, but it is not at all the same as a paper-cut.

Because the name and the technique of the silhouette are so well known, scholars have been misled into believing that the paper-cut that is pasted to one of the opening folios of Bologna, Museo Civico Bibliografico Musicale, Ms. Q 19, a stag chained to a tree, is of eighteenth-century origin.[70] Rainer Heyink, in his 1994 study of the manuscript, was more inclined to see it as close to the date of the manuscript (one piece is dated 1518), but without producing new evidence on the history of the technique. Instead, he proposed that the emblem itself was that of Lucrezia Gonzaga, a member of the Bozzolo branch of the Gonzaga family, born in 1522.[71] Leeman Perkins first drew attention to the bird perched in the tree as a possible Gonzaga emblem.[72]

Fernández de Oviedo's biographical remarks permit us to discard the theory of the eighteenth-century origin of the paper-cut, as it should now be called, in Bologna Q 19. Indeed, one is even tempted to suggest that it is one of his own works, and therefore made before, not after, the preparation of the manuscript. After his visit to Milan, Fernández de Oviedo went to Mantua, where his art impressed not only Isabella d'Este but also Andrea Mantegna ("another Leonardo da Vinci").[73] Joining the entourage of Car-

---

69. *Historia general*, ed. PÉREZ DE TUDELA, xx-xxi.

70. The first to suggest this was Ludwig Finscher, in his review of Edward Lowinsky's edition of the Medici Codex in *Die Musikforschung* 30 (1977): 477-78. There is a facs. ed. of the Ms., ed. Jessie Ann OWENS (Renaissance Music in Facsimile, 1; New York and London: Garland Publishing, 1988).

71. Rainer HEYINK, *Der Gonzaga-Kodex Bologna Q19: Geschichte und Repertoire einer Musikhandschrift des 16. Jahrhunderts* (Paderborn: Ferdinand Schöningh, 1994), 31-36, esp. 33-34. As has often been remarked, the silhouette and the initials "D P" are separate objects and not necessarily related. Heyink sees Lucrezia's father, Pirro Gonzaga, as the original owner. I do not find his evidence entirely convincing, nor Robert Nosow's argument for Padua;

see "The Dating and Provenance of Bologna, Civico Museo Bibliografico Musicale, Ms. Q 19," in *Journal of Musicology* 9 (1991): 92-108. This is still a manuscript in search of a provenance.

72. In his review of the *Medici Codex*, in *The Musical Quarterly* 55 (1969): 265-67 at 267.

73. "En Mantua, viviendo la excelente marquesa Isabel, madre del señor duque de Mantua e del señor Hernando de Gonzaga, mujer que fué del excelente marqués Francisco de Gonzaga, yo corté algunas cosas que aquellos señores dudaban que fuese posible hacerse, hasta que en su presencia me vieron cortar otras gentilezas. Y mucho más se maravillaba de eso aquel excelente pintor que entonces allí vivía, llamado Andrea Manteña, que era otro Leonardo de Avince, y aun en la pintura algunos

dinal Juan Borgia, nephew of Alexander VI and archbishop of Valencia, and newly appointed legate *a latere* to the French king, Fernández traveled to Milan, where he saw the entrance of Louis XII, then to Turin, Ferrara, Bologna, Urbino, Rome, and finally Naples, returning to Spain in 1501.[74] In all these courts he demonstrated his art. Quite possibly there are still examples of his artistic creations, tucked away in books or manuscripts of the early sixteenth century or later, preserved because of their beauty.

le hacían el principal sobre los de aquel tiempo en toda Italia. Muchas historias o imágenes corté contrahaciendo tablas de Martinus e de otros grandes varones del buril, y tan proprio que daban admiración." See *Historia*, ed. PÉREZ DE TUDELA, xxiv.

74. Ibid., xxiv-xxxi. He admired the cardinal greatly for his intelligence and magnanimity: his household included five or six bishops, and he sought out famous men of letters and musicians, giving them substantial salaries ("vivían con él cinco o seis obispos; e cuantos hombres particulares había por Italia famosos en letras, música e en otras facultades e de gentiles habilidades, todos los buscaba e daba salarios competentes" (p. xxvi). In Naples he became acquainted with Pontano, Serafino Aquilano, and Sannazaro (p. xxxi; unfortunately, no excerpts are given).

# Bruhier, Lupus, and Music Copying at Ferrara: New Documents

**M**ORE THAN TWENTY years ago, I published a set of documents on French music and its practitioners in Ferrara in the first decades of the sixteenth century.[1] These were primarily letters written by Jean Michel, long a key member of the Ferrarese musical establishment and copyist of a series of music manuscripts for local use.[2] From Jean Michel's letters, written between 1507 and 1515, we learn much about the acquisition of music by the Este patrons—mainly Duke Alfonso I d'Este but also other members of his family. Probably the main point of interest concerns contacts between these Este patrons and Jean Mouton, the leading musician at the French royal court. Along with other news, Jean Michel reports that he had obtained motets and chansons from Jean Mouton, that Mouton himself (we are in November 1515) "is going to Loreto and will pass through Ferrara," and other similar information. The context is that of the early stages of the reign of Francis I as King of France; the letters of 1515 were written from Francis' encampment at Vigevano, near Milan, during the French invasion of northern Italy in that year. The whole packet reflects a new phase in the long history of contacts between Ferrarese politics, patronage and the French court, a connection that stretched well back into the fifteenth century.[3]

My purpose here, in a volume honoring my old friend and admired colleague, Herbert Kellman, is to amplify the material that I published in 1979. This essay provides some further documentation on music copying at Ferrara in the first twenty years of the sixteenth century as well as some new material on two musicians who were active at

---

1. "Jean Mouton and Jean Michel: French Music and Musicians in Italy, 1505-1520," *Journal of the American Musicological Society* 32 (1979): 191-246, hereafter "Jean Mouton".

2. For a brief summary of what we currently know about Jean Michel at the Ferrarese court see my study cited in note 1, 1-96f. On his work as music copyist see the unpublished paper by Joshua Rifkin, "New Light on Music Manuscripts at the Court of Ferrara in the Reigns of Alfonso I and Hercules II," presented to the New England Renaissance Conference in 1974. See also Joshua RIFKIN's "Ercole's Second-Hand Coronation Mass," in Jessie Ann OWENS and Anthony CUMMINGS, eds., *Music in Renaissance Cities and Courts* (Detroit: Garland, 1996), 381-90.

3. See my *Music in Renaissance Ferrara* (Cambridge, MA: Harvard University Press, 1984), passim: hereafter this book title is abbreviated as MRF.

Ferrara in this period—Antoine Bruhier and "Lupo cantore." The main figure among the patrons, here as before, is don Sigismondo d'Este, the youngest and least known of the children of Duke Ercole I d'Este. Ercole (ruled 1471-1505) had been the major local patron of music in the late fifteenth century. That his children differed sharply from their father in cultural and musical taste is clear as crystal; what needs to be stressed is that these differences arose not merely from shifts in musical styles and genres that were coming into vogue in the early sixteenth century, but were also due to well-defined differences in manners and morals, in short, in world-outlook, that distanced Ercole's children from him and his generation. Ercole had been a shrewd and capable ruler in the fifteenth-century context, who had threaded his way through the political thickets of his time; but he had also been a profoundly religious man, a true believer, who took his role as Christian prince with the utmost seriousness. It had been quite normal for Ercole not only to build and rebuild his court chapel during his long reign,[4] but to collect sacred music, primarily Mass settings and music for Vespers, to participate with his singers in religious services, sometimes on a daily basis, and to sponsor religious life as vigorously as he could.[5]

As for his children, on the other hand, the new times that dawned as they came of age around 1500 brought new forms of political and social life. The two daughters, Beatrice (1475-97) and Isabella d'Este (1474-1539), married into allied families and moved away: Beatrice married Lodovico Sforza and became Duchess of Milan; Isabella married Francesco Gonzaga and became Marchioness of Mantua.[6] Two of the brothers took on careers expected for sons of a ruling family: Alfonso d'Este (1476-1534) inherited the dukedom in January 1505, while his brother Ippolito (1479-1520) was set up from childhood in an ecclesiastical career of extraordinary wealth and power, becoming a Cardinal at a very early age and reaping major benefices.[7]

The other brothers call for special attention. Ferrante d'Este (1477-1540) and his half-brother Giulio d'Este (1478-1561) a bastard of Ercole's, led the dissatisfied lives of

---

4. See Thomas TUOHY, *Herculean Ferrara: Ercole d'Este (1471-1505) and the Invention of a Ducal Capital* (Cambridge: Cambridge University Press, 1996), esp. 90-94. See also Werner GUNDERSHEIMER's review in *Speculum* 73/2 (April, 1998): 584-87.

5. On Ercole's religiosity see Werner GUNDERSHEIMER, *Ferrara: The Style of a Renaissance Despotism* (Princeton: Princeton University Press, 1973), 185-91; and his edition of the *De triumphis religionis* by Sabadino DEGLI ARIENTI, published as *Art and Life at the Court of Ercole d'Este* (Geneva: Librairie Droz, 1972).

6. On Beatrice a still readable study is Julia CARTWRIGHT, *Beatrice d'Este* (London: Dent, 1900), and later scholarly studies of the Sforza court, especially that of Gregory LUBKIN, *A Renaissance Court: Milan under Galeazzo Maria Sforza* (Berkeley: University of California

Press, 1994); on Isabella the literature is voluminous but a good starting point is the basic work of Alessandro LUZIO and Rodolfo RENIER, whose articles are conveniently listed by Luciano CHIAPPINI, *Gli Estensi* (Varese: Dall'Oglio, 1967), 528. On Isabella as music patron see William PRIZER, "Renaissance Women as Patrons of Music: The North Italian Courts," in Kimberly MARSHALL, ed., *Rediscovering the Muses: Women's Musical Traditions* (Boston: Northeastern University Press, 1993), 193-96 and 199-201.

7. On Alfonso see the portrait given by CHIAPPINI, *Gli Estensi*, Chapter 8, and for a preliminary view of his music patronage see my "Jean Mouton", passim. On Ippolito see my "Adrian Willaert and Cardinal Ippolito I d'Este: New Light on Willaert's Early Career in Italy," *Early Music History* 5 (1985): 85–112.

family members who were kept entirely out of power, and staged an abortive coup in 1506 that resulted in their both being incarcerated for life.[8] This leaves the brother most neglected by historians, Sigismondo d'Este (1480-1524), about whom I wrote earlier as follows: "Sigismondo at an early age contracted venereal disease, and from about 1505 until his death in 1524 he seems to have remained a semi-invalid, almost entirely in Ferrara except perhaps for occasional summer solace in nearby country residences. He seems to have had little to do but to pursue his remaining private interests, among which music seems to have ranked high; and a motet for his death in 1524 by 'Magister Symon' is in his case no formal eulogy but commemorates a genuine patron."[9] As I pointed out, Sigismondo's total personal staff between 1505 and 1524 consisted of about 35 to 40 individuals, including one or two musicians; the number increased to five in his last two years, 1523-24. He lived in the beautiful Palazzo Schifanoia in Ferrara, where the great frescoes glorified the image and career of his uncle, Borso d'Este, as ruler of Ferrara in his time (1450-71) and no doubt intensified Sigismondo's sense of lost opportunities. Among the musicians who served Sigismondo in these years were the little-known "Michelotto Cantore" and some less obscure musicians, including Antoine Bruhier, Lupo Cantore, "Jaches" Cantore [= Jaquet of Mantua], and "Simon Francese" Cantore.[10] It is primarily the first two who concern us here.

### Antoine Bruhier

What we now know of this singer, according to the most recent scholarship, is that he was a cleric of Noyon who served in 1504 at the cathedral of Langres; he may have been connected with the French court; he served from 1513 or 1514 to 1521 in the private chapel of Pope Leo X as "musicus secretus," and became a Papal singer in 1519.[11] In my earlier article, I referred to an autograph letter from Bruhier to Cardinal Ippolito I, written between 1505 and 1509, which shows that at the time of writing Bruhier was in the service of the Duke of Urbino but also that he was closely in touch with Ferrarese patronage.[12] The letter is preserved in the Archivio di Stato di Modena, Musica e Musicisti, B. I. Dated from "Urbino, xxiii febbrij 150[...]" (the last number is torn off, see below), it is addressed "Al mio Reverendissimo Signore et benefactore monsignore lo Cardinale de ferrara"; despite earlier references, until now, to my knowledge, the text has

---

8. On the plot, in which the singer Gian de Artiganova was also involved, see Roberto BACCHELLI, *La Congiura di don Giulio d'Este*, 2d. ed. (Milan: Mondadori, 1958).

9. "Jean Mouton," 198.

10. This is drawn from "Jean Mouton," 1979, 198, n. 21.

11. For the most recent information on Bruhier, I am indebted to Richard Sherr for sending me his as yet unpublished article on Bruhier for the forthcoming edition of *The New Grove.* See also "Jean Mouton", 199, n. 22; the arti-

cle "Bruhier" by Albert DUNNING in *The New Grove*, 3: 374; and Richard WEXLER, *Antoine Bruhier. Collected Works*, forthcoming from The Broude Trust, Williamstown, MA, in the series *Masters and Monuments of the Renaissance*, vol. 6. Sherr in his forthcoming article mentions the possibility that Bruhier could have been the "Antonio Brugier" who was a singer at the Milanese court in 1474.

12. "Jean Mouton," 199, n. 22.

not been available in the scholarly literature.[13] Because of its defective date, the Modena archivists thought earlier that it might be from 1503. But Bruhier was in Langres in 1504 and probably there or at least in France before that. Furthermore, he refers in the letter to the "Illustrissimo signore Duca suo fratello" [i.e., Duke Alfonso I, Ippolito's brother], and since Alfonso took power as Duke only in 1505 it cannot be earlier than that year. As to a terminal date, "150-" allows for years only up to 1509. For reasons to follow, I agree with Sherr that 1507 or 1508 is the likely date. Written in a cursive hand and with a jocular closing salutation in enormous Gothic letters, its text is as follows:

Reverendissime in Christo pater, et domine, domine ac benefactor mi praecipue, humill[issime] Comm[endo]: Per che, per li grandi obligi ho cum vostra Reverendissima Signoria, son obligato di continuo ricordarmi de quella: ritrovandome de presenti al servitio de questo Illustrissimo signore Duca di Urbino, me è venuto in fantasia de fare una sexta parte sopra Clama ne cesses; che è un altro soprano, cum sit che etiam a requisitione de predetta vostra Reverendissima signoria facessi, quando era li, la quinta parte, come quella scia. Et perche scio, che sempre le cose mie li sono piaciute: ge la mando qui alligata: insieme cum un motetto de nostra donna qual vostra Reverendissima signoria se dignarà farlo presentare al Illustrissimo signore Duca suo fratello. Item, le septe hore de la passione, a tre parte, quale et quella si dignarà farle donare al' Illustrissima signoria pur suo fratello don ["Alfonso" crossed out here] Sygismondo. Expecto che lo predetto Illustrissimo Signore Duca mio ritorni da fosimbrone che poi cum sua licentia voglio nanti vada in franza, venire a fare reverentia a vostra Reverendissima. A laquale de continuo me raccomando. Et illa felix valeat. Urbini xxiii febrij 1 50[-].
[In enormous letters:]
v[ost]re petit
[ami et?][14] serviteur
BRUHIER[15]

Most Reverend father, and lord, my lord and distinguished benefactor, to whom I humbly commend myself. Because, owing to the great obligations that I have toward your Reverend Lordship, I am obliged to continually remember myself to you, finding myself currently in the service of this Illustrious Lord the Duke of Urbino, it came into my imagination to make a sixth part on "Clama ne cesses," that is, another soprano part; although it is true that at your Reverend Lordship's request I made, when I was there, a fifth part, as you know. And since I know that my compositions always have been pleasing to you, I send it to you attached here, along with a motet for the Virgin, which Your Reverend Lordship will be pleased to present to the illustrious Duke your brother. Also the Seven Hours of the Passion in three parts, which you will be pleased to give to the Illustrious Lord, also your brother, don Sigismondo. I expect that the aforesaid Illustrious Lord my Duke, will return from Fossombrone, [and] then by his leave I will make a trip to France, and I will come to pay homage to Your Reverence. To whom I commend myself. And live happily. Urbino, 23 February i 50[-].

Your humble
[friend and] servant
BRUHIER

---

13. Its main contents are briefly summarized by SHERR in his forthcoming *New Grove* article.

14. This word or words is difficult to decipher.

15. A musical decoration or possibly a rebus of three notes, staffless but approximately spelling out *fa re fa*, comes after Bruhier's name.

The substance of the letter is clear. Written in the fulsome style typical of musicians writing to patrons in this period, Bruhier's letter provides this news:

1) Bruhier is currently in Urbino, in the service of the Duke of Urbino. This is presumably Guidobaldo I Della Rovere, who ruled Urbino 1482-1503 and died in 1508.

2) Bruhier has had previous contact with Cardinal Ippolito and the other Este brothers, Alfonso and Sigismondo, and had previously been in Ferrara. In fact we can pinpoint his previous stay, since Sigismondo's account books carry his name in the years 1505-6 and again in 1508. I believe the likeliest scenario is that Bruhier spent 1505-6 with Sigismondo, then went to Urbino in 1507 and possibly stayed through some part of 1508, then returned to Ferrara and was again with Sigismondo in 1508.[16]

3) He had previously written a Quinta pars for "Clama ne cesses," that is, the Agnus III of Josquin's *Missa L'homme armé super voces musicales*, published by Petrucci in the Liber Primus of 1502. He now sends Ippolito a sexta pars for the same movement.

4) He also sends a Marian motet for Duke Alfonso I d'Este, and a motet setting of the Seven Hours of the Passion, in three parts, for Sigismondo d'Este.

5) As soon as the Duke of Urbino returns from Fossombrone, Bruhier will request leave to go to France and will come through Ferrara to pay homage to Cardinal Ippolito.

Only one of these sacred compositions may be preserved, to judge from Sherr's work-list for Bruhier, which contains three Masses, a group of motets, and a somewhat larger group of chansons plus an untexted canon. The work that might be preserved, as Sherr suggests, is the motet *Ave celorum regina* contained in the Ms. Bologna Q 20. The two new voice-parts for "Clama ne cesses" show continued local pride over the recent presence of Josquin Desprez in Ferrara in 1503-1504, and also the continued cultivation of his music there in the years after his departure for Condé. This is evident both from musical sources and from the inclusion of the canonic Agnus dei II for three voices from the same Josquin Mass, the *Missa L'homme armé super voces musicales*, in Dosso Dossi's Allegory of Music, painted about 1520.[17]

16. The registers for Sigismondo containing references to Bruhier, the account books, in serial order, of the ruling Este family members, now in the Archivio di Stato di Modena (Archivio Segreto Estense) are as follows: LASP [Libri di Amministrazione dei Singoli Principi] No. 1465 (1505-06), f. 48ᵛ, 61ᵛ, and 75ʳ (all listing "Buriero chantore"); also LASP No. 1467, for 1508, f. 34ʳ lists "Burhiero chantore" on the date 1 August 1508, paid L. 9.9.0. Another reference is in LASP No. 1482, for 1515, f. 26ʳ (31 December 1515), and shows "Item adi ditto a Bruhyer cantore una berretta morella doppia di dui frontali" which cost 3.0.0. But this entry is retrospective and shows earlier payments for "berrette francese" that had been given to various persons by Sigismondo,

including one to "Coglia" (Girolamo de Sestola) on 22 maggio 1506 and on the same day (adi ditto) "a Bruhyer cantore." This is a typical retrospective payment entry, referring to payments made nine years earlier than the date of the entry.

17. See H. COLIN SLIM, "Dosso Dossi's Allegory at Florence about Music," *Journal of the American Musicological Society*, 43 (1990), 413-98. Most recently, the major exhibit of Dosso Dossi's works resulted in two publications that include references to this painting: Luisa CIAMMITTI, Steven F. OSTROW, and Salvatore SETTIS, eds., *Dosso's Fate: Painting and Court Culture in Renaissance Italy* (Los Angeles: Getty Institute for the History of Art and the Humanities, 1998); and the large catalogue by P. HUMFREY

## "Lupus" in Sigismondo d'Este's service

As matters stood in 1979, when I published some new documents on "Lupo francese cantore" in Sigismondo's service from June 1518 to April 1519, the "Lupus" problem remained in some entanglement.[18] I then assumed that this singer was the one we had been calling the "Italian Lupus," thought to be older than his partial namesake Lupus Hellinck (c.1495-1541) and Johannes Lupi of Cambrai (c.1505-39). I thought that this new information, placing a "Lupo francese" in Ferrara in 1518-19, helped to explain how motets, presumably by him, could find their way into Italian manuscript collections of motets (Bologna Q 19 and Florence 666) as well as Petrucci's *Motetti della Corona*, II (1519). It also fitted in with the motet by "Lupus" for Marino Grimani, Patriarch of Aquileia, in the Vallicelliana codex, probably composed in 1524.[19]

But in the meantime Richard Sherr has discovered two documents that clarify the "Lupus" problem in a new way. These are Papal supplications, dated respectively 1 and 12 April 1518.[20] Both documents give the singer's name unequivocally as "Lupus Hellinc." Sherr writes, "in the first Hellinck asks to be ordained a priest and states that he is in his twenty-fourth year, a member of the Papal household, and resident in Rome; in the second Hellinck is granted an indult because he is preparing to leave Rome."[21] As Sherr points out, this sets up a scenario in which, if there was one such musician and not two, Lupus Hellinck was in Italy and a member of the household of Leo X in April 1518, then left Rome. From June 1518 to April 1519 he could easily have been in Ferrara, and by October 1519 was "readmitted to the chapter of St. Donatian [in Bruges]."[22] The upshot of all this is that, as it now seems, there probably is no "Italian Lupus," but rather, Lupus Hellinck is that person, and all the music hitherto ascribed to the "Italian" namesake should now be attributed to Hellinck.

It now remains to spell out the dates and indicate the content of the documents from the account books of Sigismondo d'Este that I have found to refer to "Lupo cantore," to add some minor particulars to his biography. They are as follows:

**Sources:** Archivio di Stato di Modena, LASP, Account books of Sigismondo d'Este, registers as indicated

and M. LUCCO, *Dosso Dossi: Court Painter in Renaissance Ferrara* (New York: Metropolitan Museum of Art; Harry N. Abrams, 1998), No. 25.

18. "Jean Mouton," 199, n. 23. Still the basic study of the Lupus problem from the standpoint of musical styles is Bonnie BLACKBURN, *The Lupus Problem* (Ph.D.diss., University of Chicago, 1970).

19. See my "Sources of Renaissance Polyphony from

Cividale del Friuli: The Manuscripts 53 and 59 of the Museo Archeologico Nazionale," *Il saggiatore musicale* 1/2 (1994): 249-314, esp. 308-10.

20. Richard SHERR, ed., *Selections from Bologna, Civico Museo Bibliografico Musicale Ms. Q* ("Rusconi Codex"), Sixteenth-Century Motet, 6 (New York: Garland, 1989), xi-xii and xiv, notes 9 and 10.

21. Ibid., xii.    22. Ibid.

*Register No. 1474* (1518)

F. 36$^r$ [16 June 1518] "A Lupo cantore de lo Ill.mo S.N. ..." [for clothing] ... L. 1.13.0

F. 37$^v$ [19 June 1518]: "A Lupo francese cantore de lo Ill.mo S. N. ..." [for cost of cloth]. ... L. 8.10.0

F. 36$^v$ [29 June 1518] "A Lupo cantore de lo Ill.mo S.N. ..." [for cost of cloth] ... L. 2.19.0

F. 37$^v$ [30 June 1518] "A Lupo francese cantore de lo Ill. S.N. ..." [for shoes, etc.] L. 1.6.0

F. 47$^r$ [14 August 1518] "A Lupo fiamengo cantore de lo Ill. S.N. ..." [for shoes] ... L. 0.10.0

F. 48$^v$ [20 August 1518] "A Lupo fiammengo cantore de lo Ill.S.N. ..." [for shoes] L. 1.0.0

*Register No. 1475* (1519)

F. 23$^r$ [19 April 1519] "A Lupo francese cantore de lo Ill.S.N. ..." [payment] L. 18.0.0

*Register No. 1488* (1519)

[This is a large double-entry register]

F. 81$^v$ "Lupo francese Cantore dello Ill. S. Don Sigismondo da Este ..." [paid L.6.16.0 for reasons specified in another register of 1518]; two more entries on this page show payments to the same person in the amounts of L.6.0.0 (for 21 January 1519) and 18.0.0 (for 19 April 1519).

F. 82$^r$ "Lupo contrascritto debbe havere adi ultimo Decembre Lire ventiquattro marchesane per lui de spesa de salariati dello Ill. s. don Sigismondo de Este per suo servito [sic] di mesi quattro in lano 1519; che poi partitte .... adi ultimo aprile ... L. xxiiii.o.o."

And again on f. 170$^v$: "Lupo fiamengo Cantore per suo servitio di mesi quattro che poi partitte ..." L. 24.0.0

This material confirms that Lupus [Hellinck] was in Sigismondo's service from at latest 16 June 1518, until 30 April 1519, when he left.

## Music Copying in Ferrara c. 1503-23

That Ferrara was a hive of music copying in this period is already amply clear, but the documentary basis for the claim in these decades has yet to be spelled out. I gave some evidence in my earlier article, and now aim to supplement that material with a series of documented payments for music copying, culled from the account books of these same Este patrons: Duke Alfonso, Cardinal Ippolito I, and Sigismondo. The order here is chronological rather than by individual patron, and I number the entries consecutively for ease of reference. When the detailed history of music at Ferrara in the years of Alfonso's reign (1505-34) is eventually written, including as well the musical patronage of his brothers Ippolito and Sigismondo as active local patrons, these documents will form part of the basic source material. They also serve to indicate, along with previously known evidence, how far the actual music copying done in these years exceeded what is now preserved.

*1503*

LASP Alfonso 1 Reg. 35 (1503-1504)

1) F. 1$^v$: Payment to "Zo Michiel Cantore ... per haver facto regare piu libri di notare piu canti per sua signoria"

2) Ibid., f. 6$^v$: Payment to "Zo Michiele per fare la rigadura de Carta per notare mese per sua Signoria."

3) Ibid., f. liv[r]: Payment to "Carlo notadore" [presumably same as "Charles de Fiandra notadore," who is paid in this register on ff. 12[v]-12 and 18[v]]

4) Ibid., f. 9[v]: Payment to "m. Girolimo Cartolaro de L'Aquila per haver ligato uno libro de canto grande notado de mese como una bale in una arme per sua signoria"

5) Ibid., f. 21[v]: Payment to "uno m.o cartolaro che arigo quinterni sei de carta reale dati a carlo notadore per fare mese per sua signoria"

### 1504

6) Ibid., f. 40[v] (5 August 1504): Payment to "il capelano de li frati deli capuzoli (Capucins) per haver notado una mese che feze Juschi[no] Cantore"; this document appeared in my paper, "Josquin at Ferrara: New Documents and Letters," E. LOWINSKY, ed., *Proceedings of the International Josquin Festival-Conference* (Oxford, 1976), p. 137 (last item). I include it again here to put it into the context of music copying at Ferrara at this time.

7) Ibid., f. 43[v]: Payment to an unspecified recipient "per fare rigare uno quinterno de carta per notare mese"

8) Ibid., f. 45[r] (31 October): Payment "al fiolo de Tomaso Bursetto per pagare la rigadura de uno quinterno de carta e per vernixe per notare"

### 1505

LASP, Alfonso 1, Reg. No. 36 (1504-05)

9) F. 30[v] (5 April) Payment by "sua signoria per fare rigare quinterni sette de carta reale dati a zoanne michel cantore e zoanne maria burseto per notare messe"

10) Ibid., f. 31[r] (15 April) Payment "per fare rigare uno quinterno de carta real e per vernixe e ingiostro dati a Zoanne maria Borseto per notar"

LASP, Sigismondo d'Este, Reg. No. 1465

11) F. 51[v]. Payment to "Zoan Maria [name not clear] per charta da notare et da schrivere per Buriero chantore de sua signoria"

### 1506

12) Ibid., f. 64[r] (7 August 1506) Payment "a don Simon che nota per avere notado al prefato S. Li infraschriti chanti, vz

| mese novo | L.9.0.0 |
| muteti tri a cinque | 3.18.0 |
| muteti tri a cinque | 1.4.0 |
| magnifichat a uno | 0.15.0 |
| hijni dui | 0.4.0 |
| chantorini tre[23] | 0.4.6 |

per havere rigado quinterni undiexe et 2 de charta reale da notare … 4.7.6
charte che lui arefato che fanno in summa 20.11.0"

### 1508

LASP Ippolito 1 Reg. No. 772

13) F. 20[v] (4 June 1508) Payment to "prie michiele per uno libro de canto"

14) Ibid., f. 20[v] (9 November 1508) Payment to "prie michiele per carta regada per fare la moteta per il signore"

15) Ibid., f. 20[v] (10 November 1508) Payment to "Borguro per comprare carta regada per fare certe cosse per el signore"

23. 3 *cantorini*, that is, books with canticles and psalms with their tones, hymns, and tones of introits and responsories

16) Ibid., f. 20$^v$ (5 December 1508) Payment to "Borguro. . . . per comprare carta reale per fare motetti per lo Ill. S. Cardinale nostro"

*1512*

LASP Ippolito 1, Reg. 784 (1512)

17) F. 72$^v$ (24 March(?) 1512) Payment to "m.o pre michele Cantore contanti per comprare libri quatro da notare canti li quali lui fa per lo Ill. S. Cardinale"

*1513*

LASP Ippolito 1, Reg. 786 ("Compto Generale de Roma"; July 1513-14)

18) F. 1$^v$ (30 July 1513) Payment to "franzoso Cantore per comprare uno Libro per notare canti per lo Ill. S. Cardinale . . ."

19) F. 13$^v$ (24 September 1513) Payment to "pre Micgiele per comprare libri sei de Canto per uxo de lo Ill. S. Cardinale"

20) Ibid., f. 40$^v$ (26 December 1513) Payment to "pre micqiele . . . per comprare uno libro de Canto per el signore nostro"

*1514*

LASP, Sigismondo d'Este, Reg. No. 1471 (1514)

21) F. 15$^r$ (5 March 1514). Payment "A spese de donare L. Desedoto s.Desedoto demarchesane e per epsa a Constancio Festa Chantore per avere donato certi muteti a lo Ill. Signore Nostro I quali porto Lururio [?] stafiero in chaxa de messer Bidone, in Libro H. . . . 18.18.0"

[This document was published earlier in 1979 in the *Journal of the American Musicological Society*, p. 230, where the first amount paid in the English translation should be "18" not "58"; see also the facsimile of this page in ibid., Figure 6, p. 231.]

LASP, Ippolito I, Reg. No. 790 (1514)

22) F. 92$^r$ (2 September 1514) Payment to "Benaria franzoso musico per comprare uno quinterno de Carta Reale regada per notare Canzoni per lo Ill. Et Rev. S. Cardinale estense"

23) Ibid., f. 96$^r$ (15 September 1514) Payment to "Benaria Musicho per comprare folii 25 de carta reale regada per notare canti per lo Ill. Et Rev. S. Cardinale"

24) Ibid., f. 104$^v$ (6 October 1514) Payment to "Benaria Musicho . . . per pagare folii vintecinque de carta reale regada per notare canti per il S. Nostro Ill.mo"

25) Ibid., f. 107$^r$ (12 October 1514) Payment to "Boneria Musico per comprare piu cordette per metere a uno libro de canti de Signore nostro Ill.mo"

*1516* [24]

LASP, Sigismondo d'Este, Reg. No. 1472

26) F. 13$^r$ (16 January 1516). Payment "a m.o domenego cartolaro per it chusto de quinterni quattro de carta reale per fare notare canti I quali ge porto contanti a botese Joanne Antonio Venturi . . ."

Guardaroba, Memoriale D [This register belongs to the household of Cardinal Ippolito I; see *Early Music History*, 5 (1986), 110], 1516.

27) F. 60$^v$ (17 May 1516): ". . . ligato dui libri da Canto in octavo" [could be manuscript or prints].

LASP, Ippolito I, Reg. 796 (1516)

---

24. For the years 1516, 1517, and 1524 I published earlier, in "Jean Mouton," 225, n. 83, a series of entries showing payments to "Jaches Cantore" (Jaquet da Mantua) for furniture, clothing, and other material needs, all connected with his work in these years as music copyist for Sigismondo. These entries are not repeated here.

28) F. 69$^r$ (24 May 1516): Payment to "M.o Lorenzo libraro ... per haver ligato uno libro de canto coperto de cordoano, viz. de sfogezado con cordelli de seda negra ..."

Guardaroba, Memoriale D [of Ippolito I] (1516)

29) F. 16$^r$ (7 June 1516). Payment for the "factura de una burssa de cordoano per uno libro de canto ..."

30) Ibid., f. 126$^v$ (26 August 1516). Payment to Cesare de le Vieze "per minare un Calendario de Sua Signoria ..."

*1517*

LASP, Alfonso I, Reg. No. 41 (1517)

31) F. 5$^r$ (31 January 1517). Payment to "Cesare de le Vieze per quinterni 30 de carta harigato per fare libri de Canto per il Signore et per pagare quinterni 2"

32) Ibid., f. 12$^r$ (20 March 1517). Payment to "Cesare de le Vieze ... per quanto de meniadur lui fa per libri de Canto del S ..." [Published earlier by H.J. HERMANN, "Zur Geschichte der Miniaturmalerei zum Hofe der Este in Ferrara", *Jahrbuch der Kunsthistorischen Sammlungen der Allerhoechsten Kaiserhauses*, 21 (1900), 117-21. Now Hermann Julius HERMANN, *La Miniatura Estense*, rev. and translated from the original German edition of 1900 by Federica TONIOLI, Giordana MARIANI CANOVA, and Giovanna VALENZANO (Modena: Franco Cosimo Panini Editore, 1994), p. 281, Doc. 331].

33) Ibid., f. 14$^r$ (1 April 1517). Payment to "Cesare de le Vieze per havere legato e coperto de veluto negro 4 libretti de canto che manda a donar el signore nostro al fiolo del vice re ... 2.16.0" [Published by HERMANN, *La Miniatura Estense*, p. 281, Doc. 331. In the Italian edition of Hermann, "vice re" is given mistakenly as "civire."]

34) Ibid., f. 16$^r$ (7 April 1517). Payment to "Cesare de le Vieze per havere miniato lettere 172 in libri de Canto che manda a donar il signore al vicere de napuli ... 4.6.0" [Published by HERMANN, *La Miniatura Estense*, p. 281, Doc. 331, where the date is given as 8 April].

35) Ibid., f. 26$^r$ (26 June 1517). Payment to "m.o Cesare de le Vieze per haver rigado quinterni 48 de carta per notare moteti ... 1.5.0" [Not in Hermann]

Guardaroba. Memoriale E [of Ippolito I] (15 17)

36) F. 165$^r$ (20 July 1517). Payment "per havere rigato uno Quinterno di cartha mezana da notare Canti, e ... dui a Zoa[nne] Lour[del] per comprare vernice per bisogno di notar canti sopra ditti quinterni ..."

LASP, Ippolito I, Reg. No. 800 (1517)

37) F. 52$^r$ (31 July 1517). Payment to "Zoanne Lourdello ... per comprare vernice per vermigare dicta cartha da notare canti"

LASP, Alfonso I, Reg. No. 41 (1517-18)

38) F. 35$^r$ (8 August 1517). Payment to "Lorenzo Cartolaro per havere ligato dui libri di contrapunti per li Illustrissimi fioli del signore ... 0.10.0"

39) Ibid., f. 36$^r$ (14 August 1517). Payment to "Cesare da le Vieze per havere legato quinterni 60 de carta de capretto per it signore per fare libri de canto ... 3.0.0" [Incomplete in HERMANN, *La Miniatura Estense*, p. 281, Doc. 331]

Guardaroba, Memoriale E [of Ippolito I] (1517)

40) F. 256$^r$ (10 October 1517). Payment "per il precio de cinque libri di frotol a stampa"

41) Ibid., f. 271$^r$ (19 October) "per fare li chiappi a tri libri de canti che ha notado Za Lourdel Cantore (= Jean Lourdel)"

42) Ibid., f. 274$^v$ (20 October 1517). Payment for "tri libri de canto"

43) Ibid., f. 285$^r$ (24 October 1517). Payment for "burssetta de cordoano negro ... per tri libretti di canto"

44) Ibid., f. 286$^v$ (24 October 1517). Payment for "uno quinterno di cartha per notare ... consegnato a Za Lourdel Cantore"

LASP, Alfonso I, Reg. No. 41 (1517-18)

45) F. 51$^r$ (23 November 1517). Payment to "Cesare da le Vieze contanti per havere rigato quinterni 9 de carta per copiare libri de canto de don herc [name crossed out] ... 0.8.0" [Not in Hermann]

46) Ibid., f. 54$^r$ (9 December 1517). Payment to "Cesare da le Vieze per havere regato quinterni 13 de carta per fare uno libro da canto da camara ... 0. 13.0" [Incomplete in Hermann, Doc. 331]

*1518*

47) Ibid., f. 59$^r$ (29 January 1518). Payment to "m.o Cesare da le Vieze per havere regato quinterni 30 de carta da notare bali per il signore nostro ... 1 .0.0" [Incomplete in Hermann, Doc. 331]

48) Ibid., f. 59$^r$ (4 February 1518). Payment to "Cesare da le Vieze per havere regato folii 16 de carta reale per il Signore ..."

49) Ibid., f. 64$^r$ (16 March 1518). Payment to "Cesare da le Vieze per havere regato quinterni 13 de carta reale per copiare de canto"

50) Ibid., f. 84$^r$ (28 September 1518). Payment to "Cesare da le Vieze per quinterni 3 de carta reale hauta da lui per fare libri de canto per il signore don Hercule ... 1 .1.0" [Incomplete in Hermann, Doc. 331]

51) Ibid., f. 85$^r$ (5 October 1518). Payment to "Cesare da le Vieze per havere regato quinterni 50 de carta reale per fare libri de canto per il signore don Hercule"

52) Ibid., f. 89$^r$ (4 December 1518). Payment to "Don Biso Capellano per uno graduale per cantare la messa e per uno antiphonario ['psalmista' is crossed out] per cantare vespro ... 27.0.0"

*1520*
Libro Z della fabrica

53) F. 78$^r$ (24 December 1520). Payment to "Polo Chonchela per farlo notare e scrivere uno libro novo da messe e canto figura[to]"

*1523*[25]
LASP, Sigismondo d'Este, Reg. No. 1479 (1523)

54) F. 28$^v$(23 March 1523). Payment "spexa de uno libro da messe in Canto et per essa a m.o Cesare scritor lira una soldi 10 marchesane le quali disse per vernice et rigadura per il dicto"

55) Ibid., f. 41$^v$ (10 June 1523). Payment to "m.o Cesare da le Vieze scritor ... per uno libro de messe in canto che'l fa per lo signore Nostro ill.mo"

56) Ibid., f. 46$^v$ (3 July 1523). Payment "A spese del libro de le messe in Canto figurato et per essa a m.o Cesare da le Vieze scritore lire tre s. 15 de marchesane li quali allui li fu datti per il bancho de Jacomo Boiardo per suo resto e sua mercede de havere regatto fogli n.o 237 de carta reale a uno maresetto [?] il figlio. Et per havere facto letere de una messa che furno n.o 72 a denari 6 marchesane l'una ... 3.18.6"

---

25. For the year 1523 I published in "Jean Mouton," 200, n. 24, an entry concerning payments to "Simon Francese" for "tre libretti rigatti per notarli suso Cosse a tre" (three little books ruled to be notated for three voic-es) for Sigismondo (31 October) and another (for 19 October) paying Jean Michel 30 *soldi* for copying masses for him. These are not repeated here.

William F. Prizer

# Charles V, Philip II, and the Order of the Golden Fleece

THE ORDER of the Golden Fleece was a chivalric, lay confraternity that played an important role in the sacred music of Burgundy and the Low Countries from 1430 to 1559. I first published a study of the Order and music in 1985.[1] There I demonstrated that the confraternity, mostly through its sovereign, was always a major patron and consumer of sacred music, though I concentrated on the period of Duke Philip the Fair in the late fifteenth and very early sixteenth centuries. I should like to continue here, discussing the Order in the years after Philip's death in 1506 until its last full-scale meeting in 1559. I will demonstrate that the Order and its services continued unabated in this period and that it continued to adopt major polyphonic works for its services and festivities. By doing so, I hope to provide a more detailed cultural context for sacred vocal music in the Low Countries and Spain in the sixteenth century.

On 10 January 1430, the day of his wedding to Isabelle of Portugal, Duke Philip the Good of Burgundy issued a proclamation announcing the foundation of a new chivalric confraternity that was to include the major nobles of his lands.[2] This confraternity, the Order of the Golden Fleece, flourished in Burgundy, the Low Countries, and, later, the Empire from this date until 1559. The Order of the Golden Fleece took its

1. William F. PRIZER, "Music and Ceremonial in the Low Countries: Philip the Fair and the Order of the Golden Fleece," *Early Music History* 5 (1985): 113-53. In the same year, I delivered a paper on the Order in the fifteenth century at the Annual Meeting of the American Musicological Society in Vancouver, British Columbia. I published no more because the Archives of the Order were at that time closed to scholars. Since then, they have been reopened, and Barbara Haggh studied their contents in "The Archives of the Order of the Golden Fleece and Music," *Journal of the Royal Musical Association* 120 (1995): 1-43, and 121 (1996): 268-70. Subsequently, I too worked in the archives, thanks to the kindness of Dr. Otto von Habsburg, the present sovereign of the Order, and can

once again turn to the topic of the Order and music. I am also grateful to my colleague Alejandro Enrique Planchart for his many fruitful suggestions made during the course of this study. The following abbreviations are used in this article:

V-AOGF   Vienna, Archives of the Order of the Golden Fleece, Haus- Hof- und Staatsarchiv
B-BR   Brussels, Bibliothèque Royale
H-KB   Den Haag, Koninklijke Bibliotheek

2. The following general information is intended as a brief review of relevant facets of the Order. For more detail and additional literature, see PRIZER, "Music and Ceremonial."

name originally from the fleece of Jason, although slightly later the symbol was extend-ed to the fleece of Gideon and to four other fleeces. The confraternity at first had twenty-five members including the duke himself as sovereign, each of whom received a ceremonial collar. Philip established the Order "for the perfect love that we have for the noble estate and order of chivalry … in praise of our Almighty Creator and Redeemer, in reverence of his glorious Virgin Mother, to the honor of St. Andrew, glorious Apostle and Martyr, to the exaltation of the faith and the Holy Church, and the practice of virtues and good habits."[3] At the third meeting in Dijon in 1433, Philip increased the number of chevaliers to thirty-one.[4]

In addition to the chevaliers, there were four officers of the Order who were not themselves members: the *Chancelier*, a major prelate from the duke's lands, the *Tresorier*, the *Greffier* or secretary, and the *Toison d'or* or King of Arms, an official herald. These officers were charged with the society's business, including the keeping of rolls and the noble deeds of the members, the announcing of each meeting to the members wherever they were, the preparation of the church selected for the meeting, and the delivery of the cer-emonial collars to newly elected members not present at the meetings.[5]

Any discussion of the Order of the Golden Fleece and music must consider three separate official functions. The first and most obvious of these are the official meetings, or "fêtes," which the sovereign convened periodically from 1431 until 1559, when Philip II discontinued them. At first the celebrations began on the Vigil of St. Andrew's day (29 November), but in 1451 were moved to the beginning of May because of the inclement weather at the time of the feast. They remained in May through the meeting of 1491, but then were held at any time of the year convenient to the sovereign. The Order held them in different towns belonging to the sovereign, ranging from Dijon in Burgundy to 's-Hertogenbosch and Utrecht in the Netherlands to Barcelona in Spain. These meetings included a *chapitre*, an official conclave that elected new chevaliers, examined the behavior

3. "Pour la tres grande et parfaite amour que avons du noble estat et ordre de chevalerie, … nous, a la gloire et loenge du tout puissant notre Creatur et Redempteur, en revereance de sa glorieuse Vierge Mere et a l'onneur de monsiegneur Saint-Andrieu glorieux apostre et martir, a l'exaltacion de la foy et Sainte Eglise et excitacion de ver-tus et de bonnes meurs …" H-KB, MS 76. E. 12, f. [4r]. This is one of a number of copies of the statutes of the Order that were given to each new member, both within the archives of the Order and elsewhere. I have adopted this one, the original portion of which was copied in around 1470 and which also includes an armorial of the chevaliers. There is also a published facsimile of a copy of the statutes in the Österreiches Nationalbibliothek, ed. Hans GERSTINGER, *Le livre des Ordonnances de l'Ordre de la*

*Toison d'Or* (also published as *Das Statutenbuch des Ordens vom Goldenen Vlies*), 2 vols. (Vienna: L'Imprimerie d'État, 1934).
4. HAGGH, "The Archives of the Order," p. 3n, states erroneously that the number was raised to thirty-one before the first meeting in Lille. She also errs in stating that there were originally twenty-six members. The cor-rect information can be found in the *Chronique de Jean Le Févre, seigneur de Saint-Remy*, ed. François MORAND, 2 (Paris: Librairie Renouard, 1881), 284-85. V-AOGF, Schachtel I, Reg. 1, f. 8r lists separately the two new chevaliers who replaced deceased members and the six that Philip added to the original twenty-five ("Et sy accreust monseigneur son ordre des chevaliers consens").
5. On the officers and their duties, see F. KOLLER, *Au service de la Toison d'or (Les officiers)* (Dijon: Lelotte, 1971).

of old ones, and discussed other matters of importance. They also included an official banquet on the first full day of the *fête*, which the sovereign was to offer to the members and assembled dignitaries. Since the Order was a religious confraternity, the meetings also had a sequence of church services that were prescribed by statute to be celebrated each time the members gathered officially. On the first evening, there were to be Vespers and Compline of St. Andrew. The next day there would be a mass for the same saint in the morning followed in the evening by the Office of the Dead. The third day was dedicated to a Requiem Mass, and the fourth day witnessed a solemn mass of Our Lady.

Originally, these were the only services celebrated. In 1458 a Marian Office was added, and by this time too, because of the removal of the ceremony from St. Andrew's day, a Mass of the Holy Ghost was substituted for the Mass of St. Andrew. Charles the Bold, at the meeting in 1473 in Valenciennes, restored the Mass of St. Andrew, moving the Mass of the Holy Ghost to after that of Our Lady. By the time of Philip the Fair, an Office of the Holy Ghost had been added as well, although, as we shall see, the Order does not seem to have continued celebrating it, and, in fact, was less than consistent in celebrating the Holy Ghost Mass.

The second function involves the services at the Sainte-Chapelle at Dijon, which Philip the Good dedicated as the official chapel of the Order in January 1432. In honor of the confraternity, Philip established a daily, perpetual celebration of the polyphonic mass. To assure that the services were celebrated there, Philip also increased the number of canons to twenty-five, all to be "persons instructed in the art of music sufficient for the divine service." Although Burgundy had been lost to the French in 1477, both Charles V and Philip II continued to support the foundation there, and, in fact, continued to use the title of "Duke of Burgundy."

The third function came about with the removal of the official celebration from St. Andrew's Day. Gradually, it became the custom for the sovereign to gather around him the officers and the chevaliers who were present and to have an informal meeting, called a "petit chapitre," or "conseil" each St. Andrew's Day (30 November). The *petits chapitres*, too, had their prescribed services beginning on 29 November. On this day Vespers of the Saint were celebrated. On the following morning was the great mass of St. Andrew. This was followed by a banquet for those members present and then by the Office of the Dead. On 1 December, the Requiem was performed as an anniversary mass for all the deceased chevaliers. There is even some trace of this practice in the earliest days of the Order. In 1434 Philip the Good canceled the official meeting but required that the services be celebrated.[6]

These functions had long been established by the time the future Charles V was born in Ghent in 1500 and became a chevalier of the Order at the *fête* in Brussels in 1501.

6.   V-AOGF, Schachtel I, Reg. I, 14ᵛ-15ʳ.

His father Philip the Fair died on his second trip to Spain in 1506 and left Charles, then six, as heir to his titles. This caused a hiatus in the meetings of the Order and in the election of new members. The Order had last met in full session in 1501. Philip had called a meeting for 1505, but was forced to leave for Spain without celebrating the required services. Not until 1516 did the Order again hold an official meeting and chapter. In the meantime, the Emperor Maximilian had resumed the duties of sovereign, which he had already held after the death of Charles the Bold and until Philip the Fair was old enough to assume his hereditary title in 1491. The future Charles V became sovereign at the age of sixteen after being named king of Spain.

If the meetings of the Order were suspended, the *petits chapitres* were not. Although the St. Andrew's Day meeting and services were presumably held each year, they are securely documented in Brussels in 1510 and in Mechelen in 1513.[7] Indeed, Charles took the *petits chapitres* particularly seriously. No matter where his travels took him, he made it a point to celebrate the services. Several examples will suffice: they were held at Valladolid in 1517, at Worms in 1520, at Toledo in 1525, at Mantua in 1532, in Madrid in 1534, and at Brussels in 1544.[8] Philip II continued the tradition, which was required by statute of the Order.[9] These were occasions of particular magnificence, as is witnessed by the description of the 1549 ceremonies from the archives of the Order:

> The emperor being in his city of Brussels the eve of St. Andrew's Day 1549 with his son monsieur [Philip] the Prince of Spain, he held the accustomed ceremonies. After the chevaliers of the Order, his brothers in the confraternity, had assembled at court around his majesty, he went to hear Vespers and Compline in the court chapel, celebrated by prelate, the Abbot of St. Bernard, with the officers [of the Order] processing in front. . . .
> The next day, [the feast of] St. Andrew, his majesty, accompanied by the said chevaliers, went to the mass in his said chapel, which was [again] sung by the Abbot of St. Bernard

---

7.    Louis GACHARD, *Collection des voyages des souverains des Pays-Bas*, 2 (Brussels: Hayez, 1881): 9 and 12.

8.    Ibid., 22 (Valladolid), 29 (Worms), and 38 (Toledo) Charles writes from Mantua on 5 December 1532, "Chiers et Feaulx. Nous avons fait en ce lieu la solempnité de feste Saint Andrey, patron de nostre dit Ordre" F. J. DE BORS D'OVEREN, *Histoire chronologique de l'ordre de la Toison d'or*, 2 (B-BR, Ms. 20852), ff. 21ʳ-23ᵛ). Charles writes a similar letter from Madrid on 7 December 1534 (ibid., 24ʳ). V-AOGF, Codex 40, f. 15ʳ, documents the 1544 meeting: "Estant sa majesté a Bruxelles le jour Sainct Andrieu audit an [1544] ayant celebré la feste a l'accoustumé, tint conseil de son ordre apres les vespres ... [the chevaliers present] sans aultres avoyent esté aux vespres de la veille, a la messe et au disner dudit jour." For a detailed description of the St. Andrew's Day ceremonies in 1519, see the addendum at the end of this study.

9.    For example, they were held in Antwerp in 1556. DE BORS D'OVEREN, *Histoire chronologique*, f. 103ᵛ.

10.   "L'empereur stant en sa ville de Bruxelles la veille Sainct Andrieu 1549 avec monsieur le prince d'Espaigne son fils, tint les ceremonies accoustumées, et apres que les chevaliers ses confreres de l'ordre estient assemblez en court vers sa majeste il allist oyr les vespres et complyes en la chappelle de sadicte court observoit de prelat l'abbé de sainct Bernard et marcherent les officiers devant.... Lendemain jour Sainct Andrieu, sa majesté acompaignée de tous les susdits ses confreres allist a la messe en sadicte chappelle, laquelle messe fut chantée par ledit abbé de St-Bernart fort solemnellement et y eust divers sortes de musiques tant de voix que d'instrumens.... Et fut ledit disner fort triomphant de nachiers, trompettes, aultres sacquebouttes, cornez, violons et chantres, chantans fort bonne musique." V-AOGF, Codex 40, f. 159ᵛ.

very solemnly, and there were diverse types of music, both vocal and instrumental. . . . The banquet [afterward] was very lavish, with nakers, trumpets, trombones, cornetts, viols, and singers singing wonderfully good music.[10]

Afterwards Charles held the *conseil* itself, but did not hold Vespers for the Dead "because it was so cold this day that his majesty believed that they could be excused from going to Vespers." His place at the Requiem the next day was taken by another chevalier.[11] These were clearly, then, musical occasions in which polyphony was heard both at the church services and at the banquet itself.

One can document the same kinds of performances at the official meetings of the Order, which were at least as sumptuous as the annual St. Andrew's Day celebrations. Charles himself presided over four meetings of the Order, held in Brussels, Barcelona, Tournai, and Utrecht (See Table 1). Philip II, who succeeded his father as sovereign after the latter ceded him the title of Duke of Burgundy, held only two meetings, in Antwerp in 1556 and Ghent in 1559. In 1560 Philip obtained a bull from Pope Gregory XIII canceling the ancient method of electing the new members by the chevaliers themselves and canceling, as well, the examination of the behavior of each chevalier in the *chapitre*. Instead, Philip was granted the right to name the new chevaliers himself. This was in part

**Table 1**  Meetings of the Order of the Golden Fleece under Charles V and Philip II

| Year | City | Church | Sovereign |
|------|------|--------|-----------|
| 1516 | Brussels | Sainte-Gudule | Charles V |
| 1519 | Barcelona | Santa Eulalia | Charles V |
| 1531 | Tournai | Notre-Dame | Charles V |
| 1546 | Utrecht | Sint-Martin | Charles V |
| 1556 | Antwerp | Onze Lieve Vrouw | Philip II |
| 1559 | Ghent | Sint-Baaf | Philip II |

a reaction to the growing tide of Protestantism in the Low Countries, and in part, surely, the result of the increasing centralization of power in the hands of the king himself and his unwillingness to have his behavior examined by his subjects in the *chapitre*.[12]

While they lasted, the meetings were occasions for elaborate displays for the benefit of the assembled ambassadors, nobles, and townspeople, and included official banquets, jousts, and processions, as well as the church services and *chapitre*. Many of these displays were ordained by statutes of Philip the Good. Indeed, one of their more

11. "Et pour ce qu'il faisoit ung tres grand froit fut sadicte majesté d'avis que ce jour l'on pourroit vient excusé d'aller aux vespres." Ibid., ff. 161ᵛ, 174ᵛ.

12. Henri KERVYN DE LETTENHOVE, *La Toison d'or: Notes sur l'institution et l'histoire de l'ordre (depuis l'année 1429 jusqu'à l'année 1559)* (Brussels: Van Oest, 1907), 84-85, also believes that part of the motive may have been Philip's lack of willingness to travel as his father had.

notable aspects is their stability. The displays of magnificence, the church services, the dress of the chevaliers, and the chapters remain virtually the same for the entire period of the Order's activity. The towns in which the meetings were held were also expected to contribute to the magnificence of the occasion. For the meeting in Tournai in 1531, the city especially decorated the houses along the route of the Order's processions, present- ed a series of *tableaux vivants*, and celebrated the *fête* with fireworks.[13] Antwerp, for the meeting in 1556, constructed a series of triumphal arches, which had instrumentalists playing from them. One of them, sponsored by the Genoese nation, collapsed, injuring several musicians. Godelieve Spiessens has shown that so many foreign musicians came to the city for the meeting that they had to request citizenship en masse in order to fol- low the Antwerp musicians' guild rules.[14]

The meetings are, of course, described in varying degrees of detail, even in the doc- uments of the Order in Vienna. Most of the services for the meeting at Brussels in 1516 can be documented, and one contemporary describes the Mass of St. Andrew in terms that at least suggest a polyphonic performance: "the singers of the [Royal] chapel sang a lovely mass in honor of God and St. Andrew."[15] It would seem unlikely that a chronicler in 1516 would describe a simple mass in chant as a "belle messe." Important at this meeting, how- ever, was the chevaliers' granting Charles' request to increase the number of members to fifty-one in order to allow more members from Charles' new kingdom of Castile.[16] There is a fair amount of detail about the ceremonies in Barcelona, including the participation of the Royal Chapel and organ in the services and the presence of trumpets and trom- bones in the processions, as well as the clergy of the Cathedral singing hymns.[17]

The meeting at Tournai in 1531 is also described in some detail, and it is apparent that the services for this meeting were unusual. This was because the *fête* began on 2 December. Charles had already been in Tournai and had celebrated the St. Andrew services on 29 and

13. M. VOISIN, "Chapitre de la Toison-d'or tenu à Tournai en 1531," *Bulletin de la Société historique et littéraire de Tournai* 8 (1862): 6-22. On this meeting see also Adolphe HOCQUET, "Un chapitre de la Toison d'or et les entrées de Charles-Quint à Tournai," *Revue Tournaisienne: Histoire, Archéologie, Art, Folklore* 2 (1906): 131-33. See also GACHARD, *Collection des voyages* 2: 564-67, where documents from the State Archives in Tournai concerning the expenses of the city are reproduced.

14. Godelieve SPIESSENS, "Bijdrage tot de studie van de Antwerpse speellieden in de XVIde eeuw," *Antwerpen in de XVIde eeuw* (Antwerp: Mercurius, 1975), 523-24.

15. "Là fut par les chantres de la chapelle chantée une belle messe à l'honneur de Dieu et de monseigneur sainct Andrieu." Chronicle of Laurent Vital, cited from Louis GACHARD and Charles PIOT, *Collection des voyages des souverains des Pays-Bas*, 3 (Brussels: Hayez, 1881), 20. At the banquet

after the mass, Vital specifies that "player[s] of several ins- truments came before the king and the chevaliers, and several pretty chansons were sung by the singers" ("Durant ce convie, vindrent devant le Roy et la siegneurie jouer[s] de plusiers sortes de instrumens, et y furent plusieurs bonnes chansons chantées par les chantres.") (Ibid., 23-24).

16. Charles wanted to increase the number of chevaliers to between fifty and sixty. The members voted to increase the number by twenty, i.e., to fifty-one. B-BR Ms. 20830, pp. 160-64. See also GACHARD, *Collection des voyages*, 2: 56.

17. On this meeting see Ramón de VILANOVA DE ROSSELLÓ, *Capitulo del Toison de oro celebrado en Barcelona el año 1519* (Barcelona: Verdaguer, 1930); Joan AINAUD DE LASARTE, *El Toisó d'Or a Barcelona* (Barcelona: Aymà, 1949). The meeting has now been admirably described by Emilio ROS-FÁBREGAS, "Music and Cermony during Charles V's 1519 Visit to Barcelona," *Early Music* 23 (1995): 375-91.

30 November. Accordingly, Vespers and Mass of the Holy Ghost were moved to the beginning of the meeting and were celebrated in place of those of St. Andrew. The archives of the Order, in fact, specify that after Charles and the other chevaliers were seated below their coats of arms in the choir of the Cathedral of Notre Dame, "the trumpets sounded and the 'Te Deum' was sung, after which the Vespers of the Holy Ghost [were sung] by the singers of his Majesty."[18] After this, the normal order of services was followed: Office and Mass for the Dead, and Vespers and Mass for the Virgin. This is the only mention of the Vespers of the Holy Ghost during the entire tenure of Charles and Philip, and it therefore would seem that the service was not normally celebrated at the meetings during this period. In fact, writing at some point after having been named Chancellor of the Order in 1563, Viglius de Aytta of Zuichem (1507-1577) wrote specifically that on the day of the Marian mass the chevaliers "do not go to Vespers [of the Holy Ghost] after dinner, but the next day ... they go to Mass of the Holy Ghost, which has neither offering nor sermon.[19]

The most detailed descriptions of the meetings under Charles V, however, are those of the meeting in Utrecht, in January 1546. A certain amount of information is included in Codex 40 of the Order's archives, but the most helpful description is that of a printed, six-page pamphlet, probably published shortly after the meeting. This is found in the same box as Ms. 76.E.10 of the Royal Library in Den Haag; the manuscript itself is a highly illuminated copy of the statutes of the Order, begun in 1470 and continued until the admission of Philip the Fair in 1481.[20] The pamphlet would appear to be an early copy of the description written by Jean de Vandenesse, in his "Journal des Voyages de Charles-Quint."[21] The two are virtually identical, except for what appears to be a typographical error in the pamphlet: it dates the beginning of the meeting as "janvier 1545, stile de Rome." This is clearly an error, and, in fact, Vandenesse's account, agreeing with other early sources, specifies "janvier 1546, stil de Rome."[22] Like earlier such descriptions, notably that of the Brussels meeting in 1501, the pamphlet demonstrates clearly how much these meetings were intended to show the sovereign's subjects the magnificence and power of their ruler and, by extension, his Order.

18.  "Sa majesté venue en l'eglise s'est mise en son siege soubs les armes et les aultres chevaliers aussy chascun selon son ordre, puis ont esté sonnées les trompettes et a esté chanté 'Te Deum' et an apres Vespres de St-Esprit par les chantres de sa majesté." V-AOGF Codex 35, vol. iv (Recueil D), ff. 55ʳ-56ᵛ. Also cited in HAGGH, "The Archives of the Order," 13n.
19.  "Lendemain vont... a la messe de Notre Dame.... Ledit jour ne vont apres disner aux vespres, mais le lendemain... yront oyr la messe du St-Esprit, a la quelle messe ny a offerande ny sermon." B-BR Ms. 20857, *Memoires dressez par messire Viglius de Zuichem, prévost de St-Bavon et chancellier de l'ordre de la Thoison d'or*, f. 21ᵛ. On

Viglius's biography, see KOLLER, *Au service de la Toison d'or*, 30-31.
20.  The pamphlet, entitled *Ceremonies de l'orde de la Toison d'or tenues en la ville d'Utrecht par l'empereur Charles V*, is now published in facsimile in the catalogue of an exhibition of the treasures of the Order in 1987, the *Trésors de la Toison d'or* (Brussels: Crédit Communal, 1987), 43-47.
21.  Published in GACHARD, *Collection des voyages* 2: 313-30.
22.  *Trésors de la Toison d'or*, 126, and GACHARD, *Collection des voyages*, 2: 323. In fact, the pamphlet itself shows that "1545" is an error. It states that the meeting began on "Sammedy second jour dudit mois [janvier]"; 2 January fell on Saturday in 1546, but not 1545.

On Saturday, 2 January, the chevaliers and the officers of the Order assembled at the rooms of Charles. All were clad in their long red robes and caps, the same style of robes worn by the members in the fifteenth century. They were met by a large number of the clergy, including the bishops of Utrecht, Cambrai, Nice, and Tournai, eight mitered abbots, and others. They processed toward the Cathedral, the clergy and the prelates leading on foot. After them came the gentlemen, lords, barons, counts, marquises, and princes, also on foot; they were followed on horseback by the trumpets, heralds, and kings-of-arms, all with their coats-of-arms. After them came the *Toison d'or*, the *Greffier*, the Treasurer, and the Chancellor of the Order wearing their mantles. Next came the chevaliers on horseback according to their length of membership, the newest coming first. After them came Charles himself, followed by his chief officials, amongst them the Duke of Alba. Last came the troops of the sovereign. This impressive procession wound its way to the church of Sint-Martin.

The church itself was elaborately decorated. It was hung with the series of tapestries depicting the story of Gideon and his fleece, which had been commissioned a century before by Duke Philip the Good of Burgundy for his new Order. The walls of the choir, where the chevaliers were to sit, were covered in satin and damask. The seats of the members were decorated and over each was his coat of arms on a plaque. The seat of the emperor was covered in gold cloth. The chevaliers genuflected to the altar and bowed to Charles and then were seated. In a balcony above them sat many of the spectators who were to be impressed by the ceremony, including the ambassadors of the pope, France, England, Portugal, Poland, and Venice. On the other side sat the prelates. Above the entry to the choir sat the Queen Regent with the Archduke of Austria, the Prince of Piedmont, and other noblewomen. The officers of the Order sat on a low bench in front of Charles. The Vespers were celebrated by the Bishop of Utrecht and were sung by the "singers of the chapel of his majesty."[23]

After the service, all processed in the same order back to the rooms of the Emperor, where, except for the clergy who waited at the church, they met the next morning at nine and again processed to Sint-Martin for the Mass of St. Andrew. First Charles, then each chevalier came forward separately for the offertory, each called by name and title by the *Toison d'or*. After the service they returned to Charles' lodging where they were given a thirteen-course banquet. Trumpets announced the courses and "there was abundant music and instruments."[24] The members of Charles' chapel ate together in a

23. "Chacun chevallier mis en son lieu, furent encommencées les vespres par l'Evesques d'Utrecht et chantrées par la chappelle de sa majesté." *Ceremonies de l'ordre de la Toison d'or tenues en la ville d'Utrecht*, 3.

24. "Et durant ledit disner y avoit force musique et instrumens." Vandenesse specifies that the chevaliers had decided in a meeting before the beginnning of the fête, that the *trompettes*, *chantres*, and *aultres instrumens* should be present at the banquet. GACHARD, *Collection des voyages* 2: 315.

separate room. At four, clad in black robes and caps, they processed again, now without the trumpets, to Sint-Martin for the Office of the Dead. They were to process with trumpets to and from each service, except for the Office of the Dead and the Requiem.

The Requiem Mass followed at 9:00 the next morning. At the Offertory, each chevalier presented himself with a lighted candle bearing his arms. The *Toison d'or* called representatives of the chevaliers who had died, and extinguished the candle of each. The Mass was followed by another banquet, now of fourteen courses. After the meal, the Order held a chapter until about 4:00, when they donned white robes and processed back to the church for Vespers of the Virgin. The following day saw the celebration of the Lady Mass, after which Charles announced the election of several new chevaliers. Finally, on 6 January, the Order celebrated the Mass of the Holy Ghost, though Charles did not attend, since he was suffering from his habitual gout. After the service, however, he did join the chapter with the chevaliers. Here, other new members were named.

Aside from a slight difference in services already explained and the sovereign's absence from the final mass, very little has changed from the time of the founding of the Order in 1430 and virtually nothing has altered since the changes instituted by Charles the Bold in the 1460s. This sense of continuity is underlined in two details. The first is the decoration of the church with tapestries commissioned by the founder of the Order. The other is that at the Requiem mass each meeting, including that of Utrecht, an officer preached a sermon on the founding and history of the Order and read the by-now long list of deceased members from 1430 to the date of the latest meeting.

The emphasis on grandeur and ceremony continued during two meetings under Philip II. The meeting in Antwerp is described in great detail in several sources, and it is clear that it proceeded much as had the previous meeting in Utrecht. The same services were celebrated, the same processions wended their way through the streets, the chevaliers wearing the same robes and caps. Now we find, however, that the singers are part of the procession returning from the church: "Tuesday his majesty the king went to hear Vespers in the said church [Onze Lieve Vrouw] in which all the prelates come to be present at the celebration of the said service assembled, as also the canons, chaplains, and clergy of the church and those of the chapel of the king, all dressed in rich vestments. They marched processionally, singing antiphons, to the abbey of St.-Michael, where his majesty was staying."[25] The Vespers of St. Andrew are described in a way that makes polyphony seem certain: "The divine service was sung with great honor and admirable

---

25. V-AOGF Codex 35, Recueil D, f. 84ᵛ "Le mardy que sa majesté du Roy alla oyr vespres en ladictte eglise, en laquelle s'assemblerent tous les prelats venus assister a la celebration dudict service, comme aussy peirent les chanoines, chapellains et habituez d'icelle eglise et ceulx de la chapelle du Roy, tous lesquels vestus de riches chappes, marcherent processionellement, chantans antiennes jusque a l'abbaie de St.-Michel, en laquelle sa majesté royalle estoit logié." The chapel was a part of the procession by statute of the Order, but there is no mention of them in the Utrecht descriptions.

devotion. The singing and the music were in marvelous resonance and it seemed that all the joys of the world had come there."[26] The mass of St. Andrew the next day also had both "sonnades" from the trumpets and the performance by Philip's chapel "accompanied by the organist like the day before."[27] At the banquet, the same singers sang "many melodious chansons" for the entertainment of the chevaliers and their guests.[28] The church was still decorated with Philip the Good's Gideon tapestries, and we are told that it was now decorated with tapestries celebrating Charles V's victory in Tunisia, as well.[29]

The meeting in Ghent in 1559, the Order's last *chapitre* to elect new members, also featured polyphony. One manuscript description of the event, from the Royal Library in Brussels, is particularly full of detail. According to this "both the Royal singers and [Royal] musicians" processed to the church from Philip's residence; the "trumpets, drums, and nakers, resounding, . . . entered [the church] first with great melodiousness" for the Vespers of St. Andrew. The next day, they went in the same order to Sint-Baaf "to the sacrifice of the mass, which was sung with very great ceremony and no less harmony, both vocally and with musical instruments." The chronicle also describes the services for the dead, specifying that they processed "as they had done before, though without any sounding of trumpet or other instrument of joy, because of the grief that they were demonstrating for the death of the deceased chevaliers of the said Order."[30] The chronicle also notes that a Mass of the Holy Ghost was celebrated and that the chevaliers returned to church for a mass after they had elected their new members. At this time, they also gave another banquet for the new chevaliers, "who were treated and fêted with equal magnificence and music as had been present at the banquet of the first and principal day."[31]

26. Ibid., f. 77ʳ "Le service divin fu chanté en moult grant honneur et admirable devotion, la chanterie et la musique fut en admirable resonnance et sembloit que toutes les joyées du monde s'estoyent illec venues posées . . . ."
27. DE BORS D'OVEREN, *Histoire chronologique*, f. 108ʳ "Sadicte majesté entrant et s'en mettant en son siege durant quoy les dittes trompettes sonnerent plusieurs sonnades et ce fait noterent es alées au desir des carolles d'icelle eglise. . . la messe commencée. . . laquelle fut solemnellement chantée par les chantres de laditte chapelle du roy qui furent assistés par l'organiste comme le jour precedent."
28. DE BORS D'OVEREN, *Histoire chronologique*, f. 111ʳ "Et durant ledict convive ceulx de la chappelle de sa majesté realle chanterent plusieurs melodieuses chansons. . . pour d'orner plus grande melodie. Lesdits prelats eurent leur table converté en ung aultre lieu a part comme aussy eurent ceulx de ladicte chapelle. . . ."
29. "Le nef de ceste eglise estoit tendus de moult riches tapisserie toute d'or et de soye ou estoit (selon la feste de la Toison d'or) les histoires de Gedeon et ses victoires. Ceste riche tapisserie estoit faicte du regne du duc Philippe fondateur du noble ordre de la Toison d'or car ses

armes et bannieres se demonstroyent partout. La croisiere de ceste eglise estoit enrobée plus richement—tapisserie que n'estoit la nef ces tapis estoyent tout d'or et de soye. . . . En ceste tapisserie se demonstre les victoires de grand renomme du tres puissant empereur Charles, cincquieme de son nom." AOGF Codex 35, (Recueil D), f. 75ᵛ.
30. "Retentissans les trompettes, tabours et attabales, qui alloient les premiers de tous en grant melodies." "[Ils alloient] au sacrifice de la grand Messe, la quelle se chanta avec tres grande ceremonie e non moindre harmonie tant de voix que d'instrumens musicaulx." "S'en allerent de rechef a l'eglise pour ouir les Vespres en rang et en compaignie comme aux autres fois precedentes, sans toutes fois qu'on y ouyt aucun son de trompette ou d'autre instrument de joye, a cause du doeil qu'ils representoient de la mort des chevaliers du mesme ordre decedés." B-BR Ms. 14509-10, f. 2ʳ-6ʳ: *Chapitre ou feste de l'Ordre de la Thoison d'or tenue par Philippes deuxieme du nom, Roy d'Espagne, en sa ville de Gand, l'an 1559.*
31. "Apres leur retour de laditte eglise au palais, y souperent tous ensemble, en congratulation de leurs nouveaux compagnons et confreres et furent traictez et

It is clear from the sum of these descriptions that polyphony was an integral part of both the services and the entertainment music for the banquets, just as it had been at the time of Philip the Fair, Charles the Bold, and, I believe, Philip the Good. What, then, was performed at the services? Long ago I pointed out the lack of settings appropriate to the most important of these, the St. Andrew Mass, celebrated both at meetings and on the Saint's feast in November. I also stated that I believed that the most obvious candidates for this service, and for the Mass of the Holy Ghost, were the constellation of *L'homme armé* masses. Indeed, if the cantus firmus had any significance at all in the choice of a polyphonic setting of the Ordinary for the services at the meetings, it is difficult to see what other choices were possible. This tune would have been particularly fitting for an Order composed entirely of "armed men" (knights or chevaliers), and it would have held a strong emblematic significance in an Order dedicated to a crusade against the Turks. This argument has since been taken up by Richard Taruskin, with special reference to Busnoys' *Missa L'homme armé*, and by other scholars in a more general way, among them Herbert Kellman, Alejandro Planchart, Barbara Haggh, and Kate van Orden.[32] Emilio Ros-Fábregas has now suggested that the copying of Busnoys' mass into the manuscript Barcelona M. 454 was related to its performance at the Barcelona meeting in 1519.[33]

There are also *L'homme armé* masses that can be associated specifically with Charles V, though they come from an at-first-unlikely source: Cristóbal de Morales.[34] Morales is the composer of two masses on the *l'homme armé* tune: a five-voiced paraphrase mass and a four-voiced cantus-firmus mass. Although the former had already been published in 1540, both were included in the two books of Morales' masses published under the composer's close supervision by Valerio Dorico in 1544.[35] The contract for the publica-

festoyez avec pareille magnificence et melodie, qu'avoit estée celle du disner du premier et principal jour." B-BR Ms. 14509-10, f. 5ʳ. The chronicler may be conflating two separate masses into one. He mentions the Holy Ghost Mass on the day that should have been the Marian Mass. It seems more likely that the Holy Ghost Mass was celebrated later, after the new chevaliers had been elected.

32. Herbert KELLMAN, Introduction to *Vatican City, Biblioteca Apostolica Vaticana, MS Chigi C VIII 234* (New York: Garland, 1987), viii-ix; idem, ed., *The Treasury of Petrus Alamire: Music and Art in Flemish Court Manuscripts, 1500-1535* (Ghent: Ludion, 1999), 127; Richard TARUSKIN, "Antoine Busnoys and the *L'Homme armé* Tradition," *Journal of the American Musicological Society* 39 (1986): 255-93; Alejandro Enrique PLANCHART, "Guillaume Du Fay," forthcoming in *The New Grove*, 2d. ed; HAGGH, "Archives of the Order," 28-37; Kate VAN ORDEN, "The Reign of Music," in Francis MAES, ed., *The Empire Resounds: Music in the Days of Charles V* (Leuven: Leuven University Press, 1999): 74-77.

33. ROS-FÁBREGAS, "Music and Ceremony," 385-86, and idem, "The Manuscript Barcelona, Biblioteca de Catalunya, M. 454: Study and Edition in the Context of Iberian and Continental Manuscript Traditions" (Ph.D. diss., City University of New York, 1992) I: 110-14. Ros-Fábregas also suggests that Anchieta's *Missa de nostra dona salve* from the same manuscript may have been associated with the Marian mass at the meeting. For an alternate suggestion, see below.

34. I am in large part reporting the discoveries of Professor Alison Sanders McFarland of Louisana State University, whose recent dissertation, "Cristóbal de Morales and the Imitation of the Past: Music for the Mass in Sixteenth-Century Rome" (Ph.D. diss., University of California, Santa Barbara, 1999) discusses the findings in detail.

35. *Christophori Moralis hyspalensis. Missarum, liber primus* (Rome: Dorico, 1544); *Christophori Moralis hyspanlensis. Missarum, liber secundus* (Rome: Dorico, 1544).

tion of these masses exists, and it is clear that the project was initiated by Morales him-self: he went to Dorico with a plan to publish fifteen masses, and according to the contract he was responsible for the order of the masses and their decorated initials. Either Dorico or Morales suggested as a model Antico's 1516 mass print in folio, and this was used as a general guide to the layout.[36] Morales' masses, however, were lengthier than those published by Antico, and the original one-volume project became two.

In Dorico's volume the large "K" initials that begin each mass are carefully chosen to illustrate the subject of the mass' basis. That of the *Missa de Beata Virgine*, for example, depicts the Madonna and Child; the "K" for the *Missa Si bona suscepimus*, based on a Verdelot motet whose text is taken from the book of Job ("If we have received good from the Lord, should we not also receive evil?"), shows Job kneeling, covered with boils and a banderole bearing the phrase "Dominus dedit; Dominus abstulit" ("The Lord giveth and the Lord taketh away"). Of special importance is that three of the masses show connections to Charles in their initials. The *Missa Mille regretz*, based on the chanson by Josquin known in Spain as the "cancion del emperador," displays the imperial symbol of the bicipital eagle in its opening initial.[37] The four-voiced *Missa L'homme armé* is particularly clear. Its initial depicts an aged armed man above whom is Charles' personal device: the two Pillars of Hercules with ban-deroles displaying "Plus ultra."[38] The five-voiced *Missa L'homme armé* shows a younger knight without a banderole, and Alison McFarland argues that this, too, must be associated with Charles.[39] Owen Rees, in fact, believes that Charles was himself the "armed man" in his role as sovereign of the Order of the Golden Fleece. According to Rees, Charles adopted "Plus ultra" as his device specifically for his first meeting as head of the confraternity in 1516, thus demonstrating his resolve to lead the Order against Islam ("le doubté Turcq" of the fif-teenth-century *L'homme armé* chanson) and to retake the Holy Land. He also argues that Charles knew Morales' five-voiced mass so well that, when Guerrero had his own *L'homme armé* Mass sung for him, he could recognize that it was closely based on Morales' work.[40]

A problem with this theory is that Morales himself had not believed to have had any particular association with Charles or his circle. Professor McFarland, however, has produced new documentary proof that he did. As a member of the papal chapel from 1535 to 1545, Morales would have met Charles several times: at Charles' entry into Rome in April 1536, at Nice for the meeting between Charles and Paul III, at Bussetto for anoth-er meeting between the two in 1543, and perhaps in Genoa earlier in the same year. Charles

---

36. *Liber quindecim missarum electarum quae per excellentissimos musicos compositae fuerunt* (Rome: Antico, 1516). Suzanne Cusick, *Valerio Dorico, Music Printer in Sixteenth-Century Rome* (Ann Arbor: UMI, 1981), 64-67 and 95-101.

37. This was already shown by Owen REES, "*Mille regretz* as Model: Possible Allusions to 'The Emperor's Song' in the Chanson Repertory," *Journal of the Royal Musical*

*Association* 120 (1995): 44.

38. Owen REES, "Guerrero's *L'homme armé* Masses and Their Models," *Early Music History* 12 (1993): 50.

39. McFARLAND, "Cristóbal de Morales," 50-52.

40. REES, "Guerrero's *L'homme armé* Masses," 47-48 and 50-54.

was resident in the city at a time when Morales was given a leave of absence from the choir specifically to go there. Even more important is McFarland's discovery that Morales held a second position while a member of the papal chapel. From 1534 he was chaplain to Ferdinando de Silva, Count of Cifuentes. De Silva, a Spaniard resident in Rome, was Charles V's ambassador to the Holy See.[41] It is my contention that the four-voiced *Missa L'homme armé*, with its "Plus ultra" initial and the five-voiced mass, which Charles apparently knew well, were both composed for him, and that they are likely associated with various of the annual St. Andrew's Day celebrations.

There is a further mass that could well be associated with the Marian mass of the confraternity's meeting. This is Pierre de la Rue's *Missa Sancta Dei genetrix*, which occurs uniquely in Jena, Universitätsbibliothek, Chorbuch 21.[42] Since this source was copied after 1521, it may well be a late work of the master. The editor of this work, Herman Keahey, has drawn attention to a strange citation of the end of the A section of the *L'homme armé* tune in the Credo of this mass (see Example 1, Bassus). As Professor Keahey points out, it is difficult to believe that listeners, singers, or composer would not have been aware of this passage.[43] Indeed, it must have held a particularly strong emblematic significance to be included within the Credo of a Marian mass. It would seem possible, then, that La Rue composed this work shortly before his retirement in 1516 for Charles V's first meeting of the Order in the same year.

Suggestions can also be made about the repertory of music not related to the Ordinary of the mass. Before the meeting in Utrecht, Charles asked the chevaliers to convene to make suggestions as to ceremony for the coming meeting, probably because the Order had not met for fifteen years and also because Charles himself had intended to begin the meeting in December, but was unable to travel from 's-Hertogenbosch to Utrecht because of his gout.[44] Those suggestions that were accepted were incorporated into special copies of the statutes that included the ceremonies for the meetings and St. Andrew's day. One of these copies is extant in the Royal Library in Brussels, Ms. II 5799. This includes both the original fifteenth-century ceremonies and, beginning on folio 72ʳ, the "Ceremonies of the most noble Order to the Golden Fleece Commanded by the Emperor Charles V."[45] Actually there is little that seems new in these instructions; virtually all of them can be found as having been traditional parts of the

41. McFarland, "Cristóbal de Morales," 43, 50 and passim. Morales's trips are described there in a revised biography of the composer (Ibid., 14-60).

42. On this manuscript see Herbert Kellman, ed., *The Treasury of Petrus Alamire*, 103.

43. Nigel St. John Davison, J. Evan Kreider, and T. Herman Keahey, eds. *Pierre de la Rue. Opera Omnia*, 6 (American Institute of Musicology, Neuhausen-Stuttgart: Hänssler, 1996): XVIII. I am grateful to Professor Keahey for calling my attention to this passage before the publication of the edition.

44. Gachard, *Collection des voyages*, 2: 313-14.

45. "Ceremonies du tres insigne Ordre du Thoison d'or ordonnées par L'Empereur Charles Cincquiesme de ce nom.... L'an mil cinq cent quarante cinq au chappitre par luy tenu en sa cité d'Utrecht." B-BR Ms. II 5799, f. 72ʳ.

Example 1   Pierre DE LA RUE, *Missa Sancta Dei genetrix*, Credo, mm. 25-29

(after Nigel St. John DAVISON, J. Evan KREIDER, and T. Herman KEAHEY, eds. *Pierre de la Rue. Opera Omnia*, 6 (American Institute of Musicology, Neuhausen-Stuttgart, Hänssler-Verlag, 1966), 9

meetings. There are two articles, however, that allow us to suggest specific polyphonic works that must have been performed.

The first of these is Article 28, which concerns the celebration of Vespers and Compline of St. Andrew: "The prelate ordered to say Vespers must begin and, at the Magnificat, must carry the incense to the chief and sovereign alone, and when Vespers are finished Compline and a motet are sung."[46] I pass over the Magnificat, which surely could have been sung polyphonically, to concentrate on the motet.[47] There are not

46. B-BR Ms. II 5799, f. 81ʳ "xxviij. Et ce faict le prelat ordonné a dire vespres les doibt commencher et au Magnificat d'icelles honnestement assister porter l'encens au chief et souverain seul et les vespres finies se chantent les complies et ung motet." HAGGH, "The Archives of the Order," 11n, quotes a portion of this same passage from V-AOGF, but does not emphasize the prescriptive nature of the article. It is not only a description of what happened at the Utrecht meeting, but it is rather a directive for what should happen at all meetings.

47. For the Magnificat, one could propose, however, any of the many settings by Morales or Gombert. Clement A. MILLER, "Jerome Cardan on Gombert, Phinot, and Carpentras," *The Musical Quarterly* 58 (1972): 415, suggests that the Gombert's motets were written to obtain the composer's release from a galley. Most recently, Alan LEWIS, "Nicolas Gombert's First Book of Four-Voice Motets: Anthology or Apologia," in MAES, ed., *The Empire Resounds*, 50, believes them to be later works.

many works that stem from imperial circles that could have been appropriate to an office of St. Andrew, but there are three that I believe must have been intended for this purpose, though at different moments of the service. The first is the anonymous *Maxsimilla Cristo amabilis* contained in Ms. Royal 8 G. vii of the British Library. This source, as Herbert Kellman has shown, is one of the Netherlands complex of manuscripts, probably copied after 1516.[48]

The four-voiced *Maxsimilla* is a setting of an antiphon for the Vespers of St. Andrew and is stylistically a surprise (see Appendix). It contains little trace of the structural imitation established by La Rue, Josquin, and their generation as the basis of motet and mass composition. It is not, on the other hand, an ineffective work: there is, for example, the three-fold statement of the opening material (mm. 1-6, 7-13, and 23-28), the pleasant shift to triple meter (mm. 45-52), and a concluding section in imperfect tempus (mm. 53-59) featuring block harmonies with only slight elaboration in the antepenultimate and penultimate measures and almost syllabic text declamation. Nor does the work seem earlier than the sixteenth century. Rather, at fifty-nine measures it is much shorter, simpler, and more straightforward in style than a typical motet. In fact, *Maxsimilla* does not seem to be a motet, in the sense of a work sung, as Article 28 suggests, after the celebration of Vespers and Compline and itself the central object of the attention of those at the service. *Maxsimilla* appears instead to be actual liturgical music, a true antiphon intended to adorn the service, but not to the extent of demanding the full attention of the devout. One chronicle shows that both antiphons and motets were performed at the service, in a way that at least hints at polyphonic settings of the former. In 1559 at Ghent "they began to sing Vespers and Compline with all possible ceremony with their antiphons and motets in homage to God and to his apostle St. Andrew, chosen protector of the said Order."[49]

A further possibility exists: the unusual character of *Maxsimilla* may have to do with performance practices. The text does not fit the lower voices nearly as well as it does the Cantus: in order to underlay the text to these voices, the editor must divide several notes and place syllables under more than one note in ligatures. It may be, therefore, that only the Cantus was sung, accompanied by organ. This would certainly explain the lack of imitation in the lower voices, and, at least twice during the sixteenth century, there is documentation of organ performance in the Office of St. Andrew. Ainaud de Lasarte, citing from an

48. KELLMAN, introduction to *London, British Library, MS Royal 8 G. vii* (New York: Garland, 1987), vii; and idem., *The Treasury of Petrus Alamire*, 111. As Kellman points out in the latter source, a date of *c.*1513 was recently proposed by Honey MECONI, "Another Look at Absalon," *Tijdschrift van de koninklijke vereniging voor nederlandse muziekgeschiedenis* 48 (1998): 3-29. Kellman was the first to point out the sig-

nificance of *Maxsimilla* for the Order.

49. "Lors se commencerent a chanter les Vespres et Complies en toutte celebrité avec leurs antiphons et motets a la hommauge de Dieu e de son apostre St-André, choisi protecteur dudit ordre." B-BR Ms. 14509-10, f. 3ʳ.

anonymous local chronicle, says that, for this service, the principal organ of the cathedral accompanied the Royal Chapel at the meeting in Barcelona in 1519.[50] The same is true of the meeting in Antwerp in 1556. As we have seen, the Imperial Chapel sang the Mass of St. Andrew there "accompanied by the organist like the day before."[51] If this is the case, then a further function for *Maxsimilla* can be suggested: it may also have been used as processional music. It is simple enough to have been sung by the members of the chapel, accompanied by the core of sackbuts, as the procession made its way from the Emperor's residence to the church, as was required in the official Ceremonial of the Order.[52]

The second work for Vespers of St. Andrew seems much closer to the intention of Article 28. This is Thomas Crecquillon's *Andreas Christi famulus*, the text of which is a compilation of an antiphon for Second Vespers for the Feast of St. Andrew, an antiphon for Matins on the same feast, and a free prayer which in Phalesius' print dedicated to Crecquillon's motets reads "Sancte Andrea, ora pro nobis."[53] Although it is ascribed to Morales in the index of a peripheral German print of 1564,[54] Barton Hudson believes the motet to be by Crecquillon,[55] who was in the Flemish chapel of Charles in the 1540s and perhaps the 1550s as well. Based on my study of the Order at the time of Philip the Fair, in fact, Hudson proposes that the motet was written for a meeting of the Order, and suggests the meeting of 1556. I concur with Hudson's attribution, though I prefer the meeting of 1546, when Crecquillon was definitely in imperial service and when a new article of the Order's Ceremonial specifically required a motet to be sung.

*Andreas Christi famulus* is an extraordinary work, everything that *Maxsimilla Cristo amabilis* is not. It is in two large *partes*, totaling 131 measures in Hudson's transcription. It is for eight voices, one of only two motets by Crecquillon for such a large ensemble.[56] Here, furthermore, Crecquillon composes eight real voices, not divided into smaller choirs of four voices each, but rather all eight constantly involved in the polyphony. Only at the mention of suffering ("et in passione socius") does the composer move to a kind of antiphonal play, first lower voices, then higher. Otherwise this motet is unrelievedly

50. Ainaud de LASARTE, *El Toisó d'or*, 100; see also Ros-FÁBREGAS, "The Manuscript Barcelona, Biblioteca de Catalunya" 1: 112.

51. See the discussion of the Antwerp meeting above. The service the day before was, of course, Vespers of St. Andrew.

52. B-BR Ms. II 5799, ff. 39ᵛ-40ʳ: "et yra ladite procession chantant respons et anthiennes jusques a l'eglise, a laquelle procession, service et solempnité dudit monsieur Sainct Andrieu pourront estre pour contemplacion et honneur de monseigneur Sainct." This is the original part of the Ceremonial, not that modified by Charles V.

53. *Opus sacrarum cantionum (Quas vulgo moteta vocant) Thoame*

*Criquillon augustissimi Caroli Quinti Imperatoris chori Magistri celeberrimi...* (Leuven: Phalesius and Bellerius, 1576).

54. *Thesaurus musicus continens selectissimas octo, septem, sex, quinque et quatuor vocum harmonias...* (Nuremburg: Montanus and Neuber, 1564). The ascription to Morales is included only in the index, not over the music.

55. Barton HUDSON, ed., *Thomasii Crequillonis, Opera Omnia*, 5 (American Institute of Musicology, Neuhausen-Stuttgart: Hänssler, 1990): XXI. The motet is scored on pp. 1-9 there.

56. Crecquillon's other eight-voiced motet, *Pater pecavi* (sic), is often attributed to Clemens. See ibid., XXVI.

polyphonic and imitative. Nevertheless, Crecquillon enlivens it with constantly shifting points of imitation so that, even though the style is the typical, pervasive imitation of Low-Countries sacred music, a sense of variety is produced. Particularly impressive is the conclusion of the motet, which dedicates the final twenty-six tempora to the corporate prayer, "Sancte Andrea, ora pro nobis."

If Crecquillon is the more likely author of this *Andreas Christi famulus* because of the centrality of the source that ascribes it to him, Morales is the composer of another *Andreas Christi famulus*, for five voices, which combines the antiphon of the incipit and the same corporate prayer with different antiphons for St. Andrew. Instead of "Dilexit Andream Dominus in odorem suavitatis" at the *secunda pars*, Morales chooses "Videns Andreas crucem cum gaudio dicebat: Salve crux preciosa, quae in corpore Christi dedicata es. O bona crux."[57] Given the ties between Morales and Charles V demonstrated by McFarland and discussed above, and the likelihood that his two *L'homme armé* masses were written for Charles (and for his confraternity), it seems at least possible that Morales' work could be related to the Order.

The source picture reinforces this possibility considerably. The work is found in one contemporaneous Spanish manuscript, Toledo, Biblioteca Capitular de la Catedral Metropolitana B 17; Morales, of course, was *maestro de cappilla* there from 1545 to 1547, and the manuscript was copied in 1550 and 1551, probably for use at the Cathedral itself.[58] Morales' motet is printed only once, however: in Antwerp. It appears in 1556 in the fourth book of the *Sacrum cantionum* for five and six voices of Waelrant and Laet.[59] Morales is not well represented in the printed music books of the Low Countries, and at this date, he had had only two works published there: Susato had issued his *Tu es Petrus* in 1546, and Phalesius had published the "Et in spiritum sanctum" from his *Missa Mille regretz* in an arrangement for two lutes in 1552.[60] Weaver, in his study of Waelrant, rightly wonders how the printer obtained this single motet by the Spanish composer.[61] The appearance of *Andreas Christi famulus* so far from the area of its composer's activity (Italy and Spain), and at the center of

57. Modern edition in Higinio ANGLÉS, ed., *Cristóbal de Morales. Opera Omnia*, 2 (Barcelona: Consejo Superior de Investagaziones Científicas, 1953), 157-65.

58. Charles HAMM and Herbert KELLMAN, *Census-Catalogue of Manuscript Sources of Polyphonic Music, 1400-1550*, 3 (American Institute of Musicology, Neuhausen-Stuttgart: Hänssler-Verlag, 1984): 206. It is also found in the slightly later Spanish manuscript Valladolid, Parroquia de Santiago, Ms. s.s. ("Diego Sánchez Codex") with the text "Hoc est praeceptus meum." See ibid., 4 (Neuhausen-Stuttgart, 1988), 8-9.

59. *Sacrarum cantionum (vulgo hodie moteta vocant) quinque et sex vocum. . . . Liber quartus* (Antwerp: Waelrant and Laet, 1556). I exclude here the intabulation for two lutes pub-

lished by Valderrabano. See below for this version.

60. *Tu es Petrus* was published in the *Liber secundus sacrarum cantionum, quinque vocum* (Antwerp: Susato, 1546); the "Et in spiritum," in *Hortus musarum in quo tanquam flosculi quidam selectissimorum carminum collecti sunt* (Leuven: Phalesius, 1552). In 1569 Phalesius was to issue three more motets ascribed to Morales in books two and three of his *Selectissimarum sacrarum cantionum . . . flore, trium vocum*. See Henri VANHULST, *Catalogue des éditions de musique publiées à Louvain par Pierre Phalèse et ses fils, 1545-1578* (Brussels: Académie Royale de Belgique, 1984), 143-45.

61. Robert Lee WEAVER, *Waelrant and Laet: Music Publishers in Antwerp's Golden Age* (Warren, MI: Harmonie Park Press, 1995), 300.

the Order's sphere of influence, surely argues for its function as a motet for the group's worship. This argument is considerably strengthened by the fact that *Andreas Christi famulus* was published in 1556 in Antwerp itself, where the Order had met in January of the same year.

The nature of the work also argues for its use by the Order. Both settings—by Crecquillon and Morales—include the particularly apt corporate prayer, "Sancte Andrea ora pro nobis," which would be especially fitting for a religious confraternity whose patron was St. Andrew. Morales, moreover, sets the prayer in the manner of an ostinato, repeating it some eighteen times in the Quintus.[62] He sets up a rigid pattern for these repetitions. For the ostinato's melodic material, he selects the passage from the Litany of the Saints that is actually intended to set "Sancte Andrea, ora pro nobis."[63] The ostinato is heard alternately on g' and d"; each statement spans four tempora and each is preceded by three tempora of rests. Morales is clearly concerned that the prayer be audible. He chooses to make the Quintus a Cantus part so that the pattern will not be buried within the five-voiced texture. When the pattern enters on d", it is invariably the highest sounding voice, Cantus I either resting or singing below it. When the pattern enters on g', Morales most often has another voice rest in order to thin the texture, and he frequently chooses to have Cantus I as that voice, thus throwing the ostinato into even higher relief.

If Waelrant did obtain the motet through the Order's meeting in his city, then it must have been in use by the confraternity for some time. Morales had died in 1553, and the motet had already appeared in an intabulation for two vihuelas in 1547 in Valderrabano's *Silva de sirenas.*[64] It must, therefore, have been written before the Order's meeting in Utrecht in 1546 and it thus easily stretches back to the time of Charles V as sovereign of the Order. Any of the several occasions between 1535 and 1543 that McFarland's research has shown that Morales and Charles probably met would be possible occasions for the presentation of a motet dedicated to the patron saint of the Order of the Golden Fleece to its sovereign.

Article 50 of the Ceremonial contains information concerning another motet, again to be sung after the service: "The same day [as the celebration of the Requiem Mass] the chief and sovereign, the chevaliers, and the officers, clad in their long robes of white damask [and] their caps of red velour, in order and accompanied as they were the day before, must go to the solemn Vespers and Compline, which shall be sung to Our Lady. When it is finished an

62.  Waelrant changed this to "Sancte Andrea gaudet in coelis," apparantly to make a pair with the motet *Sanctus Wilhelmus amicus Dei,* which contains in the Quintus the text "Sanctus Wilhelmus gaudet in coelis." The latter motet opens the book because of its aptness for the dedicatee Wilhelm Trainer. Since Morales's motet immediately follows this, the two form a set with the same discrete text in the Quintus. See WEAVER, *Waelrant and Laet,* 169, as well as idem, *A Descriptive Bibliographical Catalog of the Music Printed by Hubert Waelrant and Jan de Laet*

(Warren, MI: Harmonie Park Press, 1994), 48-52.
63.  See, for example, *Liber usualis* (Paris: Desclée, 1964), 836.
64.  Enrriquez de VALDERRABANO, *Libro de musica de vihuela intitulado Silva de sirenas* (Valladolid: Francisco Fernandez de Cordoba, 1547), ff. 49ᵛ-50ʳ. Valderrabano treats the corporate prayer as though it were the actual Litany of the Saints, changing the name of the saint with each repetition, beginning with "Sancte Andrea" and concluding with "Sancta Maria."

'Inviolata' is sung."[65] This is almost assuredly the Marian *prosa* "Inviolata, integra et casta es," known to us through the famous setting of Josquin Des Prez, though there are numerous settings of the text. I do not reject the possibility that the chapel could have sung Josquin's work, though there is another that seems more likely for the mid-sixteenth century: the five-voiced setting by Nicolas Gombert, who had been the *maître des enfans* in Charles' chapel in the 1530s. The work was first published in Gombert's first book of five-voiced motets, issued by Scotto in 1539, just at the time the composer was released from imperial service.[66]

Gombert's *Inviolata* is a worthy partner to *Andreas Christi famulus*. Like Crecquillon's and Morales' motets, Gombert's elaboration of the Marian *prosa* is a highly ornate work. It is in two large *partes*, here totaling 162 measures in transcription.[67] With its tranquil surface, its lack of simultaneous cadences, its relentlessly imitative fabric, and the asymmetrical entry of voices, it would have been a serene and fitting conclusion to the Office of the Virgin at the Order's meetings. Indeed, the placement of a Marian motet after the evening offices neatly parallels the widespread tradition in the Low Countries of the Marian *lof*, an informal service that featured the singing of a Marian motet like the *Salve Regina* or, perhaps, the *Inviolata*.[68]

The pattern established by the earlier sovereigns of the Order of the Golden Fleece thus continues under its sovereigns in the sixteenth century. The meetings and St. Andrew's Day ceremonies continue to be ornamented by major polyphonic works, some of which they merely adopted, like the Requiem Mass of Du Fay, and others they commissioned especially for the services of the Order, like Crecquillon's *Andreas Christi famulus*. Whatever the original purpose of the pieces, the Order's services seem to have included works by Du Fay, Busnoys, Josquin, La Rue, Morales, Gombert, and Crecquillon, among others. During the reign of Charles V and the first years of the reign of Philip II, they remain important consumers and patrons of sacred music. Since the annual St. Andrew's feast persisted even after the dissolution of the official chapters, they continued to adopt polyphony for their at services at least throughout his reign.

---

65. B-BR Ms. II.5799, f. 86ᵛ. "Le mesme jour le chief et souverain, les chevaliers, les officiers habillez de robbes longues de dams blancq et de leurs chapperons de velours cramoisi a bourlette en l'ordre et accompagnés comme le jour precedent doibvent aller aux Vespres solempnelles et complyes que se chanteront de Notre Dame, lesquels finis, se chant 'Inviolata.'" Cited from V-AOGF in HAGGH, "Archives of the Order," n.I I. Haggh again does not emphasize the prescriptive nature of the article, treating it as a description of the Utrecht meeting.

66. *Musica excelentissimi Nicolai Gomberti (vulgo motecta quinque vocum nuncupata)... Liber primus quinqe vocum* (Venice: O.

Scotto, 1539). For Gombert's release from imperial service and his condemnation to the galleys, see MILLER, "Jerome Cardan on Gombert," 413-15 and, most recently, Alan LEWIS, "Nicolas Gombert's First Book of Four-Voice Motets.".

67. Joseph SCHMIDT-GÖRG, ed., *Nicolai Gombert. Opera Omnia*, 7 (American Institute of Musicology, 1968): 47-54.

68. For the *lof* tradition in Antwerp, see Kristine K. FORNEY, "Music, Ritual, and Patronage in the Church of Our Lady, Antwerp," *Early Music History* 7 (1987): 8-12.

## Addendum

After having submitted this essay, I left for Italy to work on other topics. While there, however, I found a new, highly detailed description of the ceremonies of the Order of the Golden Fleece for St. Andrew's Day, 1519. This account was written by Count Nicola Maffei (*c.*1487-1536), the distinguished representative of a noble Mantuan family, who was to serve as Federico II Gonzaga's *maestro di camera* from 1520. In 1519 Federico sent Maffei to Spain and Portugal on political matters and to extend his respects to Charles V at the time he was to be officially named Holy Roman Emperor in Molin de Rey, near Barcelona. On 1 December, the day of the last ceremonies, Maffei wrote a letter of some seven pages detailing the festivities of the Order. The letter has been partly published by Guido Rebecchini in a local Mantuan journal,[69] and I transcribe it here for three reasons: because of its value to the understanding of the Order's ceremonies, because Rebecchini's article is perhaps not widely available, and because it does not exist in an English translation. Although the document is not the equal of Niccolò Frigio's description of the 1501 *fête* (see above), in that it does not mention specific works, this new account complements it by supplying an analogous description of the St. Andrew's Day ceremonies. Maffei, like Frigio, is essentially interested in reporting the pageantry of the occasion. For the Mantuan diplomat, as for his contemporaries, the splendor of the proceedings, the dress of the participants, and the brilliance of the banquet were designed to be direct and conscious reflections of the power and magnificence of the court. For the music historian, their grandeur demonstrates clearly the way in which music itself had become an integral part of this process.

### Letter from Count Nicola Maffei to Marchese Federico II Gonzaga
### Molin de Rey, Spain, 1 December 1519
Archivio di Stato di Mantova, Archivio Gonzaga, Busta 585, ff. 110r-111r bis.[70]

*Illustrissimo et Excellentissimo Signor mio observandissimo . . . . Here per tempo retornai a Molin de Rey per veder la cerimonia del Tosone che celebra ogni anno questo invictissimo Re nel giorno di Sancto Andrea, la quale non mi par tacer a Vostra Signoria.*

*Venero la matina a corte tutti li cavallieri del Ordine predicto del Tosone con pompa grandissima de gentilhomini et servitori vestiti a livree loro sopra ginetti et mule richamente guarnite, che furono a numero dodeci che più non si ne trova al presente drieto la corte, et circa alle deceotto, hore italiane, uscitte il Re de la camera sua ove sta ad dar audientia, et vene in una sala tutta aparata de muraglie finissime fatte in figure, in capo de la quale si vedea una sedia regale tutta guarnita di brocato d'oro rizo sopra rizo et veluto cremesino a liste di largheza come era il brocato. A meggio a man dextra stava uno altare sopra il quale erano sei imagini de Apostoli de argento sopra dorato, alte forsi duo braza, con altri tanti candeleri, con torze accese et molti vasi pur di argento come è ditto, che faceano tanto più bella vista quanto che erano optimamente partiti sovra tre gradi, oltra di ciò vi era anchor un'altra imagine di Nostra Donna et una croce tutte di oro et cariche di gioie preciosissime, poste in meggio de lo altare tra le preditte cose, ma nel grado più abasso stava la croce et di sopra nel secundo la predicta imagine di Nostra Donna. A man sinistra era accommodato [110v] uno scabello longo come poteva capir tutta la sala alquanto eminente et tutto adobato di veluto cremesino, loco deputato alli*

69. REBECCHINI, "Nicola Maffei ambasciatore presso Carlo V nel 1519-1520," *Quaderni di Palazzo Te* 5 (1999): 98-103. Rebecchini does not transcribe the section at the end of the document on the Requiem Mass of 1 December. On Maffei, see Idem, "Per una biografia di Nicola Maffei," *Civiltà mantovana*, 3/103 (1996): 75-92.

70. I have added all accents, capitalization, and punctuation, and have resolved all abbreviations in this and all documents quoted in this study. The transcription presented here differs in only a few details from that of Rebecchini.

cavallieri per udir la messa, la quale fu cantata da l'Episcopo de la Indias con da circa trenta musici excellentissimi. La pianeda et tunicelle che lui, et li altri dui preti che cantorono la epistola et evangelio, haveano in dosso erano di brocato d'oro rizo sopra rizo fornite per meggio et li collari di varie e molte gioie de grande valuta per quanto si potea comprendere.

Stava il Re in la sedia sua vestito d'una robba di panno di argento texuto a schachi, l'un soglio, l'altro rizo sopra rizo de la più bella maniera del mondo con fodra de zebelini di belli che sia possibile a trovar; havea il saglio di panno d'oro tirato pur a schachi ma piccoli, una di seta negra, l'altro rizo sopra rizo, tutto frappato con sotto tela di argento; teneva zupone del medemo lavoro. Li cavallieri furon posti cadauno al loco suo con questo ordine: el primo era Monsignor di Chievres con robba di raso negro fodrata di lupo cervero, et saglio di tabbé d'oro tirato in negro; seguiva Don Zoanne Emanuel, qual portava saglio et robba di veluto negro fodrata de zebelini; presso di lui era il Conte Palatino con veste di panno di argento tirato fodrata de zebelini et saglio di panno d'oro tirato tuto tagliato con sotto raso cremesino; a questo succedea il Marchese di Brandinburgo sopra li altri pomposissimo, vestiva un robba richissima di panno di argento rizo texuto a foliami d'oro rizo sopra rizo con fodra de zebellini bellissimi in excellentia, meggio il salio era del medemo panno di argento, l'altro meggio di brocato in negro fatto a friate reportato l'un sovra l'altro et tagliato, se gli vedea poi una camisa con il collare [110 bisʳ] alto di oro di martilio, et dentro vi erano ligate perle di bona grossezza et molte et varie gioie poste a ordine che molto ben comparevano, havea in la beretta uno gioiello belissimo extimato di grandissimo valore, al canto portava una spada guarnita di purissimo oro con lavoriero di mirabile artificio. Doppoi gli era Monsignor di Porsiane, nepote di Chievres con veste de tabbé di argento fodrata de zebelini et il saglio del medemo ma frappato et fodrato di raso negro; el cavallarizzo maggiore li stava appresso adobato di veste di argento tirato fatto a canestri fodrata de zebelini con saglio di brocato d'oro richissimo. El septimo era il Duca di Alva adobato di robba negra di veluto con la fodra d'una pelle nigrissima ch'è molto stimata qui, et tiene il pele longo come quello del lupo cervero, vestiva in saglio di veluto negro frapato con raso de medemo colore di sotto. L'altro era il Contestabile di Castiglia, quale havea la veste di veluto morello fodrata de ginetti con saglio d'oro tirato; drieto a lui era il Duca di Besser con robba negra di veluto fodrata di bellissimi zebelini con saglio di tabbé d'oro tirato; teneva il decimo loco il principe di Bisignano adobato di veste di panno di argento texuto a guisa de tovalia con fodra de zebelini, et portava saglio meggio del ditto panno di argento l'altro meggio di veluto negro. Seguiva doppoi Monsignor di Fienes vestito di robba di raso leonato fodrata di veluto negro con saglio di brocatello. Lo ultimo era Monsignor di Beoren, figlio di Monsignor de Ros, con veste di raso cremesino fodrata de gatti di Spagna et havea il saglio a liste di tela d'oro [110 bisᵛ] et veluto negro frapato l'un sopra l'altro. Portavano poi tutti al collo la collana d'oro richissima, fata con li azalini secundo si costuma et con il Toson pendente.

Essendo cantato lo evangelio, voltossi uno sacerdote che serviva alla messa e fece uno sermone in lingua castigliana molto dotto, benché non si extendesse in altro che in la importantia di questo ordine, el quale laudò et magnificò assai, attribuendo la origine sua ad Philippo Duca di Borgogna che lo ordinò a persecutione de scismatici, narrò doppoi tutte le cose a che sono tenuti gli cavallieri, exhortandoli con dolce et accomodate parole, che sì come il Re li havea honorati di questa dignità, così anche volessero usar bene di quella et secundo erano debitori et esser fideli ad sua Maestà, la quale pregò in fine del parlar suo ad voler amare et tener chari ditti cavaglieri et esserli exemplo di sancta vita. Molte altre cerimonie se fecero che sogliono usarse ne le misse regali, le quali non scrivo a Vostra Excellentia per haverle lei vedute molte volte.

Finite le cerimonie et missa insieme, levossi il Re et con tutti li cavallieri inanti per ordine a dui a dui andò in camera sua ove stette fin tanto che furono apparechiate le tavole per disnar in la medema sala, perché nel palazo non era loco maggior né più al proposito per il bisogno. Dove era la sedia, posero la mensa di Sua Maestà con sopra molti beli vasi di oro, ma tra li altri vi ne erano tre bellissimi et di valuta grandissima: uno si era la salinera fatta di oro purissimo in forma di galea longa circa brazo et alta meggio con il piede lavorato a fogliami di grande magisterio con molte petre preciose per dentro poste; li altri dui erano vasi da bevere, uno di cristalo, l'altro di calcidonio con li piedi d'oro alti un palmo [111ʳ] del medemo lavoro di quello de la galea. Nel loco del scabello fu preperata una altra mensa per li dodeci cavallieri che con un cubito si coniungeva con quella del Re, et vi erano sopra dodeci salinare et altre tante coppe per bever di purissimo oro. De lo altare fecero la credenza miraculosa da vedere per la infinità de vasi de oro et argento, de' quali vi ne erano sei alti duo braza, molto belli et artificiosamenti lavorati, alcuni altri puoco meno grandi, molti alquanto più piccoli di questi, et grande copia de la grandezza d'uno bichiero, tra quali ni erano assai di oro. De le taze et confettere non parlo che si ne vedea cumuli di dece, quindeci et fin in vinti, l'una sovra l'altra. Fatto questo, Sua Alteza pur con li *cavallieri avanti retornò in sala, et tutti se assetorono a tavola per ordine come stavano ala messa. Il Re havea dui ministri gentil-homini riccamente vestiti de saglij di brocato d'oro et robbe di drappo fodrate de martiri con collane d'oro al collo, che continuamente stetero alla mensa ad servirlo, et gli cavaglieri n'haveano uno per uno similmente vestito di drappo con le veste fodrate, chi de martiri, chi de lupo cervero et altri de gatti de Spagna et zanetti. Quattro volte si andò alla cusina et per ogni volta portavasi dodice vivande ad sua Maestà et sei per cadauno cavagliero, tutte varie l'una da l'altra. Le vivande veneano a questo modo: da la cusina fino alla porta de la sala erano accompagnate da vinti trombette, dece del sono che si usa in Italia, l'altre d'una altra maniera, et fino alla mensa da dui mazeri e da lo Araldo che portava in dosso* [111ᵛ] *un manto con sopra pinctate tutte le insigne de li Regni di questo dignissimo Re; seguiva poi li dui siniscalchi di sua Alteza con drieto dodeci gentilhomini riccamente vestiti con saglij et robbe di drappo fodrate di bellissime fodre, et la maior parte di loro havea le collane d'oro al collo, che portavano le vivande per la bocca di sua Maestà. El primo de questi scuderi ogni volta portò una imagine de zeladia di alteza d'uno brazo et più, molto bella e ben fatta:*[71] *la prima fu un Sancto Andrea colorato secundo bisognava per pinger uno homo con vestimenti, l'altra era una vergine tutta di bianco, in grembo de la quale stava uno unicorno dormendo, la terza era una donna che lactava un fanciullo fatta pur in bianco, et l'ultima uno homo con corona di fronde in capo a cavallo d'uno leone et li squarciava la bocca con le mani; doppoi ditti scuderi erano li dodeci siniscalchi de li cavallieri per ordine, cadauno con drieto li suoi sei scuderi con vivande di sei sorte come è ditto, che faceano bel vedere perché erano tutti gentilhomini de la familia del Re et vestiti come quelli di sopra. Il pasto fu lautissimo et abundantissimo et durò per spatio di due grosse hore in grande festa et iubilo. Si sentivano soni di cornemuse, di flauti, et di tamburi, accompagnati di arpe, che mandavano dolce armonia. Finito di disnare, lo Reverendissimo Cardinale Tortosa et il Reverendo Episcopo di Badaiosa benedissero la mensa sì come havean anche fatto nanti disnare. Fatta la benedictione, Sua Alteza levossi con tutti li cavallieri et si ridussero in una camera a far consiglio, che così è usanza, dove stetero fino* [111 bisʳ] *a l'hora del vespro che poi retornorno in sala, et assettandosi cadauno al loco suo, fu cantato un vespro molto solenne, al quale fu fatto fine, il Conte Palatino, non havendo anchora parlato al Re se non privatamente, fece publicamente reverentia ad Sua Maestà, et per uno doctore di esso conte fu fatta una elegantissima oratione in nome de tutti li electori del Imperio che durò per spatio de meza hora, a la quale fu fatta resposta dal grande cancellero; doppoi il conte predetto, basatoli prima la mano, gli presentò la electione de Sua Alteza a lo Imperio in carta membrana sottoscritta de mano de tutti li preditti electori. Fatto questo, per esser l'hora tarda, tutti gli gentilhomini et signori che si trovorono a corte andorono alli lor allogiamenti.*

*Hoggi mattina li dodici cavallieri del Toson sono retornati a Palazo in pompa come heri, ma vestito di veluto negro con la collana del Ordine, et il Re vestito similmente di veluto negro. Alle decesette hore è venuto in la sala sopradita, tutta imbrunita di veluto, et essendosi Sua Maestà posta sovra la sua sedia et li cavallieri per ordine cadauno al loco suo, si dete principio ad una messa de morti per l'anima di cavallieri defuncti che fu cantata da l'Episcopo de la Indias, aparato lui et li preti che gli ministravano di veluto negro. Ditta la messa, disnò*[72] *la Maestà del Re et si ne è andato a caccia. Alla Excellentia Vostra basando la mano humilmente, in sua bona gratia me raccommando. Da Molin de Rei a dì primo di Decembro 1519.*

*Di Vostra Excellentia fidellissimo Servitore*
*Nicola de'Maphej*

My Most Illustrious and Most Excellent and Most Revered Lord . . . . Yesterday I returned early to Molin de Rey in order to see the ceremony of the Toison [d'or] that this most powerful King [Charles] celebrates every year on St. Andrew's Day, which I should not fail to describe to you.

In the morning all the Chevaliers of the said Order of the Fleece came to court, [accompanied] with the greatest pomp by gentlemen and servants dressed in their livery [mounted] on richly decorated saddle horses and mules. There were [only] twelve [Chevaliers] because there are at present no others at court. About noon, Italian style,[73] the King came out of his chambers where he had been giving audiences and

---

71. "come qui appresso" crossed out in letter.
72. There is a hole in the letter that partially obscures the last two letters of this word, though enough of the

outlines remain to suggest that the word is "disnò."
73. In Italy, from the fourteenth century to until after the French Revolution, hours of the day were reckoned

came into the hall, decorated with the finest tapestries done with figures. At the head of the room one saw a royal throne completely covered with very rich gold brocade and crimson-bordered velvet, both the width of the throne. In the middle of the room on the right was an altar on which were six images of Apostles in gilded silver, perhaps two braccia high, with the same number of candelabra, with lit torches, and many silver vessels in the manner described [i.e., gilded], which made a wonderful sight. They were divided over three tiers. In addition to these there was also an image of Our Lady and a cross, both of gold and filled with most precious jewels,[74] placed in the center of the altar amid the aforesaid things, but the cross was on the lowest tier and the image of Our Lady was above it on the second tier. On the left side was a long bench that was the length of the room and somewhat raised and all covered in crimson velvet, the place assigned to the Chevaliers to hear the mass, which was sung by the Bishop of the Indias with at least thirty most excellent musicians. The chasuble and cassock that he and the other two priests who sang the Epistle and the Gospel wore were of the richest gold brocade decorated in the middle and the collars with many different jewels of great value, inasmuch as one could see.

The King sat on his throne dressed in a mantle of silver cloth woven in squares, one normal, the other of the richest velvet in the most beautiful manner in the world with lining of the loveliest sable it would be possible to find; he had a long cloak of sewn gold cloth also in squares but smaller, one of black silk the other of the richest cloth, all lined with silver material; he wore a doublet in the same fashion. Each Chevaliers was in his place in the following order: [Guillaume de Croy,] Monseigneur of Chièvres,[75] with a mantle of black silk lined in lynx, and a long cloak of gold tabby sewn on black; next was Don Juan Manuel [Lord of Belmonte] who wore long cloak and mantle of black velvet lined with sable; beside him was the Count Palatine [Frederick II, Duke of Bavaria] with a garment of spun silver lined with sable and a long cloak of gold-spun cloth all slit with red silk underneath; following him was [Johannes] the Margrave of Brandenburg more richly dressed than the others, attired in a most beautiful mantle of rich silver cloth woven with gold leaf in the most opulent fashion possible with a lining of very lovely and excellent sable; half of the cloak was of the same silver material, and the other half was in black brocade layered one over the other and slit, so that one saw a shirt with a *[110 bis^r]* high collar of beaten gold, and on it there were sewn pearls of a good size and many different jewels placed in a way that they appeared very attractive; he had on his beret a very beautiful jewel, estimated to have the greatest value; at his side he wore a sword inlaid with the purest gold, miraculously well worked. After him was Monseigneur of Porcean [Philippe II de Croy, first Duke of Aarschot, Prince of Chimay and Count of Porcean], relative of Chièvres, clothed with silver tabby lined with sable, and a cloak of the same but slit and lined with black silk. The principal man-at-arms stood next to him, dressed in a garment of spun silver in a basket-weave pattern lined with sable with a long cloak of the richest gold brocade. The seventh was [Fadrique Alvarez

on a twenty-four-hour schedule beginning one-half hour after sunset and continuing to twenty-four hours, the last hour of daylight. I have tried to interpret these hours according to the approximate time of sunset for the season of the year. They are therefore only a rough equivalent based on sunset around 5:30 to 6:00 P.M. in Spain at the end of November. See Gerhard DOHRN-VAN ROSSUM, *History of the Hour: Clocks and Modern Temporal Orders,* trans. Thomas DUNLAP (Chicago: University of Chicago Press, 1996), 108-14.

74. This must be the famous "Croix du serment" or Cross of Allegiance on which each new chevalier swore

his oath of allegiance to the Sovereign. See Francis SALET "La 'Croix du serment' de l'Ordre de la Toison d'or," *Comptes-Rendus de l'Académie des Inscriptions et des Belles Lettres* (1965): 116-18, and idem, "La 'Croix du serment' de l'ordre de la Toison d'or," *Journal des Savants* (1974): 73-94. The cross is still extant in the Treasury of the Order in Vienna. It is reproduced in, among other places, Rotraud BAUER, et al., *Kunsthistorisches Museum Vienna: The Secular and Ecclesiastical Treasures,* trans. by Sophie KIDD and Peter WAUGH (Vienna: Residenz Verlag, 1991), 207, and in *Trésors de la Toison d'or,* 186-87.

de Toledo] the Duke of Alba adorned in a mantle of black velvet with the lining of a very black fur that is much esteemed here, and he kept the pelt long like [the pelt of] a lynx; [he was also] dressed in a cloak of black velvet lined with silk of the same color. Another was [Iñigo de Velasco, Duke of Frias and] the Constable of Castile who wore a garment of dark red velvet lined in civet with a cloak of spun gold; behind him was [Alvaro de Zuniga et Guzman] the Duke of Béjar with a black mantle of velvet lined with beautiful sable and a long cloak of gold-spun tabby; the tenth was [Pietro Antonio San Severino] the Prince of Bisignano adorned in a vestment of silver cloth woven in the manner of table linen with a lining of sable, and he wore a cloak half of the said silver cloth and half of black velvet. Next followed [Jacques de Luxemburg] Monseigneur of Fiennes, dressed in a leonine-colored silk cape lined with black velvet with a cloak of thin gold. The last was [Adrien de Croy] Monseigneur of Bueren, son of Monseigneur de Roeulx, with a garment of crimson silk lined with white Spanish fur, and he had a striped cloak in gold cloth [110 bis$^V$] and black velvet one over the other. Around their necks, all wore collars of the richest gold made with the fire-steels according to the custom and with the fleece hanging [from them].

After the Gospel had been sung, a priest who had assisted at the mass turned and gave a very learned sermon in Castilian, although he spoke of nothing other than the importance of this Order, which he lauded and praised greatly, attributing its origin to Philip [the Good] Duke of Burgundy who ordered it for the persecution of schismatics. He then told of all the duties of the Chevaliers, exhorting them with sweet and appropriate words that, because the King had honored them as Chevaliers, thus they too should want to do well for him, since they were the faithful debtors of his Majesty, whom he asked at the end of his speech to love and hold dear the said Chevaliers and to be an example of the holy life for them. There were many other ceremonies that are normal in royal masses, which I am not writing to Your Excellency since you have seen them many times.

The ceremonies and the mass both finished, the King got up and with his Chevaliers in front of him in order two-by-two, he went to his chamber where he stayed until the tables were set for the meal in the same room, because there was no larger or more suitable place in the palace. Where the throne had been was placed His Majesty's dining table with many beautiful gold vessels on it, but there were in particular three very beautiful [objects] of great value: one was the saltcellar made of the purest gold shaped like a galley about a foot and a half long, with the base worked with leaves of marvelous artistry and many precious inset stones; the other two were drinking vessels, one of crystal, the other of chalcedony with golden feet perhaps a palm high [111$^r$] worked in the same fashion as the galley. In the place of the bench was prepared another table for the twelve Chevaliers that was connected at right angles to that of the King, and on this were twelve saltcellars and the same number of drinking cups of the purest gold. Where the altar had been was a credenza which was miraculous to see because of the infinite number of gold and silver vessels, of which there were six [that were] two braccia high, worked most beautifully and with great skill, and several others slightly smaller, many rather smaller than these, and a great number the size of a glass, among which there were many of gold. I shall not speak of the cups and sweets-boxes except to say that I saw a total of ten, fifteen and even twenty, one after the other. After [the tables were set] His Highness, again with the Chevaliers in front of him, came back into the room and all sat down at table in the same order in which that had been at mass.[76] The King had two gentlemen servers richly dressed in gold brocade capes and mantles of material lined with marten and gold chains at their necks who stood continuously at the banquet to serve him,

75. The Chevaliers are identified through the list of members in *La Toison d'or: Cinq siècles d'art et d'histoire. Exposition organisée par le Ministère de l'Éducation Nationale et de la Culture et de la Ville de Bruges . . . 14 juillet–30 septembre 1962.* *Catalogue* (Bruges: Lannoo, 1962), 38-39.

76. The Chevaliers sat, both at mass and at the banquet, in order of their seniority, the member with the longest service closest to the Sovereign.

and the Chevaliers each had one [server], all of whom were dressed similarly with lined vestments, some with marten, some with lynx, others with white Spanish fur and others in civet. They went to the kitchen four times, and each time brought twelve dishes to his Majesty and six for each chevalier, each different from the others. The dishes came in this fashion: from the kitchen up to the door of the hall they were accompanied by twenty trumpets, ten of the type found in Italy and the others of another manner, and then [were accompanied] up to the table by two mace bearers and by the Herald [Thomas Ysaac, King of Arms of the Order][77] who wore [111$^v$] a tabard with all the insignia of the realms of this most worthy King depicted on it,[78] followed by two stewards of his Highness with behind them twelve gentlemen who carried the dishes for the mouth of His Majesty; [they were] richly dressed in cloaks and mantles of material with a most beautiful lining, and the majority of them had gold chains around their necks. Each time, the first of these shield bearers carried an ice sculpture higher than a braccia, very lovely and well made: the first was a Saint Andrew colored as one would expect to depict a man with vestments; the second was a virgin all in white, in whose lap was a sleeping unicorn; the third was of a woman nursing a child also in white; the last was a man with a crown of leaves on his head riding a lion and tearing his mouth with his hands. After the said shield bearers were the twelve stewards for the Chevaliers in order, each with his six bearers behind with dishes of six sorts, as I have said, which made a wonderful sight because they were all gentlemen of the family of the King and dressed like those above. The banquet was most praiseworthy and abundant and lasted for more than two hours in great celebration and jubilation. There were also the sounds of cornemuses, recorders, and drums, along with harps that send out sweet harmony. When dinner was finished, the most Reverend Cardinal of Tortosa and the Reverend Bishop of Badajoz blessed the meal just as they had done before it. The Benediction completed, His Highness arose with all the Chevaliers and went into a room to hold a council, as is the custom [on this day], where they stayed until [111 bis$^r$] the hour of Vespers, when they returned to the hall, and each sitting his place, a most solemn Vespers was sung, and when this was done the Count Palatine, not having yet talked with the King except privately, made public reverence to His Majesty, and a doctor of the said Count gave a most elegant speech, which lasted for a half an hour, in the name of all the Electors of the Empire. When this was finished [Philibert Naturel][79] the Grand Chancellor responded, then the said Count, kissing first his [Charles's] hand, presented him the [official document of] the election of His Highness to the Empire in parchment signed by all the aforesaid Electors. When this was done, since the hour was late, all the gentlemen and lords who were at court went to their lodgings.

This morning the twelve Chevaliers of the Toison [d'or] returned to the Palace in pomp as they did yesterday, but dressed in black velvet with the collar of the Order, and the King was likewise dressed in black velvet. At 1:00 P. M. they came into the above-mentioned room, all draped with velvet in mourning, and when His Majesty was on his throne and the Chevaliers were all in order in their places, there began a Mass for the Dead for the soul of the deceased Chevaliers, which was sung by the Bishop of the Indias, both he and the priests who assisted in black velvet. When the mass was done, His Majesty the King dined and went off on a hunt. Humbly kissing the hand you Your Excellency, in whose good grace I ask to be remembered. From Molin de Rey, 1 December 1519.

The most faithful servant of your Excellency,
Nicola Maffei

---

77. KOLLER, *Au service de la Toison d'or*, 141–42.

78. This is the official tabard of the King of Arms. A later version is extant in the Order's treasury. See BAUER et al., *The Secular and Ecclesiastical Treasures*, 205.

79. KOLLER, *Au service de la Toison d'or*, 20–23.

## Appendix

Anonymous, *Maxsimilla Cristo amabilis* (beginning)
London, British Library, Ms. Royal 8 G. vii, ff. 20ᵛ-21ʳ

22
- pus A - po - - - - - - - - - - sto - li, tu -
- pus A - - - - - - - - po - - sto - li, tu - -
- pus A - - po - - - - - - - - sto - li, tu - -
- pus A - - po - - - - - - - - - - sto - - li, tu - -
30
- lit cor - - - - - pus A - po - - - - - - -
- lit cor - pus, cor - pus A - po - - - - - - -
- lit cor - - - - - - pus A - - - - - - po - - -
- lit cor - - - - - - pus A - - po - - - - - - -
37
- - - - - - sto - li, A - - po - - - - - - -
- - sto - li, A - - po - - - - sto - - - li
- - sto - li, A - - po - - - - - - -
- - sto - li, A - - - - - - - po - - - - - -

43
- sto - - li, cor - - pus A - - - - po - sto -
cor - - pus A - - - - po - sto -
- sto - - li, cor - - pus A - - - - po - sto -
- - sto - li, cor - - - - - - - - - - - - pus
48
- li, cor - - - - pus A - - po - - sto - li, op - ti -
- li, cor - - - - - - pus A - po - - sto - li, op - ti -
- li, cor - - - - - - - pus A - po - sto - - li, op - ti -
A - - - po - - - - - - - sto - - - li, op - ti -
54
- mo lo - co cum a - ro - ma - ti - b us se - - - pe - le - - vit.
- mo lo - ro cum a - ro - ma - ti - bus se - - - pe - le - - vit.
- mo lo - co cum a - ro - ma - ti - bus se - pe - le - - vit.
- mo lo - co cum a - ro - ma - ti - bus se - pe - le - - vit.

Roberta Freund Schwartz

# From *Criado** to Canonization:
# Music in the Life
# of St. Francis of Borja

THOUGH ADMITTEDLY A MINOR COMPOSER of the Renaissance, the few extant works of San Francisco de Borja, fourth Duke of Gandía and third general of the Jesuits, have generated a certain interest among scholars due to his later canonization. His compositions, though, are only one indication of the scope of Borja's musical interests, for the saint was the very model of the noble melomane: an active composer, patron, and performer, who incorporated his affection for music into every aspect of his multifaceted career. His most significant contribution, however, is the reform of music that he instituted as head of the Jesuit order, where his own affection for polyphony and instrumental music was translated into a liberalization of monastic doctrine.

Don Francisco de Borja, the eldest son of Don Juan de Borja, third Duke of Gandía and his first wife, Juana de Aragón, also the great-grandson of Pope Alexander VI, was born in the seat of his ancestral duchy on 28 October 1510. As befitting a young nobleman who would one day inherit his father's title, Don Francisco was given a humanistic education: his biographers mention specifically studies of Latin, history, philosophy, mathematics, and music.[1] Little is known of his tutor, the canon Alfonso de Avila, save that he was the organist for the ducal chapel and that he required his charge to study

---

\* A *criado* is a young noble who is raised at another court, serving a minor position (as page, for example) while receiving an education and learning how to rule.

1. The earliest biographies of San Francisco cite as a reference the *Crónica de S. Francisco* by Padre Dionisio VASQUEZ, who was Borja's confessor and companion for many years. The *Crónica* itself is assumed to be lost, though the extensive duplication of both factual and anecdotal information in the early biographies suggests that their authors drew heavily from the aforementioned work, although differing in minor details. The eighteenth-century biography by M. Alvaro CIENFUEGOS, *La Heroica Vida, Virtudes y Milagros del Grande S. Francisco de Borja,*

*antes Duque 4° de Gandía; y después 3° General de la Compañia de Jesús* (Madrid: Juan García Infanzon, 1702), is the most complete of these early sources, and replicates much of the information contained in other studies.

2. Pedro SUAU, S.J., *Historia de S. Francisco de Borja, Tercer General de la Compañía de Jesús (1510-1572)* (Saragossa: Hechos y Dichos, 1912), 30. In addition to the standard biographies of Borja, Suau also used information from the depositions of family members, particularly the saint's brother, Tomás, for the preliminary hearing to begin canonization proceedings in 1610. Tomás de Borja, also a student of Avila's, recalled the specifics of his musical education and presumed that his brother's stud-

both the theoretical and practical aspects of music.[2] From an early age the boy frequently sang with the choir during religious services – a practice he continued until the end of his life – and most probably received organ lessons as well, as later accounts state that he played the instrument capably.

At the age of twelve, Francisco was sent to the court of Don Juan de Aragón, archbishop of Saragossa, to complete his education. As a *criado* he assumed minor duties within the household, learning the business of governance as well as continuing his studies of letters, arms, and music. Later in his adolescence Borja spent approximately a year at the court of Queen Juana the Mad in Tordesillas, serving as a page to the princess Catalina. Although the dates of his tenure are uncertain - various sources list the year as 1523, 1524, and 1526 - it was certainly after the Queen's *maestro de capilla*, the famed Juan de Anchieta, had retired from active service. Nonetheless, Juana maintained a modest musical establishment, and it is likely that the young Borja continued to sing and pursue his musical studies.

Shortly after his eighteenth birthday, Don Francisco de Borja was called to serve as a *gentilhombre* of the Spanish royal court. This honor probably had more to do with the political favor enjoyed by his father than his reputation, though by this time the young man was known as a well-rounded courtier as capable of skillful feats of horsemanship as of advanced discussions of the arts and sciences.[3]

It was at the royal court where Borja, by then granted the title of Marquis of Lombay and married to Doña Leonor de Castro, a lady-in-waiting of the Empress Isabel, seriously applied himself to the study of music. By all accounts, he was already an enthusiastic and gifted vocalist, capable of singing polyphony and falsobordone at sight, but he further developed his skills under the tutelage of someone at the royal court; judging from his compositions his master was probably one of the members of the King's Flemish chapel. Alvaro Cienfuegos asserts that the young man "…had a sonorous and sweet voice, that in tenderly expressing the emotions stole all of the attention, and touched a great many of the souls who heard it; and now [at the royal court] learning the most dexterous skills of music, came to be one of the most celebrated masters in Spain." [4] It is likely that Borja's earliest compositional efforts date from this same period.

Although most of his biographers insist that the saint never performed or composed secular music, others state that he enjoyed singing and writing the "music of the streets" as well as sacred polyphony and plainchant.[5] A two-voiced song known as

---

ies had been similar. The author, making use of this information and supporting documents from numerous Jesuit archives, treats the saint's musical activities more extensively than do other biographers.

3.  Fray Justo PÉREZ DE URBEL, "San Francisco de Borja," *Hidalguía* 126 (1974): 723.

4.  "Tenía la voz sonora, y tan suave, que regalando los

afectos blandamente, robada toda la atención, y mucha parte de las almas por el oído; y aprendido ahora los más diestros primores de la música, llegó a ser uno de los mas celebrados Maestros que tuvo España." CIENFUEGOS, *La heroica vida*, 50.

5.  See URBEL, "San Francisco de Borja," 25-26, for a refutation of this argument. The statement that the Saint

the *Canción del Duque de Gandía*, popularly attributed to Borja, almost certainly dates from his tenure at the royal court.[6] The *canción* sets a fairly conventional verse on courtly love in a highly imitative fashion, and demonstrates a firm if unimaginative grasp of technique and the predominant Franco-Flemish style, implying that it is an early effort. However, it is obvious that Borja possessed a certain flair for melodic writing, as the lines are well-shaped, balanced, and emotional.

Borja was in continuous residence at the imperial court until the death of the Empress Isabel in 1538. According to popular legend, the young nobleman was so affected by the sight of the sovereign in her coffin that he immediately devoted his life to the service of God. However, Borja did not enter the priesthood at this time; rather, he, like many courtiers, assumed a more significant position. On 26 June 1539 Don Francisco was named viceroy and lieutenant general of Cataluña and established his court at the Casa del Arcediano in Barcelona.[7] Borja was quick to establish a musical chapel for his new residence that soon garnered a fine reputation; unfortunately, no list of the chapel personnel is extant, and the identity of only one singer is known. Pedro Suau relates that in 1554, Borja, by then a member of the Company of Jesus, received into his monastery one Melchoir Marcos, who had sung in his chapel in Barcelona and was at the time *maestro de capilla* of the Duchess of Medina Sidonia. Marcos became a permanent attaché to his former employer and remained his closest aide and companion until death.[8] The viceroy was intimately involved with the workings of his chapel, selecting appropriate repertoire, singing with the choir and most probably composing items to be performed in the Divine Service.[9]

Nothing else is known of Borja's musical activities in Barcelona, save for the fact that in 1540, he banned public dancing in the city, an action often sighted as evidence of his religiosity and distaste for secular music. However, in a letter to the private secretary of the King, Borja explained that this was a gesture of mourning for the Empress, and the ban was not enforced after twelve months had expired.[10]

---

was never tempted to write secular polyphony and composed only for the Divine Service seems to have originated with Cienfuegos, who may not have known of the existence of any of these works. This claim has been rigidly repeated since, despite the published transcription of the *Canción del Duque de Gandía* in Mariano Soriano FUERTES, *Historia de la Música Española desde la venida de los Fenicios hasta el año de 1850*, 4 vols. (Madrid: Martin y Salazar, 1855-59), 2: 115. Most modern biographers who mention the work contest its attribution to San Francisco de Borja.

6.   A copy of this work is housed in the Museo Borjiano maintained in the Ducal Palace of Gandía. The aforementioned transcription is fraught with errors, and this unreliability makes evaluation difficult, particularly where contrapuntal errors are present; it is impossible to determine whether they are due to lack of compositional skill, improper transcription or copyist error.

7.   The palace is now the Instituto Municipal de Historia de la Ciutat de Barcelona.

8.   SUAU, *Historia de San Francisco de Borja*, 241. Upon the orders of Saint Francis of Loyola, Borja was required to follow the orders of his former musician as if coming from a superior in all matters regarding his personal health and well being.        9.   Ibid., 53.

10.   Don Francisco de Borja, Marques of Lombay, to Francisco de los Cobos, Barcelona, 24 June 1541. The letter is reproduced in *Sanctus Franciscus Borgia, Quartus Gandiae Dux et Societatis Jesu*, 2, published as *Monumenta Historica Societatis Jesu* X 117 (1903): 262-69.

Francisco de Borja served as viceroy until 1542, when his father, the third Duke of Gandía, passed away; Francisco then returned to his estates to take control of the duchy. He brought the majority of his musicians with him from Barcelona and installed them in the chapel of San Miguel, contained within the ducal palace. Here he heard the mass ordinary celebrated daily and continued to take his place among the musicians for the service and Divine Offices.[11] According to contemporary reports, the repertoire of the chapel in Gandía was quite different from that of the choir in Barcelona, and it is likely that the new Duke contributed items for performance.[12] On feast days he worshipped in public, most likely at one of the two religious establishments founded and patronized by the ducal household: the monastery of Santa Clara and the collegiate church of Gandía. The latter effectively functioned as a secondary ducal chapel, as the foundation statutes provided funding for twelve singers, six choirboys, and several instrumentalists.[13] Borja lavished money on both establishments, and used his rights as a patron to introduce new musical traditions; the polyphonic motets for an Easter procession in Gandía, written by the Duke in 1550, are the only extant example of such reforms.[14]

After the death of his wife in March of 1546, the Duke began a life of religious contemplation, spending the majority of his time in prayer in his private chapel, surrounded by his musicians. He had not completely forsaken his love of luxury and secular pursuits, however. Huge sums were spent on household ornaments, fine livery, and the maintenance of the ducal chapel. Moreover, Borja kept all of the employees of his father in active service, including a number of secular musicians.[15] Although no *nómina* of either the chapel personnel or the minstrels of the court is extant, his musical establishment must have contained at least four string players, because a 1595 inventory of the possessions of Don Francisco remaining in the custody of his son includes a full consort of viols.[16]

In February of 1548 Borja joined the Jesuit order, though his vocation was kept secret from all but his closest associates and the King, who had requested that the Duke serve as the *mayordomo* of the court of Prince Felipe II. Later that year he founded the University of Gandía and promptly engaged in a program of religious studies, completing a doctorate in theology in May of 1550. That August Don Francisco de Borja abdicated, appointing his son Carlos as the fifth Duke of Gandía and renouncing all his material possessions; nine months later he became a priest and began to serve actively as a Jesuit.

11. Pedro de RIVADENEIRA, *Vita Francisci Borgiae tertii Societatis Jesu Generalis* (Mainz: Baltasar Lipsius, 1603), 26.
12. SUAU, *Historia de San Francisco de Borja*, 53, 174-75.
13. Archivo Histórico Nacional de la Nobleza, Sección Osuna, legajo 541, no. 19.
14. SUAU, *Historia de San Francisco de Borja*, 148. No inventories of music are extant for either establishment, so it is impossible to determine what changes were instituted

during the saint's tenure as primary patron.
15. RIVADENEIRA, *Vita Francisci Borgiae*, 30v and Archivo Historia Nacional de la Nobleza, Sección Osuna, Leg. 807, no. 1: "Cuadernos de cantidades que debía el Duque D. Francisco a partir para Roma (1550)."
16. Archivo Histórico Nacional de la Nobleza, Sección Osuna, Leg. 569, no. 1.

Borja did not remain a simple servant of the faith for long; he quickly rose through the Jesuit ranks, and was named general of the order within seven years. As the ultimate authority for doctrine, he instituted a number of reforms that had a powerful impact on the types of music cultivated in all European establishments controlled by the Order. Shortly after assuming control over the Jesuits, San Francisco issued an order which allowed polyphonic masses to be performed in monasteries, stating that "...many of the faithful complain that we don't have sung masses; these may now be performed on feast days."[17] In addition, he approved the use of wind instruments in services and increased the importance of the organ in daily worship.[18] The saint also played a role in the foundation of the Convento de las Descalzas Reales in Madrid. Doña Juana de Austria, sister of Felipe II, consulted Borja in the earliest planning stages and left to him the creation of the convent's musical establishment, including the selection of repertoire, composition of the choir, and personnel recommendations.[19] The *capilla* soon gained a formidable reputation, founded in part on the fame of one of its earliest organists, Tomás Luis de Victoria.

Even while serving as the highest official of the Jesuits, Borja continued to perform and compose; the head of the order was often found singing in the choir of various establishments, particularly during Marian services.[20] His biographers attest to his compositional activities during this period, though only one specific work is mentioned; while recovering from a grave illness, the saint wrote a polyphonic setting of Psalm 118, *Beati immaculati in via qui ambulant in lege Domini.*[21]

Although few of his works are extant, Borja composed numerous works in sacred genres during his lifetime. With the exception of the Easter processional motets, none can be dated with any accuracy, nor can their origin be ascertained. According to his biographers, his compositions were of a quality akin to that of most *maestros de capilla* of the time, and were widely sought for performance in many churches and cathedrals in Spain and Italy; Borja was extremely generous in acceding to such requests, and freely sent his compositions to any who asked for them.[22] He is known to have composed at least one mass and one magnificat, motets, psalm settings and chants for processions and the Office. Unfortunately, he never made any effort to publish his compositions, "...abandoning his works to the public without trying to conserve a monopoly...due to the generosity of the author and his devotion to true sacred music."[23] Although no extant Spanish manuscripts contain works attributed to the saint, sixteenth-century inventories of the Cathedral of

17. This portion of the order is reproduced in SUAU, *Historia de San Francisco de Borja*, 230.

18. Candido de DALMASES, *El Padre Francisco de Borja* (Madrid: Editorial Católica, 1983), 87.

19. Soriano FUERTES, *Historia de la Música Española*, 2: 116.

20. Juan Eusebio NIEREMBERG, *Vida del Santo Padre y gran siervo de Dios el B. Francisco de Borja* (Madrid, 1644): 1, chap. 17.

21. Ibid.

22. CIENFUEGOS, *La Heroica Vida*, 53.

23. SUAU, *Historia de San Francisco de Borja*, 55.

Tarazona mention a book of motets and magnificats which contained an *Exaltata est* attributed to the "Duke of Gandía", and an inventory of items kept in the ducal palace in Gandía compiled in 1670 includes "four part-books of the motets of San Francisco."[24]

It is possible that more pieces by Francisco de Borja have survived as anonymous works. It is known that a number of other pieces by the composer were housed in the collegiate church of Gandía, including several full manuscripts; these have never come to light and were most probably destroyed in the fire that razed the church in 1936.[25] However, it is possible that manuscripts and documents from the Colegiata may still exist, as wide-scale looting occurred while the church burned. It is believed that the *Cançoner de Gandía*, a large collection of religious polyphony by Bartolomé Caceres, Pedro de Pastrana and other Valencian composers of the mid sixteenth century now residing in the Biblioteca de Cataluña, was recovered in this way.[26]

The extant works attributed with some certainty to San Francisco de Borja are a mass setting a4, and the aforementioned music for an Easter procession at the monastery of Santa Clara in Gandía. Unfortunately, both exist only in second or third generation copies and are anonymous; their assignment to the saint's body of works rests largely on popular tradition. This is most pronounced in the case of the *Missa Sine Nómine*.

The mass, which was "discovered" in the archives of the Collegiate Church of Gandía by Juan Bautista Guzmán in the late nineteenth century, was still being performed on the Sundays of Advent and Lent at that time. The internal traditions of the church held that the saint himself had composed the work known as the "mass of San Borja," and the claim can be supported to a degree by the biographies of Pedro Ribadenyera, Juan Eusebio Nieremberg, and Pedro Vásquez, all of which state that the saint composed a polyphonic setting of the mass ordinary and that it was sung in Gandía.[27] Guzmán was convinced by the evidence, and his transcription of the work is attributed to San Francisco de Borja.[28]

24. Archivo Histórico de la Nobleza, Sección Osuna Cartas, Leg. 441.

25. Jesús Giner FERRER, *La Santa e Insigne Colegiata de Gandía: Historia e estado actual* (Valencia: Tipografía Moderna, 1944), 17.

26. Mariano BAIXAULL attests to the existence of compositions by the saint in the archives of the Colegiata in his article "Las Obras Musicales de San Francisco de Borja conservadas en la insigne Colegial de Gandía" *Razón y Fe* 4 (Sept.-Dec. 1902): 154-70, 273-83. The *Cançoner* of Gandía has received a great deal of scholarly attention since brought to light by Josep María LLORENS in 1980. A modern edition of the manuscript has been prepared by Josep CLIMENT (Valencia: Generalitat Valenciana, 1995), and a full codicological study appears in Maria Carmen GOMEZ, *Bartolomeu Caceres: Opera Omnia*

(Barcelona: Biblioteca de Cataluña, 1996). The origin of the manuscript has yet to be determined; Climent believes that the volume may have been compiled in Gandía, while Carmen Gomez and Bernadette Nelson strongly advocate an origin at the court of the Duke of Calabria in Valencia. In addition to the above editions, see Maria Carmen GOMEZ, "Climent, Josep. Cançoner de Gandía," *Nassarre* 12/1 (1995): 353-62, and Bernadette NELSON, "Pie Memorie," *The Musical Times* 136 (July 1995): 338-44.

27. See BAIXAULL, "Obras Musicales," 278, for a summation of the references to the mass. In 1902 Baixaull encountered a manuscript copy of the Vásquez *Crónica* in the archives of the Monastery of Santa Clara in Gandía; the work has not been seen since World War II, and may have been destroyed.

Without at least one composition that is firmly attributed to the saint, it is impossible to either prove or disprove the attribution on stylistic grounds. However, a comparison with the *Cançion del Duque de Gandía* and the motets from the Easter procession reveals nothing that would rule out Borja as the composer. All three compositions make extensive use of imitation at the octave with new voices entering close on the heels of the leading part, normally at a distance of a semibreve or breve. The points of imitation are invariably introduced at the beginning of a new text phrase and frequently break down after only a few measures. Triadic structures abound, and the bass lines frequently move by fifth, as they provide the root of each chord. This is particularly pronounced in the Gloria, Credo, and Agnus Dei, which are largely homophonic and structured by alternation of duet, trio, and quartet textures, often pitting the higher voices against the lower in a quasi-antiphonal manner. The mass is well wrought, though not entirely free from errors, particularly in the preparation and resolution of chromatic tones. Baixaull holds that such instances, particularly in the final movement, are attributable to scribal error or later interpolations by another hand; however, the aural impact of such passages is striking, and they may have been deliberate violations of contemporary technique in the service of expression.

The other extant work commonly attributed to Borja, the music for the Easter procession of the city of Gandía, is of extreme interest; not only is the music for the occasion preserved in full, but the original foundation document from the chapter acts of the monastery of Santa Clara also provides a detailed description of the ceremony as envisioned by San Francisco in 1550. The same statute lends credence to the belief that the music to accompany the procession was composed by the saint, as it states that during the event "... hymns, verses, motets and prayers will be sung, according to the way they were composed to this effect."[29]

The music for the procession is a setting of the *Quem quaeritis* dialogue. According to the foundation documents, on Holy Thursday the Host was removed from the Collegiate church and stored in a monument in the center of Gandía. On Easter morning a procession composed of all church officials, the choir, and the instrumentalists left the Colegiata at 5 AM and proceeded to Santa Clara, singing the responsory *Dum transisset Sabbatum* in plainchant.[30] When the assembly arrived at the closed doors of the

28. Guzmán's copy of the mass is housed in the Archive of the Colegio de Corpus Christi in Valencia. BAIXAULL, "Obras Musicales," contains a transcription of the Sanctus and Benedictus, prepared from an anonymous late seventeenth-century copy in the Archives of the Colegiata de Gandía. A full modern edition of the work appears in Josep CLIMENT, "Misa de San Francisco de Borja," *Tesoro Sacro Musical* 56/1 (January-March 1973): 15-16, appendix.

29. Chapter acts of the Collegiate church of Gandía,

Códice 2° "Libre I de Recorts," 4 de Agosto 1550. An excerpt is reproduced in BAIXAULL, "Las Obras Musicales," 279.

30. As with the mass, no original manuscript of the processional music survives. The music found in the collegiate church of Gandía by Guzmán was a copy prepared in 1697. A transcription of all of the items is included in BAIXAULL, "Las Obras Musicales," 159-68. The copy of the source made by Guzmán is located in the Archive of the Cathedral of Valencia.

monastery, an Auto Sacramental would commence: two nuns inside the church representing angels sang an a2 setting of *Quem quaeritis in sepulchro*, and the choir of the Colegiata responded with *Jesum Nazarenum*, set as a four-voice motet. The nuns answered *Non est hic*, composed in the same style, and the choir again responded with *Jesum Nazarenum*. The nuns then sang *Venite et videte locum*, and the choir again repeated the motet, at the end knocking on the door of the monastery three times. All of the music for the nuns is highly imitative, while the motet is strictly homophonic, providing an attractive contrast between the heavenly agents and the mortal supplicants. The procession then proceeded to the monument, where three choirboys dressed as the three Marys sang *Quis revolvit nobis lapidem ab ostio monumenti* a3; again, the setting is imitative, symbolically stressing their connection with the divine. The youth portraying Mary Magdalene then intoned *Surrexit Christus* three times while ascending the steps to the monument, with each repetition transposed up a whole tone. After the third statement the choir responded with a seven-voice *Alleluia* composed for two choirs, alternately polyphonic and homophonic. The procession then returned to the collegiate church, with the assembled officials singing the sequence *Victimae paschalis* [sic] *laudes* in plainchant, in alternation with the choir, which performed the four-voice motet *Dic nobis Maria*. The settings demonstrate no outstanding compositional skill, but the aforementioned contrasts of texture to define the relationships of the participants is clever and effective, and the music is charming and undeniably emotional.

Although always pursued as a sideline, Borja remained devoted to the art of music until his death in 1572. Even his religious commentaries are filled with musical analogies, such as his contrasting of the perfect harmonies of a well-tuned consort to the dissonance of the soul caused by sin and the conception that man should be as receptive to the will of God as the pipes of an organ are to a hand on the keyboard.[31] Clearly, the impact of music on the life and thought of San Francisco de Borja was significant. Unfortunately, due to the loss of supporting documentation, it is difficult to measure his influence as a patron; there is no record of the composers he employed, compositions he commissioned, or manuscripts he ordered compiled. However, his reformation of the musical protocols of the Jesuit order had a widespread and lasting impact, as did the creation of the outstanding musical establishment of the Convento de la Descalzas Reales in Madrid, which served as an important center for musical activity in the late sixteenth and seventeenth centuries. The contributions of San Francisco de Borja to Spanish musical life may never be known in full, but should be recognized, along with his religious leadership, for their impact on the culture of his day.

---

31.  DALMASES, *Francscio de Borja*, 65.

Jeremy Noble

# The Genealogies of Christ and Their Musical Settings

IT WOULD BE HARD to conceive of any biblical texts much less evidently attractive to a composer than those of the genealogies of Christ, as presented in the gospels according to St. Matthew (i, 1-17) and St. Luke (iii, 21-38). They consist largely of a bare recitation of "x begat y" or, in the case of Luke, "x, who was the son of y, who was the son of z"—for whereas Matthew starts with Abraham and works forwards to Joseph the husband of Mary, Luke starts with Joseph and works back to Adam, and indeed to God. In each case the list of names leads either to or from Joseph, rather than Mary, and the two lists are largely different from one another—matters which have exercised both believers and unbelievers from the earliest times, and have generated much fascinating commentary. However, it is not my purpose to discuss the theological significance of the genealogies, let alone their value as historical documents, but rather to point up their importance as items of the liturgy. At least as early as the ninth century they had come to occupy a special place at the end of Matins at the feasts of Christmas and Epiphany—that is to say, at the beginning and end of the Christmas season—where they were dignified by the use of a special chant more elaborate than that of the usual gospel tone. What seems to have started as a specifically monastic observance had become, by the end of the Middle Ages, a virtually universal practice, requiring its own special mention in liturgical customaries.[1]

As an example we may take the instruction contained in the new *ordinarium* of the cathedral church of Le Mans,[2] drawn up in the early 1480s by the canon Pierre Hennier—evidently the resident liturgical expert, since he was in charge of editing all

\* A version of this paper was originally read in 1985 at the Annual Meeting of the American Musicological Society in Vancouver. Since then, research on Josquin's biography (to our knowledge of which Herbert Kellman has contributed so much) has perhaps given new relevance to its concluding suggestions about the possible connection of his Genealogy settings with Louis XI and St. Martin's Abbey at Tours.

1. Peter WAGNER, *Einführung in die gregorianischen Melodien, III. Gregorianische Formenlehre* (Leipzig, 1921, repr. Hildesheim: Olms, 1962), 251.
2. Le Mans, Bibliothèque Municipale, Ms. 165: "Ordinarium novum, secundum usum ecclesie Cenomannensis ...", begun 1 September 1481, and completed (?) in 1485.

the early printed service books of Le Mans. This is what he has to say about the end of Matins on Christmas Eve: "And while the ninth responsory is sung, the deacon must prepare himself solemnly and change his vestments [*revestire*], together with the subdeacon and four boys to carry the cross, censer and two candles as for the reading of the gospel; and he shall proceed thus before the altar, so that the bishop may bless the incense and place it in the censer; then the deacon shall cense the altar, and having censed it shall receive the bishop's blessing; and he shall go with the others in orderly procession to the pulpitum, and shall read the gospel, 'Here beginneth the gospel according to St. Matthew: *Liber generationis Jesu Christi* ...'. At the end of this the bishop shall begin the *Te Deum*, and when that is finished the cantor shall begin the Mass, namely *Dominus dixit ad me* [the introit of the first mass of Christmas, the so-called 'midnight mass']." Seventy years later a manuscript from the cathedral of Aix-en-Provence[3] says specifically that the deacon shall sing the "Liber generationis" gospel *in cantu solempni et speciali*, and yet other places give more detailed instructions as to the magnificence of his vestments on this occasion. I think we must assume that in a feudal and aristocratic age the genealogies of Christ had taken on, in a more or less spiritual way, something of the character of a heraldic proclamation of titles, and that it was this which led them to be treated with special solemnity; and of course the same impulse that called for special vestments and ceremonial actions also led to the provision of more elaborate and varied music.

During the centuries in which this ceremony spread and developed throughout most of Christendom (the main area of resistance being that of the Roman/Franciscan rite), the music that accompanied it also developed and was embellished in many different ways, culminating in the polyphonic settings by Josquin and Prioris. The purpose of this article is to survey, in roughly chronological order, the course of that development, but it may be as well to admit that the research on which it is based was sporadic and accidental rather than systematic or orderly. It was, in fact, a by-product of a quite different project, namely a survey of early printed missals (that is to say those of the late fifteenth and early sixteenth centuries) with a view to establishing criteria for identifying local and monastic uses in the late Middle Ages and applying these to musical sources.[4] The very earliest printed missals of course contain little music themselves, if any. The technical difficulties of incorporating musical notation into a mainly verbal text were evidently a deterrent, so that we find at most

3.   Aix-en-Provence, Bibliothèque Méjanes, Ms. 12: "Liber hebdomadarius" of Saint Sauveur, dated 1554.
4.   The standard bibliography of early printed missals is still W. H. J. WEALE's *Catalogus missalium ritus latini* ..., 2d. ed. revised by Hanns BOHATTA (London, 1928); breviaries are listed in Hanns BOHATTA,

*Bibliographie der Breviere 1501-1850* (Leipzig, 1937). Both are supplemented by Robert AMIET, *Missels et bréviaires imprimés* (Paris: Éditions du CNRS, 1990). Also see the online database, Renaissance Liturgical Imprints: A Census (RELICS) at: www-personal.umich.edu/~davidcr/index.html

the celebrant's intonations for the Gloria and Creed, either provided on an inserted woodcut or else, more often, copied in by hand, very probably in the printer's shop. Soon, however, these come to be supplemented by the Prefaces, and then, here and there, by other important liturgical items: the Easter Exultet, various chants for Holy Week, the Candlemas procession for the feast of the Purification, and lastly the two Genealogies whose function has been described above.

Now precisely because of their rather anomalous position in the liturgy, situated usually between the end of the office of Matins and the beginning of the Mass, these two items appear rather unpredictably in the liturgical *manuscripts* of earlier centuries: sometimes we find them in noted missals or breviaries, sometimes as the only notated items in evangeliaries, very occasionally in processionals, and hardly ever in the big choir graduals and antiphoners. For this reason their relatively frequent appearance in the printed missals does more than merely provide us with yet further variant versions of the established chants; it gives a new solidity to our picture of their geographical distribution at the end of the Middle Ages, at least in Europe north of the Alps; it also enables us to see that while some of the large number of chants mentioned by Bruno Stäblein in *MGG* and Michel Huglo in the *New Grove* are very widespread indeed, others are of purely local occurrence.

This can easily be illustrated. Example 1 shows the third-mode chant common to the diocesan uses of Paris, Noyon, Cambrai, Rheims, Troyes, Tours, Séez, and Saintes. It is found, with only very minor variants, in the printed missals of all those dioceses. It is also clearly the same melody as is indicated by the neumes of the ninth-century Corbie evangeliary[5] illustrated in the *New Grove* under the article "Gospel", and in other manuscripts of the same early period. But whereas the above-mentioned dioceses clung tenaciously to this earliest and simplest form of the chant, in others the forces of tradition and conservatism were evidently outweighed by the desire to elaborate. Thus in the diocese of Arras, in northern France, the initial alternation of G and A is constantly ornamented with a figure that rises to C or even D (Example 2). It is surely not too fanciful to suggest that this ornamentation may be the work of the same musician who composed the hymn ("Lumen clarum rite fulget orto magno sydere …") which prefaces both genealogies in the very carefully written Arras source.[6]

Similarly, at the closely connected dioceses of Sens and Auxerre, south-east of Paris, we find not only that the second limb of the melody has incorporated a descent to the low C (something which occurs also at Chartres and Orleans); it has balanced this with an ascent to the upper C. This might be put down to the vagaries of oral transmission, no doubt, but the insertion at two points in the Christmas genealogy of

5.   *The New Grove*, 7: 546. The manuscript in question is Paris, Bibliothèque nationale de France, Ms. lat. 11958.

6.   Arras, Bibliothèque municipale, Ms. 883.

**Examples 1-8**    Chants for the Genealogies

. Basic melody

Li - ber ge - ne - ra - ti - o - nis Je - su Chri - sti fi - li - i Da - vid fi - li - i A - bra - ham:

. Arras

. Sens / Auxerre

. Bayeux

. Sarum

. Basic melody

Li - ber ge - ne - ta - ti - o - nis Je - su Chri - sti fi - li - i Da - vid fi - li - i A - bra - ham:

. Fontevrault

. St. Aubain (Namur)

**Examples 1-8 (cont'd)**

1    A - bra - ham    ge - nu - it    -sa - ac:    -sa - ac au - tem    ge - nu - it    Ja - cob:...

2

3.2

3.3    ...Da - vid au - tem rex    ge - nu - it Sa - lo - mo - nem ex    e - a    que fu - it U - ri - e...

4    A - bra - ham    ge - nu - it    -sa - ae:    -sa - ae au - tem    ge - nu - it    Ja - cob:...

5    < au-tem >

6

7

8

a new melodic segment with an altogether higher tessitura, highlighting musically the mention of King David and also of the Babylonian exile, surely bespeaks individual and conscious "composition", not to mention a desire to bring out the text's inherent structure (Example 3 with continuation).

Elsewhere the elaborative impulse works against that structure. The proper names in the Matthew genealogy are grouped in three symmetrical series of fourteen, as the evangelist himself points out in a final verse which some dioceses omit: "So all the generations from Abraham to David are fourteen generations. And from David to the Babylonian exile are fourteen generations. And from the Babylonian exile to Christ are fourteen generations." The simple alternation of two melodic phrases, which we find in the original E-mode melody, obviously poses no problems, provided no mistakes are made in fitting it to the longer verses, as happens in some sources; two into fourteen "goes", without remainder. But once musicians strive to avoid monotony by adding new musical phrases and grouping them in longer recurring units—in groups of three, four, five, or even six—problems arise, since fourteen is exactly divisible only by two and seven. However, this does not seem to have worried the musicians, whoever they were, who were responsible for amplifying these melodic formulae. At Soissons the third-mode melody was preserved virtually in its original form, but with the addition of a third phrase that confines itself entirely within the G-E ambitus. In a group of eastern French dioceses, ranging from Besançon and Lausanne in the south up to Langres and Châlons-sur-Marne in the north, we find another three-limbed third-mode melody—similar, but apparently distinct.

Musically more interesting than these are the notably florid versions current in some Norman dioceses and in their descendant or cousin across the English Channel at Salisbury. It seems clear that these all spring from a common root in the standard third-mode melody, but at Coutances, for example, this is extended by two further phrases of wider range. At Bayeux, where the process of melodic elaboration gives us a group of three notes to almost every syllable, the melody extends to five phrases, and to six in the Sarum sources (still more florid, and remarkably consistent with one another over four hundred years). (See Examples 4 and 5.) In spite of the evident relationship between the two last-mentioned, I doubt whether a clear line of descent can be established between all these versions; if it were to be attempted, it would have to be on the basis of earlier sources than those which I have been able to examine. It seems likely, in any case, that most of the various local divergences within the E-mode family of melodies date back at least to the twelfth century, and we should need to take into account monastic sources as well as diocesan ones. What can be asserted, though, I think, is that the E-mode melodies are almost all outgrowths, by a process of more or less conscious elaboration, from a single simple formula—something which Peter Wagner observed long ago,[7] but which tends to be obscured by Stäblein's rather abstract and over-systematic method of classification.[8]

But that E-mode family by no means exhausts the repertory of chants to which the Christmas (Matthew) genealogy was sung, even though it does cover the majority

7.  WAGNER, *Einführung*, 252.                  8.   *Die Musik in Geschichte und Gegenwart*, 3: cols. 1618-29.

of diocesan liturgies in France. Virtually throughout the German-speaking area of Europe, from Salzburg in the south-east to Cologne, Münster, and Utrecht in the north-west, with Bamberg as one of the very few exceptions, we find a totally different *first*-mode melody[9] (Example 6). Where exactly this D-melody originated I am not qualified to guess. It is found at Aquileia (whence no doubt it came to Salzburg). It is also found in a Narbonne manuscript of the twelfth century.[10] It was the melody prescribed in the liturgical books of the Dominican order and also, in a rather more elaborate form, in those of the Hospitallers of St. John of Jerusalem. It seems to me likely that it is a later melody than the third-mode one (which would help to explain why it suffered less radical transformations) and that it must have come to Germany from the south rather than from the west—but the pre-Roman southern sources are outside my purview, and this whole subject deserves further research.

Over and above these two principal melodies or melodic families are those which seem, on the basis of surviving sources, to have had only local currency. The mother-house of the order of Fontevrault is geographically equidistant from Tours, Angers, and Poitiers, but the very distinctive melody preserved in the order's books (and apparently only there) has nothing at all in common with theirs (Example 7). It must surely have been composed specially for the order soon after its foundation in 1100, and been jealously preserved by it through the succeeding centuries of its existence. Perhaps more recent is the very F-majorish four-phrase melody found in a fifteenth-century gradual of the collegiate church of St.-Aubain at Namur,[11] and so far nowhere else (Example 8).

When this prolonged history of *melodic* embellishment is taken into account, the various *polyphonic* settings of the genealogies can be seen simply as a continuation of the same tradition through different musical means. The manuscript setting from the Cluniac priory of St.-Martin-des-Champs in Paris, published in facsimile by Madeleine Bernard and in quasi-score by Theodor Göllner,[12] is a fifteenth-century attempt to apply to the text of the Christmas genealogy a technique more appropriately developed for the Passions: the sharing of a monophonic melody by three voices—high, middle and low—which then come together in three-part polyphony. This alternation of textures, which has an evident quasi-dramatic function in the Passion texts, is purely dec-

---

9. The Toul version from which Dom POTHIER in *Revue du chant grégorien* 5 (1896-97): 70-71 attempted to demonstrate a common origin for both E- and D-mode melodies is the result of conflation or contamination—as might be expected in a source coming from a diocese on the border between the two linguistic areas.
10. Paris, Bibliothèque nationale de France, Ms. lat. 778.

11. Namur, Evêché, Archive capitulaire, Ms.2; dated 1466.
12. Paris, Bibliothèque Mazarine, Ms. 438, ff. 7ʳ-11ʳ; 15th c., before 1436. See Madeleine BERNARD, *Répertoire de manuscrits médiévaux contenant des notations musicales*, II— Bibliothèque Mazarine (Paris: Éditions du CNRS, 1996), plates XIII-XVI and pp. 139-41; Theodor GÖLLNER, *Die mehrstimmigen liturgischen Lesungen* ...

orative when applied to a genealogy, though none the less attractive for that (Example 9). It should be noted that this shared melody from St. Martin-des-Champs, like the one from St.-Aubain, is in a modern-sounding "F major"; it evidently had no independent pre-existence as a purely monophonic piece, but was specifically composed to be combined with polyphony, since its three segments suit the compass of the three voices employed, in the descending order high-middle-low. Whether its use was peculiar to this particular Parisian priory or was widespread among other Cluniac houses

**Example 9**   St.-Martin-des-Champs

will be difficult to determine, given the scarcity of Cluniac liturgical sources with notation.

A somewhat similar technique is employed in the first fifteen of the examples collected by Göllner from Eastern Europe,[13] except that here the underlying melody (again a strongly F-majorish one) is designed to be shared by three voices in the ascending order low-middle-high. Again it seems most unlikely that this melody had an existence independent of three-voice performance; in fact the primitive technique of the interspersed polyphonic segments strongly suggests the written record of an improvisational tradition[14] (Example 10). (Here and elsewhere the initial verses, responses and title have been omitted to facilitate comparison.) The above-mentioned versions all come from Silesia, Bohemia, and Poland: it is only in one from much further south, namely from Zagreb in Croatia,[15] that we find this technique of alternating monophony and polyphony (or at least homophony) applied to one of the traditional chants, and, as we might expect, it is the D-melody so widespread throughout the German-speaking lands; in the Zagreb source the three voices join together only on the recur-

(Münchner Veröffentlichungen zur Musikgeschichte, 15 Tutzing, 1969) 1: 239-43; commentary in 2: 115-16.

13. GÖLLNER, 1: 211 ff; 344; 2: 109-15.

14. Here given after Cracow, Chapter Archive of the Wawel Cathedral, Ms. 235, pp. 180-85.

15. GÖLLNER, 1: 244-50, 348, and 2: 116-17; after Zagreb, University Library, Ms. MR 10, ff. 159r-162v.

**Example 10**    Cracow (after Göllner)

**Example 11**    Trent 91 (reduced 1:8)

**Example 12**    JOSQUIN: Christmas Genealogy (Tenor) cf. Example 1

rent phrase marked with a bracket in Example 6. If it seems likely that Zagreb would look west to Aquileia and north to Austria for its liturgical traditions, it is certain that Trent in the fifteenth century took its liturgy directly from Salzburg; the missal of Bishop Hinderbach now in the Trent, Biblioteca Comunale, Ms. 1562, proves as much. So it looks as though the through-composed three-part setting of the Christmas genealogy in Trent 91 (#1225 in the DTÖ thematic index), which uses the D-melody as its Tenor throughout, may be a local composition, or in any case not an importation from those parts of western Europe where the E-melody held sway. This is confirmed by the fact that it turns out to be identical with the piece which Göllner prints as his final example of settings of the Christmas genealogy.[16] The only significant difference is that while Trent of course uses white void notation, Göllner's source, Zwickau, Ms. XCIV, 5, although it is a few decades later, is written in a combination of Hufnagelschrift and black mensural notes—a nice instance of notational decay! (See Example 11.)

One feature that all of these polyphonic treatments or embellishments of the Christmas genealogy have in common, whether they use one of the pre-existent mono-

16. GÖLLNER, 1: 251-58, 348, and 2: 116-17; after Zwickau, Ratschulbibliothek, Ms. XCIV, 5, ff. 25ʳ-30ʳ.    The concordance with Trent 91 was not noted by Göllner.

phonic chants or not, is that they are essentially liturgical music—compositions, that is to say, whose style and structure are dictated by their function in the service. It is this that makes the sudden appearance of Josquin's extended setting of this text as a motet for four voices so extraordinary. There is absolutely nothing to prepare us for a composition which so far transcends the purely liturgical necessities, or even proprieties. It is true that Josquin starts by presenting the familiar E-mode melody in the clearest of imitation in all four voices, and that throughout the first of the motet's three *partes* it is constantly being referred to, usually in Tenor or Superius (Example 12). But thereafter the references become more distant and more sporadic; the impulse behind the composition seems to be not so much to present the text or its melody, as to provide a meditation on the one and a fantasia on the other. It is, in other words, already a paraliturgical piece, as much at home in the chamber as the church—and that in spite of the fact that no-one, I think, would wish to put it among Josquin's later works.

It would be nice to know where and in what circumstances so exceptional a piece came to be composed. Unfortunately, although Josquin lets us know very clearly which chant he is using, this tells us little about the work's provenance, precisely because the chant in question is the E-mode one in common use, as we have seen, for the Christmas genealogy in most of northern and central France. But the case is quite different with his setting of the Epiphany genealogy from St. Luke, "Factum est autem." Chants for this text are preserved in fewer sources than for the Christmas one, perhaps reflecting the slightly lesser importance of the feast itself. Among them there seems to be a wider repertory of more or less independent melodies—in other words, the melodic families are harder to sort out—but it is nevertheless clear that almost all those dioceses in northern France which used Josquin's E-mode chant for the Christmas genealogy prescribe a D-mode one for the Epiphany text. Paris, Arras, Noyon, Amiens, Soissons, Angers and Tours on the Loire, Rouen and Bayeux in Normandy, even Vannes in Brittany and Besançon in the far east of France, not to mention the Dominicans and the Hospitallers, all use a melody that begins with a distinctive upward leap of a fifth, D-A and at least start their list of names with the same pair of phrases, what ever changes fancy may lead them into later on (Example 13).

But Josquin did not choose to base his setting of the Epiphany text on this standard melody. Instead he again chooses a somber E-mode melody. Could this be simply a matter of aesthetic preference? Given Josquin's strong creative personality I suppose that that is possible, yet it seems more likely that if he were simply concerned to provide a companion-piece to his setting of the Christmas genealogy he would, all things being equal, have preferred a contrasting mode to the same one. But that of course assumes that a choice was available to him, and that he could, as we can, look at a number of alternative chants to a particular text and pick whichever suited his pur-

**Example 13-15**  Epiphany Genealogy D melody (Paris &c.)

Fac-tum  est  au-tem  cum  bap-ti-za-re-tur  om-nis  po-pu-lus,  et  Je-su  bap-ti-za-to  et  a-ran-te...

Epiphany Genealogy E melody (St.-Martin & Le Mans)

Epiphany: JOSQUIN (Tenor) cf. Example 14

Fac-tum est au-tem  cum bap-ti-za-re-tur  om-nis po-pu-lus   et Je-su bap-ti-za-to et  o-ran-te...

pose—surely an anachronistic notion. If he chose a specific E-mode melody for his setting of the Epiphany genealogy, it seems much more likely that it was because this was the melody current at the place for which he was composing the work. And if this is so, the results we get from placing Josquin's polyphonic setting in the context of the monophonic tradition are much more interesting than they were with the Christmas genealogy, for the melody he uses appears, so far as I have yet been able to discover, in only two places: the diocese of Le Mans, and the abbey of St.-Martin at Tours. This may seem surprising, since Tours has already been mentioned above as one of the dioceses which used the distinctive D-mode melody for Epiphany. (See Example 13.) But the royal abbey of St.-Martin was a law unto itself in such matters, and even made a point of publishing in 1529 its own printed folio missal (an extraordinary luxury for an individual monastic house) as if to demonstrate its independence from the diocesan use. A seventeenth-century panorama of Tours provides a view that is, alas, no longer available to us (see Plate I). On the left is the cathedral, usually known as St.-Gatien, though it is here labelled St.-Gentian, with its distinctive pepper-pot towers. On the right is the much more ancient abbey church of St.-Martin, of which all but a single tower was destroyed at the Revolution. In the 1529 missal, and in the manuscript noted breviary (Tours, Bibliothèque municipale, Ms. 149) that is our main witness to the repertory of chant performed at St.-Martin's, the melody prescribed for the Epiphany genealogy corresponds exactly to that used by Josquin, though they notate it a fourth higher than he does in his Tenor voice (Examples 14 and 15).

Now the Le Mans sources, both the printed missals and earlier manuscripts, notate this melody at Josquin's pitch, i.e. a fourth lower, so is the suggestion of a relationship with St. Martin's perhaps too speculative? It is true that nothing has yet come to light connecting Josquin with Le Mans, but that is not to say that nothing will; there are still plenty of unsolved mysteries about his career. In the complex world of fifteenth-century dynastic politics it is always possible to find *some* connection, however tenuous, and it should be noted that Le Mans was the capital of the Counts of

Maine, and that in the 1470s and '80s this title was held successively by the younger brother and the nephew of Duke René of Anjou, the "good King René" in whose service Josquin certainly was at Aix-en-Provence around 1477/78. But this connection seems far-fetched in view of the fact that no evidence has yet come to light that the Counts of Maine maintained the kind of musical establishment that might have performed such exceptional works as Josquin's two genealogy settings.

It seems to me much more likely that those settings—or at the very least, that for Epiphany—were composed for St.-Martin's at Tours, where the King of France was the titular abbot and where Ockeghem had held the important post of Treasurer since 1459. It is true that the surviving ritual of of St.-Martin's, edited and privately circulated by the Abbé Fleuret early in the twentieth century, contains no more mention of polyphony for the genealogies than does the ordinary of Le Mans which was quoted in the second paragraph of this article: they are to be sung by the deacon, accompanied by the subdeacon carrying the abbot's crozier, a thurifer, and three choirboys clad in albs, one of whom is to carry the cross. But we would hardly expect to find mention of an exceptional piece of polyphony in a code of ritual which was meant to last for ever—particularly since that polyphony was probably performed outside the context of the service itself. We do know that Louis XI, who reigned from 1461 to 1483, made Tours virtually his capital, and we know too that he lavished enormous largesse on St.-Martin's, culminating in a solid silver screen for the saint's shrine, costing 200,000 livres.[17] What could be more likely than that Josquin's genealogy settings were composed for such a context of lavish patronage and musical expertise?

Nor is it at all improbable that Josquin himself could have been present. No documentary evidence has yet been discovered for his whereabouts between March 1478, when he was certainly in Duke René's service and presumably at Aix, and February and March 1483, when he returned north to Condé-sur-l'Escaut. But Patrick Macey has plausibly suggested that even if he remained in René's entourage until the latter's death in 1480, he may well have transferred to Louis XI's service in the following year together with the rest of René's chapel. In default of further evidence I would propose that both of Josquin's genealogy motets, virtuoso works both in the demands they make on their performers and in their flamboyant elaboration of jejune basic material, may have been composed for performance by Louis' chapel during the Christmas celebrations at Tours in the early 1480s. The fact that the Matthew setting, "Liber generationis," uses a widely known chant while the Luke one, "Factum est

17. B. de MANDROT, ed., *Journal de Jean de Roye connu sous le nom de Chronique Scandaleuse 1460-1483* (2 vols., Paris, 1894, 1896) 2: 77: "Et en oultre, pour la grande et singuliere confidence que de tout temps il a eu è mons<sup>r</sup> saint Martin de Tours, voult et ordonna estre fait ung grant treilliz d'argent tout autour de la chasse dudit saint Martin, lequel y fut fait, et pesoit de xvi à xvii<sup>m</sup> mars d'argent, qui cousta, avant que estre prest et tout assis, bien cc<sup>m</sup> frans."

autem", is based on a chant which had very restricted currency is entirely consonant with the use of the royal abbey of St.-Martin. It might also explain why Prioris, master of the French royal chapel under Louis XII, a generation or so later, found it necessary to provide a setting of the Epiphany genealogy based, though more freely, on the standard D-melody current throughout most of northern France (Example 16).

**Example 16** Epiphany Genenealogy: Prioris (Tenor) cf. Example 13

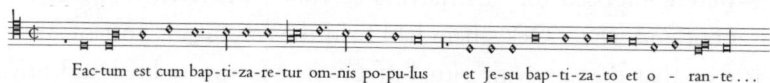

Fac-tum est cum bap-ti-za-re-tur om-nis po-pu-lus    et Je-su bap-ti-za-to et o - ran-te...

**Plate 1** Seventeenth-century panorama of Tours (left and right closeups)

Richard Sherr

# JOSQUIN'S RED NOSE

A MONG THE WORKS attributed to Josquin des Prez are a few isolated settings of the Ordinary of the Mass. Most of these were printed by Petrucci in 1505 in the collection entitled *Fragmenta Missarum* (a compilation of settings of single movements of the Ordinary by a number of composers). In the Petrucci print settings attributed there to Josquin are all grouped together. Most have conflicting attributions or are unica, and all but two were published in the *Fragmenta Missarum* volume of the Josquin *Werken*.[1] In this essay, I wish to address myself to the issues raised by one of the works with conflicting attributions, the Credo *Chascun me crie*, a work that has engendered some discussion, is extremely interesting, may even be unique, and might even be "good".[2] First, the source situation.

## Sources of the Credo *Chascun me crie*

> *Fragmenta*, No. 21, Josqn
> MunBS 53, ff. 205ᵛ-216ʳ, A. B.
> VatS 23, ff. 140ᵛ-145ʳ, Josquin Des Prez [*Patrem des rouges nes*]
> VatSM 26, ff. 250ᵛ-253ʳ, Anon.
> VienNB 11778, ff. 130ᵛ-135ʳ, Josquin Des Pres

The transmission of this Credo seems strongly to favor an attribution to Josquin. The work appears in five sources of which the earliest appears to be the Petrucci print.[3] Two manuscript sources in addition to the print ascribe the work to Josquin; more to the

* An abbreviated form of this essay appears in Richard SHERR, ed. *The Josquin Companion* (Oxford: Oxford University Press, 2000), chap. 7.

1. Albert SMIJERS and Miroslaw ANTONOWYCZ, eds. *Werken van Josquin des Prez: Fragmenta Missarum* (Amsterdam Vereniging voor nederlandse muziekgeschiedenis, 1956-63). Omitted are the *Credo La Belle se siet*, believed to be by Robert de Févin, and the *Missa de Feria*, which is most likely by Martini. The *Fragmenta* of the *Werken* plus the Credo *La Belle se siet* are now published in vol. 13 of *The New Josquin Edition*, ed. Barton HUDSON. Measure numbers in this study refer to the edition in the *Werken*.

2. The problem of attribution of the Credo is discussed by Barton HUDSON, "Josquin and Brumel: The Conflicting Attributions", in Willem ELDERS, ed., *Proceedings of the International Josquin Symposium, Utrecht 1986* (Utrecht: Vereniging voor nederlandse muziekgeschiedenis, 1991), 67-92, and by Adeline VAN CAMPEN, "Conflicting Attributions of *Credo Vilayge II* and *Credo Chascun me crie*", *Proceedings of the International Josquin Symposium*, 93-98.

3. The latest chronologies place MunBS 53 at *c.*1510, VatS 23 at after 1505 and before 1512, VatSM 26 at *c.*1520, VienNB 11778 at *c.*1521-25.

point, as Barton Hudson has shown, those manuscripts are not related and are not dependent on Petrucci's readings;[4] this is particularly true of VatS 23, which has widely variant readings at spots[5] and furthermore gives the work a different title, "Patrem des rouges nes" (red noses), in its table of contents (the work is also attributed to Josquin both in the body of the MS and in its table of contents). This weakens the force of the one conflicting attribution in the Munich manuscript (to "A. B.", who might be, but need not necessarily be, Antoine Brumel), although some caution is warranted, because it is possible for the musical readings and even the title in VatS 23 to have been independent of Petrucci while the attribution was not.[6]

Yet the piece itself seems to belie the evidence of its transmission. Everyone who has considered the Credo *Chascun me crie* has remarked on its uniqueness within the Josquin oeuvre. The problem concerns its model, its style, and also its very integrity as a Credo. Osthoff put his finger on it as he struggled to reconcile himself to a work he believed to be by Josquin (he was unaware of the conflicting attribution), but really did not want to accept because he was embarrassed by it.

> Aber sie trägt den Stempel ihrer Herkunft aus dem Bereich heiter-beschwingter Chansonmelodik allzu deutlich an der Stirn, um vor dem Credotext bestehen zu können. Es gibt kaum einen zweiten Messensatz von Desprez der so weltlich und so wenig sakral wirkt. Trotzdem sich die Worte den Noten leicht unterlegen lassen klaffen Text und Musik weit auseinander. Sieht man von der noëmatisch herausgehoben Stella "passus et sepultus est" ab, so bemerkt man kaum einige Takte die eine enge Wort-Ton-Bezeihung verraten. Wie wenig der Komponist bei dieser Arbeit der Erfordernisse des Messentextes berüksightigte, erkennt man daran, dass nicht selten die gleiche oder fast gleiche Musik sich dem Sinn nach völlig verschiedenen Sätzen verbindet. So kehrt die Musik zu dem Worten "Crucifixus etiam pro nobis" völlig unverändert wieder bei "Et resurrexit tertia die secundum Scripturas". Es tut der Bedeutung des Meisters keinen Abbruch, wenn man feststellt, dass bei dieser Komposition nur seine Routine, nicht sein "ingenium" beteiligt war. [7]

4.  Barton HUDSON, "Josquin and Brumel: The Conflicting Attributions," in *Proceedings of the International Josquin Symposium, Utrecht 1986*, 67–92. I am grateful to Barton Hudson for sharing with me his transcription of the Credo and his Critical Commentary to *The New Josquin Edition*, vol. 13, prior to publication.

5.  For instance, VatS 23 replaces the Bass notes in mm. 14–16 with rests; it is hard to see how this could have come about if the scribe was copying from Petrucci or Petrucci's exemplar.

6.  In other words, Johannes Orceau, the scribe of the VatS copy could have copied the work from an exemplar that was anonymous and then learned about the Petrucci attribution. This is also plausible, because in my opinion the Orceau copy is contemporary with or more likely postdates the Petrucci print.

7.  But it bears all too clearly on its surface the mark of its origin in the realm of fast and merry chanson melodies for it to be consistent with a setting of the Credo text. There is hardly another mass movement by Josquin in which secular feeling so overpowers the sacred. Even though the words can easily be underlaid, there is a yawning gap between text and music. With the exception of the emphasis on the text in the "passus et sepultus est" section, there is scarcely a bar in which a close word-tone relationship can be observed. How little the composer was concerned with expressing the mass text is evident when practically the same or nearly the same music is used to set completely different phrases of text, as when the music for "Crucifixus etiam pro nobis" returns entirely unchanged at "Et resurrexit tertia die secundum Scripturas". It does no injury to the

In other words if there was a red nose involved, it was Josquin's. Of course, the main problem for Osthoff arose not from his view of the value of the work as a piece of music, but from his preconceived notion of what a piece of sacred music should be like. To put it bluntly, for him the piece was much too happy to be a Credo. This view was shared by Miroslaw Antonowycz, the work's editor in the Josquin *Werken*, who was at one point driven by the need for sacred propriety to make a radical decision about musica ficta (see below).

### The Model (?)

It has long been known that a four-voice chanson with the title "Chescun me crie" was published in *Canti C* and has a concordance in the Cortona/Paris partbooks,[8] but scholars who have commented on the Credo have generally dismissed any real connection between the Credo and the chanson in *Canti C* except for some vague references to the same popular tune.[9] As I wish to argue that the relationship is closer than has been assumed, some discussion of the extant chanson is in order.

The putative original melody "Chascun me crie" can easily be extracted from the four-part arrangement in *Canti C*, since it is almost always presented in the Superius, and the text can be supplied from the Cortona/Paris partbooks (see Example 1).[10]

This polyphonic setting is a very good example of the four-part arrangement or new-style chanson as it was developed by composers like Antoine Bruhier and Ninot le Petit in the last decades of the fifteenth century and the first decades of the sixteenth century, particularly in the way the setting of a melody, with a distinctly uncourtly text presented mostly in the Superius, is parsed into distinct duet and four-voice polyphonic sections with little feeling of overlapping phrases, even though it lacks the triple time

Master's reputation to state that in this composition he employed only routine, not *ingenium*. Helmuth OSTHOFF, *Josquin Desprez*, I (Tutzing: Hans Schneider, 1962), 171-72.

8.   CorBC 95-96/ParisBNN 1817. See Anthony M. CUMMINGS, "Giulio de' Medici's Music Books," *Early Music History* 10 (1991): 65-122. No chanson called "Des rouges nes" has been found; presumably if it existed it resembled "Chascun me crie" and caused confusion or possibly this is because that phrase is part of an interior part of a chanson rather than its beginning, a question only a massive database or a photographic memory (neither of which I possess) might answer.

9.   OSTHOFF, 171: "Mit dem anonymen vierstimmigen Instrumentalsatz 'Chascun me crie' (f-jonisch) in Petruccis 'Canti C' von 1504 besteht-entgegen anderen Angaben in der Literatur-kein Zusammenhang"; HUDSON, 81: "Evidently it was written in imitation of an actual popular song arrangement, although a possible model has not been found. Petrucci's *Canti C* contains a

piece with the title *Chescun me crie*, also obviously incorporating a popular tune; it may have borne similarities to that used in the Credo. Possibly both pieces allude to the same tune; certainly they have much the same carefree character and occasionl melodic similarities."; VAN CAMPEN, 94: "The *Credo Chascun me crie* is not based on a *cantus prius factus* but is merely a series of imitation-points of which only a few refer to a chanson of the same name."

10.   I have added the text following Gustav GRÖBER, "Zu den Liederbüchern von Cortona," *Zeitschrift für romanische Philologie* 11 (1887): 371-404; and Rudolfo RENIER, "Un mazzetto di poesie musicali francesi," *Miscellenea di Filologia e Linguistica in Memoria di N. Caix e U. A. Canello*, Graziado Isaia ASCOLI, ed. (Florence, 1881), 271-88. I am grateful to Anthony Cummings for making these articles available to me. A complete transcription of the chanson is provided in Barton HUDSON's Critical Commentary to vol. 13 of *The New Josquin Edition*, 11-17.

**Example 1**    The Melody "Chascun me crie"

and excited repeated note declamation that one occasionally finds in pieces of this sort.[11] But it certainly makes great use of the clichéd chanson rhythm: ♩ ♩. ♩ ♩ ♩ ♩ and, like many examples of this type of chanson, exhibits a clear repetitive structure, not related to the formes fixes, that can be diagrammed as a large scale refrain form.

11.    For a good description of the general style of these pieces, see Lawrence BERNSTEIN, "A Florentine Chanson-nier of the Early Sixteenth Century: Florence, Biblioteca Nazionale Centrale, Ms. Magliabechi xix 117," *Early Music History* 6 (1986): 1-108, esp. 68-69.

**Example 1 (cont'd)**

*43*

A — cha - scun me cri - e ma - ri - e toi ma - ri - e

*47* — he - las je n'o - se tan suis bon com - pa - gnon

*51*

B' — en - tre vous gen - ti ga - lans ne vous ma-ri - es mi - e

*55* — cer - te si vous ma - ri - es vous fe - res grant fo - li - e ie

*59* — me re - pens de l'a - voir fet or suis ie pris au tre - bu - ciet

*63*

A' — cha - schun me cri - e ma - ri - e toi ma - ri - e

*67* — he - las je n'o - se tan suis bon com - pa - gnon he - las je n'o - se tan

*72* — suis bon com - pa - gnon he - las ie n'o - se tan suis bon com - pa - gnon.

**Diagram 1**  The Chanson "Chascun me crie" (see Example 1)

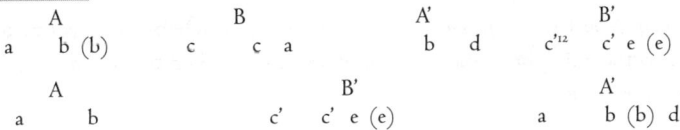

| A | | B | | A' | | B' | | | |
|---|---|---|---|---|---|---|---|---|---|
| a | b (b) | c | c a | b | d | c'¹² | c' | e | (e) |

| A | | B' | | | A' | | |
|---|---|---|---|---|---|---|---|
| a | b | c' | c' e (e) | a | b (b) | d | |

## The Credo

The Credo is divided into three Parts (Patrem, Crucifixus, Et unam sanctam) of 95, 71, and 38 measures respectively.[13]

Part I is difficult to describe. It indeed supports the contentions of those who claim that there is very little actual relationship with the chanson. A more detailed look further shows this section to be constructed in a very strange way. It relies exclusively on one phrase of music that can be divided into two subphrases as shown in Example 2, each of these subphrases subject to slight alteration and combined with the other without any discernable order or plan.

In Example 2, a is the first part of the phrase as presented in the first 10 measures of the work. As has been noticed, this has a resemblance, not to the beginning of the chanson, but to the phrase of the chanson labeled "c" in Example 1. $a^1$ appears as a diminution of a (although it might be more accurate to think of a as an augmentation of $a^1$); sometimes this phrase is preceded by an upbeat (as in mm. 14ff.).[14] $a^2$ is found in mm. 66ff. this is a transposition of a from G to C. It too has a variant found in mm. 77ff.

A problem arises with the second part of the phrase however, for here two distinct melodic shapes are used, both of which could be related to an abstraction labelled b (see Example 2b—the versions are given in order of appearance).[15] Some of these versions of b (particularly when in diminution) recall the second part of the first phrase of the chanson with its stereotyped rhythm (see $b^2$, and $b^4$ for instance), but others are closer to the abstraction than to the chanson which seems to dominate in their transposition to C ($b^4$-$b^8$). The b group is not as homogenious as the a group. There is no way to predict which variant is going to be used.

The combination of the a and b phrases forms the basis of practically everything that happens in the first part of the Credo as the following description shows:

### Part I: Description organized by phrase of the text.[16]

— Section I (All cadences on G)

1: *Patrem omnipotentem factorem caeli et terrae;* mm.1-15; $a+b^1$ (four voices; imitation T,A,B,S); cadence G;

2: *visibilium omnium et invisibilium;* mm.15-23 ; $a^1+b^2$ (begins as overlapping paired duets, B-A, T-S, then becomes duet S, A); cadence G;

3: *et in unum Dominum Jesum Christum filium Dei unigentium;* mm. 23-39; $a^1+b^3$ ( four voices; $a^1$ is in the Tenor covered by the other three voices; canon between T and S on $b^3$ in mm. 29-39); a strong cadence G ends this section.

---

12. In the four-part setting, this is in the Tenor and covered by the other voices.

13. Measure numbers refer to the score published in the *Josquin Werken:* see Example 10.

14. This upbeat is implied in the T and S in mm. 6-7 of the presentation of a.

15. Could it be in this abstraction that we find the elusive "des rouges nes" (sort of like "faisant regretz")?

16. See Example 10.

**Example 2 a-b**  Thematic Elements in the Credo *Chascun me crie,* Part I

— **Section II**

4. *Et ex patre natum ante omnia secula;* mm. 39-44; $a^1+b^2$ (duet B,T); weak cadence on G;

5: *Deum de Deo lumen de lumine Deum verum de Deo vero;* mm. 44-52 (new material loosely based on $b^3$; duet S,A); cadence G;

6: *genitum non factum;*[17] mm. 52-56; $a^1$, $a^1$ ( the repetition [mm. 52-53 (S,A,T)=mm. 54-55 (S,A,B)] and close cadences on G have the effect of turning the **a** phrase from the beginning of something to the end of something ) cadence G;

7: *genitum non factum consubstantialem patri;* mm. 54-59; $a^1+b^4$; (here, the $a^1$ of mm. 54-56 is simultaneously the end of section 6 and the beginning of section 7; that is, the ending quality that had begun to be associated with **a** is negated by the expected appearence of a **b** phrase; nonetheless, the two parts of the tune begin to disassociate); no strong cadence which leads into a kind of transition

8: *consubstantialem patri;* mm. 58-62 (based on $b^4$; duet S,A; here the repetition of the **b** phrase turns it into a beginning rather than an ending phrase); the cadence on D in m. 62 (the first cadence not on G) is inconclusive (this is not the end of a text phrase either), leading directly to the next section

— **Section III**

This section is characterized by cadences on C (the only cadences on C in the entire Credo), the introduction of four-voice imitation, and an ambiguity about the status of the **a** and **b** phrases.

9: *per quem omnia facta sunt;* mm. 62-66; $b^4$ hinted in the S+ $b^5$ in the B (4-part imitation S,A,T at octave, but B at lower fifth ending on C in m. 67); cadence on G/E ( but the Bass is not finished presenting $b^5$ so this cadence is very weak and allows the section to run into the next);

10: *qui propter nos homines;* mm. 66-71; $a^2$ (four voices with three-part imitation T, S, B; the cadence at m 71 makes the **a** phrase appear as the ending of a section rather than the beginning of a section); strong cadence on C;

11: *et propter nostram salutem descendit de caelis;* mm. 71-77; $b^4$ in the S+$b^6$ in the B(four-part imitation S,A,T,B [A and B at lower fifth]; mm. 71-77 are a loose repetition of mm. 62-66;); cadence G/E (with the same ambiguity as the previous G/E cadence);

12: *Et incarnatus est;* mm. 77-82; $a^2$ (four voice imitation A,T, S, B; mm. 77-82 are a loose repetition of mm. 66-71); cadence C. The version of $a^2$ used here does not contain the move up a step on the fourth note; this, perhaps not coincidentally, makes the pitches the same as the setting of "Et incarnatus est" in the chant Credo I; the counterpoint leave little doubt that this was intended (see m. 81); cadence C

13: *de spiritu sancto ex Maria virgine;* mm. 82-88; $b^7$ in all voices (four voice imitation, S, A, T, B) followed by $a^2$ in B; cadence C.

14: *et homo factus est;* mm. 88-95; $b^8$ in all voices (mm. 88-94 are a loose repetition of mm. 83-86; four voice imitation S,A,T, B); cadence, G (tacked on, and therefore somewhat inconclusive sounding); end of section.

17.  The text at this point in VatS 23 is *de deo vero.*

**Diagram 2** The Thematic Structure of Part I

*Patrem omnipotentem. . . homo factus est* (mm. 1-95)

| I | | II | | | III | | | | | | | | | | |
|---|---|---|---|---|---|---|---|---|---|---|---|---|---|---|---|
| 1 | | 15 | 23 | 39 | 44 | | 52 | 54 | 56 | 58 | | 62 | | 66 | 71 | 77 | 82 | 86 | 88 |

$$a+b^1 \quad a^1+b^2 \quad a+b^3 \quad a^1+b^2 \quad [b^3?] \quad a^1 \quad a^1 \quad b^4 \quad [b^4] \quad b^4+b^5 \quad a^2 \quad b^4+b^6 \quad a^2 \quad b^7 \quad a^2 \quad b^8$$

I would summarise my impression of Part I of the Credo as follows. It is more complicated than it appears at first glance and in fact is highly integrated. There seems to be a cantus prius factus behind this section (even if it was a cantus prius factus made up just for this Credo) and it is very "chanson-like" if not directly related to a known chanson melody, yet this tune is not treated in an organized manner. The general impression the listener gains is of a piece which begins straightforwardly, neatly presenting the tune in a series of discrete duets and four-part sections, but becomes murky about 2/3 of the way through when the tune is transposed and interlocking imitation begins. And there is the constant feeling that not merely a tune, but blocks of polyphony are being repeated, even though no literal repetition takes place; further, none of the quasi-repeats are related in any way to the expression of the text. To repeat tunes and polyphony is a characteristic of the new style French chanson of the late fifteenth and sixteenth centuries, but to introduce ambiguity in repeats by constantly altering them in some way, further, to introduce a canon out of nowhere (cf. mm. 29-39), and to alter phrase a so that it becomes a quote of Credo I; these are stylistic characteristics that could be ascribed to Josquin des Prez.

But in Part II of the Credo all bets are suddenly off. The complicated intertwined imitative polyphony and the obsessive and unpredictable restatement of the a and b phrases of the chanson which underly the first part of the Credo are now completely abandoned in favor of discrete separated melodic/contrapuntal blocks contrasting short duets with four-voice sections, also adding sonorities (four-voice homophonic declamation and fauxbourdon) that had not been heard in Part I. These very compositional techniques are in fact precisely those of the new style chanson, and it is perhaps therefore not a coincidence that it is here that the relationship to the chanson *Chascun me crie* is made crystal clear. The thematic elements in this section are presented in Example 3.

**Part II: *Crucifixus ... per Prophetas*; mm. 96-166 (71 measures). Description organized by phrase of text** (See Example 10)

— Section I

In this section the relationship to the extant chanson is the closest.

1: *Crucifixus / etiam pro nobis / sub Pontio Pilato*; mm. 96-106; three clearly demarcated phrases; the beginning is very close to the "a" phrase of the chanson (containing a rising third from the tonic and following it with the stereotyped rhythmic phrase that also recalls b² of Part I and is further treated in fauxbourdon (the first appearance of that sonority in the Credo) (see Examples 1, 2, and 3); cadence G. It is here, in Example 10, that Antonowycz intervened in the "happy" Credo by adding ficta b-flats to create a "g-minor" sonority at "Crucifixus", the only possible reason being that he wanted the music to express the words, since there is no principle of musica ficta that can be invoked to motivate the accidentals.

2: *passus et sepultus est*; mm. 106-108 ; four-voice homophony (the first occurrence); cadence D

3: *Et resurrexit / tertia die / secundum Scripturas*; mm. 109-119; a repetition of 1 (the first direct repetition in the Credo and a clear reference to a major stylistic trait of the new style French chanson) altered only by creating fauxbourdon sections out of the final duet; furthermore, it cannot be claimed that this repetition is engendered by the text;[18] cadence G

4: *et ascendit in caelum sedet ad dexteram patris*; mm. 119-124; this starts out as a repetition of the opening motive of the Credo , yet it also has affinities with the "c'" section of the chanson as presented in mm. 35-38 of Example 1 (see Example 3), cadence G

**Example 3**    Thematic Elements in the Credo *Chascun me crie*, Part II

18. I am not convinced by van Campen's attempt to explain this away with reference to a similar repetition in the Credo of the *Missa de Beata Virgine*. The repeat in that Credo does not extend beyond the first 4 measures of the two texts and indeed responds to the repeat of the chant while the repeat in this Credo is much longer and is not based on chant. See VAN CAMPEN, 97. Note that here, in Example 10, there are no ficta b-flats, forcing a contrast between the "sad" Crucifixus and the "happy" Et resurrexit.

5: *et iterum venturus est / cum gloria judicare / vivos et mortuos*; mm. 124-130; the relationship of the motive in 4. to the c' section of the chanson is reinforced now by a direct quotation of the "e" phrase of the chanson, which follows "c'" (see Example 3 and mm. 38-42 of Example 1), also encumbered in Example 10 by "expressive" b-flats. Furthermore the duets in mm. 124-128 mirror the duets of the four-part arrangement (which also contains a statement of "e" in four voices); at this point, it can no longer be maintained that the Credo has little relationship to the chanson or that any perceived relationship is accidental; cadence G.

## — Section II

Suddenly, in this section all relationship to the extant chanson is abandoned.

5: *cuius regni non erit finis*; mm. 130-134; three voice polyphony; new material not found in extant chanson setting but possibly derived from a cantus prius factus leads to first sesquialtera passage; cadence D

6: *et in spiritum sanctum Dominum / et vivificantem*; mm. 130-142; begins in sesquialtera (mm. 130-137) with new material (duet A,B then four voices); then four voice polyphony with new material; cadence G

7: *qui ex patre filioque procedit*; mm. 142-146; three-voice fauxbourdon statement of the phrase in 5; cadence G; I: mm. 146-150; repetition of text with new four voice harmonization of the phrase; cadence D

8: *qui cum patre et filio / simul adoratur / et conglorificatur*; mm. 150-157; begins as rising duet B, T; then becomes four-part homophony; then becomes descending duet S,A; weak cadence D; mm. 157-159; repeat of text and music of duet at 155-157 at lower fifth, T, B; weak cadence G

9: *qui locutus est per prophetas*; mm. 159-166; starts as duet S,A with material of previous duets beginning on g" and d"; then becomes four voice section to end section; inconclusive cadence on D prepares the way for the third section.

Part III of the Credo is the least distinctive and the shortest, seemingly making references to things that went on in the two preceding sections. Its purpose seems to be to bring things to a close as quickly as possible.

**Part III: *et unam sanctam. . . Amen*; (38 measures). Description organized by phrase of text**

(See Example 10)

1: *Et unam sanctam catholicam et apostolicam ecclesiam*; mm. 169-175; begins by recalling the beginning of Part I, **a**, followed by what could be heard as a reference to **b²** or the second part of the beginning of Part II; cadence G

2: *confiteor unam baptisma*; mm. 175-181; sesquialtera section which also makes reference to **a**; imitation (A, T, B); cadence G

3: *in remissionem peccatorum expecto*; mm. 180-189; begins with paired duets, S,A and T, B with material not related to the extant chanson, but very "chanson-like"; cadence D/B in m. 186 is inconclusive; cadence D

4: *resurrectionem mortuorum*; mm. 189-195; begins by repeating mm. 180-185 reversing the order of voices (now, T,B followed by S,A); cadence D

5: *et vitam venturi seculi*; mm. 195-200; four-voice sesquialtera section; cadence G

6: *Amen*; mm. 200-205; four voices with a reference to **b²** in the S; concludes the Credo with a cadence on G.

Following this parsing of the music, it appears that this Credo in its totality was not composed according to any particular guiding plan; indeed the compositional techniques used in its three sections seem quite different. The first section is based on some sort of cantus prius factus that is used in a manner that is at once obsessive and almost chaotic and further emphasises a move to C; the second section abandons that cantus prius factus and drops the idea of cadences on C in favor of G and D, with clear reference to the style of the four-part arrangement as well as direct quotation of the chanson *Chascun me crie*, and possibly even its extant polyphonic setting; the third section returns to the cantus prius factus of the first, but abandons it immediately and rushes to a conclusion. Nonetheless, there is a feeling that the three Parts were meant to hang together in some way (witness the final cadences of Parts I and II both of which are inconclusive and seem to lead into the next section). The result, with its constant G-major qualities (*pace* Antonowycz) and its lively rhythms is not unpleasing, in fact is quite effective. It is indeed happy, but even one who might not agree with Osthoff about the need for proper reverence for a sacred text would have to admit that this mixture of compositional techniques in the course of one movement simply is not the way a composer born before 1500 constructs a piece of sacred music, particularly a setting of a text from the Ordinary of the Mass. As far as I know, it is not the way a composer born after 1500 constructs such a piece of sacred music. Can this hodgepodge really have "nothing that is inconsistent with his [Josquin's] style" as Hudson claims?[19] In that regard, I would like to point out another aspect of this Credo which adds yet another layer of mystification and seems to have been overlooked by everybody who has discussed the piece. I refer to the unmistakeable, unambiguous, atrocious declamation of: *visibilium omnium* (mm. 14-19), *ante omnia secula* (mm. 42-44), *consubstantialem patri* (mm. 56-61), *etiam pro nobis* (mm. 99-102), *tertia die* (mm. 112-16), as well as the declamation of *sedet ad dexteram patris* (mm. 123-24), and *et apostolicam ecclesiam* (mm. 170-75) (see Example 4).[20]

It is hard to imagine that any composer who had the slightest knowledge of ecclesiastical Latin would have knowingly committed so many obvious solecisms in the course of a single work. A search of Credo settings concentrating on the most egregious examples of bad declamation, *vi-SI-bi-li-um o-mni-um, con-SUB-stan-ti-a-lem Pa-tri*, and *e-TI-am pro no-BIS*, reveals that the rhythm assigned to these words in the Credo *Chascun me crie* appears in no other setting attributed to Josquin, while a survey of the Masses and separate Credos of Josquin's contemporaries and later French composers shows that the rhythms for these words adopted in the Credo *Chascun me crie* cannot be explained as part of some sort of generalized perverted response to Latin accentuation, since they almost never occur.[21] Nor are they representative of the "French accent" in Latin pronunciation,

---

19. HUDSON, 81.
20. The setting of *Crucifixus* isn't so terrific either.

21. Unlike *lumen de lumine*, which often appears set to exactly this rhythm as *lu-mén de lu-mi-né*.

**Example 4**    Bad Declamation in the Credo *Chascun me crie*

vi – si – – bi – li – um    om – ni – um

an – te    om – ni – a    se – cu – la

con – sub – stan – ti – a    lem    pa – – – tri

e – – ti – – am pro    no – bis

ter – ti – – a di – – e

se – det    ad dex – te – ram pa – tris

et    a – – po – sto li – cam

as this tends to emphasize the final syllable of a word. Naturally some of the same sole-cisms can occasionally be found, but generally no more than one such solecism appears in any single work.[22] Thus, it can be claimed that the Credo *Chascun me crie* is in fact the only setting of the text in the entire fifteenth and sixteenth centuries that has so many occurrences of this type of declamation error in the same piece. This is a clear sign to me that the person who produced this Credo was not at all interested in correct declamation of basic Latin words.

It could be argued that the solecisms, all of which are related to the clichéd chan-son rhythm: ♩♩. ♩♩♩ would come about naturally in any piece closely related to the new style chanson. But it was, in fact, perfectly possibly to avoid them even in pieces more clearly related to the new style chanson than is this Credo. As an example, take an anonymous and untitled Mass in VatS 49 which, however, appears to be based on a pop-

---

22. Settings of *etiam pro nobis* in the rhythm of the Credo *Chascun me crie*, are present in the *Credo Sine nomine* (mm. 34-35) of COMPÈRE and in the Credo of the *Missa A l'om-bre d'un Buissonet* (mm. 45-46) of BRUMEL; although in the COMPÈRE, the setting is followed immediately by one in which the declamation is corrected Settings of *visibilium*

*omnium* using this rhythm can be seen in the Credos of OBRECHT's *Missa Pfauenschwantz*, m. 11 (possibly—S only); A. FÉVIN's *Missa O Quam glorifica luce*, mm. 5-6 (only in A and B); MOUTON's *Missa Quem dicunt homines*, mm. 5-9 (only T and B); LA RUE's *Missa Alleluia*, mm. 8-10; SERMISY's *Missa Plurium Motettorum*, mm. 10-11.

ular tune or a four-part arrangement, in this case the chanson *Adieu Madame*, part of which underlies the Agnus II of Bruhier's *Missa Carminum* (see Examples 5-7).[23]

**Example 5** Phrases of *Adieu Madame* in Agnus II of BRUHIER's *Missa Carminum*

**Example 6** The Patrem of the *Missa Adieu madame*, beginning

23. See A.-K. LAIRD and Nors S. JOSEPHSON (eds.),    Wolfenbüttel, 1979).
*Antoine Bruhier, Missa Carminum* (Das Chorwerk 127;

**Example 7** The Crucifixus of the *Missa Adieu madame*, beginning

The chanson-like elements in the *Missa Adieu madame* Credo are very pronounced: the repetition of segments, the short paired duets, the clichéd rhythm; in fact, one could almost reconstruct a four-part arrangement from this setting of the Credo text, and this may indeed be an early imitation Mass. Yet at the words *visibilum* and *etiam pro nobis*, the rhythmic cliché is not allowed to interfere with correct declamation. This chanson-based Credo has none of the chaotic elements of the Credo *Chascun me crie*.

In fact, such clearly bad Latin declamation is usually the sign of a contrafactum.[24] As an example, take the motet *Salve mater pietatis* found in the Gaffurius codices (the text of the prima pars is given below and the beginning of the musical setting in Example 8).

| | |
|---|---|
| Salve mater pietatis | Que totius trinitatis |
| Et totius trinitatis | Sicut mater honestatis |
| Nobili triclinium | Baiulasti unitatem |
| Verbi tamen incarnatis | Fons gratie fons salutis |
| Speciale maestati | Confer virgo sanitatem |
| Preparans hospitium | Salubre iuvamentum |
| O regina castitatis | Nec nos sinas tempestatis |
| Fac nos tue sanctitatis | Inimici rugientis |
| Concipere veritatem | Sentire impedimentum. |

Here we find exactly the bad declamation of the Credo *Chascun me crie*. But here, this is explained by the realization that *Salve mater pietatis* seems to be a contrafactum of a previously unknown setting of *E la la la*, a chanson that we have known only from the four-voice arrangement by Ninot le Petit; the music and words of the chanson in the Superius of Ninot's version fit the Superius of the first part of the motet almost perfectly (see Example 9).[25]

**Example 8**  *Salve mater pietatis*, beginning (MilD 2267, ff. 198ᵛ-200ʳ)

24. Bonnie Blackburn gives similar examples of bad declamation in known contrafacta of Josquin's chansons as motets. See Bonnie J. BLACKBURN, "Josquin's Chansons: Ignored and Lost Sources," *Journal of the American Musicological Society* 29 (1976): 30-76.

25. In the same codex, by the way, is an untexted piece attributed to Coppini that turns out to be a setting of *Vecy la Danse Barbery*; another chanson awaiting a sacred text no doubt (ff. 189ᵛ-190ʳ).

Example 8 (cont'd)

**Example 8 (cont'd)**

[musical notation, measure 25]

- tis con - ci - pe - re ve - ri - ta - tem

- tis con - ci - pe - re ve - ri - ta - em        que to - ti

- tis con - ci - pe - re ve - ri - ta - tem    que to - ti - us tri - ni - ta - tis

- tis con - ci - pe - re ve - ri - ta - tem        que to - ti - us tri - ni - ta -

**Example 9**  Superius of *Salve mater pietatis,* Part I with Superius of *E la la la*

[musical notation]

E la la la la la la la          fai - ctes luy

Sal - ve ma - ter pi - e - ta - tis    et to - ti - us tri - ni - ta - -

[measure 6]

bon - ne chie - - re        mi le - vay par ung ma - tin      la fres - che

- - - - tis          no - bi - le tri - cli - ni - um      ve - bi ta -

[measure 12]

ma - ti - ne - - e          m'en en - tray en no jar - din pour coeul - lier

- tem in - car - na - tis        spe - ci - a - le ma - ie - sta - ti pre - pa -

[measure 19]

gi - rou - fle - - e    e la la la la la la la

- rans ho - spi - ti - um      o - re - gi - na ca - sti - ta - tis      fac nos tu -

24
fai - ctez luy bon - ne chie - - re
e san - cti - ta - tis con - ci - pe - re ve - ri - ta - tem si -
31
m'en en - tray en no jar - din pour coeul - lier gi - ro - fle - - - - -
- cut ma - ter ho - ne - sta - tis bai - u - le - sti u - ni - ta -
36
- - - - - - - e la trou-vay ly mien a - my qui l'a - voit a - mas -
- - tem fons gra - ti - e fons sa - lu - tis con - fer vir - go sa -
41
- se - - e e la la la la
- ni - ta - tem nec no si - ne tem - pe - sta - tis
46
- tez luy bon - ne
i - ni - mi - ci ru - gi - en - tis sen - ti - re im - pe - di -
51
chie - - re a la bel - le ber - ge - - re
- men - tum sen - ti - re im - - pe - di - men - - - - - - - tum

The other voices, however, are mostly new, although they too occasionally seem to quote from the Ninot version. This may mean that *E la la la* really was a popular melody, although it is also possible that we have here a "parody chanson" based on Ninot, or Ninot reworking an earlier work. The point is that without the Latin text this piece would immediately have been recognized as a chanson, and it seems impossible to believe that any composer actually beginning with the Latin words would have produced with such a setting.[26]

Many examples exist of motets created from chansons by contrafactum, although they tend to appear almost exclusively in German or Austrian sources.[27] There are also examples of what might be called contrafacta worked into Masses; again these tend to occur in mid fifteenth-century German or Austrian sources, indeed seem to represent German or Austrian taste, and are generally connected with cantus firmus procedures anyway.[28] Sometimes these consist of entire sections (as in the *Missa Quand se viendra* that has been attributed to Busnois or in the *Missa O Praeclara (La mi la)* of Isaac.[29]) But Adelyn Peck Leverett also points to examples where such contrafacta are used within sections of Masses.[30] This technique, that of occasional "block quotation", may describe what is going on in the Credo *Chascun me crie*, the composer constructing the Credo around direct borrowing of sections of a polyphonic chanson model of some sort (as in the beginning of the Crucifixus), adding new material in order to set the whole text, because there can be little doubt that the Credo *Chascun me crie* in its totality is not a contrafactum; there simply is no extant type of chanson that would fit. (I know of no new-style chansons in three parts, for instance). What sets it apart from the Masses Leverett discusses or the Masses by Johannes Martini which also use this technique is the lack of a clearly defined cantus firmus underlying the entire movement.[31]

If this is true, if the Credo *Chascun me crie* actually uses the technique of contrafactum of a polyphonic model mixed with free writing to make up for the lack of a

---

26. Nothing like this occurs in Ninot's known motets, for instance.

27. See BLACKBURN, "Josquin's Chansons."

28. Adelyn P. LEVERETT, "Song Masses in the Trent Codices: The Austrian Connection," *Early Music History* 14 (1995): 205-56 refers to "block quotation" and "contrafact" as compositional procedures used in song-based Masses in Austria in the mid-fifteenth century.

29. Perhaps only coincidentally, both of these examples occur in Credos. In the *Missa Quand se viendra*, the Et in spiritum is a contrafact of the four-voice version of the chanson of that title. See Richard TARUSKIN (ed.), *Antoine Busnois Collected Works*, Part 3: The Latin-Texted Works, Commentary (Masters and Monuments of the Renaissance 5; New York, 1990), 94-95. In the *Missa O*

*praeclara*, the instrumental piece *La mi la sol* is used; Part I as the Patrem, Part II as the Et unam sanctam. See Martin STAEHELIN, *Die Messen Heinrich Isaacs* (Publikationen der Scweizerischen Musikforschenden Gesellschaft, ser. 2, 28/3 ; Bern, 1977), 63-67. The late fourteenth-century Italian examples of contrafacta in Ordinary movements cannot have much relevance in this context. See Kurt von FISCHER, "Kontrafakturen und Parodien italienischer Werke des Trecento und frühen Quattrocento," *Annales musicologiques* 5 (1957): 43-59

30. LEVERETT, "Song Masses," 228-37.

31. LEVERETT, "Song Masses," and J. Peter BURKHOLDER, "Johannes Martini and the Imitation Mass of the Late Fifteenth Century," *Journal of the American Musicological Society* 38 (1985): 470-523

governing cantus firmus, the work may represent a unique response to a problem that confronted composers of Masses at precisely this time (the late fifteenth and early sixteenth century) which was in fact: "How does one compose a setting of the Ordinary of the Mass that is based on a model but does not have the comfort of the cantus firmus anchor"? They were confronted with this problem because, as Lewis Lockwood has shown, the musical construction of the pool of contemporary models was changing from one with easily extractable complete musical lines to one based on separable sections, be they points of imitation, chains of duets, homophonic passages etc., that were to be sewn together by the composers to create the setting of the text.[32] The solution that Mass composers eventually adopted was the imitation or parody Mass, based on motets, something that is conceptually different enough from the older idea of contrafactum within cantus firmus procedure that it should be viewed as the result of a specific response to a specific problem that arose at a specific point in time.

The Credo *Chascun me crie*, then, might be a very topical experiment in Mass composition based on a polyphonic model but without cantus firmus, distinguished, however, by a lack of clear organization and an unnuanced use of the block quotation technique rather than by the newer idea of recomposition and recombination of imitative motives in some sort of recognizeable order, as was behind the imitation Mass. And this finally (or unfortunately) brings us back to the question of authorship. If my hypothesis is wrong, if the composer of this Credo was not experimenting with the contrafactum technique and actually wanted to set the words mentioned above the way he did, then this composer was not Josquin des Prez; he might as well be the mysterious A.B..[33] But if my hypothesis is correct, then this becomes a different order of piece, one that might have come out of the head of an inventive composer such as Josquin, who was alive to contemporary musical developments, even as the only example of such a work.

---

32. Lewis LOCKWOOD, "A View of the Early Sixteenth-Century Parody Mass," in Albert MELL (ed.), *Queens College Twenty-Fifth Anniversary Festschrift (1937-1962)* (New York, 1964), 53-78. We have normally associated this change entirely with the motet, but as my examples show, at this period, this sectionalized method of construction was applied equally to secular French music and to sacred music to the point that stylistically, in the hands of some composers (the composers of the *Missa Adieu Madame* and other examples that I do not have space to mention) and some consumers of music (the editor of the Gaffurius Codices), they were effectively the same thing.

33. There were in fact at least two composers with the initials "A.B." who were indeed capable of producing a work like this. For instance, Antoine Brumel's *Missa Sine Nomine*, seems to have been based on a chanson or chan-

sons that come from the same family as *Adieu Madame*, presenting the material not as a cantus firmus but as recognizeable phrases, mostly in the superius, and employing the chanson rhythm as well as the duets, imitation, four-voice homophony, and sesquialtera associated with the new-style chanson. And we must not forget the composer of the *Missa Carminum* in which the *Adieu madame* tune appears, that master of the new-style chanson Antoine Bruhier ("A.B."). As it happens, both Brumel and Bruhier (and another "A.B." Antoine Bidon [Collebault]) were active in Ferrara precisely around the time of the publication of Petrucci's *Fragmenta Missarum*. Brumel or Bruhier could have been the composer of the *Missa Adieu Madame*. Yet it should be stressed that the Masses by Bruhier and Brumel even at their most chanson-like are more cogently structured than the CREDO *Chascun me Crie*.

Finally, I want to return to Osthoff's and Antonowycz's objections to the Credo as not being Credo-like in its jaunty happy style. In a posthumously published volume entitled *De Ceremoniis Cardinalium et Episcoporum* (Rome, 1564). Paris de Grassis, papal master of ceremonies for popes Julius II and Leo X, discusses two Credos, the Apostle's Creed, recited in the Offices of Prime and Compline, and the Credo of the Mass (the revision of the Nicene Creed presumably adopted at the Council of Constantinople in 381).[34]

> *Duo inquit symbola sunt, quae per vocabulum Credo invocantur; unum scilicet Apostolicum a duodecim Apostolis in totidem versibus per rithmos Hebraicos cirditum quod cum nec dum missarum canendarum usus haberetur in simplicibus missis quae a primitiva Eccelsia sine cantu legebantur absolute, ut nunc quoque in Prima & Completorio recitabatur. Verum missae cantandae usu demum reperto, quia ipsum Apostolicum symbolum propter versuum & rithmorum concinnitatem sub hilari tripudio cantari vix poterat; ideo per Constantinapolitanam synodum illud ex Hebraeo in Graecum sermonem primo, & mox sub Damaso Papa in Latinum sic translatum fuit, ut cum iucunditate, & tripudio delectabili inter missarum solemnia decantari posset.*[35]

Here de Grassis does not adduce what were presumably the real reasons for the adoption of the Nicene Creed (the need to clarify the expression of faith in the face of heresies), but opts instead for an explanation that seems to depend on the desire to provide a happy musical moment in the celebration of the Mass, one that even may have inspired people to physical movement.[36] Now it happens that de Grassis lived in a time when the chant Credo was indeed sung to a definite rhythm that could take on a "jaunty" aspect depending on the tempo chosen.[37] Was this intended to get the people to sing along and stomp their feet also? At least it might explain why the happy Credo *Chascun me crie*, as the *Patrem des rouges nez*, made its way into the repertory of the papal choir at the very time de Grassis was overseeing the papal ceremonial. We must assume that there was probably at least one occasion in the papal chapel when slightly tipsy (?) "red noses" believed to be Josquin's prevailed over the more solemn recitation of the profession of faith that we know from his other works.

34. See Joseph A. JUNGMANN, *The Mass of the Roman Rite: Its Origins and Development*, 1 Francis A. BRUNNER, trans., (New York: Benziger, 1951), 1: 461-74.
35. *De Ceremoniis Cardinalium et Episcoporum*, 101.
36. "Tripudio" usually means "dance", although in this context it may simply mean "joy" or "happiness".
37. See my article, "The Performance of Chant in the Renaissance and its Interactions with Polyphony," in Thomas KELLY ed. , *Plainsong in the Age of Polyphony* (Cambridge: Cambridge University Press, 1992), 178-208.

**Example 10**  Credo *Chascun me crie*
(from the *Werken, Fragmenta Missarum*, 121-32, including text underlay and ficta)

20
in - vi - si - bi - li - um. Et in
- si - bi - li - um. Et
Et in u - num
Et in u - num
25
u - num Do - mi - num, Je - sum Chri - stum,
in u - num Do - mi - num, Je - sum Chri -
Do - mi - num, Je - sum Chri - stum. Fi -
Do - mi - num, Je - sum Chri -
30
Fi -
stum, Fi - li -
li - um De - i u - ni - ge -
stum. Fi - li - um De -
34
li - um De - i u - ni - ge -
um De - i u - ni - ge -
ni - tum. u - ni - ge -
i u - ni - ge -

38
- - - - ni - tum.
- - - - - - ni - - - tum.
- - - ni - tum. Et ex Pa - tre na - tum, an -
- ni - tum. Et ex Pa - tre na - tum, an - te om -
43
De - um de De - - o, lu - men de lu - mi - ne, De -
De - um de De - - o, lu - men de lu - mi -
te om - ni - a sæ - cu - la.
- ni - a sæ - cu - la.
48
- um ve - - rum de De - o ve - - - - - - - - - - -
- ne, De - um ve - - rum de De - o ve - - - - - - -
52
- ro. Ge - - - - ni - tum non fac - tum,
- - - - - - - - - - - ro. Ge - ni - tum, non fac - tum,
Ge - ni - tum non fac - tum, con - sub - stan-
Ge - ni - tum non fac - tum. con -

57
con - sub - stan-ti - a lem Pa - - - - -
con sub - stan-ti - a - lem Pa - - - - - - - -
- ti - a lem Pa - tri,
- sub - stan-ti - a - lem Pa - tri.
62
- tri, per quem om - - ni - a fac - ta sunt.
- tri, per quem om - ni - a fac - - ta sunt.
per quem om-ni - a fac - ta sunt. Qui prop-
per quem om - ni - a fac - ta
67
Qui prop-ter nos ho - mi - nes
Qui prop - ter nos ho - -
- ter nos ho - mi - nes
sunt. Qui prop - ter nos ho - mi -
71
et prop - ter no-stram sa - lu - tem de - scen - -
- mi - nes et prop - ter nos-tram sa - - lu - - tem
de scen - - - - -
- nes

85
et ho - - mo
ex Ma - ri - - - a Vir - gi - ne. et ho -
Sanc - to, ex Ma - ri - - - a Vir - - - - - - gi - ne,
- ri - tu Sanc - to, ex Ma - ri - a Vir - gi - ne.
90
fac - - - - tus est.
- mo fac - - - tus est.
et ho - - - mo fac - - - tus est.
et ho - - - mo fac - - - - tus est.
96
Cru - - ci - fi - - xus e - ti - am pro no -
Cru - - ci - fi - xus e - ti - am pro no -
Cru - - ci - fi - xus
Cru - - ci - fi - xus e -
101
- bis, sub Pon - ti - o Pi - la - - - - - -
- bis, pro no - - - bis.
pro no - - - bis, sub Pon - ti - o Pi - la - - - - -
- ti - am pro no - - - bis.

106
- to pas - sus et se pul - tus est. Et re - sur - re -
pas - sus et se - pul - tus est. Et re - sur - re - xit
- to pas - sus et se - pul - tus est. Et re - sur - re - xit
pas - sus et se - pul - tus est. Et re - sur -
112
- xit ter - ti - a di - - e, se - cun - dum
ter - ti - a di - - e, ter - ti - a di - - e, se - cun - dum
ter - ti - a di - - e, se - cun - dum
- re - xit ter - ti - a di - - - - - - e.
117
Scrip - - tu - - - - - ras.
Scrip - - tu - - - - - ras. Et a - scen - dit in cæ - lum, se - det
Scrip - - tu - - - - - ras.
Et a - scen - dit in cæ -
122
Et i - te - rum ven - tu - rus est
ad dex - te - ram Pa - tris. cum glo - ri -
Et i - te - rum ven - tu - rus est
- lum. se - det ad dex - te - ram Pa - tris. cum glo - ri -

127
vi - vos et mor - tu - os, cu - jus
- a ju - di - ca - re vi - vos et mor - tu - os, cu - jus
vi - vos et mor - tu - - os, cu - jus
- a ju - di - ca - re vi - vos et mor - tu - os.
131
re - gni non e - rit fi - - - - - nis.
re - gni non e - rit fi - - - - nis. Et in Spi - ri -
re - - gni non e - rit fi - - - - - nis.
Et in Spi - ri -
136
Sanc - tum, Do - mi - num et vi - vi - fi - can - - -
- tum Sanc - tum, Do - mi - num et vi - vi - fi - can - - tem,
Sanc - tum, Do - mi - num et vi - vi - fi - can - - - - - -
- tum Sanc-tum, Do - mi - num et vi - vi - fi -
141
- - - - - - tem,
qui ex Pa - tre Fi - li - o - que pro - ce -
- - - tem, qui ex Pa - tre Fi - li - o - que pro - ce -
- can - - tem, qui ex Pa - tre Fi - li - o - que pro - ce -

145
qui ex Pa - tre Fi - li - o - que pro - ce -
- - - - - - dit. qui ex Pa - tre Fi - li - o que pro - ce -
- - - - - - - - - - - - - - dit, pro - - ce -
dit.
149
- - - - - dit. si - mul
- - - - - dit. si - mul
- - - - - dit. Qui cum Pa - tre et Fi - li - o si - mul
Qui cum Pa - tre et Fi - li - o si - mul
154
ad - o - ra - tur et con - glo - ri - fi - ca - tur.
a - do - ra - tur et con - glo - ri - fi - ca - tur,
ad - o - ra - tur et con - glo - ri - fi - ca -
a - do - ra - tur et con - glo - ri - fi - ca -
159
qui lo - cu - tus est per Pro - phe - - - - - - - tas.
qui lo - cu - tus est per Pro - phe - - - - - - - - -
- tur, per Pro - phe - tas, per
- tur. per Pro - phe - tas.

174
- - - - si - am.
- si - am. Con - fi - te - or u - nam bap - tis - ma,
- cle - - si - - am. Con - fi - te - or u - nam bap - tis - -
- cle - - si - - am. Con - fi - te - or u - nam
180
in re - mi - si - o - nem pec - ca -
in re - mi - si - o - nem pec -
- - - - ma. in re - mi - si - o -
bap - tis - - ma. in re - mi - si - o -
185
- to - - rum. Et ex - pec - - - - - - - - to
- ca - to - rum. Et ex - - pec - to
- nem pec - ca - to - rum. Et ex - pec - - to re -
- nem Et ex pec - to re -
190
re - sur - rec - ti - o - nem mor - tu - o - - -
re - sur - rec - ti - o - nem
- sur - rec - ti - o - nem mor - tu - o - -
- sur - rec - ti - o - nem

195
- rum. Et Vi - tam ven - - tu - - ri sæ - cu - li. A -
Et vi - tam ven - tu - ri sæ - - - - - - cu - li. A - -
- rum. Et vi - tam ven - tu - ri sæ - cu - - li.
Et vi - tam ven - tu - - ri sæ - - - - cu - li. A - -
201
- - - - - - - - - - - - - - - - - men.
- - - - - - - - - - - - - - - - - men. a - - - men.
A - - - - - - - - - - - - - - men.
- - - - - - - - - - - - - - - - - men.

David Fallows

# WHO COMPOSED

## *MILLE REGRETZ?*

**A**T FIRST GLANCE the case looks easy. The song that for over a century has counted for vocal groups and their audiences as the most famous and moving work of Josquin des Prez really cannot be by him. Among twenty-four sixteenth-century sources, the only ones to credit it to Josquin are Narváez's vihuela tablature of 1538 and just two of the four partbooks of Susato's *Unziesme livre* published in 1549. The earliest known sources of the piece are from 1533, already twelve years after the composer's death. If one thing has become increasingly clear from Josquin research of the last half century, it is that these late sources must be viewed with extreme scepticism. As early as 1540, Georg Forster had remarked that "I remember a very great man saying that after his death Josquin had composed more works than in his lifetime."[1]

It is also a classic example of how new information can be added into the factual record without reflection on how it changes the balance of probabilities. Already Eitner had reported in his *Quellenlexikon* that there was an Attaingnant print of 1533 crediting the piece to "J. Lemaire"; but nobody later had seen the print. It came to public knowledge only in the 1960s, in the private collection of the pianist Alfred Cortot. In many ways that print still awaits full investigation: it is one of the few key documents of early western music still to remain in private hands, now in the collection of the pianist's nephew, Jean Cortot; and only the discantus partbook survives.

It would be quite wrong to say that the partbook and its information have been ignored: at the time they were well and seriously discussed by both Daniel Heartz and Martin Picker.[2] But there are two important points that these two men, who surely count

---

1. "Memimi summum quendam virum dicere, Josquinum iam vita defunctum, plures cantilenas aedere, quam dum vita superstes esset." From his preface to his motet collection RISM 1540⁶, a volume that contains nothing ascribed to Josquin. Helmuth OSTHOFF, *Josquin Desprez*, (Tutzing: Hans Schneider, 1962-65), 2:9, quotes this passage, suggesting that the "very great man" could well have been Martin Luther, formerly a close acquaintance and moreover famously enthusiastic about Josquin's music.

2. Daniel HEARTZ, *Pierre Attaingnant* (Berkeley: University of California Press, 1969), 97, and a fuller statement in HEARTZ, "The Chanson in the Humanist Era," *Current Thought in Musicology*, ed. John W. GRUBBS (Austin: University of Texas Press, 1976): 193-230, at 199-202. Martin PICKER, "Josquin and Jean Lemaire: Four Chansons Re-examined," in Sergio BERTELLI and Gloria RAMAKUS (eds.), *Essays Presented by Myron P. Gilmore* (Florence: La Nuova Italia, 1978): 447-56.

among the most professional and most discriminating of recent researchers into Renaissance music, failed to make. First, if a piece survives with many ascriptions to a very famous composer and just one to an almost unknown figure, it very often turns out that the almost unknown figure is the composer. Second, in all such cases it is wise to pay particular attention to the earliest source or the earliest ascription. Both considerations undermine what was in any case a wobbly ascription.

Some of Heartz's and Picker's conclusions, with thirty years' hindsight, are less than compelling. They asserted that the work was in the purest Josquinian style: that they said little to support that view is less worrying than the way such assertions look in the late 1990s, when we can see how many works have now been eliminated from Josquin's *oeuvre*, and how much earlier views on what was "Josquinian" were based on works that are probably not his. If we are looking for a better picture of what Josquin did, we must for the moment resist stylistic or aesthetic judgments and look hard at the documentary case for each piece. For *Mille regretz*, that case looks very thin indeed.

Heartz and Picker also both suggested that the ascription "J. Lemaire" referred to the famous poet Jean Lemaire de Belges. Heartz conceded that there is no other known case of an Attaingnant print (or indeed any early music print) containing an ascription for the text rather than the music. He also noted that if the poem was indeed by Jean Lemaire de Belges, then it cannot have been written for the Emperor Charles V as implied by the title *Cancion del emperador* in Narváez's intabulation of 1538, since Charles became emperor three years after Lemaire's death. One might add, as a gloss to Heartz's remarks, that this consideration further weakens the credibility of the ascription of the piece to Josquin in the Narváez print.

Martin Picker took the discussion in a different direction by putting *Mille regretz* alongside the anonymous setting of a poem demonstrably by Jean Lemaire de Belges, *Sous ce tumbel*, his famous lament at the death of the *Amant vert*, Margaret of Austria's pet parrot. He proposed, following a much earlier suggestion of Droz and Thibault, that *Sous ce tumbel* was by Josquin and that the similarity of the two works both supports his connection with Jean Lemaire de Belges (already known from Josquin's *Plus nulz regretz*, setting a poem unquestionably by Lemaire) and endorses the surviving Josquin ascriptions for *Mille regretz*.

Picker's case for *Sous ce tumbel* being by Josquin rests on three main factors: its position immediately before two unquestionable Josquin works, *Plus nulz regretz* and *Entree suis*, in the Brussels chansonnier 228, a manuscript that shows occasional evidence of organization by composer; the apparent quote at the outset from Josquin's lament at the death of Ockeghem, *Nymphes des bois*; and the stylistic similarity of *Mille regretz*.

Any composer could easily have copied the opening of *Nymphes des bois*, with an obvious allusion that would be wittily appropriate for the *Amant vert* of the poem. Recent discoveries show that *Nymphes des bois* was more widely diffused than was once thought;[3]

and it is hard to think that such a glorious work should not have been known. Since there is considerable doubt as to who composed *Mille regretz*, attention must focus on the song's context in Brussels 228.

First, it must be observed that the song immediately precedes the only other known Lemaire setting in the manuscript, namely *Plus nulz regretz*: if the matter of groupings is to be invoked, that must stand as the *prima facie* explanation for the position of *Soubz ce tumbel*. As Kellman has shown, Josquin seems not to have been well known at the court of Burgundy; Lemaire, on the other hand, was the official court poet and Brussels 228 comes from the collection of Margaret of Austria.

Second, though, *Plus nulz regretz* stands in a rather special place in Brussels 228. It has the most elaborate decoration of any song apart from the opening group and the piece that opens the three-voice section (*Pour ung jamais* on ff. 50ᵛ-51ʳ); it is the only piece in the manuscript with an ascription; and it stands on the first opening of gathering E. All three features would seem to suggest a new beginning. That *Soubz ce tumbel* precedes it, on the junction between two gatherings, hardly encourages the view that the pieces form a planned group and gives no fuel whatsoever to the notion that this is a group of Josquin pieces.[4]

What should be said here is that the Attaingnant ascription "J Lemaire" could easily refer not to the famous poet, who had died eighteen years before the date of the print, but to a composer who is otherwise unknown.[5] There are after all many composers known only from a single piece: those even among the pre-1536 Attaingnant prints listed by Heartz include Adorne (41-17), Barbette (31-27), Beaumont (18-1), Bridam (41-21), Couillart (46-2), Fescam (45-27), Françoys (15-12), Jodon (68-3), L'enfant (61-7), de Lestanc (45-15), Lombart (14-8), G. Louvet (61-11), Colin Margot (68-9) and Vassoris (3-?). Nor am I aware of biographical support for the existence of any of these composers.

There is little need to elaborate on the observation that *Mille regretz* has nothing in common with what is otherwise known of Josquin's four-voice works. Given that the most common reason for misascription is the existence of an authentic piece with a similar text incipit, it is hard to ignore the many German sources that give the title of *Plus nulz regretz* as "Plus mille regretz".[6] An intriguing gloss on that is the existence of another piece called *Mille regretz*. It is in the isolated printed discantus partbook in Paris (Rés.

3. A later source with a Latin text commemorating Josquin himself is reported in Henri VANHULST, "Le manuscrit C¹," *Yearbook of the Alamire Foundation* 2 (1997): 95-102; for a new French poem to the same music in *S'ensuivent plusieurs belles chansons* (Geneva: Jacques Viviane, [c.1520]; only known copy in *CH-Gpu*, Se 9765 Rés); see the discussion in *Die Musik in Geschichte und Gegenwart*, 2d. ed., ed. Ludwig FINSCHER (Kassel: Bärenreiter, 1994-99), s.v. "Genf," by Raymond MEYLAN, vol. 3, col. 1257.

4. It is true that there are some groupings by composer in this manuscript, notably Pierre de la Rue: the opening group of four-voice pieces, nos. 2-12 (though nos. 6 and 11 are not ascribed to him anywhere), and the opening group of three-voice pieces, nos. 44-46, immediately followed by three pieces of Compere. But these are at the beginnings of the two main sections of the manuscript, and there is little sign of such organization otherwise.

5. A point made in Joshua RIFKIN's unpublished paper, "A Singer Named Josquin," n. 15.

6. These two points are also made in RIFKIN, loc. cit.

Vm⁷ 504) reliably attributed to the publisher Christian Egenolff and currently dated ca. 1535, on ff. Gg6-Gg7 (no. V). It appears there straight after Josquin's *Plus nulz regretz* (no. III) and *Adieu mes amours* (no. IV). Given that all pieces in this collection lack the composer's name and that there is elsewhere some evidence of grouping (nos. 17-33 are all taken directly from Petrucci's *Canti B* of 1502), there seems at least a marginal possibility that this is Josquin's setting. It is therefore presented herewith (Ex. 1). Plainly it does not belong to the group of later pieces based on the "Josquin" *Mille regretz*, such as those of Gombert and Susato, which use its materials. As the edition shows, the text can be fitted effortlessly to the music; the shorter phrases in bars 11-13 and particularly 31-33 seem to indicate a ten-syllable line (since such lines in French always have a caesura after the fourth syllable); and the design of the melody seems well suited to a four-line stanza. While there are many French poems with that structure, there seems nevertheless a good chance that this is indeed a setting of the same poem. It is obviously dangerous to attempt an evaluation of a four-voice piece when only the top line survives, so it needs to be stressed at this point that the Egenolff piece is anonymous and that it shows no more contact with what we think of a Josquinian style than does the more famous setting.

Attaingnant printed hardly any Josquin before his late chanson print of 1549 (itself mostly culled from Susato's 1545 volume). Among his thirteen books of motets, he has only two by Josquin, some would think the greatest motet composer of them all: *Virgo salutiferi* and the five-voice *Salve regina*, both of them widely distributed and widely attested as by Josquin. Otherwise, apart from *Mille regretz* with its ascription to Lemaire, there is only the four-voice chanson *Cueurs desolés*, ascribed to "Josquin des pres" in 1529³ but beyond all reasonable doubt by Benedictus Appenzeller.[7]

Susato, as well, seems to have almost entirely ignored Josquin except in his famous collection of Josquin songs in the *Septiesme livre* of 1545 (1545¹⁵). Otherwise his only ascriptions to Josquin are for *Mille regretz* and for *N'esse pas ung grant desplaisir* (in 1544¹³; and repeated in his 1545 print). The ascription of *Mille regretz* in Susato's *L'unziesme livre* is particularly tricky. It reads "Io. de Pres." (S) and "Io. de Pres" (T), the other voices being anonymous.[8] In general "Io" is the standard abbreviation for Johannes, not Josquin. Even though Susato gives Josquin Baston as "Jo Baston" elsewhere several times, the ascription here nevertheless demands caution.

7.   To these we must add the two four-voice canonic songs *Basiés moy* and *En l'ombre d'ung buissonnet* presented anonymously in one of Attaingnant's earliest prints, *Chansons et motetz en canon a quatre parties sur deux* (*c.*1528; HEARTZ no.3), of which a complete copy has now been located in the private library of Graf Schweinitz (on loan to *D-W*), see Ludwig FINSCHER, "Attaingnantdrucke aus einer schlesischen Adelsbibliothek," in Axel BEER and

Laurenz LÜTTEKEN (ed.), *Festschrift Klaus Hortschansky zum 60. Geburtstag* (Tutzing: Hans Schneider, 1995), 33-42. But this early volume of Attaingnant is taken almost wholesale from Antico's *Motetti novi et chanzoni franciose a quatro sopra doi* (RISM 1520³).

8.   These ascriptions are precisely the same in both known editions of Susato's *Unziesme livre* (the only known copy of the later edition is in *A-Wn* S.A. 76.F.44).

| Example 1 | Paris, Bibliothèque nationale de France, Musique, Rés. Vm⁷ 504, no. V |

Moreover the piece has a very odd place in the book. All other songs take up a full page in each partbook, just occasionally continuing on to the top line of the facing page; and the composer's name is printed in large letters at the top of the page in all four partbooks. Just this opening is different, containing three songs: Rocourt's *Plaindre n'y vault*, with the full-size name; then *Mille regretz*, going from bottom left to top right, with the ascription in tiny letters in only two partbooks; and finally Susato's "response", *Les miens aussi*, with an ascription again in tiny letters but in all four partbooks (twice "Tylman Susato", twice "Tylma Susato"). The reason for the "Jo de Pres" ascription being omitted from two partbooks was lack of space: there was too much material on this opening.[9] But the general picture here is plainly unpromising.

Our understanding of the evolution of the "Parisian" chanson is bedevilled by the shortage of printed or manuscript sources between about 1510 and the first Attaingnant prints of 1528; but the existing picture would certainly encourage the notion that *Mille regretz* comes from the later 1520s. It may be a marvellous piece, but how much is that view influenced by the assumption that it is by Josquin des Prez? *Mille regretz* must owe at least part of its popularity to being the single "Josquin" work that fits beautifully to the needs of an amateur SATB group. Technically speaking, there is nothing here that is beyond the wit of a far lesser figure.

9. The technique and problems of ascription here are similar to those in Italian madrigal prints outlined in Stanley BOORMAN, "Some Non-Conflicting Attribu- tions, and Some Newly Anonymous Compositions, From the Early Sixteenth Century," *Early Music History* 6 (1986): 109-57.

At this point I should mention that I have held the views expressed above since first reading Daniel Heartz's book on Attaingnant in 1970 and learning that the 1533 print had actually been found. The details of the case may have accumulated gradually in my mind over the years (often in conversation with people who have felt likewise, though I do not believe anybody has made these doubts public[10]); but the discovery of the 1533 print seemed to me already then severely to undermine the dubious case presented by the other sources and the style of the piece. How could a late work by the man who was by then unchallengeably the most famous composer who had ever lived have circulated so widely without an ascription? And it was only in the course of an attempt to edit the piece for the New Josquin Edition that things began to look different. As a preliminary to the discussion, it seems necessary to present the full listing of sources for *Mille regretz*, giving the source abbreviations to be used in the New Josquin Edition.

### Manuscripts

**Bs¹**    Basel, Öffentliche Bibliothek der Universität, MSS F.IX.59-62, SATB f. 29ʳ (no. 59), Anonymous

**Bs²**    Basel, Öffentliche Bibliothek der Universität, MSS F.X.17-20, S f. 10ʳ; AB f. 10ᵛ; T f. 11ᵛ (no. 21), Anonymous

**Bl**    Berlin (West), Staatsbibliothek Preussischer Kulturbesitz, MS Mus. 40194, ff. 12ᵛ-13ʳ [T partbook only], Anonymous

**Ca**    Cambrai, Médiathèque Municipale, MSS 125-128 (*olim* 124), SATB f. 131ʳ, Anonymous. Full text in S partbook

**Gd**    Gdańsk (Danzig), Biblioteki Polskiej Akademii Nauk (Library of the Polish Academy of Sciences), MS 4003 (*olim* Mus. q.20), SATB f. 16ᵛ, Anonymous. All voices carry full text

**Mu¹**    Munich, Bayerische Staatsbibliothek, Musiksammlung, Musica MS 1501 (= Maier 207), S f. 20ᵛ; ATB f. 21ᵛ (no. 40), Anonymous

**Mu²**    Munich, Bayerische Staatsbibliothek, Musiksammlung, Musica MS 1516 (= Maier 204), SATB no. 22, Anonymous

**Re**    Regensburg, Fürst Thurn und Taxis Hofbibliothek, MS Freie Künste Musik 3/I, no. 46 [B partbook only], Anonymous

### Early Printed Editions

**At**    *Chansons musicales a quatre parties* (Paris: Pierre Attaingnant, April 1533) [S partbook only], f. 11ʳ, J le maire. Fully texted

**Su**    *L'unziesme livre contenant vingt et neuf chansons amoureuses a quatre parties* (Antwerp: Tylman Susato, 1549), SATB, ff. 9ᵛ-10ʳ, Jo de Pres (ascription in S and T partbooks only; A and B are anonymous). All voices carry full text

10. They have been outlined in Louise LITTERICK, "Forgotten Works," in the informally circulated book of essays for the conference *New Directions in Josquin Scholarship*, ed. Rob C. WEGMAN (Princeton University Department of Music, 1999): 122-31, esp. 125-27; she repeats the doubts in her chapter for *The Josquin Companion*, ed. Richard SHERR (Oxford: Oxford University Press, 2000). They are also outlined in Joshua Rifkin's unpublished paper "A Singer Named Josquin."

Intabulations

Am     Amsterdam, Toonkunst-Bibliotheek, MS 208. A. 27 (*olim* Maatschappij tot Bevordering der Toonkunst, Bibliotheek, MS V. B. 13), ff. 27ᵛ-28ʳ, Anonymous. In German lute tablature

Kl      Klagenfurt, Kärtner Landesarchiv, MS GV 4/3, ff. 23ᵛ-24ʳ, Anonymous. In German keyboard tablature

Mu³   Munich, Bayerische Staatsbibliothek, Musiksammlung, Musica MS 266 (= Maier 248), f. 41ʳ, Anonymous. In Italian lute tablature

Mu⁴   Munich, Bayerische Staatsbibliothek, Musiksammlung, Musica MS 272 (= Maier 253), f. 47ᵛ, Anonymous. In German lute tablature

Wr     Wrocław (Breslau), Biblioteka Kapitulna, MS 352, ff. 54ᵛ-56ʳ (no. 54), Anonymous. In German lute tablature

Ger    *Tabulatur auff die Laudten ... Durch Hanns Gerle ...* (Nuremberg: Hieronymus Formschneider, 1533), ff. 40ᵛ-41ʳ (no. 32), Anonymous. In German lute tablature

New   *Der ander theil des lautenbuchs ... durch mich Hansen Newsidler* (Nuremberg: Johann Petreius, 1536), ff. Ee3ᵛ-Ee4ᵛ, Anonymous. In German lute tablature

Nar    *Los seys libros del Delphin de musica ... por Luys de Narbaez* (Valladolid: Diego Hernandez de Cordova, 1538), ff. 40ᵛ-42ʳ, Jusquin. In Spanish vihuela tablature. Ascription is on preceding page (f. 40ʳ): "Comiençan las canciones Francesas y esta primera es una que llaman la cancion del Emperador del quarto tono de Jusquin."

Ph¹    *Carminum quae chely vel testudine canuntur, trium, quatuor, et quinque partium liber secundus* (Louvain: Pierre Phalèse, 1546), ff. e3ᵛ-e4ʳ, Anonymous. In French lute tablature on 5-line staves. This intabulation concords with **Gerle 1533⁴**

Ph²    *Des chansons reduictz en tabulature de luc a trois et quatre parties livre deuxieme* (Louvain: Pierre Phalèse, 1546), ff. e3ᵛ-e4ʳ, Anonymous. In French lute tablature on 5-line staves. This is bibliographically identical with **Ph¹** and similarly concords with **Gerle 1533⁴**.

Ph³    *Hortus musarum in quo tanquam flosculi quidam selectissimorum carminum collecti sunt* (Louvain: Pierre Phalèse, 1552), pp. 52-53, Anonymous. In French lute tablature on 5-line staves

Hec¹   *Lautten Buch ... Durch Wolffen Heckel von München ...* (Strasbourg: Urban Wyss, 1556), "Discant" [= 1st lute part], pp. 66-69, Anonymous; no copy survives of the "Tenor" partbook. In German lute tablature

Hec²   *Lautten Buch ... Durch Wolffen Heckel von München ...*, (Strasbourg: Christian Müller, 1562), "Discant" [= 1st lute part], pp. 66-69, Anonymous; "Tenor" [= 2nd lute part], pp. 55-57, Anonymous. In German lute tablature

Ph⁴    *Theatrum musicum* (Louvain: Pierre Phalèse, 1563), f. 22ʳ, Anonymous. In French lute tablature on 5-line staves. This concords with **Phalèse 1552²⁹**

Of these sources, four tablatures could be dropped immediately as having no independent value: Ph¹ and the identical Ph² are both derived straight from Ger; Ph⁴ comes directly from Ph³; and the incompletely surviving Hec¹ was reprinted almost exactly in Hec². But in any case examination needed to begin with the staff-notation sources.

Obviously it seemed wise to start by attempting to reconstruct the earliest surviving version, that in the Attaingnant discantus print of 1533 (At). Apart from anything else, all previous modern editions have used the late Susato print (Su), and it would be good to explore the possibility of presenting the music differently. Musically, there were just two variant readings in the surviving discantus partbook: even minims rather than the dotted figure in bar 4 (see Ex. 2), and a lightly embellished suspension in bar 21 (see Ex. 3). It was good to note that these readings were supported by various manuscript sources: for bar 4, Bs¹, Bs², Gd and Mu²; and for bar 21 all these apart from Gd.

Those findings were satisfying, because they offered a good case for thinking that the lower voices of those manuscripts could be used to reconstruct the remainder of the At version. Long ago Bruce Whisler's doctoral thesis on Mu² had established that a very large proportion of its pieces were copied directly from Attaingnant.[11] There was no such clear case here, because these untexted sources occasionally tie notes that are separate in their exemplars; but there was a good case for thinking that they at least belonged to the same part of the stemma and were perhaps taken straight from At.

The resulting reconstructed four-voice version had two added advantages: first, at least two of the manuscripts directly imitated the suspension at bar 21 with the same figure in the tenor at bar 23 (see Ex. 3), which was to be expected; second, and far more interesting, all four, together with the isolated tenor partbook Bl, had the tenor falling a fourth to E in bar 25 rather than the more familiar G (Ex. 4). This last was a turning point in the investigation. The E at that point would offer a reading in my edition that was seriously and fascinatingly different from all previous modern editions; and its falling fourth was in many ways part of a pattern that obtained throughout the song. For all those variants, only Ca and Mu¹ agreed with Su, whereas the other staff-notation sources resoundingly endorsed the version derived from the At part of the stemma.

**Example 2** Variants in bar 4

---

11.   Bruce A. WHISLER, *Munich, Mus. Ms. 1516: A Critical Edition* (Ph.D. diss., University of Rochester, 1974).

**Example 3**  Variants in bar 21 and 23

**Example 4**  Variant in bar 25

But this turning-point actually turned in a rather surprising direction. It was time to consider the tablature sources. All were embellished, so there was little hope of finding either endorsement or contradiction of such tiny variants. So it was a surprise to find that all the tablatures apart from Nar unambiguously supported the tenor G at bar 25 rather than the E; that is, they all clearly had a first-inversion chord in the first half of the bar, with G as the bass, adding the E root only for the second half of the bar. That gave pause for thought, since it is reasonable to expect an intabulation to prefer the easiest solution—the root-position chord throughout the bar. The reading of all but one of the tablatures (agreeing with the staff-notation sources Su, Ca, and Mu[1]) is definitely a *lectio difficilior* in tablature terms and should be taken seriously. In that context it needs to be remembered that At is not quite so absolutely the earliest surviving source: the tablature Ger was published in the same year, 1533.

Returning to bar 4, there were more surprises. None of the sources in staff-notation of the bassus matched the non-dotted figure in the At discantus: they all had the dotted rhythm familiar from editions based on Susato. Perhaps that should not be too worrying: the momentary dissonance that results is in some ways rather attractive. But again it was notable that most of the tablatures endorsed the dotted rhythm in both voices, among them the earliest, Ger.

At the very least, it was now beginning to seem as though it would be irresponsible to present an edition based on At and related sources. To do so would merely be to offer something else for the sake of being different—something to justify the labour of exploring the work's full source basis for the first time. There was a further point here that now seemed relevant: the text presented in the Attaingnant print cannot be correct, since its fourth line does not rhyme with the first. For most purposes it is better to consider the stemma for the text separately from that for the music; but in this new context it began to look like yet another indication that Attaingnant printed a corrupt version of the song.

In fact the picture now was of two main branches in the song's transmission: a "Parisian" one in At and sources perhaps copied from him; and a "Flemish" one in Su (Antwerp), Ca (Bruges) and Mu¹ (origin not determined, but perhaps south German). Of those traditions it was the "Flemish" one that looked far better; the "French" one had a corrupt text and several musical variants that did not withstand full scrutiny.

The next and (in my mind) decisive turning-point came with an examination of the lute tablatures at the cadences in discantus bar 21 and tenor bar 23. In general tablatures embellish all cadences, so there would be no reason to expect them to offer any useful insights here. But it happens that two of the tablatures emphatically do not embellish the cadence at bar 21 (Mu⁴ and Ph³) and two do not in bar 21 (Mu⁴ and Hec²). It was the last thing I expected to find. In that context it suddenly became significant that the staff-notation sources have a slightly (if only slightly) inconsistent pattern here: Gd has a simpler suspension at both cadences (supported in bar 23 by the isolated tenor partbook Bl); and Bs¹ embellishes the two voices differently.

That in its turn led to two conclusions that may seem obvious enough but needed resisting at the early stage of source comparison. The first conclusion is that in staff-notation sources the insertion of a suspension or the decoration of a cadence is the easiest and the first kind of corruption that can arise; moreover, the simplification of a cadence like this is emphatically not the kind of thing you would expect a scribe to do on his own initiative. On top of the growing doubts about the "Parisian" readings in bar 4 and bar 25, the findings here finally convinced me that a responsible new edition of *Mille regretz* would once again need to take Su and the two related sources as its basis. The second conclusion, surely one that would be endorsed by all musicians who have ever loved the piece, is that the stark unembellished and unsuspended cadence is astonishingly beautiful, in some ways one of the most ineffably moving touches in this tiny piece.

Those conclusions inevitably change the balance of probabilities about who composed the piece. The case for the prosecution presented at the start of this essay continues to look fairly formidable. But if Attaingnant really did have a version of *Mille regretz* that was corrupt in both its text and its music, perhaps he was working from a distant copy that named the poet rather than the composer, or simply got the composer's name wrong. It remains true that in the twenty years of his publishing activity prior to the 1549 Josquin collection (itself mainly taken from Susato), he published only two motets by Josquin and ascribed to him one song that is demonstrably by Benedictus Appenzeller. He really cannot be considered a reliable informant on Josquin des Prez.[12]

But the situation with Susato can be read differently. The Josquin songs he printed in his 1545 volume may not all be unanimously accepted as his today, but in most cases he was the first person to print them; the collection does betoken an active interest in Josquin. Moreover we know that Susato had a special interest in *Mille regretz*: he composed a three-voice parody of the song, printed in his 1544 volume; he printed an adaptation of it to become a pavane in his *Derde musyck boexken* of 1551; he composed two settings of the *response* to the poem, *Les miens aussi*, that in three voices printed after his own three-voice *Mille regretz*, that in four voices after the "Josquin" setting. Put those details on top of the stemmatic evidence that he printed the best surviving version of the song, and it begins to look as though his ascription should not be taken lightly.

The last two considerations are ones that particularly concern your own work, my dear Herbert, since I first heard you speak at the 1974 Annual Meeting of the American Musicological Society in Chicago, on the occasion when you revealed for the first time—alongside much else about Josquin's last years—the special place of his motet *Pater noster-Ave Maria* in Josquin's obsequies and the likelihood that it is one of his last works.[13] Because, with the view for the first time in my adult life that *Mille regretz* could really be by Josquin, I naturally began turning the pages and ransacking my aural memories for anything comparable in his work. *Mille regretz* shares nothing significant with the other famous Phrygian piece considered to belong to his last years, the mass *Pange lingua*; but then I have recently argued that this could well be from far nearer to 1510 than 1520.[14] But there are the most astonishing parallels in the six-voice *Pater noster*: in its 120 bars there

---

12. It is of course true that in these years Attaingnant concentrated his efforts mainly on the publication of new works — a matter that is even more true of his Lyons contemporary Moderne, who printed not a note of Josquin's music.

13. A view challenged in Daniel E. FREEMAN, "On the Origins of the *Pater noster - Ave Maria* of Josquin Des Prez," *Musica disciplina* 45 (1991): 169-219.

14. "Approaching a New Chronology for Josquin: an Interim Report," forthcoming in *Schweizer Jahrbuch für Musikwissenschaft* NS 19 (1999): 1-20.

are only four suspensions; and, despite its six voices, the motet gloriously exemplifies the astonishingly restrained textures, the gentle repeated notes, and the phrase parallelism of *Mille regretz*. The exploration of those similarities must be a task for another day, perhaps when its forty known sources have been fully explored. So too must be the point that emerges so clearly from these pieces, as from so much else of Josquin, namely that a major part of his genius was in the ability to cut down the number of notes, rather as Debussy was to recommend four hundred years later. Both *Mille regretz* and *Pater noster* seem to achieve that in the most magical way.[15]

The second detail concerns our first personal conversation, some six months later, when you described some details of your paper for the 1972 Josquin Festival-Congress, most particularly the matter of the famous payment record reporting that two singers from Condé, one of whom was called Joskin, had visited the emperor Charles V in September 1520 and been paid a reward for *aucunes chansons nouvelles*.[16] Your brilliant analysis of the document and of earlier views about it indeed serves to reinforce the point that Josquin des Prez was not particularly well known at the Netherlands court, or at least not to the accountant who later reimbursed the treasurer for this sum and made a record to explain the payment. But, as we have often discussed since, this is perhaps the weakest of your arguments for this particular case, since it could be mere chance that the accountant abbreviated the entry rather than spelling out Josquin's full name and titles. Besides, there is the further issue of Josquin's age: back then it looked as though Josquin would be about eighty years old at the time and hardly likely to be making such trips. Now we seem to be agreed that Josquin was born later than once thought; in fact my current view is that he was born in about 1455 and would therefore have been almost exactly sixty-five at the time—still young enough to travel, to sing, and to write peerless masterpieces.

Whether *Mille regretz* was one of them we shall probably never know; but I am now inclined to think that the *cancion del emperador* was indeed one of Josquin's very last works and written for Charles V.

---

15. Hermann FINCK, *Practica musica* (Wittenberg: heirs of Georg Rhaw, 1556), f. Aii[r], remarked that Josquin's music was *in compositione nudior, hoc est, quamvis in inveniendis fugis est acutissimus, utitur tamen multis pausis* (quoted from OSTHOFF, *Josquin Desprez*, 1:92, who however misprints

"invendis" for "inveniendis").

16. Herbert KELLMAN, "Josquin and the Courts of the Netherlands and France: the Evidence of the Sources", in *Josquin des Prez*, ed. Edward E. LOWINSKY (London: Oxford University Press, 1976): 181–216, at 186–89.

Stefano Mengozzi

# JOSQUINIAN VOICES AND GUIDONIAN LISTENERS

*Nam siquis manus non habeat,*
*ergo cantum discere non potest?*
*Id credere stultum est.*

For shall we conclude that a person without [a left] hand
can not learn how to sing?
It is foolish to believe so.

Johannes GALLICUS (*De ritu canendi vetustissimo et novo, c.*1460)

## The Guidonian System as "Second Nature" for Late Medieval and Renaissance Musicians

THE IDEA THAT WESTERN ART MUSIC was "hexachordally coded" for a sizeable portion of its long history—roughly from the late middle ages to the Renaissance—is now customarily accepted by music scholars in the field.[1] A series of studies that began to appear about thirty years ago has slowly but inexorably led to the conclusion that the six-note segment known as the "Guidonian hexachord" served not only as the basis of a widely adopted system of solmization, but also as the main pillar of the entire musical system of Western art music at least from the fourteenth to the sixteenth century. Support for this view relies on a vast and diverse body of evidence that is gathered from careful scrutiny of music-theoretical writings, analyses of compositional structures, interpretations of notational conventions, and information on the early training of medieval and Renaissance composers and singers.

In a landmark study that in many ways set the tone for subsequent research on this subject, Gaston Allaire chose as his point of departure the now widely accepted idea of the hexachord as a sort of second nature for practicing musicians. Since the hexachordal system was internalized by Renaissance singers at an early stage of their musical training—so Allaire's theory claimed—in later times they would instinctively process musical intervals and pitches in accordance with the rules of that system.[2] More recent-

---

1. I borrow the expression "hexachordally coded" from Thomas BROTHERS, *Chromatic Beauty in the Late Medieval Chanson* (Cambridge: Cambridge University Press, 1997), 39.

2. Gaston ALLAIRE, *The Theory of Hexachords, Solmization and the Modal System* (Rome: American Institute of Musicology, 1972), 44.

ly Jeffrey Dean has proposed the "solmization-as-second-nature" argument in support of his hexachordally-based analysis of modal strategies in Ockeghem's music.[3]

In the same year that saw Allaire's contribution, Richard Crocker portrayed Hermannus Contractus' major sixth as a scalar module that was essential to negotiate the relationship between the tetrachord of the modal finals and the Greater Perfect System, thus substantiating his view of the hexachord as "the central concept for both chant and polyphony up through the sixteenth century."[4] Crocker had anticipated some of his views in his discussion of Gioseffo Zarlino's renumbering of the modes.[5] More recently, the same author has offered the following summary of the development of the diatonic system in the West:

> [The] use of the tetrachord of the finals continued as the cornerstone of European history: the *Musica [enchiriadis]* had, in effect, added a whole tone to one end of the tetrachord or the other (C + D-E-F-G or D-E-F-G + a). Guido of Arezzo, a century later, added *both* these whole tones to make the hexachord (C-D-E-F-G-a), the basic tonal construct that was used in European music until replaced by the major scale (C-D-E-F-G-a + b), sometime in the seventeenth century.[6]

Other scholars, such as Margaret Bent, have interpreted the virtually ubiquitous presence of the Guidonian syllables in late medieval and Renaissance musical treatises as an indication of the essential role played by hexachords in defining the relationship between individual pitches and the steps of *musica recta*. According to Bent,

> [I]t was only when yoked with hexachordal syllables that the letters acquired unequivocal tone-semitone definition, even within the norms of *musica recta*. Only when coupled with the superstructure of overlapping hexachords could letters convey the normal, customary

3.   Jeffrey DEAN, "Ockeghem's Attitude Toward Modality: Three-Mode and Eight-Mode Typologies," in Ursula GÜNTHER, Ludwig FINSCHER, and Jeffrey DEAN, eds., *Modality in the Music of the Fourteenth and Fifteenth Centuries*, Musicological Studies and Documents 49 (American Institute of Musicology; Neuhausen-Stuttgart: Hänssler-Verlag, 1996): 203-46, esp. 210.

4.   Richard L. CROCKER, "Hermann's Major Sixth," *Journal of the American Musicological Society* 25 (1972): 19-37 (the citation is from p. 37). Echoing Crocker's argument quoted above, Richard FREEDMAN has recently described some of Luca Marenzio's harmonic procedures as resting "in an extreme application of the most basic of Renaissance musical conceptions, the semitone *mi-fa* as a central determinant of the hexachord and, therefore, of musical space" (see his "Marenzio's *Madrigali a quattro, cinque et sei voci* of 1588: A Newly-Revealed Madrigal Cycle and its Intellectual Context," *Journal of Musicology* 13 [1995]: 318-49, citation at 327). Finally, Norman CAREY

and David CLAMPITT have recently expanded on Crocker's reading of Hermannus in their "Regions: A Theory of Tonal Spaces in Early Medieval Treatises," *Journal of Music Theory* 40 (1996): 113-47, especially section IV, pp. 125-32. The very distinction between *cantus durus* and *cantus mollis* that is frequently encountered in the musicological literature rests on the idea of the musical space as articulated in interlocking hexachords.

5.   "Perchè Zarlino diede una nuova numerazione ai modi?," *Rivista italiana di musicologia* 3 (1968): 48-58.

6.   Richard CROCKER, review of *Musica enchiriadis and Scolica enchiriadis*, translated with introduction and notes by Raymond ERICKSON (New Haven: Yale University Press, 1995), in *Notes* 53/1 (September 1996): 61, emphasis in the original text.

relationships in *musica recta*. E-F was a semitone only by virtue of, or by being understood normally to have, the hexachord articulation mi-fa.[7]

Finally, this interpretation of hexachordal syllables as "space-definers" figures prominently also in recent textbooks of Renaissance music, a sure indication of the wide reception enjoyed by this theory today.[8]

In spite of the conspicuous body of evidence that has been presented in support of the general orientation outlined above, the hypothesis that the Guidonian hexachord may have operated as a central cognitive structure for Renaissance musicians is not without difficulties, as the present article aims to show. In the first place, other normative systems of pitch organization—such as the diatonic modes and counterpoint—were based on a theory of diatonic intervals that privileged the octave, while it assigned a very marginal role to segments of six notes. It is misleading to downplay the cognitive weight of the octave by arguing that this interval had merely a nominal or theoretical significance for medieval and Renaissance musicians, or that it was too large and too complex for them.[9] On the contrary, the interval of the *diapason* appears to be central to eminently *practical* treatises on modes (often described with reference to the seven letters only) and discant.[10] The hexachordal

---

7.  Margaret BENT, "Diatonic Ficta," *Early Music History* 4 (Cambridge: Cambridge University Press, 1984): 9-10.

8.  "One of the practical difficulties faced by the musicians of the Middle Ages came in correctly placing the semitones of the diatonic scale as they sang the melodies of the liturgy. This led to the invention of one of the most widely used didactic devices to come out of the musical tradition of that age: solmization by hexachords." (Leeman L. PERKINS, *Music in the Age of the Renaissance* [New York: W.W. Norton, 1999], 987); "What the gamut did was define the diatonic scale and, with the aid of the solmization system, locate the relative placement of whole steps and half steps along the way.... The solmization syllables remained the same from one hexachord to another. Their main purpose was to locate the relative position of the whole steps and half step; the half step in each hexachord always came between the syllables *mi* and *fa*" (Allan ATLAS, *Renaissance Music: Music in Western Europe, 1400-1600* [New York: W.W. Norton, 1998], 34-35). Along the same lines, Lionel PIKE has recently described the hexachord as "a means of identifying notes" in his *Hexachords in Late-Renaissance Music* (Aldershot: Ashgate, 1998), 13. (I have reviewed this study for *Music Theory Online*, 4/3 [May 1998], URL: http://smt.ucsb.edu/mto/issues/mto.98.4.3/toc.4.3. html.) Among the numerous studies that have attempted to articulate analytic approaches to medieval and Renaissance music grounded on hexachordal theory, see

in particular Eric T. CHAFE, *Monteverdi's Tonal Language* (New York: Schirmer, 1992); Christian BERGER, *Hexachord, Mensur, und Textstruktur: Studien zum Französischen Lied des 14. Jahrhunderts*, Beihefte zum Archiv für Musikwissenschaft, 35 (Stuttgart: Franz Steiner Verlag, 1992); as well as Pike's study mentioned above. For a critical response to Christian Berger's study, see Sarah FULLER, "Modal Discourse and Fourteenth-Century French Song: A 'Medieval' Perspective Recovered?," *Early Music History* 17 (1998): 61-108.

9.  This is the line of argument proposed by Christian Berger, when he writes that "Die Oktaveinteilung bleibt aber während des ganzen Mittelalters eine bloß theoretische Gliederung, die in der Praxis keine große bedeutung hat.... Als musikalische Intervall wird die Oktave erst in der Verbindung von Quinte und Quarte greifbar.... Die *litterae* sind eben wie in der Grammatik bloß 'partes vocum significativarum et ipse nichil [sic] significant'," in *Hexachord, Mensur, und Textstruktur*, 97. Richard Crocker refers to the octave as "too large a module" for Frankish theorists, and stresses the fact that the pitch names of the Greater Perfect System tended to obscure the notion of octave equivalence ("Herman's Major Sixth," 29).

10.  To mention only one example, after listing the six types of consonances (*species discantus*)—unison, minor third, major third, fifth, major sixth, and diapason—the anonymous author of the *tractatus secundus* of the Berkeley manuscript (*c.*1375) offers the following explanation:

system may have become second nature for some musicians in particular areas of musical practice, but the first "nature"—presumably learned in the cradle, *cum lacte*—was certainly not easily shed or rendered ineffective through the various stages of musical training.

Secondly, the fact that several fifteenth- and sixteenth-century theorists openly criticized the hexachordal system as unnecessarily complicated and even counterproductive as a pedagogical device should warn us against the acritical tendency to view the Guidonian system as a conceptual frame that was accepted by all musicians from all corners of Western Europe for half a millennium. I am referring here in particular to treatises by Johannes Ciconia, Johannes Gallicus, and Bartolomeo Ramos de Pareja—all active in northern Italy throughout the fifteenth century—but the list becomes significantly longer if we include other more or less radical attempts to reform the Guidonian system that were proposed mostly north of the Alps in the sixteenth century. One easily concedes that the numerical consistency of this group of theorists and musicians pales in comparison with the countless legions that solmized, mutated, and permuted with Guido's syllables for centuries on a daily basis. But if we start from the premise that the Guidonian system was a *sine qua non* for the musicians and the theorists of that time, then we need to explain how it was possible for some of them to reject that system altogether, what induced them to do so, and why their proposed alternatives were preferable, in their eyes, to the traditional method.

Thirdly, it could be argued that the few extant commentaries of Renaissance music by contemporaneous listeners—most notably those by Henricus Glareanus, dating from

---

"The six species stated above are called simple, because they are comprised inclusively within the diapason. It must be known concerning the aforesaid that since, according to the Pythagoreans, every simple consonance is embraced within the diapason and everything outside can be called a reiteration, it was not necessary to present here more species than the aforesaid ones. The tenth is counted like the third since it is composed of a diapason and a third. The twelfth (that is, the diapason-with-diapente) is counted like the fifth, the thirteenth like the sixth, the double octave like the diapason, and so on for the others" ("Supradicte vero 6 species dicuntur simplices, eo quod infra dyapason inclusive sunt comprehensi. Et sciendum circa predicta, quod cum, secundum Pitagoricos, omnis consonancia simplex infra dyapason amplectitur, et quicquid exterius est reiteracio potest dici, non fuit necessarie plures in hoc opere ponere species quam predictas. Decima enim reputatur quasi tercia, quia componitur ex dyapason et tercia. Duodecima, id est dyapason cum dyapenthe, reputatur quasi quinta, terciadecima quasi sexta, duplex octava quasi dyapason, et sic de aliis." See *The Berkeley Manuscript: University of California Music Library, MS. 744 (olim Philipps 4450)*, ed. and trans. by Oliver B. ELLSWORTH (Lincoln:

University of Nebraska Press, 1984), 112-15. Similar passages are found in many treatises of the late middle ages, such as those by Johannes de Muris, Ugolino of Orvieto, Prosdocimo, Hothby, Tinctoris, Gaffurius, Aron, and others. I should like to point out that an hexachordal reading of these pairs of intervals will only occasionally confirm this relation of "reiteration." The interval of a third, for example, does not necessarily correspond to the same hexachordal syllables that would indicate a tenth. The dichotomy between letters and syllables in this case is further emphasized by the equivalence at the octave (*aequisonare* is Gaffurius' term) of pitches reached by contrary motion. This is the familiar "rule of the 9," which Guilielmus Monacus (late fifteenth century) formulated in a language that seems to hold hexachordal considerations in no regard: "unisonus accipitur pro octava, *tertia bassa accipitur pro sexta alta*, tertia alta accipitur pro decima, *et ipsa quarta bassa accipitur pro quinta alta*, et ipsa quinta alta aliquotiens accipitur pro duodecima, et ipsa *sexta aliquotiens accipitur pro tertia bassa*, et ipsa octava bassa accipitur pro unisono," *De preceptis artis musice et pratice compendiosus libellus*, ed. Albert SEAY, Corpus scriptorum de musica, 11 ([Rome]: American Institute of Musicology, 1965), 35, emphasis mine—and more on this later.

the first half of the sixteenth century—do not support the hypothesis of the hexachord as an essential diatonic structure for either listeners or composers. A close examination of Glareanus' own descriptions of his "modal hearings" is beyond the purpose of the present paper and must remain the subject for a future study. Here I will limit myself to suggesting that Glareanus' concepts of *phrasis*, ambitus, and modal "transposition" point to the octave, rather than the hexachord, as the main scalar module of the diatonic space, in spite of Glareanus' frequent reliance on Guidonian syllables throughout his treatise.[11]

The entire argument about the possible cognitive primacy of the Guidonian system—or, better said, about the extent to which that system had cognitive primacy for medieval and Renaissance musicians and listeners—depends on the crucial issue of the functional relationship between two rather different models of diatonic space that seem to emerge from contemporary musical treatises. On the one hand, a conceptualization of the diatonic space as consisting of interlocking segments of six Guidonian *voces* is no doubt very common, especially from the thirteenth to the sixteenth century. On the other hand, however, an alternative model conceived as a continuum of musical "quantities" expressed by the seven *litterae* not only occurs prominently in the music-theoretical literature of the time, but it also provides the default ordering of musical pitches for the codification of vital practical matters, such as intervals, modes, counterpoint, and tuning. In sum: given the undeniable fact that the two "segmental" and "circular" models of the diatonic system went hand in hand through centuries of musical theory and practice, the question for modern scholars becomes one of determining which one of the two models had structural and cognitive priority over the other—since it does not seem likely that two uneven diatonic sets such as those of the *voces* and the *litterae* may have been equally responsible for the conceptualization of musical space at any given time.

The present paper will attempt to offer an answer to this basic question by exploring the aural significance of the Guidonian hexachord, or, more precisely, by measuring the extent to which the Guidonian syllables may have operated as a referential system in the minds of Renaissance listeners. My main concern is to try to understand the mechanism by which such listeners may have made sense of a polyphonic mass or motet by mentally allocating pitches and intervals to underlying hexachordal scale degrees, expressed by solmization syllables. It seems logical, even tautological, to assume that the act of listening—in its active, passive, and silent variants—must have been an essential step in the process of internalizing the Guidonian system, for it is not clear how anything musical could be internalized at all by any other means. And inasmuch as listening is the goal of composing music, it is hard to believe that composers would write hexachordal-

---

11.  I have dealt extensively with Glareanus' commentaries on chant and polyphony—albeit not in the context of the present topic—in my "Between Rational Theory and Historical Change in Glareanus' *Dodecachordon*" (Ph.D. diss., University of Chicago, 1998).

ly—whatever that concept might imply—if hexachords were not, somehow, aurally perceived by at least the musically-educated portion of the audience. In short, the issue of listening sits at the very core of the modern theory of "hexachord as second nature," and it is the category of hexachordal listening that seems particularly in need of definition and clarification, if current theories on this thorny issue are to be properly evaluated.

For the purpose of this paper, I will consider only the "hexachordally-trained" listeners, that is to say, largely the singers themselves who were familiar with the nuts-and-bolts of the Guidonian system and who had presumably acquired an hexachordal mind-set after years of daily practicing with the system. My analyses will concentrate on the music by Josquin Desprez, given this composer's penchant for introducing hexachordal references and puns of various sorts in his music—a tendency that is often conveyed by the very titles of his compositions. My general thesis is that solmization and listening often followed distinct paths, since the conversion of aural musical data into hexachordal patterns too frequently would have proved to be a forbidding task even for hexachordally-trained listeners.

## Intervals Expressed as Guidonian Syllables

An important chapter of chant modal theory offers a convenient point of departure for our investigation of the possible aural significance of Guidonian hexachords. A widespread mnemonic formula assisted medieval and Renaissance singers in identifying the mode of a given piece and—more importantly—in choosing the appropriate psalm-tone after a given antiphon. The formula associated each of the eight modes with two syllables, of which the first indicated the end of the antiphon, and the second the beginning of the words "saeculorum amen" that closed the intonation of the psalm:

> Primus re la, secundus re fa
> Tertius mi fa, quartus mi la;
> Quintus fa fa, sextus fa la
> Septimus ut sol, octavus ut fa.

This pithy mnemonic formula may conceal a much-needed answer to the key question on the functional relationship between modes, hexachordal syllables, hexachords, and interval species. I would like to suggest that the Guidonian syllables in this context indicate interval species, rather than hexachords. The point of the formula is to convey the information that, for example, the third species of fifth *fa-fa* (often changed into *ut-sol* by turning B natural into B flat) is characteristic of mode 5, and that the fourth *mi-la* is typical of mode 4. The fact that these intervals correspond to different "hexachordal degrees"—a concept that is in any case significantly absent from the theoretical literature—seems altogether irrelevant: the decisive factor, for the singer and listener, is not the position of a given pitch within the hexachord, but rather the intervallic context around a given pitch which is established as a *finalis* through a combination of rhythmic and melodic features. That such intervallic context may be expressed by Guidonian syllables is not necessarily an indication that those intervals and pitches are part of an underlying hexachordal grid. Indeed, I am aware of no medieval source suggesting that the process of modal recognition activated by that formula would proceed from the syllable to the hexachord and from the hexachord to the mode.

In other words, the formula is not there to remind the singers and listeners that one of the characteristic notes of mode 1 falls on the second degree of the hexachord. Rather, it reminds them that this pitch corresponds to the lowest note of a particular species of fifth that is conveniently, but not necessarily, expressed by a solmization sylla-ble. In accordance with this view is the fact that around the middle of the fifteenth century Johannes Gallicus not only qualified the seven letters as *dominae* and the six syllables as *sub-ditae*, but also offered mnemonic formulae that bypassed the syllables altogether:

> *Rhythmi faciles ad cuius toni sit antiphona discernendum:*
> Pri[mus] per D A cognoscitur, Se[cundus] per D F discernitur.
> Ter[tius] per E C, Quar[tus] per E A, Quin[tus] per F C, Sex[tus] per F A.
> Sept[imus] per G D videbitur, Oc[tavus] per G C similiter.
> Sed per A D si finiat in A talis antiphona.[12]
> *Hi docent per singulos tonos omnes inchoare psalmos:*
> Primus tonus inchoatur per F G A, sed acutum,
> Et secundum per C D F graves quidem intonatur.
> Tertius et per G A C duabus iunctis notulis,
> Quartus autem per A G A, sed inchoans in acutis.
> Quintus vero per F A C primam habens in gravibus,
> Sextus quoque sicut primus, tertiam tangens acutam.
> Septimus C♮C, quae tamen erunt acutae.
> Octavus et per G A C divisis quippe voculis.
> Verum in A finientes per D C D, sed acutas.[13]

In the notated examples of the psalm tone formulae that follow, Gallicus has inserted the same capitalized letters in front of each corresponding note, so that the reader can find an immediate confirmation of his mnemonic stanza.

---

12. "Easy verses to recognize the mode of the antiphon: The first mode is known through D A, the second through D F. The third through E C, the fourth through E A, the fifth through F C, the sixth through F A. The seventh appears through G D, likewise the eighth through G C. But the interval is A D if the antiphon ends in A." See Johannes GALLICUS, *De ritu canendi vetustis-simo et novo*, ed. SEAY (Colorado Springs: Colorado College Music Press, 1981), part 2, p. 39, translation mine.
13. "These verses teach how to begin all the psalm tones

in each of the eight modes: the first tone begins with F G A, in the range of the *acutae*, the second is intoned C D F in the *graves*. The third is sung with G A C, with two of them [A C] tied together, the fourth with A G A, but beginning in the *acutae*. The fifth mode begins as F A C, with the first note in the *graves*, the sixth is like the first, touching the third of the *acutae*. The seventh C♮C, but in the range of the *acutae*. The eighth goes G A C, with the notes divided. Those that end in A begin with D C D, but in the *acutae*" (GALLICUS, *De ritu canendi vetustissimo et novo*, ed. SEAY, part 2, p. 39, translation mine).

It is easily conceded that Gallicus' "*rhythmi faciles*" may be more cumbersome to memorize—or even to read—than their "Guidonian" counterpart. Moreover, they obscure the fact that in practice these melodic formulae are not tied to specific pitches, but may instead be freely transposed. To express the characteristic intervals of modes and psalm-tones by means of Guidonian syllables does have the advantage of reflecting the flexible conventions of pitch of a largely oral performance practice. On the other hand, Gallicus' letters do allow some freedom of transposition in that they are by no means tied to specific pitch frequencies. They should be taken as indications of nominal pitches, rather than absolute ones: a certain modal type is introduced as long as certain characteristic intervals are established, at whatever pitch level.

It is interesting to compare the "Guidonian" rule for mode 3 and Gallicus' own version. In Guidonian terms, the characteristic syllables of this mode (*mi/fa*) encompass the range of a minor sixth, E-c, an interval that implies a mutation from *naturalis* (E*mi*) to *durus* (C*fa*). But Gallicus' polemical avoidance of the syllables suggests that such an operational switch carried no musical meaning. Surely, had he perceived hexachordal shifts as "beautiful" or "relevant" musical events, he would not have gone as far as to propose his Occam's razor method based on identifying letters and intervals only.[14] Thus, Gallicus' treatment of the Guidonian syllables as dispensable elements constitutes by itself an unequivocal statement about "pitch conceptualization" from the early Renaissance, while it also points to "non-Guidonian" singing practices that may have been more common than is customarily believed today.[15]

## The Guidonian Syllables in Prosdocimo's *Contrapunctus*

The modern confusion as to whether hexachords or octaves constituted the foundation of the late-medieval musical system should come as no surprise, since the very sources that contain the key for an answer to this crucial problem are often themselves ambiguous. Theorists tend to gloss over the issue of the relationship between the six syllables and the seven letters; at best, they deal with this subject only in indirect or cryptic ways.

14. I should like to add here that one of the chief goals of solmization manuals of this period is to teach singers how to *make* mutations in the most rational way, rather than to *locate* them in their notated part ("*fare* le mutationi" is the typical wording used by Italian theorists). To my knowledge, no medieval theorist has ever proposed rules for the *recognition* of hexachords similar to those that were customarily taught for the eight modes. Of course, identifying the *proprietas* (*durus, mollis, naturalis*) of a given *cantus* was necessary in order to correctly associate syllables with letters. I would like to suggest, however, that the purpose of this identification was merely operational,

that is, to ascertain the status of the B key within the *cantus* regardless of its distinct role in relation with the other pitches. In other words, because the *proprietates* did not reflect pitch emphases, their identification was relevant only for the purpose of solmization.

15. Gallicus himself explicitly denies using hexachordal solmization while teaching chant to his Carthusian brothers. I briefly survey this and other documented cases of non-Guidonian musical training in my "The Ciconian Hexachord", *Johannes Ciconia, musicien de la transition*, ed. Philippe VENDRIX (Paris: Klincksieck, forthcoming).

To make things even worse for modern scholars, some of their statements in this regard appear to be in flagrant contradiction with each other. Consider, for example, the third chapter of Prosdocimo's *Contrapunctus* (written *c.*1410). In the opening paragraph it is the six *voces* musicales that literally "generate" consonant and dissonant sounds. In the paragraph that follows, however, the basic intervals are listed as spanning from the unison to the octave, and all the additional intervals (which today we call "compound") are measured with an octave-long yardstick:

> I say that an interval is the combination of two syllables producing a sound consonant or dissonant to the ears; and by "syllables" I understand the musical syllables, of which there are six, ut, re, mi, fa, sol, la. Furthermore, I say that the intervals customarily named in this art by all our predecessors are read out in great number: the unison, the second, the third... and the octave, which has the force of the unison, since every song that begins with a unison can also begin with an octave, and vice versa; likewise the ninth, which has the force of the second for the reason stated; the tenth, which... is considered similar to the third... the sixteenth, similar to the second and the ninth... the twenty-second, similar to the unison, the octave, and the fifteenth; and so forth, proceeding in this way to infinity, if the syllables or instruments could be extended to infinity.[16]

In the following chapter, and elsewhere in his treatise, Prosdocimo goes as far as to describe intervals an octave apart as *equivalentes*.[17] This relation of equivalence at the octave remains at odds with the argument that those same intervals result from the combination of the six Guidonian syllables, since two pitches an octave apart will only occasionally correspond with the same syllable, as I have already observed. There is little doubt, however, that the concept of octave equivalence shapes the content of Prosdocimo's *Contrapunctus* far more extensively than the alternative definition of musical intervals as generated by the Guidonian syllables.[18]

To be sure, Prosdocimo's definition of unison does not corroborate this interpretation. In his view:

> the unison occurs when both syllables making up the counterpoint are found on the same part of the musical hand and with the same syllable, because two syllables could be on the

16. "Dico quod vocum combinatio est duarum vocum consonantiam vel dissonantiam auribus reddentium insimul agregatio, et intelligo per voces, voces musicales, que sunt sex, scilicet ut, re, mi, fa, sol, la. Ulterius dico quod combinationes vocum in hac arte nominari solite ab omnibus nostris predecesoribus quamplures esse recitantur, scilicet unisonus, secunda, tertia... et octava, que tantum valet quantum unisonus, quoniam omnis cantus inceptus in unisono inchoari potest in octava, et e contra; item una nona, que tantum valet quantum una secunda propter causam dictam; et una decima... uni ter-cie assimilatur... et decima sexta, secunde et none... et vigesima secunda, unisono, octave, et quinte decime; et sic ulterius isto modo in infinitum procedendo, si in infinitum voces vel instrumenta elongari possent." See Prosdocimo DE BELDEMANDIS, *Contrapunctus*, a new critical text and translation by Jan HERLINGER (Lincoln: University of Nebraska Press, 1984), 34–37.

17. PROSDOCIMO, *Contrapunctus*, ed. HERLINGER, chap. 3 (pp. 38, 40, and 42); chap. 4 (p. 58 and 60).

18. *Contrapunctus*, 37, n. 3.

same part of the musical hand and nonetheless not be in unison, like the fa and mi found in ♭fa ♮mi, which, though they be on the same part of the musical hand, as is evident, are nevertheless not in unison, because they are not and cannot exist on the same syllable.[19]

But the case of ♭fa ♮mi singled out by Prosdocimo constitutes the exception rather than the rule, since in most of the remaining "parts of the musical hand" multiple syllables did correspond with the same pitch, expressed by one single letter (e.g., E *la-mi*; c *sol-fa-ut*). In all these instances, one suspects that Prosdocimo's distinction between "omosyllabic" and "eterosyllabic" unisons was irrelevant from the perspective of performing and compositional practices, both monophonic and polyphonic. As Herlinger points out in his discussion of this passage, late medieval theorists usually described the unison as two notes occupying the same position on the staff.[20]

In his lengthy treatment of the distinction between consonance and dissonance, for example, Prosdocimo avoids any mention of the six syllables. At the same time, he maintains that such a distinction has a direct impact on an hypothetical listener (*auditor*) who, upon hearing vertical sonorities, will respond to the related connotations of sweetness and harshness (*dulcor* and *duritia*):

> The second rule is this: that counterpoint ought to begin and end only with perfect intervals—with the unison, the major fifth, the major octave, and their equivalents; the reason for this is if the listener is to be charmed by these harmonies, he should at first be moved by the harmonies that are sweeter and more amicable by nature; these are the perfect consonances named above, and thus they are to be placed first. Finally, the listener ought to be sent away with the sweetness and harmony delectable to nature, lest the listener's spirit, moved by the sweet preceding consonance, be repelled by the harshness of the final consonance from that toward which harmony is directed, enjoyment and delight.[21]

It is of course not at all surprising to realize that Prosdocimo's *auditor* would be no less sensitive to the vertical aspect of any given "cantus" (that is, to octave-based *contrapunctus* or *armonia*), than he or she would be to the horizontal one. Even less remarkable is the prescription that a polyphonic piece begin and end on perfect consonances. More inter-

---

19. "Unisonus est quando ambe voces contrapunctum facientes in eadem parte manus musicalis et voce reperte sunt et dicitur notanter in eadem parte manus musicalis et voce, quoniam possent esse due voces in eadem parte manus musicalis et tamen non unisone, sicut est de fa et mi que in ♭fa ♮mi reperiuntur, que, licet sint in eadem parte manus musicalis, ut apparet, non tamen sunt unisone, quia in eadem voce non sunt nec existere possunt" (PROSDOCIMO, *Contrapunctus*, ed. HERLINGER, 36-37).
20. Idem, 37, n.3.
21. "Secunda regula est hec, quod contrapunctus nunquam incipi vel finiri debet nisi in combinationibus

perfectis, scilicet in unisono vel in quinta maiori vel octava maiori vel in hiis equivalentibus, et ratio huius est quoniam si auditor per armonias mulceri habet, oportet ipsum primitus admoveri per armonias dulciores et nature amicabiliores, que sunt consonantie perfecte superius nominate, et sic ipse preponende sunt. Demum etiam ipse auditor dimitti debet cum dulcore et armonia nature delectabili, ne ipsius auditoris anima dulci consonantia precedente mota duritie consonantie finalis ab eo quod per armoniam intenditur, scilicet gaudio et delectatione, amoveatur" (PROSDOCIMO, *Contrapunctus*, ed. HERLINGER, 58-61).

esting for the purpose of this paper is the suggestion that the Guidonian system plays no role in discriminating between consonances and dissonances. In this passage and throughout the *Contrapunctus*, the distinction between the two seems to be exclusively a matter of intervallic *lengths*, rather than one of establishing certain correspondences between sounds and syllables.

In sum: Prosdocimo's puzzling argument about the constituent role of the six syllables in counterpoint needs to be understood in the context of the treatise as a whole, as well as of traditional contrapuntal theory. But it is certainly possible to accept it at face value and to address the questions that it inevitably raises. To wit: if hexachordal syllables are responsible for producing consonant and dissonant sound, as Prosdocimo at times seems to suggest, how was it possible—if it was possible at all—for a late medieval or Renaissance listener to *hear* musical sound as hexachordally-coded in the context of an octave-based system of counterpoint? How could such a listener understand musical pitches *embedded in counterpoint* in terms of their hexachordal position? By which factors, or according to which rationale, could the aural information derived from the hexachordal placement of musical pitch override the sense of cyclical diatonicism conveyed by octave-based counterpoint? The following analyses will attempt to formulate preliminary answers to these questions.

## Josquin and the Hexachord: *Stabat mater dolorosa*

The opening phrase of Josquin's *Stabat mater dolorosa* provides a good example for the essential ambiguity of Prodoscimo's hexachordal approach to counterpoint (Ex. 1). Upon hearing the head motive in the parts of Bassus and Superius, an hexachordally trained listener would no doubt think of two statements of the syllables *sol-sol-mi-ut-fa-mi-re-ut* an octave apart (with slight modifications). Because the Superius answers at the octave, the contrapuntal relations between this part and the Bassus are conveniently expressed by the syllables: the *mi* and *ut* of the Bassus are respectively a minor and a major tenth lower than the *sol* and *mi* of the Superius, and these are the same syllables that would still obtain if the two parts moved in parallel thirds, rather than tenths.

Within an "hexachordal" context so clearly established in the outer voices, how would a Guidonian listener negotiate the cantus firmus part in the Tenor? From an hexachordal point of view, the beginning of this melody—borrowed from the Tenor of Binchois' *Comme femme desconforteé*—is also straightforward, as it suggests the syllables *ut-re-fa*. These syllables, however, belong to the hexachord that is complementary to the one being established by Bassus and Superius. At some point, our listener would have to realize that the Tenor part resides in an hexachordal portion of the gamut that lies a fourth below the Superius and a fifth above the Bassus, as in *naturalis-durus-naturalis* or *mollis-naturalis-mollis*. But here we may pause and wonder: given the fact that these three parts would be most likely

**Example 1**  JOSQUIN, *Stabat mater dolorosa*, beginning

solmized as indicated above, would Guidonian listeners—or even the singers themselves—also hear these parts as *belonging to* different hexachords? If so, how would they be able to *perceive* different hexachords at the same time, and how would they mentally shift between them?

More importantly, it is necessary to evaluate this hypothetical perceptive model based on solmization syllables in the context of the contrapuntal relations between the three parts. Since the Tenor starts at the unison with the Bassus (*pace* Prosdocimo), there seems to be no reason for mentally labeling its opening pitch as *ut: sol* would seem to be a better choice, especially considering that, as the Tenor holds this note, the Bassus reaches the third and the fifth lower, corresponding with the syllables *mi* and *ut*. Likewise, the *fa* of the Bassus on the B flat of measure 3 automatically qualifies the upper D of the Tenor as *la*. As for the third note of the Tenor, the fact that it lies a major third below the *mi* of the Superius and a full octave above the *ut* of the Bassus strongly points to this note as *ut*, rather than *fa* (which, again, remains the most plausible syllable from the point of view of a singer who is solmizing this part).

On the other hand, one cannot rule out the possibility that an hexachordal listening of the passage might start from the Tenor, rather than from the Superius and Bassus, on account of the well-known structural importance of this part in Renaissance polyphony. Measured from the standpoint of the Tenor, the hexachordal status of the Superius changes considerably: the third semibreve turns from *mi* to *la* (a major sixth from the *ut* of the Tenor), the fourth one from *ut* to *fa*, and the A of "do-lo-<u>ro</u>-sa" from *mi* to *la* (against the *fa* of the Tenor).

To summarize my argument: for the purpose of solmization the hexachordal position of any given pitch depends exclusively on horizontal considerations (that is, on the hexachordal placement of the neighboring pitches within the same melodic line); however, to ascribe cognitive significance to the Guidonian system is to go far beyond the limited domain of solmization, as the hexachordal position of any given pitch depends in this case not only on that of the other pitches in the same part, but also on the contrapuntal relationships between all the parts involved. Thus, I would like to propose that the neat demarcation between hexachords that often results from solmizing the various parts of a given polyphonic excerpt becomes easily blurred when the reciprocal relations among these parts are taken into account. The additive arithmetics of counterpoint, which by definition assumes a seamless model of diatonic space, by itself obliterates the idea of co-existing hexachordal "regions" that is suggested by the practice of solmization. On the basis of these considerations (as well as others to be exposed below), it seems unlikely that the daily practice of solmization may have shaped—even in the long run—the innermost cognitive structures of Renaissance musicians. On the contrary, a scenario in which pitches may be associated with more than one syllable and mutations may be introduced, eliminated, or displaced at will inevitably qualifies the six syllables as rather shaky and at best superficial signposts of the diatonic space.

### Salve regina a 5

Interpreted in cognitive terms, the Guidonian syllables can be positively misleading. In Josquin's five-part *Salve regina* (Ex. 2), the first four notes on the word "Salve" in the Superius quote the well-known Gregorian tune, which—as any musically trained listener would have known—is solmized *la-sol-la-re* (D-C-D-G in the Josquin). When the Quinta Vox answers at the lower fifth by entering on the last G of the Superius, the syllables become *sol-fa-sol-ut* (G-F-G-C), an hexachordal spelling that is also prepared by the opening melisma in the Altus part. However, to *hear* this entrance as *sol-fa-sol-ut* implies both a mental transposition of the structural hexachord down a *fourth* (such as from *mollis* to *naturalis* or from *naturalis* to *durus*) and a shift of hexachordal degrees from 6-5-6-2 in *mollis* to 5-4-5-1 in *naturalis*.

Now, I am puzzled by the idea of a listener, who, facing a run-of-the-mill instance of transposition down a fifth, would mentally perform a "systemic" transposition down a fourth plus a concomitant shift of the melodic material one scale degree lower (even without mentioning the problem of the exact sequence of this two-step computation). It is perhaps more instructive to attempt to understand just why those two consecutive statements of the Gregorian incipit of *Salve regina* would be solmized that way. The decisive factor is that none of the three constituent intervals of this head motive (a descending second followed by an ascending second and a descending fifth) is a semitone. Of course, a

**Example 2**  JOSQUIN, *Salve regina*, beginning

semitone is necessarily located somewhere in the "empty" space between the second and the fourth note of the motive, but the fact that this interval is not directly stated allows the motive to be presented in a variety of diatonic contexts while preserving its characteristic contour. Contrarily, had the motive featured a semitone among its constituent intervals, it would have always been solmized in the same way under transposition.[22]

Within the gamut "per B flat" there are five different positions in which the *Salve regina* motive may occur, namely, E, D, C, A, and G; the remaining two *claves*, F and B flat, are not available in that they are located at the upper edge of a semitone. It seems to me that this conclusion alone corroborates Johannes Gallicus' view of the letters as *dominae* and of the syllables as *subditae*: the possibilities of transposition of the *Salve regina* motive are determined not by its hexachordal position, but rather by the intervallic context of each of the seven letters. It is the variety of diatonic contexts in which the motive may appear—contexts that are determined by the individual position of each letter within an octave-based gamut—that is responsible for the number and the types of possible solmizations of the motive.

Thus, it is possible to argue that the two different solmizations of the *Salve regina* motive at the beginning of Josquin's motet do not point to the cumbersome transpositional computations that I have described above. Rather, they convey the important information that different diatonic species are being employed in the two statements (the descending fifth, in particular, is implicitly "minor" in the first statement, and implicitly "major" in the second one). Such a conclusion is in line with my argument above that in the rules for the recognition of the modes the Guidonian syllables express intervallic "qualities" pre-determined by the letters. To argue the other way around— that is, that the syllables were a necessary tool for the definition of the relative position of the letters within the gamut—is simply to place the cart before the horses.

---

22.  The *soggetto cavato* of the *Hercules* Mass illustrates precisely this point.

**Example 3** JOSQUIN, *Petite camusette,* first entrance of Bassus

## Petite camusette

Other examples from the Josquin *oeuvre* show that the association of specific sylla-bles to musical intervals may be quite problematic, when established on the basis of listening alone. Since the determining factor in the identification of the underlying "hexa-chord" is the position of the semitone *mi-fa*, any ambiguity on the exact location of the semitone within a given subject will cause a listener to wonder as to precisely which sylla-bles (here in the "hard" sense of "hexachordal scale degrees") are being performed. The first entrance of the Bassus in Josquin's six-part *Petite camusette* is a good example of this type of ambiguity. In this part the head motive of the chanson maintains the two characteristic leaps of a fifth, but avoids the upper neighbor figure of Superius and Quinta pars (b-E-b-c-b) (Ex. 3). A textbook solmization of the Bassus line would obviously require one to label the opening B as *mi* and immediately to perform the characteristic mutation *mi/mi* required by the second species of fifth. A singer who resolves to adopt such a strategy will have no problems performing the remainder of the first phrase. The main advantage of this choice of solmization lies in its placing the syllable *ut* on the C that introduces the final run of six-teenth notes, a labeling that has almost the entire melisma—with the only exception of the upper b*mi*—fall within the span of the natural hexachord.

From the perspective of a Guidonian listener, however, the first phrase of the Bassus part may well cause a headache, because the only reliable clue that would allow him to translate correctly the opening fifth into Guidonian syllables—namely, the semitone *mi-fa* that *must* be placed somewhere in that "empty" space—makes only a quick appearance at the end of the phrase, almost buried by the melisma. In this case, not only would our listener not know whether he is hearing *cantus durus* or *cantus mollis* (as it is generally the case), but he would not even know which syllables, or "hexachordal scale degrees," correspond to the notes he is hearing. More precisely, our listener would have no way of telling whether the opening fifth corresponds with *mi/mi*, or rather with *la-re*, as it indeed happens when the motive is stated in the Tenor and Sexta pars beginning on E.

In the context of this discussion it is particularly interesting to observe that these two alternative aural interpretations are essentially identical in their intervallic structure—that is, in a non-Guidonian scenario—as the only possible difference between them may affect exclusively the pitch level of the fourth note of the final melisma (either F or F♯). From the point of view of the constituent intervals of the phrase, nothing earth-shattering happens when this tiny little note finally occurs (at either pitch level): the opening fifth at the beginning of the piece will retain its structural weight no matter where the semitone turns out to be, so much so that a trained listener may even guess that the two opening notes correspond respectively to the *confinal* and the *final* of the chanson, or at least of its opening section. The arrival of the semitone may no doubt contradict the expectations of a non-Guidonian listener to some extent, but it will not call for a reassessment of the diatonic positions and relative weights of the notes heard until that point.

On the other hand, such a reassessment may be precisely what a Guidonian listener would have to perform, were the crucial *mi-fa* to appear in the unexpected place. If he had mentally processed the opening fifth as *la-re*, rather than *mi/mi*, upon hearing the semitone several breves later he would have to reinterpret the first note of the subject from *la* to *mi*, the second one from *re* to *mi*, and so on, following the correct intervallic configuration. Of course, our listener would more likely choose a combination of the two basic hexachordal readings suggested above, or perhaps even different ones. But it is hard to believe that such a frustrating operation of retroactive pitch-reckoning would take place in someone's mind. It seems more reasonable to conclude that even expert listeners would have heard the beginning of *Petite camusette* without superimposing syllables to pitches.

### The Christe from the *Missa la sol fa re mi*

Paradoxically, uncertainties about the precise hexachordal status of diatonic pitches persist even in the relatively rare cases of subjects derived from hexachordal syllables, the so-called *soggetti cavati dalle vocali*. The Christe from Josquin's *Missa la sol fa re mi* (Ex. 4) opens with the subject first introduced in the Superius beginning on A-*la*, immediately imitated by the Altus beginning on E-*la* (bars 15-22 of the Josquin Edition).[23] Tenor and

---

23.  For a discussion of the origins of this mass and an overview of Josquin's treatment of the *ostinato*, see James HAAR, "Some Remarks on the 'Missa La sol fa re mi'," in *Josquin Desprez: Proceedings of the International Josquin Festival*

**Example 4** JOSQUIN, *Missa la sol fa re mi*, beginning of Christe

Bassus soon repropose the same point of imitation at the lower octave (bars 21-29). The entrance of the Altus in bar 16, however, would not have sounded unequivocally as *la* to a Guidonian listener, because that note is also the *mi* of the hexachord that is simultaneously being "established" by the Superius. Again, if we assume that the hexachord functioned as a sort of cognitive yardstick for Renaissance musicians and listeners, then we have to conclude that those same listeners would have perceived the first three notes of the Altus also as part of the same hexachordal "region" introduced by the Superius. In sum: the first three notes of the Altus (just like the Tenor of *Stabat mater dolorosa* discussed above) feature what I would call a dual hexachordal status: contrapuntally, they function as *mi, re, ut* in *naturalis*, whereas thematically they are obviously *la, sol, fa* in *durus*—the latter reading corresponding with their proper, in this case unequivocal, solmization.[24]

The notion of "dual hexachordal status," however, is not exactly in line with Renaissance theories of solmization. True, the theory of hexachordal mutation results from the fact that most musical pitches in the system of *musica recta* correspond to multiple "degrees" in different hexachords. A mutation, however, is a systemic switch that introduces a new hexachord at the same time when the old one is abandoned. When a mutation is performed, it is not necessary to preserve a memory of the old segment once the new one has been adopted. On the contrary, the kind of dual hexachordal status that I am discussing here is a real co-existence of the two hexachordal segments that is prolonged for a relatively long stretch of time.

Thus, we need to investigate the cognitive implications of an hexachordal hearing that interprets a series of notes at the same times as *mi/la, re/sol,* and *ut/fa*. In my opinion, it is highly unlikely that even the best Guidonian listener would associate each of these three notes with two different "hexachordal degrees," especially because such a choice would flatly contradict basic principles of the practice of solmization that (supposedly) would be informing his listening. Rather, I would like to suggest that each of the two hexachordal positions represents a different portion of the intervallic continuum that surrounds those pitches. To hear the note E as both *mi* and *la* is to hear the perfect fourth above it (*mi-la*) and the fifth below it (*la-re*) joined together in a portion of the diatonic space that spans an octave. This means that even an hexachordally-trained listener would in fact hear these two statements of *la, sol, fa, re, mi* not as segments compartmentalized into two different hexachords, but rather as open-ended portions of a diatonic continuum, in which the distance of a fourth between the two entrances lies *on the same layer* with the pitches and intervals of the two statements of the subject. Paradoxically, then, the hypothetical hexachordal grid behind the scene of this point of

---

(*21-25 June 1971*), ed. Edward E. LOWINSKY in collaboration with Bonnie J. BLACKBURN (London: Oxford University Press, 1976): 564-88.

24. Likewise, the A of the Tenor in bar 21 functions not only as *la*, but also as *re* in the context of the *durus* statement of the subject in the Altus.

imitation collapses onto an undivided series of tones and semitones that establish the octave, rather than the hexachord, as the governing module of *musica recta*.

I am arguing that a non-Guidonian analysis and listening of this Christe is not only theoretically justifiable, but also quite appealing in its simple linearity. The main advantage of such an interpretation lies in its revealing the fundamental unity between contrapuntal/vertical and melodic/horizontal space—that is to say, between the descending melodic fourth a-E in the Superius (the *la-sol-fa-re-mi* of bars 15-18) and the descending "harmonic" fourth a-E generated by the entrance of the Altus in bar 16. A non-Guidonian listener would hear the E in the Altus simultaneously as the lowest pitch of a structural fourth a-E and as the highest pitch of a structural fifth E-A. Such a strategy would highlight the fact that the various occurrences of the subject are of course identical, but not completely symmetrical in relation to the main diatonic axis A-E: when stated by the Superius and the Tenor, the subject seems to end on the bottom note of the structural fourth (as in a-G-F-D-E); when stated by the two other voices, on the other hand, it concludes off the axis, on the pitch *above* the root of the fifth (as in E-D-C-AA-B). In a similar manner, Josquin uses the two pitches F and C in quite different contexts, in spite of the fact that they both correspond to the syllable *fa* of their respective "hexachords": whereas F normally functions as the upper neighbor of E (see the "Phrygian" cadences of bars 19-20 and 25-26, as and the pre-cadential F chord in bar 34), the primary role of C is that of "third-above-A" (see for example Altus and Tenor in bar 21; the descending 3-2-1 line in the Tenor of bars 27-29 and in the Superius of bar 34; and the double C in the Superius and Altus over A of the Tenor in bar 29).

The melodic function of E-*mi* and B-*mi* are also quite different in spite of their identical position within their respective hexachords. The strong connotation of B as the *superfinalis* (or, at any rate, as the note immediately above the root of the structural fifth) is confirmed by the cadence of bars 29-30, where B goes to A either through a descending second in the Tenor, or even through the unusual step of an ascending seventh in the Bassus; the function of E as the *confinalis* of A is most clearly defined by the very four entrances of the subject, as well as by the cadential E sonority of bar 35.

Perhaps even more interesting is another type of asymmetry that illustrates the extent to which different presentations of Josquin's "hexachordal" subject define each other's location within the diatonic continuum. The two opening statements in the Superius and Altus complement each other in terms of pitch content, in that the second and third pitches of the Superius (G and F) do not occur in the Altus, whereas the notes C and B in the Altus are not found in the Superius. But whereas the G of the Superius is symmetrical to the C of the Altus, in that they are both the implied *ut* of the reciprocal statement of the subject (that is, G is *ut* for the Altus just as C is *ut* for the Superius), F and B occupy *asymmetrical* positions outside the "hexachords" of which they are not part.

In fact, in the context of the hexachordal range of the Altus, the note F lies a semitone above E-*la* and a whole tone below the unstated G-*ut*; vice-versa, in the context of the hexachordal range of the Superius, the note B lies a whole step above A-*la* and a semitone below the unstated C-*ut*. To put it another way, the Superius and Altus define each other as similar in terms of melodic contour, yet remain at variance in terms of their respective placement within the diatonic continuum. Their hexachordal *affinitas* is quickly overridden by the arrival of the *seventh* pitch of the diatonic collection that is provided by the complementary statement of the subject (see Table 1):

**Table 1**   Asymmetrical placements of the *La sol fa re mi* motive

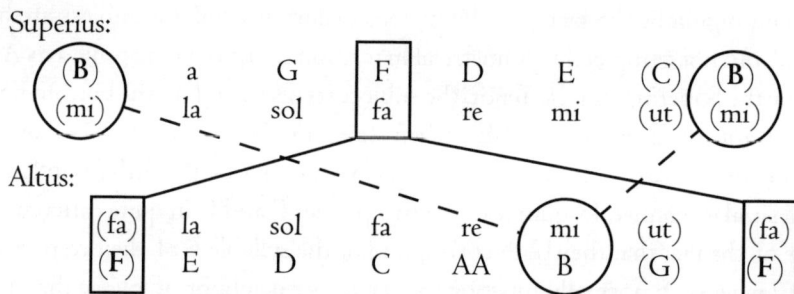

Of course, it could be argued that the asymmetry discussed here is perfectly in line with the hypothesis of a system of interlocking hexachords. The F in the Altus can always be explained as the *fa* of the hexachord on C next to the one on G, and the B in the Superius as the *mi* of the hexachord on G next to the one on C. But more important is the fact that there is only *one* pitch that needs to be "borrowed" at all, after which the diatonic series begins a new cycle, that is to say, encounters another *ut* (or *la*) of the same hexachord that has just been "extended." It is precisely this idea of "filling the hole" with a seventh pitch that bespeaks the dependency of the segmented space based on interlocking hexachords from the continuous space based on recurring patterns of tones and semitones distributed within an octave

The point of the previous discussion is to argue that an hexachordal analysis (and hearing) of the "Christe" would likely miss different kinds of pitch emphasis, asymmetries, and *accent* that seem not only structurally relevant, but also eminently audible. Because, as I hope to have shown above, hexachords highlight only one portion of the intervallic context of each individual note, they often label as *identical* pitches that are only *similar*, leaving it to the three kinds of *proprietates* the task of accounting for the differences in the relative positions between them. The functional split between diatonic "regions" and their individual members—between *proprietates* and *voces*—may result in a convenient, indeed highly efficient solmization system such as the Guidonian one, but it becomes grossly inadequate when interpreted as the conceptual basis of diatonic space in the middle ages and Renaissance, let alone as systems of music perception and cognition. We do hear *la sol fa re mi* (just as Renaissance listeners no doubt did) every time we hear the subject of Josquin's mass at whatever pitch level. But we also miss a great deal if we try to hear these sounds *solely* as the corresponding "hexachordal degrees" suggested by the solmization syllables of the subject—a model of listening that has, at any rate, little historical merit.

### Missa L'homme armé super voces musicales

The *Missa L'homme armé super voces musicales* is no doubt the most impressive of Josquin's "hexachordal" compositions, as each movement of the mass leads to the next one following a master plan of truly monumental proportions.[25] The preposition *super* in the title of the work announces the structural role of the hexachord even more explicitly than in the case of the *Missa la sol fa re mi*: the six syllables—it seems to suggest—constitute the very scaffolding, or the backbone, of this vast musical edifice.[26] As every musicologist knows, the title refers to the fact that the *L'homme armé* tune appears in the Tenor part throughout the Mass at progressively higher pitch levels, from *C* in the Kyrie to *a* in the final Agnus Dei, thus outlining the six syllables *ut-la* of the natural hexachord. Previous composers who had used the *L'homme armé* tune as a cantus firmus, such as Busnois, had modified its modal set-up by changing the constitutive species of fourths and fifths, also using retrograde and inverted forms of the tune. In dialogue with this tradition, Josquin presents his mass as a *ne plus ultra* of compositional artifice by turning the original tune into a sort of *catholicon*—to use Glareanus' term—that can be performed in all possible modal combinations.

A detailed analysis of this highly complex mass would go beyond the purpose of the present paper. Here I will limit myself to several comments on the relationship between the cantus firmus and the large-scale structure of the composition. My observations center for the most part on a slight incongruity—albeit a revealing one, as I would like to argue—that affects the ascending series of opening pitches of the cantus firmus. As Table 2 shows, the *L'homme armé* tune always begins on the same pitch within each movement with the notable exception of the third Agnus Dei, where it starts on *a* instead of the more logical G.

Of course, it could be argued that there *has to* be a statement of the cantus firmus on a somewhere in the Agnus Dei, if the title of the Mass is to be vindicated. Careful listeners may even *expect* a statement of the cantus firmus on *a* in the third Agnus Dei, since

25. For a modern edition of this mass, see Josquin DESPREZ, *Opera omnia, editio altera*, ed. Albert SMIJERS (Amsterdam: Alsbach & Co., 1957), i, fasc. i: 1–41.

26. Obviously, the title also serves the purpose of distinguishing this work from the other mass on the same tune written by Josquin, the *Missa L'homme armé sexti toni.*

**Table 2**  Beginning and end of the cantus firmus in JOSQUIN's *Missa L'homme armé super voces musicales* (Tenor part)

|              | Begins on      | Ends on |                 | Begins on | Ends on |
|--------------|----------------|---------|-----------------|-----------|---------|
| Kyrie        | C              | C       | Et in spiritum  | E         | E       |
| Christe      | c              | G       | Confiteor       | E         | E       |
| Kyrie II     | C              | C       |                 |           |         |
|              |                |         | Sanctus         | F         | c       |
| Gloria       | D              | D       | Hosanna         | F         | F       |
| Qui tollis   | D (retrograde) | D       |                 |           |         |
|              |                |         | Agnus Dei I     | G         | d       |
| Credo        | E              | E       | Agnus Dei III*  | a         | a       |
| Et incarnatus| E (retrograde) | E       |                 |           |         |

\* Cantus firmus in the Superius

this section constitutes the last resort for completing the hexachordal ascent from *ut* to *la* that Josquin has patiently constructed up until this point. Yet, this final rush to complete the span of the hexachord would seem unconvincing, if not amateurish, if the whole point of breaking the rigorous pattern of cantus firmus pitch levels were merely one of spelling out the last syllable of the hexachord.[27] Why would Josquin give the impression of having to "fix things up" at the eleventh hour in a work that exudes compositional bravura from the first to the last note? Why would he appear to be tangled up in his own scheme in a work that no doubt aimed to outdo the extraordinary contributions to the *L'homme armé* tradition by artists of the caliber of Busnois and Ockeghem? Surely, from the composer of *Ut phoebi radiis* and the *Hercules* mass one might expect a more elegant and compelling musical tribute to the six venerable Guidonian syllables.[28]

For an overview of the two masses, see Nicoletta GUIDOBALDI, "Le due messe *L'homme armé* di Josquin," *Rivista italiana di musicologia* 18 (1985): 193-202.

27.  Incidentally, because the *L'homme armé* tune begins with an ascending fourth, each statement of the cantus firmus throughout Josquin's mass is bound to begin on one of the three "ascending syllables" (*ut*, *re*, or *mi*). Thus, the correct solmization syllable of the first note of the cantus firmus in the Agnus Dei III is *re*, not *la*, just as it is *ut* instead of *sol* in the Agnus Dei I and *ut* instead of *fa* in the Sanctus. Only when taken in isolation, and separated from the intervallic context in which they appear, do the opening pitches of the cantus firmus of the Mass outline the complete series of *voces musicales*.

28.  As Paula Higgins has pointed out, a recurrent element in Josquin's mass *super voces musicales* is a direct reference to "hexachordal" works by Busnois and Ockeghem that were well-known in Josquin's time. It is the famous descending motive that accompanies the words "Haec Okeghem" in Busnois' *In Hydraulis* and constitutes the head motive in Ockeghem's *Ut heremita solus*. In the *Missa l'homme armé super voces musicales* it occurs at the very beginning of the first Kyrie in the Altus, at the beginning of the Gloria in the Superius, and once again at the beginning of the first Agnus Dei in the Superius. In this way Josquin self-consciously pays homage to the old masters, while indirectly selecting them as the yardstick for evaluating his own composition. See Paula HIGGINS, "*In hydraulis*" Revisited: New Light on the Career of Antoine Busnois," *Journal of the American Musicological Society* 39 (1986): 78-79.

Josquin may be playing more than one game at the same time here. Indeed, the third Agnus Dei marks not only the completion of the structural "hexachord," but also an important point of convergence in the complex relationship between the different versions of the cantus firmus and the overall mode of the Mass. As it is well known, throughout this work Josquin counterbalances the modal restlessness of the cantus firmus with the solid modal structure of the remaining parts, which remain firmly anchored on D (Mode 1) throughout the entire five movements. This means that the cantus firmus is modally at odds with the other voices for most of the Mass (in spite of the old truism that the mode of the Tenor part is what determines the mode of the entire polyphonic complex). Of course, in the Gloria the *finalis* of the cantus firmus does match the mode of the Mass. It is quite significant, however, that Josquin does not make any effort to underscore this particular modal convergence. Instead, it's business as usual: the Tenor enters a few bars after the beginning of the piece and closes a few bars before its end, just as in the other movements of the Mass where such a strategy is necessary in order to establish the "right" mode.

The third Agnus Dei, however, breaks the pattern, for in this case Josquin seems quite eager to emphasize the modal convergence between the cantus firmus and the remaining three parts involved. To begin with, the cantus firmus stretches throughout the movement without rests, from the first to the last breve. Secondly, the durational values of the cantus firmus are twice as long as in the previous movements. Thirdly, the cantus firmus, presented here at its highest pitch level, appears in the more prominent part of the Superius, rather than in the Tenor. Fourthly, this movement also marks a contrapuntal climax within the mass as a whole, as it features a stricter kind of imitation among the voices, more lively rhythmic figurations, sequences, and in general a dense contrapuntal network that effectively contrasts with the stillness of the Superius. By virtue of such modal/contrapuntal details, the third Agnus Dei functions more as the "sixth movement" of the mass than as the final section of the "fifth movement," thus providing an appropriate context for the introduction of the last *vox musicalis*.

To clarify my point, I am arguing that Josquin's hexachordal game in the *Missa L'homme armé super voces musicales* rests on a complex modal narrative that develops throughout the entire work. The five movements of the mass are able to outline the six notes of the "hexachord" and still preserve an aura of system, because the sixth note (*la*) is called for by the modal expectations that are built into the mass as a whole. Without the sense of fulfillment of these expectations conveyed by the third Agnus Dei—a sort of modal *lieto fine*—the large-scale "hexachordal" path through the five movements could not have been nearly as compelling.

The primacy of mode over hexachord in this work comes to the fore from the very first entrance of the cantus firmus in the first Kyrie, that is, from the first statement of the borrowed tune on C (Ex. 5). By the time the Tenor joins the other three parts in bar 7, the movement is already solidly anchored around the regular final of the *protus* mode (D), thanks to the strong "Dorian" flavor of the brief cantus firmus references in the outer voices (bars 1-5), to the two cadences on D in bars 3 and 5, and to the cadence on A in bar 7 that provides the context for the very entrance of the Tenor. The Bassus part in bars 5-6, with its repeated motive (D)-G-F-D (*re-sol-fa-re*) is even reminiscent of the opening moments of the *Hercules* mass, which is also in Mode 1. In brief, when the C of the Tenor appears in bar 7, this note is heard as the one that lies immediately below the *finalis*, rather than as the first scale degree of a supposed "hexachord." Furthermore, since this note lies a minor third above the note in the Bassus (A), its hexachordal color would seem to be *fa*, rather than (or in addition to) *ut*—an hypothesis that is also confirmed by the fact that the following C in the Bassus line would most certainly be solmized (and heard!) as *fa*. The final sonority of the first Kyrie no doubt produces the same impression, for it inevitably creates an "harmonic context" that makes the corresponding C in the Tenor sound once again as *fa*, rather than (or in addition to) *ut*.[29]

Thus, we encounter here another case of a "dual hexachordal status," analogous to the one described above in the "Christe" of the *Missa La, sol, fa, re, mi*: from a melodic standpoint, the first and last C's of the Tenor part correspond to *ut* of a natural "hexachord"; on the other hand, in contrapuntal sense they correspond to *fa* of a *durus* "hexachord" on G. Again, it seems to me that such a reading undermines the very possibility of an hexachordal listening of these pitches—in spite of the fact that they can be solmized unequivocally as *ut*—if by "hexachordal listening" one means the act of understanding musical sound as organized in overlapping layers of six notes. On the contrary, Renaissance listeners may certainly have heard the Tenor part as both opening and closing one whole step below the *finalis*, simply by virtue of the emphasis that the cadences of the Kyrie place on D. It may seem ironic that the very first pitch of the hexachordal edifice that shapes the large-scale structure of Josquin's mass actually corresponds,

---

29. Of course, the C in the Tenor at the end of this Kyrie may very well be performed as C♯, as in the recording of the mass by The Tallis Scholars (Gimell, CDGIM 0019). Needless to say, such an interpretation has interesting, and rather complex, hexachordal implications. On the one hand, a C♯ in the final sonority of the Kyrie would correspond to *mi* of a *fictus* A-hexachord both in an horizontal sense (that is, in relation to the previous D in the Tenor), and in a vertical one (that is, in relation to the A in the Bassus). In this way, though, it is the low A in the Bassus that comes to acquire the dual hexachordal status of *la* (from the syllable of the previous a͟ in the upper octave) and *ut* (as determined by the *mi* in the Tenor). On the contrary, the two upper parts of Altus and Superius remain unaffected by this hexachordal transformation, continuing to sound, or function, respectively as *la* and *mi* of the natural hexachord (although they are also *re* and *la* of *durus* from the perspective of their intervallic distance). These may very well be the new "hexachordal functions" triggered by the chromatic alteration in the Tenor part, but I am highly skeptical that any Renaissance listener would have heard this familiar series of consonant sounds as simultaneously belonging to two hexachords located three *proprietates* away from each other. Even more, it is highly unlikely that the A in the Bassus would be aurally recognized as *simultaneously* the top pitch of *naturalis* (*la*) and the bottom pitch (*ut*) of the *fictus* A-hexachord.

**Example 5**  JOSQUIN, *Missa l'homme armé super voces musicales*, beginning

Example 5 (cont'd)

aurally and conceptually, to the seventh degree of the mode. However, the hymn *Ut queant laxis* that inspired Guido's system of solmization is also a mode 1 piece that begins on the *subfinalis*. In this historical sense at least, Josquin's homage to the *voces musicales* could not have been more compelling.

The argument that late-medieval and Renaissance composers thought of music in hexachordal terms is appealing to modern scholars, because it appears to capture music in its most elusive moment—that of its very *making*. A modern reading of a motet or a chanson may well sound speculative and dry until it incorporates the flesh-and-bones perspective of *musica prattica*, that of the singers who once turned musical notation into breath, sound, and life. And because the Guidonian syllables were an integral part of the musical training of a Renaissance singer (at least in its earlier stages), it seems plausible to view them as a fundamental ingredient of the musical mind-set of that period. Yet the cognitive and perceptual significance of the Guidonian method has been thus far simplistically assumed, rather than convincingly demonstrated. After all, nobody would argue that Renaissance keyboard players would measure the diatonic space by the num-

ber of fingers in their hands, and the history of hymn singing from the sixteenth century to the present—both in Europe and in the United States—suggests that solmization
systems based on four, six, or seven syllables may be equally adequate to perform what
we would call "tonal" melodies.

In short, it is the significance of the practice of solmization, as pervasive as it may
have been, that needs to be carefully evaluated, preferably in the context of other pedagogical and compositional practices such as mode and counterpoint. This was precisely
the goal of the examples discussed in this study, which in my view undermine the now
fashionable argument that the custom of singing musical pitches with the help of hexachordal labels points *ipso facto* to the existence of underlying hexachordal structures. In
*Stabat mater dolorosa*, the hexachordal position of the beginning of the cantus firmus,
viewed in the context of the other parts, is different from the hexachordal position of the
same notes taken in isolation—that is, from the perspective of a singer who is about to
solmize them. Even motivic ideas that seem to have been derived hexachordally, such as
those that constitute the ostinato subject of Josquin's *Missa la sol fa re mi*, may in fact be
described as belonging simultaneously to two hexachords (or as having a "double hexachordal status," as I have labelled it). In *Salve regina*, the level of transposition suggested by
two consecutive statements of the cantus firmus (down by fifth) does not correspond
with the level of transposition of the hexachordal regions to which those statements supposedly belong (down by fourth). In the not infrequent cases in which multiple
solmizations of a given melody are possible, such as in the opening Bassus phrase of *Petite
camusette*, the yoking of pitches to syllables that an hypothetical Guidonian listener would
have to perform in his mind turns essentially into a guessing game. Finally, there are reasons to interpret even the structural "hexachord" in the Tenor part of Josquin's *Missa
l'homme armé super voces musicales* as a mere portion of the octave, that is, as a segment that
contemporary theorists often describe as a *tonus cum diapente, sexta major, hexachordum major*,
and so on.

The evidence gathered from these examples point to the conclusion that
Guidonian singers and listeners in many cases did not and could not have heard music in
the same way as they solmized it, nor, vice-versa, solmized it in the same way as they
heard it. Consequently, it is highly unlikely that Renaissance listeners and singers shared
a notion of "hexachordal space" that governed the very foundations of their music perception, as it is often suggested today. Yet the skeptical observations presented in this
essay, if confirmed, should spell good news for modern performers, scholars, and listeners of medieval and Renaissance music: if *they* did not hear hexachordally, then there is
no need for *us*, centuries later, to attempt to do so.

# JOSQUIN AND MUSICAL REPUTATION

I N 1997 JESSIE ANN OWENS asked why Josquin rather than any earlier composer (such as Machaut, Dufay, or Ockeghem) achieved the unprecedented acclaim that he did.[1] Owens showed that only in Josquin's generation—and most specifically with the advent of music printing—did this type of lasting renown become possible. This essay addresses the corollary question: given that the preconditions for an enduring reputation were in place in the early sixteenth century, why did Josquin rather than any of his contemporaries catapult into prominence? This question assumes even greater significance in light of recent reattributions of some famous "Josquin" works to other composers, e.g. *Absalon fili mi* to Pierre de la Rue,[2] *De profundis* ($4_v$, low clefs) to Champion,[3] and *Missa Mater patris* (to Brumel?)[4]

Assessing a composer's reputation half a millennium after the fact is no easy task. Relevant factors could include employment record (prestige of a given job, responsibilities of the job, pecking order within the institution served, salary, prebends and benefices, extra payments, receipt of horses, whether head-hunting occurred), dissemination of music (how many sources and their trustworthiness, chronological and geographical spread, frequency of attribution, existence of multiple copies, occurrence of reprint and pirated editions, number of inauthentic works assigned, conflicting attributions, frequency of prints or manuscripts devoted largely or exclusively to the composer), and

* An earlier version of this essay was prepared in connection with the symposium "New Directions in Josquin Scholarship," Princeton University, 29-31 October 1999.

1. Jessie Ann OWENS, "How Josquin Became Josquin: Reflections on Historiography and Reception," in *Music in Renaissance Cities and Courts: Studies in Honor of Lewis Lockwood*, edited by eadem and Anthony M. CUMMINGS (Warren, Michigan: Harmonie Park Press, 1997), 271-80.

2. Most recently discussed in Honey MECONI, "Another Look at Absalon," *Tijdschrift van de koninklijke vereniging voor nederlandse muziekgeschiedenis* 48 (1998): 3-29.

3. Demonstrated by Patrick MACEY in "Conflicting Attributions for *De profundis*: Josquin and Champion," paper prepared in connection with the symposium "New Directions in Josquin Scholarship," Princeton University, 29-31 October 1999.

4. See M. Jennifer BLOXAM, "Masses Based on Polyphonic Songs and Canonic Masses," in *The Josquin Companion*, ed. Richard SHERR (Oxford: Oxford University Press, forthcoming) for an effective dismissal of Josquin's authorship and a discussion of Brumel as a possible composer.

public recognition (use of compositions as models and the geographical and chronological extent of derived works, theorists' remarks or use of compositions as examples, citations in literary works [including lists of musicians], appeals to the composer's expertise, literary and musical eulogies on the composer's death or homages during lifetime, treatment by posthumous historians, both near-contemporary and modern).

All of these criteria are potentially misleading. With very few exceptions, we have no way of knowing whether composers were hired or wooed for their composing or their performing. Manuscripts' datings are approximate and disputed, pieces circulate without attribution, and what survives may be an atypical representation of what existed. Public recognition could be prompted by factors not discernable to us today, including personal friendship, chauvinism, simple parroting of earlier material, or other reasons. Unfortunately we have few alternatives to these kinds of data. The following discussion will focus (though not exclusively) on the distribution of music in manuscript and printed sources as being the factor with the most obvious connection to a musician's compositional reputation.

The Appendix gives the pre-print distribution of Josquin and his most widely-disseminated contemporaries: Agricola, Compère, Isaac, and Obrecht.[5] 1500 was chosen as the cut-off point both because the printing of polyphonic music commenced the following year and because the number of surviving manuscripts explodes at the same time—a not unrelated phenomenon. The charts include every attribution that appears in the manuscripts surveyed, whether we currently think the piece was by the composer or not; they also include anonymous appearances of works now believed authentic. They leave out works considered inauthentic that are anonymous in these sources, and they also omit pieces surely written during this period whose sources are from 1501 or later. Bold face calls attention to problems with ascriptions.

It goes without saying that these lists exhibit a certain level of subjectivity, and not only as far as the datings (and choices) of manuscripts go. If we considered works such as *Hellas madame* and *Madame hellas* to be early works of Josquin, for example, the charts would unquestionably look different. We are also obviously missing sources; no manuscript of sacred music from this time survives from the French court, for example. But bearing these caveats in mind, we can make the following observations.

Josquin initially appears to make a relatively poor showing in comparison with his major contemporaries.[6] T. Elizabeth Cason recently showed that his *Ave Maria* was copied

5.   Comparable tables were compiled for Brumel, Ghiselin, Prioris, and Weerbeke but were not included because of the far smaller early circulation of their works (Brumel: 27 appearances; Ghiselin: 11 appearances; Prioris, 22 appearances; Weerbeke, 47 appearances). Similarly, La Rue, Mouton, and Févin, all

major presences in the early sixteenth century, were omitted because of a minuscule pre-print distribution.
6.   David Fallows was the first to examine the early source distribution of Josquin in connection with questions about his biography; see "Josquin and Milan," *Plainsong and Medieval Music* 5 (1996): 69-80.

**Table 1**  An Approximation of Pre-Print Distribution

| AGRICOLA | |
|---|---|
| 204 appearances | 1 Isaac work attributed to someone else? |
| 105 attributions (51% attribution rate) | 11 non-Isaac works attributed to him? |
| 6 Agricola works attributed to others | JOSQUIN |
| 9 non-Agricola works attributed to him | 93 appearances |
| COMPÈRE | 57 attributions (61% attribution rate) |
| 144 appearances | 2 Josquin works attributed to someone else? |
| 68 attributions (47% attribution rate) | 6 non-Josquin works attributed to him |
| 2 Compère works attributed to someone else? | OBRECHT |
| 6 non-Compère works attributed to him | 78 appearances |
| ISAAC | 47 attributions (60% attribution rate) |
| 143 appearances | 2 Obrecht works attributed to someone else? |
| 94 attributions (66% attribution rate) | 1 non-Obrecht work attributed to him? |
| | "?" indicates a work or works of uncertain authenticity |

in MunBS 3154[7] possibly as late as 1484, thereby putting Josquin's manuscript "debut," at least as far as what survives, some years later than previously thought.[8] Compère's music is in circulation earlier: *Omnium bonorum plena* shows up in both VatSP B80 and TrentC 91 in the earlier 1470s, while his chanson *Puisque si bien* was copied in the previous decade. If FlorR 2356 and Paris BNF 15123 date from the 1470s rather than the 1480s, as is certainly possible,[9] Agricola, too, has secular music in circulation earlier than Josquin. Compère and Agricola are also much more heavily represented in fifteenth-century chansonniers than Josquin. Agricola has nineteen pieces in RomeC 2856 to Josquin's five, thirteen in FlorR 2794 to Josquin's two, ten or twelve in the early layer of LonBLR 20 A. xvi in contrast to none by Josquin and so on; Compère also overshadows Josquin, though to a somewhat lesser extent. Obrecht's sacred music clearly has earlier and better representation than does Josquin's.[10] By the time Josquin's first mass shows up, Obrecht has had four in MunBS 3154, two in LinzBS 529, two in BerlS 40021, two in VatS 35, and one in VatS 51.

But there are other ways of looking at this material. Table 1 gives an approximate summary of this pre-print material.[11] Though Josquin is outnumbered by all except

7.  All manuscript abbreviations and most dates for sources are taken from *Census-Catalogue of Manuscript Sources of Polyphonic Music, 1400–1550*, 5 vols., vol. 1 ed. Charles HAMM and Herbert KELLMAN, vols. 2-5 ed. Herbert KELLMAN, Renaissance Manuscript Studies, 1 (American Institute of Musicology; Neuhausen-Stuttgart: Hänssler-Verlag, 1979-88).

8.  T. Elizabeth CASON, "The Dating of Munich 3154 Revisited," paper presented at the Josquin Symposium, Duke University, 19-20 February 1999. 1476 was the date previously accepted for the section of MunBS 3154 containing *Ave Maria*.

9.  See Honey MECONI, "Poliziano, *Primavera*, and Perugia 431: New Light on *Fortuna desperata*," in *Antoine Busnoys: Method, Meaning, and Context in Late Medieval Music*, ed. Paula HIGGINS (Oxford: Clarendon Press, 1999), 479.

10.  The same is true for Weerbeke, who has masses in VatS 14 (prob. 1474), VerBC 755 (c.1475-1480), ModE M.1.13 (1480 or 1481), BerlS 40021 (1485-1488), VatS 35 (c.1487-1490, two masses), and VatS 51 (c.1484-1491), all before the appearance of Josquin's first surviving mass.

11.  The approximate nature of this summary should be obvious; changing an opinion on what is authentic would clearly shift the numbers and percentages.

Obrecht, his early surviving works appear with attributions more often than those of the more prominently-represented Agricola and Compère. Certain of these attributions are also suggestive. *Domine non secundum peccata,* for example, is one of very few pieces added to VatSP B80, a manuscript with a very much earlier repertoire, and it is added with the attribution to Josquin (only four pieces in the collection are attributed). His *Que vous madame/In pace* is also in the later section of LonBLR 20 A. xvi, again with attribution (again rare in this manuscript).[12] VatS 197 consists exclusively of Josquin's (attributed) *Missa L'homme armé super voces musicales.*

Also worthy of attention is the collection of "Josquin" pieces in FlorBN Magl. 178. In addition to a solid selection of readily-accepted Josquin works, scribes have placed the composer's name on four others of much more dubious authenticity. Two ascriptions are patently false, and two others are very shaky stylistically. With *Cela sans plus,* further, numerous closely-related sources attribute it correctly to Lannoy. Misattribution of works is by no means limited to Josquin's output, but it is striking to see that the practice we typically associate with posthumous German sources has its antecedents in supposedly much more reliable Italian manuscripts compiled during Josquin's lifetime while he was employed nearby.

Attributions—or the lack thereof—are of course open to many interpretations. In some instances, such as the La Rue chansons in BrusBR 228, attributions were unnecessary; the owner of the chansonnier, Marguerite of Austria, clearly knew that her court composer had written those works. In other cases an attribution may appear because the composer is completely unfamiliar to the scribe. But while we can rarely discern the impetus behind a present or missing attribution, an ascription tells us that from that point on users of the manuscript would know the presumed composer of a work. By this measure, then, the surviving sources suggest that Josquin may have had a higher name recognition than Agricola and Compère at the dawn of music printing.

Another factor is the geographical distribution of works. Josquin's music made it to major musical centers throughout Europe before printing changed the picture; this is also true for Obrecht, Agricola, and Compère, but not for Isaac. His music, though widespread, is absent from surviving French sources (with the possible exception of BrusBR 11239).

An additional component is genre. As the Appendix makes clear, Agricola's music was overwhelmingly secular. Compère's was predominantly so as well, with a selection of sacred music, but almost no masses. Sacred music dominates Obrecht's output, with the secular music concentrating on works that survive only with Flemish incipits. Isaac and Josquin are the two with the greatest balance and variety in their sacred and secular works.

All of these factors taken together suggest that Josquin was, in fact, an excellent contender for canonization as the fifteenth century drew to a close. If we consider what

---

12. Josquin is the only composer of his generation to receive an attribution here.

would presumably be predictors for success—a significant number of compositions, a higher than average rate of attribution and thus name recognition, widespread geographic distribution, and a balance among different compositional genres—we see that only Josquin really matches all these criteria.

Is this statement perhaps too hasty? Except for an apparent vacuum in fifteenth-century French sources, after all, Isaac meets or exceeds Josquin in all these predictors for success. Yet any possibility that Isaac rivaled Josquin vanishes once printing comes into the picture. Simply put, for the first twenty-five years of polyphonic music printing—until just a few years after his death—Josquin dominated the presses to an extent that no other composer of his generation even approached. One can scarcely overestimate the effect that printing had on the dissemination of music (and hence a composer's reputation). Even a print run of only a hundred copies would have a hundred times the impact that a manuscript would, and printing propelled Josquin's music farther than that of any of his peers in the early sixteenth century.[13]

The figures for the first five years of printing for our composers are approximately as follows; Isaac is the least well represented.[14]

| | |
|---|---|
| Agricola: | 52 pieces in 11 prints |
| Compère: | 74 pieces in 11 prints |
| Isaac: | 20 pieces in 6 prints |
| Josquin: | 76 pieces in 15 prints |
| Obrecht: | 36 pieces in 10 prints |

Compère comes close to Josquin in total pieces, largely owing to the two reprint editions of *Odhecaton* (which included sixteen of his works). But Josquin easily surpasses him in frequency of prints; in fact, only two anthologies from this period don't contain at least one Josquin composition, further testimony to his compositional versatility. Further, Compère fades as the years pass; from 1506 to 1510 he has two pieces in a single print; Josquin has ten in five prints. This discrepancy increases; between 1516 and 1520 Compère is represented by a single printed work; Josquin has twenty-six in seven collections.

The difference is even more dramatic if we consider collections dedicated to single composers. Petrucci's famous series of mass prints included those devoted to Obrecht (1503), Brumel (1503), Ghiselin (1503), La Rue (1503), Agricola (1504), de Orto (1505), Isaac (1506), Weerbeke (1507), Mouton (1515) and Antoine Févin (1515; despite the print's title,

13. It is important to stress that no universal preference for Josquin is to be found, whether in manuscripts or prints. *Motetti A*, for example, contains four Josquin motets but nine by Weerbeke. The reason for Josquin's ultimate success is that printers (and compilers of manuscripts) turned more often and more consistently to Josquin than to his peers.

14. Even Brumel (23 pieces in 11 prints) and Weerbeke (23 pieces in 7 prints) were more prominent. Prints become important for the circulation of Isaac's music only posthumously.

works by Robert Févin and La Rue were included as well). But the series started with Josquin, in 1502, in only the fourth volume of polyphonic music ever printed. While other composers received a single volume (and composers such as La Rue, Isaac, and Obrecht could easily have filled multiple volumes), the Josquin series ran to a second book (1505) and a third (1514), with reprints of the second and first books (1515 and 1516 respectively). Printing was an expensive and potentially disastrous business venture, and Petrucci surely commenced with Josquin, because he thought the composer would sell.

Somewhere between 1495 and 1502, then, Josquin went from presumably being virtually unknown as a mass composer to being the one most likely to attract buyers. The date 1502 is important for another reason. This is the year of the famous letter to Duke Ercole d'Este of Ferrara by his agent Gian de Artiganova, where Josquin is acknowledged as a better composer than Isaac.[15] As far as we know, Gian—whom the music-loving duke surely trusted in his quest—had nothing invested in praising Josquin's abilities. He didn't even want him to be hired. So a confirmed contemporary preference for Josquin's music, by someone connected with one of the most sophisticated musical establishments in Western Europe, should be included among factors influencing the growth of a reputation.

Still another element is Josquin's position in compositional trends. Though not always on the cutting edge—La Rue and Févin are more important in the development of the "parody" mass, for example—he certainly became a stylistic leader in secular music, especially with the fading presence of Agricola and Compère.[16] A related matter is who among Josquin's contemporaries borrowed from whom. Normally the material reused was from the previous generation, but Table 2—an extremely cursory survey of

**Table 2**  Partial List of Contemporary Borrowings

| Borrowed from Agricola | Borrowed from Josquin |
|---|---|
| BRUMEL: Missa Je n'ay dueil | BRUMEL: Missa A l'ombre d'un buissonet |
| GHISELIN: Missa Je n'ay dueil | BRUMEL: Missa Bergerette savoyenne |
| OBRECHT: Missa Si dedero | FÉVIN: Faulte d'argent |
| | FÉVIN: Missa Ave Maria |
| Borrowed from Compère | FÉVIN: Missa Mente tota |
| FÉVIN: Missa Dictes moy toutes | MOUTON: Dulces exuviae |
| MOUTON: Missa Dictes moy toutes | OBRECHT: Missa Fortuna desperata |
| Borrowed from Isaac | |
| LA RUE: Credo Angeli archangeli | |

15. For a recent translation see Rob C. WEGMAN, "From Maker to Composer: Improvisation and Musical Authorship in the Low Countries, 1450-1500," *Journal of the American Musicological Society* 49 (1996): 466.

16. This statement is not to deny the accomplishments of Agricola and Compère, but rather to put them in perspective. Agricola's death in 1506 and Compère's gradual cessation of compositional activity around the same time left the secular field to those composers still experimenting and producing (La Rue and others as well as Josquin). Josquin's precise significance in the stylistic development of the motet awaits stronger contextualization than it has heretofore received.

borrowing from contemporaries—puts Josquin in the lead as a source for model mater-ial.[17] This table certainly suggests that Josquin's cohorts were more likely to turn to his music than that of anyone else of their generation, whether they knew it was by him or not. This partial list shows works based on very popular favorites. Were other composers trying to cash in on Josquin's success?

We should also not neglect the possible impetus of Josquin himself towards a posi-tion of dominance. I have argued elsewhere that *Nymphes des bois* was an intentional attempt on the composer's part to align himself with Ockeghem, the most famous composer of the fifteenth century.[18] His possible participation in the flurry of end-of-century Vatican manuscripts could demonstrate another calculated career move,[19] as might his purported practice of witholding compositions, thereby increasing the perception of their value (we want what we can't have).[20] This habit might also account for the somewhat smaller num-ber of fifteenth-century sources than we might otherwise expect.

If Castiglione[21] is to be believed, Josquin had achieved his unassailable reputation by 1507, which further events in the sixteenth century merely solidified. But if nothing else, this overview of musical reputation and factors contributing to it should demonstrate that Josquin's ascent to unquestioned heights was neither monolithic nor inevitable but rather cumulative. Agricola, Compère, Obrecht, and especially Isaac all produced quanti-ties of widely-disseminated and clearly valued music. But only with Josquin do we find the precise combination of elements contributing to phenomenal success: an apparently long and productive life resulting in a large number of compositions spread over a wide variety of genres, often written in the newest and freshest styles, found throughout Europe both in manuscript versions and even more significantly in hundreds of printed copies, more often than not clearly identified as his. Add to this the connoisseurs' high assessment of his music, his role as a musical model for his contemporaries and followers, and possibly some self-promotion as well, and we have an unbeatable formula for fame. At the dawn of the twenty-first century, aided by technological advances that will surely rival the inven-tion of the printing press in their impact, we can look back five hundred years and watch this process unfold.

---

17. I have not included a rather substantial list of works by La Rue that were clearly influenced by Josquin, as the borrowing therein only rarely involves a direct melodic quotation. These influences are discussed in Honey MECONI, *Pierre de la Rue* (Oxford: Oxford University Press, forthcoming).

18. Honey MECONI, "Ockeghem and the Motet-Chanson in Fifteenth-Century France," in *Johannes Ockeghem: Actes du XLᵉ Colloque international d'études human-istes, Tours, 3-8 février 1997*, ed. Philippe VENDRIX (Paris: Klincksieck, 1998): 381-402.

19. For Josquin's possible role as scribe see Richard SHERR, "The Papal Chapel *c.*1492-1513 and its Polyphonic Sources" (Ph. D. diss., Princeton University, 1974), 192.

20. Josquin's delay in releasing compositions was reported in Heinrich Glarean, *Dodekachordon* (Basel: Henrichus Petri, 1547), 363. He also supposedly acquired a reputation among the *cognoscenti* before reaching a broader public (ibid., 440).

21. As cited in WEGMAN, "From Maker to Composer," 467-68.

# Appendix

## JOSQUIN (?-1521)

### early 1480s

**SevC 5-1-43** (probably Naples)
*Une musque de Biscaye*, 4v (anon)

### c.1481[1]

**RomeC 2856** (Ferrara)
*Adieu mes amours*, 4v (Jossim)
*En l'ombre d'un buissonet au matinet*, 4v (**Bolkim**)
*Ile fantazies de Joskin*, 3v
*Que vous madame/In pace in idipsum*, 3v (Joskin)
*Une musque de Biscaye*, 4v (Josquin de pres)

### c.1480-1490

**VerBC 759** (Verona)
*Salve regina*, 4v (fragment) (anon)

### 1484?[2]

**MunBS 3154** (probably Innsbruck; perhaps also Augsburg)
*Ave Maria...virgo serena*, 4v (anon)

### probably pre-1488

**FlorR 2794** (probably French royal court)
*Adieu mes amours*, 4v (Josequin)
*Entré je suis en grant pensée*, 3v (Josquin des pres)

### c.1487-1490[3]

**VatS 35** (Rome)
*Domine non secundum peccata*, 4v (attributed to Josquin)

### 1488-1490[4]

**BerlS 40021** (Leipzig?)
*Ave Maria...virgo serena*, 4v [contrafactum] (anon)

### late 1480s/early 90s[5]

**UppsU 76a** (southwestern France). Scribe A
*Entré je suis en grant pensée*, 3v (anon)
*Mon mari m'a diffamée*, 3v (anon) S only

### early 1490s

**FlorBN Magl. 178** (Florence)
*Adieu mes amours*, 4v (Josquin Depres)

*Belle pour l'amour de vous*, 4v (Josquin)
*Cela sans plus*, 3v (Josquin) **by Lannoy**
*Comment peult haver joye*, 4v (Josquin)
*Helas madame*, 3v (Josquin Depres) **doubtful**
*J'ay bien nourri sept ans*, 3v (Josquin Depres) **by Japart**
*Je me*, 3v (Josquin) **doubtful**
*Je n'ose plus*, 3v (Josquin Depres)
*Que vous madame/In pace in idipsum*, 3v (Josquin Depres)
*Se congié prens*, 4v (Josquin)
*Une musque de Biscaye*, 4v (Josquin)

### 1490-1498

**ParisBNF 2245** (France)
*En l'ombre d'un buissonet au matinet*, 4v (Josquin)

### 1490s

**LonBLR 20 A.xvi** (France)
second layer : *Que vous madame/In pace in idipsum*, 3v (Josquin)

### c.1490-1504

**LeipU 1494** (Leipzig?)
*Ave Maria...virgo serena*, 4v (anon)

### 1492-1493

**FlorBN BR 229** (Florence)
*Adieu mes amours*, 4v (Josquin)
*Que vous madame/In pace in idipsum*, 3v (Josquin)
*Scaramella va alla guerra*, 4v (Josquin)
*Une musque de Biscaye*, 4v (Josquin)

### 1492-1494

**VatG XIII. 27** (Florence)
*Adieu mes amours*, 4v (Iosquin)
*Comment peult haver joye*, 4v (Josquin depres)
*Que vous madame/In pace in idipsum*, 3v (Josquin)
*Recordans de my segnora* [=*Se congié prens*], 4v (Josquin)
*Que vous madame/In pace in idipsum*, 3v (Josquin)
*Une musque de Biscaye*, 4v (Josquin)

---

1. I incline to the outside limit suggested in *Census-Catalogue*, 4: 471.
2. T. Elizabeth CASON, "The Dating of Munich 3154 Revisited," paper presented at the Josquin Symposium, Duke University, 19-20 February 1999.
3. Refinements for datings of Vatican manuscripts are taken from Richard SHERR, *Papal Music Manuscripts in the Late Fifteenth and Early Sixteenth Centuries*, Renaissance Manuscript Studies, 5

(Neuhausen-Stuttgart: Hänssler-Verlag, 1996).
4. Dates for BerlS 40021 are from Martin JUST, *Der Mensuralkodex Mus. ms. 40021 der Staatsbibliothek Preuflischer Kulturbesitz, Berlin: Untersuchungen zum Repertoire einer deutschen Quelle des 15. Jahrhunderts*, 2 vols. (Tutzing: Hans Schneider, 1975).
5. UppsU 76a dates are from *Uppsala Universitetsbiblioteket Vokalmusik i handskrift 76a*, ed. Howard Mayer BROWN, Renaissance Music in Facsimile, 19 (New York : Garland, 1987).

### 1493-1495

**BerlS 40021** (Leipzig?)

*Magnificat tertii toni*, 4v (Josquini)

*Mente tota*, 4v (5a pars of *Vultum tuum deprecabuntur*)
(anon)

### c.1495

**VatS 197** (Rome)

*Missa L'homme armé super voces musicales*, 4v (Josquin)

### c.1495-1497

**VatS 49** (Rome)

*Missa ad fugam*, 4v (anon)

**VatS 15** (Rome)

*Alma redemptoris mater/Ave regina caelorum*, 4v (anon)

*Ave maris stella [Monstra te esse matrem]*, 4v (Josquin des
pres)

*Illibata Dei virgo nutrix/La mi la*, 5v (acrostic)

*Nardi Maria pistici [Honor decus]*, 4v (Josquin des pres)

### c.1495-1498

**VatS 41** (Rome)

*Missa La sol fa re mi* (Josquin)

### after 1495[6]

**SegC s.s.** (Spain)

*Ave Maria...virgo serena*, 4v (Josqui[n] du preß)

*Bergerette savoyenne*, 4v (Josquin du prez)

*Fortuna disperata*, 3v (Josqui[n] du pres) **doubtful**

*Intemerata virgo*, 4v (3a pars of Vultum tuum)
(Josqui[n] du preß)

*Magnificat primi toni*, 4v (Josquin du pres) **doubtful**

*Missa L'homme armé sexti toni*, 4v (Josquin du pres)

*O Maria nullam*, 4v (4a pars of Vultum tuum) (anon)

*Que vous madame/In pace in idipsum*, 3v (Josquin du
press)

**SienBC K.I.2** (Siena)

*Gloria* from *Missa L'ami Baudichon*, 4v (anon)

### 1497

**BerlS 40021** (Leipzig?)

*Missa Une musque de Biscaye*, 4v (Josquini)

### after 1497[7]

**BolC Q17** (probably in or near Florence)

*Adieu mes amours*, 4v (Josquin)

*Comment peult haver joye*, 4v (Josquin)

*En l'ombre d'un buissonet tout au loing d'une rivière*, 3v
(Josquin)

*Que vous madame/In pace in idipsum*, 3v (Josquin)

*Une musque de Biscaye*, 4v (Josquin)

### late 15th century

**BarcOC 5** (unknown)

*Missa Fortuna desperata*, 4v (anon)

**VatS 41** (Rome)

*Credo De tous biens*, 4v (Josquin des pres)

*Missa Fortuna desperata*, 4v (Josquin des pres)

### late 15/early 16th c.

**HradKM 7** (Bohemia)

*Ave Maria...virgo serena*, 4v (anon)

*Christum ducem*, 4v (anon)

*Missa L'ami baudichon*, 4v: Credo (**attributed to
Tinctoris**)

*Virgo prudentissima*, 4v (anon)

**PozU 7022** (Lwów?)

*Missa L'ami baudichon*, 4v (anon)

*Missa L'homme armé sexti toni*, 4v (anon)

### by c.1500

**VatSP B80** (Rome)

*Domine non secundum peccata*, 4v (Jusquin)

### c.1500[8]

**BrusBR 11239** (N. France? Savoy?)

*Belle pour l'amour de vous*, 4v (anon)

*Que vous madame/In pace in idipsum*, 3v (anon)

**LonBLE 3051** (N. Italy? Florence?)

*In te domine speravi*, 4v (anon)

**MilD 3** (Milan)

*Alma redemptoris mater/Ave regina*, 4v (Jusquin Despret)

*Missa Ave maris stella*, 4v (Josquin)

*Missa Hercules dux ferrarie*, 4v (GCS) (Josquin)

*Missa L'homme armé sexti toni*, 4v (GCS) (Josquin)

*Salve sancta facies*, 4v (anon)

**ParisBNF 1597** (probably Paris)

*A l'ombre d'un buissonet au matinet*, 3v (anon)

*Que vous madame/In pace in idipsum*, 3v (anon)

*Si j'ay perdu mon amy*, 3v (anon)

**VerBC 757** (Verona)

*Cela sans plus*, 3v (anon)

**VerBC 758** (Verona)

*Ecce tu pulchra es*, 4v (anon)

*O bone et dulcis domine Jesu/Pater noster/Ave Maria*, 4v
(anon; really by Josquin?)

---

6. For SegC s.s. see Honey MECONI, "Art-Song Reworkings:
An Overview," *Journal of the Royal Musical Association* 119 (1994):
16; for SienBC K.I 2 see Rob C. WEGMAN, *Born for the Muses:
The Life and Masses of Jacob Obrecht* (Oxford: Clarendon Press,
1994), 100.

7. See Honey MECONI, "The Manuscript Basevi 2439 and
Chanson Transmission in Italy," in *Atti del XIV congresso della*

*Società Internazionale di Musicologia* (Bologna 1987), ed. Angelo
POMPILIO, Donatella RESTANI, Lorenzo BIANCONI, and F.
Alberto GALLO (Turin: EDT, 1990), 3: 171.

8. On BrusBR 11239 see Honey MECONI, "Pierre de la Rue
and Secular Music at the Court of Marguerite of Austria,"
*Jaarboek van het Vlaamse Centrum voor Oude Muziek* 3 (1987): 50.

**WarU 2016** (Silesia or Bohemia)
*Ave Maria...virgo serena*, 4v (anon)
*Mente tota*, 4v (5a pars of *Vultum tuum deprecabuntur*) (anon)
*Que vous madame/In pace in idipsum*, 3v (anon)

**WashLC M6** (Florence? Northern Italy?)
*Adieu mes amours*, 4v (anon)

*Que vous madame/In pace in idipsum*, 3v (anon)
*O mater dei et hominis* (Tu solus), 4v (anon)

### c.1500-1503

**VatC 234** (Brussels/Mechelen)
*Missa L'homme armé sexti toni*, 4v (K,G, C) (Josquyn)
*Stabat mater*, 5v (Josquyn)

## AGRICOLA (*c.*1446-1506)

### 1470s?[9]

**FlorR 2356** (Florence)
*Ay je rien fet* (anon)
*Lheure est venue/Circumdederunt me* (anon)
*Si dedero* (anon)

**ParisBNF 15123** (Florence)
*Ay je rien fet* (anon)

### early 1480s

**SevC 5-1-43** (probably Naples)
*Cest mal cherche* (Agricola)
*Cest trop sur* (anon)

### 1481

**ModAS s.s.** (Ferrara)
*Missa Je ne demande* (C & S) (anon)

### c.1481

**RomeC 2856** (Ferrara)
*Ay je rien fet* (Agricola)
*Cest mal cherche* (Agricola)
*Comme femme*, 3v (Agricola)
*Dictes moy toutes* (anon)
*En actendant* (Agricola)
*En dispitant* (Agricola)
*En men venant* (Agricola)
*Il me fauldra maudire* (Agricola)
*Il nest vivant* (Agricola)
*In minen zin* (Agricola)
*Je nay dueil* (Agricola)
*Lheure est venue/Circumdederunt* (Agricola)
*Oublier veul* (Agricola)
*O venus bant II* (Agricola)
*Pourquoy tant/Pour quelque* (Velu per) (anon)
*Pour voz plaisirs* (Agricola)
*Serviteur soye* (Agricola)
*Si dedero* (Agricola)
*Vostre hault bruit* (anon)

### 1482-1484

**MunBS 3154** (prob. Innsbruck; also Augsburg?)

*Regina coeli* (anon)

### c.1483-1488

**LonBLR 20 A.xvi** (France) [first layer]
*A la mignonne de fortune* (anon)
*Cest mal cherche* (anon)
*Cest trop sur* (anon)
*En actendant* (anon)
*En effait* (suggested as Agricola; anon)
*Il nest vivant* (anon)
*Lheure est venue/Circumdederunt me* (anon)
*Par ung jour* (anon)
*Pour faire larlkymie* (suggested as Agricola; anon)
*Se je vous eslonge* (anon)
*Si vous voullez* (anon)
*Soit loing* (anon)

### 1484?

**MunBS 3154** (prob. Innsbruck; also Augsburg?)
*Cecus* (Gaudent in caelis) (anon)

### c.1485-1495[10]

**WashLC L25** (Loire Valley?) [Scribe 3]
*En actendant* (anon)
*Pour voz plaisirs* (anon)

### 1487

**BolC Q16** (Naples or Rome)
*Dictes moy toutes* (anon)
*Jay beau huer* (anon)
*Si dedero* (anon)

### probably pre-1488

**FlorR 2794** (probably French royal court)
*A la mignonne* (anon)
*In minen zin* (Le second jour d'avril) (agricola)
*Jay beau huer* (anon)
*Je nay deuil* (Agricola)
*Lamentations* (Quomodo sedet only) (anon)
*Lheure est venue/Circumdederunt me* (Agricola)
*Pour voz plaisirs* (anon)
*Se je fais bien* (anon)

---

9. See Honey MECONI, "Poliziano, *Primavera*, and Perugia 431: New Light on *Fortuna desperata*," in *Antoine Busnoys: Method, Meaning, and Context in Late Medieval Music*, ed. Paula HIGGINS (Oxford: Clarendon Press, 1999): 479.

10. Dates for WashLC L25 are from Martella GUTIÉRREZ-DENHOFF, "Untersuchungen zu Gestalt, Entstehung und Répertoire des Chansonniers Laborde," *Archiv für Musikwissenschaft* 41 (1984): 113-46.

*Se je vous eslonge* **(Heyne) by Agricola**
*Serviteur soye* (Agricola)
*Si dedero* (anon)
*Si vous voullez* (Agricola)
*Soit loing* (anon)

### 1488-1490

**BerlS 40021** (Leipzig?)
*Cecus (Regali quem decet)* (anon)

### 1489-1493

**BerlS 40021** (Leipzig?)
*Jam fulsit* (anon)

### late 1480s/early 1490s

**UppsU 76a** (southwestern France) [Scribe A]
*In minen zin (Le second jour d'avril)* (Agricola)

### early 1490s

**FlorBN Magl. 178** (Florence)
*Cest mal cherche (Id est trophis)* (Alexander)
*Cest trop sur* (Alexander)
*Dictes moy toutes* (Alexander)
*En actendant* (Alexander Agricula)
*Et qui la dira* (Alexander)
*Gentils galans* (Alexander)
*Ha quil mennuye* (Alexander) **by Fresneau**
*Il nest vivant* (Alexander)
*In minen zin* (Alexander)
*Jars du desir* [*Mom pere*] (Alexander) **NG: dubia**
*Jay beau huer* (Alexander)
*Je nay dueil* (Alexander)
*Je ne puis plus (Je nem puis)* (Alexander)
*Je ne suis point* (Alexander)
*Lheure est venue/Circumdederunt me* (Alexander)
*Mauldicte soit* (Alexander)
*Se je fais bien* (Alexander)
*Se je vous eslonge* (Alexander)
*Si dedero* (Alexander)
*Si vous voullez (Je vous)* (Alexander)
*Vostre hault bruit* (Alexander Agricola)

### 1490-1498

**ParisBNF 2245** (France)
*In minen zin* (agrico[la])

### 1490s

**LonBLR 20 A.xvi** (France) [second layer]
*Je nay dueil* (anon)
*Royne des flours* (anon)

### 1492-1493

**FlorBN BR 229** (Florence)
*A la mignonne* (Alexander agricola)
*Cest mal cherche* (Alexander agricola)
*Cest trop sur* (Alexander agricola)
*Cest ung bon bruit* (anon)

*Dictes moy toutes* (Alexander agricola)
*En actendant* (anon)
*Et qui la dira* (Alexander agricola)
*Garde vostre visage* (anon)
*Gentil galans* (Alexander agricola)
*Il nest vivant* (Alexander agricola)
*In minen zin* (Alexander agricola)
*Jay beau huer* (anon)
*Je nay dueil* (Alexander agricola)
*Je ne puis plus (Je nem puis)* (anon)
*Je ne suis point* (anon)
*Mauldicte soit* (anon)
*Notres assovemen* (Alexander agricola) **by Fresneau**
*O venus bant I* (anon)
*Par ung jour de matinee* (anon)
*Pour voz plaisir* (anon)
*Royne des flours* (anon)
*Se je fais bien* (Alexander agricola)
*Si dedero* (Alexander Agricola)
*Si vous voullez* (anon)
*Soit long* (Alexander)
*Vostre bouche dist* (anon)
*Vostre hault bruit* (Alexander agricola)

### 1492-1494

**VatG XIII.27** (Florence)
*A la mignonne* (anon)
*Allez regretz (No me canteys)* (Agricola)
*Comme femme, 3v* (Agricola)
*De tous biens plaine, 4v* (anon)
*Dictes moy toutes* (anon)
*En actendant* (Agricola)
*Et qui la dira* (Agricola)
*Guarde vostre visage* (Agricola)
*Il nest vivant (Pensee vivant)* (Loyset Compere) **by Agricola**
*Je nay dueil* (Agricola)
*Je ne suis point* (anon)
*Lheure est venue/Circumdederunt me* (anon)
*O venus bant I* (anon)
*Se je fais bien* (Agricola)
*Si dedero* (Agricola)
*Soit long (Aint long)* (anon)

### 1492-1495

**BerlS 40021** (Leipzig?)
*A la mignonne* (anon)
*A solis ortis cardine* (Alex. Agri.)
*Ave maris stella* (A.A.)
*Missa sine nomine (Re fa mi)* (anon)

### 1493-1494

**BerlS 40021** (Leipzig?)
*Comme femme, 3v (Virgo sub aetheris)* (anon)
*Comme femme, 4v (Ave quae sublimaris)* (anon)

**1493-1495**

**BerlS 40021** (Leipzig?)
*Salve regina II* (Allexr)

**c.1495**

**ParisBNF 1596** (Cognac)
*Oublier veul* (anon)

**after 1495**

**SegC s.s.** (Spain)
*Cecus* **(Ferdinandus et frater ejus) probably by**
**Agricola**
*Comme femme, 2v* (Alexander agrico[la])
*De tous biens plaine* (Alexander agricola) **by Bourdon**
*De tous biens plaine IV* (Alexander agrico[la])
*De tous biens plaine V* (Alexander agrico[la])
*Dung aultre amer IV* (Alexander agricola)
*Gaudeamus omnes* (Alexander agrico[la])
*Helas madame* (Elaes) (Alexander agricola) **NG: dubia**
*In minen zin* (Alexander agricola)
*Jay beau huer* (Loysette Compe[re]) **by Agricola**
*Je nay dueill* (Alexander Agricola)
*Je ne puis plus* (Loysette Compe[re]) **by Agricola**
*Magnificat quarti toni* (Alr. Agricola) **by Brumel**
*Mijn alderliefste moeschkin* (Alexander agrico[la])
*Mijn liefskins* (**attribution to Agricola crossed out;**
**Pipelare put in; by Pipelare**)
*Missa sine nomine* (Alexander Agricola) **by Aulenus**
*Oublier veul* (Oublier suis) (Alexander Agrico[la])
*O venus bant I* (Alexander agricola)
*O venus bant II* (Alexander agricola)
*Princesse de toute beaulte* (Al agricola)
*Si dedero* (Alexander Agrico[la])
*Soit loing* (Alexander agricola)
*Tandernaken* (Alexander agricola)

**SienBC K.1.2** (Siena)
*Magnificat secundi toni*[11] (Agricola)

**after 1497**

**BolC Q17** (probably in or near Florence)
*Amours amours* (A agricola)
*Cecus* (anon)
*Cest trop sur* (Cest mal ser) (A agricola)
*Je nay dueil* (A Agricola)
*Lheure est venue/Circumdederunt me* (Alexander
Agricola)
*Oublier veul* (A agrico[la])
*Par ung jour de matinee* (A agricola)
*Si dedero* (A agrico[la])

*Soit loing* (A agricola)

**late 15th/early 16th c.**

**HradKM 7** (Bohemia)
*Cecus* (as Ave ancilla) (Isaac) **probably by Agricola**
*Credo and Sanctus sine nomine* (Allexander)
*O virens virginum* (Agrico[la])

**c.1500**

**BrusBR 11239** (N. France? Savoy?)
*Les grans regretz* (agricola) **by Hayne**
*Revenez tous regretz/Quis det ut veniat* (Alexand[er] agricola)
*Si dedero* (anon)

**MilD 3** (Milan)
*Missa sine nomine* (attributed to Agricola)

**ParisBNF 1597** (probably Paris)
*Comme femme II* (anon)
*Da pacem* (anon)
*Il nest vivant* (anon)
*Lheure est venue/Circumdederunt me* (anon)
*O quam glorifica* (anon)
*Royne des flours* (anon)
*Se je vous eslonge* (anon)
*Se mieulx* (anon)
*Si conge prens* (anon)
*Si dedero* (anon)
*Si vous voullez* (anon)

**TurBN I. 27** (Turin or vicinity)
*A la mignonne* (anon)
*Amours amours* (anon)
*Jay beau huer* (anon)
*Si conge prens* (anon)

**VerBC 757** (Verona)
*Cest mal cherche* (anon)
*De tous biens plaine, 4v* (anon)
*En actendant* (anon)
*Jay beau huer* (Agricola)
*Je nay dueil* (anon)
*Si dedero* (anon)
*Vostre hault bruit* (anon)

**WarU 2016** (Silesia or Bohemia)
*Lamentations, 3v* (anon)
four other works (all anon)

**c.1500-1503**

**VatC 234** (Brussels/Mechelen)
*Missa In myne zin* (Allexander)

---

11. This is a different work from the *Magnificat secundi toni* normally identified with Agricola.

COMPÈRE (*c.*1445-1518)

### c.1460-1467
**WashLC L25** (Loire Valley?) Scribe I
*Puisque si bien* (anon)

### 1470s?
**Paris BNF 15123** (Florence)
*Mes pensees* (L compere)

### 1472-1474
**TrentC 91** (Trent)
*Omnium bonorum plena* (name in text)

### before July 1476
**VatSP B80** (Rome)
*Omnium bonorum plena* (name in text)

### 1480-1482
**MunBS 3154** (probably Innsbruck; perhaps also Augsburg)
*Magnificat sexti toni* (incomplete; attributed to Compère)

### c.1480-1500
**MonteA 871** (Gaeta)
*Mes pensees* (Loyset Co[m]pere)

### 1480s (or late 15th c.)
**DijBM 517** (Loire Valley?)
*Dictes moy toutes* (Loyset [Com]pere)
*Ne doibt en prendre* (Loyset [Com]pere)

### c.1481
**RomeC 2856** (Ferrara)
*A qui diraige ma pensee* (Compere)
*Au travail suis* (Loiset Co[m]pere)
*La saison en est* (Compere)
*Le renvoy* (Compere)
*Pleut or adieu* (Compere)
*Tout mal me vient* (Compere)

### c.1484-1490
**MilD 1** (Milan)
*Ave domine Jesu Christe* (anon)
*Ave salus infirmorum* (from *Missa Galeazescha*) (anon)
*Ave sponsa verbi summi* (from *Missa Galeazescha*) (anon)
*Ave virgo gloriosa*, 5v (from *Missa Galeazescha*) (Loyset)
*Hodie nobis de virgine* (Loyset)
*Magnificat primi toni* (Loyset)
*Magnificat sexti toni* (Loyset)
*O admirabile commercium* (Loyset)
*O genitrix gloriosa* (2a pars only: Ave virgo, 4v) (anon)
two to four more (anon)[12]

### c.1485-1495
**WashLC L25** (Loire Valley?) Scribe III
*Dictes moy toutes* (anon)
*Mes pensees* (anon)

### 1487
**BolC Q16** (Naples or Rome)
*A qui diraige ma pensee* (anon)
*Dictes moy toutes* (anon)

### c.1487-1490
**VatS 35** (Rome)
*Missa Lhomme arme* (attributed to Compère)

### probably pre-1488
**FlorR 2794** (probably French royal court)
*Au travail suis* (anon)
*Des trois la plus* (Loyset Compere)
*Dictes moy toutes* (anon)
*Faisons boutons* (anon)
*La saison en est* (L. Compere)
*Le renvoy* (anon)
*Mes pensees* (anon)
*O genitrix gloriosa* (anon)

### late 1480s/early 1490s
**UppsU 76a** (southwestern France) Scribe A
*Mes pensees* (anon)
*Puisque si bien* (anon)

### early 1490s
**FlorBN Magl. 178** (Florence)
*En attendant* (anon)
*La saison en est* (Loyset Comper)
*Le renvoy* (anon)
*Mes pensees* (Loyset)
*Vostre bargeronette* (Loyset Comper)
*Vray dieu quel payne* (anon) **possibly by Weerbeke**

### 1490-1498
**ParisBNF 2245** (France)
*Disant adieu a madame II* (attributed to Compère)
*Faisons boutons* ([Com]pere)
*Jay un syon* (attributed to Compère)
*La saison en est* (attributed to Compère)
*Pensant au bien* (attributed to Compère)
*Pour estre ou nombre* (Compère)
*Se pis ne vient* (attributed to Compère)
*Vaten regret* (attributed to Compère)
*Vous me faites morir* ([Com]père)

---

12.    As suggested in *Census-Catalogue*, 4: 438.

**1490s**

**LonBLR 20 A.xvi** (France) second layer
*Mes pensees* (anon)

**c.1490-1500**

**MilD 2** (Milan)
*O genitrix gloriosa* (2a pars only: Ave virgo, 4v) (anon)
*Sanctus* (anon)

**c.1490-1504**

**LeipU 1494** (Leipzig?)
*Magnificat sexti toni* (anon)

**1492-1493**

**FlorBN BR 229** (Florence)
*Beaulte damours (Seraige)* (anon)
*Disant adieu I (Ne vous hastem pas)* (Loyset Compere)
*En attendant* (Loyset Compere)
*Le renvoy* (anon)
*Mes pensees* (Loyset Compere)
*Ung franc archier* (anon)

**1492-1494**

**VatG XIII.27** (Florence)
*De le mon getes (Voles oir)* (attributed to Compère)
*Dictes moy toutes* (anon)
*Il nest vivant (Pensees vivant)* (attr. to Compère) (**by Agricola**)
*Je suis amie du fourrier* (attributed to Compère)
*Mes pensees* (anon)
*Vostre bargeronette* (anon)
*Vray dieu quel paine* (anon) **possibly by Weerbeke**

**1492-1495**

**BerlS 40021** (Leipzig?)
*Magnificat sexti toni* (anon)

**mid to late 1490s**

**UppsU 76a** (southwestern France) Scribe B
*En attendant* (anon)

**c.1495**

**ParisBNF 1596** (Cognac)
*Vaten regret* (anon)

**VatS 15** (Rome)
*Magnificat primi toni* (Loyset Compere)

**c.1495-1497**

**VatS 15** (Rome)
*Ave Maria* (Loyset Compere)
*Crux triumphans* (anon)
*Propter gravamen* (anon)
*Quis numerare queat/Da pacem* (anon)
*Sile fragor* (anon)

**after 1495**

**SegC s.s.** (Spain)

*Ave Maria* (2a pars only: *Sancte Michael*) anon
*Beaulte damours* (loysette [Com]pere)
*Bergeronette savoysienne* (loysette [Com]pere)
*Cayphas* (loysette [com]pere; **Joha[n]nes Martini**)
*En attendant* (loysette [com]pere)
*Guerises moy* (loysette [com]pere)
*Hellas (as Elaes)* (loysette [com]pere) **by Tinctoris**
*Jay beau huer* (loysette co[m]pe[re]) **by Agricola**
*Je ne fais plus* (loysette co[m]pere) **by Busnois or Mureau**
*Je ne puis plus* (loysette [com]pe[re]) **by Agricola**
*Mon pere ma donne mari* (loysette [com]pere)
*Puisque si bien* (loysette [com]pere)
*Reveille toy franc cueur* (Loysette [com]pere)
*Se jay parle* (Loysette [com]pere)
*Veci la dansa* (Loysette co[m]pere) **by Vaqueras**
*Vive le noble roy de France* (Loysette [com]pere)

**SienBC K.I.2** (Siena)
*Ave Maria* (anon)
*Gloria sine nomine* (anon)
*O genitrix gloriosa* (anon)

**1497-1498**

**BerlS 40021** (Leipzig?)
*Ave Maria* (anon)

**after 1497**

**BolC Q17** (probably in or near Florence)
*Che fa la ramacina* (Loyset [Com]pere)
*Le renvoy* (Loyset [Com]pere)
*Lourdault (Nino petit)* **by Compère?**
*Mes pensees* (Loyset [Com]pere)
*Plaine dennuy/Anima mea* (Loyset [Com]pere)
*Royne du ciel/Regina celi* (**Prioris**) same as Compère's work except ,for first 4 mm.
*Se jay parle* (anon)
*Tant ay dennuy/O vos omnes* (Loyset [Com]pere)
*Venes regrets* (Loyset [Com]pere)
*Vostre bargeronette* (Loyset [Com]pere)
*Vray dieu quel payne* (anon) **possibly by Weerbeke**

**late 15th/early 16th c.**

**HradKM 7** (Bohemia)
*Sile fragor* (anon)

**c.1500**

**BrusBR 11239** (N. France? Savoy?)
*Plaine dennuy/Anima mea* (anon)
*Vaten regret* (Compere)
*Venes regrets* (Compere)

**MilD 3** (Milan)
*Ave Maria* (2a pars only: *Sancte Michael*) (Loyset)
*Gloria and Credo sine nomine* (Loyset)
*Missa Galeazescha* (anon)
*O genitrix gloriosa* (anon)

**Paris BNF 1597** (probably Paris)
*Crux triumphans* (anon)
*Faisons boutons II* (anon)
*La saison en est* (anon)
*Lourdault* (anon)
*Mes pensees* (anon)
*Tant ay ennuy/O vos omnes (O devotz cueurs)* (anon)
*Vaten regret* (anon)

**TurBN I. 27** (Turin or vicinity)
*Dictes moy toutes* (anon)
*En attendant* (anon)
*Guerises moy* (anon)
*Magnificat primi toni* (anon)
*Magnificat sexti toni* (anon)

**VerBC 757** (Verona)
*Le renvoy* (anon)

*Tant ha bon oeul* (anon)

**VerBC 758** (Verona)
*Ave Maria* (anon)
*Crux triumphans* (anon)
*Sile fragor* (anon)

**WarU 2016** (Silesia or Bohemia)
*Ave Maria* (anon)
*Crux triumphans* (anon)

### c.1500-1503

**VatC 234** (Brussels/Mechelen)
*Missa Lhomme arme* (Loyset Compere)
*Sile fragor* (anon)

### c.1500-1520

**WashLC L25** (Loire Valley?) Scribe IVb
*La saison en est* (L. Compere)

## ISAAC (c.1450-1517)

### 1470s-c.1500

**LucAS 238** (additions after 1472 in Lucca)
*Missa Charge de deul* (anon)

### 1480-1490; c.1485?

**PerBC 431** (Naples)
*Je suys malcontent (Serviteur suis)* (Henricus Isahc)
*Morte que fay* (anon)

### 1484?

**MunBS 3154** (probably Innsbruck; perhaps also Augsburg)
*Argentum et aurum* (attributed to Isaac)
*Ecce sacerdos magnus* (anon)
*Inviolata integra et castas* (anon)

### 1485-1488

**BerlS 40021** (Leipzig?)
*Adieu fillette de regnon* (anon)
*Missa Et trop penser* (anon)

### c.1487-1490

**VatS 35** (Rome)
*Missa Quant jay au cueur* (Ysaac)

### 1488-1489?

**MunBS 3154** (probably Innsbruck; perhaps also Augsburg)
*Credo XII* (anon)
*Missa Comment poit avoir joie* (Wohlauf gut Gsell), 6v (Ysaac)
*Missa Comment poit avoir joies* (Wohlauf gut Gsell), 6v (Ysac)

### 1488-1490

**BerlS 40021** (Leipzig?)
*Ecce sacerdos magnus (Ecce dilectus meus)* (anon)

### 1490

**BerlS 40021** (Leipzig?)
*Missa Quant jay au cueur* (anon)

### early 1490s

**FlorBN Magl. 178** (Florence)
*Corri fortuna* (attributed to Isaac)
*Fille vous avez mal garde* (Enriqus Ysac)
*Helogierons nous* (Yzac)
*Jay pris amours*, 4v, II (Ysaac)
*Je suys malcontent (Serviteur suis)* (anon)
*La morra* (Enrigus Yzac)
*Missa charge de deul*
  *Christe = Ami de que* (Ysac)
  *Qui tollis = A fortune content* (Ysac)
*Sempre giro piangendo* (attributed to Isaac)

### c.1490-1495

**LinzBS 529** (Innsbruck?)
*Argentum et aurum* (anon)
*Le serviteur* (anon)

### c.1490-1500

**MilD 2** (Milan)
*Missa Charge de deul* (Isach)
*Missa La bassadanza* (Enricus Isaac)
*Missa Quant jay au cueur* (Isac)

### c.1490-1504

**LeipU 1494** (Leipzig?)
*A la battaglia (as O praeclarissima)* (attributed to Isaac)
*Angeli arcangeli (as O Regina)* (anon)
*Argentum et aurum* (anon)
*Ecce sacerdos magnus (Ecce dilectus meus)* (attributed to Isaac)
*La morra* (H.Y.)

*La morra (Reple tuorum)* (anon) = 2nd appearance in ms.
*Missa Et trop penser (Crucifixus)* (H.Y.)
*Missa La spagna (Agnus II only; La spagna)* (anon)
*O decus ecclesiae,* **4 versions** (anon)

### 1491-1495

**BerlS 40021** (Leipzig?)
  *O decus ecclesiae (Vocum modulatio)* (anon)

### 1492

**BerlS 40021** (Leipzig?)
  *Missa Une musque de Biscaye* (Ysaac de manu sua)

### 1492-1493

**FlorBN BR 229** (Florence)
  *Donna di dentro* (Henricus Yçac)
  *Et ie boi dautant* (Yzac)
  *Helas que devera (Helas que pourra)* (Henricus Yzac)
  *Helogierons nous* (Henricus Yzac)
  *Jay pris amours, 3v* (Henricus Yzac)
  *Je ne puis vivre* (Henricus Yzac)
  *Je suys malcontent (Serviteur suis)* (anon)
  *La martinella I* (Henricus Yçac) )
  *La morra* (Henricus Yzac)
  *Le serviteur* (Henricus Yçac)
  *Maudit soit* (Henricus Yçac)
  *Missa Charge de deul (Christe)* (Henricus Yzac)
  *Missa Quant jay au cueur (Benedictus)* (Henricus Yzac)
  *Mon pere ma done mari* (Henricus Yzac)
  *Moyses* (Barle) **possibly by Isaac**
  *My my* (Henricus Yzac)
  *Salve regina II (Ad te clamamus only)* (Henricus Yzac)
  *Textless 1* (Henricus Yçac)
  *Textless 2* (Henricus Yçac)
  *Textless 3* (Henricus Yçac)
  *Textless 4* (Henricus Yçac)
  *Textless 5* (Yzac)
  *Textless 6* (Henricus Yzac)
  *Textless 7* (Henricus Yçac)

### 1492-1494

**VatG XIII.27** (Florence)
  *Coment poit avoir yoye* (Ysach)
  *Des biens amours* **originally attr. to Ysach; scribe B rubbed out** (really by Martini)
  *Digau alez donzelles (Pour vostre amours)* (Ysach) **by Brumel?**
  *Fille vous avez mal garde* (Ysach)
  *Fortuna desperata, 3v* (Ysach)
  *Helas que devera mon cuer* (Ysach)
  *Helogierons nous* (Ysach)
  *La morra (Donna gentil)* (Ysach)
  *Martinella* **originally attr. to Ysach and called** *Serviteur;* scribe B rubbed out both; really anon

*Maudit soit* (Ysach)
*Missa Comme femme (Benedictus, as Gracias a vos donzella)* (anon)
*Missa Quant jay au cuer (Benedictus)* (Ysach)
*Palle palle* (H. Isach)
*Par ung chies do cure* (Ysach)
*Quis dabit capito meo aquam* (anon)

### 1492-1495

**BerlS 40021** (Leipzig?)
  *Salve regina I* (h. Isaac)
  *Salve regina II* (Heyn Ysack)
  *Salve regina III* (h. Isaac) **NG: dubia**

### after 1495

**SegC s.s.** (Spain)
  *Ave regina caelorum* (Ysaac)
  *De tous biens [Et qui la dira]* (Ysaac)
  *Fortuna desperata* (Ysaac) **by Martini**
  *Fortuna desperata/Sancte Petre* (Ysaac)
  *Gentile spiritus* (Ysaac)
  *Gracias refero tibi domine* (Ysaac)
  *Hellas que devera mon cuer (Elaes)* (Ysaac)
  *Het es alghedaen* (Ysaac) **by Barle**
  *Jay pris amours, 4v, II* (anon)
  *La martinella II* (Ysaac)
  *La morra (Elaes)* (Ysaac)
  *La stangetta (Ortus de caelo)* (Ysaac) **by Weerbeke**
  *Missa Charge de deul (Christe, as Vostre amour)* (Ysaac)
  *Missa Comment poit avoir joie [Wohlauf gut Gsell], 6v (incomplete)* (anon)
  *Missa Quant jay au cueur* (Ysaac)
  *Morte que fay* (Ysaac)
  *Moyses* (Ysaac) **possibly by Barle**
  *My my* (Ysaac)
  *Pour mieux valoir (Comt hier)* (Ysaac) **by Rubinet**
  *Salve regina, 4v, II* (Ysaac)
  *Salve virgo sanctissima* (Ysaac) **NG: dubia**

**SienBC K.I.2** (Siena)
  *Missa Quant jay au cueur* (anon)

### c.1495-1497

**VatS 49** (Rome)
  *Missa Comme femme* (anon)
  *Missa Tmeiskin was jonck* (anon)

### after 1497

**BolC Q17** (probably in or near Florence)
  *Fille vous avez mal garde* (Yzac)
  *Helogierons nous* (Yzac)
  *O venus bant* (Yzac)
  *Sanctus fortuna desperata* (Ysac)

### 1497-1506?

**BerlS 40021** (Leipzig?)
  *In Gottes namen faren wir* (Isaac de manu sua)

### 1498

**BerlS 40021** (Leipzig?
*La la ho ho* (*Allahoy*) (anon)

### 1498-1501

**BerlS 40021** (Leipzig?)
*Sanctissime virginis votiva festa* (Ysaac de manu sua)

### late 15th century

**BarcOC 5** (this part of unknown origin)
*Missa Argentum et aurum* (Henericus Yzaac)
*Missa Comme femme* (Henericus Yzaac)
*Missa La spagna* (Henericus Yzaac)

### late 15th/early 16th c.

**HradKM 7** (Bohemia)
*Cecus* (*Ave ancilla*) (Isaac) **probably by Agricola**
*Missa Charge de deul* (*Missa Rosarum*), C & S only (anon)

### c.1500

**AugsS Mus. 25** (probably of southern German provenance)
*Je suys malcontent* (*Serviteur suis*) (attributed to Isaac)
**BrusBR 11239** (N. France? Savoy?)
*Et qui la dira* (H Ysac)
**MilD 3** (Milan)
*Missa Comment poit avoir joir* (*Wohlauf gut gsell*), 4v (Enricus Isaach)
**TurBN I. 27** (Turin or vicinity)
*Missa Quant jay au cueur* (Benedictus) (Isach)

### VerBC 757 (Verona)

*Helas que devera* (*Helas que pourra*) (anon)
*Je suys malcontent* (*Serviteur suis*) (anon)
*La morra* (anon)
*Missa La Spagna* (Agnus) (anon)
*Missa Quant jay au cueur* (Benedictus) (anon)
*Par ung chies do cure* (anon)

### WarU 2016 (Silesia or Bohemia)

*A la battaglia* (*Ave sanctissima*) (anon)
*Missa Charge de deul* (anon)
*Missa La Spagna*
  Qui tollis (as Agnus for *M. Charge*) (anon)
  Agnus II (anon)
*Missa Quant jay au cueur* (Ysaac)
  Also: separate textless *Et incarnatus* also in ms (anon)
*Salve regina I* (anon)
*Salve regina II* (anon)

### WashLC M6 (Florence? N. Italy?)

*Missa Comme femme* (Benedictus) (anon)
*Missa Quant jay au cueur* (Benedictus) (anon)
*Palle palle* (anon)

### 1500-1502

**MunBS 3154** (probably Innsbruck; perhaps also Augsburg)
*Cibavit eos* (attributed to Isaac)

### c.1500-1503

**VatC 234** (Brussels/Mechelen)
*Angeli archangeli* (Yzaac)

## OBRECHT (1457/1458-1505)

### c.1480

**BerlPS 40098** (Silesia; possibly Glogau or Sagan)
*Lacen adieu* (anon)

### c.1481

**RomeC 2856** (Ferrara)
*Fuga*, 4v (Hobrecht)
*Se bien fait* (Hobreth)

### 1480-1490; c.1485?

**PerBC 431** (Naples)
*Nec mihi nec tibi* (*Helas*) (anon)

### late 1487/early 1488

**VatS 51** (Rome)
*Missa Salve diva parens* (anon)

### c.1487-1490

**VatS 35** (Rome)
*Missa Plurimorum carminum I* (K & S only) (Hobrecht)
*Missa de Sancto Donatiano* (Ia. Hobrecht)

### 1487-1491

**MunBS 3154** (probably Innsbruck; perhaps also Augsburg)
*Missa Je ne demande* (anon)

### 1488-1490

**MunBS 3154** (probably Innsbruck; perhaps also Augsburg)
textless (Oppcht)

### 1489-1493

**BerlS 40021** (Leipzig?)
*Missa Fortuna desperata* (anon)

### late 1480s/early 1490s

**UppsU 76a** (southwestern France) Scribe A
*Parce domine* (anon)

### early 1490s

**FlorBN Magl. 178** (Florence)
*Meskin es hu* (*Adiu adiu*) (Jacobus Obret)
*Tmeiskin was jonck* (Japart; **really by Obrecht?**)

### c.1490-1495

**LinzBS 529** (Innsbruck?)
*Missa plurimorum carminum I* (C &S) (anon)
*Missa Salve diva parens* (anon)

### c.1490-1500

**MilD 2** (Milan)
*Missa Adieu mes amours* (Obret)

### c.1490-1504

**LeipU 1494** (Leipzig?)
*Missa Salve diva parens* (anon)
*Missa Si dedero* (anon)

### 1491-1493

**MunBS 3154** (probably Innsbruck; perhaps also Augsburg)
*Missa Beata viscera* (hobrecht)
*Missa plurimorum carminum II* (Hobrecht)
*Missa Rosa playsante* (anon)

### 1492

**BerlS 40021** (Leipzig?)
*Missa Naray je jamais* (anon)

### 1492-1493

**FlorBN BR 229** (Florence)
*La tortorella* (Jacobus Obrech)
*Meskin es hu* (Jacobus Obrech)
*Nec mihi nec tibi* (anon)
*Tmeiskin was jonck* (anon) **Japart? Obrecht?**
textless (Jacobus Obrech)

### 1492-1494

**VatG XIII.27** (Florence)
*La tortorella* (Jacobus Obrech)
*Nec mihi nec tibi* (Virgilius) **not Obrecht?**
*Wat willen wy* (Maule met) (J. Obrech)

### after 1495

**SegC s.s.** (Spain)
*Als al de weerelt in vruechden leeft* (Jacobus Hobrecht)
*Ave maris stella* (Jacobus Hobrecht)
*Benedicamus in laude* (Jacobus Hobrecht)
*Cuius sacrata viscera, 3v* (Jacobus Hobrecht)
*Cuius sacrata viscera, 4v* (Jacobus Hobrecht)
*Den haghel ende* (Jacobus Hobrecht)
*Ic draghe de mutse clutse* (Jacobus Hobrecht)
*Ic en hebbe gheen ghelt* (Jacobus Hobrecht)
*Ic hoerde de clocskins luden* (Jacobus Hobrecht)
*Ic weinsche alle scoene* (Jacobus Hobrecht)
*Inter praeclarissimas virtutes* (Jacobus Hobrecht)
*Lacen adieu* (Jacobus Hobrecht)
*Laet u ghenoughen* (Jacobus Hobrecht)
*Meskin es hu* (Jacobus Hobrecht)
*Mille quingentis / Requiem aeternam* (Jacobus Hobrecht)
*Missa Adieu mes amours* (Jacobus Hobrecht)

*Missa Fortuna desperata* (Jacobus Hobrecht)
*Missa Libenter gloriabor* (Jacobus Hobrecht)
*Missa Rosa playsante* (Jacobus Hobrecht)
*Missa Si dedero* (Christe) (Jacobus Hobrecht)
*Moet my laten* (Jacobus Hobrecht)
*Nec mihi nec tibi* (Jacobus Hobrecht)
*Omnis spiritus laudet* (Jacobus Hobrecht)
*Regina caeli* (Jacobus Hobrecht)
*Salve regina, 4v* (Jacobus Hobrecht)
*Sullen wij langhe* (Jacobus Hobrecht)
*Tmeiskin was jonck* (Jacobus Hobrecht) **by Japart?**
*Tsat een meskin* (Jacobus Hobrecht)
*War sij di han* (Jacobus Hobrecht)
*Wat willen wy* (Jacobus Hobrecht)
*Weet ghij* (Jacobus Hobrecht)

**SienBC K.I.2** (Siena)
*Missa Beata viscera* (anon)

### 1497

**BerlS 40021** (Leipzig?)
*Missa Malheur me bat* (anon)

### after 1497

**BolC Q17** (probably in or near Florence)
*Parce domine* (anon)
*Tmeiskin was jonck* (De tous en bousc) (anon) by Obrecht?
    by Japart?

### 1498

**BerlS 40021** (Leipzig?)
*Missa Je ne seray* (anon)
*Wat willen wy* (anon)

### late 15th century

**BarcOC 5** (unknown)
*Missa Salve diva parens* (anon)

### late 15th/early 16th c.

**HradKM 7** (Bohemia)
*Lacen adieu* (anon)
*Missa Je ne seray* (anon)
*Nec mihi nec tibi* (anon)
*Wat willen wy* (Precantibus) (anon)

### c.1500

**AmiensBM 162** (presumably of French origin)
*Parce domine* (anon)

**BrusBR 11239** (N. France? Savoy?)
*Si sumpsero* (anon)

**Paris BNF 1597** (probably Paris)
*Si sumpsero* (anon)

**TurBN I. 27** (Turin or vicinity)
*Nec mihi nec tibi* (anon)

**VerBC 757** (Verona)
textless (Obreth)
textless (Jacob Oberti)

Craig J. Westendorf

# Josquin in the Early German Baroque: Seth Calvisius' Parody of *Præter rerum seriem*

A T THE END of the time of the transmission of Josquin's works, Erhard Bodenschatz published in 1603 Seth Calvisius' reworking of the incomparable *Praeter rerum seriem*, subtitled *"Parode ad Josquini."*[1] From this one historical fact arise several enigmas requiring further investigation. Not only does this parody appear when Josquin has been entirely supplanted by later composers in the larger central German manuscripts, it appears after the period typically associated in the secondary literature with the great mass parodies. Further, it is printed by a publisher hardly given over to arcane or antiquarian exercises, for Bodenschatz's collections enjoyed use well into the eighteenth century.[2] Of what interest could a reworked motet no longer matching contemporary musical style be to a printing industry attuned to works of immediate liturgical application? This modest study will make some suggestions to explain why Calvisius was prompted to re-present Josquin to his own generation.

In studies of the contrapuntal parody of this era, the secondary literature of the last two decades has dealt almost entirely with the masses of Lassus and Palestrina.[3] While this repertoire is deserving of ever more study as a means to explain compositional procedures, there is a neglect of later appearances of parody, with the exception of the works of Claudio Monteverdi[4] and Heinrich Schütz.[5] Studies during the twentieth century have concentrated on the introduction of the figured bass in Germany and the concertizing styles dependent on it, far outweighing studies into the persistence of the counterpoint

1. *Florilegium selectissimarum cantionum* (Leipzig, 1603), RISM 1603¹.

2. Günther STILLER, *Johann Sebastian Bach and Liturgical Life in Leipzig*, ed. Robin LEAVER (St. Louis: Concordia, 1984), 86-87.

3. See especially Rufina ORLICH, *Die Parodiemessen von Orlando di Lasso* (Munich: Wilhelm Fink Verlag, 1985); Quentin QUEREAU, "Aspects of Palestrina's Parody Procedure," *Journal of Musicology* 1/2 (April, 1997): 199-216.

4. Lewis LOCKWOOD, "Monteverdi and Gombert: The

*Missa In illo tempore* of 1610," *De musica et cantu: Studien zur Geschichte der Kirchenmusik und der Oper—Helmut Hucke zum 60. Geburtstag* (Hildesheim: Olms, 1993), 457-69; and Anthony NEWCOMB, "A New Context for Monteverdi's Mass of 1610," *Studien zur Musikgeschichte. Eine Festschrift für Ludwig Finscher* (Kassel: Bärenreiter, 1995), 163-73.

5. Werner BREIG, "Heinrich Schütz' Parodiemotette *Jesu dulcissime*," *Convivium musicorum. Festschrift Wolfgang Boetticher zum sechzigsten Geburtstag am 19. August 1974* (Berlin: Merseburger, 1974), 13-24.

dependent on longer note values, as composers of the time described the *Allabreve* style.[6] Heinrich Schütz may have been a prophet of the current research situation when he admonished younger composers to crack the hard nut of counterpoint.[7] The parody mass remained more popular at the beginning of the seventeenth century than has been recognized, with Northern Italian examples by Balbi, Croce, Merulo, Guami, Banchieri, Vecchi, Gastoldi, Pallavicino, and Massaino.[8] Some of the larger and most representative manuscripts of central German provenance from this time also contain parody masses worthy of consideration. Krakow, Biblioteka Jagiellonska, Mus. ms. 40044, with masses by Jacob Praetorius and Joseph Botticher on models by Vecchi, Hassler, and Hieronymus Praetorius. Mus. ms. 40111 from the same library has an extensive mass repertoire with masses principally by Sebastian Rauffufius on models by Dressler, Lassus, Meiland, Handl, and Schandelius; and Mus. ms. 40345 transmits anonymous masses on Vulpius' *Pater noster* and Hassler's *Verbum caro factum est.* Thus Calvisius' *Praeter rerum seriem* is a rarified exemple only in that it is a parody motet and not a parody mass. That he turns a motet into another motet is of great benefit to modern analysis. A parody mass often involves the introducion of new motives because of the length of the text of the mass ordinary. Such is not the case here, and the reworking of motivic material is easy to justify, since the texts and the motivic material to which they are joined remain almost identical.

The appearance of Georg Quitschreiber's *De ΠΑΡΩΔΙΑ*, *tractatus musicalis musicae studiosis propositus* in 1611[9] is proof of the vitality of the parody tradition precisely within Calvisius' milieu. This small tract of only four leaves, with the body of the text only four pages long, is not a theoretical treatise, but rather a defense of parody procedure overall.[10] The argument is built to answer his leading question, whether parody is legimate in musical composition: *An Parodia Musicalis concedatur?*[11] Before citing examples of parody, he establishes that the well-schooled composers are creating many innovations and inventions,[12] giving examples from Marenzio and Landgraf Moritz of Hesse. As a faithful German humanist, Quitschreiber draws his ultimate justification of musical parody from Quintilian, who defines this procedure as *canticum ad alterius imitationem modulatum.* (*Imitatio,*

---

6. Werner BRAUN, *Der Stilwandel in der Musik um 1600* (Darmstadt: Wissenschaftliche Buchgesellschaft, 1982), 14-17.

7. Als bin ich hierdurch veranlasset worden derogleichen Wercklein ohne Bassum Continuum auch einsten wieder anzugehen/ und hiedurch vielleicht etliche/ insonderheit aber theils der angehenden Deutschen Componisten anzufrischen/ das/ ehe Sie zu dem concertirenden Stylo schreitten/ sie vorher diese harte Nuß (als worinnen der rechte Kern/ und das rechte Fundament eines guten Contrapuncts zusuchen ist) auffbeissen … . Heinrich SCHÜTZ, *Geistliche Chormusik*, 1648. *Neue Ausgabe sämtliche Werke* (Kassel: Bärenreiter, 1955), 5: vi.

8. NEWCOMB, 163.     9. Jena: Johann WEIDNER.

10. There is a very helpful summary by Klaus NIEMÖLLER, "Parodia—Imitatio: Zu Georg Quitschreibers Schrift von 1611," *Studien zur Musikgeschichte. Eine Festschrift für Ludwig Finscher* (Kassel: Bärenreiter, 1995): 174-80. Niemöller gives very helpful paraphrases and bibliography to Quitschreiber's classical allusions.

11. F. Aii[r].

12. "Et nostra aetas illustribus inventis & maximis foecunda est, ut quasi hodie cum Musica ludere (at honeste) illi dicantur, qui in Schola Musica bene educati sunt, …. F. Aii[r].

rather than *parodia*, was the most frequently used term through the sixteenth century; it is obvious here that Quitschreiber makes no distinction between the two terms.[13] The tract then describes precise examples of parody procedure, the first of which is the piece under consideration, Calvisius' parody of Josquin's *Praeter rerum seriem*. Reduction of voices is considered parody procedure. Quitschreiber cites Lippius' seven-voice adaptation of Alessandro Striggio's *Ecce beatam lucem* and Sweelinck's five-voice reduction of Lassus' six-voice *Magnificat Susanne un jour*, accomplished by retaining the original discant, discarding the other five voices, and then adding four new voices. Expansion of texture is also part of parody. Giovanni de Antiquis and Francesco Sorrentino added a bass to the bicinia of Rocco Rodio. Palestrina expands voices as he parodies himself (Quitschreiber uses the verb *parodizavit*) in the *Missa Vestiva i colli*, based on his own three-voice madrigal, and there are "a great number" of masses in imitation of motets. At the midpoint of his argumentation, Quitschreiber exclaims that in defense of musical parody nothing could be clearer than the light of noon.[14] Michael Praetorius is praised for his manifold treatments of chorales and his plans to compose in the style of Lassus, Marenzio, and as Quitschreiber presumes, Victoria.[15] Contrafacta also fit within the realm of parody, exemplified by Valentin Haußmann's *Canzonette* (Nürnberg, 1606), in which German texts replace the Italian-texted pieces of Horatio Vecchi and Geminiani Lupi.[16]

Parody technique is defined above all in the modern secondary literature in relation to the parody mass, since this was the predominant repertoire of the sixteenth and early seventeenth centuries.[17] Titles beginning with *Missa ...*, *Missa super ...*, or *Missa ad imitationem ...*, followed by the name of the contrapuntal model dominate modern analysis. The concentration on the parody mass is certainly justified. Of the 104 Mass cycles by Palestrina, at least half have contrapuntal models; of the approximately 63 masses of Lassus, 53 have contrapuntal models.[18] The parody masses remain closely tied to their models, much in the way that Pietro Cerone describes in *El melopeo y maestro* (Naples, 1613): the Kyrie, Gloria, Credo, Sanctus, and Agnus Dei should begin with the same motivic material, the Christe should be drawn from a subsidiary motive from the model, endings of certain movements should correspond to the close of the model, and so on.[19] The parodies of Josquin's *Praeter rerum seriem* for the most part certainly conform to the pattern of parody as mass cycle.[20] The Bayerische Staatsbibliothek preserves in manuscript masses by

13.  Lewis LOCKWOOD's study remains definitive for the use of *parodia* and *imitatio*. "On 'Parody' as Term and Concept in 16th-Century Music," ed. Jan LaRUE, *Aspects of Medieval and Renaissance Music. A Birthday Offering to Gustave Reese* (New York: Norton, 1966): 560-75.

14.  " Sic pleraeque Missae, ut vocant, ad imitationes Mutetarum concinnatae, decantantur. Sed quid opus est demonstrationibus cum res luce meridiana sit clarior?" F. Aii^v.

15.  NIEMÖLLER, 179.    16.    RISM V, 1034.

17.  "... the parody technique, primarily associated with the mass ... ." Michael TILMOUTH, "Parody," *The New Grove*, 14: 238.

18.  ORLICH, 7.

19.  The pertinent section is translated in Oliver STRUNK, *Source Readings in Music History* (New York: Norton, 1950), 265-68.

20.  Marie Louise GÖLLNER, "*Praeter rerum seriem*: Its

Mattheus Le Maistre, Ludwig Daser, and Cipriano de Rore, as well as a parody Magnificat by Orlandus Lassus;[21] George de la Hèle is yet another composer of a mass on Josquin's model. The parody mass dominates the entire parody repertoire, and Quitschreiber does indeed acknowledge masses *ad imitationes Muterarum*. Yet it is important to keep in mind his more inclusive definitions of parody as described above, and that Calvisius' *Praeter rerum seriem*, a parody motet, has a special place of honor in his treatise.

If tabulations are not considered as parodies, only Calvisius reworks Josquin's motet as a *motet* and not as a parody mass.[22] Indeed, when one considers all of the parodies of the sixteenth and early seventeenth centuries, there are no examples of this procedure (outside of contrafacta) that come immediately to mind. Also rare are parodies of any kind which are based on so much older models. For Palestrina, parody models not of his own composition come mostly from the 1530's; the corresponding decade for Lassus is the 1540s. Thus for Lassus and Palestrina, models taken from other composers are rarely more than 35 years old.[23] By the time Calvisius published his parody, his model could have been almost 120 years old.[24] Perhaps the modern assessment of Calvisius' unique procedure has been so negative precisely because it is so rare. Göllner calls it a "strange arrangement and simplification."[25] Werner Braun is harsher: Josquin's actual compositional concept is lost.[26] Yet it is precisely simplification which Quitschreiber praises. Calvisius is given as the first example of the highly valued definition of *imitatio* quoted from Quintilian: "In the same manner [as Quintilian] Seth Calvisius, the brilliant chronologist and musician of Leipzig, has now made a parody on Josquin de Pres' six-voice motet *Praeter rerum seriem* etc., and having taken out the more difficult passages has again returned it to six voices with the inscription *Parode Josquini*."[27] In a treatise with little theoretical definition the phrase *omissis difficilioribus clausulis* becomes quite significant. The term *clausula* can mean both cadence and "contrapuntal section" in seventeenth-century German theory.[28] That clausula here means "passage" and not "cadence" can be taken from Quitschreiber's own context. He praises Melchior Vulpius' five- and six-voice parodies of the "clausulas" from Hieronymus Praetorius' 44 pieces on

History and Sources," *Von Isaac bis Bach. Studien zur älteren deutschen Musikgeschichte. Festschrift Martin Just zum 60. Geburtstag* (Kassel: Bärenreiter, 1991): 41-49. This article is very helpful in listing sixteenth-century parodies and intabulations.
21. Göllner, 48-49.    22. Göllner, 48.
23. Orlich, 303-4.    24. Göllner, 47-48.
25. Göllner, 49.
26. Werner Braun, *Die Musik des 17. Jahrhunderts. Neues Handbuch der Musikwissenschaft*, 4 (Wiesbaden: Akademische Verlagsgesellschaft Athenaion, 1981), 305.
27. "Ejusmodi Parodiam confecit aliquando Sethus

Calvisius, Chronologus & Musicus argutissimus Lipsiae, super Mutetam 6. vocum Josquini de Pres. Praeter rerum seriem &c. & omissis difficilioribus clausulis, iterum 6. Vocibus eam reddidit, cum inscriptione, Parode Josquini." F. Aii$^v$.
28. Werner Braun outlines how *clausula* can mean "motive," "imitative section," "ritornello," or "cadence" in the sense of all voices coming to rest in a consonance after passing through dissonance. Werner Braun, *Deutsche Musiktheorie des 15. bis 17. Jahrhunderts. Zweiter Teil: Von Calvisius bis Mattheson* (Darmstadt: Wissenschaftliche Buchgesellschaft, 1994), 234-35.

*Miserere mei, Deus.*[29] Quitschreiber does know the term *clausula* as cadence, but confines this usage to the very precise *clausula formalis*.[30] In a time when both theory and the larger printed and manuscript collections were created for immediate and practical use, modernization towards simplification was praiseworthy.

What exactly did Calvisius do to be so exalted by his contemporaries and so criticized by commentators of our time?[31] In the beginning of his *Parode Josquini*, nothing has changed except for the mensuration. Josquin's *modus perfectus cum tempore imperfecto*—in this case three breves per tactus, with each breve divided into two semibreves—has been simplified to alla breve. At this point Calvisius is certainly in line with the mensural theory of his time. The older system of prolatio-tempus-modus-proportio-augmentatio-diminutio so exhaustively described and illustrated by Sebald Heyden is simply not needed at the beginning of the seventeenth century.[32] There was then simply a two-part division of the tactus or a three-part division of the tactus. For a two-part division there is by 1620 hardly any distinction between open C and slash-C; Michael Praetorius simply says an open C is beat more slowly than a slash-C, since an open C signifies a madrigal with overall shorter note values.[33] A triple meter is likewise either slow or fast, depending on the note values.[34] It is difficult to say if Calvisius' simplified mensuration with its halving of note values meant a substantial change in the actual speed of the notes because of the ambiguity of mensural theory. There was most likely no substantial change, especially when one considers the ubiquitous admonitions by both theorists and compilers of *Kirchenordnungen* that motets were to be done *gravior* because of the solemnity of the texts and the density of the counterpoint. In any case, because of the original tempus imperfectum, there is no sense of accentual shift if Calvisius' parody is done at a moderate to moderately slow tempo. His mensuration change is thus an adaptation to modern exigencies.

Calvisius' faithfulness to Josquin's model at least at the outset is in line with parody technique well established by 1550 and codified by Cerone. The initial point of imitation is the most identifiable feature of any motet, and its use at the beginning of mass movements with sparing alterations is the most practical way to signal the identity and style of the model. Josquin's use of parallel thirds in a relatively low register seemed to captivate later composers, especially for sections that are not so syllabic. Cipriano de Rore

29. "Quis igitur Musurgo prohibeat, ne, quoad Tonum vel sonum ex Hieron. Praet. 44. cant. 5. Voc. Clausulam imitetur: Miserere mei Deus, ut Vulpius fecit in I. parte, num. 5. & 6. vocibus videre est?" F. Aiii^r.

30. "Nam, ex reliquis utilitatibus cognitionis Musicae poeticae, haec ultima est: contrapunctos triplices ad vocem, choralem vel figuralem, ex tempore singere, modulari vel componere; quod praestari potest, cognita consonantiarum, modorum, syncopationum & clausularum formalium proprietate." F. Aiii^r.

31. A critical edition is found in Albrecht TUNGER, ed., *Sethus Calvisius, Geistliche Chormusik. Das Chorwerk alter Meister,* 4/13 (Stuttgart: Hänssler Verlag, 1965), 5-12.

32. Sebald HEYDEN, *De arte canendi* (Nürnberg, 1540; facs. New York: Broude Brothers, 1969), 55-135.

33  Michael PRAETORIUS, *Syntagma musicum Tomus tertius* (Wolfenbüttel, 1619; facsimile ed. Wilibald GURLITT Kassel: Bärenreiter, 1978), 48.

34. Michael PRAETORIUS, 52-54.

**Example 1**    Cipriano DE RORE, Credo from *Missa Præter rerum seriem*

uses this as a "signal" sonority in his mass based on *Praeter rerum seriem* (Ex. 1).[35]

In Calvisius' generation this texture was exploited especially for motets setting German Bible verses for texts. Especially when one word of the text is repeated, it is a means of creating sonority during what is overall static harmony. Heinrich Hartmann's *Ich hab dich ein klein Augenblick verlassen*[36] exploits this both for text expression and to brake the forward propulsion before going into the sesquialtera section (Ex. 2). The persistence of this texture may have been one reason for the resiliency of Josquin's motet well past the normal life expectancy of transmission.

As Calvisius proceeds, it is difficult at first to grasp what was meant by Quitschreiber's encomium that the "more difficult" passages were omitted. Most obvi-

---

35. *Cipriano de Rore Opera Omnia*, 7, ed. Bernhard MEIER (American Institute of Musicology, 1966), 69. De Rore further expands his texture by adding a seventh voice, a

cantus firmus in honor of the duke of Ferrara.

36. *Confortativae sacrae symphoniacae, Erster Theil*, No. 16 (Coburg: Justus Hauck, 1613; RISM H 2197).

**Example 2**   HARTMANN, *Ich hab' dich ein klein Augenblick verlassen*

ous are features that have been added. The texture actually becomes denser more quick-ly, because a fourth voice, in this case the Altus II, enters earlier than it does in the origi-nal motet. But the most obvious and distinctive departure from Josquin's motet is the regular introduction of *clausulas formales*, that is, cadences marked by suspensions, at the end of virtually all phrases of text. In the *prima pars*, Josquin uses only four suspensions: a 7-6 "Burgundian" cadence before the first entrance of the Superius, a 7-6 suspension midway through the presentation of *Virgo mater*, a 4-3 suspension at the end of *Virgo mater* to prepare for the entrance of the new motive on *Nec vir tangit*, and a 4-3 suspension mid-way through the presentation of *Nec prolis originem*. By the time Calvisius reaches the end of his *prima pars*, he has used 25 suspensions, two pairs of which use intervening 6/4 sonorities. Where Josquin creates tonal direction and the overall tonal scheme by ostina-to-like reiteration of motives in ultimate reliance on the cantus firmus, Calvisius relies on formal cadences. Of all of the suspensions in the *prima pars*, only one instance does not reinforce either the *finalis* or the *confinalis* (respectively 'G' or 'D' in the Dorian mode transposed by one flat). The one exception is near the end of the development of *Virgo mater*, with a resolution on the supertonic of the transposed Dorian. In the rhetorical thinking of the early German Baroque, this structural definition through frequent cadences is laudable, as it parallels the *ornamenta* of well-conceived oratory. Cadences defined by suspensions give sense to musical construction just as the orator must create clarity by means of commas, colons, and periods. As Calvisius explains in his own ΜΕΛΟΠΟΙΙΑ (1630) without such organization there is only clamor and confusion.[37] Formal cadences "ornament" the music in the rhetorical sense of adding delight and allowing the text to be instructive, and should be used as frequently as the harmony (that is, according to the *finales* and *confinales* of the twelve modes) and the text allow.[38] This predilection for more frequent cadences permeates all of Calvisius' parody, a phenome-non already noted by Werner Braun.[39]

The rhythmic modification necessary to prepare a suspension creates significant and audible differences between the model and the parody. Not even the cantus firmus is spared, as Calvisius alters it freely in his cadence. That even the opening phrase *Praeter rerum seriem* is treated in this way seems to establish a pattern, and even a program, for the

37. "Quemadmodum in oratione, etiamsi omnia, quae ad bonitatem ejus requiruntur, & qua ad docendum, delectandum, & movendum auditorem faciunt, ad-fuerint, atque abundaverint: nisi commatis, colis, & periodorum comprehensionibis distinguatur, & exorne-tur, confusus oritur sensus, & incertus ab ore differentis pendet auditor: Ita in Harmonia, etiamsi omnia, quae hactenus tradita sunt, ad amussim observentur, Conso-nantiae optimae eligantur, perfectae cum imperfectis recte misceantur, & Dissonantiis per Syncopen & celeri-tatem admissis varientur: tamen nisi clausulis in partes quaedam Harmonia quasi secetur, & distinguatur, con-fusus exoritur, concinentium occinentium, intercinen-tiumque clamor, & auribus pariter atque animo affertur lassitudo." Seth Calvisius, ΜΕΛΟΠΟΙΑ (Magdeburg: Johann Franck, 1630), chap. 13.

38. "Etsi Clausula Harmoniam magnopere exornant, ut diximus, & frequenter usurpantur … idque & ratione Harmoniae & ratione textus." ibid., chap. 14.

39. Braun, *Die Musik des 17. Jahrhunderts*, 305.

entire parody (Ex. 3a and 3b). The cadence formed at the end of *Parit Deum et hominem* is an even more drastic example (Ex. 4a and 4b).

Calvisius' predilection for cadences sometimes leads to complete abandonment of the model, as a comparison of the model and new setting of *Nec vir tangit virginem* will show. Here the rhythmic pattern required by the preparation of the suspension also creates the imitative motive (Ex. 5a and 5b).

Calvisius concludes with ever more densely placed suspensions ultimately coming to rest not on the final, as do the original chant and Josquin's motet, but on the confinalis. This is a major change in large-scale construction from that of the Renaissance to that of the early Baroque. Very deliberate development around the confinalis—that is, the dominant—takes precedence over development of motives with a logical linear development around the final.

The simplification praised by Quitschreiber, characterized in this parody by the elimination of motivic material, is even more obvious in the *secunda pars*. Josquin requires 52 breves before the beginning of the triple mensuration, while Calvisius uses exactly half that number at 26 breves. For a specific example, Josquin uses nineteen breves for *Initus et exitus partus tui penitus;* Calvisius uses less than a third of that, presenting this phrase in only five breves. The internal rhyme of *initus* and *exitus* prompts Josquin to use the same motives for each word, with time for a series of parallel 3rds and 10ths in addition to a motive derived from the original hymn (chant original when transposed, $b^b$-$a$-$b^b$-$c'$-$b^b$-$a$-$g$; Josquin changes this to $b^b$-$b^b$-$b^b$-$c'$-$b^b$-$g$-$a$-$g$) used in imitation. The presentation of *partus dei penitus* foregoes the melodic extension of parallel 3rds and 10ths, relying on imitation of a motive derived from the chant. Here Calvisius deviates further from his model than at any other point in his parody, with only the vaguest reference to Josquin's motives and building of sonority through parallel 10ths. Greater reference to the model is restored at *quis scrutatur*, where Calvisius uses Josquin's bass. Again, where Josquin will use the same motive at the same pitch level three times, Calvisius will economize and only use it once. Immediately before the triple mensuration, Josquin has an almost inconspicuous 4-3 suspension in the lower voices; Calvisius, again true to his own style, has a formulaic 6/4 sonority to prepare for the 4-3 suspension.

The parody of the section in triple mensuration closely matches the model, probably because it is the most "modern" sounding section to begin with. Calvisius actually makes it a bit longer, and in so doing uses a slightly thicker texture. He also changed the text in favor of evangelical theology (a contrafactum well within Quitschreiber's definition of parody): *Dei providentia quae disponit omnia tam suave, Tua puerperia transfer in mysteria, Mater ave* becomes *Dei providentia haec disponit omnia tam suave, et pios coelestia transfert in palatia, Puer ave.* The mystery of virgin birth is suppressed in favor of the saving grace of the fruit of this birth; Marian adoration is abandoned in order to praise the redemption brought

**Example 3a**  JOSQUIN, *Præter rerum seriem*

**Example 3b**  CALVISIUS, *Præter rerum seriem*

**Example 4a**  JOSQUIN, *Præter rerum seriem*

**Example 4b**  CALVISIUS, *Præter rerum seriem*

**Example 5a**  JOSQUIN, *Nec vir tangit virginem*

**Example 5b**  CALVISIUS, *Nec vir tangit virginem*

about by God through the child. Calvisius pays ultimate homage to Josquin, however, by not inserting any cadences at the conclusion of the *secunda pars*. Both model and parody share the same motives, and the final sonority is identical in both ($G$-$d$-$g$- $b^b$-$d'$-$b^{b\prime\prime}$). The practicality of Cerone's instructions is again substantiated. Just as the opening is one of the sections most faithful to the model, so at the end a its close recollection allows the listener to identify Josquin's motet most easily.

If cadences are added freely to define even short textual phrases and to establish the final, Calvisius nevertheless eliminates the *notae cambiatae*. The section *Parit Deum hominem virgo mater* in the *prima pars*, which abounds in *cambiatae* in the model, has been stripped of this figure by Calvisius in favor of conjunct motion, with scalar motives through an ascending fifth. The *nota cambiata* may have been what Quitschreiber considered one of the "more difficult" features of Josquin. Although still to be found in Palestrina,[40] it disappeared from the counterpoint of the early German Baroque.

Another consistent characteristic of Calvisius' reshaping of his model is the expansion of tonal "space," that is, the expansion of the interval between the outermost voices. This was a compositional procedure very much part of the self-conscious innovations of the early German Baroque, as Quitschreiber attests. He praises Moritz of Hesse for expanding the scale to $b^{b\prime\prime\prime}$ in instrumental music and Nicolaus Rhostius for expanding the vocal ambitus to four octaves, from $C$ to $c^{\prime\prime\prime}$.[41] Lassus, whose works were still very much a part of the performing repertoire of the early German Baroque, would also expand the tonal space in his parodies, even when the model was a modest chanson.[42] The exploitation of this new sonority may be one reason for the rapid increase in the number of polychoral works in German prints and manuscripts of this time; a double-choir motet by Heinrich Hartmann is a particularly helpful illustration. Within an eight-voice texture, the lower-voiced choir sings by itself what is at first apparently a lament from Isaiah 54:7, *Ich hab' dich ein klein Augenblick verlassen*. However, at the crucial syntactic juncture of the promise of mercy—*Aber mit großer Barmherzigkeit*—the texture explodes to a nineteenth, reinforced by a harmonic change from an a-minor triad to a C-major triad (Ex. 6). The treatment of *nec prolis originem* combines the retention of parallelism with the expansion of tonal space. Where Josquin uses parallel sixths, Calvisius has used parallel tenth (Ex. 7a and 7b).

The opening of the *secunda pars* is particularly illustrative of how the expansion of tonal space is combined with the well-defined pattern of frequent cadences and

---

40. Knud JEPPESEN, *The Style of Palestina and the Dissonance*, 2d. ed. (Copenhagen: Levin & Munksgaard, 1946), 213.
41. "Et Illustrissimus Princeps Mauritius Landgravius &c. saepe propter instrumenta in bbb. Acutissimum tendit, ut & Nicolaus Rhostius aulicus olim Phonascus id in Cantilena quadam natalitia observavit; imo hodierna Scala in Tetradiapason a ad ccc. extenditur. QUITSCHREIBER, F. Aii$^r$.
42. OHRLICH, 296-300.

**Example 6**    HARTMANN, *Ich hab' dich ein klein Augenblick verlassen*

exploitation of parallelism. At the outset, the ascending parallel thirds are retained, but Calvisius expands the tonal realm from an octava to a tenth. Josquin's trademark of ostinato-like repetition of motives is not wasted on Calvisius, but where Josquin brings the lines to a logical linear conclusion, Calvisius has already introduced a 4-3 suspension. As the lower voices are introduced, all of these techniques are used again. The tonal space of a twelfth is expanded to a seventeenth, and motives are reshaped to conform to cadential formulas. Melismas are also substantially shortened. Josquin also exploited tonal space, but its expansion was reserved for truly architectonic purposes, rather than as a constant compositional device. The *prima pars* of the model concludes with a climactic and dramatic opening of the tonal space to a seventeenth near the beginning of the *novit pater* motive. The satisfying conclusion is brought out by reiterated motives circulating around the confinalis, rather than cadencing on the confinalis itself as Calvisius does.

Although Josquin was still a master to be revered and emulated at the beginning of the seventeenth century, Calvisius' parody reflects much more the taste of his own time. The most noticeable change is the manner in which harmonic progress is defined. Josquin achieves this by reiterated motives around various degrees of the mode, creating a logic closely allied with the logic of the cantus firmus. Calvisius abandons this repeti-

**Example 7a**    JOSQUIN, *Nec prolis originem*, from *Præter rerum seriem*

**Example 7b**    CALVISIUS, *Nec prolis originem*, from *Præter rerum seriem*

tion of motives in favor of the *clausula formalis* as a device to reinforce almost relentlessly the final and confinalis of the mode. These frequent cadences correspond to a clear rhetorical definition, with even short textual phrases receiving this treatment. While he expands the tonal space according to the taste of his time, the density of the contrapuntal texture has remained essentially the same. It is the combination of all these features which allowed Calvisius' parody to be understood as a worthy "simplification." Repeated voice pairings of the same motives and a wide variety of dissonance treatment to define the ends of larger sections, features so typical of Josquin, have been eliminated in favor of condensation and a clear structure around a modern tonic and dominant of the mode. This clarity, when added to the exploitation of luxurious sonority created by parallelism, became a hallmark of German contrapuntal composition in the first three decades of the seventeenth century.

Jessie Ann Owens

# A Robert Jones Autograph?

THE MANUSCRIPT Folger Shakespeare Library, Ms. V.b.278, presents interesting problems. It contains a song, "The loue of change," which bears the name 'Ro Iones'. The manuscript may be an autograph of the English composer Robert Jones (*fl.* 1597-1615), but it could also be a copy written by someone else. The very attempt to answer the question of who wrote the manuscript leads to other questions concerning compositional process and practice in the English lute song repertory.

The manuscript consists of a single bifolium; the thin paper bears an indistinct and deteriorated watermark, a bunch of grapes surmounted by a crown (?).[1] Each of the two conjugate leaves measures approximately 32 x 21.5 cm. The manuscript has neither pagination nor foliation. As it is presently folded, what might be considered "fol. 1ʳ" contains a six-line poem—"For whe [*sic, recte* who] can change yᵗ [that] likes his former choyce"—that turns out to be the second stanza of a known poem. The back page ("fol. 2ᵛ") contains the first stanza of the poem, "The loue of Change hath chang'd the world through outt." The inside of the bifolium (= "fol. 1ᵛ-2ʳ") is blank.

The present configuration of the manuscript obscures the simple logic of its original structure. The current inner opening, which is quite dirty, was once probably the outside. In the original configuration, the inside opening of the bifolium contained the music (with the text of the first stanza) on the left, facing the second stanza on the right, as shown in Plates 1-2. A series of folds suggests that the bifolium was folded in half, and then in half again; notable differences in the amount of dirt found on the sections of the blank opening correspond to these folds. This manuscript shows one of the characteristic ways that music circulated, in single fascicles, folded small enough to be enclosed with a letter.

---

\* This article is in some ways a footnote to the excellent study by Joseph Quincy Adams cited in note 3. It is too slight an offering for my dear friend and colleague, Herbert KELLMAN, but perhaps he will enjoy the hunt and be amused that the prey continues to elude my grasp.

1. A somewhat similar mark can be found in Edward HEAWOOD, *Watermarks, Mainly of the 17ᵗʰ and 18ᵗʰ Centuries* (Hilversum: Paper Publications Society, 1950), no. 2343 from 1599.

**Plate 1**  Robert JONES, Song "The loue of change hath chang'd," 1602
The Folger Shakespeare Library, Ms. V.b. 278, recto

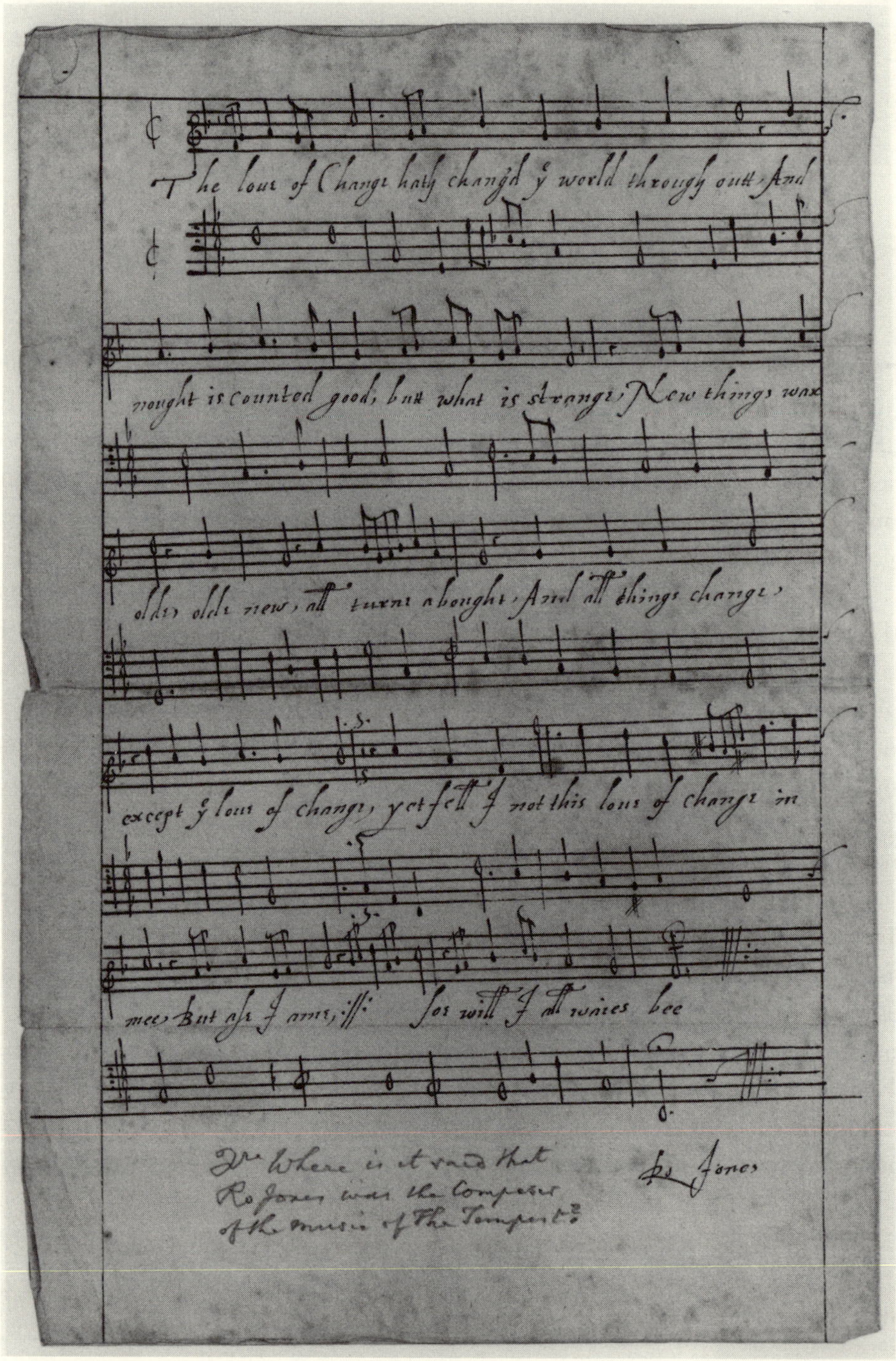

Robert JONES, Song "The love of change hath chang'd," 1602
The Folger Shakespeare Library, Ms. V.b. 278, verso

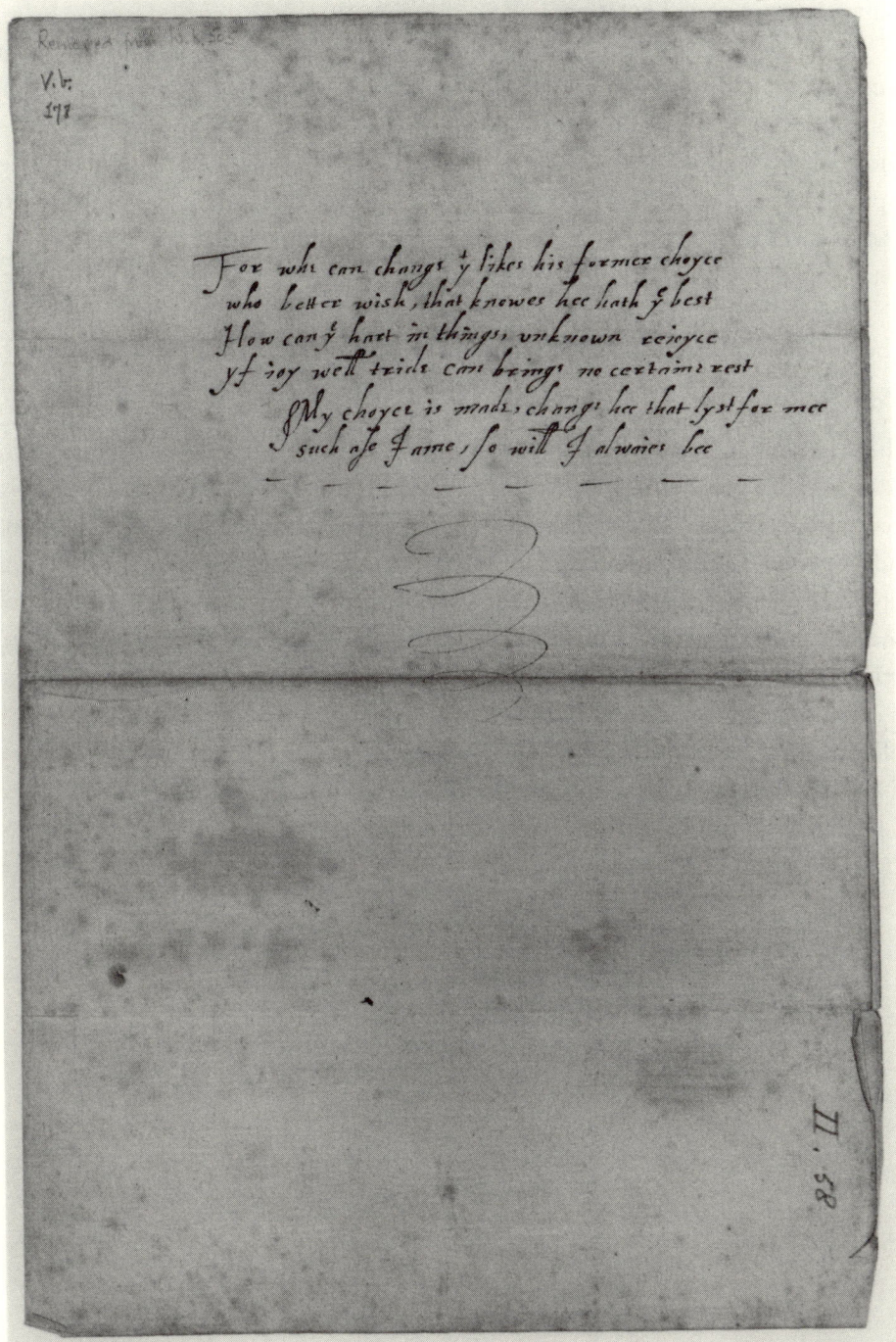

The poem is set to music as a strophic song or "ayre." The musical setting, which survives only in this single source, consists of two lines, a treble and bass, notated in score format, using mensural notation.

The name "Ro Iones" appears beneath the final sonority, written in the same hand that wrote the text and presumably the music as well. There is no reason to doubt that this is an attribution to Robert Jones or that he composed the song. At issue is whether he himself wrote the Folger manuscript and signed his own name or whether a copyist or scribe wrote down the song and added the name. The Folger manuscript resembles at least one other composer autograph from this period, the quintus part of "Grace my louely one" ("Sir: frances Seeward, his Canzonett"), signed "tho: Weelkes"; the signature can be authenticated as autograph by comparison to other documents.[2] However, since anyone can write a name on a song, the mere presence of Jones' name in the Folger manuscript can scarcely be considered reliable evidence that it is autograph.

The manuscript was brought to the attention of scholars in this century by John Quincy Adams (1881-1946), distinguished Shakespeare scholar and director of the Folger Shakespeare Library.[3] In a 1940 article he accepted the manuscript without question— and even without any discussion of the possible evidence—as a Robert Jones autograph.[4] In this he was following the view of the manuscript's previous owner, John Payne Collier (1789-1883). Collier was a scholar of Elizabethan theater who had been accused in 1859 of forging documents concerning theater history as well as marginalia in an early Shakespeare edition.[5] In 1871-72, his reputation ruined, Collier published two volumes of memoirs for the years 1832-33 under the title *An Old Man's Diary*.[6] He includ-ed a description of the Jones manuscript in the entry for 22 September 1832 (vol. 1, part II, p. 58), changing "Robert" to "Richard" by mistake:

> Richard Jones is said to have been the composer of the music to *The Tempest*, on its first pro-
> duction: no scrap of it has, I believe, come down to our day; but I have before me a song
> by the very same musician, in his own handwriting, and with very clever words: I do not
> suppose that he wrote the words as well as the music, but he put his name, "Ri. Jones", to

2. For facsimiles, see Thomas WEELKES, *Collected Anthems*, ed. David BROWN, Walter COLLINS and Peter LE HURAY, *Musica Britannica*, 23 (London: Stainer and Bell, 1966), xviii.

3. Charles BOYCE, *Shakespeare A to Z* (New York: Facts on File, 1990), 3.

4. "A New Song by Robert Jones," *Modern Language Quarterly* 1 (1940): 45-48. He included a partial facsimile that omits the later additions to the manuscript.

5. Collier seems to be undergoing a rehabilitation of sorts, as the evidence concerning his possible forgeries is studied more thoroughly. For a sympathetic view, see

Dewey GANZEL, "Collier, John Payne," *Dictionary of Literary Biography*, 184: (Detroit MI: Gale Research Co., 1997), 56-68. See also idem, *Fortune and Men's Eyes: The Career of John Payne Collier* (New York: Oxford University Press, 1982).

6. The full title of the first section reads: *An Old Man's Diary, forty years ago; for the first six months of 1832* [drawing of Collier] Omne meum: nihil meum *for strictly private cir-culation* (London: Thomas Richards, 1871). According to GANZEL (*Fortune and Men's Eyes*, 377), only twenty-five copies were printed.

7. Collier added the pencil annotation "II.58" to the

the whole. I copy the stanzas as a relic of the time of Shakespeare: for aught we know, they may be his, but they read more like a fancy by Sir Walter Raleigh.

Collier then provided the two six-line stanzas from the manuscript: "The love of change hath chang'd the world throughout..." and "For who can change that likes his former choyce?" He concluded: "There is no date either to words or music."

By the time he wrote his memoir, Collier was understandably insistent about the authenticity of his sources, and he kept many of them, the Jones song among them, in his own unbound and annotated copy of *An Old Man's Diary*.[7] This copy, purchased by Henry Clay Folger (1857-1930) at the Christie sale of 18 June 1902 (no. 191), became part of the Folger Shakespeare Library, catalogued as W.b.504-505 and 506-507.[8] It contains an index in Collier's hand, the relevant entry of which is "Jones, Richard author of the music of The Tempest ii.58." On p. 58 of his own copy, Collier added an insertion mark in pencil to the line "Richard Jones is said [insertion mark] to have been the composer..." In the margin, using his distinctively shaped question mark, he wrote "where?" Collier also left traces of his bibliographic uncertainty on the manuscript itself, as Adams noted. On the bottom of the page with music (see Plate 1) he wrote: "*Query* Where is it said that Ro Jones was the Composer of the music of The Tempest?"

It was not just the first name—Robert versus Richard—that gave Collier trouble, but also the last. Adams provided a plausible explanation for Collier's query, namely, that he had confused Robert *Jones* with Robert *Johnson*, a composer in royal service from 1610 until his death in 1633.[9] It was Johnson, not Jones, who composed music for *The Tempest*.[10]

Adams passed without comment, however, over Collier's confusion between Richard and Robert Jones. There was in fact good reason for a historian of theater in Shakespeare's London to have confused the two Joneses. Both appear in legal documents associated with composer and theater entrepreneur Philip Rosseter.[11] *Richard* Jones was named in a 1610 license for The Children of the Queen's Revels.[12] *Robert* Jones appeared

manuscript, a reference to the volume and page number of his memoir. A slip of paper that accompanies the manuscript contains Collier's note: "Song by the celebrated musician Robert Jones, music + words in two stanzas, in his own hand writing + subscribed by himself." The manuscript also has two pencilled annotations associated with the Folger Shakespeare Library: the current call number "V.b.278" and the indication "removed from W.b.505."

8.  For a history of the Folger collections, see Betty Ann KANE, *The Widening Circle: The Story of the Folger Shakespeare Library and Its Collections* (Washington: Folger Shakespeare Library, 1976).

9.  ADAMS, "A New Song," 48. On Johnson, see *A*

*Biographical Dictionary of English Court Musicians 1485-1714*, compiled by Andrew ASHBEE and David LASOCKI, assisted by Peter HOLMAN and Fiona KISBY (Aldershot: Ashgate, 1998), 2: 630-32, with bibliography.

10.  See in addition R. COVELL, "Seventeenth Century Music for The Tempest," *Studies in Music* (Australia) 2 (1968): 43-65, esp. 45-47.

11.  *A Biographical Dictionary*, 2: 973-75. I have not been able to consult John JEFFREYS, *The Life and Works of Philip Rosseter* (Aylesbury: Roberton, 1990).

12.  The 4 January 1610 patent is published in *Collections* (Malone Society), Part III (1909), 271-73. While the published transcription clearly names *Richard*, not Robert Jones, many scholars have mistakenly credited

with Philip Rosseter, Ralph Reeve, and Philip Kingman in the 1615 patent for the failed venture to build a theater at Blackfriars.[13] Unfortunately for our purposes, there are autograph documents by Richard Jones, but nothing so far by Robert Jones.[14] Rosseter, Kingman, and Reeve all left wills as residents of the London parish of St Dunstan in the West; we can only hope that a document in the hand of their colleague Robert Jones will turn up there as well.[15]

None of the usual means of determining authenticity can help us. We don't know the context—why the song was composed or for whom—or what its path had been from the early seventeenth century to the early nineteenth when it came into Collier's possession. Nor can we link it to any other manuscript or document known to be in Robert Jones' hand. The only other avenue open to us is to consider the song itself both as it appears in the manuscript and in the larger context of Jones' songs.

The text of the Folger song consists of two six-line stanzas, one underlaid beneath the music, the other on the facing page:

> The loue of Change hath chang'd the world through outt,
> And nought is counted good, butt what is strange,
> New things wax olde, olde new, all turne abought,
> And all things change, except y$^e$ [the] loue of change,
> yet fell I not this loue of change in mee,                    5
> But ase I ame, *but ase I ame* soe will I all waies bee
>
> For whe [*sic*] can change y$^t$ [that] likes his former choyce
> who better wish, that knowes hee hath y$^e$ [the] best
> How can y$^e$ [the] hart in things, vnknown reioyce
> yf ioy well tride can bringe no certaine rest                 10
> My choyce is made, change hee that lyst for mee
> such ase I ame, so will I alwaies bee

These two stanzas are the beginning of a longer poem that was first published in 1602 in Francis Davison's anthology, *A poetical rapsody* (STC 6373).[16] Anonymous in all four early

*Robert* with this venture (for example, ADAMS, "A New Song," 47; BROWN, "Jones, Robert (ii)"; and Linda AUSTERN, *Music in English Children's Drama of the Later Renaissance* [New York: Gordon and Breach, 1992], 10).

13. The 3 June 1615 patent is published in *Collections* (Malone Society), Part III (1909), 277-79. Susan P. CERASANO, "Competition for the King's Men?: Alleyn's Blackfriars Venture," *Medieval and Renaissance Drama in England* 4 (1989): 173-86, has explored the force of this patent in light of a later lawsuit by Edward Alleyn. See ADAMS, "A New Song," 47-48 and idem, *Shakespearean Playhouses; A History of English Theatres from the Beginnings to the Restoration* (Boston, 1917; repr. Gloucester, MA: P. Smith,

1960), 342-47.

14. My thanks to Susan Cerasano for searching for Robert's hand among the theatrical documents. I have not seen the original documents; it might be worth verifying the transcriptions to see if there are any mistakes such as the one Collier made between "Ri" and "Ro."

15. E. A. J. HONIGMANN and Susan BROCK, *Playhouse Wills 1558-1642* (Manchester: Manchester University Press, 1993).

16. Modern edition: *A Poetical Rhapsody 1602-1621*, ed. Hyder Edward ROLLINS, 2 vols. (Cambridge, MA: Harvard University Press, 1931).

editions, it bears the title "That he is vnchangeable" and concludes with "Iamais aultre," possibly a motto, possibly a succinct statement of the message of the poem.[17] Its six stanzas all employ the same rhyme scheme (ababcc) and are further linked by the near exact repetition of the final line. The first two stanzas, as printed in the first edition, are close but not identical to the Folger manuscript:

> The loue of change hath chang'd the world throwout
> And nought is counted good, but what is strang;
> New things waxe olde, olde new, all turne about,
> And all things change except the loue of change.
> Yet feele I not this loue of change in mee,　　　5
> But as I am, so will I alwayes bee.
>
> For who can change that likes his former choice,
> Who better wish, that knowes he hath the best?
> How can the heart in things vnknowne reioyce,
> If ioy well tride can bring no certaine rest?　　　10
> My choyce is made, change he that list for mee,
> Such as I am, such will I alwaies bee.[18]

There are differences in spelling and punctuation as well as a minor change of wording in line 12.

Jones might have been working from the 1602 edition, although the second edition (1608 [STC 6374]) uses his reading of lines 12 ("Such as I am, so will I alwaies be"). He might also have encountered the poem in manuscript.[19] We know that it was in circulation before the 1602 edition since Richard Carlton included a five-voice setting as the first piece in his 1601 publication, *Madrigals to Fiue Voyces*.[20]

That Jones chose a poem published in *A poetical rapsody* is no surprise: he was conspicuous among composers of his time for his extensive use of Davison's anthology. Of the 105 songs that he published in five books, twenty-one in each book, and of the eighteen madrigals in his "first" set, seventeen have texts published by Davison. Nine of them are among the songs of his third book, *Vltimum vale* (1605) and eight in his *First set of madri-*

17. My thanks to Alison RAWLES, Peter STALLYBRASS, and Georgianna ZIEGLER for their help in trying to identify the phrase. See ibid., 2: 145: "*Iamais aultre*. The "emblem," *jamais autre*, merely repeats the refrain of the poem." The motto is a reminiscent of Queen Elizabeth's well-known "semper eadem."

18. sig. G9-10. Ibid., 1: 143, no. 90.

19. I am not as confident as ADAMS ("A New Song," 45) that Jones "transcribed [the text] directly from that anthology." Nor do I see the "exact fidelity" he finds.

20. Edmund FELLOWES, *English Madrigal Verse, 1588-1632*

(Oxford: Clarendon Press, 1920), 68; the third edition, revised and enlarged by Frederick W. STERNFELD and David GREER (Oxford: Clarendon Press, 1967), 686, includes a reference to the Folger manuscript. Winifred MAYNARD, *Elizabethan Lyric Poetry and Its Music* (Oxford: Clarendon Press, 1986), 91. Edition: *Richard Carlton's Madrigals to Five Voices (1601)*, ed. Edmund H. FELLOWES, revised by Thurston DART, The English Madrigal School, 27 (London: Stainer and Bell, 1923, revised ed., 1960). Carlton sets only the first stanza, and alters "feele" in line 5 to "find."

*gals* (1607).[21] The settings from Davison's anthology seem to be concentrated in a brief period, at least as reflected by the dates of publication.[22] The Folger manuscript adds yet another song to the list of texts from *A poetical rapsody*. Perhaps it, too, dates from the period between 1605 and 1607.

"The loue of change," which is presented here for the first time in a modern edition (see Example 1), is a strophic setting of the text. To judge from the result, Jones' main compositional task was to create three musical phrases, each corresponding to two lines of poetry. Phrase 1 (mm. 1-4, lines 1-2), which begins after a "Minnum" and "Chrochet" rest—to use Jones' own terminology[23]—reaches the high point in the melody at the end of mm. 2, coinciding with the end of line 1 of the poem, and continues to a close on F, coinciding with the end of line 2 in mm. 4. Phrase 2 (mm. 5-8, lines 3-4) is composed of five brief segments, each of which is separated by a "Chrochet" rest, begun off the beat, and ended with a "Minnum" on the beat. The phrase ends with a close on Bb. Phrase 3 (mm. 9-14, lines 5-6) mirrors Phrase 1 in the rhythm of its beginning. Harmonically, its cadences (first on C, then on FF) mirror the cadences of Phrases 1-2 (first on F, then on Bb) and bring the opening F full circle.[24]

Jones expanded the final line of text to permit a sequential rising third motive in the melody (he repeated "But ase I ame"), thus extending the phrase from four measures (as in the first two phrases) to six.[25] He also brought out the refrain structure of the final couplet of each stanza, and especially the repeated final line, by introducing a musical

21. MAYNARD, *Elizabethan Lyric Poetry*, esp. 70-75; *A Poetical Rhapsody*, vol. 2, p. 86-87. The number of settings in *Vltimum vale* increases to ten (and the overall number to eighteen) if "Cynthia, queen of seas and lands," is included; it appeared for the first time in the second edition of Davison. Jones may have composed it as early as 1602, if it is the setting used for "A Lotterie," an entertainment presented before Queen Elizabeth in that year (MAYNARD, *Elizabethan Lyric Poetry*, 71). Jones' songs and madrigals are available in modern edition: Edmund FELLOWES, ed., The English School of Lutenist Song Writers, vols. 4, 5, 6, 14, 15 (London: Stainer and Bell, 1925); and Edmund FELLOWES, ed., The English Madrigal School, 35 (London: Stainer and Bell, 1924). A facsimile edition of the five songbooks, edited by David GREER, can be found in the series, *English Lute Songs 1597-1632*, vols. 26-30 (Menston, England: Scholar Press, 1967-71). The texts of the songs have been edited by Edward DOUGHTIE, *Lyrics from English Airs 1596-1622* (Cambridge, MA: Harvard University Press, 1970); this excellent edition also provides full bibliographic information for each print.

22. Edward DOUGHTIE (*Lyrics from English Airs*, 203) points out that *Vltimum vale* is often erroneously listed as

1608, but the discovery of a copy with the original title page confirms the date as 1605. See the facsimile edition mentioned in the previous note.

23. Jones uses the rhythms of mensural notation for his lyra viol tablature in the 1601 songs and provides an explanation for his reader. See DOUGHTIE, *Lyrics from English Airs*, 149.

24. "The loue of change" is Jones' only song notated in F (with a flat in the signature), one of the "fa" tones or airs, to use Butler's terminology. (On Butler, see my "Concepts of Pitch in English Music 1560-1640," *Tonal Structures in Early Music*, ed. Cristle Collins JUDD (New York: Garland, 1998), 183-246, esp. 216-30.) Jones composed 7 other "fa" pieces (-C), 41 "ut" (-G), 42 "sol" (7 -D and 35 bG), 14 "re" (13 –A, 12 bG), and 1 "la" (2bD).

25. Concerning Jones' use of sequence, see David GREER, "'What if a day': An Examination of the Words and Music," *Music & Letters* 43 (1962): 304-19, esp. 313-14; and Deborah TEPLOW, "Lyra viol accompaniment in Robert Jones' Second Booke of Songs and Ayres (1601)," *Journal of the Viola da Gamba Society of America* 23 (1986): 6-18; Edward DOUGHTIE, *English Renaissance Song* (Boston: Twayne Publishers, 1986), 133-34 and 149-52.

Example 1

The love of change hath changed the word through outt,
3
And nought is coun - ted good, butt what is strange
5
New things wax olde olde new, all tur - - ne a -
7
- bought, And all things change ex - cept the love of change,
9
yet felt I not this love of change in
11
mee, But ase I ame, But ase I ame Soe will I all waies bee

refrain consisting of the repetition of phrase 3 (lines 5-6). This repetition is indicated by a *signum congruentiae* in each part.[26] Because the music had to fit two sets of words, Jones did not engage in much word painting. The only possible examples are the "Quauer" turning figures at "all *turne* abought" and "this loue of *change*."

The bass seems to be an independent line, not simply a chordal underpinning for the melody. There is imitation between bass and melody at "and nought is counted good"; the bass anticipates in longer note values the gesture at "all turne"; and a lengthy imitation between bass and melody begins Phrase 3. There are also places, however, where it seems an afterthought. The sequence that ends Phrase 3, even with its rhythmic displacements, scarcely conceals frequent parallel octaves and fifths.[27] (See Example 2.)

**Example 2**   Reduction of bars 11-14

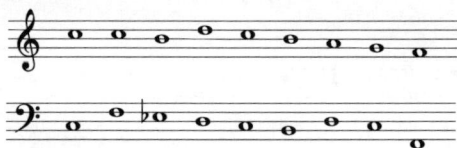

Here the discussion becomes tricky. For the Folger manuscript is both a physical object, which may or may not be a Jones autograph, and a song preserved in a particular state relative to the norms of transmission and performance of English songs. These two strands interact and make complex the question of the manuscript and its function.

The manuscript has none of the telltale signs of an autograph used in composition: revisions, changes of mind revealed through erasures, or crossed-out notes.[28] If it were an autograph, it would be considered a "fair copy"—no different in appearance and function from a copy made by someone other than the composer.

Several features of the writing are worth noting. There is a mensuration sign (or time signature), C/, written to the left of the first staff in both parts, in the space where an initial letter is often found. The music is generally barred every breve. There are exceptions, however. There is no barline after mm. 2, possibly to avoid drawing a line through the semibreve D in the melody. The strong line that runs down the right-hand side of the entire page seems to function as a barline at the end of mm. 7 and 10, but falls in the middle of mm. 3 and 5. The barring in the actual manuscript is thus far less regular in

26. The lower part is easy enough to understand as notated, but the upper part is not. There is a line drawn through the stem of the final dotted "Minnum," which can mean ignore the stem and read the note as a dotted "Semibreefe." In fact, the note must be read as a plain "Minnum" for the return marked by the signum to make sense. There is, of course, no way of knowing whether the

decision to mark the repetition by means of a signum was Jones' (if the manuscript is autograph) or the copyist's.
27. See note 23.
28. See my *Composers at Work: The Craft of Musical Composition 1450-1600* (New York: Oxford University Press, 1997).

appearance than the edition (and music) suggest. There are no ties; instead, a dot after a barline indicates the continuation of a note across the barline (the minim C in mm. 1-2 and F at the parallel place in mm. 9). The lower voice, in contrast, has three instances where a barline cuts a semibreve or minim in half. In these and other instances it appears that the barlines were added soon after (and sometimes over) the notes.

The spacing suggests that the text was written out first: the writing is fluent and evenly spaced. It looks as though the melody was written down next, with the notes directly over the appropriate words. The bass line seems to have been written last. It is frequently out of alignment with the melody; the spaces between notes are uneven and the barlines do not line up with those in the upper part.

It is hard to know what to make of these observations. Does the misalignment reflect a composer thinking of the two lines as distinct entities, occupying separate spatial and functional realms? Or is it perhaps an indication of practices of writing and reading different from our own, in which alignment is relatively unimportant?[29] Might it reflect a process of bringing two lines notated separately—the melody with its customary barlines and the (instrumental) bass line without barlines—into score for convenient transmission and possibly even for performance?

Whether the song is autograph or not, the way it is presented in the manuscript is distinctive: "The loue of change" is unique among Jones' songs in consisting only of texted melody and untexted bass. The other songs, all of which were published, include one or more forms of accompaniment.[30] The titles pages spell out for the consumer the various arrangements and possible performing forces.[31] Book I ("so made that all the parts together, or either of them seuerally may be song to the lute, orpherian or viol de gambo") contains the melody with lute tablature and three additional texted parts. Book II ("set out to the lute, the base violl the playne way, or the base by tableture after the leero fashion") contains the melody with lute tablature, a texted bass, and a lyra viol tablature.[32] Book III has three different arrangements: melody with lute tablature and untexted bass ("for the lute, the voyce, and the viole degambo"); melody with lute tablature and three additional texted voices ("for the lute, the viole, and foure partes to

---

29. See, for example, the alignment in printed editions of Purcell songs.

30. Edmund H. FELLOWES ("The Text of the Song-Books of Robert Jones," *Music & Letters* 8 [1927]: 25-37) characterizes the accompaniments as follows (p. 35): "Of the 105 songs in his five books 52 are solo songs without any four-part vocal alternative, 14 are duets and 39 have the part-song alternative. Books II. and V. consist entirely of solo songs; Book I. entirely of songs with the four-voice alternative, and Books III. and IV. include both types and also duets." I count 51 solo songs, 14

duets, and 40 with a four-voice version.

31. See DOUGHTIE, *Lyrics from English Airs* or the facsimiles edited by Greer. The specific wording may be the printer's, not the composer's. The wording of the titlepage of Dowland's first book (1597) is essentially identical to Jones' (1600); both were printed by Peter Short, using the same woodcut title-page.

32. TEPLOW, "Lyra viol accompaniment." The lyra viol, derived from Italian practice, is found there for the first time in an English publication.

sing"); and melody with lute accompaniment and a second texted treble line ("for two trebles, to sing either to the lute, or the viole or to both, if any please"). Book IV also has three arrangements: melody with lute accompaniment, a second texted vocal line, and an untexted bass ("for the lute, two voyces, and the viole de gambo"); melody with lute tablature, with three additional texted voices ("for the lute, the viole and foure voices to sing"); and melody with lute tablature and untexted bass ("for one voyce alone, or to the lute, the basse viole, or to both if you please"). Book V ("onely for the lute, the base-vyoll, and the voyce") has a melody with lute tablature and an untexted bass.

In editing Jones' songs, Fellowes noted that the accompaniments frequently contained mistakes, and he concluded that the songbooks had been "very carelessly produced."[33]

> The text must be corrupt. So fine a song-writer could not have tolerated such discordant sounds. So good a musician as he proved himself to be by his book of madrigals, even though he was scarcely in the second rank of English madrigalists, could not have written such impossible chords.

Fellowes compared the nature of the lute accompaniments, enumerated the errors, and concluded that at least in the case of Book V the lute parts were "very probably by some hack who was an indifferent lutenist and poor musician."

His remarks have unfortunately been taken into the literature as a general condemnation of Jones' competence as a composer. Thus, David Brown: "At times Jones seems harmonically almost illiterate, though it is clear that some of the crudities arise from the large number of printer's errors that fill all Jones' publications."[34] And Ian Spink: "His output as a whole shows him to have been an uneven composer, becoming increasingly careless and unselfcritical, prone to tediousness in serious mood yet with a lively rustic vein."[35] And David Greer: "After an inauspicious start Jones' composing career proceeded downhill all the way."[36]

I wonder if the Folger manuscript—whether autograph or not—might help us see Jones in a different light. The manuscript preserves the only known example of a

33. FELLOWES, "The Text," 28.
34. "Jones, Robert (ii)," *The New Grove.*
35. Ian SPINK, *English Song Dowland to Purcell* (1974; paperback ed., New York: Taplinger, 1986), 29.
36. David GREER, "Five Variations on 'Farewell dear love'," *The Well Enchanting Skill: Music, Poetry, and Drama in the Culture of the Renaissance: Essays in Honour of F. W. Sternfeld*, ed. John CALDWELL, Edward OLLESON and Susan WOLLENBERG (Oxford: Clarendon Press, 1990), 213-29, at 214. Greer may have been influenced by his realization that Jones had evidently used a popular melody as the model for one of his own songs (GREER, 'What if a day',"

317-18). Another possible source of the prevailing negative views could be Jones' own remarks "to the reader," in which he defends himself against criticism; this stance could well be a matter of artistic convention. Peter WARLOCK [pseud.], whose survey, *The English Ayre* (London: Oxford University Press, 1926), preceded Fellowes' publication, had a far more positive view of Jones' accomplishments (p. 63-81). In fact, at least one of his tunes ("Farewel dear loue") became an international hit (GREER, "Five Variations"), and another was well-enough known to be parodied (AUSTERN, *Music in English Children's Drama*, 266-67).

Jones song in its elemental form as a melody and a generic bass. It seems to be the work of a songwriter who composes a song that he then gives to another musician to arrange. Like the published songs it would be transformed through the addition of appropriate kinds of arrangements. This particular song, in contrast to a number of others, would not lend itself to partsong arrangement, with four distinct texted lines, nor could the bass line be sung. It could have a lute accompaniment, like all of the others, or a lyra viol accompaniment like the songs in the second book, or it could be accompanied on the bass viol.[37] Rather than a Dowland *manqué*, Jones should perhaps be regarded as a tune-smith, analogous to composers of American musical comedy who crafted the tunes but farmed out the task of making instrumental arrangements.[38]

Fellowes sought an explanation for the apparent contradiction between the musical quality he saw in Jones' madrigals and the infelicities in the songs. He offered an interesting account of Jones' compositional process, based on the distinction he observed between two classes of songs: "(1) those that had an alternative setting for four voices; and (2) those that were designed only as solo songs."[39] He imagined that "in the first of these two classes the four-part vocal version was written first, the air or melody being simply harmonised, and contrapuntal imitations being very sparsely introduced." The lute accompaniment would then be derived from the vocal lines, giving precedence first to the bass and then to the others as the instrument's technical possibilities allowed. In the second, while there might sometimes be an implied vocal version, "the plan seems to have been to write a bass to the melody and upon that bass to build an independent lute part."[40] Though Fellowes did not know of its existence, the Folger song seems to fit his second scenario rather well.

An interesting question, too large to be considered here, is whether Fellowes' assumptions about compositional process in the lute song will prove valid. The kind of arrangement a song is given may not in fact reflect how it came into existence. Campion, for example, wrote in the preface to his 1613 songs, "These Ayres were for the most part framed at first for one voyce with the Lute, or violl, but upon occasion, they have since been filled with more parts, which who so please may use, who like not may leave..."[41] Jones himself may have written something similar in his confessional remarks about his musical style in "To the Reader" from *The First Booke of Songes or Ayres* (1600): "I will not saie my next shall be better, but I will promise to take more paines to shew more points

---

37. TEPLOW ("Lyra viol accompaniment") describes the lyra viol accompaniments as being of two types: a simpler one in which the viol offers chordal support to the melody but few motivic gestures, and a contrapuntally more elaborate one in which the viol is an equal partner in presenting and developing melodic ideas.

38. My thanks to M. Jennifer Bloxam for this suggestion.

39. FELLOWES, "The Text," 29.

40. FELLOWES, "The Text," 31.

41. Cited from SPINK, *English Song*, 26.

of musicke, which now I could not do, because my chiefest care was to fit the Note to the Word…"[42] Of the several possible interpretations that this passage admits, one surely is that his focus was more on text and melody than on counterpoint.

A second, equally unanswerable question concerns the quality of the arrangements. It is worth pointing out that even Dowland's partsong arrangements of his songs have been labeled "aesthetically inappropriate" and "technically…unsatisfactory."[43] It may in fact be unfair to condemn Jones when we understand too little about the ways in which lute songs were arranged. The unfortunate reality is that Fellowes' editions of the lutenist songwriters present a kind of composite accompaniment, designed to enable pianists to accompany singers, that makes it impossible to compare the versions of accompaniments given in each print.[44]

I close without an answer to the question posed in the title. Without a better understanding of its context or the fortuitous discovery of a document in Robert Jones' hand, we will never know whether the Folger manuscript is in fact an autograph. But the search for answers has helped raise even more interesting questions that deserve further study. What is the role of the copyist as a witness and participant in the creative process? How are we to understand the nature of the compositional process and its relation to performance and transmission in the English song repertory?

42. Jones' remarks "To the reader" in his six publications are very interesting. See DOUGHTIE, *Lyrics from English Airs*; the quotation is from p. 115.

43. SPINK, *English Song*, 18.

44. It would be helpful to have an edition that shows the partsong version as well as the lute and lyra viol accompaniments.

* I have incurred a number of debts during my work on this article. I am grateful to the National Endowment for the Humanities and to the Folger Shakespeare Library for a fellowship in 1998-99 that allowed me to begin research on this topic. I am pleased to acknowledge the help of Peter STALLYBRASS, Susan P. CERASANO, Laetitia YEANDLE, Alison RAWLES, Georgianna ZIEGLER, Linda AUSTERN, Fiona KISBY, Douglas FREUNDLICH, John MILSOM and Anne Lake PRESCOTT, all of whom graciously answered my questions. Laetitia YEANDLE, M. Jennifer BLOXAM, and Ellen HARRIS read the final draft with great care and made a number of suggestions that I have incorporated.

Stacey Jocoy

# THE ROLE OF THE CATCH IN ENGLAND'S CIVIL WAR

I N ENGLISH SOCIETY, the end of the eighteenth century witnessed an important revision of ideas about politeness, manners, and morals. One aspect of this revision was the criticism and denigration of what was considered earlier indecency. Coarse humor, bawdy language, and especially any utterance related to the intimate workings of the body became conversational taboo, whereas in the seventeenth century such topics and prurient discourse had been openly discussed. One of the casualties of this new morality was the catch, which had long been regarded as a pleasant, convivial form of entertainment. As late as 1776 Charles Burney still described catches as "humourous and convivial effusions."[1] However, by the end of the century one often heard articulated the view that the catch was "ever three parts obscenity, and one part music."[2] By the end of the nineteenth century this opinion had gained so much ground that William Alexander Barrett, in his history of English glees and part-songs, called catches "an ever-shameful monument of the licentiousness of the age which gave them birth,"[3] and Edward F. Rimbault, in the preface to his anthology *Rounds, Catches, and Canons of England*, went so far as to claim that he and his assistant editor had been forced to "wade through seas of filth to extract a few drops of sweet perfume for the adornment of our volume."[4]

Victorian definitions of filth, over time, obscured the original purpose of such music, of which lewdness was only part of the picture. In their day, catches were not just bawdy songs for their own sake, but rather constituted a genre similar to the broadside ballad, in which current events, humor, and sexual attitudes were addressed.

1.  *A General History of Music, From the Earliest Ages to the Present Period* (1789) (New York: Harcourt, Brace & Co., 1957), 2: 316

2.  William Jackson of Exeter described the catch thus in 1783; *Stainer and Barrett's Dictionary of Musical Terms*, ed. and rev. Sir J. STAINER (London: Novello, 1898), 78.

3.  *English Glees and Part-Songs, an Inquiry into their Historical Development* (London: Longmans, Green & Co., 1886), 138-39.

4.  *The Rounds, Catches, and Canons of England* (London: Cramer, Wood & Co., 1865). On the reception history of the catch, see my forthcoming dissertation, *Decoding Musical Resistance: Popular Music of England's Civil Wars* (University of Illinois at Urbana), chap. 1.

This is especially true for catches dating from the middle of the seventeenth century, for they reflect the chaos of the Civil War and partisan politics. Intimately connected to the royalist side of the conflict, catches acted as propaganda, expressing loyalist views, concerns, fears, and, as I will also argue here, promulgated a version of the royalists' cavalier image—namely that of the noble outlaw trying to make the best of his defeat and exile.

Thus, the ripe humor and scatological references in catches were not simply the product of wantonness, but rather part of a reaction by royalist sympathizers against the puritanical stance of Parliament. This reaction helped create an anti-puritan aesthetic. For, like the character Robin Hood, still popular in romances of the period, the royalists saw themselves as outlaws, flouting the laws and rules of the usurping middle-class Parliament. Lois Potter has aptly noted this social phenomenon in writing, "The association of virtue with Puritan hypocrisy naturally seemed an inducement for vice to display itself openly."[5] Thus the good royalist would embody the antithesis of puritan morals, and would and did advertise this antithesis in poetry and music, including catches. This is not to say that catches were not amusing and fun to sing— they were—but they also fulfilled a political function that has hitherto remained relatively unexplored.

What has been recognized in recent scholarship, is the place of popular literature during this period of English history. Pamphlets called drollery books, which contained short stories, poems, and song lyrics were popular and highly sought after during the wars and the ensuing protectorate, both by royalist sympathizers—to read and enjoy—and by parliamentary supporters—to confiscate and burn. For, despite their seemingly innocent mask of humor and bawdry, the sedition inherent in seventeenth-century drollery books was understood by his original audience. Parliament deemed these collections so dangerous that most drollery books were condemned for their "scandalous and seditious" content, and their printers were fined or imprisoned.[6] As J. Woodfall Ebsworth, the editor of a nineteenth-century reprint of *Choyce Drollery* noted in 1876, the danger of such books lay in their ability to revive loyalty to the crown.[7] Some of the means by which this was accomplished in catches are hidden from us, for we lack the full context and this hinders analysis concerning the events of the 1640s-60s and of the language in currency, especially the slang of these decades.

---

5. See her *Secret Rites and Secret Writing, Royalist Literature 1641-1660* (Cambridge: Cambridge University Press, 1989), 104.
6. Among the printers fined in the these years were Richard Royston, John Crouch, and Richard Overton. For more on the history of war-time printing, see Joseph George MUDDIMAN, *A History of English Journalism to the Foundation of the Gazette* (London: Longmans, Green & Co., 1908) and POTTER, *Secret Rites*, chap. 1.
7. Joseph Woodfall EBSWORTH, ed., *Choyce Drollery: Songs and Sonnets* (Boston: R. Roberts, 1876), xv.

In addition to this, due to suppression of the royalist presses, some royalist tactics for creating sympathy and raising morale were intentionally veiled in a kind of coded language which literary historians have only just begun to unravel. These codes involved the use of symbolic words and phrases, literary and classical allusions, references to specific persons, and to a nostalgically-remembered past. Interestingly, music books of the period contain many of the same codes, and these, as my work thus far of deciphering the imagery has revealed, bring a new view of the catch into focus.

Since music books share poetry and lyrics with drolleries, it should come as no surprise that these codes exist in both kinds of collections. In many cases the texts are the same, and it is difficult to say whether the musical version or the textual version came first, because much of this material circulated in manuscript long before it ever reached print. Like drolleries, song books were condemned by parliament. One documented case is that of Thomas Weaver's 1654 song book, mentioned by the seventeenth-century antiquarian and music-lover Anthony à Wood. Wood later made a point to document the fact that Weaver had been arrested on account of his songbook. The songs in Weaver's collection were highly inflammatory pro-royalist texts: based on traditional (and familiar) I say "simple" because on the whole the tunes were traditional ones that most everyone would have known (like "Greensleeves"), and these tunes were mainly used as vehicles for the delivery of scandalous texts. Catches, on the other hand, held both textual and musical interest.

At first blush, most catches seem deceptively simple due to their brevity and their use of major key areas. The first phrases are usually melodic and memorable, though the following phrases often become more difficult introducing wide leaps, large ranges, and ornamentation that demands some musical skill to perform. Inherent in the term catch is the notion of the voices catching each other lik as in a round. But catch, of course, also implies a textual meaning akin to a joke, and many catches were indeed designed to reveal a humorous or bawdy message when all the voices were heard. Although the first catch book, Thomas Ravenscroft's *Pammelia*, was published in 1609, it took almost forty years until the next collection of catches, John Hilton and John Playford's *Catch That Catch can* (1652) appeared. From then until the end of the century, about fifteen books containing roughly 500 pieces were issued.[9] In the remainder of this essay I would like to offer some preliminary observations about the imagery in the 1652 and 1658 editions of *Catch That Catch Can*, the two editions published during the protectorate.[10]

8. Anthony À Wood, *Athenae oxonienses*, 5 vols. (London: F.C.&J. Rivington, 1813), 3: 622-23.

9. The majority of these books are editions of *Catch That Catch can*, to which were added new songs while others were eliminated with each revision. For a listing of song books published during this period, see Cyrus Laurence Day and Eleanore Boswell Murrie, *English Song-Books, 1651-1702* (London: The Bibliographical Society, 1940).

10. On differences between these editions other than imagery see my *Decoding Musical Resistance*.

Due to judicious handling by both Hilton and Playford, these collections seem to have avoided the condemnation of Parliament. Hilton states in the dedication of *Catch that Catch can* of 1652 that the music was "not snatcht up at randome, nor catcht at with an uncivill and rude hand, but gathered with a reverend and carefull collection, to avoyd offence and scandall." Although, his introduction is addressed "to all Lovers of Musick," he also makes a point of referring to people, presumably puritans, who "catch at them with detraction," which he notes is a "catching disease." This verbal playfulness, a trait of the ideal royalist-cavalier who avoids direct speech, preferring wit and allusion, must to some degree have contributed to keeping these catch anthologies in the marketplace while other, more direct royalist efforts were banned by Parliament. But another factor in their popularity was surely their music—playful music by definition—which mediated the text, in many cases altering or softening the overall impression with jaunty new tunes or word-displacement.

As in the drollery books, there is much discussion here of wine, women, and song which helps to locate these texts firmly within the royalist aesthetic. Of those three subjects, the discussion of wine tends to dominate in the 1652 and 1658 editions. Several scholars have mistaken the cavaliers' love of wine for alcoholism, and taken the references in the texts to imply that the cavaliers were merely irresponsible and depressed. However, as I have already emphasized, this forced gaiety was an intentional image promulgated in reaction to the perceived hypocrisy of Parliamentary virtue. For instance, the good cheer and feasting seen in the anonymous piece "'Mongst all those pretious juices" obviously satires the Puritan zeal for fasting:

> 'Mongst all those pretious juices afforded for our uses,
> ther's none to be compar'd with Sack,
> for the body or the mind, no such Phisick you shall find;
> therefore see boy wee doe not lack:
> Wouldst thou hit a lofty straine, with this liquor warme thy braine,
> and thou Swaine shalt sing as sweet as Sidney;
> Or wouldst thou laugh and be fat, there's not any like to that,
> to make Jack Sprat a man of Kidney.

Aside from establishing sack as the preferred drink of the cavaliers, this song also, in the last line, mentions being fat. This is not a derogatory reference to fatness, but rather projects a positive image of jolliness akin to that seen in Shakespeare's Falstaff, a character who, in fact, figures prominently in the texts of royalist anthologies. As in the nursery rhyme, "Jack Sprat" Jack, who could eat no fat, undoubtedly symbolized the good average citizen who, since he was trying to follow the dictates of Parliament, could not indulge himself. In these years, Parliament had in fact decreed national fasts once a month.[11] The royalist prescription is, of course, that Jack should come and join the cavaliers in drinking sack, as it is a "Phisick", which would make him a "man of Kidney"—which in the seventeenth century was slang for a man of honor.[12] The identifying markers of the royalist image are also stated in Hilton's piece, "Your merry Poets":

> Your merry Poets old boys of *Aganippes* wel,
> ful many tales have told boys, whose liquor doth excell,
> and how that place was haunted by those that lov'd good Wine,
> who tippl'd there and chaunted, & chaunted amongst the Muses nine,
> where still they cri'd, drinke deere boys, and you shall quickly, quickly, know it,
> that tis not lowly Beers boys, but Wine that makes a Poet.

This is especially evident in the last line where "lowly Beers", the plebeian drink of parliamentarians, is compared quite unfavorably to wine, which, "makes a poet." Encapsulated in this imagery, "makes a poet" is a more subtle allusion, and that is to the reality that many cavaliers were themselves poets.

However, there is another side of drinking which is expressed as a cheerless resignation that verges on melancholy escapism, and this is the sentiment seen in "A pox on the jalor," also by Hilton:

> A Pox on the Jalor, and on his fat Goales,
> ther's liberty lies in the bottome of Bowles:
> A Fig for the Raskall, what e're he can do,
> his Dungeons are deepe, so are our Cups too:
> then drink we a health in dispight of our foes,
> and make our cold Irons cry clink in the close.

Recognizing their gloomy predicament, the cavalier response here is to seek solace in the "bottome of Bowles," which, in this context is a reaction to imprisonment. Such a reference in a catch, then, merges with other prison literature and imagery of the period. Taking a larger view, we can draw the conclusion that in many ways royalists felt as though they were in a prison because of the newly reformed society around them. Yet it is significant that the literary conceit plays more on an earlier image, one of noble and fashionable melancholy. Thus the cavalier protagonist, even in his justifiable depression, maintains an aura of stately control, and this allows him to raise his glass and proclaim, "drink we a health in dispight of our foes," at the end of the song.

---

11. The second Tuesday of each month became the official fast day, but other special occasions for fasting were frequently observed. The literature on England during the period of the Civil Wars is, of course, vast; some studies which discuss parliamentary decrees including fasting are Christopher HILL, *A Nation of* *Change and Novelty* (London: Routledge, 1990) and John F. WILSON, *Pulpit in Parliament* (Princeton: Princeton University Press, 1969).

12. See Francis GROSE, *A Classical Dictionary of the Vulgar Tongue*, 3d. ed. (New York: Barnes and Noble, 1963), 211.

These songs also promote the image of the promiscuous cavalier, unfettered by puritan standards of morality. One of the best known examples of this type is William Cranford's "Here dwells a pretty Mayd":

> Here dwells a pretty Mayd,
> whose name is *Sis*,
> you may come in and kisse:
> Her whole estate is seventeen pence a yeare,
> yet you may kisse her, if you come but neare.

In the fashion of later catches, the surface meaning is fairly innocent, but when the voices combine, the composite message is quite bawdy; the image has gone from that of a young man, perhaps coyly, kissing a maid to one that is explicitly sexual. Of course one might argue that the surface meaning is not so different, for, if the maid is available to be kissed, and she is alone, such that one can talk of her humble estate, then she is probably a woman of loose morals, quite likely a prostitute. A document given by Percy Scholes records an incident involving a man singing this song in a private gathering around 1650. The singer was a captain in Cromwell's army. The glimpse we get of him from the report of the incident is sketchy, though we can assume his behavior (in singing such a song) was not looked upon with favor. Although we are not directly informed of his dismissal, he appears again in a petition to the House of Commons a few years later bemoaning his wretched state and asking for financial relief.[13] Apparently for some, even private performance held no guarantees against government informants.

There are other examples of bawdy language in these catch collections. Two such songs in which vulgar parlance occurs are William Lawes' "See how in gathering of their May," which repeatedly mentions "love's <u>holy</u> day," and William Ellis's "My lady and her Maid," which features a flatulence contest. It is notable that the participants in the contest are women. That this is the case is surely both for the shock value and for the titillation of the consumers of the songs. But as overtly sexual as cavalier literature is, it is notable that bawdy songs are not as common in the catch repertory as one may think; indeed they only comprise about fifteen percent of the 1652 and 1658 *Catch That Catch can* editions.

The image of the cavalier as outlaw can also be also be found in these collections. The piece, "Come follow mee" by Hilton, has been the source of some confusion over the years. The text reads:

> Come follow mee,
> whither shall I follow thee?
> To the Gallow tree.

---

13. SCHOLES, *The Puritans and Music in England and New England* (London: Oxford University Press, 1947), 146-48.

> Wee have oft been Rogues together,
> Now we must hang 'twixt winde and weather:
> We have oft time nipt a Bung boy
> Neatly, in a throng boy, [repeat].

In the late nineteenth and early twentieth century the sentiment was deemed too dark, and the word "gallow" was replaced with "greenwood" and the second verse completely omitted, thus creating a rural pastoral scene. Interestingly, "greenwood" was not an altogether bad choice, for while it changes the meaning entirely, it, too, is related to the figure of Robin Hood, which royalist writers were using as a model for the role of nobility in exile.[14] Another outlaw prince, Shakespeare's Prince Hal from Henry IV, was also evoked by royalist writers in the service of this image. The phrase "Wee have oft been Rogues together" can be read as Falstaff talking to Hal, that is to say, as cavaliers celebrating their adventures, rather than the reminiscences of common thieves. Although the text is not completely clear as to whether these characters are in imminent danger of hanging, the word "now" in the second line of the second stanza seems to imply that this is the case. The jaunty tune in F major might strike us today as more appropriate to the "greenwood" substitution introduced in the nineteenth century than with a march to the gallows. But the convention of setting catch texts in major keys aside, it also bears consideration that the key, like the imagery, could have been deliberately chosen to highlight the resigned behavior mentioned in association with prison literature. Forced to the gallows for his crimes against a government that he does not acknowledge, the cavalier falls back on his assumed posture of gaiety, for he is already beyond despair.

So far in this music, I have considered the traits of the cavalier persona and the literary codes that identify these traits, but other more direct codes can be found both in drolleries and catch collections. One of the most obvious references to Charles I is in the anonymous piece, "The Silver Swan", which is a new musical setting of an older poem, earlier set as a madrigal by Orlando Gibbons:

> The Silver Swan, who living had no Note,
> till Death approcht, unlockt her silent throat,
> leaning her brest against the Reedy Shore,
> thus sung her first and last, and sung no more,
> farewell all joyes: Oh Death come close mine eyes,
> more Geese then Swans now live, more fooles then wise.

14. In the 1929 *Euterpe Round Book*, a well-known collection edited by Charles Kennedy Scott, this substitution is among those made. For further on the significance of Robin Hood tales and the outlaw image in seventeenth-century English literature, see Potter, *Secret Rites*, 103, and Nigel Smith, *Literature and Revolution in England, 1640-1660* (New Haven: Yale University Press, 1994), 49. For discussion of the musical settings of outlaw and prison literature during the Civil Wars see my *Decoding Musical Resistance*.

Although it is an older text, the metaphor of the swan song developed here accords well with events surrounding the end of Charles I's life. Thus the presence of this song in both the 1652 and 1658 editions seems more than a coincidence. The line identifying the swan as one "who living had no Note," also identifies Charles I, who, despite his love of music and dance, was never a singer and was reluctant to speak because of a speech impediment.[15] The swan song that here "unlockt her silent throat" seems to relate directly to events before the king's execution when it was reported that he told several supporters about his desire to reveal his thoughts and motivations to the English people. Just such a testimony came out in the form of the anonymous tract *Eikon Basilike* ("the image of the King"), shortly after Charles's death. Allegedly written by Charles himself, this was one of the most important pieces of royalist propaganda after his execution, and helped to secure his place as the martyr king. Lamenting the current state of affairs in that "more geese than Swans now live, more fools than wise," the swan gives itself over to death as it seems that the time for its grandeur has passed. This was the stance taken by many royalist writers, who felt that Charles's fate was more the fault of the coarse and vulgar elements of society, which failed to appreciate his innate royal worth. We might see the music as also emphasizing the word "fools" by the leap of an octave in the final cadence. Set in the key of d minor, this tune truly has a somber air. To state the obvious, the use of dotted notes here, in a slow tempo, creates a stately atmosphere which is in sharp contrast to most of the pieces in the *Catch That Catch can* anthology, for in those the music serves to deny the seriousness of the text.

Literary allusions and references to specific persons present in drolleries are also present in catches. Catch texts sometimes quote from a specific text, mention a recognizable literary character, or even refer to a writer by name. Since authors alluded to in this way were usually figures from an earlier period, their words had some significant social weight but alluding to them broadly could also elicit a sense of nostalgia in the hearts and minds of the consumers of catches. An example of this kind of "loaded" image and what it would likely have recalled to certain listeners of royalist sympathies is the reference to Sir Phillip Sidney that appears in the piece mentioned earlier, "'Mongst all those pretious juices". In the song, the narrator who favors sack claims that its consumption will make one "sing as sweet as Sidney." Evoked here is a sense of Sidney's reputation as a poet and of the quality of his poetic style which is clearly held in high regard. But the encapsulated image may have stirred in the minds of a royalist audience a more general longing for, and fond remembrance of, the vibrant artistic culture and the economic and political stability of their lives twenty years earlier. Another example of a literary allusion is in the anonymous piece "Ha we to the other World" in which there appears the figure of "the man in the moon":

15. Charles I announced his "disability" during his first speech to Parliament in 1625, Maija JANSSON and William B. BIDWELL, eds., *Proceedings in Parliament 1625* (New Haven: Yale University Press, 1987), 492-93.

Ha we to the other World,
where 'tis thought they very merry be,
there the man in the Moon drinks Claret,
a health to thee and mee.

He is a character from Robert Burton's *Anatomy of Melancholy* (1621). In Burton's text, "man in the moon" was intended to be interpreted as "every man" but in the middle of the seventeenth century the expression came to be associated directly with the royalist pamphleteer John Crouch, who used it as his *nom de plume*.[16]

Nostalgia was also created by other allusions. By citing older material of a pastoral or jocular vein, compilers could evoke the idea of the Golden Age, which, since the beginning of the protectorate, had also come to include the period of Stuart rule. An older text that has been set to music is "Here lies a woman" by John Hilton. The text was written by the infamous jester for the court of Charles I, Archie Armstrong. Aside from its reference to the Stuart reign, it is also significant because Armstrong had been dismissed from court in 1637 for insulting Archbishop Laud, a highly unpopular figure who was blamed by royalists for misadvising Charles and thus contributing to his downfall.[17] Several other examples of older songs could be cited. These songs collectively, I would submit, contributed to a sense of nostalgia. It is significant that while all of the songs that appeared in 1652 were new,[18] the 1658 edition included eleven songs from the anthologies of Ravenscroft published forty years earlier.[19] These pieces including "Three blind mice," "Birch and Green Holy," and "New Oysters" are all anonymous, and they appear innocent, seemingly free from political associations. However, the presence of the song "Hold thy peace" the text of which was sung in Shakespeare's *Twelfth Night*, would have been associated not only with a great writer of the past, but may well have evoked memories of a time when such amusements were seen on the public stage. This was a clearly royalist sentiment, but one with which many London citizens, not only sympathizers of the House of Stuart, would have identified—especially in 1658 with the death of Cromwell and the crumbling of the protectorate.[20]

---

16. For further on Crouch, see David UNDERDOWN, *A Freeborn People, Politics and the Nation in Seventeenth-Century England* (Oxford: Clarendon Press, 1996), 95.

17. For more on Armstrong and his relationship with Laud, see *A Banquet of Jests and Merry Tales, by Archie [Archibald] Armstrong, Court Jester to King James I. and King Charles I 1611-1637* (London: Hamilton, Adams & Co., 1889), introduction.

18. The only exception are ten songs in the collection that had been printed the previous year at the end of Playford's publication *A Musicall Banquet*.

19. In his collections *Pammelia* (1609), *Deuteromelia* (1609), and *Melismata* (1611). For more on Ravenscroft's career with relation to music and theater, see Linda Phyllis AUSTERN, "Thomas Ravenscroft: Musical Chronicler of an Elizabethan Theater Company", *Journal of the American Musicological Society* 38 (1985): 238-63.

20. The public theaters were closed from 1642 to 1660. On political sentiment in London during the later years of the protectorate, see David UNDERDOWN, *Revel, Riot, and Rebellion, Popular Politics and Culture in England 1603-1660* (Oxford: Clarendon Press, 1985) and J. T. CLIFFE, *The Puritan Gentry Besieged, 1650-1700* (London, 1993).

Although the political significance of certain kinds of music, particularly Broadside Ballads, has always been understood, the social significance of other kinds of musical entertainment from the 1650s has not. Victorian emphasis on the bawdry of seventeenth century English music created the impression—to a certain degree still held today—that this music was slight at best, but mostly trash enjoyed by a coarser age and now to be avoided. But this view fails to grasp the import of these pieces. The kind of political messages and subversions that were present in the poems of the period were also present in these seemingly simple, drinking songs. The performance of such pieces, while they provided pleasure and amusement for their performers and sympathetic audiences, was in direct violation of the prescribed morals of the day and would have been understood by contemporary audiences as an attack against Parliament and against Puritan zeal.

*    An earlier version of this essay was presented at the Newberry Library Center for Renaissance Studies Conference, Chicago, Illinois, 9 June 2000. I wish to thank the Newberry Consortium and the University of Illinois Graduate College and School of Music for support of this research.

Jennifer Thomas

# The Core Motet Repertory of 16ᵗʰ-Century Europe:
# A View of Renaissance Musical Culture

T HE REPERTORY of the sixteenth-century motet is so vast—comprising perhaps as many as 18,000 different motets—that we cannot comprehend it in its entirety. We necessarily become familiar with a limited repertory that represents to us the musical practices of the period. How well does this microcosm symbolize the whole? Core-repertory methodology suggests a fruitful approach to this elusive genre.[1] It aims to discover a repertory representative of a particular musical culture by surveying the musical sources directly, and by defining the "core repertory" as the nucleus of works that appear most often in surviving sources. A perfect knowledge of the sixteenth-century motet core repertory is beyond our grasp: manuscripts and prints have been forever lost, some works have probably been perpetuated by idiosyncratic standards, and others have been suppressed. The methodology, nevertheless, attempts to determine in a quantifiable way what was valued—what was preserved by people of the time. It helps guard against anachronistic value judgments—an inevitable handicap of hindsight—and it helps place less representative works in context

Besides its size, one of the hallmarks of the complete motet repertory is rarity of repetition: most motets appear in only one source. Repeated works are conspicuous, and works that appear numerous times are not only rare, but noteworthy as well. The motet

---

\*    This article supplements the findings in my dissertation, "The Sixteenth-Century Motet: A Comprehensive Survey of the Repertory, and Case Studies of the Core Texts, Composers, and Repertory" (University of Cincinnati, 1999). The basis for the dissertation, and for this study, is a comprehensive motet catalogue in database form, which I compiled from the inventories of over 1400 manuscripts and printed anthologies (1475-1600). The dissertation itself demonstrates methodologies that mine the database to survey the entire repertory as well as to examine specific aspects of it. The compilation of the *Census-Catalogue of Manuscript Sources of Polyphonic Music 1400-1550* provided the final necessary antecedent

for the completion of such a project (5 vols., ed. Charles Hamm and Herbert Kellman, Stuttgart: Hänssler-Verlag, 1979-88). The database catalogue does not yet include single-composer prints; I hope eventually to add these prints to the catalogue. Their absence affects some aspects of the discussion in this article and is addressed in the pertinent places.

1.    Developed by Richard Crawford, *The Core Repertory of Early American Psalmody* (Madison: A-R Editions, 1984). Crawford has also applied the methodology to his study of recorded jazz.

core repertory comprises fifty-four works by twenty-three composers that appear at least twenty times in extant sources. Over the course of more than a century, 539 extant sources participated in the dissemination and preservation of these motets. The works made their appearances gradually, beginning in the 1480s and continuing into the 1560s. Though very broad dating for many sources obscures the precise period of circulation for some works, it is clear that all of the motets, even the most short-lived of the group, not only appeared in numerous sources, but were known and circulated far longer, and in most cases more widely, than was typical. All but two, Alexander Agricola's *Si dedero* and Josquin's *Miserere mei deus*, stayed in circulation into the 1570s,[2] most remained until the 1590s, and at least fifteen circulated after 1600. Over the course of the century, this reper-tory coalesces: increasingly, the motets cluster together in single sources and in small groups of related sources. This suggests that core-repertory methodology accurately discerns a phenomenon of the period.[3] The works that comprise the core repertory did in fact form a cohesive repertory during their lifetimes and do not constitute merely an anachronistic virtual repertory. A chronological survey of the core repertory illuminates the source picture and musical taste of sixteenth century, the geographic shift of Renais-sance motet sources from Italy and western Europe to the Habsburg Germanic[4] regions and eastern Europe, and the scholarly problems that have occupied modern study of the motet.

Table 1 arranges the core repertory motets according to frequency of appearance in sources. All *pars* are listed according to the practice in the database catalogue (see pre-liminary note) of labeling the *prima pars* as "a," the *secunda pars* as "b," and so on. Rank numbers will identify the core repertory motets in the tables throughout this article. Motets attributed to Josquin appear with the catalogue number assigned to them in the *New Josquin Edition*, e.g. 23.6 is the number assigned to *Ave Maria*, 25.8 to *Stabat mater*, and so on.[5] Several works dubiously attributed to Josquin or now believed to be by other com-posers still carry these numbers, e.g. Verdelot's *Sancta Maria virgo virginum* 25.6.

---

2.    The latest database sources for *Si dedero* are SGallS 463, dated from 1540 and GreifU 640-1, dated 1539-88. It seems unlikely that a forty-year period would have elapsed between the penultimate and final sources, thus GreifU 640-1 may well be dated much closer to 1539 than to 1588. The next motet to cease active circulation was probably *Miserere mei deus*, which appears to have stayed in circulation into the 1560s; its latest sources are VatS 38, dated 1563 or KlagL 4/3, dated *c.*1560-70.

3.    For listings of the sources for each work and for the repertory as a whole, see THOMAS, "The Sixteenth-Cen-tury Motet." The sources of the core repertory motets are listed in chronological order, along with their date and provenance, in Appendix VI.A (vol. 3). The Core

Repertory Catalogue (vol. 2) includes a complete list of sources for each core-repertory motet, ascriptions in the sources, and descriptions of each source.

4.    I use the term "Germanic" instead of "German" to refer to sources from the German-speaking regions of central Europe including Germany, Austria, Switzer-land, Bavaria, and Saxony. Political boundaries changed frequently over the course of the century, and prove-nance for many sources is only broadly identified. This general adjective avoids a too-specific designation that could be misleading.

5.    *The New Josquin Edition*, ed. Willem ELDERS et al., (Utrecht: Vereniging voor nederlandse muziek-geschiedenis, 1987-).

**Table 1**  Motet Core Repertory

| Rank | Number of Sources | Composer | Motet | Number of Voices |
|------|------|------|------|------|
| 1 | 76[6] | Josquin Desprez | a. *Benedicta es caelorum 23.13*<br>b. *Per illud ave*<br>c. *Nunc mater* | 6<br>2<br>6 |
| 2 | 54 | Josquin Desprez | a. *Stabat mater 25.8*<br>b. *Eia mater* | 5 |
| 3 | 54 | Josquin Desprez | a. *Praeter rerum seriem 24.12*<br>b. *Virtus sancti spiritus* | 6 |
| 4 | 50 | Philippe Verdelot | *Si bona suscepimus* | 5 |
| 5 | 46 | Caen/ Lupus/ Hellinck<br>(probably not Caen) | a. *Jerusalem luge*<br>b. *Deduc quasi* | 5 |
| 6 | 45[7] | Antoine de Févin-Arnold von Bruck | *Sancta trinitas 26.12* | 4 (6) |
| 7 | 44 | Clemens non Papa | a. *Maria Magdalene*<br>b. *Cito euntes* | 5 |
| 8 | 43 | Jacquet of Mantua | *Aspice domine quia facta* | 5 |
| 9 | 40 | Josquin Desprez[8] | a. *Pater noster 20.9*<br>b. *Ave Maria gratia plena 20.9* | 6 |
| 10 | 39 | Hellinck/ Senfl/ Verdelot<br>(probably Hellinck) | a. *In te domine speravi*<br>b. *Quoniam fortitudo* | 5 |
| 11 | 36 | Jacques Arcadelt | *Dum complerentur* | 5 |
| 12 | 36 | Jean Mouton | a. *Quaeramus cum pastoribus 26.10*<br>b. *Ubi pascas ubi cubes* | 4 |
| 13 | 36 | Dominique Phinot | *Iam non dicam* | 8 |
| 14 | 34 | Adrian Willaert | a. *Pater noster*<br>b. *Ave Maria* | 4 |
| 15 | 32? | Philippe Verdelot | *Sancta Maria virgo virginum 25.6* | 6 |
| 16 | 32 | Clemens non Papa | a. *Deus in adjutorium*<br>b. *Ecce in tenebris* | 6 |
| 17 | 30 | Ludwig Senfl | a. *Vita in ligno*[9]<br>b. *Qui prophetice*<br>c. *Qui expansis* | 4 |
| 18 | 30 | Clemens non Papa | a. *Venit vox de caelo*<br>b. *Respondit miles* | 5 |
| 19 | 29 | Jean Richafort | a. *Quem dicunt homines*<br>b. *Petre diliges me* | 4 |
| 20 | 29 | Hollander[10] | a. *Dum transisset*<br>b. *Et valde* | 5 |
| 21 | 29 | Alexander Agricola | *Si dedero* | 4 |
| 22 | 28 | Josquin Desprez | a. *Inviolata integra 24.4*<br>b. *Nostra ut pura*<br>c. *O benigna* | 5 |
| 23 | 28 | Clemens non Papa | a. *Concussum est mare*<br>b. *Factum est silentium* | 5 |
| 24 | 27 | Josquin Desprez | *Ave Maria gratia plena 23.6* | 4 |

6. This total includes sixteen sources that contain only *Per illud ave*, the *secunda pars* duet.

7. This total includes both Févin's original four-voice version and Bruck's six-voice reworking of the motet.

8. The *secunda pars* of *Pater/Ave* pairs frequently appears independently. For Josquin's setting, some sources that include both *pars* list *Ave Maria* as a separate work.

9. *Qui prophetice* occurs as the *prima pars* in several sources.

10. "Hollander" is the catalogue's standardized form for the names of Sebastian and Christian Hollander, two names that probably represent one person, a Netherlander. Their attributions overlap almost entirely, so the two names have been conflated in the database.

| Rank | Number of Sources | Composer | Motet | Number of Voices |
|------|------|----------|-------|------|
| 25 | 26 | Antoine de Longueval | a. *Passio domini*<br>b. *Apprehendit ergo eum*<br>c. *Orabat autem Jesus* | 4 |
| 26 | 26 | Orlande de Lassus | *Surrexit pastor* | 5 |
| 27 | 25 | Walter/ Verdelot | *Deus qui sedes* | 4 |
| 28 | 24 | Dominique Phinot | *O sacrum convivium* | 8 |
| 29 | 24 | Dominique Phinot | *Sancta trinitas* | 8 |
| 30 | 24 | Dominique Phinot | *Tanto tempore* | 8 |
| 31 | 24 | Orlande de Lassus | *Angelus ad pastores* | 5 |
| 32 | 24 | Orlande de Lassus | *Veni in ortum* | 5 |
| 33 | 23 | Josquin Desprez | a. *Qui habitat in adjutorio 18.7*<br>b. *Non accedat ad te* | 4 |
| 34 | 23 | Gombert/ Josquin Desprez (almost certainly Gombert) | a. *Tulerunt dominum*<br>b. *Alleluia Noli flere Maria*<br>In addition to the main text, there are several contrafacts:<br>a. *Lugebat David Absalom*<br>b. *Porro rex operuit*<br>*Tu sola es virgo pulcherrima*<br>*Sustinuimus pacem*<br>*Ecce quam bonum* | 8 |
| 35 | 22 | Lupus Hellinck | a. *Panis quem ego*<br>b. *Locutus est populus* | 4 |
| 36 | 22 | Orlande de Lassus | a. *In te domine speravi*<br>b. *Quoniam fortitudo* | 6 |
| 37 | 22 | Jean Maillard | *Ascendo ad patrem* | 5 |
| 38 | 22 | Clemens non Papa | *Ego flos campi* | 7 |
| 39 | 22 | Giaches de Wert | *Transeunte domino* | 5 |
| 40 | 21 | Jean Richafort | a. *Christus resurgens*<br>b. *Mortuis est enim* | 4 |
| 41 | 21 | Nicolas Gombert | *Ave sanctissime Maria*<br>One contrafact version exists for this motet:<br>*Ave sanctissime Jesu* | 4 |
| 42 | 21 | Thomas Stoltzer | *O admirabile* | 5 |
| 43 | 21 | Clemens non Papa | *Ego me diligentes* | 5 |
| 44 | 21 | Maistre Gosse/ Senfl | *Ecce dominus veniet 14.5* | 5 |
| 45 | 21 | Ducis/ Maffoni | a. *Dilexi quoniam*<br>b. *O domine libera* | 4 |
| 46 | 21 | Orlande de Lassus | *Tristis est anima* | 6 |
| 47 | 21 | Jacobus Meiland | *Gaudete filiae Jerusalem* | 6 |
| 48 | 21 | Jean Mouton | *Tua est potentia MA 84* | 5 |
| 49 | 21 | Clemens non Papa | a. *Jerusalem surge*<br>b. *Leva in circuitu* | 5 |
| 50 | 21? | Josquin Desprez/ Lebrung/ Richafort | a. *Congratulamini mihi 26.3*<br>b. *Tulerunt dominum* | 4 |
| 51 | 20 | Josquin Desprez | a. *Miserere mei deus 18.3*<br>b. *Audi auditui 18.3* | 5 |
| 52 | 20 | Arnold Feys | a. *Emendemus in melius*<br>b. *Peccavimus cum patribus* | 5 |
| 53 | 20 | Orlande de Lassus | a. *Congratulamini mihi*<br>b. *Tulerunt dominum* | 6 |
| 54 | 20 | Jacobus Meiland | a. *Non auferetur sceptrum*<br>b. *Lavabit in vino* | 6 |

## The Growth of the Core Repertory and Its Representation in Musical Sources[11]

**Table 2** *1480–1500*

| | | |
|---|---|---|
| 24 | Josquin Desprez | *Ave Maria gratia plena 23.6* |
| 21 | Alexander Agricola | *Si dedero* |
| 2 | Josquin Desprez | *Stabat mater 25.8* |

The earliest core repertory motets, Alexander Agricola's cantilena motet *Si dedero sompnum oculis meis* and Josquin's *Ave Maria gratia plena . . . virgo serena* 23.6 and *Stabat mater* 25.8, appeared a combined total of twelve times in twelve sources in the decades before 1500. The most notable aspect of this early period is the isolation of the works in the sources: only one early source contains two core repertory works, and one of these was a later addition. This trait rapidly vanishes: as the core repertory becomes widely disseminated, sources often collect several of these works. In this early era, however, the works circulate not only in separate manuscripts, but in distinct regions. Fully half of the sources emanate from Italy. These, along with the single French source, FlorR 2794, preserve Agricola's motet, while the German, Netherlandish, and Bohemian sources preserve Josquin's motets. *Si dedero* appears in seven sources within about a decade; subsequently, it remains largely separate from the other works in the repertory, ultimately appearing in only seven sources shared by other core repertory works. It probably ceases circulation by the 1540s, much earlier than the others (see footnote 2). The Josquin motets, on the other hand, mix freely for nearly a century with many other core repertory motets in an international array of sources. *Ave Maria* last appears in a Spanish tabulature print, *Obras de musica para tecla arpa y vihuela*[12] in 1578[24]; the last source for *Stabat mater* is LonBL 32377, an English manuscript dating from around 1584.

Noteworthy among the early sources is the manuscript MunBS 3154. Possibly the earliest core repertory source, it contains Josquin's *Ave Maria* and probably originated at the Habsburg Imperial Court.[13] Though German sources do not become generally prominent until after 1530, two more include *Ave Maria* before 1500:[14] LeipU 1494 and BerlS 40021,[15] along with a Bohemian manuscript, HradKM 7. In this earliest period,

---

11. The motets that enter the repertory in each decade are listed with their rank number from Table 1, which identifies them in subsequent tables.

12. Dates for prints are indicated by the RISM *sigla* (as in 1578[24]) which, in addition to dating prints, positively identify them.

13. Motets in this source date from 1476–84, according to the watermark of the paper used in the manuscript. Thomas Noblitt assigned a date of 1476 to Josquin's *Ave Maria*, but Elizabeth Cason has challenged that date, sug-

gesting 1484 as more likely. Thomas NOBLITT, "Die Datierung der Handschrift Mus. ms. 3154 der Staatsbibliothek München," *Die Musikforschung* 27 (1974): 35-56, and Elizabeth CASON, paper presented at the International Josquin Symposium at Duke University, 20 February, 1999.

14. See discussion of Josquin's early Germanic sources in THOMAS, "The Sixteenth-Century Motet," 177-87.

15. One of the scribes involved in the copying of MunBS 3154 was involved with both of these sources; see NOBLITT, "Die Datierung," 45.

then, core repertory sources from Bologna, Ferrara, Florence, Rome, Innsbruck, Leipzig, Brussels, and unnamed cities in Bohemia, Germany, and France foreshadow the international presence that characterizes the repertory in later decades. (See Appendix I.)

The composers as well as the sources impart an international stamp to the repertory. Both Josquin, from France, and Agricola, from the Netherlands, were internationally known and esteemed. Their works circulated internationally, and both composers enjoyed varied careers, sharing ties to the French royal court, conceivably during the same time, and to Galeazzo Maria Sforza and the Medici family. Since Agricola also worked for the Habsburg family and in the Netherlands, it is ironic that his motet is not the one included in the Habsburg and Netherlandish sources. The general dearth of French Renaissance sources undoubtedly manifests itself here in the absence of sources from the French Royal Court for these two composers.

Févin's *Sancta trinitas* is not considered along with the other motets of this period even though it appears along with Josquin's *Stabat mater* in VatC 234, the Chigi Codex, a Netherlands court manuscript dated 1498-1503 with additions apparently made in Spain around 1514. As Herbert Kellman points out in his thorough study of the manuscript, Févin's motet was one of the later additions, while *Stabat mater* belongs to the earlier layer; thus, the pairing of these two motets in a single source does not accurately represent their chronology.[16] The earliest extant source for *Sancta trinitas* is probably CambriP 1760,[17] a manuscript representing the composers and repertory of the French court, and dated 1503-16, aligning *Sancta trinitas* with the next generation of core repertory motets.

**Table 3** *1500-1510*

| | | |
|---|---|---|
| 6 | Antoine de Févin (–Bruck) | *Sancta trinitas* 26.12[18] |
| 19 | Jean Richafort | *Quem dicunt homines* |
| 25 | Antoine de Longueval | *Passio domini* |

*1510-1520*

| | | |
|---|---|---|
| 3 | Josquin Desprez | *Praeter rerum seriem* 24.12 |
| 1 | Josquin Desprez | *Benedicta es cælorum* 23.13 |
| 50 | Josquin/Lebrung/Richafort | *Congratulamini mihi* 26.3 |

16. Herbert KELLMAN, "The Origins of the Chigi Codex," *Journal of the American Musicological Society* 11 (1958): 6-19; see also *The Treasury of Petrus Alamire: Music and Art in Flemish Court Manuscripts, 1500-1535*, ed. Herbert KELLMAN (Ludion: University of Chicago Press, 1999), 125-27.

17. This manuscript serves as an antecedent to many of the works included in manuscripts emanating from the Netherlands scriptorium. See case study of the Netherlands Court in THOMAS, "The Sixteenth-Century Motet," chap. 5, 300-33.

18. *Sancta trinitas* circulates either anonymously or correctly ascribed to Févin until Petreius attributes it to Jean Mouton in his 1536[13] print, *Der ander theil des Lautenbuchs*. Subsequently, it is attributed to several other composers: Nicolas Craen in BerlGS 7/KönsSU 1740, Const. Festa in TrevBC 5, and Morales in SaraP 34. Because of its attribution to Josquin in a mid-century German source, EisS s.s., it carries a catalogue number in the *New Josquin Edition*. Arnold de Bruck later adds two voices, and this form of the motet pervades the Germanic sources in the latter decades of its circulation.

*1510-1520* (cont'd)

| | | |
|---|---|---|
| 22 | Josquin Desprez | *Inviolata integra* 24.4 |
| 51 | Josquin Desprez | *Miserere mei deus* 18.3 |
| 45 | Ducis/Maffoni (almost certainly Ducis) | *Dilexi quoniam* |
| 48 | Jean Mouton | *Tua est potentia* MA 84 |
| 40 | Jean Richafort | *Christus resurgens* |

In the first two decades of the sixteenth century, more than half of the core repertory sources are still Italian, though Spanish, Bohemian, Savoyard, French, and Netherlandish manuscripts also figure into the source pool. Most of the new motets are introduced in Italian sources; the two exceptions are *Quem dicunt* in BarcOC 5, a Spanish manuscript, and *Sancta trinitas* in CambriP 1760, a manuscript of French origin and English destination.

Prints begin to appear in 1501 with Petrucci's first offering, *Odhecaton A,* which contains *Si dedero;* the next year his *Motetti A* includes *Ave Maria.* Févin's *Sancta trinitas* may have been introduced in a print, and two more motets, Josquin's *Inviolata integra* and *Miserere mei deus,* reached print shortly after their initial manuscript appearances; both appear in *Motetti de la corona,* book 3 (1519²), the year after their inclusion in FlorL 666, the Medici Codex.

Of the thirty-four sources preserving core repertory motets between 1500 and 1520, ten contain more than one. From 1500 to 1510, sixteen sources carry twenty occurrences of core repertory motets, and from 1510 to 1520, eighteen sources carry thirty occurrences, a slight increase in density resulting from a growing tendency for these works to be found in pairs or clusters (see Appendix II.) When this occurs, the grouping of motets in one musical source seems to provoke continued grouping of the same motets. *Stabat mater* and *Sancta trinitas,* paired in VatC 234, subsequently share seven more sources; *Praeter rerum seriem* and *Benedicta es caelorum,* both introduced in VatS 16, share eighteen more sources; *Inviolata integra, Miserere mei deus,* and *Tua est potentia* all share FlorL 666 (the Medici Codex) as the earliest extant source, and at least ten later sources include at least two of the three together. All of these works, including those by Mouton and Févin, were attributed to Josquin at some point, perhaps because so many sources adopted clusters of works by Josquin. Scribes may not have noticed that works by other composers were nested among the Josquin motets. We find that this clustering of motets continues in later periods and for works by other composers as well, most notably the four core repertory motets by Dominique Phinot.

The addition of four new Josquin pieces to the list (five including *Congratulamini mihi* with its conflicting attribution), along with the two from the previous period, shows Josquin's dominance of the repertory during this era. Perhaps even more intriguing is the obvious influence of the French court: the other new core repertory works are all by composers associated with that court—Févin, Richafort, Longueval, and Mouton. Whereas in the first period, the core repertory draws attention to Josquin and Agricola, both of whom enjoyed varied international careers, it now highlights the stature and international influence of the French court, which in fact may have been the influential factor in the previous generation of sources as well, since both Josquin and Agricola served that court.

Given the centrality of Italian sources, we may have expected to find a more Italian bias, but in fact, Italian sources before 1520 contain mainly works of French and Netherlandish composers: most prominent for that period are three French composers, Josquin, Compère, and Mouton. (Both Josquin and Compère, of course, worked in Italy as well as in France.[19]) Thus, the strongly French orientation for this period does project Italian taste. Of course, a complete accounting of all the sources that existed during this time would only strengthen the position of the French repertory, since the French sources constitute the largest lacuna for the period.

**Table 4**    *1520–1530*

| 12 | Jean Mouton | *Quæramus cum pastoribus* 26.10 |
|----|-------------|---------------------------------|
| 9 | Josquin Desprez | *Pater noster* 20.9 |
| 14 | Adrian Willaert | *Pater noster* |
| 4 | Philippe Verdelot | *Si bona suscepimus* |
| 15 | Philippe Verdelot | *Sancta Maria virgo* 25.6 |
| | | contrafacts: *Ave Jesu Christe* and *Christus resurgens* |
| 35 | Lupus Hellinck | *Panis quem ego* |
| 33 | Josquin Desprez | *Qui habitat in adjutorio* 18.7 |
| 17 | Ludwig Senfl | *Vita in ligno* |

The number of sources conveying the core repertory in this decade equals the number for the previous two decades combined, and the number of motet occurrences surpasses that of 1500-20, totaling at least sixty-four. Thirteen of the thirty-two musical sources, over one third, are not Italian, though all but one or two of the motets' first appearances are in Italian sources. MunBS 10 (dated 1525-30) introduces the two exceptions, Senfl's *Vita in ligno* and perhaps Josquin's *Qui habitat in adjutorio*, though VienNB 15941, dated 1521-31, has an equal claim as its earliest extant source.[20] Prints still play only a marginal role in introducing the new motets, but they now make up a larger share of

19.    Though most of his career was spent at the French royal court, Loyset Compère was employed by Galeazzo Sforza in the 1470s; he contributes 117 database records to Italian sources before 1520. Like Compère, Josquin had both French and Italian connections (René d'Anjou, Louis XII, Ascanio Sforza, Ercole I d'Este, Papal chapel) and he contributes 296 records to Italian sources before 1520. Mouton, with no known Italian employment, but clearly a favorite of Pope Leo X, contributes 189 Italian records for

the same period. In the decades before 1500, Italian sources are largely lacking in attributions. The most prominent composers among the few attributions that do exist before 1500 are to Dufay, Binchois, Busnois, Tinctoris, Gaffurius, Weerbeke, Agricola, Compère, and Josquin.

20.    Both sources are late for Josquin. About this same time, *Qui habitat* appears in a cluster of broadly-dated sources. It is probable that none was the original site of the motet, since all date from the 1520s.

the source pool. Nine of the sources are prints; they represent the firms of Grimm and Wyrsung (Augsburg), Antico (Venice), Antico and Scotto (Rome or Venice), Pasoti (Rome), Pasoti and Dorico (Rome), and Attaingnant (Paris). (See Appendix III.)

With each succeeding decade, the new core-repertory motets disseminate to their numerous sources more rapidly. Perhaps the profile of motet and source production during this period has a bearing on this new dissemination pattern. These mid-century decades saw dramatic increases in the number of motet sources, the number of motets produced, and the number of repeated motets. Editors and scribes may have been presented simultaneously with both a demand to produce motet sources and the motets with which to fill those sources.[21] We may well wonder what propelled such an increase in both music and sources. What might the abundant creation and promulgation of motets, a phenomenon which continued through the middle decades of the century, reveal about the context in which they were used?

For the first time, the earliest extant sources for all of the new motets (with the possible exceptions of Mouton's *Quaeramus cum pastoribus* and Josquin's *Qui habitat*) also contain previously established core repertory motets. As we find new and older motets increasingly included in the same sources, we may wonder about the motivation of the editors: were they filling a demand for motet books by publishing or copying some new motets, but padding their anthologies and manuscripts with older works; or were they using older, well-accepted works to promote unfamiliar ones? That is, were the core repertory motets in circulation already prized, and if so, did their prestige transfer to other motets in the source?[22] It is difficult to shed an anachronistic prejudice in favor of these motets, knowing that they eventually accumulate an astonishing number of source appearances, and it is certainly possible that they carried elevated status after just a few decades of circulation—their appearances in prestigious prints such as the 1520[4] Grimm and Wyrsung print, *Liber selectarum cantionum quas vulgo Mutetas appellant* lends support to this notion. In fact, the core repertory motets gather with increasing frequency in individual musical sources, so that well before the century's end, we find most of the motets of the core repertory behaving as a coherent repertory: they are efficiently collected in a few sources, as well as being simultaneously dispersed over a large number of sources. We continue to find that motets grouped together in one source are likely to appear together in subsequent sources, though they may also be transmitted singly.

It is hard to tell whether Grimm and Wyrsung's *Liber selectarum cantionum* displays a certain prescience, wields a strong influence, or simply exploits hindsight. It contains five of Josquin's well-established core repertory motets, all of which continue to circulate wide-

---

21. See THOMAS, "The Sixteenth-Century Motet," 31-37, for a discussion of the relationship between manuscripts and prints.

22. See the discussion below of BERG and NEUBER's 1558-59 *Novum insigne opus musicum* for confirmation of both of these motivations.

ly: *Praeter rerum, Benedicta es, Miserere mei deus, Inviolata integra,* and *Stabat mater.*[23] Three years later, Antico takes a different approach with his *Motetti novi,* book three (published in 1524, but with RISM siglum of 1521[7]), confirming his title by presenting works that are mostly new; the print includes just one core repertory motet, Richafort's *Christus resurgens.*[24]

*Motetti novi* is not the first source of *Christus resurgens,* however; the pattern for this work is typical for one whose earliest surviving sources are really second-generation sources. This is most clearly demonstrated by the dissemination patterns of the works of composers, such as Richafort and Mouton, who were employed at the French royal court. For many of these composers, the earliest extant sources for their motets are Italian, and the sources appear in a cluster several years after we might have expected a first appearance. For Richafort's *Christus resurgens,* for example, we find at least seven appearances within the decade of the 1520s. Normally, the original source of a work stands alone, but the second generation of sources may form just such a cluster. For Mouton, Richafort, and other French composers, the explanation is obvious: because French royal manuscripts have almost all vanished, the earliest surviving sources for their works are usually removed from their time and place of origin.[25]

The composers of the new core repertory motets are a more diverse group than in previous decades. They represent a younger generation—composers born after 1480—and several nationalities. Benedictus Ducis, the likely composer of *Dilexi quoniam* (which bears an attribution to Hieronymous Maffoni in one tabulature print), was a German Protestant pastor with probable ties to the musical circle of the Imperial Court. Senfl was probably the most prominent German composer of the century. Lupus Hellinck, born and employed throughout his professional life in the Low Countries, is not well-known in our day, but was well-represented internationally in musical sources of his own time. The French Verdelot and the Flemish Willaert, both actively engaged in the composition of vernacular music as well as motets, spent their entire careers in Italy. New works by Josquin and Mouton also appear in this decade,[26] and the core repertory works already circulating continue to enjoy a lively commerce.

23. Of this group, *Miserere mei deus* is the most limited in circulation, appearing in twenty sources and apparently exiting the sources in the 1560s; either KlagL 4/3 or VatS 38 is its last source. The other four motets are among the most frequently reproduced motets in the entire repertory. *Benedicta es* appeared in only one previous source, but the others had all accumulated between two and five sources before 1520. Stephanie SCHLAGEL discusses the print, its humanistic orientation, its historicist function, and its Josquin motets in "Josquin des Prez and His Motets: A Case Study in Sixteenth-Century Reception History" (Ph.D. diss., University of North Carolina, Chapel Hill, 1996), 27-46.

24. A few of the motets appeared previously in PETRUCCI's 1519 *Motetti de la corona,* and *Christus resurgens* appeared earlier in ANTICO's own 1521[3] *Motetti libro primo.* Several of the motets included in *Motetti novi* appear in manuscripts dated around the same time, though none are dated definitively earlier. For most, scholars have suggested dates that encompass the 1520 publication date of *Motetti novi.*

25. Another example is JOSQUIN's *Ave Maria,* which appears in three German sources and one Bohemian source prior to 1500.

26. As previously noted, the late dates of these sources relative to the life span of the composers points strongly to lost earlier sources.

| | | |
|---|---|---|
| **Table 5** | *1530-1540* | |
| 5 | Caen/Lupus/Richafort | *Jerusalem luge* |
| | (Probably not Caen) | |
| 8 | Jacquet of Mantua | *Aspice domine quia facta* |
| 11 | Jacques Arcadelt | *Dum complerentur* |
| 41 | Nicolas Gombert | *Ave sanctissima Maria* |
| 27 | Walter/Verdelot | *Deus qui sedes* |
| 44 | Maistre Gosse/Senfl | *Ecce dominus veniet 14.5* |
| 34 | Gombert/Josquin | *14.7:/ Lugebat David/Porto rex operuit* |
| | (Almost certainly Gombert) | *Tolerunt dominum/Alleluia Noli flere* |
| | | *Tu sola es virgo pucherrima/* |
| | | *Sustinuimus pacem/* |
| | | *Ecce quam bonum*[27] |
| 43 | Clemens non Papa | *Ego me diligentes* |
| 10 | Hellinck/Senfl/Verdelot | *In te domine speravi* |
| | (Probably Hellinck) | |

Works from this period are much more likely to share sources than previously. The total number of sources has nearly doubled to sixty-three, and the number of prints has tripled to at least twenty-five. Thirty-one core repertory motets circulate with 168 appearances in this decade. Twenty-three motets appear singly, but many sources include two, three, or four motets, and several sources include many more. Because of the progressively shifting national origins of the works and their sources, the mingling of old and new works also results in an international mixture of music within single sources: the first layers of works, of French origin, are now preserved in Germanic sources that also introduce or preserve works by Germanic composers. (See Appendix IV.)

Formschneider's 1537[1] *Novum et insigne opus musicum* is the first print to include a rather broad spectrum of the core repertory motets—eleven works originally introduced over at least three decades.[28] The print, with fifty-seven motets, is unusually large. German composers predominate—Senfl is the most common—but Josquin also holds an important place. The source preserves several works with spurious or conflicting attributions to Josquin; some of these problematic attributions may originate here and some are known from other sources. The list of the contents of this source places the core repertory works in a context typical of this decade, when Germanic sources become increasingly numerous (see Table 6.)[29]

27. This motet appears in various combinations of *pars* and with multiple texts.

28. Volume two of the series, *Secundus tomus novi operis* of 1538[3], adds three more

29. SCHLAGEL discusses this print and its relationship to Grimm and Wyrsung's 1520[4], an earlier print that both summarized and influenced other sources, in "Josquin des Prez and His Motets," 47-56. See also her discussion of the misattributions in Formschneiders's 1537[1] in "Perceived Authenticities: A Defense of Misattributions to Josquin in Hans OTT's *Novum et insigne musicum*," in a paper presented at the International Josquin Conference held at Princeton University, 29-31 October 1999.

**Table 6**   Contents of FORMSCHNEIDERS' 1537[1] *Novum et insigne opus musicum*
(Core repertory motets appear in **bold type**.)

| Standard composer | Motets (listed according to the order of the source) | Standard composer | Motets (listed according to the order of the source) |
|---|---|---|---|
| Mathurin Forestier | Veni sancte spiritus 26.16 | Ludwig Senfl | De profundis 15.14 |
| **Josquin Desprez** | **Pater noster 20.9** | Johannes Heugel | Laudate pueri |
| Antoine de Févin/Arnold von Bruck | Sancta trinitas 26.12 | Matthias Eckel | Cantabo domine qui bona |
| | | Josquin Desprez | In exitu 17.4 |
| **Josquin Desprez** | **Praeter rerum seriem 24.12** | **Josquin Desprez** | **Qui habitat in adjutorio 18.7 4** |
| Ludwig Senfl | Verbum caro | Josquin Desprez | Benedicite omnia opera 14.2 |
| Ludwig Senfl | Ave Maria gratia plena | Ludwig Senfl | Virga Jesse floruit |
| Ludwig Senfl | Haec est dies quam fecit | Josquin Desprez | Virgo prudentissima 25.11 |
| Ludwig Senfl | Hodie in Jordane | Ludwig Senfl | Beati omnes qui timent |
| Ludwig Senfl | Philipe qui | Ludwig Senfl | Ecce quam bonum |
| **Josquin Desprez** | **Benedicta es caelorum 23.13 6** | Ludwig Senfl | Deus in adjutorium |
| Arnold von Bruck | Fortitudo dei regnantis | Matthias Eckel | Deus in nomine tuo |
| Josquin Desprez | Haec dicit dominus 30.6 | Jean Courtois | Domine quis habita |
| **Josquin Desprez** | **Miserere mei deus 18.3** | Carpentras | Cantate domino canticum |
| Josquin Desprez | Propter peccata quae peccastis | Thomas Stoltzer | Beatus vir qui non abiit |
| Nicolas Gombert | Vias tuas domine | Leonhard Paminger | Confitemini domino |
| **Hellinck/ Senfl/ Verdelot** | **In te domine speravi** | Johannes Galliculus/ J. Förster | Quare fremuerunt gentes |
| **Philippe Verdelot** | **Si bona suscepimus** | Ludovicus Heydenhamer | Expectans expectavi |
| Adrian Willaert | In diebus illis erat | Appenzeller/ Vinders | Domini est terra 16.12 |
| Costanzo Festa | Jerusalem quae occidis | Maistre Jhan | Lauda Jerusalem 17.9 |
| **Ludwig Senfl** | **Vita in ligno** | Moulu/ Mouton | In illo tempore accesserunt |
| Ludwig Senfl | Nisi dominus aedificaverit | Sampson | In illo tempore litigabant |
| Ludwig Senfl | Ave rosa sine spinis | **Josquin Desprez/ Lebrung/Richafort** | **Congratulamini mihi 26.3** |
| | Domine non est exaltatum | Balthasar Arthopius | Cognoscimus domine |
| | O sacrum convivium | Josquin Desprez | Misericordias domini 18.4 |
| | Attendite universi | Josquin Desprez/ Verdelot | |
| **Maistre Gosse/Senfl** | **Ecce dominus veniet 14.5** | | Tribulatio et angustia 18.11 |
| Leonhard Paminger | Si deus pro nobis | Pierre Moulu | Quam pulchra es amica 14.10 |
| Nicolas Gombert | Felix Austriae domus | Andreas de Silva | Te deum laudamus |
| Jean Le Brung | Recumbentibus undecim discipulis | | |

The shift to Germanic sources as the earliest sites of core repertory technically begins earlier in the decade with a 1533[4] Formschneider print, *Tabulatur auff die Laudten . . . Durch Hanns Gerle Luttinisten*, but the position of this print as a first source for one motet raises a cautionary flag that extends to many other manuscripts and prints that appear as "first sources." In this case, it is unlikely that a motet would make its first appearance in tabulature form; the editor almost certainly gleaned the work from an earlier vocal model.[30]

30. Published intabulations of many of the core repertory motets become numerous as the century goes on; most motets do not appear in tabulature until after they appear in many vocal sources.

For some other motets, the provenance of the earliest source does not fit what we know about the composer's whereabouts: for instance, we may suspect that Josquin's *Ave Maria* appeared in another manuscript before being copied into MunBS 3154 in 1484, since Josquin is not known to have been associated with the Imperial Court at that time. Likewise, some of the earliest database sources for motets of Lassus, whose works generally appeared first in prints devoted to his works, may have had antecedents, either in those single-composer prints (not yet included in the database catalogue) or in lost manuscripts. For example, CopKB 1873, a Danish source dated 1566, is early enough to be a first source for his *Congratulamini mihi*, but unless this appearance represents a special commission from the Danish Court, it is unlikely to have been the earliest site of a Lassus motet. Similarly, while WarU 7.41.5.14, a Polish source possibly dated as early as 1559 (but also with a date of 1587 in the manuscript), may be the earliest database source for *Angelus ad pastores*, it is unlikely that it was actually the first site of this work. Other possibilities seem more probable: the motet may have appeared in a single-composer print, or, given the uncertainties of manuscript dating, other sources from the early 1560s, for instance StuttL 1 or RegB 853-4, may be plausible original sources of this work.

The uncertainty of chronology resulting from imprecise dates for manuscripts is compounded by the absence of many lost original sources. Clearly, though the vast number of motets preserved in Germanic sources represents the work of many Germanic composers (some known only in a limited region, some more widely known), these sources also received a significant proportion of their repertory from earlier Italian, French, and Netherlandish sources. When motets of composers known to have had careers outside the Habsburg empire appear posthumously for the first time in Germanic sources, we often question the authenticity of the attribution, but we should equally suspect transmission from vanished earlier sources. For example, the appearance of new Josquin and Mouton motets late in the 1520s raises questions either of authenticity or of absent sources. Close examination of nearly any group of motets is almost certain to invite suspicion of lost antecedent sources. For many of the earliest core repertory motets composed by musicians of the French court, we must acknowledge the *lacuna* of French sources discussed earlier. The dearth of Italian manuscripts and printed anthologies after the 1530s seems abrupt and puzzling, given the strong tradition of Italian musical sources, both manuscript and printed, in earlier decades. Did single-composer prints usurp their place, did they cease to be produced, are they missing, or did other genres supplant the motet? While the ease of manipulating information from the database catalogue does not eradicate these frustrating gaps in source history, it does make them easier to identify and evaluate as large-scale repertorial patterns emerge. These large-scale patterns may point not only to source gaps, but to cultural changes—who produced music for whom, where, and in what form.

Uncertain authorship clouds our understanding as much as uncertain chronology. Nearly half of the new core repertory works carry conflicting attributions, no doubt a result of the quickly growing number of sources in which the works appear. The problem is a pervasive one for motets that gained circulation in multiple sources—the works most likely to come to the attention of scholars.[31] However, the problem presents more than an inconvenience to scholars trying to understand the authorship of the works or the output of specific composers. We should also regard the phenomenon as a legitimate reflection of contemporaneous practices and seize the opportunity to gain insight into the possible perceptions and motives of the scribes and publishers who did not know the correct composer; who had incorrect information; who felt that no attribution, or only a partial one, was necessary; who exercised judgment about the musical style of the motet and perhaps set out to change the perception of authorship; or who may have deliberately mislabeled the work.

In some cases, a survey of all the sources for a work bearing a conflicting attribution suggests one composer as much more likely than others who share the attribution. An example is the five-voice *In te domine speravi*, attributed to Ludwig Senfl, Philippe Verdelot, Johannes Lupus, and Lupus Hellinck as well as appearing in numerous sources anonymously. Hellinck appears to have the best claim on the piece:

- the earliest sources, Moderne's 1532[9] and RomeV 35-40 (dated 1530-31) cite him;
- six of the seven prints cite him; the seventh, Phalèse's 1571/16, contains no attribution;
- both Verdelot and Senfl made other settings of the text which may have caused confusion; this appears to have been the only setting attributed to Hellinck;
- the attribution to Johannes Lupus is just one of many instances of confusion between these two composers.

**Table 7**    *In te domine speravi:* Attributions and Sources

| Attribution | Source | Publisher or Scribe | Date |
|---|---|---|---|
| Lupus | RomeV 35-40/I | Antonius Morus | 1530-31 |
| Senfl | MunU 401 | | 1530-40 |
| | UlmS 237 | | 1530-40 |
| Lupus | *Mottetti del fiore 5 vc Bk 2* | Moderne | 1532[9] |
| Phil. Verdelot | KasL 24 | Johann Heugel | 1534-50 in MS |
| Lupus | *Liber nonus XVIII… musicales psalmos* | Attaingnant | 1535[1] |
| Lupus | *Novum et insigne opus musicum* | Formschneider | 1537[1] |
| Lupus | *Mottetti del fiore 5 vc Bk 2* | Gardane | 1539[6] |
| | NurGN 83795 | Walter, Johann+[32] | 1539-48 |

31. Though this is an issue that rarely affects unique or anonymous works, occasionally a work may be attributed to one composer in the index and another on the page where the music appears, creating a conflict within a single source.

32. "+" indicates that other, unnamed scribes also participated.

| Attribution | Source | Publisher or Scribe | Date |
|---|---|---|---|
| | BerlPS 40013 | WALTER, supervisor | 1540 |
| Lupus | BolC Q 27/1 | | c.1540 |
| Senfl | WeimB B | | 1540-44 |
| | PiacD (5) | | c.1540-60 |
| | RegT 2-3 | Jo. SCHINEIS+ | c.1540-60 |
| | MunU 326 | Narcissus ZÄNCKL | 1543 |
| | MunU 327 | | 1543 |
| Lupus Hellink | ErlU 473/3 | Johannes HARTUNG | 1545 |
| | GothaF A98 | | 1545 |
| Lupo | StuttL 34 | Nikolaus PEUSCHEL | c.1545 |
| Lupus | LeuvU 163 | 1+1[33] | 1546 |
| Philippus Verdelot | ZwiR 73/II | Jodocus SCHALREUTER | 1547 |
| Lupus | *Libro de musica de vihuela intitulado Silva* | CORDOVA | 1547[25] |
| Lupus | RegB C 99 | Johannes STENGL | 1548 title page |
| Lupus Hellinck | BrusC 27088 | | pre-1549; 1563 in MS |
| Lupus | ToleBC 17 | Martín PÉREZ | 1550-1 |
| Philippe Verdelot | DresSL 1/D/3 | | 1550-60 |
| Lupus | *Liber primus collectorum modulorum* | | |
| | *(qui moteta vulgo dicuntur)* | CHEMIN & GOUDIMEL | 1553[2] |
| | *Horti musarum secunda pars* | PHALÈSE | 1553[33] |
| | CopKB 1873 | | 1556 |
| | HradKM 29 | | 1556-62 in MS |
| Lupus | *Secunda pars magni operis* | BERG & NEUBER | 1559[1] |
| | DresSL 1/D/501 | | c.1560 |
| | *Theatrum musicum* | PHALÈSE et BALLÈRE | 1571[16] |
| Johannes Lupus | *Teütsche Lautenbuch darinnenn kunstliche Muteten* | Bernhard JOBIN | 1574[13] |
| | HradKM 26 | | 1575-1600 |
| Lupus | RokyA 22 | | 1575-1600 |
| | LüneR 150 | 41 scribes | 1575-1620 in MS |
| Lupus | *Obras de musica para tecla arpa y vihuela* | SANCHEZ | 1578[24] |
| Lupus Hellinc | *Novum pratum musicum* | PHALÈSE | 1592[6] (Brown) |

For some works, the sources provide little help in determining a correct attribution. The Walter/Verdelot conflict for *Deus qui sedes* exemplifies just how ambiguous the source evidence can be for the cases most difficult to resolve (see Table 8). The motet circulates in various German locales without attribution until 1556, when a Pirna manuscript carries an attribution to Philippus Verdelot; the next source, a Bavarian manuscript dated 1557-59, bears an attribution to Johann Walter. Only three more sources include any attribution, two to Walter, one to Verdelot. With such inconclusive source evidence, the composer assignment for this motet will have to rely on a scholarly judgment that can take into account biographical, archival, and stylistic evidence.

The problem is more complex for the Caen/ Lupus/ Richafort attribution for *Jerusalem luge* (see Table 9). It is fairly easy to dismiss Arnold Caen, a German composer,

---

33. A numeral without a name indicates the number of unnamed scribes.

**Table 8**    Attributions for WALTER/VERDELOT: *Deus qui sedes*

| Attrib. | Source | Publisher or Scribe | Date |
|---|---|---|---|
| | *Tabulatur auff die Laudten...* | | |
| | *Durch Hanns Gerle Luttinisten* | FORMSCHNEIDER | 1533[4] |
| | StuttL 35 | Nikolaus PEUSCHEL | c.1540 |
| | BerlPS 40013 | WALTER, supervisor | 1540 |
| | WeimB B | | 1540-44 |
| | GothaF A98 | | 1545 |
| | KrakPAN 1716 | JOHANNES OF LUBLIN | 1537-48 |
| | NurGN 83795 | Johann WALTER[+] | 1539-48 |
| | WarSM 564 | I | |
| | 1548 in MS | | |
| | LeipU 51/2 | Michael HEGER, director? | 1555+ |
| Philippus Verdelot | DresSL Pirna VII | Albert WEISSENBERGER | 1556 |
| Johann Walter | RegB 940-1 | Wolfang KÜFFER[+] | 1557-59 |
| | RegT 2-3 | Jo. SCHINEIS[+] | c.1540-60 |
| | RegB 1018 | | 1563 on covers |
| Verdelot | RosU 42/1 | | 1555-70 |
| | AmstT 27 | | c.1580 |
| | UppsU 76g | | 1575-85 |
| | StockKM 33 | | 1593 in MS |
| | RosU 71/2 | | 1550-1600 |
| | UlmS 236 | | 1550-1600 |
| Joh. Walter | WrocS 1 | | 1550-1600 |
| Joh. Walter | WrocS 12 | | c.1600 |

probably employed at the Burgundian court, who flourished at the beginning of the century. His earliest source for this motet, a 1558 German tabulature print, is dated more than two decades after the earliest sources credit Lupus and far beyond Caen's own time and place of activity. It is even easier to disregard Verdelot, whose only attribution appears in a 1547 Spanish tabulature print. The difficulty lies in sorting out the claims of Lupus, who is credited in the earliest sources (1530, 1534[10], and 1536), from Richafort, whose attributions follow rather quickly (the earliest are 1539[6], 1540[6], 1541, and 1530-40). Richafort's are more numerous than Lupus': Lupus' name drops from circulation after it appears in VatG XII.4 in 1536 and is not seen again in conjunction with this work, while Richafort's name, along with Caen's, circulates internationally with the piece until the very end of the century.

Aside from problems of simple error, many factors could have figured into this pervasive problem.[34] It is surely no accident that it manifests itself so markedly as the number of multiple sources for individual motets increases so rapidly.

34. The most thorough treatment of the problem is found in Young-Han HUR, "Conflicting Attributions in the Motet, 1500-1550" (Ph.D. diss., New York University, 1991). Hur himself declines to resolve conflicts, but he compiles and summarizes attribution information and scholarly opinion. See also the discussion of the conflicting attributions in THOMAS, "The Sixteenth-Century Motet," chap. 5.

**Table 9**  *Jerusalem luge*: Attributions and Sources

| Attribution | Source | Publisher or Scribe | Date |
|---|---|---|---|
| **Lupus** | **RomeV 35-40/I** | Antonius MORUS | 1530-31 |
| | *Motetti del fiore, 5 vc, bk 2* | MODERNE | 1532[9] |
| Lupus | Liber octavus | ATTAINGNANT | 1534[1] |
| Lupus | VatG XII.4 | Johannes PARVUS | 1536 |
| **Richafort, Jean** | ***Mottetti del fiore 5 vc Bk 2*** | MODERNE | 1539[6] |
| Richafort, Johannes | *Selectissimarum mutetarum partim 4-5 vc Bk 1* | PETREIUS | 1540[6] |
| Richafort | MunU 401 | | 1530-40 |
| | UlmS 237 | | 1530-40 |
| Richafort | ErlU 473/1 | Johannes HARTUNG | 1541 |
| | CopKB 1872 | Mathhias KRÜGER? | 1541-43 |
| | MunU 326 | Narcissus ZÄNCKL | 1543 |
| | MunU 327 | | 1543 |
| | *Das Dritt Buch Ein new kunslich Lauten Buch* | Hans GÜNTHER | 1544[25] |
| | *Chansons & motetz reductz en tabulature de luc* | PHALÈSE | 1547[23] |
| | *Carminum ad testudinis usum compostiorum liber 3* | PHALÈSE | 1547[24] |
| **Verdelot, Philippe** | *Libro de musica de vihuela intitulado Silva* | CORDOVA | 1547[25] |
| | NurGN 83795 | Johann WALTER+ | 1539-48 |
| Richafort, Jean | *Intabulatura Valentini Bacfarc translivani coronensis, bk 1* | MODERNE | 1552[30] |
| Richafort | *Liber primus collectorum modulorum (qui moteta vulgo dicuntur)* | CHEMIN & GOUDIMEL | 1553[2] |
| Richafort, Jean | DresSL Pirna VII | Albert WEISSENBERGER | 1556 |
| | *Troisieme livre de tabulature de leut* | FEZANDAT | 1558[19] |
| Richafort | LeipU 49/50 | Michael HEGER, dir.? | 1558 |
| **Caen, Adrian** | ***Tabulaturbuch auff die Lauten von Moteten*** | Johann KOHLEN | 1558/20 |
| Richafort | RegB 940-1 | Wolfang KÜFFER+ | 1557-59 |
| Caen, Arnoldus | *Secunda pars magni operis musici* | BERG & NEUBER | 1559/1 |
| Richafort | RegT 2-3 | Jo. SCHINEIS+ | c.1540-60 |
| | PiacD (5) | | c.1540-60 |
| | SionA 87-4 | Simon ZMUTT | 1550-60 |
| | LeidGA 1442 | Johannes FLAMINGUS+ | c.1540-60+ |
| | | | 1564-67 |
| | HradKM 29 | | 1556-62 in MS |
| | LüneR 376 | | 1566 or later |
| | *Cantionum gallicarum et motettarum liber* | PHALÈSE et BALLÈRE | 1573[26] |
| Caen, Arnold | *Teütsche Lautenbuch darinnenn kunstliche Muteten* | Bernhard JOBIN | 1574[13] |
| Richafurt | *Zwey Bücher. Einer neüen kunslichen Tabulatur auff Orgel und Instrument* | Bernhard JOBIN | 1577[12] |
| Richafort, Jean | *Obras de musica para tecla arpa y vihuela* | SANCHEZ | 1578[24] |
| Caen, Arnold | WrocU 54 | | 1578 |
| Caen, Arnoldus | RegB 891-2 | Erasmus ZOLLNER? | 1570-80 |
| Richafort | *Tabulaturbuch auff Orgeln...* | Johann BEYER | 1583[24] |
| Richafort | DresSL Lob 8/70 | Christoph NOSTWITZ + 29 scribes | 1593 |
| | RosU 71/1 | | 1550-1600 |
| Caen, Arn. | WrocS 1 | | 1550-160 |
| | ZwiR 46/120 | Cornelius FREUNDT | 1567-1600 |
| Richafort | ZwiR 74/1 | Johann STOLL | 1575-1600 |
| Caen, Arnoldus | RokyA 22 | | 1575-1600 |
| Caen, Arn. | WrocS 12 | | c.1600 |
| Caen, Arnold | LüneR 150 | 41 scribes | 1575-1620 in MS |

**Table 10**    *1540-1550*

| | | |
|---|---|---|
| 23 | Clemens non Papa | *Concussum est mare* |
| 16 | Clemens non Papa | *Deus in adjutorium* |
| 7 | Clemens non Papa | *Maria Magdalena* |
| 13 | Phinot, Dominique | *Iam non dicam* |
| 30 | Phinot, Dominique | *Tanto tempore* |
| 42 | Stoltzer, Thomas | *O admirabile* |

In this decade, six new motets enter the core repertory, and one, Agricola's *Si dedero*, exits (see footnote 2). In the 1540s the number of prints holds steady, and the number of manuscripts rises only slightly: seventy-three sources preserve at least 180 occurrences of the core repertory motets, now numbering thirty-seven. The sources, from France, the Netherlands, Spain, Eastern Europe, Italy, and the Germanic region, represent a truly international array, though Germanic sources are easily the most numerous. (See Appendix V.) Accordingly, all of the composers whose works are new to the growing core repertory are heavily represented in Germanic sources, even if, like Dominique Phinot, they are not known to have worked in the region. Perhaps some of them, like Phinot, have prints devoted to their motets alone. For Phinot, and perhaps others, these single-composer sources were the first sites for his core repertory motets, which later found audiences in the Habsburg regions.

Phinot's core repertory motets are sparsely represented in Italian manuscripts and printed anthologies. Only three of the twenty-four sources for *Tanto tempore* are Italian. Two of these are early and essentially identical prints, both titled *Materna lingua moteta* and published simultaneously in 1549 by Scotto and Gardane. Slightly later, the same motet appears in the Treviso manuscript TrevBC 7, dated 1555-71. The only Italian database source for *O sacrum convivium*, Amadino's 1595[5] Venetian print *Augustini Zineroni bergomensis*, contains no composer attribution and was issued very late in the source history of the motet.

Jacob Clemens non Papa's motets enter the repertory during this decade. They remain largely confined to Germanic, eastern European, and Netherlandish regions, not spreading to France, Italy, the Iberian peninsula, or England. Clemens's employment history is unclear, but this dissemination pattern is typical for composers whose employment was primarily German. In general, works do not migrate from German sources west to French or Italian ones, but east and north, to eastern Europe and Scandinavia.

**Table 11**    *1550-1560*

| | | |
|---|---|---|
| 38 | Clemens non Papa | *Ego flos campi* |
| 49 | Clemens non Papa | *Jerusalem surge* |
| 18 | Clemens non Papa | *Venit vox de caelo* |
| 52 | Feys, Arnold | *Emendemus in melius* |
| 20 | Hollander | *Dum transisset* |

**Table 11 (cont'd)**

| | | |
|---|---|---|
| 31 | Lassus, Orlande de | *Angelus ad pastores* |
| 53 | Lassus, Orlande de | *Congratulamini mihi* |
| 32 | Lassus, Orlande de | *Veni in ortum* |
| 37 | Maillard, Jean | *Ascendo ad patrem* |
| 28 | Phinot, Dominique | *O sacrum convivium* |
| 29 | Phinot, Dominique | *Sancta trinitas* |
| 39 | Wert, Giaches de | *Transeunte domino* |

The source picture for this decade is distinctly international and, for the first time, print-dominated: of eighty-three sources, fifty are prints. The thirty-one Germanic sources dominate, followed by Netherlandish (23), French (9), Swiss (7), Spanish (6), Italian (5), eastern European (4), Scottish (1), and Danish (1) sources. This is the most significant decade for Netherlandish sources and for printed anthologies. However, even with this high proportion of prints, eight of the ten sources that introduce the dozen new core repertory motets are manuscripts. This decade sees the largest number of motets enter the repertory. (See Appendix VI.)

As Josquin dominated the first decades of the core repertory and Clemens the middle, we will find Orlande de Lassus—the most prolific and famous composer of the last portion of this century, according to the witness of the sources—dominating the last decades of the core repertory's formation; he introduces three core repertory motets in this decade. The position of each of these composers in the core repertory perfectly reflects their position in the complete motet repertory as the three most frequently represented composers of motets in the sixteenth century.

Clemens non Papa and Dominique Phinot, both prominent in the previous decade, again introduce a total of five motets. The Netherlandish Giaches de Wert, like the French Dominique Phinot, spent his career in Italy and published several books of motets devoted to his works. Also like Phinot, despite his Italian employment, Wert's earliest and most abundant motet database records are in Germanic sources. Gardane's 1568³ *Novi atque catholici thesauri musicus* book 2, the first extant Italian database source for Wert's core repertory motet *Transeunte domino*, is preceded by four earlier sources:

- RegB 940-1, dated 1557-59; from Regensburg or Wittenberg
- WarU 7.41.5.14, with dates 1559 and 1587 in the MS; from Olkusz, Poland
- RegB 1018, dated 1563 on the covers; from southern or central Germany
- Ansbach 18, with dates 1566-67 in the MS; from Ansbach, Germany

Three composers of varying degrees of obscurity to most modern scholars complete the roster with their new core repertory motets in this decade. Jean Maillard, a French composer with 138 database catalogue records, flourished in the middle part of the century. According to Ronsard's *Livre des mélanges*, he was a pupil of Josquin, though

Ambros questions the statement.[35] His work was known to Palestrina, who based masses on two of his motets, one of them the core repertory work *Ascendo ad patrem*. In addition to his database sources, Maillard published three individual books of motets. The name "Hollander" refers to Sebastian and Christian Hollander (see footnote 10); no individual prints exist. Arnold Feys is the mystery composer of the core repertory, unknown except for his setting of the text *Emendemus in melius*; no individual prints exist. The name does not appear with any other texts in the database and *New Grove* contains no entry for him.

The motets continue to converge in the sources—that is, an increasing number of sources carry an increasing number of core repertory works. By the end of this decade—1558-59—a group of just four German sources carries thirty-four of the forty-nine motets so far included in the core repertory (see Table 12). In the dedication of one of these sources, Berg and Neuber's three volume *Novum et insigne opus musicum*, the publisher, Berg, confirms and explains the trend we have seen growing for several decades: the mingling of old and new music. He writes that he chose the motets that fill these volumes for "one reason":

> so as to make my work pleasing to those who are captivated by an admiration for the new and are now almost completely tired and have had their fill of the old. And by joining the new with the old, in one work and one effort I have aimed to win favor from both those who love antiquity and esteem the old more highly than the new, and from those who are tired of returning again and again to the same song and prefer to seek their pleasure from the new rather than the old.[36]

Howard Mayer Brown, who edited the Garland Facsimile edition of this series, acknowledges the trend in his introduction:

> Even if a case cannot be made that the "early music movement" actually began in the second half of the sixteenth century, it nevertheless seems clear that throughout the century compositions written by the great masters active during its first decades continued to be performed, studied, and appreciated. Older compositions formed a basic repertory against which new creations were tested.[37]

Brown's later observation speaks to the preservation of music by so many composers whose works appeared in the earliest periods of the core repertory, as well as the growing international character of the repertory:

35. See the Ronsard reference in Oliver STRUNK, *Source Readings in Music History* (New York: W. W. Norton, 1950), 289, and the cautionary note in A.W. AMBROS, *Geschichte der Musik* (Breslau: F. E. C. Leuckart, 1868), 3: 328. See also J. Heywood ALEXANDER's preface to his edition of Chemin's 1554[7] *Moduli Undecim Festorum* (Madison, WI: A-R Editions, 1983), viii. Alexander mentions the Ronsard and Ambros statements, and also a statement in the printing privilege granted to another Parisian printing establishment, Le Roy and Ballard, that calls Maillard

"one of the composers especially in demand." Alexander's assessment of the purpose and context for *Moduli Undecim Festorum*, which opens with Maillard's *Victimae paschali luades* and *Ascendo ad patrem*, points to Maillard's importance in his own time.

36. Howard Mayer BROWN, *Novum et insigne opus musicum, sex, quinque, et quatuor vocum*, Renaissance Music in Facsimile, 27-29, (New York: Garland, 1986), vii.

37. Ibid., v.

There are about as many composers represented in the three volumes of the *Novum et insigne opus musicum* who had died by 1558 as there are composers still living then. And the collection includes music by composers active almost everywhere in Europe: Germany, Italy, France, the Netherlands, and most especially, at the Imperial Court. Berg and Neuber's gigantic anthology offers, in short, a dazzling array of samples from the works of the greatest and many of the lesser composers of the early and mid-sixteenth century.[38]

Berg's praise of Josquin in the introduction corroborates the status we have seen conferred upon him:

> Furthermore if anyone who esteems the talent and skill of Josquin has the desire to learn the extent to which he excels other composers who flourished before and after him, they will have at their disposal a large quantity of exceptional songs. A comparison of these songs will easily reveal Josquin's excellence to those who perform and practice them.[39]

This important series of prints includes twenty core repertory motets; significantly, it combines old and new works, overtly praises Josquin, and embraces an international *corps* of composers—precisely the characteristics revealed in the unfolding core repertory. Thus, the legitimacy of the core repertory as a concept and as an actual body of music is attested by contemporaneous participants in the music and its culture.

**Table 12**  Convergence of the Core Repertory in Four Sources

| Composers | Motets | A | B | C | D |
|---|---|---|---|---|---|
| FÉVIN, Antoine de (-Bruck) | *Sancta trinitas 26.12* | A | | C | D |
| JOSQUIN DESPREZ | *Stabat mater 25.8* | A | | | D |
| RICHAFORT, Jean | *Quem dicunt homines* | | | C | |
| LONGUEVAL, Antoine de | *Passio domini* | | B | | |
| JOSQUIN DESPREZ | *Praeter rerum seriem 24.12* | A | | | D |
| JOSQUIN DESPREZ | *Benedicta es caelorum 23.13* | A | | | D |
| JOSQUIN/ LEBRUNG/ RICHAFORT | *Congratulamini mihi 26.3* | | | C | |
| JOSQUIN DESPREZ | *Inviolata integra 24.4* | A | | | D |
| JOSQUIN DESPREZ | *Miserere mei deus 18.3* | | | | D |
| MOUTON, Jean | *Tua est potentia MA 84* | A | | | D |
| DUCIS/ MAFFONI | *Dilexi quoniam* | | | C | |
| MOUTON, Jean | *Quaeramus cum pastoribus 26.10* | | | | D |
| JOSQUIN DESPREZ | *Pater noster 20.9* | A | B | | D |
| WILLAERT, Adrian | *Pater noster* | | B | C | |
| VERDELOT, Philippe | *Si bona suscepimus* | A | | C | D |
| HELLINCK, Lupus | *Panis quem ego* | | B | | |
| JOSQUIN DESPREZ | *Qui habitat in adjutorio 18.7* | A | | C | D |
| SENFL, Ludwig | *Vita in ligno* | A | | | D |
| CAEN/ LUPUS/ RICHAFORT | *Jerusalem luge* | A | B | C | D |
| JACQUET OF MANTUA | *Aspice domine quia facta* | | | | D |
| ARCADELT, Jacques | *Dum complerentur* | | B | C | |
| GOMBERT, Nicolas | *Ave sanctissima Maria* | | B | | |
| WALTER/ VERDELOT | *Deus qui sedes* | | | C | |
| GOSSE, MAISTRE/ SENFL | *Ecce dominus veniet 14.5* | | | C | D |

38. Ibid, ix.  39. Ibid, vii.

**Table 12 (cont'd)**    Convergence of the Core Repertory in Four Sources

| Composers | Motets | A | B | C | D |
|---|---|---|---|---|---|
| GOMBERT/ JOSQUIN DESPREZ | 14.7: Tulerunt dominum/Lugebat David, etc | | B | | |
| CLEMENS NON PAPA | Ego me diligentes | | | | D |
| HELLINCK/ SENFL/ VERDELOT | In te domine speravi | | | | D |
| CLEMENS NON PAPA | Maria Magdalena | | | C | |
| STOLTZER, Thomas | O admirabile | | B | | |
| CLEMENS NON PAPA | Concussum est mare | | B | | D |
| CLEMENS NON PAPA | Jerusalem surge | | | C | D |
| HOLLANDER | Dum transisset | | | C | |
| CLEMENS NON PAPA | Venit vox de caelo | | | | D |
| WERT, Giaches de | Transeunte domino | | | C | |

### Key to Source Codes

| | Source | Date | Pub Scribe | City | Country |
|---|---|---|---|---|---|
| A | Tabulaturbuch auff die Lauten von Moteten | 1558[20] | Johann KOHLEN | Heidelberg? | S.W. Germany? |
| B | LeipU 49/50 | 1558 | Michael Heger, dir.? | Leipzig | E. Germany |
| C | RegB 940-1 | 1557-59 | Wolfang Küffer+ | Regensburg/ Wittenberg | S. Germany (Bavaria) |
| D | Novum et insigne | 1558[4] | Berg & Neuber | Nürnberg | C. Germany |
| D | Secunda pars magni operis musici | 1559[1] | Berg & Neuber | Nürnberg | C. Germany |
| D | Tertia pars magni operis musici | 1559[2] | Berg & Neuber | Nürnberg | C. Germany |

**Table 13**    1560-1570

| 36 | Lassus, Orlande de | In te domine speravi |
|---|---|---|
| 26 | Lassus, Orlande de | Surrexit pastor |
| 46 | Lassus, Orlande de | Tristis est anima |
| 47 | Meiland, Jacobus | Gaudete filiae Jerusalem |
| 54 | Meiland, Jacobus | Non auferetur sceptrum |

The last of the core repertory motets enter the sources during this decade (see Appendix VII). Of the fifty-five sources, those of Germanic origin prevail, numbering twenty-six, followed by fourteen Italian, six Netherlandish, three eastern European, three French, one English, and one Spanish source. Seventeen of this decade's sources are prints issued variously by Phalèse of Louvain, Gardane of Venice, Le Roy and Ballard of Paris, Berg and Neuber of Nürnberg, and Andreae of Kraków. Two of the motets, Lassus's *In te domine speravi* and Meiland's *Non auferetur sceptrum*, were introduced in a print, Berg and Neuber's 1564[3] *Thesauri musici*, book three for six voices (both composers published motets in single-composer prints that may have contained these works previously, however).

Though not well-known today, Jacob Meiland, with 173 database records[40] and six individual motet books, is hardly a minor figure; his works are found mainly in Ger-

---

40. The database catalogue greatly expands upon *The New Grove* source list for Meiland, and thus the implied list of works; the *New Grove* article does not contain such a list, but simply an enumeration of the number of

manic, eastern European, and Swedish sources. Walter Blankenburg notes that Meiland was a pupil of Johann Walter, one of Protestant Germany's most important and influential composers, that he was influenced by Clemens non Papa, and that his compositional innovations in Passion settings were historically significant.[41]

Many sources of *c.*1570-1600 are imprecisely dated, so last sources are in some cases as difficult to determine as earliest (see Appendix VIII). In the last three decades of the century, at least 164 sources carry the core repertory motets in a total of at least 550 appearances, and the repertory continues to converge. Most of the motets in the core repertory remained in circulation at least until the 1580s, at least thirty-nine of the motets were still in circulation as late as 1592, and at least fifteen continued to appear in sources after 1600:

- Josquin Desprez — *Praeter rerum seriem* 24.12
- Gombert/ Josquin Desprez — *Lugebat David/ Tulerunt dominum*, 14.7:
- Adrian Willaert — *Pater noster*
- Dominique Phinot — *Iam non dicam*
- Dominique Phinot — *Tanto tempore*
- Giaches de Wert, — *Transeunte domino*
- Clemens non Papa — *Deus in adjutorium*
- Arnold Feys — *Emendemus in melius*
- Orlande de Lassus — *Angelus ad pastores*
- Orlande de Lassus — *Congratulamini mihi*
- Orlande de Lassus — *Surrexit pastor*
- Orlande de Lassus — *Tristis est anima*
- Orlande de Lassus — *Veni in ortum*
- Jacobus Meiland — *Gaudete filiae Jerusalem*
- Jacobus Meiland — *Non auferetur sceptrum*

A few central sources often contain the bulk of any given repertory, attracting clusters of works, even as these same works continue to be dispersed singly and in pairs.[42] These summarizing manuscripts or prints efficiently gather the repertory that is spread over dozens of sources. In just this way, the core repertory can be extracted from a body of central sources without eliminating any works. Of the 539 sources that carry all the occurrences of the core repertory, most contain fewer than five core repertory motets: just ninety-two contain five or more. Thus, most participate only minimally in the preservation of this repertory. At the other extreme are sources that contain large numbers of the core repertory motets. Because of these sources, we can reduce the source

works of particular genres he wrote in various sources. The database indexes twenty-six motets; most occurred in several sources.

41. Walter Blankenburg, "Jean Maillard," *The New Grove*, 12: 71.

42. This tendency is reflected in repertorial case studies of Rome, of the Low Countries, of Mouton, and of the shared sources of Mouton and Josquin, reported in Thomas, "The Sixteenth-Century Motet," chaps. 4 and 5.

pool to eighteen central sources and still retain fifty-three of the motets (see Table 15), losing only Agricola's *Si dedero*, which, as previously noted, does not follow the patterns of most of the core repertory motets. We can further reduce the pool to just seven key sources or source groups and lose only eight motets (see Table 16). Finally, we can reduce the source pool even further, to DresSL Gl 5, a large manuscript, probably copied in Saxony from 1583 until the end of the century,[43] and a group of thirteen Regensburg manuscripts, probably copied by the scribe Erasmus Zollner in the 1570s,[44] and still retain forty-two of the core repertory motets (see motets in italics in Table 15; these last sources are represented in bold type in the same table).

The convergence of the motets in the sources signals a repertorial phenomenon: the earliest works appear independently, only gradually becoming associated with each other. As the repertory builds, we find grouping of the works increasing as they become recognized by musicians of the period as worthy of continued reproduction. The value placed on each of them individually eventually brings them together as scribes and editors continue to group highly valued works together within a unified context. This convergence of the repertory dispels any notions that core repertory methodology is an anachronistic construct imposed upon this music and confirms its aptness as a tool for presenting us with a more accurate view of the values that governed the high culture of Renaissance music.

**Table 14**   Key to Source Codes

| | | | | | |
|---|---|---|---|---|---|
| A | *Novum et insigne opus musicum* | 1537[1] | O | RegB 775-7 | 1579 in MS |
| B | MunU 401 | 1530-40 | O | RegB 875-77 | 1568-79 |
| C | CopKB 1872 | 1541-43 | O | RegB 786-837 | 1569-78 in MS |
| D | MunU 326 | 1543 | O | RegB 891-2 | 1570-80 |
| D | MunU 327 | 1543 | O | RegB 893 | 1570-80 |
| E | NurGN 83795 | 1539-48 | O | RegB 960-3 | 1570-80 |
| F | *Liber primus collectorum modulorum* | 1553[2] | O | RegB 930-9 | 1572-78 |
| G | CopKB 1873 | 1556 | O | RegB 863-70 | 1572-79 |
| H | *Tabulaturbuch auff die Lauten* | 1558[20] | O | RegB 844-8 | 1573-77 |
| I | LeipU 49/50 | 1558 | O | RegB 883-86 | 1573-79 |
| J | RegB 940-1 | 1557-59 | O | RegB 871-74 | 1576-79 |
| J | *Secunda pars magni operis musici* | 1559[1] | O | RegB 861-2 | 1577 in MS |
| K | *Tertia pars magni operis musici* | 1559[2] | O | RegB 887-90 | 1577-78 |
| L | HradKM 29 | 1556-62 in MS | P | *Obras de musica… arpa y vihuela* | 1578/24 |
| M | RegB 1018 | 1563 on covers | Q | *Tabulaturbuch auff Orgeln und Instrument* | 1583/24 |
| N | WrocS 2 | 1573 | R | WrocS 11 | 1583 on covers |

43. For more information about the source, see *Census-Catalogue*.

44. RegB 775-5, 786-37, 844-8, 861-62, 863-70, 871-74, 875-77, 883-86, 887-90, 891-92, 893, 930-39, and 960-63. See *Census-Catalogue*.

**Table 14 (cont'd)**   The Core Repertory in Eighteen Representative Sources

(sources arranged chronologically)

| Motet | A | B | C | D | E | F | G | H | I | J | K | L | M | N | O | P | Q | R |
|---|---|---|---|---|---|---|---|---|---|---|---|---|---|---|---|---|---|---|
| 9 | A | B | C | | E | | | H | I | | | | | | O | | | |
| 1 | A | B | C | | | F | | H | | | | L | | | | PX2 | | |
| 3 | A | B | C | | | | | H | | | | L | | | O | | | R |
| 4 | A | | C | D | E | F | | H | | J | K | L | M | | OX2 | P | Q | |
| 6 | A | | C | | | | G | H | | J | | L | | | O | | | |
| 44 | A | | C | | | | G | | | J | K | | | | O | | Q | R |
| 17 | A | | | D | | | | H | | | K | | | | O | | Q | R |
| 51 | A | | | D | | | | | | | K | | | | O | | | |
| 33 | A | | | | | | | H | | J | K | | | | | | | |
| 50 | A | | | | | | | | | J | | | M | NX2 | O | | | |
| 2 | | B | C | D | | F | G | H | | | K | | | | | PX2 | | R |
| 5 | | B | C | DX2 | E | F | | H | I | J | K | L | | | | P | | |
| 40 | | B | | | | F | | | | | | | | N | | | | |
| 8 | | B | | | | | | | | | K | | | | O | P | | |
| 15 | | B | | | | | | | | | | | M | N | OX2 | P | | |
| 22 | | | C | D | | | | H | | | K | L | | | | PX2 | | |
| 13 | | | C | | | | G | | | | | | M | | | | | |
| 7 | | | | D | E | | G | | | J | | L | M | NX2 | | | Q | |
| 24 | | | | D | E | | | | | | | | | | O | P | | |
| 14 | | | | D | | F | | | I | J | | L | | | O | | | |
| 11 | | | | D | | | | | I | J | | L | | | | | Q | |
| 45 | | | | D | | | | | | J | | | M | | O | | | |
| 25 | | | | D/J | E | | | | | | | | | | O | | | |
| 10 | | | | DX2 | E | F | G | | | | K | L | | | O | P | | |
| 42 | | | | | E | | | | I | | | L | | | O | | | |
| 27 | | | | | E | | | | | J | | | M | | | | | |
| 19 | | | | | | F | | | | J | | | | | O | | | |
| 12 | | | | | | F | | | | | K | | | | | PX3 | | |
| 48 | | | | | | | G | H | | | K | L | | | | | | |
| 53 | | | | | | | G | | | | | | | NX4 | | | Q | |
| 38 | | | | | | | G | | | | | | | | OX2 | | | |
| 34 | | | | | | | G | | I | | | | | N | | | | |
| 23 | | | | | | | | | I | | K | L | | | OX2 | | | |
| 35 | | | | | | | | | I | | | | | | O | | | |
| 41 | | | | | | | | | I | | | | | | | | | |
| 49 | | | | | | | | | | J | K | L | | | O | | Q | R |
| 39 | | | | | | | | | | J | | | M | | OX3 | | Q | |
| 20 | | | | | | | | | | J | | | | NX2 | O | | | |
| 18 | | | | | | | | | | | K | L | M | | O | | | |
| 43 | | | | | | | | | | | K | L | | | | | | |
| 52 | | | | | | | | | | | | L | | | O | | Q | |
| 16 | | | | | | | | | | | | L | | | | | Q | |
| 37 | | | | | | | | | | | | | | N | | | | |
| 26 | | | | | | | | | | | | | | NX2 | O | | | |
| 30 | | | | | | | | | | | | | | NX2 | OX2 | | | |
| 31 | | | | | | | | | | | | | | | O | | Q | R |
| 28 | | | | | | | | | | | | | | | O | | | R |
| 46 | | | | | | | | | | | | | | | O | | | R |
| 32 | | | | | | | | | | | | | | | O | | | |
| 36 | | | | | | | | | | | | | | | OX2 | | | |
| 29 | | | | | | | | | | | | | | | OX2 | | | |
| 47 | | | | | | | | | | | | | | | OX3 | | | |
| 54 | | | | | | | | | | | | | | | | | | R |
| 21 | no sources | | | | | | | | | | | | | | | | | |

**Table 15** The core repertory in seven representative sources
(**Bold type** denotes DresSL Gl 5 and Regensburg source group. Motets that appear in these sources are in italics.)

| Composer | Motet | A | B | **C** | D | E | **F** | G |
|---|---|---|---|---|---|---|---|---|
| Févin, Antoine de (-Bruck) | *Sancta trinitas 26.12* | A | | C | D | | F | G |
| Hellinck, Lupus | *Panis quem ego* | | | Cx2 | | | | |
| Josquin Desprez | *Stabat mater 25.8* | A | | C | | E | | |
| Josquin Desprez | *Benedicta es caelorum 23.13* | | | C | Dx2 | | | |
| Mouton, Jean | *Quaeramus cum pastoribus 26.10* | | | C | | | | |
| Richafort, Jean | Christus resurgens | | B | | | | | G |
| Willaert, Adrian | *Pater noster* | | | C | | | | |
| Josquin Desprez | *Inviolata integra 24.4* | | | C | | | | |
| Josquin Desprez | *Praeter rerum seriem 24.12* | | | C | | E | F | |
| Josquin Desprez | *Pater noster 20.9* | | | | D | | F | |
| Josquin Desprez/ Lebrung/ Richafort | *Congratulamini mihi 26.3* | | Bx2 | | | | F | G |
| Mouton, Jean | Tua est potentia MA 84 | A | | | | | | |
| Josquin Desprez | *Ave Maria gratia plena 23.6* | | | C | | | | |
| Longueval, Antoine de | Passio domini | | | C | | | | |
| Arcadelt, Jacques | Dum complerentur | | | | | | F | G |
| Caen/Lupus/Richafort | *Jerusalem luge* | | | C | | | | |
| Clemens non Papa | *Ego flos campi* | A | | C | D | | | |
| Clemens non Papa | *Deus in adjutorium* | | | Cx2 | D | | | |
| Clemens non Papa | *Concussum est mare* | | | Cx2 | | | F | G |
| Clemens non Papa | *Maria Magdalena* | A | Bx2 | | | | F | G |
| Clemens non Papa | Jerusalem surge | | | | | E | | |
| Clemens non Papa | Venit vox de caelo | | | | | | F | |
| Feys, Arnold | *Emendemus in melius* | | | C | | | F | |
| Gombert/Josquin | *14.7: Alleluia Noli/ Ecce quam/ Lugebat David/ Tulerunt dominum* | A | B | C | Dx2 | Ex2 | | G |
| Gosse, Maistre/Senf | *Ecce dominus veniet 14.5* | A | | | | E | F | |
| Hellinck/Senfl/ Verdelot | In te domine speravi | A | | | | | | |
| Hollander | *Dum transisset* | | Bx2 | C | | | F | G |
| Josquin Desprez | *Qui habitat in adjutorio 18.7* | | | C | | | | |
| Lassus, Orlande de | *Angelus ad pastores* | | | C | | | F | |
| Lassus, Orlande de | *In te domine speravi* | | | C | D | | | |
| Lassus, Orlande de | *Surrexit pastor* | | Bx2 | C | | | | G |
| Lassus, Orlande de | *Tristis est anima* | | | C | | E | F | |
| Lassus, Orlande de | *Congratulamini mihi* | A | Bx4 | Cx2 | D | | | Gx2 |
| Lassus, Orlande de | *Veni in ortum* | | | Cx2 | | | | |
| Maillard, Jean | Ascendo ad patrem | | B | C | | | F | G |
| Meiland, Jacobus | Non auferetur sceptrum | | | C | D | E | | |
| Meiland, Jacobus | Gaudete filiae Jerusalem | | Ox3 | | D | | F | |
| Phinot, Dominique | *Iam non dicam* | A | | C | D | | F | G |
| Phinot, Dominique | O sacrum convivium | | | C | D | E | F | |
| Phinot, Dominique | Sancta trinitas | | | C | D | | F | G |
| Phinot, Dominique | Tanto tempore | | Bx2 | C | D | | | G |
| Senfl, Ludwig | *Vita in ligno* | | | | | E | F | |
| Stoltzer, Thomas | O admirabile | | | | | | F | |
| Verdelot, Philippe | *Si bona suscepimus* | | | C | | | | |
| Verdelot, Philippe | *25.6 Sancta Maria/ Ave Jesu/ Christus* | | B | Cx2 | | | | G |

**Table 15 (cont'd)**   Key to the Sources

| | | | | | |
|---|---|---|---|---|---|
| A | CopKB 1873 | 1556 | | RegB 844-8 | 1573-77 |
| B | WrocS 2 | 1573 | | RegB 883-86 | 1573-79 |
| C | RegB 775-7 | 1579 in MS | | RegB 871-74 | 1576-79 |
| | RegB 875-77 | 1568-79 | | RegB 861-2 | 1577 in MS |
| | RegB 786-837 | 1569-78 in MS | | RegB 887-90 | 1577-78 |
| | RegB 891-2 | 1570-80 | D | MunBS 1536 | 1583 on covers |
| | RegB 893 | 1570-80 | E | WrocS 11 | 1583 on covers |
| | RegB 960-3 | 1570-80 | F | DresSL Gl 5 | 1583-8; 1600 |
| | RegB 930-9 | 1572-78 | G | WrocS 5 | c.1575-1600 |
| | RegB 863-70 | 1572-79 | | | |

## Overview Of Sources And Dissemination

Manuscripts rather than prints played the dominant role as the most numerous as well as the earliest extant sources for core repertory motets. Manuscripts make up 71 percent of the core repertory sources (383) and prints 29 percent (157). Of the thirty-nine sources that introduced core repertory motets, just eight, or only 20 percent, are prints. Only in the 1550s do prints dominate.[45] Thus, it appears that manuscripts were disproportionately important in introducing the core repertory motets. In many instances, however, the extant sources represent the actual entry of these motets into the repertory inadequately—for instance, motets by composers employed in Italy appear first, and sometimes nearly exclusively, in Germanic sources. This evidence may suggest that many such works are preserved only in second-generation sources at best. Before concluding that we have lost large numbers of prints and manuscripts, however, we must incorporate the evidence of the single-composer prints, which grew in importance over the course of the sixteenth century. No doubt consideration of these will, at least in part, offset the disparity between manuscripts and printed anthologies as the earliest sources for many of these works. We frequently lack plausible first sources for core repertory motets from 1550 to 1580, decades which saw the production of large numbers of these prints. Even if single-composer prints fill some of the gaps apparent in later Italian music production, we must still wonder what became of manuscript production, which continued to flourish elsewhere; why publishers chose not to continue to issue anthologies, so popular in mid-decade; or, if anthologies were issued, why they did not survive.

Many of the core-repertory motets circulated not only frequently and over a long period of time, but widely, appearing in sources far from their point of origin. The breadth of geographic representation for many works depended on when they were

---

45. See THOMAS, "The Sixteenth-Century Motet," chap. 2, for a close comparison of manuscripts and printed anthologies.

introduced. Over the course of the century, the geographic center of source distribution shifts unmistakably, not only for the core repertory, but for the entire repertory. In this regard, the core repertory accurately represents the general musical culture. Italian sources are overwhelmingly dominant numerically and proportionally from 1480 to the early decades of the 1500s; after that time, Germanic sources increase their numbers and their proportion of the whole as Italian sources recede. Judging from repertorial relationships among sources, Germanic sources acted as a musical conduit to Scandinavian and especially to eastern European sources. Thus, the surviving music that emerged in the late fifteenth or early sixteenth centuries was almost certain to have originated in Italian sources (or lost French sources) and in time spread to the east and north. Music originating after 1530 was increasingly likely to have appeared first in German sources[46] and then to move east or north, but far less likely to move west.

A comparative listing of the provenance statistics for the entire database with those of the core repertory is supplied in Table 16. The most significant differences between the entire repertory and the core repertory is the percentage of Germanic and Italian records in each: the percentage of Germanic records is disproportionately high for the core repertory, while that of Italian records is disproportionately low. The most likely explanation for the discrepancy is the role that Germanic sources played in preservation of this body of music. While Italian sources introduced and preserved the motets for only a few decades, these same works were preserved for many more decades in multiple Germanic sources. By contrast, Roman sources, for example,[47] demonstrated a marked reluctance to repeat works already in circulation within the city; this reluctance may have been prevalent in other parts of Italy as well. As the number of Italian sources dwindled and the role of introduction shifted to Germanic sources in the 1530s, these Germanic sources also preserved and transmitted the new motets in multiple manuscripts and prints.

Table 16 reveals the degree to which the core repertory entered the sources of various regions. England, known for its insularity in most eras, demonstrates little awareness of the core repertory. Scandinavian sources preserve less than one percent (.88) of the complete motet repertory found in manuscripts and printed anthologies as compared with two percent of the core repertory records. Though a difference of 1.2 percent may seem slight, it more than doubles the Scandinavian participation in the core repertory as compared with its proportion of the repertory as a whole. In addition, core repertory records make up eleven percent of the Scandinavian total, as opposed to about five

---

46. Undoubtedly, some works that appear first in the database in German sources actually appeared in single composer prints; some of these sources emanate from non-Germanic regions.

47. See THOMAS, "The Sixteenth-Century Motet," chap. 5 for discussion and a table of the Roman repertory, especially 259-61 and 290-99.

percent of the German, three percent of Italian, and about seven percent of the eastern European and French records. A cursory investigation of the repertory of Scandinavian sources indicates that their repertory was culled largely from Germanic sources. Compilers of the Scandinavian sources may have selected core repertory works for the same reasons that they were passed along from source to source elsewhere. Moreover, Scandinavian sources received these works late in the century, after the filtering process had already been underway for decades, so the repertory that these sources drew from was disproportionately weighted with core repertory works.

**Table 16**  Geographic Distribution of Core Repertory Motets

| Place code | Database records | % of database | Geographic area | CR records | % of CR |
|---|---|---|---|---|---|
| 1 | 20,614 | 41 | Germany/ Austria/ Switzerland/ Bavaria/Saxony | 1142 | 46 |
| 2 | 11,208 | 22 | Italy | 372 | 15 |
| 3 | 5,666 | 11 | Bohemia/ Poland/ Silesia/ Moravia/Slovakia/ Czechoslovakia/ Rumania/ Ukraine/Prussia/ Slovenia | 285 | 11.4 |
| 4 | 3,181 | 6 | Belgium/Netherlands | 230 | 9.37 |
| 5 | 1,832 | 3.6 | Spain/Portugal | 114 | 4.6 |
| 6 | 1,662 | 3.3 | France | 100 | 4 |
| 7 | 1,793 | 3.5 | England/Scotland/United Kingdom | 40 | 1.6 |
| 8 | 441 | 0.88 | Denmark/Sweden | 52 | 2 |

## Core Repertory Composers

The composers who created the core repertory are not entirely those indicated by our modern standard repertory. Modern scholars of the Renaissance would expect the names of Josquin Desprez and Orlande de Lassus to be as prominent as they are, but might also have expected at least some works by Isaac and Palestrina. Isaac produced an enormous amount of music and was highly regarded in his lifetime; the absence of his works in the core repertory can be explained by the infrequent reproduction and the narrow dissemination of his motets.[48] Palestrina's absence may be partially explained by the omission of single-composer prints from consideration and by the fact that his works began to appear later in the century, thus did not have the opportunity to circulate as widely, to be selected for anthologies, and to be as frequently reproduced in general sources as works which appeared earlier.[49] These same constraints, however, did not prevent Lassus' appearance in the core repertory. Composers like Lassus, whose natural out-

48. See THOMAS, "The Sixteenth-Century Motet," chap. 4, especially discussion surrounding Table 4.26, for a summary of the distribution and dissemination of the motets of Isaac and Palestrina.

49. The smaller number of manuscripts and printed anthologies emanating from Italy during the latter half of the century surely contributed to the narrower dissemination of Palestrina's music.

let was Germanic sources, were much more likely to see their works widely circulated in manuscripts and anthologies during the second half of the century. The core repertory, then, at least partly reflects the pure numerical strength of Germanic sources in the latter part of the century.

We are not surprised to see works of Gombert, Jacquet of Mantua, Mouton, Richafort, and Verdelot in this repertory, but perhaps did not expect to find Clemens non Papa, a composer acknowledged but little lauded today, second only to Josquin in his representation in the core repertory. More surprising yet is the appearance of a motet by the unknown Arnold Feys along with those of several other composers who, though known, are not conspicuous in modern Renaissance scholarship: Lupus Hellinck, Jean Maillard, Jacobus Meiland, Dominique Phinot, and Thomas Stoltzer. Some composers, such as Ludwig Senfl, are well known to modern Renaissance scholars, but perhaps not expected to have achieved the wide-spread recognition of Lassus or Josquin. Their appearance in this repertory calls for a new assessment of what their music contributed to their culture and of the role of Germany in extending the life of the motet during the Renaissance. Are the qualities represented by the core repertory similar to those of composers we already know well, or will our study of it add depth to our perception of the ideal Renaissance style? What qualities in the works of these composers commanded the attention of their contemporaries?

## Conclusions

We find that the core repertory motets span not only the entire sixteenth century, but that they have their roots in the last decades of the fifteenth century and extend into the seventeenth. Decade by decade, the core repertory motets reflect the source issues and musical taste of the period, the problems that confront modern scholars, and a geographic shift in production and preservation of motets from west to east and north. Even as new works continue to enter the repertory, many of the earliest core repertory motets thrive in the sources, often the same ones that introduce the new works, to the very end of the century and beyond. Thus, the sixteenth-century motet as a genre not only spoke to the musical and spiritual tastes and needs of specific times, places, and people, but transcended temporal, regional, and even religious boundaries, becoming the first art music (excluding plainchant) to endure over a long span of time and to symbolize the new awareness of Europe as a cohesive geographic, commercial, and cultural entity.

Though the reconstruction of the core repertory depended on a technology anachronistic to the repertory—using the computer database catalogue to create artificial contexts of expanded time and geography—the employment of the methodology has identified a body of music that behaved as a coherent and valued repertory in its own time, as attested by Berg in his 1558-59 collection, *Novum et insigne opus musicum*. It merits serious and extensive consideration. Works preserved in two, or perhaps even ten, sources may persist or vanish through accidents of preservation, but the survival of a work claiming fifty, forty, or even twenty extant sources cannot be called an accident of preservation. It is true that once works reached a certain level of circulation in the sources, their presence in scattered areas would have created an exponential increase, since more exemplars would have allowed for the creation of many more copies widely distributed in time and place. Even so, given the rarity of repetition in this repertory,[50] such persistent and wide-spread repetition and preservation constitutes a phenomenon of conscious choice and perseverance. Clearly, these works embody a musical legacy.

Of the core repertory motets, only Josquin's *Ave Maria* and Lassus's *Tristis est anima mea* are commonly found in modern music anthologies. Many of the most highly valued works from the core repertory are now little heard or discussed: Verdelot's *Si bona suscepimus* and *Sancta Maria virgo virginum*, Clemens's *Maria Magdalena*, Stoltzer's *O admirabile*, Fèvin's *Sancta trinitas*, Jacquet's *Aspice domine quia facta*, Maillard's *Ascendo ad patrem*, not to mention works whose authorship is uncertain—*In te domine speravi, Dilexi quoniam*, and *Deus qui sedes*. This music surely has much to reveal that we have not yet heard. Musical analysis of these motets may introduce a greater awareness of the most sought-after musical characteristics of their era. This understanding will afford an intelligent assessment of the modern standard repertory as well as local repertories and unfamiliar works of all kinds from the period, an overview of compositional evolution, and a greater ability to determine persistent musical values.

The assertion that this repertory was one that drew the attention of musicians of the time is borne out by the many parodies of certain of these works (*Si bona suscepimus, Benedicta es, Stabat mater, Praeter rerum*), by the fact that many of these settings seemed to engender settings of the same texts by other composers (*Miserere mei deus, Inviolata integra, Benedicta es*), posthumous collaborations (the Fèvin-de Bruck *Sancta trinitas*, the Josquin-Guyot *Benedicta es*), and by stylistic imitation. In addition, key sources, such as Grimm and Wyrsung's 1520[4] print, *Liber selectarum cantionum quas vulgo Mutetas appellant*, preserve a retrospective selection of highly prized works. Edited by Senfl, *Liber selectarum* was an important touchstone of the musical values leading up to that time as well as a portal to succeeding sources, not only in Germany, but in Italy and Spain as well. This print may be emblematic of the means by which the core repertory formed: an influential and well-placed musician, Ludwig Senfl, assembled from motets already in circulation a collection arguably designed to demonstrate the humanistic values of the Habsburg Court under Maximilian I. That print, whether because of the repertory it contained, because of its association with an important court, or both, wielded considerable influence on

---

50. See THOMAS, "The Sixteenth-Century Motet," 389 and 397-99.

subsequent musical sources, many of which relied on *Liber selectarum's* musical readings.[51] The same process that created this print elevated the status of this core repertory of fifty-four motets: knowledgeable musicians recognized and selected a valued set of motets for preservation in sources that extended the lives of these motets far beyond the typical limitations of time and place. The increasing convergence of the works in particular sources testifies that a consistent set of values perpetuated them.[52] The core repertory, then, offers us a view of the musical values embraced by knowledgeable participants in the culture of the Renaissance.

51. See SCHLAGEL's discussion of this print and its descendents as well as of the concept of historicist anthologies in her dissertation, "Josquin des Prez and His Motets," chap. 2. These historicist volumes play a pivotal role in perpetuating the core repertory.

52. The specific musical and textual nature of these works and the particular path each of them took will be taken up in several future studies.

## Appendix I    Core Repertory Sources to 1500

| Motets | Source | Date | Country | City | Scribe* |
|---|---|---|---|---|---|
| 24 | MunBS 3154 | 1484 | Austria or S. Germany | Innsbruck/Augsburg | |
| 21 | FlorR 2356 | 1480-5 | N.C. Italy | Florence | |
| 21 | RomeC 2856 | 1485-90 | N. Italy | Ferrara | Alessandro Signorello[+] 2 |
| 21 | BolC Q 16 | 1487[1]; 1490s | C. Italy | Rome | Marsilius[+] |
| 21 | BolC Q 17 | 1490s | N. Italy | Bologna | Spataro[+] 1 |
| 21 | FlorBN Magl. 178 | 1492-94 | N.C. Italy | Florence | |
| 21 | VatG XIII.27 | 1492-94 | Italy | Rome | |
| 24 | BerlS 40021 | 1495 in MS | Germany | | |
| 24 | HradKM 7 | 1475-1500 | Bohemia | | |
| 24 | LeipU 1494 | 1490-1504 | E. Germany | Leipzig | |
| 2, (6) | VatC 234 | 1498-1503; + 1514 | Belgium | Brussels/Mechelen | Martin Bourgeois[+]; illum. wkshp. Hortulus Master |
| 21 | FlorR 2794 | 1480s | France | | Pietrequin[+] |

## Appendix II    Core Repertory Sources 1500-20

(motets introduced during the period are indicated by **bold type**)

| Motets | Source | Date | Country | City | Publisher or Scribe |
|---|---|---|---|---|---|
| 21 | BrusBR 11239 | c.1500 | Savoy | | |
| 21 | ParisBNF 1597 | c.1500 | N. France | Paris | |
| 21 | VerBC 757 | c.1500 | N. Italy | Verona | One main + 2 |
| 24 | WarU 2016 | c.1500; on cover | Bohemia | | |
| 2, 6 | VatC 234 | 1498-1503; + 1514 | Belgium | Brussels/Mechelen | Martin Bourgeois+ |
| **19**, 24 | BarcOC 5 | 1475-1525 | Spain | | |
| **6**, 24 | BarcBC 454 | 1475-1525; (1525-32 in MS) | Spain | | |
| 21 | Odhecaton A | 1501 | N. Italy | Venice | Petrucci |
| 24 | Motetti A | 1502[1] | N. Italy | Venice | Petrucci |
| 21, 24 | SegC s.s. | 1502 | Spain | Toledo | |
| 21 | ParisBNC 676 | 1502 in MS | N. Italy | Mantua/Ferrara | Lodovicus Millias (Milliare?) |
| 21 | Odhecaton A | 1503[2] | N. Italy | Venice | Petrucci |
| **2** | BrusBR 9126 | 1505 | Belgium | Brussels/Mechelen | Martin Bourgeois+ |
| 21 | BolC Q 18 | 1502-6 | N. Italy | Bologna | Spataro + |
| 21 | Intab. de lauto bk 2 | 1507[6] | N. Italy | Venice | Petrucci/ Spinacino |
| 24, **25** | VatS 42 | 1507 in MS; 1503-12 | Italy | Rome | Johannes Orceau |
| **6** | Mot. corona 1 | 1514[1] | Italy | | Petrucci |
| 2, 24, **25** | FlorBN II.I.232 | 1515 | N.C. Italy | Florence | |
| **3** | UppsU 76b | c.1515? | N.E. France | Troyes? or vicinity | |
| **6** | CambriP 1760 | 1503-16 | France | | |
| **1, 3** | VatS 16 | 1512-17 | Italy | Rome | Claudius Gellandi |
| **2** | BrusBR 215-16 | 1503-18 | Belgium | Brussels/Mechelen | Petrus Alamire |
| **50** | BolC Q 19 | 1518 | N. Italy | Bologna/Cento | |
| 22, **48, 51** | FlorL 666 | 1518 | Italy/France | Rome | Gellandi; Bouchet |
| 2, **3, 51** | Mot. corona 3 | 1519[2] | Italy | | Petrucci |
| 22 | Mot. corona 4 | 1519[3] | Italy | | Petrucci |
| **6** | FlorBN Magl. 117 | 1505-20 | Italy/to England | Florence? | |
| **3** | SGallS 464 | 1510-20; + 1540 | Switzerland | Basel | Aegidius Tschudi (1540) + 5 others |
| 6, 21 | ChiN C25 | c.1515-20 | N. Italy | Venice | "Vidal," pupil of Vincenzo Capirola |
| **48** | VatS 26 | 1515-21 | Italy | Rome | Gellandi |

## Appendix III  Core Repertory Sources 1520-30

| Motets | Source | Date | Country | City | Publisher or Scribe |
|---|---|---|---|---|---|
| 40 | *Motetti novi libro tertio* | 1520[2] | N. Italy | Venice | Antico |
| 1, 2, 3, 22, 51 | *Liber selectarum vulgo Mut.* | 1520[4] | Germany | Augsburg | Grimm & Wyrsung |
| 6 | BolC Q 27/2 | 1520 | N. Italy | Bologna | |
| 45 | FlorBN II.I.350 | c.1520 | N.C. Italy | Florence | |
| 3, 22 | RegB C120 | c.1520s | Germany or Austria | | |
| 24 | MilD 4 | c.1520s | N. Italy | Milan | Gafurius et al |
| 12, 22, 48, 51 | *Motetti libro primo* | 1521[3] | N. Italy | Venice | Antico |
| 1, 6, 9, 19, 50 | PadBC A17 | 1522 | N. Italy | Padua | Passetto |
| 12 | ModD 3 | 1520-24 | N. Italy | Modena | Eustachius de Monte Regali + |
| 12, 22 | *Moteti novi* | 1521][7] (publ. 1524) | C. Italy | Rome/Venice? | Antico and Scotto? |
| 24 | BerlS 40026 | 1520-24 | Germany | Esslingen and Pforzheim | |
| 6 | LonBLR 8 G. viii | 1513-25 | Belgium | Brussels/Mechelen | Petrus Alamire |
| 21 | FlorBN Panc. 27 | 1500-25 | N. Italy | | |
| 12 | BolSP 38 | c.1525 | N. Italy | Bologna | Giovanni Spataro |
| 21 | CopKB 1848 | c.1525 | France | Lyon (copied at) | Charneyron et al |
| 6 | Mot. corona 1 | 1526[1] | C. Italy | Rome | Pasoti & Dorico |
| 2, 3, 51 | Mot. corona 3 | 1526[3] | C. Italy | Rome | Pasoti |
| 22 | Mot. corona 4 | 1526[4] | C. Italy | Rome | Pasoti & Dorico |
| 2, 3, 51 | Mot. corona 3 | 1527 | C. Italy | Rome | Pasoti |
| 24 | MunU 322-5 | 1527 | Switzerland | Basel | Glareanus, supervisor |
| 12, 19 | VatS 46 | 1508-27 | Italy | Rome | Claudius Bouchet; Claudius Gellandi |
| 9 | VatS 55 | 1512-27 | Italy | Rome | Gellandi Bouchet |
| 12 | *Motetz a quatre et cinq voix* | 1529[1] | N. France | Paris | Attaingnant |
| 4, 14, 15 | ChiN M91/2 | 1525-29 | Italy/to England | Florence | Gianpiero Masacone |
| 25 | DresSL 1/D/505 | 1510-30 | Germany | Annaberg; prob. copied at Wittenberg | |
| 6, 21 | SGallS 462 | 1510-30 | N. France | Paris | Johannes Heer + |
| 2, 3 | VatV 11953 | 1515-30 | Germany | | |
| 4, 14, 19, 50 | VatVM 571 | 1520-30 | C. Italy | Rome | |
| 6, 14, 19, 35, 45 | VerBC 760 | 1520-30 | N. Italy | Verona | |
| 12 | ModD 11 | 1520-30; l. 16th c | N. Italy | Modena | |
| 17, 33, 51 | MunBS 10 | 1525-30 | S.Germany | Munich | Lucas Wagenrieder |
| 4, 6, 9, 15, 22, 24 | ModD 9 | 1518-31 | N. Italy | Modena | Several |
| 33 | VienNB Mus 15941 | 1521-31 | Belgium | Brussels/Mechelen | Petrus Alamire |
| 21, 24 | SGallS 530 | 1512-21; + 1531 | Switzerland | Constance, St. Gall | Fridolin Sicher |

## Appendix IV  Core Repertory Sources 1530-40

| Motets | Source | Date | Country | City | Publisher or Scribe |
|---|---|---|---|---|---|
| 2, 9 | MunBS 12 | 1530 | S. Germany | Munich | Senfl; Wagenrieder |
| 35 | ModE L.11.8 | c.1530? | N. Italy | | |
| 1, 2, 6, 12, 19, 35, 40 | UppsU 76c | c.1530? | France | | |
| 8 | TrevBC 36 | 1530,+ | N. Italy | Treviso | Dominus Maur? |
| 14, 40 | VatP 1976-9 | c.1528-31 | Belgium | Brussels/Mechelen | Petrus Alamire |
| 48 | 's HerAB 72C | 1530-31 | Belgium | Brussels/Mechelen | Petrus Alamire |
| 3, 4, 5, 8, 9, 10, 11, 15 | RomeV 35-40 | 1530-31 | N.C. Italy | Florence | Antonius Morus |
| 6 | *Treze Motetz* | 1531[5] | N. France | Paris | Attaingnant |
| 4, 5, 8, 10 | *Motetti del fiore bk 2* | 1532[9] | E. France | Lyons | Moderne |
| 14, 19, 35 | *Primus liber 4 vc* | 1532[10] | E. France | Lyons | Moderne |
| 41 | *Motetti del fiore 4 v bk 2* | 1532[11] | E. France | Lyons | Moderne |
| 22, 27, 33 | *Tabulatur...Hanns Gerle* | 1533[4] | C. Germany | Nürnberg | Hieronymus Formschneider |

| | | | | | |
|---|---|---|---|---|---|
| 5 | *Liber octavus* | 1534[10] | N. France | Paris | Attaingnant |
| 14 | *Musicales 4 v motetos bk 2* | 1534[4] | N. France | Paris | Attaingnant |
| 40, 50 | VienNB Mus 18825 | 1515-34 | Belgium | Brussels/Mechelen | Petrus Alamire |
| 14 | LonRC 2037 | 1527-34 | N. Italy | Ferrara | |
| 48 | VienNB 9814 | 1515-34 (1519-25) | Belgium | Brussels/Mechelen | Petrus Alamire |
| 2, 3, **8**, 15 | RomeM 23-4 | 1532-34 | C. Italy | Rome | Johannes Ochon |
| 15 | FlorBN Magl. 125bis | 1530-34 | N.C. Italy | Florence | |
| 22, 51 | LonBL 19583 | *c.*1535 | N. Italy | Ferrara | Jean Michel |
| 51 | ModE F.2.29 | *c.*1535 | N. Italy | Ferrara/to Modena 1598 | Jean Michel |
| **10** | *Liber nonus XVIII.* | 1535[1] | N. France | Paris | Attaingnant |
| 21 | BasU F IX 22 | 1513-35 | Switzerland/ E. Germany | Basel or Freiburg | Kotter, Wecker, Amerbach, Zyr + 1 |
| 1, 3, 9, 19, 25, 33 | ToleF 23 | 1520-35 | Belgium | | |
| 2, 3, 6, 12, 24 | LonRC 1070 | 1510-36 | England | London | |
| 2, 9 | *Intab. di Liuto de Diversi* | 1536[11] | N. Italy | Venice | |
| 6, 21 | *Der ander theil des Lautenbuchs* | 1536[13] | C. Germany | Nürnberg | Petreius |
| 2, 9 | *Intab. di Liuto de Diversi* | 1536[15] | N. Italy | Venice | |
| 2, 9 | *Intavolatura de viola* | 1536[16] | Italy | Naples | Johannes Sultzbach |
| 2, 3, 4, **5** | VatG XII.4 | 1536 | Italy | Rome | Johannes Parvus |
| **34** (two versions) | VerA 218 | 1536 | N. Italy | Padua, prob. | |
| **11** | VatS 19 | 1535-37 | Italy | Rome | Johannes Parvus |
| 1, 3, 4, 6, 9, **10**, 17, 33, **44**, 50, 51 | *Novum et insigne opus musicum* | 1537[1] | C. Germany | Frankfurt am Main | Formschneider |
| 19, 45 | WittenL 1048 | 1524-38 | C. Germany | | |
| 25 | *Selectae Harmoniae 4 vc de Passione Domini* | 1538[1] | E. Germany | Wittenberg | Rhau |
| **11**, 15 | *Tertius liber mottetorum* | 1538[2] | E. France | Lyons | Moderne |
| 2, 22, 41 | *Novi operis bk 2* | 1538[3] | C. Germany | Nürnberg | Formschneider |
| 14, 19 | *Modulationes...vulgo modetas* | 1538[7] | C. Germany | Nürnberg | Petreius |
| 19, 35 | *Symphoniae iucundae 4 v* | 1538[8] | E. Germany | Wittenberg | Rhau |
| 35, **44**, 48 | RegB B211-15 | 1538 | S. Germany/Austria | | |
| **11**, 15 | *Tertius liber mottetorum* | 1539[4] | E. France | Lyons | Moderne |
| **44** | *Mottetorum ad 5-6 v bk 4* | 1539[5] | E. France | Lyons | Moderne |
| 4, 5, **10**, **11** | *Mottetti del fiore 5 vc Bk 2* | 1539[6] | N. Italy | Venice | Gardane |
| 4, **11** | *Cantiones 5 v selectissimae* | 1539[8] | E. France | Strasbourg | Peter Schoeffer |
| 45 | *Motetti del fiore 4-5 v bk 2* | 1539[9] | C. Germany | Nürnberg | Johann Petreius |
| 14, 19, 35, 41 | *Mottetti del fiore 4 vc bk 1* | 1539[12] | N. Italy | Venice | Gardane |
| 40 | *Officia Paschalia* | 1539[14] | E. Germany | Wittenberg | Rhau |
| 24 | FlorBN Magl. 164-7 | 1515-40 | N.C. Italy | Florence | |
| 1, 2, 3, **5**, **8**, 9, **10**, 15, 40 | MunU 401 | 1530-40 | Germany/Austria | Augsburg? | |
| 12, 19, 40, 50 | CasAC D(F) | 1521-*c*26;1538-*c*45 | N. Italy | Montferrat | |
| 33 | AmstM I | 1520-40? | Belgium | | 1 + |
| **5**, **10**, 24 | UlmS 237 | 1530-40 | C. Germany | | |
| 4, 8 | ParisBN 32 | 1530-40? | N. Italy | Padua | |
| 6 | CivMA 59 | 1535-40, 45 | N.E. Italy | Cividale del Friuli | |
| 24 | MunBS 19 | pre-1531; 1531-40 | S.Germany | Munich | Lucas Wagenrieder |
| **10**, 24, 25, **27** | BerlPS 40013 | 1540 | E. Germany | Torgau | Walter, supervisor |
| 3, 12, 19, 21, 22, 24, **43**, 45, 51 | SGallS 463 | 1540 ff | Switzerland | Glarus | Aegidius Tschudi |
| 4, **8**, **10** | BolC Q 27/1 | *c.*1540 | N. Italy | Bologna? | |
| **8**, **27** | StuttL 35 | *c.*1540 | S.W. Germany | Stuttgart | Nikolaus Peuschel |
| 4, 17 | StuttL 43 | *c.*1540, | S.W. Germany | Stuttgart | Nikolaus Peuschel |
| 8 | MilC 186 | *c.*1540? | N. Italy | Mantua | |

## Appendix V  Core Repertory Sources 1540-50

| Motets | Source | Date | Country | City | Publisher or Scribe |
|---|---|---|---|---|---|
| 5, 8, 11, 48 | *Selectissimarum mutetarum 4-5 vc Bk 1* | 1540[6] | C. Germany | Nürnberg | Petreius |
| 5, 6 | ErlU 473/1 | 1541 | S.W. Germany | Heilbronn | Johannes Hartung |
| 41 | *Gombert excell. 4 vc Bk 1* | 1541[4] | N. Italy | Venice | Scotto |
| 6 | StuttL 25 | 1542 | S.W. Germany | Stuttgart | Chamerhueber |
| 11, 15 | *Tertius liber mottetorum* | 1542[4] | E. France | Lyons | Moderne |
| 6, 19, 33, 35, 40, 41, 48, 50 | CambraiBM 125-8 | 1542 in MS | Belgium | Brugge | g h |
| 14 | *Adriani Willaert 6 vc Bk 1* | 1542[10] | N. Italy | Venice | Gardane |
| 1, 2, 3, 4, 5, 6, 9, **13**, 22, 44 | CopKB 1872 | 1541-43 | Prussia | Königsberg | Mathhias Krüger? |
| 5, 10, 14, 22, 24, 25 | MunU 326 | 1543 | Germany | Augsburg | Narcissus Zänckl |
| 2, 4, 5, 7, 10, 11, 17, 45, 51 | MunU 327 | 1543 | Germany | Augsburg | |
| 10, 25, 27 | WeimB B | 1540-44 | E. Germany | Torgau/Wittenberg | |
| 9, 50 | BerlPS 40043 | 1542-44 | E. Germany | Torgau | Walter, supervisor |
| 1, 9 | TóleBC 18 | 1543-36 | Spain | Toledo | Martín Pérez |
| 6, 45 | BerlGS 7/KönsSU 1740 | 1537-44 | Prussia | Königsberg | Mathhias Krüger |
| 5, 17, 45 | *Das Dritt...Lauten Buch* | 1544[25] | C. Germany | Nürnberg | Hans Günther |
| 45 | IserV F124 | 1544 | N.W.Germany | Westphalia | |
| 14 | VienNB Mus 15500 | 1544 | Germany | | |
| 14, 14, 45 | CasAC N(H) | 1538-45 | N. Italy | Montferrat | |
| 2, 8, 15, 19, 22 | ToleBC 10 | 1544-45 | Spain | Toledo | Martín Pérez |
| 40 | *Concentus 8, 6, 5, 4 vc* | 1545[2] | Germany | Augsburg | Ulhard |
| 14, 19, 35, 41 | *Flos florum 4 vc Bk 1* | 1545[4] | N. Italy | Venice | Gardane |
| 1 | *Bicinia gallica, latina, germanica, ex praestantissimis* | 1545[6] | E. Germany | Wittenberg | Rhau |
| 45 | BergBC 1209 | 1545 | Bavaria | | Gaspar de Albertis |
| 4, 10, 25, 48 | ErlU 473/3 | 1545 | S.W. Germany | Heilbronn | Johannes Hartung |
| 3, 4, 9, 10, 24, 25, 27, 33 | GothaF A98 | 1545 | E. Germany | Torgau/Jena/Weimar | |
| 10, 50 | StuttL 34 | c.1545 | S.W. Germany | Stuttgart | Nikolaus Peuschel |
| 1, 2, 3, 10, 11 | LeuvU 163 | 1546 | Netherlands? | | 1+1 |
| 7 | *Sacrarum cantionum 5 v Bk 1* | 1546[6] | Belgium | Antwerp | Tylman Susato |
| 14 | *Alonso Mudarra...vihuela* | 1546[23] | S. Spain | Seville | Juan de Leon |
| 41 | *Intab. lautto ... Dominico Bianchini* | 1546[24] | N. Italy | Venice | Gardane |
| 12 | *Joan Maria intab. lauto Bk 1* | 1546[25] | N. Italy | Venice | Gardane |
| 2, 9 | *Intab. lauto ...Milano Bk 2* | 1546[29] | N. Italy | Venice | Gardane |
| 1, 24, 40 | *Dodecachordon* | 1547[1] | Switzerland | Basel | Heinrich Petrus |
| 1, 2, 3, 8, 9, 15, 17, 48 | *Intab. lauto ...Gintzler* | 1547[22] | N. Italy | Venice | Gardane |
| 1, 4, 5, 9, 12, 41 | *Chansons & motetz reduictz* | 1547[23] | Belgium | Louvain | Phalèse |
| 1, 4, 5, 9, 12, 41 | *Carminum ad testudinis bk 3* | 1547[24] | Belgium | Louvain | Phalèse |
| 1, 5, 9, 10, 12, 14, 22, 35 | *Libro de musica de vihuela intitulado Silva* | 1547[25] | Spain | Valladolid | Cordova |
| 4 | BasU F X 22-24 | 1547 | Switzerland | Basel | Piperinius |
| 10, **42** | ZwiR 73/II | 1547 | N.Germany | Magdeburg/ Wittenburg | Jodocus Schalreuter |
| 22 | VatS 24 | 1545 in MS 1538-50 | Italy | Rome | Johannes Parvus |

| | | | | |
|---|---|---|---|---|
| 17, 17, 27, 27 WarSM 564 | 1548 in MS | S. Poland | Kraków | 1 |
| 10, 14, 19, 48 RegB C 99 | 1548 on title page | Bavaria | Regensburg | Johannes Stengl |
| 2, 17, 27, 35 KrakPAN 1716 | 1537-48 | Poland | Crasny | Johannes of Lublin |
| 4, 5, 7, 9, 10, NurGN 83795 24, 25, 27, **42** | 1539-48 | E. Germany | Torgau | Johann Walter + |
| 3 HofG 3713 | 1548-49 | N.Germany | Brunswick | Heinrich Faber? |
| 30 *Materna lingua moteta 4 vc* | 1549[9] | N. Italy | Venice | Gardane |
| 50 *Electiones...motetorum 4 v* | 1549[12] | N. Italy | Venice | Gardane |
| 30 *Materna lingua moteta 4 vc* | 1549[9a] | N. Italy | Venice | Scotto |
| 12 *Opera intitolata...lauto* | 1549[39] | N. Italy | Venice | Scotto |
| 17 *Das Ander ...Lauten Buch* | 1549[6] | C. Germany | Nürnberg | Newsidler |
| 19 LeidGA 1438 | 1549 | Netherlands | Leiden | |
| 7, 10, **16**, 23 BrusC 27088 | pre-1549 1563 in ms | N. France | Beaumont | copied at 1 |
| 1 MunBS 260 | 1539-50 | Belgium | | |
| 17, 33 LüneR 1196 | 1525-50; 1549 in MS | | | 1 |
| 12 BolC Q 25 | 1525-50 | Italy/France | | |
| 1, 3 BolC R142 | 1515-50 | N. Italy | | |
| 8, 9, 9, 15, 40 VallaC 15 | 1525-50 | Italy? | | |
| 10, 33, 51 KasL 24 | 1534-50 in MS | C. Germany | Kassel | Johann Heugel |
| 22, 40 BarcBC 681 | 1500-50 | | | |
| 6, 25, 44 EisS s.s. | 1540-50 | E. Germany | Eisenach | Wolfgang Zeuner |
| 25 StuttL 39 | 1540-50 | S.W. Germany | Stuttgart | Nikolaus Peuschel |
| 12 PadBC D27 | 1541-50 | N. Italy | Padua | Passetto |
| 14, 41 HerdF 9821 | 1545-50 | prob. Germany | | |

## Appendix VI    Core Repertory Sources 1550-60

| Motets Source | Date | Country | City | Publisher or Scribe |
|---|---|---|---|---|
| 3, 17, **32**, 33 MunBS 272 | 1550 | Germany | | 1 |
| 3, 17, 42 BudOS 2 | 1550 (pt I) | E. Germany? | Bártfa | |
| 40, 48, 48 BudOS 23 | 1550 in MS | E. Germany | Wittenberg/ Bártfa | |
| 6 RegB C 96 | 1550 in MS | Bavaria | Regensburg | |
| 11 *Carmina vere divina 5 vc* | 1550[2] | C. Germany | Nürnberg | Berg & Neuber |
| 3 BerlDS 1175 | c.1550 | Germany | A.S.? | |
| 7, 25, 42 DresSL Grimma 59 | c.1550 | E. Germany | Leipzig | Wolfgang Figulus + |
| 7, **20**, 25, ColnU 57 37, 49 | post-1550 | Germany | | |
| 2 HradKM 41 | post-1550 | E. Bohemia | Hradec Králové | 2 |
| 4, 10 ToleBC 17 | 1550-1 | Spain | Toledo | Martín Pérez |
| 37 *Primus liber septem decim* | 1551[1] | N. France | Paris | Chemin |
| 41 *Nicolai Gomberti musici ecclesiasticarum cantionum* | 1551[2] | N. Italy | Venice | Gardane |
| 1 *Le troysieme livre ...Simon Golier* | 1551[22] | N. France | Paris | Granjon and Fezandat |
| 8 BolSP 39 | 1552 | N. Italy | Bologna | |
| **18**, 43, 49 MunBS 13 | 1552 | S.Germany | Munich | Ludwig Daser |
| 1, **18**, **20**, 38 WhalleyS 23 | 1552 in MS | Belgium | | Christophe Plantin, binder |
| 24 MunBS 41 | 1552-60 | S.Germany | Munich | Ludwig Daser; Peter Steydl |
| 1, 2, 9, 48 *Hortus musarum* | 1552[29] | Belgium | Louvain | Phalèse |
| 5, 8 *Intabulatura ...Valentini Bacfarc* | 1552[30] | E. France | Lyons | Moderne |
| 12, 14, 14, *Libro de...vihuela* 34, 51 *...Diego Pisador* | 1552[35] | W.C. Spain | Salamanca | Pisador |
| 6 ToleBC 13 | 1553-54 | Spain | Toledo | Martín Pérez |

| Motets | Source | Date | Country | City | Publisher or Scribe |
|---|---|---|---|---|---|
| 1, 2, 4, 5, 10, 12, 14, 19, 40 | Liber primus collectorum modulorum (qui moteta vulgo dicuntur) | 1553[2] | N. France | Paris | Chemin & Goudimel |
| 51 | Psalmorum selectorum | 1553[4] | C. Germany | Nürnberg | Berg & Neuber |
| 23, 43, **49** | Cantionum sacrarum bk 4 | 1553[11] | Belgium | Louvain | Phalèse |
| 8 | Iachet musici suavissimi | 1553[17] | N. Italy | Venice | Gardane |
| 1, 2, 10 | Horti musarum secunda pars | 1553[33] | Belgium | Louvain | Phalèse |
| 23, 32, 43 | LonBL 31438 | 1553 | Belgium | | |
| 2 | Musices practicae erotematum bk 2 | 1553 | Switzerland | Basel | |
| **18, 20, 49** | Cantionum sacrarum bk 1 | 1554[1] | Belgium | Louvain | Phalèse |
| 52 | Cantionum sacrarum bk 2 | 1554[2] | Belgium | Louvain | Phalèse |
| 23, 43 | Cantionum sacrarum bk 4 | 1554[4] | Belgium | Louvain | Phalèse |
| 37 | Moduli undecim festorum | 1554[7] | N. France | Paris | Chemin |
| 7, **20**, 34, 40 | Evangeliorum/I | 1554[10] | C. Germany | Nürnberg | Berg & Neuber |
| 37 | Primus liber motetorum | 1554[12] | Switzerland | Geneva | Guéroult Du Bosc |
| **18** | Secundum liber modulorum | 1554[13] | Switzerland | Geneva | Guéroult Du Bosc |
| **18** | Motetti del laberinto 4 v bk 4 | 1554[16] | N. Italy | Venice | Scotto |
| 1, 3, 4, 8, 14, 41 | Libro... vihuela, ...Orphenica lyra | 1554[32] | S. Spain | Seville | Montesdaca |
| 3 | DresSL Pirna IV | 1554 | E. Germany | Pirna | |
| 1, 3, 9, 22 | SevBC 1 | 1554 | S. Spain | Seville | |
| **18, 20, 49** | Cantionum sacrarum bk 1 | 1555[2] | Belgium | Louvain | Phalèse |
| 52 | Cantionum sacrarum bk 2 | 1555[3] | Belgium | Louvain | Phalèse |
| 16, **38** | Cantionum sacrarum bk 8 | 1555[5] | Belgium | Louvain | Phalèse |
| 16 | Sacrarum cantionum bk 3 | 1557[7] | Belgium | Antwerp | Waelrant, Laet |
| **20** | Ecclesiasticarum cantionum bk 10 | 1555[8] | Belgium | Antwerp | Susato |
| 40, 43 | Ecclesiasticarum cantionum bk 11 | 1555[9] | Belgium | Antwerp | Susato |
| 11, 13, 30, **37** | Evangeliorum/II | 1555[10] | C. Germany | Nürnberg | Berg & Neuber |
| 6, **28, 29**, 35 | Evangeliorum/III | 1555[11] | C. Germany | Nürnberg | Berg & Neuber |
| 23, 41, 43 | Tertius liber modulorum | 1555[13] | Switzerland | Geneva | Guéroult Bosc |
| 3 | Cinquiesme livre ...tabulature (leut) | 1555[36] | N. France | Paris | Fezandat |
| 14, 19, 27 | LeipU 51 | 1555[+] | E. Germany | Leipzig | Michael Heger, dir.? |
| 2, 6, 7, 10, 13, 34, **38, 44, 48, 53** | CopKB 1873 | 1556 | Denmark | Copenhagen | |
| 5, **18**, 27, 42, **52** | DresSL Pirna VII | 1556 | E. Germany | Pirna | Albert Weissenberger |
| 15 | ZwiR 96/1 | 1556 | E. Germany | Wittenberg | Johann Wircker |
| 16, **38** | Cantionum sacrarum bk 8 | 1556[2] | Belgium | Louvain | Phalèse |
| 16 | Evangeliorum/VI | 1556][9] | C. Germany | Nürnberg | Berg & Neuber |
| 52 | Evangeliorum/V | 1556[8] | C. Germany | Nürnberg | Berg & Neuber |
| 30, **37** | Sextus liber modulorum | 1556[10] | Switzerland | Geneva | Bosc |
| 1, 11, 45 | Tabulatura...insignes et selectissimas | 1556[32] | E. Germany | Franfurt (an der Oder) | Johann Eichorn |
| 1 | Lautten Buch von mancherley schönen und lieblichen Stucken | 1556[34] | E. France | Strasbourg | Christian Müller |
| 23, 43 | Cantionum sacrarum bk 4 | 1557[5] | Belgium | Louvain | Phalèse |
| 4, 8 | Libro de cifra nueva para tecla, harpa, y vihuela...Luys Venegas de Henstrosa | 1557[2] | Spain | Alcala | Brocar |
| 3, 4, 11, 12, 35, 40 | FlorD 11 | 1557 in MS | N.C. Italy | Florence | Gianpiero Masacone |
| 1 | EdinU 64 | c.1557 | S.W. Scotland | Dumfries | |
| 1, 3, 6, 9 | Novum et insigne opus musicum 6v | 1558[4] | C. Germany | Nürnberg | Berg & Neuber |

| Motets | Source | Date | Country | City | Publisher or Scribe |
|---|---|---|---|---|---|
| 16, **38** | Cantionum sacrarum bk 8 | 1558[7] | Belgium | Louvain | Phalèse |
| 23, 41 | Primus liber modulorum | 1558[8] | Switzerland | Geneva | Arbillius |
| 5 | Troisieme livre tabulature de leut | 1558[19] | N. France | Paris | Fezandat |
| 1, 2, 3, 4, 5, 6, 9, 17, 22, 33, 48 | Tabulaturbuch auff die Lauten von Moteten | 1558[20] | S.W. Germany? | Heidelberg? | Johann Kohlen |
| 1, 5, 9, 11, 14, 23, 25, 34, 35, 41, 42 | Sixiesme livre de tabulature | 1558[21] | France | | |
| 4, 5, 6, 7, 11, 14, 19, **20**, 27, 33, **39**, 44, 45, **49**, 50 | RegB 940-1 | 1557-59 | Bavaria | Regensburg/ Wittenberg | Wolfang Küffer[+] |
| 2, 4, 5, 8, 10, 17, **18**, 22, 23, 43, 44, 48, **49**, 51 | Secunda pars magni operis musici | 1559[1] | C. Germany | Nürnberg | Berg & Neuber |
| 12, 33 | Tertia pars magni operis musici | 1559[2] | C. Germany | Nürnberg | Berg & Neuber |
| 23, 43 | Cantionum sacrarum bk 4 | 1559[3] | Belgium | Louvain | Phalèse |
| **18**, 37 | Quartus liber modulorum | 1559[5] | Switzerland | Geneva | Sylvius |
| 1, 7, 15, **18**, **20**, 49 | LeidGA 1439 | 1559 | Netherlands | Leiden | Anthonius de Blauwe |
| 2, 3, 11, 23 | LeidSM 1440 | 1559 | Netherlands | Leiden | Anthonius de Blauwe |
| 15 | VienNB Mus 16195 | 1559 title pg | E. Germany | | Caspar Peschel |
| 42 | BudOS P4 | post-1559 | E. Germany? | Bártfa | |
| 15, **31**, **32**, **39**, **49**, **53** | WarU 7.41.5.14 | 1559/1587 in MS | Poland | Olkusz | |
| 1, 3, 4, 5, 6, 7, 10, 11, 14, 16, **18**, 22, 23, 42, 43, 48, **49**, **52** | HradKM 29 | 1556-62 in MS | E. Bohemia | Hradec Králové | |
| 15 | MunBS 59 | 1556-63 | N.E.Germany | Borna or Wittenberg | Johann Wircker |
| 8, 11 | LucBS 775 | c.1540-60, | Belgium | | |
| 5, 8, 10, 15 | PiacD (5) | c.1540-60 | | Piacenza, prob. copied at | |
| 1, 5, 10, 19, 27, 45 | RegB B220-2 | c.1540-60 | Austria | Salzburg? | |
| 2, 3, 5, 7, 14; 1, 9, 22, 41 | LeidGA 1442 and 1441 | c.1540-60, + 1564-57 | Netherlands | Leiden | Johannes Flamingus [+] |
| 10, 51 | DresSL 1/D/ 3 | 1550-60 | E. Germany | Wittenberg | |
| 5, 17, 25, 27, 45, 50 | SionA 87-4 | 1550-60 | Silesia | Wroclaw | Simon Zmutt |

## Appendix VII  Core Repertory Sources 1560-70

| Motets | Source | Date | Country | City | Publisher or Scribe |
|---|---|---|---|---|---|
| 44, 51 | DresSL Grimma 59a | c.1560 | E. Germany | Meissen | Wolfgang Figulus[+] |
| 4, 8, 14 | ModE C.313 | c.1560 | N. Italy | Ferrara | Hernando Bustamante? |
| 31 | BudOS P3 | post 1560 | E. Germany? | Bártfa | |
| 38, **46** | OxfBT 341-44 | post 1560 | England | | |
| 16, **38** | Cantionum sacrarum vulgo moteta bk 8 | 1561[1a] | Belgium | Louvain | Phalèse |
| 2, 9 | Intabulatura di lauto di Francesco da Milano | 1561[17] | N. Italy | Venice | Gardane |
| 31, 42 | RegB 853-4 | 1561 in MS | Bavaria | Regensburg | Erasmus Zollner |
| 1 | Lautten Buch von mancherley schönen und lieblichen Stucken | 1562[24] | E. France | Strasbourg | Christian Müller |
| 1 | Cinquiesme livre de tabelature de luth contenant plusieurs motetz, et fantasies. | 1562[28] | N. France | Paris | Le Roy et Ballard |
| 23 | BerlS 40213 | 1562 in book | S.E. Germany | Halle | |
| 26, 31, 32 | StuttL 1 | 1562-63 | S.W. Germany | Stuttgart | Johann Chamberhueber |

| Motets | Source | Date | Country | City | Publisher or Scribe |
|---|---|---|---|---|---|
| 2, 9 | *Intabolatura de lauto di Francesco da Milano* | 1563[20] | N. Italy | Venice | Gardane |
| 1, 2, 9 | *Theatrum musicum* | 1563[25] | N. France | Paris | Phalèse |
| 4, 8, 15, 33, 51 | VatS 38 | 1563 | Italy | Rome | Johannes Parvus |
| 7, 47, 49 | BerlPS 40272 | 1563 on covers | Germany | | |
| 4, 7, 13, 15, 18, RegB 1018 27, 39, 45, 50 | | 1563 on covers | S. or C. Germany | | |
| 13, 28, 29, 30, 34 | *Thesauri musici Bk 1* | 1564[1] | C. Germany | Nürnberg | Berg & Neuber |
| 38 | *Thesauri musici 7 vc Bk 2* | 1564[2] | C. Germany | Nürnberg | Berg & Neuber |
| 42 | *Thesauri musici 5 vc Bk 4* | 1564[4] | C. Germany | Nürnberg | Berg & Neuber |
| 36, 54 | *Thesauri musici 6 vc Bk 3* | 1564[3] | C. Germany | Nürnberg | Berg & Neuber |
| 14, 19, 35, 41 | *Mottetti del fiore 4 vc Bk 1* | 1564[6] | N. Italy | Venice | Gardane |
| 14 | FLorD 27 | 1564 in MS | N.C. Italy | Florence | Gianpiero Masacone |
| 4, 23, 49, 52 | ZwiR 79/2 | 1564 in MS | E. Germany | Zwickau? | Schrei and Morgenstern |
| 28, 29, 30 | StuttL 22 | 1564-68 (1571) | S.W. Germany | Stuttgart    Chamerhueber | |
| 33 | *Valentini Greffi Bakfarci bk 1* | 1565[22] | S. Poland | Kraków | Andreae |
| 18, 23, 49 | DresSL Lob 12 | 1565 | Austria? | Vienna? | |
| 13, 22, 28, 29, 30, 34, 38 | KasL 38 | 1535-66 in MS | C. Germany | Kassel | Johann Heugel |
| 26 | *Il secondo libro intabolatura di liuto di Melchior Neysdler* | 1566[30] | N. Italy | Venice | Gardane |
| 25 | RosU 49/3 | 1566 | N.E.Germany | Hamburg | Jacob Praetorius |
| 13, 28, 29, 30 | KasL 143 | 1566 in MS | C. Germany | Kassel | Johann Heugel |
| 5 | LüneR 376 | 1566 or later | N.Germany | Lüneburg? | |
| 13 | StuttL 5 | 1566-67 | S.W. Germany | Stuttgart | Johann Chamberhueber |
| 23, 36, 39 | Ansbach 18 | 1566-67 in MS | | Germany | Ansbach    Friederich Lindner |
| 1, 3 | RomeSM 26 | 1566-67 | C. Italy | Rome | Johannes Parvus |
| 3, 3, 15, 42, 42 | WrocS 6 | 1567 | | | |
| 36 | TrevBC 6 | 1560-68 in MS | N. Italy | Treviso | |
| 1, 39 | *Novi atque catholici thesauri musicus bk 4* | 1568[5] | N. Italy | Venice | Gardane |
| 1, 2 | *Luculuntum theatrum musicum* | 1568[23] | Belgium | Louvain | Phalèse |
| 33 | *Valentini Greffi Bakfarci bk 1* | 1569[36] | S. Poland | Kraków | Andreae |
| 35 | KasL 43 | 1534-70 in MS | C. Germany | Kassel | Johann Heugel |
| 15, 36 | MunBS 266 | 1550-70 | Germany | Augsburg or vic. | Many |
| 16, 20, 27, 37 | RosU 42/1 | 1555-70 | N.E.Germany | Rostock | |
| 1, 17, 22, 33 | MunBS 267 | c.1550-70 | 7 scribes | | |
| 13, 16, 28, 29, 34, 38, 44 | StockKB 229 | 1560-70 | Sweden | Stockholm | |
| 13, 28, 29, 34 | StockKM 45 | 1560-70 | Sweden | Stockholm | |
| 7, 37, 43 | DresSL Pirna VIII | 1560-70 | E. Germany | Pirna | Albert Weissenberger |
| 2, 9, 48, 51 | KlagL 4/3 | c.1560-70 | | | |
| 19, 30, 30, 35, 40 | TrevBC 7 | 1555-71 | N. Italy | Treviso | |
| 16, 18 | KasL 91 | 1544-71 in MS | C. Germany | Kassel | Johann Heugel |

## Appendix VIII   Final Core Repertory Sources

| Motet | A | B | C | D | E | F | G | H | I | J | K | L | M | N | O | P | Q | R | S | T | U | V | W | X | Y |
|---|---|---|---|---|---|---|---|---|---|---|---|---|---|---|---|---|---|---|---|---|---|---|---|---|---|
| 47 | Ax3 | | | | E | | | | | | | | | | | | | R | | | | | | X | Y |
| 54 | | | | | | | | | I | J | K | | | | | | | R | | | | | | | Y |
| 13 | | | | | | | G | | I | J | | | | | | | | R | | | | | | | Y |
| 16 | | | | | E | | | | I | | | | | | | | | | S | | | | W | X | |
| 3 | A | | | | E | | | | | | K | L | | | | | | R | | | | | | X | |
| 46 | A | | | | | | | | | | K | | | | | P | | R | | | U | | W | | |
| 52 | A | | | | E | | | | | | | | | | | | | R | S | | | | W | | |
| 34 | | | | | | | G | | | | | | | | | | | Rx2 | | | | | W | | |
| 53 | | | | | | | Gx2 | | | | | | | | | | | | | | | | W | | |
| 31 | A | | | | | | | | I | J | K | | | | | | | R | | | U | V | | | |
| 39 | Ax3 | | | | | | | | | | | | | | | | | R | | | | V | | | |
| 26 | A | | | | | | G | | I | | | | | | | | | | | | | V | | | |
| 30 | Ax2 | | | | | | G | | | | | | | | | | | | | | | V | | | |
| 14 | A | | | D | | | | | | | | | | | | | | | | | | V | | | |
| 32 | A | | | | | | | | | | | | | | | | | | | | U | | | | |
| 42 | A | | | | E | | | | I | | | L | | | | | | R | | T | | | | | |
| 44 | A | | | | | | | | I | J | K | | | | | | | R | | T | | | | | |
| 37 | | | | | | | G | | | | | | | N | | | | R | S | | | | | | |
| 11 | | | | | E | F | G | | I | J | | | | | | | | R | S | | | | | | |
| 27 | | | | | | | | | | | | | | | | P | | | S | | | | | | |
| 4 | Ax2 | B | C | D | E | | | | I | | | | | | | | | | S | | | | | | |
| 20 | A | | | | | | G | | | | | | | | | | Q | R | | | | | | | |
| 28 | A | | | | | | | | | | K | | | N | | P | Qx2 | R | | | | | | | |
| 17 | Ax2 | | | | | | G | | I | J | | | M | | | | | R | | | | | | | |
| 18 | A | | | | E | | | H | I | | K | L | | | | | | R | | | | | | | |
| 23 | A | | | | E | | | H | I | J | | | | | | | | R | | | | | | | |
| 6 | A | | | | | | G | | | J | | | | | | | | R | | | | | | | |
| 7 | E | | | | | | G | H | I | | | | | | | | | R | | | | | | | |
| 50 | A | | | | | | G | H | | | | | | | | | | R | | | | | | | |
| 9 | A | | | | | | | | | | | | | | | | | R | | | | | | | |
| 38 | Ax2 | | | | | | | | | | | | | | | P | Q | | | | | | | | |
| 48 | | | | | | | | | | | | | | | | P | Q | | | | | | | | |
| 1 | | Bx2 | | D | E | | | | | | | | | | | P | | | | | | | | | |
| 5 | | B | | | | | | | | | | | | | | P | | | | | | | | | |
| 51 | A | | | | | | | | | | | | | | | P | | | | | | | | | |
| 2 | | Bx2 | | | E | | | | | | K | | | | O | | | | | | | | | | |
| 25 | A | | | | | | | H | | | | | | | O | | | | | | | | | | |
| 8 | A | B | | D | | | | | | | | | | | O | | | | | | | | | | |
| 29 | Ax2 | | | | | | | | | | | | | N | | | | | | | | | | | |
| 33 | A | | | | | | | | | | | | M | | | | | | | | | | | | |
| 49 | | | | | | | | | | | | | M | | | | | | | | | | | | |
| 45 | | | | | | | | | | | | L | | | | | | | | | | | | | |
| 43 | A | | | | E | | | H | | J | K | | | | | | | | | | | | | | |
| 10 | E | | | | | | | H | I | | | | | | | | | | | | | | | | |
| 36 | A | B | | | E | | | | I | | | | | | | | | | | | | | | | |
| 15 | Ax2 | | | | | | | | I | | | | | | | | | | | | | | | | |
| 40 | Ax2 | B | | | | | G | | | | | | | | | | | | | | | | | | |
| 35 | | | | | | | G | | | | | | | | | | | | | | | | | | |
| 41 | A | | | | | F | | | | | | | | | | | | | | | | | | | |
| 12 | | | | | | F | | | | | | | | | | | | | | | | | | | |
| 19 | | Bx3 | C | | | | | | | | | | | | | | | | | | | | | | |
| 24 | A | | C | | | | | | | | | | | | | | | | | | | | | | |
| 22 | A | B | | | | | | | | | | | | | | | | | | | | | | | |
| 21 | Bx2 | | | | | | | | | | | | | | | | | | | | | | | | |

| Appendix VIII (cont'd) | Source Key |
|---|---|

| | | |
|---|---|---|
| A | RegB 775-7    1579 in MS | |
| A | RegB 875-77 | 1568-79 |
| A | RegB 786-837 | 1569-78 in MS |
| A | RegB 891-2 | 1570-80 |
| A | RegB 893 | 1570-80 |
| A | RegB 960-3 | 1570-80 |
| A | RegB 930-9 | 1572-78 |
| A | RegB 863-70 | 1572-79 |
| A | RegB 844-8 | 1573-77 |
| A | RegB 883-86 | 1573-79 |
| A | RegB 871-74 | 1576-79 |
| A | RegB 861-2 | 1577 in MS |
| A | RegB 887-90 | 1577-78 |
| B | *Obras de musica para tecla arpa y vihuela* | 1578/24 |
| C | MadM 6832 | 1575-1600 |
| D | ParisBNC 851 | 1575-1600 |
| E | RokyA 22 | 1575-1600 |
| F | CoimU 32 | c.1575-1600 |
| G | WrocS 5 | c.1575-1600 |
| H | WrocS 8 | c.1575-1600 |
| I | LüneR 150 | 1575-1620 in MS |
| J | LübBH 203 | 1586-1613 |
| K | WrocS 11 | 1583 on covers |
| L | DresSL Grimma 57 | 1560-86 |
| M | GreifU 640-1 | 1539-88 |
| N | Novum pratum | 1592/6 (Brown) |
| O | ChelmE 2 | c.1596 |
| P | StockKM 15 | 1581, 1598 in MS |
| Q | VastS 68 | 1598 |
| R | DresSL Gl 5 | 1583-8; 1600 |
| S | WrocS 12 | c.1600, |
| T | WrocS 14 | c.1600 |
| U | NYorkP 4302 | 1613-19 ("Sambrook Manuscript") |
| V | RomeSC 792-5 | 1590-1620 |
| W | DresSL Grimma 7 | 1590-1621 |
| X | LevocaE 13990a | 1603-23 |
| Y | VastS 67 | 1597-1626 |

Mary Tiffany Ferer

# The Feast of
# St. John the Baptist and its
# Celebration in the Renaissance

When the season of spring appears to gladden all the world, every man bethinks him how to make fair the day of St. John, which follows at Midsummer … Marriages and other joyous occasions are deferred until that time, to do the festival honor … The whole city is in a hustle for the preparation of the festa; and the hearts of young men and women, who take part therein, are set on nought but dancing, playing, singing, banqueting, jousting, and other fair amusements, as though nought else were to be done in those weeks before the coming of St. John's eve.[1]

Thus, Goro di Stagio Dati, writing at the beginning of the fifteenth century, provides a vivid account of the celebration in Florence of the feast of the Nativity of St. John the Baptist, patron saint of the city.

The feast of the Nativity of St. John the Baptist on 24 June emerged in the fourth century as one of the most significant and widely celebrated feasts of the Christian year.[2] Cathedrals and chapels were dedicated to St. John in every region of the Christian world, and his relics were venerated throughout Western Europe and the Near East. St. John was celebrated in painting and sculpture and his name invoked against disease and misfortune.[3]

---

*. A version of this essay was read at the Allegheny Chapter Meeting of the American Musicological Society on 23 April 1977. The research is based on the author's dissertation, *The Feast of St. John the Baptist: Its Background and Celebration in Renaissance Polyphony* (University of Illinois at Urbana, 1976). It is with great affection and immeasurable gratitude that this essay is dedicated to Herbert Kellman, mentor and friend since 1967.

1. Goro di Stagio Dati, *Istoria di Firenze dall'anno MCC-CLXXXX all'anno MCCCCV* ; cited in Cesare Guasti, *Le feste di S. Giovanni Batista in Firenze* (Florence: Giovanni Cirri Editore, 1884), 4-9. This passage is quoted from John Addington Symonds, *Renaissance in Italy: Italian Literature in Two Parts*, Part 1 (New York: Henry Holt, 1888), 52.

2. During the fourth century fourteen oratories and churches were dedicated to St. John the Baptist in Constantinople. The basilica of St. John in the Lateran at Rome was perhaps the first sanctuary dedicated to the saint by the Western church. In the early years of the church basilicas and cathedrals in honor of the saint were also erected in Albano, Ostia, Ravenna, Naples, Monza, and Turin. St. John was frequently named the patron saint of baptisteries. There is some evidence that the baptistry in Florence was dedicated to the precursor as early as 589. St. John's ascetic life in the wilderness was taken as a model by several of the early monastic orders. An oratory at Montecassino and a monastery at Subiaco dedicated to St. John were erected by St. Benedict, founder of the Benedictine order.

3. It was first brought to my attention by Herbert Kellman that archival account books often begin their fiscal year with the feast of St. John the Baptist. In the preface to *Music in Late Medieval Bruges* (Oxford: Oxford

In 506, the Council of Agde ranked the feast of the Nativity of St. John the Baptist with the feasts of Easter, Christmas, Epiphany, Ascension, and Pentecost. All the faithful were required to attend Mass and to abstain from work.[4] Homilies of the fourth century likewise confirm the celebration of the feast in this period. St. Augustine provides seven sermons for the feast and implies that it had been celebrated prior to this period.

> This day of the nativity is handed down to us and is this day celebrated. We have received this by traditions from our forefathers and we transmit it to our descendants to be celebrated with like devotion.[5]

The pilgrimages of Westerners to the shrines associated with the life and ministry of St. John the Baptist also have their beginning in the fourth century. That St. John had been venerated prior to this period is indicated by the presence of sanctuaries at these sites.[6] The appearance of the name of St. John the Baptist in the martyrologies and calendars of the early church is indicative of the diffusion of the feast throughout Western Europe, and the rather fully developed cycle of masses for the feast in the earliest extant sacramentaries of the seventh century suggests an origin prior to this period.[7]

The first chapter of the gospel of Luke recounts the annunciation of the birth of St. John to the high priest Zechariah while the latter was serving in the temple. Since Zechariah was not allowed to enter the Holy of Holies, where he had the vision of the

---

University Press, 1985), vii-viii, Reinhard STROHM reports that "account books and similar registers often begin the year with 24 June or another feast day ..." In the fifteenth century the fiscal year at the Cathedral at Cambrai began on 24 June (Alejandro Enrique PLANCHART, "The Early Career of Guillaume Du Fay," *Journal of the American Musicological Society* 46 [1993]: 352). Craig WRIGHT in "Antoine Brumel and Patronage at Paris," *Music in Medieval and Early Modern Europe: Patronage, Sources and Texts* (Cambridge, 1981): 41, informs us that the sixteen unbeneficed clerks (or clerks of matins) of the cathedral choir at the Cathedral of Notre Dame in Paris "were required to resign *en masse* annually at the first capitular meeting after the feast of St. John the Baptist to be reappointed at the pleasure of the chapter."

4. *Sacrorum Conciliorum Nova et Amplissima Collectio,*8: Anno 492-536, ed. Joannes Dominicus MANSI, (Florence: Antonii Zatta Veneti, 1762; repr. Paris, 1901), 328.

5. *Sancti Aurelii Augustini, Hipponensis Episcopi, Opera Omnia,* Patrologiae Cursus Completus Series Latina, 38 (1865): 1320 (Sermon 292), translated in Sabine BARING-GOULD, *The Lives of the Saints,* (Edinburgh: John Grant, 1914), 6: 332.

6. Sanctuaries at the birthplace of St. John at '*Ain Karim,* the tomb at *Sebaste,* the grotto in the desert, and several baptismal sites in the region of the river Jordan existed from an early period and were the objects of pilgrimages from the West which began in the fourth century. Early pilgrimages are described in a letter of St. Jerome and in the *Peregrinatio Aetheriae,* an account by Egeria, a Spanish nun. See *Egeria: Diary of a Pilgrimage,* ed. and trans. George E. GINGRAS (New York: Newman Press, 1970).

7. The *Calendar of Carthage* compiled *c.*450 contains one of the earliest registers of a feast associated with St. John the Baptist. The following calendars and martyrologies compiled between the sixth and the ninth centuries include various feasts in honor of St. John:

- *Martyrologium Hieronymianum,*
- *Calendar of St. Willibrordus,*
- *Martyrology of the Venerable Bede,*
- *Martyrology of Florus,*
- *Small Roman Martyrology of Ado,*
- *Martyrologium Romanum.*

Mass formularies for St. John the Baptist appear in the Leonine, Gelasian, and Gregorian sacramentaries.

angel, except at the feast of the Tabernacles, the early church determined that the annunciation took place in September. The gospel account continues to report that in the sixth month the angel of the Lord appeared to the Virgin Mary to announce the conception of Christ. The Biblical account interprets the phrase "in the sixth month" as six months following the conception of John. Thus it follows that the celebrations of the births of St. John and Christ must likewise be rendered six months apart, with the feast of the Nativity of St. John in June preceding by six months the feast of the Nativity of Christ in December.

It is significant that the feast of the Nativity of Christ and the feast of the Nativity of St. John the Baptist coincide with the solar solstices. The choice provided the early church with the symbolic interpretation of St. John's words, "He must increase, but I must decrease," (John 3:30), as one reads in a sermon of St. Augustine.

> At the nativity of Christ the days increase in length, on that of John they decrease. When the Saviour of the world is born, the days lengthen; but when the last prophet comes into the world, the days suffer curtailment.[8]

The fourteenth-century writer, Jacobus da Voragine, in the *Golden Legend*, also elaborates on the mystical connection between the solstices and the nativity feasts.

> The fame of John who was taken for Christ must also sink. John says, He must increase, but I must decrease. At the time of the birth of St. John the days begin to grow shorter, whereas at the time of the birth of Christ, they grow longer, and it is written: *Solstitium decimo Christum praeit atque Johannem*, which means, the solstice is ten days before the birth of Christ and St. John. It was the same in their death; Christ's body was raised up on the Cross; the body of John was shortened by a head.[9]

The determination by the early church of the date of 24 June for the celebration of the feast of the Nativity of St. John the Baptist could well represent an attempt to Christianize the pagan midsummer festivities, which were celebrated throughout Western Europe annually on that date. James Frazer, in his exhaustive study of European folklore and customs, *The Golden Bough*, presents a vivid picture of those rituals, some of which persist to this day in parts of rural Western Europe.[10]

Seasonal flowers, herbs, and greenery gathered for the feast day and fashioned into wreaths, garlands, and a type of maypole erected on the village square, were often endowed with magical and therapeutic qualities. They were believed to provide protection from the ravages of the weather, witchcraft, and disease. Rituals often centered on the gathering and consuming of the pods of the locust or carob tree, which had nour-

8. BARING-GOULD, *The Lives*, 332.

9. Jacobus DA VORAGINE, *The Golden Legend*, trans. Granger RYAN and Helmut RIPPERGER (London: Longmans, Green and Co., 1941), I: 327.

10. James George FRAZER, *The Golden Bough: A Study of Magic and Religion*, abridged edition in one volume (New York: Macmillan, 1942).

ished St. John during his sojourn in the desert, as well as vegetation which took their popular names from the saint.[11]

The festivities frequently centered on the ritual burning of bonfires. Peasants gathered and danced around the flames, which were ignited in village squares, at the crossroads of primitive highways, and on the mountain heights. The fires purified the air and dispelled evil spirits. They provided a defense against witchcraft, thunder, hail, and disease. They were regarded as a prognosticator of the weather, the harvest, or success in marriage. Exposure to the flames and ashes of the St. John's fire promoted fertility, both human and agricultural, while the charred remains of the fire were believed to be endowed with therapeutic and curative qualities. Vestiges of human and animal sacrifice are suggested by the frequent bonfires—as the name implies—of bones. They are also reminiscent of the burning of the bones of St. John, which occurred during the reign of Julian the Apostate.[12]

Therapeutic qualities also extended to bathing rituals practiced on the feast day. It was believed that the water prevented illness and misfortune during the following year. In 1330 Petrarch described bathing on the feast day in the Rhine at Cologne. As Frazer suggests, "the parallel between ritualistic bathing and the redemptive rite of baptism instituted by St. John is suggestive and may explain why the church, in throwing its cloak over the old heathen festival, chose to dedicate it to St. John the Baptist."[13]

In no city was the veneration of St. John the Baptist more elaborately displayed than in Florence. A *cassone* painting by the early fifteenth-century Florentine Francesco di Antonio, depicting a marriage between the Adimari and Ricasoli families, provides a glimpse of Florence "decorated" for the feast day. The Baptistry appears in the background and the piazza is covered with a white and red awning. Trumpeters playing instruments with pennants decorated with the lily of Florence are positioned under the *Loggia del Bigallo*. The figures in the foreground, dressed in damask, velvet, and furs, and adorned with jewels and elaborate headgear, appear to be dancing. The painting calls to mind Dati's report that "marriage and other joyous occasions are deferred until that time, to do the festival honor."[14]

In Renaissance Florence the feast day was celebrated by processions, exhibitions, feasting, and the annual *palio* or horse race. These events often spanned several days, begin-

11. Rituals connected with the pagan celebration of midsummer as well as with the Christian celebration of the feast of St. John the Baptist are discussed in the author's dissertation and in FRAZER, *The Golden Bough*.

12. Jacobus DA VORAGINE, *The Golden Legend*, 326-27.

13. Paolo TOSCHI, "Giovanni Battista," *Enciclopedia Cattolica*, 6 (1951), 525; FRAZER, *The Golden Bough*, 154.

14. Bernhard BERENSON, *Italian Pictures of the Renaissance:* *The Florentine School in Two Volumes* (New York: The Phaidon, Press, 1963), plate 733. The painting, which is now in the *Accademia* in Florence is described in SYMONDS, *Renaissance in Italy*, 52. Anthony M. CUMMINGS in *The Politicized Muse: Music for Medici Festivals 1512-1537* (Princeton: Princeton University Press, 1992) devotes one chapter to a discussion of the celebration of the feast in Florence in 1514.

ning with those preceding the 24 June and climaxing with the presentation of the palio, the cloths that were specially woven for the occasion, to the winner of the horse race. The sixteenth-century diarist, Luca Landucci, reports that in 1514 the feast day was celebrated with a joust and the running of the palio, followed by fireworks in the evening.[15]

The processions and the elaborate *edifizi* or floats captured the attention of art historians and chroniclers alike. Vasari in his life of *Il Cecca* (Francesco d'Angelo) describes the *edifizi* exhibited by the guilds and confraternities in the processions which moved through the streets of Florence annually on the 24 June throughout the sixteenth century.

> The piazza of the Duomo was covered in with a broad blue awning—similar, we may suppose, to that veil of deeper and lighter azure bands which forms the background to Fra Lippi's "Crowning of the Virgin." This was sown with golden lilies, and was called a Heaven. Beneath it were the clouds, or *Nuvole*, exhibited by various civic guilds. They were constructed of substantial wooden frames, supporting an almond-shaped aureole, which was thickly covered with wool, and surrounded with lights and cherub faces. Inside it sat the person who represented the saint, just as Christ and Madonna are represented in the pictures of the Umbrian school. Lower down, projected branches made of iron, bearing children dressed like angels, and secured by waistbands in the same way as the fairies of our transformation scenes. The wool-work and the wires were hidden from sight by wool and cloth, plentifully sprinkled with tinsel stars. The whole moved slowly on the backs of bearers concealed beneath the frame . . . [16]

Matteo Palmieri's *Historia Fiorentina* describes a procession of *edifizi* in 1454, which lasted sixteen hours. Actors were seated on twenty towers or wooden cars, each depicting tableau scenes from Biblical history:

> On the 22nd day of June, the Cross of S. Maria del Fiore moved first, with all the clergy and children, and behind them seven singing men. Then the Companies of James the wool-shearer and Nefri the shoemaker, with some thirty boys in white and angels. Thirdly, the Tower (*edifizio*) of S. Michael, whereupon stood God the Father in a cloud (*nuvola*); and on the piazza, before the Signoria, they gave the show (*rappresentazione*) of the Battle of the Angels, when Lucifer was cast out of heaven . . . [17]

A similar account of the celebration of the feast in Florence in 1439 appears in the report of the general church council convened in the city at that time.

> The eve of the feast, 23 June, was also a public holiday, enlivened by a gigantic procession and a series of pageants. Various religious episodes were portrayed by illustrating the life

---

15. Luca LANDUCCI, *A Florentine Diary from 1450 to 1516*, translated by Alice DE ROSEN JERVIS, (London: Dent, 1927), 274.

16. Giorgio VASARI, *Lives of the Most Eminent Painters, Sculptors and Architects*, trans. Gaston DU C. DE VERE

(London: Philip Lee Warner Publisher to the Medici Society, 1912-14), 3: 193-200, as cited in SYMONDS, *Renaissance in Italy*, 318-19.

17. Matteo PALMIERI's chronicle written in 1454, *Historia Fiorentina*, as cited in SYMONDS, *Renaissance in Italy*, 316.

of Our Lord—the scene of Bethlehem with shepherds, Magi and a star, and beasts near the manger; a miracle of raising to life and the history of the Passion. The procession, to the sound of drums and trumpets, with holy relics, banners, crosses, contained besides grotesque figures of more than human size—hermits on high stilts, and huge paste-board effigies carried on the shoulders of men hidden in folds of drapery below—a St. Augustine on a kind of dais some 25 feet high haranguing the people and a St. George in deadly combat with the dragon. On the feast itself the city and its citizens displayed their riches of gold, silver, and precious fabrics. In the church of the Precursor some hundred banners were dedicated and ... more than a hundred lamps, high and low in the church, burned all night and dissipated the darkness.[18]

That midsummer celebrations of this kind took place throughout Western Europe is paralleled by the widespread appearance of polyphony associated with the feast of St. John the Baptist in the musical sources of the Renaissance. Polyphonic settings intended for the liturgical celebration of the feast in churches, chapels, and cathedrals appear in manuscript sources copied as early as c.1400 and as late as the end of the sixteenth century. Those manuscript sources considered in this study include the principal extant sources of fifteenth-century sacred polyphony as well as thirteen groups of sources associated with particular ecclesiastical institutions in the sixteenth century.

### The Fifteenth-Century Repertory

The repertory as found in the primary sources of fifteenth-century sacred music appears in Table 1. Settings appropriate for Mass and Vespers are found, and international as well as local composers are represented.

The repertory includes a Mass Ordinary cycle, a Mass Proper cycle, introits, antiphons, a responsory, hymns, and motets. The settings are almost without exception based on pre-existent chants traditionally assigned to the feast of the Nativity of St. John in the Gregorian as well as the Sarum traditions. Although St. John was honored by the church on several occasions during the liturgical year, the texts and pre-existent melodic material of the settings are derived entirely from the feast of the Nativity of St. John celebrated on 24 June.[19]

18. See Joseph GILL, *The Council of Florence* (Cambridge: University Press, 1959), 282–83. Geoffrey CHEW, "The Early Cyclic Mass as an Expression of Royal and Papal Supremacy," *Music & Letters* 53 (1972): 269, has suggested that the anonymous cyclic *Missa Fuit homo missus*, discussed in the following remarks as part of the fifteenth-century musical repertory for the feast, was composed for and performed at feast day festivities while the council was in session in 1439.

19. Throughout its history the church has honored St. John the Baptist with a number of feast days during the liturgical year: ; 23 September: Conception of St. John the Baptist (celebrated by the Eastern church); 24 September: Conception of St. John the Baptist (celebrated by the Western church); 24 February: Invention of the Head of St. John the Baptist; 25 May: Invention of the Head of St. John the Baptist; 29 August: Decollation of St. John the Baptist; 26 September: Translation of the Relics of St. John the Baptist; 13 January: Commemoration of the Baptism of Christ (celebrated by the Western church); 11 January: Commemoration of the Precursor (celebrated by the Eastern church).

The anonymous *Missa Fuit homo missus* is a *cantus firmus* mass. A gradual assigned to the feast in the Sarum liturgical sources appears with the same rhythmic configuration in the tenor of each mass movement. Stylistic features suggest an English origin contemporary with the masses of Leonel Power and Dunstable.[20] An anonymous Sanctus on the Vespers antiphon *Iste puer magnus* appears in MunBS 3154; however, the other sections of this mass have not been located, and no other complete Mass Ordinary cycle in the fifteenth-century sources that can be assigned to the feast has been identified.

The five sections of the anonymous Mass Proper cycle in TrentC 88 exhibit a liturgical unity, rather than cyclical procedures. There is no common *cantus firmus* unifying movements. In each section the pre-existent melody paraphrased in the superius corresponds to a chant bearing the same text. The cycle is one of sixteen proper cycles found in TrentC 88 whose composition and liturgical destination remains a subject of controversy.[21] Although attributed to Dufay in the first modern edition, the proper cycles of TrentC 88 were long thought to be the work of an anonymous composer.[22] More recent research suggests that the anonymous proper cycles may in fact have been composed by Dufay in the early 1440s for Cambrai.[23]

The Vespers hymn, *Ut queant laxis*, appears in every large collection of hymns from this period. Twenty-six survive. As is characteristic of the other liturgical settings appropriate for the feast, one of the monophonic melodies associated with the hymn is used as a structural voice. The settings in the Italian sources generally employ the chant which Bruno Stäblein in *Die mittelalterlichen Hymnenmelodien des Abendlandes* assigns No. 151; the settings in the German and Bohemian sources primarily use either Stäblein's No. 72 or No. 422.[24] The settings in the Trent codices derive from both the Italian and the German

20. Charles HAMM, "A Catalogue of Anonymous English Music in Fifteenth-Century Continental Manuscripts," *Musica Disciplina* 22 (1968): 54, 62, and 71; Gareth CURTIS in "Musical Design and the Rise of the Cyclic Mass," *Companion to Medieval and Renaissance Music*, (Berkeley: University of California Press, 1992): 155, suggests the dates of late 1420s or 1430s for this work.

21. Philip Stephen CAVANAUGH, *A Liturgico-Musical Study of German Polyphonic Mass Propers, 1490-1520* (Ph.D. diss., University of Pittsburgh, 1972), 1-7, and idem, "Early Sixteenth-Century Cycles of Polyphonic Mass Propers-An Evolutionary Process or the Result of Liturgical Reforms?" *Acta musicologica* 48 (1976): 151-65; see also Robert E. GERKEN, *The Polyphonic Cycles of the Proper of the Mass in the Trent Codex 88 and Jena Choirbooks 30 and 35* (Ph.D. diss., Indiana University, 1969).

22. Charles E. HAMM, *A Chronology of the Works of Guillaume Dufay Based on a Study of Mensural Practice* (Princeton: Princeton University Press, 1964), 131-36. The attribution to Dufay was first called into question

by Manfred BUKOFZER in his review of the Feininger 1947 edition of the Mass Propers, *The Musical Quarterly* 35 (1949): 335-37.

23. David FALLOWS, *Dufay* (London: J.M. Dent & Sons, 1982), 188-91; see also David FALLOWS, "Dufay and the Mass Proper Cycles of Trent 88," *I codici musicali trentini a cento anni dalle lore riscoperta: Atti del Convegno Laurence Feininger* (Trent, 1986): 46-59, and Alejandro Enrique PLANCHART, "Guillaume Du Fay's Benefices and His Relationship to the Court of Burgundy," *Early Music History* 8 (1988): 117-71.

24. Bruno STÄBLEIN, ed., *Die mittelalterlichen Hymnenmelodien des Abendlandes*, Band 1 of *Monumenta Monodica Medii Aevi* (Kassel: Bärenreiter, 1956). The identification of hymn settings in the sources was facilitated by three studies by Tom WARD: *The Polyphonic Office Hymn from the Late Fourteenth Century until the Early Sixteenth Century* (Ph.D. diss., University of Pittsburgh, 1969); "The Polyphonic Office Hymn and the Liturgy of Fifteenth Century Italy," *Musica disciplina* 26 (1972): 161-88; and *The Polyphonic*

traditions. Thus, it appears possible to establish a correlation between the monophonic model used and the origin of the polyphonic setting.

The Mass and Office items—the Ordinary and Proper cycles, as well as the individual antiphons, introits, hymns, and responsory—were most certainly prescribed for the same liturgical use as that of the chants on which they were based and were most likely sung as substitutes for chant. The liturgical function of the motets is less clear. Four-voiced and organized by isorhythmic techniques, the motets, with the exception of *Gaude tu baptista Christi*, are polytextual. The texts of the upper voices are sacred, however non-liturgical, and do not correspond to the texts prescribed for the Mass and Office on the feasts associated with St. John the Baptist.[25] A liturgical tenor has been identified only for Dunstable's *Preco preheminencie*.[26] The style of the tenors of the other motet settings suggests that they may also have liturgical origins as yet unidentified.

The liturgical use of the motets is thus problematic. The musical and textual style would seem to preclude the possibility of their substitution for chant in the Mass and Office. Ceremonial motets, like Dunstable's setting of *Preco preheminencie*, very likely performed at a service of thanksgiving at the Cathedral of Canterbury on 21 August 1416 in the presence of Henry V and the Emperor Sigismund, were composed for state occasions.[27] Those of a more devotional character were most likely performed at some point in the Mass or Hours of the feast day. For example, it has been suggested that the 71 motets in ModE X.1.11. were sung during Vespers, inserted into the prescribed liturgy.[28] In his study

*Office Hymn from 1400 to 1520: A Descriptive Inventory*, Renaissance Manuscript Studies 3 (Rome: American Institute of Musicology, 1979).

25. The text of *Gaude tu Baptista Christi* has been identified as Chevalier 6979 and is printed in *Analecta hymnica* 39: 173. Sources for the texts of *Preco preheminencie* and *Elisabeth Zachariae* have not yet been located. The condition of the manuscript (BolC Q15) prevents an accurate reading of *O baptista mirabiles*.

26. It is the antiphon, *Inter natos mulierum*, prescribed for the feast of the Nativity of St. John in the Sarum tradition (AS 436).

27. Margaret BENT in *Dunstaple* (London: Oxford University Press, 1981), 8, reports that the service of thanksgiving most likely was in response to reports which had arrived at Canterbury on 21 August 1416 "that the Duke of Bedford had broken the siege of Harfleur and won the Battle of Seine." According to Nicolas SANDON, "Fragments of Medieval Polyphony at Canterbury Cathedral" *Musica disciplina* 30 (1976): 42, Dunstable's motet is among the few which appear in an English source (Cant C3). Sandon also reports that two altars at the cathedral were dedicated to St. John and that the head of the saint was among the relics venerat-

ed there. The appearance of the motet in two continental sources, (ModE X.1.11. and TrentC 92), might possibly be explained by the presence of the Emperor Sigismund at the service at Canterbury. Reinhard STROHM in "European Politics and the Distribution of Music in the Early Fifteenth Century" *Early Music History* 1 (1981): 305-23, has explored the role of political events and diplomatic ties in the transmission of repertory in this period. Ann Besser Scott in "English Music in Modena, Biblioteca Estense, α X.1.11. and Other Italian Manuscripts," *Musica disciplina* 26 (1972): 148, suggests that the English repertory in some of the northern Italian sources of this period was collected by the emperor during this visit to England and transmitted to the Italians either at the Council of Constance or during his subsequent visit to Italy in 1431-1433.

28. Charles HAMM and Ann BESSER SCOTT, "A Study and Inventory of the Manuscript Modena, Biblioteca Estense, X.1.11.α (Mod B)," *Musica disciplina* 26 (1972): 102. The function and place of motets within the liturgical context of the Mass and Office has been explored in a number of studies. Although by no means a complete list, the following have provided useful information and valuable insights: Jeremy NOBLE, "The Function of

of PragP 47 Robert Snow proposed that the motets in this period were "intended for use either within the traditional liturgy at places where no sung items were prescribed officially (during the Canon of the Mass, at the conclusion of this service or of Office Hours, etc.) or at those places within newer services (stations within processions, devotional services at shrines, etc.) where the use of a sung item was prescribed, but the text to be used, either optional or fixed, new or borrowed from the traditional liturgy, had no melody associated with it specifically intended for use with it in only that situation."[29]

The fifteenth-century repertory provides a vivid picture of the celebration of the feast in this period. It indicates not only that polyphony was performed on the feast day in a number of ecclesiastical centers and locations, but it also indicates somewhat precisely which parts of the Mass and Office received polyphonic treatment. Some conclusions about the repertory and the liturgical practice of the period begin to emerge. The Mass Ordinary cycle and the Mass Proper cycle exist as isolated phenomena. The period exhibits little predilection to set these items polyphonically as a cycle. The introit appears in four additional settings. This suggests that while the other Mass items continued to be performed in plainsong, the introit for this particular feast began to receive polyphonic treatment. The repertory that is extant also would appear to indicate that Vespers was the only Office celebrated polyphonically on this feast in this period. The number of hymn settings in comparison with the other Vespers settings indicates that while the hymn repeatedly received polyphonic treatment, other Vespers items were rarely set.

The late fifteenth century was witness to the tendency to compile collections that would supply settings for every liturgical occasion on which polyphony might be used during the course of a year. It is significant that settings for the feast of the Nativity of St. John the Baptist appear in the major collections of hymn cycles in sources throughout the century, as well as in the yearly cycles of introits in AostaS D19, TrentC 90, and PragP 47; the Mass Proper cycles in TrentC 88; and the extensive collection of antiphons and motets in ModE X.1.11. It is a measure of the importance of the feast that it received a rather extensive polyphonic treatment in the fifteenth century.

Table 2 provides the date and provenance of each manuscript source for the fifteenth-century repertory. The sources were copied from about 1400 into the first decades of the sixteenth century. They were compiled as private anthologies and also as choirbooks that received extensive monastic and ecclesiastical use. With the exception of

Josquin's Motets," *Tijdschrift van de koninklijke vereniging voor nederlandse muziekgeschiedenis* 35 (1985): 9-22; Anthony M. CUMMINGS, "Toward an Interpretation of the Sixteenth Century Motet," *Journal of the American Musicological Society* 34 (1981): 43-59; James H. MOORE, *Vespers at St. Marks: Music of Alessandro Grandi, Giovanni Rovetta, and Francesco Cavalli*, 2 vols. (Ann Arbor: UMI Research Press, 1981); Richard SHERR,

*The Papal Chapel c.1492-1513 and Its Polyphonic Sources* (Ph.D. diss., Princeton University, 1975); and Bonnie J. BLACKBURN, *Music for Treviso Cathedral in the Late Sixteenth Century: A Reconstruction of the Lost Manuscripts 29 and 30* (London: Royal Musical Association, 1987).

29. Robert J. SNOW, *The Manuscript Strahov D.G. IV. 47* (Ph.D. diss., University of Illinois, 1968), 139.

CantC 3, the sources were copied on the continent, many in the region of northern Italy and southern Germany/Austria. Two manuscripts were copied in the peripheral region of Bohemia/Silesia. Correlations between the repertory and the date and provenance of the sources emerge:

1. The Vespers hymn, *Ut queant laxis,* appears in the sources throughout the fifteenth century and in virtually every major collection of hymns during this period. It emerges as the only liturgical item for the feast to receive extensive polyphonic treatment.

2. The polyphonic Mass Ordinary items and the polyphonic Mass and Office Propers are found in sources copied before *c.*1465, or in post-1465 sources whose contents are retrospective, (BerlPS 40098, PragP 47, and MunBS 3154). [30] The Mass Ordinary cycle and Brassart's setting of the introit for the feast most likely date from before 1450. The Vespers antiphons likewise date from the first half of the century and are found in manuscripts copied by *c.*1450 (TrentC 87 and ModE. X.1.11).

3. The liturgical settings, with the exception of the antiphons in ModE X.1.11, appear in sources of German provenance or in sources which show Germanic influence (for example, the Trent codices). [31]

4. The Vespers responsory, *Inter natos mulierum,* is found only in BerlPS 40098, copied in Silesia.

5. Motet settings for the feast were most likely composed by *c.*1435 and appear in sources copied by *c.*1450. The motets disappear from the repertory after mid-century.

6. Concordances have been identified for only the limited number of settings by composers of international reputation. A large portion of the repertory emanates from local composers and consequently did not have a wide circulation.

It is thus possible to reconstruct the liturgical composition of the feast as it was celebrated polyphonically in the fifteenth century. The manuscript sources would seem to indicate that prior to *c.*1440 polyphonic performance was limited to hymns and motets in a few local repertories. The period 1440-65 corresponds to the introduction of polyphonic antiphons, introits, Mass Ordinary and Mass Proper cycles in a large number of sources of sacred music copied in the region of southern Germany and northern Italy. Motet settings gradually disappear in the sources. After 1465 new settings of the hymn continue to appear in all of the sources, while other liturgical settings appear primarily in peripheral sources whose contents are retrospective. It is uncertain whether the liturgical settings copied in manuscripts about mid century continued in use after 1465.

---

30. The Mass Propers copied by scribe 1 in PragP are of the "middle to late Dufay-Binchois period 1440 to 1460," SNOW, 51.

31. WARD has noted in "The Polyphonic Office Hymn and the Liturgy of Fifteenth Century Italy," *Musica disciplina* 26 (1972): 176, that polyphonic introits in this period are found almost exclusively in German sources.

The liturgical settings in particular reveal not only the liturgical composition of the feast and the extent to which it was celebrated polyphonically, but would also seem to indicate the particular locations where the feast was celebrated in the fifteenth century. A number of sources may be associated with ecclesiastical situations. As indicated in Table 2, AptSA 16bis was copied for the papal chapel at Avignon during the Great Schism, while VatS 15 was compiled for the papal chapel at a later period. ModE X.1.11. is associated with the Este court chapel at Ferrara. MonteA 871 is associated with the Aragonese court at Naples. AostaS D19, section IV, and MunBS 3154 may contain part of the repertory of the imperial court chapel at Innsbruck, while TrentC 92-I and AostaS D19, sections II and II, have recently been shown to represent the repertory of the chapels at the Council of Basel.

Certain fifteenth-century sources can be shown to have been associated with the careers of several fifteenth-century composers. FlorBN 112bis was most likely compiled and copied by Antonius Janue, named in a 1456 payment order in Genoa and the recipient of thirteen attributions in the manuscript.[32] Johannes de Lymburgia is likewise closely associated with BolC Q15, a source which contains all his extant works. BolC Q15 may have been copied in Piacenza, a city which cannot be connected with the career of Lymburgia, however.[33] Nicholas Merques, known to have been a member of the chapel of the Council of Basel from November 1433 until at least 1436, is named as the composer of a setting of *Ut queant laxis* in TrentC 92-I, a source now believed to transmit the repertory used by the chapels at the Council of Basel (1431-49) and the court of the antipope Felix V, the former Amadeus VIII, Duke of Savoy.[34] Johannes Brassart's cycle of introits in AostaS D19 may also be part of the repertory used at the Council of Basel. Brassart's introit for the feast, *De ventre matris meae,* appears in the first portion of the manuscript copied *c.*1430-35 in Bologna in connection with the papal chapel. Brassart is known to have been a member of the papal chapel in 1431. This section of AostaS D19 was most likely taken to the Basel-Strasbourg area during the years of the council where later sections of the manuscript were copied and compiled. Documentary evidence places Brassart at the council in 1433. Brassart's introit for the feast more likely dates from his tenure at the papal chapel and the council than from his later tenure as a member of the imperial chapel of the Emperor Sigismund and his successors.[35]

32. Richard LOYAN, "Janue, Antonius," *The New Grove,* 9: 503-504.

33. Keith E. MIXTER, "Johannes de Lymburgia," *The New Grove,* 9: 666-67.

34. Tom R. WARD, "The Structure of the Manuscript Trent 92-I," *Musica disciplina* 26 (1975): 142-44; Tom R. WARD, "Merques, Nicolas," *The New Grove,* 12: 186-87.

35. Marian W. COBIN, *The Aosta Manuscript: A Central*

*Source of Early Fifteenth-Century Sacred Polyphony* (Ph.D. diss., New York University, 1978), 69-72. As Cobin points out, Keith MIXTER's conclusion in *Johannes Brassart and His Works* (Ph.D. diss., University of North Carolina, 1961), 83-85, that the introits were composed after *c.*1434 when Brassart became a member of the imperial chapel, is based on the assumption that AostaS D19 was copied entirely at the imperial court.

Several other settings have also been somewhat closely dated. Liturgical and stylistic evidence now suggest that Dufay's hymn cycle, of which *Ut queant laxis* is a part, was written not as previously proposed during the period of Dufay's tenure with the papal choir in 1428-33, but later between 1433 and 1435, coinciding with Dufay's residence in Cambrai and Savoy.[36] The anonymous *Elisabeth Zachariae*, attributed to Dufay, has been, on the basis of stylistic evidence, assigned a date of composition about 1430.[37]

The manuscript sources demonstrate that the feast was celebrated widely throughout western Europe as well as in the peripheral areas of Silesia and Bohemia. The pivotal role of the church councils in the transmission of music in this period is borne out by the polyphony for the feast in sources compiled during the councils.[38] The absence of concordances for all but a few works may attest to the particular popularity or merit of these works or it may simply indicate their random survival in multiple sources. The appearance of settings in sources whose provenance is geographically distant from the composer's sphere of activity raises considerable questions about the transmission of music in this period. The appearance of works by Binchois and Dunstable in ModE X.1.11., a source copied in Ferrara, a city which neither composer is recorded to have visited, may suggest that the works in question were considered distinguished enough to have been transmitted to a region remote from their place of origin. It may also indicate that these settings may have existed in other sources no longer extant. It would also imply that these particular items were sung as part of the liturgical celebration of the feast at the Este court in Ferrara. Does it also suggest that Binchois' setting of the antiphon, *Inter natos mulierum*, was also part of the repertory of the Burgundian court chapel during Binchois's tenure, although it survives in no extant manuscript associated with that court?

In the case of ModE X.1.11. Lewis Lockwood may have explained part of the missing link when he proposes that although this source seems to have been copied at Ferrara, "much of its basic contents may have been accumulated from outside and brought to the court,"[39] and that Benoit, who spent between 1438 and 1448 in Florence,

36. Heinrich BESSELER, "Dufay in Rom," *Archiv für Musikwissenschaft* 15 (1958): 10. Charles HAMM in "Dating a Group of Dufay Works," *Journal of the American Musicological Society* 15 (1962): 68-70, revised Besseler's earlier dating, reasoning that the hymn cycle was composed between 1433 and 1435 during Dufay's residence in Cambrai or Savoy. The argument that the cycle was composed in Savoy was strengthened by the work of Ward in "The Polyphonic Office Hymn and the Liturgy of Fifteenth Century Italy," *Musica disciplina* 26 (1972): 185-86, which found the cycle to be inconsistent with the melodic and liturgical traditions of the papal chapel as well as with those of Cambrai.

37. Charles E. HAMM, *A Chronology of the Works of Guillaume Dufay Based on a Study of Mensural Practice* (Princeton: Princeton University Press, 1964), 70, 72-73.

38. Geoffrey CHEW suggests in "The Early Cyclic Mass as an Expression of Royal and Papal Supremacy," *Music and Letters* 53 (1972): 269, that the anonymous *Missa Fuit homo missus* was possibly intended for the celebration of the feast in Florence during the Council of Florence.

39. Lewis LOCKWOOD, "Dufay and Ferrara," *Papers Read at the Dufay Quincentenary Conference, Brooklyn College, December 6-7, 1974* (New York: Department of Music, School of Performing Arts, Brooklyn College, CUNY, 1976): 9.

but subsequently returned to Ferrara, "could well have brought music back to Ferrara when he returned."[40] Among Benoit's six extant works apparently composed in the 1430s and 1440s are two settings appropriate for the feast. Both may date from Benoit's tenure in Florence, possibly composed for the Florentine celebration of St. John, patron saint of the city, before they were brought to Ferrara.[41] It becomes apparent that the feast was more widely celebrated polyphonically than the manuscript sources would indicate.

## The Sixteenth-Century Repertory

Polyphony appropriate for the feast of St. John the Baptist appears in a large number of sixteenth-century sources. Thirteen groups of manuscripts that may be associated with particular ecclesiastical institutions in this period are considered here. The sources are frequently liturgically organized and rubrics occasionally appear with the settings. The repertory includes items for the Mass and the Office of Vespers: hymns, antiphons, responsories, introits, sequences, Mass Proper cycles, and motets. Three large groups of manuscript sources emerge: the Italian cathedral sources, the German pre-Reformation sources, and the Lutheran sources.

## The Italian Cathedral Sources

Manuscripts copied at the cathedrals of Casale Monferrato, Florence, Modena, Padua, and Treviso were selected for this study as representative of the liturgical situation at Italian cathedrals during the sixteenth century. All except the Treviso and the Florence choirbooks were copied in the first half of the sixteenth-century and are pre-Tridentine. It is in fact questionable whether the Treviso sources, copied between 1552 and 1572 and contemporary with the Council of Trent, were influenced to any great extent by the reforms of the council. The following is a summary of these sources:

Casale Monferrato (CasAC): seven paper choirbooks copied at Casale Monferrato for use by the cathedral choir by 60 or more scribes associated with the cathedral between 1515 and 1545. These manuscripts contain only sacred music. Except for the cycle of hymns in manuscript C, the items are not arranged in liturgical order. A number of the settings appear to have been copied from prints. The choirbooks copied before 1533 may show the influence of the ruling Paleologo family and the close alliance of Casale Monferrato with the Duchy of Savoy and the French court. These sources contain works by Franco-Flemish composers. After 1533 Casale Monferrato came under the political con-

40. Lewis Lockwood, *Music in Renaissance Ferrara: 1400-1505: The Creation of a Musical Center in the Fifteenth Century* (Cambridge: Harvard University Press, 1984), 57 and 62. Benoit may be "Benotto di Giovanni" who was hired in Ferrara in 1438 as well as the musician identified as "Benedette di Giov. dito Benoit, chantadore de la

chapela" listed in 1448 as a musician in the ducal chapel of Ferrara. See also Hamm and Scott, 113 and 120, and Frank D'Accone, "The Singers of San Giovanni in Florence During the 15th Century," *Journal of the American Musicological Society* 14 (1961): 310-13.

41. Tom R. Ward, "Benoit," *The New Grove*, 2: 505.

trol of the Gonzagas of Mantua. The choirbooks copied during this period contain works by local composers as well as northern composers employed in Italy. Polyphony for the feast of St. John the Baptist appears in manuscript C (copied 1538-*c*.1545) and manuscript D(F) (early layer copied 1521-*c*.1526; later layer copied 1538-*c*.1545).[42]

Florence (FlorD): a group of choirbooks copied in Florence between *c*.1480 and 1570. The scribe for manuscripts 4, 11, 27, and 28 was connected with the Medici court and the church of San Lorenzo. Settings for the feast are found in manuscript 4 (copied 1563), manuscript 11 (copied 1557), manuscript 28 (copied mid sixteenth century), and manuscript 46 (third quarter of the sixteenth century).[43]

Modena (ModD): A group of choirbooks copied in Modena for use by the cathedral choir. The main scribe of choirbook III is Eustachius de Monte Regali, *maestro di cappella* at the cathedral between 1520 and 1524. Choirbooks IV and IX show evidence of being composites of originally separate fascicles which were combined at the end of the sixteenth century. Polyphony for the feast of St. John the Baptist is found in manuscript III (copied 1520-1524, with later additions *c*.1524-1530), manuscript IV (copied *c*.1520-1530), and manuscript IX (copied *c*.1520-1530, with late sixteenth-century additions).[44]

Padua (PadBC): four choirbooks copied during the first half of the sixteenth century for use at the cathedral of Padua. Manuscripts D25 and D26 contain polychoral psalms for Vespers. Polyphony for the feast appears in manuscripts A17 and D27. Both were copied by the same scribe, identified as Fra Giordano Pasetto, *maestro di cappella* at the cathedral from 1520 until his death in 1557. Choirbook A 17 bears the date 1522. Choirbook D27 was probably copied between 1541 and 1550. PadBC A17 preserves works by the Josquin generation; PadBC D27 preserves works by the post-Josquin generation. Both contain a number of settings copied from prints. The two choirbooks complement each other and together represent the repertory in use during Pasetto's tenure at the cathedral.[45]

Treviso (TrevBC): choirbooks copied at Treviso during the second half of the sixteenth century for use at the cathedral. Seven choirbooks were destroyed by a bombing raid on Treviso in 1944; eleven are still extant. The contents of these destroyed manuscripts are known through the notes and incipits made by the cathedral librarian, Giovanni d'Alessi, prior to World War II. Several of the manuscripts are ordered according to the

42. Information about these sources as well as the others discussed in this essay is from *Census Catalogue of Manuscript Sources of Polyphonic Music 1400-1550*, 5 vols., Renaissance Manuscript Studies, 1 (American Institute of Musicology, 1979-82). David CRAWFORD, *Sixteenth-Century Choirbooks in the Archivio Capitolare at Casale Monferrato*, Renaissance Manuscript Studies, 2 (American Institute of Musicology, 1975).

43. David A. SUTHERLAND, "A Second Corteccia Manuscript in the Archives of Santa Maria del Fiore," *Journal of the American Musicological Society* 25 (1972): 79-85.

44. David CRAWFORD, *Vespers Polyphony at Modena's Cathedral in the First Half of Sixteenth Century* (Ph.D. diss., University of Illinois at Urbana, 1967).

45. John George CONSTANT, *Renaissance Manuscripts of Polyphony at the Cathedral of Padua* (Ph.D. diss., University of Michigan, 1975).

liturgical year. Precise dating of the choirbooks is occasionally possible where the local scribes recorded not only the year but also the day and hour of copying. Polyphony for the feast appears in manuscripts 3 (copied 1556-70), 4 (copied 1559-69), 5 (copied 1559-72) , 7 (copied 1558-71), 8 (copied 1556-69), 13 (copied 1562 and 1565) and 25 (copied *c.*1560-75). Manuscripts 3, 4, and 5 were among the choirbooks destroyed in 1944.[46]

The repertory for the feast in the selected Italian cathedral manuscripts is found in Table 3. It includes polyphonic settings of Mass and Vespers propers as well as motets. The frequent use of pre-existent material, the strict adherence to the liturgical text, and the frequent inclusion of liturgical rubrics with the proper settings suggest that they were very likely substituted for the chant propers in the celebrations of the feast.

The Mass Proper cycle for the feast in FlorD 46 is part of the fourteen cycles to which Francesco Corteccia, Florentine organist and composer, may have referred in the preface of his *Hinnario* (Biblioteca Mediceo-Laurenziana Pal.7). The cycles were probably completed *c.*1544, contemporary with Corteccia's tenure as *maestro di cappella* at the court of the Duke Cosimo de Medici as well as at the Baptistry of S. Giovanni Battista and the Cathedral of Santa Maria del Fiore.[47] The "counterpoints newly made on the *canto fermo* of the Solemn Masses" to which Corteccia refers are the proper settings in which the *cantus firmus* appears in non-mensural black notation in the bassus.[48] Several anonymous liturgical settings appropriate for the feast in TrevBC 5 exhibit a similar style. The notes compiled by Giovanni d'Alessi prior to the destruction of the manuscript in 1944 indicate that the *cantus firmus* bearing voice in the following propers is also notated in non-mensural black notation:

| Incipit | Liturgical Function | Chant Notation |
|---|---|---|
| Pro eo quod non credisti | Unknown | Bassus |
| Ingresso Zacharia | Magnificat antiphon | Tenor |
| Puer qui natus est nobis | Magnificat antiphon | Bassus |
| De ventre matris meae | Introit | Bassus |
| De ventre matris meae | Introit | Bassus |
| Ingresso Zacharia | Magnificat antiphon | Tenor |
| 2p. Puer qui natus est nobis | | |

The even note values (unbroken semibreves) of the tenor *cantus firmus* in an additional setting (*Puer qui natus est nobis* in TrevBC 25) imply that this setting like those above

46. Giovanni d'ALESSI, "I Manoscritti Musicali del Sec.XVI° del Duomo di Treviso (Italia)," *Acta Musicologica* 3 (1931): 148-55; Bonnie J. BLACKBURN, *Music for Treviso Cathedral in the Late Sixteenth Century: A Reconstruction of the Lost Manuscripts 29 and 30* (London: Royal Musical Association, 1987).

47. SUTHERLAND, "A Second Corteccia Manuscript," 79-85.

48. Ibid., 81 and 84. Apparently each pitch in the bassus was sung to the value of a semibreve. Thus the bassus in these settings is simply the unaltered and unelaborated chant associated with the text in the monophonic tradition.

may also have been substituted for the corresponding chant, the Magnificat antiphon on which it is clearly based.

The use of pre-existent chant in the Italian cathedral settings is limited to the polyphonic settings of the Mass and Vespers propers discussed above and to the six settings of the Vespers hymn assigned to the feast in CasAC C, FlorD 28, ModD 3 and 4, and TrevBC 3, 13, and 25.

The liturgical role of the motets in the ecclesiastical celebration of the feast is less clear. All are based on liturgical texts. However, the independence from pre-existent material which characterizes these settings, as well as the manipulation of, rather than strict adherence to, the prescribed texts for the feast most likely precludes the possibility that these motets were substituted for Gregorian items in the Mass and Office.

Some conclusions about the repertory begin to emerge:

1. The sources contain *cantus firmus* based liturgical settings which could be substituted for the monophonic portions of the Mass and Office as well as motets based on liturgical texts. The liturgical settings include Vespers hymns, the Mass Proper cycle, and polyphonic antiphons and introits. Mass propers are found in the Florence and Treviso choirbooks; Vespers propers appear in the Florence, Treviso, Casale Monferrato, and Modena choirbooks.

2. Motets appropriate for the feast are found in all the Italian cathedral sources considered here. Motets and hymns appear in the Casale Monferrato and Modena sources; motets, hymns, and liturgical propers are found in the Florence and Treviso choirbooks. The repertory for the feast in the Padua choirbooks consists exclusively of motets.

3. There are no Mass Ordinary cycles or sections specifically designated for the feast in the Italian cathedral sources considered here.

4. Franco-Flemish composers who spent part of their careers in Italy as well as Italians are represented in the repertory. The liturgical settings are primarily the work of native Italians, often local composers. The motets are primarily the work of Franco-Flemish composers of international reputation.

5. Polyphony for the feast appears together in the choirbooks copied for the cathedrals at Treviso, Padua, and Florence. These sources are liturgically organized.

6. The settings in the choirbooks copied at Casale Monferrato, Modena, and Padua are contemporary with the copying of these manuscripts. In some cases the polyphony for the feast in these sources predates its appearance in print. On the other hand, several of the motets by well-known international composers in the Florence and Treviso choirbooks are retrospective. Most liturgical settings in these sources, especially those by local composers (Corteccia in Florence, and N. Olivetus and Jan Nasco in Treviso) are contemporary with the copying of these sources.

The Italian cathedral manuscripts provide a vivid picture of the liturgical celebration of the feast at five locations in sixteenth-century Italy. The repertory of each collection of sources, whether copied from existing prints and manuscripts or composed expressly for a local celebration of the feast, represents an attempt to meet the liturgical requirements as they existed in this period. A number of settings may have been composed at Florence, a city which held St. John the Baptist in particular veneration. Three of the composers represented in the repertory—Corteccia, Isaac, and Verdelot—spent all or a large part of their careers in Florence, and while it is possible to establish that the liturgical and motet settings by Corteccia and Isaac in the Italian cathedral sources considered here were composed during their tenures in Florence,[49] it is tempting to propose that Verdelot's setting of *Gabriel archangelus* was also composed during his tenure in Florence. Documentary evidence places Verdelot in Florence as early as 1521.[50]

The liturgical settings had a limited circulation in Italy. The *cantus firmus* based settings in TrevBC 5, the hymn settings in TrevBC 3 and 13, Chamatero's polyphonic antiphon in TrevBC 25, as well as Corteccia's Mass Proper cycle in FlorD 46 are unica. Print and manuscript concordances exist only for the settings of *Ut queant laxis* in CasAC C, TrevBC 25, ModD 3 and 4, and FlorD 28.

Jacquet of Mantua's setting of the hymn in CasAC C (copied between 1538 and c.1545) may predate any of its printed sources. Carpentras' setting in ModD 3 and 4 may also precede Channay's publication at Avignon in c.1535. Corteccia's setting of *Ut queant laxis* most likely composed between 1542 and 1544 is found in four Florentine sources. It appears in FlorL Med. Pal. 7 as part of a cycle of hymns entitled *Hinnario di Francesco Corteccia secondo l'uso della Chiesa Romana et Fiorentina* dedicated to his patron, Duke Cosimo de Medici. An earlier version of the *Hinnario* without attribution was copied in FlorD 28, part of the collection of choirbooks that contain the repertory of the cathedral. Both sources date from Corteccia's tenure at the baptistry and the cathedral. The two later sources were compiled after Corteccia's death in 1571 and attest to the popularity of this setting into the early years of the seventeenth century.[51] Only Jacquet of Mantua's setting of *Ut queant laxis* appears more than once in the manuscript groups considered here. Apparently each cathedral to some extent preferred liturgical settings by local composers and the hymns available in a small number of prints in this period.

49. Martin Just, "Heinrich Isaacs Motetten in Italienischen Quellen," *Analecta musicologica* 1 (1963): 4-5, assigns the composition of *Prophetarum maxime* to c.1484-1494/96, the period in which Isaac was employed by the Medici at Florence.

50. Richard Sherr, "Verdelot in Florence, Coppini in Rome, and the Singer 'La Fiore'," *Journal of the American Musicological Society* 37 (1984): 402-404. According to

Norbert Böker-Heil, *Die Motetten von Philippe Verdelot* (Frankfurt am Main, 1967), Verdelot's setting of *Gabriel archangelus* was most likely composed between 1527 and 1530, and first printed in 1532.

51. Frank A. D'Accone, ed., *Music of the Florentine Renaissance*, vol. 12, Corpus Mensurabilis Musicae, 32 (Rome: American Institute of Musicology, 1996), xix-xxiv.

Motets appear in all of the Italian cathedral manuscript groups considered here. The composers represented include members of the Josquin as well as post-Josquin generation. Composed between c.1480 and 1550 primarily by Franco-Flemish composers who either spent part of their careers in Italy or traveled there in the retinue of a patron, many of the motets had a wide and extensive distribution in the sources of the sixteenth century. Most likely copied from prints, their appearance in the Italian cathedral sources reflects their widespread popularity and circulation in the prints of the period.

## The German Pre-Reformation Sources

Table 4 presents the repertory for the feast as it is found in two groups of German pre-Reformation sources, the two choirbooks copied at the cathedral in Annaberg and the seven paper manuscripts copied for All Saints Church at Wittenberg. Both groups of sources were copied during the first quarter of the sixteenth century in Saxony, an area which became predominantly Lutheran in the early years of the Reformation. As such they may be considered representative of the liturgical situation in Germany immediately prior to the Reformation.

Annaberg Choirbooks (DresSL): two choirbooks probably copied in the early sixteenth century at Wittenberg and taken to Annaberg for use at the *St. Annenkirche*. Brought to the Dresden *Sächsische Landesbibliothek* in 1968, they appear to have been copied between 1510 and 1530. The contents of the choirbooks are exclusively sacred, and for the most part liturgical settings for the Mass and Office. The majority of the anonymous settings are probably the work of German composers from the end of the fifteenth century. Many of the ascribed pieces are by Netherlanders.[52]

The Annaberg choirbooks contain two settings of the Vespers hymn, *Ut queant laxis*, and one setting of *Sancti Baptistae Christi*, a sequence appropriate for the feast. The hymns follow the fifteenth-century procedure of using the same polyphonic setting for each verse. Both hymns use the same *cantus firmus*, Stäblein's melody No. 72, a source for a number of polyphonic hymns in the German manuscripts of the fifteenth century. Adam von Fulda's setting may date from his tenure between 1490 and 1505 at the court of Friedrich the Wise and the University of Wittenberg.[53] The two anonymous settings are contemporary with the copying of the choirbooks or date from the end of the fifteenth century. They are in all probability, because of their style and liturgical nature, the works of local German composers.[54]

---

52. Thomas L. NOBLITT, "Manuscript Mus. I/D/505 of the Sächsische Landesbibliothek Dresden (*olim* Annaberg, Bibliothek der St. Annenkirche, Ms. 1248)," *Archiv für Musikwissenschaft* 30 (1973): 275-310; Idem, "Manuscript Mus. I/D/506 of the Sächsische Landesbibliothek Dresden (olim Annaberg, Bibliothek der St. Annenkirche, Ms. 1126)," *Musica disciplina* 28 (1974): 81-127.

53. Klaus Wolfgang NIEMÖLLER, "Adam von Fulda," *The New Grove*, I: 102.

54. NOBLITT, "Manuscript Mus. I/D/505," 278.

Jena Choirbooks (JenaU): seven paper manuscripts (JenaU 30, 31, 32, 33, 34, 35, and 36) at the *Universitätsbibliothek* at Jena, copied between 1500 and 1520 for All Saints Church at Wittenberg. The physical characteristics and the repertory of these choirbooks suggest a group of sources distinct from the parchment choirbooks copied at the Netherlands court in Brussels/Mechlin, also found in the same collection. Scribal concordances exist among manuscripts 30, 31, 32, and 33 and between manuscripts 34 and 35. Choirbooks 30, 33, and 35 contain propers for the temporal and sanctoral cycles arranged in the order of the liturgical year. JenaU 30 contains 82 Mass proper sections, many of which, on the basis of stylistic grounds, may be the work of Adam Rener, who from 1507 until 1520 was in the service of Friedrich the Wise. JenaU 30 includes a Mass Proper cycle for the feast of the Nativity of St. John the Baptist and a Mass Proper cycle for the Decollation of St. John.[55] Both are unattributed and each contains four items—introit, alleluia, sequence, and communion. A plainchant *cantus firmus* functions as a structural basis for each setting. The cycles apparently enjoyed a long popularity for several of the items are found in the late sixteenth-century Lutheran sources, DresSL Pirna VI and RosU 49.

The repertory in the German pre-Reformation sources considered in this study exhibits the following characteristics:

1. The settings are liturgical and were most likely substituted for the monophonic portions of the Mass and Office. No motets appear in the sources.

2. The settings are all *cantus firmus* based.

3. With the exception of Adam von Fulda, the composers of the repertory are unnamed. The unattributed settings are probably the works of local German composers.

4. In its dependence on pre-existent materials and liturgical character, the repertory presents a conservative musical style consistent with that of the repertory for the feast in the fifteenth-century manuscripts of German provenance.

A number of the settings for the feast in the German pre-Reformation manuscripts are unica. Several other settings had a limited circulation in manuscripts copied in Saxony contemporary with the Annaberg and Jena choirbooks (as for example, LeipU 1494) or in sources originating at Lutheran centers later in the sixteenth century (as for example, RosU 49 and DresSL Pirna VI). No concordances for this repertory have been found in sixteenth-century prints.

---

55. Kathryn Ann P. DUFFY, *The Jena Choirbooks: Music and Liturgy at the Castle Church in Wittenberg Under Frederick the Wise,* *Elector of Saxony* (Ph.D. diss., University of Chicago, 1995).

## The Lutheran Sources

The celebration of the feast of St. John the Baptist in a number of Lutheran centers in the sixteenth century is indicated by the appearance of a repertory appropriate for the feast in six representative groups of sources copied between c.1540 and 1570 in Germany.

The Heilsbronn Choirbooks (ErlU): four choirbooks now in the *Universitätsbibliothek* at Erlangen, copied at the Cistercian monastery at Heilsbronn between 1540 and 1548. The repertory is Lutheran, reflecting the sympathetic attitude toward the Reformation at the monastery. The Heilsbronn choirbooks, along with the Stutttgart choirbooks also examined in this study, form the most important group of sources of polyphonic sacred music in Protestant South Germany. Originally part of a group of seven manuscripts, the Heilsbronn choirbooks were copied by Johannes Hartung, *Klosterrichter* at the monastery. An addition to manuscript 473/4 was probably made by Hartung's son-in-law, composer Caspar Othmayr, in 1545. The choirbooks are devoted to sacred music arranged approximately in the order of the liturgical year. The liturgical character of the choirbooks suggest that they were compiled for ecclesiastical use, rather than as a private collection, and that the repertory may have been sung by the *Lateinschule* of the monastery. The Heilsbronn choirbooks preserve a Lutheran repertory, much of it copied from the prints of Rhau, Petreius, Formschneider, and others. Largely represented are German and Netherlandish composers of the Josquin and Senfl generations. The choirbooks contain six Mass Proper cycles from the second part of Isaac's *Choralis Constantinus*, for which no other dated manuscript source prior to the Formschneider print of 1555 is known. Settings appropriate for the feast of St. John the Baptist appear in manuscript 473/2 (dated 1548), and manuscript 473/4 (copied in 1540-41, with an addition made in 1545).[56]

Leipzig *Thomaskirche* Partbooks (LeipU): two sets of partbooks copied at Leipzig during the middle of the sixteenth century, perhaps under the direction of Melchior Heger, cantor at the *Thomaskirche* from 1553 to 1564. Scribal concordances exist between both sets of partbooks. The repertory in LeipU 49/50 is arranged by genre and ordered according to the liturgical year. LeipU 51 consists of two extant partbooks (tenor and bassus) bound in 1555, and may have been compiled for use by the students of the *Thomasschule*. Although it is uncertain whether the partbooks were used at the *Thomaskirche*, the repertory is representative of Lutheran service music favored at Leipzig and other centers in Saxon Germany. Many of the settings in LeipU 51 appear to have been copied from contemporary German prints.[57]

56. Franz KRAUTWURST, "Die Heilsbronner Chorbücher der Universitätsbibliothek Erlangen (Ms. 473, 1-4)," *Jahrbuch für Fränkische Landesforschung* 25 (1965): 273-324; 27 (1967): 253-82.

57. Laura YOUENS, *Music for the Lutheran Mass in Leipzig, Universitätsbibliothek, MS. Thomaskirche 49/50* (Ph.D. diss., Indiana University, 1978); Thomas NOBLITT, "A Reconstruction of Ms. Thomaskirche 51 of the Universitätsbibliothek Leipzig (*olim* III, A. α 22-23)," *Tijdschrift van de koninklijke vereniging voor nederlandse muziekgeschedenis* 31 (1981): 16-72.

Pirna Choirbooks (DresSL Pirna): nine choirbooks copied for the *Stadtkirche St. Marien* at Pirna between 1550 and 1580. Moved to the *Sächsische Landesbibliothek* at Dresden in 1899, the single dated work in the extant choirbooks is a six-voice Mass by Scandello in Pirna I, dated 1562. Pirna VI contains two settings appropriate for the feast of St. John the Baptist.[58]

Rostock, *Universitätsbibliothek*, MS Mus. Saec. XVI-49 1-6 (RosU 49): six paper partbooks, the so-called *Opus musicum* of Jacob Praetorius, organist and *Kirchenschreiber* at St. Jacob and St. Gertrud in Hamburg from 1555 until 1586. The partbooks are dedicated to Johann Albrecht I (d.1576), Duke of Mecklenburg-Schwerin, and his brother Duke Ulrich III (d.1603). Copied by Praetorius, largely from Rhau prints, the pieces are grouped according to liturgical categories. The title page bears the date 1566. The partbooks bear the characteristics of a presentation manuscript and their excellent condition suggests that they were never used for practical music making. However, the repertory, which is sacred, fulfills the liturgical requirements of the Lutheran Reformation, which Johann Albrecht had supported in Mecklenburg. The title page indicates that the repertory follows the rite of the church in Saxony. The majority of composers represented are Protestants who wrote for Wittenberg. The Mass Ordinary cycles are by Netherlandish composers. Almost exclusively Latin-texted, the partbooks represent a comprehensive collection for liturgical use by the Lutheran church.[59]

Stuttgart Choirbooks (StuttL): a set of choirbooks, copied in Stuttgart between 1538 and 1570 for use at the court chapel of Ulrich, Duke of Württemberg (1487-50). The court became Lutheran in the early 1530s. The choirbooks were copied by three principal scribes, Nikolaus Peuschel, Johann Chamerhueber, and Heinrich Leitgeb. Settings appropriate for the feast of St. John the Baptist are in manuscript 33 (copied after 1544), and manuscript 35 (copied *c.*1540).[60]

Torgau-Walter Manuscripts: a group of six manuscripts (choirbooks and partbooks) related by scribal concordances and similar repertories. These sources were probably copied at Torgau, some under the direction of Johann Walter, between *c.*1539 and 1548. The five manuscripts, now housed in various libraries are: BerlPS 40013, BerlPS 40043, GothaF A98, NurGN 83795, and WeimB B. Scribal concordances exist among WeimB B, GothaF A98, BerlPS 40013, the first part of BerlPS 40043, and some of the paper manuscripts in the *Universitätsbibliothek* at Jena. The main scribe of the tenor partbook of NurGN 83795 was Walter.

BerlPS 40013 was copied for use at the *Pfarrkirche* in Torgau and WeimB B perhaps for use at Wittenberg *Schlosskirche*. NurGN 83795 also was apparently copied for use at the

---

58. Lothar HOFFMANN-ERBRECHT, "Die Chorbücher der Stadtkirche zu Pirna," *Acta musicologica* 27 (1955): 121-37.

59. Lothar HOFFMANN-ERBRECHT, "Das *Opus musicum* des Jacob Praetorius von 1566," *Acta musicologica* 28

(1956): 96-121.

60. Clytus GOTTWALD, *Codices Musici (Cod. Mus. Fol. I 1-71)*, Vol. 1 of *Die Handschriften der Württembergischen Landesbibliothek Stuttgart* (Wiesbaden, 1964).

*Pfarrkirche* or the *Schlosskirche* at Torgau. The title page of GothaF A98, which is dated 1545, includes a dedication to Johann Friedrich, Elector of Saxony, and indicates that this choirbook was copied for the Torgau *Schlosskirche*. Liturgical items for the feast of St. John the Baptist are found in NurGN 83795 (copied *c.*1539-48 with later additions), BerlPS 40013 (copied *c.*1540), and WeimB B (copied 1540-44).[61]

The repertory as it appears in these Lutheran sources is found in Table 5. It includes several motets as well as a large number of *cantus firmus* based liturgical settings, presumably substituted for monophonic items in the Mass and Office on the feast day.

The Mass items include Johann Walter's introit setting for the Vigil of the feast, *Ne timeas Zacharia*, in the Walter Torgau sources; an anonymous sequence for the Decollation of St. John, *Psallite regi nostro*, in LeipU 49; the anonymous introit, *De ventre matris meae*, in DresSL Pirna VI and RosU 49; and the anonymous alleluia and sequence settings for the Decollation in RosU 49. The appearance of Isaac's Mass Proper cycle (introit, alleluia, and communion) from the second volume of the *Choralis Constantinus* in ErlU 473/4, copied between 1540 and 1545, precedes its publication by Formschneider in 1555.

The Vespers items for the feast include four responsory settings, two polyphonic hymns, and a setting of the Magnificat antiphon, *Ingresso Zacharia*, anonymous in LeipU 51 but attributed in *Symphoniae iucundae atque adeo breves quatuor vocum* ...Wittenberg, G. Rhaw, 1538 to Benedictus Ducis, Protestant pastor of a parish at Schalckstetten near Ulm from 1535 until 1544.[62]

The four responsory settings of *Inter natos mulierum* have a common *cantus prius factus*. Johann Walter's setting in the Walter Torgau sources and the Rostock partbooks was most likely composed to meet liturgical requirements at Wittenberg and Torgau. Ulrich Brätel's setting in StuttL 35 was presumably written for liturgical use at the *Württembergisches Hofkapelle* during Brätel's period of residence at the court between *c.*1534 and 1545.[63] The earliest of the settings was composed by Thomas Stoltzer in the first decades of the sixteenth century, but is extant only in LeipU 49 and BudOS 22, both copied about mid-century.[64] The setting by Balthasar Resinarius in ErlU 473/2 and StuttL33 was apparently copied from Rhaw's publication of the composer's eighty responsories shortly after it appeared in 1543.[65]

Vespers responsories for the feast days of the church year had appeared as early as 800. In the years preceding the period under consideration, however, the responsory had

61.  Carl GERHARDT, *Die Torgauer Walter-Handschriften: Eine Studie zur Quellenkunde der Musikgeschichte der deutschen Reformationszeit* (Kassel: Bärenreiter, 1949).

62.  Louise E. CUYLER, "Ducis, Benedictus," *The New Grove*, 5: 671.

63.  Wilfried BRENNECKE, "Brätel, Ulrich," *The New Grove*, 3: 214. The common *cantus prius factus* for the *Inter natos*

mulierum settings has been identified in *Responsoria noviter* ... Stuchs, Nürnberg, 1509, 82v.

64.  Lothar HOFFMAN-ERBRECHT, *Thomas Stoltzer* (Kassel: Johann Philipp Hinnenthal Verlag, 1964), 65.

65.  *Responsorium numero octoginta de tempore et festis iuxta seriem totius anni, libro duo* ... Wittenberg: Georg Rhaw, 1543; see Table 5.

declined in importance and had disappeared from use in many areas. Luther's *Deutsche Messe* of 1526 as well as an order prepared in 1525 by Johannes Bugenhagen for the Collegiate Church of All Saints in Wittenberg failed to include the responsory in the order for Vespers. A church order prepared for the friars of Pomerania in 1535 indicated that the responsory was to be used "occasionally." Georg Rhaw's publication of eighty responsories by Bathasar Resinarius in 1543 represents an attempt to restore the responsories "to their former prominence and use."[66]

The Vespers hymns in the Lutheran sources include Sixtus Dietrich's *Ut queant laxis* in ErlU 473/2 and Walter's setting of *Aeterno gratias patri* in the Torgau Walter sources, RosU 49, and LeipU 49. *Ut queant laxis* uses the same *cantus prius factus* as the pre-Reformation German settings of the hymn, (Stäblein No. 72), and was apparently copied about 1548 in ErlU 473/2 from Rhaw's 1545 publication of the composer's hymns. Trained as a Roman Catholic priest, Dietrich joined the Protestant movement in 1527.[67] Walter's setting of *Aeterno gratias patri*, a hymn text written by Philipp Melanchthon in 1544,[68] represents a departure in several Lutheran centers from the traditional practice of assigning *Ut queant laxis* to the feast.

The repertory in the Lutheran sources considered here is Latin-texted and drawn from a newly-emerging Lutheran tradition as well as from Roman Catholic practice both in Italy and pre-Reformation Germany. The repertory includes motets as well as liturgical settings (hymns, responsories, antiphons, introits, alleluias, sequences, and communions) appropriate for the feast of the Nativity of St. John the Baptist celebrated on 24 June as well as for the feast of the Decollation of St. John celebrated on 29 August. Many of the liturgical pieces are *cantus firmus* based and have liturgical rubrics. The restoration of the Vespers responsory and the replacement of the traditional hymn assigned to the feast with the Lutheran *Aeterno gratias patri* emerge as the only Lutheran modifications of the Roman Catholic celebration of the feast.

Liturgical settings are found in the Heilsbronn choirbooks, the Rostock partbooks, and the Walter-Torgau manuscripts. Liturgical settings as well as motets appear in the Stuttgart choirbooks, the Pirna choirbooks, and the Leipzig *Thomaskirche* partbooks. The liturgical settings include those that were newly composed for the Lutheran services as well as three settings from Isaac's *Choralis Constantinus II*, commissioned by the Cathedral at Constance in 1508. There do not appear to be any motets that were newly composed for the Lutheran service. All are motets drawn from the Roman Catholic tradition.

66. Inge Maria SCHRÖDER, "Foreward," *Georg Rhau Musikdrucke* I: xi-xii.

67. *Novum opus musicum tres tomus sacrorum hymnorum …* Wittenberg: Georg Rhau, 1545; see Table 5. Manfred

SCHULER, "Dietrich, Sixt," *The New Grove*, 5: 469-70.

68. Philip WACKERNAGEL, *Das Deutsche Kirchenlied von der ältesten Zeit bis zu Anfang des XVII. Jahrhunderts*, I (Leipzig: B.G. Teubner, 1864), 269.

Composers represented include German Protestants, responsible for the liturgical settings designed to meet the requirements of the emerging Lutheran church, and well-known international composers whose motets were most likely copied from prints that had a wide circulation. A number of the liturgical settings may also have been copied from prints.

The motets in this repertory had a wide circulation in Italian as well as German prints and manuscripts. Several were composed a number of years before their appearance in the Lutheran sources considered here and some remained popular throughout much of the sixteenth century. The liturgical settings had a rather limited circulation within German prints and manuscripts, and although conservative in musical style, they are often contemporary with the copying of the manuscripts in which they appear. However, the Mass propers in RosU 49 and DresSL Pirna VI, sources copied in 1566 and *c*.1570, are concordant with settings found in the much earlier pre-Reformation Jena choirbooks, copied *c*.1500-20.

The appearance of a large number of settings for the feast of St. John the Baptist in sources throughout the fifteenth and sixteenth centuries attests to the universality of the feast and confirms its significant role in liturgical life at ecclesiastical centers in Italy and Germany both before and after the Reformation. As each center attempted to meet its own particular liturgical requirements for the feast, distinctions in genre and musical style emerge. Some distinctions between centers may be attributed to the availability of settings in prints and manuscripts. Others may be related to doctrinal and geographic preferences. The manuscript sources provide the evidence for these distinctions and confirm the widespread polyphonic celebration of the feast in Roman Catholic as well as Protestant ecclesiastical centers throughout Europe in the Renaissance.

# Appendix

## Sources

Parentheses indicate chant intonations, or, as in the case of the hymn, *Ut queant laxis,* when they surround the title, they indicate that the first verse is in chant, but those following in polyphony. Parentheses around the name of a composer indicate that the setting is anonymous in the source cited and that the attribution appears elsewhere. Abbreviations of manuscript sources follow the sigla found in the *Census Catalogue of Manuscript Sources of Polyphonic Music 1400-1550,* 5 vols., Renaissance Manuscript Studies 1 (American Institute of Musicology, 1979-82). Abbreviations of print sources follow RISM except for the following:

C1571     *Canticorum liber primus, cum quinque vocibus* ... Venice, Gardane, 1571 = RISM C4156

D1545     *Novum opus musicum tres tomos sacrorum hymnorum* ... Wittenberg, Rhau, 1545 = RISM D 3018

G1535     *Liber hymnorum usus Romanae ecclesiae authore Carpentras* ... Avignon, Channay, *c.*1535 = RISM G 1573

G1539     *Musica quatuor vocum ... liber primus* ... Venice, Scotto, (1539) = RISM G 2977
Reprint: Venice, Gardane, 1541

I 1555     *Tomus secundus Choralis Constantini (ut vulgo vocant) continens partem primam historiarum de sanctis, quae diebus festis in templis canuntur,* Augsburg, Willer (Nürnberg, Formschneider), 1555 = RISM I 90

J1539a     *Motecta quinque vocum ... liber primus* ... Venice, Scotto, 1539 = RISM J 6 Repr.: 1540 and 1565

J1539b     *Motecta quatuor vocum ... liber primus* ... Venice, Scotto, 1539 = RISM J 9 Repr.: 1544, 1545, 1554, 1565

J1566     *Himni vesperarum totius anni secundum Romanam curiam ... cum quatuor et quinque vocibus* ... Venice, Scotto, 1566 = RISM J 22

L1542     *Chori Sacrae Virginis Mariae Cameracensis magistri, musice cantiones ... liber tertius* ... Paris, Attaingnant & Jullet, 1542 = RISM L 3089

R1543     *Responsoriorum numero octoginta de tempore et festis iuxta seriem totius anni, libro duo* ... Wittenberg, Rhau, 1543 = RISM R 1196

W1544     *Wittembergisch deudsch Geistlich Gesangbüchlein* ... Wittenberg, Rhau, 1544 = RISM W 171

W1551     *Wittembergisch deudsch Geistlich Gesangbüchlein* ... Wittenberg, Rhau, 1551 = RISM W 173

### Liturgical sources cited

AS     *Antiphonale Sarisburiense*

GS     *Graduale Sarisburiense*

LU     *Liber Usualis*

MO     Moberg, Carl A., *Über die schwedischen Sequenzen*

ST     Stäblein, Bruno, *Die mittelalterlichen Hymnenmelodien des Abendlandes*

ZR     *Responsoria noviter ... de tempore et de sanctis per totum annum* ... Stuchs, Nürnberg, 1501-Zwickau, Ratschulbibliothek, No. 194

### Modern editions cited

BincS     Kaye, Philip, ed. *The Sacred Music of Gilles Binchois.* Oxford: Oxford University Press, 1992.

BrassO     Mixter, Keith E., ed. *Johannis Brassart: Opera Omnia.* CMM [=Corpus Mensurabilis Musicae], 35. American Institute of Musicology, 1965-71.

CW     Blume, Friedrich et al., eds. *Das Chorwerk.* Berlin and Wolfenbüttel, 1929-.

ClemensO    KEMPERS, K.Ph. BERNET and MAAS, Chris, eds. *Jacobus Clemens non Papa: Opera Omnia.* CMM, 4. American Institute of Musicology, 1951-76.

CorteCS    D'ACCONE, Frank A., ed. *Francesco Corteccia: Collected Sacred Works.* Vols. 11 and 12 of *Music of the Florentine Renaissance.* CMM, 32. American Institute of Musicology, 1981- 96.

DTO    ADLER, Guido et al., eds. *Denkmäler der Tonkunst in Österreich.* Graz and Vienna, 1894-.

DufayO    VAN, Guillaume de, and BESSELER, Heinrich, eds. *Guillaume Dufay: Opera Omnia.* CMM, 1. American Institute of Musicology, 1948-66.

EDMR    GEERING, Arnold et al., eds. *Das Erbe Deutscher Musik.* Leipzig, Kassel, Wolfenbüttel, and Wiesbaden, 1935-.

GasMA    GASTOUÉ, A., ed. *Le Manuscrit de Musique du Trésor d'Apt.* Vol. 10 of Series I of Publications de la Société Française de Musicologie. Paris, 1936.

GehrenM    GEHRENBECK, David Maulsby. *Motetti de la Corona: A Study of Ottaviano Petrucci's Four Last-Known Motet Prints.* D.S.M.diss., Union Theological Seminary, 1971.

GenetO    SEAY, Albert, ed. *Elziarii Genet (Carpentras): Opera Omnia.* CMM, 58. American Institute of Musicology, 1972-3.

GerkPC    GERKEN, Robert E. *The Polyphonic Cycles of the Proper of the Mass in the Trent Codex 88 and Jena Choirbooks 30 and 35.* Ph.D. diss., Indiana University, 1969.

GombertO    SCHMIDT-GÖRG, Joseph, ed. *Nicolai Gombert: Opera Omnia.* CMM, 6. American Institute of Musicology, 1951-75.

JachetO    JACKSON, Philip, and NUGENT, George, eds. *Jachet of Mantua: Opera Omnia.* CMM, 54. American Institute of Musicology, 1971-.

JanueO    KANAZAWA, Masakata, ed. *Antonii Janue: Opera Omnia.* CMM, 70. American Institute of Musicology, 1974.

JosqMT    SMIJERS, A., ed. *Werken van Josquin des Prez: Motetten.* Amsterdam, 1926-64.

KanP    KANAZAWA, Masakata. *Polyphonic Music for Vespers in the Fifteenth Century.* Ph.D. diss., Harvard University, 1966.

LowMCE    LOWINSKY, Edward E., ed. *The Medici Codex of 1518: A Choirbook of Motets Dedicated to Lorenzo de Medici, Duke of Urbino.* Vols. 3-5 of *Monuments of Renaissance Music.* Chicago, 1968.

MB    LEWIS, Anthony et al., eds. *Musica Britannica: A National Collection of Music.* London, 1951-.

MPLSER    FEININGER, Laurence, ed. *Monumenta Polyphoniae Liturgicae Sanctae Ecclesiae Romanae.* Rome, 1947-.

MarM    MARIX, J., ed. *Les Musiciens de la Cour de Bourgogne au XV^e Siècle.* Paris, 1937.

MilO    MILLER, Ronald L. *The Musical Works of Marbriano de Orto: Transcription and Commentary.* Ph.D. diss.., Indiana University, 1974.

NieS    NIEMANN, W. "Studien zur deutschen Musikgeschichte des XV. Jahrhunderts," *Kirchenmusikalisches Jahrbuch* 17 (1902), pp. 1-46.

ParrS    PARRIS, Arthur. *The Sacred Works of Gilles Binchois.* Ph.D. diss., Bryn Mawr College, 1964.

PopeMC    POPE, Isabel, and KANAZAWA, Masakata, eds. *The Musical Manuscript Montecassino 871:A Neapolitan Repertory of Sacred and Secular Music of the Late Fifteenth Century.* Oxford, 1978.

PruettM    PRUETT, Lilian Pibernik. *The Masses and Hymns of Costanzo Porta.* Ph.D. diss., University of North Carolina, 1960.

ReaneyE    REANEY, Gilbert, ed., *Early Fifteenth-Century Music.* CMM, 11. American Institute of Musicology, 1955-.

RedmS    REDMOND, Mary. *A Set of Part-Books for Giuliano de' Medici: Cortona, Biblioteca Comunale, Mss. 95, 96 and Paris, Bibliothèque Nationale, Nouvelle Acquistion 1817.* Master's thesis, University of Illinois, 1970.

RhauMD ALBRECHT, Hans, ed. *Georg Rhau Musikdrucke aus den Jahren 1538-1545 in praktischer Neuausgabe.* Kassel: Bärenreiter, 1955-.

RigsG RIGSBY, O. Lee, *The Sacred Music of Elzéar Genet.* Ph.D. diss., University of Michigan, 1955.

ShineMM SHINE, Josephine M. *The Motets of Jean Mouton.* Ph.D. diss., New York University, 1953.

SmijT SMIJERS, A., and A. TILLMAN MERRITT, eds. *Trieze Livres de Motets parus chez Pierre Attaingnant en 1534 et 1535.* Paris: Oiseau-Lyre, 1934-64.

WalterW SCHRÖDER, Otto et al., eds. *Johann Walter: Sämtliche Werke.* Kassel: Bärenreiter, 1953-70.

WillaertO ZENCK, Hermann, Walter GERSTENBERG and B.H. MEIER, eds. *Adrian Willaert: Opera Omnia.* CMM, 3. American Institute of Musicology, 1950-77.

WolfS WOLF, Johannes, ed. *Sing und Spielmusik aus älterer Zeit.* Leipzig, 1926 and 1931.

WrdH WARD, Tom Robert. *The Polyphonic Office Hymn from the Late Fourteenth Century Until the Early Sixteenth Century.* Ph.D. diss., University of Pittsburgh, 1969.

## Table 1   The Fifteenth-Century Repertory

| Incipit / Title | Composer | Source | Genre | Cantus Firmus | Modern Edition |
|---|---|---|---|---|---|
| Missa Fuit homo missus | Anon. | TrentC 88<br>TrentC 90<br>TrentM 93 | Mass Ordinary Cycle | GS 188-tenor | |
| Sanctus Iste puer magnus | Anon. | MunBS 3154 | Mass Ordinary Section | LU 1496-tenor | EDMR LXXXI, p.148 |
| (De ventre) matris meae | Anon. | TrentC 88 | Mass Proper Cycle - Introit | LU 1499-superius | MPLSER II/I, p.58 |
| (Priusquam) te formarem | Anon. | TrentC 88 | Mass Proper Cycle - Gradual | LU 1500-superius | MPLSER II/I, p.60 |
| Alleluia Tu puer propheta | Anon. | TrentC 88 | Mass Proper Cycle - Alleluia | LU 1501-superius | MPLSER II/I, p.63 |
| (Justus) ut palma | Anon. | TrentC 88 | Mass Proper Cycle - Offertory | LU 1193-superius | MPLSER II/I, p.65 |
| (Tu puer) propheta | Anon. | TrentC 88 | Mass Proper Cycle - Communion | LU 1502-superius | MPLSER II/I, p.67 |
| De ventre matris meae | Anon. | TrentC 90<br>TrentM 93 | Introit | LU 1499-superius | |
| (De ventre) matris meae | Anon. | TrentC 90<br>TrentM 93 | Introit | LU 1499-superius | |
| (De ventre) matris meae | Brassart | AostaS D19 | Introit | LU 1499-superius | BrassO I, p.8 |
| (De ventre) matris meae | Anon. | PragP 47 | Introit | LU 1499-superius | |
| (Puer) qui natus est nobis | Benoit | ModE X.1.11. | Antiphon | LU 1505-superius | ReaneyE III, p.103 |
| (Inter natos) mulierum | Binchois | TrentC 87 | Antiphon | AS 573-superius | MarM, p.209 · ParrS, no.29 · BincS, p.218 |
| Inter natos mulierum | Binchois | ModE X.1.11. | Antiphon | | MarM, p.210 · ParrS, no.28 · BincS, p.219 |
| Inter natos mulierum | Anon. | BerlPS 40098 | Responsory | ZR 82-superius | EDMR LXXXVI, p.286 |
| (Ut queant laxis) | Adam von Fulda | DresSL I/D/505<br>LeipU 1494 | Hymn | ST 72-superius<br>MO 23-vagans | EDMR XXXII, p.8 ·<br>CW XXXII, p.21 / NieS, p.11 |
| (Ut queant laxis) | Adam von Fulda | LeipU 1494<br>WrocU 428 | Hymn | ST 72-tenor | EDMR XXXII, p.35 · NieS, p.17 |
| Ut queant laxis | Cristofferus Anthony | TrentC 90 | Hymn | ST 72-superius | KanP II, p.105 |
| Ut queant laxis | Binchois | MunBS Lat.14274<br>VenBN 7554 | Hymn | ST 151-superius | MarM, p.226 · WolfS No.13, p.38 ·<br>ParrS, no.59 · BincS, p.257 |
| (Ut queant laxis) | Dufay | BolC Q15<br>ModE X.1.11.<br>TrentC 92 · VatS 15 | Hymn | ST 151-superius | DufayO V, p.61 · DTO 14-15, p.167 ·<br>CW XLIX, p.16 |
| (Ut queant laxis) | Antonius Janue | FlorBN Magl.112bis | Hymn | ST 151-superius | JanueO, p.14 · WrdH, p.520 |
| Ut queant laxis | Ray de Lan(tins) | MunBS 3224 | Hymn | ST 72-superius | KanP II, p.61 |
| Ut queant laxis | Nicolas Merques | TrentC 92 | Hymn | ST 151-superius | |
| (Ut queant laxis) | Marbrianus de Orto | VatS 15 | Hymn | ST 151-superius | MilO II, p.388 |
| Ut queant laxis | Anon. | AptSA 16bis | Hymn | ST 151-superius | GasMA, p.64 |
| Ut queant laxis | Anon. | BerlPS 40098 | Hymn | ST 422-superius | EDMR LXXXVI, p.293 |
| Ut queant laxis | Anon. | FlorBN Magl. 112bis | Hymn | ST 151-superius and tenor | JanueO, p.45 |
| (Ut queant laxis) | Anon. | FlorBN Magl. 112bis | Hymn | ST 151-superius | JanueO, p.46 |
| (Ut queant laxis) | Anon. | LeipU 1494 | Hymn | ST 72-superius ·<br>LU 1503-bassus | EDMR XXXII, p.6 |
| (Ut queant laxis) | Anon. | LeipU 1494 | Hymn | ST 151-superius | EDMR XXXII, p.7 |
| (Ut queant laxis) | Anon. | LeipU 1494 | Hymn | ST 72-tenor | EDMR XXXII, p.12 |
| Ut queant laxis | Anon. | MonteA 871 | Hymn | ST 151-superius | PopeMC, p.268 |
| (Ut queant laxis) | Anon. | ParisBNC 862 | Hymn | ST 151-superius | |
| Ut queant laxis | Anon. | PragP 47 | Hymn | ST 422-superius | |
| (Ut queant laxis) | Anon. | PragP 47 | Hymn | ST 72-superius | |
| Ut queant laxis | Anon. | TrentC 89 | Hymn | ST 72-superius | |
| Ut queant laxis | Anon. | TrentC 89 | Hymn | ST 72-superius | |
| Ut queant laxis | Anon. | TrentC 91 | Hymn | ST 151-tenor | KanP II, p.173 |
| Ut queant laxis | Anon. | TrentC 92 | Hymn | ST 151-superius | |
| Ut queant laxis | Anon. | VatSP B80 | Hymn | ST 151-superius | |
| Ut queant laxis | Anon. | VerBC 759 | Hymn | ST 151-superius and tenor | KanP II, p.202 |
| Elisabeth Zachariae | (Dufay) | TrentC 87 | Motet | | DTO 76, p.16 |
| O Baptista mirabiles | Lymburgia | BolC Q15 | Motet | | |
| Preco preheminencie | Dunstable | CantC 3 · ModE X.1.11.<br>·TrentC 92 | Motet | AS 436-tenor | DTO 76, p.46 · MB VIII, p.78 |
| Gaude tu Baptista Christi | Benoit | BolC Q15 | Motet | | ReaneyE III, p.98 |

**Table 2**  Sources for the Fifteenth-Century Repertory

*c.*1400-1430

| | | |
|---|---|---|
| AptSA 16bis[1] | copied 1400-1425; some of the repertory may be retrospective | probably copied at Avignon or Apt; connected with the papal residence during the Great Schism (1377-1417) |

*c.*1430-1450

| | | |
|---|---|---|
| CantC 3[2] | *c.*1430-40 | probably copied at Canterbury Cathedral |
| BolC Q15 | *c.*1420-35 | probably copied in Padua or Vicenza |
| VenBN 7554 | Part I: *c.*1420-40 Part II: mid 15th century | copied in Venice or vicinity, presumably at Franciscan monastery |
| AostaS D19[3] | compiled before 1446; repertory dates *c.*1414-43; section I copied *c.*1430-5; sections II and III copied *c.*1435-43; section IV copied *c.*1443-6 | Section I copied in Bologna; sections II and III copied in the Basel-Strasbourg area and compiled with section I; section IV copied in Innsbruck; some of the repertory probably used by the chapels at the Council of Constance (1414-18) and the Council of Basel (1431-49); repertory in section IV composed at the imperial court chapel at Innsbruck |
| MunBS 3224 | *c.*1440-45 | copied in northern Italy |
| MunBS Lat.14274[4] | *c.*1436-59 | copied in Vienna, Regensburg, and Leipzig; three gatherings possibly copied at the convent of St. John the Baptist and St. John the Evangelist at Munich |
| TrentC 87[5] | *c.*1430-45, with one addition *c.*1465 | parts I-II perhaps copied in Venice or vicinity or Basel-Strasbourg region; part III copied in Ciney, Namur province |
| TrentC 92[6] | *c.*1430-45, with additions to early 1450s | part I copied in Basel-Strasbourg region possibly for use at the chapels associated with the Council of Basel (1431-49) and the court of the antipope Felix V, the former Amadeus VIII, Duke of Savoy; parts II-III possibly copied in Venice or vicinity or Basel-Strasbourg region |
| ModE X.1.11.[7] | *c.*1440-48; additions *c.*1450-60 and *c.*1471-80 | copied in Ferrara for the court of Leonello d'Este (Marquis of Ferrara, 1441-50); later additions during the reigns of Borso d'Este (Duke of Ferrara, 1450-71) and Ercole I d'Este (Duke of Ferrara, 1471-1505); manuscript apparently copied for use at Vespers by the court chapel; repertory may have been collected from elsewhere and brought to Ferrara in the late 1430s and throughout the 1440s |

*c.*1450-1465

| | | |
|---|---|---|
| FlorBN Magl.112bis | 1460-70 | probably copied in Genoa; one of the scribes was Antonius Janue, a musician at the Genoese ducal palace in 1456 |
| TrentC 88 | *c.*1460-65 | copied in Trent; portions copied by Johannes Wiser, rector of the cathedral school at Trent 1459-65, later chaplain to Johannes Hinderbach, Bishop of Trent 1465-86 |

1.  Information on sources from the *Census-Catalogue of Manuscript Sources of Polyphonic Music 1400-1550*, 5 vols., Renaissance Manuscript Studies, 1 (American Institute of Musicology, 1979-82). Additional studies are also cited.

2.  Nicholas SANDON, "Fragments of Medieval Polyphony at Canterbury Cathedral," *Musica disciplina* 30 (1976): 37-53.

3.  Marian W. COBIN, *The Aosta Manuscript: A Central Source of Early-Fifteenth Century Sacred Polyphony* (Ph.D. diss., New York University, 1978).

4.  Ian RUMBOLD, "The Compilation and Ownership of the 'St. Emmeram' Codex (Munich, Bayerische Staatsbibliothek, Clm 14274," *Early Music History* 2 (1982): 161-235; Tom WARD, "A Central European Repertory in Munich, Bayerische Staatsbibliothek, Clm 14274," *Early Music History* 1 (1981): 325-43.

5.  Peter WRIGHT, "The Compilation of Trent 87 and 92," *Early Music History* 2 (1982): 237-71.

6.  Tom R. WARD, "The Structure of the Manuscript Trent 92-I," *Musica disciplina* 29 (1975): 127-47.

7.  Charles HAMM and Ann Besser SCOTT, "A Study and Inventory of the Manuscript Modena, Biblioteca Estense, α X.1.11 (ModB)," *Musica disciplina* 26 (1972): 101-43.

| | | |
|---|---|---|
| TrentC 89 | c.1460-80 | copied in Trent; portions copied by Johannes Wiser (see preceding entry); composite of originally separate fascicles |
| TrentC 90 | c.1452-59 | copied in Trent; portions copied by Johannes Wiser (see TrentC 88 entry); part of the repertory concordant with and probably copied from TrentM 93 |
| TrentC 91 | c.1460-80 | copied in Trent; portions copied by Johannes Wiser (see TrentC 88 entry) |
| TrentM 93 | c.1450-56 | copied in Trent; portions copied by Johannes Wiser (see TrentC 88 entry); portions of the repertory concordant with that of TrentC 90; composite of at least two originally separate manuscripts |
| PragP 47[8] | c.1460-80; repertory dates from c.1445 | probably copied in Bohemia or Silesia; possibly copied in Moravia for use at Olomouc Cathedral; acquired by Strahov Premonstratensian monastery in Prague; identified watermarks are of southeast German provenance; concordances exist primarily with manuscripts of south-German origin; compiled as a liturgical manuscript with polyphonic settings for the principal feasts of the temporal and sanctoral cycles |
| VatSP B80[9] | 1474-75 with additions to c.1500 | copied in Rome for the Basilica of St. Peter at the Vatican; source of much of the repertory believed to be two earlier manuscripts (c.1458-63) no longer extant |

### c.1465-1490

| | | |
|---|---|---|
| MonteA 871[10] | copied c.1480-1500; repertory c.1430-1480 | probably copied at the Benedictine monastery of Sts. Severino and Sossio in Naples or the Benedictine monastery of St. Michele Arcangelo de Planciano in Gaeta |
| BerlPS 40098 | c.1475-85 | Of Silesian origin; possible copied in Glogau or Sagan; once owned by the cathedral at Glogau |
| VerBC 759[11] | c.1480-90 | copied in Verona; the local repertory of the Vesper settings reflects the liturgical practice in late-fifteenth century Verona |

### c.1490-1530

| | | |
|---|---|---|
| MunBS 3154[12] | copied between 1466 and 1511; some of the repertory may be earlier; fascicle manuscript portions may have circulated as independent fascicles before they were bound in 1511 | probably copied in Innsbruck (and Augsburg?); copied by scribes probably members of Maximilian's imperial court chapel in Innsbruck; manuscript once owned by Nikolaus Leopold of Innsbruck; transmits some of the repertory of the imperial court chapel |
| LeipU 1494 | c.1490-1504 | possibly copied in Leipzig; the manuscript was bound in Leipzig on 1 September, 1504 for Nikolaus Apel |
| ParisBNC 862 | c.1503-05 | manuscript addition to Petrucci print, RISM 1503[1]; possibly copied in Venice or Milan |
| VatS 15[13] | c.1495-1500 | copied in Rome for the use of the Sistine Chapel |
| DresSL I/D/505 | 1510-30; c.1530 | copied for the St. Annenkirche in Annaberg |
| WrocU 428 | c.1510-30, perhaps c.1516 | copied in Frankfurt an der Oder or vicinity |

8.    Robert Joseph SNOW, *The Manuscript Strahov D.G. IV. 47.* (Ph.D. diss., University of Illinois, 1968).

9.    Christopher REYNOLDS, "The Origins of San Pietro B 80 and the Development of a Roman Sacred Repertory," *Early Music History* 1 (1981): 257-304.

10.    Isabel POPE and Masakata KANAZAWA, eds., *The Musical Manuscript Montecassino 871: A Neapolitan Repertory of Sacred and Secular Music of the Late Fifteenth Century* (Oxford: Oxford University Press, 1978).

11.    Masakata KANAZAWA, "Two Vesper Repertories from Verona, c.1500," *Rivista italiana di musicologia* 10 (1975): 155-73.

12.    Thomas L. NOBLITT, "Das Chorbuch des Nikolaus Leopold (München, Staatsbibliothek, Mus. Ms. 3154): Repertorium," *Archiv für Musikwissenschaft* 26 (1969): 169-208; Thomas L. NOBLITT, "Die Datierung der Handschrift Mus. Ms. 3154 der Staatsbibliothek München," *Die Musikforschung* 27 (1974): 35-56.

13.    Richard SHERR, *Papal Music Manuscripts in the Late Fifteenth and Early Sixteenth Centuries,* Renaissance Manuscript Studies 5 (Rome:

**Table 3**  The Italian Cathedral Sources

| Manuscript | Incipit / Title | Composer | Genre | Concordance | Modern Edition |
|---|---|---|---|---|---|
| CasAC C | (Ut queant laxis) | (Jacquet of Mantua) | Hymn | TrevBC 25 · 1542[11] · 1550[3] · J 1566 | WillaertO VII, p.96 · JachetO II, p.57 |
| CasAC D(F) | Descendit angelus Domini 2p. Ne timeas quoniam | (Hilaire Penet) | Motet | LeipU 51 · MadM 6832 · MunU 401 · PadBC D27 · RegB 861-2 · RegB 875-7 · TrevBC 7 · 1532[10] · 1539[12] · 1540[6] · 1545[4] · 1564[6] | PruettM, supp., p.209 |
| FlorD 4 | Elisabeth Zachariae 2p. Fuit homo missus | (Corteccia) | Motet | C 1571 | |
| FlorD 4 | Precursorem Domini 2p. Hic est enim propheta | Anon. | Motet | | |
| FlorD 11 | Gabriel archangelus | (Verdelot) | Motet | LeipU 51 · MadM 6832 · RegB 861-2 · TrevBC 5 · 1532[10] · 1534[3] · 1538[8] · 1539[12] · 1545[4] · 1559[2] · 1564[6] | RhauMD III, p.155 · SmijT, p.99 |
| FlorD 11 | Inter natos mulierum 2p. Fuit homo missus | (Josquin)[14] | Motet | BolC R142 · RomeV 35-40 · VatS 38 | JosqMT 84/49, p.125 |
| FlorD 28 | (Ut queant laxis) | (Corteccia) | Hymn | FlorD 39 · FlorL Med.Pal. 7 · FlorSL O | CorteCS XII, p.97 |
| FlorD 46 | (De ventre) matris meae | (Corteccia)[15] | Introit | | |
| FlorD 46 | Alleluia (Tu puer propheta) | (Corteccia) | Alleluia | | |
| FlorD 46 | (Tu puer) propheta | (Corteccia) | Communion | | |
| ModD 3 and ModD 4 | (Ut queant laxis) | Carpentras | Hymn | G 1535 | GenetO III, p.147 and 241 · RigsG II, p.72 |
| ModD 9 | Elisabeth Zachariae 2p. Inter natos mulierum | Jean de La Fage[16] | Motet | BolC Q20 · DresSL 1/D/501 · FlorL 666 · LeipU 51 · PadBC A17 · RegB 861-2 · RegB 940-1 · RegB C120 · VatS 46 · 1519[1] · 1520[1] · 1526[2] · 1538[8] · 1546[23] · 1559[2] | RhauMD III, p.93 · LowMCE IV, p.100 · ShineMM I, p.259 · GehrenM IV, p.1593 |
| PadBC A17 | Puer qui natus est nobis | Anon. | Motet | | |
| PadBC A17 | Elisabeth Zachariae 2p. Inter natos mulierum | (Jean de La Fage) | Motet | BolC Q20 · DresSL 1/D/501 · FlorL 666 · LeipU 51 · ModD 9 · RegB 861-2 · RegB 940-1 · RegB C120 · VatS 46 · 1519[1] · 1520[1] · 1526[2] · 1538[8] · 1546[23] · 1559[2] | RhauMD III, p.93 · LowMCE IV, p.100 · ShineMM I, p.259 · GehrenM IV, p.1593 |
| PadBC A17 | Inter natos mulierum 2p. Elisabeth impletum | Mouton | Motet | BolC Q20 · VatS 46 | ShineMM I, p.400 |
| PadBC A17 | Prophetarum maxime 2p. Concede nobis tuas digne 3p. Inter natos mulierum | (Isaac) | Motet | CorBC 95-6 · FlorBN II.I. 232 · FlorBN Magl. 164-7 · ParisBNN 1817 · SGallS 530 · VatV 11953 · 1520[4] | RedmS, p.319 |

---

American Institute of Musicology, 1996).

14.  Attributed to Josquin in BolC R142 and RomeV 35-40, *Inter natos mulierum* is excluded from the *New Josquin Edition* as spurious; see *New Josquin Edition: Motets on Texts from the New Testament*, 19: 109-13.

15.  David A. SUTHERLAND in "A Second Corteccia Manuscript in the Archives of Santa Maria del Fiore," *Journal of the American Musicological Society* 25 (1972): 79-85, attributes the anonymous Mass Propers in FlorD 46 to Corteccia.

16.  Although attributed to Mouton in later manuscripts and prints, this work is usually regarded as a motet by La Fage.

| Manuscript | Incipit/Title | Composer | Genre | Concordance | Modern Edition |
|---|---|---|---|---|---|
| PadBC D27 | Fuit homo missus<br>2p. Hic praecursor | (Gombert) | Motet | CambraiBM 125-8 · MunU 401 · 1532[11] · 1539[12] · G 1539 · J 1539a · 1545[4] · 1547[25] · 1552[35] · 1564[6] | GombertO V, p.81 |
| PadBC D27 | Descendit angelus Domini<br>2p. Ne timeas Zachariae | (Hilaire Penet) | Motet | CasAC D(F) · LeipU 51 · MadM 6832 · MunU 401 · RegB 861-2 · RegB 875-7 · TrevBC 7 · 1532[10] · 1539[12] · 1540[6] · 1545[4] · 1564[6] | PruettM supp., p.209 |
| *Trev BC 3[17] | (Ut queant laxis) | Jan Nasco | Hymn | | |
| *TrevBC 4 | Misso Herodes spiculatore | Olivetus | | | |
| *TrevBC 5 | Gabriel angleus | Janequin | | | |
| *TrevBC 5 | Gabriel archangelus | Verdelot | Motet | FlorD 11 · LeipU 51 · MadM 6832 · RegB 861-2 · 1532[10] · 1534[3] · 1538[8] · 1539[12] · 1545[4] · 1559[2] · 1564[6] | RhauMD III, p.155 · SmijT I, p.99 |
| *TrevBC 5 | Angelus Domini apparuit | Jacquet de Berchem[18] | | BrusC 27088 · L 1542 · 1543[3] · 1569[2] | |
| *TrevBC 5 | Vox clamantis in deserto | Anon. | | | |
| *TrevBC 5 | Audite insulae<br>2p. Et exposuit os meum | Jacquet de Berchem | | | |
| *TrevBC 5 | Precursor Domini | Anon. | | | |
| *TrevBC 5 | Pro eo quod non credisti | Anon. | | | |
| *TrevBC 5 | Ingresso Zacharia | Anon. | | | |
| *TrevBC 5 | Puer qui natus est nobis | Jan Nasco | | | |
| *TrevBC 5 | De ventre matris meae | Anon. | | | |
| *TrevBC 5 | De ventre matris meae | Anon. | | | |
| *TrevBC 5 | Puer qui natus est nobis | Anon. | | | |
| *TrevBC 5 | Ingresso Zacharia<br>2p. Puer qui natus est nobis | Anon. | | | |
| TrevBC 7 | Descendit angelus Domini<br>2p. Ne timeas quoniam | (Hilaire Penet) | Motet | CasAC D(F) · LeipU 51 · MadM 6832 · MunU 401 · PadBC D27 · RegB 861-2 · RegB 875-7 · 1532[10] · 1539[12] · 1540[6] · 1545[4] · 1564[6] | PruettM supp., p.209 |
| TrevBC 7 | Puer qui natus est nobis | (Jacquet of Mantua) | Motet | LeipU 51 · StuttL 35 · 1538/5 · J 1539b · 1540[6] · 1547[22] · 1552[29] | JachetO IV, p.61 |
| TrevBC 8 | Factum est verbum Domini<br>2p. Ego vox clamantis | Jacquet de Berchem | Motet | 1542[10] · 1558[4] | WillaertO IV, p.75 |
| TrevBC 13 | (Ut queant laxis) | Anon. | Hymn | | |
| TrevBC 13 | (Ut queant laxis) | N.O.[19] | Hymn | | |
| TrevBC 25 | (Ut queant laxis) | Jacquet of Mantua | Hymn | CasAC C · 1542[11] · 1550[3] · J 1566 | WillaertO VII, p.96 · JachetO II, p.57 |
| TrevBC 25 | (Puer qui natus est nobis) | H.C.[20] | Antiphon | | |

17.   An asterisk indicates that the manuscript was destroyed in 1944.

18.   This motet is probably by Lupus; see George Edward NUGENT, *The Jaquet Motets and their Authors* (Ph.D. diss., Princeton University, 1973), 207.

19.   N.O. may refer to Nicolo Olivetto, who was employed at the cathedral at Treviso between 1528 and 1537; see, Giovanni d'ALESSI, "Precursors of Adriano Willaert in the Practice of Coro Spezzato," *Journal of the American Musicological Society* 5 (1952): 206.

20.   H.C. may refer to Ippolito Chamatero.

**Table 4** The German Pre-Reformation Sources

| Manuscript | Incipit/Title | Composer | Genre | Concordance | Modern Edition |
|---|---|---|---|---|---|
| DresSL 1/D/506 | (Ut queant laxis) | Anon. | Hymn | | |
| DresSL 1/D/505 | (Sancti Baptistae Christi) | Anon. | Sequence | | |
| DresSL 1/D/505 | (Ut queant laxis) | (Adam von Fulda) | Hymn | LeipU 1494 | EDMR XXXII, p.8 |
| | | | | | NieS, p.11 |
| | | | | | CW XXXII, p.21 |
| JenaU 30 | (De ventre matris meae) | Anon. | Introit | RosU 49 • | GerkPC III, p.60 |
| | | | | DresSL Pirna VI | |
| JenaU 30 | Alleluia Erat Johannes | Anon. | Alleluia | | GerkPC III, p.67 |
| JenaU 30 | (Sancti Baptistae Christi) | Anon. | Sequence | | GerkPC III, p.73 |
| JenaU 30 | (Tu puer) propheta | Anon. | Communion | | GerkPC III, p.84 |
| JenaU 30 | (In virtute tua) | Anon. | Introit | | GerkPC III, p.286 |
| JenaU 30 | Alleluia Vox clamantis | Anon. | Alleluia | RosU 49 | GerkPC III, p.293 |
| JenaU 30 | (Psallite regi nostro) | Anon. | Sequence | RosU 49 | GerkPC III, p.299 |
| JenaU 30 | Magna est gloria eius | Anon. | Communion | JenaU 33 | GerkPC III, p.315 |

**Table 5** The Lutheran Sources

| Manuscript | Incipit/Title | Composer | Genre | Concordance | Modern Edition |
|---|---|---|---|---|---|
| ErlU 473/2 | Inter natos mulierum | Resinarius | Responsory | StuttL 33 · R 1543 | RhauMD II, p.51 |
| ErlU 473/2 | (Ut queant laxis) | Sixt Dietrich | Hymn | D 1545 | EDMR XXIII, p.72 |
| ErlU 473/4 | (De ventre matris meae) | (Isaac) | Introit | I 1555 | DTO XVI/32, p.75 |
| ErlU 473/4 | Alleluia. Inter natos mulierum | (Isaac) | Alleluia | I 1555 | DTO XVI/32, p.76 |
| ErlU 473/4 | (Tu puer) propheta | (Isaac) | Communion | I 1555 | DTO XVI/32, p.81 |
| LeipU 49 | Inter natos mulierum | Stoltzer | Responsory | BudOS 22 | EDMR LXXXXIX, p.63 |
| LeipU 49 | (Psallite regi nostro) | Anon. | Sequence | | |
| LeipU 49 | Aeterno gratias patri | Walter | Hymn | BerlPS 40013 · GreifU 640-1 · | WalterW III, p.69 |
| | | | | NurGN 83795 · RosU 49 · | |
| | | | | WeimHP B · ZwiR 81/2 | |
| LeipU 51 | Elisabeth Zachariae | (Jean de La Fage) | Motet | BolC Q20 · DresSL 1/D/501 · | RhauMD III, p.93 · |
| | 2p. Inter natos mulierum | | | FlorL 666 · ModD 9 · PadBC A17 · | LowMCE IV, p.100 · |
| | | | | RegB 861-2 · RegB 940-1 · RegB | ShineMM I, p.259 · |
| | | | | C120 · VatS 46 · 1519¹ · 1520¹ · 1526² · | GehrenM IV, p.1593 |
| | | | | 1538⁸ · 1546²³ · 1559² | |
| LeipU 51 | Ingresso Zacharia | (Benedictus Ducis) | Antiphon | 1538⁸ | RhauMD III, p.124 |
| LeipU 51 | Gabriel archangelus | (Verdelot) | Motet | FlorD 11 · MadM 6832 · RegB 861-2 | RhauMD III, p.155 · |
| | | | | · TrevBC 5 · 1532¹⁰ · 1534³ · 1538⁸ · | SmijT I, p.99 |
| | | | | 1539¹² · 1545⁴ · 1559² · 1564⁶ | |
| LeipU 51 | Descendit angelus Domini | (Hilaire Penet) | Motet | CasAC D(F) · MadM 6832 · | PruettM supp., p.209 |
| | 2p. Ne timeas quoniam | | | MunU 401 · PadBC D27 · RegB | |
| | | | | 861-2 · RegB 875-7 · TrevBC 7 · | |
| | | | | 1532¹⁰ · 1539¹² · 1540⁶ · 1545⁴ · 1564⁶ | |
| LeipU 51 | Puer qui natus est nobis | (Jacquet of Mantua) | Motet | StuttL 35 · TrevBC 7 · 1538⁵ · J 1539b | JachetO IV, p.61 |
| | | | | · 1540⁶ · 1547²² · 1552²⁹ | |
| DresSL Pirna VI | (De ventre matris meae) | Anon. | Introit | JenaU 30 · RosU 49 | GerkPC III, p.60 |

## Table 5 (cont'd)  The Lutheran Sources

| | | | | | |
|---|---|---|---|---|---|
| DresSL Pirna VI | *Innuebant patri ejus* <br> 2p. *Apertum est os Zachariae* | (Clemens non Papa) | Motet | BerlS 40329 · DresSL Grimma 56 · HradKM 30 · LeuvK 4 · LubBH 203 · RegB 861-2 · ZwiR 74 · 1556⁶ · 1559¹ | ClemensO XVII, p.65 |
| RosU 49 | *Inter natos mulierum* | (Walter) | Responsory | BerlPS 40013 · BudOS 23 · NurGN 83795 · W 1544 · W 1551 | WalterW II, p.111 |
| RosU 49 | (*De ventre matris meae*) | Anon. | Introit | DresSL Pirna VI · JenaU 30 | GerkPC III, p.60 |
| RosU 49 | *Alleluia. Vox clamantis* | Anon. | Alleluia | JenaU 30 | GerkPC III, p.293 |
| RosU 49 | (*Psallite regi nostro*) | Anon. | Sequence | JenaU 30 | GerkPC III, p.299 |
| RosU 49 | *Aeterno gratias patri* | (Walter) | Hymn | BerlPS 40013 · GreifU 640-1 · LeipU 49 · NurGN 83795 · WeimHP B · ZwiR 81/2 | WalterW III, p.69 |
| StuttL 33 | *Inter natos mulierum* | Ulrich Brätel | Responsory | | |
| StuttL 33 | *Inter natos mulierum* | Resinarius | Responsory | ErlU 473/2 · R 1543 | RhauMD II, p.51 |
| StuttL 35 | *Puer qui natus est nobis* | Jacquet of Mantua | Motet | LeipU 51 · TrevBC 7 · 1538⁵ · J 1539b · 1540⁶ · 1547²² · 1552²⁹ | JachetO IV, p.61 |
| BerlPS 40013 · NurGN 83795 · WeimHP B | (*Ne timeas Zacharia*) | (Walter) | Introit | | WalterW VI, p.98 |
| BerlPS 40013 · NurGN 83795 | *Inter natos mulierum* | (Walter) | Responsory | BudOS 23 · RosU 49 · W 1544 · W 1551 | WalterW II, p.111 |
| BerlPS 40013 · NurGN 83795 · WeimHP B | *Aeterno gratias patri* | (Walter) | Hymn | GreifU 640-1 · LeipU 49 · RosU 49 · ZwiR 81/2 | WalterW III, p.69 |

# PER FARE IL VESPRO MENO TEDIOSO:
# DON PIETRO MARIA MARSOLO
# AND THE "ANTIPHON PROBLEM"

THE "ANTIPHON PROBLEM" of the sixteenth and seventeenth centuries is one of those issues for modern musicology that results from our own difficulty in understanding how musicians of an earlier age worked. The "antiphon problem" may have been no problem for them at all.

As discussed in the musicological literature, the "antiphon problem" turns on the relationship between antiphons on the one hand and psalms and Magnificats on the other in sixteenth and seventeenth-century music for Vespers. Considerable ink has been spilled over this issue, beginning with the question of whether or not the *sacri concentus* in Monteverdi's 1610 publication of the *Missa in illo tempore* and the *Vespro della Beata Vergine* were intended as substitutes for the "liturgically correct" plainchant antiphons.[1]

The relationship between antiphon and psalm or Magnificat is relatively unproblematic in a service entirely in plainchant. Since the antiphon is proper to the particular feast being celebrated, the psalm or Magnificat tone is chosen to fit the mode of the antiphon. But if the psalms are set to polyphony, this is no longer possible, since the tone of the psalm is fixed and cannot be adapted to the antiphon (polyphonic Magnificats were often published in all eight tones so that tone could still serve as the criterion for selecting the Magnificat setting to fit a particular antiphon). A further complication is

---

1. For the principal literature on this issue, see Stephen BONTA, "Liturgical Problems in Monteverdi's Marian Vespers," *Journal of the American Musicological Society* 20 (1967): 87-106; Wolfgang OSTHOFF, "Unità liturgica e artistica nei Vespri del 1610," *Rivista italiana di musicologia* 2 (1967): 314-27; Thomas D. CULLEY, *Jesuits and Music: I, A Study of the Musicians connected with the German College in Rome during the 17th Century and of their Activities in Northern Europe* (St. Louis: St. Louis University, 1970), 78 and 85; idem, "Musical Activity in Some Sixteenth Century Jesuit Colleges," *Analecta musicologica* 19 (1979): 1-29, here 7; Anthony M. CUMMINGS, "Toward an Interpretation of the Sixteenth Century Motet," *Journal of the American Musicological Society* 34 (1981): 43-59; James H. MOORE, *Vespers at St. Mark's: Music of Alessandro Grandi, Giovanni Rovetta and Francesco Cavalli* (Ann Arbor: UMI Research Press, 1981), 151-52; idem, "The Liturgical Use of the Organ in Seventeenth-Century Italy: New Documents, New Hypotheses," in *Frescobaldi Studies*, ed. Alexander SILBIGER (Durham: Duke University Press, 1987): 351-83, here 358; and James ARMSTRONG, "The Antiphonae, seu sacrae cantiones (1613) of Giovanni Francesco Anerio: a Liturgical Study," *Analecta musicologica* 14 (1974): 89-150.

introduced when antiphons are composed in polyphony and cannot be assigned unambiguously to a "mode." Monteverdi's print presents yet another complication in that the texts of the *sacri concentus* do not match those of any of the liturgically assigned antiphons for any of the feasts represented by the class of services (Marian feasts) the print is designed to accommodate. Nor does the set of tones represented by Monteverdi's psalms and Magnificat settings match the set of modes of the liturgically correct antiphons for any of the eight Marian feasts listed in breviaries of Monteverdi's day.

Thus, we have a "problem" to be resolved. But the perception of this state of affairs as a "problem" rests on two principal assumptions: 1) that sixteenth- and seventeenth-century musicians were still concerned with the relationship between the tone of a polyphonic psalm or Magnificat and the mode of the proper antiphon (the identification of the tones of many polyphonic psalms in the repertoire suggests that they might have been); and 2) that musicians adhered to the liturgically appropriate antiphon texts as printed in official liturgical books. If we accept these assumptions, then indeed there was a problem which musicians of the time had to resolve in one or more ways, and the task of musicology has been to try to understand just how they did so.

What is curious, however, is that we have no discussions of this "problem" in sixteenth- and seventeenth-century Italian sources, whether theoretical or practical. We do have evidence in practical sources of a number of different ways composers treated the relationship between antiphons and psalms or Magnificats, which point to no single "solution" but to several possible practices. Perhaps there was no "problem" of antiphon-psalm or antiphon-canticle relationship for Italian musicians in the period in question. Perhaps they simply did whatever was most convenient or seemed most suitable to them at any given time—ignoring tonal relationships between antiphons and psalms or Magnificats; they could transpose antiphons either literally or tonally, thereby either destroying the intervallic structure of the original mode or retaining it and thus generating chromatic clashes between the antiphon and the polyphonic psalm or Magnificat setting; reorder antiphon texts within a service freely, or even move antiphon texts from one service to another; substitute new texts for official antiphon texts; compose polyphonic antiphons or antiphon-substitutes without regard to modal-tonal identity; or substitute instrumental compositions for antiphons. In fact, there is evidence to support any and all of these practices, though the evidence for some is more plentiful and persuasive than the evidence for others.[2]

Thus, sixteenth- and seventeenth-century Italian musicians may not have had an "antiphon problem" based on modal-tonal relationships or on liturgically correct texts

---

2. The various possible practical solutions to this "problem" as shown by seventeenth-century sources are considered in Jeffrey KURTZMAN, *The Monteverdi Vespers of* *1610: Music, Context, Performance* (Oxford: Oxford University Press, 1999), chap. 2, "The Liturgy of Vespers and the 'Antiphon Problem'," 56-78.

at all. They may have felt free to handle the relationship between antiphon and psalm or Magnificat in any number of ways, and the "problem" is merely modern musicologists' difficulty in understanding what they did and why they did it from the limited and conflicting source materials and information now at our disposal.

Ironically, there is indeed an "antiphon problem" discussed in one source of the early seventeenth century, but of an entirely different nature from the "problem" briefly outlined above. The source is Don Pietro Maria Marsolo's second book of motets:

> MOTECTA/ QVINQVE TANTVM VOCIBVS/ Decantanda in totius Anni sol-/lemnioribus diebus./ LIBER SECVNDVS/ D. PETRI MARIAE MARSOLI I.V.D./ SICVLI, NOB: MESS./ In Cathedrali, nec non in Illustrissima INTREPIDORVM/ Academia FERRARIAE MVSICES PRAEFECTI/ *OPVS VNDECIMVM*/ Recenter compositum; & impressum./ Cum declaratione in calce cuiusq; libri apprime necessaria/ *CATHOLICO REGI DICATVM*./ CVM PRIVLEGIO./ [Vincenti device]/ *Venetijs Apud Iacobum Vincentium. 1614.*

The part-books comprise Cantus ($A^7 = 28$pp.), Tenor ($B^7 = 28$pp.), Altus ($C^7 = 28$pp.), Bassus ($D^6 = 24$pp.), Quintus ($E^7 = 28$pp.) and Basso pro Organo ($F^6 = 24$pp., without dedication or *ai lettori*).

Don Pietro Maria Marsolo was a Sicilian nobleman from Messina, a doctor in civil and canon law, whose musical activities are first traceable at the court of Ferrara in 1604.[3] From December 1608 to May 1610 he served as *maestro di cappella* at the cathedral of Fano, after which he returned to Ferrara. He was *maestro di cappella* of the Ferrarese Accademia degli Intrepidi, and by September 1612 (and perhaps from as early as 1610) held the same post at the Duomo of Ferrara. In that month he corresponded with Duke Francesco Gonzaga in an unsuccessful effort to compete for the position at the court of Mantua recently vacated through the dismissal of Claudio Monteverdi.[4] Marsolo was still *maestro di cappella* at the Duomo in Ferrara in 1614, but is recorded as *maestro di cappella* in Piacenza in the following year. Nothing further is heard of the composer after 1615.

The bulk of Marsolo's extant repertoire consists of five books of madrigals for five voices and two books of four-voice madrigals, all published between 1604 and 1614, the years in which he is documented in Ferrara and Fano. The last of these prints, the *Secondo libro de' madrigali a quattro voci, opera X*, is a unique collection of four-part expansions

---

3. The biographical information reported here is derived from the exhaustive study of Lorenzo BIANCONI in his introduction to *Pietro Maria Marsolo: Madrigali a Quattro Voci sulle monodie di Giulio Caccini e d'altri autori, e altre opere*, ed. BIANCONI, in *Musiche Rinascimentali Siciliane* 4 (Rome, Edizioni de Santis, 1973), and from BIANCONI's subsequent article, "Marsolo, Pietro Maria," *The New Grove* 11: 709-10.

4. The four letters by Marsolo in which he sought to have himself appointed at Mantua are all reproduced in BIANCONI, ed., *Pietro Maria Marsolo: Madrigali a Quattro Voci*, xxxii-xxxv. Monteverdi's dismissal that summer is described in Susan PARISI, "'Licenza alla Mantovana': Frescobaldi and the Recruitment of Musicians for Mantua, 1612-1615," *Frescobaldi Studies*, ed. Alexander SILBIGER (Durham: Duke University Press, 1987), 55-91.

of monodies by Giulio Caccini and a few other composers. This last print has been published in modern edition by Lorenzo Bianconi.[5]

Marsolo's first sacred collection consisted of a mass, motets and Vesper psalms for eight voices, dated 1606, and there followed a book of motets for five voices in 1608. The present collection, the composer's second book of motets for five voices, marks his final extant opus.

Marsolo's ambition to secure a more lofty position, revealed through his letters to Duke Francesco Gonzaga, is evident from the dedication of this second book of motets to Philip III of Spain, perhaps in hope of obtaining an appointment in Philip's domains in Italy or elsewhere.

> PHILIPPO REGI CATHOLOCO/ PETRVS MARIA MARSOLO. F.P./
>
> Videri queam tibi confidentior, Rex Augustissime, qui omnium mi-/nimus Patronum mihi deligam eum, cuius tanta est Maiestas, &/ amplitudo, vt quam noster Mundus non potest, ei noui fuerint/ aperiendi, qui capiant. Sed nescio quomodo cúm mea meique ope/ris humilitas, tùm tua tuae que pietatis celsitudo animos mihi ad-/dunt, iubentque bene me de tua pari Maiestati benignitate clemē/tiaque confidere. Nam & opus scio esse eiusmodi, cui repere humi/ necesse sit, nisi Maiestas tua, quæ Diuinæ similis in rebus abiectis/ erigendis maxime cernitur, adminiculetur; & pietatem tuam tam insignem, vt, qua tuis/ inregnis quae DEI sunt, vnde Catholici cognomen habes, tueris vniuersa, eadem, quæ ip-/se de Deo eiusque Sanctis viris Cantiones concinnaui tuiturum certò te defensurumque confido. Accipe igitur Rex Optime, & Maxime munus, si rem donantemque spectes exi-/guum, si donantis animum & voluntatem tàm magnum, vt, sicut Cæli Rex facere solet,/ qui in muneribus nostris non rem pensat, sed affectum, non debeas aspernarì. Tam & si/ cùm homo Siculus te naturalem mihi Dominum considero, non tàm videor quod meum/ est offerre tibi quàm quod tuum est reddere. Quæ res haud dubitanter efficìet, vt gratius,/ etiam tibi accidat, quod ipse quasi rem tuam, tuæque rei veluti annuum redditum, fru-/ctumque perpenderis. Crescat interim tua in dies magis Maiestas & Celsitudo, diuque-/ tuis Regnis, Christianoque Orbi Vniuerso ìs, cuius in manu vitæ nostræ momenta decur-/runt, incolumem ad sui nominis gloriam, propagatìonemque tueatur.
> Venetiis Kalendis Aprilis MDCXIV.

The dedication gives us nothing more than the expected encomiums to the chief secular defender of the Catholic faith, whose rule extended as far as nearby Milan. A more specific rationale for this publication is explained, however, in a note to readers printed in both Latin and Italian on the final page of each vocal part-book following the index:

> LECTORI.
>
> *IN Metropolitanis, Cathedralibus, Colleggiatisque Ecclesiis solet in fine, vel in principio cuius que Psalmi, eius Psalmi antiphona ab vno, vel pluribus Organo, vel alio instrumento comite decantari. Quæ res quoniam efficit vt Vesperæ abeant propè in infinitum, tedijque non parum ea prolixitate pariatur; visum est Auctori quinque*

---

5.    See n. 3 above.

Psalmorum Antiphonas in vnam, quæ infine vltimi Psalmi cantetur, contrahere. Quo fiet vt & diuino officio satisfiat, & leuetur magna ex parte tedium, & locus detur, si quando vti inter Psalmis libuerit, instrumentis.

## AL LETTORE.

NElle Metropolitane, Catedrali, & Colleggiate si suole dopò ciaschedun Salmo del Vespro, ò innanti cantare da vna ò piu voci nell'Organo ò altro instrumento L'Antifona che correa à tal Salmo, per la qual cosa il Vespro diuiene longo, ne si da loco a instrumento alcuno, onde acciò non succeda tale inconueniente, hà l'Autore in ciascheduno Motetto abbracciate tutte le cinque antifone di Salmi, qual Motetto si cantarà dopo l'ultimo salmo, che così si sodisfara all'officio, il Vespro sara meno tedioso, & se alcuno instromento vorra sonare hara loco commodamente.

"To the Readers"

"In the Metropolitan, Cathedral, and Collegiate [churches] it is customary either before or after each Vesper psalm to sing the antiphon that goes with that psalm with one or more voices with organ or another instrument. Because of this the Vespers becomes long, nor does it leave room for any instrument [instrumental composition]. To avoid such inconvenience, the author has included in each motet all five psalm antiphons; thus one sings the motet after the last psalm, which satisfies the Office, the Vesper will be less tedious, and if one desires to play an instrument, there is enough room for it."

For Marsolo, the "antiphon problem" is the length of Vespers when an antiphon setting is performed before or after every psalm and the Magnificat, wearying the congregation and leaving no room for instrumental music.

This brief lament is remarkable for what it implies. It suggests that all five psalm antiphons were commonly performed in some kind of setting in modern style ("with one or more voices with organ or another instrument"), extending the duration of each antiphon well beyond a simple plainchant presentation and thereby elongating Vespers beyond tolerable limits.

Monteverdi's five elaborate, few-voiced *sacri concentus* in his 1610 print have heretofore been viewed in the literature as unusual when considered as substitutes for the liturgically appropriate plainchant antiphons.[6] Indeed, apart from a print by Paolo Agostini from 1619, there is virtually no indication in a publication of Vespers music that any of the limited number of motets included in many such collections were intended to serve as antiphons or antiphon-substitutes.[7] Most of our evidence that this was done

---

6.    See the literature cited in n. 1 above.

7.    Paolo AGOSTINI, *Salmi della Madonna Magnificat à 3. voci. Hinno Ave Maris Stella, Antifone A una 2. & 3. voci. Et Motetti Tutti Concertati. Di Paolo Agostino Maestro di Cappella in San Lorenzo in Damaso, Discepolo, & Genero di Gio. Bernardino Nanini. Con il Basso continuo per sonare. Divisa in due parti. Libro Primo. In Roma, Per Luca Antonio Soldi. 1619.* RISM A411.

Agostini's print contains multiple settings of the five psalms of the Marian *cursus*, each psalm setting followed by a motet. One of the motets in each group associated with a single psalm text is labeled *antifona prima, antifona seconda*, etc. These *antifone* are polyphonic settings of the liturgically correct antiphon texts from the Feast of St. Mary of the Snow, which became the Common of the

consists of a few eyewitness accounts or references in service manuals or theoretical treatises.[8] On the other hand, some large collections of polyphonic antiphons for the entire liturgical year had already been published by the time of Marsolo's print.[9] It has already been demonstrated by James Armstrong that in one of these publications, Giovanni Francesco Anerio's *Antiphonae* of 1613, a sizable number of antiphons have been reordered or exchanged within a particular service and among different services in comparison with their order in the Roman breviary.[10] In this context, Marsolo's lament suggests that the practice of performing antiphons or antiphon-substitutes in few-voiced polyphony was much more widespread than scholars have been able to deduce from the limited evidence in the scholarly literature.

What is equally striking about Marsolo's comments, however, is the desirability of playing instrumental music within the service, between one or more psalms (*si quando uti inter Psalmis liberit*, in the Latin version), and very probably at the end.[11] Marsolo seems to take for granted that the use of instrumental music at Vespers service was common as well. Polyphonic antiphons not only made the service too long, they also left no room for instrumental music.[12]

Marsolo's solution to this "antiphon problem" is a unique one. In this collection he presents a set of 21 motets for 21 different Vespers of feasts in the Temporale and Sanctorale. Each motet contains the texts of *all five* psalm antiphons proper to that feast (Marsolo does not include any of the Magnificat antiphons). Thus the liturgical function of the psalm antiphons is fulfilled, but with only one polyphonic setting, not five,

---

B.V.M., while the texts of most of the other motets, apparently serving the same function in relation to the psalms as the *antifone*, are not liturgical antiphons at all.

8.    See the BONTA, OSTHOFF, and MOORE citations in note 1 above.

9.    See Guglielmo SITIBONDO, *Antiphonae ad Magnificat Festorum Omnium per annum occurrentium secundum tonos ab Ecclesia Romana observatos, Authore Guyilelmo Sitibundo Ancon. Liber Primus. Cum Quinque Vocibus. Venetiis, Apud Ioannem Barillettum. 1574.* RISM S3550; Girolamo LAMBARDI, *Antiphonarium Vespertinum Dierum Festorum Totius anni iuxta ritum Romani Breviarij iussu Pij V. reformati, nunc nuper pulcherrimis contrapunctis exornatum atque auctum. A Reverendo D. Hieronymo Lambardo Canonico Regulari sancti Spiritus prope Venetias. In Tres Partes Distributum, quarum una complectitur dies festos Domini altera Proprium sanctorum, tertia Commune. Impressum in Caenobio Sancti Spiritus prope Venetias. 1597.* RISM L366; and Giovanni Francesco ANERIO, *Antiphonae, seu Sacrae Cantiones, quae in totius anni Vesperarum ac Completorii solemnitatibus decantari solent; in tres partes distributae; Quarum prima Nativitatis Domini, Circumcisionis, Epiphaniae, & omnium Sanctorum. Secunda, Festa mobilia, & Communia Sanctorum.*

*Tertia, Praecipua Mendicantium Religionum festa complectitur. Binis, Ternis, & Quaternis vocibus concinendae. Una cum Basso ad Organum. Auctore, Io: Francisco Anerio Romano. In Ecclesia Sanctissimae Virginis ad Montes Capellae Magistro. Romae, Apud Io: Baptistam Roblectum. 1613.* RISM A1104.

10.    See article cited in n. 1.

11.    Stephen BONTA and David BLAZEY have both called attention to Adriano Banchieri's suggestion in *L'organo suonarino* of 1605 to play a 'Franzesa Musicale,' or something else if he likes' after the Magnificat, as well as to Giovanni Battista Fasolo's instructions from his *Annuale* of 1645 to play a short organ piece called *fuga sopra l'obligo* as a substitute for the Magnificat antiphon (*post Magnificat loco antiphonae*). See BONTA, "Liturgical Problems," 99; and BLAZEY, "A liturgical role for Monteverdi's *Sonata sopra Sancta Maria," Early Music* 18 (1989): 175-82.

12.    It seems unlikely that Marsolo anticipated inserting an instrumental piece between each of the psalms, since this too would have made the service too long.

13.    Praetorius' calculations work out to quarter note = *c*.MM 85. See Michael PRAETORIUS, *Syntagmatis Musici... TomusTertius* (Wolffenbüttel: Elias Holwein, 1619; facsim-

thereby shortening the service and leaving room for instrumental music.

The index of the print lists only the text incipits of the 21 motets; I have interpolated in italics each motet's caption within the part-books:

INDEX MOTECTORVM QVINQVE VOCIBVS [Canto Part-Book]

| | | | |
|---|---|---|---|
| TEcum principium<br>*Natale di N. Sig. & per l'otta.* | 1 | Audite insule<br>*Nella Nativita di S. Gio. Battista* | 13 |
| O admirabile comercium<br>*Nella sollenità della Circuncisione del Signore* | 2 | Petrus ascendebant<br>*Nella festivita di SS. Apostoli Pietro & Paulo* | 14 |
| Ante luciferum<br>*Nella solennita di Pasqua Epifania* | 3 | Exurgens Maria abiit<br>*Nella Visitatione della sempre Vergine Maria* | 15 |
| Simeon iustus<br>*Nella purificatione della Madre di Dio Maria* | 4 | Laurentius ingressus est martir<br>*Nella solennita di S. Lorenzo* | 16 |
| Missus est<br>*Nella Annuntiatione della B.V.M.* | 5 | Assumpta est Maria in Celum<br>*Nella Assumptione della sempre Vergine Maria* | 18 |
| Agelus [sic] autem<br>*Nella festività di Pasqua di Resurrettione* | 7 | Natiuitas gloriosæ Virginis<br>*Nella Nativita della sempre Vergine Maria* | 19 |
| Cum complerentur<br>*Nella Pentecoste & nell'ottava* | 8 | Stetit Angelus iuxta aram<br>*Nella festivita di S. Michele Archangelo* | 21 |
| Gloria tibi<br>*Nella festivita della Santissima Trinità* | 9 | Vidi turbam magnam<br>*Nella solennità di tutti i Santi* | 22 |
| Sacerdos in æternum<br>*Nella festivita del Corpus Domini & nell'Ottava* | 10 | Dixerunt discipuli<br>*Nella solennita di S. Martino* | 23 |
| Domine ostende<br>*Nella festività di SS. Filippo è Iacobo* | 11 | Salue Cruce precîosa.<br>*Nella sollenita di S. Andrea* | 24 |
| O magnum pietatis<br>*Nella solennità dell'inventioni della Croce* | 12 | FINIS. | |

These motets are not unusually brief. They range from a minimum of 37½ tempora to 72 tempora. Only two of the twenty-one motets are less than 40 tempora; eleven fall in the range of 40-50 tempora; two are between 55 and 60 tempora; while five are between 60 and 65 tempora. According to Michael Praetorius' method of timing the length of compositions at a moderate tempo, these motets would require nearly four minutes for the shortest and nearly seven minutes for the longest in performance.[13] Of course, Praetorius' method is designed only for approximation, and the note values and texture in each motet will affect the tempo and length of performance. Nevertheless, these figures illustrate that for each feast Marsolo has composed a substantial motet to fulfill the liturgical requirement of reciting all five antiphons for the five psalms. For this motet to have

ile ed. Wilibald Gurlitt, Kassel: Bärenreiter, 1958), 87-88. English trans. in Hans Lampl, "A Translation of *Syntagma Musicum III* by Michael Praetorius" (DMA diss., University of Southern California, 1957), 149-50. Praetorius' wording is "*Denn weil ich nothwendig* observiren *müssen/ wie viel* tempora, *wenn man einen rechten mittelmässigen* Tact *beit/ in einer viertel Stunde* musiciret *werden können.*"

14.   The Basso pro Organo part-book contains a rubric indicating that the *Alleluia* at the end of each antiphon is sung only if the feast falls in the period after Easter.

saved time in Vespers—enough time to insert some significant instrumental music without the service becoming tedious—the individual few-voiced antiphons they were replacing must have been much longer than a simple plainchant antiphon. Indeed, it usually takes Marsolo longer, sometimes substantially longer, to traverse the text of a single antiphon in his motets than it would to sing the antiphon in plainchant, and even Marsolo's shortest motet takes longer than would all five plainchant antiphons. (If the antiphons were sung before *and* after the psalm, however, then they would take longer than Marsolo's shorter motets.)

A straightforward progression through the five antiphon texts is only one of several ways Marsolo proceeds in these motets, and there is considerable variety in the manner in which he treats each individual antiphon. Sometimes the end of one antiphon overlaps with the beginning of another, according to the traditional practices of imitative polyphony. Sometimes there is a firm cadence at the end of one antiphon and a brief pause before the beginning of the next. The third motet, *Ante luciferum*, for Epiphany, exemplifies the separation between antiphons, for each antiphon comes to a full cadence before the next begins, in all but one instance only after a brief pause. This motet is thus a series of five mini-motets strung together. On the other hand, the fourth motet, *Simeon iustus*, for the Purification of the Virgin, is continuous from beginning to end, even though the conclusion of each antiphon is articulated by a cadence. Nor does Marsolo confine himself to a single pattern in any given motet, for some antiphons are treated as distinct entities, while others within the same composition may have considerable polyphonic overlap.

Textures also vary substantially within a single motet. Some antiphons are set as monodies with organ continuo; others are set for from two to five voices, with duet textures quite common. Sometimes only a portion of an antiphon, especially a quotation within an antiphon, is set for solo voice, while the remainder employs the full five-voice texture. Imitation prevails in the thicker textures, but there are passages of homophony as well. Varying textures between antiphons are the rule and are likewise common within a single antiphon. Although the predominant meter is duple, passages in triple meter are not unusual, especially for settings of the word *alleluia*. In sum, each motet presents a variety of textures and techniques representative of the range of early seventeenth-century few-voiced composition.

But Marsolo is even more creative with respect to treatment of the text in a few of the antiphons. For example, in the fifth motet, *Missus est Angelus Gabriel*, for the Feast of the Annunciation, the text of the first antiphon, *Missus est Angelus Gabriel*, is repeated as a refrain before the third and fourth antiphons, each time with different music. The words of Gabriel in the second, third and fourth antiphons are all treated as monodies, as is the beginning of Mary's response in the fifth antiphon. Thus the narrative text,

*Missus est Angelus Gabriel* serves as a polyphonic introduction to each of Gabriel's speeches, and the entire motet becomes a small dramatic *scena*.[14]

The twelfth motet, *Audite insulae*, for the Nativity of John the Baptist, also has a refrain, but the refrain is not drawn from one of the antiphons; rather it is derived from Isaiah 49:1, which serves as the source for collect of the chapter at the Mass and Vespers for the Feast of John the Baptist.[15] Marsolo uses only a portion of the Vespers chapter as his refrain, which opens the motet and is inserted either wholly or partially before each of the antiphons and again in full after the final antiphon. Indeed, the final version of the refrain is reinforced by reiteration of the second half of the text (from *de ventre*), the first time with the rubric *piano* and then with the repeat marked *forte*.

This refrain repeats in its music as well as its text. Repetitions of the refrain do involve exchanges of some vocal parts, but the most interesting change is to notation of the first half of the text, which is set in triple meter and is notated differently upon each reiteration (*de ventris. . .* is in duple meter under C). The refrains and their mensurations are as follows: Refrain 1: mensuration C3/1 in semibreves; Refrain 2: mensuration 3 in minims; Refrain 3: *de ventris. . .* in C only; Refrain 4: mensuration ₵3 in minims (first half of refrain only); Refrain 5: *de ventris. . .* in C only; Refrain 6: mensuration 3/1 in semibreves.

Because each of these refrains comprises the same music and bears the same relation to the second half of the refrain in C, whose mensuration and note values remain unchanged, it is clear that Marsolo has simply found a different way to notate the same rhythm each time the first portion of the refrain returns in triple meter. In other words, C3/1 in semibreves, 3 in minims, ₵3 in minims, and 3/1 in semibreves are all equivalent to one another. And in each case the proportional relationship between the triple meter and the duple meter is one three-note group equalling two minims, whether the triple groupings are in semibreves or minims.[16] This is a much clearer statement of equivalencies among various triple notations and their proportional relationships to C than one

15.   See the *Liber Usualis* with Introduction and Rubrics in English (Tournai: Desclée, 1963; henceforth *LU*), 1500, 1504. Marsolo's refrain text is as follows: *Audite, insulae, et attendite universi populi; de ventre matris meae recordatus est Dominus nominis mei.* Isaiah 49 reads: *Audite, insulae, et attendite populi de longe: Dominus ab utero vocavit me, de ventre matris meae recordatus est nominis mei.* This is the text for the Chapter at Vespers. The Chapter of the Mass contains a longer excerpt.

16.   There is a further metrical complication under ₵3, which is introduced *before* the refrain begins, on the last word, *gaudebunt*, of the preceding antiphon. This antiphon, which is a monodic setting for solo tenor, concludes with a melisma in semiminims under the new mensuration. The note groupings are in melodic

sequences of six sudivided into units of three, so that the passage is clearly in 6/4. Moreover, the last unit consists of a semiminim and a blackened semibreve followed by a white semibreve and minim rest. The blackened semibreve makes it clear that all of the preceding seminimins are in actuality blackened minims and that the entire passage is in diminution. Thus the white semibreve followed by a minim rest is a semibreve imperfected by the rest, the whole being equivalent to a 6/4 metric unit. The question then becomes, "Are the white semibreve and the white minims of the refrain also diminished notes, i.e., diminished breves and semibreves?" The answer must be "no," since diminishing semibreves would involve blackening them, not reducing them one level. It then becomes clear that the purpose of the black notation prior to the refrain

finds in most theoretical writing. It is as if Marsolo were saying, "Look, there's no real difference among all of these different ways of notating triple time."[17]

Yet another refrain structure is found in the seventeenth motet, *Nativitas gloriosae Virginis* for the Feast of the Nativity of the B.V.M. In this case Marsolo takes the fourth antiphon of the set, *Corde & animo,* and uses it as a refrain before the second and third antiphons and after the fifth as well as giving it a normal function as the fourth antiphon (also an introductoring introductory refrain to the fifth antiphon). In these refrains, too, the music also remains essentially the same, with exchanges of Cantus and Quintus voice parts and slight rhythmic differences between the version that serves as fourth antiphon and first refrain, and the one that serves as the second and last refrain. As in the twelfth motet, the final refrain is also lengthened through repetition of the last part of the text (in the version from the first refrain).[18]

Marsolo's versions of his antiphon texts follow closely those found in contemporary breviaries with some minor exceptions.[19] Moreover, early seventeenth-century breviaries agree with the versions found in the *Liber Usualis* with minor exceptions apart from the fourth antiphon for the Feast of the Purification of the Virgin, which reads in both Marsolo and contemporary breviaries: *Revertere in terram Iuda: mortui sunt enim qui quaerebant animam pueri.* The fourth antiphon in the *Liber Usualis* is *Lumen ad revelationem.*[20] Appendix A lists all of the differences between Marsolo, contemporary breviaries and the *Liber Usualis.*

To this point, I have not had an opportunity to research Ferrarese sources for the deviations in Marsolo's texts from those in contemporary liturgical books. It is quite likely that he took his texts from liturgical books at hand in the cathedral of Ferrara, perhaps even quite old ones that transmitted versions antedating the publication of the

---

is to generate the ⁶⁄₄ meter, which contrasts with the ³⁄₂ of the refrain (notated in groups of three minims). In terms of equivalency, each pair of blackened minims (diminished) is indeed equal to a single white minim (undiminished) of the refrain. Marsolo has therefore used the dot in the middle of a mensuration sign in its traditional sense of diminution to reinforce the diminution signaled by the black notation, but not as a way of imposing diminution on everything that follows. A similar usage of ₵3 comprising simultaneous units of ⁶⁄₄ and ³⁄₂, with the ⁶⁄₄ notated in groups of one white minim and one black semiminim (not a blackened minim) is found in the fifth antiphon for the Visitation, *Ex quo facta est.*

17.  BIANCONI quotes a similar example of triple meter notational equivalencies in a refrain from Marsolo's *Motecta Quinque Vocibus. . . Venezia, 1608; Vincenti* is quoted by BIANCONI in *Pietro Maria Marsolo: Madrigali a Quattro Voci,* xxxvi.

18.  The relationship between this last refrain and the

earlier versions is a bit more complicated than this, since the second half of the text is first reduced in texture from five voices to three (based on the second refrain version) before the text is repeated in the version from the first refrain.

19.  The breviaries used for comparison were the following: 1) *Antiphonarium Romanum ad ritum breviarij, ex decreto Sacrosancti Concilij Tridentini restituti, Pii Quinti Pontificis Maximi iussu editi, & Clementis Octavi auctoritate recogniti. Ea omnia continens, quae tum ad Divinum Officium decantandum, tum ad religiosorum commodum, necessaria sunt. De licentia superiorum. Venetiis, M.DC.VII. Apud Nicolaum Misserinum.;* and 2) *Antiphonarium Romanum Ad Ritum Breviarij, ex decreto Sacros. Concilij Tridentini restituti, Pij Quinti Pontificis Maximi iussi editi, Et Clementis viij. auctoritate recogniti, Ad usum omnium Ecclesiarum Cathedralium, et Collegiatarum nuper iuxta regulas Directorij Chori magno studio, ac labore redactum. Venetiis, Apud Iuntas. M DC XXIII.*

20.  *LU* 1366.

reformed breviaries of the late sixteenth and early seventeenth centuries. If his texts reflect local practices and liturgical books, the question is, "Why would he issue for widespread distribution through such a major publisher as Vincenti motets with texts that differed in some details from the official liturgy?" The answer, perhaps, is already contained in the very nature of the collection itself and in what it tells us about liturgical functions in the early seventeenth century.

Marsolo considered that the performance of all five antiphons in a single motet at the end of the sequence of five psalms was sufficient to fulfill the presciptin of the liturgical rite, even though the rite calls for performance of the antiphons both before and after each psalm. Obviously, deviations in such details were unimportant to him and to any user of his publication. When one observes how freely antiphon texts were interchanged within and between feasts in Anerio's *Antiphonae* of 1613, it is not difficult to accept that minor deviations between the texts of Marsolo's motets and those of official liturgical books were simply of no consequence to him or to anyone else who might wish to take advantage of his solution to the "antiphon problem."

We have no way of knowing how widely employed Marsolo's solution to the "antiphon problem" was. Apart from the potential use of Marsolo's own collection, there may be other motet collections as yet unstudied which duplicate Marsolo's method or find some related solution. After all, Marsolo does not announce his purpose on his title page and other composers may not have done so either. But until any further publications with similar purpose are uncovered, Marsolo's *Motecta Quinque tantum vocibus . . . Liber Secundus* remains a unique witness to the "antiphon problem" as understood in the early seventeenth century and offers a unique solution by a composer of not insignificant stature occupying the chief musical posts in a city which boasted major composers throughout the century, from Marsolo's successor at the cathedral of Ferrara, Alessandro Grandi (d.1630), to Giovanni Battista Bassani (d. 1716 at its end).

*Note for the following table:*
21. In the breviaries cited in n. 19 above, the antiphon at the *Benedictus* begins *Cum audisset salutationem.*

| | Marsolo | 17<sup>th</sup>-century breviaries | Liber Usualis |
|---|---|---|---|
| Feast of Circumcision, 5th antiphon: Ecce Maria | | | |
| | *tollit* | *tollis* | *tollit* |
| Epiphany, 1st antiphon: Ante luciferum | | | |
| | *alleluia* added | no *alleluia* | no *alleluia* |
| Epiphany, 2nd antiphon: Venit lumen tuum | | | |
| | *& reges in splendore ortus tui* inserted before *alleluia* | no comparable text | no comparable text |
| Purification of B.V.M., 4th antiphon: Revertere in terram | | | |
| | *Revertere in terram Iuda: mortui sunt enim qui quaerebant animam pueri* | *Revertere in terram . . .* | *Lumen ad revelationem* |
| Annunciation of B.V.M. | | | |
| | Pascal Time *Alleluia* at end of each antiphon | no *Alleluias* | Pascal Time *Alleluia* at end of each antiphon |
| Easter, 3rd antiphon: Erat autem aspectus | | | |
| | *autem* inserted in *vestimenta autem eius sicut nix* | no *autem* | no *autem* |
| Pentecost, 1st antiphon: Cum complerentur dies | | | |
| | *Cum complerentur dies . . . pariter in eodem loco* | *Cum complerenter dies . . . pariter in eodem loco* | *Dum complerentur dies . . . pariter dicentes* |
| Holy Trinity, 2nd antiphon: Laus & perennis | | | |
| | *Laus & perennis* ends in *saeculorum saecula* | *in saeculorum saecula* | *in saecula saeculorum* |
| Holy Trinity, 4th antiphon: Laus Deo Patri | | | |
| | *pariterque (pitilique) proli* | *parilique proli* | *parilique proli* |
| Visitation of the B.V.M., 3rd antiphon: Ut audivit salutationem | | | |
| | *Cum audisset salutationem* | *Ut audivit salutationem*[21] | *Ut audivit salutationem* |
| Visitation of the B.V.M., 4th antiphon: Benedicta tu in mulieribus | | | |
| | *Benedicta tu inter mulieribus* | *Benedicta tu in mulieribus* | *Benedicta tu in mulieribus* |
| St. Lawrence, 1st antiphon: Laurentius ingressus est | | | |
| | *martir et confessus est* | *martyr et confessus est* | *martyres confessi sunt* |
| St. Michael, Archangel, 2nd antiphon: Dum praeliaretur Michael | | | |
| | *Dum predicaretur Michael* | *Dum praeliaretur Michael* | *Dum praeliaretur Michael* |
| All Saints, 3rd antiphon: Redemisti nos | | | |
| | series of *ex* in place of *et* | series of *et* | series of *et* |
| St. Martin, 4th antiphon: oculis ac manibus | | | |
| | repeated *alleluia* at end | single *alleluia* at end | repeated *alleluia* at end |
| St. Andrew, 5th antiphon: Qui persequebantur iustum | | | |
| | *in infernum* | *in inferno* | *in inferno* |

Jonathan Glixon

# IMAGES OF PARADISE OR WORLDLY THEATERS?
## TOWARD A TAXONOMY OF MUSICAL PERFORMANCES
### AT VENETIAN NUNNERIES

T HE ROLE OF MUSIC in cathedrals, court chapels, and confraternities can be quite easily categorized and has therefore attracted the vast majority of musicological studies. In such establishments, sacred music for religious or ceremonial occasions, was performed by professional musicians paid by the directors of the institution, and intended, at least in some respects, for public consumption. This was certainly the case at the major Venetian establishments, the Ducal Basilica of San Marco[1] and the great lay confraternities known as the *scuole grandi*.[2] At another famous group of Venetian institutions, the *ospedali*, the situation was only slightly different: the performers were the resident women (both young and not-so-young, orphans and paying students), with the assistance of their paid male *maestri*; the music was still sponsored by the institution itself, and the intended audience was certainly the public.[3]

1.  For music at San Marco through 1562, see Giulio ONGARO, "The Chapel of St. Mark's at the Time of Adrian Willaert (1527-1562): A Documentary Study" (Ph.D. diss., University of North Carolina, Chapel Hill, 1986). The years through the mid-1580s are discussed in Rebecca EDWARDS, "Claudio Merulo: Servant of the State and Musical Entrepreneur in Later Sixteenth-Century Venice," (Ph.D. diss., Princeton University, 1990), 68-158. For the early seventeenth century, see James H. MOORE, *Vespers at St. Mark's: Music of Alessandro Grandi, Giovanni Rovetta, and Francesco Cavalli*, (Ann Arbor: UMI Press, 1981). The later period is treated in Francesco PASSADORE, Franco ROSSI, and Claudio MADRICARDO, *San Marco: vitalità di una tradizione*, 1 (Venice: Edizioni Fondazione Levi, 1996), and in the articles published in Francesco PASSADORE and Franco ROSSI, *La cappella musicale di San Marco nell'età moderna* (Venice: Edizioni Fondazione Levi, 1998).

2.  Musical activities at the Scuole Grandi were first uncovered by Denis ARNOLD in two articles: "Music at the Scuola di San Rocco," *Music & Letters* 40 (1959): 229-41, and "Music at a Venetian Confraternity in the Renaissance," *Acta musicologica* 37 (1965): 62-72. Another treatment of the material on San Rocco appeared as Chapter Eight of Denis ARNOLD, *Giovanni Gabrieli and the Music of the Venetian High Renaissance* (London: Oxford University Press, 1979). The first broad study was Jonathan GLIXON, "Music at the Venetian *Scuole Grandi*, 1440-1540," (Ph.D. diss., Princeton University, 1979). Other general studies of mine include: "Music at the Venetian *Scuole Grandi*, 1440-1540," in Iain FENLON, ed., *Music in Medieval and Early Modern Europe*, (Cambridge: Cambridge University Press, 1981), 193-208, and "Music at the Scuole in the Age of Andrea Gabrieli," in Francesco DEGRADA, ed., *Andrea Gabrieli e il suo tempo* (Florence: Leo F. Olschki, 1987), 59-74. A complete history of musical activities at the Venetian confraternities from their origins to the fall of Venice will be published as *Music at the Venetian Confraternities, 1260-1805* (New York: Oxford University Press, forthcoming).

3.  See Jane L. BALDAUF-BERDES, *Women Musicians of Venice: Musical Foundations, 1525-1855* (Oxford: Clarendon Press, 1993) and Pier Giuseppe GILLIO, "La stagione d'oro degli ospedali veneziani tra i dissesti del 1717 e 1777," *Rivista internazionale di musica sacra* 10 (1989): 227-307.

For Venetian male monasteries, the differences are predictable: many of the musicians were not external professionals, but the monks themselves. Additionally, there is some limited evidence of private music-making by individual monks. Similarly, at some of the smaller confraternities, in addition to paid professionals, the brothers themselves sometimes sang and played (though this practice was far less common in Venice than in many other cities).[4]

The world of music at Venetian nunneries, however, was a far more complex one.[5] Some added complications brought about by the cloistered status of all Venetian convents is not surprising, but there is more involved than simply a division between internal and external portions of the convent (that is those areas within the cloister and those still under the control of the convent but open to the public). A scholar studying these institutions is confronted (as were the nuns themselves) by several different kinds of patronage, involving not only the convent administrations but also private individuals, both inside and outside the walls, and with conflicting layers of external control, by both governmental and diocesan authorities. In order to make sense of the confusing variety of documented musical performances, I decided to construct a taxonomy of music in and around the nunneries. In the following pages, this taxonomy will be explained and illustrated with documents from several archives.

There were, during the existence of the Venetian republic, about fifty-five nunneries in the city and surrounding islands, of ten orders (most prominently Benedictines, with twenty-one houses, Augustinians, with eighteen, and Franciscans, with seven) (see Table 1).[6] Some were quite large and wealthy, populated in part by daughters of the noble families of Venice, but others were small and rather poor. The

4.   On music at the smaller confraternities, the *scuole piccole*, see Jonathan GLIXON, "*Con canti et organo*: Music at the Venetian *Scuole Piccole* in the Renaissance," in Jessie Ann OWENS and Anthony CUMMINGS, eds., *Music in Renaissance Cities and Courts: Studies in Honor of Lewis Lockwood* (Warren, MI: Harmonie Park Press, 1997), 123-40, and GLIXON, "*Far il buon concerto*: Music at the Venetian Scuole Piccole in the Seventeenth Century," *Journal of Seventeenth-Century Music* 1/1 (1995) (http://www.sscm.harvard.edu/jscm/). An important new study of music at all the "minor" institutions of Renaissance Venice, including parish churches, monasteries, and the *scuole piccole*, is Elena QUARANTA, *Oltre San Marco: Organizzazione e prassi della musica nelle chiese di Venezia nel Rinascimento* (Florence: Leo S. Olschki Editore, 1998).

5.   Research for this study was conducted with the support of the Gladys Krieble Delmas Foundation and the University of Kentucky. An earlier version was presented at the Annual Meeting of the American Musi-

cological Society, Baltimore, MD, November 1996. The following abbreviations will be employed in the footnotes: Vas=Archivio di stato di Venezia; Vasp=Archivio storico del patriarcato di Venezia; Vmc=Biblioteca del museo civico Correr; PC=Provveditori di commun; PSM=Provveditori sopra monasteri; PV=Eleanor SELFRIDGE-FIELD, ed., *Pallade Veneta (1687-1751): Writings on Music in Venetian Society* (Venice: Fondazione Levi, 1985); B=Busta; R=Registro. In the transcriptions of the documents, spelling has been left unchanged, but punctuation and capitalization have been regularized, and abbreviations have been expanded.

6.   The most comprehensive surveys of all the churches of the dioceses of Venice and Torcello are Flaminio CORNER, *Ecclesiae Venetae antiquis monumentis nunc etiam primum editis illustratae ac in decadis distributae* (Venice: Pasquali, 1749) and CORNER, *Ecclesiae Torcellanae antiquis monumentis nunc primum editis illustratae* (Venice: Pasquali, 1749).

**Table 1**  Nunneries of Venice and its Lagoon

| Order | Diocese of Venice | Diocese of Torcello |
|---|---|---|
| Augustinian | S. Alvise | S. Bernardo di Murano |
| | S. Andrea de Zirada | S. Giacomo Maggiore di Murano |
| | S. Catterina dei Sacchi | S. Maria degli Angeli di Murano |
| | S. Daniele | |
| | Gesù e Maria | |
| | S. Girolamo | |
| | S. Giuseppe di Castello | |
| | S. Giustina | |
| | S. Lucia | |
| | S. Maria delle Vergini[1] | |
| | S. Maria del Pianto | |
| | S. Maria Maddalena, Le Convertite* | |
| | S. Marta | |
| | SS. Rocco e Margherita | |
| | Spirito Santo | |
| Benedictine | S. Anna di Castello | S. Antonio Abbate di Torcello |
| | SS. Biagio e Cataldo alla Giudecca | S. Catterina di Mazzorbo* |
| | SS. Cosma e Damiano alla Giudecca* | S. Eufemia di Mazzorbo* |
| | S. Croce alla Giudecca* | S. Giovanni Evangelista di Torcello* |
| | S. Giovanni Laterano* | SS. Marco e Andrea di Murano |
| | S. Lorenzo* | S. Maria del'Orazione di Malamocco* |
| | S. Margherita di Torcello[2] * | S. Maria della Valverde di Mazzorbo* |
| | S. Maria dell'Umiltà* | S. Matteo (S. Maffio) di Murano* |
| | S. Matteo (S. Maffio) di Mazzorbo[3] * | S. Mauro di Burano* |
| | Ognissanti* | S. Vito di Burano* |
| | S. Zaccaria* | |
| Capucin | Cappucine di Castello* | S. Maria delle Grazie di Mazzorbo* |
| Carmelite | Terziarie di S. Maria del Carmine | SS. Giuseppe e Teresa di Murano |
| | S. Teresa | |
| Cistercian | S. Maria della Celestia | |
| Dimesse | | S. Maria della Concezione di Murano |
| Dominican | Corpus Domini | |
| | Terziarie di S. Martino | |
| Hermit | Eremite in S. Trovaso | |
| Franciscan | S. Chiara* | S. Chiara di Murano |
| | S. Francesco della Croce | |
| | S. Maria dei Miracoli* | |
| | S. Maria Elisabetta (terziarie) | |
| | S. Maria Maggiore | |
| | S. Sepolcro* | |
| Hieronymite | | S. Martino di Murano |
| Ursuline | Orsoline at S. Nicolò dei Mendicoli | |

*  The archives of these nunneries were not examined for this study.

1.  Although this church was in the geographical boundaries of the Diocese of Venice, the Doge had *jus patronatus* and the Primicerio of San Marco had rights of ecclesiastical supervision.

2.  Although on one of the islands subject to the Bishop of Torcello, this nunnery was, from the early sixteenth century, assigned to the Patriarch of Venice.

3.  Although on one of the islands subject to the Bishop of Torcello, this nunnery was, from the mid-sixteenth century, assigned to the Patriarch of Venice.

documentary records of these institutions, preserved primarily in the State Archives, are far from complete. Much appears to have been lost at the time of the suppression of the nunneries shortly after 1800, following the fall of Venice to Napoleon, and only a portion of the extant material has been indexed. Unlike the situation for convents in other Italian cities, few detailed chronicles or records of daily activities survive; rather, much of the material is financial in nature, especially account books recording living expenses, and primarily from the later centuries of the republic (that is, the seventeenth and eighteenth centuries). Undertaking a detailed history of music at one convent or limiting a study to the Renaissance, for example, would, therefore, be impractical undertakings. A more useful approach is to make a single broader study, one more comprehensive and global: to examine all the surviving records of all the convents, and then to attempt to construct a general picture from the widely scattered data.[7]

Unlike male monasteries, which reported to the superiors of their orders, primarily in Rome, convents of nuns were under the direct authority of the local bishops. In the area considered in this study there were two dioceses: Venice itself was under the direction of a Patriarch, and the surrounding islands were led by the Bishop of Torcello. Therefore, as in other cities, the diocesan archive also contains much of value for a study such as this one. In Venice, however, the authority of the bishops was not unchallenged. Always cautious about any extension of ecclesiastical power within their borders, and unwilling to trust the Patriarch and Bishop to work for the best interests of the state, the Council of Ten, the feared government body charged with state security, kept a watchful eye on the convents. Governmental control was made more explicit, and more direct, with the establishment, in the late sixteenth century, of the Provveditori sopra Monasteri, which usurped much of the day-to-day supervision undertaken elsewhere by representatives of the bishop. As with the diocesan archive, the records of this magistracy provide much of interest for this study.[8]

---

7. As of 1999 I have completed my studies of about 60% of the nunnery archives (thirty-five of the fifty-six separate *fondi* in the Archivio di Stato), as indicated in Table 1. Work in the remainder will be completed in the near future. In the discussion that follows, references to events at nunneries whose archives I have not consulted come from documents of diocesan and governmental authorities, where my research has already been completed.

8. Some seventeenth-century documents from this archive concerning music were presented in a recent article (published after most of the research for the present study had been completed) by Gastone VIO, "I monasteri femminili del seicento: gioie e dolori per i musici veneziani," in Francesco PASSADORE and Franco ROSSI, eds., *Musica, scienza e idee nella Serenissima durante il seicento*

(Venice: Edizioni Fondazione Levi, 1996), 295-316. For studies of nunneries in many other cities, the documents of the Sacra Congregazione dei Vescovi e Regolari in the Archivio Segreto Vaticano in Rome, the ecclesiastical body to which nuns could appeal decisions of the local bishop, are invaluable, as in, for example, Craig A. MONSON, *Disembodied Voices: Music and Culture in an Early Modern Italian Convent* (Berkeley: University of California Press, 1995). However, the Venetian government enacted legislation that forbade any communications from Venetian monasteries, male or female, to Rome without prior approval by the Senate. This law appears to have been effective. I have not consulted the archive myself, but understand that there is little there concerning Venice (Craig Monson, personal communication).

**Figure 1**  Plan of a Typical Venetian Nunnery

**Key**

A  public square
B  main entrance to the nunnery
C  courtyard
D  entrance to the cloister
E  main door of the church
F  external church
F'  choir of the external church
G  entrance for the priests
H  sacristy
I  nuns' choir (above)
J  public areas of the parlatories
K  nuns' areas of the parlatories
L  internal church
M  cloister
a  altars
x  grates
y  *ruota* (for giving communion to the nuns)
z  organ

Shaded areas are those locations within the walls open to the general public.

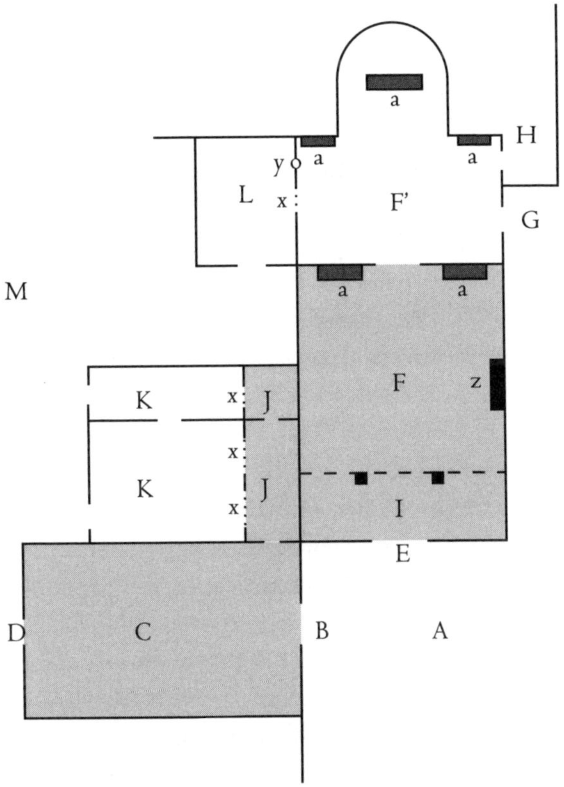

In order to understand fully the taxonomy proposed here, and the documents that will be employed as illustrations, a basic familiarity with the layout of a convent is necessary. Figure 1 is a schematic drawing of a Venetian nunnery, based on several sixteenth- and seventeenth-century plans in the Venetian State Archives. The entire complex is surrounded by a wall, which encloses both the buildings of the convent (including the church) and its gardens. Only the shaded areas were open to the public. These included the courtyard (C) and the main body of the church (F). Note that the nuns themselves did not enter the external church, but remained in the inner chapel, shielded from the public by a screen. The specific arrangement varied; very often in Venice, as in this illustration, the nuns' choir was a large grated balcony, like a choir loft, over the main doorway (I), with a second area on the ground floor near the high altar (L) where the nuns take communion (through a rotating shelf [y]) from the celebrant; in other cases, the interior church was directly behind the altar.

Other than the external church itself, there was only one other group of rooms open to the public, the parlatories (J). These spaces, entered either directly from the courtyard or through a reception room, adjoined directly the enclosed area of the convent, from which they were separated by grates (x), which allowed limited contact between the nuns and those on the outside. In most convents there were several such rooms, offering various levels of privacy. One was usually reserved specifically for guests of the Abbess or Mother Superior, who needed to consult frequently with the male financial and legal agents of the convent.

The interior spaces (not shown in the illustration), such as the cloister, the refectory, the infirmary, and the cells themselves, were off-limits to men, with very few exceptions. These exceptions, carefully controlled by the authorities, included the nuns' confessor (a priest certified by the bishop), and, when absolutely necessary, a doctor to minister to the sick or workmen to make essential repairs to the convent buildings. After the Council of Trent, the separations between interior and exterior were strengthened, and restrictions on entry by outsiders, even into the parlatories, were increased, but, as will be shown, enforcement of such regulations varied.

The taxonomy of musical performances offered here (see Table 2) has as one of its principal criteria for classification the geography of the convent. The first division is between the internal (I) and external (II) spaces. Each of these is then divided further into three classes. First, for both, are the respective portions of the church (A). Second, are the next most important locations for music: within the cloister, the nuns' cells, outside, the parlatories (B). Third, are other spaces, including, for the interior, the refectory and the nuns' portions of the parlatories, and for the exterior, spaces entirely outside the precincts of the convent (C). Each of the geographical subdivisions contains the same two classifications, by source of funding, whether by the convent itself (1), or by individuals, which include primarily single nuns or novices and their families (2). Finally, each of those classifications is subdivided into those activities permitted by the authorities (a), and those declared illegal (b). It should be noted that these final subdivisions are not all rigid—some vary from convent to convent, others change over time, particularly according to the succession of Patriarchs and bishops. In addition, much of the illegal music consists, as will be shown, of activities usually permitted that have gone wrong. The range of musical performances reflects, of course, the wide range of motives for sponsoring them in the first place. Some performances resulted from a desire to glorify God, in particular as part of the regular or occasional liturgy. Others, however, were brought about by ambition, in order to make an impression or to increase status, either individual or corporate, or simply because the sponsors wanted to be entertained. The desire for music, and particularly for splendid music, was often strong enough to drive the nuns and their collaborators to push, and even exceed, the boundaries set by the authorities, at the risk, sometimes, of rather severe penalties.

**Table 2** A Taxonomy of Musical Performances at Venetian Nunneries

I. Internal
  A. Church
    1. CONVENT-SUPPORTED
    a. *legal*
      1–nuns singing chant with organ
        (a) sometimes: spinet and/or violone allowed
      2–purchase of chant books
    b. *illegal*
      1–polyphony
      2–instruments other than organ
      3–in certain convents: chant
      4–dramatic performances
        (rappresentazioni, recreazioni)
    2. PRIVATE PATRONAGE [none]
  B. Cells
    1. CONVENT-SUPPORTED [none]
    2. PRIVATE PATRONAGE [nuns; resident students]
    a. *legal*
      1–in some convents: keyboard instruments
      2–in some convents: sacred singing
    b. *illegal*
      1–instruments other than keyboard
      2–secular songs
      3–any music at night
  C. Other [see also external--parlatories]
    1. CONVENT-SUPPORTED
    a. *legal*
      1–chant for episcopal visits
      2–sometimes: dramatic performances
        (recreazioni, rappresentazioni)
    b. *illegal*
      1–in dramatic performances
        (recreazioni, rappresentazioni)
        (a) nuns dressed as men
        (b) nuns in secular outfits
        (c) in sight of public
    2. PRIVATE PATRONAGE
    a. *legal* [none]
    b. *illegal*
      1–nuns singing in parlatory

II. External
  A. Church
    1. CONVENT SUPPORTED
    a. *legal*
      1–purchase, maintenance of organ
      2–salaried organist to accompany mass
      3–hired singers/instrumentalists for annual festivals
      4–musicians for monacations and investitures
        (partial support)
      5–music lessons (especially organ) with license
    b. *illegal* (all regarding outside musicians)
      1–activities of outside musicians
        (a) changing/substituting/rearranging sacred texts
        (b) inappropriate dress
        (c) misbehavior
        (d) singing with women
        (e) performing without a license
      2–nuns providing food for musicians
    2. PRIVATE PATRONAGE
    a. *legal*
      1–by confraternities housed in church
        (a) construction of organ music for confraternity
        events
      2–by families of nuns/novices
        (a) music for monacations, etc.
        (b) sacred music
        (c) oratorios
    b. *illegal* [see above, for convent-supported
        external church music]
  B. Parlatories
    1. CONVENT-SUPPORTED
    a. *legal*
      1–sometimes: music lessons through grate
    2. PRIVATE PATRONAGE
    a. *legal*
      1–sometimes: music lessons through grate
    b. *illegal*
      1–singing by visitors
      2–playing of instruments
      3–dancing
      4–teaching music to nuns through grate
        without license
  C. Other
    1. CONVENT-SUPPORTED [none]
    2. PRIVATE PATRONAGE
    a. *legal* [none]
    b. *illegal*
      1–performance of music for nuns
        from outside the walls
      2–*serenate* or *mattinate* from boats
      3–musical performances outside that disturb
        the quiet of the convent

## Music Lessons in Parlatory and Church[9]

There were only two locations in the convents where direct interactions, including musical ones, between nuns and outsiders were possible: in the parlatories and at the windows separating the internal and external portions of the church, the porous boundaries between two worlds. These interactions, however, were strictly controlled, both by physical barriers—iron grates—and by law. Legal musical activities in these locations were severely limited, with control maintained by officers of the Provveditori, who made regular rounds, especially in the evening, reporting to their superiors any violations they might discover. The magistracy also relied on secret denunciations, paid informants, and other varieties of espionage. Teaching was the one sort of musical interaction ever sanctioned, but even this permission was not consistently granted. The earliest regulation that has come to light, a patriarchal decree from 1575, banned all teaching by outsiders, not only of polyphony or instruments, but even by priests instructing the nuns in plainchant.[10] Restrictions seem to have been loosened by the early seventeenth century, with teaching now permitted as long as a license was first obtained from the Provveditori. Whether this represents an actual change of policy, or rather an example of conflicting authority, is unclear.

A case considered by the Provveditori in 1610 reveals that some of the music lessons went beyond what the Patriarch had declared acceptable.[11] The Captain of the Provveditori, their chief policeman, reported that

> it has been made known secretly that misser Zuane, the assistant organist at the Frari, was locked alone in the church of the Spirito Santo, where he taught the reverend nuns to sing and play, and he has done this for a long time without any sort of license.[12]

The accused, Zuane Picchi, was brought before the Provveditori in April of that year, and questioned:

> Q: Do you know the reason why these Most Excellent Lords have had you brought before them?
> A: Yes sir, because I went to teach the nuns of the Spirito Santo.
> Q: What things did you teach them?
> A: I went to teach them to sing and to play the organ and the viola da gamba; to three

---

9. While the systematic taxonomy as presented in Table 2 is arranged essentially from the inside out, beginning with the most central activities of the nuns, their religious observances, and working from there outward, the following discussion treats the materials in a different order, both to make explanations easier and for purposes of narrative.

10. Vasp, Curia Patriarcale, Archivio Segreto, Visite Pastorali a Monasteri Feminili, R.2, 1560-89, ff. 47ᵛ-48ᵛ, 2 September 1575, Mandatum generalis.

11. Vas, PSM, B.263, Processi criminali e disciplinari, 1600-1613, 28 April 1610. Dicussed briefly in Vio, *I monasteri femminili*, 302.

12. "... sechretamente si fa saper ale vostre Signorie Illustrissime che a ore 20 in circha era sarato solo in giezia misser Zuane soto organista dei Frari et muzicho, che insegnava a sonar et a chantar a quele reverende madre, et a frequentato molto tenpo avanti senza lisentia di sorte alchuna." Ibid.

> I taught the viola da gamba, and to one the violin, and to two the organ, but one of
> them was not yet a nun.
> Q: For how long have you done this?
> A: I began … last September, if I'm not mistaken, and continued until the captain found
> me.
> Q: Did you have a license from this magistracy to teach those nuns?
> A: I did not, because I did not know I needed one.[13]

Picchi's plea of ignorance was apparently believed: he was simply reprimanded and told to be sure to get a license in the future. That he had been teaching instrumental performance went unremarked by the authorities.

In 1616 the magistracy revoked all the licenses it had issued for teachers, declaring that no more would be forthcoming, to teach either the nuns themselves or the wealthy, usually noble girls residing in the convents as paying students (known as *educande*). However, an exception would be granted to teach novices and their superiors what they needed to prepare for the ceremonies surrounding the taking of their vows.[14] It was for precisely such an occasion that a license was issued for teaching at Santa Maria delle Vergini just one year later. The Abbess of the Vergini applied to the Doge, who held the *jus patronatus* of this nunnery, for permission for pre Paulo Bozi, a chaplain at the parish church of San Severo, "to teach singing to six young nuns who have to make their profession in the said monastery."[15] The abbess certified that pre Paulo was a sober and responsible man, and the Doge agreed to a thirty-day license, as long as conditions to be established by the *Primicerio* (the clergyman whose role was equivalent to the bishop for those churches under the direct control of the Doge) were obeyed. The rules were quite strict:

> this is to be done only during daylight hours, and never at night, or even near evening,
> and in the parlatories, confessional, or church, that is at the grates in those places, and
> in the presence of the oldest nuns of the monastery, that is, those especially designated
> by the Most Reverend Mother Abbess, and not otherwise.[16]

13. "Li domanda: Sapete la causa per la quale questi Signori Eccelentissimi vi habbiano fatto venir qua alla loro presenza? Risponde: Signor si, perché andaria ad insegnar alle madre al Spirito Santo. Li domanda: Che cosa ghe andavi ad insegnar? Risponde: Ghe andava ad insegnar a cantar, et a sonar di organo et di viola: a tre di viola, ad una di violin, et a doi di organo, ma una di esse non era ancora monaca. Li domanda: Per quanto tempo haver continuado di andarvi? Risponde: Cominciai [crossed out: doppo una sagra] avanti una sagra che fu questo settembre, salvo il vero, passato, et ho continuado fino che mi trovò [crossed out: il Capitano] l'homo del Capitano di questo Magistrato. Li domanda: Havete havuto licenza da questo Magistrato di andar ad inse-

gnar alle dette Monache? Risponde: Mi non ho havudo niente perché mi non ho sapudo." Ibid.

14. Vas, PSM, B.12, Filza Ordini, Proclami, ff. nn., April 1616.

15. "di far insegnare a cantar a sei giovini monache, ch'hanno da far professione in detto monastero" Vas, Doge, B.80, Atti 1615-23, p. 76.

16. "che cio sii solamente nelle hore di giorno, et non mai di notte, né verso la sera, et questo nei luochi delli parlatorii, confessionale, o chiesa, cioè alle finestre di quelli, et con l'assistenza di quele monache più vecchie del Monasterio, che a cio dalla Molta Reverenda Madre Abbadessa saranno specialmente deputate, et non altrimente." Vas, Doge, B. 196, Atti del Primicerio, 1609-19, f. 460ᵛ.

The absence of references to teaching over the following decades, while possibly indicating that the 1616 ban remained in effect, is just as likely to be the result of gaps in the records, for in 1645, without any revocation of the edict, the Provveditori issued a series of licenses to musicians (including Francesco Cavalli) for the teaching of the organ to noble girls receiving their educations in the convents (this represents an example of privately supported, legal activity in the parlatory, II.B.2.b).[17] In the latter half of the seventeenth century, licenses for the teaching of chant to nuns, especially for the ceremonies of the taking of vows, were granted fairly frequently, usually for brief periods from one to thirty days. On one occasion, in 1699, permission was extended by the bishop of Torcello to the teaching also of the organ at San Mauro of Burano, undoubtedly so that the nuns could accompany themselves during daily Office.[18]

Regulations regarding the teaching of sacred music to the nuns were relaxed, apparently, in the eighteenth century. From as early as 1720 and continuing through at least the 1750s, the convent of Corpus Domini employed salaried teachers of singing, organ, and instruments, particularly the violone (sometimes two of these posts being held by the same person).[19] These men appear to have conducted regular and frequent lessons: a 1727 payment to the singing teacher refers to the "many times he taught the nuns,"[20] and a 1755 entry specifies that in the four months ending in October, the *maestro del canto* had held 48 classes ("*scuole*"), that is two or three times a week.[21] The Provveditori continued to be worried about the possible moral dangers surrounding the teaching of secular music to *educande*, and in 1724 issued new regulations, requiring that prospective teachers present themselves personally before the magistrates so that their character could be evaluated, also presenting documentation that they had reached the age of forty.[22]

### Other Music in the Parlatories

The parlatories were also the scene of a wide variety of musical activities considered illegal, beyond that of teaching without a license (that is, activities classified

17. Vas, PSM, B.312, R. 104, Licenze 1643-51. The license to Cavalli, dated 30 December, was to teach organ to an *educanda* of the Grimani family at Santa Maria delle Gratie; the license was extended in 1646. Also in 1645, Giovanni Battista Chinelli, a San Marco musician, was licensed to teach the daughter of Michiel Caotorta at San Lorenzo (also renewed for another six months in 1646), and on 20 February 1646, the instrumentalist Marco Caorlini was given a fifteen-day license to teach a nun and several *educande* at the Spirito Santo.
18. Vasp, Episcopato di Torcello, Actorum, B.21, 1692-1705, f. 113^{r-v}.
19. Vas, Monastero del Corpus Domini, B.27, Libro Cassa, 1718-31, B. 24, Quaderno 1718-31, B. 25, Quader-

no 1731-44, B. 22, Cassa spesi…camerlenga, 1755-61, and Vas, Monastero di Santa Chiara di Venezia, B. 43, Cassa di spese 1744-55 [this registro of accounts for the Corpus Domini has been placed erroneously in the *fondo* of Santa Chiara].
20. "per ser Santo Mastro di Canto // a detta £44 per molte volte che insegnò alle religiose…" Vas, Monastero del Corpus Domini, B. 27, Libro Cassa, 1718-31.
21. "Al Maestro del canto per scuole numero 48, mesi 4 …"Vas, Monastero del Corpus Domini, B. 22, Cassa spesi…camerlenga, 1755-61.
22. Vas, PSM, B. 85, Mixtorum, 1723-30, ff. 33^{r}-34^{r}, 11 September 1724.

II.B.2.b). There were frequent (and therefore probably regularly ignored) admonitions, from both Patriarch and Provveditori, that dancing, singing, and playing instruments were not to be permitted in the parlatories at any time. Especially condemned were performances after dark or with the participation of courtesans. Such events were much desired, especially during carnival, in order to provide entertainment for the noblewomen, the sisters, nieces, and aunts of the Venetian Patricians, who were cloistered in these nunneries and who had few other opportunities for amusement. These rules were therefore, of course, regularly violated, as in this report made in 1675 by the Captain of the Provveditori:

> Last Friday I went to observe what they were doing at a late hour in the parlatory of Santa Catterina. With all possible diligence, I was never able to recognize anybody, because they were all wearing masks. Just at that moment, I heard from another parlatory, the door of which was locked, singing and playing of music. Since I could not get in, since, as I said, the doors were locked, I endeavored to climb up the wall to look into a window into the parlatory, to discover who it was who was singing and playing there, but I could recognize only one person, the one who was playing the harpsichord, Antonio Sartorio, a musician, and I could not see the others, except for a woman who was singing operatic songs, and this went on until an hour after dark ... [23]

No record of any further investigation or punitive action is extant.

The most remarkable case of such illegal activities to come to light happened in 1666 at the convent of San Daniele, when some of the most worldly music possible, opera, came right to the edge of the cloistered realm of the nuns.[24] Following up on a report by an officer, the Provveditori interrogated two singers, Antonio Formenti and Francesco Galli. Galli admitted that in February, during the rehearsals of the second opera at Teatro San Luca, Sartorio's *Seleucco*, the Patrician sponsors of the opera told them they would rehearse at another location than the theater, because too many outsiders were there to watch. When, the next day, he was picked up as usual for the rehearsal, Galli was brought, he claimed against his will, to the parlatory of San Daniele, where, in addition to the noblemen and their wives, there were several other singers, including Antonio da Ferrara, Steffano del Bentivoglio, Paulo Rivani (who sang the part of the old woman), a boy who sang the part of the page, and a soprano (that is,

---

23. "...venerdì decorso, fu li 14 febraio 1675, fui ad'osservare quelli li quali praticano tardi nelli parlatori di Santa Cattarina di questa città, si che per ogni diligenza possibile ussata non fu mai possibile il riconoscer alcuno, stante che erano tutti mascherati, e nell medemo punto o sentito in un altro parlatorio, che era serato le porte, a sonare e cantar di musicha, onde per non poter entrar nell detto parlatorio, poi che come dico le porte erano chiuse, m'ingiegniai ad rampegarmi suso dell muro per vedere per una fenestra nell' parlatorio per riconoscere quelli li quali ivi sonavano e cantavano; solamente da me fu conosciuto quello il quale sonava di spineta esser Antonio Sartorio pur musico, e non potei veder altri che una dona, la quale cantava delle canzonzine di opera; e questo è stato in sino ad una hora passata di note..." Vas, PSM, B. 261, Riferte dei Capitani e Denuncie, 1631-85.

24. Vas, PSM, B. 261, B. 272, Processi. See also Vio, *I monasteri femminili*, 306-307.

a castrato) from Livorno, whose name, he thought, was Alessandro; in other words, most of the male singers in the company.[25] Though Galli was told he would only sing one or two songs, the singers ended up staying for several hours, accompanying each other on a spinet, and performing nearly the entire opera. By the date of the investigation, most of the singers had left the city, but Galli, Formenti, and the noblemen were sternly admonished never to do anything like that again.

In the eighteenth century, though the regulations against music in the parlatories remained in effect, and musicians and other participants were regularly arrested and punished, there seem to have been some occasions on which such practices were allowed, nonetheless. The diarist Pietro Gradenigo remarks on one such event in 1771:

> In one of the vast parlatories of the nuns known here as the Celestia, a sumptuous and grandiose ball was tolerated until five hours after sunset, with the most beautiful women, generous refreshments, and many lights, all at the expense of the nobleman Andrea Memo, but the next day, by order of the Magistracy sopra Monasteri, it was prohibited in all the nunneries to ever again permit such dances.[26]

The monastery of Santa Maria delle Vergini, since it was under the direct control of the Doge, and therefore out of the reach of the Provveditori, seems to have enjoyed special privileges in this matter, as recognized by Gradenigo just a year after the incident at the Celestia:

> A ball with the leading women and gentlemen, conducted until six hours after sunset in the spacious parlatory of the most noble nuns called the Vergini in Castello, and this with the gracious permission of the Most Serene Doge Alvise Mocenigo, who possesses over this monastery a most ancient *jus patronatus*.[27]

## Music Outside the Walls

One type of musical performance that might not really seem to belong in this taxonomy at all, but that, in fact, can be found discussed frequently in the records of the Provveditori, provides a glimpse at the strictness with which the authorities attempt-

---

25. Steffano del Bentivoglio was probably Stefano Costa, and the soprano from Livorno can likely be identified as Alessandro Moscanera (Beth L. Glixon, personal communication).

26. "In uno de vasti parlatori delle Monache qui chiamate della *Celestia*, fu tolerato sino 5 ore della notte un sontuoso et grandioso *Ballo* delle più belle giovani dame con generoso *Rinfresco* e quantità di lumi, il tutto a spese del NV ser Andrea Memo, ma nel giorno seguente fu proibito a tutti li chiostri di non più permettere tali danze, per ordine del Magistrato sopra Monasteri." Vmc, Codice Gradenigo 67, tomo 32, f. 25ʳ, 18 February 1771. For more

on Pietro Gradenigo and his diaries, see Berthold OVER, "Notizie settecentesche sulla musica a San Marco: i *Notatori* di Pietro Gradenigo," in Francesco PASSADORE and Franco ROSSI, *La cappella musicale di San Marco nell'età moderna* (Venice: Edizioni Fondazione Levi, 1998), 23-38.

27. "Festa di ballo fra le primarie dame e Cavalieri, eseguito sino alle ore 6 della notte nel spazioso parlatorio delle nobilissime Monache, dette le *Vergini*, a Castello, e cio previo il grazioso assenso del Serenissimo Doge Alvise Mocenigo, di cui quell'illustre Monastero è antichissimo Juspatronato." Vmc, Codice Gradenigo 67, tomo 35, f. 84ᵛ, 5 February 1772.

ed to enforce the separation between the nuns and the outside world. These are musical events that happened entirely outside the precincts of the convent (classified in the taxonomy as II.C) that often, in fact, involved the nuns, if at all, purely by chance.[28]

It was the Venetian practice, during carnival and especially on fine summer evenings, to gather with friends on a boat and row through the canals of the city eating, drinking and generally making merry. When wealthy men celebrated, they often hired professional musicians. Occasionally, the Provveditori sopra Monasteri would investigate complaints of singing outside convent windows and find that it had all been entirely accidental. In one instance, the boat had gotten stuck in a traffic jam, and then was stranded by the low tide. The revelers decided to have dinner while they waited for higher water, and the musicians sang and played to amuse the guests; as the boat happened at the time to be under the window of the convent of the Celestia, the sponsors and musicians were hauled before the Provveditori, interrogated, and admonished for having disturbed the nuns.[29] Sometimes, on the other hand, the investigators discovered that the location of the music was indeed intentional. In October of 1665 the musician Antonio Sartorio (once again), during an investigation regarding music in the canal outside the convent of San Giuseppe, admitted that he and a young female student had once been brought by a wealthy young man and his wife in a gondola to sing outside the window of the convent where the wife's sister was a nun. After ascertaining that Sartorio's student had sung only one song, and of the most modest type, all were let off with only a severe admonition never to involve themselves in such activities again, under threat of severe penalties.[30] They were fortunate: in 1611 a young apprentice fruit vendor was caught singing obscene songs outside a nunnery, and was sentenced to six months in prison.[31]

Usually, these performances seem to have been ignored by the nuns, and the complaints were made by outsiders. In 1623, however, when the Patriarch made one of his periodic inspections of the Benedictine nunnery of San Lorenzo, he received a litany of complaints from one of the nuns, Suor Contarina Contarini, about the behavior of the nuns' confessor. Among his misdeeds, according to Suor Contarina, was that in late July, he had come with a singer named Donatello, and had sung a "*mattinada*" under the windows of some of the nuns with whom he was friendly.[32] No record survives of his punishment. In 1668 an anonymous nun of San Giuseppe filed a complaint with the Provveditori, describing an incident in which at least some of the nuns appeared to welcome a serenade by one of the best-known Venetian singers of the day:

28. For brief discussions of some of the following incidents, and a few others, see Vio, *I monasteri femminili,* 297-300.

29. Vas, PSM, B. 263, Processi criminali e disciplinari, ff. nn., 22 January 1568.

30. Vas, PSM, B. 272, Processi, ff. nn., 1 October 1665.

31. Vas, PSM, B. 12, Filza Ordini, Proclami; 27 July 1611.

32. Vasp, Curia Patriarcale, Archivio Segreto, Visite Pastorali a Monasteri Feminili, B. 4, No. 11.

Monday night, the seventeenth of the current mon th of September, there was music performed under the windows of our monastery of San Giuseppe, and scandalous songs were sung by Antonio Formenti, Perin, and others, with diverse [instrumental] sounds. All the nuns ran to the windows and spoke with those who were in the *peota* [a type of large boat, usually used for carrying cargo] and gondolas. I be Your Excellencies to do something about this, since it was Suor Lucieta who was the cause for all the scandal.[33]

## Legal Performances in the External Church

Of all the music making in the convents, the most public took place in the external church on various occasions throughout the year: during regular weekly or monthly mass, vespers, or compline, at the annual celebrations for the patron saints of the convents, and at ceremonies during which new nuns swore their solemn vows and accepted the veil. While the musicians for the regular services and annual saints' days were paid by the convent. The families of the new nuns usually paid all or part of the expenses for the music at the veiling and profession ceremonies.[34] On ordinary Sundays, the external musicians at nunneries were usually limited to an organist and perhaps some priests to sing chant; the music was clearly intended specifically for the nuns themselves. Both the annual celebrations and monacations, however, were opportunities for the nunnery, individual nuns, or the relatives of novices to enhance their prestige through the use of elaborate music. These events attracted large audiences, and were often commented on both by visitors and in the seventeenth- and eighteenth-century newsletters that described events in the city. For example, the *Pallade Veneta* of March 1688 described the feast of San Giuseppe in that convent:

In the wonderful and rich church dedicated to San Giuseppe . . . one saw a most noble apparatus, made by the illustrious and most reverend nuns, and one enjoyed very lovely music, sung under the masterly direction of Don Paolo, by a quantity of voices selected from the best of these learned singers, embellished by plucked lutes, with a supporting choir of bowed instruments, with trumpets and *cornetti*, which succeeded to the full satisfaction of the nobility who came there, and, one could almost say, to all the people of Venice . . .[35]

---

33. Vas, PSM, B. 261, Riferte dei Capitani e Denuncie, 1631-85. "Lunedì notte adì 17 del corente di settenbrie è stata una musica sotto delli balconi del nostro Monastero di San Iseppo, e sono state cantate canzone scandolose da Antonio Formenti, Perin, et altri con suoni diversi, concorendovi tutte le monache alla finestre e parlando con chi stava in peota e nelle gondole. Supplico Vostre Eccellentie del rimedio, esendo Suor Lucieta la causa di tutto il scandolo." Suor Lucieta has not been identified, but was undoubtedly a rival of the complaining nun. The singer Perin can most likely be identified as Pietro (or Pierino) Lucini (Beth L. Glixon, personal communication).

34. Excluded entirely here (but listed in the taxonomy) are performances sponsored by confraternities whose altars were in the nuns' churches. Except when these coincided with the festivities of the monastery, the nuns were not in any way involved. For more on these see the references in n. 4 above.

35. "Il dì dicenove, consagrato alle feste spirituali ed ai celesti trionfi del Patriarca Giuseppe, si vide nobilissimo apparato nella vaga e ricca chiesa dedicata al suo nome, fatto da quelle illustrissime e reverendissime signore monache; e si gode una musica molto gratiosa, cantata sotto la mano maestra del Signor Don Paolo, da quantità di voci trascielte fra le più disciplinate di que-

In part because of the popularity of these events, and because of the possibility that outside musicians could embarrass the nuns or distract from the solemnity of the churches, the Patriarchs issued detailed regulations in the early seventeenth century about the performances. In the rules of 1628, perhaps in reaction to the extravagances of the new, Baroque style, the Patriarch seemed particularly concerned with the texts and the way they were set:

> The confessors and chaplains of the churches of nuns must not allow that in their churches, oratories, or chapels, in the musical performances done there, that other words than those of the Holy Scriptures accepted by the Holy Roman Catholic Church be sung, the words following one after another as they are in the text itself, without transposition of one before another, and without combining various words collected from several various places in those Holy Scriptures, breviaries, and missals ...[36]

The guidelines of 1633 recapitulated some of the 1628 rules, and were more explicit in other areas:

> 1. It is ordered that the words that are sung should be chosen entirely from the Holy Scriptures, with the exception of the Song of Songs, which is completely forbidden in the musical performances.
> 2. If it is necessary to sing other words than those of Holy Scripture, they must first be seen and approved by His Eminence or by the vicar in charge of nuns.
> 3. Such instruments as lute, theorbo, harp, and the like may be used.
> 4. That the [intonations] *Gloria in excelsis Deo* and *Credo in Deum* should not be repeated, but [the music] should follow immediately where the celebrant finishes, and similarly for psalms, hymns, and every other thing.
> 5. The names of the musicians must be brought to His Eminence [the Patriarch], so that they may be recognized and approved if they are worthy of nuns' churches.
> 6. That the musicians should use that reverence that is called for by the holiness of the place in which they find themselves, and that modesty which is proper to their office, and acting otherwise they shall be prohibited immediately from singing or playing in nuns' churches.
> 7. That the platforms for the music may not be built near the enclosure of the nuns, but should be as far away as possible.
> [8.] That when the nuns give the wages to the musicians, or offer them some gift, this should not be the cause of disturbances which would bring scandal to religious and pious persons.[37]

sti dotti cantanti, rifiorita da tasteggiare tiorbe, con un sotto coro d'instrumenti da arco, con trombe e cornette, che riuscì con piena satisfattione della nobiltà concorsa, e quasi dissi, di tutto il popolo di Venetia...."
*Pallade Veneta*, March 1688 (PV#78).

36. "... confessori, et capellani delle chiese di monache ... non debbino permettere che nelle lor chiese, oratorii, o capelle nelle musiche che si faranno si cantino altre parole che quelle della Sacra Scrittura admesse dalla santa Chiesa Cattolica Romana seguenti una doppo l'al-

tra come che stanno nel Testo istesso, senza trasportatione di una inancti dell'altra, et senza concatenatione di varie parole raccolti da più et varii luochi di essa sacra scrittura, breviarii, et messali...."Vasp, Curia Patriarcale, Actorum Generalium Curiae Patriarcalis, R.5, 1620-31, f. 85ᵛ, 1628.

37. "1. Si ordina che le parole che si cantano siano tolte puramente dalla sacra scrittura, eccettuata però la Cantica, la quale si prohibisce del tutto nelle musiche. 2. Che dovendosi cantare altre parole che dalla sacra scrit-

The final refinement, published in 1640, extended the controls to all churches in the diocese, not only those of nuns, and made the religious objections to the modern style quite clear. Churches, the Vicar General of Patriarch Federico Corner wrote, should be "images of Paradise," but had become instead "almost worldly theaters, with the diminution of the Divine Cult, distracted many times by the most vain things …" The liturgical services were to be performed as described in the approved books, without introduction of other materials, except during the Secret or the Elevation, when "the musicians or singers may use a motet, but with devout words used by the Holy Church, and not made up in their heads." The refined regulations regarding instruments seem designed to exclude much of the more elaborate music of the period:

> The use of trumpets or drums, warlike or other unusual instruments is not permitted. And universally when instruments are introduced, either by themselves or accompanied, the sense of the words must not be divided, and much less, under the pretext of performing concerti, should vain things be played. And in the churches of nuns it is also intended that theorbos be prohibited.[38]

This last decree also reaffirmed the requirement that nunneries obtain licenses for the use of musicians, with the application listing all the names of those proposed. These licenses are the sole documents other than descriptions by audience members that can provide information on who performed at these special occasions, since the nuns or families of novices contracted only with the maestro, who would supply all the needed musicians. Unfortunately, they survive only for a brief period in the 1640s, scattered in various registers of the Patriarch's archive.[39] Many of these indicate that only

tura, si vedino prima, et si ammettino da sua Eminenza o dal suo vicario sopra le monache. 3. Che si possino adoperare tutti gli stromenti dal liuto, tiorba, et arpa da poi. 4. Che non si repliche il *Gloria in excelsis Deo*, né il *Credo in Deum*, ma si seguiti subito dove sia terminato il celebrante, il simile de salmi, himni, et ogn'altra cosa. 5. Che si portino i nomi de musichi a sua Eminenza a fine che li possa riconoscere et approvare per le chiese di monache, se meritaranno. 6. Che li musichi usino quella riverenza che ricerca la santità del luoco dove si trovano, e quella modestia che è propria dell'officio, et essercitano altrimenti saranno privi di più presto cantare o sonare in chiese de monache. 7. Che li palchi della musicha non si possino fabricare vicini alle serrate delle monache, osia più lontani che sarà possibile. Che nel dar le monache la mercede a musichi, o nel regalarli di qualche gentilezza, non si cagioni streppiti con scandolo delle persone religiose et pie. Dati dal Palazzo Patriarchale il dì 16 zugnio 1633." Vasp, Curia Patriarcale, Sezione Antica, Monialium, Atti particolari, B. 4, 1632-39, f. 13$^{r-v}$.

38. "…Simolacri di Paradiso; restano quasi in theatri del secolo, con diminutione del culto Divino, distratti molte volte a cose vanissime…potranno li Musici, o Cantori usare qualche Motteto, ma di parole divote usate da Santa Chiesa, & non fatte di testa…Non permettano l'uso delle Trombette, o Tamburi, instromenti bellici, o d'altri insoliti. Et universalmente nell'introdurre gl'instromenti, o soli, overo accompagnati, non si divida il senso delle parole: e tanto meno, sotto pretesto di Concerti, si suonino cose vane. Et nelle Chiese di Monache s'intendino prohibite anco le Tiorbe." Broadside published 22 February 1640; copies in many archives, including Vas, Sant' Alvise, B. 16.

39. Some of these licenses are in the sorts of general registers in which one would expect such items: Vasp, Curia Patriarcale, Sezione Antica, Diversorum, B. 13, 1644-49, Vasp, Curia Patriarcale, Sezione Antica, Actorum, Mandatorum, Praeceptorum, B. 105, 1644-46, and Vasp, Curia Patriarcale, Sezione Antica, Monialium, Atti Particolari, R.6, 1644-46. A larger series, however, is found among the interrogations regarding men and women whose situations required special permission to

a small ensemble of three or four singers and an organist was employed. Others, such as one from 1645, give an idea of the splendor that must have been usual at the wealthier nunneries on major occasions: the nuns of Santa Catterina, for the celebrations for their patron saint, proposed a list of musicians headed by Francesco Cavalli as first organist, that included another organist, two spinet players, three violins, two violas, three trombones, and thirteen singers, some of whom were among the best in the city.[40]

In the late seventeenth and eighteenth centuries, the authorities apparently abandoned their attempts to reduce the level of display and splendor in the musical performances at convents. The only limits now were economic ones, and the desire to excel led to rivalries among the richest of the convents, notably San Lorenzo, San Zaccaria, and the Celestia, joined by Santa Catterina after 1758, the year when Carlo della Torre Rezzonico, whose sister was then Abbess, was elected Pope Clement XIII. Another factor that kept the level of splendor high was related to the method of funding the annual patronal feast: in the wealthiest nunneries, the responsibility for organizing and financing the decorations and music was placed on the shoulders of the *sagrestana*, the nun elected for the year to supervise the activities of the church. As these were always daughters of the most important Venetian patricians, no expense would be spared to maintain the prestige of the family or the convent. The results were, indeed, spectacular. In the late seventeenth century, the Benedictine nunnery of San Lorenzo had perhaps the greatest reputation for the lavishness of its music, as can be seen from a description in the *Pallade Veneta* of 1687 of the feast of their patron saint:

> There was music with five choirs, filled with as many voices and as many instruments as there are, the best in this great city, a fine work by Signor Legrenzi, choirmaster in the ducal basilica of San Marco, which brought the ear such content that I do not know if the harmony of the spheres in their sweet spinning could give more joy.[41]

Sometimes, the excess of musicians did not work as well, as recounted in a 1673 letter to the Duke of Hanover, describing a similar event, again at San Lorenzo (note that even the ban on warlike instruments was no longer being observed):

> Yesterday we had the famous feast of San Lorenzo, which the nuns celebrated with infinite generosity. The apparatus could not be more magnificent or more wonderful. The

get married, in registers that otherwise have nothing to do with nuns: Vasp, Curia Patriarcale, Sezione Antica; Examinum Matrimoniorum, Matrimoniorum 1644-45 and Matrimoniorum 1645-46.

40. Vasp, Curia Patriarcale, Sezione Antica, Monialium, Atti Particolari, R.6, 1644-46, f. 33ʳ, 14-11-1645.

41. "...Una musica a cinque cori, ripiena di tante voci e di tanti instrumenti quanti appunto erano i migliori di questa gran dominante, opera studiata del Signor Legrenzi, maestro di cappella nella ducale di San Marco, tratteneva l'orecchio in tanto contento che non so se l'armonia delle sfere col suo dolce girare possa dispensarne di più." *Pallade Veneta*, October 1687 (PV#41). An eighteenth-century celebration at San Lorenzo, with similar numbers of musicians, is depicted in a painting by Gabriel Bella, now in the Querini-Stampalia collection in Venice, reproduced in Umberto FRANZOI and Dina di STEFANO, *Le chiese di Venezia* (Venice: Alfieri, 1976), plate 681.

music [however], was chaos, a Babylon of all the musicians of Venice, five organs, all the instruments, trumpets, trombones, and everything there is in Venice; but you could not hear anything except a rumble, without being able to understand a single word.

The writer continued with the hope that the music at the upcoming festa for the monastery of the Celestia, San Lorenzo's rival, would be better: "Soon we have that of the Celestia, a monastery that competes with that of San Lorenzo, and we will see an even larger crowd; but if the musicians do not do any better, they [the Celestia] will lose all their prestige."[42] In the year 1700, the Celestia certainly succeeded, as recorded in the *Pallade Veneta*, where credit was given both to the *sagrestana*, "la Nobil Donna Lugrezia Pizzamano" and to "Signor Carlo Pollaroli, who, with his musical miracles, rendered by now more enviable than imitable, formed a tuneful echo to the untiring accents of the heavenly musicians, who perhaps listened to the sweet manner of those compositions which carry in themselves a portion of Paradise."[43]

It is interesting to note that while these elaborate musical performances were clearly designed to make an impression on the public, at the two convents with the grandest reputations in the eighteenth century, San Lorenzo and the Celestia, accommodations were also made to satisfy the nuns. On the day of the patronal feast (as at most nuns' churches in Venice), the music was performed from the specially built platforms, with singers and instrumentalists facing toward the audience. However, as the diarist Pietro Gradenigo explained, the same music was repeated at the octave of the feast in a different arrangement:

> This morning of the octave of the martyr St. Lawrence, the Reverend Benedictine nuns have a solemn mass celebrated in the temple dedicated to that glorious Levite, and the same music that was performed at the festivity [on the saint's day] was repeated by the singers on the floor [of the church] next to the grate ...; when this was finished the musicians were all given cakes and sweets, and thus received payment for their efforts.[44]

42. "Hieri habbiamo hauto la famosa festa di San Lorenzo; quelle signore moneghe l'hanno celebrata con infinita generosità; l'apparato non poteva eser più magnifico e più vago; la musica è stata un caos, un Babilonia tutti li musici di Venetia, cinque organi tutti li istromenti, trombe, tromboni, e tutto quanto era in Venetia; ma, non vi è goduto altro che il mormorio, senza esserne potuta intendere una parola [...] Habbiamo ancor prossima quella della Celestia, monastero che gareggia con quello di San Lorenzo, e vedremo un concorso anco maggiore; ma se li musici non fanno meglio, perderanno affatto il lor credito." Letter dated 11 August 1673 in Hannover Archive (PV#A29). The last phrase could alternatively refer to the prestige of the musicians themselves.

43. "...il Signor Carlo Pollaroli, con li suoi miracoli

musicali resossi ormai più invidiabili ch'immitabile, formò eccho canora agl'accenti instancabili de' celesti musici, che forse seguivano la maniera dolcissima di quelle compositioni che portano in se una porzione di paradiso." *Pallade Veneta* 14-21.VIII.1700 (PV#107).

44. "In questa mattina dell'Ottava del Martire San Lorenzo, le Reverende Monache Benedittine fanno celebrare Messa solenne nel Tempio a quel glorioso *Levita* qui dedictato, e viene appresso il pavimento contiguo alla *Grata* replicata da cantori la musica stessa che fu eseguita nella Festività, cioè a 10 corrente, la quale terminata tutti li filarmonici vengono regalati di ciambelle e dolci, indì ricevono il pagamento delle loro fatiche..." Vmc, Ms Gradenigo 67, tomo 37, f. 122ʳ, 17 August 1773.

At the Celestia in 1772, this repeat performance was done with the musicians "seated in a circle on the floor [of the church] next to the high altar," that is, once again, right next to the grate behind which the nuns could listen from the interior church, which in this case was located immediately behind the altar.[45]

### Illegal Music in the Church

As can be imagined, there were many opportunities for problems to arise in the planning or execution of the musical portion of church ceremonies, and illegal activities often resulted. The records of the Provveditori and Patriarch are filled with violations of the above-mentioned rules, as well as others. Difficulties included the musicians being served refreshments (a restriction usually ignored), fighting after the performance, wearing inappropriately fancy clothes, singing too long,[46] or having the specially built platform over-decorated with elaborate materials or architectural ornaments.

One of the most frequent types of abuse was the performance of music without the appropriate license. In 1683, for example, a priest named Michiel Rocca fled the city rather than face the consequences of having dared to direct music (he was the "*maestro del batter*") at the convent of Santa Marta without a license, with the added scandal that he had performed the *Tantum ergo* with violins, which was against regulations, and had sung motets "in a premeditated fashion, with total disrespect for all public order" with "pernicious consequences."[47] The Provveditori declared that he should be imprisoned for a year if caught.

Even when the necessary license had been obtained (or the circumstances did not require one), the music itself could be a problem. Among the more interesting cases is one involving a priest named Francesco Dei, who was accused in 1617 by the nuns of San Daniele of creating a scandal while singing from the organ loft in their church. Apparently attempting to sing some motets based on texts from Song of Songs, he did such a bad job, garbling so many words, that not only did the motets sound obscene (these texts are perilously close to that in any event, which is why they were banned several years later), but everybody began to laugh, certainly not an appropriate reaction. Under interrogation, he admitted having sung in the church a few times, when nobody else was available, but said that he had only performed some of his favorite, most devout motets, which he had copied into a book, and that these were the only ones he knew how to sing. Giovanni Battista Savii, an organist at San Marco, testified that he had, in

45. "ma sedenti in circolo nel pavimento appresso l'altare maggiore..." Vmc, Ms Gradenigo 67, tomo 34, f. 21$^{r-v}$, 14 August 1772.
46. On performances continuing illegally after sunset, see Vio, *I monasteri femminili*, 303-34.

47. "...con quelle perniciose conseguenze...havendo commesso sicente, pensata, deliberatamente in onta e sprezzo de publici ordini..." Vas, PSM, B. 276, Processi, 1683-84, February 1683.

fact, taught some motets by Viadana to Dei, and the priest's brother produced seven printed books of works by Viadana plus the two hand-copied books. Since Dei was also accused of unlawful dalliances with a nun, he was sentenced to a year in prison and banned from convents for life.[48]

Whereas Francesco Dei's transgression was, at least in part, caused by incompetence, even correctly sung motets could be illegal, if they were used inappropriately. This was the case with another priest, pre Battista Mida da Castello, who apparently had maintained improper relationships with some nuns (in an unnamed convent), and compounded his error by expressing his feelings through the performance of certain motets, as described in his indictment, of 1617:

> That he, together with other musicians, his companions, at the recurrence of feasts in the church of the said convent, had sung motets, that although they seemed as if they were in praise of His Divine Majesty, were rather, through the abuse of phrases from Holy Scriptures, sung solely to name some of those nuns.[49]

He was sentenced to two-years' banishment or imprisonment, and a lifetime exclusion from all nunneries.

Quite common also were problems of the behavior of musicians, usually involving fighting, improper language, or inappropriate garb. The events graphically (and crudely) described in a secret and unsigned denunciation that was delivered to the Provveditori in 1658, however, were of a different sort altogether:

> In the music at Santa Marta directed by Giovanni [da Pesaro], some of the musicians … went into a corner of the music platform, and there, between the organs and the wall, they lowered their trousers and displayed their shameful parts, touching each other's asses, and displaying their pricks, taking them in their hands in front of the nuns, who were standing nearby to hear the music; they did all this just so they would be seen by the nuns … Heaven is offended, these virgins are contaminated, the church has been profaned, and worldly justice has been given a slap in the face. The music master admonished these singers, and knows all about this, and he would know how to bring them to justice, if you want to avenge an offended church and scandalized nuns.[50]

48. Vas, PSM, B. 265, Processi Criminali e Disciplinari, 1614-18, February 1618.

49. "Che habbi cantato insieme con altri musici suoi compagni con occorenze di feste nella Chiesa del sodetto Monasterio, motetti, che se bene pareva che fussero in lode di Sua Divina Maestà, abusando detti della scrittura sacra, erano solo per nominare alcune di quelle monache…"Vas, PSM, B.12, Filza Ordini, Proclami, 20 September 1617.

50. "Nella musica di Santa Marta fatta da D. Giovanni sono stati così arditi fra Piero di Carmeni, Tonini, Formenti, Tinti, et Amato di ridursi in un angolo del palco, che stava appoggiato al muri, et ivi tra li organi et muro, alciandosi suso le braghesse, mostrar tutte le parti vergognose, toccandosi il culo l'un l'altro, et mostrandosi li cotali, pigliandosili in mano in faccia delle monache che stavano affaciate sopra detto palco per udire la musica, havendo tutto fatto appunto per esser veduti da dette monache… Il Cielo è offeso, contaminate quelli vergini, proffanata la Chiesa, et sprezzata la giustizia del mondo. Il Maestro di Capella ha fatto la monition, è molto ben informato, et saperà lui renderli pagha la Giustizia si vorrà vendiciar una chiesa offesa, et monache scandalizate."Vas, PSM, B. 270, Processi, August 1658.

The maestro, Giovanni da Pesaro, and the first organist, pre Sebastian Enno, were brought before the Provveditori, but denied that any musicians under their charge had misbehaved. The nuns themselves made no complaint, and, without further evidence, the case was dropped; there is the real possibility that the events never happened, and that the anonymous denunciation was, in fact, an instance of mischief resulting from professional jealousy among musicians.

## Music Performed by the Nuns in Church

Studies of convent music in other Italian cities have pointed out the great attraction that music performed by nuns held for the public.[51] This held true, at least to some extent, in Venice, as well (activities of this type fall into category I.A in the taxonomy). Certainly, around 1500, at least two convents were renowned for their singing nuns. Marin Sanudo, in his detailed description of the government and wonders of the city, put this practice high on the list of notable things shown to foreign dignitaries. Visiting princes were greeted in the *bucintoro*, the great ceremonial boat of the Doge, taken to an audience with the Doge, and then shown the Palace, the Basilica of San Marco with its jeweled relics, the famous markets, the Arsenal, and "the singing of nuns, either at Le Vergini or at San Zaccaria."[52]

In later years, as the Venetian *ospedali* became world-famous for their musical performances by young women, those by the city's nuns became less noticeable. Another factor might also have been involved. The professed nuns at most of the Venetian monasteries were, as has been mentioned, daughters of Patricians, the ruling class of the Venetian Republic. These families were extraordinarily concerned with their reputations, and it was rare for either men or women to display any artistic talents they might possess outside of small circles of family and friends—doing so more publicly might be seen as acting like lower class, paid professionals. Such an attitude might well have been carried into the cloister. While the nuns would not necessarily hesitate to sing among themselves, performing in public, as was not uncommon in other cities, might have been seen as a threat to their good names.

Among the numerous seventeenth- and eighteenth-century references in the periodical *Pallade Veneta* to music at convents, only three mention performances by the nuns themselves, all at the same convent, and all, such as this, from 1698, regarding the singing of chant:

---

51. See MONSON, *Disembodied Voices*; Robert KENDRICK, *Celestial Sirens: Nuns and their Music in Early Modern Milan* (Oxford: Clarendon Press, 1996), Colleen REARDON, "Veni sponsa Christi: Investiture, Profession and Consecration Ceremonies in Sienese Convents." *Musica disciplina* 50 (1996) [pub. 1998]: 271-97 and REARDON, *Holy Concord*

*within Sacred Walls: Nuns and Music in Siena, 1575-1700* (New York: Oxford University Press, forthcoming).

52. "Cantar monache, o alle Verzene o a San Zaccaria," Marin SANUDO il giovane, *De origine, situ et magistratibus urbis Venetae, ovvero la città di Venetia* (1493-1530), ed. Angela CARACCIOLO ARICÒ (Milan: Cisalpino-La Goliardica, 1980), 62.

> The reverend mothers known as the Terese [venerated Saint Teresa] with their inimitable plainchant, which makes the other choirs in this city [specializing] in this harmonic profession blush honorably ...[53]

On the same feast in 1739, attended by the Doge, who was the patron of the convent, the anonymous author of the *Pallade* praises the "mass sung by those cloistered nuns, who in the singing of Gregorian chant are worthy of all attention and applause ..."[54]

While not much evidence of public attention to singing nuns in Venice has emerged, the convents themselves, and the civil and religious authorities, made a number of attempts to define what was and was not appropriate. In 1575 the Patriarch issued a decree to the abbesses that made all singing of polyphony illegal, and only reluctantly permitted plainchant in some convents:

> Under penalties ... at our discretion you [and your nuns] may not learn polyphony [*canto figurato*] nor to play any sort of instrument, nor sing such songs in your churches or convents; but where it is the custom to sing plainchant, you [and your nuns] may be taught to sing that chant by teachers who are nuns in your own convents, and not by others; where it is the custom to say psalms in speech, we wish that custom be observed without fail.[55]

A slight modification in the decree, but also a recognition that violations must have been fairly common, is evident in a Patriarchal admonition to the Benedictine nuns of San Lorenzo in 1617, which reminded them that polyphony was prohibited, and that only the organ was allowed as accompaniment to plainchant.[56] Additional flexibility was apparently allowed if the convent's finances did not allow the purchase of an organ for the nuns' choir (since the principal organ in all Venetian monasteries was in the external church): a spinet was sometimes substituted.

In some cases, the nuns themselves held passionate views about what type of music was appropriate for their services. In 1625 an anonymous nun at San Geronimo urged the Patriarch to move to an earlier date his planned visitation to the convent to help quell a dispute over certain forbidden *"canti figurati"* (that is, polyphonic works)

---

53. "[...] come pure fecero le reverende madri dette le Terese con il di loro inimitabile canto fermo, che fa onorato rossore ad altri chori della città in tal harmonica professione [...]" *Pallade Veneta*, 11-18.X.1698 (PV#101).

54. "alla messa cantata da quelle claustrali che nel canto gregoriano sono degne d'ogni attenzione ed applauso" *Pallade Veneta*, 10-17.X.1739 (PV#351).

55. "né dobbiate imparar a cantar canto figurato, né a sonar alcuna sorte d'instrumento, né cantar tali canti nelle vostre chiese over monasterii, ma dove è costume di cantar canto fermo possiate imparar a cantar detto canto dalle vostre monache maestre del monasterio et non da altrii, et dove è costume di salmizar in parole

volemo sia osservato detto costume per ogni modo." Vasp, Curia Patriarcale, Archivio Segreto, Visite Pastorali a Monasteri Feminili, R.2, 1560-89, ff. 47ᵛ-48ᵛ, 2 November 1575, Mandatum generalis.

56. "che nella celebratione dei divini offitii non possiate in alcun tempo usar altra forma di canto et d'instrumento musicale, che il canto fermo et l'organo, prohibendo espressamente il canto figurato et ogn'altro instrumento da sonar, essendo così necessario di fare per convenienti rispetti, et per levare ogni occasione di scandolo." Vasp, Curia Patriarcale, Sezione Antica, Monialium, Atti Particolari, B.2, 1609-19, f. 49ʳ⁻ᵛ, 20-2-1617.

that were being sung. This dispute had recently manifested itself in the form of broadsides that had been attached to the walls of the convent by the opposing sides in the dispute, each accusing the other of unspecified scandalous behavior.[57]

As mentioned above, even the singing of plainchant was not universal, and a special dispensation was required if it was to be added to the otherwise spoken observances of a convent. In 1721 the Franciscan nuns of Santo Sepolcro, who were experiencing financial difficulties, obtained permission to receive instruction from a priest in the singing of "plainchant for the Psalm *Miserere*, the hymn *Pange lingua*, and the Greater Litany, for the sole reason of relieving the convent … of the heavy expenses of hiring singers on the occasion of several functions in their church …" Once they had learned the chant, the nuns were given permission to sing in the church (from out of sight, of course) when outsiders were present on the occasion of Expositions of the Holy Sacrament, "with the express condition that they were never, under any circumstances, to alter the proper, modest, and devout Gregorian chant, so that it might serve as edification, and to promote greater devotion by those secular persons that might be present in the church …"[58]

For a brief period in the early seventeenth century, the nuns of one Venetian monastery emerged from the musical shadows and made a broader, even international mark. Problems at the Benedictine house of Santi Marco and Andrea on the island of Murano, a late foundation (it was established in 1496) of modest size and income, came to the attention of the Bishop of Torcello as early as 1619. In that year he issued a stern decree castigating the nuns for singing and playing in the parlatory and church, and forbade them to do it again.[59] It seems that the nuns continued to sing secretly for themselves in church, despite the warning, for word of their excellence spread. In September of 1622, the Englishwoman Aletheia Talbot, Countess of Arundel,[60] nearing the

---

57. Vasp, Curia Patriarcale, Archivio Segreto, Visite Pastorali a Monasteri Feminili, B.4, #15, January 1625.

58. "…la licenza di poter imparare il canto fermo per il salmo *Miserere*, hinno *Pange lingua*, e Litanie Maggiori a solo fine di sgravare il monastero…dalle spese gravose solite farsi nel provedere di cantori nell'occasioni d'alcuni funtioni della loro Chiesa…con espressa conditione, che non debbano mai in alcun tempo alterare il canto proprio Gregoriano modesto e divoto, acciò servi d'edificatione, e promovi la maggior divotione e veneratione alle persone secolari che fossero presente in Chiesa…" Vasp, Curia Patriarcale, Sezione Antica, Monialium, Atti Particolari, B.9, 1717-1725, 15-9-1721.

59. Vasp, Episcopato di Torcello, Cause Criminalium 1 (23), Criminalia monialium 1600-1689, #8, 1622, decree dated 16 December 1619.

60. She is named in the documents only as the Princess

of Rondel, but the identification with Lady Aletheia Talbot, Countess of Arundel, wife of Thomas Howard, Earl of Arundel, traveler and art collector (who had been to Venice about ten years earlier, and was patron of such men as Rubens, van Dyck, and Inigo Jones), seems almost certain. Aletheia went to Italy (via Antwerp where Rubens painted her portrait) in 1620, while her husband was busy alternately holding high positions at court and being locked up in the Tower, to visit her two sons who were studying at the University of Padua. She rented both the Palazzo Mocenigo on the Grand Canal and a villa on the Brenta canal in Dolo. In 1622, not long before her visit to the nuns in Murano, the painter van Dyck came to stay with her. That same year, Tizianello, the grandson of Titian, dedicated his biography of the great painter to the Countess. The Countess's entourage left Venice sometime after 23

end of a two-year stay in Venice, insisted that she be permitted to hear the nuns of SS. Marco and Andrea sing. The abbess replied that a license from the Bishop would be required, since such performances had been outlawed, but the Countess declared (false-ly, it turned out) that she had obtained the necessary permission. While the Abbess was troubled by the absence of a written license, she was eventually persuaded to proceed, and the Countess, along with two gentlewomen, was allowed into the locked church to listen to the singing of Suor Gratiosa and Suor Regina.[61] The Abbess realized a few days later that she had been hoodwinked. She told the monastery's confessor what had happened, and then admitted everything to the Bishop's Vicar; apparently her honest admission and contrition were deemed sufficient, and no punishment was issued. The Countess herself, of course, was long gone, so the potential international incident her violation of Venetian law might have caused was avoided.[62]

Within a few years, another nun at the same monastery, Suor Maria Felice Sbaraschi (from Poland, and therefore clearly not a member of the Venetian Patriciate), became renowned for her singing. The organist Carlo Filago dedicated to her his book of *Sacri concerti a voce sola* (published in 1642), which contained, according to the dedica-tion, works of his that she had earlier performed, evidently accompanying herself on organ or theorbo.[63] This dedication, while filled with the superlatives usual in such cases, does give an indication of Suor Maria Felice's talents:

> Like an echo, these, my few musical compositions, return to her who gave them life ...
>
> She, who many times, as a Siren of this Adriatic Sea, wished to make our era happy by

September (when she took formal leave of the Doge), for Mantua, Milan, Turin, Genoa, Marseilles, and final-ly, before returning to England, Ghent, where, in 1624, her eldest son, James, died of smallpox. See Mary F. S. HERVEY, *The Life, Correspondence & Collections of Thomas Howard, Earl of Arundel* (Cambridge: University Press, 1921 [reprint New York: Kraus Reprint, 1969]), in par-ticular chap. 16; Christopher BROWN, *Van Dyck* (Oxford: Phaidon, 1982), 61-62; *Thomas Howard, Earl of Arundel* (Oxford: The Asmolean Museum, 1985), 8; Christopher WHITE, *Anthony van Dyck: Thomas Howard, The Earl of Arun-del* (Malibu, CA: Getty Museum Studies on Art, 1995), portraits of Aletheia Talbot at pl. 18 (by Daniel Myrtens) and pl. 41 (by Rubens); and *The Lives of Philip Howard, Earl of Arundel, and of Anne Dacres, His Wife. Edited from the Orignal MSS by the Duke of Norfolk, E. M.* (London: Hurst and Blackett, 1857), esp. 232-33. Some important documents concerning the Countess' stay in Venice are published in translation in Allen B. HINDS, ed., *Calen-dar of State Papers and Manuscripts Relating to Venetian Affairs Existing in the Archives and Collections of Venice...*, Vol. XVII, 1621-23 (London: His Majesty's Stationery Office, 1911).

I would like to thank Sarah Davies, of New York Uni-versity, whose suggestion led me to this identification.

61.  These women have not yet been identified more precisely, but since they were referred to as "suor" rather than "madre," it is possible that they were not Patrician professed nuns, but so-called *converse*. These were non-noble women who entered the convent either as young unmarried women or as widows, who took vows but had no voice in the Chapter, and who were exempted from service in the choir, but carried out the manual jobs in the cloister.

62.  Vasp, Episcopato di Torcello, Cause Criminalium 1 (23), Criminalia monialium 1600-89, #8, 1622.

63.  SACRI CONCERTI / A Voce sola. / Con la Partitura Per l'organo / DI/ CARLO FILAGO / RODIGINO / Organ-ista Della Serenissima Republica / di Venetia In S. Marco. / *Opera Quarta*. ... /IN VENETIA MDC XXXXII / Appresso Bartolomeo Magni. This print is described, and excerpts transcribed, in Francesco PASSADORE, *Musi-ca e musicisti a Rovigo tra rinascimento e barocco* (Rovigo: Associazione Culturale Minelliana, 1987), 107-17.

animating these [compositions] with her singing, made it necessary for me to convert my uncultured scribblings with this printing. But it is no miracle that she, who with the zither still knows how to compete with Apollo, could make the rocks that come from my pen resound musically; that she, who with sacred accents brings souls to heaven, could also raise up my compositions so that they could be printed ... Just as Orpheus with his singing and playing inspired the Argonauts on their daring path toward the Golden Fleece, you, not only with your singing and sweetest playing, but even more with your grace, have, I believe, persuaded me to ever greater efforts ...[64]

The publication contains sixteen solo motets, thirteen for soprano (presumably for Maria Felice herself), two for alto, and one for tenor. These latter three (and perhaps some of the ones for soprano) may have been composed for other nuns in the monastery, whom Filago referred to in a dedicatory sonnet as "other twins, also singing sirens, servant throats, [who] form a heaven in the happy and peaceful sea."[65]

## Private and Recreational Music in the Cloister

The Patriarch occasionally expressed concern about music making in the nuns' cells (category I.B in Table 2), issuing regulations or condemnations against performing secular music or owning instruments. A 1592 rule, which also prohibited the possession of profane pictures, dogs, and parrots, banned the ownership of "instruments that one can play while walking," that is those string and wind instruments most closely associated with dancing and other secular pursuits, effectively limiting the nuns to keyboard instruments, as well as, perhaps, theorbo or violone.[66]

The violone does, in fact, appear, in documents relating to the final category to be considered here, music for the nuns' recreations (mostly classified as I.C.I). A 1597 Patriarchal decree reads, in part, as follows:

64. "Qual Eco, ritornano a chi gli die' la vita queste mie poche Compositioni Musicali; mentre al glorioso Nome di V.S. Illustrissima divotamente le consacro. Ella che più volte come Sirena di questo MARE Adriatico ha voluto FELICITARE il nostro secolo animandole con il Canto, necessita la mia incolta penna a ridurle con queste stampe. Ma non è maraviglia che colei che con la Cetra ancora sa gareggiare con Apollo faccia risuonare musicalmente qual altra pietra la mia penna; che colei, che con sacri accenti imparadisa l'anime sollevi anco alle stampe le mie compositioni. [...] Gradisca questo picciolo tributo della mia perpetua obligazione, con quella benignità appunto con la quale non isdegna la mia continuata servitù; perchè s'Orfeo con il canto e con il suono animò gl'Argonauti all'intrapreso cammino per il Vello d'oro, non solo con il di Lei canto, e suavissimo, suono, ma con la grazia ancora, mi stimerò persuaso a

maggiori imprese, e riverentemente le bacio le mani." Ibid.

65. "...altre gemelle / Pur Sirene canore gorghe ancelle / Formano un Ciel ne MAR FELICE, e immoto..." Ibid.

66. "Non possa portar alcuna figliuola in monasterio quadri che habbino alcuna pittura profana, né instrumenti che mentre si suona si può caminare, né cani, né papagalli." Vasp, Curia Patriarcale, Sezione Antica, Monialium, Atti patriarcali riguardanti le monache, R.1, 1591-99, ff. 33ᵛ-35ᵛ, 2 November 1592. Although this regulation is aimed specifically at the *educande*, those young laywomen resident in nunneries as students, it is safe to assume that similar, if not even more severe restrictions would have applied to the nuns themselves. The rules against paintings, dogs, and parrots, do, in fact appear quite regularly in decrees directed to the nuns.

> Since it would not be a good idea to ban the honest and virtuous recreations of the nuns, it is a good idea to be vigilant, and make sure that on such occasions they do nothing to offend God, or that could damage their souls or bring scandal to the convent. Therefore, to avoid any difficulties, on occasions on which are made or performed demonstrations or plays in your convent, we issue the following rules ...[67]

He went on to declare that they could perform whatever they wished, as long as it had a religious and honest subject (later versions specify the lives of the saints), but that they must do it in their regular habits, not in secular dress. Other regulations specified that performances could not be held in the church, but must be in a more appropriate setting, such as the refectory, and that expenditures be limited.

The Bishop of Torcello issued similar regulations for the nunneries within his diocese in 1679, nevertheless allowing the nuns more freedom to dress as they pleased, as long as nobody outside the community saw them in costume:

> ... we are content to allow that in the customary performances that are sometimes done for their honest recreation, with our license, and which must be either about the lives of Saints or stories from Holy Scripture, they may wear the costumes of the characters called for in the work ... Nonetheless, we rigorously prohibit them from letting themselves be seen by any person whatsoever, even under the pretext of close family ties, in the parlatories or at the grates or windows, or in any other place ...[68]

In 1693, the Bishop issued licenses to two nunneries for such performances (undoubtedly there were more, but these are the only two that are extant): to Sant'Eufemia di Mazzorbo for "la tragedia di Santa Dimpina" in 1693, and to Santa Maria della Valverde for "l'operetta intitolata *Il Trionfo dell' Innocenza*".[69] The nuns, however, were not always satisfied with such sober and spiritual plays, especially during carnival, as the Bishop had become aware just a few years earlier:

> ... in some of the aforesaid nunneries they ignore at such time the evident peril of damnation, and they go so far as to perform totally profane, obscene, and lascivious operas, such as *Medea, Medoro, Gallieno*, and others that, for modesty, will not be mentioned.[70]

---

67. "Sicome non è conveniente impedire le honeste et virtuose ricreationi delle monache, così è necessario invigilare et avvertir bene che con simili occasioni le monache medesime non faccino cosa che offendi il Signor Dio, e che insieme possi apportar danno alle anime e scandolo al monasterio. Per tanto affine che sia ovviato a qualunque inconveniente potesse occorrer per occasione di fare o recitare dimostrationi o rappresentationi nel vostro monasterio col presente nostro ordine..." Vasp, Curia Patriarcale, Sezione Antica, Monialium, Atti patriarcali riguardanti le monache, R.1, 1591-99, f. 102ʳ, 1-1597.
68. "si contentiamo tolerare che nelle rappresentationi solite alcuna volta con nostra licenza recitarsi da loro per

honesta ricreatione, et che non devono esser che della vita de Santi, o Sante, o pur historie della Sacra Scrittura, possano vestire l'habito de Personaggi ricercati dall'opera... Nulla dimeno, prohibiamo rigorosamente a lasciarsi vedere in simil habito a qualunque persona sia chi si voglia, anco sotto più stretto congionto o parente, ne' parlatori, grati, fenestre o in qualunque altro luogo..." Vasp, Episcopato di Torcello, Actorum, B.21, 1692-1705, ff. 32ᵛ-33ᵛ, 22 January 1679.
69. Ibid., f. 33ᵛ.
70. "in alcuno de predetti monasteri si trascura a tal tempo il pericolo evidente della danatione e si arriva a termine tale di recitare opere totalmente profane, oscene,

In this case, as in nearly all others, musical performance is not specified, but the language and context of the decree make it probable that they performed for themselves the operas that they could not attend in the public theatres.

The Patriarch of Venice never referred to such violations in his own official decrees, but they were undoubtedly fairly common in nunneries within his jurisdiction as well. Complaints about them occur occasionally in the interviews the Patriarch conducted with all the nuns on his periodic visits of inspection, as in this sample:

> At Santa Maria dei Miracoli in 1595: "Sometimes the nuns sing profane things, and they play the lute and guitar, and they sometimes dress as men for the plays."[71]

> At San Lorenzo in 1623: "At Carnival they do plays, and this year they did two good ones and one bad one that was printed, and these books should be taken away and burned. The things that they perform are all lascivious, and about love, and the *intermedi* are about love."[72]

> At San Gerolamo in 1714: "Another problem is that during Carnival time, for a whole month we do not eat in the refectory, because that is where the operas are done; it is a good thing that the young ones enjoy themselves, but there are other places ...[73]

> At the Convertite in 1715: "When they perform these recreations, the nuns let themselves be seen by the workmen, whom the Mother Superior allows to stay in the convent until late at night, and they see on the stage all the gestures of the nuns as will be done in the opera, and this is not good."[74]

It is quite clear that these performances were usually done with the blessing, and perhaps even participation, of the Abbess, and were not simply expressions of willfulness by a few rebellious younger nuns. In 1636, for the celebrations of the election of a

e lascivi, come *la Medea, il Medoro, il Gallieno*, et altre che per modestia si tacciono..." Vasp, Episcopato di Torcello, Actorum, B. 20, 1683-92, f. 333ʳ, 8 February 1689. "Medea" was undoubtedly *Medea in Atene*, with a libretto by Aurelio Aureli and music by Antonio Gianettini, which had been performed at Teatro San Moisè in the 1675/76 season, and again at Teatro Sant'Angelo in 1678/79. "Galieno" was certainly the opera by Matteo Norris, set to music by Carlo Pallavicino, and performed at Teatro Santi Giovanni e Paolo in 1676/77. "Medoro" is harder to identify. The only opera by that title, with music by Francesco Lucio to a libretto by Aurelio Aureli, had not been performed for forty years, and was unlikely to still have been known or available. The character Medoro, however, does appear in an opera with a different title, *Carlo il Grande*, with libretto by Adriano Morselli and music by Domenico Gabrielli, performed at Teatro San Giovanni Grisostomo in 1688; it is likely that this is the work the Bishop referred to in his decree.

71. "Che alcune volte le monache cantano cose profane,

e chi si suona di citara e liuto, e si vestono tal volta da l'uom per far dimostrationi." Vasp, Curia Patriarcale, Archivio Segreto, Visite Pastorali a Monasteri Feminili, B.3, 1592-96, f. 369ʳ, 9 January 1595.

72. "Il Carneval si fa delle comedie, st'anno si han fatto due commedie bene, et una cattiva stampada, e che di questa li tolsi li libri, et brusiai... Le cose che recitano sono tutte lassive, et d'amor, et con intermedii d'amor." Ibid., B.4, No. 11, interview with Suor Franceschina Zen.

73. "[...] un altro inconveniente nel tempo de Carneval che si tralassia per un mese de andar in reffetorio, perché si fa dentro l'opere, sono cosa giusta che tanta gioventù se devertisca, ma vi sonno altri lochi [...] Ibid., Visite, R.6, 1711-25.

74. "[...]Quando poi si fa dimostrationi, le monache si lasia vedere da i operari stravestite, e la Superiora fano stare li huomeni in casa sin quatro o cinque hore, e in sena vedono tutti li gesti delle monache come porta l'opera, e non par bon [...]" Ibid., complaint by Suor Pisana Celeste Pisani.

new Abbess of Sant'Anna, the official documents of the monastery record a performance that would most certainly not have pleased even the most permissive Patriarch:

> … they performed a little pastorale with six people, rather pleasant and well devised: one was Suor Girletta who played the part of Venus, another was Suor Barbara who played two roles, one that of Momus and the other that of Vulcan; it was Suor Paulina who did the part of Juno; the others were Suor Agustina, who did the part of Pallas, Cataruzza, who did the role of the god of love, and Biancheta, [who] recited two choruses.[75]

In most cases, concrete documentation of such dramatic performances does not survive. One exception involves the convent of Corpus Domini in the eighteenth century. An account book beginning in 1718 lists regular expenses for such items as "libretti of the operas for recreations," "copying the operas," "composition of intermedi," "libretti of operas and intermedi," "expenses for the operas and scenarios for the intermedi," "to the carpenter and painter for the scenes," for "tickets for the operas," "for a trumpet, sword, and dagger for the operas," and for the purchase, repair, and maintenance of at least two violoni (which were also used along with a harpsichord, in the church during Holy Week). Unfortunately, no trace has survived of either texts or scores of works that might have been performed by these nuns, and there is no evidence that they violated the long-standing rule that such entertainments must remain private and not be witnessed by anybody other than the cloistered women themselves.

On at least one occasion, however, a secular musical-dramatic performance within a nunnery was observed and remarked upon by a member of the general public, thus violating in one moment, many Patriarchal and governmental rules. In his diary, Pietro Gradenigo described a 1755 performance by the *educande* of San Lorenzo (along with at least one nun) as follows:

> The nuns of San Lorenzo allowed several of their noble *educande* to perform in the presence of their relatives several sections of the musical drama entitled *Il Demetrio*, which they decided to sing in the cloister. These actresses were thus seen dressed with pomp in the heroic manner, according to theatrical practice, to their own satisfaction, and to that of the Abbess D. Marina Vendramin and their relatives and lady friends; here are their names [at this point, Gradenigo apparently begins to quote from a program or announcement]:
>
> N.D. Lugrezia Michiel will play the part of Olinto
> N.D. Ellena Mocenigo will play the part of Fenicio
> N.D. Maria Grimani will do the part of Cleonice
> Suor Geltruda will play the part of Mitrane

---

75. "recitato un pastoraleta de sie persone assai vaga et ben compartita, una fu suor Girletta, et fece la parte di Venere; l'altra suor Barbara, et fece due parte, una de Momo et l'altro de Vulcano; l'altra fu suor Paulina, fece la parte de Giunone; l'altra fu suor Agustina et fece la parte de Palade; Cataruzza fece la parte del dio d'amore, et Bianchete recita dui cori." Vas, Sant' Anna, B.II, Registro cassa 1636-39, p. 6, 2 April 1636.

N.D. . . . . . . will play the part of Barsene

N.D. . . . . . . will play the part of Alceste[76]

That this staged and costumed performance was permitted is not necessarily owing to a general relaxation of the rules that had been in place for centuries, but rather is a testament to the power and influence of both the parents of the *educande* and the nuns themselves, all of whom were members of the most important Venetian noble families.

Whatever else might be said about the nuns of early modern Venice, it is clear that their lives were far from quiet. They were surrounded by and involved in music of many kinds on a daily basis, and seem to have willingly, and often, stretched the limits of legality in attempts to enrich their cloistered lives.

76. "Le monache di San Lorenzo acconsintendo che alcune delle loro nobili educande recitino alla presenza de loro parenti alcuna parte del dramma in musica intitolato *il Demetrio*, che esse stabilirono cantare nel chiostro. Queste attrici si videro adunque pomposamente vestite all'eroica, secondo il mettodo teatrale e la sodisfazione loro, non che della Abbadessa D. Marina Vendramin e consanguines e dame amiche della medesima. Ecco li nomi: Cioè N.D. Lugrezia Michiel farà la parte d'Olinto; N.D. Ellena Mocenigo farà la parte de Fenicio; N.D. Maria Grimani farà la parte di Cleonice; Suor Geltruda farà la parte di Mitrane; N.D. .............farà la parte da Barsene; N.D. ............. farà la parte d'Alceste." Vmc, Ms Gradenigo 67, Tomo 3, f. 43$^v$, 6 November 1755. While it would seem most likely this was the same *Demetrio* (with neither composer nor librettist indicated) that had been performed by the girls of the Ospedale dei Mendicanti in 1749 (see Irene ALM, *Catalog of Venetian Librettos at the University of California, Los Angeles* [Berkeley: University of California Press, 1993] No. 669), the printed libretto does not include the character Mitrane, who does appear in the text by Metastasio upon which the 1749 libretto was based. Settings of the original libretto had been performed several times recently in Venice, notably in 1747, at Teatro San Giovanni Grisostomo with a score by Hasse, and in 1751, at Teatro San Samuele, with music by David Perez.

Darrell M. Berg

# THE DEATH AND RETURN OF THE COMPOSER: CARL PHILIPP EMANUEL BACH AS AUTHOR OF HIS MUSIC

THE IDEA OF AUTHORSHIP has evolved considerably since the Renaissance and has undergone conspicuous metamorphosis in the twentieth century. One of the most important moments in its history is located around the end of the eighteenth century, when the idea of the "original genius" came into vogue and, as a corollary, the concept of an author-god demanding absolute ownership of his text. Eventually modern critical theory raised a strong protest against what it perceived as the nineteenth-century apotheosis of the author. The most radical—and probably the most celebrated—expression of this reaction was formulated by Roland Barthes in his essay, "The Death of the Author" (1967), in which he undertook to deprive the text's writer of any significant role in its creation.[1] Studies that extend issues of authorship to technical fields and copyright law have contributed further to the separation of the author from the text.[2] Although the voices of twentieth-century theorists who would counter nineteenth-century views and wrest the text from its "scriptor" have been loud and famous, other voices have been audible. Some refuse to engage in genuine debate over the question of authorship;[3] on rare occasions they attempt to mediate between polar views about the author's role and to restore to him or her a share in his or her text (Barthes himself retreated from his most extreme position once he had declared it).[4] Restoration of

---

1. "The Death of the Author," repr. of an article originally published in *Aspen Magazine*, fall-winter 1967, *Authorship from Plato to the Postmodern*, ed. Seán BURKE (Edinburgh: Edinburgh University Press, 1995), 125-30.

2. See, for example, John CAUGHIE, ed., *Theories of Authorship: A Reader* (London: Routledge and Kegan Paul, 1981) and Donald F. McKENZIE, *Bibliography and the Sociology of Texts*, The Panizzi Lectures: 1985 (London: The British Library, 1986).

3. See, for example, Cedric WATTS, "Bottom's Children: The Fallacies of Structuralist, Post-structuralist and Deconstructionist Literary Theory," in Lawrence

LERNER, ed., *Reconstructing Literature* (Oxford: Basil Blackwell, 1983), 20-35; William GASS, "The Death of the Author" *Habitations of the Word* (New York: Simon and Schuster, 1985), 265-88; and Steven KNAPP and Walter BENN MICHAELS, "Against Theory," *Against Theory: Literary Studies and the New Pragmatism*, ed. W.J.T. MITCHELL (Chicago: University of Chicago Press, 1985), 11-30.

4. See, for example, Roland BARTHES, *Writing Degree Zero* (1967), trans. Annette LAVERS and Colin SMITH (London: Cape, 1967), and *Sade, Fourier, Loyola* (1971), trans. Richard MILLER (London: Cape, 1977), transl. of edition of 1971.

partial vesting to the author is the subject of a book by Seán Burke, *The Death and Return of the Author*, from which the present essay derives its title.[5]

Burke's monograph, a critique of the works of Barthes, Michel Foucault, and Jacques Derrida, expresses disappointment and impatience with the kind of critical assessment that these authors have received. Protesting that their writings have been either accepted unquestioningly or dismissed as "another conceit of a continental avant-gardism," Burke sets out to subject them to the rigorous analysis that he believes they require.[6] He uncovers weaknesses in each writer's argument against authorial presence and control, and finds contradictions, large and small, in the writings of each. He perceives Barthes' author-god as a straw man, a manifestation of the Absolute Subject, an abstraction who has never existed, but had to be constructed in order to be destroyed. He calls attention to Barthes' description of a text as ". . . a multidimensional space in which a variety of writings, *none of them original* [italics mine], blend and clash" and points out that because Sade, Fourier, and Loyola are "founders of languages," and presumably original, Barthes allows them privileges that other authors may not have. Burke points out Barthes' inconsistency and partiality in not mandating the authorial death of Sade, Fourier, Loyola, and other writers whose discourse he considers non-representational.[7]

In Burke's reading of Foucault and Derrida, the death of the author is less explicit. According to Foucault's *thesis*, says Burke, the death of man, whom Foucault has seen as the subject of knowledge since 1800, accompanies the Nietzschean death of God; the death of the author is implicit in these two deaths. But the transcendence that Foucault assumes, asserts Burke, makes him the author of his own text. He refers to Foucault's essay "What is an Author?" (1969), which designates a "transdiscursive" position for authors of a theory, tradition, or discipline, e.g., Homer, Aristotle, and the Church Fathers.[8] This transdiscursive role, Burke points out, is diametrically opposed to Foucault's thesis that an author is determined by the discourse of his time.[9] Derrida also demands the symbolic death of the author, says Burke, by privileging writing over authorial intentions. Burke concludes that the "death of the author emerges as a blind-spot in the work of Barthes, Foucault and Derrida, an absence they seek to create and explore, but one which is always already filled with the idea of the author."[10]

Contrary to the notion, both Platonic and Marxist, that all art is a reflection of an overriding reality, has the same history, and reflects societal structure in the same way, there can be no exact parallel between the situation of authors and that of composers. Literary

5. Seán BURKE, *The Death and Return of the Author* (Edinburgh: Edinburgh University Press, 1992).
6. BURKE, *Death and Return*, 17-19.    7. Ibid., 33-46.
8. Michel FOUCAULT, "What is an Author?" in *Language, Counter-Memory, Practice: Selected Essays and Interviews*, ed. Donald F. BOUCHARD, trans. idem and Sherry SIMON (Ithaca, NY: Cornell University Press, 1977), 113-38, particularly, 131-32.
9. BURKE, *Death and Return*, 92.    10. Ibid., 154.

critics may be transformed into authors, but music critics are almost never transformed into composers. The concept of composership has its own history, often diverging from the history of the concept of authorship in interesting ways.[11] In the present study, I will examine issues of *composership* from the Renaissance to the present and consider analogies and differences between the positions of composers and authors. Because the career of Carl Philipp Emanuel Bach (1714-88) is situated at a pivotal moment in the history of composership and constitutes a particularly felicitous entry for examination of the changing concept of the composer, I will focus upon Emanuel Bach's role as composer.

As a prelude to this examination, it may be useful to review briefly the evolution of the concept of the composer before the Renaissance. Like other medieval readers, musicians of the Middle Ages venerated certain authoritative writings about music, many endowed with the names of legendary or historical figures. Donald Pease, influenced perhaps by Foucault's "transdiscursive" authorial category (see above, p. 453), classifies such figures, "whose words commanded respect or belief," as *auctores*, naming Cicero, Aristotle, Ptolemy, the Bible, Boethius.[12] Authorities revered by cultivated musicians of the Middle Ages also included names of *auctores* or "transdiscursive" authors: Pythagorus, Plato, Aristotle, Augustine, Boethius—all writers, or alleged writers, *about* music, but not composers. It was not until certain repertories of medieval music were notated and codified that legendary composers, e.g. Gregory the Great (540-604), Leonin and Perotin (*fl.*1160-1225), and Alfonso the Wise of Castile and Léon (1252-84), were assigned to actual music in the same way that legendary *auctores* were associated with particular writings.[13]

That the concept of authorship changed with the arrival of the Renaissance seems indisputable, however the date of that arrival and the occasion for the change are construed.[14] Pease places the new concept in the late fifteenth century, relating it not only to an awareness of the individual subject, but also to the discovery of the New World and the concurrent emergence of alterity—awareness of the "other." Authors from this time on, Pease implies, display not only authority, but also individuality and subjectivity.[15] Not surprising-

11.  Two studies that examine the subject of composership are Lydia GOEHR, *The Imaginary Museum of Musical Works: An Essay in the Philosophy of Music* (Oxford: Clarendon Press, 1992), which deals with the concept of the *work of art* and by implication with the composer as owner of his work, and John SPITZER, "Authorship and Attribution in Western Art Music," (Ph.D.diss., Cornell University, 1983).

12.  Donald PEASE, "Author," *Critical Terms for Literary Study*, ed. Frank LENTRICCHIA and Thomas McLAUGHLIN, 2d. ed. (Chicago: The University of Chicago Press, 1995), 105-17.

13.  It might be argued that legendary composers, such as King David, were known to the Middle Ages. But no *music* by such composers survives—only, in the case of David, texts and iconographical representations of performers of his melodies.

14.  See Rob C. WEGMAN, "From Maker to Composer: Improvisation and Musical Authorship in the Low Countries, 1450-1500," *Journal of the American Musicological Society* 49 (1996), 409-79, an extended and thoughtful examination of the changes in the concept and status of the "composer" during the fifteenth century.

15.  PEASE, "Author," 107-10.

ly, the idea of the *composer* as individual and subject also emerged during the Renaissance, one of the most vivid manifestations of this development being the well-known description of Josquin des Prez as a unique and sought-after composer, albeit an incorrigible individual.[16] The history of music in the sixteenth-century is sprinkled with names of other musicians who can be regarded as composer-subjects—individuals with distinctive styles of composing. Writings about seventeenth-century music contain even more such names.[17] Yet from the time of the Renaissance, the history of composership differs in an important respect from that of authorship. Composers of music, like authors of texts to be performed (e.g., the dramas of Shakespeare), did not achieve the same status as did authors of texts for readers alone. Unlike literature intended to be read, most music involved collaboration between composer and performer.[18] Although names of certain composers were touted throughout the seventeenth and the first half of the eighteenth centuries, the contributions of performers of this period were still considered an important aspect of the creation of music, and the status of the composer was discernibly ambiguous.

The history of the twelve solo violin sonatas of Arcangelo Corelli's Opus 5 illustrates the complexity of one composer's situation. Rumor has it that Corelli published these works only after he had labored long over them, perhaps hoping to live up to the expectations of his public.[19] Evidence of the eighteenth-century reception of Corelli's solo violin sonatas indicates that, whatever the truth of such allegations, the twelve works that were finally published in Rome in 1700 as Opus 5 proved to be a model for composers of sonatas for melody

16. See the letter of 2 December [1502] from "Gian," a member of the court of Ercole I of Ferrara quoted and translated in Lewis LOCKWOOD, "Josquin at Ferrara: New Documents and Letters," *Josquin des Prez* ed. Edward E. LOWINSKY and Bonnie J. BLACKBURN (London: Oxford University Press, 1976), 103-37, particularly 133: "To me he [Isaac] seems very well suited to serve Your Lordship, much more so than Josquin, because he is a better nature among his companions and will compose new works more often. It is true that Josquin composes better, but he composes when he wants to, and not when one wants him to, and he is asking 200 ducats in salary while Isaac will come for 120—but Your Lordship will decide what should be done."

17. Interestingly, the "discourse" (music) of Claudio Monteverdi, one of the most stellar of these, had the properties that Foucault calls "trangressive" (see *Language, Counter-Memory, Practice*, 33-36, ): it affirmed "the limitlessness into which it" leaped as it opened a "zone [intense musical expression of texts] to existence for the first time." Monteverdi's "transgression" violated time-honored contrapuntal rules and was attacked vigorously by a contemporary. See the translated excerpts from the Monteverdi-Artusi controversy in *Source Readings in Music*

History, ed. and transl. Oliver STRUNK, rev. ed. Leo TREITLER (New York: Norton, 1998), 526-44.

18. Because there was also much improvisation in dramas of this time, the history of the concept of authorship is bifurcated one of its lines concerned with issues of collaboration between author and performer (as is the history of the concept of composership), the other concerned with the concept of an author as the sole creator of his music).

19. See Charles BURNEY, *A General History of Music from the Earliest Ages to 1789*, 3d. ed., (Baden-Baden: Heiz, 1958), 3: 442: "I was told by Mr. Wiseman at Rome, that when he first arrived in the city, about twenty years after Corelli's decease, he was informed by several persons who had been acquainted with him that his *opera quinta*, on which all good schools for the violin have since been founded, cost him three years to revise and correct." See also Marc PINCHERLE's speculation about Corelli's Opus 5, based, perhaps, on Burney's history, in *Corelli: His Life, His Work* (1954), transl. by Hubert E.M. RUSSELL (New York: W.W. Norton and Company, 1956), 85: "He attached extreme importance to it [Opus V], as though he had prescience of the preference which posterity would bestow on this work...."

instruments. Yet Corelli's audience expected to hear performances of these works overlaid with materials of the players' invention, since the printed sonatas consisted only of a melodic skeleton over a harmonic foundation. It was assumed that, even on first reading, performers would not adhere completely to this skeleton, and that they would improvise considerable embellishment for repetitions of structural sections.

A number of embellishments of works of Opus 5 have survived along with the names of their performers, among them, those of Francesco Geminiani (1687-1762) and Matthew Dubourg (1703-67); embellishments were, reportedly, written for the entire opus by Nicola Matteis the younger (d. 1749), but these can no longer be found.[20] A different kind of treatment of Corelli's sonatas, actual expansion of their length and "modernization" of their phrase structure, survives in the *Dissertazioni* of Francesco Maria Veracini (1690-1768).[21] Posterity regards Geminiani, Dubourg, and Veracini as contributors to Corelli's solo violin sonatas and, in varying degrees, as composers in their own right.

Corelli's œuvre was not eclipsed by such elaborations, however; unlike some of his contemporaries, he was able to attain and preserve distinction as a composer during the eighteenth century. The *Sonates Corellisantes* (1735-36) of Georg Philipp Telemann, although not based directly on Corelli's compositions, acknowledge his trio sonatas as models. This invocation of the name of the composer of famous solo and trio sonatas constituted even greater homage than did the treatments of Geminiani, Dubourg, and Veracini, for it endowed Corelli with the status of founder of a school. Estienne Roger's edition of Opus 5 published in 1710, allegedly with embellishments that Corelli had been heard to improvise, also established his authority as composer-subject and affirmed his ownership of his musical property.[22] It is not known whether this edition was reflexive, as the publisher claimed, for outside of Roger's

20. The ornaments by Francesco Geminiani to Sonata 8 in A Major are published in Sir John Hawkins' *A General History of the Science and Practice of Music* (1789), repr. of the edition of 1853 (New York: Dover Publications, 1963), 2: 904-907. Geminiani also arranged all of the sonatas of Opus 5 as concerti grossi which he published in two volumes (1726, 1727). Examples of a few of the alleged 19 movements with ornaments by Matthew Dubourg are to be found in David D. Boyden, "Corelli's Solo Violin Sonata 'Grac'd' by Dubourg," *Festskrift Jens Peter Larsen*, ed. Nils Schørring, Henrik Glahn, and Carsten E. Hatting (Copenhagen: Wilhelm Hansen Musik-Forlag, 1972), 113-25. Johann Joachim Quantz claimed to have seen the ornaments by Nicola Matteis 30 years before the publication of his *Versuch* See J.J. Quantz, *Versuch einer Anweisung die Flöte traversiere zu spielen* (Berlin: Voß, 1752), 3d. ed. (Breslau: Johann Friedrich Korn, 1789) *Documenta Musicologica*, 1/2 (Kassel: Bärenreiter, 1953), 151-52.

"Dieser," writes Quantz of Matteis, "hat zwar etwas mehr gethan, als Corelli selbst, indem er dieselben mit einer Art von kurzer Auszierung beschlossen. Sie sind aber noch keine Cadenzen ad Libitum, wie man itziger Zeit machet, sondern sie gehen nach der Strenge des Tactes, ohne Aufhalten des Basses fort."

21. The *Dissertazioni* by Francesco Maria Veracini (1690-1768) are contained in a manuscript, unpublished in Veracini's lifetime and presently housed in the Civico Museo Bibliografico Musicale in Bologna, Italy, and are published in a modern edition, *Zwölf Sonaten nach Arcangelo Corelli, Op. 5, für Violine und Basso continuo*, ed. Walter Kolneder (Mainz: Schott, 1961). The only existing evidence of a date of this reworking of Corelli's opus is stylistic—although it could have followed the publication of Opus 5 as early as 1710, its style suggests a time after pre-classical periodicity had begun to replace the *Fortspinnung* of the baroque.

22. *Sonate a Violino e Violone. . . troisième Edition ou l'on a joint les*

assertion, there is no evidence that Corelli was the author of these embellishments.[23] Their attribution to him nevertheless gave Roger's edition an aura that has persisted to the present.

Let us glance briefly at a different representation of composership in the early eighteenth century. Benedetto Marcello's satire, *Il Teatro alla moda* (1720), disparages the composer as a mere servant of the impresario, the poet, the prima donna, and, most of all, the castrato.[24] Even more telling, Marcello does not give the composer much claim to ownership of his music or grant him much originality in writing it. He is, Marcello implies, a regular feeder at a trough of musical commonplaces and a purveyor of stock motives and stereotypical devices which he prepares far in advance of any actual assignment or commission. As a rising musician, he typically plagiarizes the music of the "more celebrated composer" for whom he copies music.[25] *Il Teatro alla moda*, which mentions this "more celebrated" victim of plagiarism only in passing, does not say whether he was a plagiarizer or whether his work was largely his own invention. Celebrated composers of Marcello's day—Vivaldi and Handel, for example—were in fact not above plagiarizing the works of others; Handel recycled his own compositions without hesitation. It is a truism that in Handel's day there was no stigma attached to borrowing and no premium on originality. Why, then, were certain composers "more celebrated"? Was it because their work bore an individual stamp or simply because they somehow contrived to be more successful than their colleagues? Marcello's satire only suggests that wholesale borrowing is to be despised; it does not offer answers to these questions; nor do comments of contemporary listeners.

Music theorists of the first half of the eighteenth century wrote more volubly, however, about matters of borrowing and invention. Their views of these matters and their portrayal of the composer's status are often full of contradictions, but their views of borrowing and invention included an assumption that would be articulated by literary critics of the late nineteenth and twentieth centuries, most notably, Roland Barthes, in "The Death of the Author":

> The text is a tissue of quotations drawn from the innumerable centres of culture… the writer can only imitate a gesture that is always anterior, never original.[26]

*agréemens des Adagio de cet ouvrage, composez par Mr. A. Corelli, comme il les joue* (Amsterdam: Estienne Roger, 1710).

23. Many scholars have come to believe that the embellishments are not Corelli's. But in his study of the publication history of Corelli's Opus 6, Rudolf Rasch presents evidence of Roger's great integrity as a businessman, which he hints, indicates that Roger's claim of Corelli's authorship of the embellishments may have been truthful. See Rudolf RASCH, "Corelli's contract: Notes on the Publication History of the *Concerti Grossi… Opera sesta* [1714]," *Tijdschrift van de koninklijke vereniging voor neder-*

*landse musiekgeschiedenis,* 46 (1996), 83-136.

24. Benedetto MARCELLO, *Il Teatro alla moda* (*c.*1720) trans. with commentary by Reinhard PAULY, "Benedetto Marcello's Satire on Early 18th-Century Opera," *The Musical Quarterly* 34 (1948): 222-33; idem, "Il Teatro alla moda," *The Musical Quarterly* 34 (1948): 371-403, and 35 (1949): 85-105.

25. *Pauly,* "Il Teatro Alla Moda," (1948), 380-88, particularly, 381.

26. BARTHES, "The Death of the Author," 128.

Early eighteenth-century music theorists typically recommend judicious imitation of good models as long as clever use is made of borrowed material. Johann Kuhnau's reference to borrowing in his *Musikalischer Quack-Salber*, (1700) is wholly approbatory:

> It would still probably have been possible to make a melody out of this material if he had only understood the art by which the most beautiful invention can often be extracted from the best songs, especially if a person knows how to apply the *artem combinatoriam* to music.[27]

Johann Mattheson recommends collecting musical themes or *Haupt-Sätze* that can serve as stock melodic formulae:

> But these [particular things] must not be procured by writing down for oneself a catalogue of such scraps, and, in pedantic fashion, making of them a veritable invention-chest, but in the way in which we acquire a store of words and expressions from a speech—not necessarily on paper or in a book, but in our minds and memories, by means of which our thoughts, be they oral or written, can most easily be brought to light without consulting a dictionary every time.[28]

Passages from the writings of Mattheson also show him as an advocate of originality in composing:

> All elaboration (*elaboratio*), however beautiful, can be compared only to interest, but invention (*inventio*) can be compared to capital itself. I have wanted to write this, not only for myself, but for the encouragement of the world famous Keiser of whom one has spoken all the more often, the richer in invention he becomes. [29]

Other eighteenth-century theorists express respect for musical invention (*inventio* or *Erfindung*) or for distinctive use of borrowed material.[30] It is possible, even likely, that admiration for composers whose work somehow reveals them as individual subjects is implicit in such discussions. But theorists' praise is usually oblique; they did not, in fact,

---

27. Johann KUHNAU, *Der musikalische Quack-Salber* (Dresden: Miethe and Zimmerman, 1700), 147, transl. John H. ROBERTS in "Why did Handel Borrow?" *Handel Tercentenary Collection*, ed. Stanley SADIE and Anthony HICKS (Ann Arbor: UMI Research Press, 1987), 86.

28. Johann MATTHESON, *Der vollkommene Capellmeister* (Hamburg: Christian Herold, 1739), 132: "Diese Specialien müssen aber nicht so genommen werden, daß man sich etwa ein Verzeichniß von dergleichen Brocken aufschreiben, und, nach guter Schulweise, daraus einen ordentlichen Erfindungs-Kasten machen müste; sondern auf dieselbe Art, wie wir uns einen Vorrath an Wörtern und Ausdrückungen bey dem Reden, nicht eben nothwendig auf dem Papier oder in einem Buche, sondern im Kopffe und Gedächtniß zulegen, mittelst dessen hernach unsre Gedancken, es sey mündlich oder schrifftlich, am bequemsten zu Tage gebracht werden können, ohne des-

wegen allemahl ein Lexicon um Rath zu fragen."

29. Johann MATTHESON, *Critica Musica* (Hamburg: Mattheson, 1722), 72: "Alle *elaboratio*, sie sey so schön wie sie wolle/ ist nur mit Zinsen; die *inventio* aber mit dem Capital selbst zu vergleichen. Dieses habe ich nicht nur mir selbst/ sondern hauptsächlich dem weltberühmten Keiser/ zum Trost schreiben wollen/ als welchen man desto mehr und öffter zugesprochen hat/ je reicher er an schönen Erfindungen ist."

30. See, for example, Johann David HEINICHEN, *Der Generalbaß in der Composition* (Dresden: Heinichen, 1728; repr. Hildesheim: Georg Olms, 1969), 29, and Johann Joachim QUANTZ, *Versuch einer Anweisung die Flöte traversiere zu spielen* (Berlin: Johann Friedrich Voß; repr. Kassel: Bärenreiter, 1983), 13-14. I am grateful to Steven Zohn of Temple University for pointing out several of these theoretical sources to me.

glorify originality or even use the word "original" until after 1759, the year of publication of Edward Young's *Conjectures on Original Composition* (a work to which we will return later), and consequently did not grant composers an authoritative or god-like role in the creation of music. Johann Adolf Scheibe seems to have been one of the first to praise originality in composing outspokenly. In his *Theorie der Melodie und Harmonie* of 1773 Scheibe writes approvingly of Handel and Hasse for treating borrowed materials in such a way as to transform them into "original" ideas; more significantly, he calls Keiser the greatest "original genius" Germany has known.[31]

Carl Philipp Emanuel Bach (1714-88) was born and educated during this period of ambiguity in the status of the composer. From his earliest years, he was steeped in a tradition of collaboration which he never outgrew: between composer and performer, and between one composer and another. This tradition is evident in several genres in his works: 1) sets of variations on themes of other composers (a kind of collaboration found in music composed from long before Bach's lifetime and long after); 2) choral pasticcios that he made in response to the exigencies of his position as music director of five churches in Hamburg (in pasticcios the role of the composer is murky—it is often uncertain what is borrowed material, who was its author, and where in the collected works of a composer it may reasonably reside);[32] 3) the varied reprises that Emanuel Bach composed for his sonatas and the cadenzas that he wrote for his concertos. This third kind of collaboration, unlike the first two, but like the embellishments attributed to Corelli, consisted of music that was, typically, improvised by a performer. In the varied reprises to his sonatas and cadenzas to his concertos, Emanuel Bach was both composer and, presumably, performer.

Like other famous written-out "improvisations," Emanuel Bach's cadenzas and varied reprises are of interest because they constitute a valuable example of mid-eighteenth-century performance practice. His first published collection of written-out varied reprises is of great relevance to the present study, not only because it was published by the composer himself, but also because its publication provided the occasion for a manifesto. Bach's remarks in the preface to the first volume of *Sonatas with Varied Reprises*, Wq 50 (published 1760), indicate that his embellishments for the repetitions of these sonatas were intended to serve as ready-made "improvisations" for students who were deserving in certain ways, but incapable of improvising ornaments, and—interestingly—for professional musicians in whom the springs of invention had temporarily gone

---

31. Johann Adolphe SCHEIBE, *Ueber die musikalische Composition*, 1: *Die Theorie der Melodie und Harmonie* (Leipzig: 1773), liii: "[Handel and Hasse] verstunden aber die Kunst, sich diese Erfindungen so zuzueignen, daß sie unter ihren Händen in neue und Originalgedanken... Kaiser [sic] war in der Musik vielleicht das größte Originalgenie, das Deutschland jemals hervorgebracht hat."

32. I am grateful to Stephen L. Clark of Skidmore College for information on the subject of Emanuel Bach's borrowing and self-borrowing. Dr. Clark points out that since the performances of Bach's pasticcios were for local occasions, and since these works were never intended to be published, there was little reason for Bach to identify sources of borrowed material.

dry.[33] For these published embellishments there was a more exact precedent than the Roger edition of Corelli's Opus 5: the *Methodical Sonatas* (published 1728 and 1732) by Emanuel Bach's godfather, Georg Philipp Telemann. This publication, like Bach's first volume of *Sonatas with Varied Reprises*, was an offering planned by the composer himself, presumably as a model for those who had not learned to improvise embellishments. Thus Bach was not the first eighteenth-century composer to provide written "improvisations" for his own compositions, nor the last: his contemporary and colleague, Franz Benda, wrote ornaments for his violin sonatas, although he did not publish them; Haydn and Mozart often furnished written-out varied repetitions on local levels—phrases and even measures, and Mozart wrote, but did not publish, cadenzas for his piano concertos.

It is instructive to consider how Emanuel Bach's varied reprises, published and unpublished, differ from previous written "improvisations," including Telemann's, and from those by composers who followed Bach. In the collection of *Sonatas with Varied Reprises* that he published in 1760, Bach contrived, as had other composers, to introduce paradigms; unlike others, he provided the collection with a preface in which he declared his plan and defended it. His preface has resonated to the present day; it contains some of the most frequently quoted passages among his writings. Bach's written-out varied reprises also differ from those of his predecessors in their sheer quantity; more of these varied reprises, published and unpublished in his lifetime, have survived than have embellishments by any other composer. The great number of these offerings is obviously related to the growing number of amateur performers in Bach's lifetime. His publication of the *Versuch über die wahre Art das Clavier zu spielen* (*Essay on the True Art of Playing Keyboard Instruments*) was directed in large part to such players, and the number of keyboard works of all degrees of difficulty that Bach composed from the mid-1750s to the end of his life indicates that the appearance of the *Versuch*, won him a considerable clientele of keyboardists who were in need of written "improvisations." Without denying Bach's didactic purpose in providing these written "improvisations," it is possible to discern a third, and even more significant, way in which Bach's varied reprises differ from those of earlier composers: in their author's intention—often suggested in his writings—to maintain the greatest possible control of his works and the manner in which they were performed. In this purpose, it might be noted, he had a precedent in the works of his father. Johann Sebastian Bach left no verbal declaration of ownership of his music, it is true. But he often insured control of his works by tacitly ornamenting them so as not to allow performers the opportunity to produce their own embellishments.

---

33. It seems likely that Bach had been writing down "improvisations" for students before 1753, the date of the first published example of such "improvisations" (the last movement of the fifth *Probestück*), although no firm evidence exists to confirm this supposition beyond the last movement of the sonata in G Major, Wq 65/12 (H 23), composed, according to Bach's *Nachlaß-Verzeichnis* (see n. 37), in 1740.

Emanuel Bach's efforts to maintain control of other aspects of his works—their production and circulation, as well as their style of performance—were unprecedented (whether Sebastian Bach or any of his contemporaries were as proprietary as Emanuel Bach, will probably never be known, for no direct evidence of their attempts to exercise authority over these aspects of their works survives). Manuscripts by copyists in Emanuel Bach's circle—the two Berlin copyists known only as Anonymous 301 and Anonymous 303 and the Hamburg copyist, Johann Heinrich Michel—are models of accuracy; many of them bear Bach's autograph corrections and additions. It is difficult to know whether occasional errors in his published works are attributable to his lack of diligence as a proof reader or to the publisher's carelessness. But in his attempt to supply collectors of his works with accurate copies, he was more conscientious than most of his contemporaries. Bach was able to suppress many early works and thus determine the extent and quality of his œuvre. As his career progressed, his notation of his texts became more explicit, leaving as little as possible to the whims and lack of understanding of the performer. His dynamic markings, for example, became more specific. Most of Bach's manuscripts of the 1740s contain no other dynamics than *forte* and *piano*; later manuscripts partake of many dynamic options—*ff, f, mf, mp, p, pp*—and point the way to more precise directions for performance in scores by Beethoven and by most composers of the nineteenth century.

Emanuel Bach's correspondence is further evidence of his determination to supervise the distribution of his works. His letters contain only sparse details about his personal life and few direct references to his aesthetic ideals, but they stipulate the manner in which his works are to be dealt with. Posterity has often taxed Bach with money-grubbing, because his correspondence is full of concern for the profit which could be derived from the sale of his music. But his letters also indicate a desire to supply collectors with correct exemplars of his works.[34] He kept careful account of the circulation of his compositions—not only in approved manuscripts and prints, but in the pirated editions, which he deplored and against which he cautioned his buyers.[35] As early as 1772, Bach, possibly inspired by Charles Burney's request that he list all of his works, drew up a catalogue of his keyboard compositions.[36] An even more valuable account of his works and of those of members of the Bach family, the catalogue of his musical estate published by his widow in 1790, is generally believed to have derived directly from his records.[37]

---

34. See, for example, Stephen L. CLARK, ed. and trans., *The Letters of C. P. E. Bach* (Oxford: Clarendon Press, 1997), letters #18, p. 22; #66, p. 62; #78, pp. 77-78; #81, p. 80; #148, p. 134.

35. There is, for instance, a note of consternation in his letter of 5 April 1785, in which he informs an unknown collector that he has never seen an edition to which the writer refers. See CLARK, *Letters of C. P. E. Bach*, 225-26.

36. This catalogue has recently been found in the collection of the Berlin Singakademie, now housed in Kiev, Ukraine. See Christoph WOLFF: "Carl Philipp Emanuel Bach eigenhändiges Verzeichnis seiner Clavierwerke von 1733 bis 1772," *Über Leben, Kunst und Kunstwerk: Aspekte musikalischer Biographie*, ed. Christoph WOLFF (Leipzig, 1999), 217-35.

37. *Verzeichniß des musikalischen Nachlasses des verstorbenen*

Bach's works have a subjective aspect not found in the music of earlier composers and demand a subjective style of performance. In his *Versuch*, he implies that music is often full of changes of mood and directs performers to situate themselves in each successive state of mind in order to move their listeners.[38] Bach might have been writing of his own music, for it has frequent and abrupt changes of rhythm and harmony that seem to depict the fluctuations of mood described in the *Versuch*, whether the mood might belong to the composer or to his imagined high-strung subject. The programmatic titles of several of Bach's works—*Gespräch zwischen Melancholicus und Sanguineus, Abschied von meinem Silbermannischen Claviere*, and *C. P. E. Bachs Empfindungen*, for example—indicate that the composer did intend for such musical changes to represent soliloquies or dialogues between two subjects.

Reception of Emanuel Bach as a composer changed significantly in the 1770s, when the concept of "original genius" with its divine aspect attained great prestige.[39] From early in his career Bach had been recognized as a musician of strong will and superior accomplishment. But only after the beginning of his tenure in Hamburg (1768) did writers praise him as a composer of originality and of more than human inspiration.[40] Burney devoted more attention to him than to any other German composer, describing his ecstatic moments as an improviser.[41] Forkel painted him as a lonely, almost Byronic, figure, towering above the crowd.[42]

*Capellmeisters Carl Philipp Emanuel Bach* (Hamburg: Gottlieb Friedrich Schniebes, 1990), published by his widow. For a discussion of Bach's authorship of this catalogue, see Ernst SUCHALLA, *Die Orchestersinfonien Carl Philipp Emanuel Bachs* (Augsburg: W. Blasaditsch, 1968), 153; Darrell M. BERG, "Towards a Catalogue of the Keyboard Sonatas of C. P. E. Bach," *Journal of the American Musicological Society* 32 (1979): 280, and Rachel W. WADE, *The Keyboard Concertos of Carl Philipp Emanuel Bach*, Studies in Musicology, 48 (Ann Arbor: UMI Research Press, 1981), 5-8.

38. *Versuch über die wahre Art das Clavier zu spielen* (Berlin: in Verlegung des Auctoris, gedr. Christian Friedrich Henning, 1753, repr. Leipzig: Breitkopf & Härtel, 1981), 122: "Indem ein Musicus nicht anders rühren kan, er sey dann selbst gerührt; so muß er nothwendig sich selbst in alle Affeckten setzen können, welche er bey seinen Zuhörern erregen will; er giebt ihnen seine Empfindungen zu verstehen und bewegt sie solchergestallt am besten zur Mit-Empfindung."

39. See Edward YOUNG, *Conjectures on Original Composition in a Letter to the Author of Sir Charles Grandison* (London: Printed for A. Millar and R. and J. Dodsley, 1759), 26-27: "A genius differs from a good understanding, as a magician from a good architect; that raises his structure by means invisible; this by the skilful use of common tools. Hence genius has ever been supposed to partake

of something divine...."

40. See, for example, Charles BURNEY, *The Present State of Music in Germany, the Netherlands and United Provinces* (London: 1775), repr. in Monuments of Music and Music Literature in Facsimile, 2/117 (New York: Broude, 1969), 2: 256: "... however, each candid observer and hearer, must discover, in the slightest and most trivial productions, of every kind, some mark of originality in the modulation, accompaniment, or melody, which bespeak a great and exalted genius"; Christian Friedrich Daniel SCHUBART, *Ideen zu einer Ästhetik der Tonkunst* (1784/85), ed. L. SCHUBART (Wien: J.V. Degen, 1806), 178: "Man hat unzählige Clavierstücke von diesem Meister, die alle das Gepräge des ausserordentlichsten Genies tragen."

41. BURNEY, *The Present State*, 2: 246: "He tried a new *piano forte*, and in a wild, careless manner, threw away thoughts and execution upon it, that would have set up any one else...", 270: "During this time, he grew so animated and *possessed*, that he not only played, but looked like one inspired..."

42. Johann Nikolaus FORKEL, *Musikalisch-Kritische Bibliothek*, 3 vols. (Gotha: C. W. Ettinger, 1778-79), 2: 275: "Nichts stellen wir uns in der That trauriger vor, als wenn ein Mann mit seinem Wissen, oder mit seiner Kunst, sich über die Sphäre seiner Zeitverwandten so hoch hinauf geschwungen hat, daß er nur von wenigen

Even in his lifetime, Emanuel Bach was not able to maintain absolute ownership of his works, however heroic his efforts. Publishers, patrons, buyers of all sorts and conditions, and performers of his music had a share in its origin and a degree of ownership. Despite his fame as a composer of original genius, he did not survive the eighteenth century as a composer-god. At the end of the century, he died two symbolic deaths. The first was the loss of popularity his music suffered and its subsequent descent into virtual oblivion. This death had much to do with the ascendancy of the style of Haydn, Mozart, and Beethoven, but it was also related to Bach's biological death (1788). For as long as he lived, he was able to find reputable publishers and adequate numbers of subscribers to his published works. After 1788, however, the circulation of his music was largely dependent on the distribution of manuscripts to collectors, for only a few publishers took an interest in it. Although his name did not disappear entirely during the nineteenth century, it inhabited lexicons as that of a historical figure.

Bach's other symbolic death is similar to the authorial fate depicted in Donald F. McKenzie's *Bibliography and the Sociology of Texts*.[43] In a chapter titled "The book as an expressive form," McKenzie discusses the role played by editors and publishers in separating authors from their texts. With delicious irony, he presents an excerpt from William Congreve's prologue to *The Way of the World* as it appears in "The Intentional Fallacy," an essay by two New Critics, W. K. Wimsatt, Jr. and Monroe C. Beardsley. McKenzie points out that in the essay by these two writers, who are firm believers in the sacredness of the text, the font, spelling, punctuation, and even the words of Congreve's authorized version of 1710, are changed to such an extent that the author's meaning is drastically altered. Alterations that texts of Emanuel Bach's compositions underwent after his death are analogous to shifts of meaning described by McKenzie. During the last decade of the eighteenth century, the publisher J.C.F. Rellstab made sweeping changes in Bach's music. Rellstab's editions contain not only the careless mistakes for which he was famous, but also deliberate alterations of pitch, register, and time signatures as well as transpositions from original keys.[44] Publishers of the few other editions of Bach's works that appeared in this decade also undertook to "modernize" the notation of his music in various ways, with the result that editions published between 1790 and 1800 have a very different appearance from those published in Bach's lifetime.[45] During most of the nineteenth century,

---

erreicht, begriffen und genossen werden kann. Ob sich gleich ein solcher Geist, durch den innern Genuss seines Wissens oder seiner Kunst, hinlänglich belohnen kann, und allenfalls nicht nöthig hat, ängstlich um den Beyfall des grossen Haufens innerer Genuss zur Mittheilung gegen andere dringt. Wie traurig und niederschlagend muß es dan seyn, nicht verstanden zu werden, wenn man redet, und nur so wenige Nebengeschöpfe zu finden,

von denen man sagen kann, daß sie Fleisch von unserm Fleisch, und Bein von unserm Bein sind."

43. See above, n. 2.

44. Notably, *Preludio e sei sonate pel organo...* (Berlin: Rellstab [1790]) and *Œuvres posthumes de C. P. E. Bach. Trois Sonates pour le clavecin* (Berlin: Rellstab, 1792).

45. See, for example, *Grande Sonate pour le clavecin ou fortepiano* (Vienna: Hoffmeister, and Leipzig: Hoffmeister &

Emanuel Bach's music held no interest for most publishers, and consequently his texts suffered little violence. Aristide Farrenc's editions of selected keyboard works by Bach (1861-1874), undertaken to provide an anthology of works for the "piano" that included works by composers of earlier centuries, are remarkably free of editorial intervention.[46] Editions published toward the end of the of the century and in the first quarter of the twentieth century, however, abound in editorial "improvements": changes in beaming, stemming, and ornaments, and fingerings intended for the modern piano which deflect from an understanding of Bach's original aesthetic.

The deaths of Emanuel Bach's reputation and of his compositions have been no more final than the death of the author posited by Barthes, Foucault, and Derrida. In the last half of the present century, Bach has been "returned to partial vesting" in his œuvre, just as have other composers, by means of scholarly editions that seek to remove all modern editorial accretions from eighteenth-century texts (and reintroduce as few as possible); by facsimiles that present these texts as they appeared to the composer and his eighteenth-century clientele; and by performances that attempt to recover the rhetoric and performing media of the time of origin. It is true that today's scholarly edition can never entirely recapture Bach's original texts, for it is obliged to modernize his notation to some extent. Neither can historically informed performance of his music insure that it is played and heard as it was in the eighteenth century. Nor, for that matter, can it be determined precisely what part Bach's publishers, patrons, and students played in the creation of his works.

Yet Emanuel Bach can be restored to a place as composer of the music that bears his name, more successfully, perhaps, than can many composers of the past. Bach in fact always owned his music to a remarkable degree, and it always carried the potential to rise from the ashes. It is true of music, as of literature, that much—although not everything—has been said and done before, and that the composer's music is to some extent a "tissue of quotations," none of them original. Granted that Bach, like most eighteenth-century composers, had to avail himself of musical materials none of which was entirely new, we can nevertheless identify a considerable residue of originality in his music. The formulae that Bach borrowed were the tiniest of kernels. His combination of musical gestures on all but the smallest levels is so idiosyncratic as to be immediately recognizable as his. This is not to say that other composers have not also developed distinctive styles and do not have considerable vesting in their music. But it is Emanuel Bach's career and the reception of his music that illustrate most vividly, and with their peculiar chronology, the life, death, and return of the composer.

Kühnel, [c. 1802]).

46. Louise and Aristide FARRENC, eds., Le Trésor des pianistes (Paris: L. and A. Farrenc, 1861-74, repr. New York: Da Capo,

# Schubert's Problematic Relationship with Johann Mayrhofer: New Documentary Evidence

The study of the unique quality of significant men remains forever the most interesting, the most fruitful, the most worthy pursuit. I at least know of no other higher task than the attempt to understand greatness.[1]

THUS BEGINS the posthumous edition (1843) of the poems of Johann Mayrhofer (1787-1836), edited by his friend and fellow poet Ernst von Feuchtersleben (1806-49). But the proclamation of Mayrhofer's greatness fell on deaf ears and this significant Biedermeier-era poet soon joined the ranks of the neglected and forgotten. That his name is at all familiar today is due to the song settings Franz Schubert made of 47 of his poems—next to Goethe the largest number of texts chosen from any single poet—and to the fact that Mayrhofer shared living quarters with Schubert for two years. Although this poet-friend has in the past attracted minimal attention among Schubert scholars, the situation has changed recently. David Gramit's 1993 article discusses the aesthetics of Mayrhofer's *Heliopolis* cycle, a group of twenty poems dated "September and October 1821" and dedicated to another of Schubert's poet-friends, Franz von Schober.[2] Gramit argues that we ought not "to isolate Schubert so completely"[3] from his friends if we are to understand the motivation behind his choice of poetic texts. Susan Youens chose Mayrhofer as one of four poets for an in-depth study in her 1996 book on Schubert's poets.[4] She assumes rightly that Mayrhofer's poems are often autobiographical and attempts to read the symbolic language of selected poems to find evidence of the poet's relationship with Schubert, in particular of Mayrhofer's "putative homosexuality."[5] A recurring refrain in her dis-

1.   Johann Mayrhofer, *Gedichte [ . . . ] neue Sammlung*, ed. Ernst von Feuchtersleben (Vienna: Ignaz Klang, 1843) [henceforth Feuchtersleben], 1. The original German language of long quotations from unpublished documents is found in the Appendix.

2.   See David Gramit, "Schubert and the Biedermeier: The Aesthetics of Johann Mayrhofer's 'Heliopolis'," *Music & Letters* 74 (1993): 355-82.

3.   Ibid., 355.

4.   See Susan Youens, *Schubert's poets and the making of lieder* (Cambridge: Cambridge University Press, 1996) [henceforth Youens], in particular the section "Chromatic melancholy: Johann Mayrhofer and Schubert," 151-227.

5.   Ibid., 159. Youens bases this reading of Mayrhofer's sexual orientation on Maynard Solomon's unfounded speculation that Schubert may have taken on "the

cussion is "one would like to know more."[6] Taking up this challenge, the following study interprets many new documents from Austrian archives, adding significantly to our knowledge of Mayrhofer's character and his collaboration and friendship with Schubert. It will also answer some of the questions surrounding the eventual estrangement between these two important artists.

## Ignaz Spenn's Diary (1812)

The first mention of Mayrhofer in the Schubert documents collected by Otto Erich Deutsch is in connection with the unpublished diary from 1811-12 of Ignaz Spenn (1791-1813), a schoolfellow of Schubert's at the Royal Seminary in Vienna.[7] One of Schubert's early school friends, Josef Kenner, wrote later as follows: "I owe my acquaintance with Schubert to *Hofrat* von Spaun and to Ignaz Spenn, *Konzepts-Praktikant* in the Imperial Court and State Archives, who died in 1813."[8] Indeed, the name "Schub" (most likely Schubert) is recorded in at least six of Spenn's diary entries between May and August 1812.[9] Spenn was also the mathematics coach for the younger boys at the Seminary, and it may be that Spenn's death from tuberculosis on 6 January 1813 ultimately resulted in Schubert's failing grade in this subject and his subsequent decision to leave the elite school.[10] Spenn's diary is especially important here, because it records Mayrhofer's early friendship with key members of the Schubert circle, in particular with Josef von Spaun (1788-1865), Josef Kenner (1794-1868), and Franz von Schober (1796-1882):

> The 3rd [September 1812] In the evening [we attended Schiller's] *Braut von Messina*: I, Schilder, Spaun, Kenner, Arnet, Mayrhofer [...]

ephebe's role with [...] Vogl [...] and Mayrhofer." See SOLOMON, "Franz Schubert and the Peacocks of Benvenuto Cellini," *19th Century Music* 12 (1989): 203. See also the evidence I present against Solomon's position in: STEBLIN, "The Peacock's Tale: Schubert's Sexuality Reconsidered," *19th Century Music* 17 (1993): 5-33; STEBLIN, "Schubert's Relationship with Women: An Historical Account," in: *Schubert Studies*, ed. Brian NEWBOULD (Aldershot: Ashgate, 1998), 159-82; and STEBLIN, "In Defense of Scholarship and Archival Research: Why Schubert's Brothers Were Allowed to Marry," *Current Musicology* 62 (1998): 7-17.

6.   YOUENS, 153.

7.   See Otto Erich DEUTSCH, *Schubert: A Documentary Biography*, trans. Eric BLOM (London: Dent, 1946) [henceforth *Documentary Biography*], 23, and idem, *Schubert: Die Dokumente seines Lebens* (Kassel: Bärenreiter, 1964) [henceforth *Dokumente*], 18.

8.   Otto Erich DEUTSCH, *Schubert: Memoirs by His Friends*,

trans. Rosamond LEY and John NOWELL (London: Adam and Charles Black, 1958) [henceforth *Memoirs*], 85, and idem, *Schubert: Die Erinnerungen seiner Freunde* (Leipzig, 1957; Wiesbaden: Breitkopf & Härtel, 1983) [henceforth *Erinnerungen*], 99.

9.   A somewhat unreliable transcript of Spenn's diary, which also includes research conducted by Deutsch in 1962, was made by Ignaz Weinmann in 1959 and is located in the latter's important estate of Schubertiana (still for the most part uncatalogued) in the Wiener Stadt- und Landesbibliothek Handschriftensammlung [Vienna City Library] (henceforth WStLB-HSS). For the passages cited in the present article I consulted the original diary, which is in private possession. The Spenn diary will be dealt with more fully in a separate publication.

10.   This theory derives from Weinmann's research notes on Spenn, which I purchased from a Viennese bookshop (Antiquariat Löcker) in August 1993.

8th [September 1812] [...] In the afternoon [I went] with Spaun, Kenner, Mayrhofer and my brother to Kahlenberg where we drank milk; then to Leopoldsberg and home via Nußdorf

30th [September 1812] In the evening Schober was at our place with Spaun and Mayrhofer

1st October [1812] In the morning at Schilder's. In the evening Spaun, Kirchstättern, Schober, Mayrhofer at our place

2nd [October 1812]. In the morning [I went] with Spaun and Schober to the art gallery. In the evening Schilder accompanied me and [stayed] at our place

3rd [October 1812]. With Schober, Kenner, Mayer[hofer], Kirchstättern, Spaun at Kahlenberg. We ate in Heiligenstadt, had some milk at Leopoldsberg and conversed well among ourselves in the usual way. In the evening I showed Schober the way to Hernals that led me to Siboni's garden.[11]

The Swedish-born Schober, who was studying at the Kremsmünster Seminary, spent his school holidays in the fall of 1812 in Vienna, where his mother now lived. Among Spenn's many poems appended to the diary is a farewell to Schober, dated 31 October 1812, which refers to the latter as a new favoured star in the group of friends and bears witness already at this early date to Schober's charismatic powers.[12] This controversial figure was later condemned by Kenner as a "false prophet, who embellished sensuality in such a flattering manner," "won a lasting and pernicious influence over Schubert's honest susceptibility," and helped lead him astray "down to the slough of moral degradation."[13] Schober was subsequently to become a sore point in Mayrhofer's relationship with Schubert.

Mayrhofer appears as an active, congenial member of Schubert's youthful circle of friends. Born twenty-five years earlier in Steyr in Upper Austria, he had completed his primary schooling in Linz, where he was on good terms with the Spaun family, and had then served for four years as a cleric-in-training at the monastery of St. Florian.[14] Having decided to devote himself to a secular life in the public service, he came to Vienna in 1810 to study law. Here he roomed for several years with Josef von Spaun[15]

11. For the original German see the Appendix. Schober's sister Ludwiga had married the actor Giuseppe Siboni in 1811 and was accidentally killed in a shooting accident on 23 November 1812. A rather piquant entry for 12 May 1812, a day on which Spenn encountered one bad event after another, reads: "Abends entdeckte ich dß ich—die Krone des Tages—mein Perspektiv verlohren—und hatte noch Verdruß bis ins Bett *avec notre jolie Grà*—." [In the evening I discovered— to top it all—that I had lost my field-glass—and had still other annoyances until I went to bed *with our pretty Grà*—].

12. This poem, entitled "Abschied an Schober," was transcribed fully by Weinmann. For the other poems Weinmann notated only the titles.

13. *Memoirs*, 86; *Erinnerungen*, 100.

14. For basic biographical information on Mayrhofer, see FEUCHTERSLEBEN, 1-26, and the edition of *Johann Mayrhofers Gedichte [...] 1824* by Michael Maria RABENLECHNER (Vienna: Wiener Bibliophilen-Gesellschaft, 1938) [henceforth RABENLECHNER], 209-62.

15. See Carl GLOSSY, "Aus den Lebenserinnerungen des Joseph Freiherrn von Spaun," *Jahrbuch der Grillparzer-Gesellschaft* (Vienna) 8 (1898) [henceforth GLOSSY], 294. See also Josef von SPAUN, "[Chronik meiner Familie],"

and finished his legal studies with brilliant success.[16] Among his close friends in 1812 was Theodor Körner, engaged to marry the actress Antonie Adamberger and known as the poet of the Wars of Liberation, who died on the battlefield in 1813. (According to Spaun, it was Körner who encouraged Schubert to devote his life to music.)[17]

Mayrhofer himself recounted that he was first introduced to Schubert in late 1814 by Spaun, who had given the composer the poem "Am See" (D 124) to set (composed on 7 December 1814).[18] The association between composer and poet began slowly; Schubert wrote only two other lieder on texts by Mayrhofer before September 1816: "Liane" (D 298) in October 1815 and "Fragment aus dem Aeschylus" (D 450) in June 1816. More important during this period was Schubert's collaboration with Mayrhofer on a comical Singspiel in two acts, "Die Freunde von Salamanka" (D 326), composed between 18 November and 31 December 1815. There is little trace of the later "melancholic" poet in the romantic plot of this work: a love story involving three couples who end up marrying after overcoming various obstacles.[19]

## Mayrhofer's Letter to Franz von Schober (1816)

Schubert's involvement with Mayrhofer's poetry intensified in September 1816 with the composition of four lieder ("Liedesend" D 473, "Abschied" D 475, "Rückweg" D 476 and "Alte Liebe rostet nie" D 477). Another three lieder (D 490-492) followed in the next month. An important letter from Mayrhofer to Schober,

unpublished typescript by Fridolin von Spaun (Dorfen, 1980), 291. I wish to thank Dietlinde Rakowitz (Schubert Museum Atzenbrugg) for giving me a copy of this typescript, which was made from the Kurrentschrift version of Joseph von Spaun's 1864 manuscript, written out by Marie von Spaun *née* Zach (1811-1875), the widow of Maximilian Gandolf von Spaun (1797-1844). A photocopy of the latter entitled "Spaun-Chronik" is located in the Vienna Nationalbibliothek (1,181.217-D). Unfortunately, Fridolin's typescript, which modernizes the spellings, is full of serious errors. A hastily-written article by the Austrian student Ilija Dürhammer, "'Was ich gefühlt', has Du gesungen'—Neue Dokumente zu Johann Mayrhofers Leben und Schaffen," *Mitteilungen der Österreichischen Gesellschaft für Musikwissenschaft* 31 (March 1997), 13-45, appendix 4, bases the "Spaun-Familienchronik" on Fridolin's 1980 typescript, not on the 19th-century handwritten copy, and adds many new errors. Dürhammer criticizes Deutsch for altering Spaun's spelling, but his own spelling changes deviate much more from the original than those minor ones made by Deutsch in the excerpts published in *Memoirs*, 354; *Erinnerungen*, 408.

16. See Feuchtersleben, 4. See also the following passage in Ferdinand Luib's handwritten notes, "Oester-

reichs musikalischer Pantheon," dating from the late 1850s and located in the WStLB-HSS (Ja 38.712), p. 226ʳ: "[...] um erst in Wien die juridischen Studien zu beginnen. Er vollendete dieselben wieder mit glänzendem Erfolge und wurde am 28. November 1814 bei dem k. k. Bücher-Revisionsamte, in welchem er sich seit 1 Jahre als Praktikant in Verwendung befand, angestellt." Youens writes incorrectly on p. 154: "Mayrhofer gave up his legal studies." She is also mistaken in reporting that Mayrhofer "worked for a while in a tobacconist's shop." According to Spaun, the poet decided against taking a job with the "Tabakgesellschaft" [recte: "Tabakgefälls"] after reading "Tabaksbrüder Narr" [recte: "Tabacks Luder Narr"], a sermon on the follies of smoking by Abraham a Sancta Clara. See Spaun, "Chronik meiner Familie," 292, and ["Spaun-Chronik," 415]. This "Chronik" contains important biographical information omitted by Glossy and Deutsch, for example, that Mayrhofer served as a teacher for the family of Baron Isdenji.

17. *Memoirs*, 129; *Erinnerungen*, 151.

18. *Memoirs*, 13; *Erinnerungen*, 18.

19. See the plot synopsis in Elizabeth Norman McKay, *Franz Schubert's Music for the Theatre* (Tutzing: Hans Schneider, 1991), 126-29.

dated 7 September 1816 and mentioning Schubert, was excerpted by Deutsch.[20] It is published here in its entirety to give the context of the passage involving the composer (the segment cited by Deutsch is in italics):

Vienna, 7th September 1816.

Dear Brother:

When K[enner] left Vienna an instruction from you weighed heavily on his mind, which on account of his exams and for lack of time he was unable to accomplish. To reassure him I had to promise that I would carry it out myself, which I also did. Your good nature is praiseworthy, K's willingness friendly. But the manner in which the aforementioned is supposed to be realized will be time-consuming, and I know that you will take into account the way in which K. or I would now easily appear—I believe with some right—in a false light. And to get rid in part of just one great writer, for example Plut[arch] or Goethe, would take almost a month. By that time, as your friends hope, you will already be back. I am now of the opinion that you yourself should decide on the manner in which your pretty plan is to be carried out. If you insist on the sale I will not spare any effort on my part to satisfy your wish. Write me or, even better, let me know by word of mouth. I will keep your letter to K. But if you are impatient in your good-natured way, be assured that K. tried to do whatever was possible, and so remonstrate only with me. Dear Friend! Your noble mother, whom I have more and more reason to respect, has told me all about your letters. I have travelled with you to the distant north in my thoughts and hope to follow you to the more beautiful south. Just think, this trip has been a fortunate occasion for you. How I am looking forward to seeing you again: enriched with [new] knowledge of people, furnished with an altered, clearer view of life. Tomorrow (the 8th of September) I am going with the younger Watteroth to the mountains for 4 to 5 days: to Lilienfeld, Baden, Heiligenkreuz, to rejuvenate myself with fresh air. I am looking forward to this as a child would. My time is spent as always with office work, my own [work], etc. I am writing more poetry than usual and you will hear several new poems that are not unworthy of a striving soul. *Schubert and several friends are to come to me today, and the fogs of the present time, which is somewhat leaden, shall be lifted by his melodies.* And so with this live happily as I would wish it, and recommend me to your uncle.

Faithfully yours, J. Mayrhofer.

The single letter "K" probably refers to Josef Kenner, who, after being educated at Kremsmünster and then at the Royal Seminary, left Vienna in late August 1816 for a government post in Linz.[21] The exact nature of Schober's request, which Mayrhofer was trying to fulfil, is unclear. Perhaps he had wanted Kenner to sell off some of his books. Since approximately June 1816 Schober had been travelling in his birthplace Sweden

---

20. See *Documentary Biography*, 70; *Dokumente*, 48. The letter is located in WStLB-HSS I.N. 36.345. For the original German see the Appendix.

21. An unpublished letter dated 19 August 1816 from Spaun to Schober (WStLB-HSS I.N. 36.630) records that Kenner was to leave Vienna for Linz in two days time.

with his uncle, the syndic Franz Derffel, on family business.[22] The "younger Watteroth" was Hermann (1801-1822), second son of the Professor Heinrich Watteroth, for whose name-day in June 1816 Schubert had written the subsequently lost cantata "Prometheus" (D 451). Mayrhofer was in love with Hermann's sister Wilhelmine, as will be explained below. In May 1816 Schubert recorded on a manuscript of "Six Ecossaises" (D 421) that he was living in the Watteroth house in the Viennese suburb of Erdberg. Both Spaun and Mayrhofer also resided here together with Watteroth's future son-in-law, Josef Witteczek (1787-1859), for an unspecified period of time in 1816.[23] In his commentary to the above excerpt from Mayrhofer's letter, Deutsch specified that the poet was now living in the Wipplingerstraße next to the old city hall, in quarters previously occupied by Körner. Mayrhofer had an old pianoforte in his room, and it is possible that Schubert came here to lift "by his melodies" the fogs of the bleak present.

Precisely on the day this letter was written, 7 September 1816, the unsuccessful candidates for the post of music master in Laibach were to have been notified by the Civic Guard in Vienna of their failure to secure the position. Schubert had applied for this job six months previously and had he been successful, he would have been able to marry his first love, Therese Grob.[24] Schubert's heartrending diary entry of 8 September cries out against the "monarchs of today"—who had instituted the harsh marriage-consent law the previous year—and the misfortune he must bear without complaint.[25] It is surely significant that Mayrhofer's poem "Secret. To Franz Schubert," written in September 1816, repeats the same images and even wording— "aus trüber Gegenwart [...] verschleiert im Nebel" [out of the bleak present time ... masked in fog]—as found in the passage about Schubert in his letter to Schober— "die Nebel der Gegenwart, die etwas bleiern ist" [the fogs of the present time, which

22. See *Documentary Biography*, 65; *Dokumente*, 45. Dürhammer also transcribes Mayrhofer's letter (his appendix 2, 36), but mistakes one of the letters "K" for an "S," thus substituting Spaun's name for Kenner's, misreads "mir" for "dir," thus changing the meaning of the phrase "this trip has been a fortunate occasion for you" to read "this trip has been a fortunate occasion for me," and mistranslates the last line as follows: "Und sonst [instead of *somit*] lebe glücklich wie ich es wünsche und empfiehl mich deinem Vater [instead of *Onkel*]." Schober's father had died in 1802 and so could not possibly have been the travelling companion on the trip to Sweden in 1816. Dürhammer (p. 20) criticizes Gramit for minor transcription errors "which are obviously explained by the fact that the author had not enlisted the proofreading services of a 'native speaker'."

23. The conscription form dated 1816 for Watteroth's house records both Johann Mayrhofer (as *k. k. Bücher*

*Revident* [meaning Imperial-Royal book censor]) and Josef Ritter von Spaun (as *k. k. Hofkonzipist bei der Lotto*) sharing living quarters with Josef Witteczek (as *Doctor Juris* and *Hofkonzipist*), who in 1819 was to marry Wilhelmine Watteroth. See Wiener Stadt- und Landesarchiv [WStLA], Konskriptionsbogen Landstraße 105/3ʳ. See also Spaun's account in *Memoirs*, 357; *Erinnerungen*, 411. For Hermann Watteroth's death date (5 April 1822) see WStLA Totenbeschauprotokoll.

24. For independent accounts of Schubert's love for Therese Grob, see *Memoirs*, 59-61 (Anton Holzapfel) and 70, 182 (Anselm Hüttenbrenner); *Erinnerungen*, 69-71, 209.

25. See the interpretation of this diary entry and Schubert's thoughts on marriage in STEBLIN, "Franz Schubert und das Ehe-Consens Gesetz von 1815," *Schubert durch die Brille* 9 (June 1992): 32-42 and in STEBLIN, "The Peacock's Tale," 6-8.

is somewhat leaden]. In both, Schubert sings and his melodies bring sunlight and spring to the gloomy present. The poem reads as follows:

| Geheimnis | Secret |
|---|---|
| An Franz Schubert | To Franz Schubert |
| Sag an, wer lehrt dich Lieder | Tell us, who teaches you |
| So schmeichelnd und so zart? | Such tender, flattering songs? |
| Sie rufen einen Himmel | They evoke a heaven |
| Aus trüber Gegenwart. | From these cheerless times. |
| Erst lag das Land, verschleiert, | First the land lay veiled |
| Im Nebel vor uns da— | In mist before us— |
| Du singst—und Sonnen leuchten | Then you sing, and the sun shines, |
| Und Frühling ist uns nah. | And spring is near. |
| | |
| Den Alten schilfbekränzten, | You do not see the old man, |
| Der seine Urne gießt, | Crowned with reeds, emptying his urn; |
| Erblickst du nicht, nur Wasser, | You see only water |
| Wie's durch die Wiesen fließt. | Flowing through the meadows. |
| So geht es auch dem Sänger, | So, too, it is with the singer. |
| Er singt, er staunt in sich; | He sings, he marvels inwardly; |
| Was still ein Gott bereitet, | He wonders, as you do, |
| Befremdet ihn, wie dich. | At God's silent creation.[26] |

Schubert set this poem in October 1816 as the lied "Geheimnis" (D 491). Deutsch found it necessary to justify Schubert's "harmless composition of this song in praise of himself" by citing other composers (Handel and Haydn) who also set "adulatory" poems.[27] But perhaps we should consider Schubert's action from another point of view: as confirmation of the importance of biographical circumstances on his musical creativity. Here is evidence that his choice of texts was not isolated from the events of his daily life, but directly influenced by his personal relationships. It has been noted that Schubert's outpouring of lieder between 1814 and 1816, mainly on texts dealing with romantic love, was inspired by his desire to marry Therese.[28] The "Therese Grob Notebook," dating from about November 1816 and containing two set- tings of the text "Klage" [lament], was perhaps meant as a parting gesture, to signify the end of what now seemed a hopeless relationship. From this point on Schubert turned increasingly to setting texts on themes of classic mythology, undoubtedly under the influence of Mayrhofer. Until 1824, when the rift between the two had become irreparable, "Mayrhofer's poetry stood in the centre of Schubert's creation of lieder."[29]

26. Translation after Richard WIGMORE, *Schubert: The Complete Song Texts* (London: Victor Gollancz, 1992), 216.

27. *Documentary Biography*, 72; *Dokumente*, 50.

28. See Reinhard van HOORICKX, "Schubert's Remi- niscences of His Own Works," *The Musical Quarterly* 60

(1974): 379.

29. Walther DÜRR, Arnold FEIL, Walburga LITSCHAUER, *Reclams Musikführer: Franz Schubert* (Stuttgart: Philipp Reclam Jr, 1991), 60.

In 1816 Mayrhofer was working out of necessity—his father had died in 1798, leaving the family destitute—in the censorship office of the Austrian government. Before his suicide twenty years later in 1836, he had advanced to the official post of second censor. Mayrhofer carried out his duties with a strict, conscientious sense of patriotic fidelity, even though in serving the repressive aims of Metternich's regime he was betraying his own strongly-held beliefs in the freedom and equality of mankind, beliefs inspired by the rational ideals of the enlightenment. Spaun described him as "extraordinarily liberal, indeed democratic in his views and passionate about freedom of the press."[30] According to Anton Holzapfel, this continual conflict in his soul was one of the factors that led to the extreme hyponchondriacal condition that eventually culminated in his death.[31] Mayrhofer was struggling against the traditional "sense of difference," that of the rigid class system—upheld so ruthlessly by the Hapsburgs— whereby those of aristocratic standing enjoyed immense privileges.[32]

In 1817-18 Mayrhofer was a chief contributor to the two-volume literary journal *Beiträge zur Bildung für Jünglinge*, published in Vienna by members of the Linz circle or "brotherhood." This group had been founded in Linz in 1811 "because of our common love of the good" and included Anton von Spaun, Anton Ottenwalt, Josef Kenner and Josef Kreil.[33] It tried to influence the artistic development of younger talented boys, including Schober. The aesthetic aims and high moral tone of this publication is out-lined in David Gramit's dissertation, where the foreword to the *Beiträge* is summarized as follows: "through diligent study of the good, the true, and the beautiful, youths would mature to men who were manly, noble, and beneficial to society as a whole."[34] In the end, the members of the Linz circle achieved their aims: they married—several of them to each other's sisters (Ottenwalt to Marie von Spaun, Kenner to Anna Kreil), attained important positions in government service, and produced children who also achieved high distinction.[35]

30. Glossy, 295.

31. *Memoirs*, 63; *Erinnerungen*, 73.

32. Modern writers often underestimate the impor-tance of this historical condition. Youens, 151, makes incorrect use of the aristocratic "von" in citing names from the Schubert circle. She omits it from the names of Franz von Bruchmann and Eduard von Bauernfeld, but inserts it where it does not belong, in citing "Anselm von [sic] Hüttenbrenner."

33. Youens, 155, is not correct in her statement "The 'brotherhood' thus began at the Royal Seminary where Schubert received his schooling until October 1813." The group was centred at Linz and Schubert had never even met Anton Ottenwalt until his trip to Upper Austria in 1819. See, for example, Ottenwalt's letter to Josef von Spaun in Vienna, dated Linz, 7 October 1817: "My greet-ings to our Mayrhofer and, alas! as yet unbeknown, to Schubert" (*Documentary Biography*, 80; *Dokumente*, 54). Youens has confused the city of Linz in Upper Austria with Vienna. She also moves the castle Tillisburg (which she misspells "Tillisberg") from a spot near St. Florian (Upper Austria) to "the hills surrounding Vienna" (167).

34. See David Gramit, *The Intellectual and Aesthetic Tenets of Franz Schubert's Circle* (Ph.D. diss., Duke University, 1987), 37-38. See also Walther Dürr, "Der Linzer Schubert-Kreis und seine 'Beiträge zur Bildung für Jünglinge'," *Historisches Jahrbuch der Stadt Linz* (1985): 51-59.

35. See, for example, Constant von Wurzbach, *Biog-raphisches Lexikon des Kaiserthums Oesterreich*, 60 vols. (Vienna: k.k. Hof- und Staatsdruckerei, 1856-1891), under "Kenner," 11 (1864): 166-68 and "Spaun," 35 (1877): 71-86.

## Die Unsinnsgesellschaft

During the same two years that the Linz circle was publishing the serious-minded *Beiträge*, a group of artists in Vienna called the "Unsinnsgesellschaft" [Nonsense Society] was producing a weekly handwritten newsletter for private circulation called "Archiv des menschlichen Unsinns" [Archive of Human Nonsense]. The famous Burgtheater actor Heinrich Anschütz wrote in his memoirs (1866) that Schubert was one of the most active members of this merry men's club.[36] In early 1994 I discovered 73 watercolour pictures and almost 300 pages of accompanying written materials documenting the activities of this group.[37] Among the Nonsense Society members were two Anschütz brothers, Eduard and Gustav, three Kupelwieser brothers (including Josef, the later librettist of Schubert's opera *Fierrabras*), many well-known Biedermeier artists (Peter Goebel, Johann Nepomuk Hoechle, August Kloeber, August Kopisch, etc.) and such members of the ensuing circle around Schubert as Ludwig Kraißl, Carl Smirsch and Franz Goldhann. The writings include 29 issues of the newsletter and poetic/prose descriptions of two festive events (a party on New Year's Eve 1817 and the first birthday celebration on 18 April 1818). One of the pictures shows that Schubert, whose code name was evidently "Ritter Juan [Don Giovanni] de la Cimbala," brought two young women, most likely Babette and Therese Kunz, to this New Year's Eve party.[38] Another picture, painted by Schubert's artist-friend Leopold Kupelwieser and dated 16 July 1818, parodies the artist himself as a student riding an early bicycle and Schubert as a fierce schoolmaster holding a stick and peering through a kaleidoscope.[39] The composer is also featured in two dramas: in the children's ballet "Insanius auf Erden" as the ABC school teacher "Hymen Halbgott," who runs around the stage in search of his stick, and in the verse drama "Heil, Zeisig Heil" as a "Genius," a winged creature that flies out of a *Schub*lade [drawer] to the accompaniment of music and is subsequently transformed into a stick. This stick, an important character in the play, is used ironically to warn against succumbing to the enticements of a (female) prostitute.

This mass of hitherto unknown documents holds new information about Schubert's personality, in particular about his pursuit of women, and also reveals details about his relationship with Mayrhofer. When Schubert returned to Vienna from Zseliz, Hungary in mid November 1818, he moved out of the schoolhouse run by his father and into Mayrhofer's apartment at Wipplingerstraße No. 2. The follow-

36. See *Memoirs*, 223; *Erinnerungen*, 255.

37. See STEBLIN, *Die Unsinnsgesellschaft: Schubert, Kupelwieser und ihr Freundeskreis* (Vienna: Böhlau Verlag, 1998), where all of this material is transcribed and annotated.

38. See STEBLIN, *Babette und Therese Kunz: Neue Forschungen zum Freundeskreis um Franz Schubert und Leopold Kupelwieser*

(Vienna: Vom Pasqualatihaus, 1996).

39. See STEBLIN, "Schubert durch das Kaleidoskop," also in English translation "Schubert Through the Kaleidoscope," *Österreichische Musikzeitschrift* 52 (Schubert Special, 1997): 52-61.

ing account about permitted and prohibited books, written by Josef Kupelwieser for an "Unsinnsgesellschaft" newsletter dated 26 November 1818, is clearly a spoof on Mayrhofer's duties as a government censor of books:

> *Advertisement.* The following prohibited and permitted works are on public sale at the editor's publishing house:
>
> 1.) Prohibited
>
> *Multiplication tables from 1 to 1000* and back again in reverse order.
> *ABC book* with pictures by a priest of the Jacobin order.
> *Eipeldauer's* [country bumpkin's] complete writtings [sic] with fie-losophical comments from a sceptical sh—r.
> *List of all the numbers* drawn in the lottery.
> Also, in addition to printed meal, laundry, theatre and fireworks tickets, numerous other [tickets] of highly unusual contents.
>
> 2.) Permitted Books
>
> *Introduction* to the art of revolution. Paris 1792.
> *Infallible means* for the falsification of state papers.
> *N.B.* Purchasers of this work will also receive a [hangman's] rope as a free bonus.
> *On the art* of deceiving the course of nature, for the benefit of the population, by a misanthrope.
> *Universal letter stealer*, or the art of acquiring letters filled with money in a clever but very easy way.
> *Introduction to the art of defrauding people*, along with thorough instructions on how to declare a false bankruptcy. Vienna, Police House, 1818.
> *Preparations* for suicide, along with a commentary on how one can beat another person to death without much effort.
> *New, much improved encyclopaedia* in the language of thieves.
> *Collection* of excuses and lies, especially for criminals before the court; furthermore, various forms to fill out when selling one's body and soul to the devil, & & & & & & & & &.
>
> *Blas Leks* [Josef Kupelwieser]

By way of commentary, it should be pointed out that the house at Wipplingerstraße No. 2 (next to the old city hall), where Schubert now lived with Mayrhofer, had been "originally the place of rendezvous of the Jacobins,"[40] the religious order responsible for the regime of terror (1793-94) during the French Revolution. The "ABC book" in the same entry is a reference to Schubert's hated former job as assistant teacher of the ABC (primary) class in his father's school. Josef von Spaun was now working in the government's lottery office, and "misanthrope" was a word used by Mayrhofer's friends to describe his character.

It is unlikely that Mayrhofer himself was a member of the "Unsinnsgesellschaft." As an employee of the state it would have been extremely dangerous for

---

40. See Heinrich KREIßLE VON HELLBORN, *The Life of Franz Schubert*, trans. Arthur Duke COLERIDGE (London: Longmans, Green, and Co., 1869) [henceforth KREIßLE], 1: 48.

him to belong to such a secret society, one that poked fun at the police in such an obvious way. That he enjoyed hearing about its activities, however, is suggested by the following passage in the memoirs of Feuchtersleben. The latter had inherited Mayrhofer's diaries and mentions Schubert in leading up to this passage:

> The unaffected, healthy, robustly pure [kräftig-rein] person [Schubert] was [Mayrhofer's] favourite kind of person. Every morning he entered the jokes of one such instinctive, humorous, natural person, who was the soul of wit of a merry evening society, into his diary; there they stand next to excerpts from Young's Night Thoughts and Hermes Trismegistos.[41]

A reference to "Nachtgedanken" [Night Thoughts]—in connection with Abelard—also occurs in an "Unsinnsgesellschaft" newsletter (from 28 May 1818). *The Complaint, or Night Thoughts on Life, Death and Immortality* (1742-43) was a series of poems written by the English poet Edward Young (1683-1765), distraught at fate after his wife, daughter, and best friend died in rapid succession. Mayrhofer seems to have been particularly attracted to Young's work, perhaps because he too had suffered from cruel blows of fate. Feuchtersleben writes:

> And how could love have been missing from the life of the poet? How could it have appeared in the life of *this* poet other than in the form of pain? And so it winds itself then, disguised and with enigmatic magic, throughout his poems.[42]

The following lines from Mayrhofer's poetry suggest that he was speaking from personal experience—that he had perhaps been betrayed by an unfaithful woman: "Once I loved a maiden, as blooming as roses, as lilies so pure [...] Wherever she turned, she saw herself encircled by touching indications of a most faithful heart. Yet now it is different!"; "If I, like Abelard, were to find a heavenly wife, I would believe myself favored by Fortune"; "Should you be well-behaved, pleasant, and refined, dearest maiden, then you will be famed for it and profit thereby, yet the rough man defies you. Will you be faithful and truthful, oh dearest maiden, then you'll have nabbed him!"[43] One finds underlying the philosophy of both poets the same moralizing tone—in opposition to the sensuality of the time—and a similar belief in the existence of God and the spiritual world. Both poets show an appreciation for the beauty of nature and the value of ancient classical texts. Obviously a study of Mayrhofer's poetry—or the

---

41. FEUCHTERSLEBEN, 23: "Der unbefangene, gesunde, kräftig-reine Mensch war ihm der liebste. Die Späße eines solchen, unwillkürlich witzigen Naturmenschen, der einer lustigen Abendgesellschaft manche Stunde würzte, trug er jeden Morgen darauf in sein Tagebuch ein; da stehen sie, neben Auszügen aus *Youngs* Nachtgedanken und *Hermes* Trismegistos."

42. Ibid., 14: "und wie hätte die Liebe im Leben des Dichters fehlen sollen? wie hätte sie im Leben *dieses* Dichters anders erscheinen können, als in der Gestalt des Schmerzes? und so geht sie denn auch, verhüllt und mit räthselhaftem Zauber, durch seine Gesänge."

43. See YOUENS, 161-63.

attempt to read therein aspects of the poet's biography—should also examine Young's work for its influential effect.[44]

The above reference to Schubert's healthy sense of humour, wittiness, and natural manner is corroborated in the memoirs of many of his friends. Eduard von Bauernfeld, writing in 1858 under the pseudonym "Rusticocampius,"[45] compares Schubert with Moritz von Schwind as follows:

> [Schwind] was made of a robust, primeval nature,
> As if cast out of resounding brass;—
> So too Schubert—only more cheerful—
> These were my dearest friends!
> Soon a wreath of friends was woven:
> Art, the confidence of youth,
> Humour bound us—also present were
> Charming girls and women.[46]

Shortly after making Schubert's acquaintance Bauernfeld had written in his diary: "Schubert is always the same, always natural."[47] Mayrhofer, on the other hand, was described as serious, gloomy and bad-tempered [*verdrießlich*] with a bitter, caustic, sarcastic sense of humour that Schubert could not stand.[48] The poet's character was also specified as being morally pure [*sittenrein*],[49] in contrast to Schubert's sensuous, pleasure-loving [*genußliebend*] nature. The difference between their personalities was described by Mayrhofer himself as follows:

> While we lived together our idiosyncrasies could not but show themselves; we were both richly endowed in that respect, and the consequences could not fail to appear. We teased each other in many different ways and turned our sharp edges on each other to our mutual amusement and pleasure. His gladsome and comfortable sensuousness and my introspective nature were thus thrown into higher relief and gave rise to names we called each other accordingly, as though we were playing parts assigned to us. Unfortunately, I played my very own![50]

Josef von Gahy was often witness to the following scene: Mayrhofer would go after Schubert with a stick, crying in Upper Austrian dialect "Was halt mich denn ab,

---

44. And Hermes Trismegistos, Wilhelm Meyern and Ignaz Feßler as well. See KREIßLE, 1: 45-47.

45. "Rusticocampius" is the Latin for "Bauernfeld." Youens mistakenly treats this pseudonym as if it were the title of a book. See her confusing discussion on 171-74.

46. [Eduard von BAUERNFELD], *Ein Buch von uns Wienern in lustig-gemüthlichen Reimlein von Rusticocampius* (Leipzig: C. L. Hirschfeld, 1858), 27, from the poem "Jugendfreunde": "[Schwind] Ist eine derbe Ur-Natur, / Wie aus tönendem Erz gegossen; - / So war auch *Schubert* - heiterer nur - / Das waren mir liebste Genossen! / Bald sich ein Kranz von Freunden flicht: / Kunst, jugendliches Vertrauen, /

Humor verbanden sie - fehlten auch nicht / Anmuthige Mädchen und Frauen."

47. See *Documentary Biography*, 410; *Dokumente*, 281.

48. See in particular Schober's account in *Memoirs*, 266; *Erinnerungen*, 305.

49. See GLOSSY, 293: "Er war ein sittenreiner, liebenswürdiger Jüngling," and FEUCHTERSLEBEN, 5: "mit dem ihm inwohnenden Ernste und sittlichen Gehalte" and p. 6: "so sittlich zart bis zum Krankhaften war sein Gemüth."

50. See *Memoirs*, 14; *Erinnerungen*, 19.

du kloaner Raker" [What's stopping me from beating you up, you little rake] to which Schubert would reply "Waldl, Waldl, wilder Verfasser" [Waldl, Waldl, wild author].[51] Mayrhofer's nickname "Waldl"—also used in a letter from Schober to Spaun dated 4 November 1821—was possibly derived from his poem "An die Freunde" [To My Friends], set by Schubert as the lied D 654 in March 1819, that begins with the line "Im Wald, im Wald, da grabt mich ein" [In the woods, in the woods, bury me there].[52] With the new knowledge of Schubert being associated with a stick in material written for the "Unsinnsgesellschaft," the anecdote about Mayrhofer attacking the composer with a stick (the poet now being the stern teacher?) takes on a new meaning. Perhaps the role Schubert played in these scenes with Mayrhofer was that of "Don Giovanni," the composer's assigned role in the "Unsinnsgesellschaft." This would correspond with Mayrhofer's description of Schubert as being "sensuous" and no doubt reflected on the poet's disapproval of Schubert's womanizing.

That Mayrhofer disliked frivolous, immoral women is clear. The poet gives his view of ideal femininity in his historical essay "Kunigunde" (1817): "whose purpose, announced at the outset, was to acquaint readers with an outstanding woman from among the roll-call of great Austrian rulers of the past. [...] Having borne eight children, she retired into a convent upon her husband's death and died as an example of female saintliness."[53] Mayrhofer's attitude towards women obviously soured over time. Bauernfeld, writing as "Rusticocampius," attributes the following words to Mayrhofer:

> What a good man wants to create,
> Is hindered by female men—women.
> Yes, women! They are not worthy
> Of the cosmos, of the universe;
> If it were only possible for the earth
> To propagate without women![54]

Perhaps it was only a matter of course that a man displaying such sentiments would be typecast a homosexual. To quote Youens: "It seems likely, if inaccessible to irrefutable proof (seldom forthcoming in these matters), that Mayrhofer was homosexual."[55] Underlying her discussion of Mayrhofer's personality is the unstated equation: misogyny = homosexuality. Youens, following Solomon, bases most of her dis-

---

51. See KREIßLE, vol. 1, 51n.
52. YOUENS, following the *Documentary Biography*, 197, writes: "'Waldl' a south German name for a dog" (157). But this explanation seems unlikely and was later omitted by Deutsch in the *Dokumente*, 140. Deutsch explains elsewhere that the nickname "Gahidi" for Gahy may come from the opening line "Ahidi! ich liebe" of the lied "Hänflings Liebeswerbung" (D 552). See *Documentary Biography*, 574; *Dokumente*, 390.

53. YOUENS, 155.
54. [BAUERNFELD], 180, from the poem "Ein Wiener-Censor": "Was ein tücht'ger Mann will schaffen, / Hindern weib'sche Männer - Weiber. / Ja, die Weiber! Diese taugen / Nicht zum Kosmos, zum Welt-Ganzen; / Wär's nur thunlich, diese Erde / Ohne Frauen fortzupflanzen!" In this context the poetic expression "weib'sche Männer" means women, not effeminate men.
55. YOUENS, 159.

cussion on such reductive homosexual stereotypes. For example, she attributes Mayrhofer's use of themes from classical myths, in particular his poem "Hiacinthe," as well as his love of beauty to his alleged homosexuality. She writes: "the charged word 'Schöne' [beauty] in the final line [of 'Hiacinthe'] recalls the cult of Beauty in homosexual artistic circles" (p. 160). But, beauty was not the prerogative of homosexual subcultures in the nineteenth century, nor was the intense interest in ancient Greek myth limited to this particular minority. Youens also believes that Mayrhofer must have had a mother-fixation, although any evidence for this is lacking. Thus she interprets his poem "Alte Liebe rostet nie" (set by Schubert as the lied D 477) as follows: "[the poem] makes one wonder about Mayrhofer's mother and his subsequent rejection of women. 'Since I lost her [Youens's interpolation: my mother]', the poetic persona states, 'I have travelled far and wide, but I remain unmoved by the fairest flower of womankind'" (p. 162). But the poem actually begins with the words: "Alte Liebe rostet nie, Hört ich oft die Mutter sagen" [Old love never tarnishes, I often heard my mother say]. This is a common German saying, an old wives' tale, and the poem itself has nothing to do with love for one's mother.[56] Having based her argument on a shaky premise, Youens then tries to account for heterosexual allusions in such poetic lines as "Once I loved a maiden" by the curious interpretation: "it is possible [...] that the seeming 'women' in the poems are actually youths or men, veiled in an identity that would pass muster with the censors" (p. 160). Radical alterations of meaning such as this must first be supported by convincing evidence, especially in view of so much contradictory documentation, but Youens makes an insufficient attempt to situate the discussion in its proper historical context. For example, homosexual practice is described in early nineteenth-century medical and legal texts by such terms as "Unzucht gegen die Natur" [sexual offense contrary to nature] or "unsittlich, unrein" [immoral].[57] If the hypothesis proposed by Youens is to be accepted, she must explain why such a morally pure ["sittenrein"] person as Mayrhofer would have approved of "same sex activities."

That Mayrhofer appreciated talented, artistic women is revealed in an unknown anecdote by the Viennese antiquarian bookseller and journalist Franz Gräffer (1785-1852) about a joint visit in 1823 to Helmina von Chézy (1783-1856), the librettist of Schubert's *Rosamunde* (D 797):

> Helmina von Chézy lived at the Wasserkunstbastei. I invited the poet Mayrhofer, my immediate neighbour—in his way so peculiar—to come with me there. Mayrhofer, somewhat shy, appeared to think it over; but, since it involved getting to know person-

56. Schubert set this poem in September 1816; Mayrhofer's mother did not die until October 1823.

57. Sebastian Jenull, *Das Oesterreichische Criminal-Recht* (Graz: Franz Ferstl, 1809), 193. See also Joachim S. Hohmann, ed., *Der unterdrückte Sexus: Historische Texte zur*

*Homosexualität* (Lollar/Lahn: Andreas Aschenbach, 1977), passim.

58. Franz Gräffer, *Kleine Wiener Memoiren und Wiener Dosenstücke*, 2 (Munich: Georg Müller, 1922), 21.

ally a poetess whose genius he highly respected, he decided to come along. [...]
Mayrhofer had a good talk with Helmina. She respected him a great deal. She knew his
poem "In the Smithy" by heart and surprised him by reciting it. She made it clear to
him in a delicate way that he had been influenced a little too much by Goethe, and in
particular was neglecting form. One could clearly see that it had pleased her to get to
know Mayrhofer in person; the same could be said about him; he really warmed up to
her. She pressed him to stay for tea and they chatted about censorship matters.[58]

Helmina's son Wilhelm (1806-65), a poet and journalist with keen skills of
observation, had been introduced to the Schubert circle by Feuchtersleben. In Chézy's
memoirs, published in 1863, he reported the following character descriptions of
Mayrhofer and Schubert:

> Mayrhofer was morose, shy and inaccessible to people he did not know. He ended his
> life by suicide. In complete contrast to him was the small, thick-set musician [Schubert];
> though to outward appearances a lump of dough, his eyes had such a sparkle that the
> inner fire was revealed at the first glance. Unfortunately Schubert, with his liking for the
> pleasures of life, had strayed into those wrong paths which generally admit of no return,
> at least of no healthy one [...] He took a certain ... shall I say pride in the misfortunes
> which befell him on his wild caperings. Anyhow he rather preened himself on them.[59]

In 1841 Wilhelm von Chézy had published an earlier version of this passage, unnoticed
until recently in the Schubert literature, that reads as follows:

> [Mayrhofer] was morose, hypochondriac and shy. In contrast to him, a perpetual fire
> burned, hidden under a phlegmatic exterior, in the small, thick-set musician. Schubert
> adored women and wine. Unfortunately this taste had caused him to stray into those
> wrong paths from which he could no longer find his way back alive.[60]

This is a clear reference to Schubert's having acquired syphilis (from relations with the
wrong kind of woman). Chézy had also noticed Schubert preening with pride (like
Don Juan?) about his wild adventures.

Gräffer too produced precise prose-portraits of Mayrhofer and Schubert. He
obviously knew the poet well, and as his neighbour had been able to observe him and
Schubert at a close distance:

> Mayrhofer was always ailing, of sickly complexion, quite bony, but with an abnormal
> nervous system, totally without elasticity; rigid, icy-cold. Thus also his poetic spirit: ele-

59. *Memoirs*, 261; *Erinnerungen*, 299. See also Wilhelm von
CHÉZY, *Erinnerungen aus meinem Leben*, 2 (Schaffhausen: Fr.
Hurter, 1863), 292.
60. Wilhelm von CHÉZY, *Deutsche Pandora*, 4 (Stuttgart:
Literatur-Comptoir, 1841), 182-83: "[Mayrhofer] war
mürrischen Gemüthes, hypochondrisch und scheu, woge-
gen in dem kleinen breiten Musikus ewig das Feuer
sprühte, das sich unter einer phlegmatischen Außenseite

barg. Schubert verehrte Mädchen und Wein, doch hatte
leider diese Neigung sich in falsche Richtungen verirrt,
aus denen er lebend nicht mehr sich zurechtfand." I wish
to thank Gerrit Waidelich for informing me in a personal
communication dated 22 January 1995 of this passage. He
has now published this excerpt in: *Rosamunde. Drama in fünf
Akten von Helmina von Chézy. Musik von Franz Schubert*, ed. Till
Gerrit WAIDELICH (Tutzing: Hans Schneider, 1996), 53.

giac, misanthropic, rancorous, scolding, sarcastic, symbolically inclined [...] Schubert
was full of feeling, like our dear [Ignaz] Castelli—a Lower Austrian, a Viennese: sin-
cerity, warmth, sweetness, profundity, but those from above the Enns [Upper Austria],
more clarity, calm, reflection.[61]

The contrast in character between the two artists, attributed here to geography
(an historically correct way of "celebrating difference") inevitably led to a break in
their relationship. (Castelli was a notorious womanizer.) As far as we know, it was in
early 1821 that Schubert moved out of Mayrhofer's apartment and into his own place
nearby (Wipplingerstraße No. 15).[62] He lived here alone until his departure in late
summer 1821 with Schober for St. Pölten, where the two worked together on the opera
*Alfonso und Estrella* (D 732). This was the period (September-October 1821) of the
*Heliopolis* cycle of twenty poems dedicated to Schober, the period that Gramit called
"a turning-point in Schubert's relationship with Mayrhofer." Gramit also writes: "We
have no record of the circumstances leading to the breakup of [their] household, but
the corpus of Schubert's songs indicates one result: he set only seven more texts by
Mayrhofer during the rest of his life."[63]

Mayrhofer himself merely wrote: "The cross-currents of circumstances and
society, of illness and changed views of life kept us apart later."[64] It may be that the
*Heliopolis* cycle, with its emphasis on turning to the sun for redemption, and dedicated
to Schober (Schubert's "seducer" in the pursuit of sensuousness), was a message to
both artists to see the light and mend their ways. Since the two were labelled as Franz
*Schobert*, the mini-cycle of three poems under the collective title "An Franz," published
by Feuchtersleben posthumously in 1843, could perhaps apply to either one.[65]

## "Geheimnis" in Gräffer's Conversationblatt (1821)

It has always been assumed that Mayrhofer was very shy about publishing his
literary work. Other than his contributions to the *Beyträge zur Bildung für Jünglinge* in
1817-18 ("Kunigunde" was also printed in Hormayr's *Archiv* in 1818) and the poem "Am
Erlaf-See" which appeared together with Schubert's lied setting D 586 in Sartori's
*Mahlerisches Taschenbuch* of 1818, no publications by Mayrhofer were known until, encour-

---

61. GRÄFFER, "Zur Karakteristik österreichischer
Schriftsteller," *Sonntagsblätter*, ed. Ludwig August FRANKL,
3 (1844): 134. Translation with minor corrections from
YOUENS, 152.
62. See Rudolf KLEIN, *Schubert Stätten* (Vienna: Verlag
Elisabeth Lafite, 1972), 45.
63. See GRAMIT, "Schubert and the Biedermeier," 358.
64. *Memoirs*, 13-14; *Erinnerungen*, 19.
65. See YOUENS, 166: "Whoever 'Franz' was, he was
younger and seems to have shared the same aesthetic-
political ideals as the older poet who hymned him - this

does not, of course, preclude Schubert, although
Mayrhofer's fellow-writer Schober (the dedicatee of
*Heliopolis*) is also a viable alternative. As so often in this
tale, one would like to know more, but definitive answers
are not forthcoming at present. We may never know."
66. See Karl GOEDEKE, *Grundriß zur Geschichte der deutschen
Dichtung*, 12 (Dresden: L. Ehlermann, 1929), 244-45.
67. This find, which I made in Vienna early in 1996, led
me to write the present article. Dürhammer, who was
privy to my research, hastily published this find as well as
other discoveries of mine, including the autograph of

aged by friends, he brought out his *Gedichte* in early 1824. Thereafter a few isolated poems appeared each year in various literary journals and almanacs.[66] Thus it was a great surprise for me to stumble upon three poems by Mayrhofer in Gräffer's *Conversationblatt* of 1821.[67] But the even greater surprise was to find that the first poem, appearing on 29 August 1821, was none other than "Geheimnis," the poem dedicated to Schubert.[68] The other two poems, "[Die] Sternennächte" and "[Der] Alpenjäger," appeared on 12 September and 26 September respectively, and had likewise been set as lieder by Schubert (the former, D 670, in October 1819 and the latter, D 524, in January 1817). It must surely be significant that these poems appeared publicly at exactly the same time as Mayrhofer was compiling the *Heliopolis* cycle for Schober. Was there a secret message here for Schubert? Was this the poet's attempt at a rapprochement?

At the same time as these poems, the *Conversationblatt* published a long article "Über die Harmonie in der Tonkunst" [On Harmony in Music] in six parts between 15 August and 1 September 1821 by the talented critic and Beethoven-friend Friedrich August Kanne.[69] Shortly thereafter, on 19 January 1822, the first detailed criticism of Schubert songs appeared in the Vienna *Allgemeine Musikalische Zeitung*, according to Deutsch, most likely written by Kanne. Deutsch writes: "the author seems to have known Schubert and Mayrhofer, for he speaks of manuscript songs and accurately quotes from the poem 'Antigone and Oedipus,' which appeared in print only in 1824 among Mayrhofer's collected poems."[70] Schubert is praised in Kanne's review for his "excellent talent," his "rich lyrical gift", and "for making the poet's fancy so profoundly impressive for the receptive listener's heart." But he is also taken to task for changing some of the poet's words and thus "wholly disfiguring the sense." Kanne writes: "the treatment of a text should show the same respect for a poet's work with which we honour a composer's creation."

Had Mayrhofer complained about Schubert's distortions? Or was this criticism solely on Kanne's part? It seems likely that the poet had arranged for this first glow-

---

Mayrhofer's poem "Die Wolke" (in "Was ich gefühlt," 19-20), without giving me due credit. I later found that Moritz Bauer had known that there were probably Mayrhofer poems in the *Conversationblatt*, but that he had not yet been able to examine this journal. See Moritz BAUER, "Johann Mayrhofer," *Zeitschrift für Musikwissenschaft* 5 (1922-23): 79-99, in particular p. 97, where he writes: "Das 'Konversationsblatt' habe ich noch nicht einsehen können. Ich beabsichtige später über die noch nicht aufgefundenen Arbeiten zu berichten."

68. This Schubert document (the subtitle "An Franz Schubert" is omitted in the *Conversationblatt*) was overlooked both by Deutsch and the new IFSI edition of Schubert documents. See *Franz Schubert. Dokumente*, vol. 1, ed. Till Gerrit WAIDELICH (Tutzing: Hans Schneider,

1993), nos. 31, 54, 59, 90, and 111, where reviews and announcements of several of Schubert's works are cited from the *Conversationblatt* in the years 1820-21.

69. Just a few months earlier, on 16 May 1821, Kanne had published satirical verses on Anselm Hüttenbrenner's "Erlkönig Waltzes" in the Vienna *Allgemeine Musikalische Zeitung*, which Schubert copied out and sent to the composer in Graz. See *Documentary Biography*, 179; *Dokumente*, 127-28. See also Christopher GIBBS, *The Presence of "Erlkönig": Reception and Reworkings of a Schubert Lied* (Ph.D. diss., Columbia University, 1992), 301-2.

70. *Documentary Biography*, 208; *Dokumente*, 146. There is no reason to doubt Kanne's authorship of this review, especially in the light of his dealing with similar musical issues, in particular text setting, in the *Conversationblatt* series.

ing review of Schubert's lied production, making manuscript pieces (and original poems) available to the reviewer. Mayrhofer seems to intimate as much by singling out this review in his obituary notice on Schubert as follows: "Criticism, however, usually superficial, and beneficial neither to those who create nor to those who enjoy, in 1822 made a valiant and gratifying beginning towards a better understanding of Schubert's songs. This refers to No. 6 of the 'Allgemeine musikalische Zeitung' [the review in question]."[71] Perhaps this review had been another attempt at a reconciliation.

In April 1822, shortly after this review appeared, Schubert set three poems from the *Heliopolis* cycle (D 752-754), the first of which, "Nachtviolen," departs substantially from Mayrhofer's text. For example, he omitted line 9: "Ja so fesselt ihr den Dichter" [Just so you captivate the poet] and changed the word "sein" [his] to "mein" [my] in line 11: "Trefet ihr sein treues Herz" [you strike his loyal heart]. Obviously Schubert disregarded the reviewer's reservation about making changes to the poem. Gramit finds these alterations very striking: "Schubert quite literally eliminates the poet ('der Dichter' of line 9) from the text and substitutes 'my loyal heart' for 'his'." Gramit hypothesizes further that "the altered 'Nachtviolen' may be one of Schubert's responses to his altered relationship with Mayrhofer."[72] There is much work to be done before we understand the effect of these changing dynamics within the Schubert circle on the composer's creative impulse.

In the remaining years of his life Schubert set only four more poems by Mayrhofer, all composed in March 1824 to texts from the volume of poems that Mayrhofer had published earlier that year. That Schubert's name is missing from the list of subscribers has often been used as evidence of a serious rift between the two former friends. The following lines, entered by Schubert on 27 March 1824 into a lost notebook, were thought by Deutsch to be connected with this estrangement:

> There is no one who understands the pain or the joy of others! We always imagine we are coming together, and we always merely go side by side. Oh, what torture for those who recognize this![73]

If Deutsch is correct, then perhaps a subsequent entry, from 29 March 1824, may also refer to Mayrhofer:

> O imagination! thou greatest treasure of man, thou inexhaustible wellspring from which artists as well as savants drink! O remain with us still, by however few thou art acknowledged and revered, to preserve us from that so-called enlightenment, that hideous skeleton without flesh and blood![74]

Mayrhofer was known as a defender of enlightenment ideals, while Schubert had now turned towards the new Romanticism (setting, for example, poems by Schlegel and Novalis). Perhaps the fleshy, sensuous Schubert was railing out at the "bony," "icy-cold"

71. *Memoirs*, 14-15; *Erinnerungen*, 20.
72. GRAMIT, "Schubert and the Biedermeier," 359.
73. *Documentary Biography*, 336; *Dokumente*, 232.
74. *Documentary Biography*, 337; *Dokumente*, 233.

moralist Mayrhofer. The latter had even written the line "I created—it was a poor skeleton; Have I ever caught the spirit?" in the first poem of the mini-cycle called "An Franz."[75]

If we return again to Mayrhofer's explanation for the estrangement from Schubert—"the cross-currents of circumstances and society, of illness and changed views of life kept us apart later"—we see that he identifies illness as one of the chief causes. The poet's hypochondria is well-known and was even referred to by Schubert in a letter dated 8 September 1818, before the two became roommates: "Dear Mayrhofer, my longing for November will hardly be less than yours. Cease ailing, or at least dabbling in medicines, and the rest will come of itself."[76] Just how extreme Mayrhofer's case of hypochondria was, is revealed by documents housed in the Viennese state archive.[77] The poet suffered from one illness after another, including perpetual dizziness, rheumatic fever, and gout resulting from chronic liver ailments. He was often granted lengthy leaves during which he was allowed to carry out his censorship duties from home. In a letter dated 13 December 1824 Mayrhofer personally asks his employer, the I.-R. Court Censorship and Police Office, for a loan of 40 f C.M., explaining that for several years his poor health has caused him to spend almost half of his yearly income of 700 f on doctor and medicine bills and that he was now unable to make his monthly payments of 8 f 45 xr on a previous loan. (Count Sedlnitzky, the hated Chief of Police, at first granted Mayrhofer the requested 40 f, later reduced by the Pay Office to 30 f).[78]

Mayrhofer's hypochondria eventually developed into a paranoid fear of catching diseases from others and ultimately led to his suicide.[79] After his death, the doctors who examined his body reported that they could find no sign of illness. It was Schubert, on the other hand, who was seriously ill with a real disease, most likely syphilis. He was openly ill in 1823, and even lost his hair. In early 1824, at about the time Mayrhofer brought out his edition of poems, Schubert had suffered a serious relapse of the disease and was in confinement, probably undergoing a mercury treatment. With Mayrhofer's particular paranoia about disease, perhaps he was also referring to Schubert's illness as a cause of their estrangement.

## Feuchtersleben's Letter to Schober (1834-36)

After Schubert's death Mayrhofer was befriended by Feuchtersleben, who, as a medical doctor and fellow poet, felt particularly drawn to this eccentric genius. There

---

75. See YOUENS, 165.
76. *Documentary Biography*, 100; *Dokumente*, 67.
77. I am grateful to Christine Blanken for sharing with me her research notes on these documents, made in connection with her forthcoming dissertation (University of Göttingen) on Schubert's oratorio *Lazarus*. These documents are also summarized in Fritz LIST, *Johann*

*Mayrhofer: ein Freund und Textdichter Franz Schuberts* (Ph.D. diss., University of Munich, 1922), 17-18.
78. Allgemeines Verwaltungsarchiv (Vienna), Polizei-Hofstelle, Akt 1771/1824.
79. Spaun attributes Mayrhofer's suicide to paranoia over a recent outbreak of cholera. See GLOSSY, 297.

are many letters from Feuchtersleben to Schober that reveal interesting details about the older poet's last few years and shed more light on his complex personality.[80] A few excerpts from these letters follow:[81]

Vienna, 19 May 1834

Mayrhofer and I, we understand each other completely. How splendid his nature is! I have never found on the empty flea market of life such pure moral dignity, without effeminate meekness and religious fads. But if I, as a doctor, am not mistaken, there is something else in his character, apart from his stance against the outside world, that is destroying him. By the way, he is writing poetry again, at my instigation, and can be very cheerful. He loves you a great deal, although he bore a grudge against you for some time, which I can also understand. I am also supposed to greet you.[82]

The grudge Mayrhofer bore against Schober may be the same one that Kenner bore: holding Schober responsible for seducing Schubert into the wrong paths that eventually caused his illness and death.

Vienna, 9 July 1835

[…] Mayrhofer has now gone to Fusch[l] (in the Salzburg region) for 5 weeks, in order to free himself from all kinds of spleen and to write poems for me; I say for me, and it pleases me that my joy over his muse has this wonderful influence on him. He is writing all sorts of things again, even a lengthy epic poem, and shares everything with me. And since then he is much more cheerful, more sociable. Also, in his inner reflexes, his thoughts lead him now into a promising field of standing crops instead of, as before, into a desert of death. I tell you: he is the most wonderful phenomenon (I hope this does not sound too much like natural history) that I have ever observed in the realm of humankind. Nowhere can one see more clearly that the human spirit is only a limited revelation of an infinite spirit. There is something else in M[ayrhofer] besides *he* himself,—or should I call this other quality the actual *He*? He appears as the wrinkled, patched-up agent of a godly being. He listens to his own works with amazement,—as if he were a prisoner in his cell listening to a song from his homeland that is sounding outside the door. He should only move in pure ether; he moves awkwardly in our air. Enough of this; this will sound hardly mystical to *you*; but *it is so*.[83]

Feuchtersleben repeats some of the mystical ideas in this letter as well as some of the biographical information about the trip to Fuschl in the introduction to his

---

80. The hundreds of letters in the Schober estate in the WStLB-HSS undoubtedly hold many answers to questions about relationships within the Schubert circle. Gramit examined some of the earlier material with beneficial results, but the remainder awaits detailed study.

81. The following three letters are published in their entirety in Egon SCHRAMM, "Unveröffentlichte Briefe Feuchterslebens," *Euphorion* 46 (1952): 421-39. Of the eleven Feuchtersleben letters published by Schramm, eight are addressed to Schober (dated between 10

December 1833 and 10 February 1836).

82. WStLB-HSS I.N. 5.198 (Schober Nachlaß). Feuchtersleben, who was happily married and whose wife Helene often adds a few words of greeting, begins the above letter with words of consolation and advice for Schober, who had just been snubbed in his courtship of a Hungarian countess. She had demanded that he first establish his own household.

83. WStLB-HSS I.N. 5.199.

posthumous edition (1843) of Mayrhofer's poems. In a letter dated 14 October 1835 Feuchtersleben thanks Schober for sending him his own poems to read and correct. (Schober's poems were eventually published in 1842.) Feuchtersleben's extensive changes and suggestions for organizing these poems are worthy of further study since they reveal his criteria for editing poems, as well as showing how Schober's poems relate to the circle of friends, especially Schubert and Mayrhofer.[84] In an undated note accompanying these suggestions (probably from late October 1835) Feuchtersleben wrote: "Mayrhofer has attempted to commit suicide again; he was observed, treated and now feels better."[85] This second suicide attempt (in 1830 he had tried to drown himself in the Danube) is unreported in the literature. On 5 February 1836 he finally succeeded in killing himself, the details of which Feuchtersleben reports to Schober as follows:

Vienna, 10 February 1836

What had been forewarned for a long time by so many ominous events I now have to report to you as accomplished; and what was not really a surprise has—I confess to you—upset me more deeply than I expected. On the 5th of this month Mayrhofer threw himself from the highest floor of the building where the censor office is located and after an hour was dead.[86] For about the last month he had been less sociable than usual, without showing signs of what one would normally call melancholy. He spent the evening of the 4th playing a game of cards with Spaun, drank beer with him, *expressed concern that he had made a mistake in his diet*, and appeared completely normal. The next morning he came as usual to the office, went out without drawing the least attention to his movements after handing over the books he had censored to the office boss Hölzel, and a few minutes later the house servants found his body. The autopsy showed nothing abnormal other than the internal and external injuries caused by the fall. He was granted a funeral which took place yesterday. Spaun, who asked me to send you greetings when I write to you, placed a stone on his mound so that one could locate the place where his remains lie buried. He had no will[87] and left 400 fl C.M. in cash, and now the remaining objects in his estate are locked up by the *police* because of the unnatural death. Perhaps you know that his sister lives in poverty in Upper Austria. I have actively decided to take over his poetic relics, and you can imagine that I will not let go of these sacred items. I will not allow them to be scattered

---

84. Ibid., I.N. 5.203. This letter was not published by Schramm. On p. 1 of this letter Feuchtersleben writes, in connection with the original order of Schober's poems (as indicated by the numbers): "Im Ganzen ist der Faden der: N. 1 dient als Prologus; was sich auf Dichten u. Singen bezieht, schließt sich angemessen an; daß Schubert hier her beschworen wird, ist so natürlich, als daß ihm Mayrhofer auf dem Fusse folgt; diese Erinnerungen an Freunde veranlassen, sich über Freundschaft überhaupt zu ergehn; dem ungeachtet meldet sich das Liebesbedürfniß (12), dem Erwiederung u. seliger Genuß folgt; nur leider, allzukurz! Schmerzen (19) bleiben nicht aus - und das Scheiden spricht sein

unerbittliches Wort aus."
85. WStLB-HSS I.N. 74.371: "Mayrhofer hat sich wieder umbringen wollen; er ward beobachtet, behandelt, u. befindet sich besser."
86. KREISSLE, I: 53, reports incorrectly that Mayrhofer "survived for forty hours afterwards."
87. A will dated 3 October 1829 was later found and made public on 16 February 1836. Here Mayrhofer stipulated that his friend Hölzl was to receive all his books and 25 ducats in cash and his sister Franziska in Ottensheim, Upper Austria was to inherit the remaining money, furniture, and clothes. See WStLA Testament Mayerhofer 98/1836.

in the common beggarly way to all corners of the globe. If only these items do not *disappear* from under the hands of the police, then I will come to an agreement with those who might have a claim on them. I want to edit them and make sure that they appear before the public in a way that will do them justice, and so the heiress [his sister] does not come away empty-handed. It will be worth the effort because I know what must be there. Before his trip to the Fuschl baths he wrote many lyric poems, partly at my instigation; bitter poems that he called "Sermons," and he had conceived a complete epic the first part of which was finished; it outlined the conflict in the Middle Ages between the world of knights and priests and that of the common people. Once I had these things I would have to see how I come out with the censors and with the editor of his first collection (for it is my wish that these half-forgotten items also be regenerated). Now I am happy that fate has provided me with so much credit in the literary world that I can attempt to undertake this project with the hope of success. You would also have to hand over your notebooks. Should nothing be found (he could have destroyed everything!) then even [your] items together with what I have would [be enough to] make up a volume.[88]

This hitherto little regarded report is of significance for giving a first-hand account of Mayrhofer's death and burial as well as for outlining Feuchtersleben's plan to publish the remaining poems. That Schober was willing to share his Mayrhoferiana for this project, although he had reservations about its suitability for a larger audience, is clear from a letter by Feuchtersleben to Schober dated 20 April 1836. Feuchtersleben at first thanks him for sending the items requested (probably including *Heliopolis*) and then continues: "You are perhaps right that there is little here for the public at large; to enjoy them requires sympathetic interest."[89] It is to Feuchtersleben's credit that he was eventually able to bring out the poems (in 1843). However, it is unfortunate that in spite of his expressed desire to preserve Mayrhofer's written materials (which included his diaries and the librettos to his two Schubert operas) they have since disappeared.[90]

---

88. WStLB-HSS I.N. 5.204. This letter was published by Schramm in *Euphorion*, 435-36. Dürhammer's transcription of this letter (his appendix 3, 39-40), which he presents as an unpublished document, is filled with modernized spellings. For example, he adds an extra "e" to such words as "begehn," "andern," "innern," "äußern," "testirte," etc., spells "Uiberreste" with "Ü" and prints "Erbinn" with a single "n." More serious, however, is his misreading of the word "Ritter" as "Luther" in the phrase "es hatte den Konflikt des Ritter- und Pfaffenthum's mit dem Menschlichen, im Mittelalter, zum Vorwurf" and his subsequent nonsensical discussion of Mayrhofer's support of Lutheranism in the Middle Ages. Similarly, he mistranslates the word "Hefte" as "Hilfe" in the phrase "Du müsstest auch Deine Hefte dazu hergeben" and thus fails

to realize that the notebooks referred to here probably comprise the *Heliopolis* cycle owned by Schober.

89. WStLB-HSS I.N. 5.205: "Dir dank' ich für die Bereitwilligkeit, mit der Du Deine Mayrhoferiana mittheiltest; Du hast wohl Recht, es ist wenig für's grössere Publicum damit zu machen; es gehört ein verliebtes Theilnehmen zum Geniessen."

90. According to Kreißle, 1: 72, Feuchtersleben's servants probably destroyed this material after his death in 1849.

91. Frankl later interviewed Schober (in 1868) and noted that he had earlier heard from Hölzl that Schubert had composed the "Müllerlieder" while in hospital "where he found himself as the result of excessively indulgent sensual living and its consequences." See *Memoirs*, 266; *Erinnerungen*, 304.

## Hölzl's Account (1865)

Perhaps the most interesting account of the poet was made by his superior in the censorship office, Heinrich Josef Hölzl, in an interview conducted in 1865 by the journalist Ludwig August Frankl.[91] (See Plate 1.) This report, preserved in the Vienna City Library and published here for the first time, holds valuable new information on Mayrhofer, in particular about his love for two women:

> Had an unusually anxious and shy nature. Was in love with Miss Watteroth, later the wife of Court Councillor Witteczek. [Also in love with] Louise Strauß, the oldest daughter of the district doctor for the poor in Leopoldstadt. Did not dare to get married. In 1830, in fear of [catching] cholera, he jumped off the bridge by [the suburb of] Weißgärber. Saved, he was brought to the dispensary (Funkelstern's) across from Stierböck's Café. After Hölzl had dashed over, Mayrhofer had no other remark save: "The water was quite warm." Everyone laughed. On the day when he threw himself off [his office building] he took care of all of his duties punctually and then went out. H[ölzl] asked, where is M[ayrhofer]? "He should be right back." Soon after the porter came and announced the fall. H[ölzl] hurried outside. M[ayrhofer] lay there, some of his ribs broken, cheek and eye highly swollen. A (nearby) Dominican [priest] was sent for. "Are you sorry that you have done this?" "No!" The priest was indignant: "You see, he regrets nothing!" H[ölzl]: "I will ask him." "Are you sorry my dear M[ayrhofer?]" "I am sorry." Half an hour later he was dead and was brought to the general hospital for autopsy. H[ölzl] gave me two of his unpublished poems and will search for more.[92]

The news that Mayrhofer was in love with Wilhelmine Watteroth (1800-47) comes as quite a surprise (especially in light of so much speculation about his sexual orientation). In 1816 he had lived in the Watteroth house, together with Spaun and Witteczek, and had taken her brother Hermann with him on his September trip to the mountains. Perhaps it was her marriage in 1819 to Witteczek that Feuchtersleben was referring to, when he wrote that the tale of unhappy love "winds itself then, disguised and with enigmatic magic, through his poems." Wilhelmine's continuing presence in the Schubert circle—issuing for example the humorous invitation under the name "Nina" [sic][93] on 6 February [1827] to Schubert and Schober to appear for a "musical, declamatorical and dancical evening entertainment"—must have been a constant reminder of his lack of success in matters of love.

I have identified Louise Strauß as Aloisia Carolina Strauß (born *c.*1820),[94] the oldest daughter of Franz Strauß (1791-1874), a medical doctor in Leopoldstadt (now

92. WStLB-HSS I.N. 102.290.

93. See my identification of the writer of this note as Mina = Wilhelmina Witteczek in STEBLIN, "The Peacock's Tale," 23-25.

94. This information comes from the marriage registry of the church of St. Johann Nepomuk in Leopoldstadt.

See Tom. 4, Fol. 84, where the marriage of the "28-year-old" Aloisia Carolina Strauß to Moritz Franz Joseph Hörnes, doctor of philosophy and assistant at the k. k. Hof-Naturalien-Cabinette, is registered on 1 February 1848. A second daughter, Sidonie Anna, was born on 3 June 1827; see the baptismal records of the church of St.

**Plate 1** Heinrich Josef Hölzl's Account of Mayrhofer for Ludwig August Frankl, 1865
Wiener Stadt- und Landesbibliothek Handschriftensammlung, I.N. 102.290
(Reproduced with permission)

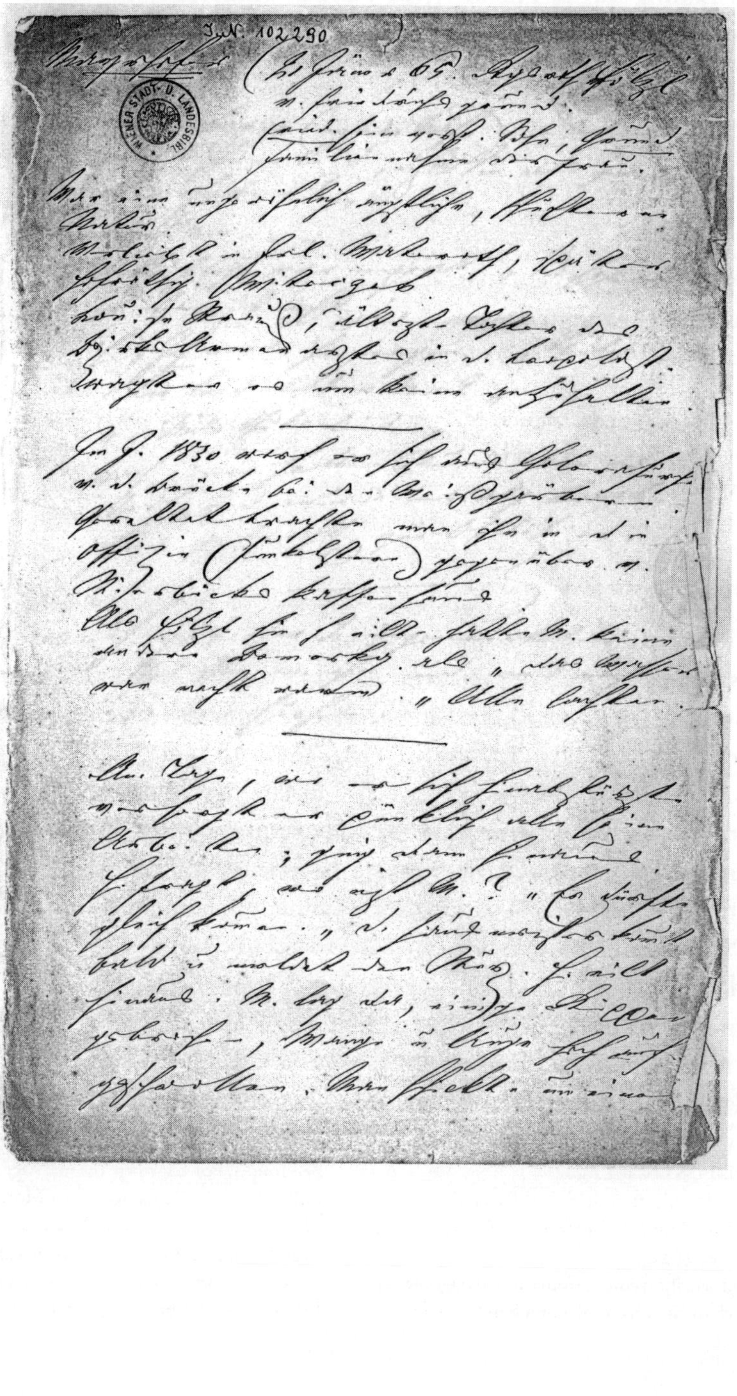

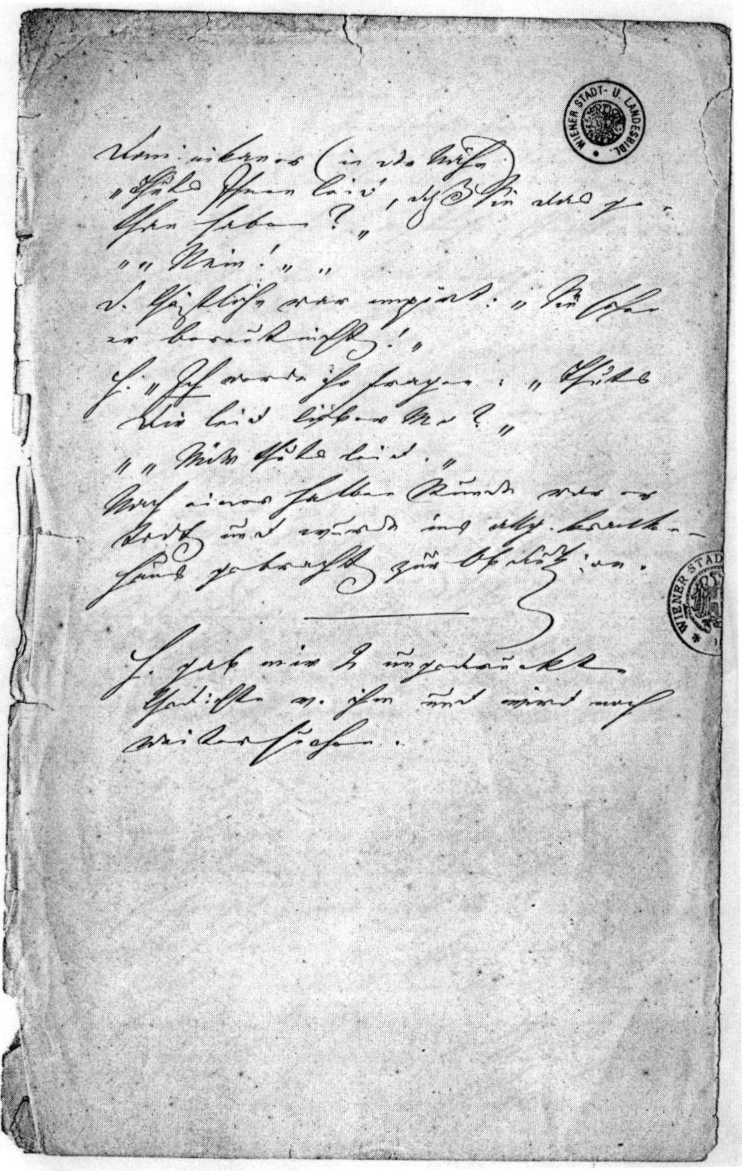
WIENER STADT- U. LANDESBIBL.

part of the 2nd district in Vienna). Strauß was later attached to the police department in this district and was awarded the Franz Joseph Medal in April 1867 for his many years of service. A conscription form dated 1830 for the house "Leopoldstadt 249" (Große Sperlgasse 2) shows that the unmarried book censor "Johann Mayerhofer [1]787 kk: Bücher Revisor, ledig" was living here (in apartment 2) together with the family of "Franz Strauß [1]791 Med^{ae} Doct u kk: Polizey Arzt," the latter's wife "Ehw: [Eheweib] Aloysia [1]798" and three daughters "Tochter Aloysia [1]819", "Sidonia [1]827" and "Wilhelmina [1]830." See Plate 2. The Staats-Schematismus, the annual address book listing employees of the state, confirms that Mayrhofer (and Dr. Strauß) were living at this address in the years 1830-1835.[95] At the time of his death Mayrhofer was still living in the home of this family, now at the new address Leopoldstadt 498 (Zirkusgasse 36).[96] Louise would have been about sixteen years old in 1836, the same age as Wilhelmine Watteroth when Mayrhofer was living in her family's home. Any connection between Louise and the poet's death, however, falls in the realm of speculation.

In conclusion, the new documentary evidence should help to balance the picture of this often misunderstood Schubert poet and give a more historically informed view of his personality. For it is only in understanding the historical context that the truth about relations between Schubert and this important friend will become clear, that the rift between the pleasure-seeking composer and the melancholy, hypochondriac poet, whose condition was exacerbated by political events, can be explained. It may even be that "history" turns out to be more important than hitherto imagined. Bauernfeld wrote in his diary on 6 February 1836: "Yesterday the poet Mayrhofer threw himself out of the window. A victim of the Austrian system."[97] This was the system that had produced genius and allowed it to flower, but through increasing repression was destroying its best talents. And the same historical conditions also applied for Schubert. The repressive marriage-consent law of 1815 almost surely led him to pursue

---

Josef in Leopoldstadt, Tom. 5, Fol. 99. A third daughter, Wilhelmina Anna, was born on 4 January 1830 (Tom. 5, Fol. 170) and died on 7 January 1834 (Sterbe-Buch, Tom. 2, Fol. 244).

95. *Hof- und Staats-Schematismus des österreichischen Kaiserthums* (Vienna: k. k. Hof- und Staats-Aerarial-Druckerey, 1835), 589, 602. Mayrhofer's name no longer appears in the Staats-Schematismus for 1836.

96. See WStLA Verlassenschaftsabhandlung [estate settlement] Fasz. 2-1281/1836, where Mayrhofer's address is given as Leopoldstadt No. 498. Both Dr. Strauß, at this same address, and Heinrich Hölzl signed the police order, dated 13 February 1836, that by law locked up Mayrhofer's effects after his death. The estate documents contain a detailed itemization of the poet's

possessions (total value 1144 fl 45 x C. M.) and similar documents concerning his father's death in Steyr on 21 June 1798. One also learns of the deaths of his brother Anaklet in Steyr on 15 January 1815, his brother Richard in Pest [Budapest] on 7 March 1819, and his mother in Ottensheim on 23 October 1823. See FEUCHTERSLEBEN, 14, for an account of how grieved Mayrhofer was over the death of a beloved family member in Pest in 1819. According to these estate documents this must have been his brother Richard.

97. Carl GLOSSY, "Aus Bauernfelds Tagebüchern," *Jahrbuch der Grillparzer-Gesellschaft* 5 (Vienna, 1895), 75: "Gestern stürzte sich der Dichter Mayrhofer übers Fenster. Ein Opfer des Oesterreicherthums."

the wrong paths that led to his disease and early death. This was the tragedy of Schubert's death, one that he shared with Mayrhofer: Schubert too was killed by this destructive regime.

**Plate 2** Conscription Form dated 1830 for Leopoldstadt No. 249, Apartment 2
Wiener Stadt- und Landesarchiv, Konskriptionsbogen Leopoldstadt 249/6
(Reproduced with permission)

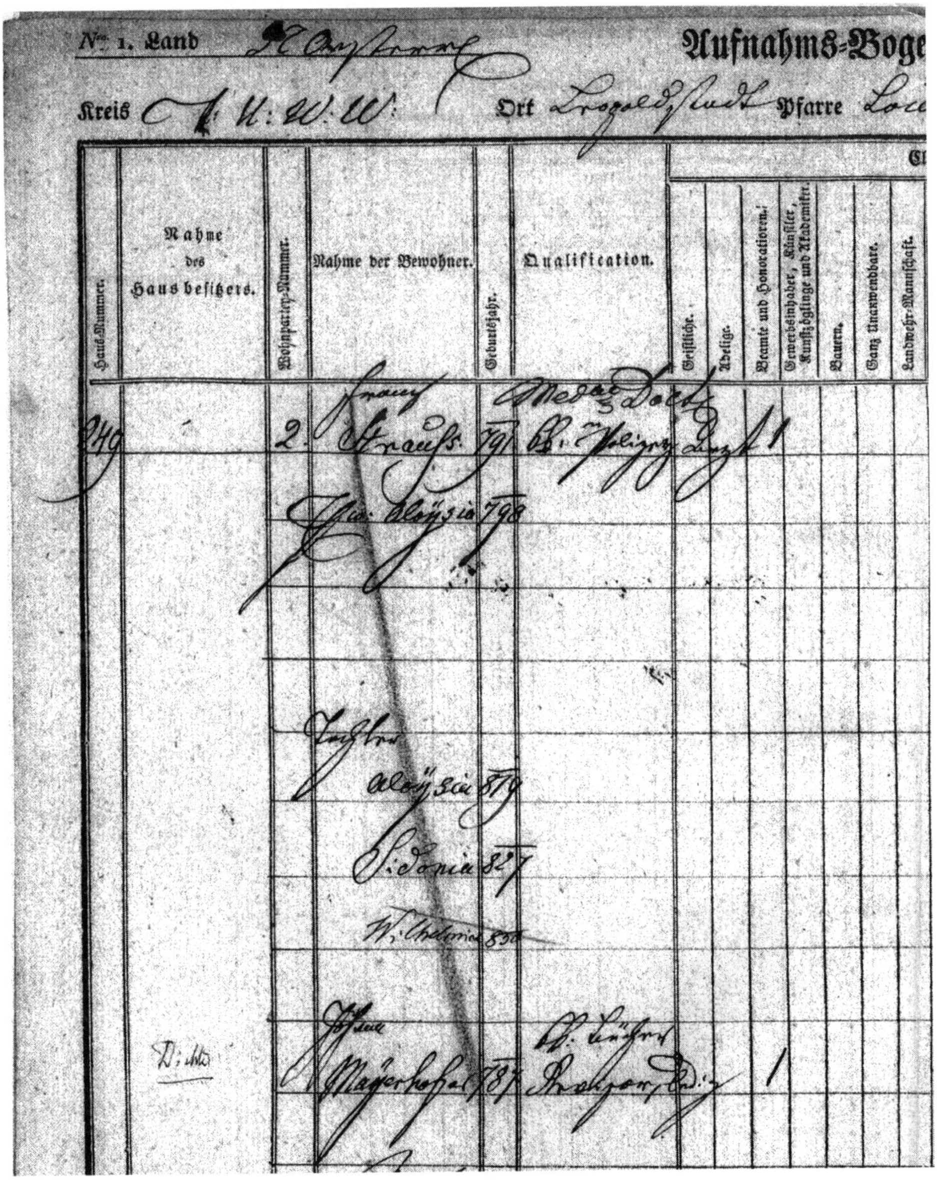
No. 1. Land
Aufnahms-Boge
Kreis
Ort
Pfarre

| Haus-Nummer. | Nahme des Haus besitzers. | Wohnparteyen-Nummer. | Nahme der Bewohner. | Geburtsjahr. | Qualification. | Geistliche. | Adelige. | Beamte und Honoratioren. | Gewerbsinhaber, Künstler, Kunstzöglinge und Akademiker. | Bauern. | Ganz Unanwendbare. | Landwehr-Mannschaft. |
|---|---|---|---|---|---|---|---|---|---|---|---|---|
| 249 | | 2 | Strauss | 791 | | | | 1 | | | | |
| | | | Aloysia | 798 | | | | | | | | |
| | | | Aloysia | 819 | | | | | | | | |
| | | | Sidonia | 827 | | | | | | | | |
| | | | | 830 | | | | | | | | |
| | Ditto | | Mayrhofer | 787 | | | | 1 | | | | |

# Appendix

### Ignaz Spenn's Diary, Unpublished Transcription by Ignaz Weinmann in the WStLB-HSS

Den 3t [September 1812] Abends in der *Braut von Messina* [von Schiller] Ich Schild[er] Spaun Kenner Arnet Mayrhofer [...]

8t September [...] nachmittag mit Spaun Kenner Mayrhofer u mein[em] Bruder auf dem Kahlenberg wo wir Milch tranken dann auf dem Leopoldsberg und über Nußdorf nach Hause [...]

30t [September 1812] Abends war[en] Schob[er] mit Spaun u Mayerhofer bey uns

1t Oktober [1812] Früh bey Schild[er] Abends war[en] Spaun Kirchstättern Schober Mayerhofer bey uns

2t [Oktober 1812] Früh mit Spaun u Schober in d[er] Bildergallerie. Abends begleitete mich Schilder u blieb bey uns

3t [Oktober 1812] Mit Schober Kenner Mayer[hofer] Kirchstättern Spaun auf den Kahlenberg wir speisten zu Heiligenstadt nahmen auf den Leopoldsberg Milch zu uns und unterhielten uns nach unserer Weise recht wohl Abends zeigte ich Schober den Weg nach Hernals der mich zu Sibonis Garten führte.

### Johann Mayrhofer's Letter to Franz von Schober.
Original located in the WStLB-HSS, I.N. 36.345

Wien am 7 Sept. 1816.

Lieber Bruder!

Als K von Wien schied, lag ihm sehr auf dem Herzen ein Auftrag von dir, den er vermög seinen Prüfungen und der Kürze der Zeit nicht gehörig ausrichten konnte. Ich mußte ihm zu seiner Beruhigung versprechen, es über mich zu nehmen, was ich auch that. Deine Gutmüthigkeit ist löblich. K Bereitwilligkeit, freundschaftlich, die Art aber wie das Bewußte ausgeführt werden soll, langwierig und ich weiß, daß du gerecht bist, von der Art daß K oder ich nun leicht in einem falschen Lichte und ich glaube mit einigem Rechte erscheinen würden. Und nur einen größeren Schriftsteller, z. B. Plut. Göthe theilweise wegzuschaffen raubt schon fast einen Monath und während dem bist du, wie deine Freunde hoffen, wieder da. Meine Meinung ist nun, daß du über die Art, wie dein schöner Vorsatz ausgeführt werde, selbst entscheidest, bestehst du auf der Veräusserung, so lasse ich mich gewiß keine Mühe reuen, dich zu befriedigen. Schreibe mir oder thue es mir noch besser mündlich kund. Das Schreiben an K. verwahre ich. Bist du aber in deiner gutherzigen Ungeduld, so glaube, daß K. das Seine möglichst gethan und rechte bloß mit mir. Lieber Freund! Deine edle Mutter, die ich immer mehr zu achten Ursache habe, hat mir deine Briefe mitgetheilt, ich bin mit dir in Gedanken zum fernen Norden gezogen und hoffe dir in den schöneren Süden zu folgen. Bedenke, daß dir ein großes Glück durch die Reise ward, wie freue ich mich dich wieder zu sehen, mit Menschenkenntniß bereichert, ausgestattet mit veränderter und klarerer Ansicht des Lebens. Morgen / 8 Sept :/ gehe ich mit dem jüngeren Watteroth auf 4 – 5 Tage in die Gebirge, Lilienfeld Baden Heiligenkreuz, um mich mit frischer Luft zu erquicken, ich freue mich darauf wie ein Kind. Meine Zeit verfließt wie gewöhnlich mit Büro Arbeiten, eigenen pp ich dichte mehr als sonst, und du wirst einige neue Gedichte hören, die eines strebenden Geistes nicht unwerth sind. *Schubert kommt heute und mehrere Freunde zu mir, die Nebel der Gegenwart, die etwas bleiern ist, sollen sich unter seinen Melodien heben.* Und somit lebe glücklich wie ich es wünsche und empfiehl mich deinem Onkel.

Dein treuer J Mayrhofer

## Josef Kupelwieser's Article on Censorship in the Unsinnsgesellschaft Newsletter "Archiv des menschlichen Unsinns" from 26 November 1818

Original located in the WStLB-HSS, I.N. 68.011/18

*Anzeige.* Im Verlage der Redaction werden folgende verbotene und erlaubte Werke öffentlich verkauft, als:

1.) Verbotene

*Das Einmaleins von 1 bis 1000* und wieder zurück in verkehrter Ordnung.

*A.B.C. Buch* mit Bildern von einem Jakobiner-Ordenspriester.

*Eipeldauers* sämmtliche Schrieften mit Vieh-losophischen Anmerkungen von einen Zweifels Sch—r.

*Zahlenverzeichniß* aller in der Lotterie gezogenen Nummern.

Dann nebst mehreren andern auch gedruckte Speis- Wäsch- Theater- und Feuerwerkszettel höchst gewöhnlichen Inhalts.

2.) Erlaubte Bücher

*Anleitung* zur Revolutionskunst. *Paris 1792.*

*Untrügliches Mittel* zur Verfälschung der Staatspapiere.

*NB.* Die Käufer dieses Werks bekommen noch als Zugabe einen Strick *gratis.*

*Ueber die Kunst,* die Natur in ihrem Lauf zu betrügen, zum Behuf der *Population* von einem *Misantropen.*

*Allgemeiner Briefsteller* oder die Kunst mit Geld beschwerte Briefe auf eine geschickte aber sehr einfache Art an sich zu bringen.

*Anleitung zum Leut' anschmieren* nebst gründlicher Anweisung einen falschen *Bankerout* zu machen. Wien Polizeyhaus 1818.

*Vorbereitung* zum Selbstmorde nebst einem Kommentar wie man einen andern ohne viele Mühe todtschlagen könne.

*Neues, um vieles verbessertes Lexikon* in der Diebessprache.

*Sammlung* von Ausflüchten und Lügen, zunächst für Kriminalinquisiten, dann verschiedene *Formularien* sich dem Teufel mit Leib u Seele zu verschreiben & & & & & & & & &.

Blas Leks

## Excerpts from Feuchtersleben's Letters to Schober (1834-36).

Originals in the WStLB-HSS

*I.N. 5.198*

Wien. 19 5/34. [19. Mai 1834]

Mayrhofer und ich, wir verstehen uns völlig. Wie herrlich ist seine Natur! mir ist auf dem leeren Trödelmarkt des Lebens noch nie so reine sittliche Würde, ohne weibische Demuth und religiöse Grillen-sucht, vorgekommen. Aber es ist, wenn ich als Arzt nicht irre, außer der Stellung gegen die Außenwelt (&c) noch etwas in seiner Complexion, was ihn untergräbt. Uibrigens dichtet er wieder, auf meine Veranlassung, und kann sehr heiter sein. Er liebt Dich sehr, wiewohl er Dir eine Zeitlang gram war, was ich auch begreife. Ich soll Dich auch sehr grüßen.

*I.N. 5.199*

Wien. 9 Jul. 1835.

[...] denn nun ist Mayrhofer nach Fusch (in's Salzburgische) auf 5 Wochen gegangen, um sich von allerlei Spleen zu befreien, und Gedichte für mich zu machen; ich sage für mich, und es freut mich, daß meine Freude an seiner Muse diesen schönen Einfluß auf ihn hat; er macht wieder Allerlei, sogar ein größeres, episches Gedicht, und theilt mir alles mit. Und er ist seitdem viel heiterer, geselliger, und auch in seinem innern Reflexionskreise führen ihn nun die Gedanken statt, wie früher, in eine Todeswüste, nun in ein hoffnungsvolles Saatgefild. Ich sage Dir: er ist die wunderbarste Erscheinung (wenn das nicht gar zu naturhistorisch herauskommt) die ich im Reiche der Menschenorganisationen gewahr ward; nirgends kann man es klarer seh'n, daß der menschliche Geist nur eine begrenzte Offenbarung eines unendlichen ist. In M. ist etwas anders als *er*,—oder nenn' ich dies Andre den eigentlichen *Er*? er erscheint, wie das zerknitterte, verkleisterte Organ eines göttlichen Wesens. Mit Staunen hört er seinen eignen Werken zu,—wie ein Gefangener in seinem Kerker einem Lied aus seiner Heimath, das vor den Thoren schallt. Er sollte sich in einem reinern Aether bewegen; in unserm bewegt er sich ungeschickt. So viel davon; es wird *Dir* wohl kaum mystisch vorkommen; aber *es ist so*.

I.N. 5204

*Wien. 10ᵗ Febr. 836 [10. Februar 1836]*

Was durch so viele vorbedeutende Ereignisse seit Langem verkündet war, habe ich Dir nun als geschehen zu berichten; und was mich keineswegs überraschte, hat mich - ich gestehe Dir's - tiefer erschüttert, als ich erwartete. Mayrhofer hat sich am 5ᵗᵉⁿ d. M. vom höchsten Stockwerke des Gebäudes, in welchem die Censur-büreau's sind, herabgestürzt, und ist nach einer Stunde gestorben. Er war seit vielleicht einem Monate, ohne Spuren dessen zu zeigen was gemeinhin für Melancholie gilt, weniger zugänglich als sonst. Den Abend des 4ᵗᵉⁿ d. M. brachte er bei einer Spielpartie mit Spaun zu, trank mit ihm Bier, *äußerte Besorgniß einen Diätfehler zu begehn*, und erschien völlig so, wie man sein gewohnt war. Des andern Morgens kam er wie gewöhnlich in's Amt, entfernte sich, ohne daß seine Bewegungen im Geringsten auffielen, indem er die revidirten Bücher dem Amtsvorsteher Hölzel übergab, und nach wenigen Minuten fanden die Hausknechte seinen Leichnam. Die Section zeigte, außer den durch den Sturz bedingten innern und äußern Verletzungen, nichts abnormes. Es ward ihm ein Leichenbegängniß zugestanden, welches gestern statt fand. Spaun, der mich bat, wenn ich Dir schriebe, Dich von ihm zu grüßen, setzt ihm einen Stein auf den Hügel, daß man doch die Stelle bezeichnet finde, wo seine Uiberreste ruh'n. Er testirte nicht; hinterließ an Baarem 400 fl CM., und nun sind die übrigen Gegenstände seines Nachlasses, des ungesetzlichen Falles wegen, unter *polizeilicher* Sperre. Du weißt vielleicht, daß in Oberöstreich seine unbemittelte Schwester lebt. Ich habe mich auf's Lebendigste seiner poetischen Reliquien angenommen, und Du kannst Dir denken, daß ich diese meine Heiligthümer nicht fahren lasse, und nicht gestatte, daß sie in die Winde, oder auf eine gemeine, bettelhafte Weise in die Welt gestreut werden. Wenn sie nur nicht unter den Händen der Polizei *verschwinden*, so will ich mich mit denen, die etwa darauf Anspruch machen können, in's Einvernehmen setzen; ich will sie redigiren; und dafür sorgen, daß sie auf eine Art wie sie's verdienen, vor's Publikum gelangen, und die Erbinn dabei nicht leer ausgeht. Es ist der Mühe werth, denn ich weiß, was alles da sein muß; er hat vor der Fuscher-Badereise vieles Lyrische gemacht, zum Theil mit mir um die Wette; bittere Gedichte, die er "Sermone" nennt, und ein episches Ganzes concipirt, dessen erster Gesang fertig ist; es hatte den Konflikt des Ritter- und Pfaffenthum's mit dem Menschlichen, im Mittelalter, zum Vorwurf. Hätte man die Sachen nur erst, dann müßte man, und wollte man gerne sehen, wie man über die Censur, und über den Verleger der ersten Sammlung (denn es sollte nach meinem Wunsch diese halb verlor'ne mit regenerirt werden) hinauskäme. Jetzt bin ich froh, daß mir der Zufall so viel Credit in der literarischen Welt verschafft hat, daß ich so was mit Hoffnung des Erfolgs unternehmen darf. Du müsstest auch Deine Hefte dazu hergeben. - Sollte wirklich nichts zum Vorschein kommen (er könnte auch Alles vernichtet haben!) so würden sogar diese letztern, sammt dem, was ich habe, ein Heft geben.

## Heinrich Josef Hölzl's Account to Ludwig August Frankl (1865)

Original located in the WStLB-HSS, I.N. 102.290

Mayrhofer (21 Jäner 65. Rgsrth Hölzl) [...]

War eine ungewöhnlich ängstliche, schüchterne Natur.

Verliebt in Frl. Wateroth, später Hofräthin Witeczek.

Louise Strauß, älteste Tochter des Bezirks Armenarztes in d[er] Leopoldst[adt].

wagte er es um keine anzuhalten.

Im J[ahre] 1830 warf er sich aus Cholorafurcht v[on] d[er] Brücke bei den Weißgärbern.

Gerettet brachte man ihn in die Offizin (Funkelstern) gegenüber v[om] Stierböcks Kaffeehaus.

Als Hölzl hie[r] h[er] eilte, hatte M[ayrhofer] keine andere Bemerk[un]g als "das Wasser war recht warm." Alle lachten.

Am Tage, wo er sich hinabstürzte versorgte er pünktlich alle seine Arbeiten; ging dann hinaus. H[ölzl] fragt, wo ist M[ayrhofer]? "Er dürfte gleich kommen."

d[er] Hausmeister kommt bald u[nd] meldet den Sturz.

H[ölzl] eilt hinaus. M[ayrhofer] lag da, einige Rippen gebrochen, Wange u[nd] Auge hoch aufgeschwollen. Man schickte um einen Dominikaner (in der Nähe)

"Thuts Ihnen leid, daß Sie das gethan haben?"

"Nein!"

d[er] Geistliche war empört: "Sie sehen er bereut nichts!"

H[ölzl] "Ich werde ihm fragen: "Thuts Dir leid lieber Mayrhofer?"

"Mir thuts leid."

Nach einer halben Stunde war er todt und wurde ins allg[emeinen] Krankenhaus gebracht zur Obduktion.

H[ölzl] gab mir 2 ungedruckte Gedichte v[on] ihm und wird noch weitersuchen.

° I wish to thank Erich Benedikt, David Buch, Marie-Agnes Dittrich, and Morten Solvik for their perceptive comments on the 1996 version of this paper submitted to *Music & Letters*, and Michael Lorenz for helpful suggestions, including the bibliographic sources Luib and

*Euphorion*. I am also grateful to the Österreichische Nationalbank Jubiläumsfondsprojekt-Nr. 5923 for the financial support in 1996 that enabled me to research and write this article.

# THE SIGNIFICANCE OF THE LUDLAMSHÖHLE
## FOR FRANZ SCHUBERT

O F THE MANY convivial social circles that met regularly in Vienna during the 1810s and 20s, one of the most intriguing is the Ludlamshöhle, which flourished *c.*1817-26. Comprised of influential, well-educated men employed in the city's court theaters and government offices, the club achieved a notoriety for its satirical jokes, nonsensical songs and comic sketches at a time when the government banned all student fraternities and secret societies. Remarkable also was the society's inclusivity and religious tolerance, welcoming Viennese locals, Austrian provincials, and foreign visitors (among whom were Jews and Protestants) within a larger society known for its etiquette and exclusive social conventions.

The Ludlamshöhle easily might have been ignored by historians had it not been raided by the police in April 1826 and some of its prominent members arrested and fined.[1] When a formal five month investigation yielded no proof that the group was politically dangerous, the police's overreaction became a source of public embarrassment. For the involved writers and artists, however, the incident was another example of the injustice of Metternich's regime.

Many Viennese contemporaries mention the society in their letters, diaries and memoirs.[2] But police and court records of the affair disappeared in 1927, and as early as 1831 Hermann Meynert reported that he was unable to locate much factual information about the group and that former Viennese members were reluctant to discuss the matter.[3] The earliest scholarly inquiry, not published until *c.*1895, was conducted by literary and cultural historians interested in the group's relation to Franz Grillparzer.[4] More

1. Alice M. HANSON, *Musical Life in Biedermeier Vienna* (Cambridge: Cambridge University Press, 1985), 56-60.
2. Among the most important eyewitness accounts include: Ignaz CASTELLI, *Memoiren meines Lebens* (Munich: Winkler Verlag, 1969); August LEWALD, *Ein Menschenleben* (Leipzig: F.A. Brockhaus, 1844); and Karl ROSENBAUM,

"Tagebücher 1821-1829," manuscript diaries in the Austrian National Library, Handschriften Sammlung, Sn 203-204.
3. Hermann MEYNERT, *Herbstblüthen aus Wien Gesammelt in den Spätmonaten 1830* (Leipzig: C.H. F. Hartmann, 1832), 236-38.
4. See: August SAUER, *Aus dem alten Oesterreich: Kleine*

comprehensive research was presented by Dr. Otto Zausmer in 1935, which, he explained, was a condensation of a lecture he had given the previous year based on a thousand pages of materials about the Ludlamshöhle in the hands of a private collector.[5] Unfortunately his article lacked scholarly citations so that his work is impossible to verify today.

During the 1980s and 90s a resurgence of interest in Biedermeier Vienna, this time by musicologists has led to many discoveries and a re-evaluation of the Ludlamshöhle and other similiar societies of the period. In 1991 in Vienna Lucia Porhansl located some of the (still) privately owned papers from Ignaz Castelli's estate described by Zausmer.[6] She presented a facsimile of the elaborate Ludlam calendar and the official list of members' names, their Ludlam titles as well as a few of the prominent non-members (called "Shadows"), explaining how many of them had ties to Franz Schubert as librettists, poets, performers, or friends.

Most recently Rita Steblin discovered another Viennese "Nonsense Society" ("*Unsinnsgesellschaft*") (*c.*1817-18) in which Schubert participated.[7] By revisiting the research of art historians on the Biedermeier painter Leopold Kupelwieser, and by applying her experience with Schubert iconology, she not only was able to identify many of the figures who appear in that club's newspapers drawn by Kupelwieser (and other artists in the group), but also she has shown their relationship to the composer. Thus she has cleared up a long held misinterpretation of a comment in Heinrich Anschütz's memoirs that supposedly linked Schubert to the Ludlamshöhle some time before 1820.[8]

Both Porhansl's article and Steblin's book provide useful, updated biographical information about the two clubs' members. In addition, Steblin's transcription of the archaic handwriting in the society's manuscript newspapers and her editorial explanations of the topical allusions and colorful Viennese expressions now make these materials accessible to modern readers.

In 1816, at the age of nineteen and living on his own as a school teaching assistant, Schubert socialized with old friends and like-minded artistic men about his own age. His new friendship with Leopold Kupelwieser as well as his living quarters' proximity to the inn "zum rothen Hahn" at this time probably brought him into contact with the "Nonsense Society".[9] The group was run mostly by art students, a few writers and local businessmen. The witty nicknames and teasing banter recorded in the club's newspaper and their elaborate New Year's skits testify to the group's relatively carefree, "arty", and

*Beiträge zur Lebensgeschichte Grillparzers und zur Charakteristik seiner Zeit* (Prague: n.p., 1895); and Carl GLOSSY, "Grillparzer und die Ludlamshöhle," *Jahrbuch der Grillparzer Gesellschaft* 8 (1898): 251-55.

5.  Otto ZAUSMER, "Der Ludlamshöhle Glück und Ende," *Jahrbuch der Grillparzer Gesellschaft* 33 (1935): 86-112.

6.  Lucia PORHANSL, "Auf Schuberts Spuren in der 'Lud-lamshöhle'," *Schubert durch die Brille* 7 (June, 1991): 52-78.

7.  Rita STEBLIN, *Die Unsinnsgesellschaft* (Vienna: Böhlau Verlag,1998).

8.  Heinrich ANSCHÜTZ, *Erinnerungen aus dessen Leben und Wirken* (Vienna: Leopold Sommer, 1866), 264.

9.  STEBLIN, *Unsinnsgesellschaft*, 16-17.

youthful nature. Their glib, humorous comments about world events also suggest that a degree of free speech was possible in Vienna after the Napoleonic wars.

But by 1826 this situation changed. Schubert already had a serious confrontation with the police because of his association with the outspoken political poet Johann Senn; his health had deteriorated, and he now was an established composer. Thus, when he and his young friend Eduard Bauernfeld decided to join the madcap Ludlamshöhle that year, most likely it was for professional not for social reasons.

Around 1825 the active members of the Ludlamshöhle certainly were older, more established and influential men than those of the "Nonsense Society". Among the more than 150 persons mentioned in memoirs, police documents and the group's own list (described by Porhansl), were some of the German-speaking world's most respected men of the theater.[10] Notable among its composers and conductors were Antonio Salieri (1774-1825), retired Kapellmeister of the court opera and Schubert's composition teacher, and the Czech composer, Adalbert Gyrowetz (1765-1850), who vied for Salieri's post the next year. Wenzel Würfel [Werfel] (1790-1832), who launched his successful opera *Der Rübezahl* in Prague in 1824, had just moved to Vienna in 1826 to assume the post of Vice Kapellmeister of the Kärntnerthor Theater. Belgian-born conductor Heinrich von Lannoy (1787-1853) directed concerts for the Friends of Music and the Concert Spirituels during the 1820s.

About the same time other Ludlamites actively participated in various court musical establishments, including pianists Ignaz Moscheles (1794-1870), Josef Fischhof (1804-1857) and Ignaz Assmayer (1790-1862), a student of Salieri who held the post of second court organist in 1826.[11] The flutist Johann Sedlatschek had just finished fifteen years of service for the court orchestra, while Joseph Mayseder (1789-1863) played violin and Joseph Merk (1795-1862) played cello in the court orchestra. Ludlamite vocalists included many operatic professionals such as tenors Anton Forti (1790-1859), Anton Haitzinger, and Ludwig Tietze (1797-1850). Singer Johann A. Stöger also managed a theater in Graz by 1823. Johann Mosevius founded a Singakademie in Breslau in 1825.

Also potentially useful to Schubert could have been acquaintance with the dramatists, theater critics and writers who were club members. In fact, as Porhansl points out, Schubert had already set many of their works to music. For example, Ignaz Castelli (1781-1862) provided the libretto to Schubert's opera *Die Verschworenen* (1823) and poems by Ludwig Rellstab, Ludwig Deinhardstein and Theodor Hell [pseud. of Karl G. Winkler] were used in a number of his Lieder.[12] He may have met other Ludlamites when his works were performed. For example, Gyrowetz's ballet *Die Zwei Tanten* shared the theater bill with Schubert's *Zwillingsbrüder* on 14 June 1820 as did Karl Blum's ballet

---

10.  PORHANSL, "Schuberts Spuren," 54-70.        11.  Ibid., 64-65.        12.  Ibid., 67.

*Achilles* on 4 July 1820. Gyrowetz conducted a public charity concert on 7 March 1821 during which Schubert's vocal quartet "Das Dörfchen" premiered, and Ludlam singers Sedlatschek and Götz sang his quartets at other public recitals.

Schubert probably was aware of the precedent for migrating from the "Nonsense Society" to the Ludlamshöhle. For example he knew Georg Kettel, a Burgtheater actor whose specialty was romantic lead roles. When the former society disbanded in 1819, Kettel joined the Ludlamshöhle and participated in it until he left Vienna in 1826.[13] Likewise Josef Kupelwieser, eldest brother of Leopold (Schubert's close friend), was employed as theater secretary at the Kärntnerthor theater in 1821. After he wrote the libretto *Fierrabras* for Schubert in 1823 he became a full member of the Ludlamshöhle, although he left Vienna soon thereafter to take a theater position in Pressburg.[14]

Schubert probably had witnessed how Ludlam members had contributed toward Carl Maria von Weber's success in Viennese theaters. In 1822 when Weber came to Vienna to oversee the premiere of his newly commissioned German Romantic opera, *Euryanthe,* he and his assistant Julius Benedict were invited to attend a meeting of the Ludlamshöhle. Weber hated the experience at first but was aware of its usefulness:

> It must have been the devil that thrust me into that wasps nest.
> Were it not for the necessity of keeping well with the critics
> who wallow in such filth, Satan himself could never drag me there again.[15]

But his investment paid off, because the Ludlamites appeared as a mighty claque at the premiere performance on 25 October 1823 and gave the production good reviews. Ignaz Moscheles recalled later in his memoirs:

> Ludlam succeeded infusing the orthodox German spirit into the press.[16]

Both Weber and Benedict were feted after the performance in the Ludlamshöhle and voted by acclamation as members. Miraculously soon thereafter Benedict received the post of director of the opera theater, which he held until 1825. Certainly Schubert never experienced such ease in penetrating the Austrian court theater bureaucracy.

The evidence that actually ties Schubert to the Ludlamshöhle society is slim and second hand. His name does not appear in any of the extant lists made by Rosenbaum, Castelli or the police report of 1826. But he was known to have eaten at the Haidvogel, the society's meeting place. Music historian Otto E. Deutsch reports that in the fall of 1822 Franz Lachner met Schubert there for lunch and they became friends.[17] But whether either stayed for supper and the entertainments later is unknown.

13. STEBLIN, *Unsinnsgesellschaft,* 83–84.
14. Ibid., 100.
15. John WARRACK, *Carl Maria von Weber: Writings on Music* (Cambridge: Cambridge University Press, 1981), 316.

16. Charlotte MOSCHELES, *Life of Moscheles* (London: Hurst & Blackettl, 1873), 87.
17. Otto E. DEUTSCH, *Schubert: A Documentary Biography* (New York: Da Capo Press, 1977), 314.

The most important, and now only evidence linking Schubert to the society comes from Eduard Bauernfeld's memoir article that appeared in the *Neue Freie Presse* (27 April 1877)—fifty years after the fact. He wrote:

> Schubert and I were just about to join that gay band of people
> and our names were already on the notice board, when the
> authorities intervened, closed the meeting place, seized what
> papers they could lay their hands on, called the members
> themselves to account.[18]

In February 1825 Bauernfeld made friends with Schubert. The next month he proposed writing an opera libretto on the tale of the Graf von Gleichen, which he finished in August 1826. His diary records their first year's whirl of parties, Schubertiades, and concerts they attended together. But by February a year later, his friends called him "Spelunk" because he rarely left his room in order to study for his law exams and to finish his Shakespeare translation.

Since the police raid of the Ludlamshöhle was on 16 April 1826, he and Schubert just missed being involved with the investigation because Bauernfeld left on 15 April to join a map surveying project in southern Austria. Upon his return to Vienna in September he secured a position in the civil service (with the Lower Austrian provincial government) in the office that was assigned to review the Ludlamshöhle investigation. He wrote:

> Had the police delayed their intervention but a single day
> Schubert and I would also have become 'Ludlamites'
> and I might have had to assist at my own enquiry. What irony![19]

In 1826 Schubert and Bauernfeld both had good reasons to join the Ludlamshöhle. In April the previous year Schubert had applied for the post of assistant conductor at the Kärntnerthor Theater, Bauernfeld was eager to promote his translation of Shakepeare's *Leichtsinn und Liebe* [Much Ado About Nothing], and both planned the production of their opera venture *Graf von Gleichen*.

If Bauernfeld is correct about their names having been posted on the notice board of the Ludlamshöhle club, he and Schubert were up for election as members to the society. Since most elections were done by ballot, both men probably had participated in earlier meetings (in March or April 1826) in order to prove themselves worthy by demonstrating their wit and sense of humor. Schubert would have been expected to compose some drinking songs or humorous male vocal quartets on Ludlamite texts. Accordingly, the Deutsch thematic catalogue and John Reed's updated research both suggest that the

18.  Otto E. DEUTSCH, *Schubert: Memoirs by His Friends*    19.  Ibid.
(London: Adam and Charles Black, 1958), 241.

great number of consecutively numbered songs, ie. D. 865-871 and 878-881, reputedly composed in the spring of 1826, were all on texts by Ludlamites (see Table 1).[20]

**Table 1** Songs by Ludlamites

| | | | |
|---|---|---|---|
| D. 865 | "Widerspruch"- Seidl | 1826?, | pub. op. 105 #1 by Czerny quartet TTBB in Vienna, 21 Nov 1828 |
| D. 866 | Refrain Lieder - Seidl "Die Unterscheidung" "Bei dir allein" "Die Männer sind méchant" "Irdisches Glück" | summer 1828? | pub. op. 95 by Weigl in Vienna August 1828 |
| D. 867 | "Wiegenlied"- Seidl | 1826?, | pub. Op. 105 #2 by Czerny |
| D. 868 | "Das Echo"-Castelli | undatable (Deutsch); 1826-28 (Reed) | pub. Op. post 130 by Weigl in Vienna July 1830 |
| D. 869 | "Totengräber-Weise"-Schlechta | 1826, | pub. by Diabelli in Vienna 4 Jan 1832 |
| D. 870 | "Der Wanderer an den Mond"-Seidl | 1826, | pub. Op. 80 #1 by Haslinger in Vienna 25 May 1827 |
| D. 871 | "Das Zügenglöcklein"-Seidl | March 1826; | pub. Op. 80 #2 by Haslinger in Vienna 1827 |
| D. 878 | "Am Fenster"- Seidl | March 1826; | pub. Op. 80 #3 by Czerny in Vienna 21 Nov 1828 |
| D. 879 | "Sehnsucht" - Seidl | | Op. 105 #4 by Czerny in Vienna 21 Nov 1828 |
| D. 880 | "Im Freien"- Seidl | March 1826, | pub. Op. 80 #3 by Haslinger in Vienna 1827 |
| D. 881 | "Fischerweise"-Schlechta | March 1826, | pub. Op. 96 #4 by Schober (in 2 versions) |

Johann Gabriel Seidl (1804-75) had known Schubert as early as 1824, for in a letter to the composer dated 1 July 1824 he urged him to remember his promise to compose music for *Der kurze Mantel* (Seidl's first court theater play). He maintained friendly ties with Schubert because Bauernfeld invited him to attend a Schubertiade at the home of Franz von Schober on 10 January 1825. In February of that year two volumes of Seidl's poetry were published.

The two works by Franz von Schlechta (1796-1875) also are connected to that time because of their dating in the Witteczek-Spaun song catalogue. Schubert met Schlechta during their school days, but easily could have renewed their acquaintance at the Ludlamshöhle because the poet was an active member in the spring of 1826. In fact he was arrested with Grillparzer, but released when he demanded his right to a military rather then a civilian court hearing.

Conspicuous in the list is the song "Das Echo" on a text of Ignaz Castelli, one of Ludlam's liveliest participants and staunchest supporters. In 1995 in an article about

20. Otto E. DEUTSCH, *Schubert. Thematisches Verzeichnis seiner Werke in chronologischer Folge* (Kassel: Bärenreiter, 1978) and John REED, *The Schubert Song Companion* (New York: Universe Books, 1985).

Schubert's settings of Castelli texts, Porhansl noticed that the song is very unusual for Schubert because of its comic tone.[21] But her major discovery was that the seven-strophe poem was first published in the almanac *Aglaja: Taschenbuch für das Jahr 1826*. Hence the song could have been composed as early as that year.

The song presents a humorous dialogue between a mountain girl, her mother, and a mischievious echo.[22] The girl must explain why a strange man just kissed her and why they are now engaged to be married. Each strophe relates the romantic overtures of the man on another hillside, the virtuous protestations of the girl and the echo between them that distorts her message into an encouragement. Schubert's piano introduction prefigures the singer's melody and acts as the echo. If this song had been intended for performance in the Ludlamshöhle, its dialogue sung by men in falsetto and acted out in scenes could have been hilarious.

Castelli provides another tantalizing, albeit ambiguous, link of this song to his society. At the end of his memoirs' lengthy description of the Ludlamshöhle, he names some of the club's song titles, among which he calls song 37 "Ludlam's Echo"—text and music by a Shadow.[23] Since Schubert was not yet a member, he would have been considered a Shadow. Even though he did not compose the text, he might have written his own parody of it—a common practice in that club. Only the examination of the Ludlam score, in the end, will settle the matter but the coincidences are many.

Thus, in 1826 seeking a court appointment and success for his newest opera, Schubert needed allies with clout in the theater and court musical institutions. Like Weber, he knew that the Ludlamshöhle could help. Schubert had previous experience with similar artistic societies and he already knew many Ludlamites. If he wanted to join the club, he had to demonstrate his wit and provide some service to the group. Accordingly that spring he set a number of poems by Ludlamites, one of which is uncharacteristically humorous and written by an important theater critic and a club leader. Whereas membership in the Ludlamshöhle might have sparked a turning point in Schubert's theater career, its own swift and unexpected demise led instead to further disappointments. Schubert did not get the theater post and Bauernfeld's opera libretto was banned by the censors in October 1826.[24]

21. Lucia PORHANSL, "Schuberts Textvorlagen nach Ignaz Castelli," *Schubert durch die Brille* 14 (Jan 1995): 102-104.

22. Franz SCHUBERT, "Das Echo," in *Franz Schubert: Complete Works*, 16 (New York: Dover Publications, 1964), 258-59.

23. CASTELLI, *Memoiren*, 128.

24. DEUTSCH, *Biography*, 548.

Judith Radell

# Sphere of Influence:
# Clara Kathleen Rogers
# and Amy Beach

Wishing you great happiness in the future, & that your artistic career may prove as brilliant in its' (sic) fulfilment as it now is in promise.[1]

WITH THIS MESSAGE the singer, pianist, and composer Clara Kathleen Rogers (1844–1931) signed the young Amy Cheney's autograph album in December 1881. Although they were born a generation apart, Amy Marcy Cheney Beach (1867–1944) and Rogers both began publishing their music in the early 1880s with Arthur P. Schmidt as their primary publisher. While their social circles were not identical, they had in common many friends and acquaintances, including the poets Oliver Wendell Holmes, Henry Wadsworth Longfellow, Thomas Bailey Aldrich, Margaret Deland, and Celia Thaxter. Their townhouses were not far apart; it is an easy walk through the Back Bay area from Beach's home at 28 Commonwealth Avenue to Rogers' at 309 Beacon Street. It was customary at the time to communicate invitations, acceptances, and messages of congratulations in writing. Yet no correspondence from Rogers is found among Beach's papers. Moreover, Rogers' posthumously-published memoir, *The Story of Two Lives*, contains anecdotes about most of Boston's prominent musicians and musical patrons during the late 1880s, but ignores the well-known prodigy, Amy Beach.[2]

Three newly discovered letters from Beach to Rogers, held in the Collection of Clara Barnett Rogers and Henry Munroe Rogers in Harvard University's Theatre Collection, provide new insight into the relationship between the Second New England School's pioneer woman composer and its most famous woman member. Of particular interest is

---

1. Amy BEACH, Autograph Album, Beach Collection, Douglas and Helena Milne Special Collections and Archives, Dimond Library, University of New Hampshire, 25. Adrienne Fried BLOCK mentions the inscription in her article, "Arthur P. Schmidt, Music Publisher and Champion of American Women Composers," *The Musical Woman*, 2, ed. Judith LANG ZAIMONT, Catherine OVERHAUSER, and Jane GOTTLIEB

(Westport, CT: Greenwood Press, 1984-85), 159. This article provides insight into Schmidt's path-breaking work with American women composers; the article's scope does not extend to an exploration of the relationships between the composers.
2. Clara Kathleen ROGERS, *The Story of Two Lives* (Norwood, MA: Privately printed, The Plimpton Press, 1932).

Beach's letter of 4 October 1893, in which she expresses admiration for Rogers' Sonata for Piano and Violin (Arthur P. Schmidt and Co., 1893), especially for its first movement.[3] Three years later Beach began work on her own violin sonata, which was published by Schmidt in 1899. In its structure and in its themes, the first movement of this sonata appears to show the influence of Rogers' earlier work. Evidence from the music and from the letters suggests the possibility that Beach may have consulted the work of her senior colleague in creating her first major piece of chamber music. Moreover, the similarities between the composers' careers and life paths before 1911 may imply that Clara Rogers' life, as well as her music, influenced the young Amy Beach.

Fully a generation older than Beach, Clara Kathleen Barnett was born in Cheltenham, England, in 1844. She was the daughter of an opera composer, John Barnett, and the granddaughter of a violoncellist, Robert Lindley. From 1857 to 1860 she attended the Leipzig Conservatory, where her original principal interest was the piano.[4] She studied with Louis Plaidy, Ignaz Moscheles and, later, with Hans von Bülow. Following her vocal training in Milan with Antonio San Giovanni, she took the stage name, Clara Doria, and sang in Italian opera (1863–67) and on the British concert stage (1867–71). Between 1871 and 1873 she performed in the United States, first as a member of the Parepa-Rosa Opera Company and then with the Max Maretzak Company. Following her Boston appearance with the latter company in the winter of 1872–73, she met Otto Dresel, a pianist and a friend of Robert Franz. In February 1873, Dresel wrote to her in New York, inviting her to join the more sophisticated cultural environment of Boston.[5] She thus began a long career as a singer, pianist, composer, teacher, and writer in America's reigning musical city.

Like Amy Beach, Clara Barnett had been a composer since her early childhood. At the Leipzig Conservatory, she had studied harmony, a discipline that included training in part-writing and voice-leading.[6] Coeducation did not exist at the Leipzig Conservatory at mid-century; separate classes for male or female students were held in each subject. There was no class in composition for women. Clara Barnett, with the aid

3. Amy BEACH to Clara ROGERS, 4 October 1893. In Clara ROGERS, Scrapbooks, vol. 1, The Collection of Clara Barnett Rogers and Henry Munroe Rogers, Courtesy of the Harvard Theatre Collection, the Houghton Library, Harvard University.

4. Clara Kathleen ROGERS, *Memories of a Musical Career* (Boston: Little, Brown and Co., 1919). Rogers' books of memoirs are frequently vague about dates. Where Rogers does not provide a date, I have used timelines based on the events in the memoirs, and I have confirmed them, where possible, with the dates of documents and of historical events. For example, Rogers states that she entered

the Leipzig Conservatory in 1857 (*Memories of a Musical Career*, 130), at the age of twelve (ibid., 101). Clara Barnett's *Inskriptionsverzeichniss des Konservatoriums*, held in the *Hochschulbibliothek, Bereich Archiv, Hochschule für Musik und Theater*, Leipzig, confirms the year of entrance, but incorrectly lists her birth year as 1845. It is quite possible that her parents provided the later birth date to make her accomplishment as a prodigy appear greater.

5. Otto DRESEL to Clara ROGERS, 1 February 1873. In Rogers, Scrapbooks, vol. 1, op. cit., (n. 3).

6. ROGERS, *Memories of a Musical Career*, 175.

of her fellow student, Arthur S. Sullivan, was instrumental in changing this policy. Inspired by Sullivan's reputation as the composer of a quartet, she wrote at least one movement of her String Quartet in D Minor. Sullivan copied the parts, arranged an impromptu performance, and alerted the faculty. Subsequently, a composition class for women students was formed.[7]

Clara Barnett appears to have worked on the quartet until at least 1867; the draft of the third and fourth movements, held in Harvard's Rogers Collection, bears that date. Several other compositions in the collection probably date from the 1850s and 1860s, including songs and part-songs in German and Italian and a *Tarantella* for piano (1860). None of her compositions appeared in print until 1882.

In the 1880s and 1890s Clara Barnett Rogers' commitment to composition intensified. Prompted by the interest of her mentor, Otto Dresel, and by praise from other Boston musicians, she decided to offer her works for publication.[8] An important factor in this decision was her marriage in 1878 to the prominent Boston attorney, Henry Munroe Rogers. In *The Story of Two Lives*, she relates her attempt to reconcile her own musical needs with the expectations of society:

> … the mere thought of giving up that which from earliest childhood had been the one and only deep interest in my life was like death to me … I felt … that it would be right for me to retire from public life … but the thought of settling down into a mere house-wife and social creature with the prospect of no other than a dilettante-ish expression in Art was abhorrent to me!"[9]

Clara and Henry Rogers agreed that she would continue in her teaching career and in amateur performing. She herself found publishing her compositions to be a satisfying substitute for the concert stage.[10] Schmidt published fifty-seven songs by Rogers, often re-issuing them in albums. He brought out only two of her instrumental works, a small Scherzo in A Major and the Sonata for Piano and Violin. In addition to her Schmidt publications, she contributed two piano pieces to an anthology, *Half-Hours With the Best Composers*.[11] Rogers' entire published output dates from 1882 to 1906, a time span that roughly corresponds to Amy Beach's tenure as a Boston composer (1883-1911).

While most of Rogers' music is unpublished or out of print, Amy Beach's *œuvre* is regaining its place in the concert repertoire. Adrienne Fried Block's comprehensive biography, *Amy Beach, Passionate Victorian: The Life and Work of an American Composer, 1867-1944*, has begun to make Beach's life story equally familiar to musicians and scholars.[12] Born in Henniker, New Hampshire in 1867, Amy Cheney moved to Chelsea, Massachusetts

7.  Ibid., 165-68.
8.  ROGERS, *The Story of Two Lives*, 80-83.
9.  Ibid., 4.    10.   Ibid., 80.
11.  *Half-Hours With the Best Composers*, ed. Karl KLAUSER

(Boston: J.B. Millet, 1894).

12.  Adrienne Fried BLOCK, *Amy Beach, Passionate Victorian: The Life and Work of an American Composer, 1867-1944* (New York: Oxford University Press, 1998).

in 1871, and spent the remainder of her childhood and her young adulthood in the Boston area. Unlike Clara Rogers, Amy did not study at a European conservatory, but received her musical training locally. From 1876 to 1882 Amy Cheney was the pupil of the pianist Ernst Perabo, who had been a contemporary of Clara Barnett at the Leipzig Conservatory.[13]

Rogers does not mention Perabo in her memoirs, but it is likely that they had met in Leipzig. Both had been piano students of Moscheles. Since Clara Barnett was often chosen to perform on the conservatory's evening recitals, Perabo probably heard her play. He certainly heard her sing in Boston; Clara Doria and Perabo were frequent performers on the Harvard Symphony concerts, and they appeared on the same program at least once, in November 1873.[14] Perabo may have introduced his promising student to his former conservatory classmate.

If Perabo did not introduce them, it is possible that Rogers and Amy Cheney met at one of Amy's performances. In 1880 Amy played for Henry Wadsworth Longfellow in much the same way that the young Felix Mendelssohn had played for Goethe.[15] In her memoirs, Rogers describes such an event:

> I recall, when once at (Longfellow's) request I went to Craigie House to hear two little "child wonders" play the piano, how he had prepared beforehand some neat little packages of sweets for the children … I still see with my mind's eye the venerable picture of that gentle, fatherly face bending over the little ones perched on his knee.[16]

Could one of the "child wonders" have been Amy Cheney?

The Cheney family would almost certainly have heard Clara Rogers sing during the 1870s, and they would have known her reputation as a teacher, and, perhaps, as a composer. They themselves may have suggested that Amy seek Clara's autograph for her album. In fact, the many similarities in the careers of the two composers suggest the possibility that Clara Rogers' life or work may have been offered to Amy Cheney as a model.

Both young women played similar repertoire during their years as prodigy-pianists. At the time of her debut, Amy Cheney was a pupil of Carl Baermann, a pianist whose training differed from that of Perabo; he had studied with Liszt rather than with Moscheles.[17] Nevertheless, Amy performed Moscheles' Concerto in G Minor at her first public concert on 24 October 1883. Clara Barnett had studied the same Moscheles concerto with Louis Plaidy in Leipzig. Moreover, Clara had played the first movement

13.  Block lists Perabo's years of study in Leipzig as 1858–65 (BLOCK, *Amy Beach, Passionate Victorian*, 319, n. 13). Details of Amy Beach's early life may be found in BLOCK, 21–33, and in Walter S. JENKINS, *The Remarkable Mrs. Beach, American Composer: A Biographical Account Based on Her Diaries, Letters, Newspaper Clippings, and Personal Reminiscences*, ed. John H.

BARON (Warren, MI: Harmonie Park Press, 1994), 5–13.
14.  John Sullivan DWIGHT, "First Symphony Concert," *Dwight's Journal of Music* 33/15 (15 November 1873): 126.
15.  BLOCK, *Amy Beach, Passionate Victorian*, 28.
16.  ROGERS, *Memories of a Musical Career*, 458–59.
17.  BLOCK, *Amy Beach, Passionate Victorian*, 28.

of the Chopin Concerto in F Minor on a *Haupt-Prüfung* concert in the Gewandhaus on 23 April 1860. In her memoirs, she mentions performing that work before Alfred Jäell and Salomon Jadassohn, and receiving a handwritten score and a complimentary letter from Jadassohn the next day.[18] It was this concerto that Amy Cheney performed with the Boston Symphony in April 1885. The Moscheles concerto was an obvious selection for a European-trained teacher to make for a student playing her debut concert. The musically sophisticated Chopin concerto was a less obvious choice. One wonders whether the story of the teenaged Clara's triumph with that concerto might have been a factor in Amy's choice of the Chopin.

In December 1885 the eighteen-year-old Amy Cheney married Henry Harris Aubrey Beach, a prominent surgeon and a widower who was twenty-four years her senior. Like the Rogerses, the Beaches were married at Trinity Church, and both couples were friends of its famous rector, Phillips Brooks. At the outset, Amy Beach's life at least superficially resembled that of Clara Rogers. Both Rogers and Beach married well-known professional men; following their marriages, both women found ways to reconcile marriage and art. Unlike Amy Beach, Clara Rogers continued to teach after her marriage. Both women agreed to curtail their concert performing. The thirty-four-year-old Rogers sang only for benefit and amateur events. Beach, whose professional career was only two years old, severely limited her solo performances after 1885, although she continued to participate in ensemble programs and in concerts in which she played her own compositions. While she kept the royalties she earned from her compositions, she donated her concert fees to charity.[19] Both Clara and Amy held musicales in their music rooms and, with their husbands' encouragement, both musicians came to view composition as a serious vocation.

In 1885 both women were composers of songs. By 1900 their careers diverged significantly. Following her recognition at the World's Columbian Exhibition (1893), Amy Beach became known nationally, even internationally, as a composer of large choral and orchestral works, while Rogers remained a locally or regionally respected vocal composer. Rogers believed that her lack of early training put her at a disadvantage:

Had I acquired early in life a good technique in writing for instruments (as a student in

---

18. Rogers describes her study of the Moscheles concerto (*Memories of a Musical Career*, 125) and mentions performing two Chopin concerti, the F Minor before Jadassohn and Jäell (ibid., 132) and the E Minor at her final examination recital (ibid., 190). Her student records verify her performance of the Concerto in F Minor, first movement, on 23 April 1860 (*"Einladung und Programm zur Haupt-Prüfung im Conservatorium der Musik zu Leipzig," Hochschulbibliothek, Bereich Archiv, Hochschule für Musik*

*und Theater*, Leipzig.)

19. In her excellent alternative analyses of the relationship between Amy and Henry Beach ("Two Ways of Looking at a Marriage"), Block states that Amy performed one annual solo recital after her marriage (*Amy Beach, Passionate Victorian*, 47–48). A third, slightly different picture of the marriage and its effect on Amy Beach's performing career is offered in Jenkins, 19-23.

Germany) I really think I might have accomplished something worth while in orchestral composition .... I have had to content myself with writing music in the simpler forms, the most ambitious of my achievements – since my callow attempt at a quartette for strings when I was thirteen—being two sonatas in classic form.[20]

But Beach had received even less formal training than had Rogers. Her early works comprised small piano pieces, chorales, and songs. There was no youthful string quartet to suggest an unusual gift for composition. Aside from a year's study of harmony with Junius Hill in Boston, Beach was entirely, but systematically, self-taught. Her notebook, held in the Boston Public Library, attests to the rigor of her program of study, and also to her independence of thought.[21] In the early 1890s she began to compose in the larger forms. The final decade of the nineteenth century saw the premieres of her Mass in E-flat Major, op. 5 (in 1892), her "Gaelic" Symphony, op. 32 (in 1896), and her violin sonata, op. 34 (in 1897).

While Clara Rogers never attempted to compose orchestral music, she did compose major works in sonata form. Her published and unpublished works in this genre were familiar to her peers. The critic Louis Elson describes her work in *The History of American Music*:

> Among foreign women-composers who have settled in the United States, Mrs. Clara Kathleen Rogers ... holds high rank .... Her compositions comprise a string quartette, a violin sonata, a violoncello sonata, a large number of songs, and a few piano works."[22]

The violin and cello sonatas and a *Fantasia for Viol d'Amor and Harp or Piano* probably date from the last two decades of the nineteenth century.

With the exception of piano character-pieces and songs, Roger and Beach rarely composed in the same genres. Within their vocal *œuvres*, they set the same text only three times. Both composers set the popular Browning verses, "Ah, Love, But a Day" and "The Year's at the Spring." A less obvious choice of text was Victor Hugo's "*L'aube naît et ta porte est close*," which both women set in translation. In instrumental music, their only common genre was the violin sonata. That Beach found Rogers' sonata to be a significant work is demonstrated by her letter of 1893.

Clara Rogers preserved the three letters from Amy Beach in the first of two scrapbooks of correspondence. On a slip of paper in the first scrapbook, she notes that the books are not autograph albums, but, rather, are "records of interesting friendships and acquaintances."[23] The Beach - Rogers correspondence took place over a brief three-year

---

20. ROGERS, *The Story of Two Lives*, 81.
21. Amy BEACH, Notebook, Music Department, Boston Public Library. A discussion of her self-tutelage, as revealed in the notebook, is found in BLOCK, *Amy Beach, Passionate Victorian*, 54-57.

22. Louis C. ELSON, *The History of American Music* (New York: Macmillan, 1925, repr., New York: Burt Franklin, 1971), 307.
23. ROGERS, Note in Scrapbooks, vol. 1, op. cit. (n. 3).

period, 1892-95, and ended with a cordial invitation (17 May 1895) to Rogers to join the New York Manuscript Society, of which Beach was corresponding secretary.[24]

The purpose of Beach's first letter, dated 31 January 1892, was to send Rogers a copy of Beach's Mass, in which Rogers had, "according to the reports of several friends," expressed "so kind an interest."[25] To the twentieth-century reader, the letter is surprising in two ways. First, it is obvious that Beach and Rogers did not know each other well; Beach had learned of Rogers' interest through their mutual friends rather than from the composer herself. Second, it is interesting that both inquiry and response occurred at so late a date, one week before the work's scheduled performance by the Handel and Haydn Society (7 February 1892). Beach had completed the Mass in 1889, and the piano-vocal score had been in print for two years. Its publisher was also Rogers' publisher, Arthur P. Schmidt. Beach's letter does allow for the possibility that Schmidt had sent Rogers a score, but their mutual acquaintances must have told her that Rogers had none, otherwise there would be no purpose to the letter. It seems curious that Rogers did not express her interest earlier, and it seems equally curious that Beach did not send her colleague a copy until the week before the work's premiere.

More than twenty months later, on 4 October 1893, Beach sent a second letter in response to a present sent by Clara Rogers—a copy of Rogers' violin sonata. This letter is warmer in tone. In it, Beach calls the sonata "a most delightful welcome" for her as she returned to Boston, and praises the work for its "practicable" violin and piano parts, and for the fact that the "interest. . .continues so steadily to the end." The second paragraph is especially interesting. Here, Beach praises specific aspects of the sonata: "I find the melodious second theme of the first movement often singing in my ears, and the contrast of that with the first theme, as well as the working out, are alike effective."[26]

Even more significant in the second paragraph is the following statement: "It is delightful to know that much-abused woman is equal to such work as this, and I am proud of it and of you." This is a statement that could only be made by a woman who had become a prominent woman composer, as well as a champion of women's rights to be composers. It is the statement of a composer of stature to an able composer of lesser stature. It is apparent that the events of 1892-93 had altered the professional lives of Clara Rogers and Amy Beach.

The World's Columbian Exposition in Chicago was dedicated in October 1892. Official opening ceremonies took place in the Women's Building on 1 May 1893, and the Women's Musical Congress convened at the Memorial Art Palace on 5 July of that year. Bertha Palmer, chairman of the Board of Lady Managers, had originally commissioned

24. Block, Amy Beach, Passionate Victorian, 91.

25. Beach to Rogers, 31 January 1892. In Rogers, Scrapbooks, vol. 1, , op. cit. (n. 3). Printed by permission of The MacDowell Colony, Inc. (Copyright 1999, The MacDowell Colony, Inc.)

26. Beach to Rogers, 4 October 1893. Printed by permission of The MacDowell Colony, Inc. (Copyright 1999, The MacDowell Colony, Inc.)

Beach to write a choral work for the October dedication ceremonies.[27] Over Palmer's protest, Beach's *Festival Jubilate* was removed from the dedication program and was performed instead at the May opening ceremonies for the Women's Building. In spite of the controversy over the *Jubilate*, it received both public and critical acclaim, as did the works Beach presented on the three days of the Women's Musical Congress. Four of Clara Rogers' *Browning Songs*, Op. 27, appeared on the 6 July program for the congress, and she was mentioned in at least one contemporary newspaper.[28] However, most reviews focused their attention on Beach, as America's "representative musical woman."[29] Rogers' own account may reflect her reaction to Beach's celebrity. Her description of the fair in *The Story of Two Lives* omits any mention of the exposition's music.[30]

Beach herself had paved the way for her acceptance as "representative musical woman" in her public reply to Antonín Dvořák shortly after the dedication of the fair. On 30 November 1892, three days before the premiere of Beach's aria from *Maria Stuart* in New York, an interview with Dvořák appeared in the *Boston Post*. In it, Dvořák, who had come to New York to direct the National Conservatory of Music, challenged the ability of American women, indeed, of women generally, to compose music:

> I have been asked frequently what I think of America musically.... You have plenty of music here but I find that the musicians are all Germans. What America wants is education, musically....That is the work of the conservatory not to produce amateurs—but musicians who follow it as an art, as a profession. Here... all the ladies play. It is well, it is nice. But I am afraid they cannot help us much. They have not the creative power....There (in Bohemia) everybody plays, and especially the men.[31]

Beach's reply, published in an interview in the *Boston Daily Traveller* on 10 December 1892, was politely scathing:

> Mr. Dvořák, like Rubinstein, takes the position... that women are lacking in the creative power. So broad and sweeping a statement from one occupying so prominent a position... naturally carries weight, but it is reasonable to suppose that Mr. Dvořák, in the turmoil incident to his locating in an entirely new country... has scarcely had time to consider the subject in all its bearings.[32]

27. For an account of the Exposition's gender and musical politics, see Ann E. FELDMAN, "Being Heard: Women Composers and Patrons at the 1893 World's Columbian Exposition," *Notes* 47/1 (September 1990): 7-20. Block discusses the controversy in *Amy Beach, Passionate Victorian*, 77-83.

28. Clipping, *Boston Times*, 16 July 1893. In BEACH, Box 11, Green Scrapbook, 14, Beach Collection, Dimond Library, University of New Hampshire.

29. Typical is the clipping from *The Beacon*, 8 July 1893, in which Beach is called "pre-eminent" in the "cultivation of the finer qualities," as well as "gifted" and "devoted

to her art." In BEACH, Box 11, Green Scrapbook, 14, Beach Collection, Dimond Library, University of New Hampshire.

30. ROGERS, *The Story of Two Lives*, 226.

31. "Women Can't Help. Dvořák Says They Have Not Creative Talent. He's Talking About Music," *Boston Post*, 30 November 1892 (Massachusetts Genealogical and Investigative Research Services, http://www.mass-doc.com).

32. "American Music... Some Testimony on Woman's Ability as a Composer," *Boston Daily Traveller*, 10 December 1892. Clipping, without title, in BEACH, Box 12, Blue

The reply continued with a carefully researched argument in defense of women composers. In her discussion of Beach's response, Adrienne Fried Block writes, "To her newly won status as America's leading woman composer, she now added the role of advocate and spokesperson for women...."[33]

The letter to Rogers on 4 October, 1893 attests to Beach's acceptance both of her status and of her role. It also attests to her admiration for Rogers' work as the composer of well-constructed music in a serious form, that of the sonata for piano and violin.

Beach appears not to have known Rogers' sonata before October 1893. She herself had not yet written a work in sonata form. The "Gaelic" Symphony was still in the future; she would begin its composition in March 1894. Beach composed her own violin sonata between the symphony's completion and its premiere; specifically, between 11 March and 6 June 1896.[34] Could she have kept the Rogers sonata in mind, and used it as a model for her own sonata for violin and piano?

Although it was published in 1893 Clara Rogers' sonata was probably composed during the spring of 1886. In *The Story of Two Lives*, Clara Rogers states that she wrote her violin sonata to "express in music my new state of mind" after her discovery of Theosophism.[35] She gives no date, but she implies that she began work on the sonata shortly before her trip to Bayreuth in the summer of 1886. With the violinist Charles Martin Loeffler, she performed the sonata on many occasions, most notably at a meeting of the Boston Manuscript Club on 19 January 1888. A program signed by the composer may be found in the archives of the Isabella Stewart Gardner Museum.[36]

Since the sonata is not yet well known, it is useful to give a brief description of its organization. The opening *Allegro* is a dramatic sonata-allegro in D Minor (Rogers originally called the work "*Sonata Dramatico*"). A slow movement in A Major, marked *Andante con espressione*, follows, and the work concludes with a modified sonata-rondo, marked *Allegro giojoso* (sic), in D Major. The first movement's principal theme contains three seminal elements. The first element is the descending fourth that opens the movement. In the opening phrase the fourth descends from d' to a, returning to d' after a trill on the leading tone. The key relationship of the three movements is thus stated at the outset. Initially, the falling fourth is also combined with the second seminal element, a dotted figure, which in the first movement occurs almost exclusively on the first beat of the measure. In measure 5, the soprano voice contains the triad that serves as the third unifying element (example 1). These three elements are the building blocks for thematic material in all three movements.

---

Gilded Scrapbook, 84-85, Beach Collection, Dimond Library, University of New Hampshire. Cited in BLOCK, *Amy Beach, Passionate Victorian*, 72, 332, n. 42.

33. BLOCK, *Amy Beach, Passionate Victorian*, 73.

34. Ibid., 86, 113.

35. ROGERS, *The Story of Two Lives*, 155.

36. Papers of Charles Martin Loeffler, Isabella Stewart Gardner Library.

**Example 1**    Clara Kathleen ROGERS, *Sonata in D Minor for Piano and Violin*, op. 25. I, mm. 1–8 (Arthur P. Schmidt, 1893)

Rogers' pithy first movement themes fit Percy Goetschius' description of Amy Beach's melodies. Writing in *The Musician*, he compares the latter to Brahms' "rugged, almost uninviting" themes, chosen to "supply the elements of pregnancy and strength, while the beauty, interest and force of the composition must be the reward of skillful manipulation."[37] It is in these very "rugged" themes that the Beach and Rogers first movements most resemble each other.

Rogers begins her sonata with the downbeat dotted figure shown in example 1. The figure returns in the second measure (the second measure is an exact replication of the first) and in the third measure. While Beach's sonata opens with a slow, static principal theme, she begins her transition, marked *Animato* (m. 33), with a vigorous dotted figure on the downbeat, similar to Rogers' principal theme. Like Rogers, Beach repeats the rhythm in the second measure of the phrase (m. 34), although she uses a contrasting rhythm in measure 35. While Beach's dotted motive does not encompass a descending

37. Percy GOETSCHIUS, "Their Works (clipping from article)," *The Musician* (September 1899). In BEACH, Box 12, Blue Gilded Scrapbook, 132-33, Beach Collection, Dimond Library, University of New Hampshire.

fourth, her repetition of the figure in m. 34 begins an augmented fourth above its original statement. Thus, Rogers' principal theme and Beach's transition are motivically linked
(example 2).

**Example 2**  Amy BEACH, *Sonata in A Minor for Pianoforte and Violin*, op. 34, I,
mm. 33–36 (Arthur P. Schmidt, 1899)

Although Beach delays the emphatic, downbeat employment of the dotted figure
until the transition, similarities do exist between the two sonatas' principal groups. Like
Rogers, Beach begins her sonata in a minor key, in triple meter, and at a metronome
marking of 120 to the quarter note. Beach's principal theme opens with an ascending
fifth, the complement of Rogers' falling fourth. The dotted rhythm appears in mm. 5
and 6, foreshadowing its more decisive statement in m. 33 (example 3). Moreover, just as
Rogers touches briefly on the relative major in m. 5 (example 1), Beach begins the sequence
in m. 17 in the relative major.

Perhaps the most important similarity between the two sonatas is formal. In both
sonatas, the transitional section is marked by an abrupt change to a quicker tempo. Beach's
tempo indication is *Animato* (example 2); in the Rogers work, the transition is marked
*Molto più mosso* (example 4). Both transitional sections are relatively weighty. Rogers' brief,
sixteen-measure principal theme leads to a transition section thirty-one measures long;
Beach balances her principal group of thirty-two measures with an equally long transition. In both cases, the active, dramatic section is the transition; the principal group has
an almost introductory character.

Finally, both composers employ modal themes in their sonatas. The opening
octaves of Beach's first movement (example 3) outline a principal theme that could easily
be in the Aeolian mode, since no defining leading tone appears until m. 12. In the answering phrase, the A Minor tonality becomes clear. While the opening phrase of Rogers'
first movement is decisively in minor, the second phrase begins in the relative major
(example 1, mm. 5 and 6). Taken without its harmonization, however, the motive in mm.

**Example 3** BEACH, *Sonata for Pianoforte and Violin,* I, mm. 1–20

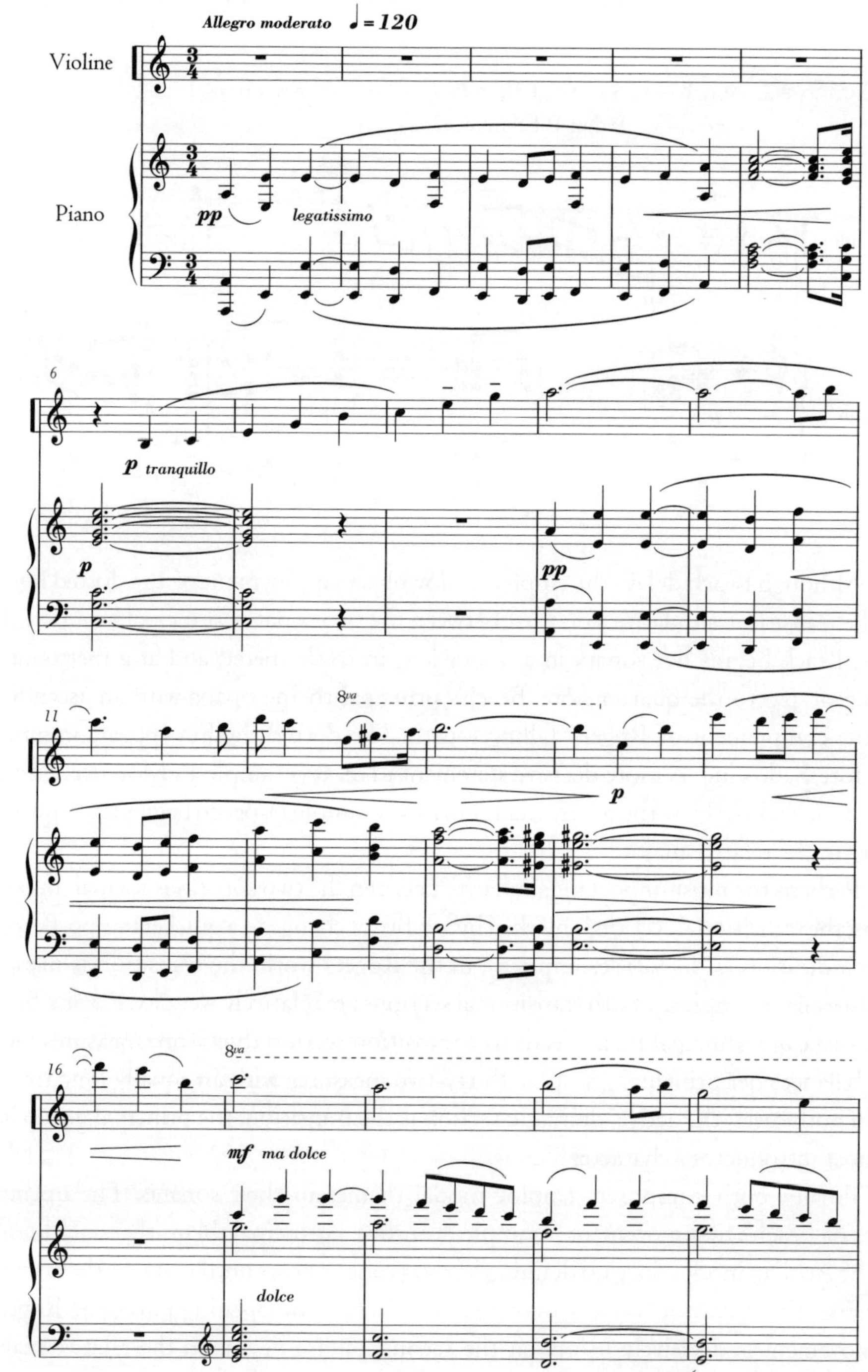

**Example 4** ROGERS, *Sonata for Piano and Violin*, I, mm. 16–23

5 and 6 is pentatonic. It is this motive that Rogers uses in the modal B theme of her second movement (example 5, mm. 42–44).

Beach does not repeat her modal principal theme in the other movements. However, like Rogers, she re-introduces the modal element in her second movement (example 6). Thus, both composers employ a tonal-modal (or modal-tonal) contrast in the second movement.

It is even possible that Clara Rogers' violin sonata was one of Beach's early models for the use of folk-like melodies in the context of sonata form. Its delivery to Beach in the autumn of 1893 was certainly timely. During the previous May, in a *Boston Herald* article, Beach had advocated the use of English, Irish, and Scottish folk music as a basis for American art music.[38] Beach encountered Rogers' sonata less than five months after expressing this opinion, two months before the premiere of Dvořák's "New World" Symphony,

38.  Clipping, *The Boston Herald*, 28 May 1893. In BEACH, Box 12, Blue Gilded Scrapbook, 61, Beach Collection, Dimond Library, University of New Hampshire.

**Example 5**    ROGERS, *Sonata for Piano and Violin*, II, mm. 40–44

and only three months before she began the research for her own "Gaelic" symphony.

The similarities between the two sonatas are the more striking when one considers that the general style of the two composers is quite different. Although both are associated with the Second New England School, Rogers represents an earlier, mid-Romantic approach. Her training in part-writing led her to treat the piano as a quartet-texture in chamber music. Beach, on the other hand, used a late-Romantic pianism even in vocal accompaniments and chamber music. In analyzing her style, Jeanell Wise Brown found that Beach preferred Lisztian piano textures such as "thick block chords," octaves, and perpetual figuration in her piano music, using counterpoint only as a "secondary texture."[39] With the exception of the dramatic *fugato* section in the last movement, Beach employs such piano textures in the violin sonata. In the Rogers sonata, the piano is an equal partner; in the Beach work, it more than rivals the violin's virtuosity.

Franz Kneisel and Amy Beach first performed the Beach sonata on 4 January 1897, two years before its publication but nine years after the Manuscript Club performance of the Rogers sonata. Beach remained an important force in American music for many years thereafter, and she continued to write chamber music. Block points out that the Quintet for Piano and Strings, op. 67 shows the influence of Brahms' piano quintet in much the same way that this author believes the violin sonata reflects Rogers' sonata.[40]

Clara Rogers' interest in composition waned around 1902, when, buoyed by the success of her book, *The Philosophy of Singing*, she joined the faculty of the New England Conservatory of Music.[41] At that time she had published most of her songs. The unpublished autographs of her chamber works, along with her scrapbooks of letters, became

39. Jeanell Wise BROWN, *Amy Beach and Her Chamber Music: Biography, Documents, Style* (Metuchen, NJ: The Scarecrow Press, 1994), 156-61.
40. BLOCK, *Amy Beach, Passionate Victorian*, 127-29.
41. Clara Kathleen ROGERS, *The Philosophy of Singing* (New York: Harper and Brothers Publishers, 1893). In an e-mail communication, Jeanne A. Morrow, Director of Libraries, New England Conservatory, stated that Rogers was a faculty member from 1902 to 1903 and from 1905 to 1913.

**Example 6**   BEACH, *Sonata for Pianoforte and Violin*, II, mm. 73–76

part of Henry Rogers' bequest to Harvard University's Widener Library.

Rogers' influence on Beach seems to have existed, if briefly, during the early portion of Beach's career. The coincidences of details in their Boston careers and private lives may imply that someone—a teacher or a parent—considered Clara's life as a musician, composer and "housewife" to be worthy of Amy's emulation. In 1911, following the deaths of her husband and mother, Beach left that life behind and became a concert artist and composer of international reputation.

Beach's letters to Rogers imply a closer connection between the composers. One can read in the letters that their relationship was professional, not social; that both composers took their art and their profession seriously; and that they shared a belief that "much-abused woman" was capable of great things. During the 1880s and 1890s, at least, Clara Rogers was a valued colleague, if not a personal friend, of Amy Beach.

Ultimately, Rogers' greatest influence upon the younger composer was musical. In using Rogers' sonata to provide a springboard for her own, Beach chose a model that was creative in its manipulation of form and of motives, and modern in its use of folk-like melodies. Further study of the chamber works of both composers will no doubt yield a greater understanding of the roles played by Amy Beach and Clara Rogers in the development of American chamber music.

* I would like to thank my colleagues, Delight Malitsky and Dieter Wulfhorst, for their collaboration in the ongoing research into the life and music of Clara Kathleen Rogers, and for their inspired performances of her works. Fredric W. Wilson, Curator of the Harvard Theatre Collection, and Annette Fern, Research and Reference Librarian of that collection, have my gratitude for their assistance with the Collection of Clara Barnett Rogers and Henry Munroe Rogers. I wish to thank Daniel O. Cheever of the Douglas and Helena Milne Special Collections and Archives, Dimond Library, University of New Hampshire, for his assistance with the Amy Beach Collection. I am grateful to Cheryl A. Young, Executive Director of the MacDowell Colony, for permission to quote from Amy Beach's letters.

H. Colin Slim

# Stravinsky's *Scherzo ... à la russe* and its Two-Piano Origins

ALMOST HALF A CENTURY AGO (and admittedly more than slightly tongue-tied), I happily drove with Igor Stravinsky on Sunday morning, 5 October 1952, from the Hotel Vancouver to the Orpheum Theatre to hear him rehearse the Vancouver Symphony in, among other works, his *Scherzo ... à la russe.* The several signed business contracts by which he sold this *Scherzo* (and his *Sonata for Two Pianos*) in 1944 came my way in 1981 at London.[1] Some years later, in 1995, I successfully bid at Christie's in London for his holograph arrangement of the *Scherzo* for two pianos,[2] which he signed on its final page: "I Str. / June 44 / Hollywood."

That Stravinsky composed at the piano is well known. In 1935 he affirmed, "I do compose at the piano and I do not regret it," and in 1962 he deemed the instrument, "the center of my life and the fulcrum of all my musical discoveries."[3] Almost as well known is his practice of making arrangements of his own orchestral works for four hands or for two pianos so that he might test them. Three instances may suffice, one found in his correspondence, one in his conversation books with Robert Craft, and a third hitherto undisclosed. In letters to Willy Strecker in 1938 about compositional and editorial progress on his *Concerto in E flat* ("Dumbarton Oaks"), on 28 January, well before finishing its third movement, he writes: "What about the 4-hand transcription of my concerto?... I would like to play that transcription with him [his pianist son, Soulima] before fixing its final form for the edition..." And, on 20 March, "I am busy finishing the instrumentation of the second movement" (for which the two-piano reduction has just been completed)."[4] In 1963 he told Craft: "All my life I have tried out

1. Purchased from Burnett Simeone, London, 17 June 1981.

2. Purchased through J & J Lubrano, Great Barrington, MA, bidding for me at Christie's, *Important Autograph Letters, Manuscripts and Music from Richard Monckton Milnes Collection and other properties* (London: 29 June 1995),

lot 476.

3. See Charles M. JOSEPH, *Stravinsky and the Piano* (Ann Arbor, MI: UMI Research Press, 1983), 239-40.

4. *Stravinsky, Selected Correspondence*, ed. Robert CRAFT, 3 vols. (New York: Alfred A. Knopf, 1982-85), 3:256-59. In Vera STRAVINSKY and Robert CRAFT, *Stravinsky in Pictures*

my music as I have composed it, orchestral as well as any other kind, four hands at one keyboard."[5]

My late good friend, Dorothy Ellis McQuoid Hopper (1911-98), documented this practice for me in 1994. She had first met Stravinsky at Los Angeles' Union Station in mid December 1939 through his long-time friend and his then secretary, Alexis Fyodorovich Kall (1878-1948), her piano teacher since 1923. She and her first husband, Edwin McQuoid (1910-50), befriended the Stravinskys shortly after they arrived on 23 May 1940 at Kall's decrepit house, 143 South Gramercy, Los Angeles.[6] A formidable pianist and sight-reader even in her mid 80s, she recalled playing that summer of 1940 with Stravinsky in his rented bungalow at 124 South Swall, Beverly Hills, portions of his *Symphony in C* (including its final movement) from his piano four-hand manuscript, she taking mostly piano primo. Although unfinished, such a manuscript indeed survives and may well be the very one they used.[7]

Just when Mrs. McQuoid's four-hand performance with the composer took place cannot be exactly determined. The Stravinskys did not move to South Swall until 6 June 1940 (his piano arrived the following day) and she herself was away from Los Angeles during the last ten days of that month and the first ten of July.[8] In Mexico with Vera from 18 July until 9 August, Stravinsky only completed the last movement ten days later after returning to Los Angeles.[9] That their performance may have taken place in June could result from the number of times "Dorothy" appears in Vera's diary in June (the last one on the 17th, none at all in July, and only a few times in late August, September, and October).[10] The Stravinskys were away from Los Angeles 6-13 September and departed for Chicago on 2 November, not returning until early the ensuing February. Whatever the precise date may have been, Stravinsky's desire that summer to play his new symphony *à quatre mains* during or shortly after its composition was evidently satisfied.

and Documents, (New York: Simon and Schuster, 1978), 340, Craft rightly observes that this two-piano transcription "offers a view into Stravinsky's working methods."

5. Igor STRAVINSKY and Robert CRAFT, *Dialogues and A Diary* (Garden City, NY: Doubleday, 1963), 74.

6. *Dearest Bubushkin: The correspondence of Vera and Igor Stravinsky, 1921-1954, with excerpts from Vera Stravinsky's diaries, 1922-1971*, ed. Robert CRAFT and trans. Lucia DAVIDOVA (New York: Thames and Hudson, 1985), 23, 26 May and 9 June 1940; plate 90 reproduces a cropped photograph of Vera and the McQuoids taken by Stravinsky in mid June, of which Mrs. Hopper owned a complete exemplar. Kall (who in 1940 recalled knowing Stravinsky since 1900) lived on South Gramercy from 1935 through 1941, offering hospitality there during Stravinsky's visits to Los Angeles in 1935, 1937, and 1939. See Dorothy ELLIS

[McQUOID], "Dr. Alexis Kall, a Gentleman and a Scholar," *The Baton of Phi Beta Kappa* (March 1939): 19-21, 26; and M. T. ZAROTSCHENZEFF, "Fingalova Peshchera. K 70-letnemu yubileyu professora A.F. Kal'," *Novaya Zarya* [Los Angeles] (28 January 1948): 1-3.

7. Paris, Bibliothèque nationale de France, Réserve, Vma Ms. 1039, cited by Christian GOUBAULT, *Igor Strawinsky*, (Paris: H. Champion, 1991), 252.

8. On her, see *Who's Who in California* 1 (2 years, 1942-43) (Los Angeles, CA: 1941[sic]), 277, and Robin HINCH, "Music was theme of Dorothy Hopper's life; Obituary," *The Orange County Register* (28 February 1998), Metro section: 7.

9. Stephen WALSH, *The Music of Stravinsky* (Oxford: Clarendon Press, 1993), 304, no. 79.

10. This information stems from Vera's diary for 1940, preserved in the Paul Sacher Foundation, Basle.

Thus the *Scherzo . . . à la russe* which he edited and had published in three versions (jazz band, symphony orchestra, and two pianos) can scarcely be considered atypical, except perhaps in the abundance and dispersal of its materials. Tiresome obstacles to studying its surviving sketches, versions, drafts, transparencies, ozalids, and editions lie in their geographical dispersal to Basle, Washington, and Laguna Beach (the latter collection, soon to be in Vancouver, Canada, however). The largest cache of relevant holdings was acquired in 1983 by the Paul Sacher Foundation at Basle from the Stravinsky sale that year.[11] Pertinent materials now held by the Library of Congress in Washington were donated to it and described by Robert Craft *c.*1989 in his typed catalog there of his library.[12] The fourteen pages of holograph transparencies of the *Scherzo* for two pianos which I own here in Laguna Beach have not hitherto been studied. Only brief descriptions have appeared in auction sales catalogs.[13]

Essential information about the formation of the *Scherzo . . . à la russe* first appeared in 1978.[14] Craft postulated a compositional order for the *Scherzo*'s two trios as: trio 2, and then trio 1, and opined that the scherzo proper, the "opening portion of the *Scherzo*, in its first form, was a piece for two pianos, the opus. . . actually made up of three separate numbers." Although acknowledging that Stravinsky "initially envisioned [the *Scherzo*] as a two-piano piece and in fact performed [it] as such with [Nadia] Boulanger," Charles M. Joseph said nothing further about it in his 1983 book about Stravinsky's piano music.[15]

New discoveries by Richard Taruskin about the *Scherzo*'s origins appeared in 1996. He discussed some sketch materials, linked the genesis of trio 2 with music once intended for the 1943 movie, *The North Star* (on a script by Lillian Hellman), and located the thematic content for the entire *Scherzo* in a late nineteenth-century anthology of Russian folk melodies purchased by Stravinsky in Los Angeles, probably late in 1942.[16]

Also in 1996, Christoph Flamm signed his two virtually identical prefaces to his editions of the *Scherzo*'s versions for orchestra.[17] Including two facsimiles, his prefaces give useful information about materials now held by the Paul Sacher Foundation.

11. See *Igor Strawinsky Musikmanuskripte*, ed. Hans Jörg JANS (Winterthur: Amadeus Verlag, 1989), 34.

12. See its parts IV and V.

13. See Sotheby's *Music and Continental Manuscripts* (London: 16-17 May 1991), lot 475 and above, n.2, respectively.

14. *Pictures and Documents*, 373.

15. *Stravinsky and the Piano*, 227.

16. *Stravinsky and the Russian Traditions. A Biography of the Works Through Mavra* (Berkeley: University of California Press, 1996), 2 vols. continuously paginated, 1623-32. In addition, the beginning of no. 51 in Bernard's collection surely influenced the central E-flat section of trio 2. For a probable date that Stravinsky purchased the anthology, see

Bubushkin, 4 November 1942, affirmed by CRAFT, *Stravinsky: Glimpses of a Life* (London: Lime Tree, 1992), 300.

17. *Scherzo . . . à la russe. Version for Jazz ensemble* (1944), and its *Symphonic Version* (1945), both ed. Christoph FLAMM (London: Ernst Eulenburg, 1999). The latter, first printed in 1945 by Associated Music Publishers, New York, was reprinted *c.*1954 (though reset) by B. Schotts Söhne, Mainz, London, and New York. Despite GOUBAULT, *Strawinsky*, 260, who cites an AMP 1945 edition of the former and WALSH, *Stravinsky*, 304, no. 89, who gives a 1949 edition, no such editions apparently exist. I thank Mr. Walsh for generously sending me copies of Flamm's two editions.

Both Taruskin and Flamm paid more than passing attention to Stravinsky's various drafts for two pianos. Even so, the history and editing of the two-piano version, published only in October 1945 (at the same time as the arrangement for symphony orchestra), remains to be told. Connections of sketches to versions for two pianos, chronological relationships of the two-piano versions to those for orchestra, and their own internal evolution as shown by Stravinsky's back-and-forth editing between and among my transparencies and his several ozalid copies made from them, need clarification. The following discussion of the *Scherzo* for two pianos refers to Craft's, Taruskin's, and Flamm's remarks about it and the arrangements for jazz band and symphony orchestra. Necessarily, some of their steps will be retaken and some of their findings restated.

Based on my research trips to Washington and Basle in 1999, a summary of holdings there (many of which preceded even the first fair copy for two pianos) will prove useful. The order in which these are taken up here, namely, scherzo proper, trio 1, and trio 2, is solely for convenience. My order of discussion will not necessarily be the order in which Stravinsky composed them.

## Sketches

The earliest surviving sketches and their initial elaborations now at Basle support Craft's assertion that the *Scherzo* originated as "three separate numbers." Sketches for the scherzo proper appear in a folder inscribed and underlined by Stravinsky (perhaps in 1949 when he and Craft began cataloging his manuscripts): "Scherzo a la Russe / Some Sketches / 1943." It includes a single undated sheet copied in pencil of seven measures in G major.[18] By means of clever manipulation and rhythmic shifts, the tune in this sketch (except for its discarded third measure of repeated notes) was later to generate the entire scherzo proper (see Example 1).

Trio 1 is represented only by a sketch page with its main theme. Stravinsky copied it in ink and even in the same key (F major) directly from an anthology of harmonized Russian folk melodies he had purchased in Los Angeles.[19] Taruskin has identified this anthology as the source not only for the scherzo proper (including the G-major sketch discussed above) and for both its trios, but also for the contemporaneous *Sonata for Two Pianos* (the latter begun in August 1943).

For trio 2, the Sacher Foundation Library in Basle holds a large folded sheet on the outer side of which Stravinsky wrote: "*Detskii khorik* / IStr / Jan 43 / 2nd TRIO /

18.  *Stravinsky*, [1634], Ex. E.9a. Professor Taruskin graciously allowed me access to his original transcriptions. Made in 1982-83 when the Stravinsky manuscripts were still in New York, they contain a few minor errors and omissions. Compare, for example, his example E.5 at

[1624] with the facsimile printed by FLAMM, *Scherzo*, [XI].
19.  TARUSKIN, *Stravinsky*, 1632-33, apparently missed the sketch page itself ("sketches do not survive in the Archive"), although in Ex. E.8a he correctly identified its source.

**Example 1**    Stravinsky, *Scherzo à la russe* (1943-44), mm. 1-37

'Scherzo a la Russe' /. The inner page contains 63 measures of an A-major duet for the "little children" copied in pencil on staves which Stravinsky had ruled with his rastrum. Dating this sheet: "1–18"[1943], he designated the voice parts as: "Disc.[anti]" and "Alti." He gave two metronome markings and their timings: $\downarrow$ = 112 – 1'04", written above: $\downarrow$ = 108 – 1'08"; he repeated the latter timing at the bottom of the page.[20] Taruskin suggests that these timings refer to the projected use of the "Little Children's Chorus" in the movie *The North Star*, film music for which Stravinsky was approached by the Samuel Goldwyn Studios in 1942 (probably at the end of November). Vera Stravinsky's diary reports the collapse of the project on 18 January 1943,[21] the very day Stravinsky dated his sketch for trio 2.

## Elaborations–Particells

Unfortunately, Stravinsky did not date compositional elaborations he made from these early 1943 sketches. The order here proposed for his elaborations is therefore provisional. It is based partly on the assumption that music copied on one type of paper might be chronologically related, and partly on common sense.

The scherzo proper has two elaborations, one similar to the other. The earlier must surely be the one virtually complete (but with some notational short-hand for reiterated triads) on a single page copied in pencil at first on three staves and then continuing on two staves, all of them ruled by Stravinsky's rastrum. This page comprises some 32 measures in G major of the scherzo, its upper triads on one stave in the treble clef, its lower ones on a stave in the bass clef. Below these two staves, another begins with reiterated pedal octave D's notated in the bass clef, but the latter stave disappears by the third measure where the D pedal is simply marked "etc."

This virtually complete statement of the scherzo proper he copied once again, but this time in ink and complete on four pages, the first one blank except for his heading in Russian: "Harmonies / 3 pages /." This particell (short-score) comprises three ensuing pages of twelve-staved commercially printed paper on which Stravinsky notated neatly the entire 37 measures of the scherzo proper, in the same three-stave grouping described for the earlier elaboration, but this time employing three staves throughout. He heads his first page of music: "Allegro e Forte / $\downarrow$ = 116" and gives a timing of 36" at the close of the last page. This "Allegro" survives through various two-piano versions of the scherzo joined to trio 1 until the spring of 1944 (the time of scoring for jazz band), when he alters it to "Con moto." To this elaboration he has added some markings in pencil and in green pencil which he surely made subsequent to his careful ink manu-

---

20. See above, n.17.

21. See *Bubushkin*, 30 November 1942 and 18 January 1943, respectively.

script. The markings include "8ve," some extra chords, and on its second page: "Ck, Sym", which is followed by some octave doublings. This is the final elaboration extant of the scherzo before it appears on the first four pages of a seven-page ozalid for two pianos which also includes trio 1 (about which see ozalids 1 and 2 below).[22]

From the F-major tune which Stravinsky copied for later use in trio 1, there survives but a single two-page elaboration, in B major without indication for instrumentation (also called a particell by Jans). It is well on the road to its final form as an accompanied two-voiced canon. Intermediate elaborations presumably once existed because this sole survivor already includes not only the modulation at the close of trio 1 in order to return to the dominant of the returning scherzo, but also the latter's opening measure.

Stravinsky copied his elaboration in ink and pencil on three staves of two pages of nine-staved commercial paper, formed into three groups of three staves. Each group of three staves has printed clefs—treble, treble, and bass. As in the first and subsequent ozalids (see below), this particell also lacks the opening F-sharp octave in piano 2 in the 1945 edition (at rehearsal [9]),[23] an addition not earlier than the spring of 1944. He reveals some uncertainty about barring his canon. His original ink barring (which would fall in the middle of measures of the first known two-piano ozalid) is altered by his dotted pencilled rebarrings (conforming to that ozalid). Whatever the date of this elaboration may be, its connecting materials to and its quotation of the returning scherzo's first measure demonstrate that it precedes the two-piano ozalid already mentioned, the seven pages of which contain both scherzo proper and trio 1 as one unit.

A short transition in the above elaboration from trio 1 to the scherzo proper disturbs the prevailing triadic diatonicism of the *Scherzo ... à la russe* ([15], 4th beat ff.). After all, the simplest way to modulate from B major to G major would include the former key's subdominant, then an A-minor pivot, followed by a dominant triad of G. Fundamentally, Stravinsky proceeds in just this manner.

His transition might also be regarded, however, as a brief (although partial) excursion into octatonicism employing solely Collections II and III.[24] An arpeggiated chord of six pitches from Collection II: D-sharp, B, F-sharp, C, A, and G-sharp, moves to a double-forte chord drawn from Collection III: C-sharp, A, E, C, and G. C-natural in the bass causes us to hear this chord as a slightly dissonant dominant seventh which then resolves to D major to prepare for the returning G-major scherzo proper. During the transition repeated D-sharps alternate with E's in sixteenth notes. The move from one collection to another occurs by D-

---

22. A facsimile of the title page of Ozalid 2 is in FLAMM, *Scherzo*, [XII].

23. *Scherzo ... à la russe for orchestra. Transcribed for Two Pianos by the Composer* (New York: Associated Music Publishers,

1945), 4, reprinted (London, Mainz, New York, Tokyo: Schott, n.d.), 4.

24. Pieter C. VAN DEN TOORN, *The Music of Igor Stravinsky* (New Haven: Yale University Press, 1983), 50-51.

sharps (common to both collections), giving way to gradually lengthening E's, the latter only in Collection III. Stravinsky's brief injection here of chromaticism into trio 1 surely qualifies for what van den Toorn characterizes as "octatonic-diatonic interaction."[25]

In the case of trio 2, source material for its three elaborations (all of which Jans called particells) is more plentiful than for trio 1, but slightly more confusing. Two elaborations are in A major, and a third one in C major. The earliest must be one in A major on the same nine-staved paper with three printed clefs Stravinsky used for Trio 1. Unlike the latter, however, this particell contains no return to the scherzo. Such a lack could well incline one to think it was copied before any elaboration of trio 1.[26] In any event, this initial elaboration has just the first 23 measures of trio 2 (part A). It probably directly followed the A-major little children's duet of January 1943 because its two pages copy in ink the corresponding two voices of that duet on the uppermost printed treble clef of its three staves. Directly below, in pencil on the pair of staves with printed treble and bass clefs, Stravinsky copied a variant of the duet. On these two lower clefs he also harmonized the tune, wavering between a four- and a five-voiced texture, even venturing occasionally to six voices for rhythmic emphasis. No hints of instrumentation are given for this particell. At the close of the second page on its right edge Stravinsky wrote a series of numbers: "126/41/85" and "1.28/1.25/1.8," totalling the second group as: "3.56" [sic]. Unless these numbers were added after he had copied this particell, 3.56 suggests that he already had the entire *Scherzo* in his mind because this total closely approximates its timing of 3'52".

The next stage in the evolution of trio 2 also appears on the same kind of nine-staved paper with printed treble, treble, and bass clefs. Of 62 measures and still in A major, this elaboration (particell) occupies six pages, is entirely in ink, is rather strictly written in four voices. Stravinsky heads it: "2ᵈ TRIO." Unlike its predecessor, it contains not only the previously missing parts of trio 2 and its transition for returning to the scherzo proper, but also the initial three measures of that G-major scherzo, the last measure being marked: "etc."

A final stage in the evolution of these elaborations for trio 2 is another six-page particell neatly written in ink on the same type of nine-staved paper with three printed clefs. Headed by Stravinsky "TRIO 2°" and chiefly *a4*, it also closes with the scherzo's initial measures, as in the A-major particell immediately preceding it. Crucial distinctions from its two predecessors, however, are its transposition to the ultimate key of C major and the composer inscribing: "Scherzo da capo" at its close. At some point, this C-major particell also served Stravinsky for his jazz band version because it contains his (presumably later) indications in pencil and in red and green pencil: "Flauto and Guit[ar]

---

25. Ibid., xv; mentioned at 353, the *Scherzo* ... *à la russe* is not scrutinized for octatonic content.

26. Perhaps this feature prompted Craft's belief that Stravinsky composed trio 2 before trio 1.

combinne" [sic], "Saxophones," as well as reiterated sixteenth-note decorations. This brings us to the end of the various elaborations of sketches on the way to the fully integrated work as a scherzo with two trios.

Aside from the various stages of trio 2 for two pianos, and of my parent transparencies and of their several ozalid offspring for the arrangement of the entire *Scherzo* for two pianos, two scorings at Basle for symphony orchestra remain to be mentioned. One is for part of trio 1, the other for part of trio 2. Both must precede Stravinsky's copying in the summer of 1945 of the complete work for symphony orchestra on 23 pages of transparencies. The single page for trio 1 merely scores its close ([15] through second measure after [16]), copied in pencil on 20-stave commercial music paper with a printed heading of: <u>Title</u>      <u>Page</u>      .

Of these two symphonic orchestrations, the one for trio 2 (an ABA' structure) deserves further comment. Of sections A and B only, it is in pencil on three huge folded double sheets of paper with printed names of various instruments preceding each of its 27 staves. Stravinsky inscribes it: "Piano as in the old score," perhaps referring to the piano part in his 1944 orchestration for jazz band. On the lower left side of each verso is also printed <u>EARNEST ANDERSSON</u>, which name Stravinsky inked out on one verso, perhaps in recognition of Andersson's death. Father-in-law of the then young conductor James Sample (who led the first performance of Stravinsky's arrangement of *The Star-Spangled Banner* in mid October 1941), Andersson was Stravinsky's only composition student. They began some 215 lessons together in March 1941, which only terminated with Andersson's sudden death two years later, on 24 June 1943.[27] Cancelling his pupil's name on this music paper may well suggest that this orchestral scoring of two-thirds of trio 2 postdates Andersson's death. Indeed, Stravinsky apparently did not begin his complete symphonic orchestration of *Scherzo . . . à la russe* before mid 1945, well after he had finished the one for jazz band.

## Versions for Two Pianos

Before considering my own fourteen pages of autograph transparencies of his two-piano arrangement, I must mention a pair of two-piano drafts for trio 2 copied in pencil at Basle, each comprising solely its parts A and B. These are preceded by a wrapper marked in Russian by Stravinsky: "Tr[anscription] [for] 2 Klaveré" (or, less likely:) "Tr[io] 2 Klaveré." Jans' catalog states both drafts are copies by some other person with corrections by Stravinsky. Inspection in Basle of both manuscripts, however, convinces me that both are entirely in Stravinsky's hand, albeit a rough and rapid one. Neither draft has any tempo indication. Taruskin discusses each of them and prints a conflation of both.[28]

27. Craft, *Pictures and Documents*, 359; Bubushkin, 24 and 30 June 1943.
28. *Stravinsky*, [1627-29], Ex. E.6. Taruskin kindly confirms that "(D.C.)" at its close is his own editorial addition.

As Taruskin first observed, the earlier draft is on twelve-stave paper issued by a film studio (not identified). Each page bears a printed heading: <u>Prod.[ucer]</u>_____ <u>Title</u> _____ and is numbered (1 through (5 in pencil by Stravinsky. Taking advantage of the printed headings of <u>Title_____</u>, he twice wrote in the underlined blank spaces: "Trio II" (on pp. 1 and 2) and: "Scherzo" (on p. 5). Such annotations show that he already considered this first surviving draft of trio 2 for two pianos (however rough and incomplete) a component of the entire *Scherzo*, rather than a separate work. Taruskin believes that he used this studio music paper either during or soon after his negotiations with Goldwyn about music for *The North Star*, that is, late 1942 to early 1943. If so, his handwritten additions following the printed headings show that a two-piano scherzo with two trios was conceived this early. Given Stravinsky's parsimonious ways, however, he may simply have hoarded the studio-issued paper and used it later (as was perhaps the case with music paper belonging to his deceased student, Earnest Andersson). He presumably then copied more neatly, though still in pencil, a slightly more refined version of this incomplete draft onto twelve-stave Maestro no. 108 transparencies which he paginated: (1 through (4. If he had ozalid copies made from these four pages of transparencies, they have not survived, although this version certainly preceded the complete trio 2 as copied on the final seven pages of my transparencies.

### Transparencies

These transparencies, beautifully copied in black ink with occasional traces of preparatory pencil, are themselves the prime source for at least four stages of ozalids variously reedited by the composer, ultimately leading in 1945 to the printed edition. A detailed description becomes imperative. Their differing page sizes and numbers of printed staves: ten (pp. 1-6; 8-9), eleven (p. 7), and twelve (pp. 10-14) show that they have been re-copied and reassembled in various ways. Pages not so affected, 1-2, 6, and 8-14, are each 30.2 x 24.2 cm. Only the lengths of pages 3-4 have been trimmed to 29.7 cm. Page 5 (though like its predecessors of ten staves) has been reassembled and also page 7 (uniquely into eleven staves), both to 30.5 x 24.2 cm. To separate his two-piano systems, Stravinsky mostly left staves 5 and 6 blank. Copying pages 10-11 so densely without leaving blank staves between the systems, however, was surely for a practical reason, for he could easily have redistributed his three systems on each of these two pages onto three pages each having two systems. But that would have necessitated an extra page-turn for the pianists.

Throughout trio 1 (pp. 4-7) Stravinsky carefully drew additional, small staves (inserted between piano 1 and piano 2, except on reassembled p. 7) on which he notated a two- and three-voiced much more agitated texture in sixteenth notes. These extra notes also appear in the 1944 jazz band version, assigned to violins, violas, and muted trumpet, and of course in the symphonic arrangement of 1945. Inscribing "Scherzo a[sic] la Russe" in a kind of art-deco lettering at the top of page 1, he signed: "Igor Strawinsky" directly above "1943" at the upper right edge. A metronome indication of $\downarrow = 116$ is supplemented by: "allegro e forte," the latter written cursively between piano 1 and piano 2. (As mentioned above, the same metronome and tempo marks appear on an early three-stave short score of just the scherzo proper.) In a still different style—this time almost a formal kind of printing—he wrote at the lower left side of the page: "Copyright by Igor Strawinsky 1944." Below the last bar on the final page (14) he wrote: "I Str." above "June 44," and below the month, "Hollywood."

Except for its first page, the entire manuscript has autograph page numbers: -2- through -14-, inscribed in the center of the upper margin on each page. Yet, even the naked eye can discern traces of a previous set of erased autograph page numbers: -2- through -7- on the upper corners of these pages only. On the lower right side of page 4 (between the staves of piano 2 at the close of the scherzo proper) is a mostly erased: "I Str." Below it are some numbers barely legible even under ultra-violet light. They are perhaps "21:44-43," or "2/:4-43." (Either of these might signify a copying date in 1943.) Immediately following on the same page, both F-sharp dotted half notes in piano 1 (which open trio 1 here) were originally inscribed much closer to the right bar line, marked (as ultra violet light reveals): "sub. p." The final measure of page 6 in piano 2 also reveals erasures at the close of Stravinsky's added stave (using his rastrum).

After the double bar ending trio 1 on page 7 (which also has an erasure of a triad above the final notes in the left hand of piano 1), Stravinsky wrote: "S[c]herzo da capo al fine." Placing an *al fine* here surely implies that at the time he finished copying page 7 (in 1943?) there was then no trio 2 attached by means of pages 8-14 (remember that page numbers for trio 2, unlike the earlier ones of 1-7 at the upper corners for scherzo and trio 1, appear only in the center of each page).

## The Sonata for Two Pianos

Before turning to the various ozalids generated from my transparencies, a brief excursus to a much more numerous, but collateral, set of transparencies is in order. The latter not only shed some light on the formation of the former, but also help a little to date them. The forty-one transparencies of the *Sonata for Two Pianos* were auctioned at the same sale in 1991 which attracted the first buyer, the dealer John Wilson of Oxford (now Cheltenham), for my transparencies of *Scherzo . . . à la russe*. The Sotheby's transparencies are now in the Pierpont Morgan Library, Lehman deposit. Sotheby's 1991 auction catalog reproduces their first page and furnishes a brief description.[29] The Paul Sacher

29. See above, n.13.

Foundation owns not only short-scores of the three movements of the *Sonata*, but also a complete set of ozalids with the composer's corrections, the latter made from his transparencies.[30]

Using some observations by Craft in 1978, discoveries by Lawrence Morton in 1982, and an account by Charles Joseph in 1983 (for which Taruskin had provided much information), Taruskin found virtually all the thematic material for the *Sonata* in the same 1886 Russian anthology which served Stravinsky for the *Scherzo ... à la russe*.[31] Like the *Scherzo*, the *Sonata* also began life as music for the film, *The North Star*, a project Stravinsky abandoned by mid January 1943. Beginning work on the *Sonata* in mid August of that year, he completed its three movements on 11 February 1944. By mid March he had copied the *Sonata*'s transparencies and had sent ozalid copies to pianist friends in New York.[32]

The *Sonata*'s transparencies auctioned in 1991 thus date from no later than mid March, 1944. The style of the autograph title page of the *Sonata* is virtually identical to that of the *Scherzo*—similar art-deco lettering for their titles, the same style of signature at the upper right and the date below (except that the Sonata unites its "1943" with "-44") and an almost identical inscription of the 1944 copyright at the bottom. All but two of the forty-one pages of the *Sonata* are copied on ten-stave paper, identical to that used in the first six pages and pages 8-9 of the *Scherzo* before the latter's seventh page was reconstituted from twelve staves into one with only eleven. Moreover, *all* pages of the *Sonata* are numbered in their upper corners. This is additional evidence that Trio 2 (pp. 8-14) was copied at a time different both from the *Sonata* and from the *Scherzo* proper and its Trio 1. Because both two-piano works were apparently conceived and composed at the same time (during 1943), one might postulate that both were copied on their transparencies early in 1944. Thus June 44 on the final page of the *Scherzo* could refer solely to the copying of trio 2, rather than to all the transparencies making up the whole manuscript.[33] Stravinsky's presumed recourse to twelve-staved paper from that of ten staves for his reconstituted page seven and for copying the last five pages of trio 2 could well have resulted from having run out of ten-staved transparencies in 1944 after (or perhaps even before) having used 39 pages for the Sonata and at least nine more pages for the *Scherzo*.

Also noteworthy is the distinction Stravinsky makes about the time of composition: on their title pages he dates the *Scherzo* as 1943, but the *Sonata* as 1943-44 (distinctions

30. JANS, *Stravinsky Manuskripte*, 36.

31. His findings, announced in Lawrence MORTON, "Stravinsky at Home," *Confronting Stravinsky: Man, Musician, and Modernist*, ed. Jann PASLER (Berkeley: University of California Press, 1986), 336, n.5, appeared only in 1996, in his *Stravinsky*, 1632-46.

32. CRAFT, *Pictures and Documents*, 373.

33. Stephen WALSH, *Stravinsky, A Creative Spring: Russia and France, 1882-1934* (New York: Knopf, 1999), 612, n.61, observes, however: "Stravinsky was in the habit of dating his fair copies according to the actual date of completion, without regard to the date of copying." Mr. Walsh very kindly allowed me a prepublication copy of his book.

lost when these works were printed in 1945). For the former we have no certain dates in 1943 (aside from those on its sketches) but his composition dates on the short-scores of the *Sonata* explain his need to extend 1943 into 1944 when he copied its transparencies.

### Ozalids, states 1-4

Study of the several sets of ozalid copies at the Library of Congress and at the Paul Sacher Foundation (all made at one time or another from my transparencies) also helps to differentiate between the copying dates of the scherzo and its first trio on the one hand, and that of trio 2 on the other. Three identical seven-page exemplars of a first set of ozalids are held by the Library of Congress. They were made from pages 1-7 (scherzo plus trio 1) of an earlier (probably the first) state of my transparencies and are paginated solely at their upper corners as: -2- through -7-, just as in the latter's original state (see above). Unlike my transparencies, however, these LC ozalids have no small notes added anywhere during trio 1. Moreover, they display almost all the features already noted as revealed by Stravinsky's ineffectual erasures to the transparencies—on page 4 positioning to the far right in the first bar of piano 1 at the opening of trio 1 and its octave marked sub. p; a page 7 orginally copied on 12-staved paper; and the final notes of trio 1 on page 7 differently apportioned between the two pianos. That is, the left hand of piano 1 was assigned the diminished triad now divided between the hands of piano 2, and the left hand of piano 2 had the last graced-octave of piano 1 (concluding its motion from its previous bar). Henceforth these three identical ozalid copies will be referred to as Ozalid 1. I believe this set precedes the commission Stravinsky received from Paul Whiteman at the beginning of April, 1944. If Stravinsky later added its copyright in 1944, his copying of LC's Ozalid 1 could be sometime in 1943, justifying "1943" on the title page. Justification for this belief proceeds from Ozalid 2.

Ozalid 2 survives in but a single exemplar, at Basle. Folded accordion-style, its pages are joined together with brown-paper tape. Again of but seven pages (scherzo and trio 1) and likewise paginated only in their upper corners, this set of ozalids is the immediate predecessor of the present state of the corresponding pages of my transparencies. The chief musical difference of Ozalid 2 from Ozalid 1 and from the transparencies is Stravinsky's addition on Ozalid 2 of the small notes for trio 1 by hand in *pencil* on *available* printed staves. These notes he was subsequently to add in *ink* mostly on *additional* staves which he himself ruled in my transparencies. His notational hand in Ozalid 2 for these additions to trio 1 is much rougher than what he later employed when copying the transparencies.

Just when he pencilled in these small notes on Basle's Ozalid 2 can be determined by the many pencil indications he also added to the music of the two pianos as verbal reminders about how to score the *Scherzo* for jazz band. A facsimile of the first page of Basle's Ozalid 2 shows his method of naming directly on the music the instruments he intended to employ.[34] (Additional indications for jazz band appear on Ozalid 2 at pp. 3, at the close of 6, and 7.) Page 7 of Ozalid 2 (like p. 7 of Ozalid 1) has twelve staves. It was thus made before page 7 of my transparency was reassembled to eleven staves. (Given its predecessors and immediate followers, however, the earliest version of p. 7 could well have also been copied on ten-stave paper.) In Ozalid 2, blank staves 5-8 on page 7 bear pencil notations for the string section of the jazz band.

Ozalid 2 comes from around the time of Paul Whiteman's commission, first broached early in April 1944, to which Stravinsky responded on 23 April that he would compose "4½ minutes of music" for later recording on one side of a 78-rpm disc. Ozalid 2 must, however, just precede the actual scoring for jazz band upon which Stravinsky embarked early in May and by 4 June had "nearly finished."[35]

Ozalid 3 is held by the Library of Congress (again in three exemplars). Unlike its two predecessors, Ozalid 3 reveals Stravinsky's *calligraphic* additions of small notes to trio 1, made mostly on small *additional* staves he ruled *between* pianos 1 and 2. And unlike Ozalids 1 and 2, Ozalid 3 includes all of trio 2. All three exemplars of Ozalid 3 are identical to and were made directly from my transparencies.

Two of the three sets of Ozalid 3 in the Library of Congress are virtually the same, except for Stravinsky having added in ink to one set a necessary pair of F-sharps for piano 1 and piano 2 at the final measure of page 14. We may better designate these two sets as Ozalid 3a because the third set is quite different.

LC's Ozalid 3b was Stravinsky's personal copy and thus affords insight into his per-formance practice. Its fourteen pages are bound together with brown paper and Scotch tape so that the pages (accordion-folded) could gradually be extended along the music rack of a piano. On the (blank) verso cover of the first page, he wrote: "Igor Strawinsky / Scherzo … à la Russe / arrangement / for / two pianos by the / author." Modern per-formers should pay attention to this copy. It contains many autograph fingerings for piano 2 (obviously the part he played), additional slurrings (especially in the central E-flat portion of trio 2, section B), as well as the necessary final F-sharps in both pianos. Moreover, in trio 2 he made extensive alterations and deletions to piano 2 by white-out, simplifying its many rapid and difficult double- and triple-note passages. Spelling his name with "w" rather than "v" may indicate that he first used this copy before 1945 when he adopted the "v" (Discussion of Ozalid 4 may be profitably delayed until we learn more about Stravinsky playing the *Scherzo* himself.)

---

34. See above, n.22. "Severine" inscribed by Stravinsky at the upper left on the title page of Ozalid 2 may be Severin Kavenoki, an employee (1933-35) of Alexander Bernardovich Merovich, Stravinsky's New York agent, who in 1935 succeeded him in the same capacity until at least December, 1938; see their correspondence in the Paul Sacher Foundation; *Selected Correspondence* 2:304,n.43, 306, 503,n.4; and *Pictures and Documents*, 340.

35. See *Selected Correspondence* 3:293-94 and the telegrams and letters about negotiations with the Blue Network in FLAMM, *Scherzo*, VI-VII.

## Stravinsky as Duo Pianist

Probable occasions for which he made these changes in Ozalid 3b can be suggested. "Nadia [Boulanger] and Igor work together the whole day" (in Hollywood), so wrote Vera in her diary on 22 October 1944. They were surely practicing the *Scherzo . . . à la russe*, the *Sonata for two pianos*, and the *Circus Polka*, all for their forthcoming two-piano concert at Mills College, Oakland, where the composer gave a lecture. Three days later, on a Wednesday evening, 25 October, the premiere of the two-piano *Scherzo* indeed took place. At least one additional performance of the *Scherzo* by Stravinsky and another pianist occurred when Stravinsky addressed the Philadelphia Arts Alliance on 21 February 1945. This time he was joined by Vincent Persichetti (1915-87) who had rehearsed it with him in New York on 8 February.[36] Almost certainly Stravinsky's performing experience of the *Scherzo* in 1944 and early 1945 influenced his later editing of the arrangement for symphony orchestra. As we shall learn next, the latter arrangement was, in turn, to influence the editing of the two-piano arrangement when it came to be published.

## Ozalid 4 and Publication

A final ozalid held by the Library of Congress could with perfect justice be called Ozalid 3c because, like Ozalids 3a and 3b, it, too, began life from my transparencies. Much greater editorial attention, however, ultimately transformed it into a proof copy for the first edition by Associated Music Publishers in October 1945. Thus it is more aptly called Ozalid 4 in order to distinguish it securely from its predecessors and from its parent transparencies.

A printed slip, <u>Proofs Arthur Mendel AMP</u>, accompanies Ozalid 4.[37] At the top of a new manuscript page 1 is notated in red: "AM/7/31/45 (with IS's answers to questions)." The 1945 two-piano edition was edited according to an opening 19 measures, copied in an unprofessional hand on two pages of manuscript paper.[38] On the manuscript's first page appear the same headings as in my transparencies except that the bottom of this page now reads as in the printed edition: "A.C. 19455 Copyright 1945, by Chappell & Co. Inc." The remaining pages, 3-14, are made from my transparencies. These are heavily edited ozalids (some with changes in Stravinsky's hand), except for a small manuscript of three measures in the same unprofessional hand pasted over the two final bars of one ozalid (p. 4, beginning of trio 1). On this pastedown Mendel asked Stravinsky in French about adding an additional measure from the "score," to which the composer agreed in English.

---

36. See *Bubushkin*, 22-25 October 1944, 8 and 21 February 1945.

37. Arthur Mendel (1905-79), appointed Professor and Chairman of Music at Princeton University in 1952, was editor for Associated Music, 1941-47. See *Selected*

*Correspondence* 3:284, 286-88, 294, 299, and 305.

38. Craft's typed catalog (see above, n.12) identifies the hand as that of Stravinsky's friend then living in New York, the violinist, Samuel Dushkin (1891-1976).

This pastedown was necessary so as to insert an initial F-sharp octave for piano 2 in trio 1, an introductory octave first present (for harp) in the 1944 transparencies for jazz band (and also, of course, in the 1945 transparencies for symphony orchestra). All this editing in Ozalid 4, chiefly articulation and additional dynamic marks, stems not from the 1944 jazz-band transparencies, but from Stravinsky's quite different editing of the *Scherzo* in his May 1945 transparencies of the symphonic version.[39] Hence Mendel's reference to a "score" is to the latter. The 1945 printed edition for two pianos by AMP follows edited Ozalid 4 scrupulously except for a printer's error in misreading a final—and correct—D in the bass of piano 1 (2 measures before [20]), printing instead an incorrect F.

No agreements for publishing the two-piano arrangement of the *Scherzo* are in the three signed business contracts of mid July, September, and October 1944 which I acquired in 1981. These contracts concern the forthcoming broadcast premiere on the Blue Network from New York on 5 September 1944 of the jazz band arrangement, its "publication," and that of the *Sonata for Two Pianos* by Associated Music Publishers (the *Sonata* not printed until early in 1945). The *Scherzo* arrangement for jazz band, however, was not printed until Flamm edited it more than half a century later. In fact, a note (held by the Paul Sacher Foundation) to an unidentified enquirer two weeks after the latter's premiere and signed "I Str 25 Sept/44" relates: "Je n'ai pas un seul exemplaire available sous le main sans quoi je vous l'aurai envoyé. L'Associated Music Publisher a mon manuscrit en ce moment et va le publier probablement en photostats."

As mentioned above, it was the act of orchestrating and editing the arrangement for symphony orchestra during May 1945 that engendered the simultaneous publication of it and the one for two pianos that October.[40] The latter's title page, "Scherzo… à la Russe for orchestra / Transcribed for Two Pianos / by the composer," and its first page of music are a little misleading. The two-piano arrangement existed for some time, even before the arrangement in 1944 for jazz band. Furthermore, relative to the 1945 orchestral arrangement, "edited" would be more accurate than "transcribed." And by replacing the transparencies' "1943" below Stravinsky's name with "1944" and altering their "Copyright 1944" to "Copyright 1945," the 1945 edition severed the connection of the work not only with music for a film about Russia, but also with its origin in Russian folk tunes.

Flamm has observed that a year earlier Stravinsky was already denying any extramusical connections. He assured Associated Music Publishers on 22 August 1944 that

39. Easily seen by comparing Flamm's two editions cited above, n.17. These editions contain several errors. The final measure of the jazz band version at p. 33 (also lacking an F-sharp in trombone 2) is repeated redundantly at 34, which latter bar omits slurs for both trombones and French horn (see at 13); the symphonic version, p. 25, last bar, lacks a treble clef in the left hand of the piano.

40. The New York Public Library's copy of a fall supplement to the 1945 AMP checklist—the former advertises both arrangements—is stamped: Oct 16 1945.

the *Scherzo ... à la russe* had "no story to it," was "composed... without use of a special folk tune," and that his inspiration in composing "lies, as always in music itself and never in things exterior to the music."[41]

## Recordings and Early Performances by Others

Unlike his performances of the *Concerto for Two Solo Pianos* with his son Soulima in February 1938 and with Adele Marcus (1906-95) in March 1940,[42] no recordings are extant of his two-piano performances of the *Scherzo* with Boulanger in October 1944 and with Persichetti in February 1945 (or indeed, of any of his performances of its companion work, the *Sonata for Two Pianos*). As if in compensation, many recordings exist of him conducting the symphonic arrangement of the *Scherzo*, the earliest, timed as 3'40", dating from 1946, made with the New York Philharmonic for a Voice of America Broadcast to Europe[43] and the last one, a commercial recording on 17 December 1963 with the Columbia Symphony Orchestra, of 3'57"(CBS CD, MK 42432). Among these are his slowest one of 4'03" made in 1957 with the Rome Symphony Orchestra and his fastest, 3'35" made a decade earlier with the RCA Victor Symphony Orchestra in Hollywood.[44]

From early in 1946 come the first hints of endorsements by the composer— perhaps even his actual coaching—of two-piano teams wishing to play the *Scherzo*. Arthur Gold and Robert Fizdale, two young duo-pianists, had played the *Sonata* (although not the *Scherzo*) at their Town Hall debut on 15 February 1946. Three days later they came to Stravinsky's New York hotel "to play Igor's music."[45] By April he gave his blessing for a recording by Gold and Fizdale of the *Scherzo*, along with the *Sonata* and the *Five Easy Pieces*.[46] If they made a recording of the *Scherzo*, however, it was never issued.[47]

The first New York performance of the *Scherzo* was by the experienced team of Vitya Vronsky and Victor Babin in Carnegie Hall, on 3 December 1946. At the very least, he probably influenced their interpretation. Good friends of the Stravinskys, they had already played their own arrangements of his *Circus Polka* and *Tango* in January 1943 "to his great delight."[48] They also made the first commercial recording of the *Scherzo* (Columbia 37789)—on 19 May 1947, at the same time as the *Concerto for Two Solo Pianos*, both issued

41. FLAMM, *Scherzo, Jazz ensemble*, VI, quoting *Selected Correspondence* 3:298.

42. Philip STUART, *Igor Stravinsky—The Composer in the Recording Studio. A Comprehensive Discography* (New York, Westport CT, London: Greenwood Press, 1991), 30, no. 27 and 73, App. C, respectively. On Marcus, another piano student, *c.*1920-22, of Stravinsky's long-time friend, Alexis Kall, see the obituary by Bernard HOLLAND, *The New York Times*, 5 May 1995.

43. See Ulf SCHARLAU, *Igor Strawinsky. Phonographie*

(Frankfurt am Main: Deutsches Rundfunkarchiv, 1972), 125-26, no. 70.

44. STUART, *Recording Studio*, 71, App. C and 34, no. 50, respectively.

45. *Bubushkin*, 18 February 1945.

46. *Selected Correspondence* 3:305.

47. Their recording of the *Sonata* and of *Five Easy Pieces*, however, appeared in June 1947; see *Saturday Review of Literature* 30 (21 June 1947):47.

48. *Bubushkin*, 11 January 1943.

on a 78-rpm set (MM 837). Unlike the *Concerto*, however, their *Scherzo* recording (on a sixth side) did not survive into the LP era.[49]

Whether Vronsky and Babin had learned and were recording the *Scherzo* from one of Stravinsky's ozalids or from the published edition (available from October 1945) is difficult to decide. On the one hand, their slurrings and articulation seem mostly to follow my transparencies rather than the edition. Playing the correct D (rather than the erroneous published F in trio 2 mentioned above) suggests they used an ozalid copy rather than the 1945 edition. On the other hand, their recording includes the extra F-sharp octave in piano 2 which opens trio 1 in the printed edition. Perhaps these features stemmed from Stravinsky's editorial supervision. Even though overdubbing was technically possible by 1947,[50] their recording did not include the small notes which Stravinsky had added to trio 1 (as Ozalid 2 reveals) during his arrangement for jazz band.

Pearl Kaufman and Dale Reubart played the *Scherzo* for a first time in Los Angeles at a Monday Evening Concert on 5 March 1956.[51] Professor Reubart kindly informed me by letter (16 May 1996) that he and Ms. Kaufman played from the printed edition which contained, however, a manuscript insert (unidentified) by Stravinsky's close associate, Ingolf Dahl (1912-70). Reubart does not know whether Stravinsky attended the concert, although Robert Craft did (in his capacity as conductor).

During the composer's lifetime one more two-piano recording was made—by Michael Tilson Thomas and Ralph Grierson, early in 1969 at Hollywood and issued in the middle of that year (Angel LP S-36024). For the first time, the small notes of trio 1 (unplayable with just four hands otherwise occupied) are overdubbed. Coached by Lawrence Morton (1904-87), another Stravinsky intimate, their recording probably reflects some of the composer's wishes, for Thomas recalled that at the time of recording its companion work, the four-hand version of the *Sacre*, he had conversations with Stravinsky about it.[52] Even though the tempo of the *Scherzo* is slower than indicated, Mr. Grierson kindly informed me (8 April 1996) that Stravinsky heard this recording and signalled his approval of it to Craft and to Morton.

Arguably the finest recorded performance is by two Russian pianists, Vladimir Ashkenazy and Andrei Gavrilov, made in January 1990 and issued two years later (London CD 433 829-2). Also employing overdubbing for trio 1, the pair are within five seconds of the timing prescribed by Stravinsky's metronome mark. Obviously having

49. STUART, *Recording Studio*, 33, no. 47x (omitting mention of the *Scherzo*).

50. On 19 October 1946 Jascha HEIFETZ had recorded the *Bach double violin concerto* for RCA Victor by overdubbing.

51. See Arthur and Herbert MORTON, *Monday Evening Concerts 1954-1971: the Lawrence Morton years* (Los Angeles: A & H Morton, 1993), 52.

52. Michael TILSON THOMAS, *Viva Voce. Conversations with Edward Seckerson* (London: Faber, 1994), 83. George Sponhaltz, the producer, kindly informs me that both works were recorded at the same sessions.

heard his several orchestral recordings, they also observe rather strictly his 1945 edition for two pianos (itself derived from the contemporaneous edition for orchestra).

## Obfuscations

The same AMP flyer in October 1945 which advertised the two-piano edition described the miniature orchestral score thus: "originally written for Paul Whiteman's Blue Network Orchestra, it now appears, completely rescored and partly recomposed, in what the composer considers its definitive version, for symphony orchestra." "Rescored" from the 1944 jazz band version is accurate and "definitive" seems fair enough. But what about "partly recomposed?" For some months before he scored the *Scherzo* for jazz band (spring of 1944), it had existed as scherzo and trio 1 for two pianos, to which he very likely in June added its already composed trio 2 (my transparencies, pp. 8-14). For both the orchestral arrangement and the 1945 two-piano edition influenced by it, "partly recomposed" should read "newly edited." Thus to the deceptions which Stravinsky practiced about the *Scherzo . . . à la russe* (so thoroughly exposed by Taruskin), should be added its origins as a two-piano work and even its ultimate editing.

When and how did these transparencies leave his personal collection? Probably already by 1949, the year he and Craft first cataloged manuscripts which he still owned and in the list of which they do not appear.[53] Craft has observed helpfully: "All of his life, Stravinsky disposed of his manuscripts at every opportunity... in a letter of June 15 1950, Stravinsky lists manuscripts, with minimum prices, that he wants [his son, Théodore] to try to sell." And in 1952 he commissioned his younger son, Soulima, to offer certain manuscripts for sale.[54] No information has surfaced as to the whereabouts of my transparencies between 1945 and 1991. Their reappearance at auction the latter year (lot 475) in such close juxtaposition to transparencies for the *Sonata For Two Pianos* (lot 473) may well suggest that both had been owned by a two-piano team or by an enthusiast for two-piano music.

## Critical Responses

Reviewing the *Scherzo . . . à la russe* in 1946, Olin Downes dismissed it as "an amusing skit."[55] In 1980 Eric Walter White included it among "frankly lightweight works."[56] And in 1996 Taruskin called it "a little potboiler."[57] Without wishing to overvalue the

53. See Eric Walter WHITE, *Stravinsky: the Composer and His Works* (Berkeley: University of California Press, 1979), App C, no. 79a; the list was updated in 1952, see CRAFT, *Glimpses*, 321. Fuller details of White-Craft, nos. 79a-b, in Sigmund Rothschild's 1970 typed catalog, 2: 155-56, initialled by Craft on 1 February 1983 (a copy in the Music Division, New York Public Library), do not describe my two-piano transparencies; see TARUSKIN, *Stravinsky*, [1142-43], n.C.1.

54. *Pictures and Documents*, 576.

55. Review of Vronsky and Babin recital 3 December, *The New York Times*, 4 December 1946, 44.

56. WHITE, "Stravinsky, Igor," *The New Grove*, 18:256.

57. *Stravinsky*, 1632.

*Scherzo*, one might still take issue with these verdicts. Taruskin employs such terms as internal repetition, subtle dislocations, rhythmic distension, and isomelism in discussing the *Sonata for Two Pianos*. I turn to its companion work, or rather, just to the scherzo proper, to point out a few of these same features in it (see Example 1). Appearing within an unchanging meter and regular pulsation, they produce several surprises. Stravinsky's first compositional act is to shear off the repeated G's in the third measure of his sketch (m. 3a). He does so not only because of their redundancy, but because in conjunction with the pickup to the initial three B's they would otherwise form a plodding sequence.

As their alignment in the Example reveals, the various motives of his now fully-"composed" tune never appear in the same order that he first proposes for them (mm. 1-6) until the very end of the scherzo proper (mm. 30-35). Even there they are joined by a repetition (36-37) from within (mm. 20-21; 22-23). If we allow that the revised sketch (minus its bar at m. 3a) with an extension at m. 7 constitutes an antecedent phrase, part of the charm is trying to discover a consequent to it. Just when one thinks one hears it, it dissolves into yet another slightly altered antecedent (mm. 12-21).

But his most cunning feat occurs at mm. 26-29. So much dwelling upon and circling about dominant D and subdominant A pitches half-way through (mm. 16-25) must signal either a return or the anticipated consequent. Indeed, with the anacrusis to m. 26, a more active piano 2 (here both orchestral arrangements are heavily scored) and double-forte dynamics all support such expectations. But three details are awry. First, one of the repeated B's from mm. 1-2 is lacking during mm. 26-27; second, the pair of B's offered here are not short eighth notes as at the outset, but sustained quarters; and third, extension of the D and E from m. 7 are not present. This small nest of rhythmic and melodic deceptions persists until the "recapitulation" of mm. 1-7 as an antecedent (not a consequent) at mm. 30-37. And even here, the repeated final measure throws one back immediately to an unsettling recall of the identical dominant-submediant alternation at the work's very center, mm. 16-17.

Rarely are the above techniques known, let alone used, by hack writers of "skits," "lightweight works," and "potboilers." Such techniques more appropriately betoken the subtleties bestowed on miniatures by master composers. Never disdaining miniatures, they took the utmost care with them. Just so with Stravinsky and his *Scherzo ... à la russe*.

# Astor Piazzolla:
# Tangos, Funerals, and "Blue Notes"

I N OCTOBER 1959, the Argentine composer and bandoneon virtuoso Astor Piazzolla
(1921-92)—famous as the creator of the so-called *tango nuevo* and, with Carlos Gardel
(1887-1935), one of the two most important figures in the history of the tango[1]—
commemorated the death of his father by composing what is undoubtedly his
best-known and (to judge from the applause that greets and follows it on recordings of
live concerts) most beloved composition: *Adiós nonino.*[2]

---

[1]. For the latter assessment, see Ramón PELINSKI,
"Nomadic Tango," in *Latin American Music: An Encyclopedic
History of Musics from South America, Central America, Mexico,
and the Caribbean*, 2 vols., ed. Malena KUSS (forthcoming);
this essay is a revised and enlarged version of "Le Tango
nomade," which originally appeared in *Tango nomade*, ed.
Ramón PELINSKI (Montréal: Triptyque, 1995), 25-70,
where both the separate section on Piazzolla and the
assessment quoted are lacking; Pelinski does, however,
refer to Piazzolla in the earlier essay as the "figure dominante du tango des cinquante dernières années" (p. 53).
Recent years have seen a spate of Piazzolla biographies,
by far the most authoritative of which is María Susana
AZZI and Simon COLLIER, *Le Grand Tango: The Life and Music
of Astor Piazzolla* (New York: Oxford University Press,
2000), which, despite its title, has little about the music
itself (and which appeared too late to be worked into the
notes that follow); among the others, mainly anecdotal
in character: Natalio GORIN, ed., *Astor Piazzolla: A manera
de memorias*, 2d ed. (Buenos Aires: Libros Perfil, 1998),
with an English translation scheduled for publication by
Amadeus Press; Oscar LÓPEZ RUIZ, *Piazzolla: Loco, loco, loco*
(Caracas: Ediciónes de la Urraca, 1994); Diana
PIAZZOLLA, *Astor* (Buenos Aires: Emecé, 1987); López
Ruiz was Piazzolla's guitarist for many years; Diana
Piazzolla is the composer's daughter. Far more searching
in its treatment of Piazzolla's aesthetic and stylistic roots
is Carlos KURI, *Piazzolla: La música límite*, 2d ed. (Buenos

Aires: Corregidor, 1997). In addition, one should consult
Horacio FERRER's monumental *El libro del tango: Arte popular de Buenos Aires*, 3 vols. (Buenos Aires: Antonio Tersol,
1980), with biographical material on Piazzolla at I, pp.
524-30, 560-73, 587-93, 637, 667-81, 751-56; III, pp. 814-30.
For an exhaustive discography, see Mitsumasa SAITO,
*Astor Piazzolla: El luchador del tango* (Tokyo: Seido-sha, 1998)
which, despite the Spanish title, is in Japanese.

[2]. Among the many performances of *Adiós nonino*
recorded live at Piazzolla concerts, three—all with his
Quinteto Tango Nuevo—strike me as particularly bril-
liant: *Astor Piazzolla: Live at Cine Teatro Gran Rex, Buenos
Aires* (20 December 1981), West Wind Latina 2212 (1992); *Astor
Piazzolla y su Quinteto Tango Nuevo: The Vienna Concert* (1984),
Messidor 15922-2; and *Piazzolla: Central Park Concert* (6
September 1987), Chesky Records JD 107 (1994). The
personnel on the Buenos Aires and Vienna recordings
consists of Piazzolla, bandoneon; Pablo Ziegler, piano;
Fernando Suárez Paz, violin; Oscar López Ruiz, electric
guitar; and Héctor Console, bass; on the Central Park
recording, the guitarist is Horacio Malvicino.
Finally, we can gage the popularity of *Adiós nonino* from
the following statistic: as of late Fall, 1998, *Adiós nonino*
was available—performed by Piazzolla himself in conjunction with various groups—on no fewer than
thirty-six CDs (out of slightly fewer than one hundred
that are available), albeit with duplication of performances from one CD to another; in addition, the piece

The piece consists of two, sharply contrasting sections: *A*, a relatively up-tempo, rhythmically driving section based on the opening of an earlier work, *Nonino*, which Piazzolla had composed and dedicated to his father in 1954;[3] and *B*, a slower, lyrical section, which features the haunting melody for which the piece is famous. Example 1 (opposite) gives the opening measures of both sections (meas. 1-5 and 18-25), as well as the short bridge (as much the conclusion of *A*) that connects them (meas. 15-17).[4]

Though the two sections might seem to be related along the lines of introduction and main theme, they did not function as such when Piazzolla performed the work with one or another of his small groups: quintet or sextet. Rather, each of the performances cited in note 2 (and others as well) follows an expansive (between 8'00" and 8'30") rondo-like scheme:[5]

*B'*   worked into a rhapsodic, improvisatory-sounding "introduction" for solo piano, with the theme embellished;[6]

*A*   the entire group;

*B*   played in its most straightforward manner by the violin;

*A*   the entire group;

*B"*   played in its most profusely embellished version by the bandoneon;

*B"'*   coda-like function; the entire group, and with the tempo picked up.

can be heard performed by others—from Daniel BARENBOIM (*Mi Buenos Aires querido*, Teldec 0630-13474-2 [1996]) to the New Danish Saxophone Quartet (*Astor Piazzolla-Tango*, Kontrapunkt 32196 [1994]) to a harpsichord duo (Mario RASKIN and Oscar MILANI, *Tangos pour 2 clavecins* (Pierre Verany Disques PV.789102 [1989])—on forty-two CDs; see César LUONGO, "Piazzolla CD Compilation" on the Piazzolla website: <http://www.piazzolla.org/works/astorcd.html>. Mr. Luongo is currently compiling a Piazzolla data base, surely the first step in bringing the present, virtually bewildering Piazzolla bibliographical-discographical situation under control.

3.   See FERRER, *El libro del tango* 1: 564, which provides the opening four measures, and 2: 11-12. For what may be a third manifestation of this theme, see the website entitled "Piazzolla Film Compilation," compiled by César A. LUONGO: <http://www.piazzolla.org/works/astfilm.html>, who notes that the same theme appears on the soundtrack of the film *Sucedio en Buenos Aires* (1954), for which Piazzolla wrote the music. On the possibility of a second self-quotation within the *A* section, see my forthcoming book: *The Music of Astor Piazzolla: An Introductory Survey*.

4.   I give the music after the edition first issued by Editorial Julio KORN (Buenos Aires, 1960), Plate No. 7872—reprinted by Les Éditions Universelles (Paris,

1962)—which, however, prints the piece in F minor (*A* section) and Ab major (*B* section). My transposition to F# minor (*A*) and A major (*B*) is based on the authority of the three recordings cited in note 2, all of which offer it in that pair of keys. In addition, I have substituted a metronome indication for the "Lentamente" at the beginning of the *A* section, and added the "rallentando" at measures 16-17, both emendations made after the same recordings. For a score and parts—two bandoneons, two violins, electric guitar, bass, and piano—see *Astor Piazzolla: 20 de ses plus grands tangos* (Paris: Éditions Universelles, n.d.), No. 1.

5.   Piazzolla would depart from this scheme when playing the piece with orchestra, which, apparently, afforded him less flexibility. Thus at what turned out to be his last live concert, that in Athens, 3 July 1990 (one month before he suffered a stroke—Paris, 4 August—from which he never recovered), with the Athens Colours Orchestra, Manos Hadjidakis, cond., he simply followed the *A B* sequence twice through in a rather uninspired arrangement; *Astor Piazzolla: Bandoneón Sinfónico*, Milan 73138/35758-2 (1996).

6.   Despite its improvisatory sound and "feel," the introduction is largely written out. Piazzolla composed two introductory "cadencias" for the piece, one for the pianist Dante Amicarelli, the other for Pablo Ziegler (see n. 2); see Ziegler's comments in the notes to *Asfalto, Street*

**Example 1**    *Adiós nonino:* (a) mm. 1-5, (b) mm. 15-25

*Tango: Pablo Ziegler & his Quintet for New Tango*, RCA 09026-63266-2 (1998), where he plays both versions.

7.   On the power of *Adiós nonino* to move audiences, see the comments of Daniel Piazzolla, the composer's son,

We should consider the lyrical main theme ($B$) for a moment, since it is the poignant character of that melody that makes *Adiós nonino* both memorable and moving.[7] No doubt, what especially moves us are the "blue notes": the $g'$ and $a'$ that form dissonant flatted ninths with the bass at measures 21 and 25, respectively. (They can, of course, also be heard as flatted sevenths *in* I and *on* ii, respectively.) Moreover, their sense of grief is heightened by their unexpected appearance in a context that seems otherwise bathed in innocence.

There is another—admittedly speculative—point that might be made about the theme. On all but two of the Piazzolla performances that follow the rondo-like scheme (and with which I am familiar), the bandoneon's—thus Piazzolla's—turn at the melody is always reserved for section $B''$, the final "panel" (not including the up-tempo coda).[8] One reason for this is no doubt related to the purely musical dynamics of the piece: it is the bandoneon—that unmistakable "signature timbre" of any tango ensemble[9]—that subjects the melody to its most elaborate round of virtuoso embellishment; and that, obviously, is best reserved for the culminating statement (again, the coda not included).

There may, however, be another reason for Piazzolla's seeming reluctance to take up the melody. Perhaps it had to do with the melody's associations; he had, after all, composed the melody as a memorial to his father, and perhaps his insistence on waiting until almost the bitter end, before turning it into a solo vehicle for himself, reflects the continued recollection of grief that his father's death occasioned.[10] Yet whether the underlying reason was purely musical or tinged with psychological complications (or was a combina-

who describes a performance by Piazzolla and his group in Paris at which the Argentines in the audience broke down and cried; cited in Diana PIAZZOLLA, *Astor*, 205-206. In March 1998, I had the privilege of playing the piece (the "English" concertina is not the worst substitute for the bandoneon) with pianist David Cannata at a memorial concert in honor of Barry S. Brook; here, too, music and occasion combined to produce some tears in the audience.
8.    The exceptions occur on the recordings of the BBC and Lausanne concerts of June and November 1989, respectively, where the bandoneon takes a crack at the melody during the central panel ($B$). These performances, however, differ from those cited in note 2 in two important respects. First, the group at both concerts is a sextet (instead of a quintet), with two bandoneons, and I am not sure if it is Piazzolla or the "second" bandoneon that plays the melody there. Second, the sextet, featured a cello in place of the quintet's violin; and when the bandoneon plays the melody in the central panel, it is precisely at the spot at which, in performances with quintet, the violin would normally take the theme for a second time, but now up an octave. Obviously, the cello would not "soar" quite as dramatically. The BBC performance can be heard on *Astor Piazzolla: 57 Minutos con la Realidad*, Intuition INT

30792 (1996), that from Lausanne on *Astor Piazzolla: The Lausanne Concert*, Milan 73138/35649-2 (1993).
9.    On the bandoneon in the tango tradition, see the superb notes by Maria Dunkel that accompany the recording *Bandoneon Pure: Dances of Uruguay-René Marino Rivero*. International Institute for Traditional Music, Traditional Music of the World 5, Smithsonian Folkways SF 40431 (1993); see also DUNKEL, *Bandonion und Konzertina: Ein Beitrag zur Darstellung des Instrumententyps*, 2d ed., Berliner musikwissenschaftliche Arbeiten 30 (Munich: Emil Katzbichler, 1996), 19, 30, 149-53; and FERRER, *El libro del tango*, 1: 79-86; 2: 78-81. For a recording that presents a survey-like history in sound of the bandoneon as a tango instrument from the early twentieth century through "early" Piazzolla in the 1940s, see *Los grandes bandoneones de la Guardia Vieja y la época de oro del tango*, El Bandoneón EBCD 100 (1998).
10.    We might note that he shows no reluctance to lead the way in the *A* sections, which, as noted above, is based on the earlier *Nonino*, composed and dedicated to his father at a happier time in their lives. On Piazzolla's father, Vicente (1897-1958), himself an amateur accordionist, and the father-son relationship, see Diana PIAZZOLLA, *Astor*, 19-31 and *passim*.

tion of the two), there can be no doubt that Piazzolla associated the haunting melody of *Adiós nonino*—and its blue notes in particular—with the idea of death.

Indeed, Piazzolla revisited the association of blue notes and death a decade later, when, in 1967-1968, he collaborated with the Montevideo-born poet Horacio Ferrer to produce his only dramatic work, the "operita" (as they called it) *María de Buenos Aires*, which had its premiere in Buenos Aires on 8 May 1968.[11]

Derived from—and in a way a sequel to—a *porteño*[12] legend about a young girl, María, who, circa 1900, leaves her factory job to become a tango singer, only to sink into a life of prostitution and die shortly thereafter, Ferrer's libretto depicts a surrealistic, 1960s fantasy world in which María, clearly a personification of both the tango itself and the city of Buenos Aires,[13] is surrounded by a set of colorful characters that includes El Duende (the goblin-narrator), the Chief Old Thief (Ladrón Antiguo Mayor), a choir of psychoanalists (Coro de los Analistas), and the Three Marionettes Drunk on Things (Tres Marionetas Borrachas de Cosas). The opera begins with El Duende standing at María's asphalt-covered grave; there he evokes her voice—in which she is embodied—in order to lure her to a cruel life-after-death in which she is seduced by "a fistful of this bandoneon voice that still burns in her throat,"[14] and thus destined to suffer another life

11.    On both the genesis of the work and a sketch of its performance history, see FERRER, *El libro del tango*, 3: 676-77; see also, FERRER, *The Golden Age of Tango: An Illustrated Compendium of its History* (Buenos Aires: Manrique Zagos, 1996), 160-61 and 213, and "How *María de Buenos Aires* Came to be Written," notes (21-23) for the Teldec recording cited below. In recent years *María* has enjoyed major revivals in both the United States and Europe (see the comments about the recordings, below). I know of four recordings of the work: (1) Trova TLS-5020/2 (1968), the "original cast" recording, with Piazzolla, Ferrer as narrator, Amelita Baltar as María, and Héctor de Rosas in the various male roles (my thanks to Malena Kuss for having made this out-of-print recording available to me); (2) Teldec 3984-20632-2 (1997-1998), with Gidon Kremer and the Kremer_ATA Musica, Ferrer as narrator, and Julia Zenko and Jairo as the two vocalists; this recording, the only one to provide the entire libretto—with translations into English, French, and German—uses a revised orchestration by Leonid Desyatnikov (see below) and offers the work as Kremer has been performing it on tour; (3) Dynamic CDS 185/1-2 (1997), with I Solisti Aquilani, Vittorio Antonellini, dir., Nestor Garay as narrator, and Marina Gentile and Paolo Speca as vocalists; this recording offers an Italian revival of 1996-97; and (4) Milan 73138/35602-2 (1989-90), with a version that constitutes a Piazzola- approved (later regreted) "adaptation" presented at a 1987 French revival

that added choreography, scenery, and extra characters, expanded the instrumental forces, and altered the very substance of the music. (It is not recommended to those coming to the work for the first time.)

The original version of the opera called for the following forces: a narrator for the role of El Duende (see below); two singers, female and male, for the roles of María and the various male characters, respectively; a small chorus (for recitations only); and an instrumental ensemble of bandoneon, two violins, viola, cello, double-bass, flute, electric guitar, piano, and two percussion parts. The reorchestration by Desyatnikov for the Kremer revival reduces the instrumental parts to eight, doing away with one violin, one percussion part, and the guitar.

Piazzolla and Ferrer collaborated a number of times during the years just after *María*, most notably on the wildly successful *Balada para un loco* (1969) and other short songs, as well as on the more ambitious oratorio *El pueblo joven* (1972); on the Piazzolla-Ferrer collaborations, see Pierre MONETTE, "Astor Piazzolla: De New York à New York," in *Tango nomade*, 388-89.

12.    The term denotes someone or something from the port city of Buenos Aires.

13.    We should note that, having discovered the city in the sixteenth century, Spanish sailors named the site Nuestra Señora Santa María del Buen Aire.

14.    "... un puñado de esa voz bandoneonera/que aùn quema en tu garganta" (*cuadro* 1, lines 17-18). More than

of degradation. Having descended into the city's sewers, María dies, now to be resur-
rected as her own "shade" (La Sombra de María), in which guise—and to the strains of
a chant-like dirge sung by A Voice of that Sunday (Una voz de ese Domingo)—she eventually gives birth to another María (and another and another?), whose fate, no doubt,
will be yet another hellish cycle of grinding poverty (or will it?).

Ferrer and Piazzolla cast *María de Buenos Aires* in two *partes* of eight *cuadros* each.[15] It
is *cuadro* 9—the "Contramilonga a la funerala (por la primera muerte de María)"—that
interests us here.[16] As its title implies, the scene presents the funeral for María's "first
death"; more specifically, according to the "synopsis" for *cuadro* 9 that appears in the
score: "El Duende describes the funeral that the night creatures make for the first death
of María," beginning his narration to the accompaniment of the music shown in
Example 2 (see next page).[17]

Then, at the words "Mystery there, misereireing on the tightrope of an obscene
jingle in sacramental solitude,"[18] Piazzolla shifts gears, and we hear the following
beneath El Duende's droning recitation (see Example 3).

just another instrument in the ensemble, the bandoneon
takes on the role of a protagonist who lures María into
the sordid underworld of tango life.

15.   To these, the Kremer recording (see note 11) adds
another as *cuadro* 3a, which borrows its music (but not its
text) from *cuadro* 15; I do not know if it is authentic.
Ferrer originally wrote—but did Piazzolla set?—eighteen scenes.

16.   Briefly, the *milonga* was originally a song-type introduced to Buenos Aires around the mid-nineteenth
century by the *payadores* (popular singer-improvisors) of
the countryside. Once established in its urban setting,
the *milonga* picked up and parodied the dance steps of
the *rioplatense* African community, and, by *c.*1880 at the
latest—and by now transformed into a dance-type—
gained popularity with the slum-dwelling *compadritos* (the
Pampa *gauchos* who flocked to the outskirts of Buenos
Aires), among whom it soon evolved into the tango. As
for the prefix "contra": this seems to point to nothing
more than the *milonga's* country origins. On the *milonga*
and its evolution into the tango, see FERRER, *El libro del
tango*, III: 714-16; see also, Isabel ARETZ, *El folklore musical
argentino* (Buenos Aires: Ricordi Americana, 1952), 157-59;
and Simon COLLIER, "The Birth," in *Tango: The Dance, the
Song, the Story*, ed. Collier (London: Thames and Hudson,

1995), 40-41, 44-45. For a brilliantly concise summary of
the much-debated (often along ethnic lines) origins of
the tango, see Marta E. SAVIGLIANO, "Fragments for a
Tango-centric History," in *Latin American Music: An
Encyclopedic History*, (forthcoming); see also, Gerard
BÉHAGUE, "Tango," in *Die Musik in Geschichte und Gegenwart*,
rev. ed., ed. Ludwig FINSCHER, (Kassel: Bärenreiter, 1998),
Sachteil 9, cols. 221-23. Finally, the term *milonga* could also
designate the place—a cabaret, for example—at which
the dance was done, as well as the women, *milonguitas*, who
worked there.

17.   There are two piano-vocal scores available for the
opera. I follow that published by Editorial Lagos
(Buenos Aires, 1973), where the synopsis for *cuadro* 9—
there is one for each *cuadro*—reads: "El Duende relata el
funeral que las criaturas de la noche hacen por la primera
muerte de María" (p. 73). The other piano-vocal score,
which I have not seen, is that issued by Tonos, Plate No.
20067; cited in "Piazzolla's Published Score List," a
website compiled by Noritake YONEZAWA: <http://
www.yonezawa.com/piazzolla/scores.htm>. Finally,
an orchestral score, which can be rented from Editorial
Lagos, is not commercially available.

18.   "Misterio allà, misereteando en la maroma/de un
jingle obsceno en soledad de sacramento ..."

**Example 2**    *Cuadro 9, mm. 1-16 (p. 36)*

The reference to the *B* section of *Adiós nonino* can, I think, hardly be missed: (1) for the first seven measures (mm. 47-53), both the harmonies and the bass line of María's funeral music are identical to those with which the *B* section of *Adiós nonino* begins (mm. 18-24—see Ex. 1b), while an inner voice in the following measure (m. 54) echoes the melody of its earlier analogue (m. 25); (2) the blue notes that make *Adiós nonino* so memorable also permeate the melodic/harmonic fabric of the

| Example 3 | *Cuadro* 9, mm. 47-62 (pp. 37-38) |

"Contramilonga" (mm. 49-50, 55-56, 59-60), and do so in precisely the same metric context; and (3) what else is the opening motive of the *María* excerpt—$\hat{1}$ $\hat{2}$ $\hat{5}$—than a scrambling of *Adiós nonino's* $\hat{5}$ $\hat{2}$ $\hat{1}$ $\hat{5}$, even if we become aware of the connection retroactively, after hearing the blue notes.

One may, of course, argue that at least some elements of the resemblance may be coincidental, especially since Piazzolla used both the harmonic pattern and its underlying bass line on other occasions. Indeed, he uses them in two later *cuadros* in *María de Buenos Aires*: (1) throughout the second part of *cuadro* 12—the "Aria de los Analistas"—where they take on an almost-refrain-like function as they accompany either the sorrowful melody of the "analista primera" (mm. 128-135, 150- 159, 172-179, 192-199, 223-231) or, in one instance, a guitar obbligato (mm. 205-212); and (2) near the end of *cuadro* 13—the "Romanza del Duende"—in order to accompany a snippet of narration by the Three Marionettes Drunk on Things (Ex. 4a-b, pp. 547-48).

Now, however, the biting blue notes are either little more than a faint memory (*cuadro* 12, meas. 130, where, without the suspension over the barline, the minor ninth is lost), or absent entirely (*cuadro* 13). And indeed, the reference in the "Romanza" presents us only with that aura of "innocence" (as I called it above) through which the blue notes otherwise cry out and jar us in both *Adiós nonino* and María's funeral music.

There is another aspect of these references to *Adiós nonino* that calls for comment. Though various published editions of *Adiós nonino* present it in either F minor-Ab major or D minor-F major (the two keys for *A* and *B*, respectively), the three great performances at Buenos Aires (1981), Vienna (1984), and Central Park (1987) present the work in F# minor-A major,[19] with the poignant melody of the *B* section in the latter key. And it is almost exclusively in A major that Piazzolla refers to it in *María de Buenos Aires*: it appears only in that key in both the "Contramilonga" for María's first funeral—where, significantly, A major makes its first appearance in the work—and El Duende's "Romanza," as well as in the first four (of six) recollections in the "psychoanalysist's aria. Thus not only did the harmonies, bass line, and blue notes of *Adiós nonino* have significance for Piazzolla, but so too, apparently, did the key of A major.[20]

Why should Piazzolla have returned to the harmonies, bass line, blue notes, and tonality of *Adiós nonino* in *cuadro* 9 of *María de Buenos Aires*? The answer is obvious: the music of both pieces refers to similar extra-musical contexts, as both are concerned with funerals and the mystery of death. And if, in *María*, we fancifully interpret (and what else is "interpretation" but "fanciful") the dissonant blue notes as a response to El Duende's "obscene jingle," perhaps we may hear the transformation of *Adiós nonino*'s opening $\hat{5}\ \hat{2}\ \hat{1}\ \hat{5}$ into the somewhat more open-ended $\hat{1}\ \hat{2}\ \hat{5}$ as a reflection of both the "mystery" and the "sacramental solitude" of the scene. Less clear, at least to me, is the significance of the recollections in *cuadros* 12 and 13, especially since they are now stripped—partially in the

---

19. See n. 2 and 4.
20. There is, I believe, still another instance in which Piazzolla looks back to the harmonies, bass line, and "blue notes" of the *Adiós nonino* theme; it occurs—once

again in A major—in the third movement, "Nightclub 1960," of his *Histoire du Tango* for flute and guitar, measures 36-43 and 87-94; I discuss the quotation in my article cited in footnote 3.

**Example 4a**    *Cuadro* 12, mm. 128-35 (pp. 50-51)

former, entirely in the latter—of the emotive power of the dissonant blue notes. Perhaps the safest recourse is not to attribute any semantic significance to them at all.

I should like to end this short essay with an even shorter plea. Although the self-quotation in *cuadro* 9, especially the very audible blue notes, must seem obvious to anyone who comes to *María de Buenos Aires* with *Adiós nonino* already in the ear—indeed, the blue notes set off a whispered buzz of "es *Adiós*" among the Piazzolla cogniscenti who surrounded me and my wife at a performance of *María* at the Brooklyn Academy of Music in October 1998—the literature on Piazzolla does not, so far as I know, make a single reference to it. And this, I think, sends a signal: and that is that although biographical-

**Example 4b**    *Cuadro* 13, meas. 111-118 (p. 58)

anecdotal, sociological-anthropological, and aesthetic matters certainly have an important place in Piazzolla research (as does the journalistic approach that has prevailed so far), it is time to stop concentrating on them exclusively. Rather, the music itself—piece by piece, genre by genre, period by period—must begin to share center stage.[21] It is, after all, Piazzolla's music that engages and fascinates us. And if the present essay calls forth others that take a close look at the music, it will have more than served its purpose.[22]

21.  This, of course, would be greatly facilitated if more of Piazzolla's original full scores and arrangements were generally available. They should be as easily available as those by composers already ensconced in the "canon." Thankfully, Tonos Verlag (Darmstadt) and Editorial Lagos (Buenos Aires) have begun to issue some of the works for small ensemble, such as the quintet.

22.  A start in that direction occurred at the conference *Astor Piazzolla: A Symposium*, sponsored by the Center for the Study of Free-Reed Instruments at the Graduate Center, The City University of New York, on 13 March 2000. In addition to the paper printed here, other contributors and their titles were: David B. CANNATA, "Piazzolla's New York Concerts"; Ulrich KRÄMER, "Harmony and Form in *María de Buenos Aires*"; Malena KUSS, "The Referential Poetics of Astor Piazzolla"; Martín KUTNOWSKI, "Instrumental Rubato and Phrase Structure in Astor Piazzolla's Music"; and Ramón PELINSKI, "Wandering Ostinato Figures and the Pleasure of Repetition in Astor Piazzolla's Music." My thanks to Ulrich Krämer, Malena Kuss, and Ramón Pelinski for having read and commented on an early draft of this essay.

Ted Solís

# "Let's Play One *Seis caliente*": Coalescence and Selective Adaptation in a Diasporic Puerto Rican Musical Style

A DIASPORIC COMMUNITY, the Hawaii Puerto Ricans, have created a musical dialect in some ways unique, but recognizably Puerto Rican and "Latin." The community has drawn upon "root" Puerto Rican, situational Hawaiian, U.S., pan-Latin, and hegemonic Cuban musical sources, mediated through a combination of chronological and geographical circumstances, and ethnic self-image. The Jíbaro, "white" peasant farmers of the Puerto Rican hinterland (whose life styles and cultural production today exist largely in memory and in deliberately "folkloric" contexts), are the most potent symbol of that self-image among Hawaii Puerto Ricans. The term *seis caliente* found in the title symbolizes the musical culture's uniqueness. The two Spanish words are not normally found together in other parts of the Puerto Rican diaspora or in Puerto Rico itself; as a phrase, "seis caliente," they represent a coalescence of the traditional (a traditional dance/song genre with many variants brought from Puerto Rico to Hawaii) and the diasporically adapted *seis caliente*, a homogenization and amalgam in Hawaii of these variants. Such processes of homogenization have characterized the musical history of this community since its inception, but here I consider its development from the early 1900's through the 1950's, a period during which the aesthetic ideals of the style crystallized and endured despite its long period of isolation from Puerto Rican primary cultural streams.

## The Hawaii Puerto Rican Community

Hawaii Puerto Ricans are, along with the Nuyoricans of New York, the most distinctive subgroup of the Puerto Rican diaspora. Deriving their cultural roots in Puerto Rico primarily from the highland Jíbaro peasants, they came to Hawaii early in this century as contracted plantation laborers, and now number some 15-20,000. The largest and earliest Puerto Rican groups, some 5,000 men, women, and children, migrated to Hawaii in 1900 and 1901. A smaller, distinct importation occurred in 1921. Until relatively recently (the late 1960s), they have experienced little contact with their ancestral homeland.

The isolation of Hawaii Puerto Rican culture ensured that it would develop differently from cultures of Caribbean and U.S.-mainland Puerto Ricans. Owing both to isolation and cultural self-image, Hawaii Puerto Ricans preserve as everyday music older Jíbaro genres and performance practices of music and dance, which in Puerto Rico have either been lost or preserved in self-consciously revivalist or "folkloric" contexts. Unique in the Hawaiian subculture of the Puerto Rican diaspora, Jíbaro music has provided and remained the foundation for popular music and dance.

Hawaii Puerto Ricans define themselves ethnically through the music and dance complex, wherein the most potent symbols are certain genres, performance practices, and musical instruments. My general hypothesis is that the maintenance of this ethnic identity involves what I have elsewhere called a "Jíbaro filtering process" : i.e., changes in music and dance must be legitimized by "being Jíbaro."[1] Through musical culture this community has grappled with the complexities of its ethnic self-image vis-a-vis broader ethnic categories such as "Hispanic" and "Latino."

## Music and Migration

The Hawaii Sugar Planters' Association in the nineteenth century was perennially in search of new sources of labor. Each imported ethnic group, beginning in the 1850s with Chinese, followed by the Japanese, Portuguese, Koreans, Filipinos, and others provided plantation laborers, but within a few years workers inevitably began to drift to urban areas, demanding higher wages and better working conditions. Then another outside ethnic group would be targeted for recruitment to defuse the power of the preceding assertive group or groups. Puerto Rico was considered a potentially important source of labor at the turn of the century, since the island had been devastated in 1899 by the great hurricane San Siriaco of 1899, which destroyed crops and infrastructure.

Jíbaros made up the overwhelming majority of the Puerto Rican sugar labor importations to Hawaii in the early 1900s. Their small highland coffee and tobacco landholdings in Puerto Rico had been devastated, and many left the land for the cities, accelerating the process begun earlier in the nineteenth century with the encroachment of haciendas and plantations. Their agricultural expertise and ability to endure hard agricultural labor made them prime candidates for recruitment by sugar emissaries from Hawaii.

Most Jíbaros brought to Hawaii in 1900 cut ties with their homeland rather abruptly and completely; visits to Puerto Rico were prohibitively expensive for these plantation workers. In effect, they either stayed or left, but almost never returned to Hawaii if they re-visited Puerto Rico even once. Splitting of families, with assignments to any of the sugar plantation Hawaiian islands, and name confusion even among fami-

---

1.   See Theodore SOLÍS, "Jíbaro Image and the Ecology of Hawaii Puerto Rican Musical Instruments," *Latin* *American Music Review* 16/2 (Fall/Winter 1995): 123-53, here passim.

ly members, were common. Widespread illiteracy among the first generation exacerbated this general isolation. In addition, Jíbaros were well known in Puerto Rico for independence and hospitality, but also insularity and defensiveness; these attitudes were readily re-directed to Hawaii plantation owners, functionaries, workers, and other non-Hispanic, non-Catholics outsiders. This set the stage for the kind of selective adoption of genres, styles, and musical instruments leading to the unique musical world which developed in Hawaii.

In the more than ninety years since the principal migrations to Hawaii, extensive urbanization and cultural homogenization in Puerto Rico have blurred its Hispanic-African cultural polarity. The great cultural gap between the highland Hispanic Jíbaros and lowland Afro-Puerto Ricans which existed at the time of the first migration has considerably narrowed in Puerto Rico itself since that time, under the pressure first of the large incorporated plantations (largely U.S.-owned), and later of industrialization. These processes had the effect of drawing Jíbaros from their individual shareholdings, and ultimately of urbanizing the island and throwing disparate racial groups together.[2] The result was an inevitable acceleration of the physical and cultural mixing which had been taking place since the early colonial period.

Much of this process bypassed Hawaii Puerto Ricans, who still cling tenaciously to their perceived Hispanic and Taino Amerindian heritage,[3] and have implicitly (and sometimes explicitly) rejected overtly African or Afro-Latin musical and dance features. That general attitude has influenced the musical selection procedure at every level, with regard to genre, improvisation practices, dancing style, or musical instruments.

For Hawaii Puerto Ricans, overtly Puerto Rican ethnic symbols are relatively limited. Icons of Puerto Rican identity such as the Spanish language have over the decades eroded; most third and fourth generation Hawaii Puerto Ricans can neither speak nor understand much Spanish. This has brought into relief the few areas which remain unique symbols of Puerto Rican identity: a *compadrazgo* (co-godparent) system, in which, through the terms *comay* [*comadre*: "godmother"] and *compay* [*compadre*: "godfather"], they clearly acknowledge religious/familial relationship obligations and mutual respect; certain popu-

2.   For an excellent discussion of this process as it applies to musical acculturation see Jorge DUANY, "Toward an Anthropology of Salsa," *Latin American Music Review* 5/3 (Fall/Winter 1984): 187-215; for an exploration of further musical acculturation in New York City, see Ruth GLASSER, *My Music is My Flag: Puerto Rican Musicians and Their New York Communities, 1917-1940* (Berkeley: University of California Press, 1995).
3.   Caribbean Taino Amerindian ancestry is commonly used by Hawaii Puerto Ricans to explain dark skin or "nonwhite" features. See Jorge DUANY, "Ethnicity, Identity, and Music: An Anthropological Analysis of the Dominican Merengue," *In Music and Black Ethnicity: The Caribbean and South America*, ed. Gerard H. BÉHAGUE (New Brunswick, NJ: Transaction Publishers, 1994): 65-90, and Michael LARGEY, "Composing a Haitian Cultural Identity: Haitian Elites, African Ancestry, and Musical Discourse," *Black Music Research Journal* 14/2 (1994): 99-117, here 112, who refer to this same rationalization for the Dominican Republic and among Haitian creoles respectively.

lar foods such as *pasteles, arroz de gandule, ensalada de bacalao,* and *arroz con pollo,* which remain of the richly varied Caribbean Puerto Rican cuisine; and, most importantly, music and dance.

## Plantation Musical Culture of the Immigrants

The kinds of music and dance heard on early 1900's plantations were those popular in parts of Puerto Rico which the immigrants had recently left. The basic ensemble consisted of a trio: the *cuatro* plucked melodic lead creole guitar;[4] an ordinary six-string Spanish guitar strummed an accompaniment; and a *güiro* gourd scraper steadily subdivided the main metric pulses.

The *sinfonía* button accordion was also played on plantations and sometimes replaced the cuatro as the melodic lead instrument. The standard instrumentation for most groups now is one Spanish guitar, plus electric bass, cuatro, güiro, and *bongós* and/or *congas* (and sometimes a *timbales* drum set). As the most tangible musical artifacts of culture, instruments have served as vital ethnic symbols of this community, its history and attitudes. I have earlier examined changing instrumentation as ethnic metaphor.[5] In this paper, however, I will limit myself primarily to a discussion of genres, their hierarchies, and interactions.

The musical genres, described in detail in the glossary, included the *danza, guaracha, seis, vals, polca, mazurca,* and *aguinaldo* or Christmas song. All but the very last are dances, some of which are also sung; the aguinaldo, generally religious, was sung but not danced. The repertory of such genres came from the old country, and new pieces were composed in those styles. Other song/dance genres were added to this nucleus over the years, notably the coastal Puerto Rican *plena* in the 1920s, Cuban *bolero* in the 1930s, and the Dominican *merengue* in the 1950s. Of the above, the vals, guaracha, *seis,* bolero, and merengue still comprise the core of any Hawaii Puerto Rican dance, while danzas and plenas are frequently heard, albeit in greatly altered form, and (as we will see) often not recognized as such.

The Plantation context worked to both internalize and reify pre-existing attitudes and cultural production. Plantation camps were often segregated by ethnicity ("Puerto Rican Camp," "Filipino Camp," etc.), partly because plantation owners feared a unified labor force. The poverty, isolation, and relative self-sufficiency of the Puerto Rican plantation workers threw them upon their own devices with regard to amusement: the Saturday evening dance, generally held in individual homes, was their primary recreation in the early years.

Camps were in rural areas, far from music stores and phonograph records (which

---

4. The old cuatro had four single strings or double courses and was very different from the curvaceous modern, five double-coursed, violin-like instrument (see Figure 1) which supplanted it in Puerto Rico from the 1930s on.

5. See Solís, "Jíbaro Image," 123-53.

**Figure 1** Nuclear trio of güiro, strummed Spanish guitar, and plucked lead modern cuatro, accompanied by timbales
Kapa'a, island of Kauai, Hawaii, 7/15/90 (photo: Ted Solís)

L-R: timbales; Johnny TORRES, güiro; George ORTIZ, guitar; Bobby CASTILLO, cuatro

were at any rate, for the first years, at least, beyond their financial means), and it was not until the early 1920's that radio broadcasts were common in the U.S. Musicians therefore drew upon their traditional repertory—guaracha, *seis*, vals, polca, mazurca, and danza—and composed music and texts in those styles. The oldest in this community attest to the survival, earlier in this century, of the venerable Puerto Rican *trovador* tradition of sung *décima* improvisation in Spanish.[6] The décima is a traditional Iberian ten-line, octosyllabic or hexasyllabic poetic form found throughout Latin America. A number of décima schemes exist, but the most common in Puerto Rico is the *espinela*, whose rhyme scheme is ABBAACCDDC. (Lines 1, 4, and 5 rhyme, as do 2 and 3, 6, 7, and 10, and 8 and 9.) The octosyllabic form was set to the secular *seis*, and the hexasyllabic, to the sacred aguinaldo.[7] Using this extremely demanding verse form, true *trovadores* were expected to improvise in real time upon both topics and a *pie forzado* ("forced foot," a final line: see glossary), which were presented to them *ad hoc*.

6. These are for the most part elderly children or grandchildren of the immigrant generation, although a few very aged, treasured individuals were born in Puerto Rico and came when very young.

7. See Appendix II, Example 1: Two verses of décima

espinela in *controversía* (competitive dialogue) form between a man and woman, recorded on the island of Kauai in 1990. These were not, however, improvised, but learned verbatim long before.

## Plantation Musical Acculturation

De facto camp segregation notwithstanding, Puerto Ricans came in close contact with members of other ethnic groups on the plantations and later in the towns. It is not surprising, therefore, that some were able to sing and play musics of these groups. Polynesian Hawaiian music, for example, has long served as an *au courant* source of adapted repertoire; over the decades, Puerto Ricans have combined currently popular Hawaiian genres with syncretically suitable genres of their own. Like most musicians in Hawaii of whatever ethnic group, Puerto Rican musicians can usually sing at least some folk and popular Hawaiian songs. Many can play the ukelele and some are adept at playing folk Hawaiian "slack key" guitar, using its characteristic *scordatura* technique.

For "slack key" guitar [Hawaiian: *ki ho 'alu*] performance, the six strings of the Spanish guitar are loosened so that open strings play some form of a major triad. Performers reiterate brief melodic and rhythmic patterns derived from the "traditional" (primarily pre-"Tin Pan Alley") hula tradition, frequently using parallel chords, harmonics, "hammering" onto the string, ostinati, and (as opposed to dotted) even note values with syncopated phrasing. I have collected examples of slack key guitar pieces played as guarachas.[8] The guaracha makes typical use of the last three stylistic features; as we will see, it is, of all the traditional immigrant generation genres, the least distinctive in style, and frequently serves as a sort of "catchall" category into which more specialized genres have been subsumed.

Both the media-generated dreamy Waikiki-style ballad of the "Sweet Leilani" variety and the Cuban bolero (the slow-medium tempo, duple meter romantic vocal genre, not to be confused with the triple meter Spanish dance) were introduced to Hawaii in the 1930s. All boleros and most Waikiki ballads share duple meter, slow-medium tempo, relatively sophisticated harmonies (in the Puerto Rican case, by comparison with the *seis* and guaracha), and the use of a lyrico-dramatic voice production. The barred glissando parallel chord technique used by some cuatro players, especially in boleros, is very likely borrowed from that of the Hawaiian steel guitar.[9]

## The Guaracha as Mediator

Over the years, some genres have absorbed others, and some have undergone coalescence and homogenization within their own general categories. The guaracha has served as an important point of mediation among a number of these genres, absorbing here, contributing features there. That this influence has extended to the danza, *seis*, and

8. See Theodore SOLÍS, *Puerto Rico in Polynesia: Jíbaro Traditional Music on Hawaiian Plantations*, CD and liner notes (Original Music OMCD 020, 1994).
9. For an example of this technique, and of a Hawaiian ballad, "Pua Elena" played as a bolero, see Theodore SOLÍS, *Puerto Rican Music in Hawaii: Kachi-Kachi*, CD/Cassette and liner notes (Smithsonian/ Folkways CD SF40014, 1989).

plena, which are socio-historically and musically so different from one another, is indicative of the guaracha's powerfully evocative musical qualities, as well as its adaptability and relative looseness of parameter.

Most likely originating in Colonial Mexico, the guaracha was brought to Cuba and later to Puerto Rico (a closely-associated Caribbean colonial partner) in the nineteenth century. In Cuba and Puerto Rico it is most commonly performed as a duple meter song and dance in medium to fast tempo, usually strophic, with a verse and chorus structure.[10] Guaracha texts are usually light and/or amorous. Rhythmic patterns based upon the *tresillo* figure permeate its texture, and inform its step and bass patterns.[11] The güiro today generally plays a *guarachada* ("guaracha style") pattern using alternating down and up strokes.[12] (The term guarachada is used in Puerto Rico, but not Hawaii.) The first of each set of four sixteenth notes is a longer down stroke, thus imparting a stress accent. The guitar accompaniment reflects güiro rhythm and technique: it consists of strummed block chords in alternating sixteenth note up and down strokes, the first in each set of four strokes being damped with the heel of the right hand.[13] In Puerto Rico and among some of the oldest Hawaii Puerto Ricans the pattern is called *habana[d]o*, (for Havana) probably in recognition of the Cuban origin of the Puerto Rican guaracha. In Cuba, Puerto Rico, New York, and other areas in contact with the Latin mainstream, under the powerful influence of the Afro-Cuban son, both the bass pattern (and often the guitar strum) were sometimes characterized by what has been called the "anticipation" principle.[14] This technique demands a considerable musical sophistication, involving the ability of the bassist to: (1) play the first, tresillo measure of the typical two-measure *son clave* pattern;[15] (2) mentally reduce this to a two, rather than three-stroke pattern in which the first beat of the clave is silent;[16] and (3) anticipate by one beat the harmonic structure of the next measure. This layered, "out-of-phase" rhythmic texture helps impart an important harmonico-rhythmic drive to such Cuban and Cuban-influenced musics.

In addition to denoting traditional pieces actually known to be guarachas the term is used in Hawaii more generically to describe fast Latin dance pieces of uncertain category (i.e., "uncertain" to the average Hawaii Puerto Rican, not necessarily to a

---

10. In Cuba, under the growing influence of the *rumba*, *son*, and other Afro-Cuban genres the guaracha acquired a final *montuno* section, in which a harmonic ostinato, choral response, and more "Afro," complex percussion accompany solo vocal improvisation. Consistent with the (at least initial) general rejection of overtly "Afro" stylistic gestures and instrumention, this montuno section (which, significantly, became part of the guaracha complex after the 1900 migration) is seldom heard in Hawaii except as performed by self-consciously Cuban-oriented groups. In general, therefore, the montuno may

be discounted as a typical stylistic feature and does not play a role in the mediative process between guaracha and other genres there.

11. See Appendix II, Example 2.

12. See Appendix II, Example 3.

13. See Appendix II, Example 4.

14. See Peter MANUEL, "The Anticipated Bass in Cuban Popular Music," *Latin American Music Review* 6/2 (Fall/Winter 1985): 249-61.

15. See Appendix II, Example 5.

16. See Appendix II, Example 6.

*Caribeño* (Caribbean Latino), who may be perfectly aware she or he is listening or danc-ing to, or performing a plena, guaracha, son or rumba).[17]

## "Plenas y Porquería"

That the plena is often confused with the guaracha is not surprising, as they share some basic elements: duple meter, simple harmony, and a verse-chorus (the chorus being sung by a group) structure. Although plenas became popular in Puerto Rico during World War I, it is unlikely many were heard in Hawaii before being brought by immi-grants in 1921. In 1990 Miguel Rodrigues (1904-96) remembered members of this second, smaller labor importation from Puerto Rico as having brought *"plenas y porcería"* [plenas and other such junk]; the implication is that of an "un-Jíbaro" accretion to the traditional repertory introduced by more recent arrivals, unwelcome reminders of the racial-cultural intermingling which had occurred in Puerto Rico during the 20 years since the first generation had left. The plena grew out of the Afro Puerto Rican coastal tradition (in and around the southern Puerto Rican coastal town of Ponce) and thus retained some of the "dangerous" Afro connotation. Its typical accompaniment in Puerto Rico included vertical barrel drums and a set of jingle-less frame drums (*pan-deretta*), which were the most tangible evidence of Afro heritage denial.[18]

## The Danza: Faded Colonial Memories

The danza, by contrast, shared very few elements with the Caribbean guaracha, either in context or musically. The *danza Puertorriqueña* is related to the great Euro-Caribbean continuum originating in the French *contredanse*, which was then taken up by other European nobility and their colonial subjects. (For the Spanish, this meant the Philippines and many colonies in Latin America.) The contredanse evolved in the Spanish colonies into a myriad varieties of *contradanza*; in Cuba, the contradanza evolved into the danza, *danzón* (closely related to the Puerto Rican danza), and *mambo* ultimately into the *chachachá*. Rural folk versions of the danza evolved in nineteenth-century Puerto Rico from this essentially upper-class ballroom dance. At the time of the first Hawaii migration, danzas were among the most popular Jíbaro dances.

Like its Cuban relative the danzón, but unlike the guaracha, the danza is usually instrumental only, with long melodies, sectional structure, relatively complex harmonies (often with shifts in tonal center and modality), and melodic phrases typically built around

17. Although the *seis* has borrowed musical and choreo-graphic features from the guaracha, its harmonic and poetic structures are quite distinctive and it is seldom if ever confused with the guaracha. Likewise, although the Dominican merengue (like the guaracha) is a medium to fast duple meter dance, it has such distinctive rhythmic patterns—the percussion pickup phrase (see Appendix, Example #7) and the march-like "two-step" bass, cor-responding to its simple steps—that it has not been heavily influenced by the guaracha (although some güiro players have adopted the guarachada stroke pattern).

18. See SOLÍS, "Jíbaro Image," 123-53, here passim.

the *cinquillo* (see glossary). In the slower introductory section, couples promenaded side by side, counterclockwise, moving to "closed" ballroom position when the faster danza proper began. In Puerto Rico the promenade is called *paseo*; in Hawaii, the term *despaseo* (which may through the process of "folk etymology" combine paseo "promenade" with *despacio* "slowly") is more common. More danzas are remembered than paseos, and a single paseo may serve to precede several distinct danzas. The paseo is all but extinct at dances; only the oldest Hawaii Puerto Ricans remember the danza in its original form, in which the paseo alternated, sometimes several times, with the danza. Danzas are now played in a style approximating that of the guaracha, having adopted its guitar and güiro accompaniment patterns, and dance steps. Many musicians, especially younger ones, play danzas without realizing that they are anything other than instrumental, long-melodied, sectional guarachas.[19] (Such a definition of guaracha is of course oxymoronic at every level, at least with regards to the "classic" guaracha features outlined above.) The following danzas were, however, so recognized as such by the performers. Most of the danzas I collected are of the category known in Puerto Rico as *danzas festivas* ("lively danzas"). Most were traditional pieces acquired from older musicians, learned long ago, and seldom played in recent years. The names of most danzas have long been forgotten, perhaps because they typically have no texts. Probably because of their relatively complex melodic/harmonic structures (relative to, e.g., guarachas and *seis*) they are normally played with little improvisation.

### Becoming a "Regular *Seis*"

The *seis*, with its very distinct harmonic pattern, melodic instrumental accompaniment patterns, and frequently nationalistic décima poetry, has shown no signs of disappearance as a genre. In its great diversity (named variously for descriptive qualities, towns, performers, composers, or hybrids with other forms) and narrative-expressive décima poetry, often replete with Jíbaro imagery and *Weltschmerz*, the *seis* is the genre with which Jíbaros most typically identify and to which they remain the most fiercely loyal. At the sound of the characteristic rising arpeggiated pickup phrase of a *seis caliente*[20] played by the lead cuatro one hears from the assemblage a collective welcoming sigh of warm anticipation.

Some older Puerto Ricans, especially, are familiar with specific *seis* genre names, each distinguished by characteristic ostinato accompaniments, tempi, instrumental interlude

---

19. Conversely, those Hawaii Puerto Rican musicians who do have some conception of danza as an independent genre sometimes conflate other long pieces with it. When requested to play an "old danza," three sets of musicians on two recordings (see Solís 1989 and 1994 recordings) quite independently played "danza" versions of "Lágrimas Negras" (two of the three not remembering its name), actually originally a classic bolero song by Cuban composer Miguel Matamoros popularized by the Trio Matamoros and others. It is likely that the relatively complex harmonies and sectional structure of this particular piece led to its misidentification as a danza.

20. See Appendix II, Example #8.

formulae and other features. Tanilau Dias (1908-98) for example, included the following *seis* types among those he remembered from the plantation: *Lorenzillo, Cagueño, de Andino, la una y una*, and *bombeada*. Raymond Rodrigues (1904-93) cited *villarán, chorreao, milonga, marumba, garrao, valseao*, and what he called "regular *seis*" (i.e., the typical modern amalgamated *seis caliente*). Only a half generation later, however, those distinctions were already blurring: Frank Fraticelli (b.1918), speaking of the 1920's and thirties, said "We used to say just "*seis*," not "*seis montuno*," "*seis Fajardeño*," [etc.]... We learned the types from Ramito records." Beginning in the 1950s, New York or Puerto Rico-recorded Jíbaro LP's featuring iconic Jíbaro singers such as "Ramito" and "Chuito" began to find their way to Hawaii. Many featured flamboyant record jackets with stereotypical Jíbaro symbols such as machetes, straw hats, cock fights, sugar cane fields, and so on.[21] These recordings included most of the traditional Jíbaro musical genres mentioned above, many of which had not been heard (other than the repertory of the immigrant generation retained in fading memory).

For Hawaii Puerto Ricans, these pieces formed the basis for a resurgence of, and re-contact with contemporary Puerto Rico. That resurgence included a renewed awareness of specific *seis* types. It has now become somewhat difficult in many cases to ascertain which pieces have come down from "the parents," and how much from later contact with visiting musicians from Puerto Rico, and from their recordings. I have found that, at least in some cases, informants who were sincerely convinced that they had learned pieces in the laps of their Puerto Rican-born parents had actually drawn verses or whole pieces from recordings.[22] In practice, however (except for a few somewhat obsessively folkloric heritage-minded musicians) the rich variety of *seises* to be found in Puerto Rico is but a memory to most contemporary Hawaii Puerto Ricans. What Raymond Rodrigues referred to (above) as "regular *seis*" is the typical idiosyncratic Hawaii up-tempo amalgam of rhythmic, harmonic, and melodic gestures drawn from *seis chorreao, seis con décimas, seis de Andino, seis Fajardeño*, and others, often generically referred to (uniquely by Hawaii Puerto Ricans) as a as "*seis chorreao*", or, most typically, as "*seis caliente*."[23]

---

21. Jíbaro culture declined very much in the countryside, but Jíbaros were in the process of becoming nationally what Kirshenblatt-Gimblett (quoted in Chris GOERTZEN and María Susana AZZI, "Globalization and the Tango," *Yearbook for Traditional Music* [1999]: 45-54 ) calls "museums of themselves" (see Barbara Kirshenblatt GIMBLETT, "Theorizing Heritage," *Ethnomusicology* 39/3 [1995]: 367-80.) Successive Puerto Rico governments have found Jíbaros (in their domesticated folkloric roles) a safe and useful national symbol.

22. The picture began to take on a shape similar to that of a "Saturday Night Live" episode I saw years ago, as follows: Dolly Parton (SNL guest host) is surrounded by her "children," speaking in faux-Appalachian accents.

They are begging her to "tell us a story, Mama!!" She assents. We are clearly about to hear an Old Folk Tale From The Hills. She begins: "Once upon a time, far, far away, there was a girl named 'Lucy'; she had the loveliest red hair. She was in love with a boy named 'Desi'..."(and it goes on from there). The point (not necessarily an original one) is that the "folk background" of "the folk" inevitably becomes intertwined with the whole cloth of their experience, including mass media.

23. For a discussion and recorded examples of a variety of *seis* types in Hawaii, see SOLÍS, *Puerto Rico in Polynesia: Jíbaro Traditional Music on Hawaiian Plantations*, CD and liner notes (Original Music OMCD 020, 1994).

The intricate group step patterns of the colonial period *seis*[24] have been amplified; the *seis* in Hawaii is now a couple dance, whose steps, like those of the danza, have been assimilated to those of the guaracha; all three, as well as the plena, are danced identically in Hawaii.

Most of the above-named *seis* categories were characterized by distinct guitar strums and güiro patterns. One especially common güiro stroke pattern in Puerto Rico (still maintained there) is the *café con pan*, so-called for its mnemonic rhythm derived by beginning the pattern on the sixteenth note (see Appendix I: Glossary). This *seis* güiro pattern is virtually extinct in Hawaii, having been supplanted by the guarachada pattern described above.

## Urbanization And The "Dangers" Of "New Repertoire"

By the mid to late 1930s a large proportion of the Hawaii Puerto Rican population had moved from the plantations to Honolulu and smaller urban centers. This urban migration represented the end of an era of relative social cohesiveness. Gymnasiums, social halls, and ballrooms replaced living rooms as dance settings. Plantation life served to preserve traditional musical culture, while urbanization accentuated and accelerated the process of adaptation of Hawaii and mainstream American musical values.

The musical acculturation of Hawaii Puerto Ricans in the 1930s, involving a considerable degree of adaptation of musical instruments, performance techniques, and genres significantly different from those of their immigrant parents, was well underway. Those remaining Puerto Rico-born musicians with acute memories of the old country would have been in their sixties or older; however, most active musicians were now of the second generation, had never seen or even communicated with Puerto Rico, spoke only English in daily discourse (whether or not they had any Spanish), and may have seen, but probably never played an old "keyhole cuatro."[25]

We can probably safely assume that the sometimes traumatic process of redefining "suitable" repertory in Hawaii began as soon as the newcomers arrived in 1901. Younger Puerto Ricans were in a "double bind" as the years passed: chastized both for preferring English to Spanish and for attempting Spanish in a way increasingly viewed to be incompetent. Attitudes toward the introduction of new musical practices, genres, and instruments have likewise proven complex and often ambiguous.

---

24. The *seis* was originally a Spanish Catholic liturgical altar dance named for the six (*seis*) young acolytes who typically participated in it. I was able to witness this dance in Sevilla (still regularly performed in the Cathedral) at Christmas in 1984. The nineteenth century social dance which developed out of it in the Caribbean is described in Manuel A. ALONSO, *El Jíbaro* [orig. *El Gíbaro*] (San Juan, Puerto Rico: Cultural Puertorriqueña., 1986).

25. In the mid 1930s musicians adapted cuatro tuning and performance practice to the American tenor guitar (see Figure 2), which replaced it until the late 1960s, when they became aware of the modern Puerto Rican cuatro. See SOLÍS, "Jíbaro Image."

Many members of the immigrant generation, musicians and non-musicians alike, appear in general to have had their musico-aesthetic preferences "frozen" in the time frame of that immigration. Musicians repeatedly attest to the strong-willed opposition to change, characteristic of most of the old-timers. Frank Fraticelli (b. 1918), discussing reactions to his music and that of others who, embraced musical genres and performance practices not characteristic of the period of the first immigrations, recalls their saying "Se Dañaron [they got spoiled]," or "Dañaron la música" [they spoiled the music]." This sort of interaction naturally takes place between contiguous generations: each generation reassesses its music and identity, creating new schisms and new confrontations between those persons willing to change and those adhering to established genres, musical instruments, and performance practices. Thus, attitudes may diverge widely to a "canon" repertory, such as *salsa* music and dance, which is actually the coalescence of musical practices that have accrued in Hawaii over generations. musical practices which had, even though having accrued in Hawaii over the years, became the "canon" repertory (even though attitudes about *salsa* music and dancing still differ considerably).[26] We can thus logically assume that even in the early 1900s musically adventurous Puerto Ricans met with disapproval from at least some of their peers and elders for cross-cultural musical attempts.

In the 1930s, excepting the smaller 1921 labor importation (see earlier discussion of the plena), musicians had been culturally isolated from Puerto Rico for three decades. The economic lot of Hawaii Puerto Ricans had improved at least to the extent that even some plantation workers could afford gramophones and 78 records. Plantation stores stocked Latin records in small numbers, sometimes by order. Such Latin American recordings as were available in Hawaii were for the most part produced in Mexico, Cuba, or New York, where the largest Latin American recording industries existed. Tanilau Dias, trained as an electrician and active as a band leader in the 1930s, habitually listened via short-wave radio to a Havana station, which offered the 78's they played for sale, and ordered many of the selections he heard (mostly Cuban) by mail. Old pieces "learned from their parents" apparently still formed the nucleus of the early 1930s repertory. However, due to the language assimilation discussed above, the creation of new compositions became increasingly rare. Thus, newly acquired recordings were important in contribution to the expansion of the corpus. Eventually these records represented the overwhelming majority of music performed.[27]

26. At any given time, two or three salsa bands mostly composed of Latino servicemen exist, playing mostly for dances at service clubs. These dances are advertised in the networks of local Puerto Ricans, who attend these dances only sporadically. For an exploration of local Hawaii Puerto Rican attitudes toward salsa instruments and music, see Solís 1995, ibid.

27. Theodore Solís, "'It's All From Records': The Musical 'Americanization' and 'Latinization' of Diasporic Puerto Ricans in Hawaii and California" (Unpublished paper, Annual meeting of the Far West Popular Culture and Far West American Culture Associations, Las Vegas, NV, 2 June 99).

Relatively few of the 78's reaching Hawaii featured specifically Puerto Rican genres, although many of the guarachas, canciones, waltzes, boleros, and other Cuban/Pan Latin genres were composed and/or performed by Puerto Ricans. Manuel[28] has addressed the degree to which Puerto Ricans have identified with overtly or adapted Cuban musics. Even most 1920s and 30s Puerto Rican musicians who had performed Jíbaro or Afro-Puerto Rican genres in Puerto Rico were obliged to accede to the demand for Cuban music in New York, whether in dance clubs or in the recording industry. Caught between a drastically declining local creative production and the lack of availability of recordings of Jíbaro music, Hawaii Puerto Ricans found themselves obliged to adapt repertoire. It is a measure of their allegiance to traditional repertory that Hawaii Puerto Ricans forced such vital and distinctive genres as Mexican *corridos* and Cuban popular orchestral rumbas, *sones* (such as the 1930 Cuban "rhumba" mega-hit "El Manisero," (actually a *son-pregón*) to the procrustean bed of the plantation-style guaracha.

The Puerto Rican waltz was then and still is an indispensable part of the corpus, second perhaps only to the *seis* in terms of its communal associative qualities. I have documented very few waltzes of Caribbean origin on 78 records, however. Thus, numerous Mexican and some South American waltzes (the latter often creolized varieties such as the *marinera*, *pasillo*, or *vals criollo*) were adapted to Puerto Rican style. Many of the Mexican "waltzes," although in danceable triple meter, were actually sung as narrative trophic *corridos* or emotional barroom-style *rancheras* that were primarily intended for listening rather than dancing. "Puerto Ricanization" often consisted of eliminating the lyrics, which tended to be Mexican referent-specific and highly charged emotionally, and because most Puerto Rican waltzes were purely instrumental. The guitar and güiro accompaniment patterns of the Puerto Rican waltz are closely related; they bear the same relationship to one another as they do in guaracha technique (see above). The güiro maintains a steady eighth note down/up pattern, six strokes per 3/4 measure. Each measure begins with a long stroke, thus imparting a stress accent. The guitar rhythmic pattern is essentially identical; the first chord in each set of six strums is damped with the heel of the right hand. This technique is quite different from that used by Hawaii Puerto Rican musician who wish, for whatever reason, to impart an exotic "Mexican" quality to a waltz. They then play only three main accents per measure, plucking the bass on beat one, and strumming chords on beats 2 and 3. Such songs are sometimes sung with enthusiastic stereotypical Mexican-style *gritos* ("yells") which irritate some traditionalists who consider the practice undignified and un-Puerto Rican. Musicians also seem to have converted Mexican polka-rhythm corridos into guarachas, eschewing the polka's march-like two-step bass and very binary, un-syncopated rhythms for the pervading tresillo and Caribbean syncopations of the guaracha.

28. See Peter MANUEL,"Puerto Rican Music and Cultural Identity: Creative Appropriation of Cuban Sources from Danza to Salsa," *Ethnomusicology* 38, 2 (Spring/Summer 1994): 249–80.

Figure 2 Expanded "rhumba [sic] band" style: "Jolly 'Ricans" band, Honolulu, 1945
Note bongós, claves, multiple guitars, "exhibition rhumba" dancers
(photo: courtesy of Raymond Pagan)

*Front*, L-R: John TRUSDELL, bongós. – Raymond PAGAN, guitar. – Louis PAGAN, guitar. – George
ACIA, Rickenbacker electric tenor guitar. – Albert PAGAN, guitar. – Frank LOPEZ, claves. – Firmin
PAGAN, güiro. *Rear*, L-R: John SANTIAGO, maracas. – Hattie PAGAN, vocal. – Danny RIVERA and Alice
FLORES, dancers. – Beatrice PAGAN, vocal.

The "exhibition rhumba" was largely derived from the Havana cabaret style,[29]
which first appeared in New York in 1930,[30] and was most likely promulgated in Hawaii
via escapist Hollywood musicals of the late 1930s and early 1940s, with their cameo
appearances by Cugat, Carmen Miranda, *et al.* A "specialty" feature of many social dance
intermissions, pre-prize fight entertainment, and other public occasions, it was usually
danced barefoot in Hawaii by one man and woman in typical ruffled "rhumba [sic] costumes," accompanied by enlarged ensembles (Hawaii versions of Cuban and American
cabaret "rhumba bands") with several guitars, maracas, and claves.

The exhibition rhumba's flamboyant "Afro" and individualistic (i.e., open, solo
position) qualities were the opposite of those of the established Jíbaro dance culture
(which emphasized "Iberian" erect bearing, and closed position, highly coordinated
couple dancing), and it was never performed as a social ballroom dance. It does, however, indicate the (conflicted and frequently resisted) attraction for this community of
Afro-Cuban music and dancing. These cinematic Cuban rhumbas nearly always featured

29. Robin MOORE, "The Commercial Rumba:
Afrocuban Arts as International Popular Culture," *Latin
American Music Review* 16, 2 (1995): 165-98, here 175.

30. John Storm ROBERTS, *The Latin Tinge: The Impact of
Latin American Music on the United States* (New York: Oxford
University Press, 1979, 76).

"white" performers, whether Latin or Anglo; the high society bands seen in these films mirrored the self-imposed de facto segregation of Havana tourist spots, including the bands which played in them. This also aided in the Hawaiians' ongoing avoidance of the acknowledgement of Africanisms in musics to which they were attracted.

## Conclusion

We have seen how an immigrant people based their musico-aesthetic choices upon ethnic self-image, creating a rigid yet mutable set of criteria which informed their repertoire, musical instruments, and performance practice. The Puerto Rican immigration to Hawaii in the early 1900s, consisting mainly of Jíbaro peasant farmers, preceded the geographic and cultural integration in Puerto Rico of highland "whites" and lowland "blacks." This integration in Puerto Rico and later, in New York, resulted in Latin popular musics of great vitality, but initially by-passed the Hawaii Puerto Ricans. The Hawaii diasporic Jíbaro community felt itself doubly besieged culturally: first, as immigrants cut off from communication with their homeland, far off in another ocean; and later, as "white" maintainers of a perceived Iberian background faced with the musical hegemony of an Africanized Cuba.

They dealt with these perceptions by iconicizing certain genres that were symbolically charged for them, maintaining and strengthening them through homogenization, simplification, and coalescence. The *seis* complex, for example, with its multifarious varieties, seemed to benefit by amalgamating and drawing unto itself the most desirable qualities from a number of its sub-genres. The guaracha, on the other hand, facilitated the adjustment to sociologically changed conditions by lending enough of its familiar, Jíbaro features to more "dangerous" genres, such as the Afro-Puerto Rican plena, to render them acceptable, and by allowing more complex genres, such as the danza, to exist within it (albeit at times almost unrecognizably) in simpler, more modern and manageable forms.

In addition, the degree to which musicians—during the five decades when they were essentially without contact with the mother culture—adapted available musics (sometimes as different as the Mexican corrido) to their symbolically central genres, demonstrated the vitality and symbolic importance of these musics. Through the adaptation process, they were able to both maintain ethnic identity and channel their creativity from the generation of material in an old traditional style to the imaginative reinterpretation of "exotic" materials.

The contacts finally re-established between Hawaii and Puerto Rico in the 1950s resulted in a resurgence of traditionalism in musical repertoire, style, and instrumentation. The coalescence and adaptation which had insured the survival of musical ethnic identity during that hiatus had, however, become integral processes in the creation of a distinct Hawaii Puerto Rican musical dialect, for which the *seis caliente* was—and is—a potent metaphor.

# Appendix I

## Glossary

*café con pan*  mnemonic for ♪. ♪ ♪ ♪ *güiro* rhythmic pattern

*cinquillo*  Caribbean non-symmetric "quintuplet") pattern ♪ ♪ ♪ ♪ ♪

*controversía*  competitive poetic dialogue, usually improvised, in *décima espinela* (q.v.) form

*cuatro*  10-stringed Puerto Rican plucked lead guitar (for modern version, see Figure 1). Early versions had four single or double strings

*danza*  instrumental dance in sectional form, with modulations, often including a *paseo*

*décima*  10-line poetic form of Spanish origin (see Appendix II)

*espinela*  décima with A B B A A C C D D C rhyme scheme (see Appendix II)

*guaracha*  strophic song/dance introduced from Cuba, in medium to fast tempo, usually with verse/chorus structure

*guarachada*  "in the style of the *guaracha*" (esp. ♪♪♪♪ ♪♪♪♪ or ♪ ♪♪ ♪ ♪♪ *güiro* and guitar accompaniment patterns)

*habanao*  "Havana style" *guarachada* guitar strum (related to *guarachada güiro* pattern).

*Jíbaros*  Puerto Rican rural white or mestizo small farmers

*paseo*  promenade with which many *danzas* begin, and which may return between repetitions of the *danza*

*pie forzado*  "forced foot": recurring last line of a *décima* stanza; sometimes provided beforehand as a challenge to a performer, who is expected to improvise the preceding nine lines within the complicated rhyme scheme

*seis chorreao*  fast *seis* with tonic-subdominant-dominant harmony

# Appendix II

## Musical and Textual Examples

*Example 1* First two verses of a Décima Espinela, sung to fast *seis*, in *controversía* (competitive dialogue form), between man and a woman. Note that in each verse the last two lines are repeated, with variations. These two "extra" lines do not affect what is considered to be a 10-line verse scheme. Note also the "flawed" *espinela* rhyme scheme in verse 1, in which the singer has apparently omitted (probably due to faulty memory) a fifth line which would originally have rhymed with "*comel*," and also a sixth line, which would have rhymed with "*echada*."

Such textual alterations are common due to the generally low level of competence in Spanish among Hawaii Puerto Ricans nowadays.

(Verse 1: Angel Santiago)

*Esta contraya [maldita] mujel(r)*
This accursed woman

*ya me trae en un patín*
makes me nuts

*y como barril sin fín*
and like a bottomless barrel

*no piensa más que [en] comel(r)*
she only thinks about eating

*siempre está en la cama echada*
she's always lying in the bed

*y no quiere trabajal(r)*
and doesn't want to work

*de mi se quiere burlal(r)*
she wants to mock me

*que mujel(r) abandonada (Pie Forzado)*
What a shiftless woman!

*oye mi pelu[d]a*
listen, my hairy one

*que mujel[r] abandona*
What a shiftless woman!

(Verse 2: Rose Santiago)

*Cuando usted me enamoró*
When you fell in love with me

*muy tranquila me sentía*
I felt very reassured

*con ruegos y majaderías*
with entreaties and nonsense

*siempre así me convenció*
always thus you convinced me

*de mi casa me sacó*
you got me out of my home

*con afán desesperao*
with desperate burning desire

*y sí aun no la [la comida] he preparado*
and if I haven't prepared it [dinner]

*y que no hago nada*
and that I do nothing

*y como [m]e siento cansada*
and as I feel tired

*tienes que aquantal[r] callado (Pie Forzado)*
you'll have to endure keeping quiet

*mira mi infeliz*
look, my unhappy one

*tienes que aquantal[r] callado*
you'll have to endure keeping quiet

*Example* 2 *tresillo* figure ♩. ♩. ♩

*Example* 3 *guarachada* ('*guaracha* style") güiro stroke pattern ♪♪♪♪ ♪♪♪♪ Strokes one, five, etc. are
accented

*Example* 4 *habana[d]o* guitar strum, used in the accompaniment of guaracha, *seis*, and other fast genres
(excepting merengue)
4/4 ×♪♪♪ ×♪♪♪

*Example* 5 *son clave* pattern
4/4 | ♩. ♩. ♩ | ⁞ ♩ ♩ ⁞ |

*Example* 6 "anticipated bass" rhythm
4/4 | ⁞. ♩. ♩ |

*Example* 7 characteristic merengue phrase
4/4 ♪♪♪♪ | ♪ ⁊ ♪♪♪ ⁊

*Example* 8 typical cuatro pickup phrase (rhythm only) of a *seis caliente*
4/4 | ⁊♪♪♪ ♪♪♪♪ ♪♪ ♪ ♪♪ |

Marcello Sorce Keller

# Why Do We Misunderstand Today The Music of All Times and Places and Why Do We Enjoy Doing So?

## Appreciating the "Bad", Misunderstanding the "Good"

SOME YEARS AGO, I was offered the opportunity to express the opinion that it is possible, and indeed in my view desirable, to gain pleasure even from the contemplation of "bad" art and "bad" music".[1] By "bad music" I meant at the time, as I do now, music which the competent listener easily recognizes to be unprofessionally made, by someone who does not thoroughly master the sonic material he is using, and is therefore unskilled and awkward in "putting together" the composition. In other words: when we as competent listeners know what a musician would like to do, but does not succeed in doing—then the result is, in this sense of the word, "bad music". Such music can be, nonetheless, quite revealing from a sociological standpoint (no less than Marcel Proust once explained how important *la mauvaise musique* could be in the life of people).

I would like now to go a step further and explain why I feel that today, whether we like it or not, we often cannot help but to "misunderstand" the music we listen to—as good or bad as it might be. In fact, my impression is that of late a considerable number of people have indeed developed a talent for enjoying bad music. Even more intriguing, they have learned to give a "sense" of their own making to music, which, because of its origins, they could not possibly comprehend on its own terms.

No anthropological expertise is necessary for us to recognize the original significance of music coming to us, like a meteorite, from a totally unfamiliar cultural universe (be it the European Middle Ages or a tribal culture in Papua New Guinea), can hardly be accessible to most of us. I find it therefore fascinating that so many people today, while missing the original import of much of the music they listen to, nonetheless "misunderstand" it in quite a successful way: they gain gratification from it. If so many people can indeed enjoy the sounds of alien musics, that must be thanks to a new *esprit* capable

---

1. M. Sorce Keller, "Some Considerations on Aesthetics Taken from the Viewpoint of Ethnomusic- ology," *The Music Review* 49 (1988): 138-44.

of "producing meaning" for alien musical styles and genres, which even educated Westerners of a few decades ago did not possess. Not many Westerners of our parents' or grandparents' generation could have taken seriously, as music, the sound of an Australian didjeridu, an American Indian song, or the Inuit "throat games."

## World Music: An Optimistic View

Let me recall how, many years ago, the newly born field of ethnomusicology took upon itself the task of convincing the Western world that all cultures produce music deserving to be heard. Now, at least in principle, the message has been received. Various kinds of music—Indian, African, and others—are accessible today through the mass-media, and this colorful rainbow of sounds is becoming more and more a part of our everyday experience. It is indeed a much more colorful *musique d'ameublement* than Eric Satie could ever have imagined. Of course, "ethnic music" is also easily available on CDs. Such records are bought by people of different extraction (albeit with the almost sole exclusion of conservatory teachers and classical musicians) and listened to with little or no under-standing of the reasons that put those musics into existence. It is intriguing that such musics are nonetheless enjoyed in some way by casual listeners.

There is of course at least something to be said for the widely shared idea that music is "naturally accessible", that sound speaks for itself, and that one only needs to lis-ten with an open mind. No less than Hugo Riemann, with his dissertation *Über das musikalische Hören* of 1873,[2] was one of the first scholars to point out that music is natural-ly accessible only when certain cultural pre-conditions exist and that, otherwise, listening is no simple and straightforward activity. Although he was only considering the Western art-music of his time, it takes little effort to realize that any attempt at "listening" to sound objects that do not belong to our tradition can only be more problematic. For example: how can we really tell a good performance of classical Indian music from a bad one? How do we know what the musician set out to do? Do we realize under what con-straints his creativity is working? Have we heard enough of that music to be able to make comparisons, and understand—for instance—whether the performer is having a bad day? If such pre-conditions are not met, how can we appreciate the music in such a way that the performer would recognize an adequate response to his work?

At any rate, this widespread belief that music is naturally accessible is now applied to musics regardless of their geographical and cultural origin (this, of course, is somewhat linked to the Romantic idea that true art, although rooted in a given time and local cul-ture, is ultimately universal). It is to be found among the compulsive listeners of today, and it is also supported—to same extent—by ethnomusicologists, who deserve the cred-

2.   Universität Göttingen.

it of bringing to the attention of the wider public the existence of these worlds of music in the first place. Of course ethnomusicologists know full well that things are not so simple. They know better than most the challenges inherent in cross-cultural listening. They have explained very well how the musics of the world should be understood "on their own terms", something that is hardly possible for the majority of music lovers. Nonetheless most ethnomusicologists seem to be rather optimistic and share the notion that it is possible, with progressive efforts and adequate exposure, to enlarge our musical horizon to embrace the world. The idea seems to be that, starting with some knowledge and appreciation of the music of our native environment (our musical mother-tongue, so to say), as Kodály also maintained, we could (and perhaps we all should, as educated people) move on to the appreciation of musics further and further removed from our cultural horizon.[3] In order to do so, there should be nothing wrong in starting with the simple appreciation of "exotic sounds", to whet the appetite and trigger further curiosity.

No quarrel with that, of course. Musical tourism hurts nobody. And so much the better for those who feel like going beyond superficial contacts. Each musical tradition is a remarkable achievement in its kind, and understanding the characteristics of such achievements is always worthwhile. I am less convinced, however, that we can actually understand all musics for what they intend to be, and even if we did, that we should actually come to like all of them.[4] And if we should indeed succeed in liking them all, then I suspect we would in a way be unfair to those musics which embody a worldview that is incompatible with that of other cultures. An all-embracing awareness of world musics forces single traditions to coexist with each other, and interact in our consciousness with "neighbors" that could not even exist or be imagined when some of them came into being. Our taking cognizance of the musics of the past, and of other cultures takes place within a new horizon which is just not compatible with the original "sense" and function of which these musics are carriers. I cannot help but seeing this as an act of violence on our part rather than an expression of broadmindedness.

## The Rainbow Soundscape

And here I come to my main point: my feeling that during the second half of the twentieth century, musical creativity in the Western world has been expressed even more in the area of "listening" than in that of composition or performance. In other words:

3.   I expressed my view of how problematic that can be in "Multiculturalism: Can We Really Face a Different Music?" *The Quarterly Journal of Music Listening and Learning* 3/4 (1992): 5-9.

4.   I argued that we do not have to like all musics, and that we are actually justified in disliking some of them in "Multiculturalism,", op. cit., and also in "Of

Minority Musics, Preservation and Multiculturalism: Some Considerations", *Traditionelle Musik von Minderheiten/Ethnische Gruppen* (=*Traditional Music of Ethnic Groups/Minorities*), Ursula HEMETEK and Emil LUBEJ, eds. (Vienna: Böhlau Verlag, 1996), 41-46, which also appeared in *Sonus* 16/2 (1998): 33-41.

5.   Oscar CHILESOTTI (1848-1916) is best known for his

music listening today is a more widely diffused activity than it ever was and also a more creative one. What we had in the past was not really "music lovers," but, rather, lovers of just one kind of music, genre, or style. Today it is not rare to meet people who like many kinds of music and who—when necessary—even create new meaning for musics, whose original import is quite beyond their cultural or historical reach. One could also look at it differently and say that, because of their lack of expertise, they miss the original sense of music (or maybe intentionally ignore it, even when it is attainable). But that is not necessarily bad. It can be a safety measure. There are meanings and ideas, in the music of other cultures, which, if properly grasped, would probably antagonize the Western listener. After all, most cultures are ethnocentric and intolerant of the other cultures. Understanding alien cultures on their own terms is tantamount to a comprehension of why, from their point of view, our own culture may be nonsense or even an abomination.

Be that as it may, our parents and grandparents were not as capable of listening to music lying beyond their historical or cultural horizon. It is well known how, during the nineteenth century, one could either like Verdi or Wagner, but not both of them. During the second half of that century, the distinguished Italian musicologist Oscar Chilesotti could not appreciate Dufay and Ockeghem, even though he was ecstatic about the music of... Tromboncino.[5] We also know that, up until quite recent times, no educated Westerner had any tolerance for Indian, Chinese, or Arabic music—let alone the music of tribal, or (what in those times were called) "primitive" societies. Today, on the other hand, it is generally acceptable to bathe in a soundscape where the Western tradition is present in its entirety—where Hildegard von Bingen, Machaut, and Josquin have become, in a sense, contemporaries of Vivaldi, Verdi, Bartók, Stockhausen, Philip Glass, and others. And then, at the same time, music from the most diverse contemporary cultures of our planet is progressively creeping in and becoming part of this already rich musical rainbow that we are exposed to, in which the sounds of each single tradition contribute to create a context for the sounds of the other traditions.

That is why, in suggesting that we have no other choice than to misunderstand much of the music reaching our ears, I do not have in mind solely the art-music of the Far East or that of some tribal society. It is much too obvious that an Indian *rag* listened to in, say, a Manhattan apartment can only be misconstrued and only enjoyed by a creative act of the mind; one capable of giving it some sense that is compatible with the kind of life and experiences one is having in New York. But I also have in mind music that does belong to the Western tradition and which, in such an intricate context in which we perceive it, is likely to be "understood" in ways that would probably surprise and puzzle its

transcriptions for guitar of Renaissance lute tablatures. See, for the purpose of my argument, his: *L'evoluzione della musica. Appunti sulla teoria di Herbert Spencer* (Turin: Fratelli    Bocca Editori, 1911).

makers. This can perhaps be seen in the worldwide popularity of pieces that are part of the Western tradition itself, even though their position in it is quite marginal. It may be at times *mauvaise musique*, or, at other times, quite respectable music re-contextualized and re-functionalized in surprising manners.

## The "Gray Zone": Where the "Good", the "Bad", and the "Ugly" Meet

It is intriguing to consider how, in our multicultural world, musical pieces, styles, and genres of geographically or historically diverse origin become part of the same "global soundtrack" available everywhere. Of course, this is too big a topic for me to deal with satisfactorily in this essay. But I can, perhaps, at least touch upon the especially notable "gray area", where I feel good music loses much of its original import and lives side by side with bad music, which, bad as it is, seems nonetheless to become a carrier of some kind of sense. It is an area where the most diverse products meet, selected by a process in which serendipity seems to play quite an important role, indicative perhaps of how points of reference can easily be lost in a condition of musical over-stimulation and overexposure.

One such case is, for instance, the "Andante" from Mozart's *Piano Concerto K. 467*. Its melody is universally popular, thanks to its role in the sound track of a world famous film of some thirty years ago. And the melody is now remembered by the broad public through the film character it was meant to identify—like a leitmotif: Elvira Madigan.[6] A second instance might be the "Aria" from Bach's *Third Suite*, already popularized by the violin transcription of August Wilhelmj, which, because of its sad thoughtfulness, has now become devotional music for funeral ceremonies the world over.[7] Absorbed as they are in our contemporary life experience, such "musical asteroids" coming from the musical past, are insufficient to give a picture of what the planet they once were part of looked like. In other words: their ties with their tradition of origin have been severed, and, as they are now used, they no longer convey the values that made distinctive their tradition or provenance. On the contrary, such fragments of our musical past are absorbed into a present which erases their original meaning while failing to give them a substitute "sense" comparable in depth and "thickness" to the one they lost.

It is also increasingly frequent that musical artifacts by "second rate" authors (... *absit iniuria verbis*) are absorbed into the mainstream of background music or "easy listening" that we come across in our everyday life. The music of such minor composers is also taken out of its original context and absorbed into a "collective memory" that ignores authorship and either makes the music "anonymous", or attributes it, unwar-

6.  *Elvira Madigan*, 1967.
7.  August WILHELMJ (1845-1908), German violinist, a friend of Richard Wagner's, and first violin of the Bayreuth orchestra in 1876, made a solo arrangement "On the G String" of the air in D major from the *Suite no. 3* by J.S. Bach.

rantedly, to composers whose names are, for a number of reasons, more evocative or easier to remember. I find significant in this connection the *Concierto de Aranjuez*, just because it is essentially insignificant for the history of twentieth-century music, and the name of its author, Joaquin Rodrigo—the Spanish composer who recently passed away (on 6 July 1999), is almost solely remembered for this one title of his. From the *Concierto de Aranjuez* comes the fortunate *Adagio*, which entered the repertoire, not so much of the concert hall, but rather of that pervasive soundtrack of our life which includes records, radio stations, wall-paper musics in supermarkets, airports, and other public buildings. This is perhaps sufficient to highlight how much of the music disseminated across the planet is not selected by the quality and originality the author was capable of, but rather in the coincidence of fortuitous factors (in this case Spanish exoticism, archaic, "quasi-Baroque" ornamentations of the melody, and so on.).

A rather similar fate occurred to a composition appearing more or less at the same time: the well-known *Adagio* by Albinoni. Of course, any genuine lover of eighteenth-century music can easily guess that it is not by Albinoni at all. It is, rather, by Remo Giazotto, the Italian musicologist that many readers of this *Festschrift* may know for his contributions to the study of of eigthteenth-century Italian opera, who also died, like Joaquin Rodrigo, at the age of 89, in 1999.[8] His death was almost totally ignored by the mass-media, even in his native Italy, because his composition (in which only a short fragment of a bass line by Albinoni is to be found) only owes its popularity to its connection to the name of the Venetian composer, a name carrier of associations of various kinds (mostly sentimental Italian films set in Venice in which baroque music, such as the Oboe concerto by Alessandro Marcello, not Benedetto, is in the soundtrack).[9] The fact that Rodrigo's *Adagio* and the *Adagio* by Giazotto present many analogies probably indicates that they both meet some need of contemporary popular taste, which may be at the origin of other similarly arbitrary choices.[10]

Not entirely dissimilar is the case of what is possibly the most famous Neapolitan song of all times, *Io te voglio bene assaje*, which owes its popularity not only to the fact that it is indeed a good song (at least as good as many others in that rich tradition) but to the legend that it was composed not by a Neapolitan, but by that very prolific Northern Italian composer, Gaetano Donizetti. And legend it is, since not one scrap of historical evidence supports the claim.[11] But music publishers and record companies have a vested

8.  Remo GIAZOTTO (1910-99) in his musicological work also gave much attention to Caccini, Stradella, Vivaldi, Albinoni, and Viotti.

9.  This is the oboe concerto which was borrowed by Bach and made into a harpsichord solo piece (BWV 974), transposing the key from D minor to C minor and adding figurations and ornaments. It is oftentimes erro-

neously attributed to Benedetto Marcello rather than to his brother Alessandro.

10.  The world-wide popularity of such "second rate" musics is further discussed by Carlo PICCARDI, "Bontà della cattiva musica," *L'onda*, 74/1-2 (1999), Lugano, Radio della Svizzera Italiana.

interest in upholding legends. And they act accordingly, by printing on record labels they produce the indication "by G. Donizetti," or, in the best of cases, "attributed to Donizetti".

When confronted with such phenomena one is tempted to react with that aristocratic disdain so eloquently expressed by Theodor Adorno about a half century ago. Adorno rejected the logic of mass-society *in toto*. Yet cases such as Mozart's theme for *Elvira Madigan*, Bach's *Aria on the G String*, Rodrigo's *Concierto de Aranjuez*, Albinoni's *Adagio*, and Donizetti's *Io te voglio bene assaje*, can only in part be blamed on the perverse manipulatory potential of the mass-media. I see them, rather, as symptoms of a disorientation easy to occur in times of musical overabundance. Different is perhaps the case of the tedious association of Charpentier's *Te Deum* with the TV Eurovision Logo, or that of Gounod's "Funeral March of a Marionette" with Alfred Hitchcock's fortunate TV series. The repeated association of the musical theme with a situation with which it originally had nothing to do is in this case responsible for the fact that a particular piece of music can no longer be listened to as music, in its own right.

## … and What About Beethoven?

In approaching my conclusion, let me summarize: 1. I take it as easy to comprehend that almost inevitably we misunderstand and create new meaning for the music of cultures that are substantially alien to our own; 2. I take it as equally apparent that even pieces of European music are often charged with associations that obscure our perception of how they once related to the mainstream of their tradition; and at the same time 3. In modern society, much room is made for *mauvaise musique* to take place side by side with more dignified compositions.

One may wonder at this point whether we are at least on safer grounds, or whether we can depend on more reliable points of aesthetic reference, when we listen to Beethoven or some other great master of the past. I am not sure we can. And I am not saying so because of the occasional misuses their music has also been subjected to (Beethoven, too, has become a jingle in the 47-measure arrangement of the *Ode an der Freude* produced by Herbert von Karajan in 1972 for the Conseil de l'Europe…). But such occasional incidents are of minor significance if one considers the magnitude of the production left by Beethoven and the other first-rate masters of the Western tradition. Quite aside from such occasional mishaps, I believe that drastic action might still be justified. I mean that musicologists have sufficient grounds to take upon their shoulders the sad task of finally telling music lovers what up to now has been kept secret: that even Beethoven, the "real Beethoven" (if it ever made sense to speak of such an entity), is lost

11.  Marcello SORCE KELLER, "*Io te voglio bene assaje*: A Famous Neapolitan Song Traditionally Attributed to        Gaetano Donizetti", *The Music Review* 45/3-4 (1984): 251-64.

for ever. And there is no lack of evidence to justify the news. Since Beethoven's time, too much has changed: performance practice, social context, all cultural terms of reference, soundscape. The piano that we use today is also only a relative of the fortepiano of Beethoven's times. Quite different are as well the places, modes, and social motivations for the making and listening of music. Different is the historical memory of the listeners (who not only have in their ears Haydn, Mozart, Brahms, Mahler, and Ravel but also Morricone, Madonna, Philip Glass, and Eric Clapton). And in the living room they have a gadget capable of producing music at the touch of a button and with a sound quality that Beethoven could never have dreamed of.

One could go on and on, but overemphasizing the issue might be counterproductive and only stimulate more efforts at philological restorations and reconstructions. The essential point is, rather, elsewhere. No musical work of the past ever arrived into our hands in its pristine form and shape. On the contrary, it carries layers of physical and psychological sediments collected in the course of time. Each epoch leaves its own mark. Each epoch, in turn, guards and preserves those marks, which, in its judgement, are part of the work's "essence." Ultimately what we inherit from the past is a constellation of footprints in which earlier ones are seldom distinguishable from those made later. What we perceive as the "unity" of the work of art is an interpretation of metamorphoses that erase any trace of borderline between a hypothetical original authenticity and the history of its occurring in time. What we call the "Musical Work" *is* that history. Already in 1906 Gaston Rageot observed, although few took notice at the time, that it is more significant to study "what happens" to a work of art in the course of history than to study the work of art in "itself", or how it came into existence.[12] In sum, there is more than enough evidence to bring to dust the totem of faithfulness to "the Original," because… there is ultimately no Original to be faithful to. On the contrary, one may do justice to music by "letting it happen" once again, as the historical conditions of the time allow— and not by reconstructing its hypothetical past identity. In other words: one does justice to a musical work by "misunderstanding" it, by discovering with our intelligence and creativity what kind of sense it can still have in our time—if it can at all.

Indeed in the world of art paradoxes occur. Among others, this one: a creative misunderstanding of music is the basis for our personal growth. Music is indeed a listener's art. And not only as Harold Bloom once suggested, that each work of art results from the misunderstanding of previous art-works. But even our appreciation of the art of times past can only be a misunderstanding of it,[13] and that misunderstanding may in itself be a "Work of Art".

---

12.  Gaston RAGEOT, *Les succès, auteur et public, essai de critique sociologique* (Paris: Alcan, 1906).

13.  Harold BLOOM, *A Map of Misreading* (New York: Oxford University Press, 1975), 19 *et passim*.

• ALLAN ATLAS ——————————————
is professor of music at The Graduate Center of The City University of New York. Among recent publications are: *The Wheatstone English Concertina in Victorian England* (Oxford, 1996) and *Renaissance Music* for W.W. Norton's Introduction to Music History series (New York, 1998); he is currently working on a "popular" book on the music of Astor Piazzolla, and serves as editor of *The Free-Reed Journal*. His friendship with Herbert Kellman stretches back to the early 1970s.

• ELIZABETH AUBREY ——————————
is professor of music at the University of Iowa, in Iowa City. Her friendship with Herbert Kellman began at a meeting of the Midwest Chapter of the American Musicological Society nearly twenty years ago, and it has flourished across many miles, from Chicago to Champaign to Southampton to London.

• DARRELL M. BERG ————————————
is Visiting Associate Professor of Musicology at Washington University in St. Louis, Missouri. She has known Herbert Kellman since 1965 when he was a professor at the State University of New York at Buffalo and she was a graduate student. She is the author of many articles concerning the life and works of Carl Philip Emanuel Bach and was recently appointed Co-Executive Editor of the forthcoming edition of Bach's works—*Carl Philipp Emanuel Bach: Collected Works*.

• BONNIE J. BLACKBURN ————————————
is a member of the Faculty of Music, Oxford University. She has written on music and music theory of the fifteenth and sixteenth centuries and co-edited *A Correspondence of Renaissance Musicians* (Oxford 1991). She is General Editor of the series, "Monuments of Renaissance Music." Her acquaintance with Herbert Kellman goes back some thirty years to the time of the International Josquin-Festival Conference in 1971.

• BRUNO BOUCKAERT ————————————
is Postdoctoral Fellow of the Fund for Scientific Research—Flanders (Belgium) and is working for the Alamire Foundation, International Centre for the Study of Music in the Low Countries (Katholieke Universiteit Leuven). In 1998 he completed a doctoral dissertation music at the collegiate churches of St.-Bavo and St.-Veerle in Ghent (*c.*1350-*c.*1600)

• DAVID FALLOWS ————————————
is professor of music at the University of Manchester, where he has taught since 1976, and is a member of the British Academy. He is the author of *Dufay* (1982, 1987), *A Catalogue of Polyphonic Songs, 1415-1480* (1999), and of numerous articles and reviews about early music, most recently on Josquin.

• MARY TIFFANY FERER ————————————
received her Ph.D. from the University of Illinois in 1976, where she was a student and graduate assistant of Herbert Kellman, who served on her dissertation committee. She is now assistant professor of music at West Virginia University in Morgantown and editor of five volumes of the Thomas Crecquillon *Opera Omnia* published by the American Institute of Musicology.

• JONATHAN GLIXON ————————————
associate professor of music at the University of Kentucky, received his PhD from Princeton in 1979, with a dissertation on musical activities at Venetian confraternities in the Renaissance. He has published widely since then and is now completing a monograph on music in Venetian confraternities to 1800, and, with Beth Glixon, a book on opera production in seventeenth-century Venice. He first met Herbert through his advisors at Princeton.

• BARBARA HAGGH ————————————
is associate professor of music at the University of Maryland, College Park. She edited *Musicology and Archival Research* (1994) and *Two Offices for St Elizabeth of Hungary* (1995), and writes about sacred music in the Low Countries and northern France. Herbert Kellman advised her masters' thesis (1980) and her dissertation on music in Brussels, 1350-1500 at the University of Illinois (Ph.D., 1988), and she was his research assistant for several years.

• ALICE M. HANSON ————————————
is professor of music at St. Olaf College. Herbert Kellman

advised for her master's thesis (1973) and Ph.D. dissertation, the latter on music and its cultural context in Biedermeier Vienna (1979). The dissertation was published by Cambridge University Press in 1984, by Bohlau Verlag in Vienna in 1987, and was translated into Japanese in 1988.

- EDWARD HOUGHTON ————————————
is professor of music and dean of the Division of the Arts at the University of California, Santa Cruz. He is collaborating with Herbert Kellman on a critical edition of the Chigi Codex (Vatican City, Biblioteca Apostolica Vaticana, MS Chigi C VIII 234).

- STACEY JOCOY————————————————
is a Ph.D. candidate in musicology at the University of Illinois at Urbana and is research assistant to Herbert Kellman in the Renaissance Archives. He is advising her dissertation, *Decoding Musical Resistance: The Popular Music of England's Civil Wars, 1600-1660*.

- JEFFREY KURTZMAN————————————
is Professor of Music at Washington University in St. Louis, Missouri. He first met Herbert Kellman when he was a graduate student at the University of Illinois and Kellman arrived from Buffalo to join the faculty. Kurtzman assisted Kellman in unloading and moving his furniture into his new three-story house, which formed the foundation of a lifelong friendship.

- LEWIS LOCKWOOD ——————————————
is the Fanny Peabody Professor of Music at Harvard University. He has known Herbert Kellman since 1958, when Lockwood was a first-year instructor at Princeton University and Herbert Kellman was a graduate student in musicology.

- HONEY MECONI————————————————
is Director of Medieval Studies at Rice University. She received her Ph.D. at Harvard University in 1986, under Lewis Lockwood, and now writes frequently on Pierre de la Rue and music at the Habsburg-Burgundian court. She has benefitted greatly from the expertise and generosity of Herbert Kellman for almost two decades.

- STEFANO MENGOZZI ———————————————
is assistant professor of music at Baylor University. He holds a lute diploma from the conservatory of Verona, a *laurea* in musicology from the University of Bologna, and a Ph.D. in musicology from the University of Chicago. A seminar that Herbert taught in Chicago in 1993, with characteristic passion and incisiveness, introduced him to Josquin's *ingenium*. Dr. Mengozzi is presently investigating the role played by historical music theories in shaping our modern approach to the musical repertories of the Middle Ages and Renaissance.

- JEREMY NOBLE ————————————————
who studied Classics at Oxford, has divided his career

between music criticism and the teaching of music history. A shared love of Renaissance music, and particularly that of Josquin, led to a collaboration and friendship with Herbert Kellman that has lasted more years than either can readily calculate. Since his retirement from the State University of New York at Buffalo, Jeremy Noble has lived in London.

- JESSIE ANN OWENS ——————————————
is professor of music and Dean of Arts and Sciences at Brandeis University. In November 2000 she will begin a two-year term as President of the American Musicological Society. She specializes in Renaissance music, particularly compositional process, analysis, and history of theory. Her book *Composers at Work: The Craft of Musical Composition 1450-1600* (New York: Oxford University Press, 1997; paperback 1998) won the 1998 ASCAP Deems Taylor Prize.

- WILLIAM F. PRIZER————————————
is professor of music and immediate past departmental chair at the University of California, Santa Barbara. He is former editor of the *Journal of the American Musicological Society*. He has known Herbert Kellman since 1974 and vividly remembers the pleasant December we and our present wives passed together in Florence many years ago.

- JUDITH RADELL ————————————————
is associate professor of music at Indiana University of Pennsylvania. She holds the DMA in Piano Performance from the University of Illinois (1980). Herbert Kellman chaired her doctoral committee and supervised her thesis on the performance implications of the sketches of Beethoven's "Diabelli" variations. She is active as a soloist and chamber musician; currently she is recording chamber music by Clara Kathleen Rogers and is editing Rogers' chamber works with Dieter Wulfhorst.

- ALMA COLK SANTOSUOSSO ————————————
is professor of music at Wilfrid Laurier University in Waterloo, Canada, and received her Ph.D. in musicology at the University of Illinois in 1979 (Herbert Kellman served on her committee). She is the author of *Letter Notations in the Middle Ages* (1989) and of several studies on manuscripts of medieval music theory. The most recent is the first volume of a series of three facsimiles of manuscripts from medieval Normandy.

- ROBERTA FREUND SCHWARTZ ————————————
is a Ph.D. candidate in musicology at the University of Illinois at Urbana. Her master's thesis won the Rita Benton award for excellence in musicological writing. She has taught at Millikin University and at the University of Illinois and is currently assistant professor of music at Luther College in Decorah, Iowa. Her dissertation in progress under Herbert Kellman considers patronage by the Spanish nobility between 1450 and 1600.

• EUGEEN SCHREURS ──────────────
studied viola da gamba at the Brussels Conservatory with Wieland Kuyken, and musicology at the Katholieke Universiteit Leuven. Since 1991 he has been postdoctoral fellow (Fund for Scientific Research, FWO-Flanders) and coordinator of the Alamire Foundation, a center for the study of the music in the Low Countries from Middle Ages to 1800. In collaboration with Herbert Kellman, the Alamire Foundation organised in 1999 an exhibition on Petrus Alamire and his time, as well as a colloquium and several publications.

• RICHARD SHERR ──────────────
is Caroline L. Wall '27 Professor of Music at Smith College in Northampton, Massachusetts. He has known Herbert Kellman as a friend and colleague for about 25 years.

• H. COLIN SLIM ──────────────
taught at the University of Chicago, 1959-65; 1972-73, and at the University of California, Irvine from 1965 until retiring in 1994. He has published widely on Renaissance vocal and keyboard music, on their relationship to the visual arts, and has edited operas by A. Scarlatti and Rossini. President of the AMS, 1989-1990, he was elected a Fellow of the American Academy of Arts and Sciences and also received an honorary Doctorate of Music from McGill University in 1993. A Harvard Ph.D. candidate in 1958, he greatly admired Kellman's first *Journal of the American Musicological Society* article, but met him only in 1971 at the Josquin Conference. Having published *A Gift of Madrigals and Motets* in 1972, he remains eternally grateful for Kellman having alerted him about his discovery in 1976 of the missing altus partbook to the *Gift*. Such scholarly generosity he hopes to repay, in part, by responding to the honoree's interest in Stravinsky.

• TED SOLÍS ──────────────
received his Ph.D. in ethnomusicology from the University of Illinois in 1982, with Herbert Kellman serving on his comittee. He is Associate Professor of Music (Ethnomusicology and Music History) in the School of Music, Arizona State University, where he has taught since 1989. He also directs "Marimba Maderas de Comitán," ASU's Latin marimba band. He has published articles and reviews on Latin America and India in *Ethnomusicology, Garland Encyclopedia of World Music, Latin American Music Review, World of Music, Ethnomusicology On-Line,* and Smithsonian/ Folkways Records.

• MARCELLO SORCE-KELLER ──────────────
is professor of music history and ethnomusicology at the Conservatorio della Svizzera Italiana – Scuola Universitaria di Musica (Lugano, Switzerland) and a regular contributor to Swiss Radio. He is a founder of the Societa Italiana di Analisi Musicale and has edited its journal, *Analisi.* He is also the founder and current president of the Swiss-Italian Chapter of the Schweizerische Musikforschende Gesellschaft, and member of its board of directors. He was Herbert Kellman's student in 1974 and 1975 and received a Ph.D. in ethnomusicology from the University of Illinois in 1986.

• RITA STEBLIN ──────────────
received her Ph.D. in musicology in 1981 at the University of Illinois, after taking four graduate seminars with Herbert Kellman and serving as his research assistant. Also a harpsichordist, she studied at the Hochschule für Musik in Vienna from 1977 to 1979, and has lived and worked in Vienna for the past nine years. Her dissertation, *A History of Key Characteristics in the Eighteenth and Early Nineteenth Centuries,* was published in 1983 and reprinted in 1996; she has since published widely on Beethoven and Schubert and is the author of *Die Unsinnsgesellschaft* (1998).

• JENNIFER THOMAS ──────────────
earned her Ph.D. in 1999 at the College-Conservatory of Music at the University of Cincinnati with her dissertation, "The Sixteenth-Century Motet: A comprehensive Survey of the Repertory and Case Studies of the Core Texts, Composers, and Repertory." She conducted much of her research at the University of Illinois Musicological Archives for Renaissance Studies, where Herbert Kellman became a valuable friend and mentor. Her research and writing continue to mine the motet database catalogue with regard to specific motets and repertories as well as largescale phenomena.

• CRAIG J. WESTENDORF ──────────────
is currently organist-choir director at St. Anthony on the Desert Episcopal Church, Scottsdale, Arizona, and artistic director of the Central Phoenix Oratorio Choir. He has enjoyed Herbert Kellman's friendship and tutelage as both a doctoral student and visiting assistant professor at the University of Illinois at Urbana-Champaign. His DMA dissertation on the *Spruchmotette* won the Julius Herford award in 1986.

• RICHARD WEXLER ──────────────
is professor of music at the University of Maryland, College Park, where he has been a member of the historical musicology faculty since 1976. He is the editor, with Dragan Plamenac, of the motets and chansons of Johannes Ockeghem (*Collected Works,* III, 1992), and he is currently completing editions of the works of Antoine Bruhier and the music of the Laborde Chansonnier. Herbert Kellman has been an inspiration to him and a friend for more than three decades.